D0996755

A MANUAL FOR

TOWNSHIP GOVERNMENT

PREVIOUS PUBLICATIONS

A HANDBOOK FOR TOWNSHIP OFFICIALS — 1957
A MANUAL FOR TOWNSHIP OFFICIALS — 1963

A MANUAL FOR
TOWNSHIP GOVERNMENT

for the

State of Michigan

Joseph A. Parisi

Executive Director
MICHIGAN TOWNSHIPS ASSOCIATION

Price $15.00

Ordered published by action of the
BOARD OF DIRECTORS OF
MICHIGAN TOWNSHIPS ASSOCIATION
on January 12, 1973

To that valiant group of more
than 700 township officials who founded
the Michigan Townships Association
in Lansing, Michigan on
October 6, 1953

There are two kinds of township officials who create problems for their township:

New ones who know nothing about township government
Old ones who think they know everything about it

If you are one of these, this book will be a revelation to you.

The best defense against takeover of township government responsibilities by big government is the kind of job at the local level that leaves no room for adverse criticism. Government is growing. Public officers must grow with it. Townships which do nothing give bureaucrats a toehold. What was good enough fifty years ago may not be, and generally is not good enough for today. It is much more difficult to be a good township supervisor, or clerk, or treasurer, or trustee now than it used to be. If one is not willing to give what the office requires, he/she should not take the office, good salary or bad.
— *D. Hale Brake*

A rural township official may think the township's isolation means it doesn't have the problems of its metropolitan neighbors, but may be surprised on getting up some morning to find that the township is well on the way to becoming part of a teeming community of tomorrow. The average township official reading this book is going to realize that township government is big business and that he/she had better begin to act like it.

These wards, called townships in New England, are the vital principle of their governments, and have proved themselves the wisest convention ever devised by the word of man for the perfect exercise of self-government and for its preservation.
— *Thomas Jefferson*

To you in township government, I say ... stand tall, erect and proud of your accomplishments ... look ahead to the future ... resolve and dedicate yourself to total commitment ... promise yourself to seek responsibility rather than avoid it ... vow never to miss an opportunity to speak out in a courageous forthright manner ... commission yourself to do everything possible to bring others into the arena of public concern ... all so that by your attitudes and persuasion local government shall forever be a solid, workable form of government.

— *Joseph A. Parisi*

CONTENTS

TABLES

ILLUSTRATION

FOREWORD

This *Manual for Township Government* will do much to promote efficiency in township government in the State of Michigan. It is informative and broad in scope, dealing with problems township boards face both today and in the future as they implement statutes with which they are charged by the legislature.

A unique feature is that officials at all levels of government will find it useful in gaining better understanding of how township officials serve their constituent citizens. This is due to the author's expertise and complete understanding of his subject.

Further credit is due the author for the excellent compilation, layout and design of his material. Certainly the manual will be an asset to anyone's library and I am sure township officials will find the textbook both useful and practical.

On behalf of the Board of Directors and members of the Michigan Townships Association, I want to thank Col. Parisi for his untiring efforts on behalf of township government, both in his duties as Executive Director of the Association and in the preparation of this manual.

John "Bud" Gilmour

John "Bud" Gilmour, President
Michigan Townships Association

PREFACE

Most historians believe that township government was brought to England by the Anglo-Saxons. The first written reference to it dates back to the year 890. In 1620, by order of the Mayflower Compact, it became the first form of government in America when the Pilgrims established a colony at Plymouth. At this same time the famous French explorer Champlain was mapping New France, which included the area of Michigan. Men working under his orders lived in Indian villages to learn the native language and habits and to chart the land for future exploration. It is believed that Eugene Brule was the first European to navigate Lakes Erie, Huron and Superior and that he was the first white man to set foot on Michigan soil.

New France was surrendered to the British at the end of the French and Indian War, remaining under British rule until the Americans assumed control in 1796. Although the Revolutionary War officially ended with the signing of the Treaty of Paris on September 3, 1783, a bronze inscription on the Federal Building in Detroit states that the war ended July 11, 1796, the British having continued to instigate small Indian scrimmages against the inhabitants for thirteen years after the treaty. The British ceded to America what was then called the Northwest Territory (from the Pennsylvania border to the Mississippi River and from the Ohio River to the Great Lakes). This area was explored by George Rogers Clark and parts of it were later claimed by the states of Virginia, Massachusetts, Connecticut and New York.

The Continental Congress, unable to pay its soldiers after the Revolutionary War, decided to aid the veterans by land grants in the Northwest Territory. Congress passed the Ordinance of 1785, providing for the survey and sale of land given back to the nation by those four states. The territory was divided into townships, usually six miles square. The townships were then subdivided into thirty-six sections, each containing 640 acres. Each township and section was numbered so that all tracts could readily be located by the migrating pioneers. In some townships, section sixteen was set aside for a school district. (Due to annexation and changing natural boundaries, townships today have no uniform legal size.)

Congress then passed the Ordinance of 1787, officially creating the Northwest Territory and dividing it into counties. Wayne County was formed with boundaries encompassing most of what is presently Michigan, as well as large portions of Wisconsin, Illinois, Ohio and Indiana. The Territory of Michigan was formed in 1805 and President Jefferson named William Hull of Massachusetts as its territorial governor. The Ordinance of 1787 also provided that any territory with 60,000 or more inhabitants was eligible to become a state. By 1835, Michigan's population was in excess of 85,000 and it became the 26th state by Act of Congress in 1837. Stevens T. Mason, a twenty-four year old Democrat, was elected the first governor, unopposed because the Whig Party could not agree on a candidate.

In the beginning, townships were the only form of government in Michigan. Each was named by its inhabitants, sometimes after an early settler or a creek or river, or some old world location such as London, Berlin, Paris, Vienna, Rome, Venice and Athens. There were virtually no roads, and hostile Indians resented the intrusion of the white man. Tasks were many and hardships common as these hardy pioneers wrestled a living from lands covered by a portion of the greatest unbroken forest on the face of the globe.

Against this rugged background, the officers of the newly formed townships had the responsibility of maintaining good government for the migrants. Many perished as they attempted to serve the people and their names are mostly forgotten for they had no skills in writing memorials. But their achievements are recorded in every cleared acre of Michigan farmland, and their blood is our inheritance. Originally the officers-- trustees, constables, clerks and overseers of the poor -- were appointed, but later were established as elected officials.

As Michigan's population increased, additional governmental services were demanded. Cities and villages began to crop up within the townships. Industries began locating in the cities and there was a gradual internal migration from farm to factory. As the cities grew they extended their boundaries by annexing parts of the townships. Big business and tax revenue fed the growing cities while townships, their basic organization remaining fairly stable, were left to perform virtually the same services with less tax revenue.

In 1947 the State Legislature provided for certain qualified general law townships to become incorporated as charter townships, with powers comparable to those of a city, short of actually becoming a home rule city. However, in 1952 there came the threat of political annihilation when certain theorists advocated abolition of township government "because it no longer served the needs of the majority of the people." The Michigan State Tax Aid Survey, sometimes referred to as the "Sly Report," was introduced in the legislature.

This was the spark that brought about concerted action toward co-operation among the townships. Although there had been townships in Michigan for over two hundred years, the officials decided that if they wanted this form of local government to continue in existence, they would have to work together. Many individuals assisted the author as he and men like Roy Brigham, one of the organization's earliest presidents, traveled more than 6,000 miles rallying support in every county in Michigan, and their efforts to weld township governments into a statewide association culminated in establishment of the Michigan Townships Association in 1953. Today, two decades later, the association is still the only official organization representing the overall needs of township government.

A township's size and the services it provides determine the number of elected or appointed officials and employees required. A typical rural township is governed by a board consisting of a supervisor, clerk, treasurer and two trustees; appointed officials include a board of review, volunteer firemen, traffic officers, etc. In contrast, a typical urban township has an elected board consisting of a supervisor, clerk, treasurer and four trustees. The board appoints the same officials indicated above, as well as others such as a police commissioner, building superintendent, zoning board, director of public works, chief engineer, fire commissioner, police chief, attorney, auditor and so on. Any general law township may appoint a township manager and a charter township may appoint a township superintendent. Supportive clerical staff are employed as needed and finances permit.

Modern township officials are not much different from their pioneer predecessors in that they are still faced with the basic problems of serving the people. Michigan townships spend upwards of $200 million annually, under statutory regulations, for such things as planning, zoning, building and mechanical inspection, cemeteries, street lighting, roads, water, sanitary and storm sewers, drains, sidewalks, fire and police protection, elections and other miscellaneous services such as health, libraries, parks and recreation and the operation of township public buildings.

Today more than a third of the state's population resides in the 1,245 townships of Michigan's eighty-three counties. Recent figures from the state treasurer's office show that annual township expenditures vary according to population, location and needs. Michigan's smallest township spends approximately $200 per year while the largest metropolitan township has a budget of over $3.5 million yearly. The majority, however, range from $75,000 to $500,000 annually.

Revenues are derived from a per capita distribution of the state sales, income and intangible taxes and from federal and state revenue sharing, including a portion of state liquor license fees; and, at the local level, from special assessment taxes, ad valorem property taxes, ordinance enforcement fees and local license fees.

Of a total township budget, the cost of maintaining general government normally amounts to 15 percent, fire protection 20 percent, cemeteries 8 percent, services and utilities 42 percent and miscellaneous 15 percent. With revenues generally exceeding expenditures, the township concept continues to be a sound, sensible and economic means of maintaining government to serve the people of rural and suburban Michigan.

Most township officials augment their incomes by working at other jobs. Occupations vary greatly--from attorneys to business executives, homemakers, factory workers, farmers, operators of small businesses and so on. By living and working in close contact with the people they serve, there is a personal touch that is rarely found in any other form of government.

ACKNOWLEDGEMENTS

I am sincerely grateful to a number of persons, agencies and business concerns for their material and substantive contributions to the preparation and writing of this manual. Much of the content was determined upon as a result of the urgently expressed needs and desires of many long-term township officials too numerous to mention. I am also indebted to the following:

Mrs. Margaret Hoogendoorn for her loyalty and dedication to the difficult task of shielding me from many routine duties, meetings and public speaking engagements while writing the text ... **Robert R. Robinson, Herbert Norton** and **Robert M. Edwards,** all MTA staff members, for taking care of much of the correspondence, telephone requests and speaking engagements normally done by me ... to the **Honorable D. Hale Brake,** Director of the Educational Division of MTA for his wise counsel, suggestions and recommendations ... to **John H. Bauckham** of Bauckham, Reed, Lang and Schaefer, MTA Legal Counsel, for his assistance in answering many questions and reviewing content ... **Philip Siegfried** of Siegfried, Crandall,Voss and Egly, Certified Public Accountants and Auditors for MTA for help in matters involving finance, budgeting and accounting ... to Wilkins and Wheaton Engineering Co. for wise counsel over the years on engineering services, and particularly in the field of creating special assessment districts ... to **Robert S. D'Amelio, Alfred L. Westol** and **Albert C. Blankenship** of the Bureau of Local Government Services, Michigan Department of State Treasury, for their contributions in matters involving finance, accounting, taxation and regulatory ordinances associated with the Subdivision Control Act and zoning ... to **Mrs. Marjorie Draher** for her untiring efforts in research; her tremendous assistance in grammatical structure and editorial comment; her ability to type and retype scores of thousands of words with accuracy and efficiency and many, many other responsibilities too numerous to account for here ... **Mrs. Kaye Rebney** who varityped much of the contents, as well as providing editorial, design and layout assistance ...**Marie, Ruth, Sandra, Elizabeth, Debbie** and **Sandy** who provided assistance in varityping, layout and the all-important proof-reading ... **Donald T. Strong** of Doubleday Brothers and Co. of Kalamazoo, who provided a great deal of advice and technical assistance in makeup, sequence of presentation and layout ... to **MTA officials** and **members of township government boards, agencies** and **commissions** for their patience and understanding in waiting for this manual to be made available to them ... to **Ann Arbor Task, Inc.** for assistance in preparation of the index ... to **Edwards Brothers, Inc.** of Ann Arbor and their account representatives for their much appreciated assistance in styling the manual through selecting grade and quality of paper, printing, binding, cover and color ... **to my family and many friends** for their loving understanding and indulgence of an author's needs under the pressure of compiling, writing and editing a textbook... **Finally, man can accomplish no works of any kind without the sustenance and strength he can derive from only one source -- his Creator. This book could not have been accomplished without God's will.**

HOW TO USE THIS MANUAL

The scope of the subject and the size of this text should not intimidate the reader. Every effort has been made to clearly and concisely present the voluminous material necessary for township government. It is intended on one level as an instruction book, and on another level as a reference book. The materials presented are intended to be used as a readily available source of reference materials for the township officials interested in achieving a high degree of proficiency in the conduct of their offices. It should also be an invaluable aid to civics and political science teachers and to those who wish to prepare themselves for office in township government.

The text itself is structured so as to clearly show the logical evolution of governmental authority. Authority is based on law. The Introduction and Chapters I and II are concerned with the Constitutional and legal bases for township government and the POWERS AND DUTIES thereof. Every concerned township official and citizen should be thoroughly acquainted with these basic chapters as they affect their roles in good government.

Chapter III is devoted to the conduct of elections and the citations related to this matter.

The remaining chapters are devoted to various areas of governmental function that may fall under the authority of township government. The statutes cited therein provide the basis for legislative action. It should be noted at this point that there may be some overlapping of citations when they affect more than one parameter of life or government. In chapters where the material is particularly complex we have attempted to preface actual citations with a brief discussion of the materials presented, as well as examples where useful.

It is also hoped by the author that the method of presentation will evidence the living or organic nature of the law, its responsive growth and and modification to modes of life in flux. The ability of legislators to respond to the problems of their environments and their constituents, and the ability of law to evidence that response, are one index to how healthy and responsive government is in a democracy.

The book may be advantageously utilized by both township officials and township attorneys. For the official, there is a wealth of material which can easily be found through the index. For a complete cross index of a subject matter, the reader should go to the more comprehensive indexes provided in the law volumes. For the township attorney, research time should be considerably reduced because of the comparison-type manner in which identification of the statutes is provided. Almost without exception the P.A. (public act) number and name are given, followed by the MCLA (Michigan Compiled Laws Annotated) number at the left margin preceding the section heading and the MSA (Michigan Statutes Annotated) number following the section heading. In some instances only the reference numbers are given.

In the interest of complete identification of the laws under which township government must operate, or those which may be jointly used with other units of government, little regard has been given to repeating the entire content except for the title and sections providing definitions and method of implementation. Hundreds of sections are only partially cited. It should be noted that all actual wording of the law is in italic type. Headings and sub-headings are done in bold-face (heavy) type. Any footnote is for purposes of editorial clarification, and bold-face words or phrases within the law wording are for editorial emphasis. Three periods (. . .) indicate that portions are omitted. Occasionally, for purposes of clarification, a word or phrase is enclosed within parentheses and done in regular type -- these should not be considered as wording from the law itself. Historical information as to amendments and additions to act titles and sections is included only in the first chapter.

This method of presentation was employed because the author felt it was important for the township official to be aware of the many laws which can be used by township government, the complete text of which can be found in the law books themselves. Reading, analysis, interpretation and opinion as to the advisability of use of any statute must remain the responsibility of the township attorney.

The text itself is ample evidence of the complexity of laws affecting township government. While we sincerely hope it will enable township officials to more efficiently perform their statutory duties, it is not intended to replace those necessary and crucial services performed by a township attorney or legal consultant. It is intended to augment the knowledge of all those who participate in the effort to achieve good township government. To that end the Michigan Townships Association (and the author) has dedicated itself and this effort.

Introduction

DEVELOPMENT OF TOWNSHIP GOVERNMENT

Before elaborating upon the construction of township government, let us consider the words of former Governor Cass of the State of Michigan, who said:

> *In proportion, as government recedes from the people, they become liable to abuse. Whatever authority can be conveniently exercised in primary assemblies, may be deposited there with safety. They furnish practical schools for the consideration of political subjects, and no one can revert to our revolutionary struggle without being sensible that to their operation we are indebted for much of the energy, unanimity, and intelligence which was displayed by our government and people at that important crisis.*

Add to this the equally important comment by Thomas Jefferson regarding township government:

> *These wards, called townships in New England, are the vital principle of their governments, and have proved themselves the wisest convention ever devised by the word of man for the perfect exercise of self-government and for its preservation.*

The basic structure of township government in Michigan was first projected by the Public Acts of 1827 and, with some change, remains the same today. The changes which have occurred have come about to meet the needs of the twentieth century. Very little was written into the law from the period 1827 to 1850, but in 1850 the constitution was amended to provide for the mandatory election of township officers as follows:

> There shall be elected annually, on the first Monday of April in each organized Township, one Supervisor, one Township Clerk, who shall be ex-officio School Inspector, one Commissioner of Highways, one Township Treasurer, one School Inspector, not exceeding four Constables, and one Overseer of Highways for each highway district, whose powers and duties shall be prescribed by law.

This same wording, except that school inspectors were eliminated, appeared as Section 18 of the Constitution of 1908. In 1943, Section 18 was amended to extend the term of elected township officials from one year to two years (members of the board of review and justices of the peace, four years), and justices of the peace were later eliminated entirely.

Section 18 of Article VII of the present constitution, adopted by the people on April 1, 1963, provides as follows:

> In each organized Township there shall be elected for terms of not less than two nor more than four years as prescribed by law, a Supervisor, a Clerk, a Treasurer, and not to exceed four Trustees, whose legislative and administrative powers and duties shall be provided by law.

Members of the township board (supervisor, clerk, treasurer and trustees) are all constitutional officers. Although functions of the township board have kept pace fairly well with the times, administrative organization has changed little since the early days.

TOWNSHIP GOVERNMENT TODAY

Until 1947, townships were organized only under provisions of the constitution and general law. Then, in 1947, the Charter Township Act (Public Act No. 359) was enacted into law, providing that a township having a population of 5,000 or more inhabitants, or a township bordering on a city of 25,000 population with a township population of 2,000 or more, could incorporate as a charter township, which "shall be a municipal corporation." Recent amend-

2

ments now make it possible for any township with a population of 2,000 or more to become a charter township.

The supervisor, the clerk, the treasurer and two trustees, all elected, comprise the township board of a general law township. There may be four trustees in townships having a population of 3,000 or more registered electors. Charter townships, regardless of population, shall have a township board composed of a supervisor, clerk, treasurer and four trustees.

There are presently 1,245 townships in Michigan, although the number varies slightly from time to time. Increases are caused by subdividing larger townships and decreases come about when townships incorporate as cities. The standard township is usually six miles square, although some may be as much as eight times larger and many much smaller. Royal Oak Township in Oakland County is the smallest in geographic size (six tenths of a square mile) yet the most densely populated in the state (approximately 6,000 persons). Populations run from a handful (six) in Pte. Aux Barques Township in Huron County to more than 80,000 persons in Redford Township in Wayne County. State equalized values, as of 1970, vary from $241,800 in Henderson Township, Wexford County, to $323,804,140 in Redford Township, Wayne County.

Each incorporated village is part of at least one township, and sometimes of two or more. The exception is that when village boundaries become coterminous, township government passes out of existence and only village governments remain. However, no city is part of any township nor is any township part of any city.

Townships as governmental units (along with cities, villages and counties) have only such jurisdiction and power as may be granted by specific constitutional or statutory authority or reasonably implied therefrom. Use of the term "home rule" for cities or counties is misleading since all of us have one thing in common -- that is, being creatures of the legislature. The legislature can take away at any time that which it has previously granted. It was only recently that the courts were directed (Section 34 of Article VII of the 1963 Constitution), to take a broad liberal construction of statutes as they apply to **townships:**

> *The provisions of this constitution and law concerning counties, townships, cities and villages shall be liberally construed in their favor. Powers granted to counties and townships by this constitution and by law*

*shall include those fairly implied and not prohibited by
this constitution.*

Only historians can judge the value of this important constitutional directive to the courts of this state.

MICHIGAN CONSTITUTION OF 1963 - ARTICLE VII, LOCAL GOVERNMENT

Article VII of the Michigan Constitution of 1963 covers the basic structure and organization of the four major areas of local government, takes into account a number of responsibilities regarding delivery systems for public services and utilities, matters regarding metropolitan governments and authorities, cooperative or joint operation of services, and the important arena of franchises and licenses.

If the reader does not already have a copy of the complete constitution, one should be obtained and carefully read, and then kept convenient for use with this manual.

ARTICLE VII
Local Government

Sec. 1. **Counties; corporate character, powers and immunities.** Each organized county shall be a body corporate with powers and immunities provided by law.

Sec. 2. **County charters.** Any county may frame, adopt, amend or repeal a county charter in a manner and with powers and limitations to be provided by general law, which shall among other things provide for the election of a charter commission. The law may permit the organization of county government in form different from that set forth in this constitution and shall limit the rate of ad valorem property taxation for county purposes, and restrict the powers of charter counties to borrow money and contract debts. Each charter county is hereby granted power to levy other taxes for county purposes subject to limitations and prohibitions set forth in this constitution or law. Subject to law, a county charter may authorize the county through its regularly constituted authority to adopt resolutions and ordinances relating to its concerns.

Election of charter commissions. The board of supervisors by a majority vote of its members may, and upon petition of five percent of the electors shall, place upon the ballot the question of electing a commission to frame a charter.

Approval of electors. No county charter shall be adopted, amended or repealed until approved by a majority of electors voting on the question.

Sec. 3. **Reduction of size of county.** No organized county shall be reduced by the organization of new counties to less than 16 townships as surveyed by the United States, unless approved in the manner prescribed by law by a majority of electors voting thereon in each county to be affected.

Sec. 4. **County officers; terms, combination.** There shall be elected for four-year terms in each organized county a sheriff, a county clerk, a county treasurer, a register of deeds and a prosecuting attorney, whose duties and powers shall be provided by law. The board of supervisors in any county may combine the offices of county clerk and register of deeds in one office or separate the same at pleasure.

Sec. 5. **Offices at county seat.** The sheriff, county clerk, county treasurer and register of deeds shall hold their principal offices at the county seat.

Sec. 6. **Sheriffs; security, responsibility for acts, ineligibility for other office.** The sheriff may be required by law to renew his security periodically and in default of giving such security, his office shall be vacant. The county shall never be responsible for his acts, except that the board of supervisors may protect him against claims by prisoners for unintentional injuries received while in his custody. He shall not hold any other office except in civil defense.

Sec. 7. **Boards of supervisors; members.** A board of supervisors shall be established in each organized county consisting of one member from each organized township and such representation from cities as provided by law.

_____

It should be noted here that Act No. 261 of the Public Acts of 1966 eliminated the county board of supervisors composed of township supervisors and substituted therefor a board of county commissioners apportioned and elected under the concept of "one man - one vote." Therefore, all references herein to "county board of supervisors" shall be interpreted as meaning "board of county commissioners." MCLA 46.601 [MSA 5.359(1)].

_____

Sec. 8. **Legislative, administrative, and other powers and duties of boards.** Boards of supervisors shall have legislative, administrative and such other powers and duties as provided by law.

Sec. 9. **Compensation of county officers.** Boards of supervisors shall have exclusive power to fix the compensation of county officers not otherwise provided by law.

Sec. 10. **Removal of county seat.** A county seat once established shall not be removed until the place to which it is proposed to be moved shall be designated by two-thirds of the members of the board of supervisors and a majority of the electors voting thereon shall have approved the proposed location in the manner prescribed by law.

Sec. 11. **Indebtedness limitation.** No county shall incur any indebtedness which shall increase its total debt beyond 10 percent of its assessed valuation.

Sec. 12. **Navigable streams, permission to bridge or dam.** A navigable stream shall not be bridged or dammed without permission granted by the board of supervisors of the county as provided by law, which permission shall be subject to such reasonable compensation and other conditions as may seem best suited to safeguard the rights and interests of the county and political subdivisions therein.

Sec. 13. **Consolidation of counties, approval by electors.** Two or more contiguous counties may combine into a single county if approved in each affected county by a majority of the electors voting on the question.

Sec. 14. **Organization and consolidation of townships.** The board of supervisors of each organized county may organize and consolidate townships under restrictions and limitations provided by law.

Sec. 15. **County intervention in public utility service and rate proceedings.** Any county, when authorized by its board of supervisors shall have the authority to enter or to intervene in any action or certificate proceeding involving the services, charges or rates of any privately owned public utility furnishing services or commodities to rate payers within the county.

Sec. 16. **Highways, bridges, culverts, airports; road tax limitation.** The legislature may provide for the laying out, construction, improvement and maintenance of highways, bridges, culverts and airports by the state and by the counties and townships thereof; and may authorize counties to take charge and control of any highway within their limits for such purposes. The legislature may provide the powers and duties of counties in relation to highways, bridges, culverts and airports; may provide for county road commissioners to be appointed or elected, with powers and duties provided by law. The ad valorem property tax imposed for road purposes by any county shall not exceed in any year one-half of one percent of the assessed valuation for the preceding year.

Sec. 17. **Townships; corporate character, powers and immunities.** Each organized township shall be a body corporate with powers and immunities provided by law.

Sec. 18. **Township officers; term, powers and duties.** In each organized township there shall be elected for terms of not less than two nor more than four years as prescribed by law a supervisor, a clerk, a treasurer, and not to exceed four trustees, whose legislative and administrative powers and duties shall be provided by law.

Sec. 19. **Township public utility franchises.** No organized township shall grant any public utility franchise which is not subject to revocation at the will of the township, unless the proposition shall first have been approved by a majority of the electors of such township voting thereon at a regular or special election.

Sec. 20. **Townships, dissolution; villages as cities.** The legislature shall provide by law for the dissolution of township government whenever all the territory of an organized township is included within the boundaries of a village or villages notwithstanding that a village may include territory within another organized township and provide by law for the classification of such village or villages as cities.

Sec. 21. **Cities and villages; incorporation, taxes, indebtedness.** The legislature shall provide by general laws for the incorporation of cities and villages. Such laws shall limit their rate of ad valorem property taxation for municipal purposes, and restrict the powers of cities and villages to borrow money and contract debts. Each city and village is granted power to levy other taxes for public purposes, subject to limitations and prohibitions provided by this constitution or by law.

Sec. 22. **Charters, resolutions, ordinances; enumeration of powers.** Under general laws the electors of each city and village shall have the power and authority to frame, adopt and amend its charter, and to amend an existing charter of the city or village heretofore granted or enacted by the legislature for the government of the city or village. Each such city and village shall have power to adopt resolutions and ordinances relating to its municipal concerns, property and government, subject to the constitution and law. No enumeration of powers granted to cities and villages in this constitution shall limit or restrict the general grant of authority conferred by this section.

Sec. 23. **Parks, boulevards, cemeteries, hospitals.** Any city or village may acquire, own, establish and maintain, within or without its corporate limits, parks, boulevards, cemeteries, hospitals and all works which involve the public health or safety.

Sec. 24. **Public service facilities.** Subject to this constitution, any city or village may acquire, own or operate, within or without its corporate limits, public service facilities for supplying water, light, heat, power, sewage disposal and transportation to the municipality and the inhabitants thereof.

Services outside corporate limits. Any city or village may sell and deliver heat, power or light without its corporate limits in an amount not exceeding 25 percent of that furnished by it within the corporate limits, except as greater amounts may be permitted by law; may sell and deliver water and provide sewage disposal services outside of its corporate limits in such amount as may be determined by the legislative body of the city or village; and may operate transportation lines outside the municipality within such limits as may be prescribed by law.

Sec. 25. **Public utilities; acquisition, franchises, sale.** No city or village shall acquire any public utility furnishing light, heat or power, or grant any public utility franchise which is not subject to revocation at the will of the city or village, unless the proposition shall first have been approved by three-fifths of the electors voting thereon. No city or village may sell any public utility unless the proposition shall first have been approved by a majority of the electors voting thereon, or a greater number if the charter shall so provide.

Sec. 26. **Cities and villages, loan of credit.** Except as otherwise provided in this constitution, no city or village shall have the power to loan its credit for any private purpose or, except as provided by law, for any public purpose.

Sec. 27. **Metropolitan governments and authorities.** Notwithstanding any other provision of this constitution the legislature may establish in metropolitan areas additional forms of government or authorities with powers, duties and jurisdictions as the legislature shall provide. Wherever possible, such additional forms of government or authorities shall be designed to perform multi-purpose functions rather than a single function.

Sec. 28. **Governmental functions and powers; joint administration, costs and credits, transfers.** The legislature by general law shall authorize two or more counties, townships, cities, villages or districts, or any combination thereof among other things to: enter into contractual undertakings or agreements with one another or with the state or with any combination thereof for the joint administration of any of the functions or powers which each would have the power to perform separately; share the costs and responsibilities of functions and services with one another or with the state or with any combination thereof which each would have the power to perform separately; transfer functions or responsibilities to one another or any combination thereof upon the consent of each unit involved; cooperate with one another and with state government; lend their credit to one another or any combination thereof as provided by law in connection with any authorized publicly owned undertaking.

Officers, eligibility. Any other provision of this constitution notwithstanding, an officer or employee of the state or any such unit of government or subdivision or agency thereof, except members of the legislature, may serve on or with any governmental body established for the purposes set forth in this section and shall not be required to relinquish his office or employment by reason of such service.

Sec. 29. **Highways, streets, alleys, public places; control, use by public utilities.** No person, partnership, association or corporation, public or private, operating a public utility shall have the right to the use of the highways, streets, alleys or other public places of any county, township, city or village for wires, poles, pipes, tracks, conduits or other utility facilities, without the consent of the duly constituted authority of the county, township, city or village; or to transact local business therein without first obtaining a franchise from the township, city or village. Except as otherwise provided in this constitution the right of all counties, townships, cities and villages to the reasonable control of their highways, streets, alleys and public places is hereby reserved to such local units of government.

Sec. 30. **Franchises and licenses, duration.** No franchise or license shall be granted by any township, city or village for a period longer than 30 years.

Sec. 31. **Vacation or alteration of roads, streets, alleys, public places.** The legislature shall not vacate or alter any road, street, alley or public place under the jurisdiction of any county, township, city or village.

Sec. 32. **Budgets, public hearing.** Any county, township, city, village, authority or school district empowered by the legislature or by this constitution to prepare budgets of estimated expenditures and revenues shall adopt such budgets only after a public hearing in a manner prescribed by law.

Sec. 33. **Removal of elected officers.** Any elected officer of a political subdivision may be removed from office in the manner and for the causes provided by law.

Sec. 34. **Construction of constitution and law concerning counties, townships, cities, villages.** The provisions of this constitution and law concerning counties, townships, cities and villages shall be liberally construed in their favor. Powers granted to counties and townships by this constitution and by law shall include those fairly implied and not prohibited by this constitution.

TOWNSHIP POPULATION STATISTICS

On December 31, 1972, records in the Secretary of State's office indicated that there were 1,245 townships in Michigan. According to the 1970 federal census, these townships fall into eleven major population categories, as listed in the chart below. There are 400 townships presently qualified for charter status since the Charter Township Act requires a minimum of 2,000 population to become chartered.

Township Population by Thousands

Population Category	Number of Townships
10,000 and over	52
9,000 and over	58
8,000 and over	68
7,000 and over	89
6,000 and over	93
5,000 and over	128
4,000 and over	160
3,000 and over	228
2,000 and over	400*
1,000 and over	756
Under 1,000	489

*Eligible to become charter townships

Number of Townships within Population Category

Population Category	Number of Townships
10,000 and over	52
Between 9,000 and 10,000	6
Between 8,000 and 9,000	10
Between 7,000 and 8,000	21
Between 6,000 and 7,000	4
Between 5,000 and 6,000	35
Between 4,000 and 5,000	32
Between 3,000 and 4,000	68
Between 2,000 and 3,000	172
Between 1,000 and 2,000	356
Under 1,000	489
Total townships	1,245

Chapter I

CHARTER TOWNSHIP ACT

In 1947 the Michigan legislature adopted one of the finest laws ever devised for the benefit of township government. The charter township act is a result of the great vision of such outstanding former legislators as Robert M. Montgomery, William Romano, Roy H. Brigham and others who recognized the need for not only expanding the powers of township government, but of increasing their efficiency and economical operation. Pennsylvania passed a similar statute called the First Class Township Act. Michigan and Pennsylvania are the only states progressive enough to allow townships to operate with the same powers as cities. Experience has proven in both states that townships can provide more and better services to their constituents at less cost than city government.

On the basis of the 1970 United States census, more than 400 Michigan townships which have a population of 2,000 or more can qualify to become charter townships following a referendum of their electorate. When a city incorporates, drafting a charter is an expensive item, since it must be done by a charter commission. With a township, however, there is no expense, since the act itself is the charter.

Becoming a charter township does not prohibit the township from using most of the statutes provided for general law townships, because the law states: "Each...charter township, its inhabitants, and the officers thereof, shall have, except as otherwise provided in this act, all the powers, privileges, immunities and liabilities possessed by townships, their inhabitants, and by the officers of townships by law and under the provisions of chapter 16 of the Revised Statutes of 1846.'' Careful study of the rest of the act will bring out that there are additional advantages as well.

Charter townships may still employ professional staff of all kinds. In fact, a high degree of professionalism can be brought to the governmental operation through employment of a township superintendent, whose duties are specified by law. This differs from the general law township manager, whose duties are delegated through the political decision of the township board.

Charter township boards may, by resolution, levy up to five mills without a vote of the electorate. With approval of the electorate, this may be raised to as much as ten mills. (Incidentally, the maximum city charter limitation is twenty mills.) Although the township board may purchase property without a vote of the people if the money is available within the millage limitation and the annual budget appropriation, any project calling for more than that must be decided by referendum of the people. Adoption of the act does not automatically cut off the one mill allocated to a general law township. However, this is a decision which must be made by the county allocation board following request of the township board, and would be counted as part of the charter limitation of five mills. Since federal revenue sharing and state aid monies are allocated on factors other than form of government, organizing as a charter township would have no effect on those amounts.

One of the most tangible benefits is that the charter township fiscal year is from January 1 through December 31, with provisions for a well-planned, well-prepared and well-timed budget to be brought before the people. By July 1 the supervisor must have a budget prepared based on figures submitted by department heads. During July he/she reviews and revises wherever necessary and prepares the budget for presentation to the board, which makes its own review and revisions. This is followed by a public hearing, with the budget available for public inspection at least one week prior.

Contrary to the once-a-year financial report required of the general law township, the charter township must prepare **a quarterly statement for each fund,** showing how much money was available at the beginning of the quarter, how much was taken in, how much was spent, and the balance at the end of the quarter. Furthermore, no expenditures may be made which are not appropriated in the budget, unless there is special authority and action of the **entire board,** and then only in emergency situations. There is no similar provision at any other level of government.

Every township official should welcome the legal checks and balances which insure that the charter township government will be fiscally responsible and responsive to township residents. Not only does it instill confidence in their actions, but the fact that it permits pledging the full faith and credit of the township without a vote of the people provides a great advantage in the bond market. Bond buyers look at the amount of outstanding debt and tax base of a township, as well as the nature of the project being financed. Charter township bond issues attract more buyers, resulting in less interest and premium costs.

The improved financial situation of the charter township permits township residents to enjoy more and better services at less cost than in general law townships, or for that matter, than in cities and villages. The township board may still declare public necessity for a project, and may join with other units of government to do any number of things. Its ordinance-making powers are comparable to those of cities, and greater than those of the general law township. It is interesting to note that all ordinances in the charter township, as well as the regular law township, are adopted by resolution of the township board **by roll call vote**; another provision establishing personal responsibility to the people.

There are some who fear that adoption of the act would "cement" the structure of charter government and the boundaries of the township for all time. This is simply not true. As a matter of fact, the statute specifies that any part of the township may be annexed to or consolidated with a nearby city or village, or incorporated as a city. Furthermore, if experience with charter government is not satisfactory, it is possible to return to general law township status by referendum of the electorate after a four-year trial period. Based on the experience of the present nineteen charter townships, however, disincorporation is not likely to occur. Disincorporation elections may not be held more than once every four years.

The courts are instructed to take a broad, liberal construction of the provisions of the Charter Township Act in the interests of public peace, health, welfare and safety of persons and property within the township. This is further strengthened by the constitutional provision, in section thirty-four of article seven, that the constitution and any law governing local governments shall be liberally construed in their favor.

The charter township act is a self-help tool for the best in township government. Given the additional powers of the act, Michigan's townships can adequately meet all the challenges and unusually high demands for services which are sure to come as we approach the year 2000 and all of the problems which the increased population will bring.

In spite of all these advantages, the charter township act languishes in a cauldron of suspicion, apprehension and misunderstanding, in townships as well as in cities. And the legislature, which provided it in the first place, now resists every effort to bring about liberalizing amendments to the act which would enable townships to even better meet their burgeoning needs in today's modern society.

The 1970 federal census reveals that suburbs now exceed cities as the sites of jobs and homes ("Surprises From the 1970 Census" by Trevor Armbrister in **Reader's Digest,** July 1973). This means that cities have lost much of their tax base and see their only recourse as annexation of the suburbs where people and business went when they left the city. The only trouble is that annexation removes the tax base from townships. Cities know that when townships meet needs, it slows down annexation, so they bar no holds as they fight against anything that will help townships.

Seeking ways to convince township residents to vote down adoption of the charter township, cities and villages play on the fact that townships generally have failed to provide adequate services and so entice annexation by promising to give them what they want and do it cheaper than the township could. Much to their distress and regret, once annexed and the services provided, township residents usually find that "cheaper" bit doesn't hold water.

Also, since township citizens fear loss of control over their money because a charter township may levy up to **five mills** without a vote of the electorate, cities and villages in their effort to defeat charter township act adoption, play on this fear. Trouble is, when the inevitable annexation comes, the citizen finds himself under a government which operates on a **twenty mill** limitation without a vote of the electorate!

The communications media, mostly city-based and thus city-oriented, perhaps fail to recognize that they usually present a pretty one-sided view when it comes to a difference of opinion between cities and villages on the one hand and townships on the

14

other. The fact remains, however, that they do so--and too many, even in townships and the legislature--look at that one side and go along with it without realizing they don't have all the facts. What is most needed is for all levels of government to sit down together and look calmly and carefully at the whole picture, and then work cooperatively to meet the needs in the best possible way, wherever they may be. In other words, forget **self**-interest, remember **everybody's** interest.

Act No. 359, P.A. 1947 - Charter Townships Act

AN ACT to authorize the incorporation of charter townships; to provide a municipal charter therefor; and to prescribe the powers and functions thereof.

Amended by Act 70, P.A. 1949 and Act 238, P.A. 1967.

MCLA 42.1 Charter townships, incorporation; powers and privileges, officers; special census, enumerators, expense. MSA 5.46(1)

Sec. 1. Any township, having a population of 2,000 or more inhabitants according to the most recently made regular or special federal or state census of the inhabitants thereof, or to any such census hereafter taken shall have power to incorporate as a charter township which shall be a municipal corporation, to be known and designated as the charter township of —————————, and each township which incorporates as a charter township shall be subject to the provisions of this act, which act shall constitute the charter of such municipal corporation. Each such charter township, its inhabitants, and the officers thereof, shall have, except as otherwise provided in this act, all the powers, privileges, immunities and liabilities possessed by townships, their inhabitants, and by the officers of townships by law and under the provisions of chapter 16 of the Revised Statutes of 1846. A special census of the inhabitants of any township desiring to incorporate under the provisions of this act shall be taken by the secretary of state upon receipt of a petition signed by not less than 100 registered electors of the township. Within 5 days after receipt of such petition, the secretary of state shall appoint an enumerator or enumerators to enumerate inhabitants of such township who shall qualify for the office of enumerator, enumerate the inhabitants of such township, and make a return thereof in the manner provided in section 6 of Act No. 279 of the Public Acts of 1909, as amended, being section 117.6 of the Compiled Laws of 1948. Such census, when accepted by the secretary of state shall fix the population of any township so enumerated for the purposes of this act. All expenses incident to such special census shall be paid for by the township so petitioning.

> Amended by Act 70, P.A. 1949 and Act 163, P.A. 1964.

MCLA 42.2 Same; referendum; duties of township clerk; finality of proceedings; term of incumbents; disincorporation. [MSA 5.46(2)]

Sec. 2. Any eligible township shall become a charter township when the inhabitants thereof shall, by a majority vote of the electors thereof, voting on such proposition, declare in favor thereof at any general or special election at which the proposition to incorporate as a charter township shall be submitted to the electors of the township. At such election the township clerk shall prepare a ballot for the submission of such proposition in accordance with the general election laws of the state and setting forth such proposition as follows:
> "Shall the township of ————————— incorporate as a charter township which shall be a municipal corporation subject to the provisions of Act No. 359 of the Public Acts of 1947, as amended, which act shall constitute the charter of such municipal corporation?
> Yes ☐
> No ☐ "

If on the vote being canvassed on the question of incorporation as a charter township, the result is determined to be in favor of such incorporation, the township clerk shall file with the secretary of state and with the county clerk of the county within which the township is located a copy of the petition or resolution initiating the move to become a charter township, together with the notice of the election at which such question was submitted to the electors of the township, the ballot upon which such question was submitted, and a certificate of the board of canvassers showing that the purposes of such petition or resolution have been approved by a majority of the electors of the township voting thereon, which certificate shall also give the number of votes cast on such proposition and the number cast for and against the same. From the date of such filing, the township shall be duly and legally incorporated as a charter township. After the filing of such petition or resolution and the other papers hereinabove required, neither the sufficiency thereof nor the legality of the incorporation of the township as a charter township may be questioned in any proceeding except by proceedings in the nature of quo warranto which shall be brought within 40 days after the date of such filing. All officers of any township which shall elect to become a charter township shall serve in the offices to which they have been elected or appointed for the balance of the terms for which they were elected or appointed and until their successors elect or to be elected shall qualify for and assume their respective offices. Any charter township may be disincorporated and returned to its previous status as a township governed under the provisions of chapter 16 of the Revised Statutes of 1846, as amended, being sections 41.1 to 41.103 of the Compiled Laws of 1948, by following the same procedures therefor as provided herein for adopting the provisions of this act. No election to disincorporate shall be held until 4 years after incorporation nor oftener than once each 4 years.

Amended by Act 163, P.A. 1964.

MCLA 42.3   Same; submission of question, vote of township board, petition of electors; duties of township clerk. [MSA 5.46(3)]

Sec. 3.   The proposition to incorporate as a charter township shall be submitted at the next general or at a special election in the event that, on or before August 30, or, in the event of a special election, not less than 60 days, preceding such election, the township board shall vote to submit such proposition to the electors of the township, or in the event that there shall be filed with the township clerk on or before such date petitions requesting the submission of such proposition which have been signed by a number of electors of the township which shall not be less than 10% of the total vote cast for supervisor in the township at the last election in which a supervisor was elected. The township clerk shall check the signatures on such petitions with those of the electors signing such petitions as they appear on the registration cards of the township and, if such petitions bear the required number of signatures of electors of the township, shall do and perform all acts required for the submission of the proposition to become a charter township at the next general or special election.

Amended by Act 70, P.A. 1949; Act 169, P.A. 1954 and Act 163, P.A. 1964.

MCLA 42.4   Same; nomination of candidates; petitions; duties of township clerk; election board. MSA 5.46(4)

Sec. 4.   All candidates for township office in charter townships shall be nominated at the general primary election held in such township prior to each general election at which township officers are to be elected, which primary election shall be conducted in accordance, as near as may be, with the provisions of Act No. 116 of the Public Acts of 1954, as amended, being sections 168.1 to 168.992 of the Compiled Laws of 1948.   To obtain the printing of the name of any candidate of any political party for a township office under the particular party heading on the official primary election ballot of the township, there shall be filed with the township clerk of the township up to 4 p.m., eastern standard time, of the seventh Tuesday before the day designated for holding any such primary election, nomination petitions bearing the signatures of a number of registered and qualified voters of such township equal to not less than 1% nor more than 4% of the total number of votes cast for the office of supervisor in the township in the last election in which a supervisor was elected.   All the duties which devolve upon the county clerk in the conduct of primary elections shall be performed by the township clerk with respect to the nomination of township officers, and the duties of the county board of election commissioners shall be performed for each township by a board of township election commissioners to be composed of the township clerk, and the 2 trustees appointed by the township board.   At the election on the proposition to incorporate as a charter township, the township board shall designate 2 of the justices of the peace* to act on such board.

----

*References to justices of the peace, although still a part of the charter township act, obviously are no longer pertinent, since by mandate of the 1963 Michigan Constitution (Article VI, Section 26) the office of justice of the peace has been abolished.   In their place, the legislature established the district court system.

Amended by Act 70, P.A. 1949; Act 188, P.A. 1953; Act 169, P.A. 1954 and Act 163, P.A. 1964.

MCLA 42.5 Charter township board, election; ... [MSA 5.46(5)]

Sec. 5. Except as otherwise provided in this act, all legislative authority and powers of each charter township shall be vested in and shall be exercised and determined by a township board of 7 members composed of the supervisor, the township clerk, the township treasurer and 4 trustees who shall be electors in and taxpayers* to the township. In the event the provisions of this act

----

*Attorney General's Opinion No. 4723, March 24, 1971: *The statutory requirement that a candidate for office must be a property owner and taxpayer is a violation of the equal rights clause of the federal constitution.*

----

shall be adopted, the township board as constituted at the time of the adoption of this act shall constitute the township board until the first general election at which township officers are elected after the adoption of this act. All members of the township board shall be elected under the provisions of Act No. 116 of the Public Acts of 1954, as amended. ...

Township board, powers; supervisor, president pro tem; record of proceedings. *Such township board shall be the successor to the prior township board of the township and shall possess the powers and perform the duties of township boards in townships in addition to the powers granted by law to charter townships. As a member of the township board, the supervisor shall be the presiding and executive officer thereof and shall have an equal voice and vote in the proceedings of the board. He shall authenticate by his signature such instruments as the board and the laws of the state or the federal government may require. In the event of the absence of the supervisor from any meeting of the township board, said board shall appoint 1 of its members president pro tem for such meeting. The township clerk shall be clerk of the township board and shall keep a full record of all the proceedings of the township board. In the absence of the clerk, such board shall appoint 1 of its members as temporary clerk for such meeting.*

Amended by Act 188, P.A. 1953 and Act 20, P.A. 1962.

MCLA 42.6 Charter township board; members, compensation, expenses. [MSA 5.46(6)]

Sec. 6. Each trustee may receive, in addition to other emoluments provided by law for his service to the township, not to exceed the sum of $15.00 per meeting of the board actually attended by him, but not to exceed in total $1,000.00 per year, to be paid upon authorization of the township board. The supervisor, the township clerk and the township treasurer shall receive no additional compensation for attending meetings of the board. Reasonable expenses may be allowed to members of the township board when actually incurred on behalf of the township.

Amended by Act 70, P.A. 1949.

MCLA 42.7 Same; regular and special meetings, notice; quorum, rules, journal, voting; public attendance; members, attendance. [MSA 5.46(7)]

Sec. 7. (a) The township board shall provide by resolution for the time and place of its regular meetings and shall hold at least 1 regular meeting each month. If any time set for the holding of a regular meeting of the township board shall be a holiday, then such regular meeting shall be held at the same time and place on the next secular day which is not a holiday.

(b) Special meetings of the township board shall be called by the township clerk on the written request of the supervisor or of any 2 members of the township board, on at least 24 hours written notice to each member of the township board, designating the time, place and purpose of any such meeting and served personally or left at his usual place of residence by the township clerk or someone designated by him. Notwithstanding the foregoing requirements for the calling of special meetings, any special meeting of the township board at which all members of the said board are present or have, in writing, waived the requirements that notice be given at least 24 hours prior to the time specified for the holding of such meeting and at which a quorum of the said board is present, shall be a legal meeting.

(c) No business shall be transacted at any special meeting of the township board unless the same has been stated in the notice of such meeting. However, if all the members of the said board are present at any special meeting thereof, then any business which

might lawfully come before a regular meeting of the said board may be transacted at such special meeting.

(d) All regular and special meetings of the township board shall be open to the public and its rules of order shall provide that citizens shall have a reasonable opportunity to be heard.

(e) Four members of the township board shall be a quorum for the transaction of business at all meetings, but, in the absence of a quorum, 2 members may adjourn any regular or special meeting to a later date.

(f) The township board shall determine its own rules and order of business and shall keep a journal of all of its proceedings in the English language which shall be signed by the supervisor and the township clerk. The vote upon the passage of all ordinances, and upon the adoption of all resolutions and ordinances shall be taken by "Yes" and "No" votes and entered upon the record, except that where the vote is unanimous, it shall only be necessary to so state. Each member of the township board who shall be recorded as present shall vote on all questions decided by the said board unless excused by the unanimous consent of the other members present. Any citizen or taxpayer of the township shall have access to the minutes and records of all regular and special meetings of the said board at all reasonable times under supervision of the clerk.

(g) The township board may, by vote of not less than 2 of its members, compel the attendance of its members and other officers of the township at its regular and special meetings and enforce orderly conduct therein; and any member of the said board or other officer of the township who refuses to attend such meetings or conduct himself in an orderly manner thereat shall be deemed guilty of misconduct in office. The township marshal shall serve as the sergeant-at-arms of the township board in the enforcement of the provisions of this section.

Amended by Act 70, P.A. 1949.

MCLA 42.8 Same; publication of proceedings, notices and ordinances. [MSA 5.46(8)]

Sec. 8. The proceedings of the township board shall be published at least once each month. The publication of a synopsis of such proceedings, prepared by the township clerk and approved by the supervisor, showing the substance of each separate proceeding of the said board shall be a sufficient compliance with the requirements of this section. The said board shall determine the method of publication of all notices, ordinances, and proceedings for which a mode of publication is not prescribed by this act or ordinance. The said board shall determine that such publication shall be made in a newspaper as defined by state law, which is published and circulated in the township, if there be one so published and circulated, or in the event that there be no such newspaper, then in one published in the county in which the township is located, or that such publication shall be made by posting in the office of the clerk and in 5 other public places in the township. In case publication is made by posting, a notice of such posting, setting forth by a descriptive phrase the purpose or nature of the notice, ordinance, or proceeding posted, and location of the places where posted, shall be published at least once in a newspaper, as above required, within 7 days after such posting was done.

MCLA 42.9 Officers, powers and duties; resolution creating additional officers, limitations. [MSA 5.46(9)]

Sec. 9. The township supervisor, township clerk, township treasurer, and constables in each charter township shall have and perform the duties and functions required of such officers by state law. The township board may, by resolution, upon the recommendation of the supervisor, or of the township superintendent, if one shall be appointed, create such additional officers as may be necessary to administer the affairs of the township government, or may combine any administrative offices in any manner not inconsistent with state law, and prescribe the duties thereof. No creation of any additional administrative office or combination thereof shall abolish the offices of township clerk or township treasurer nor diminish any of the duties or responsibilities of those offices which are prescribed by state law.

Amended by Act 70, P.A. 1949.

MCLA 42.10 Same; township superintendent, appointment, powers and duties. [MSA 5.46(10)]

Sec. 10. The township board in each charter township shall have power to appoint a township superintendent and may delegate to him any or all of the following functions and duties which functions and duties, unless so delegated, shall be exercised by the supervisor:

(a) To see that all laws and township ordinances are enforced;

(b) To manage and supervise all public improvements, works, and undertakings of the township;

(c) To have charge of the construction, repair, maintenance, lighting and cleaning of streets, sidewalks, bridges, pavements, sewers, and of all the public buildings or other property belonging to the township;

(d) To manage and supervise the operation of all township utilities;

(e) To be responsible for the preservation of property, tools, and appliances of the township;

(f) To see that all terms and conditions imposed in favor of the township or its inhabitants in any public utility franchise, or in any contract, are faithfully kept and performed;

(g) To attend all meetings of the township board, with the right to take part in discussions, but without the right to vote;

(h) To be a member, ex officio, of all committees of the township board;

(i) To prepare and administer the annual budget under policies formulated by the township board and keep the said board fully advised at all times as to the financial condition and needs of the township;

(j) To recommend to the township board for adoption such measures as he may deem necessary or expedient;

(k) To be responsible to the township board for the efficient administration of all departments of the township government;

(l) To act as the purchasing agent for the township or, under his responsibility, delegate such duties to some other officer or employee;

(m) To conduct all sales of personal property which the township board may authorize to be sold;

(n) To assume all the duties and responsibilities as personnel director of all township employees or delegate such duties to some other officer or employee;

(o) To perform such other duties as may be prescribed by this act or required of him by ordinance or by direction of the township board, or which are not assigned to some other official in conformity with the provisions of this act.

MCLA 42.11 Same; term, qualifications. [MSA 5.46(11)]

Sec. 11. Such township superintendent shall hold office at the pleasure of the township board and shall be selected by the said board on the basis of training and ability alone, without regard to his political or religious preference and need not be a resident of the township at the time of his appointment but shall become a resident thereof within 90 days after his appointment and shall so remain throughout his tenure of office.

Added by Act 145, P.A. 1962.

MCLA 42.11a Assessors, compensation. [MSA 5.46(11.1)]

Sec. 11a. In any charter township, in addition to the supervisor, the charter township board may provide for the appointment of assessors, not exceeding 2, for such charter township. Such assessors, when appointed, shall be clothed with all the powers and duties of supervisors in the assessment of property for taxation within such township and shall receive for their services such compensation as may be allowed by the charter township board. Whenever assessors shall be appointed, as in this act provided, the supervisor shall be the chief assessing officer and such assessors shall in all cases be subordinate to such supervisor. Upon completion of the assessment and the making of the rolls, such rolls shall be deposited with the supervisor.

MCLA 42.12 Police force, establishment; township marshal; rules, powers and duties. [MSA 5.46(12)]

Sec. 12. The township board in each charter township may provide for and establish a police force and authorize the supervisor, or the township superintendent if one has been appointed, to appoint, subject to the approval of the said board, a township marshal and such other policemen and watchmen as may be required to protect property and preserve the public welfare and safety in that portion of the township not included within the corporate limits of any village or villages located wholly or in part within the township. No police officer of any such village shall be ineligible for appointment as a member of the township police force, except that no village police officer shall serve as township marshal. The township board shall make all necessary rules for the government of the township police force and its members and shall prescribe the powers and duties of policemen and watchmen, and may invest them with such authority as may be necessary for the preservation of quiet and order and the protection of persons and property within that part of the township not located within the corporate limits of any village.

MCLA 42.13 Fire department, establishment; township fire chief; refusal of persons to aid at fire, penalty. [MSA 5.46(13)]

Sec. 13. The township board in each charter township shall have power to provide for and establish and maintain a fire department and authorize the supervisor, or the township superintendent if one has been appointed, to appoint, subject to the approval of the said board, a township fire chief and such other firemen as may be required to protect persons and property from the hazards of fire in that part of the township located outside the corporate limits of villages. The township board shall make and establish rules and regulations for the government of the department, the employees, firemen, and officers thereof; and for the care and management of the buildings, engines, apparatus, and equipment pertaining thereto. The township fire chief, or any officer acting as such, may command and require any person present at a fire to aid in the extinguishment thereof, and to assist in the protection of property thereat. If any person shall wilfully disobey any such requirement or other lawful order of any such officer, he shall be deemed guilty of a misdemeanor.

Amended by Act 70, P.A. 1949.

MCLA 42.14 Power to acquire property. [MSA 5.46(14)]

Sec. 14. Each charter township shall have power to acquire property for public purposes by purchase, gift, condemnation, lease, construction, or otherwise, and to maintain and operate public buildings, parks, and facilities needed in the performance of the powers and functions, expressed and implied, granted, possessed, and required of them by this act, or any other statute of the state of Michigan relating to townships and may sell and convey or lease any such property or part thereof which is not needed for public purposes: Provided, That no taxes shall be levied to acquire any property, public building, park or facility, unless such levy shall be approved by a majority of the electors of the township voting thereon at any regular or special township election.

Added by Act 188, P.A. 1953.

MCLA 42.14a Public improvements; issuance of bonds, limitation; net bonded indebtedness, computation; provisions. MSA 5.46(14A)

Sec. 14a.   The township may borrow money and issue bonds on the credit of the township for the purpose of constructing or otherwise acquiring any public improvement which the township is authorized to construct or otherwise acquire by any of the provisions of this act or any other act relating to public improvements by townships, upon approval thereof by a majority of the electors voting thereon at any general or special election: Provided, however, That the net bonded indebtedness of the township incurred for all public purposes shall at no time exceed 10 per cent of the assessed value of all real and personal property in the township: Provided further, That in computing net bonded indebtedness for the purposes hereof, bonds issued in anticipation of the collection of special assessments even though they are also general obligations of the township shall not be included, and the resources of the sinking fund or debt retirement fund pledged for retirement of any outstanding bonds shall also be deducted from the amount of the bonded indebtedness: Provided further, That such bonds shall be issued subject to the provisions of Act No. 202 of the Public Acts of Michigan 1943, as amended.

Amended by Act 70, P.A. 1949.

MCLA 42.15 Ordinances to provide for peace, health and safety; licenses, fee; bond. MSA 5.46(15)

Sec. 15.   The township board of any charter township may enact such ordinances as may be deemed necessary to provide for the public peace and health and for the safety of persons and property therein, and may by ordinance prescribe the terms and conditions upon which licenses may be granted, suspended, or revoked; and may in such ordinances require and exact payment of such reasonable sums for any licenses as it may deem proper.   The persons receiving the licenses shall, before the issuing thereof, execute a bond to the township when required by any ordinance in such sum and with such securities as prescribed by such ordinance, conditioned for the faithful observance of this act, and the ordinance under which the license is granted.

Amended by Act 70, P.A. 1949.

MCLA 42.16 Streets, alleys, bridges and other public places, use and licensing; ordinance records, filing. [MSA 5.46(16)]

Sec. 16. Except insofar as limited by state law and the provisions of this act, the township board shall have power to establish and vacate and use, and to control and regulate the use of the streets, alleys, bridges, and public places of the township and the space above and beneath them, such regulation of its streets, alleys, bridges, and public places shall be deemed a matter of local concern. Nothing in this act shall be construed to repeal or nullify the provisions of Act No. 221 of the Public Acts of 1937. Any ordinance concerning the operation of motor vehicles on any road, street or highway shall not become effective until 30 days after approval by the commissioner of the Michigan state police. A record of all ordinances so approved by the commissioner shall be kept on file in his office. Such power shall include, but not be limited to, the proper policing and supervision thereof; to the licensing and regulation, or the prohibition of the placing of signs, awnings, awning posts, and other things which are of such nature as to impede or make dangerous the use of sidewalks or streets, upon or over the sidewalks or streets of the township; and the licensing and regulation of the construction and use of openings in the sidewalks or streets, and of all vaults, structures, and excavations under the same.

MCLA 42.17 Buildings, construction; public health, safety measures. [MSA 5.46(17)]

Sec. 17. Charter townships shall have and possess and may exercise the same powers and shall be subject to the same liabilities as are possessed by cities to regulate the construction of buildings for the preservation of public health and safety, to regulate the conduct of business, and to provide for the public peace and health and for the safety of persons and property.

MCLA 42.18 Joining with other governmental agency. [MSA 5.46(18)]

Sec. 18. Each charter township may join with any governmental unit or agency, or with any number or combination thereof, by contract or otherwise as may be permitted by law, to perform jointly, or by one or more, for or on behalf of the other or others, any power or duty which is permitted to be so performed by law or which is possessed or imposed upon each such governmental unit or agency.

Amended by Act 70, P.A. 1949.

MCLA 42.19 Ordinances, resolutions, rules and regulations of former township; continuation, repeal, etc. MSA 5.46(19)

Sec. 19. All ordinances, resolutions, rules and regulations of a charter township which were in effect at the time such township became a charter township and which are not inconsistent with the laws of the state applicable to charter townships shall continue in full force as the ordinances, resolutions, rules and regulations of the charter township until repealed or amended by action of the proper authorities.

Amended by Act 70, P.A. 1949.

MCLA 42.20 Legislation to be by ordinance or resolution; ordinances, form, passage, etc.; recording and compilation.
MSA 5.46(20)

Sec. 20. All legislation of charter townships shall be by ordinance or by resolution. The term "resolution" shall mean the official action of the township board in the form of a motion, and such action shall be limited to matters required or permitted to be done by resolution by this act or by state or federal law and to matters pertaining to the internal affairs or concerns of the township government. All other acts of the township board, and all acts carrying a penalty for the violation thereof, shall be by ordinance. Each ordinance shall be identified by a number and a short title. Each proposed ordinance shall be introduced in written or printed form. The style of all ordinances shall be, "The charter township of _____ ordains:." Except in the case of ordinances which are declared to be emergency ordinances, no ordinance shall be finally passed by the township board at the same meeting at which it is introduced, nor until it has been published in the form in which it was introduced at least once. No ordinance shall be revised, altered, or amended by reference to its title only, but the section or sections of the ordinance revised, altered, or amended shall be re-enacted and published at length, and all ordinances, when enacted, shall be immediately recorded by the township clerk in a book to be called "The ordinance book;" and it shall be the duty of the supervisor and township clerk to authenticate such record by their official signatures thereon. The ordinances of each charter township shall be compiled and published in loose leaf or booklet form not less than once in every 10 year period.

Amended by Act 70, P.A. 1949.

MCLA 42.21 Same; penalties; disposition of fines. [MSA 5.46(21)]

Sec. 21. The township board shall provide in each ordinance for the punishment of those who violate its provisions. No punishment for the violation of any township ordinance shall exceed a fine of $100.00 or imprisonment for 90 days, or both in the discretion of the court. All fines collected for the violation of the ordinances of a charter township shall belong to such township and shall be paid into the township treasury on or before the first Monday of the month next following receipt thereof by any justice of the peace or other judicial officer.

Amended by Act 70, P.A. 1949.

MCLA 42.22 Publication of ordinances; effective date. [MSA 5.46(22)]

Sec. 22. Each ordinance passed by a township board shall be published at least once and all such ordinances shall become effective immediately upon the publication thereof, unless a date upon which such ordinance shall become effective, which is subsequent to the date of the publication thereof, is specifically provided in the ordinance itself. The publication of any ordinance in full after its final passage as a part of the published proceedings of the township board shall constitute publication of such ordinance as required herein.

Amended by Act 70, P.A. 1949.

MCLA 42.23 State law or standard codes in ordinance, adoption; identification; distribution to public; fee. [MSA 5.46(23)]

Sec. 23. The township board may adopt any provision of state law or any detailed technical regulations as a township ordinance or code by citation of such provision of state law or by reference to any recognized standard code, official or unofficial: Provided, That any such provision of state law or recognized official or unofficial standard code shall be clearly identified in the ordinance adopting the same as an ordinance of the township. Where any recognized official or unofficial standard code is so adopted, it may be published by providing to the public not less than 50 copies in book or booklet form, available for public distribution at a reasonable charge, and any amendment to or revision of such adopted code or detailed technical ordinance may be published in the same manner.

MCLA 42.24 Budget for next fiscal year; submittal by township officers; time. [MSA 5.46(24)]

Sec. 24. On or before the first day of August in each year, each township officer shall submit to the supervisor, or to the township superintendent if such officer has been appointed, an itemized estimate of the anticipated expenditures of the township for the next fiscal year for the township activities under his charge. The supervisor, or the township superintendent, as the case may be, shall prepare a complete itemized budget proposal for the next fiscal year and shall submit it to the township board on or before the first day of September.

MCLA 42.25 Same; information to be included. [MSA 5.46(25)]

Sec. 25. The budget proposal shall present a complete financial plan for the ensuing fiscal year, which shall commence on January first of each year and end on the following December thirty-first. It shall include at least the following information:

(a) Detailed estimates of all proposed expenditures for each function and office of the township, showing the expenditures for corresponding items for the current and last preceding fiscal years, with reasons for increases and decreases recommended, as compared with appropriations for the current year;

(b) Statements of the bonded and other indebtedness of

the township, showing the debt redemption and interest requirements, the debt authorized and unissued, and the condition of sinking funds, if any;

(c) Detailed estimates of all anticipated income of the township from sources other than taxes and borrowing, with a comparative statement of the amounts received by the township from each of the same or similar sources for the last preceding and current fiscal years;

(d) A statement of the estimated balance or deficit, as the case may be, from the end of the current fiscal year;

(e) An estimate of the amount of money to be raised by taxation and from delinquent taxes and the amount to be raised from bond issues which, together with income from other sources, will be necessary to meet the proposed expenditures;

(f) Such other supporting schedules as the township board may deem necessary.

MCLA 42.26 Same; hearing, notice, public inspection.
MSA 5.46(26)

Sec. 26. A public hearing on the budget shall be held before its final adoption, at such time and place as the township board shall direct, and notice of such public hearing shall be published at least 1 week in advance by the township clerk. A copy of the proposed budget shall be on file and available to the public for inspection during office hours at the office of the township clerk for a period of not less than 1 week prior to such public hearing.

Amended by Act 70, P.A. 1949 and Act 188, P.A. 1953.

MCLA 42.27 Budget; adoption by township board; levy of taxation; limitation; increase; separate appropriation for fire or police department; collection of tax; interim budget. MSA 5.46(27)

Sec. 27. Not later than the 1st day of November in each year, the township board shall, by resolution, adopt the budget for the next fiscal year and shall, in such resolution, make an appropriation of the money needed for township purposes during the ensuing fiscal year of the township and provide for a levy of the amount necessary to be raised by taxes upon real and personal property for the municipal purposes of the township, which levy shall not exceed 1/2 of 1 per cent of the assessed valuation of all real and personal property subject to taxation in the township: Provided, That the electors of each charter township shall have power to increase such tax levy limitation to not to exceed a total of 1 per cent of the assessed valuation of all real and personal property in the township for a period of not to exceed 20 years at any one time: And provided further, That in each township in which there shall be located 1 or more villages which maintain either a fire department or a police department which is not limited solely to the village marshal, or both a fire department and such a police department, the expense of any township fire department or police department, or both of said departments, in case both are maintained by the township, shall be appropriated separately from the other expenses of the township and no tax levy therefor shall be spread upon the township assessment roll against any property, either real or personal, located in any such village. The adoption of such resolution shall constitute complete and final authority for the township supervisor to spread the levy or levies therein provided upon the tax roll for the current year, according and in proportion to the valuations entered by the board of review in the assessment roll of the township and to include the amount of each levy in his warrant to the township treasurer. The township treasurer shall collect and return the same in the manner provided by the Michigan general property tax law. Within 60 days after the incorporation of any township as a charter township under this act, the township board shall adopt an interim budget to defray the expenses of such township until the commencement of the next fiscal year as in this act established and shall, in the adopting resolution, make an appropriation of the money needed for such purposes from the funds and assets of the township available for such purposes.

Amended by Act 34, P.A. 1967.

MCLA 42.28 Budget appropriation; expenditure restrictions; transfer to unencumbered balances; reappropriation. MSA 5.46(28)

Sec. 28. No money shall be drawn from the treasury of the township nor shall any obligation for the expenditure of money be incurred, except pursuant to the budget appropriation, or pursuant to any supplemental appropriation which may be made from surplus received. The township board may transfer any unencumbered appropriation balance, or any portion thereof, from 1 fund or agency to another. The balance in any appropriation, which has not been encumbered, at the end of the fiscal year shall revert to the general fund and be reappropriated during the next fiscal year.

MCLA 42.29 Quarterly statement showing relation between estimated and actual income and expenses; reduction of appropriations; exceptions. MSA 5.46(29)

Sec. 29. At the beginning of each quarterly period during the fiscal year, and more often if required by the township board, the supervisor or the township superintendent, as the case may be, shall submit to the township board data showing the relation between the estimated and actual income and expenses to date; and if it shall appear that the income is less than anticipated, the township board may reduce appropriations, except amounts required for debt and interest charges, to such a degree as may be necessary to keep expenditures within the cash income.

MCLA 42.30 Accounts, annual audit, filing results, public inspection; annual reports. MSA 5.46(30)

Sec. 30. An independent audit shall be made of all accounts of the township government at least annually and more frequently if deemed necessary by the township board. Such audit shall be made by qualified accountants experienced in municipal accounting. The results of such audit shall be on file in the office of the township clerk and available to the public for inspection. An annual report of the township business shall be made available to the public by the township board in such form as will disclose pertinent facts concerning the activities and finances of the township government.

Amended by Act 13, P.A. 1960 and Act 34, P.A. 1964.

MCLA 42.31 Local or public improvements; determination of necessity; special assessments; duties of officers; bonds. MSA 5.46(31)

Sec. 31. Each charter township shall have the power to make local or public improvements by the paving of streets which are not a part of the county highway system, the laying of curbs and gut-

ters, the installing of elevated structures for foot travel over highways within the township with the written approval of the state highway commissioner if such highways are state highways or with the written approval of the board of county road commissioners if such highways are county roads, the laying of sidewalks, the installation of garbage disposal systems, the paving of streets which are a part of the county highway system with the consent of and according to specifications of the county road commission, the laying of storm and sanitary sewers, the installation of water systems, and the installation of street and highway lighting systems, and shall have the further power to maintain or operate the same. The township board of each such township shall have the power to determine the necessity of any such local or public improvement and to determine that the whole or any part of the expense thereof shall be defrayed by special assessment upon lands abutting upon and adjacent to or otherwise benefited by the improvement, such assessment to be made in all respects as provided for the making of special assessments under either the provisions of Act No. 3 of the Public Acts of 1895, as amended, being sections 61.1 to 75.12 of the Compiled Laws of 1948, or the provisions of Act No. 188 of the Public Acts of 1954, as amended, being sections 41.721 to 41.737 of the Compiled Laws of 1948, except that the township board, township clerk, township treasurer, and a township board of assessors created by the township board for each local or public improvement, shall perform the duties and functions required by Act No. 3 of the Public Acts of 1895, as amended, of village councils, clerks, treasurers, and boards of assessors, respectively. Each such township shall have power to borrow money and to issue bonds therefor in anticipation of the payment of special assessments, which may be an obligation of the special assessment district or may be both an obligation of the special assessment district and a general obligation of the township.

MCLA 42.32 Succession to properties of former township; suits or prosecutions; debts or liabilities; uncollected taxes or assessments. MSA 5.46(32)

Sec. 32. All charter townships created under the provisions of this act shall succeed to and be vested with all the property, real and personal, moneys, rights, credits and effects, and of all records, files, books and papers belonging to such township as it formerly existed, and no rights or liabilities of the township which existed at the time it became a charter township, and no suit or prosecution of any kind commenced prior to and continuing at such time, shall be, in any manner, affected by such change, but the same shall continue, stand, or progress as if no such change had been made, and all debts and liabilities of the township and all taxes and assessments levied and uncollected at the time of such change shall stand until discharged or collected the same as if such change had not been made.

MCLA 42.33 Liberal construction of act in interest of public health and safety. [MSA 5.46(33)]

Sec. 33. The provisions of this act shall be liberally construed in the interest of the public health and welfare and the safety of persons and property within such townships as shall incorporate under the provisions of this act.

MCLA 42.34 Charter township; incorporation as or annexation to city or village. [MSA 5.46(34)]

Sec. 34. This act shall not prevent any part of a charter township from being incorporated as a city or village or from being annexed to a city or village in accordance with provisions of law for incorporation of, or annexation to any city or village.

Chapter II

TOWNSHIP OFFICERS, BOARDS, AGENCIES AND COMMISSIONS

ELECTED OFFICIALS

Section 18, Article VII (Local Government) -- Michigan Constitution

In each organized township there shall be elected for terms of not less than two years nor more than four years as prescribed by law, a supervisor, a clerk, a treasurer and not to exceed four trustees, whose legislative and administrative powers and duties shall be provided by law.

Act No. 116, P.A. 1954 - Michigan Election Law of 1954, Chapter XVI - Township Offices

MCLA 168.341 Township officers. [MSA 6.1341]

Sec. 341. Elective township offices shall consist of a supervisor, township clerk, township treasurer, not to exceed 4 constables, and not to exceed 4 trustees.

MCLA 168.358 Township officers; election, date, conduct, officers elected,...constables, trustees. [MSA 6.1358]

Sec. 358. In every township there shall be a general November election in each even numbered year at which there shall be elected by ballot the following township officers: A supervisor, a clerk, a treasurer, 1 trustee, and at least 1 but not to exceed 4 constables. ...

36

The number of constables to be elected shall be determined by the township board at least 6 months prior to the township election. If no determination ... is made ..., 2 constables shall be elected.

In townships now or hereafter having a population of 5,000 or more, or now or hereafter having 3,000 or over qualified and registered electors, as shown by the registration records at the close of registration for the last preceding November election, there may be elected in such township 4 trustees. In other townships there shall be 2 trustees....

Note: The balance of this section provides that there must be voter approval at a regular township election or at an annual meeting for election of four instead of two trustees and establishes procedure to be used. Some ambiguity exists as to whether annual meeting action is sufficient by itself.

Act No. 359, P.A. 1947 - Charter Townships

MCLA 42.5 Charter township board, election.... [MSA 5.46(5)]

Note: A charter township board, regardless of population and notwithstanding the provisions of Sec. 168.358 above, **shall** have a seven member board (four trustees).

Note: Act No. 44, P.A. 1966 (amendment to the Election Law) eliminated the offices of township highway commissioner and justice of the peace and repealed "all acts or parts of acts inconsistent therewith." Therefore, wherever the term "township highway commissioner" or "justice of the peace"* appears in any act (even

----

*Abolished by Sec. 26, Article VI (Judicial Branch) of the Michigan Constitution.

----

those which may be cited in this book), it is to be ignored inasmuch as the office no longer exists in Michigan township government.

Act No. 261, P.A. 1966 - Apportionment of Boards of Supervisors

MCLA 46.416 References to supervisors deemed to mean commissioners. [MSA 5.359(16)]

Sec. 16. All references to county supervisors or county boards of supervisors in any other act shall be deemed to mean county commissioners and county boards of commissioners as established by this act and such county boards of commissioners shall be the county board of supervisors referred to in article 7 of the state constitution.

Note: In view of this, whenever the terms "county supervisor" and "county board of supervisors" appears in a statute, they are deemed to mean "county commissioner" and "county board of commissioners."

The change has actually been made by the author in citations quoted in this chapter.

ELIGIBILITY

Sec. 1, Article II (Elections) - Michigan Constitution

Every citizen of the United States who has attained the age of 21* years, who has resided in this state six months, and who meets

---

*MCLA 722.52 Legal Age [MSA 25.244(52)] - **Act No 79, P.A. 1971 (Age of Majority Act)**
Sec. 2. Notwithstanding any other provision of law to the contrary, a person who is 18 years of age but less than 21 years of age when this act takes effect (January 1, 1972), and a person who attains 18 years of age thereafter, is deemed to be an adult of legal age for all purposes whatsoever and shall have the same duties, liabilities, responsibilities, rights and legal capacity as persons heretofore acquired at 21 years of age.

The United States Constitution, 26th Amendment, prohibited any state from lowering the voting age below 18. Michigan ratified this amendment April 7, 1971.

---

the requirements of local residence provided by law, shall be an elector and qualified to vote in any election except as otherwise provided in this constitution. The legislature shall define residence for voting purposes.

Act No. 116, P.A. 1954 - Michigan Election Law of 1954, Chapter XVI - Township Offices

MCLA 168.342 Township officers; eligibility. [MSA 6.1342]

Sec. 342. No person shall be eligible to a township office who is not a qualified elector of the township in which election is sought....

Act No. 116, P.A. 1954 - Michigan Election Law of 1954, Chapter I - Definitions

MCLA 168.10 Qualified elector. [MSA 6.1010]

Sec. 10. The term "qualified elector", as used in this act, shall be construed to mean any person who possesses the qualifications of an elector as prescribed in section 1 of article 2 of the state constitution and who has resided in the ... township 30 days.

MCLA 168.11 Residence. [MSA 6.1011]

Sec. 11. (a) The term "residence", as used in this act,... shall be construed to mean that place at which a person habitually sleeps, keeps his or her personal effects and has a regular place of lodging. Should a person have more than 1 residence, or should a wife have a residence separate from that of the husband, that place at which such person resides the greater part of the time shall be his or her official residence for the purposes of this act....

Act No. 116, P.A. 1954 - Michigan Election Law of 1954, Chapter XXIII - Registration of Electors

MCLA 168.492 Registration of electors; qualifications of elector. [MSA 6.1492]

Sec. 492. ...an elector...must be a citizen of the United States; at least 18 years of age; a resident of the state for at least 45 days; and be a resident of the...township...on or before the fifth Friday prior to the next ensuing regular or special election or primary election.

Note: There are no further qualifications or prior conditions in seeking elective township office.

NOMINATIONS

Act No. 116, P.A. 1954 - Michigan Election Law of 1954, Chapter I - Definitions

MCLA 168.15 Nominating petitions, signatures required, basis for computation. [MSA 6.1015]

Sec. 15. Whenever the number of signatures required on a nominating petition is based on a percentage of the vote for a party's candidate for secretary of state at the last preceding election and that party did not have a candidate for secretary of state at (that) election, the vote of the party's principal candidate at the last preceding election shall be used in lieu of the vote for secretary of state.

Act No. 116, P.A. 1954 - Michigan Election Law of 1954, Chapter XVI - Township Offices

MCLA 168.349   Township officers; nominating petitions, filing. [MSA 6.1349]

Sec. 349. (For)...each candidate for nomination...for a township office...there shall be filed with the township clerk nominating petitions signed by a number of qualified and registered electors residing within said township, equal to not less than 1% nor more than 4% of the number of votes cast by (his) party in the township for secretary of state at the last general election in which a secretary of state was elected, but in no case less than 5 signatures.... in the form prescribed in section 544c.

Act No. 359, P.A. 1947 - Charter Townships

MCLA 42.4 Charter townships; nomination of candidates;... [MSA 5.46(4)]

Note: In charter townships nomination petitions must contain not less than 1 percent nor more than 4 percent of the total number of votes cast for the office of **supervisor** in the township at the last election at which a supervisor was elected.

Act No. 116, P.A. 1954 - Michigan Election Law of 1954, Chapter XXIV - Primary Elections

MCLA 168.532 Primary elections; party not casting 5% of vote may not nominate by primary method;... ‌MSA 6.1532‌

Sec. 532. Any political party whose principal candidate received less than 5% of the total vote cast for all candidates for the office of secretary of state in the last preceding state election... in any political subdivision affected, shall ... make its nominations ... by means of caucuses or conventions....

MCLA 168.544c Nominating petitions; size, form, contents. ‌MSA 6.1544(3)‌

Note: This section provides specifications as to size, form and content, as well as regulations regarding circulation and signing. Subsequent sections in this chapter of the election law further regulate how petitions are handled. Any candidate wishing to run for elective township office would be well advised to consult with both the township clerk and the county clerk regarding legal procedures.

ELECTION

Act No. 116, P.A. 1954 - Michigan Election Law of 1954, Chapter XVI - Township Offices

MCLA 168.345 Township officers; primary election, date. ‌MSA 6.1345‌

Sec. 345. A primary of all political parties shall be held in every organized township of this state on the Tuesday succeeding the first Monday in August preceding every general November election, at which time...electors...may vote for...candidates for township offices.

Act No. 116, P.A. 1954 - Michigan Election Law of
1954, Chapter XXIV - Primary Elections

MCLA 168.534 Primary elections; time,... MSA 6.1534

Sec. 534. A general primary of all political parties except as
otherwise provided in section 532 of this act shall be held in every
election precinct in this state on the Tuesday succeeding the first
Monday in August preceding every general November election,...

Act No. 116, P.A. 1954 - Michigan Election Law of
1954, Chapter XXVIII - Holding of Elections

MCLA 168.641 General November election. MSA 6.1641

Sec. 641. An election which shall be known and designated as
the "general November election" shall be held in this state on the
Tuesday succeeding the first Monday of November in every even
numbered year.

Note: Township officers are elected at this election.

TERM OF OFFICE

All township officers elected at the regular November election
shall qualify and take their oath of office not later than noon on
November 20.

Both elected and appointed township officers in various other
areas of township government shall qualify and take oath of office
and serve terms in accordance with the statute under which their
service is conducted or in accordance with rules established by the
township board.

Act No. 116, P.A. 1954 - Michigan Election Law of
1954, Chapter XVI - Township Offices

MCLA 168.352 Township officers; term. MSA 6.1362

Sec. 362. The term of office of township officers listed in
section 358 (MCLA 168.358 - MSA 6.1358]) shall be 2 years. The
term of office of township trustees shall be 4 years....

42

QUALIFYING FOR OFFICE

Each township officer shall, before entering upon the duties of his/her office, take and subscribe to the oath before the township clerk or other officer authorized to administer oaths. With right hand raised he/she shall repeat the oath as stated in the constitution (see above).

Certain township officials must also further qualify (according to law) by depositing or giving bonds in specified amounts for the duration of the term of office. These include the township treasurer, deputy township treasurer, constables and such other persons as may be designated by the township board. Amounts of bonds are determined by the township board and the persons or corporations who grant the surety. Almost without exception, **any person handling public funds is required to be bonded.**

Additional qualifications may be imposed by the township board, such as requiring the township engineer to be a professional registered engineer or the township nurse to have a degree in nursing or be accredited by a hospital licensed by the state of Michigan, etc.

Act No. 2, P.A. 1968 - Uniform Charts of Accounts and Reports - MCLA 141.421 - 141.433 [MSA 5.3228(21) - 5.3228(33)] establishes the firm qualification that **anyone who audits township funds must be a certified public accountant.**

Qualifications for other offices such as housing commissioner, zoning administrator, building inspector, and various members of boards, agencies and commissions are established by specific statutes governing particular areas of township government. Some of these are enumerated in other sections of this book.

Section 1, Article XI (Public Officers and Employment) - Michigan Constitution

All officers..., before entering upon the duties of their respective offices, shall take and subscribe the following oath or affirmation: I do solemnly swear (or affirm) that I will support the Constitution of the United States and the constitution of this state, and that I will faithfully discharge the duties of the office of ------ according to the best of my ability. No other oath, affirmation, or any religious test shall be required as a qualification for any office or public trust.

R.S. 1846, c. 16 - Township Officers

MCLA 41.55 Neglect to qualify; penalty. [MSA 5.39]

Sec. 55. If any person elected to any township office, of whom an oath of office is required, who is not exempted by law from holding the office to which he is elected, shall not, within 10 days after notice of his election, take and subscribe the oath of office required by law, and cause the same to be filed with the township clerk, or if any such officer of whom a bond or security shall be required, shall not file such bond or security within the time above limited for filing his said oath, he shall forfeit and pay the sum of 10 dollars.

MCLA 41.69 (Township clerk) **bond, contents;...** [MSA 5.61]

Note: The bond of a township clerk, unlike those of other officers, is primarily a performance bond to insure that the clerk shall accurately and diligently perform the duties of the office.

MCLA 41.77 (Township treasurer) **bond, filing, time;...** [MSA 5.69]

MCLA 41.80 (Constables) **bond; ... time.** [MSA 5.72]

Act No. 116, P.A. 1954 - Michigan Election Law of 1954, Chapter XVI - Township Offices

MCLA 168.363 Township officers; oath, filing. [MSA 6.1363]

MCLA 168.364 Township officers; township treasurer, bond, sureties, approval, filing. [MSA 6.1364]

MCLA 168.365 Township officers; constable, indemnification. [MSA 6.1365]

CONTINUITY OF GOVERNMENT

Act No. 203, P.A. 1959 - Emergency Interim Local Succession Act

MCLA 31.101 - 31.115 [MSA 5.5000(1) - 5.5000(15)]

Note: Sec. 3 of this act permits township boards to enact resolutions or ordinances providing for emergency interim successors and specify their order of succession and file a list of same, together with their order of succession, with the clerk or other recording officer of the township and with the county clerk. The officer shall also periodically review his/her list and name new persons in order to keep five qualified emergency interim successors on file at all times.

Sec. 11 provides that each interim successor named is to keep himself informed as to the duties, procedures, practices and current affairs of the office to which he/she has been designated. This, of course, implies that the officer himself has a responsibility to see that those he/she names have full opportunity to so inform themselves.

The act specifies that the persons named, in the order listed, will assume the particular office if an elected officer is "unavailable to exercise the powers and discharge the duties of the office because of a disaster ... caused by an enemy attack...."

Thousands of local government officials in Michigan, at each succeeding election, violate this law. Within three days after he/she takes his oath of office, each township official **must** designate a first, second, third, fourth and fifth choice, in that order, as his/her successor in accordance with this act.

VACANCIES IN OFFICE - OCCURRENCE

There is one situation occurring fairly often which should be discussed at this point. This is the matter of a township official who moves from the township but still owns property in the township and has indicated to a number of people that he/she expects to return.

Whether a vacancy occurs in the office depends upon the officer's intent, and intent is very difficult to resolve, even in a court of law. If an official attends board meetings* and maintains legal

---

*There is no law which **compels** a general law township trustee to attend any meetings after his election and qualification. The law does require a charter township trustee to attend board meetings and **he/she may be compelled to do so** on the order of the township supervisor.

---

voting residence in the township, then he/she is eligible to hold office. Intent generally can be established only by the officer. If there is a resignation, there is no problem. If not, then it would be best to have the township attorney investigate and advise the board on what it should do.

R.S. 1846, c. 15 - Resignations, Vacancies and Removals

MCLA 201.3 Vacancies; creation. [MSA 6.693]

Sec. 3. Every office shall become vacant, on the happening of any of the following events, before the expiration of the term of such office:
1. The death of the incumbent;
2. His resignation;
3. His removal from office;
4. His ceasing to be an inhabitant...of the township...for which he shall have been appointed, or within which the duties of his office are required to be discharged;
5. His conviction of any infamous crime, or of any offense involving a violation of his oath of office;
6. The decision of a competent tribunal, declaring void his appointment, or,
7. His refusal or neglect to take his oath of office, or to give, or renew any official bond, or to deposit such oath, or bond, in the manner and within the time prescribed by law.

Act No. 116, P.A. 1954 - Michigan Election Law of 1954, Chapter XVI - Township Offices

MCLA 168.368 Township officers; vacancy, creation. [MSA 6.1368]

Note: This section of the election law also provides that habitual drunkenness is another reason for creating a vacancy in a township office.

R.S. 1846, c. 16 - Resignations and Vacancies

MCLA 41.56 Township officers; resignations, manner. [MSA 5.40]

Sec. 56. Resignations of all officers elected at township meetings* shall be in writing signed by the officer resigning, and

---

Your attention is directed to **Act No. 116, P.A. 1954 - Michigan Election Law of 1954, Chapter XVI - Township Offices (MCLA 168.349 - [MSA 6.1349]) which requires that those who seek township elective office must be nominated by petition followed by normal election procedures.* **Township officials are no longer elected at regular or special meetings of the township.***

---

addressed to the township board; and shall be delivered to and filed by the township clerk....

MCLA 41.57 Vacation of office. [MSA 5.41]

*Sec. 57. Every township office, upon the happening of either of the events specified in chapter 15 (**MCLA 201.1 et seq** [MSA 6.691 ET SEQ])...(shall become vacant)...*

MCLA 201.1 Resignation from public office; to whom made. [MSA 6.691]

Sec. 1. Resignations shall be made as follows:
1. ...;
2. By...officers holding their offices by appointment, and not by election, to the body, board, or officer that appointed them;
3. By all other officers holding their offices by election, to the governor, if the governor is authorized to fill the vacancy created by the resignation.

Act No. 116, P.A. 1954 - Michigan Election Law of 1954, Chapter XVI - Township Offices

MCLA 168.367 Township officers; resignations, signatures, delivery, filing. [MSA 6.1367]

*Sec. 367. Resignation of any township officer **shall** be in writing, signed by the officer resigning, and addressed to the township board, and shall be delivered to and filed by the township clerk.*

VACANCIES IN OFFICE - FILLING

Vacancies are filled by appointment by the supervisor and/ or township board and in some cases by the governor, and the appointee holds office for the remainder of the term for that office.
Exceptions:

1. The only vacancy to be filled by a special election is one created by a recall election. See **MCLA 168.361** [MSA 6.1361] and **MCLA 168.369** [MSA 6.1369].

2. In the case of township trustees (with four year terms), if the vacancy occurs before the first two years of the term are completed, then the term of office of the appointee shall be only until the next regular general election at which township officials are to be elected, at which time the electors have an opportunity to extend the temporary appointment for an additional two years. See **MCLA 168.362** [MSA 6.1362].

> *Example: On November 20, 1972, Trustee John Jones took his constitutional oath of office and was sworn in. On December 1, 1972, he died of a heart attack. The township board appointed Mary Smith to the vacancy.*
>
> *Mary Smith was required by law to run for election for the remainder of Trustee Jones' term at the November 1974 general election. She was elected. Her term of office now expires on November 20, 1976. She would be qualified to run for another full four-year term of office on her own in the November 1976 general election.*

R.S. 1846, c. 16 - Township Meetings

MCLA 41.15 Township officers; vacancies, term. [MSA 5.15]

Sec. 15. Each township officer elected at a special election to fill a vacancy, shall hold his office during the then unexpired portion of the regular term of the office and no longer, unless again elected.

Act No. 116, P.A. 1954 - Michigan Election Law of
1954, Chapter XVI - Township Offices

MCLA 168.370 Township officers; vacancy, how filled.
[MSA 6.1370]

MCLA 168.370a Township officers; vacancy; term of appointee.
[MSA 6.1370(1)]

**MCLA 168.373 Township clerk or deputy; appointment of substitute
to perform election law duties.** [MSA 6.1373]

R.S. 1846, c. 16 - Resignations and Vacancies

MCLA 41.58 Temporary appointments; appointee's duties.
[MSA 5.42]

**MCLA 41.59 Temporary appointments; township treasurer; sureties,
former treasurer.** [MSA 5.43]

**MCLA 41.61 Township supervisor; clerk and assessors, appoint-
ment,...** [MSA 5.52]

THE TOWNSHIP BOARD

A miraculous thing happens after every election in a democracy. Except for judicial offices where one individual may be in
paramount control, once candidates are certified and qualified and
have taken the oath of office, they drop their individuality by forming a legislative body. In a township, five or seven individuals
with their own opinions and beliefs sit down around a table and
join forces to provide the best service possible to the township.
This is a great challenge. An individual's own feelings,
thoughts and opinions are not as important as working together with
the rest of the township board to do that which is best for the township, even though it may not be what he himself would prefer. A
township board composed of representatives of two or more political
parties which can present a united front to its people, forgetting all
differences, is the board which is going to have the best chance for
success -- and for re-election.

ELECTORS AND THE TOWNSHIP BOARD

Up to the end of World War II electors literally had the power of life and death over a township board in its conduct of the affairs of the township in which they resided. They could appropriate money for any number of services and utilities, hire and fire numerous officers and agents for the township and raise and lower salaries at will, as well as promulgate many rules, orders and regulations. All this was accomplished at the annual or special meetings of the general township electorate.

However, at the end of the war there was a tremendous increase in the demand for services by township government for their citizens. Many new statutes were introduced and others already on the books were amended, taking more and more power from direct control of the electors at annual and special meetings. As populations increased in the townships, it was recognized that electorate control could no longer be maintained and that authority had to be vested in the elected township board composed of the supervisor, clerk, treasurer and trustees.

Consequently, today most actions taken by the electorate at their meetings is advisory only. The electors, however, still look upon these meetings as the one place they can make themselves heard with their dissatisfactions over high taxes, poor services, etc., and have some say about how their money is spent. It is advisable, therefore, for the township board to allow them to have their say on matters which concern them, even to the point of making and passing motions. But the moderator must be firmly in control of the proceedings in order to prevent a takeover by any one person or group at the meeting. And it is vital that the citizens be made aware, **where appropriate,** that their action is advisory only and, although it will be taken into consideration by the township board during its deliberations, it, **in certain situations,** is not binding upon the board. Questions of legality can be decided by the moderator, may be referred to the township attorney for a final opinion during the meeting, or the meeting itself may be adjourned until some later date when more information may be available.

A simple guideline to observe is that if the enabling statute provides that "the township board at any regular or special meeting called for that purpose, may (or shall) ...," then the matter of jurisdiction is solved -- the electors have **no** responsibility or authority to act at the meeting and their only recourse is by petition and referendum in certain cases.

50

Some specific things the electors can and cannot do at annual or special township meetings are described in the next few pages. Becoming familiar with these do's and don'ts should give the moderator a good idea of the general pattern of the relationship between the electors and the township board.

ELECTORS AT ANNUAL (AND SPECIAL) MEETINGS:

1. May **approve** an increase in membership on the township board from two to four trustees (if the township has attained 5,000 in population or has 3,000 registered electors). Subsequently, however, the matter **must** be placed on the ballot at a regular or special election to determine whether all the citizens of the township want four trustees and to elect the two additional trustees.

2. May **approve** rules and regulations **not already specified by law** for the conduct of the meeting.

3. May make all such orders and by-laws for determining the time and manner in which cattle, horses, swine, sheep and other animals shall be restrained from running at large in the highways, and for directing and managing the prudential affairs of the township, as they shall judge most conducive to the peace, welfare and good order thereof.

4. May **grant authority only** for the purchase or sale of real estate, buildings, equipment, etc., or to raise money by taxation for proper charges and expenses arising in the township.

5. May vote a tax of not to exceed one twentieth of one percent of the assessed valuation of the township for the preceding year, the money so raised to be used by the township board for maintenance, upkeep or repairs of the township hall, fire station, library or other public buildings of the township. However, if the township has reached the fifteen mill limitation, a vote at an election to increase the limitation would have to be conducted.

6. May **grant and vote money for the purpose** of employing a public nurse or nurses for the township.

7. May **give authority** to the supervisor to appoint a clerk to assist him in his duties as assessor.

8. May establish office hours for the township **office employees** (but not for the elected officials).

9. May **approve or reject** the salary schedule **submitted by the township board.** They may change a township treasurer from a fee basis to a salary basis with the start of the next term of office or, **with his consent,** prior to the new term of office. However, salaries cannot be raised within sixty days prior to an election.

10. May make **comments, suggestions and recommendations** on the township budget, **if one is presented by the township board.** However, none of these are binding on the board, which shall have the final authority for adoption of the budget. In effect, the annual meeting simply acts as the medium for conducting a public hearing on the budget (with the exception, of course, of compensation of the elected officials).

ELECTORS AT ANNUAL (AND SPECIAL) MEETINGS:

1. May not abolish the annual meeting.

2. May not change any rules and regulations already specified by law for the conduct of the meeting.

3. May not establish the date, time and place of holding regular and special meetings of the **township board.**

4. May not adopt rules compelling members of the township board to attend any or all meetings of the board.

5. May not appoint a county commissioner to sit as an ex-officio member of the township board.

6. May not vote to become a charter township.

7. May not impeach members of the township board.

8. May not hire or fire members of the township board, and may not cut an official's compensation so drastically that it would, in effect, fire that official. Since township officials are elected by

all the citizens of the township, a handful of people at a meeting cannot fire any one of them, either directly or by some capricious act.

9. May not appoint a temporary supervisor.

10. May not hire an assessor to replace a duly elected and certified township supervisor.

11. May not force the township clerk, supervisor or treasurer to perform any of the duties of any one of the others.

12. May not establish the hours a township official must stay in his office.

13. May not appoint or dismiss deputy clerks or deputy treasurers.

14. May not hire or fire constables.

15. May not appoint or dismiss a township trustee as a fence viewer.

16. May not designate places or times for the township clerk to receive registrations.

17. May not divide, alter, rearrange or in any way interfere with election precincts.

18. May not tamper with, revise or in any way attempt to change the membership of the election commission or the township canvassing board.

19. May not force the township treasurer to be at any particular place to collect taxes.

20. May not pay a township treasurer who is on a fee basis an additional amount for an annual salary.

21. May not vote to waive tax collection fees on the next year's tax roll.

22. May not change the manner in which dog licenses are sold by the township treasurer.

23. May not withhold the salary of any township official who does not attend board meetings.

24. May not designate depositories for township funds.

25. May not amend state statutes.

26. May not vote millage of any kind outside the fifteen mill limitation.

27. May not hire or fire accountants to audit township financial records.

28. May not employ or discharge an appraisal firm.

29. May not hire or fire a zoning administrator.

30. May not appoint the citizen member of a zoning board of appeals.

31. May not hire or fire election inspectors.

32. May not hire or fire members of a board of review.

33. May not appoint or dismiss a commissioner of noxious weeds.

34. May not appoint or remove members of a township civil service commission.

35. May not hire or fire a township attorney.

36. May not appoint or dismiss members of a park commission.

37. May not hire or fire a township manager.

38. May not appoint or dismiss members of a township water commission.

39. May not appoint or remove members of fire and/or police administrative boards.

40. May not hire or fire a township fire chief.

41. May not hire or fire a township police chief.

42. May not appoint or dismiss traffic officers.

43. May not appoint or dismiss innumerable other employees and members of boards, agencies, commissions, committees, etc.

44. May not alter or revise a pension plan which a township board has adopted by ordinance.

45. May not order or withdraw township participation in a joint authority or commission when such authority is established in the township board by statute.

46. May not establish rules for operation of the township police and/or fire department.

47. May not create or dissolve a township improvement revolving fund.

48. May not force the township board to use federal or state revenue sharing funds to reduce property taxes.

49. May not approve annexation of township territory to another governmental unit.

50. May not vote millage for road purposes.

51. May not control the township board's activities in advancing township historical interests.

52. May not control the township board's activities in advertising agricultural and industrial benefits of the township.

53. May not approve or disapprove a junk dealer's license.

54. May not approve or disapprove a liquor license pending before the township board.

55. May not amend a zoning ordinance or any other ordinance duly adopted by the township board in accordance with appropriate statutes.

56. May not establish or dissolve an ambulance service, including inhalator services.

57. May not establish or discontinue services for spraying for Dutch elm disease or other pest control.

58. May not create or dissolve street lighting districts.

59. May not deny action adopted by the township board for weed control in inland lakes.

60. May not adopt rules regulating motorboats in waters situated in the township.

61. May not alter in any way a township traffic code.

62. May not make contributions to charitable organizations (Cancer Society, Heart Association, Muscular Dystrophy, etc.), no matter how commendable their goals may be. **Public funds may not be expended for these activities.**

63. May not deny funds appropriated for child guidance clinics by the township board.

64. May not reject sidewalk and/or paving projects approved by the township board.

65. May not create special assessment rolls.

66. May not create or dissolve plumbing and heating codes.

67. May not create or dissolve building codes.

68. May not create or dissolve electrical codes.

69. May not reject or establish plats and/or subdivisions.

70. May not adopt rules and regulations prohibiting or controlling mobile homes in the township.

71. May not reject a township sanitary land fill ordinance.

72. May not alter, revise or restructure a drain district -- this must be done by a public hearing.

73. May not exercise any control over cemeteries.

74. May not exercise any control over libraries.

75. May not order the purchase by chattel mortgage or any other manner, or the sale of, any real estate, buildings, equipment (such as fire apparatus, street cleaning or snow removing equipment, etc.) or supplies.

76. May not establish rules and regulations for use of township equipment, buildings, parks, etc.

77. May not force the township board to provide public transportation to any specific group of citizens for any purpose.

78. **A very important final caution:** Certain statutes not only provide for action by the township board but also specify that the township board appropriate monies out of the general fund. In these situations the township board designates the amounts for such activities in the general operating budget and the electors may not tamper with the appropriations therefor.

MEETINGS

A matter of immense concern in maintaining a smooth-running, conflict-free township government is the number and types of meetings which must be held throughout the year. The most controversial of these is the annual meeting of the township. Following this in order of importance are the special meetings of the township, regular and special meetings of the township board, the annual township board meeting (settlement day), meetings of the inhabitants for discussion of a particular problem and such other meetings of a joint participation type as may be called by two or more municipalities.

The following pages describe what these meetings are for and how they should be conducted, with special emphasis on the annual township meeting.

ANNUAL TOWNSHIP MEETING

Knowledge of parliamentary procedure is an invaluable asset to the township supervisor as he conducts meetings -- and the annual meeting is no different than a township board meeting in this regard. Since most meetings in Michigan are held in accordance with *Robert's Rules of Order,** every supervisor should study

---

*Other rules could include: "Each person may speak only once on each subject unless he/she has something new to offer." "Each person will be allowed only three minutes unless in the opinion of the moderator more time is needed."

---

this book thoroughly and have it available at every meeting. We also recommend the booklet "The Meeting Will Come to Order" published by Cooperative Extension Service, Michigan State University, East Lansing, MI 48823.

The display of an intelligent knowledge of good parliamentary procedure will enable the supervisor to maintain respect and order and give reasonable assurance that the needs and desires of the electors will be met. The supervisor may appoint a knowledgeable individual (the township attorney, perhaps) to act as parliamentarian, whose decision would be final in case of any conflict.

It is well to point out here that for the annual meeting the township supervisor becomes the moderator, the township clerk becomes the secretary and the treasurer and the trustees are township electors, the same as all other township electors present.

The township board may never conduct business separately from the electors during the time set for an annual or special township meeting. Neither is it possible to intersperse actions of the township board with those of the electors at such meetings by allowing only the township board members to vote on certain matters.

Temptation may be great to act on one or two things discussed at a township meeting but which only the township board could legally accomplish. However, the township would then be in a precarious legal position since this would constitute a special meeting of the township board and if it were held at that time would not come within the statutory requirements for public notice.

Furthermore, since the supervisor is moderator and the clerk secretary of township meetings, neither could handle those responsibilities and still be part of a special township board meeting at the same time.

Now let us examine, from beginning to end, the conduct of a typical annual township meeting:

AGENDA

1. Call to order.

(Date, time and place of the annual meeting must have appeared in the published/posted legal notice directing attention of the electors to the annual township meeting.)

At the time specified in the notice, the moderator says something like, *"Ladies and gentlemen, welcome to the annual meeting of ... township of ... county. This meeting will be conducted under Robert's Rules of Order. Everyone, time permitting, will be given an opportunity to be heard upon request, providing he is first recognized by the chair. When an elector has the floor, no other elector may speak. I must further inform you that under state law, if this meeting should reach a point where it is impossible for any reason to satisfactorily conduct the business before us, I shall declare a recess until (or adjourn to) some future time. Also in accordance with state law, if any person becomes unruly and a public nuisance, I will ask him to be seated and remain silent. If he further disrupts the meeting, I shall instruct the constable (or deputy sheriff or some other official) to escort him from the room. If he should return and continue to create a disturbance, he will be fined $20 for each offense. However, I am sure this will not become necessary -- this is going to be a very fine and orderly meeting. We shall now proceed with the first item of business."*

2. Roll Call.

"Madam Secretary, will you please call the roll of the township board."

3. Reading of the Minutes.

"*Madam Secretary, will you please read the minutes of last year's annual meeting*" or "*Since the minutes of last year's annual meeting were published in the official notice of this meeting, they will not be read at this time.*" The moderator will then continue, "*Are there any corrections or additions?*" "*If not, they will stand as read (or published).*" If there are changes, the secretary will duly note them and the moderator will state, "*The minutes will stand approved as corrected.*"

4. Correspondence.

"*Madam Secretary, will you please read any correspondence which should come before this meeting?*" (It will be read.) "*Does anyone else have any correspondence which should be presented at this time?*" Generally any correspondence calling for action by the electors will be referred to old or new business.

5. Presentation of Petitions.

"*Are there any petitions to be presented at this time?*" Any citizen may present a petition under several laws of this state. Petitions may be for services or utilities or an administrative matter. They are received, but very rarely acted upon at the time of filing. Petitions are accepted by the township clerk on behalf of the township board and are processed for legal sufficiency (number of signatures, etc.). With a report prepared by the clerk, final action is taken by the board in accordance with the appropriate statute.

6. Old Business.

"*Next on our agenda is old business.*" Matters for consideration here are usually found as unfinished business in the minutes of the previous year's meeting.

7. New Business.

"*We will now consider new business. The first item for consideration is the annual budget which has already been made available for your study. The township board solicits your comments on the budget, but I must point out that your deliberations at this meeting serve only as a public hearing, except in the matter of salaries of members of the township board. Any comments or motions passed will be taken into consideration by the township board but are not binding upon them.*"

The matter of salaries may be considered as part of the budget or as a separate item and may be acted upon in total or separately for each officer. We would point out, however, that if they are considered with the budget as a whole, then any action the electors take regarding salaries is legal and binding upon the township since they do by law have power to establish salaries of the supervisor, clerk, treasurer and trustees.

Following are some typical examples of subjects which might be brought up at an annual meeting and suggestions on how to handle them.

Example: *James Smith, an elector of the township, has had his hand up for some time seeking recognition from the moderator. The moderator recognizes him by stating, "Mr. Smith, you may have the floor" or "Mr. Smith, may we hear from you?" Mr. Smith arises and says, "Mr. Moderator, I move that we amend section 4 of article 3 of the ... township zoning ordinance to read as follows --" At this point the moderator interrupts and advises, "Mr. Smith, you are out of order since Act 184 of the Public Acts of 1943 stipulates that adopting or amending a zoning ordinance is a function relegated to members of the township zoning board and the township board. Since it is not a matter to be properly brought before the annual meeting, I must declare you out of order." The moderator may permit Mr. Smith to continue speaking as an expression of an opinion if he wishes or may ask him to be seated.*

Example: *Tom Brown, an elector of the township, has been recognized by the moderator and says, "Mr. Moderator, I move that the electors of this annual meeting, under section 21 of Public Act 51 of the Public Acts of 1951 (the Dykstra Act), vote that two mills be raised for road purposes." The moderator then states, "Mr. Brown, I regret to inform you that under the general property tax act of Michigan, no extra millage may be voted by simple motion or resolution at the annual meeting of a township. This must be done by petition to the township board and a referendum so that all electors (voters) of the township have an opportunity to vote on whether they want to ap-*

prove or reject two mills for road purposes. You see, Mr. Brown, the Dykstra Act is an old statute and when it was written they did not take into consideration that in due course every single county in Michigan would eventually levy the maximum fifteen mills. Since the two mills you suggest are above and beyond the fifteen mill limitation, it requires a vote of the people as extra millage. I am sorry, but I must declare you out of order."

Example: *Ms. Betty Jones, an elector of the township, arises following recognition. "Mr. Moderator, I move that the salaries of the supervisor, clerk and treasurer be raised a flat ten percent* over the present amount." Ms.*

----

*Townships with less than sixty employees do not come under the 5.5 percent salary increase limit recommended by the President's Economic Council for 1973.

Mary Adams supports the motion. The moderator, if necessary, repeats the motion (or asks the secretary to do so) and instructs the secretary to be sure that the minutes show the names of the maker and supporter of the motion.

If a motion does not receive a second, no further action is needed. If it does receive a second, then the moderator asks, "Is there any discussion?" and various electors speak on the motion if and when recognized by the chair. The moderator should show good judgment in determining the amount of time allowed for discussion on any motion.

Sometimes a motion as originally made is not worded accurately to secure the intended purpose. Rather than going through the lengthy and often confusing parliamentary procedure of amending the motion, passing the amendment and then voting on the original motion as amended, it is perfectly legal -- if the maker and supporter of the motion agree -- for a new wording to be worked out through concensus. In any case, whether amended and passed as amended, or changed by agreement, the moderator should always restate the motion as it is to be finally voted upon, or as indicated above, he may have the secretary read the motion.

If no one volunteers the request for "question" (call for a vote) within a reasonable time, the moderator should discreetly inquire,

"Do I hear a question on the motion?" Normally someone will say, *"Question."* If not, then obviously more discussion is desired. If there has been rather lengthy and/or heated debate on a motion, the moderator may limit further debate to so many people and/or so many minutes. When the question is called for, the moderator proceeds as follows:

"You have heard the question and participated in the discussion. We are now ready to vote." (He may repeat the motion again for purposes of clarification if he feels it advisable.) *"Unless there are objections, the vote will be by voice as follows -- all those in favor, signify by saying 'aye'; all those opposed, signify by saying 'no'."* If there is a clearcut indication that a majority of those present have said 'aye' he declares the motion carried; if a majority have said 'no' he declares the motion defeated. If it is not clearcut, or if the decision is immediately questioned by seven or more electors, he must make the vote certain by polling or dividing or in accordance with some other rule which may have been established by vote or by-laws.

Example: On occasion conflicts may develop during a meeting which make it advisable for the moderator to call a recess for a period of time such as ten or fifteen minutes, or to another time on another day -- or someone may make such a motion from the floor. Such a motion is not in order when another speaker has the floor, but may be made even though there is another motion in discussion. It requires a second, is not debatable, but may be amended. It requires a majority for passage and may not be reconsidered.

8. Adjournment.

A specific time for adjournment may appear on the agenda or be stipulated by the moderator at the beginning of the meeting. When that time comes, he may simply state that the meeting stands adjourned if all the business has been concluded. If there is still business to come before the electors, however, he should then declare the meeting adjourned (or recessed) **to a specific time, date and place in the future,** at which time further business will be considered. This may be continued from time to time until all business has been completed. The moderator should be very careful at this point since, once adjourned (without specifying a date to continue the meeting), the meeting is finished and the only way any further business might be conducted would be through the process of calling a special meeting of the electors. The rules regarding **how** a meeting may be adjourned are the same as those for providing for a short recess.

Depending on the situation, the moderator may state, *"There being no further business to come before this meeting, it will stand adjourned."* This concludes the annual meeting.

Or he may say, *"Due to the lateness of the hour and the fact that there is still business to be considered, this meeting will stand adjourned (or recessed) to (a specified date, time and place) when we will continue our deliberations."*

The latter statement may be made by the moderator, or moved by an elector during the meeting when it appears to be impossible to conduct business in a satisfactory manner.

R.S. 1846, c. 16 - Township Meetings

MCLA 41.8 Annual township meeting; date. [MSA 5.8]

Sec. 8. The annual meeting of each township shall be held on the Saturday immediately preceding the first Monday in April, in each year, at the time and place selected by the township board as provided in section 361 of Act No. 116 of the Public Acts of 1954*,

----

*Michigan Election Law of 1954.

----

as amended, being section 168.361 [MSA 6.1361] *of the Compiled Laws of 1948.*

Act No. 116, P.A. 1954 - Michigan Election Law of 1954, Chapter XVI - Township Offices

MCLA 168.361 Township electors annual meeting; notice, publication, posting. [MSA 6.1361]

Sec. 361. There shall be an annual meeting of the electors of each township on the Saturday preceding the first Monday in April of each year between 1 p.m. and 8 p.m. The time and place of such meeting shall be determined by the township board. The township clerk shall give notice thereof by publication at least twice in some newspaper of general circulation in the township, the last publication to be not more than 20 nor less than 14 days before the meeting day and, if deemed advisable by the township board by the posting of the number of notices that the board shall designate in conspicuous places. In townships having less than 200 registered voters, the township board may provide that notices of the annual meeting shall be by posting, as herein provided, in lieu of by publishing. The electors meeting at the place designated shall transact such business as is usually transacted at township meetings by viva voce vote.

Abolition in townships having 5,000 or more inhabitants, referendum. In all townships having 5,000 or more inhabitants the township board by resolution may, or on the filing of petitions signed by not less than 8% of the registered electors of the township shall, submit the question of the abolition of the annual meeting to the electors at the next regular primary or election. Such resolution or petition shall be filed with the township clerk at least 30 days prior to such regular primary or election day. In case a majority of the electors of the township voting on the proposal shall vote for the abolition of the annual township meeting, the annual township meeting in such township shall be abolished.

R.S. 1846, c. 16 - Township Meetings

MCLA 41.16 Meeting place [MSA 5.16]

Sec. 16. The annual ... meeting shall ... be held at such place as shall be directed in the act or proceedings by which the township was organized, or in such other place as shall be designated by the township board.

MCLA 41.19 Adjournment. [MSA 5.19]

Sec. 19. Any annual ... meeting may, by a vote of the meeting, be adjourned to any other day, and from time to time, for the purpose of transacting any proper business of the township.

MCLA 41.97 Moderator of township meeting. [MSA 5.84]

Sec. 97. In the transaction of any business in any township meeting, the supervisor, if present, shall be the moderator of the meeting; and if he shall not be present, the meeting, under the direction of the township clerk, shall elect viva voce, a moderator of the meeting: Provided, That the township clerk shall have the same powers and duties as the moderator until a moderator is chosen.

MCLA 41.98 Moderator of township meeting; powers, duties.
[MSA 5.85]

Sec. 98. The moderator shall preside in, and regulate the proceedings of the meeting; he shall decide all questions of order, and make public declaration of all votes passed; and when any vote so declared by him shall immediately upon such declaration be questioned by 7 or more of the voters, he shall make the vote certain by polling the voters, or dividing the meeting, unless the township shall, by a previous vote, or by their by-laws, have otherwise provided.

MCLA 41.99 Moderator of township meeting; permission to speak.
[MSA 5.86]

Sec. 99. No person shall address the meeting before permission is obtained of the moderator, nor while any other person is speaking by his permission; and all persons at such meeting shall be silent at the request of the moderator.

MCLA 41.100 Moderator of township meeting; disorderly conduct.
[MSA 5.87]

Sec. 100. If, at any township meeting any person shall conduct himself in a disorderly manner, and, after notice from the moderator shall persist therein, the moderator may order him to withdraw from the meeting; and on his refusal, may order the constables, or any other persons to take him into custody until the meeting be adjourned.

MCLA 41.101 Penalty [MSA 5.88]

Sec. 101. Any person who shall refuse to withdraw from such meeting, on being ordered by the moderator to do so, as provided in the preceding section, shall, for every such offense forfeit a sum not exceeding 20 dollars.

MCLA 41.102 Township electors; qualifications, challenging vote. MSA 5.151

Sec. 102. Each inhabitant of any township, having the qualifications of an elector, as specified in the constitution of this state and in statutes enacted thereunder, and no other person, shall have a right to vote on all matters and questions before any township meeting, and when any person claiming the right to vote shall be challenged by a voter, the moderator shall proceed in the same manner as on challenges at the election of township officers.

Note: A person does not have to be registered in the township in order to vote at township meetings -- only have the qualifications to be registered. If there is a challenge as to anyone's right to vote, then his qualifications should be checked according to the following.

> **Act No. 116, P.A. 1954 - Michigan Election Law of 1954, Chapter XXIII - Registration of Electors** *(Amended by Act 188, P.A. 1967; Act 17, P.A. 1972 and Act 370, P.A. 1972)*

MCLA 168.492 Registration of electors; qualifications of elector. MSA 6.1492

Sec. 492. ... an elector ... must be a citizen of the United States; at least 18 years of age; a resident of the state for at least 45 days; and be a resident of the ... township ... on or before the fifth Friday prior to the next ensuing regular or special election or primary election.

R.S. 1846, c. 16 - Powers and Duties of Townships

MCLA 41.2 Inhabitants to be a body corporate; powers. MSA 5.2

Sec. 2. The inhabitants of each organized township shall be a body corporate, and as such, may sue and be sued, ... shall have power to purchase and hold real and personal estate for the public use of the inhabitants, and to convey, alienate and dispose of the same; ...

Attorney General's Opinion 1955-56, Vol. I, No. 2260, p. 513

...(Under this section, making inhabitants of each organized township a body corporate), power to sell real estate owned by the township is vested in the inhabitants thereof ... (and such sale requires a vote of electors of township and township board has no authority to make such sale)....

Attorney General's Opinion 1961-62, No. 3619, p. 249 (specifically p. 256)

...Because townships and their various bodies have only such powers of a local, legislative, and administrative character as are conferred upon them by the state legislature in accordance with the Michigan Constitution ..., it is my opinion that, under the statutes of the State of Michigan as presently in effect, the electors at the annual township meeting are not empowered to mandate the township board to take action. ...

Note: Therefore, approval for the board to sell township lands must be granted by an affirmative vote of the electors upon resolution at the annual meeting or at a special meeting called for that purpose upon petition by twelve freeholders of the township. Although the electors may grant authority for this purpose, they may **not** mandate (force) action.

Act No. 200, P.A. 1849 - Emergency Expenses

MCLA 41.131˙ Emergency expenses, borrowing power. MSA 5.161

Sec. 1. Whenever the qualified electors of any township, at the annual township meeting, neglect or refuse to vote such sums of money as may be necessary to defray the ordinary township expenses, or to meet any emergency expenses, the township board, at any regular meeting, may vote such sums as may be necessary for that purpose, ...

R.S. 1846, c. 16 - Powers and Duties of Townships

MCLA 41.3 Inhabitants, taxing power; restrictions on officers and boards. MSA 5.3

68

Sec. 3. The inhabitants of any township shall have the power at any legal meeting, by a vote of the qualified electors thereof, to grant and vote sums of money, not exceeding such amounts as are or may be limited by law as they shall deem necessary for defraying all proper charges and expenses arising in such township, but ... (sets certain limitations according to assessed valuation and size and provides for elections in certain cases)*... No board, officer or officers shall create any debt or liability against the township, or issue any warrant, certificate or order for the payment of money, except when the creation of such debt or liability or the payment of such money has been authorized by such vote or by the provisions of law.*

Act No. 269, P.A. 1955 - School Code of 1955, Chapter 27 - Libraries

MCLA 340.905 Township library; tax for support. [MSA 15.3905]

Sec. 905. The qualified voters of each township shall have power at any annual township meeting to vote a tax for the support of libraries established in accordance with the provisions of this act.

Note: There must still be a referendum if it would put the township over the fifteen mill limitation.

Act No. 381, P.A. 1927 - Town Hall and Other Buildings *(Amended by Act 36, P.A. 1961 and Act 216, P.A. 1963)*

MCLA 41.246 Town hall; tax for maintenance, upkeep, or repairs. [MSA 5.2376]

Sec. 6. Any township of this state may at any annual township meeting vote a tax upon the property of such township of not to exceed 1/20 of 1% of the assessed valuation of such township according to the assessed valuation of all the real or personal property of said township of the preceding year and the money so raised shall be used by the township board for the maintenance, upkeep or repairs of the township hall, fire station, library or other public buildings of the township.

Note: There must still be a referendum if it would put the township over the fifteen mill limitation.

R.S. 1846, c. 16 - Powers and Duties of Townships

MCLA 41.4 Orders and by-laws. [MSA 5.4]

Sec. 4. The inhabitants of each township may, at any legal meeting, by a vote of the qualified electors thereof, make all such orders and by-laws for determining the time and manner in which cattle, horses, swine, sheep and other animals shall be restrained from going at large in the highways, and for directing and managing the prudential affairs of the township, as they shall judge most conducive to the peace, welfare and good order thereof.

MCLA 41.5 Orders and by-laws; penalties. [MSA 5.5]

Sec. 5. They may annex to such orders and by-laws suitable penalties, not exceeding 10 dollars for any 1 breach thereof, to be recovered by complaint before any (court in whose jurisdiction) the offense shall have been committed.

MCLA 41.6 By-laws; publication, effect. [MSA 5.6]

Sec. 6. The by-laws of any township shall, before the same shall take effect, be published by posting up copies thereof in 3 of the most public places in the township; and such by-laws duly made and published shall be binding upon all persons coming within the limits of the township, as well as upon the inhabitants thereof.

Note: It should be pointed out that there are many statutes placing direct responsibility upon the township board to make ordinances for the health, safety and general welfare of the township residents. **Those statutes take precedence over sections 41.4, 41.5 and 41.6 above.**

MCLA 41.61 Township supervisor; clerk and assessors, appointment, compensation,... [MSA 5.52]

Sec. 61. The supervisor shall, by virtue of his office, be an assessor of his township. At the annual meeting in any township, the electors of such township, present at such meeting, may provide for the appointment, by the supervisor, of a clerk to assist him in his duties. Such clerk shall receive such compensation as the township board may determine, ... In any township, in addition to the supervisor, the township board may provide for the appointment of assessors, not exceeding 2, for such township....

MCLA 41.95 **Township officers; compensation, township meeting.** (MSA 5.82]

Sec. 95. The officers composing the township boards, board of registration,* board of health, board of review* and inspectors of election* shall be entitled to such salary as shall be fixed by the

----

*Several statutes covering election or appointment, membership, qualifications, quorum and compensation fixes responsibility on the township board to establish salary, bonus, commission, per diem or remuneration for such other expenses as may be incurred by said officers. It becomes important to check other applicable statutes before using this section.

----

electors at the annual township meeting, and, in case of the neglect or failure of the electors to fix such salary, the officers shall be entitled to the same salary as his predecessor in office received the year before.

Same; compensation, referendum. In those townships which have abolished the annual township meeting pursuant to the provisions of Public Act No. 283 of the Public Acts of 1955, being section 168.361 [MSA 6.1361] of the Compiled Laws of 1948 (Act No. 116, P.A. 1954 - Michigan Election Law of 1954, Chapter XVI - Township Officials), the salary for officers composing the township board,* board of registration,* board of review* and inspectors of election,* shall be determined by the township board. If a petition

----

*See footnote in 41.95 above.

----

is filed within 30 days after the township board votes such salary, signed by 10% of the qualified electors of the township praying that the question shall be submitted to the electorate, the township board shall call a special election and submit the question of salary to the electors. The vote upon the question of approving such a resolution shall be by a ballot which shall be in substantially the following form:

"Vote on proposition of approving a resolution of the township board providing a salary of ..... dollars, per annum, to the ....., in lieu of all per diem charges for his services.

Make a cross in the appropriate square.

To approve said resolution. Yes ☐

To approve said resolution. No ☐"

If a majority of the electors voting upon such a resolution shall disapprove the same such officer shall draw the same salary his precedessor in office drew the year before.

Salaried officials. The salary of township officials who are paid a salary may be determined by resolution adopted by the township board. The electors at any subsequent township meeting may alter the amount of salary fixed by any such resolutions. No salaries shall be raised within 60 days prior to an election.

MCLA 41.96 Other services, compensation. MSA 5.83

Sec. 96. For services not otherwise provided for by law, rendered to townships by township officers in the duties of their respective offices, the township board shall audit and allow such compensation as they shall deem reasonable.*

----

*See footnote in MCLA 41.95 above.

Note: For example, the township board may appoint a trustee as superintendent of the water department, the township clerk as a member of a joint recreation commission, the township treasurer as a collector for utility bills, etc. For these services the **township board only** determines the amount and method of payment.

Act No. 277, P.A. 1921 - Township Nurse

MCLA 338.391 Township nurse; employment; appropriation. MSA 14.711

Sec. 1. The inhabitants of any township shall have the power at any legal meeting, by a vote of the qualified electors thereof, to grant and vote money for the purpose of employing a public nurse or nurses for said township.

SPECIAL TOWNSHIP MEETINGS

Special meetings of the township inhabitants may be called for the purpose of transacting any lawful township business. They are precipitated by the filing of a petition signed by any twelve electors of the township, specifying the purpose therefor.

The petition is served upon the township clerk who presents it to the township board. The board then gives an order to the township clerk specifying the date, time and place for the meeting and the item or items which are to be discussed. The meeting must be held not more than twenty nor less than fifteen days from the time of making the order, which shall be left with the township clerk within two days after it is made.

Within another two days, the clerk shall proceed to post copies in three of the most public places in the township, and if deemed advisable, in a newspaper of general circulation in the township. This notice shall appear at least five days before the day which has been set for the meeting.

Although the meetings are conducted in the same manner as the annual township meeting, **only** the item or items which appear in the notice of the meeting may be discussed. **No other business may be transacted.** As at the annual meeting, only the supervisor and clerk have specific responsibilities as officers; the treasurer and the trustees are simply considered township electors during the proceedings.

R.S. 1846, c. 16 - Township Meetings

MCLA 41.24 Special meetings; filling vacancies. [MSA 5.24]

Sec. 24. Special township meetings ... may be called and proceeded in, in all respects, as in the case of newly organized townships ... (when a township shall become disorganized) ...

Note: Omitted portions of the above citation are no longer applicable.

MCLA 41.25 Special meetings; lawful purposes, manner. [MSA 5.25]

Sec. 25. Special township meetings shall also be held for the purpose of transacting any other lawful business, when ordered by the township board on a request to them in writing, signed by any 12 electors of the township, specifying therein the purposes for which such meeting is to be held; and the mode of proceedings at all special meetings shall be the same as at the annual meetings.

MCLA 41.26 Special meetings; order, contents. [MSA 5.26]

Sec. 26. Every order for a special township meeting shall specify the purpose for which it is to be held, and the time when, and the place where it shall be held;...

Note: Omitted portion of the above citation is no longer applicable.

MCLA 41.27 Special meetings; order, filing. [MSA 5.27]

Sec. 27. The time appointed for holding any special township meeting shall not be more than 20, nor less than 15 days from the time of making the order therefor; and such order shall be left with the township clerk within 2 days after the making thereof, and shall be recorded in his office.

MCLA 41.28 Special meetings; notice. [MSA 5.28]

Sec. 28. The said clerk shall within 2 days after such order shall be left with him, cause copies thereof to be posted up in 3 of the most public places in the township; and if there be a newspaper printed in such township, he shall also cause a copy to be published therein if practicable, at least 5 days before the day appointed for such special meeting.

VOTING AT MEETINGS

Roll call votes may be taken upon demand -- this is not a debatable matter. Also, some votes must always be by roll call -- i.e., a resolution on bond issues, ordinances, and usually for the expenditure of large sums of money. In a roll call vote, the precedence usually is for the clerk to call for the vote in the following order: supervisor, clerk, treasurer and the trustees in order of seniority. This could be altered by local regulation. The record of a roll call vote must show one of four responses for each board member: aye, nay, abstain or absent. On other votes the record should show a total of votes cast for each response, or it may show "passed unanimously."

The supervisor has an absolute right to vote on all motions properly made at any meeting of the township inhabitants or the township board. Although he/she may break a tie vote, under no circumstances may he/she vote once and then vote a second time to break a tie that he/she has created.

TOWNSHIP BOARD MEETINGS

How effective the township board is in maintaining an efficient, well run township depends almost entirely upon the manner in which township board meetings are held. A sloppily-run, disorganized meeting with officers obviously lacking in knowledge and unprepared for discussion of matters which need attention does nothing to instill confidence in their abilities to handle township business and leaves the citizens disenchanted and unhappy.

Attitudes of board members should show real concern for each item on the agenda, no matter how insignificant nor how many. Uppermost in the minds of each should be the tremendous responsibility vested in him, both as an individual and as a member of the board, to meet the needs and demands of the citizens of the township. He should care enough to make sure that he is thoroughly informed about any matter he is voting on.

The sole purpose of the township board meeting is to coordinate and establish procedure for implementation of state and local laws and to provide utilities and services to the township residents. Like the board of directors of a great corporation, the township board must not only take care of the needs of its constituents, but must keep pace with the latest administrative and operational techniques to enable them to do it in the best possible way.

Nowhere in our democratic society is there a governing body which is under closer scrutiny of its constituents than the township board. A well conducted meeting will make friends. A poorly conducted one will cast doubt upon the board's ability to legally and properly handle the affairs of the township.

We are often asked if it is proper to begin a meeting with prayer. There is neither constitutional nor statutory prohibition

75

against this practice. It is entirely a matter of judgment on the part of the governing body itself.

Physical comfort of both citizens and township officials attending board meetings is of paramount importance. The room should be properly ventilated and large enough to provide a chair for everyone who wishes to attend. There should be enough light to enable people to read documents or take notes. Some township boards issue invitations to and make special provisions to accommodate representatives of the news media -- more of this should be done.

If a room is large and acoustically deficient, serious consideration should be given to installing a public address system, with microphones for the officials and one or more floor microphones for audience use. Anyone permitted to speak should be requested to come to the floor microphone to make his statement. Care should be taken to properly adjust the volume so it is only loud enough for comments to be heard in the farthest corner of the room. A system turned on too loud is worse than having none at all.

Another aid to good meetings is the use of electronic equipment such as a tape recorder, which should be plugged into the public address system if there is one. A tape recorder serves both to record every single word spoken at the meeting and to make it possible for the clerk to develop a more accurate set of minutes. Some townships also have a clerical employee or public stenographer on hand to operate the tape recorder or record the proceedings, which then leaves the clerk free to participate more freely in the discussion. However, the clerk should still make his or her own record of each motion passed and use the tape recorder for verification and correction.

Always start a meeting promptly at the hour announced in the notice. Nothing irritates citizens more than when they must wait for a quorum of the board to make their appearance. There is no statute permitting the supervisor to delay beginning until all board members are present -- just as soon as a quorum is on hand the meeting should start. On the other hand, it would be inappropriate and certainly a violation of law to begin a meeting before the established time.

Long drawn out meetings create disinterest, boredom and in some cases agitation among township citizens. If meetings tend to consistently have long agendas, then it would be better to have shorter meetings at closer intervals.

It is not advisable to permit citizens to enter into general discussion with the board during formal sessions. Anyone wishing to comment must request permission to speak and may not do so until recognized by the supervisor, who may also limit the amount of time that may be used by any one individual or group. Generally the public comments are accepted only during the time set aside for that purpose on the agenda.

The following statute is of tremendous significance to all government officials, including township board members. It is the most important law covering the matter of notices of meetings and providing protection to the general public regarding the right to know. It should be read carefully before proceeding with this section on township board meetings.

Act No. 261, P.A. 1968 - Public Board Meetings

AN ACT to require that meetings of the governing bodies of political subdivisions and of certain authorities and other agencies performing essential governmental functions shall be open to the public.

MCLA 15.251 Definitions. [MSA 4.1800(1)]

Sec. 1. As used in this act:

(1) "Board" means the board of commissioners of any county, the council of any city or village, the board of trustees of any township, the board of education of any school district, the governing body of any state-supported or partially supported college or university, or the board, commission or other governing body of any state or municipal authority or department created by law which has for its purpose the performance of an essential governmental function.

(2) "Public meeting" means that part of any meeting of a board during which it votes upon any ordinance, resolution, motion or other official action proposed by or to the board dealing with the receipt, borrowing or disbursement of funds or the acquisition, use or disposal of services or of any supplies, materials, equipment or other property or the fixing of personal or property rights, privileges, immunities, duties or obligations of any person or group of persons. The term "public meeting" shall not mean any meeting, the publication of the facts concerning which would disclose the

institution, progress or result of an investigation undertaken by a board in the performance of its official duties.

MCLA 15.252   Public meeting of board open to public.
[MSA 4.1800(2)]

Sec. 2.   *Every public meeting of a board shall be open to the public.*

MCLA 15.253   Public meetings; notice.   [MSA 4.1800(3)

Sec. 3.   *Every board shall hold all public meetings at specified times and places, of which public notice shall be given. Public notice of the schedule of regular meetings shall be given once for each calendar or fiscal year, and shall show the regular dates and times for meetings and the place at which meetings are held. Public notice of each special meeting and of each rescheduled regular or special meeting shall be given of the date, time and place of each meeting.   Public notice shall be given by posting a copy of the notice prominently at the principal office of the body holding the meeting or at the public building in which the meeting is to be held, or by publishing the notice once in a newspaper of general circulation in the political subdivision where the meeting will be held, at least 3 days prior to the time of the first regularly scheduled meeting in the case of regular meetings, and at least 12 hours prior to the time of the meeting in case of special or rescheduled meetings. The board holding any meeting shall supply, on request, copies of the public notice thereof to any newspaper of general circulation in the political subdivision in which the meeting will be held and to any radio station* which regularly broadcasts into the political subdivision.*

**This now would also include television stations.*

REGULAR TOWNSHIP BOARD MEETINGS

Michigan law requires that each general law township meet at least once every three months.   Charter townships are required to

78

meet at least once monthly. The resolution to establish the time, date and place for holding regular meetings of the township board is adopted by the board, usually at the first regular meeting following the annual meeting. (**Electors have no authority to establish these meeting times.**) The resolution is published by way of a notice in a newspaper of general circulation in the township. No further notice is required for regular board meetings unless one should fall on a holiday or a disaster should necessitate a change of date. Notice of a change must be handled the same as for a special meeting by publication and posting in a number of places easily accessible to the public.

A regular township board meeting is conducted in the same manner as the annual meeting -- according to Robert's Rules of Order -- except that in this instance the supervisor serves as chairman of the board. In the absence of the supervisor, the township clerk calls the meeting to order with the first order of business being to select a moderator. This position is usually relegated to the senior trustee. A typical agenda would be:

1. Roll call of officers
2. Reading of minutes of previous meeting
3. Correspondence
4. Petitions
5. Old business
6. New business
7. Public comments
8. Adjournment

There must be a quorum present before the meeting may be started. (A quorum for a five member board is three, and for a seven member board it is four.) Motions are passed by a simple majority of those present. It should be noted that this would permit a motion, under certain circumstances, to pass by less than a simple majority of the township board. For instance, three members of a five member board are at a meeting. One makes a motion, the second offers his support. Upon voice vote, those two vote "yes" and the supervisor votes "no." Thus the motion would pass with just two votes out of a five member board. This points up how important it is that all members of the board attend all meetings.

Citizens have a right to be heard at a regular township board meeting. Most township boards have a place at the end of the agenda for public comments. It is the supervisor's responsibility to decide at each meeting at what point and for how long any one person or group will be permitted to speak and what other rules will govern public comments. He simply asks, "Is there anyone in the audience who wishes to be heard?" The only other time someone from the audience might be given an opportunity to speak is if he has pertinent or vital information which the board needs to consider in its deliberations regarding some particular matter.

There is no statute requiring a prepared agenda for township board meetings. However, preparation and distribution of an agenda prior to a meeting is conducive to good, sound, orderly conduct of business. **At regular township board meetings there is no requirement that only matters on the agenda may be considered.** The township board itself, at the first organizational meeting following election of officers, could by its own resolution direct that an agenda be prepared by the township clerk in advance of each regular meeting. In the absence of a resolution or instruction to the contrary, additional items may be placed on the agenda of the regular meeting by unanimous consent of the board members in attendance at the meeting.

SPECIAL TOWNSHIP BOARD MEETINGS

The comments in the previous section regarding conduct of regular township board meetings apply equally to the conduct of special meetings.

Date, time and place of special meetings are set **only** by the supervisor or the township board. They should be called only if it is impossible to accomplish some particular order of business at a regular meeting. If a township board is holding many special meetings, then consideration should be given to having more regular meetings. (A number of township boards in Michigan hold regular weekly meetings.)

If all members of the board are present at a special meeting, any item may be discussed in addition to those which appear in the notice of the meeting, provided that a majority of those present approve the addition, and the public notice of the meeting is not too restrictive of the matters to be considered. However, if even one member of the board is absent, then the agenda is restricted to **only** those items which appear in the notice. No rules may be suspended in this regard, since both the statute and parliamentary procedure make this very specific (see **MCLA 41.72a** at the beginning of this section on Township Board Meetings).

Public notice of special meetings must be given by posting of a notice on the building where the meeting is to be held at least twelve hours prior to the meeting time. (See **MCLA 15.253** [MSA 4.1800(3)])

Although public comments must be provided for in the agenda, special meetings should never be confused with or used as public hearings for planning, zoning, services or utilities which are lawfully the responsibility of the township board. They should simply be considered as an **aid** to solving a particular problem or project, focusing attention upon such things as services not otherwise provided for by law or a decision to participate with other units of government in area-wide services. These matters often create a great deal of interest and elicit more public comment than can be handled at a regular meeting.

> **Example:** *An invitation is received by a township board to participate, along with a number of other political subdivisions, in a park and recreation service or some other mass-interest proposal for a regional service or utility. The board might logically decide that such a momentous decision should more accurately reflect the attitude of the township as a whole. Rather than calling for a costly advisory referendum, since one will be required later when the proposition is finalized, the supervisor or the township board could call a special meeting at which the inhabitants would have an opportunity to express their opinions and perhaps arrive at a genuine consensus to guide the township board in its deliberations.*

ANNUAL TOWNSHIP BOARD MEETING

The annual meeting of the (general law) township board, commonly known as settlement day, is held on the second Tuesday next preceding the annual township meeting and usually begins at the same hour established for regular meetings. As with all board meetings, it is open to the public.

The annual township board meeting should never be confused with the annual meeting of the township. Nor is there any provision in the law that would allow business of this meeting to be handled at a regular or special township board meeting -- these are separate and distinct from each other.

The purpose of the meeting is to audit and settle all claims against the township, to examine and audit the accounts of the township treasurer and to audit and settle the accounts of all other township officers authorized to handle public moneys. Provisions are to be made for the protection and preservation of township records, books and papers, and the board determines the bond and sureties required from the township clerk within thirty days preceding the annual township election. Most boards also take advantage of this time to complete preparation of the budget for the ensuing year.

JOINT TOWNSHIP BOARD MEETINGS - DIVISION AND ANNEXATION

Please note the citations for these meetings. Detailed information will be found in the section on Boundary Commission.

R.S. 1846, c. 16 - Township Board

MCLA 41.70 Township board; membership, quorum; populous townships. [MSA 5.62]

Sec. 70.   The supervisor, 2 trustees, the township treasurer and the township clerk, shall constitute the township board, any 3 of whom shall constitute a quorum for the transaction of business: Provided, That in townships now or hereafter having a population of 5,000 or over as determined by the last federal decennial census or by any federal decennial census hereafter taken or now or hereafter having 3,000 or over registered electors, the supervisor, the township treasurer, the township clerk and 4 trustees, to be elected by the registered electors of the township as provided in section 13 of chapter 1 of part 4 of Act No. 351 of the Public Acts of 1925, as amended, being section 171.13* of the Compiled Laws of 1948, ...

----

*Repealed - see now **MCLA 168.358 and 168.362** [MSA 6.1358 AND 6.1362] *(Act No. 116, P.A. 1954).*

MCLA 41.71 Raising of quorum. [MSA 5.63]

Note: Although this particular section has not been repealed, it no longer applies since it dealt with membership on the board of certain justices of the peace, who are no longer in existence.

MCLA 41.72 Annual meeting; date; claims, auditing, settling,... [MSA 5.64]

Sec. 72. The township board shall meet annually on the second Tuesday next preceding the annual township meeting for the purpose of auditing and settling all claims...

Note: The annual meeting referred to in this section is commonly known as settlement day.

MCLA 41.72a Regular meetings, time, place, ...; special meetings, notice, business; publication of proceedings. [MSA 5.64(1)]

Sec. 72a. In addition to the annual meeting of the township board, the township board shall provide by resolution for the time and place of its regular meetings, and shall hold at least 1 regular meeting every 3 months. If any time set for the holding of a regular meeting of the township board shall be a holiday, then such regular meeting shall be held at the same time and place on the next secular day which is not a holiday. ... Special meetings of the township board shall be held at such time as may be fixed by the board at any meeting or when in the discretion of the supervisor it appears advisable. Upon call of the supervisor the township clerk shall give notice of the time and place of such meeting to each member either in person or by leaving a written notice at his address. No business shall be transacted at any special meeting of the township board unless the same has been stated in the notice of such meeting. However, if all the members of the board are present at any special meeting thereof, then any business which might lawfully come before a regular meeting of the board may be transacted at such special meeting.

In every township which now has, or hereafter acquires, an assessed valuation of $25,000,000.00 or more, the township board, within 10 days after each meeting of the board, shall publish the proceedings thereof in some newspaper of general circulation in the township. The publication of a synopsis of such proceedings, prepared by the township clerk and approved by the supervisor, showing the substance of each separate proceeding of the board is a sufficient compliance with the requirements of this section.

MCLA 41.72b Township board; public meetings; executive sessions. [MSA 5.64(2)]

Sec. 72b. All regular and special meetings of the township board shall be open to the public, and the rules of the board shall provide that citizens shall have a reasonable opportunity to be heard. The board may hold executive sessions, but no final action shall be taken at any executive session.

Note: See also **Act No. 261, P.A. 1968 (MCLA 15.251 - 15.253** [MSA 4.1800(1) - 4.1800(3)]) at the beginning of the section on Meetings.

MCLA 41.73 Annual meeting; accounts of township officers, audit; powers re records, bonds. [MSA 5.65]

Sec. 73. The said board shall, at their annual meeting in each year, examine and audit the accounts of the township treasurer for all monies received and disbursed by him as such treasurer; and they shall also audit and settle the accounts of all other township officers who are authorized by law to receive or disburse any public moneys by virtue of their offices; they shall also have power and it shall be their duty to cause the provisions of the statute for the protection and preservation of township records, books, and papers to be enforced; and they shall determine the amount of the bond and the number of sureties to be required from the township clerk, as provided by law, in each year, within 30 days next preceding the annual township election.

Act No. 359, P.A. 1947 - Charter Townships

MCLA 42.7 Charter township board; regular ... meetings, notice; quorum, rules, journal, voting; public attendance; members, attendance. [MSA 5.46(7)]

MCLA 42.8 Same; publication of proceedings, notices and ordinances. [MSA 5.46(8)]

MCLA 42.24 Budget for next fiscal year; submittal by township officers; time. [MSA 5.46(24)]

MCLA 42.26 Same; hearing, notice, public inspection. [MSA 5.46(26)]

MCLA 42.27 Budget; adoption by township board; levy of taxation; limitation; increase; separate appropriation for fire or police department; collection of tax; interim budget. [MSA 5.46(27)]

Note: See the charter township act which is reproduced in full elsewhere in this book.

R.S. 1846, c. 17 - Division of Townships

MCLA 41.111 - 118 ... (provide for meetings regarding division or annexation) ... [MSA 5.2201 - 5.2208]

MCLA 41.115 Meeting of township boards, notice. [MSA 5.2205]

Sec. 5. Whenever a meeting of the township boards of 2 or more townships shall be required, in order to carry into effect the provisions of this chapter, such meeting may be called by either of the supervisors; but the supervisor calling the same shall give at least 6 days' notice in writing to all the other officers, of the time and place at which such meeting is to be held.

Note: The township board also serves as the township board of health and may serve as the township recreation commission. See the appropriate section in Duties and Responsibilities of Boards, Commissions, Agencies, etc.

DUTIES AND RESPONSIBILITIES -
ELECTED AND APPOINTED TOWNSHIP OFFICIALS
AND EMPLOYEES

How much time is a township official expected to devote to meeting his/her responsibilities to the citizens who elected him/her?

What effect does a public servant's attitude have on the citizens of the township?

There are no simple answers to these questions. First of all, a public official is expected to and should give every moment within his/her physical capacity to serving the best interests of the township. Most people agree that being a government official is not a part-time job. An elected officer is no different than a fireman or policeman who must be ready at all times to render service to the community. It is only logical to extend this, then, to state that being an elected official is a full-time, twenty-four-hour-a-day job.

Emphasis for this is found in the fact that the legislature considered local government important enough to warrant guaranteed continuity through succession to office by persons specially selected, designated and trained to succeed each local government official in the event of disaster, as well as to provide for temporary appointments to fill vacancies created because of various other situations.

A township officer must be particularly careful since there is no general law establishing a time for him/her to be available daily at office or home to serve the public. The general property tax act does require the township supervisor to be present in the township on tax day -- December 31 of each year. It also requires that the township treasurer "shall be at some central location" to collect taxes each Friday in December. The election law requires that the township clerk shall be available at certain times to take registrations, and on all national, state and local election days. Some boards and commissions also have certain specific times to meet and to be available to the public.

The temptation is great to hide behind the specific and legalistic language of these statutes and say, "The law requires that I be at my place of duty only on such and such a day" and let it go at that. It is not that simple. Public awareness that it is local government officials who are primarily responsible for assessing, levying and collecting the property tax has increased greatly during recent years because of better coverage of such activities by the news media and because additional courses on government are being taught in the schools and universities. If a person wants to keep a public position, enough time should be spent doing it to satisfy the people.

Angered citizens, or even township board members, sometimes ask how to deal with a board member who refuses to attend meetings, is constantly under the influence of alcohol, or perhaps on the few occasions when present at a meeting is a general nuisance and an actual stumbling block to progress. He/she cannot be fired. His/her salary cannot be withheld as a penalty. No statute gives the township board power to compel attendance* or punish for im-

----

*MCLA 42.7 [MSA 5.46(7)] does give such authority to a charter township board.

----

proper behavior. Of course, any official paid on a per diem (daily) basis for time actually spent on the job who does not attend meetings or perform the required duties receives no pay.

Statutes do provide that charges of misfeasance, malfeasance or nonfeasance in office may be made against any elected township official (see section on Elected Officials). Petitions for removal may be filed with the governor, there may be a recall election or on election day itself the people may remove any official by electing someone else to the office.

Township records must be available to the public at certain times (see chapter four under the heading "Preservation of Township Records and History"). However, nobody can tell a township official when and where he has to be available to the public (other than the statutory provisions mentioned above). But any person who takes an oath of office to serve the people should realize that he/she is in fact pledging to be constantly available to them. Since the township officer is closer to constituent citizens than any other government official, there is an extra degree of obligation. Arrangements should be made to be available for as much of the day as possible, even beyond normal office hours, and when out of the township on vacation or business, there should be a telephone number provided if an emergency should arise.

If an individual is not willing to do this, then he/she should not take the job in the first place. Can your constituents say with pride, "My township supervisor (clerk, treasurer, trustee) is always available when I need him/her."? If your answer is yes, then your chances for remaining in office are enhanced.

Each township official would also be well advised to become familiar with the duties and responsibilities of fellow officials. It will soon be evident that the duties of each, though specifically spelled out and distinct from each other, nevertheless are closely interrelated. One cannot serve efficiently and effectively without full and complete cooperation of the others.

Furthermore, we would point out that the basis for all understanding is adequate communication. To fail in communicating with one another is the surest way to bring about disorganization and present a bad image to the public. Basic to good communication is knowledge that is precise and accurate.

The old time politician who covered up lack of knowledge with a glib tongue and fancy clothes is no longer welcome in government. Today's citizen is too well informed to fall for that approach for very long. Public servants, more so than ever before, are judged not alone upon personal appearance (although that too is important), but more importantly upon whether they are scrupulously honest and aboveboard and whether they can be relied upon to be precise and accurate.

One of the most valuable assets a township official can possess is to be fully knowledgeable about township business, whether it is being discussed at a board or committee meeting or with a private citizen. Public servants are expected to know what they are doing. Statements such as "I reckon that's the way it is," "I guess that's the way it should be done," "I don't know anything about this, but this is the way we've always done it" or "I think I read somewhere that--" do nothing to enhance anyone's credibility.

Some would argue that precision and accuracy are involved only in matters of science. The author, however, believes that these qualities are the basis upon which sound relationships may be formed between public servants and the citizens of a community. People assume that when someone is elected or appointed to an office or employed for some specific purpose, he or she brings some degree of expertise to the office. They will not usually give a pat on the back when it is demonstrated, but surely will complain loudly when it is not present. The bigmouth practicing the art of flowery but imprecise language, speaking primarily to hear himself talk and seldom stopping to listen, may get attention for a while, but soon the lack of knowledge and concern for opinions of others will become apparent. Only those who are accurate and considerate will make the grade. If a citizen has to make a choice, the one who speaks on the basis of fact will come in far ahead of one who speaks out of speculation.

Such knowledge does not come without effort and time spent in research and study. Some may feel there is not time to do all that is indicated along this line, or may complain that there is no resource material available. This is a negative attitude, showing little concern for doing the best job possible. As the old saying goes, "Anything-worth doing is worth doing well," and township government is certainly no exception. In fact, perhaps it leads the list since so many people are affected by its decisions and actions. Ask yourself, "Do I care enough about my job to do the best I can with it? If I do, then how can I attain a high plateau of precision and accuracy?"

There never seem to be enough hours in a township official's day. Furthermore, our fast-moving, complex society does not allow the luxury of long periods in which to develop an opinion for any one problem, let alone the many faced every day in township government. Although there is need to be constantly ready to render opinions about myriads of subjects, never make the mistake of guessing. If an opinion cannot be supported by facts, it is better to say, "I don't know the answer to that right now, but I'll check into it and get back to you tomorrow."

Many periodicals published by various professional and trade associations deal with matters which, although often dull, uninteresting and full of statistical charts and analyses, will still provide local government officials with much background information needed for various aspects of government operation. Numerous publications available from state and federal government agencies are also required reading for the well informed official.

If it sounds as though the author is telling you to do your homework, that is precisely what is meant. The public servant should welcome the routing of such material to him/her and develop the discipline of setting aside time to read it. Furthermore, a course in speed-reading would be helpful since there are so many publications which can be useful. The expertise of professional consultants should also be freely called upon.

When dealing with facts, there is often great temptation to pick out a few facts that support one's position and ignore the rest. Experience has shown that a public official may get away with this a few times, but sooner or later someone will spot this weakness.

The mind should never be closed to giving proper weight to **all** facts, suggestions, recommendations and counsel that may come from reference materials or other people.

When making a presentation, chronological compilation and presentation of facts may not necessarily achieve desired results. A number of other elements are also important -- such things as correct spelling, punctuation and grammar, relevance and proper context, and supporting documents. In other words -- accuracy and precision.

A public official becomes stronger in direct relation to the strength of his philosophical belief that a statement should never be made in public which cannot be backed up with facts. If a quotation from an article or book is used, care should be taken that it is absolutely identical with the reference, and that it is properly identified. Inaccurate quotations provide poor support, sometimes even resulting in an accusation that the misquote was done deliberately for personal advantage.

The most successful public servant is one who couples native intelligence with insatiable curiosity, seeks out facts and carefully weighs them against other facts, so that a chain reaction of information leads to conclusions which are irrefutable and may be used publicly without fear of error leading to derisive criticism for a stand taken. In summary, accuracy is a state of mind that is painstaking, caring, patient and reasonable, and ultimately creative as well. Not only does it look up facts, it discovers them in the first place.

R.S. 1846, c. 16 - Resignations and Vacancies

MCLA 41.58 Temporary appointments; appointees' duties.
[MSA 5.42]

Sec. 58. Whenever there shall be a vacancy, or when the incumbent shall, from any cause, be unable to perform the duties of his office, in either of the township offices, except that of township treasurer (see section on Duties and Responsibilities of Treasurer), *the township board may make temporary appointments of suitable persons to discharge the duties of such offices respectively; and such persons, so appointed, shall take the oath of office, or file the notice of acceptance required by law, and shall continue to discharge such duties until the office is filled by election or until the disability aforesaid be removed.*

90

Act No. 359, P.A. 1947 - Charter Townships

MCLA 42.9 Officers, powers and duties; resolution creating additional officers, limitations. [MSA 5.46(9)]

*Sec. 9. The township supervisor, township clerk, township treasurer, and constables in each **charter township** shall have and perform the duties and functions required of such officers by state law. The township board may, by resolution, upon the recommendation of the supervisor, or of the township superintendent if one shall be appointed, create such additional officers as may be necessary to administer the affairs of the township government, or may combine any administrative offices in any manner not inconsistent with state law, and prescribe the duties thereof. No creation of any additional administrative office or combination thereof shall abolish the offices of township clerk or township treasurer nor diminish any of the duties or responsibilities of those offices which are prescribed by state law.*

DUTIES AND RESPONSIBILITIES - TOWNSHIP BOARD

A township is an instrumentality of the state for purposes of local government. The township board is a governing body of general, special and limited jurisdiction and in any organized general law or charter township may exercise only those powers which are conferred upon it by the constitution and the legislature, or such as may be necessary to the exercise of their corporate power. The board is concerned, therefore, with establishing policy and operational rules and regulations and providing for the general health, safety and welfare of people in the township.

All township boards are composed of a supervisor, a clerk, a treasurer and two or four trustees. In a general law township, the board must meet at least quarterly in addition to the annual meeting (which may never be changed from the date established by law). In a charter township, the board is required to meet at least monthly. Board members attend township meetings as electors, except for the supervisor and clerk who have specific duties assigned to them by law. Organization and conduct of board meetings are discussed at length in the first part of this chapter.

The board's administrative and legislative functions may include but are not limited to the following:

1. Serving as the township board of health.
2. Acting as the park commission.
3. Appointing members of other administrative boards or agencies in accordance with applicable statutory provisions (election commission, zoning board of appeals, board of review and others).
4. Establishing and collecting taxes according to statutory regulations and limitations.
5. Building and maintaining public works.
6. Establishing minimum building requirements.
7. Establishing and enforcing zoning through a planning commission or zoning board.
8. Providing police protection and/or traffic officers.
9. Providing fire protection.
10. Participating with other governing bodies or special authorities for public improvements or services.
11. Reviewing and accepting or rejecting plats submitted by land developers.
12. Examining, reviewing, approving/disapproving all claims against the township.
13. Employing personnel of all types to carry out the board's responsibilities (secretaries, clerks, bookkeepers, engineers, building inspectors, etc.).
14. Many other matters which may be properly brought before the township board.

The board makes all final decisions regarding acquisition of property, parks, cemeteries and many other things, as well as zoning of township lands for proper use, based upon specific recommendations of numerous agencies, boards, commissions and authorities. There may be public hearings or not, according to the particular statute or ordinance involved. Petitionary power being inherent with the people, township citizens may bring before the township board petitions bearing proper signatures regarding specific improvements, grievances or other matters. The board may act upon petitions calling for such things as fire protection, police protection, sale of beer, wine and liquor by the glass, lighting districts, street improvements, a township park commission, community centers, libraries and many others.

Township boards have a tremendous amount of power to adopt ordinances and regulations to secure the public's health, safety and welfare, and to provide for the establishment of various agencies and authorities to enforce its ordinances and to meet certain other requirements of the law. This may be done by the board upon its own initiation, or at the request of township citizens as indicated above. The board must always consider whether it is best to act alone within the township, or to join with another political subdivision to provide services. Of utmost importance also is determination of how much the township may legitimately contribute from its general or specially designated funds for certain purposes. If no referendum is petitioned, the township board may be called upon to make final and far-reaching decisions regarding planning and zoning, making it imperative that every factor of consideration be carefully and thoroughly developed during public hearings.

The board must be particularly aware of its limitations as to which community activities it may support, since the public is often sadly lacking in knowledge of what the law permits. For instance, a few citizens may submit a petition requesting that funds be provided for a Little League baseball program. The only way this can be done is if it is part of a township-wide recreation program which might include a general baseball program for all age groups.

Land use being one of the most critical problems facing government today, the board has great responsibility to make sure the proper individuals are appointed to the township planning commission or the township zoning board. Statutory provisions stipulating membership for these agencies should be carefully studied and followed to the letter.

Generally appointments are made by the supervisor, with the approval of the township board, although in some instances other provisions are made by statute. Such appointees may be removed in the same manner, for cause, following a hearing. Vacancies for unexpired terms are filled for the remainder of the terms.

There are statutory limitations regarding compatibility of office which spell out when a person holding a certain office may or may not be appointed to another position. It is always wise to avoid making appointments of people who might be considered in conflict of interest in a particular assignment, either because of another office held or because of his/her own financial interest.

Where the amount of compensation is not specified by statute, the township board has complete authority to establish salaries and fringe benefits and to participate in labor negotiations for and on behalf of the citizens of the township. Although township electors determine the amount of compensation for elected officials, they have absolutely no responsibility for nor right to interfere with the selection or dismissal of township employees, the establishment of compensation for them or any rules and regulations regarding their working conditions. These are entirely within the purview of the township board.

DUTIES AND RESPONSIBILITIES - SUPERVISOR

The title of the position and the fact that he/she functions within a broad spectrum of operations places the township supervisor in an area of responsibility enjoyed by few other government officials. He/she has always been looked upon as a person who can do anything for anyone at any time under any conditions and generally is expected to resolve any grievance, large or small.

In accordance with the provisions of several statutes which detail the procedure, the supervisor (on specific authorization or that which may be imposed upon him by the township board) acts as final authority for the review, sufficiency and filing of bonds for township officials in his/her township. We emphasize that **original copies of these bonds must be filed in a safe place.**

With the township clerk, the supervisor acts as agent for all development and improvement in the township, contracts with federal, state and other local units of government for many services and utilities and signs all deeds and titles for disposition of township-owned property, as well as other legal documents involving suits against or in behalf of the township, as occasion arises.

The office is comparable to that of chairman of the board of directors of any large corporation. The supervisor is charged with the conduct of all township board meetings and must see that proper action is taken regarding correspondence, petitions and such other matters as may be properly brought before the board, and also serves as moderator for township meetings. He/she has lawful right to vote at any meeting of the township inhabitants or the township board and, although he/she may break a tie vote, under no circumstances may he/she vote once and then vote a second time to break a tie that he/she has created.

The Michigan general property tax act requires that the township supervisor be the assessing officer for all taxable property in the township. However, even though not certified as an assessor by the state assessor's board, he/she would not be in any way disqualified from holding office. The statutes (see the citations at the beginning of this section) provide several methods for taking care of such a situation, including the employment of a certified supervisor from another township to do the assessing, compile the assessment roll and perform all other functions required under the tax act, in another township as well as his/her own. More detailed information about this can be found in the chapter on Finance and Taxation.

Following completion of the assessment roll, the supervisor serves as secretary of the township board of review. He/she is a member of the township board of election commissioners and may, under certain circumstances, appoint a temporary member of the board. The supervisor also serves as president (chairperson) of the township board of health.

Although no longer responsible for helping the township clerk prepare and provide lists of eligible jurors to the county clerk, the supervisor is required to forward to the county board of commissioners copies of a report prepared by the township clerk concerning monies voted to be raised in the township. He/she may also be required to take the dog census for the county board of commissioners and may have additional responsibilities in conducting hearings regarding and determining damage done by dogs to livestock or poultry. Certain tasks previously performed by the township highway commissioner have now been assigned by law to the township supervisor.

As chief law enforcement officer for the township, the supervisor prosecutes for all penalties and forfeitures incurred within the township which no other officer is specifically designated to prosecute. The supervisor may place any person under oath (and is authorized to administer the oath) on any statements made to him/her in his/her official capacity as supervisor.

Local conditions will determine the extent of other duties which the statutes, the citizens by referendum or the township board by resolution assign to the supervisor, such as administrator of a specific assignment as directed by the statute chosen for delivery of a particular service or utility; superintendent of the water district; supervisor of a sanitary sewer system; or representative of the township board on a commission, board or agency which the township operates jointly with other units of government.

The supervisor's books, assessment rolls and other papers must be kept in a safe place, under specific and quite stringent regulations, and must be delivered upon demand to his/her successor in office, whether elected or appointed. They are always open to public inspection and the supervisor is required to provide certified copies to individuals upon proper application. Further information on this matter will be found in chapter four under the heading "Preservation of Township Records and History." Any township which may be involved in selling Michigan lottery tickets should pay particular attention to that section.

R.S. 1846, c. 16 - Township Supervisor

MCLA 41.60 Prosecution of penalties and forfeitures. [MSA 5.51]

Sec. 60. The supervisor of each township shall prosecute, in the name of the people of this state, or otherwise, as may be necessary, for all penalties and forfeitures incurred within his township, and for which no other officer is specially directed to prosecute.

MCLA 41.61 Township supervisor; clerk and assessors, appointment, compensation, duties, assessment rolls. [MSA 5.52]

Sec. 61. The supervisor shall, by virtue of his office, be an assessor of his township. At the annual meeting in any township, the electors of such township, present at such meeting, may provide for the appointment, by the supervisor, of a clerk (secretary) *to assist him in his duties. Such clerk shall receive such compensation as the township board may determine, which compensation shall be paid from the general fund of the township as other township expenses are paid. In any township, in addition to the supervisor, the township board may provide for the appointment of assessors, not exceeding 2, for such township. Such assessors when appointed shall be clothed with all the powers and duties of supervisors in the assessment of property for taxation within such township and shall receive for their services such compensation as may be allowed by the township board. Whenever assessors shall be appointed, as in this act provided, the supervisor shall be the chief assessing officer and such assessors shall in all cases be subordinate to such supervisor. Upon completion of the assessment and the making of the rolls, such rolls shall be deposited with the supervisor.*

Note: Although the electors **may** provide for the appointment of a clerk to assist the supervisor, it must be emphasized that three important matters shall prevail: (1) the supervisor appoints the clerk, (2) the township board determines the compensation for the clerk and (3) the compensation **shall** be paid from the general fund of the township and **may not be deducted from the compensation of the supervisor.**

Act No. 206, P.A. 1893 - Assessment, Levy and Collection of Taxes - Of the Assessment

MCLA 211.10d   Annual property assessments, qualifications required of assessors; schools of assessment practices, establishment, supervision; certificates of qualification; lack of qualified assessor, cost of training. [MSA 7.10(4)]

Sec. 10d.   Notwithstanding any provision of any other law to the contrary, the annual assessment of property shall be made by a supervisor, assessing officer or director of an equalization department or bureau who has been certified as qualified by the (state assessor's) *board by reason of his having successfully completed training in a school of assessment practices or the passage of a test approved by the board and conducted by the board or an approved agency by the board that will enable him to properly discharge the functions of his office. The school shall be established by an approved educational institution in conjunction with the board and be supervised by the board and its agents and employees. The board may determine that a supervisor, assessing officer or a director of an equalization department or bureau who has not received the training, possesses the necessary qualifications for performing the functions of his office by the passage of an approved examination or may waive the examination if such person has at least 5 years' experience. Upon presentation of evidence of the successful completion of the qualifications the supervisor, assessing officer or director of an equalization department, or bureau shall be certified as qualified by the board. A local assessing district which does not have an assessor qualified by certification of the board may employ an assessor so qualified. If a local assessing district does not have an assessor qualified by certification of the board, and has not employed a certified assessor, the assessment shall be made by the county tax or equalization department or the state tax* commission and the cost of preparing the rolls shall be charged to the local assessing district. The local assessing district shall assume the cost of training, if a certification is awarded, to the extent of course fees and recognized travel expenditures.

Act No. 122, P.A. 1962 — Manuals for Assessing Officials

AN ACT requiring assessing officials to use manuals prepared by the state tax commission.

MCLA 211.721 Assessment of real and personal property; state tax commission manuals. MSA 7.40

Sec. 1. ... all assessing officials, whose duty it is to assess real or personal property on which real or personal property taxes are levied by any taxing unit of the state, shall use only the official manual or manuals, with their latest supplements, as prepared or approved by the state tax commission as a guide in preparing assessments.

R.S. 1846, c. 16 - Township Supervisor

MCLA 41.61a Township appraisal; assistance to supervisor as assessor. MSA 5.52(1)

Sec. 61a. Any township board may employ an independent appraisal firm to make a township-wide appraisal or to assist the supervisor as directed and authorized by the board in performing his assessing duties. Such appraisal firm shall be paid out of the general fund of the township.

MCLA 41.62 Records, preservation, turning over; certified copies, fees, evidence. MSA 5.53

Sec. 62. The supervisor shall preserve and keep all books, assessment rolls, and other papers belonging to his office, in a safe and suitable place, but not in any saloon, restaurant, public inn, hotel, place of public amusement, nor in any place where intoxicating drinks of any kind are kept or sold, or where gaming or plays of chance of any kind are carried on, or where they will be exposed to unusual hazard from fire or theft, and he shall deliver

98

the same on demand to his successor in office, and on application of any person he shall give certified copies of any such papers, or abstract from any assessment roll or books in his office; and for making any such copies or abstracts he shall be entitled to receive from the person applying therefor 6 cents for each folio; but no such copy or abstract and certificate shall be required for less than 12 1/2 cents; and such certified copies or abstracts shall be presumptive evidence of the facts therein contained.

Note: See chapter four under the heading "Preservation of Township Records and History" for further citations.

Act No. 206, P.A. 1893 - Assessment, Levy and Collection of Taxes - Of the Assessment Roll

MCLA 211.25a Real estate index number system. [MSA 7.25(1)]

Sec. 25a. ... Indexes established hereunder shall be open to public inspection.

MCLA 211.33 Secretary of board of review; record, filing, form. [MSA 7.33]

Sec. 33. The supervisor shall be the secretary of said board of review and shall keep a record of the proceedings of the board and of all the changes made in such assessment roll, and shall file the same with the township or city clerk with the statements made by persons assessed. In the absence of the supervisor, the board shall appoint 1 of its members to serve as secretary. The state tax commission may prescribe the form of the record whenever deemed necessary.

Act No. 116, P.A. 1954 - Election Law, Ch. II - Boards of Election Commissioners and Boards of Canvassers

MCLA 168.26 Townships; board of election commissioners; ... [MSA 6.1026]

Sec. 26. Unless otherwise provided by charter, the supervisor, clerk and township treasurer shall constitute the board of township election commissioners ... Should only 1 of said officers be in at-

tendance on the day appointed for a meeting of the board, the officer in attendance shall appoint a qualified and registered elector of the township to act in the absentee's stead during the period of nonattendance.

Note: The supervisor and treasurer no longer serve as members of the township board of canvassers.

R.S. 1846, c. 16 - Township Supervisor

MCLA 41.63 Attendance at meetings. [MSA 5.54]

Sec. 63. The supervisor of each township shall attend the annual meeting of the board of commissioners of the county, and every adjourned or special meeting of such board of which he shall have notice.

Note: This section appears to be no longer applicable, since it was written when the township supervisor was automatically a member of the county board of supervisors (commissioners).

MCLA 41.64 Reports to board. [MSA 5.55]

Sec. 64. Each supervisor shall lay before the (county) board of commissioners such copies of entries concerning moneys voted to be raised in his township, as shall be delivered to him by the township clerk.

Act No. 206, P.A. 1893 - Assessment, Levy and Collection of Taxes - Of Taxes, How and By Whom Certified

MCLA 211.36 Duties of township clerk, supervisor, county clerk, board of commissioners. [MSA 7.54]

Sec. 36. The township clerk of each township, on or before September 15 of each year, shall make and deliver to the supervisor of his township, a certified copy of all statements and certificates on file, and of all records of any vote or resolution in his office authorizing or directing moneys to be raised therein by taxation for township, school, highway, drain and all other purposes, together with a statement of the aggregate amount thereof, and such certified copies shall, by such supervisor, be delivered to the clerk of the county on or before October 1, and the same shall by said clerk be laid before the board of commissioners at its annual meeting and filed in his office. ...

R.S. 1846, c. 16 - Township Supervisor

MCLA 41.64a Agent, legal township business. [MSA 5.56]

Sec. 1. ... the supervisor of each township shall be the agent for his township, for the transaction of all legal business, by whom suits may be brought and defended, and upon whom all process against the township shall be served.

Act No. 359, P.A. 1947 - Charter Townships

MCLA 42.5 Charter township board, ...; supervisor, president pro tem; ... [MSA 5.46(5)]

Sec. 5. ... As a member of the township board, the supervisor shall be the presiding and executive officer thereof and shall have an equal voice and vote in the proceedings of the board. He shall authenticate by his signature such instruments as the board and the laws of the state or the federal government may require. In the event of the absence of the supervisor from any meeting of the township board, said board shall appoint 1 of its members president pro tem for such meeting. ...

MCLA 42.9 ...; resolution creating additional officers, ...
[MSA 5.46(9)]

Sec. 9. The township supervisor, ... in each charter township shall have and perform the duties and functions required ... by state law. The township board may, by resolution, upon the recommendation of the supervisor, ... create such additional officers as may be necessary to administer the affairs of the township government, or may combine any administrative offices in any manner not inconsistent with state law, and prescribe the duties thereof. ...

R.S. 1846, c. 16 - Township Business, Other than Elections

MCLA 41.97 to 41.101 [MSA 5.84 TO 5.88]

Note: These five sections have to do with the supervisor's duties as moderator of township meetings.

Act No. 168, P.A. 1877 - Administration of Oaths by Supervisors

MCLA 41.651 Administration of oaths. [MSA 5.101]

Sec. 1. ... the supervisor of any township or ward in the state of Michigan is hereby authorized to place any person under oath on any of his statements made to said supervisor in his official capacity as supervisor, which oath the supervisor is hereby authorized to administer.

R.S. 1846, c. 16 - Township Clerk

MCLA 41.69 Bond, contents; ... [MSA 5.61]

Sec. 69. Each township clerk shall, within the time limited for filing his oath of office and before entering upon the duties of his office, give a bond ... in such sum and with such sureties as the township board shall require and approve, ... which bond shall be filed in the office of the supervisor; ...

MCLA 41.77 Bond, filing, time; ... [MSA 5.69]

Sec. 77. Each township treasurer, ... shall give a bond to the township in such sum and with such sureties as the supervisor shall require and approve ... and the supervisor shall indorse his approval thereon. ...(filed with the clerk who shall)... *deliver it to the supervisor who shall file it in his office....*

Act No. 130, P.A. 1915 - Surety Bonds, Cost

AN ACT relative to the cost of bonds to be provided by township officers.

MCLA 41.601 Authorized surety bonds, township payment.
[MSA 5.131]

Sec. 1. Whenever a bond is required by the laws of this state to be given to any township officer, the township board may authorize such officer to procure the required bond from any surety company authorized by the laws of this state to execute the same; the cost thereof, not to exceed 1 per cent per annum of the amount of said bond, may, by resolution of the township board, be paid by the township out of the contingent fund of said township.

Act No. 51, P.A. 1867 - Additional Sureties, Township Treasurer

MCLA 41.611 to 41.617 [MSA 5.141 TO 5.147]

Note: This citation has to do with the supervisor's responsibilities regarding determination, notification and supervision of adequate bonding of the township treasurer under certain circumstances. See section on Duties and Responsibilities of Township Treasurer for more complete reference.

R.S. 1846, c. 16 - Constables

MCLA 41.80 Bond; contents, time. [MSA 5.72]

Sec. 80. Every (constable) *..., before he enters upon the duties of his office, and within the time prescribed by law for filing his official oath, shall execute, with sufficient sureties, to be approved by the supervisor or clerk of his township, an instrument in writing ...*

MCLA 41.81 Bond; ... filing, ... [MSA 5.73]

Sec. 81. Such supervisor or township clerk shall endorse on such instrument, his approbation (approval) *of the sureties therein named, and shall then cause the same to be filed in the office of the township clerk, ...*

Act No. 19, P.A. 1934, 1st Ex. Sess. - Bonds of Public Officials, Liability of Sureties

AN ACT relative to the bonds of public officials, and the liability of sureties thereon; and to repeal all acts and parts of acts inconsistent therewith.

MCLA 129.51 Bonds of public officials, deputies, assistants, liability of sureties. MSA 27.1431

Sec. 1. If any officer of ... any ... township ... or of any other municipal or public corporation within this state, shall be required to file an official statutory bond or bonds, either as additional security or substituted security, the surety or sureties thereon shall not be liable, directly or indirectly, for any acts or defaults committed by such public officer prior to the date of signing of such bond or bonds, or for the failure of any such public officer to pay over on final settlement or to his successor in office, if such failure to pay over be due to an act or default committed prior to the signing of such bond or bonds, or for the failure of such surety or sureties to collect from themselves or from any prior surety or sureties the amount of any loss due to any act or default committed by such public officer prior to the date of the signing of such bond or bonds. The provisions of this act shall apply to all deputies of any such officer, and to all clerks, agents and servants of any such officer.

Act No. 187, P.A. 1905 - Public Buildings and Public Works *(Amended by Act 384, P.A. 1925 and Act 167, P.A. 1927)*

AN ACT to insure the payment of subcontractors and wages earned and all materials or labor and certain supplies furnished and used in connection with and consumed in constructing, repairing or ornamenting public buildings and public works.

MCLA 570.101 Bond of contractor on public works to secure payment for materials and labor. MSA 26.321

MCLA 570.102 Notice by subcontractor, materialman or laborer. MSA 26.322

MCLA 570.103 Same; execution, sureties, conditions. MSA 26.323

MCLA 570.104 Same; recovery. MSA 26.324

MCLA 570.105 Construction of terms. MSA 26.325

Note: Responsibility for the above lies in the township board or "agent acting on their behalf," which could be the supervisor, clerk or both.

Numerous other statutes provide for bonding under certain circumstances, most of them involving the part which the supervisor shall play in his role as agent for township business. Careful note should be made of the citations in the chapter on Services, Utilities, Contracts and Ordinances.

Act No. 339, P.A. 1919 - Dog Law

MCLA 287.276 Listing of dogs; reports; compensation; animal control officers, appointment, duties. MSA 12.526

Sec. 16. The supervisor of each township and the assessor of every city, annually, on taking his assessment of property as required by law, may make diligent inquiry as to the number of dogs owned, harbored or kept by all persons in his assessing district; and on or before June 1, make a complete report to the county treasurer, for his county, on a blank form furnished by the director of agriculture, setting forth the name of every owner, or keeper, of any dog, subject to license under this act, how many of each sex are owned by him, and if a kennel license is maintained such fact shall be also stated. Every supervisor or assessor shall receive for his services in listing such dogs at a rate determined by the board of commissioners for each dog so listed, which sums shall be paid out of the general fund of the county. In any city having a population of 5,000 or more, the county board of commissioners may by resolution appoint for a term of 2 years, an animal control officer, who shall perform in and for the city all the duties which this act prescribes for the supervisors of townships, and who shall receive the same compensation as is herein provided for supervisors. The board of commissioners of any county may, by resolution, appoint for the county for a term of 2 years an animal control officer whose duties and compensation shall be such as shall be prescribed by the board of commissioners and who may be delegated the duties

105

required by this section to be performed by the supervisors and assessors without extra compensation.

MCLA 287.277 Comparison of dog lists and license records; killing of unlicensed dogs. [MSA 12.527]

Sec. 17. On June 15 of each year the county treasurer may make a comparison of his records of the dogs actually licensed in each city or township of his county with the report of the supervisor of said township or assessor of said city or animal control officer, to determine and locate all unlicensed dogs. On and after June 15 of each year every unlicensed dog, subject to license under the provisions of this act, is declared to be a public nuisance and the county treasurer shall immediately thereafter list all such unlicensed dogs, as shown by the returns in his office of the supervisors and assessors, and shall deliver copies of such lists to the sheriff and prosecuting attorney of said county and to the commissioner of agriculture. On receiving from the county treasurer the name of any owner of any unlicensed dog, the prosecuting attorney shall at once commence the necessary proceedings against the owner of said dog, as required by the provisions of this act. It shall also be the duty of the sheriff or any member of the state constabulary to locate and kill, or cause to be killed, all such unlicensed dogs. Failure, refusal or neglect on the part of any sheriff to carry out the provisions of this section shall constitute nonfeasance in office.

MCLA 287.280 Damage to livestock or poultry by dogs, remedy; complaint, proceedings; liability for damages and costs.
[MSA 12.530]

Sec. 20. Whenever any person sustains any loss or damage to any livestock or poultry by dogs, or whenever any livestock of any person is necessarily destroyed because of having been bitten by a dog, such person or his agent or attorney, may complain to the township supervisor or appointed trustee of the township within which the damage occurred. The complaint shall be in writing, signed by the person making it, and shall state when, where, what and how much damage was done, and if known, by whose dog or dogs. The township supervisor or a township trustee appointed by the township board shall at once examine the place where the alleged damage was sustained and the livestock or poultry injured or killed, if practicable. *He shall also examine under oath, or affirmation, any witness called before him. After making diligent inquiry in relation to the claim, the township supervisor or appointed trustee shall determine whether any damage has been sustained and the amount thereof, and, if possible, who was the owner of the dog or dogs by which the damage was done. If during the course of the proceedings it shall appear who is the owner of the dog causing the loss or damage to the livestock, the township supervisor or appointed trustee shall request the district court judge to forthwith issue a summons against the owner commanding him to appear before the township supervisor or appointed trustee and show cause why the dog should not be killed. The summons may be served anyplace within the county in which the damage occurred, and shall be made returnable not less than 2 nor more than 6 days from the date therein and shall be served at least 2 days before the time of appearance mentioned therein. Upon the return day fixed in the summons the township supervisor or appointed trustee shall proceed to determine whether the loss or damage to the livestock was caused by said dog, and if he shall so find he shall forthwith notify the sheriff or the animal control officer ... to kill the dog wherever found. Any owner or keeper of the dog or dogs shall be liable to the county in a civil action for all damages and costs paid by the county on any claims as hereinafter provided.*

Note: For full citations on the Dog Law, see the appropriate section in the chapter on Health.

R.S. 1846, c. 17 - Township Division

MCLA 41.115 Meeting of township boards, notice. [MSA 5.2205]

Sec. 5. Whenever a meeting of the township boards of 2 or more townships shall be required, in order to carry into effect the provisions of this chapter, such meeting may be called by either of the supervisors; but the supervisor calling the same shall give at least 6 days' notice in writing to all the other officers, of the time and place at which such meeting is to be held.

R.S. 1846, c. 35 - Local Health Boards, General Provisions

MCLA 327.1 Township board of health; ... [MSA 14.61]

Sec. 1. In every township the township board shall be the board of health. The supervisor shall be the president, ...

MCLA 327.2 Health officer; appointment, ... [MSA 14.62]

Sec. 2. Every board of health shall appoint and constantly have a health officer, who shall be a well educated physician, and act as the sanitary adviser and executive officer of the board: Provided, That in townships where it is not practicable to secure the services of a well educated and suitable physician, the board may appoint the supervisor or some other person as such health officer. The board of health shall establish his salary or other compensation, ...(appointment to be made within 30 days after the annual township meeting)...

Note: For more complete citations covering duties and responsibilities of the township board of health and its various officers, see the chapter on Health.

DUTIES AND RESPONSIBILITIES - TOWNSHIP CLERK

The township clerk serves as secretary (clerk) of the township board, the township board of health, the township board of canvassers (when there is one) and all township meetings, as chairman of the township election commission and treasurer of the township board of health with regard to cemetery perpetual care trust funds.

One of the most important of the clerk's responsibilities is voter registration and records, including sending the county clerk certification of nominating and local question petitions for voting at primary elections and lists of township elected or appointed officials and eligible jurors. A few citations from the election law are included in this section, but for more specific coverage of this subject please check the chapter on Elections.

The clerk may direct the township constable to serve warrants, notice and process for the township and, along with the supervisor, acts as agent in the conduct of township business matters.

Another significant aspect of the clerk's duties is in the area of keeping an accurate record of all financial transactions. He/she is charged with maintaining the cash receipts register (journal), posting each receipt received from the treasurer in this journal in numerical order to the proper bank account, fund and account. Monthly totals are posted from this journal to the general ledger, which is also maintained by the clerk. Normally the official township disbursements journals from which the general ledger is posted will be maintained by the township clerk, who will post to these journals on the basis of his/her copy of each three-part check drawn on township funds and general accounts.

In accordance with the provisions of **Act No. 2, P.A. 1968 - Uniform Charts of Accounts and Reports (MCLA 141.421 to 141.433 [MSA 5.3228(21) TO 5.3228(33)]**), **the regular audit of township funds is conducted on the books maintained by the clerk.** The township clerk needs to become familiar with the Uniform Accounting Procedures Manual, provided by the Local Government Division of the State Department of Treasury, and to attend one of the accounting schools provided by the Michigan Townships Association and the Continuing Education Service of Michigan State University through the Institute for Community Development and Services.

The clerk is also charged with the safe keeping of the township records, books and papers, under specific and quite stringent restrictions, and everything must be turned over to his/her successor in office. Included are items regarding township officials, such as certificates of oaths (which he/she also administers), recording and delivering bonds to the supervisor and receiving and filing written resignations from office. Related to this is keeping records of all actions involving the adoption and enforcement of township ordinances, including zoning. Under English law the township clerk serves as "recorder and keeper" of vital statistics, but in Michigan this responsibility is now vested in the county clerk. Further information on this matter will be found in chapter four under the heading "Preservation of Township Records and History." Any township which may be involved in selling Michigan lottery tickets should pay particular attention to this section.

The township clerk prepares and delivers to the township supervisor a certified copy of all statements and certificates on file, and of all records of any vote or resolution in his/her office authorizing or directing moneys to be raised by taxation for township, school, highway, police, fire, drain and all other purposes, with a statement of the aggregate amount thereof.

Occasionally the clerk temporarily performs a function for another principal executive officer. A classic illustration of this is when he/she serves as temporary moderator in starting township meetings in the absence of the township supervisor. Other duties may be imposed by the township board.

Under many statutes, particularly in the area of services, utilities, contracts and ordinances, the township board may direct the clerk to do many things. For instance, he/she might be requested to call for sealed bids for purchase of furniture and equipment, improvements, building construction, fire and police equipment, etc. **MCLA 123.501** is one illustration.

The township clerk **must** appoint a deputy clerk, under certain conditions may appoint a temporary member of the township board of election commissioners, and may appoint temporary members of the township board of canvassers. If neither the clerk nor the deputy clerk is available to perform necessary functions in connection with registrations, nominations or elections during the usual or required time, the township board shall appoint some qualified person to assume those duties until the clerk or deputy returns to duty.

It makes good sense and serves the best interests of a sound public relations program if the township clerk, the deputy clerk and, in the case of those townships which operate a full time business office, at least one other person in that office be notaries public.

R.S. 1846, c. 16 - Township Business Other than Elections

MCLA 41.97 Moderator of township meeting. [MSA 5.84]

Sec. 97. ... If (the supervisor, as moderator) *shall not be present, the* (any township) *meeting, under the direction of the township clerk, shall elect viva voce, a moderator of the meeting: Provided, That the township clerk shall have the same powers and duties as the moderator until a moderator is chosen.*

R.S. 1846, c. 16 - Township Clerk

MCLA 41.69 Bond, contents; deputy, appointment, duties. [MSA 5.61]

Sec. 69. Each township clerk shall, within the time limited for filing his oath of office and before entering upon the duties of his office, give a bond to the township in such sum and with such sure-

110

ties as the township board shall require and approve, conditioned for the faithful discharge of the duties of his office according to law, and especially for the safe keeping of the records, books, and papers of said township in the manner required by law, and for their delivery on demand to his successor in office, which bond shall be filed in the office of the supervisor; he shall also appoint a deputy, who shall take an oath of office and file the same with the clerk, and in case of the absence, sickness, death, or other disability of the clerk, such deputy shall perform the duties of such clerk, and receive the same compensation as the clerk would have been entitled to receive therefor.

Act No. 359, P.A. 1947 - Charter Townships

MCLA 42.5   Charter township board, ... record of proceedings.
MSA 5.46(5)

Sec. 5.   ... The township clerk shall be clerk of the township board and shall keep a full record of all the proceedings of the township board.   In the absence of the clerk, such board shall appoint 1 of its members as temporary clerk for such meeting.

R.S. 1846, c. 35 - Local Health Boards, General Provisions

MCLA 327.1   Township board of health; record of proceedings.
MSA 14.61

Sec. 1.   In every township the township board shall be the board of health.   The ... township clerk shall be the clerk of said board.   The clerk shall keep a record of the proceedings of the board in a book to be provided for that purpose at the expense of the township.

Act No. 95, P.A. 1909 - (Cemetery) Property Held by Township Boards

MCLA 128.71 to 128.74 MSA 5.3131 TO 5.3134

Act No. 81, P.A. 1903 - Cemetery Lots, Care Deposits

MCLA 128.81 to 128.88 [MSA 5.731 TO 5.738]

Note: The above two citations have to do with the clerk's responsibilities as **treasurer** of cemetery perpetual care trust funds, and bonding therefor.

R.S. 1846, c. 65 - Conveyances of Real Property, Alienation by Deed; Proof and Recording of Conveyances, and Cancelling of Mortgages

MCLA 565.30 Deeds of church pews and slips, recording.
[MSA 26.548]

Sec. 30. Deeds of pews or slips in any church, may be recorded by the clerk of the township in which such a church is situated, or by the clerk of the society or proprietors, if incorporated or legally organized; and such clerks shall receive the same fees as the register of deeds is entitled' to for similar services.

Act No. 288, P.A. 1939 - Probate Code, Chapter III - Guardians and Wards

MCLA 703.5 Guardian of minor, nomination and approval; certification of nomination. [MSA 27.3178(205)]

Sec. 5. When such minor, being above the age of 14 years, shall reside more than 10 miles from the place of holding the probate court, his nomination of a guardian, made in writing, and signed by himself, may be certified to the judge of probate by ... the township clerk of the township in which such minor resides, or by a notary public, which shall have the same effect as if made in the presence of the judge: ...

R.S. 1846, c. 16 - Township Board

MCLA 41.73 Annual meeting; ... bonds. [MSA 5.65]

Sec. 73. ...(The board) shall determine the amount of the bond and the number of sureties to be required from the township clerk, as provided by law, in each year, within 30 days next preceding the annual township election.

MCLA 41.77 Bond, filing, time; ... MSA 5.69

Sec. 77. ... It shall be the duty of such treasurer to file within the time above mentioned said bond with the township clerk of such township, who shall record the same in a book to be provided for that purpose. The township clerk shall, after recording same, deliver it to the supervisor ...

Act No. 116, P.A. 1954 - Election Law, Ch. XVI - Township Offices

MCLA 168.364 Township officers; township treasurer, bond, sureties, approval, filing. MSA 6.1364

Sec. 364. Each township treasurer ... (shall) file within the time ... mentioned ... bond with the township clerk of such township, who shall record the same in a book to be provided for that purpose. The township clerk shall, after recording the same, deliver the bond to the supervisor ...

Act No. 206, P.A. 1893 - Assessment, Levy and Collection of Taxes, Miscellaneous Provisions

MCLA 211.111 Deputy township treasurer, appointment, ... MSA 7.165

Sec. 111. Any township treasurer with the approval of the township board and the consent of his bondsmen, which consent shall be in writing and shall be filed with the clerk ... may appoint a deputy ....

R.S. 1846, c. 16 - Constables

MCLA 41.80 (Constable) bond; contents, time. MSA 5.72

Sec. 80. Every (constable) ..., before he enters upon the duties of his office, and within the time prescribed by law for filing his official oath, shall execute, with sufficient sureties, to be approved by the supervisor or clerk of his township, an instrument in writing ...

MCLA 41.81 (Constable) bond; ... filing, ... $\boxed{\text{MSA 5.73}}$

Sec. 81. Such supervisor or township clerk shall endorse on such instrument, his approbation (approval) of the sureties therein named, and shall then cause the same to be filed in the office of the township clerk, and a copy of such instrument, certified by the township clerk, shall be presumptive evidence ...

Act No. 116, P.A. 1954 - Election Law, Ch. XVI - Township Offices

MCLA 168.365   Township officers; constable, indemnification. $\boxed{\text{MSA 6.1365}}$

Sec. 365. Every ... constable, ... shall execute, with sufficient sureties to be approved by the supervisor or clerk of his township, an instrument (bond) in writing ...

Act No. 187, P.A. 1905 - Public Buildings and Public Works

AN ACT to insure the payment of subcontractors and wages earned and all materials or labor and certain supplies furnished and used in connection with and consumed in constructing, repairing or ornamenting public buildings and public works.

MCLA 570.101 to 570.105 $\boxed{\text{MSA 26.321 TO 26.325}}$

Note: The above act applies now only to construction and maintenance contracts of the state highway commissioner (See **MCLA 129.211** $\boxed{\text{MSA 5.2321(11)}}$). Responsibility lies in the township board or "agent acting on their behalf," which could be the supervisor, clerk or both. The following act applies to municipal public works, for contracts exceeding $5,000.

Act No. 213, P.A. 1963 — Public Works, Contractor's Bond

AN ACT to provide a procedure for bonding contractors for public buildings and public works of governmental units; and to repeal certain acts and parts of acts.

MCLA 129.201 – 129.211 [MSA 5.2321(1) – 5.2321(11)]

Act No. 116, P.A. 1954 - Election Law, Ch. XVI - Township Offices

MCLA 168.363 Township officers; oath, filing. [MSA 6.1363]

Sec. 363. All township officers shall, before entering upon the duties of their offices, take and subscribe the oath as provided in section 1 of article 11 of the state constitution before the township clerk or other officer authorized to administer oaths, ...

> **Example:** *(With right hands raised) Do you, John Smith, solemnly swear (or affirm) that you will support the constitution of the United States and the constitution of the state of Michigan and that you will faithfully discharge the duties of your office, [so help you God? (may be omitted]].*

MCLA 168.367 Township officers; resignations, signatures, delivery, filing. [MSA 6.1367]

Sec. 367. Resignation of any township officer shall be in writing, signed by the officer resigning, and addressed to the township board, and shall be delivered to and filed by the township clerk. ...

Act No. 116, P.A. 1954 - Election Law, Ch. II - Boards of Election Commissioners and Boards of Canvassers

MCLA 168.26 Township; board of election commissioners; quorum, absentee. [MSA 6.1026]

Sec. 26. Unless otherwise provided by charter, the supervisor, clerk and township treasurer shall constitute the board of township election commissioners ... The township clerk shall act as chairman of the board. Should only 1 of said officers be in attendance on the day appointed for a meeting of the board, the officer in attendance shall appoint a qualified and registered elector of the township to act in the absentee's stead during the period of nonattendance.

Note: See the chapter on Elections for other responsibilities of the township clerk in this area.

MCLA 168.30a Local board of canvassers; powers and duties, appointment, term, notice; contract with county, cost. [MSA 6.1030(1)]

Sec. 30a. (1) A 4-member board of canvassers is established in every ... township having more than 5 precincts, notwithstanding any statutory or charter provision, or any other rule or law to the contrary. ... Members of the board shall be notified of their appointment within 5 days thereafter by their ... township clerk.

(2) The ... township board of any ... township having more than 5 precincts may contract with the board of commissioners of the county in which all or the greater portion of the ... township's population resides to provide that the board of county canvassers of that county shall perform all the functions of the board of ... township canvassers. Financial arrangements of such a contract may provide that the ... township shall bear all or part of cost of such work.

Note: Appointments are made and compensation established by the township board. **(MCLA 168.30c, 168.30e** - [MSA 6.1030(3), 6.1030(5)])

MCLA 168.30d Local board of canvassers; ... officers.
[MSA 6.1030(4)]

Sec. 30d. ... The ... township clerk shall be the clerk of the board of ... township canvassers.

MCLA 168.30g Board of canvassers; ... appointment of temporary members, ... [MSA 6.1030(7)]

Sec. 30g. Whenever a board of canvassers created under this act is required to perform its statutory duties and because of illness or absence of members of the board a quorum is not present, the clerk of the political subdivision may appoint a sufficient number of temporary members to constitute a quorum. ... (who) shall serve only until the business on hand has been transacted.

116

R.S. 1846, c. 16 - Township Clerk

MCLA 41.65 Township records; contents, preservation, turning over. [MSA 5.57]

Sec. 65.   The township clerk ... shall have the custody of all the records, books, and papers of the township, when no other provision is made by law; and he shall duly file and safely keep all certificates of oaths and other papers required by law to be filed in his office, and record such as are required by law to be recorded therein; such records, books, and papers shall not be kept in any saloon, restaurant, public inn, hotel, place of public amusement, nor in any place where intoxicating drinks of any kind are kept or sold, or where gaming or plays of chance of any kind are carried on, nor where they will be exposed to unusual hazard of fire or theft, and he shall deliver the same on demand to his successor in office; he shall also open and keep an account with the treasurer of his township, and shall charge such treasurer with all funds which shall come into his hands by virtue of his office, and shall credit him with all moneys paid out by him on the order of the proper authorities of the township, and shall enter the date and amount of all vouchers in a book kept by said clerk in said office; he shall also open and keep a separate account with each of the several funds belonging to his township, and shall credit each of said funds with such amounts as properly belong to them, and shall charge them severally with all warrants drawn on the township treasurer and payable from said funds respectively.

Note: See chapter four under the heading "Preservation of Township Records and History" for further citations.

Act No. 2, P.A. 1968 - Uniform Charts of Accounts and Reports

MCLA 141.421 Uniform charts of accounts; standard procedures and forms. [MSA 5.3228(21)]

Sec. 1.   The state treasurer shall prescribe uniform charts of accounts for all local units of similar size, function or service designed to fulfill the requirements of good accounting practices relating to general government. ... The official who by law or charter is charged with the responsibility for the financial affairs of the local unit shall insure that the local unit accounts are maintained and kept in accordance with the chart of accounts. The state treasurer may also publish standard operating procedures and forms for the guidance of local units in establishing and maintaining uniform accounting.

Note: Uniform Accounting Procedures Manual is published by Local Government Audit Division, Department of State Treasury, Treasury Building, Lansing, Michigan 48922.

R.S. 1846, c. 16 - Township Clerk

MCLA 41.66 Township records, minutes of meetings, orders, rules. MSA 5.58

Sec. 66. He shall transcribe, in the book of records of his township, the minutes of the proceedings of every township meeting held therein, and he shall enter in such book, every order or direction, and all rules and regulations made by any such township meeting.

Act No. 116, P.A. 1954 - Election Law, Ch. XXIII - Registration of Electors

MCLA 168.493 Registration of electors; registration cards, contents. MSA 6.1493

Sec. 493. The clerk of each township, ... shall provide blank forms printed on cards (hereinafter termed "registration cards"), to be used in the registration of electors. Such registration cards shall contain the following: (a) Affidavit to be executed by the registrant, (hereinafter termed "registration affidavit"); (b) spaces in which to note any change of address; (c) spaces in which to write or stamp the date of each election at which registrant shall vote; (d) the ward or precinct, if any, in which the registrant resides; (e) spaces in which to note the cancellation of the elector's registration, together with the cause and date thereof and the signature of the clerk cancelling such registration; and (f) blanks for any other information which shall facilitate registration and holding of elections.

MCLA 168.494 Same; definitions. [MSA 6.1494]

Sec. 494. The term "registration cards", as used in this chapter, shall be construed as meaning either cards or loose leaf sheets, and either may be used in the discretion of the township ... clerk, ... The term "file", as used in this chapter, shall be construed as meaning either a file or loose leaf book.

MCLA 168.495 Same; registration affidavit, contents. [MSA 6.1495]

Sec. 495. The registration affidavit shall state the name, residence address, street and number, if any, and birthplace and birthdate of the elector. The affidavit shall also state that the person signing it is a citizen of the United States and is or will be, on a specified date between the date of registration and the date of the next regular or special election or primary election, at least 18 years of age, that he has or will have on the specified date lived in the state 6 months or more; that he has or will have established his residence in the township, ... in which he is applying for registration on or before the fifth Friday preceding the next regular or special election or primary election and that he is or will be on the specified date a qualified elector of the township.... The affidavit shall also contain a space in which an elector shall state the place of his last registration.

MCLA 168.498 Same; township ... clerk, when to accept applications for registration, office hours, notice, publication or posting. [MSA 6.1498]

Sec. 498. In every township, ... the clerk thereof shall be at his office or in some other convenient place therein, which place shall be designated by the township ... clerk between the hours of 8 a.m. and 8 p.m. on the fifth Friday preceding any election or primary election in such township ... unless such fifth Friday shall fall on a legal holiday, in which event registration shall be accepted during the same hours on the following day. In any township ... in which the clerk does not maintain regular daily office hours, the township board ... may require that the clerk of such township ... shall be at his office or other designated place for the purpose of receiving applications for registration on such other days as it shall designate prior to the last day for registration, not exceeding 5 days in all. Before a fall primary or November general election the clerk shall be at his office or other designated place for the purpose of receiving registrations between the hours of 8 a.m. and 5 p.m. on the first Saturday preceding the close of registration which is not a legal holiday. The clerk of each township ... shall give public notice of the days and hours thereof that he will be at his office or other designated place for the purpose of receiving registrations prior to any election or primary election by publication thereof at least twice in a newspaper published or of general circulation in such township ... and, if deemed advisable by the township ... clerk, by posting written or printed notices in at least 2 of the most conspicuous places in each election precinct, said first publication or said posting to be made not less than 10 days prior to the last day for receiving registrations.

MCLA 168.646a Local officers; nomination, primary, caucus, petition; certification. Procedure. Local or county questions, submission. Application of section, filing of affidavits or petitions. [MSA 6.1646(1)]

Note: The above citation has to do with the clerk's responsibilities regarding certification of nominating or local question petitions for voting at primary elections.

R.S. 1846, c. 16 - Township Clerk

MCLA 41.67 Election returns, contents, time. [MSA 5.59]

Sec. 67. The township clerk ... shall, immediately after the qualifying of the several officers elected or appointed in (the township) return to the (county clerk) the names of all such officers, with their respective postoffice addresses:...

R.S. 1846, c. 16 - Resignations and Vacancies

MCLA 41.59 Temporary appointments; township treasurer; ... [MSA 5.43]

Sec. 59. ... the township clerk shall immediately give notice ... (of appointment of a temporary treasurer for the remainder of the term) to the county treasurer; ...

Act No. 236, P.A. 1961 - Revised Judicature Act, Ch. 13 - Jury Board and Jurors

MCLA 600.1310 Names and addresses of registered voters, methods of furnishing. [MSA 27A.1310]

Sec. 1310. (1) The township ... clerk shall annually between April 15 and May 1 deliver to and file with the county clerk a full, current and accurate copy of the voter registration cards containing the names and addresses of the registered voters. In lieu of a copy of the registration card a full, current and accurate list of those registered together with the current addresses shown on the card may be filed.

(2) The board shall secure from the county clerk, and the county clerk shall provide, copies of the current voter registration cards or the current voter registration lists for each precinct in the county. The board shall treat the cards and lists as 1 list, with voters grouped either by precinct or by city, township or village as they may be provided.

(3) The (jury) board, in lieu of receiving a list from the county clerk of current registered voters, may, if electronic or mechanical devices are used by the township, ..., order such clerks to provide only the names and addresses selected by applying the key number and starting number designated by the (jury) board.

Act No. 116, P.A. 1954 - Election Law, Ch. XVI - Township Offices

MCLA 168.373 Township clerk or deputy; appointment of substitute to perform election law duties. [MSA 6.1373]

Sec. 373. If neither the township clerk nor any deputy township clerk shall be available to perform any necessary functions in connection with registrations, nominations or elections during the usual or required times for performing such functions, the township board shall appoint some qualified person who is a registered elector of the township to perform such functions until such time as the clerk or a deputy resume their duties. Any such person so appointed shall have all of the powers and authority of a deputy appointed by the clerk pertaining to registrations, nominations and elections.

MCLA 41.72 Annual meeting; date; claims, auditing, settling, payment. [MSA 5.64]

Sec. 72. *The township board shall meet annually on the second Tuesday next preceding the annual township meeting for the purpose of auditing and settling all claims against the township which have not previously been audited and settled by the township board at a regular meeting and they shall state on each account the amount allowed by them; and the amounts allowed shall be paid by the treasurer, on the order of the board, signed by their clerk.*

MCLA 41.72a Regular meetings, ...; special meetings, notice, ...; publication of proceedings. [MSA 5.64(1)]

Sec. 72a. *... Upon call of the supervisor the township clerk shall give notice of the time and place of such* (special meeting) *to each member either in person or by leaving a written notice at his address. ... In every township which now has, or hereafter acquires, an assessed valuation of $25,000,000.00 or more, the township board, within 10 days after each meeting of the board, shall publish the proceedings thereof in some newspaper of general circulation in the township. The publication of a synopsis of such proceedings, prepared by the township clerk and approved by the supervisor, showing the substance of each separate proceeding of the board is a sufficient compliance with the requirements of this section.*

MCLA 41.74 Clerk of board; duties. [MSA 5.66]

Sec. 74. *The township clerk shall be the clerk of such* (township) *board, and shall keep a true record of all their proceedings in his office.*

MCLA 41.75 Accounts, contents; audited accounts, filing, inspection, subject to call. [MSA 5.67]

Sec. 75. *No accounts shall be audited by such* (township) *board, except such as are made in writing, giving the particular items of such account, and verified by oath or affirmation of the claimant or some one in his behalf. If such account shall include a claim for labor or services, for which a certain rate per day is allowed by law, or demanded by the claimant, it shall set forth correctly the number of days spent in such service, the nature of the services rendered, and the date thereof as near as may be. All accounts audited by such board shall be filed and preserved by the clerk, for the inspection of any of the inhabitants of the township, or of any persons liable to pay taxes therein, and shall be produced at the next annual township meeting and there read by him, if the same shall be required by the meeting.*

Act No. 262, P.A. 1897 - Township Financial Statements

MCLA 41.171 Township financial statements, publication and distribution. [MSA 5.111]

Sec. 1. The township boards of the several townships of this state shall make and cause to be published annually, immediately upon the settlement of the township board, a statement of first, the amount of money in the hands of the township treasurer at the beginning of the fiscal year, specifying the amount in the several funds; second, the amount and source, by type, of all money placed to the credit of the township and the fund to which the same has been credited; third, the total of disbursements of money paid, and for what purposes, and from what fund the same has been paid; fourth, the balance of money remaining to the credit of township, specifying the amount in each of the several funds; fifth, the total of unpaid claims for each fund. The statement shall be written or printed and distributed to each member of the township board and 6 copies shall be posted in 6 conspicuous places within the township. Distribution and posting shall be made at least 10 days prior to every annual township meeting. The board may order further publication of the statement in 1 issue of a newspaper of general circulation in the county. The township clerk shall carry out the provisions as to publication.

Act No. 206, P.A. 1893 - Assessment, Levy and Collection of Taxes - Of the Board of Review

MCLA 211.33 Secretary of board of review; record, filing, ... [MSA 7.33]

Sec. 33. The supervisor ...(as secretary of the board of review) *... shall file* (a record of the board proceedings and all changes made in the assessment roll)*... with the township ... clerk with the statements made by persons assessed. ...*

MCLA 211.36 Duties of township clerk, ... ⟦MSA 7.54⟧

Sec. 36. The township clerk ..., on or before September 15 of each year, shall make and deliver to the supervisor of his township, a certified copy of all statements and certificates on file, and of all records of any vote or resolution in his office authorizing or directing moneys to be raised therein by taxation for township, school, highway, drain, and all other purposes, together with a statement of the aggregate amount thereof, ...

MCLA 211.41 Assessor, ... local clerk, duties; ... ⟦MSA 7.82⟧

Sec. 41. Before the supervisor or assessing officer shall deliver such roll to the township treasurer ... he shall carefully foot the several columns of valuation and taxes, and make a detailed statement thereof, which he shall give the clerk of his township ... and said clerk shall immediately charge the amount of taxes to the township treasurer ...

R.S. 1846, c. 16 - Constables

MCLA 41.82 Service of process; ... ⟦MSA 5.74⟧

Sec. 82. Constables shall serve all warrants, notices and process lawfully directed to them by the ... township clerk, ...

Act No. 191, P.A. 1939 - Township Ordinances, Publication

MCLA 41.191 Township ordinances; publication, ... ⟦MSA 5.6(1)⟧

Sec. 1. ... Publication of such ordinance shall be made by causing a true copy thereof to be inserted once in some newspaper circulating within said township, which insertion shall be made within 10 days after the passage thereof. ...

MCLA 41.192   Passage, publication, and filing of ordinances, records, time; copies of ordinances, fees. [MSA 5.6(2)]

Sec. 2. (1) Within 1 week after the first publication of any ordinance as herein provided, the township clerk shall record the ordinance in a book of ordinances kept by him for that purpose and record the date of the passage thereof, the names of the members voting thereon and how each member voted, and file an attested copy of the ordinance with the county clerk. The township clerk shall certify under the ordinance in a blank space provided therefor the date or dates of publication thereof and the name of the newspaper in which publication was made and the date of filing with the county clerk.

(2) Within 90 days after the effective date of this 1972 amendatory act (effective May 22, 1972) the clerk of each township shall file attested copies of all operative township ordinances with the county clerk. If a township has not adopted any ordinance, the township clerk shall so certify to the county clerk. The county clerk shall maintain separate files for the ordinances of each township in the county and make the files readily available to the public.

(3) The provisions of this section with regard to filing with the county clerk shall not apply to a township which maintains a township office open to the public during regular hours on each business day.

(4) The county clerk may charge a reasonable fee for the reproduction or furnishing of a copy of an ordinance.

Act No. 381, P.A. 1927 - Town Hall and Other Buildings

MCLA 41.242   Referendum proceedings; ballot, form. [MSA 5.2372]

Sec. 2. Upon the filing of ... application with ... township board the township board shall first determine whether the same has been signed by at least 12 freeholders of such township, and if the township board shall determine that the same has been signed by 12 freeholders of the township, and that the sum of money stated in such application does not exceed the percentage of assessed valuation above specified, thereupon the said township board shall by resolution provide for the submission of such proposition to the legal voters of the township at such township meeting, general election or at a special election to be held within 30 days after the adoption of such resolution, and in such resolution the township board shall prescribe the form of ballot to be used in voting upon such proposition, and shall determine whether such proposition shall be voted upon at a special election to be called by the township board for that purpose, or at the annual election and such township board shall also, in its resolution, direct the township clerk of such township to give notice of such proposition and of the vote to be taken thereon, by posting notices signed by said clerk in not less than 3 public and conspicuous places in each election district of such township, not less than 20 days before such annual township meeting or general or special election, and which said notice shall set forth the form of the ballot to be voted upon said proposition at such annual meeting or general or special election, and if such proposition is to be voted upon at a special election, the said township board in and by such resolution shall call such election and provide for the same and such notice so to be given by the township clerk shall also give notice that such special election has been called by such township board.

Act No. 170, P.A. 1933 - Bidders on Public Works

AN ACT to regulate the practice of taking bids and awarding contracts on public work construction, maintenance or repair work, except public buildings, and to provide a means of prohibiting those not qualified by experience, financial resources or any other valid reason from undertaking such public construction work.

MCLA 123.501 Bidders on public works; statement as to qualifications, notice of rejection. [MSA 5.2311]

MCLA 123.502 Same; failure to file statement; rejection of bid. [MSA 5.2312]

MCLA 123.503 Allotment of work by public officers. [MSA 5.2313]

MCLA 123.504 Questionnaire and statement; confidential treatment. [MSA 5.2314]

MCLA 123.505 Refusal to furnish data to bidder; discretion of public officers. [MSA 5.2315]

MCLA 123.506 Review of decision of public officers. [MSA 5.2316]

MCLA 123.507 False statements, penalty. [MSA 5.2317]

MCLA 123.508 Definition of person. [MSA 5.2318]

DEPUTY CLERK AND DEPUTY TREASURER - GENERAL LAW TOWNSHIP

There has been a great deal of misunderstanding and confusion regarding appointment of the deputy township clerk. For some reason there is a myth that it is a full-time position, that the salary must be approved by the electors at the annual meeting and that the deputy has no vote on the township board. These are but a few of the erroneous conceptions of the deputy clerk's status.

The statute says, *"... and in case of the absence, sickness, death or other disability of the clerk, such deputy shall perform the duties of the clerk, and receive the same compensation as the clerk ..."*

The **only** time a deputy clerk performs any of the clerk's duties is when the clerk is absent from the township or physically incapable of handling them. If the deputy is acting for the clerk, then he/she may vote on all matters coming before the township board -- this has been firmly established by opinions of the attorney general and by decisions in the courts.* While acting for the clerk, the

----

*In a charter township a deputy clerk does not have to be a qualified elector in the township. However, he/she does not have a vote on the township board.

----

deputy receives exactly the same salary as the clerk, which is paid from the general fund of the township and **may not be deducted from the clerk's salary.**

Death of the township clerk poses another problem. Under the principal law that a deputy acts in place of a principal agent, the new township clerk must appoint a new deputy clerk. It may be the former deputy or someone entirely new. Once appointed, a deputy can only be removed for cause (misfeasance, malfeasance, nonfeasance, criminal prosecution, habitual drunkenness).

Although the township clerk is charged with certain responsibilities, this does not mean that he/she must do all of the clerical and secretarial work involved. Someone may be employed to take registrations, do the bookkeeping, file and the many other things that have to be done in an office. The salary for such position(s) is established by the township board. In many townships the deputy clerk is hired to do these things, but it is important to bear in mind that **if and when the deputy is taking the place of the clerk, then the salary received is the same as the clerk's and paid from the general fund.**

In a general law township, the treasurer may appoint a deputy and assign his/her duties and responsibilities. The township board approves the appointment, may assign additional duties with the treasurer's consent, and establishes the salary (which is paid from the general fund). In the elected official's absence the deputy may be requested to handle all of the treasurer's work, including making the treasurer's report at township board meetings. However, the deputy treasurer never, under any circumstances, has any voting power at those meetings. He/she may, of course, be present at any meeting the same as any other township resident.

See the narration at the end of the section on Duties and Responsibilities - Treasurer for further explanation.

DEPUTY CLERK AND DEPUTY TREASURER - CHARTER TOWNSHIP

Although there has never been an official attorney general's opinion or a court decision, an opinion provided by a competent authority has indicated that:

1. The law does not require the appointment of a deputy clerk or a deputy treasurer in a charter township.

2. The charter township board, upon recommendation of the supervisor or the township superintendent, if there be one, may by resolution create the offices of deputy township clerk and deputy township treasurer and appoint the individuals to fill such offices.

3. The charter township board may prescribe the duties of the deputy township clerk and the deputy township treasurer and may grant them the broad authority to exercise all the powers and duties of the clerk and treasurer in their absence, **except** the right to be a voting member of the charter township board.

4. The salary or compensation for such officers may be established by the charter township board and need not necessarily be the same compensation as provided for the clerk and the treasurer.

5. In the event a township clerk is absent from a regular or special meeting of the charter township board, such board shall appoint one of its own members as temporary clerk for such meeting.

It should be pointed out that although the law does not require the appointment of these deputies, it would perhaps be desirable in order to enable the continuation of administrative functions of the offices of the clerk and treasurer in the event of their absence or inability to function.

DUTIES AND RESPONSIBILITIES - TREASURER

The township treasurer keeps records of receipts and disbursements of township funds which come into his/her hands, receives and deposits in a bank depository designated by the township board all funds which belong to the township, disburses township funds upon order of the township board, makes scheduled reports required by law and upon demand of the township board of all records of receipts and disbursements, collects all real and personal property as well as special assessment taxes, in most townships sells dog licenses and trailer camp licenses, prepares delinquent tax rolls and turns them over to the county treasurer for collection, serves as a member of the township election commission and performs such other duties as may be directed by statute or by the township board in accordance with local conditions.

The treasurer's records shall be open to public inspection at all times and, along with any township moneys in his/her hands, must be turned over to his/her successor in office, whether elected or appointed.

The majority of Michigan townships have salaried persons filling the office of township treasurer. Unfortunately there still remain a number of township treasurers who are paid on a fee basis, causing many problems for township boards because they are reluctant to deprive the officer of certain equipment and other emoluments. The problems stem from the fact that the statutes do not permit a fee basis treasurer to receive reimbursement for such things as mileage and other incidental expenses commensurate with the operation of the office. Some townships actually violate the law by providing a salary in addition to the fees allowed by statute. It must be emphasized that the only additional payment a fee basis treasurer may legally receive is per diem for attending meetings of the township board.

Act No. 2, P.A. 1968, requires that the treasurer maintain a record of all cash reflecting the beginning balance, receipts, disbursements and ending balance of each fund each month. It is significant that only the official receipts prepared by the township treasurer are posted to the official cash receipts journal from which monthly postings are made to the general ledger. The treasurer should become familiar with the Uniform Accounting Procedures Manual provided by the Local Government Division of the State Department of Treasury and should attend one of the accounting schools provided by the Michigan Townships Association and the Continuing Education Service of Michigan State University through the Institute for Community Development and Services.

Townships should take advantage of the statute which provides that a deputy treasurer may be appointed by the township treasurer with the approval of the township board and the consent of his bondsman. A deputy treasurer can render invaluable service in the event of the inability of the township treasurer to perform the duties of his/her office, especially so during the busy period of tax collection time.

Compensation for a deputy treasurer is established by the township board. If the township treasurer is paid a salary, then the deputy receives a salary, in an amount to be decided by the board, which is paid from the general fund and may not be deducted from the treasurer's salary. If the treasurer is paid on a fee basis, then the deputy's compensation is deducted from the fees collected by the treasurer.

Act No. 116, P.A. 1954 - Election Law, Ch. XVI - Township Offices

MCLA 168.364 Township officers; township treasurer, bond, sureties, approval, filing. [MSA 6.1364]

Sec. 364. Each township treasurer, within the time limited for filing his oath of office and before he shall enter upon the duties of his office, shall give a bond to the township in such sum and with such sureties as the supervisor shall require and approve ...(and file it within that time)... with the township clerk ...

R.S. 1846, c. 16 - Township Board

MCLA 41.72 Annual meeting; date; claims, auditing, settling, payment. [MSA 5.64]

Sec. 72. The township board shall meet annually on the second Tuesday next preceding the annual township meeting for the purpose of auditing and settling all claims against the township which have not previously been audited and settled by the township board at a regular meeting and they shall state on each account the amount allowed by them; and the amounts allowed shall be paid by the treasurer, on the order of the board, signed by their clerk.

MCLA 41.76 Township treasurer; duties. [MSA 5.68]

Sec. 76. The township treasurer shall receive and take charge of all moneys belonging to the township, or which are by law required to be paid into the township treasury, and shall pay over and account for the same, according to the order of such township, or the officers thereof duly authorized, and shall perform all such other duties as shall be required of him by law.

MCLA 41.77 Bond, filing, time; location of depository. [MSA 5.69]

Sec. 77. Each township treasurer, within the time limited for filing his oath of office and before he shall enter upon the duties of his office, shall give a bond to the township in such sum and with such sureties as the supervisor shall require and approve, conditioned for the faithful discharge of the duties of his office, and that he will faithfully and truly account for and pay over according to law all moneys which shall come into his hands as such treasurer, ... It shall be the duty of such treasurer to file within the time above mentioned said bond with the township clerk ... The township board of any township may provide by resolution for the depositing of any or all moneys coming into the hands of the treasurer of said township, and said treasurer shall deposit said money in such bank, banks or depository within the county, or in a subsidiary or branch of such bank, banks or depository though located outside the county, in which said township is located as such township board may direct, subject to the provisions of this act. Any interest which may accrue upon such deposit shall be paid into the general fund of such township. The township board ... shall determine in such resolution the time for which such deposits shall be made, and all details for carrying into effect the authority herein given, but all such proceedings in connection with the deposit of such moneys shall be conducted in such a manner as to insure full publicity and shall be open at all times to public inspection. When a depository is provided as authorized herein and the funds are deposited therein as herein directed the treasurer of the township and his bondsmen shall be relieved of any liability occasioned by the failure of the bank or banks of deposit or the sureties for such bank or banks, or by the failure of either of them to safely keep and repay such funds.

MCLA 41.78 Accounts. [MSA 5.70]

Sec. 78. *Each township treasurer shall keep a just and true account of the receipts and expenditures of all moneys which shall come into his hands by virtue of his office, in a book to be provided for that purpose, at the expense of the township, and to be delivered to his successor in office.*

Act No. 51, P.A. 1867 - Additional Sureties, Township Treasurer

AN ACT to provide for additional sureties from township treasurers in certain cases.

MCLA 41.611 Sureties insufficient; new bond. [MSA 5.141]

Sec. 1. *That whenever the sureties in the bond given by any township treasurer to the county treasurer, as required by law, shall become insolvent, or shall remove out of the county, or shall in the opinion of the county treasurer become in any manner insufficient, the county treasurer shall give notice thereof to the supervisor of the township, and that such township treasurer is required to give a new bond to the county treasurer.*

MCLA 41.612 Same; new bond. [MSA 5.142]

Sec. 2. *Whenever the sureties in the bond given by any township treasurer to his township, as required by law, shall become insolvent, or shall remove out of the county, or shall in the opinion* of the township board become in any manner insufficient, or when-ever the penal sum named in such bond shall by said board be deemed insufficient, the township board may require the township treasurer to give a new bond to the township, with sufficient sureties, to be approved as required by law.

MCLA 41.613 New bond; notification. [MSA 5.143]

Sec. 3. Whenever the county treasurer or township board of the township shall require a new bond of the township treasurer, as in this act provided, it shall be the duty of the supervisor forthwith to notify such township treasurer in writing of such requirement, and that he is required to give such new bond or bonds, as the case may be, within such time, not less than 5 nor more than 10 days after such notice, as the supervisor may prescribe.

MCLA 41.614 Same; issuance. [MSA 5.144]

Sec. 4. When any new bond shall be required of any township treasurer as herein provided, it shall be his duty to give the same to the township or the county treasurer, as the case may be, within the time prescribed by the supervisor; such bond to be of the amount and to be approved as now required by law in cases of bonds required to be given by such treasurers to the township or to the county treasurer.

MCLA 41.615 Refusal; new treasurer; liability of old sureties. [MSA 5.145]

Sec. 5. If any township treasurer shall neglect or refuse to give any new bond required of him as herein provided, such refusal or neglect shall be deemed a refusal to serve, and thereupon the township board shall appoint a new treasurer for the remainder of the year, who shall give like security and be subject to like duties and penalties, and have the same powers and compensation as the treasurer in whose place he was appointed; and the township clerk shall immediately give notice of such appointment to the county treasurer, but such appointment shall not exonerate the former treasurer or his sureties from any liability incurred by him or them.

MCLA 41.616 Transfers to new treasurer; accounting to board. [MSA 5.146]

Sec. 6. Whenever any township treasurer appointed as provided in the preceding section shall have given the security required by law, the former treasurer shall forthwith deliver over all moneys in his hands by virtue of his office, and the tax-roll for the year (if the same shall have been delivered to him), to such new treasurer; and shall, whenever required by the township board of the township, account to them for all moneys received or disbursed by him.

MCLA 41.617 New bond; delivery of tax roll. [MSA 5.147]

Sec. 7. When any new bond shall be required of any township treasurer, as in this act provided, the tax-roll of the township for the year, shall not be delivered to him until he shall have given the required security.

Act No. 206, P.A. 1893 - Assessment, Levy and Collection of Taxes - How To Be Assessed

MCLA 211.41 Assessor, duties; ... [MSA 7.82]

Sec. 41. Before the supervisor or assessing officer shall deliver such roll to the township treasurer ...

MCLA 211.42 Tax roll preparation; warrant; township treasurer, accounting; collection period; ... [MSA 7.83]

Sec. 42. The supervisor shall ... prepare a tax roll, ... and annex thereto a warrant signed by him, commanding the township ... treasurer to collect the several sums mentioned in the last column of such roll but the warrant shall not refer to the total or aggregate of the several sums mentioned in the last column, and to retain in his hand the amount receivable by law into the township treasury for the purpose therein specified, and to pay over to the county treasurer the amounts which shall have been collected for state and county purposes up to and including January 10 next following, and to the treasurer of each school district the amounts which shall have been collected for such school district up to and including January 10 next following, within 10 days thereafter, and notify the secretary or director of each school district of the amount paid to the school district treasurer, and the remainder of the amounts therein specified for said purposes, and account in full for all moneys received on or before March 1 next following. The warrant shall authorize and command the treasurer, in case any person named in the tax roll shall neglect or refuse to pay his tax, to levy the same by distress and sale of the goods and chattels of such person. The supervisor may make a new roll and warrant in case of the loss of the one originally given to the township treasurer; the copy of the roll with the warrant annexed shall be known as "the tax roll."

MCLA 211.43   Notice to township treasurer of apportionment of taxes; bond, exception; township tax roll; maximum amount of taxes on hand. MSA 7.84

Sec. 43. The supervisor of each township, on or before the 5th day of November in each year, shall notify the township treasurer of the amount of ... taxes ... and such treasurer, on or before the 28th day of November, **shall give to the county treasurer** *a bond running to the county in the actual amount of state, county and school taxes, except ...(conditions/payment for/possible exceptions regarding bond)... (After bond requirements completed)... on or before the 1st day of December the supervisor shall deliver to the township treasurer the tax roll of his township. The county treasurer shall file and safely keep such bond in his office, and shall give to the township treasurer a receipt stating that he has received the bond required, which receipt the township treasurer* **shall deliver to the supervisor** *on or before the 1st day of December. The supervisor after the delivery of such receipt and on or before the 1st day of December, shall deliver to the township treasurer the tax roll of his township. Such township treasurer shall at no time have on hand collections of state, county and school taxes in excess of 25 per cent of the amount of such taxes apportioned to his township and from time to time whenever such collections on hand shall reach such percentage he shall immediately account for and turn over to the county treasurer the total amount of such ... collections on hand and to the several school district treasurers the total amount of ... school tax collections on hand and notify the secretary or director of the school districts the total amount of taxes paid to the school district treasurers which notification shall show the different funds for which the taxes were collected.*

MCLA 211.43a Delay in receipt of tax roll; fees for unpaid taxes; delinquent tax return. [MSA 7.85]

MCLA 211.43b Public moneys; depository; liability. [MSA 7.86]

Sec. 43b. The governing board ... of every township ... within this state shall provide by resolution for the deposit of all public moneys which shall come into the hands of the treasurer ...(and depository)... Failure on the part of (the) *treasurer to deposit* (such public moneys) *in accordance with the terms of such resolution shall render him and his surety or sureties liable for any loss occasioned by such failure, ...*

MCLA 211.44   Tax collections; statement to taxpayers, time; ... [MSA 7.87]

Sec. 44. On receiving such tax roll the township treasurer ... shall proceed to collect such taxes. ... shall mail to each taxpayer at his last known address on his tax roll, on the receipt of such tax roll, a statement showing ... the amount of the tax thereon. ... The township treasurer shall remain in his office at some convenient place in his township on every Friday in the month of December, from 9 a.m. to 5 p.m. to receive taxes, but he shall receive taxes upon any week day when they may be offered. ...(late fees, etc.)... In townships in which the treasurer receives a salary, the township board only may waive all or part of the collection fees on taxes paid on or before February 15. All fees collected by the township treasurer ... where the treasurer receives a salary shall be credited to the contingent fund of the township. ...(payment of bond cost)*... (enforcement of collection)...*

MCLA 211.45 Collection, time limit. [MSA 7.89]

Sec. 45. All taxes shall be collected by the several township ... treasurers ... before the first day of March, in each year.

Note: For additional citations and information about the treasurer's responsibilities as tax collector, see the chapter on Finance and Taxation.

Act No. 116, P.A. 1954 - Election Law, Ch. II -
Boards of Election Commissioners and Boards of
Canvassers

MCLA 168.26 Townships; board of election commissioners; ...
MSA 6.1026

*Sec. 26. Unless otherwise provided by charter, the supervisor,
clerk and township treasurer shall constitute the board of township
election commissioners ... Should only 1 of said officers be in
attendance on the day appointed for a meeting of the board, the
officer in attendance shall appoint a qualified and registered elector of the township to act in the absentee's stead during the period
of nonattendance.*

Note: The supervisor and treasurer no longer serve as members of the township board of canvassers.

Act No. 243, P.A. 1959 - Mobile Home Park Act

MCLA 125.1042 Trailer coach park; tax revenue, disbursement.
MSA 5.278(72)

*Sec. 42. The treasurer of the municipality, in which a trailer
coach park is located, shall accept and verify the monthly reports
from licensees and collect and disburse the monthly tax payments
as hereinafter provided. The municipal treasurer shall issue a receipt in triplicate for all moneys collected under this act, the original to be given the licensee, the duplicate to be retained for
municipal records, and the triplicate, together with 50 cents per
trailer coach shall be transmitted to the county treasurer, who shall
issue a receipt therefor and credit the county general fund. The
municipal treasurer shall credit the municipal general fund with 50
cents per trailer coach so parked, and shall transmit to the school
district in which the trailer coach was parked $2.00 for each trailer
coach so parked.*

Act No. 339, P.A. 1919 - Dog Law

MCLA 287.274 Township ... treasurer, duties; fees; ... MSA 12.524

*Sec. 14. Every township ... treasurer ... shall, on or before
December first, ... of each year ..., make application to the county
treasurer for the necessary license blanks and tags for the ensuing
year and after receipting therefor may issue dog licenses and tags
in like manner, and upon like application as prescribed for the
issuing of licenses by the county treasurer. Each township ...
treasurer shall not later than March first of each year return to the
county treasurer all unused tags, together with the book or books
from which he has issued dog licenses, with the stubs therein contained properly filled out, and showing the names of each license
and the number of each license issued to him and a full description
of each dog licensed by him. He shall also on or before March first
of each year pay over all moneys received by him for issuing licenses less 15 cents for each license issued, to pay him for issuing and recording the same. ...*

Note: For full citations on the Dog Law, see the appropriate
section in the chapter on Health.

R.S. 1846, c. 16 - Resignations and Vacancies

MCLA 41.58 Temporary appointments; appointees' duties.
MSA 5.42

*Sec. 58. Whenever there shall be a vacancy, or when the in-
cumbent shall, from any cause, be unable to perform the duties of
his office, in either of the township offices,* **except that of township
treasurer,** *the township board may make temporary appointments ...*

**MCLA 41.59 Temporary appointments; township treasurer; sureties,
former treasurer.** MSA 5.43

*Sec. 59. In case the treasurer of any township shall refuse to
serve, or shall vacate his office before completing the duties thereof, or be disabled from completing the same, by reason of sickness
or any other cause, the township board shall forthwith appoint a
treasurer for the remainder of the term, who shall give like security,
and be subject to like duties and responsibilities, and have the
same powers and compensation as the treasurer in whose place he
was appointed, ...; but such appointment shall not exonerate the
former treasurer or his sureties from any liability incurred by him
or them.*

Act No. 206, P.A. 1893 - Assessment, Levy and Collection of Taxes

MCLA 211.111 Deputy township treasurer, appointment, responsibility, compensation. MSA 7.165

Sec. 111. Any township treasurer with the approval of the township board and the consent of his bondsmen, which consent shall be in writing and shall be filed with the clerk of the township, may appoint a deputy who shall possess all the powers and may perform all the duties of the treasurer. Such township treasurer and his bondsmen shall be liable for all the acts and defaults of such deputy treasurer. Such deputy shall be paid by salary or otherwise as the township board determines.

DUTIES AND RESPONSIBILITIES - TRUSTEES

Since township trustees basically function by helping make decisions in two areas -- legislation (ordinances) and policy establishment (rules and regulations) -- it is imperative that they be fully aware of the responsibilities of the township board as delineated in this manual. Familiarity with the duties of fellow board members will also enhance their efficiency.

If the supervisor is absent, a trustee may be called upon to serve as chairman at a board meeting. Additional duties may be imposed upon the trustee from time to time by statute (fence viewer) or by direction of the township board (commissioner of noxious weeds, supervisor of department of public works, member of park commission, etc.). Care should be taken, of course, that no officer is placed in a conflict of interest situation. If a conflict should arise, any official involved should refrain from participating in action regarding the matter under discussion.

It is advisable that the township board be so organized that trustees may also serve on advisory committees for budget preparation, establishment of operational procedures for various departments, information-gathering prior to making determinations regarding services, etc. Such assignments make it possible to take full advantage of the expertise and knowledge of these public servants. and better qualifies them to make decisions during deliberations of the board.

For their services, trustees receive compensation established by the electors and by applicable statutes, as well as that which may be allowed by the township board for services not defined as being within the purview of the office. Because of increased utilization of township trustees, many larger metropolitan townships have established an annual salary for the office. This is not only legal but also more efficient and businesslike from the standpoint of the trustee, the people and the township board.

In addition to salary and/or per diem payments, trustees may receive mileage and other incidental road expenses when traveling on township business. In addition, upon authorization of the township board, they may (along with other township officials) be legally reimbursed for registration fees, hotel and motel bills, food, mileage and other incidental expenses for attending educational meetings of any kind. Included, of course, would be the annual convention, district and county chapter meetings and other especially programmed educational meetings for township officials sponsored by the Michigan Townships Association.

R.S. 1846, c. 16 - Township Board

MCLA 41.70 Township board; membership, quorum; populous townships. [MSA 5.62]

Sec. 70. The supervisor, 2 trustees, the township treasurer and the township clerk, shall constitute the township board, ... Provided, That in townships now or hereafter having a population of 5,000 or over as determined by the last federal decennial census or by any federal decennial census hereafter taken or now or hereafter having 3,000 or over registered electors, the supervisor, the township treasurer, the township clerk and 4 trustees, ... shall constitute the township board, ...

Act No. 359, P.A. 1947 - Charter Townships

MCLA 42.5 Charter township board, ... [MSA 5.46(5)]

Sec. 5. Except as otherwise provided in this act, all legislative authority and powers of each charter township shall be vested in and shall be exercised and determined by a township board of 7 members composed of the supervisor, the township clerk, the township treasurer and 4 trustees ... In the event of the absence of the

140

supervisor from any meeting of the township board, said board shall appoint 1 of its members president pro tem for such meeting. ...

R.S. 1846, c. 16 - Compensation to Township Officers

MCLA 41.95 Township officers; compensation, township meeting. [MSA 5.82]

Sec. 95. The officers composing the township boards, ... shall be entitled to such salary as shall be fixed by the electors at the annual township meeting, ...

Same; compensation, referendum. *In those townships which have abolished the annual township meeting ... the salary for officers composing the township board, ... shall be determined by the township board. ...(Subject to referendum petition)...*

Salaried officials. *The salary of township officials who are paid a salary may be determined by resolution adopted by the township board. The electors at any subsequent township meeting may alter the amount of salary fixed by any such resolution. No salaries shall be raised within 60 days prior to an election.*

MCLA 41.96 Other services, compensation. [MSA 5.83]

Sec. 96. For services not otherwise provided for by law, rendered to townships by township officers in the duties of their respective offices, the township board shall audit and allow such compensation as they shall deem reasonable.

Act No. 359, P.A. 1947 - Charter Townships

MCLA 42.6 Charter township board; members, compensation, expenses. [MSA 5.46(6)]

*Sec. 6. Each **trustee** may receive, in addition to other emoluments provided by law for his service to the township, not to exceed the sum of $15.00 per meeting of the board actually attended by him, but not to exceed in total $1,000.00 per year, to be paid upon authorization of the township board. ... Reasonable expenses may be allowed to members of the township board when actually incurred on behalf of the township.*

Note: Mileage to and from a meeting may not be paid in addition to the $15.00.

TRUSTEE - FENCE VIEWER

Perhaps one of the more unusual, sometimes controversial duties of a township trustee is when he is required by law to serve as a fence viewer to resolve differences regarding fences and property lines. Line disputes are perhaps responsible for more emotional, even hysterical, reaction on the part of aggravated landowners than any other problem.

A check under the subject heading Fences in the index of the Michigan Compiled Laws will indicate the diversified situations which may embroil the fence viewer in disputes over property lines. These include but are not limited to such things as holes for mineral exploration, abandoned mines, enclosures for holding animals awaiting slaughter, brine pipe line companies and their problems, cisterns, gravel pits, highways and roads (especially private roads), fences on property lines between individual landowners or between townships and villages, and even something as new and modern as control of snowmobiling by fencing.

A trustee-fence viewer must learn the true meaning of patience, tolerance and understanding, develop a good sense of humor and be able to arrive at decisions which are equitable, just, fair and impartial as well as economically feasible to the disputants. All this for $5.00 a day while pursuing his/her duties as a fence viewer!

R.S. 1846, c. 18 - Fences and Fence Viewers

MCLA 43.1 Legal fence. [MSA 5.211]

MCLA 43.2 Partition fences, maintenance; lands under jurisdiction of conservation commission. [MSA 5.212]

MCLA 43.3 Same; neglect; remedy. [MSA 5.213]

MCLA 43.4 Same; legal share, failure to pay; remedy. [MSA 5.214]

MCLA 43.5 Same; controversy; fence viewers' determination.
[MSA 5.215]

MCLA 43.6 Same; assigned portion, neglect; remedy. [MSA 5.216]

MCLA 43.7 Same; proportionate reimbursement. [MSA 5.217]

MCLA 43.8 Same; repair. [MSA 5.218]

MCLA 43.9 Boundary in stream; controversy; fence viewers, duties. [MSA 5.219]

MCLA 43.10 Same; fence viewers' proceedings; remedy. [MSA 5.220]

MCLA 43.11 Partition of severalty land occupied in common. [MSA 5.221]

MCLA 43.12 Same; time limits, neglect; remedy. [MSA 5.222]

MCLA 43.13 Partition fence; removal. [MSA 5.223]

MCLA 43.14 Same; payment for one-half; remedy. [MSA 5.224]

MCLA 43.15 Same; township line; fence viewers. [MSA 5.225]

MCLA 43.15a Same; appointment of fence viewers where fence on boundary between city and township; procedure; report, filing; assessment of special tax. [MSA 5.225(1)]

MCLA 43.16 Same; across water; neglect, remedy. [MSA 5.226]

MCLA 43.17 Same; unimproved lands. [MSA 5.227]

MCLA 43.18 Same; erection, exceptions. [MSA 5.228]

MCLA 43.19 Designation of township trustees as fence viewers. [MSA 5.229]

Sec. 19. Two township trustees in each township shall be designated by the township board as fence viewers in their respective townships.

MCLA 43.20 Neglect, penalty. [MSA 5.230]

Sec. 20. *Any fence viewer, who shall, when requested, unreasonably neglect to view any fence, or to perform any other duty required of him in this chapter, shall forfeit the sum of 5 dollars, and shall also be liable to the party injured for all damages consequent upon such neglect.*

MCLA 43.21 Compensation; recovery. [MSA 5.231]

Sec. 21. *Each fence viewer shall be paid by the person employing him, at the rate of $5.00 a day for the time he shall be so employed; and if such person shall neglect to pay the same within 30 days after the service shall have been performed, each fence viewer having performed any such service may recover in an action of assumpsit double the amount of such fees.*

Act No. 243, P.A. 1959 - Mobile Home Park Act

AN ACT to define, license and regulate trailer coach parks; to prescribe the powers and duties of the state health commissioner and other state and local officers; ...

MCLA 125.1073 Line fences. [MSA 5.278(103)]

Sec. 73. *If the owner of improved property abutting a trailer coach park demands that a fence be built on his property lines, the operator of the park shall build a suitable fence not less than 4 nor more than 6 feet in height, constructed of woven wire or open metal or wood pickets or boards, the cost of which shall be shared equally with the abutting property owners. Barbed wire shall not be used in the construction of this fence.*

Act No. 201, P.A. 1911 - Fencing of Private Cemeteries

AN ACT to compel owners of private cemeteries to keep the same enclosed with a suitable fence to prevent encroachment of live stock.

MCLA 128.91 Private cemeteries, fencing. [MSA 5.3141]

MCLA 128.92 Same; notice to build or repair. [MSA 5.3142]

MCLA 128.93 Non-compliance, erection by township health board; expense. [MSA 5.3143]

Act No. 227, P.A. 1915 - Galvanized Wire Fence

AN ACT to provide a standard test and gauge of galvanized wire fence within this state, to provide for the grading of such fence according to such test and gauge, to regulate the use of tags or labels in connection with the sale of such fence within this state, and to provide a penalty for the violation of this act.

MCLA 290.351 Galvanized wire fence; standard test gauge. [MSA 5.251]

MCLA 290.352 Same; galvanizing test. [MSA 5.252]

MCLA 290.353 Same; standard grades. [MSA 5.253]

MCLA 290.354 Same; label. [MSA 5.254]

MCLA 290.355 Same; label, annexing conditions; fee. [MSA 5.255]

MCLA 290.356 Same; test, board of agriculture; permit; label contents. [MSA 5.256]

MCLA 290.357 Same; unlawful sales, penalty; civil liability. [MSA 5.257]

MCLA 290.358 Same; taking of samples; tests. [MSA 5.258]

MCLA 290.359 Tests, accounts, publication; expenses; unexpended balance. [MSA 5.259]

MCLA 290.360 Effective date. [MSA 5.260]

Act No. 236, P.A. 1961 - Revised Judicature Act, Ch. 29 - Provisions Concerning Specific Actions

MCLA 600.2919 Damage to land; treble damages, single damages; waste. [MSA 27A.2919] **Treble and single damages. Waste by holder of present estate, double damages. Threatened waste, in-**

junction, damages. **Waste after commencement of action, restraining order, contempt. Waste on land under levy, restraining order, contempt. Land sold on execution, liability of person entitled to possession, acts after sale not waste.** ... *If, at any time after the sale of real estate on execution and before a deed is executed in pursuance of the sale, the defendant in the execution or any other person commits waste on the real estate or removes from it any buildings, fences or other fixtures belonging to the land which would pass to the grantee by a deed of conveyance of the land, the purchaser at the sale or any person who has acquired his rights may have and maintain, against the person doing the injury and against any other person who has the buildings, fences, or fixtures in his possession after their removal, the same actions which the absolute owner of the premises would be entitled to. ... (c) ... (iv) He may apply any wood or timber on the land to the necessary repair of any fences, buildings, or erections which were on the premises at the time of sale; ...*

MCLA 600.2940 Nuisance; abatement, circuit court, injunction; damages and expenses; nature of action. ⌈MSA 27A.2940⌉ **Venue; power of circuit court. Private nuisance; damages, abatement. Same; abatement. Same; expense of abatement.** ... *materials of any buildings, fences, or other things that may be removed as a nuisance, may be sold* ... **Actions equitable in nature, damages.**

DUTIES AND RESPONSIBILITIES - CONSTABLES

Adoption of the 1963 constitution abolished the office of justice of the peace. It also considerably diminished the strength and stature of the office of constable, since that officer was the ministerial arm of the justice courts. There are still a number of things the constable may perform for county agencies and municipal courts (usually located in cities), as well as a few specifically in townships -- provided they are within his/her own county. These can be found by checking the subject index under Constables in the Michigan Compiled Laws, the Administrative Code of the State of Michigan and finally with the local prosecuting attorney.

Since the constable is by statute a traffic and peace officer, appointment to a township office such as the zoning board would not be advisable. This could place the constable in the position

146

of policing his/her own actions as an appointive officer. However, constables may be employed by the township board as liquor license inspectors and/or enforcement officers in other areas of township operation, with additional compensation for duties performed beyond those for which specific statutory fees are established for the constable.

If a constable intends to assume the responsibility of his office, he must first file a bond in an amount approved by the township supervisor or clerk. If the township board employs the constable for additional duties, the bond should reflect the increased responsibility.

Act No. 116, P.A. 1954 - Elections, Ch. XVI - Township Offices

MCLA 168.365 ... constable, indemnification. ⎡MSA 6.1365⎤

Sec. 365. Every person elected or appointed to the office of constable, before he enters upon the duties of his office and within the time prescribed by law for filing his official oath, shall execute, with sufficient sureties ... an instrument in writing by which said constable and his sureties shall jointly and severally agree to pay ... all ... sums of money as the said constable may become liable to pay ....

R.S. 1846, c. 16 - Constables

MCLA 41.80 Bond; contents, time. ⎡MSA 5.72⎤

Sec. 80. Every person elected or appointed to the office of constable, before he enters upon the duties of his office, and within the time prescribed by law for filing his official oath, shall execute, with sufficient sureties, to be approved by the supervisor or clerk of his township, an instrument in writing by which said constable and his sureties shall jointly and severally agree to pay to each and every person who may be entitled thereto, all such sums of money as the said constable may become liable to pay on account of any neglect or default of said constable in the service or return of any process that may be delivered to him for service or collection, or on account of any misfeasance of the said constable in the discharge of, or failure of said constable to faithfully perform any of the duties of his said office.

MCLA 41.81 Same; approval, filing, evidence, suits. [MSA 5.73]

Sec. 81. Such supervisor or township clerk shall endorse on such instrument, his approbation of the sureties therein named, and shall then cause the same to be filed in the office of the township clerk, and a copy of such instrument, certified by the township clerk, shall be presumptive evidence of the contents and execution thereof, and all actions against a constable or his sureties, upon any such instrument, shall be prosecuted within 2 years after the expiration of the year for which the constable named therein shall have been elected.

MCLA 41.82 Service of process; duties. [MSA 5.74]

Sec. 82. Constables shall serve all warrants, notices and process lawfully directed to them by the township board, or the township clerk, or any other officer, and shall perform such other duties as are required of them by law.

MCLA 41.83 Same; powers. [MSA 5.75]

Sec. 83. Any constable may serve any writ, process or order lawfully directed to him, in any township in his county.

MCLA 41.84 Duties as ministerial officer. [MSA 5.76]

Sec. 84. Constables shall ... attend upon the sessions of the circuit courts for their respective counties, when notified for that purpose by the sheriff.

Act No. 236, P.A. 1961 - Revised Judicature Act of 1961, Ch. 76 - Fees of ... Constables ...

MCLA 600.7611 Constables' fees and mileage in civil cases; penalty, excess fee. [MSA 27A.7611]

Sec. 7611. (1) Constables shall be entitled to the following fees in civil cases:
(a) For serving a warrant, $2.00; for serving a summons, $2.00.
(b) For a copy of every summons delivered on request, or left at the dwelling of the defendant, in his absence, 25 cents.

(c) For serving a subpoena, $2.00 for service upon each witness summoned by him.

(d) For serving an attachment or writ of replevin, $2.00; and for a copy thereof, and of the inventory of the property seized, $1.00.

(e) For serving an execution upon the body or goods and chattels of a party, $2.00.

(f) Committing a defendant to prison on execution, $5.00.

(g) For traveling in the service of process including any summons, subpoena or writ mentioned in this section, 20 cents for each mile necessarily traveled from the place of service to the place of return.

(h) Summoning a jury, $2.00.

(i) Attending upon a jury, $1.00.

(j) For collecting and paying over money on executions, 5% upon all sums.

(k) Advertising sale of property, $2.00.

(l) Selling property, $2.00.

(m) For attending circuit court at the request of the sheriff, $5.00 for each day, to be paid out of the county treasury.

(2) ...(refers to justice courts, now common pleas courts in cities)...

(3) Any constable who shall wilfully collect more fees for the service rendered than herein provided, shall upon conviction thereof be guilty of a misdemeanor.

Act No. 175, P.A. 1927 - Code of Criminal Procedure, Ch. XV - Fees

MCLA 775.3   Fees; services of constables, additional compensation. [MSA 28.1240]

Sec. 3. A constable shall be allowed for serving a warrant or other process for the arrest of any person, issued by any magistrate or court, 50 cents; for traveling to make such service, going only, 15 cents per mile, and where an arrest has been made, 15 cents per mile return travel from the place of arrest to the place of return; for taking a prisoner to jail or to the house of correction, 15 cents per mile, going only; for serving a mittimus, 15 cents; serving a subpoena, 15 cents for each witness, and 15 cents per mile for the distance actually and necessarily traveled in going to make such service; for summoning a jury, 1 dollar; for attending

*the same, 1 dollar; for attending any court by order of the magis-
trate or officer before whom a trial or examination is being held,
when not in charge of a jury, 2 dollars per day for each day and 1
dollar for each half day so actually attending. The board of commissioners of each county may allow such further compensation for
the services of process and the expenses and trouble attending the
same as they shall deem reasonable. For other services in criminal cases, for which no compensation is especially provided by
law, such sum as the board of commissioners shall allow.*

MCLA 775.10 Fees; prohibited as in civil cases. [MSA 28.1247]

*Sec. 10. The provisions of law prohibiting the taking of any
fees for services in civil cases, other than such as are allowed
by law, shall apply to the taking of fees in criminal cases beyond
the amount allowed by law for such services.*

**Township Current Legal Opinions, Vol. I, 1956 to
1969**

Opinion 12-28-62: Summary of Duties of Township Constables

**Opinion 8-21-67: Township Board may Hire Constables as Town-
ship Police Officers if it so Decides**

**Opinion 3-25-68: Townships can by Board Resolution have up to
4 Constables with Terms of 2 Years Each. Vacancies in the Office
of Constable can be Filled by the Township Board**

**Township Current Legal Opinions, Vol. II, 1970 to
1972**

**Opinion 2-24-70: Liquor License Monies Returned to a Township
can be Used to Pay Police Officer (Constable) Appointed by the
Township Board to Make Bar Inspections**

**Opinion 5-12-70: Summary of Duties and Compensation of Township
Constables**

**Opinion 5-13-70: A Township may Employ an Elected Township
Constable as a Township Policeman, However, it is not Required
to do so**

150

Opinion 4-5-71: Summary of Duties of Township Constables

Opinion 10-14-71: A Township Constable not Employed by the Township as a Township Police Officer and Performing Duties Beyond those Authorized by State Statute for Constables is Acting on his Own and the Township Should Not be Liable for those Acts, However, the Township May Nevertheless be Forced to Defend a Lawsuit (Concerning the Constable's Activities) and Should Carry Liability Insurance to Protect Itself

COMMISSIONER OF NOXIOUS WEEDS

At first thought, it would appear that the commissioner of noxious weeds has a simple job -- merely to cruise around the countryside seeking out weeds and then destroying them in any way he sees fit.

It is not that simple. There are many highly specialized medical, technical and other scientific methods of detecting hundreds of noxious weeds, plants and insects, as well as other objectionable solids created by man. Under certain circumstances, the commissioner may be required to provide control of weeds in inland lakes, as well as prevention of swimmers' itch.

A commissioner of noxious weeds must give prompt attention to these problems. A township—wide survey should be made periodically to determine where objectionable material may be, how it can best be destroyed and how to prevent future growth or regrowth and deposits. Painstaking care must be used in selecting methods for destruction or control. Township boards, as a result of irresponsible or uninformed action, could find themselves in a lawsuit situation. This could happen because of serious or fatal or toxic reaction of humans or animals to poisons and chemicals used, or damage to crops, trees and other deciduous growth.

The basic statute under which the commissioner of noxious weeds performs his duties is Act No. 359, P.A. 1941 (above). It is suggested that reference be made to the index of the Michigan Compiled Laws under the subject heading Weeds for additional references.

Act No. 359, P.A. 1941 - Commissioners of Noxious Weeds

AN ACT for the purpose of controlling and eradicating certain noxious weeds within the state, to permit townships, ... to have a lien for expenses incurred in controlling and eradicating such weeds, to permit officials of counties and municipalities to appoint commissioners of noxious weeds, to define their powers, duties and compensation, and to repeal certain acts and parts of acts.

MCLA 247.61 Commissioner of noxious weeds; appointment, term, removal, report. MSA 9.631(1)

Sec. 1. The ...(township board)... may appoint a competent person to be the commissioner of noxious weeds who shall take the oath required of township ... officers, and shall hold office for the term of 2 years and until a successor is appointed and qualified, and he shall receive for his compensation such sum as may be fixed by the appointing body. The body so appointing may, at any time, for good cause remove such commissioner from office and appoint his successor to serve the remaining portion of his term. The appointing body shall report the name and address of the person so appointed to the state department of agriculture within 10 days after making such appointment.

MCLA 247.62 "Noxious weeds" defined. MSA 9.631(2)

Sec. 2. For the purpose of this act, "noxious weeds" shall include ...(several listed)... or other plant which in the opinion of the governing body ... coming under the provisions of this act is regarded as a common nuisance.

MCLA 247.63 Eradication of noxious weeds; duty of commissioner. MSA 9.631(3)

MCLA 247.64 Same; duty of; owner, commissioner, municipality; notice; contents; penalty. State-owned lands. MSA 9.631(4)

MCLA 247.64a Same; alternative notice by publication; cutting weeds at expense of property owner; exemption as to railroads. [MSA 9.631(4A)]

MCLA 247.65 Same; means; limitation upon expense. [MSA 9.631(5)]

MCLA 247.66 Prosecution of violators of act. [MSA 9.631(6)]

MCLA 247.67 Annual report of commissioner; contents. [MSA 9.631(7)]

MCLA 247.68 Department of agriculture; duty to cooperate in enforcement. [MSA 9.631(8)]

MCLA 247.69 Auditing accounts of commissioner; payment. [MSA 9.631(9)]

MCLA 247.70 Board of commissioners; appropriations, penalties. [MSA 9.631(10)]

Sec. 10. The boards of commissioners may make appropriations from the county treasury to aid in destroying the noxious weeds in any 1 or more towns or precincts of the county; and in case they deem it expedient, they may assume control over any 1 tract or of all the noxious weeds in the county, ... Whenever the board of commissioners shall decide to assume control, and so long as they exercise it, their jurisdiction shall be superior to that of the commissioner.

MCLA 247.71 Railroads; penalty for failure to comply. [MSA 9.631(11)]

MCLA 247.72 Highways; duty of officials to prevent growth. [MSA 9.631(12)]

Note: This section places responsibility upon the state highway commissioner and the county road commissions for prevention of noxious weeds as defined in this act from growing within the right of way of any highways under their jurisdiction.

See chapter on Services, Utilities, Contracts and Ordinances for ordinance powers.

TOWNSHIP SUPERINTENDENT/TOWNSHIP MANAGER/ OTHER EMPLOYEES

The phenomenal growth and development in Michigan since the end of World War II has made it imperative that township government be conducted with a higher degree of professionalism. If they are to meet the greater demands being made upon them, township boards must avail themselves of the services of many individuals as they develop and administer local ordinances and services. In scores of townships supportive staff now number anywhere from a low of five or six to a high of 400 to 500.

Recognizing this need for a more professional approach, the legislature has made it possible for a charter township to employ a superintendent and a general law township a manager. These persons may be delegated broad administrative responsibilities, as outlined in the charter township act, including many of the activities normally performed by the supervisor and some of the other township officials. Such an administrative officer can implement governmental policy with less political recrimination than an elected official might receive. It should be noted, however, that when someone is employed in an administrative capacity, or when administrative offices are combined in any manner, care must be taken that the legal duties of the township clerk and the township treasurer are not abolished or diminished.

In addition to a superintendent or manager, the diversified duties and responsibilities now laid upon township government require the services of such professional people as attorneys, engineers, certified public accountants, building inspectors of all kinds, community planners, doctors, nurses, firemen, policemen, traffic officers and many others. Not to be overlooked, of course, are such positions as cemetery sextons, pound masters, public works and water department supervisors and many others created by the statutes listed elsewhere in this text. Behind all of these are the supportive services of competent office personnel such as secretaries, stenographers, computer operators, bookkeepers, file clerks, general clerks, receptionists, telephone operators and other positions especially designed and required because of certain functions or utilities.

This places township government in a highly competitive field if satisfactory employees are to be secured. The township board, acting as its own employment agency, must exercise caution in establishing adequate educational and experience levels for all positions. Furthermore, it is extremely important to make sure that a prospective employee is in reasonably good physical condition. This is of particular concern with regard to policemen and firemen who may be subjected to unusual physical hazard and strain. It is good practice to utilize employment application forms which contain questions about health such as diseases of the heart, lungs, kidneys, liver and gall bladder, high or low blood pressure, paralysis, epilepsy, rheumatism, cancer, ulcers, tumors, etc. Some township boards may want to require a physical examination by a doctor, at least for applicants for the more hazardous positions.

Board members must also familiarize themselves with state and federal laws and other information which will keep them up to date on employment practices, including labor relations and arbitration procedures, working conditions, minimum wages, fair employment practices, the President's guidelines on wages and many others.

For specific citations regarding employee relations and fringe benefits, please see the final chapter.

Act No. 359, P.A. 1947 - Charter Townships

MCLA 42.9 ...; resolution creating additional officers, ...
[MSA 5.46(9)]

Sec. 9. The ... township superintendent, if one shall be appointed, (may) create such additional officers as may be necessary to administer the affairs of the township government, or may combine any administrative offices in any manner not inconsistent with state law, and prescribe the duties thereof. ...

MCLA 42.10 ...; township superintendent, appointment, powers and duties. [MSA 5.46(10)]

MCLA 42.11 Township superintendent; term, qualifications.
[MSA 5.46(11)]

Note: See Chapter I — Charter Township Act

R.S. 1846, c. 16 - Township Board

MCLA 41.75a Township manager, employment, term, duties.
[MSA 5.67(1)]

Sec. 75a. The township board may employ a township manager. The manager shall serve at the pleasure of the township board and shall not perform any duties otherwise prohibited by state law.

Note: The township manager may be assigned duties similar to the superintendent in a charter township.

THE PENAL CODE AND TOWNSHIP GOVERNMENT, OFFICERS AND EMPLOYEES

Readers should become informed of the provisions in the following citations regarding the penal code as it applies to township government. Here will be found the consequences for failure to meet the duties and responsibilities imposed upon township officials and employees.

Act No. 328, P. A. 1931 — Michigan Penal Code

AN ACT to revise, consolidate, codify and add to the statutes relating to crimes; to define crimes and prescribe the penalties therefor; to provide for the competency of evidence at the trial of persons accused of crime; to provide immunity from prosecution for certain witnesses appearing at such trials; and to repeal certain acts and parts of acts inconsistent with or contravening any of the provisions of this act.

CHAPTER I. DEFINITIONS

MCLA 750.5 Crime. [MSA 28.195]

MCLA 750.6 Division of crime. [MSA 28.196]

Sec. 6. ... A crime is:
1. A felony; or
2. A misdemeanor.

MCLA 750.7 Felony. [MSA 28.197]

Sec. 7. ... The term "felony" when used in this act, shall be construed to mean an offense for which the offender, on conviction may be punished by ... imprisonment in state prison.

MCLA 750.8 Misdemeanor. [MSA 28.198]

Sec. 8. ... When any act or omission, not a felony is punish-

156

able according to law, by a fine, penalty or forfeiture, and imprisonment, or by such fine, penalty or forfeiture, or imprisonment, in the discretion of the court, such act or omission shall be deemed a misdemeanor.

MCLA 750.9   Misdemeanor.   [MSA 28.199]

Sec. 9.   ... When the performance of any act is prohibited by this or any other statute, and no penalty for the violation of such statute is imposed, either in the same section containing such prohibition, or in any other section or statute, the doing of such act shall be deemed a misdemeanor.

CHAPTER IX. ANIMALS

MCLA 750.49   Animals; fighting, baiting or shooting.   [MSA 28.244]

MCLA 750.50   Same; cruelly working, transporting, abandoning.   [MSA 28.245]

MCLA 750.51   Same; confining on railroad cars.   [MSA 28.246]

MCLA 750.52   Duty of public officers.   [MSA 28.247]

Sec. 52.   ... It shall also be the duty of all ... constables, policemen and public officers, to arrest and prosecute all persons of whose violation of the provisions of the preceding sections of this chapter they may have knowledge or reasonable notice, and for each neglect of such duty, the officer so offending shall be deemed guilty of a misdemeanor.

MCLA 750.53 Arrest of persons and seizure of animals. [MSA 28.248]

Sec. 53.   ... Persons found violating any of the provisions of the preceding sections of this chapter may be arrested and held without warrant, in like manner as in the case of persons found breaking the peace, and it shall ...

MCLA 750.54   Search warrants.   [MSA 28.249]

Sec. 54.   ... When complaint is made, on oath or affirmation, to any magistrate authorized to issue warrants in criminal cases, that the complainant believes that any of the provisions of the preceding sections of this chapter are being, or are about to be violated in any particular building or place, such magistrate, if satisfied that there is reasonable cause for such belief, shall ...

MCLA 750.55 Incorporated society, representative deputy sheriff. MSA 28.250

MCLA 750.56 Definitions. MSA 28.251

MCLA 750.57 Burial of dead animals. MSA 28.252

MCLA 750.58 Horses, unhitching and driving away. MSA 28.253

MCLA 750.59 Animals unfit for work, disposition and use. MSA 28.254

MCLA 750.60 - 750.64 MSA 28.255 - 28.259

MCLA 750.65 Bull running at large on highway or unenclosed land. MSA 28.260(1)

MCLA 750.67 Domestic animals or fowl on cemetery grounds, landing fields, airports. MSA 28.262

Sec. 67. ... Any owner or keeper of any domestic animal or fowl, who shall allow any domestic animal or fowl to run at large and enter or be upon any premises constituting a cemetery, landing field or airport in this state, shall be guilty of a misdemeanor.

MCLA 750.68 Changing, etc., brand of animals. MSA 28.263

MCLA 750.69 Rescuing animals. MSA 28.264

MCLA 750.70 Unlawfully impounding animals. MSA 28.265

CHAPTER X. ARSON AND BURNING

MCLA 750.71 – 750.78 MSA 28.266 – 28.273

MCLA 750.79 Clearing of land and disposing of refuse in townships. MSA 28.274

Sec. 79. ... Whenever in pursuance of the authority given by law, any township board shall, by order, rule or regulation, designate a period during which it shall be unlawful to set forest fires or fires for the purpose of clearing lands, and disposing by burning of refuse material and waste matter within its respective jurisdiction or any part thereof, any person who shall be found guilty of violat-

ing the orders, rules and regulations of such board by setting any such fire in such township contrary to the provisions thereof shall be guilty of a felony: ... Provided further, That said board is hereby authorized ...

MCLA 750.80 Setting fire to mines and mining material. [MSA 28.275]

CHAPTER XVI. BREAKING AND ENTERING

MCLA 750.110b Dumping of garbage, oil, or rubbish from boats; penalty. [MSA 28.304(2)]

Sec. 110b. Any person who ... is guilty of a misdemeanor punishable by imprisonment in the county jail for not more than 1 year or by a fine of not more than $1,000.00, or by both.

CHAPTER XVII. BRIBERY AND CORRUPTION

MCLA 750.117 Public officer; bribery. [MSA 28.312]

Sec. 117. ... Any person who shall corruptly give, offer or promise to any public officer, agent, servant or employe, after the election or appointment ... and either before or after ... qualified or shall take his seat, any gift, gratuity, money, property or other valuable thing, the intent or purpose of which is to influence the act, vote, opinion, decision or judgment of such public officer, agent, servant or employe, or his action on any matter, question cause or proceeding which may be pending or may by law be brought before him in his public capacity, or the purpose and intent of which is to influence any act or omission relating to any public duty of such officer, agent, servant or employe, shall be guilty of a felony.

MCLA 750.118 Same; accepting bribe. [MSA 28.313]

Sec. 118. ... Any ... officer who shall corruptly accept ... shall forfeit his office, and be forever disqualified to hold any public office, trust or appointment under the constitution or laws of this state and shall be guilty of a felony, punishable by imprisonment in the state prison not more than 10 years, or by a fine of not more than 5,000 dollars.

MCLA 750.119 – 750.120b [MSA 28.314 – 28.315 (2)]

MCLA 750.121 Public institutions; bribery of officers. [MSA 28.316]

Sec. 121. ...shall be guilty of a felony.

MCLA 750.123   Officer omitting duty for reward. MSA 28.318

Sec. 123.   ... Any ... constable, peace officer, or any other officer authorized to serve process or arrest or apprehend offenders against criminal law who shall receive from a defendant or from any other person any money or other valuable thing or ... to perform any duty pertaining to his office, shall be guilty of a misdemeanor, punishable by imprisonment in the county jail not more than 6 months or by fine of not more than 250 dollars: Provided, ...

MCLA 750.125   Bribery of agents, servants and employes. MSA 28.320

CHAPTER XX. CHILDREN

MCLA 750.141   Children in places where liquor is sold; local ordinances. MSA 28.336

Sec. 141. A minor child under 17 years of age shall not be permitted to remain in a dance hall, saloon, barroom or any place where any spirituous or intoxicating liquor, wine or beer, or any beverage, liquor or liquors containing spirituous or intoxicating liquor, beer or malt liquor is sold, given away or furnished for a beverage, unless the minor is accompanied by parent or guardian. A proprietor, ... shall be deemed guilty of a misdemeanor. This section shall not prevent a township ... from establishing, by ordinance, ...

MCLA 750.141a   Children, furnishing liquor without prescription, penalty. MSA 28.336(1)

MCLA 750.141c   Minors; false representation as to age for buying alcoholic liquor. MSA 28.336(3)

MCLA 750.141d   Same; false information by others as to age of minor for buying alcoholic liquor. MSA 28.336(4)

CHAPTER XXI. CIVIL RIGHTS

MCLA 750.146   Equal public accommodations; rooming and locker room facilities, separation according to sex permitted. MSA 28.343

MCLA 750.147 Denial of equal public accommodations, criminal penalties, treble damages, license suspensions or revocations. [MSA 28.343]

CHAPTER XXIV. CONSPIRACY

MCLA 750.157a Conspiracy to commit offense or legal act in illegal manner; punishment. [MSA 28.354(1)]

MCLA 750.157b Inciting, inducing or exhorting and aiding and abetting another to commit a crime or endangering the life of another. [MSA 28.354(2)]

CHAPTER XXIX. DISTURBING MEETINGS

MCLA 750.169 Disturbance of religious meetings. [MSA 28.366]

Sec. 169. ... Any person who, on the first day of the week, or at any other time, shall wilfully interrupt or disturb any assembly of people met for the worship of God, within the place of such meeting or out of it shall be guilty of a misdemeanor.

MCLA 750.170 Disturbance of lawful meetings. [MSA 28.367]

Sec. 170. ... Any person who shall make or excite any disturbance or contention in any tavern, store or grocery, manufacturing establishment or any other business place or in any street, lane, alley, highway, public building, grounds or park or at any election or other public meeting where citizens are peaceably and lawfully assembled, shall be guilty of a misdemeanor.

CHAPTER XXXI. EMBEZZLEMENT

MCLA 750.174 Embezzlement. [MSA 28.371]

Sec. 174. ... Any person who ... upon conviction thereof, if the money or personal property so embezzled shall be of the value of $100.00 or under, shall be guilty of a misdemeanor; if the money or personal property so embezzled be of the value of more than $100.00, such person shall be guilty of a felony, punishable by imprisonment in the state prison not more than 10 years or a fine not exceeding $5,000.00.
Prima facie proof of intent. *In any prosecution under this section, the failure, neglect or refusal of such agent, servant,*

161

employee, trustee, bailee or custodian to pay, deliver, or refund to his principal such money or property entrusted to his care upon demand shall be prima facie proof of intent to embezzle.

MCLA 750.175 Same; public officer, agent or servant. $\boxed{\text{MSA 28.372}}$

Sec. 175. ... who knowingly and unlawfully appropriates to his own use, or to the use of any other person, the money or property received by him in his official capacity or employment, of the value of 50 dollars or upwards, shall be guilty of a felony, punishable by imprisonment in the state prison not more than 10 years or by fine of not more than 5,000 dollars.

In any prosecution under this section the failure, neglect or refusal of any public officer to pay over and deliver to his successor all moneys and property which should be in his hands as such officer, shall be prima facie evidence of an offense against the provisions of this section.

CHAPTER XXXIV. EXTORTION

MCLA 750.214   Extortion by public officers. $\boxed{\text{MSA 28.411}}$

Sec. 214. ... Any person who ... shall be guilty of a misdemeanor; but no prosecution for such offense shall be sustained unless it shall be commenced within 1 year next after the offense was committed.

CHAPTER XXXV. FALSE PERSONATION

MCLA 750.215 False personation of public officer. $\boxed{\text{MSA 28.412}}$

Sec. 215. Any person who falsely assumes or pretends to be a ... constable, police officer or ..., and shall take upon himself to act as such, or to require any person to aid and assist him in any matter pertaining to the duty of a ... constable, police officer or ..., or shall falsely take upon himself to act or officiate in any office or place of authority, shall be guilty of a misdemeanor, punishable by imprisonment in the county jail not more than 1 year or by fine of not more than $500.00.

CHAPTER XXXVI. FALSE PRETENSES AND FALSE REPRESENTATION

MCLA 750.217a **Solicitation of information anent employment, residence, assets, or earnings by false personation.** [MSA 28.414(1)]

Sec. 217a. Any individual who ... is guilty of a misdemeanor.

CHAPTER XXXVII. FIREARMS

MCLA 750.222 – 750.230 [MSA 28.419 – 28.427]

MCLA 750.231 **Persons authorized to carry concealed weapons.** [MSA 28.428]

MCLA 750.231a **Same; nonresident licensees; transportation as merchandise.** [MSA 28.428(1)]

MCLA 750.231b **Sale and safety inspection, persons exempt.** [MSA 28.428(2)]

Sec. 231b. Sections 223 and 228 do not apply to a duly authorized police or correctional agency of the United States or of the state or any subdivision thereof, ...

MCLA 750.232 – 750.239 [MSA 28.429 – 28.436]

CHAPTER XXXVIII. FIRES

MCLA 750.240 False alarm of fire. [MSA 28.437]

MCLA 750.241 **Firemen, obstructing and disobeying, riot or civil disturbance.** [MSA 28.438]

Sec. 241. (1) Any person who shall knowingly and wilfully hinder, obstruct, endanger or interfere with any fireman in the performance of his duties is guilty of a felony.

(2) Any person who, while in the vicinity of any fire, wilfully disobeys any reasonable order or rule of the officer commanding any fire department at such fire, when such order or rule is given by the commanding officer or a fireman there present, is guilty of a misdemeanor.

(3) During a riot, or other civil disturbance any person who shall knowingly and wilfully hinder, obstruct, endanger or interfere with any person who is engaged in the operation, installation, repair or maintenance of any essential public service facility,

including a facility for the transmission of electricity, gas, telephone messages or water, is guilty of a felony.

MCLA 750.242 Traction engines using wood fuel, spark arresters. [MSA 28.439]

Sec. 242. Any person who shall own or operate upon the premises of any inhabitant of this state, or upon the highway, any traction or other portable steam engine, unless ...

CHAPTER XXXIX. FIREWORKS

MCLA 750.243a Fireworks, sale, possession, etc., prohibited; exceptions. [MSA 28.440(1)]

MCLA 750.243b Permit for use of fireworks; application; purpose of use; age limitation. [MSA 28.440(2)]

MCLA 750.243c Transportation of fireworks intrastate; permit. [MSA 28.440(3)]

MCLA 750.243d Storage of fireworks; wholesalers, dealers and jobbers. [MSA 28.440(4)]

MCLA 750.243e Penalty; misdemeanor. [MSA 28.440(5)]

Sec. 243e. Any person, firm, copartnership or corporation, who violates any of the provisions of section 243a to 243d, or who violates the terms of any permit issued thereunder, is guilty of a misdemeanor.

CHAPTER XL. FLAG AND COAT-OF-ARMS

MCLA 750.244 Definitions. [MSA 28.441]

MCLA 750.245 Exhibition and display. [MSA 28.442]

MCLA 750.246 Mutilation. [MSA 28.443]

MCLA 750.247 Exceptions. [MSA 28.444]

CHAPTER XLI. FORGERY AND COUNTERFEITING

MCLA 750.248   Forgery of records and other instruments, venue.
MSA 28.445

Sec. 248. (1) Any person who shall falsely make, alter, forge or counterfeit any public record, or any certificate, return or attestation of any clerk of a court, public register, notary public, ... township clerk, or any other public official ... shall be guilty of a felony, punishable by imprisonment in the state prison not more than 7 years.

MCLA   750.249   Same;   uttering   and   publishing.   MSA   28.446

Sec. 249. ... Any person who shall utter and publish ... shall be guilty of a felony, punishable by imprisonment in the state prison not more than 14 years.

MCLA 750.250   Forgery of notes, etc., issued for debt of state, political subdivisions.   MSA 28.447

Sec. 250. ... Any person who shall falsely make, alter, forge or counterfeit any note, certificate, bond, warrant or other instrument, issued by the treasurer or other officer authorized to issue the same, of this state, or any of its political subdivisions or municipalities, with intent to injure or defraud as aforesaid, shall be guilty of a felony, punishable by imprisonment in the state prison not more than 7 years.

MCLA 750.254   Possession of counterfeit bank, state or municipal bills or notes.   MSA 28.451

Sec. 254. ... Any person who shall bring into this state, or shall have in his possession, ... shall be guilty of a felony, punishable by imprisonment in the state prison not more than 5 years, or by fine of not more than 2,500 dollars.

CHAPTER XLIII.   FRAUDS AND CHEATS

MCLA 750.282   Public utility service, injury, interference, use.
MSA 28.493

Sec. 282. ... Any person who wilfully or fraudently injures, or suffers to be injured, any ... if such water, steam, electric current, gas or damage so caused shall be of the value of 50 dollars or less, be guilty of a misdemeanor. If such water, steam, electric current, gas or damage so caused, shall exceed in value the sum of 50 dollars, such person shall be guilty of a felony: Provided, That such criminal prosecution shall not in any way impair the right of such company to a full compensation in damages by civil suit. The provisions of this section shall ... if such water, steam, electric current, gas or damage so caused shall be of the value of 50 dollars or less, be guilty of a misdemeanor. ... If such water, steam, electric current, gas or damage so caused, shall exceed in value the sum of 50 dollars, such person shall be guilty of a felony: Provided, That such criminal prosecution shall not in any way impair the right of such company to a full compensation in damages by civil suit. ...

CHAPTER XLIV. GAMBLING

MCLA 750.301 − 750.306 [MSA 28.533 − 28.538]

MCLA 750.307 Prima facie evidence. [MSA 28.539]

Sec. 307. ... In a prosecution or proceeding relative to ... political nomination, appointment or election, ...

MCLA 750.308 Search warrant; gaming house; seizure of apparatus; arrest. [MSA 28.540]

Sec. 308. ... issue a warrant commanding ... any constable or police officer to enter and search ... take into his custody all the implements, apparatus or material of gaming ... including ... and persons ... The provisions of law relative to destroying or other disposition of gaming articles shall apply to all articles and property seized as herein provided for.

MCLA 750.308a   Disposition of articles or property seized. [MSA 28.540(1)]

Sec. 308a. On application of a ... chief of police of a police department, ... or other police officer, a court or magistrate of competent jurisdiction may upon due notice and hearing turn over to said ... officer, any articles or property listed under the provisions of section 308 of this chapter, lawfully seized by any such peace officer for such disposition as the court or magistrate shall prescribe, or said court or magistrate may provide for the destruction *or other disposition of said articles or property.*

Any funds derived from the disposition of any such articles or property shall be turned over to the treasurer of the ... township ... whose law enforcement officer made application for the disposition of such articles or property, ...

MCLA 750.309 Frequenting or attending gaming places. [MSA 28.541]

MCLA 750.310 Exceptions. [MS A 28.542]

MCLA 750.311 – 750.315 [MSA 28.543 – 28.547]

CHAPTER XLVIII. INDECENCY AND IMMORALITY

MCLA 750.343a – 345a (Obscene material) [MSA 28.575(1) – MSA 28.577(1)]

MCLA 750.346 Search warrants. [MSA 28.578]

Sec. 346. All municipal courts ... on complaint supported by oath or affirmation, that any person has in his possession or control any indecent books, papers, articles and things described in the next 3 preceding sections of this chapter, shall issue a warrant ...

CHAPTER LI. LABORERS, MECHANICS, EMPLOYEES AND WORKERS

MCLA 750.351 Consideration for employment. [MSA 28.583]

MCLA 750.353 Contributions to charitable purposes, deduction from wages. [MSA 28.585]

MCLA 750.353a Employee welfare plan, failure of employer to contribute as promised. [MSA 28.585(1)]

MCLA 750.354 Insurance with particular company, requirement (illegal). [MSA 28.586]

MCLA 750.354a Unlawful to compel certain employees to pay cost of medical examination, photographing or finger printing; penalty. [MSA 28.586(1)]

MCLA 750.355 Temporary water closets. [MSA 28.587]

Sec. 355. ... *Any architect who shall refuse, fail or neglect to insert a clause in the specifications for all buildings providing for suitable temporary water closets for the use of workmen employed on such buildings while in the course of erection, unless closets are already maintained on such premises; and any contractor or person erecting such building who shall refuse, fail or neglect to erect such closet within the first week after commencing work thereon, shall be guilty of a misdemeanor.*

MCLA 750.355a Consideration for employing or not discharging. [MSA 28.587(1)]

CHAPTER LII. LARCENY

MCLA 750.358 Larceny at a fire. [MSA 28.590]

MCLA 750.360 Larceny; places of abode, work, storage, conveyance, worship and other places. [MSA 28.592]

Sec. 360. Any person who shall commit the crime of larceny by stealing in any ... building used by the public shall be guilty of a felony.

MCLA 750.364 Same; from libraries. [MSA 28.596]

Sec. 364. ... *Any person who shall procure, or take in any way from any public library ... shall be guilty of a misdemeanor.*

MCLA 750.367 Taking or injuring trees, shrubs, vines, plants. [MSA 28.599]

CHAPTER LIII. LEGAL PROCESS

MCLA 750.369 Abuse of legal process. [MSA 28.601]

Sec. 369. ... *Any officer or person who shall wilfully make any arrest or institute any legal proceedings, or sue out any process for the purpose of obtaining the fees or mileage that might accrue thereto or therefor, shall be guilty of a misdemeanor.*

CHAPTER LIV. LIBEL AND SLANDER

MCLA 750.370 Falsely and maliciously accusing another. [MSA 28.602]

MCLA 750.371 Second or subsequent violations. [MSA 28.603]

CHAPTER LVI. MALICIOUS AND WILFUL MISCHIEF AND DESTRUCTION

MCLA 750.377 Maliciously destroying or injuring animals; poisoning. [MSA 28.609]

MCLA 750.377a Malicious destruction of property; personalty. [MSA 28.609(1)]

MCLA 750.377b Same; property of police or fire department. [MSA 28.609(2)]

Sec. 377b. ... Any person who shall wilfully and maliciously destroy or injure the personal property of any fire or police department, ... shall be guilty of a felony.

MCLA 750.378 Same; dam, reservoir, canal, trench, etc. [MSA 28.610]

MCLA 750.379 Same; bridges, etc. [MSA 28.611]

MCLA 750.380 Same; house, barn or building of another. [MSA 28.612]

MCLA 750.381 Same; fences or opening gates. [MSA 28.613]

MCLA 750.382 Same; trees. [MSA 28.614]

MCLA 750.383 Same; boundary markers, etc.; defacing inscriptions, buildings and sign boards; light bulbs, etc. [MSA 28.615]

MCLA 750.383a Same; wilfully cutting, breaking, obstructing, destroying or manipulating without authority utility equipment or appliances. [MSA 28.615(1)]

Sec. 383a. ... "Utility" includes any pipe line, gas, electric, heat, water, oil, sewer, telephone, telegraph, radio, railway, railroad, airplane, transportation, communication or other system, by whomsoever owned or operated for the public use.

169

MCLA 750.384 Same; logs, timber, etc. $\boxed{\text{MSA 28.616}}$

MCLA 750.385 Same; signs, bills and notices placed on private property. $\boxed{\text{MSA 28.617}}$

Sec. 385. ... Any person who shall wilfully tear down, destroy or in any manner deface any signs, bill or notices on any private lands of this state, or on any lots or premises in any township, ... shall be guilty of a misdemeanor: Provided, That such signs, bill or notices are not in violation of any general law of the state or municipal ordinance, and were placed by the owner or lessee or by their consent.

MCLA 750.386 Same; machinery and appliances (in mines). $\boxed{\text{MSA 28.618}}$

MCLA 750.387 Same; tombs and memorials to dead. $\boxed{\text{MSA 28.619}}$

Sec. 387. ... Any person who shall willtully destroy, mutilate, deface, injure or remove any tomb, monument, gravestone or other structure or thing placed or designed for a memorial of the dead, ... shall be guilty of a misdemeanor, punishable by imprisonment in the county jail not more than 1 year or by a fine of not more than 500 dollars.

MCLA 750.388 Same; personal property seized by legal process. $\boxed{\text{MSA 28.620}}$

Sec. 388. ... Any person or persons who shall remove, destroy, damage or dispose of any personal property that shall have been seized by due process of law issued from any court of competent jurisdiction in this state, while such seizure or levy is in force, without first giving the bond or other security therefor, if any, required by law, shall be guilty of a misdemeanor.

MCLA 750.389 False or malicious statements re insurance companies. $\boxed{\text{MSA 28.621}}$

MCLA 750.390 Malicious annoyance by writing. $\boxed{\text{MSA 28.622}}$

MCLA 750.391 Maliciously injuring or mutilating library books. $\boxed{\text{MSA 28.623}}$

Sec. 391. ... Any person who shall wilfully, maliciously or wantonly tear, deface or mutilate or write upon, or by other means injure or mar any ... (article) ... of any literary, scientific, historical or library society or association, whether incorporated or unincorporated, shall be guilty of a misdemeanor.

MCLA 750.392 Vessels, wilfully destroying. [MSA 28.624]

MCLA 750.393 Buoy or beacon, wilfully removing or destroying. [MSA 28.625]

MCLA 750.394 Train, car or vehicle, throwing stone or missile at. [MSA 28.626]

CHAPTER LIX. MILITARY

MCLA 750.398 Member of state militia; depriving or obstructing employment. [MSA 28.630]

Sec. 398. ... Any person who shall either by himself or another deprive a member of the organized militia of this state of employment or ... shall be guilty of a misdemeanor.

MCLA 750.399 Same; discrimination. [MSA 28.631]

MCLA 750.400 Same; molesting or abusing. [MSA 28.632]

MCLA 750.403 Desertion from military service (arrest by ... constable, etc.). [MSA 28.633]

CHAPTER LX. MISCELLANEOUS

MCLA 750.411 Reporting injuries by hospitals, pharmacies, physicians. [MSA 28.643]

MCLA 750.411a Fictitious crimes, report to police officers, bomb scares. [MSA 28.643(1)]

MCLA 750.411b Excess fees to members of legislature, for services. [MSA 28.643(2)]

MCLA 750.411c Asphyxia or death from submersion in water, reports, investigations, penalty. [MSA 28.643(3)]

CHAPTER LXI. MOTOR VEHICLES

MCLA 750.412 Definition. [MSA 28.644]

Sec. 412. ... The term "motor vehicle" as used in this chapter shall include all vehicles impelled on the public highways of this state by mechanical power, except traction engines, road rollers and such vehicles as run only upon rails or tracks.

MCLA 750.419 Operating bicycle and motor vehicle on sidewalks. [MSA 28.651]

Sec. 419. ... Any person who shall operate or ride a bicycle, motor cycle or other motor vehicle upon that part of the street or highway where sidewalks have been regularly laid out and constructed for the use of pedestrians, not including cross walks, in any ... plat or plats, not in any incorporated village or city, shall be guilty of a misdemeanor.

CHAPTER LXII. PERJURY

MCLA 750.423 Definition. [MSA 28.665]

Sec. 423. ... Any person authorized by any statute of this state to take an oath, or any person of whom an oath shall be required by law, who shall wilfully swear falsely, ... shall be guilty of perjury, a felony, punishable by imprisonment in the state prison not more than 15 years.

CHAPTER LXIV. POISONS

Note: These citations are important for commissioners of noxious weeds.

MCLA 750.437 Exposing poisonous substances where liable to be eaten by beasts. [MSA 28.692]

Sec. 437. ... Any person who shall expose any known poisonous substance, whether mixed with meat or other food or not, so that the same shall be liable to be eaten by any horses, cattle, dogs or other beasts of another, shall be guilty of a misdemeanor: Provided, That it shall not be unlawful to expose on one's own premises common rat poisons mixed only with vegetable substances, nor for any person to expose on his own premises, not within the limits of any incorporated city or village, poisons for the destruction of predatory or dangerous prowling animals.

MCLA 750.438 Fly Killers [MSA 28.693]

CHAPTER LXVIII. PUBLIC EXHIBITIONS AND ENTERTAINMENT

MCLA 750.464a Consuming intoxicating liquor in unlicensed places; liability. [MSA 28.719(1)]

MCLA 750.465 Ticket scalping. [MSA 28.720]

Sec. 465. ... It shall be the duty of owners, lessees and managers of every theatre, circus, athletic grounds used for athletic games, places of public entertainment or amusement to ...

CHAPTER LXIX. PUBLIC HEALTH

Note: Township officials who may be concerned with regulation of health conditions in private business and of their employees should be familiar with some of the citations in this chapter; others may be of interest where there is a hospital in which the township is involved.

MCLA 750.473 Transporting persons or articles infected with disease. [MSA 28.741]

Sec. 473. ... No person sick with cholera, smallpox, diphtheria, scarlet fever or any other communicable disease, dangerous to the public health, and no article which has been infected or is liable to propagate or convey any such disease, shall come or be brought into any township, ... without the special permit of the board of health or the health officer of said township, ... and then only under the supervision of the health officer of said township, ...: Provided, ...

Any person who shall violate the provisions of this section, or the order of the health officer made in pursuance thereof, shall be guilty of a misdemeanor.

MCLA 750.474 Exposing others to communicable disease. [MSA 28.742]

MCLA 750.475   Drinking cups at public drinking fountains.
[MSA 28.743]

MCLA 750.476   Expectoration on floors.   [MSA 28.744]

CHAPTER LXX.   PUBLIC OFFICES AND OFFICERS

MCLA 750.478   Wilful neglect of duty.   [MSA 28.746]

Sec. 478.   ... When any duty is or shall be enjoined by law upon any public officer, or upon any person holding any public trust or employment, every wilful neglect to perform such duty, where no special provision shall have been made for the punishment of such delinquency, shall be deemed a misdemeanor, punishable by imprisonment in the county jail for not more than 1 year or by a fine of not more than 500 dollars.

MCLA 750.479   Resisting, obstructing officer in discharge of duty.
[MSA 28.747]

MCLA 750.479a   Failure to obey direction of police officer to stop motor vehicles; assault upon police officer.   [MSA 28.747(1)]

MCLA 750.480   Refusing to deliver records and money to successor in office.   [MSA 28.748]

Sec. 480.   ... Any officer or agent ... of any ... township ... into whose hands money, books, papers, evidence of debt or other property shall come by virtue of his office or agency,   who shall wilfully refuse or neglect, or demand, to deliver the same to his successor in office or to the person authorized by law to receive or have charge of the same, shall be guilty of a felony.

MCLA   750.481   Neglecting or refusing to execute process.
[MSA 28.749]

Sec. 481.   ... Whenever any constable, ... of any township, ... shall at any time wilfully neglect or refuse to execute any lawful process of any ... shall be guilty of a misdemeanor: Provided, ...

MCLA 750.482   Neglecting or refusing to pay over moneys collected.   [MSA 28.750]

Sec. 482. ... Any officer who shall collect or receive any moneys on account of any fine, penalty, forfeiture or recognizance, and shall neglect or refuse to pay over ... shall be guilty of a misdemeanor, punishable by imprisonment in the county jail not more than 1 year or by a fine of not more than 500 dollars.

MCLA 750.483 Neglecting or refusing to aid sheriff, coroner, constable. [MSA 28.751]

Sec. 483. Any person who being required by any ... constable, shall neglect or refuse to assist him in the execution of his office, in any criminal case or in the preservation of the peace, or the apprehending or securing of any person for a breach of the peace, or in any case of escape or rescue of persons arrested upon civil process, shall be guilty of a misdemeanor.

MCLA 750.485 Accounting for county money by county and municipal officers. [MSA 28.753]

Sec. 485. ... It shall be the duty of all ... municipal officers, who may receive or pay out any sum or sums of money belonging to the county in which said officers may reside, to keep an accurate and perfect account of all such moneys, by whom paid and for what purpose, as the board of supervisors (commissioners) of the several counties of this state, or by the board of auditors, wherever authorized to transact such county business, may direct. ...

Any county or municipal officer who may be included under the provisions of this section, who shall neglect or refuse to comply with any of the provisions of this section, in the keeping of such accounts as may be prescribed by said county boards, shall be guilty of a misdemeanor.

MCLA 750.489 False statement of public finances and transfer of same. [MSA 28.757]

Sec. 489. ... Any officer, agent, servant or employe of ... any ... township, ... of this state, and any member, agent or employe of any board or commission of ... any of the municipalities above named, who shall knowingly deliver, publish or give out for publication any false statement relating to the finances, funds, moneys or balances in any fund of said ... township, ... shall be guilty of a misdemeanor.

Any officer, agent, servant or employe ... of any ... township

..., and any member, agent or employee of any board or commission of ... any of the municipalities above named, who shall transfer or juggle the funds of the ... municipal division thereof, or issue false checks, drafts, warrants, vouchers or other evidences of credit, shall be guilty of a misdemeanor.

MCLA 750.490   Safe keeping of public moneys. [MSA 28.758]

Sec. 490. ... All moneys which shall come into the hands of any officer ... of any township, ... shall be denominated public moneys within the meaning of this section.

It shall be the duty of every officer charged with the receiving, keeping or disbursing of public moneys to keep the same separate and apart from his own money, and he shall not commingle the same with his own money, nor with the money of any other person, firm or corporation. ...

The provisions of this section shall apply to all deputies of such officer or officers, and to all clerks, agents and servants of such officer or officers.

Any person who shall violate any of the provisions of this section, shall be guilty of a misdemeanor, punishable by imprisonment in the state prison not more than 2 years or by a fine of not more than 1,000 dollars: Provided, ...

MCLA 750.490a   Purchase by employee upon public credit for private use. [MSA 28.758(1)]

Sec. 490a. No officer or employee of any governmental agency as defined in this section shall purchase or cause to be purchased any goods, wares, or merchandise of any description whatsoever in the name of or on the credit of such governmental agency for any ...

Any person who shall violate any of the provisions of this section, shall be guilty of a misdemeanor, punishable by imprisonment in the county jail not more than 90 days or by a fine of not more than $100.00, or by both such fine and imprisonment in the discretion of the court.

CHAPTER LXXI. PUBLIC RECORDS

MCLA 750.491   Removal, mutilation, or destruction of public records, penalty. [MSA 28.759]

MCLA 750.492   Inspection and use of public records. [MSA 28.760]

Note: Complete citations for these two sections may be found in the chapter on Services, Utilities, Contracts and Ordinances under Preservation of Township Records and History.

CHAPTER LXXII. PUBLIC SAFETY

MCLA 750.493 Protection of exploration pits and holes (by fence). [MSA 28.761]

MCLA 750.493a Placing or throwing glass, etc., on beach, etc., a misdemeanor. [MSA 28.761(1)]

Sec. 493a. Any person who shall place or throw glass or other dangerous pointed or edged substances in or on any beach or waters adjacent thereto, highway, or walk, or on public property within 50 feet of a public highway, shall be guilty of a misdemeanor.

MCLA 750.493b Abandoning or failure to keep safely covered or fenced well or cistern; depth and width. [MSA 28.761(2)]

MCLA 750.493c Excavation or basement; failure to cover or fence. [MSA 28.761(3)]

MCLA 750.494 Bells on sleighs and cutters in upper peninsula. [MSA 28.762]

MCLA 750.495 Shafting to be erected to protect public (around running machinery). [MSA 28.763]

MCLA 750.496 Hotel or place of public abode; setting fire; posting notice. [MSA 28.764(1)]

MCLA 750.497 Detouring traffic as public safety measure; notices, posting. [MSA 28.765]

MCLA 750.498 Erection of traffic signals by township boards on trunk lines. [MSA 28.766]

Sec. 498. ... Upon request of any township board, ... or upon their own initiative, the state highway commissioner and the commissioner of public safety, acting jointly may ... Any person who shall, on any state trunk line highway in any township, ... fail to observe any parking, speed or traffic signs, signals or devices authorized as aforesaid, shall be guilty of a misdemeanor, and upon conviction shall be punished by a fine of not more than 100 dollars or by imprisonment in the county jail for not more than 10 days or by both such fine and imprisonment in the discretion of the court.

MCLA 750.502 Handling of gasoline, benzine and naphtha.
[MSA 28.770]

MCLA 750.502b Unlawful sale of kerosene; flash point; penalty.
[MSA 28.770(3/4)]

MCLA 750.502c Blind persons led by dog guide; denial of use of public accommodation, misdemeanor; credentials. [MSA 28.770(7/8)]

CHAPTER LXXIV. RADIO BROADCASTING

MCLA 750.507 Telegraph and telephones; priority of messages; defined. [MSA 28.775]

Sec. 507. ... Every telegraph and telephone company operating in this state shall give priority to ... any fire department, ambulance company, law enforcement agency, civil defense communications facility and the department of military affairs.

MCLA 750.507b Telegraph and telephone companies; interference, obstruction, etc. [MSA 28.775(2)]

Sec. 507b. Any unauthorized person who shall wilfully prevent, interfere, obstruct, or impede a public safety radio communication shall be guilty of a misdemeanor.

MCLA 750.508 Vehicles equipped with short wave length radio receiving sets. [MSA 28.776]

MCLA 750.509 False reports to police broadcasting station. [MSA 28.777]

MCLA 750.510 Broadcasting regulations, violation. [MSA 28.778]

CHAPTER LXXVII. RIOTS AND UNLAWFUL ASSEMBLIES

(See also **MCLA 752.541 - 752.546** in THE PENAL CODE - SUPPLEMENTAL CHAPTER, following.)

MCLA 750.523 Riots and unlawful assemblies; refusal to aid officer. [MSA 28.791]

Note: The officers referred to in this section were listed in a section which has been repealed. Included was the supervisor of the township and, by implication, the township board members and any township police officer.

MCLA 750.524 Same; neglect of officers to suppress. [MSA 28.792]

Sec. 524. ... Any ... supervisor (and by implication, township board member or township police officer) *... having notice of any such riotous or tumultuous and unlawful assembly as is mentioned in this chapter, in the township, ... in which he lives, who shall neglect or refuse immediately to proceed to the place of such assembly, or as near thereto as he can with safety, or shall omit or neglect to exercise the authority with which he is invested by this chapter, for suppressing such riotous or unlawful assembly, and for arresting and securing the offenders, shall be guilty of a misdemeanor, punishable by imprisonment in the county jail not more than 6 months or a fine of not more than 250 dollars.*

MCLA 750.525 Same; use of force to quell. [MSA 28.793]

MCLA 750.526 Same; armed force in dispersing to execute order of certain officials. [MSA 28.794]

MCLA 750.527 Same; death ensuing from efforts to disperse. [MSA 28.795]

Sec. 527. ... If, by reason of any of the efforts made by any 2 or more of the said magistrates or officers, or by their direction, to disperse such unlawful, riotous or tumultuous assembly, or ... shall be held guiltless and fully justified in law; and if ...

MCLA 750.528 Same; destroying dwelling house or other property. [MSA 28.796]

Sec. 528. ... Any of the persons so unlawfully assembled, who shall demolish, pull down, destroy or injure, or who shall begin to demolish, pull down, destroy or injure any dwelling house or any other building, or any ship or vessel, shall be guilty of a felony, and shall be answerable to any person injured, to the full amount of the damage, in an action of trespass.

CHAPTER LXXX. SLAUGHTER HOUSES

MCLA 750.533   Slaughter houses; within 20 rods of highway.
MSA 28.801

Sec. 533.   ... Any person who shall keep or maintain any slaughter-house, slaughter-yard or slaughter-pen, or any other place for slaughtering or killing any animals, or rendering dead animals as a business, within 20 rods of any public highway within this state, or in any other place except as provided in section 6521 of the Compiled Laws of 1929 and amendments thereto, shall be guilty of a misdemeanor: Provided, ...

MCLA 750.534   Same; water supply, sewerage and drainage; nuisance. MSA 28.802

CHAPTER LXXXI. STOLEN, EMBEZZLED OR CONVERTED PROPERTY

MCLA 750.535 – 750.538 MSA 28.803 – 28.806

Note: Several of these sections mention constable as one of the officers involved.

CHAPTER LXXXII. TELEGRAPH AND TELEPHONE

MCLA 750.539   Divulging contents of messages.   MSA 28.807

MCLA 750.539a Definitions. MSA 28.807(1)

Sec. 539a. As used in sections 539a to 539i:
(1) "Private place" means ...
(2) "Eavesdrop" or "eavesdropping" means ...
(3) "Surveillance" means ...
(4) "Person" means ...

MCLA 750.539b Trespassing for the purpose of eavesdropping or surveillance. MSA 28.807(2)

MCLA 750.539c   Eavesdropping upon private conversations. MSA 28.807(3)

Sec. 539c. Any person who is present or who is not present during a private conversation and who wilfully uses any device to eavesdrop upon the conversation without the consent of all parties thereto, or who knowingly aids, employs or procures another person to do the same in violation of this section, is guilty of a felony punishable by imprisonment in a state prison for not more than 2 years or by a fine of not more than $2,000.00, or both.

MCLA 750.539d Installation of device for observing, photographing, or eavesdropping in private place. [MSA 28.807(4)]

MCLA 750.539e Use or divulgence of information unlawfully obtained. [MSA 28.807(5)]

MCLA 750.539f Unlawful manufacture, possession or transfer of eavesdropping devices. [MSA 28.807(6)]

MCLA 750.539g Exceptions. [MSA 28.807(7)]

Sec. 539g. This act shall not be construed to prohibit: ...

MCLA 750.539h Civil remedies. [MSA 28.807(8)]

MCLA 750.539i Proof of installation of device as prima facie evidence of violation. [MSA 28.807(9)]

MCLA 750.540 Cutting, breaking, tapping, connecting line, wire or cable. [MSA 28.808]

MCLA 750.540a Party line, emergency, defined; refusal to yield or surrender use of line; pretext; penalty. [MSA 28.808(1)]

MCLA 750.540b Notice contained in telephone directory, printing; exception. [MSA 28.808(2)]

MCLA 750.540c Fraudulently avoiding charge for telecommunications service; use or sale of equipment; penalty. [MSA 28.808(3)]

MCLA 750.540d Seizure of equipment; destruction. [MSA 28.808(4)]

MCLA 750.540e Malicious use of service provided by communications common carrier. [MSA 28.808(5)]

Sec. 552a. *Any person who shall dump, deposit or place any filth, garbage or refuse on the grounds or premises of another, without the specific permission of the owner thereof, shall be guilty of a misdemeanor.*

MCLA 750.562 Fruit or vegetable containers, copyrighted or registered. [MSA 28.830]

MCLA 750.563 Livestock or poultry, duty in weighing. [MSA 28.831]

MCLA 750.564 Fruit or vegetable containers to hold quantity represented. [MSA 28.832]

MCLA 750.565 Fruit baskets to be marked as to number of pounds. [MSA 28.833]

MCLA 750.566 Binder twine, marking. [MSA 28.834]

THE PENAL CODE--SUPPLEMENTAL CHAPTER

Act No. 158, P. A. 1966 — Law Enforcement

AN ACT to require public officials to enforce the legal rights of citizens and to provide a penalty for failure to do so.

MCLA 752.11 Upholding or enforcing the law; duty of public officials. [MSA 28.746(101)]

Sec. 1. Any public official, appointed or elected, who is responsible for enforcing or upholding any law of this state and who wilfully and knowingly fails to uphold or enforce the law with the result that any person's legal rights are denied is guilty of a misdemeanor.

MCLA 752.12 Penalty. [MSA 28.746(102)]

Act No. 70, P. A. 1877 — Cruelty to Animals

AN ACT for the more effectual prevention of cruelty to animals.

MCLA 752.21 Cruelty to animals; penalty; cropping dogs ears. [MSA 28.161]

MCLA 752.25 Violation of act; arrest without warrant, seizure and impounding of animal. [MSA 28.162]

MCLA 752.26 Same; complaint on suspicion, search warrant; seizure and disposal of certain instruments. [MSA 28.163]

MCLA 752.27 Same; discovery and prosecution by appointee of certain society; designation of appointee as deputy sheriff, liability for his acts. [MSA 28.164]

MCLA 752.28 Same; duty of public officer; neglect a misdemeanor. [MSA 28.165]

Sec. 8. It shall also be the duty of all sheriffs, deputy sheriffs, constables, policemen, and public officers, to arrest and prosecute all persons of whose violation of the provisions of this act, they may have knowledge or reasonable notice, and for each neglect of such duty, the officer so offending shall be deemed guilty of a misdemeanor.

MCLA 752.29 Same; duty of prosecutor. [MSA 28.166]

Sec. 9. It shall be the duty of all prosecuting attorneys to represent and prosecute in behalf of the people within their respective counties all cases of offenses arising under the provisions of this act.

MCLA 752.30 Definitions; imputation of knowledge and act of employee to corporation. [MSA 28.167]

R. S. 1846, ch. 158 — Way through Cemetery

MCLA 752.73 Unauthorized construction of way through cemetery; penalty. [MSA 28.132]

Act No. 163, P. A. 1945 — Baby Chicks, Rabbits, Ducklings, Fowl, Game

AN ACT prohibiting the sale or offer for sale of dyed or artificially colored baby chicks, rabbits, ducklings, or other fowl or game; and providing a penalty for violation thereof.

MCLA 752.91 — 752.92 [MSA 28.482(1) — 28.482(2)]

184

Act No. 214, P. A. 1931 — Felonious Driving

AN ACT to enact a law to define the offense of felonious driving, when committed by the operation of a vehicle and to prescribe penalties therefor.

MCLA 752.191 — 752.192 [MSA 28.661 — 28.662]

Act No. 134, P. A. 1943 — Fishing Houses

AN ACT to require the removal of any fishing house, fish shanty or other structure or shelter placed on the ice of any of the waters under the jurisdiction of this state; to provide for marking such structures with the name and address of the owner; to provide for the cost of removing said structures; and to provide penalties for the violation of this act.

MCLA 752.211 Fish houses; marking with name and address of owner. [MSA 13.1702(1)]

MCLA 752.212 Same; removal. [MSA 13.1702(2)]

MCLA 752.213 Violation of act; penalty. [MSA 13.1702(3)]

Act No. 119, P. A. 1967 — Toxic Chemicals

AN ACT regulating the use of chemical agents containing toxic chemicals or organic solvents or both, having the property of releasing toxic vapors; and providing for penalties.

MCLA 752.271 Chemical agent. [MSA 28.643(11)]

Sec. 1. As used in this act, "chemical agent" means any substance containing a toxic chemical or organic solvent or both, having the property of releasing toxic vapors. The term includes, but is not limited to, glue, acetone, toluene, carbon tetrachloride, hydrocarbons and hydrocarbon derivatives.

MCLA 752.272 Introduction into respiratory or circulatory system, prohibition; anesthesia inhalation, exception. [MSA 28.643(12)]

Note: Commissioners of noxious weeds must be aware of

this act with regard to use of chemicals for control and destruction of weeds.

Act No. 38, P.A. 1950, Ex. Sess. - Overthrow of Government

AN ACT to make criminal certain activities relating to the overthrowing or destroying of government by force, violence, sabotage, or terrorism; to prescribe the penalties therefor; to define duties of the attorney general and the state police; to prevent unlawful disclosures of information and to prescribe penalties therefor; and to repeal certain acts and parts of acts inconsistent with or contravening any provisions of this act.

MCLA 752.311   Overthrowing or destroying government, preventing.
[MSA 28.243(1)]

MCLA 752.312   Certain acts deemed felony.   [MSA 28.243(2)]

Sec. 2. Whoever knowingly or wilfully advocates, aids, abets, advises, encourages or teaches the duty, necessity, desirability, or propriety of overthrowing or destroying the government of the United states or of this or any other state of the United States or any political subdivision thereof, by force, violence, sabotage, or terrorism or attempts or conspires to do so; or ...

MCLA 752.313   Duties of attorney general and state police.
[MSA 28.243(3)]

MCLA 752.314 Sections repealed; pending proceedings.
[MSA 28.243(4)]

MCLA 752.315 Severing clause. [MSA 28.243(5)]

Act No. 221, P. A. 1899 — Signal and Barricade where Ice is Cut

AN ACT to compel parties engaged in securing ice to erect suitable danger signals and barricades, designating what officials it shall be the duty of to see that the provisions of this act are complied with, and to repeal Act No. 100 of the Public Acts of 1877, entitled "An act to compel parties engaged in securing ice to erect danger signals," being sections 9119 and 9120 of Howell's annotated statutes of the state of Michigan and sections 11525 and 11526 of the Compiled Laws of 1897.

MCLA 752.351 Erection of signal and barricade where ice is cut; duty. [MSA 28.111]

MCLA 752.352 Enforcement; duty of harbor master, supervisor, or assessor. [MSA 28.112]

Sec. 352. It shall be the duty of the harbor master at all places where there is such an official having control of a stream or lake within this state, and where there is no such an official having control as aforesaid, it shall be the duty of the supervisor or other assessing officer in whose assessment district such stream or lake is situated to see that the provisions of section 1 of this act are complied with.

MCLA 752.353 Penalty. [MSA 28.113]

Sec. 3. Any person ...(not complying with)... this act shall be deemed guilty of a misdemeanor, and shall, on conviction thereof, be punished by imprisonment in the county jail not more than 3 months, or by fine not exceeding 100 dollars, or by both such fine and imprisonment, in the discretion of the court.

R. S. 1846, c. 158 — Disturbance of Religious Meetings

MCLA 752.525 Religious meeting, disturbance, carrying on certain business within two miles, obstruction of highway; prohibited acts. [MSA 28.133]

MCLA 752.526 Same; penalty, disposal of fine. [MSA 28.134]

MCLA 752.527 Same; duty to apprehend offender. [MSA 28.135]

MCLA 752.528 Same; ordering offender into custody of certain persons. [MSA 28.136]

MCLA 752.529 Same; commitment to jail if penalty not paid. [MSA 28.137]

MCLA 752.530 Same; jury trial, cost of suit. [MSA 28.138]

Act No. 302, P. A. 1968 — Rioting and Related Crimes

AN ACT to define and prescribe the penalties for the crime of rioting and related crimes; and to repeal certain acts and parts of acts.

MCLA 752.541 Riot. [MSA 28.790(1)]

Sec. 1. It is unlawful and constitutes the crime of riot for 5 or more persons, acting in concert, to wrongfully engage in violent conduct and thereby intentionally or recklessly cause or create a serious risk of causing public terror or alarm.

MCLA 752.542 Incitement to riot. [MSA 28.790(2)]

Sec. 2. It is unlawful and constitutes incitement to riot for a person or persons, intending to cause or to aid or abet the institution or maintenance of a riot, to do an act or engage in conduct that urges other persons to commit acts of unlawful force or violence, or the unlawful burning or destroying of property, or the unlawful interference with a police officer, peace officer, fireman or a member of the Michigan national guard or any unit of the armed services officially assigned to riot duty in the lawful performance of his duty.

MCLA 752.543 Unlawful assembly. [MSA 28.790(3)]

Sec. 3. It is unlawful and constitutes an unlawful assembly for a person to assemble or act in concert with 4 or more persons for the purpose of engaging in conduct constituting the crime of riot, or to be present at an assembly that either has or develops such a purpose and to remain thereat with intent to advance such purpose.

MCLA 752.544 Felony; penalty. [MSA 28.790(4)]

Note: See also MCLA 750.523 —750.528 in CHAPTER LXXVII. RIOTS AND UNLAWFUL ASSEMBLIES, above.

Act No. 26, P. A. 1970 — Disturbances at Institutions of Higher Education

AN ACT to provide penalties for certain conduct at public institutions of higher education.

MCLA 752.581 Rule violations, elements of offense, penalties. [MSA 28.790(41)]

MCLA 752.582 Creation of risk of personal injury or property damage or disruption of function of institution, elements of offense, penalties. [MSA 28.790(42)]

Act. No. 126, P. A. 1970 — Coin Operated Devices

AN ACT relating to coin operated devices, including but not limited to parking meters, coin telephones and vending machines; and providing for a penalty.

MCLA 752.811 Entry with intent to steal; possession of means of entry with intent to steal. [MSA 28.643(101)]

Act No. 105, P. A. 1951 — Signs Prohibiting Hunting, Fishing, or Trespassing

AN ACT regulating the erection of posters, signs and placards on any state, public or privately owned lands; and to prescribe penalties for violations of this act.

MCLA 752.821 Erection of posters, etc., on state, public or private lands without permission unlawful. [MSA 13.1484(1)]

MCLA 752.822 Prosecutions, time. [MSA 13.1484(2)]

MCLA 752.823 Enforcement and prosecutions (by prosecuting attorney). [MSA 13.1484(3)]

MCLA 752.824 Violations, penalty. [MSA 13.1484(4)]

MCLA 752.825 Resisting arrest. [MSA 13.1484(5)]

Act No. 106, P. A. 1963 — Littering of Property and Waters

AN ACT to define, control and prohibit the littering of public and private property and waters; to prescribe penalties for violation of this act; and to repeal certain acts and parts of acts.

MCLA 752.901 Litter; prohibition; construction of terms; removal of debris from highways. [MSA 28.603(1)]

Sec. 1. ... "public or private property or waters" includes, but is not limited to the right of way of any road or highway, any body of water or watercourse, or the shores or beaches thereof and including the ice above such waters; any park, playground, building, refuge or conservation or recreation area; and any residential or farm properties or timberlands. ...

MCLA 752.901a Litter; causing to fall on or throwing into path of vehicle prohibited; penalty. [MSA 28.603(1A)]

MCLA 752.902 Same; definition. [MSA 28.603(2)]

Sec. 2. The term "litter" as used herein means all rubbish, refuse, waste material, garbage, offal, paper, glass, cans, bottles, trash, debris or other foreign substances of every kind and description.

MCLA 752.903 Penalty; sentence. [MSA 28.603(3)]

Sec. 3. Any person violating any provision of this act shall be guilty of a misdemeanor. The court, in lieu of any other sentence imposed, may direct a substitution of litter-gathering labor, including, but not limited to, the litter connected with the particular violation, under the supervision of the court.

MCLA 752.904 Publication of act; receptacles for litter. [MSA 28.603(4)]

MCLA 752.906 Municipal ordinances. [MSA 28.603(6)]

Sec. 6. This act shall not affect or in any way limit the powers of ... townships to enact and enforce ordinances for the control and elimination of litter.

Chapter III

ELECTIONS

Many noted authorities have said that the demise of a nation is confirmed on the day that national and local issues and the selection of those who govern is no longer done by vote of the people. Thus one of the most important tools of citizenship in the United States is the power to vote on issues and candidates. However, this still is not enough if confidence is destroyed in the election process by doubt regarding counting and recording of votes. It is axiomatic, therefore, that there be honesty and efficiency in the conduct of every election from the presidency to the smallest local board or commission. Public officials must be fair, ethical and accurate, as well as efficient and accessible to their constituents if they hope to merit confidence in their ability to govern.

The open primary was long ago abandoned in Michigan, much to the discomfiture of many politicians who say it has destroyed party discipline. However, benefits to the people through the use of a single ballot in the closed or secret primary has brought about a new surge of voting by persons who in the past had considered themselves independents and thus not concerned with primary elections. Furthermore, most of the problems of counting and recording votes appeared during the open primaries. The result has been that Michigan is now pointed to as a state where election reform has been given real meaning.

Labor unions and other service organizations, such as the League of Women Voters, American Association of University

Women, Lions, Rotary, Kiwanis, Optimist, Civitan, Chamber of Commerce and the Jaycees have done much to bring about the establishment of many incentives to register and vote, such as making it easier to register, extending the hours for voting, making election day a holiday, giving employees four hours off to vote and many others which have encouraged many people to vote who never took the time before. Michigan is also one of the states which has lowered the voting age to eighteen. Many of the old school, more conservative in thought, frequently express resentment against the many conveniences for the benefit of the electorate which have come about during the last thirty years. They believe voting is an obligation and a responsibility and that it should be up to the citizen to take the initiative. However, most people feel that voting is a privilege and every possible effort must be made to arrange convenient places, times and methods which will encourage the citizen to exercise his voting franchise.

While the necessity to make federal and state election laws meaningful and enforceable is quite evident in Michigan, there is nonetheless sufficient flexibility to encourage local government officials to meet their responsibility under the law to insure that each election--primary, general or special--will be accurately counted and properly recorded so that confidence in the election process will always be maintained.

Only citation headings are provided in many instances in the following laws, allowing the reader to contact his own attorney wherever there is need for expanded information. Where a full citation has been included, it is because of the necessity for absolute understanding of what the statute has to offer.

In addition to the citations given, there is an urgency for every township election official to secure the special supplements, manuals and pamphlets prepared for the information and guidance of local election officials by the Elections Division of the office of the Secretary of State.

Act No. 161, P. A. 1969 - Actions Involving Elections

AN ACT to regulate the filing of certain actions involving elections.

MCLA 691.1031 Laches, rebuttable presumption. [MSA 27.794(1)]

MCLA 691.1032 Inapplicable legislative acts. MSA 27.794(2)

Act No. 221, P. A. 1951 - Defamatory Statements, Actions for Damages

AN ACT relating to actions for damages against the owners, licensees or operators of a radio broadcasting station or network of stations, for defamatory statements.

MCLA 484.331 Actions for damages against owners, etc., of radio broadcasting stations for defamatory statements. MSA 27.1405

MCLA 484.332 Same; defamatory statement by or on behalf of candidate for public office. MSA 27.1406

Sec. 2. The owner, licensee or operator, or the agents or employees of any such owner, licensee or operator of such a station or network of stations, shall not be liable for any damages for any defamatory statement uttered over the facilities of such station or network by or on behalf of any candidate for public office where sucn statement is not subject to censorship or control by reason of any federal statute or any ruling or order of the federal communications commission made pursuant thereto.

Act No. 36, P.A. 1933 — Township Polling Places In Cities

AN ACT to authorize township boards to provide polling places located within the limits of a city and to authorize the casting of ballots at such polling places.

MCLA 41.211 Township polling places in cities. MSA 6.331

Sec. 1. Township boards are hereby authorized to provide polling places located within the limits of a city which has been incorporated from territory formerly a part of such township, and the electors of such township may cast their ballots at such polling place.

Act No. 116, P.A 1954 — Election Law

AN ACT to reorganize, consolidate and add to the election laws; to provide for election officials and prescribe their powers and duties; to provide for the nomination and election of candidates for public office; to provide for the resignation, removal and recall of certain public officers; to provide for the filling of vacancies in public office; to provide for and regulate primaries and elections; to provide for the purity of elections; to guard against the abuse of the elective franchise; to define violations of this act; to prescribe the penalties therefor; and to repeal certain acts and all other acts inconsistent herewith.

CHAPTER I. DEFINITIONS

MCLA 168.1 Short title. [MSA 6.1001]

MCLA 168.2 Election. [MSA 6.1002]

Sec. 2. The term "election", as used in this act, shall mean and be held to include any election and primary election, at which the electors of the state or of any subdivision thereof choose or nominate by ballot public officials or decide any public question lawfully submitted to them. The term "election" is not synonymous with the term "civil appointment" as such term appears in section 9 of article 4 of the state constitution.

MCLA 168.3 General November election. [MSA 6.1003]

Sec. 3. The term "general November election", as used in this act, shall mean the election provided to be held in this state on the first Tuesday after the first Monday of November in every even numbered year.

MCLA 168.4 Biennial spring election. [MSA 6.1004]

Sec. 4. The term "biennial spring election", "spring election" or other similar term, as used in city or village charters unless otherwise defined therein, shall mean the local election to be held on the first Monday of April in every odd numbered year.

MCLA 168.5 General election. [MSA 6.1005]

Sec. 5. The words "general election", as used in this act, shall mean the general November election.

MCLA 168.6 Special election. [MSA 6.1006]

Sec. 6. The term "special election", as used in this act, shall mean any election, other than a regular election, called by competent authority for the purpose of choosing officials to fill vacancies in public office, or for submission to the electors of any public question.

MCLA 168.7 Primary or primary election. [MSA 6.1007]

Sec. 7. The term "primary" or "primary election", as used in this act, shall mean a primary election held for the purpose of deciding by ballot who shall be the nominees for the offices named in this act, or for the election by ballot of delegates to political conventions.

MCLA 168.8 Special primary. [MSA 6.1008]

Sec. 8. The term "special primary", as used in this act, shall mean a primary called by competent authority for the nomination of candidates to be voted for at a special election as defined in section 6 of this act.

MCLA 168.9 Village [MSA 6.1009]

MCLA 168.10 Qualified elector. [MSA 6.1010]

Sec. 10. The term "qualified elector", as used in this act, shall be construed to mean any person who possesses the qualifications of an elector as prescribed in section 1 of article 2 of the state constitution and who has resided in the city or township 30 days.

MCLA 168.11 Residence. [MSA 6.1011]

Sec. 11. (a) The term "residence", as used in this act, for registration and voting purposes shall be construed to mean that place at which a person habitually sleeps, keeps his or her person-al effects and has a regular place of lodging. Should a person have more than 1 residence, or should a wife have a residence separate from that of the husband, that place at which such person resides the greater part of the time shall be his or her official residence for the purposes of this act. This section shall not be construed to affect existing judicial interpretation of the term residence.

(b) No elector shall be deemed to have gained or lost a resi-dence by reason of his being employed in the service of the United States or of this state, nor while engaged in the navigation of the waters of this state or of the United States or of the high seas, nor while a student at any institution of learning, nor while kept at any almshouse or other asylum at public expense, nor while confined in any public prison. Honorably discharged members of the armed forces of the United States or of this state and who reside in the veterans' facility established by this state may acquire a residence where the facility is located.

(c) No member of the armed forces of the United States shall be deemed a resident of this state in consequence of being station-ed in any military or naval place within the state.

MCLA 168.12 Immediate family. MSA 6.1012

Sec. 12. The term "immediate family" as used in this act means a person's father, mother, brother, sister, spouse and any relative residing in the same household with that person.

MCLA 168.13 Time, computation. MSA 6.1013

Sec. 13. Notwithstanding any other provision of the law to the contrary, anything required by this act to be done by a day certain, except the final day for applying for an absentee ballot, if that day falls on a Saturday, Sunday or legal holiday, may be done within the same time limits on the next secular day.

MCLA 168.14 Locked and sealed. MSA 6.1014

Sec. 14. The term "locked and sealed", or terms of similar import, when used in this act to refer to locking and sealing of bal-lot boxes means sealed with a numbered flat metal seal furnished by the election commission and do not mean that a padlock is required.

MCLA 168.15 Nominating petitions, signatures required, basis for computation. [MSA 6.1015]

Sec. 15. Whenever the number of signatures required on a nominating petition is based on a percentage of the vote for a party's candidate for secretary of state at the last preceding election and that party did not have a candidate for secretary of state at the last preceding election, the vote of the party's principal candidate at the last preceding election shall be used in lieu of the vote for secretary of state.

CHAPTER II. BOARDS OF ELECTION COMMISSIONERS AND BOARDS OF CANVASSERS

MCLA 168.21 Secretary of state, powers and duties. [MSA 6.1021]

MCLA 168.23 Board of county election commissioners, members, officers. [MSA 6.1023]

Sec. 23. The judge of probate or the presiding or senior judge of probate, the county clerk and the county treasurer shall constitute a board of county election commissioners for each county, 2 of whom shall be a quorum for the transaction of business. The judge of probate or the presiding or senior judge of probate and the county clerk shall act as chairman and secretary of the board. In the absence of the county clerk from any meeting of the board of election commissioners, the board may select 1 of his deputies to act in his stead. In the event of the absence of any member of the board of election commissioners other than the county clerk, the members of the board who are present shall appoint some other county officer in his place, and such county officer, on being notified, shall attend without delay and act as a member of said board.

MCLA 168.24a Board of county canvassers. [MSA 6.1024(1)]

Establishment, powers, duties, jurisdiction, cost of canvass

Sec. 24a (1) A 4-member board of county canvassers is established in every county in this state. All of the powers granted to and duties required by law to be performed by all boards of canvas-

sers established by law, other than the board of state canvassers, boards of canvassers in cities having more than 5 precincts, boards of canvassers in counties having a population of 1,000,000 or more and boards of canvassers in townships having more than 5 precincts are granted to and required to be performed by the board of county canvassers. The board of county canvassers shall conduct all recounts of elections in cities, townships, villages, school districts or any other districts and be vested with all of the powers and required to perform all the duties in connection with any recount. If a city, village, school district or any other district lies in more than 1 county, and a duty is to be performed by the board of county canvassers, the board of county canvassers in the county in which the greatest number of registered voters of the city, village or district resides at the close of registration for the election involved shall perform the duty. The cost of canvass of school, city, township and and village elections shall be borne by the school district, city, township or village holding the election, and upon presentation of a bill for the costs incurred by the board of county canvassers, the school district, city, township or village shall reimburse the county treasurer.

Duties of boards of canvassers abolished

(2) All boards of canvassers provided for in law including boards of school canvassers, the duties of which are by this act required to be performed by boards of county canvassers, are abolished.

Appointment, term, notice

(3) Members of the board shall be appointed for terms of 4 years beginning on November 1 following their appointment. Of the members first appointed, 1 member of each of the political parties represented on the canvassing board shall be appointed for a term of 4 years and 1 for a term of 2 years. Members of the board shall be notified of their appointment within 5 days thereafter by the county clerk.

Application of section, charters

(4) This section shall apply to all elections, any charter provision to the contrary notwithstanding.

MCLA 168.24b Same; qualifications, oath, eligibility. [MSA 6.1024(2)]

Sec. 24b. Members of the board shall be qualified electors of the county and shall take and subscribe to the constitutional oath of office.

No person holding an elective public office shall be eligible for membership on the board of county canvassers. If any member of the board of county canvassers, during his term of office, becomes a candidate for any elective public office, his office shall be vacant.

MCLA 168.24c Same; method of selection. [MSA 6.1024(3)]

Sec. 24c. ... (Selection made by board of commissioners within certain ten day limitation, from names submitted by political parties by September 1 of each odd numbered year) ...

MCLA 168.24c Same; method of selection. [MSA 6.1024(3)]

Sec. 24d. ... (When vacancy occurs, notice to chairman of county committee as to political party entitled to fill same, who nominates three names within ten days, and county committee chairman appoints one within ten days) ...

MCLA 168.24e Same; meetings, chairman, vice-chairman, quorum, action, assistants. [MSA 6.1024(5)]

MCLA 168.24f Same; compensation and expenses in counties of less than one million population. [MSA 6.1024(6)]

MCLA 168.24g Same; actual and necessary expenses, compensation for attendance at meetings. [MSA 6.1024(7)]

MCLA 168.24h Same; compensation and expenses in counties over one million population. [MSA 6.1024(8)]

MCLA 168.24j Ballot boxes; examination; approval or disapproval, designation on box; use of unapproved boxes, offense; procurement of proper boxes. [MSA 6.1024(10)]

Sec. 24j. Before June 1 of every fourth year, beginning in 1970, a county board of canvassers shall examine the ballot boxes to be used in any election conducted under the provisions of this act. The board shall designate on the ballot box that the box does or does not meet the specifications required by this act. A ballot box which has not been approved by the board shall not be used to store voted ballots. A clerk of a city, village or township may procure, at the expense of the unit of government using the same, a sufficient number of proper ballot boxes to meet the requirements of this act. A clerk who uses or permits the use of any ballot box which has been disapproved is guilty of a misdemeanor.

MCLA 168.25 Cities; board of election commissioners; quorum; absentee. [MSA 6.1025]

MCLA 168.26 Townships; board of election commissioners; quorum, absentee. [MSA 6.1026]

Sec. 26.   Unless otherwise provided by charter, the supervisor, clerk and township treasurer shall constitute the board of township election commissioners for each township, 2 of whom shall be a quorum for the transaction of business. The township clerk shall act as the chairman of the board. Should only 1 of said officers be in attendance on the day appointed for a meeting of the board, the officer in attendance shall appoint a qualified and registered elector of the township to act in the absentee's stead during the period of nonattendance.

MCLA 168.27 Villages; board of election commissioners; quorum, absentee. [MSA 6.1027]

MCLA 168.28 Compensation of election commissioners and canvassers. [MSA 6.1028]

Sec. 28.   Members of the various boards of election commissioners and boards of canvassers and any other person charged with duties in connection with the conduct of primaries, elections, canvassing of returns and recounts shall receive such compensation as shall be determined by the legislative body of the state, county, city, township or village, as the case may be.

MCLA 168.29 Election assistants; authority, appointment, oath, compensation. [MSA 6.1029]

Sec. 29. The clerk of each township, ... is authorized and empowered to appoint such number of assistants as may be necessary to carry out the general provisions of the election law. Such assistants shall possess only the authority conferred upon them by the township, ... clerks appointing them, and shall perform only such duties that are assigned to them by such clerk. Each such assistant, before he enters upon the discharge of his duties, shall take and subscribe to the oath of office as provided in section 1 of article 11 of the state constitution, which shall be filed in the office of the township, city or village clerk and shall be properly instructed by the ... township clerk in the duties he is assigned to perform. Such assistants shall receive such compensation as shall be fixed by the township board.

MCLA 168.30a   Local board of canvassers; powers and duties, appointment, term, notice; contract with county, cost.
MSA 6.1030(1)

Sec. 30a. (1) A 4-member board of canvassers is established in every ... township having more than 5 precincts, notwithstanding any statutory or charter provision, or any other rule or law to the contrary. All of the powers granted to and duties required by law to to be performed by ... township boards of canvassers are granted to and required to be performed by the boards of ... township canvassers in ... townships having more than 5 precincts. ... Members of the board shall be appointed for terms of 4 years beginning January 1 next following their appointment. Of the members first appointed, 1 member of each of the political parties represented by the canvassing board shall be appointed for a term ending December 31, 1967, and 1 for a term ending December 31, 1965. Members of the board shall be notified of their appointment within 5 days thereafter by their ... township clerk.

(2) The ... township board of any ... township having more than 5 precincts may contract with the board of supervisors of the county in which all or the greater portion of the ... township's population resides to provide that the board of county canvassers of that county shall perform all the functions of the board of ... township canvassers. Financial arrangements of such a contract may provide that the ... township shall bear all or part of cost of such work.

MCLA 168.30b   Same; eligibility, affidavit, vacation of office.
MSA 6.1030(2)

Sec. 30b. Members of the board shall be qualified and registered electors of the ... township in which they serve. No person shall be appointed to a board of canvassers unless such person shall have filed with the ... township clerk an affidavit on a form approved by the state bureau of elections containing at least the following information: name, home address, political party affiliation, date of birth, employment and statement of physical disability, if any. The ... township clerk shall notify the county clerk of the name, address and political affiliation of board members, and the county clerk shall maintain such record for public inspection. A member of the board of canvassers vacates his office if at any time during his term of office he or any member of his immediate family serves as an election inspector or becomes a candidate for any elective public office at an election to be canvassed by his board of canvassers or serves as a member of the governing body of the unit for which his board is established.

MCLA 168.30c Same; bipartisan selection, applications, appointment. [MSA 6.1030(3)]

Sec. 30c. Selection of the members of such board shall be made from each of the 2 political parties casting the greatest number of votes for secretary of state at the preceding November election in the county or counties in which the ... township is located. No political party shall be represented by more than 2 members on the board at any one time. Persons possessing qualifications for membership on the board may submit an application for the position on a form approved by the state bureau of elections. The governing body of the ... township shall appoint from the applications on file the members of the canvassing board by December 1 of each odd-numbered year. In event of a vacancy, the governing body shall make the appointment to fill the vacancy. Any person appointed to fill the vacancy shall serve for the balance of the unexpired term. Notwithstanding section 30b, if an insufficient number of applications to fill the positions has been submitted, the governing body shall make the appointments in any manner it deems advisable.

MCLA 168.30d Same; meetings, quorum, officers. [MSA 6.1030(4)]

Sec. 30d. The board shall meet as necessary to transact their business and shall elect 1 of their members chairman and 1 vice chairman. *Any 3 members shall constitute a quorum but no action shall become effective unless 1 member from each political party represented concurs therein. The ... township clerk shall be the clerk of the board of ... township canvassers.*

MCLA 168.30e Same; expenses; incomplete canvass, completion by board of county canvassers; cost [MSA 6.1030(5)]

Sec. 30e. The members of the board of ... township canvassers shall receive actual and necessary expenses incurred in the performance of their official duties and in addition may be paid a daily rate if so ordered by the governing body of the ... township. Should the board fail to certify the results of any election for any office or proposition within the 14 days immediately following the election at which the office or proposition was voted on, the ... township clerk shall immediately deliver to the secretary of the board of county canvassers of that county, all records and other information pertaining thereto. The board of county canvassers shall meet forthwith, make the necessary determinations and certify the results of that election within the 7 days immediately following receipt of the records. The cost of such canvass shall be borne by the ... township involved.

MCLA 168.30g Board of canvassers; quorum not present; appointment of temporary members, qualifications, term. [MSA 6.1030(7)]

Sec. 30g. Whenever a board of canvassers created under this act is required to perform its statutory duties and because of illness or absence of members of the board a quorum is not present, the clerk of the political subdivision may appoint a sufficient number of temporary members to constitute a quorum. If the vacancy is on the board of county canvassers, the appointment shall be made by the county clerk from party recommendations on file, if available. If the vacancy is on the board of ... township canvassers, the appointment shall be made from applications on file, if available. The appointments shall be of the same political party as the ill or absent members of the board. Any temporary appointee to the board of canvassers must possess all of the qualifications required for regular membership on that board. Temporary appointees shall serve only until the business on hand has been transacted.

MCLA 168.31 Secretary of state; powers and duties. [MSA 6.1031]

Sec. 31. The secretary of state in addition to other powers and duties conferred upon him shall have the power and it shall be his duty:

(1) **Rules, regulations and instructions.** *To prepare rules, regulations and instructions for the conduct of elections and registrations in accordance with the laws of the state;*

(2) **Advice to local election officials.** *To advise local election officials upon request as to the proper methods of conducting elections;*

(3) **Manual of instruction.** *To publish and furnish for the use in each election precinct prior to each state primary and election a manual of instructions;*

(4) **Pamphlet copies of registration, primary and election laws; distribution.** *To publish indexed pamphlet copies of the registration, primary and election laws and to furnish to the various county, city, township and village clerks a sufficient number of copies for their own use and to enable them to include 1 copy with the election supplies furnished each precinct board of election inspectors under their respective jurisdictions, and he may furnish single copies of the publications to organizations or individuals who request the same for purposes of instruction or public reference;*

(5) **Forms, notices and supplies.** *To prescribe and require such uniform forms, notices and supplies as he shall deem advisable for use in the conduct of elections and registrations;*

(6) **Form of ballot; amendment to constitution, initiative, referendum.** *To prepare the form of ballot for any proposed amendment to the constitution or proposal under the initiative or referendum provision of the constitution to be submitted to the voters of the state;*

(7) **Reports from local election officials.** *To require such reports from the local election officials as may be deemed necessary;*

(8) **Investigation and report of election law violations.** *To investigate, or cause to be investigated by local authorities, the administration of election laws, and to report violations of the election laws and regulations to the attorney general or prosecuting attorney, or both for prosecution; and*

(9) **Legislative manual, publication of votes, further informa-**

tion. *To publish in the legislative manual the vote for governor and secretary of state by townships and wards and the vote for members of the state legislature cast at the preceding November election, which shall be returned to the secretary of state by the several county clerks on or before the first day of December following such election and it shall be the further duty of all clerks to furnish to the secretary of state, promptly and without compensation, any further information requested of them, to be used in the compilation of the manual.*

MCLA 168.32   Bureau of elections; director, powers and duties. MSA 6.1032

Sec. 32.   There is hereby continued in the office of the secretary of state the bureau of elections ... under the supervision of a director of elections, to be appointed by the secretary of state under civil service regulations. The director of elections shall be vested with the powers and shall perform the duties of the secretary of state under his supervision, with respect to the supervision and administration of the election laws. The director of elections shall be a nonmember secretary of the state board of canvassers.

Statement of purpose of proposed constitutional amendment or question. *The director of elections, with the approval of the state board of canvassers, shall prepare a statement for designation on the ballot in not more than 100 words, exclusive of caption, of the purpose of any proposed amendment or question, to be submitted to the electors as required under section 2 of article 12 of the state constitution. The powers and duties of the state board of canvassers and the secretary of state with respect to the preparation of such statement are hereby transferred to the director of elections.*

MCLA 168.33   Training schools; conduct, cost.   MSA 6.1033

Sec. 33.   The director of elections shall conduct training schools throughout the state of Michigan preceding the general November election, and preceding such other elections as the director shall deem advisable, for county clerks and their representatives with respect to the conducting of elections in accordance with the election laws. In case any county clerk shall fail to conduct in his county a training school for election boards within the county, the director of elections shall conduct such training school, the cost thereof to be charged as an obligation of the county.

CHAPTER XII. COUNTY ROAD COMMISSIONERS

MCLA 168.251 through 168.271 [MSA 6.1251 THROUGH 6.1271]

CHAPTER XIII. STATE BOARD OF EDUCATION; BOARD OF REGENTS OF UNIVERSITY OF MICHIGAN; BOARD OF TRUSTEES OF MICHIGAN STATE UNIVERSITY; BOARD OF GOVERNORS OF WAYNE STATE UNIVERSITY

MCLA 168.281 through 168.296 [MSA 6.1281 THROUGH 6.1296]

Note: *There is nothing in the ten chapters listed directly above which affects townships - directions will come from the county clerk.*

CHAPTER XV. CITY OFFICES

MCLA 168.321 through 168.327 [MSA 6.1321 THROUGH 6.1327]

Note: *Nothing affecting townships*

CHAPTER XVI. TOWNSHIP OFFICES

MCLA 168.341 Township officers. [MSA 6.1341]

Sec. 341. Elective township offices shall consist of a supervisor, township clerk, township treasurer, not to exceed 4 constables, and not to exceed 4 trustees.

MCLA 168.342 Same; eligibility. [MSA 6.1342]

Sec. 342. No person shall be eligible to a township office who is not a qualified elector of the township in which election is sought. ...

MCLA 168.343a Political party committees, membership.
[MSA 6.1343(1)]

Sec. 343a. There shall be a township party committee for each political party in every organized township in this state. The party committee shall consist of the members of the county committee from the township. If the number of members of the county com-

mittee from the township exceeds 5, the county committee members from the township shall select 5 of their members to serve as the township committee.

MCLA 168.345   Township officers; primary election, date.
MSA 6.1345

Sec. 345. A primary of all political parties shall be held in every organized township of this state on the Tuesday succeeding the first Monday in August preceding every general November election, at which time the qualified and registered electors of each political party may vote for party candidates for township offices.

MCLA 168.346   Same; inspectors of election.   MSA 6.1346

Sec. 346. The township board of election commissioners shall appoint 3 or more qualified and registered electors of such township for each precinct, who shall act as inspectors of election at such primary.

MCLA 168.347   Same; primaries; laws governing; recounts.
MSA 6.1347

Sec. 347. Except as herein otherwise provided, the laws governing nominating petitions, the conduct of general primary elections, the furnishing of ballots and the depositing, counting and canvassing of the same, shall, as near as may be, apply to primaries held under the provisions of this chapter. In case of recounts, said recounts shall be conducted by the township board of canvassers; and all duties which, under the parts of this act relating to general elections or primary elections, devolve upon the county clerk, shall be performed by the township clerk.

MCLA 168.348 Same; primary, call, notice, publication, posting, date. MSA 6.1348

Sec. 348. The township board, not less than 40 days prior to the holding of the primary herein provided for, shall issue a call for such primary designating the time and place thereof and shall give notice of the same by publishing a copy of such call in some newspaper of general circulation in the township, and if deemed advisable by the township board by the posting of the number of notices that the board shall designate in conspicuous places. In townships having less than 200 registered voters, the township board may provide that for elections at which no township question is to be submitted notices of the election shall be by posting, as herein provided, in lieu of by publishing. ...

Note: There are no requirements as to size of published election notices -- only that they be legible. Also, a considerable savings in the election expense can be realized by joining with other townships for the purpose of publishing joint election notices.

MCLA 168.349   Same; nominating petitions, filing.   [MSA 6.1349]

Sec. 349. To obtain the printing of the name of any person as a candidate for nomination by any political party for a township office under the particular party heading upon the official primary ballots, there shall be filed with the township clerk nominating petitions signed by a number of qualified and registered electors residing within said township, equal to not less than 1% nor more than 4% of the number of votes cast by such party in the township for secretary of state at the last general election in which a secretary of state was elected,* but in no case less than 5 signatures. Such nominating petitions shall be in the form prescribed in section 544c.

---

*In charter townships, nominating petitions must be signed by not less than 1% nor more than 4% of the number of votes cast by such party in the township for township supervisor. **MCLA 42.4** [MSA 5.46(4)]

The township clerk shall receive such nominating petitions up to 4 p.m., eastern standard time, of the seventh Tuesday preceding the August primary.

Within 4 days following the last day for filing nominating petitions, the township clerk shall deliver to the county clerk a list setting forth the names, addresses and political affiliation and office sought of all candidates who have qualified for a position on the primary ballot.

MCLA 168.351   Township officers; withdrawal, notice.   [MSA 6.1351]

Sec. 351. After the filing of a nominating petition by or in behalf of a proposed candidate for a township office, such candidate shall not be permitted to withdraw unless a written notice of withdrawal is served on the township clerk not later than 4 o'clock, eastern standard time, in the afternoon of the third day after the last day for filing such petitions as in this act provided, unless the third day falls on a Saturday, Sunday or legal holiday, in which case the notice of withdrawal may be served on the clerk up to 4 o'clock, eastern standard time, on the next secular day.

MCLA 168.352   Same; death of candidate; labels or stickers.
[MSA 6.1352]

Sec. 352. When any candidate of a political party for any township office, after having qualified as a candidate, shall die, after the last day for qualifying, leaving such party without a candidate for a township office, a candidate to fill the vacancy thereby caused may be selected by the members of the township committee of such candidate's political party for the township, and the candidate so selected shall be transmitted to the township officials required by law to print and distribute ballots, and such township officials shall cause to be printed a sufficient number of gummed labels or stickers bearing the name of the candidate, which shall be distributed to the various voting precincts within their respective township, and the board of election inspectors of each such precinct shall cause 1 of such stickers to be placed on each ballot, over the name of the candidate who has died, before such ballot is handed to the elector.

MCLA 168.353   Same; absent voters, provisions applicable.
[MSA 6.1353]

Sec. 353. The provisions of this act relative to absent voters shall apply to primaries held under the provisions of this chapter: Provided, That the duties of the county clerk relative to the furnishing and distribution of ballots shall be performed by the township clerk.

MCLA 168.354   Same; blank spaces on ballots.   [MSA 6.1354]

Sec. 354. If, for any reason, the number of candidates of a political party to a township office shall be equal to less than the total number to be nominated and elected, a sufficient number of blank spaces shall be provided on the official primary ballots which will afford every elector to said party an opportunity to vote for as many candidates as are to be nominated and elected by writing in the name or names of his or her selection or by the use of slips or pasters.

MCLA 168.355 Same; nominees, certification. [MSA 6.1355]

Sec. 355. The candidate or candidates of each political party to a township office receiving the greatest number of votes cast for candidates of said office, as set forth in the report of the township board of canvassers, based on the returns from the various election precincts, or as determined by the board of county canvassers as the result of a recount, shall be declared the nominee or nominees of that political party for said office at the next ensuing November election. The township board of canvassers shall certify such nomination or nominations to the township clerk within 48 hours after the closing of the polls.

Within 4 days following the primary, the township clerk shall deliver to the county clerk a list setting forth the names, addresses, political affiliation and office sought of all candidates nominated at the primary.

MCLA 168.357 Township officers; death after nomination. [MSA 6.1357]

Sec. 357. When any candidate of a political party, after having been nominated for a township office, shall die, remove from the township, or become disqualified for any reason, the township board of election commissioners shall provide a blank space or spaces on the official ballots which will afford every elector of said party an opportunity to vote for a candidate to fill the vacancy thereby caused, by writing in the name of his or her selection or by the use of a slip or paster.

MCLA 168.358 Same, election, date, conduct, officers elected, order on ballot, constables, trustees. [MSA 6.1358]

Sec. 358. In every township there shall be a general November election in each even numbered year at which there shall be elected by ballot the following township officers: A supervisor, a clerk, a treasurer, 2 trustees, and at least 1 but not to exceed 4 constables. The order of officers on the township portion of the ballots shall be the same as the officers are here listed.

The number of constables to be elected shall be determined by the township board at least 6 months prior to the township election. If no determination as to the number of constables to be elected is made by the township board,* 2 constables **shall** be elected.

----

*The number may be from one to four constables.

In townships now or hereafter having a population of 5,000 or over, or now or hereafter having 3,000 or over qualified and registered electors, as shown by the registration records at the close of registration for the last preceding November election, there may be elected in such township 4 trustees. In other townships there shall be 2 trustees. **No township shall elect 4 trustees unless the election of additional trustees is approved by the voters at a regular township election or by a majority of the voters attending at an annual meeting.** The township board of any township hereafter having a population of 5,000 or over, or having 3,000 or over, qualified and registered electors, shall cause the question of electing additional trustees to be voted on at the first township election following the township's qualifying for additional trustees. If a majority of the electors voting on such question vote in favor thereof, the township shall thereafter elect 4 trustees. If a majority of the electors voting on the question do not vote in favor thereof, the township board may resubmit the question at any subsequent township election or the question shall be submitted at the first township election held at least 49 days following the submission of a petition containing the signatures of at least 10% of the registered and qualified electors of the township as shown by the registration records at the close of registration for the last preceding November election asking that such question be submitted. At the first regular township election in any township held at least 4 months after the provisions of this section relative to additional trustees shall have been adopted, there shall be elected such number of trustees as is necessary to make a total of 4 trustees. Nothing in this section shall be construed to prohibit townships now electing 4 trustees from continuing to do so.

Note: Grave errors could result from misinterpretation of the language emphasized above. The better opinion is that the only action electors may take at an annual meeting is to decide whether there shall be an election to determine if the township is to have four trustees. To become legal and binding, there would have to be a referendum held upon the matter at a township election.

MCLA 168.358a Special elections in townships; notice.
MSA 6.1358(1)

Sec. 358a. The township board of any township may call a special election to be held in such township for the purpose of sub-mitting any proposition or propositions to the electors thereof. No such special election shall be held within 60 days prior or subse-quent to any regular township or state primary or general election. Like notice of such special election shall be given as is now re-quired of regular elections held under this act.

MCLA 168.360 Same; preservation of statement; certificate of election to person elected. MSA 6.1360

Sec. 360. The township clerk shall file in his office and pre-serve the original statement and determination of the township board of canvassers of the results of the election and shall forth-with execute and cause to be delivered to the persons thereby de-clared to be elected to township offices a certificate of election, certified by him.

MCLA 168.361 Township electors annual meeting; notice, publica-tion, posting. MSA 6.1361

Sec. 361. There shall be an annual meeting of the electors of each township on the Saturday preceding the first Monday in April of each year between 1 p.m. and 8 p.m. The time and place of such meeting shall be determined by the township board. The town-ship clerk shall give notice thereof by publication at least twice in some newspaper of general circulation in the township, the last pub-lication to be not more than 20 nor less than 14 days before the meeting day and, if deemed advisable by the township board by the posting of the number of notices that the board shall designate in conspicuous places. In townships having less than 200 registered voters, the township board may provide that notices of the annual meeting shall be by posting, as herein provided, in lieu of by pub-lishing. The electors meeting at the place designated shall trans-act such business as is usually transacted at township meetings by viva voce vote.
Abolition in townships having 5,000 or more inhabitants, refer-

endum. *In all townships having 5,000 or more inhabitants the township board by resolution may, or on the filing of petitions signed by not less than 8% of the registered electors of the township shall, submit the question of the abolition of the annual township meeting to the electors at the next regular primary or election. Such resolution or petition shall be filed with the township clerk at least 30 days prior to such regular primary or election day. In case a majority of the electors of the township voting on the proposal shall vote for the abolition of the annual township meeting, the annual township meeting in such township shall be abolished.*

MCLA 168.362 Township officers; term of notice. MSA 6.1362

Sec. 362. The term of office of township officers listed in section 358 shall be 2 years. The term of office of township trustees shall be 4 years. **All township officers shall take office at 12 noon on November 20 next following their election and they shall qualify not later than that date.** *Each township officer shall hold office until his successor is elected and qualified. ... Notwithstanding any provision of law to the contrary, all elective township officers, other than those listed in section 358, shall be elected at the November election immediately preceding the expiration of their term and shall take office on November 20 next following their election.*

MCLA 168.363 Same; oath, filing. MSA 6.1363

Sec. 363. All township officers shall, **before entering upon the duties of their offices, take and subscribe the oath** *as provided in Section 1 of article 11 of the state constitution before the township clerk or other officer authorized to administer oaths, and file the same with the township clerk who shall record the same; and such oath shall be administered without reward and certified by the officer before whom the same was taken, with the date of taking the same.*

MCLA 168.364 Same; township treasurer, bond, sureties, approval, filing. MSA 6.1364

Sec. 364. Each township treasurer, within the time limited for filing his oath of office and before he shall enter upon the duties of his office, shall give a bond to the township in such sum and with such sureties as the supervisor shall require and approve and the supervisor shall endorse his approval thereon. It shall be the duty

214

of such treasurer to file within the time above mentioned said bond with the township clerk of such township, who shall record the same in a book to be provided for that purpose. The township clerk shall, after recording same, deliver the bond to the supervisor who shall file it in his office.

MCLA 168.365 Same; constable, indemnification. MSA 6.1365

Sec. 365. Every person elected or appointed to the office of constable, before he enters upon the duties of his office and within the time prescribed by law for filing his official oath, shall execute, with sufficient sureties to be approved by the supervisor or clerk of his township,...

MCLA 168.367 Same; resignations, signatures, delivery, filing. MSA 6.1367

Sec. 367. Resignation of any township officer shall be in writing, signed by the officer resigning, and addressed to the township board, and shall be delivered to and filed by the township clerk; ...

Note: The next few sections also affect appointed officials.

MCLA 168.368 Same; vacancy, creation. MSA 6.1368

Sec. 368. The township offices in any organized township shall become vacant upon the happening of any of the following events: Death of the incumbent; his resignation; his removal from office for cause; his ceasing to be a resident of the township where his office is located; his conviction of an infamous crime, or of an offense involving the violation of his oath of office; the decision of a competent tribunal declaring his election or appointment void; habitual drunkenness; his refusal or neglect to take and subscribe to the oath as provided in section 2 of article 16 of the state constitution and deposit the same in the manner and within the time prescribed by law; or his refusal or neglect to give bond in the amount and manner and within the time prescribed by law.

MCLA 168.369 Same; removal from office, reasons. MSA 6.1369

Sec. 369. The governor shall remove all ... township officers chosen by the electors of any township, when he shall be satisfied from sufficient evidence submitted to him, as hereinafter provided that such officer has been guilty of official misconduct, or of wilful neglect of duty, or of extortion, or habitual drunkenness, or has been convicted of being drunk, or whenever it shall appear by a certified copy of the judgment of a court of record of this state that such officer, after his election or appointment, shall have been convicted of a felony; but the governor shall take no action upon any such charges made to him against any such officer until the same shall have been exhibited to him in writing, verified by the affidavit of the party making them, that he believes the charges to be true. But no such officer shall be removed for such misconduct or neglect until charges thereof shall have been exhibited to the governor as above provided and a copy of the same served on such officer and an opportunity given him of being heard in his defense: Provided, that the service of such charges upon the person or persons complained against shall be made by handing to such person or persons a copy of such charges, together with all affidavits or exhibits which may be attached to the original petition if such person or persons can be found; and if not, by leaving a copy at the last place of residence of such person or persons, with some person of suitable age, if such person can be found; and if not, by posting it in some conspicuous place upon his last known place of residence. No officer who has been removed in accordance with the provisions of this section shall be eligible to election or appointment to any office for a period of 3 years from the date of such removal.

MCLA 168.370 Same; vacancy, how filled. [MSA 6.1370]

Sec. 370. Whenever a vacancy shall occur in any elective or appointive township office, except as hereinafter specified, it shall be filled by appointment by the township board of the township, and the person appointed shall hold the office for the remainder of the unexpired term. If a vacancy occurs in any elective township office and the vacancy is not filled by the township board within 45 days of the beginning of the vacancy, the county clerk of the county in which the township is located shall notify the governor of such fact and the governor shall call a special election to fill such vacancy. The governor shall provide for the date for the filing of the petitions, which date shall also be the last date to register for such special primary election. Notwithstanding the provisions of section 358a of this act, the special primary or special general election may be held within 60 days of a state primary or a state general election. Any special primary or election called by the governor under authority of this section shall not affect the rights of any qualified elector to register for any other election. Any person elected to fill such vacancy shall serve for the remainder of the unexpired term.

MCLA 168.370a Same; vacancy; term of appointee. [MSA 6.1370(1)]

Sec. 370a. Notwithstanding the provisions of section 370, when a vacancy occurs in any elective or appointive township office and it is filled by appointment by the township board and the next general election is to be held more than 150 days after the vacancy occurs, and it is not the general election at which a successor in office would be elected if there had been no vacancy, the person appointed shall hold office only until a successor is elected at such general election, held more than 150 days after the vacancy occurs, in the manner provided by law and qualifies for the office. Such successor shall hold the office for the remainder of the unexpired term.

MCLA 168.371 Same; recount. [MSA 6.1371]

Sec. 371. The votes cast for any candidate to a township office at any primary or election shall be subject to recount as provided in chapter 33 of this act.

MCLA 168.372 Same; recall. [MSA 6.1372]

Sec. 372. Any person elected to a township office shall be subject to recall as provided in chapter 36 of this act.

MCLA 168.373 Township clerk or deputy; appointment of substitute to perform election law duties. [MSA 6.1373]

Sec. 373. If neither the township clerk nor any deputy township clerk shall be available to perform any necessary functions in connection with registrations, nominations or elections during the usual or required times for performing such functions, the township board shall appoint some qualified person who is a registered elector of the township to perform such functions until such time as the clerk or a deputy resume their duties. Any such person so appointed shall have all of the powers and authority of a deputy appointed by the clerk pertaining to registrations, nominations and elections.

CHAPTER XVII.   VILLAGE OFFICES

MCLA 168.381 through 168.383   [MSA 6.1381 THROUGH 6.1383]

CHAPTER XVIII.   JUSTICES OF THE SUPREME COURT

MCLA 168.391 through 168.406   [MSA 6.1391 THROUGH 6.1406]

CHAPTER XVIIIA.   JUDGES OF THE COURT OF APPEALS

MCLA 168.409 through 168.409n [MSA 6.1409 THROUGH 6.1409(14)]

CHAPTER XIX.   JUDGES OF THE CIRCUIT COURT

MCLA 168.411 through 168.426   [MSA 6.1411 THROUGH 6.1426]

CHAPTER XIXA.   JUDGES OF MUNICIPAL COURTS OF RECORD

MCLA 168.426a through 168.426n [MSA 6.1426(1) THROUGH 6.1426(14)]

CHAPTER XX.   JUDGE OF PROBATE

MCLA 168.431 through 168.446   [MSA 6.1431 THROUGH 6.1446]

CHAPTER XXIA.   JUDGES OF THE DISTRICT COURT

MCLA 168.467 through 168.467   [MSA 6.1467 THROUGH 6.1467(13)]

Note: The seven chapters listed above have no application in townships. Any necessary instructions will come from the county clerk.

CHAPTER XXII.   INITIATIVE AND REFERENDUM

MCLA 168.471 Initiative petitions proposing amendment to constitution, filing, time. [MSA 6.1471]

MCLA 168.472 Same; petitions to initiate legislation, filing, time. [MSA 6.1472]

MCLA 168.473 Same; referendum petitions, filing, time. [MSA 6.1473]

MCLA 168.474 Same; board of state canvassers, statement of purpose. [MSA 6.1474]

MCLA 168.475 Same; notification of board, meeting, time. [MSA 6.1475]

MCLA 168.476 Same; canvass; hearing upon complaint; adjournment; completion of canvass. [MSA 6.1476]

Sec. 476. Upon receipt of said petitions, said board shall canvass the same to ascertain if such petitions have been signed by the requisite number of qualified and registered electors, and for the purpose of determining the validity thereof, may cause any doubtful signatures to be checked against the registration records by the clerk of any political subdivision in which said petitions were circulated for properly determining the authenticity of such signatures. It shall be the duty of the clerk of any political subdivision to cooperate fully with said board in any request made to said clerks by said board in determining the validity of doubtful signatures by rechecking the same against registration records, and said clerk shall make the requested rechecks in an expeditious and proper manner. ...

MCLA 168.477 Same; declaration as to sufficiency or insufficiency of petition, when made; publicity, publication without expense. [MSA 6.1477]

MCLA 168.478 Same; notice of approval or rejection. [MSA 6.1478]

MCLA 168.479 Same; mandamus, certiorari, etc. [MSA 6.1479]

MCLA 168.480 Same; certification to county clerks; statement, furnishing; posting in voting precincts. [MSA 6.1480]

Sec. 480. Whenever a proposed constitutional amendment or other special question is to be submitted to the electors of the state for a popular vote, ... The county clerk shall furnish ... copies of such statement to the several township ... clerks in his county at the time other supplies for the election are furnished; and each such township ... clerk shall, before the opening of the polls on election day, deliver the copies of such text and statement to which each voting precinct in his township ... is entitled to the board of election inspectors of said precinct, who shall post the same in conspicuous places in the room where such election is held.

MCLA 168.481 Same; form. [MSA 6.1481]

MCLA 168.482 Same; petition, form. [MSA 6.1482]

MCLA 168.485 Questions submitted, form. [MSA 6.1485]

*Sec. 485. Any question submitted to the electors of this state
or the electors of any subdivision of this state shall, to the extent that it will not confuse the electorate, be worded in the following manner: A "yes" vote will be a vote in favor of the subject
matter of the proposal or issue, and a "no" vote will be a vote
against the subject matter of the proposal or issue. Questions
shall be worded so as to apprise the voters of the subject matter
of the proposal or issue, but need not be legally precise. The
language used shall create no prejudice for or against the issue or
proposal.*

CHAPTER XXIII. REGISTRATION OF ELECTORS

Note: The state director of elections in the office of the secretary of state issues new directives and up-to-date informational
material from time to time, which should be thoroughly and carefully studied and utilized by the township clerk. The township
attorney should be consulted regarding any unresolved questions or
problems, and letters of inquiry may also be addressed to the
director of elections.

**MCLA 168.491 Registration of electors; inspectors not to receive
vote of person not registered.** [MSA 6.1491]

*Sec. 491. The inspectors of election at any election or pri-
mary election in this state, or in any ... township, ... shall not receive
the vote of any person whose name is not registered in the registration book of the township, ... in which he offers to vote.*

MCLA 168.492   Qualifications for registration as an elector.
[MSA 6.1492]

*Sec. 492. Every person who has the following qualifications
of an elector, or who will have such qualifications at the next
ensuing election or primary election, shall be entitled to be registered as an elector in the township, ward or precinct in which he or*

she resides. *Such person must be a citizen of the United States; at least 18 years of age; a resident of the state for at least 45 days; and be a resident of the ... township ... on or before the fifth Friday prior to the next ensuing regular or special election or primary election.*

MCLA 168.493   Same; registration cards, contents.   [MSA 6.1493]

Sec. 493.   The clerk of each township ... shall provide blank forms printed on cards (hereinafter termed "registration cards"), to be used in the registration of electors.   Such registration cards shall contain the following: ...

MCLA 168.494   Same; definitions.   [MSA 6.1494]

Sec. 494.   The term "registration cards", as used in this chapter, shall be construed as meaning either cards or loose leaf sheets, and either may be used in the discretion of the township ... clerk, ...   The term "file", as used in this chapter, shall be construed as meaning either a file or loose leaf book.

MCLA 168.495   Same; registration affidavit, contents.   [MSA 6.1495]

Sec. 495.   The registration affidavit shall state the name, residence address, street and number, if any, and birthplace and birthdate of the elector.   The affidavit shall also state that the person signing it is a citizen of the United States and is or will be, on a specified date between the date of registration and the date of the next regular or special election or primary election, at least 18 years of age; that he has or will have on the specified date lived in the state 6 months or more; that he has or will have established his residence in the township, ... in which he is applying for registration on or before the **fifth Friday preceding** *the next regular or special election or primary election and that he is or will be on the specified date a qualified elector of the township,...   The affidavit shall also contain a space in which an elector shall state the place of his last registration.*

MCLA 168.497   Same; time for making application.   [MSA 6.1497]

MCLA 168.496   Same; duty of secretary of state.   [MSA 6.1496]

Sec. 496. It shall be the duty of the secretary of state to make the proper forms for use in the registration of electors, in recommending the use of the same to the several clerks of the townships, ... of this state, and in instructing the several township, ... clerks in this state as to the requirements of this act.

MCLA 168.497 Same; time for making application. MSA 6.1497

Sec. 497. Any person not already registered who possesses the qualifications of an elector as set forth in section 492, may make application for registration to the clerk of the township, ... in which he resides on any day other than Sunday, a legal holiday, the day of any regular, primary, school or special election. Any registrations taken on the days intervening between the fifth Friday preceding any such election and the day of such election, unless such fifth Friday shall fall on a legal holiday, in which event registration shall be accepted during the following day shall not be valid for such election but shall be valid for any subsequent regular, primary, school or special election held at a time so that at least 5 Fridays intervene between the date of registering and the date of the election. Except as provided in section 504, no application for registration shall be executed at any place other than the office of the township, ... clerk or a public place or places designated by him for receiving registrations pursuant to the provisions of this act, but such clerk may in his discretion receive such application wherever he may be. In case any township, ... clerk does not regularly keep his office open daily during certain hours, he shall not be required to be at his office for the purpose of receiving applications for registration on any particular day nor during any specific hours of any day, except as provided in section 498. Any registrations taken after the time of closing registrations prior to an election need not be processed until a date immediately following that election. No such registration shall be placed in a precinct registration file until a date immediately following that election. Any time a person registers at a time registrations are closed for an election, the person shall be given a notice, signed by the clerk, on a form established by the state director of elections, informing him that he is not eligible to vote in the election and indicating the first date on which he is eligible to vote. Any provisions of law to the contrary notwithstanding the provisions of this section relating to registration shall apply.

MCLA 168.498 Same; township, ... clerks, when to accept applications for registration, office hours, notice, publication or posting. [MSA 6.1498]

Sec. 498. In every township, ... the clerk thereof shall be at his office or in some other convenient place therein, which place shall be designated by the township ... clerk between the hours of 8 a.m. and 8 p.m. on the fifth Friday preceding any election or primary election in such township, ... unless ...

MCLA 168.499 Same; affidavit, oath, interpreter; false statements; acceptance of registration; fees prohibited; voter identification card. [MSA 6.1499]

Sec. 499. Any elector entitled to registration in any election precinct may become registered therein by applying in person and executing in duplicate the registration affidavit and swearing to and signing the same before the clerk or assistant clerk of the township, ... in which said precinct is located. Every clerk and assistant clerk of the several townships, ... in this state shall have power and it shall be their duty to require any applicant for registration to answer under oath any question touching his qualification as an elector, and for the performance of their duties under this act shall have power to administer oaths and to swear persons as to the truth of statements contained in affidavits. They may also ...

MCLA 168.500   Same; applicant unable to write, procedure. [MSA 6.1500]

Sec. 500. If the applicant for registration is unable to write, then he shall execute the registration affidavit by making his mark and there shall be noted upon the registration card the month, day and year of his birth and any other identifying information which shall be used in identifying said person at the time he makes application for voting as hereinafter more specifically provided.

MCLA 168.501 Same; precinct and master file of registration cards. [MSA 6.1501]

Sec. 501. The original registration cards shall be filed by precincts arranged either alphabetically or according to the numerical order of the houses located on each street, said file to be hereinafter termed the "precinct file". The duplicate registration cards shall be filed alphabetically without regard to wards or precincts, said file to be hereinafter termed the "master file": Provided, That in townships, ... having not more than 1 voting precinct the duplicate "master" registrations may be dispensed with.

MCLA 168.502 Same; custody of files. MSA 6.1502

Sec. 502. The master file and the precinct files shall at all times remain in the custody of the township, ...clerk, ... except that the precinct files shall be delivered on election day to the inspectors of election in the several precincts who shall have custody of the same during any election or primary election and who shall return such files to the clerk immediately thereafter.

MCLA 168.503 Same; loss or destruction of registration card, new affidavit, cancellation, re-registration. MSA 6.1503

Sec. 503. If either the original or duplicate registration card, or both, of any elector shall be lost, destroyed or mutilated, the clerk of the township, ... shall require the execution of a new registration affidavit by such elector. If any such elector shall refuse or neglect to execute such affidavit within 60 days after the mailing of a letter to such elector at the last address from which he has registered, then the registration of such elector may be cancelled. If either the original or duplicate registration cards, or both, of any township, ... or any ward or precinct thereof, shall be lost or destroyed, the township board ... shall ...

MCLA 168.504 Same; elector unable to make personal application, procedure. MSA 6.1504

MCLA 168.505 Same; cancellation of previous registration, form, mailing. MSA 6.1505

Sec. 505. At the time any elector is applying for registration, the registration officer shall ascertain if such elector is already registered in another township, city or village within the state. If the elector is previously registered, the clerk shall cause such elector to sign an authorization to cancel the previous registration on a form substantially as follows: "..." The clerk shall cause all such authorizations to be mailed to the proper registration officer not later than 5 days after the close of registration. Upon receipt of such notice the clerk shall forthwith cancel the previous registration.

MCLA 168.506 Same; change of residence, request, filing; change of street or house number. [MSA 6.1506]

Sec. 506. *Any registered elector may, upon change of residence within the township, ... cause his registration to be transferred to his new address by ...*

MCLA 168.507 Same; transfer of registration, request, filing; change of street or house number. [MSA 6.1507]

Sec. 507. *Any registered elector who has removed from 1 election precinct of a township ... to another election precinct of the same township, ... and has not recorded such removal with the local clerk shall execute a transfer of registration request, listing the new residence address thereon over his signature, with the election board in the precinct in which he is registered at the next ensuing primary or election.*

The inspector of election in charge of the registration records shall ...

MCLA 168.507a Same; removal to another city or township after fifth Friday prior to election, voting, cancellation of registration. [MSA 6.1507(1)]

Sec. 507a. *Any registered and qualified elector of this state who has moved from the city or township in which registered to another city or township within the state after the fifth Friday prior to any election or primary election, shall be permitted to vote in such election or primary election at the place of last registration upon the signing of a form containing an affidavit stating that he has so removed. Such form shall be approved by the state director of elections and shall state that the voter has so removed and shall authorize the clerk of the city or township to cancel such voter's registration. Any voter coming under the provision of this section shall be permitted to vote either in person or by absentee ballot.*

MCLA 168.508 Same; form, notice of transfer mailed to elector. [MSA 6.1508]

Sec. 508. *The clerk shall transfer the registration of any elector upon the receipt of reliable information that such elector has changed his residence, but in such cases he shall mail to the elector a form notice of the transfer as a means of avoiding errors* and informing the elector that he is duly registered from the new address.

MCLA 168.509 Same; revision and correction of records; notice of suspension, form; application for continuance; reinstatement.
MSA 6.1509

Sec. 509. During the month of December in each year, the clerk shall examine the registration records and shall suspend the registration for all electors who have not voted, continued their registration, reinstated their registration, or recorded a change of address on their registration within a period of 2 years. Each such elector shall be sent a notice through the mails substantially as follows:

NOTICE OF SUSPENSION OF REGISTRATION

You are hereby notified that your registration as a qualified elector will be canceled according to state law, for having failed to vote, to continue or reinstate your registration or to record a change of address within the past 2 years unless you apply for a continuation within 30 days from this date. You may continue your registration by signing the statement below and returning it to this office or by applying in person.

APPLICATION FOR CONTINUATION OF REGISTRATION

I hereby certify that I reside at the address given below and apply for continuation of my registration as a voter. My mother's maiden name was..
    Signature of elector..
    Present residence address..
After the expiration of 30 days, the clerk shall cancel the registration of all electors thus notified who have not applied for continuations. A proper entry shall be made on the registration card of each elector whose registration is canceled. Any elector whose registration has been canceled may have his registration reinstated under the same qualifications required at the time of the initial registration, in which case the clerk shall note the reinstatement date on the applicant's former registration card, affix his signature thereto and replace both the precinct and master cards in the active files, or a new set of cards may be executed in connection with such reinstatement. A reinstated registration shall be valid for the same period as a new registration.

226

MCLA 168.509a Same; members of Armed forces on active duty, noncancellation of registration. [MSA 6.1509(1)]

Sec. 509a. Notwithstanding the provisions of section 509, the clerk shall not cancel the registration of any member of the armed forces on active duty during his term of active duty and for 90 days after his discharge or release from active duty, if the member of the armed forces, his parent, guardian or spouse so notifies the clerk in writing.

MCLA 168.510 Same; deceased electors, cancellation of registration. [MSA 6.1510]

Sec. 510. At least once a month, the county clerk shall forward a list of the last known address and birthdate of all persons over 18 years of age who have died within the county to the clerk of each ... township within the county. The ... township clerk shall compare this list with the registration records and cancel the registration of all deceased electors.

MCLA 168.511 Same; authorization of cancellation. [MSA 6.1511]

Sec. 511. Upon the receipt of an authorization of cancellation of registration from the elector, the clerk shall cancel said registration.

MCLA 168.512 Same; challenge of elector; affidavits; cancellation of registration; indiscriminate challenge. [MSA 6.1512]

Sec. 512. Any elector of the municipality may challenge the registration of any registered elector by submitting to the clerk of that municipality a written affidavit that such elector is not qualified to vote, which affidavit shall specify the grounds upon which the challenged elector is disqualified. Upon receipt of such affidavit, the clerk shall ...
Any person who shall challenge under the provisions of this section, indiscriminately and without good cause or for the purpose of harassment, shall be guilty of a misdemeanor.

MCLA 168.513 Same; elector moving from municipality, notice by clerk. [MSA 6.1513]

Sec. 513. Upon receipt of reliable information that a registered elector has moved away from the municipality, the clerk shall notify such elector through the mail at his registered address, stating the source of the information, and if the elector does not apply for continuation of registration within 30 days, his registration shall be cancelled.

MCLA 168.514   Same; cancellation; destruction of records by burning. MSA 6.1514

Sec. 514. When the registration of any elector is cancelled, the clerk shall cause to be made a proper entry on the original and duplicate registration cards, indicating the date and the cause for cancellation, and shall affix his signature thereto. All copies of the cancelled registration cards shall be filed in the office of the clerk. All duplicates of the original registration cards so cancelled may be destroyed 2 years after the registrations were cancelled. The clerk may also destroy the original registration cards of any elector 10 years after the date of cancellation of the elector's registration, if the registration has not been reinstated within that period. The clerk may also destroy any cancelled original registration cards 2 years after the date of cancellation if the cancelled registration cards have been reproduced on film and the film is on file in the office of the clerk. The film may be destroyed after the statutory retention date of all records recorded thereon has expired. The destruction of all such registration records shall be by burning.

MCLA 168.515 Same; house–to–house canvass. MSA 6.1515

Sec. 515. The several township ... clerks may conduct a house–to–house canvass or use such other means of checking the correctness of registration records as may seem expedient.

MCLA 168.516 Same; record open for public inspection. MSA 6.1516

Sec. 516. The registration record shall be open for public inspection under rules and regulations prescribed by the clerk.

MCLA 168.517 Same; ward or precinct, division, transfer of precinct cards, notation, notice to registrant. MSA 6.1517

Sec. 517. Whenever any ward or precinct of any township,... shall be divided or changed pursuant to law, then the clerk of such township ... shall transfer the precinct cards accordingly and shall

228

make the proper notations upon the cards in both the master and precinct files and notify the registrant of such change.

MCLA 168.518 Same; new township, city; board, notice of holding registration, posting; publication. ⌐MSA 6.151⌐8

Sec. 518. Whenever a new township shall be organized, the persons designated to act as inspectors for the first election to be held therein shall constitute a board of registration for the purpose of making the first registration of qualified electors therein. Said board shall be authorized to procure the necessary books or files and forms to conduct such registration in accordance with the provisions of this act. Subsequent to the election, the records shall be ...

Annexation to city; transfer of township registration records. *Whenever any territory of a township is annexed to a city, the clerk of the township from which the territory was detached shall, not less than 5 days prior to the effective date on the annexation, forward to the clerk of the city to which the territory was annexed all of the current registration records or the registered electors residing in the annexed territory. Such records shall thereafter be a part of the registration records of such city and the electors whose registration records were so transferred shall be registered electors of such city.*

Statement by township clerk. *All such transfers of registration shall be accompanied by a statement signed by the township clerk certifying that all of the current registrations of persons residing within the annexed or incorporated area according to his records are included therein.*

MCLA 168.519 Same; unlawful registration. ⌐MSA 6.151⌐9

Sec. 519. No township ... clerk shall register any person whom such clerk shall know or have good reason to believe not to be a resident and so qualified, nor shall any person knowingly or having good reason to believe himself not to be such a resident and so qualified, cause himself to be registered as an elector. Every person so offending, or who shall aid or abet another in so offending, shall upon conviction be adjudged guilty of a misdemeanor.

MCLA 168.520 Same; illegal or fraudulent registration, investigation, assistance by police or sheriff; assistant examiners, expenses. ⌐MSA 6.152⌐0

Sec. 520. Whenever it shall come to the knowledge of any township, city or village clerk that there is probable illegal or fraudulent registration in his township, ... or in any ward or precinct thereof, he shall ...

MCLA 168.521   Same; removal of names; mandamus by aggrieved person, challenge.   MSA 6.1521

Sec. 521. Whenever any township, ... clerk shall determine that any name has been illegally or fraudulently entered upon the registration records of any precinct in his township, ... he shall remove such name from the registration records and shall ...

MCLA 168.522   Same; lists, furnishing, cost.   MSA 6.1522

Sec. 522. Any township ... clerk shall make, certify and deliver to any person a true copy of the names and addresses of the registered electors of any ward or precinct upon the payment to such clerk of the cost thereof.

MCLA 168.523   Application to vote; identification of elector; challenge, procedure; duplicate poll lists; notation on registration card.   MSA 6.1523

Sec. 523. At every election, each registered elector offering to vote shall, before being given a ballot, identify himself by executing an application showing his signature and address of residence in the presence of an election official.   The election official in charge of the precinct registration file shall ...
Increase of ad valorem tax rate; issuance of bonds, expenditure of public money; certificate of property ownership. *When questions involving the increase of the ad valorem tax rate limitation for a period of more than 5 years or the issuance of bonds are submitted, the application for ballots shall also contain a certificate to be subscribed to by persons entitled to vote on such questions as provided in section 6 of article 2 of the state constitution. Said certificate shall state that, in addition to having the qualifications of an elector, the elector or the husband or wife of the elector has property assessed for taxes in the district or territory to be affected by the result of such election, and voting on such questions shall be restricted to persons so qualified. If a question relating to the expenditure of public money or the issuance of bonds is submitted at a primary or election at which candidates are to be voted for*

or other propositions submitted, each elector entitled to vote on such questions shall execute a certificate as hereinbefore provided which shall be separate and distinct from the certificate required in connection with the issuance of other ballots. Such certificate may either appear in a separate division of the regular application for ballots or may be printed on a separate application.

Note: According to MTA Legal Counsel John H. Bauckham, the United States Supreme Court has determined in a case involving the city of Phoenix, that it is unconstitutional to require ownership of property as a qualification to vote on bond issues or tax limitation increases. This decision has also been construed to apply to any other type of election, including zoning, therefore such provisions in the above section are inapplicable.

MCLA 168.524 Reports of eligible voters. [MSA 6.1524]

CHAPTER XXIV. PRIMARY ELECTIONS

MCLA 168.531 Primary elections; nomination by direct vote [MSA 6.1531]

Sec. 531. Whenever any primary election shall be held in this state or in any city, county or district in this state, the nomination of candidates shall be made by direct vote of the qualified and registered electors of each political party participating therein as hereinafter prescribed.

MCLA 168.532 Same; party not casting 5% of vote may not nominate by primary method; ''principal candidate'' defined. [MSA 6.1532]

Sec. 532. Any political party whose principal candidate received less than 5% of the total vote cast for all candidates for the office of secretary of state in the 'last preceding state election, either in the state or in any political subdivision affected,* shall

----
*For information regarding charter townships, see **MCLA 42.4** [MSA 5.46(4)]*
----

not make its nominations by the direct primary method. The nomination of candidates of such parties shall be made by means of caucuses or conventions. The term ''principal candidate'' of any party shall be construed to mean the candidate whose name shall appear nearest the top of the party column.

MCLA 168.533 Same; applicability of act. [MSA 6.1533]

Sec. 533. The provisions of this act relative to the conduct of elections shall be applicable as near as may be in all particulars to all regular and special primary elections except as the contrary is indicated.

MCLA 168.534 Same; time, nominations. [MSA 6.1534]

Sec. 534. A general primary of all political parties except as otherwise provided in section 532 of this act shall be held in every election precinct in this state on the Tuesday succeeding the first Monday in August preceding every general November election, at which time the qualified and registered voters of each political party may vote for party candidates for the office of governor, United States senator, representative in congress, state senator, representative in the legislature, prosecuting attorney, sheriff, county clerk, county treasurer, register of deeds, county auditor, drain commissioner, coroners (medical examiners), county road commissioner, county mine inspector, surveyor and candidates for office in townships operating under section 344 of this act. No nomination for any office shall be made unless such official is to be elected at the next succeeding general November election.

MCLA 168.535 Same; nonpartisan; time; judges in certain courts ... [MSA 6.1535]

Sec. 535. A general primary shall be held in every election precinct in this state on the Tuesday succeeding the first Monday in August preceding every general November election, at which time the qualified and registered voters may vote for nonpartisan candidates for the office of judge of the court of appeals, judge of the circuit court, judge of probate ... in the years in which such officers are to be elected.

MCLA 168.538 Primary elections; notice, publication and posting. [MSA 6.1538]

Sec. 538. Primary notices shall be published and posted in the same manner as nearly as may be as provided in section 653 of this act for elections.

MCLA 168.539 Same; primary not held, city and county, notice. [MSA 6.1539]

Sec. 539. If, upon the expiration of the time for filing petitions in any primary for city or county, it appears that there is no opposition to any candidate for any office upon any ticket, then the city or county clerk, as the case may be, shall certify to the board of election commissioners the names of all persons whose petitions have been properly filed and the office for which such petitions were filed, and such persons shall be declared by such board of election commissioners nominees for the respective offices, and such county clerk shall forthwith notify the several clerks of the townships and cities interested, if any, and give notice that the primary will not be held as contemplated, giving the reasons therefor, and a public notice shall be given of such determination by a brief notice published by such clerk in a newspaper circulated in such county.

MCLA 168.540   Same; nonpartisan primary not held, notice.
[MSA 6.1540]

MCLA 168.541   Same; primary not held, district offices, notice by secretary of state. [MSA 6.1541]

Sec. 541. ... (notice by secretary of state to state board of canvassers)... shall give notice to the clerk of the several counties embraced in such district, and if the clerk shall find that there is no opposition for any office upon any ticket for a county office, then it shall be the duty of such clerk to forthwith give notice to the several ... township clerks interested that a primary will not be held as contemplated, but in no event shall a primary election be abandoned in any township, ... wherein there shall be opposition for any office upon any ticket.

PREPARATION AND FILING OF NOMINATING PETITIONS; FEES

MCLA 168.542 Nominating petitions; printing names on official ballots, method. [MSA 6.1542]

Sec. 542. The printing of the name of any person as a candidate for nomination by any political party for any office except a city or village under the particular party heading upon the official ballots for any primary election held in this state shall be obtained by following the provisions as set forth in the chapters of this act relative to the respective offices.

MCLA 168.544a   **Nonpartisan nominating petitions, contents.**
MSA 6.1544(1)

Sec. 544a.   *The form, size and contents of all nonpartisan nominating petitions shall be the same as is provided in section 544c for partisan nominating petitions, except that under the heading "nominating petition" shall be printed in 12-point type the word "nonpartisan". The petition shall contain no reference to any political party.*

MCLA 168.544b   **Judicial office, nomination, petition, convention.**
MSA 6.1544(2)

MCLA 168.544c   **Nominating petitions; size, form, contents.**
MSA 6.1544(3)

Sec. 544c.   *The size of all nominating petitions shall be 8½ inches by 13 inches and shall be printed in the following size type: The words "nominating petition" shall be in 24-point bold face type; "we, the undersigned, et cetera" shall be printed in 8-point type; "warning" and language contained therein shall be in 12-point bold face type and the balance of petition shall be in 8-point type. The name of the candidate, his address, party affiliation and office for which petitions are signed may be in type not larger than 24-point. The petition shall be in the following form:*

NOMINATING PETITION
(PARTISAN)

We, the undersigned, registered and qualified voters of the city or township of
(strike 1)

. . . ., in the county of . . . . and state of Michigan, hereby nom-
inate . . . . ,
(Name of Candidate)

. . . ., ... ,
(Street Address or Rural Route)   (Post Office)

as a candidate of the . . . . party for the office of . . . . ,
. . . ., to be voted for at the primary election to be held on the
(District, if any)
. . . . day of . . . ., 19. . . . .

WARNING

Whoever knowingly signs more petitions for the same office than there are persons to be elected to the office or signs a name other than his own is violating the provisions of the Michigan election law.

Name	Street Address or Rural Route	Post Office	Date of Signing Mo. Day Year		
1.					
2.					
3.					

4. 20 numbered lines as above

CERTIFICATE OF CIRCULATOR

The undersigned circulator of the above petition asserts that he is qualified to circulate this petiiton, that each signature on the petition was signed in his presence, that to his best knowledge and belief each signature is the genuine signature of the person purporting to sign the same and that the person was at the time of signing a qualified registered elector of the city or township listed in the heading of the petition and that such elector was qualified to sign the petition.

....
(Signature of Circular)

....
(Street Number or Rural Route)

....
(City or Township)

....
(Date)

Warning -- Any circulator knowingly making a false statement in the above certificate or any person not a circulator who signs as such or any person who signs a name other than his own as circulator is guilty of a misdemeanor.

The circulator of any petition shall be a qualified and registered elector of the state.

No petition sheet shall be circulated in more than 1 city or township and all the signers of that petition sheet shall be registered electors of city or township indicated in the heading thereof. The invalidity of any one or more signatures on a petition shall not affect the validity of the remainder of the signatures on the petition.

It shall be unlawful for any person to sign more nominating petitions for the same offices than there are persons to be elected to the office.

Any person who shall sign a petition with a name other than his own shall be guilty of a misdemeanor.

Any person knowingly making a false statement in a certificate on any petition or any person not a circulator who signs as such or any person who signs a name as circulator other than his own shall be guilty of a misdemeanor.

Any person who shall aid or abet another in any of the above listed acts shall be deemed to have committed the act.

The provisions of this section except as otherwise expressly provided shall apply to all petitions circulated under authority of the election law.

MCLA 168.545 Same; duties of two offices combined. [MSA 6.1545]

Sec. 545. In those instances in which the duties of 2 offices are combined, all nominating petitions shall include and name the 2 offices.

MCLA 168.546 Same; blank forms, furnishing. [MSA 6.1546]

Sec. 546. The various county clerks ... shall prepare and keep on hand blank forms of nominating petitions for use of the electors and candidates in said ... or county. Nothing herein contained shall be construed to prohibit any candidate from having his own nominating petitions printed, but they must comply substantially with the above form.

MCLA 168.547a Nominating petitions; too many signatures by voter; counting. [MSA 6.1547(1)]

Sec. 547a. If a qualified and registered voter signs nominating petitions for a greater number of candidates for public office than the number of persons to be elected thereto, his signatures, if they bear the same date, shall not be counted upon any petition, and if they bear different dates shall be counted in the order of their priority of date for only so many candidates as there are persons to be elected.

MCLA 168.548 Same; unlawful to procure more than maximum number of signers. [MSA 6.1548]

Sec. 548. It shall be unlawful for any candidate to wilfully and intentionally procure more names upon nominating petitions than the maximum number prescribed in this act.

MCLA 168.549 Same; excess names not considered. [MSA 6.1549]

Sec. 549. If any nominating petitions contain more than the necessary percentage of names, the excess over 1% shall neither be considered nor counted.

236

MCLA 168.550 Same; name not printed on ballot unless act complied with. MSA 6.1550

Sec. 550. No candidate shall have his name printed upon any official primary election ballot of any political party in any voting precinct in this state unless he shall have filed nominating petitions according to the provisions of this act, and all other requirements of this act have been complied with in his behalf, except in those counties qualifying candidates upon the payment of fees.

MCLA 168.551 Same; time for filing petitions or filing fees. MSA 6.1551

Sec. 551. The secretary of state and the various county, township ... clerks shall receive nominating petitions or filing fees filed in accordance with the provisions of this act up to 4 p.m., eastern standard time, of the seventh Tuesday preceding the August primary. The provisions of this section shall not apply to any city which does not nominate its officers under the provisions of this act.

MCLA 168.552 Nominating petitions; certification of nominees; investigation on complaint, procedure, review, appeal. MSA 6.1552

Sec. 552. The county, (township) or city clerk shall forthwith, after the last day named herein for receiving and filing nominating petitions, certify to the proper board or boards of election commissioners in such city, county, district or in the state, the names and post office addresses of all party candidates whose petitions meet the requirements of this act, ...

Secretary of state, duties as to petitions, canvass, complaints, investigation. ...may cause any doubtful signatures to be checked against the registration records by the clerk of any political subdivision in which said petitions were circulated ... It shall be the duty of the clerk of any political subdivision to cooperate fully with said board in any request made to said clerks ... in determining the validity of doubtful signatures by rechecking the same against registration records and said clerk shall make the requested rechecks in an expeditious and proper manner...(and)...complete said canvass at least 5 weeks prior to the primary election at which candidates are to be nominated.

Declaration as to sufficiency of nominating petitions, review,

certification of nominees. *An official declaration of the sufficiency or insufficiency of any such nomination petition shall be made by the said (state) board at least 5 weeks prior to the primary election at which candidates are to be nominated. ...*

MCLA 168.553   **Same; insufficient petition, notice to candidate.**
MSA 6.1553

MCLA 168.554   **Same; list of candidates publicly displayed.**
MSA 6.1554

MCLA 168.555   **Same; record; petitions open to public inspection.**
MSA 6.1555

MCLA 168.556   **Same; preservation and disposition of petitions.**
MSA 6.1556

Sec. 556. All nominating petitions filed under the provisions of this act shall be preserved by the ... township clerk, ... until the first day of January following the primary election for which the same were filed. At the expiration of that period, the ... township clerk may destroy all nominating petitions, the return of which has not been requested. In the record of nominating petitions, the various officers keeping such record shall cause entries to be made, stating the final disposition of each candidate's petition.

MCLA 168.557 Same; affidavit as to change of name; false statement, penalty; nonapplication of section. MSA 6.1557

Sec. 557. No nominating petitions shall be received for filing by the secretary of state or the various county clerks or the clerks of ... townships by or in behalf of any candidate, unless such candidate also files with the secretary of state, ... township clerk, as the case may be, within the time limited for filing such petitions, an affidavit in such form and containing such information as the secretary of state may prescribe relative to any change which may at any time have been made in the name of such candidate. ...(provisions for use of initials, full names, etc. and changes of name for naturalized citizens)...

MCLA 168.558 Nominating petitions or filing fees; affidavit of identification, contents, filing in duplicate. MSA 6.1558

Sec. 558. Any candidate filing nominating petitions or filing fee for any county, state or national office ...

Petitions or filing fees for incompatible offices, election. If petitions or filing fees are filed by or in behalf of a candidate for more than 1 office, either national, state, county, city, village or township, the terms of which run concurrently or overlap, the candidate so filing, or in behalf of whom petitions were so filed, shall select the 1 office to which his candidacy must be restricted within 3 days after the last day for the filing of petitions or filing fees unless for 2 offices that shall have been combined or for offices that are not incompatible. Failure to make such selection shall disqualify any such candidate with respect to any such office for which petitions were so filed and the name of such candidate shall not be printed upon the ballot for such office, and any votes cast for such candidate at the primary election ensuing shall not be counted and shall be void.

PREPARATION AND DISTRIBUTION OF BALLOTS

MCLA 168.559 Ballots; preparation, distribution. [MSA 6.1559]

MCLA 168.560 Same; contents, size. [MSA 6.1560]

MCLA 168.561 Same; names of candidates printed; similar surnames; married women. [MSA 6.1561]

MCLA 168.561a Same; candidate with same given and surname as incumbent. [MSA 6.1561(1)]

MCLA 168.562 Same; space for delegates to county convention. [MSA 6.1562]

MCLA 168.562a Delegate ballots, contents, form; write—in candidates, uncommitted; invalidity, grounds. [MSA 6.1562(1)]

MCLA 168.563 Same; number printed; contents, rotation of tickets; color of paper. [MSA 6.1563]

MCLA 168.564 Same; party ballot not printed upon failure to file required petitions. [MSA 6.1564]

MCLA 168.565 Same; proof copies mailed to secretary of state and candidates; corrections. [MSA 6.1565]

MCLA 168.566 **Same; official ballot, posting for public inspection.** MSA 6.1566

Sec. 566. *The official primary ballots shall be posted in a conspicuous place at the office of the ... township clerk, ... for public inspection at least 3 days prior to distribution for use at the primary election.*

MCLA 168.567 **Same; errors, correction.** MSA 6.1567

MCLA 168.568 **Same; official primary election ballot, form, contents.** MSA 6.1568

MCLA 168.569 **Same; numbering; columns.** MSA 6.1569

MCLA 168.570 **Same; primary ballots; order of names, numbering, title, distribution, sample form.** MSA 6.1570

MCLA 168.570a **Official primary ballot; candidates for township offices; order of listing; party qualification.** MSA 6.1570(1)

Sec. 570a. *The official primary ballot shall include candidates for township offices. Township offices and candidates shall follow state and county offices and candidates. Parties qualified to appear on the primary ballot for state and county offices and no others are qualified to appear and have the names of their candidates printed on the township portion of the primary ballot. Parties qualified to nominate candidates for state and county offices under the provisions of section 685 and no others are qualified to nominate candidates for township offices at the county caucuses provided in section 686a.*

All references in the election law to a February primary shall be deemed to be references to the primary provided by the election law to be held in August prior to the general November election and all references to an April election shall be deemed to be references to the general November election.

MCLA 168.572 **Ballots; place for added names.** MSA 6.1572

MCLA 168.573 **Same; wrapping; packages, seal, certificate.** MSA 6.1573

CONDUCT OF PRIMARY ELECTIONS

MCLA 168.574 Primary election; board of inspectors; membership.
[MSA 6.1574]

Sec. 574. *Each primary election shall be presided over by a board of primary election inspectors, which board shall be composed of the members of the board of election inspectors as provided in section 674 of this act.*

MCLA 168.575 Same; ballot; furnishing electors. [MSA 6.1575]

MCLA 168.576 Same; marking; voting more than 1 ticket.
[MSA 6.1576]

MCLA 168.576a Same; number of votes to which each voter is entitled. [MSA 6.1576(1)]

MCLA 168.577 Same; folding and delivery of ballot.
[MSA 6.1577]

MCLA 168.578 Same; poll list, comparison of ballot number.
[MSA 6.1578]

MCLA 168.579 Same; exposure of ballot, rejection. [MSA 6.1579]

MCLA 168.580 Same; candidates deemed voted for. [MSA 6.1580]

CANVASSING OF PRIMARY RETURNS

MCLA 168.581 Canvass of primary returns and declaration of results; board of state canvassers. [MS A 6.1581]

Sec. 581. *The returns of said primary election shall be canvassed and the results declared in the same manner and within the same time after the primary election and by the same officers as provided for general elections, except that in the case of a primary election for the nomination of a candidate for the office of United States senator, ...*

MCLA 168.582 Same; persons not deemed nominated. [MSA 6.1582]

MCLA 168.583 Same; civil process not served on elector.
[MSA 6.1583]

MCLA 168.584 Voting machines authorized. [MSA 6.1584]

MCLA 168.585 Same; use; ballots provided when machine not adequate. [MSA 6.1585]

MCLA 168.586 Same; alternation of names of candidates. [MSA 6.1586]

MCLA 168.587 Same; arrangement of machines. [MSA 6.1587]

MCLA 168.588 Number of machines in precinct. [MSA 6.1588]

CHAPTER XXV. DELEGATES, CONVENTIONS AND PARTY COMMITTEES

MCLA 168.591 State party conventions in even numbered years, time, place, call. [MSA 6.1591]

MCLA 168.592 County party convention in even years, time, place, call; temporary chairman. [MSA 6.1592]

MCLA 168.593 State party convention in odd years; time, place, call; delegates. [MSA 6.1593]

MCLA 168.594 County party convention in odd numbered years; time, place, call; temporary chairman. [MSA 6.1594]

MCLA 168.595 Delegates to state conventions; apportionment, election. [MSA 6.1595]

MCLA 168.595a Legislators as delegates at large, alternates, vote. [MSA 6.1595(1)]

MCLA 168.596 "Fall" convention, "spring" convention, defined. [MSA 6.1596]

MCLA 168.597 State central committee; selection, members, officers, term. [MSA 6.1597]

MCLA 168.598 Call for fall state convention. [MSA 6.1598]

MCLA 168.599 Political party county and county executive committees. [MSA 6.1599]

County conventions; executive committee, membership vacancies, officers. Certification, notice to selectee. Selection of officers; proxy. Selection of county committee; officers; vacancies; powers; term. *After the officers of the county committee have taken office and within 30 days the executive committee shall select a county committee for the party, which committee shall consist of not less than* **2 members from each township** *and 2 members from each ward of each city in the county, or shall consist of at least 2 members from each election precinct in the county, as the executive committee may determine. The committee shall have the right to appoint such officers as in its judgment may be proper to carry out the purposes of the committee, and shall have power to fill any vacancy which may occur in the membership of said committee or in any of its offices. Between meetings of the county committee such executive committee shall have all of the powers and perform all of the duties of the county committee, including the filling of vacancies in nominations as prescribed by law. The term of service of a county committee shall continue for a period of 2 years and until the selection of its successor.* **Nominees as delegates at large. ...**

MCLA 168.600 Congressional district convention of political party; officers, election, term. [MSA 6.1600]

MCLA 168.600a Residence requirement; exception. [MSA 6.1600(1)]

MCLA 168.601 County comprising single district, committee. [MSA 6.1601]

MCLA 168.602 County comprising more than 1 district, committee. [MSA 6.1602]

MCLA 168.603a Counties over 400,000; members of legislature as members of district committee; delegates at large. [MSA 6.1603(1)]

MCLA 168.604 Call for fall county convention. [MSA 6.1604]

Sec. 604. The chairman of the county committee of each political party shall forward by mail or deliver to the board of election commissioners, at least 25 days before the holding of the

August primary, a copy of the call for the fall county convention, showing the number of delegates to which each election district of said county will be entitled at the fall county convention of said political party, to be held in said county in said year, and there shall be elected at the August primary by direct vote of the registered and qualified electors of each political party in each county **as many delegates in each township,** *ward, ... as such political party in such township ... shall, according to the certificate issued by the county committee of such political party, be entitled to at such county convention.*

MCLA 168.605 Delegates' names not printed on ballot. [MSA 6.1605]

MCLA 168.606 Delegates to fall county convention; election, notice. [MSA 6.1606]

Sec. 606. Delegates to the fall county convention shall be elected by townships ... and the county clerk shall notify by mail each person elected as such delegate.

MCLA 168.607 Same; election; determination of tie vote by lot. [MSA 6.1607]

MCLA 168.608 Same; certification to the county clerk; record, notice to delegate and county chairman. [MSA 6.1608]

Sec. 608. The board of primary election inspectors shall certify to the county clerk the names of the electors so elected as delegates, naming the political party upon whose ballot such electors were elected ...

MCLA 168.609 Delegate not to give proxy; vacancy in delegation. [MSA 6.1609]

MCLA 168.610 National committeeman and committeewoman. [MSA 6.1610]

MCLA 168.611 Election of delegates to national convention and and presidential electors. [MSA 6.1611]

MCLA 168.612 Age limit. [MSA 6.1612]

Sec. 612. Any person of the age of 18 years or older shall be eligible to be a candidate for election as a precinct delegate or be selected as a delegate to the state or national convention of any political party.

MCLA 168.613 Presidential primary, date, eligible political parties; county convention delegates, election, term. [MSA 6.1613]

MCLA 168.614 Potential presidential candidates, listing, notice. [MSA 6.1614]

MCLA 168.615 Names of presidential candidates, printing and position on ballots, withdrawal of name; space for uncommitted vote. [MSA 6.1615]

MCLA 168.616 Results of presidential primary, certification. [MSA 6.1616]

MCLA 168.617 County conventions in presidential election years, time and place; state convention delegates, election. [MSA 6.1617]

MCLA 168.618 National convention delegates, selection. [MSA 6.1618]

MCLA 168.619 State conventions; national convention delegates. Date, election of national convention delegates at congressional district caucuses. Election of national convention delegates at state convention. State wide popular vote and national convention delegates, proportional equality as to commitment to candidates or noncommitment. Certification and voting of national convention delegates. Vacancies in elected delegates. State legislators and other public officials as delegates. [MSA 6.1619]

... Neither this provision nor any other provision of law shall be understood to restrict the opportunity of any registered elector in the state, including all public officials, to be elected as a delegate to any county, district, state or national convention of his political party.

MCLA 168.620 State central committee rules and procedures, filing, publicity, availability. [MSA 6.1620]

CHAPTER XXVI. DELEGATES—REFERENDUM

MCLA 168.621 Delegates to party convention; nomination. [MSA 6.1621]

MCLA 168.622 County convention; time, place, chairman, vacancy, rules. [MSA 6.1622]

MCLA 168.623a Certification and allotment of delegates to county conventions. [MSA 6.1623(1)]

Sec. 623a. (1, 2, 3) ...

(4) The allotment of delegates to all precincts in the state shall be made to insure, as near as is practicable, equal apportionment based upon the total vote cast for the candidate of each political party for either president of the United States or secretary of state at the last general election when elections for those offices were held, whichever is later, but each precinct shall have at least 1 delegate.

(5) The apportionment shall be based on the precincts as they exist on January 1 of the presidential election year and as they exist on May 1 in even numbered years which are not presidential election years. Notwithstanding the provisions of sections 656 and 661, the presidential primary election shall be conducted in precincts as they exist on January 1 of the year of a presidential primary election, except that for the 1972 presidential primary election, as they exist on March 1, 1972. The effective date of division of precincts provided for in sections 656 and 661 shall be the day following the presidential primary election in years in which a presidential primary election is held.

(6) As many delegates in each precinct as a political party is entitled to according to the certificate authorized by the chairman of the county committee or the board of election commissioners shall be elected at the presidential primary in presidential election years and at the August primary in even numbered years which are not presidential election years by direct vote of the registered electors of each political party in the county.

MCLA 168.624 Same; candidate for delegate; eligibility, petition; affidavit; registration or validity of signature of circulator or signer of petition, questioning, complaint, check. [MSA 6.1624]

MCLA 168.624a Precinct delegates, resignation. [MSA 6.1624(1)]

MCLA 168.624b County convention delegate candidates. Nominating petitions, indication of committed or uncommitted status. Voting by committed county convention delegates. Voting by committed

state convention delegates; release from commitment, county and state convention delegates. ⌈MSA 6.1624(2)⌉

MCLA 168.624c Filings and withdrawals by county convention delegate candidates, time; validity of signatures on petitions, time for complaints. ⌈MSA 6.1624(3)⌉

MCLA 168.624d August primary elections, inapplicable to county convention delegates; delegates elected in 1970, term, vacancies. ⌈MSA 6.1624(4)⌉

Sec. 624d. (1, 2) ...
(3) Vacancies in precincts resulting from death, written resignation to the county chairman or any other reason, may be filled for the balance of the unexpired term by a majority vote at the county convention of the delegates elected and serving. A vacancy must be filled by a registered elector of the precinct in which the vacancy occurs.

CHAPTER XXVII. SPECIAL PRIMARIES AND ELECTIONS

MCLA 168.631 Special primary election; time. ⌈MSA 6.1631⌉

Sec. 631. Whenever a special election shall be called to fill a vacancy in any office, the candidates for which are regularly nominated in accordance with the provisions of this act relating to primary nominations, a special primary for all political parties shall be held in the county, district or city ...

MCLA 168.632 Same; election for congressman in absence of choice by electors. ⌈MSA 6.1632⌉

MCLA 168.633 Same; when right of office ceases before commencement of term or vacancy occurs. ⌈MSA 6.1633⌉

MCLA 168.634 Same; vacancy in office of senator or representative, filling, notice by secretary of state. ⌈MSA 6.1634⌉

MCLA 168.635 Special election for submission of proposition on regular or special primary day. ⌈MSA 6.1635⌉

Sec. 635. It shall be lawful to call a special election for the submission of any proposition on any regular or special primary day.

MCLA 168.636   Provisions of act relative to ballots applicable to special primary. ⟦MSA 6.1636⟧

Sec. 636.   The provisions of this act relative to primary election ballots shall be applicable to the ballots prepared for use at a special primary election.

MCLA 168.637   Act applicable to all primary elections. ⟦MSA 6.1637⟧

Sec. 637.   All primary elections held in this state shall be governed by and conducted in accordance with the provisions of this act.

MCLA 168.638   Notice of special election given by secretary of state to county clerks, contents. ⟦MSA 6.1638⟧

MCLA 168.639   Special election called by municipalities; notice to committee; conflict with other elections, determination, notice. ⟦MSA 6.1639⟧

Sec. 639.   When a special election is called by a ... township ..., the proposed date of the election shall be submitted to a county election scheduling committee consisting of the county clerk and 3 other members appointed by the board of supervisors. Members appointed by the board of supervisors shall be appointed at the first meeting of the board each year and shall serve for 1 year.   Of the members appointed by the board of supervisors, 1 **shall be a township clerk,** *1 shall be a city clerk and 1 shall be a member of the board of education of a school district in the county. In counties containing no cities, the committee shall consist of 3 members.   Vacancies shall be filled by appointment by the board of supervisors.   The county clerk shall be chairman of the committee and the prosecuting attorney shall be legal advisor to the committee. ...*

CHAPTER XXVIII. HOLDING OF ELECTIONS

MCLA 168.641   General November election. ⟦MSA 6.1641⟧

Sec. 641.   An election which shall be known and designated as the "general November election" shall be held in this state on the Tuesday succeeding the first Monday of November in every even numbered year.

MCLA 168.643 General November election; state, county and township officers. [MSA 6.1643]

Sec. 643. At the general November elections, there shall be elected when required by law the following officers:
1. Presidential electors;
2. In the state at large, a governor and a lieutenant governor, a secretary of state and an attorney general;
3. A United States senator;
4. In each congressional district, a representative in congress;
5. In each state senatorial district, a state senator;
6. In each state representative district, a representative in the state legislature;
7. Justices of the supreme court;
8. Two members of the state board of education; except as provided in section 282a;
9. Two regents of the University of Michigan;
10. Two trustees of Michigan State University;
11. Two governors of Wayne State University;
12. In each county or district, judges of the court of appeals, a judge or judges of the circuit court, a judge or judges of probate, ...(judges of district court), a prosecuting attorney, a sheriff, a clerk, a treasurer, a register of deeds, an auditor, a mine inspector, a county road commissioner, a drain commissioner, ... and a surveyor. The board of supervisors in any county may unite the offices of county clerk and register of deeds in 1 office or separate the same at pleasure;
13. Township officers;
14. Such other officers as by this act or otherwise by law are now or hereafter may be required to be elected at such election.

MCLA 168.643a Questions submitted, form. [MSA 6.1643(1)]
Sec. 643a. Any question submitted to the electors of this state or the electors of any subdivision of this state shall, to the extent that it will not confuse the electorate, be worded in the following manner: A "yes" vote will be a vote in favor of the subject matter of the proposal or issue, and a "no" vote will be a vote against the subject matter of the proposal or issue. Questions shall be worded so as to apprise the voters of the subject matter of the proposal or issue, but need not be legally precise. The language used shall create no prejudice for or against the issue or proposal.

MCLA 168.644a Odd year general elections, description, authorization. [MSA 6.1644(1)]

Sec. 644a. An election to be known as the "odd year general election" shall be held on the Tuesday succeeding the first Monday in November in every odd numbered year.

MCLA 168.644b Odd year primary elections, description, authorization. [MSA 6.1644(2)]

Sec. 644b. A primary election to be known as the "odd year primary election" shall be held on the Tuesday following the first Monday in August of each odd numbered year.

MCLA 168.644c Officers to be elected at odd year general elections. (Judicial; city) [MSA 6.1644(3)]

MCLA 168.644e Nominations for odd year general elections, methods. [MSA 6.1644(5)]

MCLA 168.644f Nominating petitions; filing, time, place; signatures; primary, necessity. [MSA 6.1644(6)]

MCLA 168.644g Existing terms of office, effect on length of terms. [MSA 6.1644(7)]

MCLA 168.644h Date and time for taking office. [MSA 6.1644(8)]

MCLA 168.644i Manner of conducting odd year elections. [MSA 6.1644(9)]

MCLA 168.644j Home rule cities, conflicting charter provisions. [MSA 6.1466(10)]

MCLA 168.644k School and community college district elections, time; district boards, terms of members. [MSA 6.1644(11)]

Sec. 644k. (1) Notwithstanding any law to the contrary, if all or any portion of a school district or a community college district is wholly or partly within a city or more than 1 city that elect city officers ...
(2) The board of education of a school district or the board of trustees of a community college district may determine by resolution

250

whether the district shall hold its election as provided in this section, ...

(3) ...

MCLA 168.644*l* **Power of city to exempt itself from odd year elections; procedure; subsequent provision for odd year elections.** [MSA 6.1644(12)]

MCLA 168.646 **City and village elections; officers; judges, designation of incumbency.** [MSA 6.1646]

MCLA 168.646a **Local officers; nomination, primary, caucus, petition; certification. Procedure. Local or county questions, submission. Application of section, filing of affidavits or petitions.** [MSA 6.1646(1)]

MCLA 168.646b **Charter city or village officers, nomination or election dates.** [MSA 6.1646(2)]

MCLA 168.646c **Judges of common pleas court; election at general elections; terms; nomination; filing fee.** [MSA 6.1646(3)]

NOTICES OF ELECTION

MCLA 168.647 **Notice of election; sent by registered or certified mail.** [MSA 6.1647]

Sec. 647. Notices of election required by this act to be given by the secretary of state to county clerks, and by county clerks to city and township clerks, shall be sent by registered or certified mail with return receipt demanded.

MCLA 168.648 **Same;** (by secretary of state) **to county clerk, time, contents.** [MSA 6.1648]

MCLA 168.649 **Constitutional amendment or question; certification, form; local amendment or question, submission at general election or special election.** [MSA 6.1649]

Sec. 649. Whenever a proposed constitutional amendment or other special question is to be submitted to the electors of the state for popular vote, the secretary of state shall, not less than 49 days before election, certify the same to the clerk of each county in the state and shall at the same time prescribe the form in which such amendment or other special question shall be submitted. Any city ordinance ...

MCLA 168.649a Referendum petitions, placing on ballot, canvassing, certification. [MSA 6.1649(1)]

MCLA 168.650 Subsequent vacancy, additional notice. [MSA 6.1650]

Sec. 650. If, after such notices have been sent, a vacancy shall occur in any office which by law is required to be filled at such election, the secretary of state shall send to each county clerk an additional notice specifying the office in which such vacancy exists and that such vacancy will be filled at the next general election.

MCLA 168.651 Special election; notice to county clerks.
[MSA 6.1651]

MCLA 168.652 Same; notice to township ... clerks. [MSA 6.1652]

Sec. 652. On receipt of any such notice from the secretary of state, the county clerk shall forthwith send a copy of the notice in writing to the clerk of each ... township in his county, which notice shall contain in substance the notice so received from the secretary of state, and he shall at the same time in such notice designate all county offices to be filled and any questions to be submitted at such election. If such county shall be divided into 2 or more senatorial or representative districts, such notice, so far as it relates to the election of senators and representatives, shall be sent by the county clerk to the clerk of each ... township in each respective district.

MCLA 168.653 Same; public notice; posting, publication, form.
[MSA 6.1653]

Sec. 653. On receipt of any such notice from the county clerk, the clerk of each ... township shall give public notice of the time and place in such ... township at which such election is to be held and of the offices to be filled. Such notice shall be given by publication thereof at least twice in some newspaper or newspapers published or of general circulation in said ... township, and if deemed advisable by the ... township board, by posting notices in 2 or more conspicuous places in each election precinct, said first

252

publication or said posting to be made not less than 10 days prior to such election. Such published or posted notices shall be in substantially the following form:

ELECTION NOTICE

To the qualified electors of the .... county of ....
Notice is hereby given that a ....
            (indicate whether regular, special or primary)
election will be held in the .... of ....
            (here insert the name of city or township)
in the county of .... and state of Michigan, on ....
from ...... o'clock in the forenoon until ..... o'clock in the afternoon, eastern standard time, for the purpose of nominating or electing candidates for the following offices: ....
            (list of offices)
and to vote on the following propositions ....
....
(list constitutional amendments, bond issues and other propositions)
            ....
            ,,................................. Clerk
    It shall not be necessary for the county, city or township clerk to publish any notice other than as hereinbefore provided.

ELECTION PRECINCTS

MCLA 168.654   Election precincts; definition.   [MSA 6.1654]

Sec. 654. The words "election precinct" as used in this act shall mean a political subdivision, the area of which is embraced in its entirety within the confines of a city, ward, township or village, and for which not more than 1 polling place is provided for all qualified and registered electors residing therein. When not divided according to law into 2 or more election precincts, each organized ... township ... shall be an election precinct.

MCLA 168.655   Same; present precincts to remain until changed.
[MSA 6.1655]

Sec. 655. The election precincts in the several ... townships ... shall remain as established at the time this act takes effect until they shall be changed in accordance with the provisions of this chapter.

MCLA 168.656 Same; division, maximum number of registered electors; notice to director. [MSA 6.1656]

Sec. 656. Any ... township using paper ballots, having less than 400 registered voters, which constitutes a single election precinct, in the discretion of the election commission, or other officials charged with the performance of such duty by the charter of any ... (city or village) ... In any township, upon a petition signed by not less than 25 qualified electors of the township showing the boundaries of the proposed election precincts, the township board shall submit to the electors of the township, at the next election held therein, the question of the division of the township into election precincts, as set forth in the petition. If, upon such referendum, the electors of the township shall decide in favor of such division of the township into such election precincts, the township board shall thereupon make such division and enter the same of record in the proceedings of the township board. When in any township, ... or in any election precinct therein, using paper ballots, there shall be 400 or more registered electors, the election commission of the township ... shall by resolution divide such precincts into 2 or more precincts, or shall again divide the township ... into election precincts, so that there shall not be more than 400 registered electors in any one precinct.

The division of precincts shall be made effective not later than 90 days before the primary election next preceding the general November election. ... township election commissions shall divide precincts according to law, not later than the one hundred twentieth day prior to the primary next preceding the general November election, and shall forthwith notify the county clerk of the number of registered voters in each precinct in such ... township. The county clerk shall notify the state director of elections immediately following the one hundred tenth day prior to the primary of any precincts in his county which have not been divided according to law, and the state director of elections shall proceed to make such divisions as are necessary at the expense of the ... township involved, not later than the ninetieth day prior to the primary next preceding the general November election.

MCLA 168.657 Same; division, rearrangement. [MSA 6.1657]

Sec. 657. When any ... township ... has been divided into 2 or more election precincts, the election commission ... may by resolution divide any precinct thereof into 2 or more precincts, attach a

254

portion of any precinct to an adjoining precinct, or may again rearrange the ... township ... into election precincts as said election
commission ... may deem necessary and convenient for conducting
primaries or elections in said ... township ... in the same manner
and under the same restrictions as provided in sections 656 and 661
of this act.

MCLA 168.658   Same; return to single precinct.   MSA 6.1658

Sec. 658.   When any ... township ... has been divided into 2 or
more election precincts, pursuant to law, and it shall appear from
an examination of the precinct registration records, that there are
not more than 400 registered electors in such ... township ... using
paper ballots, or not more than 1,400 registered voters in such ...
township ... using voting machines, the election commission, ...
by resolution, may abolish the division or divisions and thereafter
such ... township ... shall constitute a single election precinct as
if no division had ever been made.   No such consolidation shall be
made later than the one hundred twentieth day prior to any primary
or election.

**MCLA 168.660   Election precincts; division, alteration, rearrange-
ment, abolition; record, contents; notice.**   MSA 6.1660

Sec. 660.   Whenever a ... township ... shall be subdivided into
election precincts, ... or the election commission ... shall enter
said action of record in its proceedings, specify the numbers of
said precincts altered or rearranged in numerical order, and describe the boundaries of each such precinct.   Notice of such subdivision, alteration or rearrangement shall be given forthwith by the
... township clerk.   Such notification shall be affected by mailing to
each qualified and registered elector affected by such subdivisions,
alteration or rearrangement a notice by first class letter postage
advising the location of his new polling place and, if deemed advisable by the ... township election commission, by posting a public
notice of such change in 2 places in each precinct affected thereby,
advising the boundaries of each of said precincts.   A notice shall
also be immediately transmitted to the county clerk, and the county
clerk shall transmit to the secretary of state, at least 110 days
prior to the primary next preceding the general November election,
the number of election precincts in his county.   The said ... township ... shall give like notice of the abolition of the division of a
... township ... into election precincts, and shall, in said notice of
abolition, state that the ... township ... is restored as a single elec-

255

tion precinct and indicate the location of the polling place therein. Notice of such abolition shall be immediately transmitted to the county clerk, and by him to the secretary of state, as in the case of the subdivision or alteration of boundaries as herein provided.

MCLA 168.661   Same; number of voting machines; division of precincts. [MSA 6.1661]

Sec. 661. In each precinct using voting machines, there shall be at least 1 voting machine for each 600 registered electors at all general November elections and at the primary immediately preceding such elections. At all other primaries and elections, the number of voting machines shall be at the discretion of the local election commission. When the registration in any precinct using voting machines exceeds 1,400, such precinct or precincts shall be divided or rearranged.

Any division of precincts shall be made effective not later than 90 days before the primary election next preceding the general November election. .... township election commissions shall divide precincts according to law, not later than the one hundred twentieth day prior to the primary next preceding the general November election, and shall forthwith notify the county clerk of the number of registered voters in each precinct in such ... township. ... Should the election commission of any ... township using voting machines decide to use paper ballots for any primary or election, the preceding limitations shall continue for that election.

POLLING PLACES, EQUIPMENT, SUPPLIES

MCLA 168.662   Polling places; designation rental or erection by legislative bodies; equipment; central polling place; authority of township boards. [MSA 6.1662]

Sec. 662. The legislative body in each ... township shall designate and prescribe the place or places of holding any primary or election in their respective ... townships, and shall provide a suitable polling place in or for each precinct located in such ... township, ... for use at each primary or election held therein. School houses, police stations and other publicly owned or controlled buildings, shall, whenever possible and convenient, be used as polling places. The legislative body in each ... township shall make arrangements for the rental or erection of suitable buildings for this purpose wherever public buildings are not available, and shall cause such polling places to be equipped with the necessary

256

facilities for lighting and with adequate facilities for heat and ventilation: *Provided*, *That in any ... township it shall be lawful for the legislative body to establish a central polling place or places for not more than 6 precincts to each such central polling place when it is possible and convenient for the electors to vote thereat, and to provide for the discontinuance and abolishment of such other polling places as may not be required as a result of the establishment of such central polling places: Provided further, That township boards are hereby authorized to provide polling places located within the limits of a city which has been incorporated from territory formerly a part of such township, and the electors of such township may cast their ballots at such polling places.*

MCLA 168.663 Same; barriers separating officials and voting area from rest of room, approval. [MSA 6.1663]

Sec. 663. The legislative body of each ... township shall provide for and cause to be erected in the room where any election is to be held in each election precinct of such ... township, a suitable barrier which shall be so placed as to separate from the rest of the room the area in which the election officials, challengers, voting machines or ballot boxes and voting booths, and persons in the actual process of voting, are located. The barrier shall be of a type approved by the secretary of state.

MCLA 168.664 Same; booths; number, walls, shelves. [MSA 6.1664]

Sec. 664. On the inside of said railing, the said officers shall cause 1 or more booths or temporary rooms to be erected. At least 1 such booth shall be provided at each polling place and not less than 1 for each 100 persons entitled to vote thereat, as shown by the registration book of the precinct. Each such booth shall be built with walls not less than 6 feet high and in such manner that the person preparing his ballot shall be concealed from all other persons. In each booth there shall be provided a shelf of sufficient size with smooth surface on which ballots may be placed to be marked.

MCLA 168.665 Same; forms, stationery and supplies; furnishing, delivery, approval required. [MSA 6.1665]

Sec. 665. All forms, stationery and supplies required by the several boards of precinct election inspectors for all federal, state, district and county primaries and elections shall be furnished in accordance with sections 666, 667, 668, 669 and 670 of this act. ...

The provisions of this section shall not apply to forms printed on the direct order of any ... township clerk or election commission.

MCLA 168.666 Same; election law and manual of instructions; self–sealing metal sealing devices, words stamped upon; gummed paper seals, inscription; printed instructions; blank forms. MSA 6.1666

Note: Furnished by the secretary of state through the county clerk.

MCLA 168.666a Sealing of ballot boxes, sealing devices. MSA 6.1666(1)

MCLA 168.667 Board of county election commissioners, equipment furnished at county expense. Forms for election returns; certificate of board of precinct election inspectors, form. Tally sheets. Envelopes for statement of returns. Containers for wrapping ballots cast. Pencils. MSA 6.1667

MCLA 168.668 Elections; posting of portions of election law; delivery of register and supplies. MSA 6.1668

Sec. 668. ... (by county to each election precinct) ... and the board of election inspectors shall cause the said posters to be posted in conspicuous places in the polling places so that the same can be plainly seen and read by all persons at any election. It shall be the duty of the clerk of any ... township ... in which this act is operative to deliver to the board of election inspectors of each election precinct within his jurisdiction, before the time for opening of the polls on election day, the register of electors and the blanks for poll lists and returns and any other supplies necessary to carry out the provisions of this act not herein otherwise provided for.

MCLA 168.669 Same; supplies furnished by boards of election commissioners; flag. MSA 6.1669

Sec. 669. At any federal, state, district or county primary or election, the various ... township boards of election commissioners shall furnish, at the expense of their respective ... townships, the following:

(a)   There shall be provided and kept by the township clerk for each election precinct in a township ... at the expense of the township, ... a sufficient number of suitable ballot boxes with lock and key, each of which ballot boxes shall have an opening ... (specifications) ...

(b)   The boards of election commissioners of the ... township boards of the several townships ... shall procure for each polling place therein a flag of the United States, ... and shall deliver them in proper time to the several boards of election inspectors whose duty it shall be to cause the flag to be displayed at or in each polling place during the progress of elections. Immediately thereafter, the boards of election inspectors shall return the flags, which shall be used only for the purpose herein mentioned, to the respective clerks who are charged with the proper care and custody thereof.

MCLA 168.669a   Ballot containers, approval by secretary of state, sealing.   [MSA 6.1669(1)]

MCLA 168.670   Elections; local primaries and elections, supplies, furnishing.   [MSA 6.1670]

Sec. 670.   For all local primaries and elections, the election commissioners of the various ... townships ... shall furnish, at the expense of their respective ... townships ... all ballots, forms, stationery and supplies required for the proper conduct of such primaries and elections.   These supplies shall conform generally with the supplies furnished for general primaries and elections.

MCLA 168.671   Same; blank forms for use by inspectors, self-sealing metal sealing devices.   [MSA 6.1671]

Sec. 671.   At the time of delivering the official ballots and other election supplies to the several township ... clerks, or in case of ... township elections, to the several ... or precincts, there shall be delivered with such supplies a sufficient number of such blank forms for use by inspectors of election in making returns of such general or special elections as are required by law, and there shall also be delivered at such times with such supplies a sufficient number of self-sealing metal sealing devices for the use of the inspectors of election in sealing the ballot boxes after the close of the election, and a record of the number of such sealing devices so delivered shall be preserved.

MCLA 168.672 Board of inspectors of elections; number.
MSA 6.1672

Sec. 672. At every election, there shall be a board of at least 3
inspectors of election, constituted as in this chapter provided, in
and for each election precinct. Not less than a majority of the
inspectors shall be present in the precinct polling place during
the time the polls are open.

**MCLA 168.674 Precinct election inspectors; appointment, division
between parties; chairman; vacancies.** MSA 6.1674

Sec. 674. Notwithstanding any provisions of law to the contrary, the ... township election commission ... at least 21 days but
not more than 40 days before each election, but in no case less
than 5 days prior to the date set for holding schools of instruction,
shall appoint for each election precinct at least 3 inspectors and as
many more as in its opinion is required for the efficient, speedy and
proper conduct of such election and shall designate 1 such inspector as chairman: Provided, however, That not more than 50%, as
nearly as possible, of the total number of such inspectors as are
appointed in each election precinct shall be of the same political
party. Should a vacancy occur in the office of chairman or in the
office of election inspector prior to election day, the chairman of
the election commission shall designate some other properly
qualified applicant or inspector as chairman or some other qualified
applicant as election inspector, as the case may be. Should a
vacancy occur in the office of chairman on election day, the remaining inspectors shall designate 1 of their number as chairman.

MCLA 168.675 Same; vacancy filled by electors present.
MSA 6.1675

Sec. 675. In case 3 inspectors shall not attend at the opening
of the polls or shall not remain in attendance during the election,
the electors present may choose, viva voce, such number of said
electors as, with the inspector or inspectors present, shall constitute a board of 3 in number; and such electors so chosen shall be
inspectors of that election during the continuance thereof: Provided, however, That not more than 2 of the members of the board of
inspectors of election when constituted shall be of the same
political party.

MCLA 168.677   Precinct election inspectors; qualifications; application, contents; candidates. ☐MSA 6.1677☐

Sec. 677. *Precinct election inspectors shall be qualified and registered electors of the ... township ... in which they serve, of good reputation, with sufficient education and clerical ability to perform the duties of the office. No person shall be appointed to any election board unless such person shall have filed with the ... township ... clerk an application in his own handwriting containing the following minimum information: Name, home address, ward and precinct registration, date of birth, length of residence in ... township ..., political party preference, education, employment, other experience qualifications and statement of physical disability, if any. The form of this application shall be approved by the state director of elections. No person shall be knowingly appointed or permitted to act as a precinct election inspector if such person or any member of his immediate family is a candidate for nomination or election to any office at such election or who has been convicted of a felony or election crime, nor shall any person be permitted to act as an election inspector if he shall have failed to attend a school of instruction or taken an examination as provided in section 683 of this act. The provisions of this section shall not prohibit the candidate for or delegate to a political party convention from acting as an election inspector in a precinct other than the precinct in which he resides. No election shall be invalidated merely because of the violation of the provisions of this section.*

MCLA 168.678 Same; authority. ☐MSA 6.1678☐

Sec. 678. *Each board of election inspectors shall possess full authority to maintain peace, regularity and order at its polling place, and to enforce obedience to their lawful commands during any primary or election and during the canvass of the votes after the poll is closed.*

MCLA 168.679   Counting board, membership, duty, provisions governing, duties assumed. ☐MSA 6.1679☐

Sec. 679. *The legislative body of any ... township ... may, by resolution, provide that for any primary or election in any or in each precinct of such township, ... there shall be an additional board of 3 or more inspectors of election, which shall be known as the counting board, and whose duty it shall be to count the ballots* cast in such precinct at any primary or election and make returns thereof. ...

MCLA 168.680 Oath of inspectors. ⟦MSA 6.1680⟧

Sec. 680.   Each precinct election inspector shall, before entering upon the discharge of his duties, take and subscribe the following constitutional oath of office, which oath any of the inspectors may administer: "I do solemnly swear (or affirm) that I will support the constitution of the United States and the constitution of this state, and that I will faithfully discharge the duties of the office of inspector of elections according to the best of my ability."

MCLA 168.681 Inspector may vote at place of duty. ⟦MSA 6.1681⟧

Sec. 681.   Any precinct election inspector in any township **shall have the right to vote in the election precinct where he acts** *as such election officer, even though he resides in another election precinct of the same township.*

MCLA 168.682   Compensation of election officials ⟦MSA 6.1682⟧

Sec. 682.   Any person employed as an inspector of election, or in any other official capacity at any election, primary election, or on any board of canvassers or board of registration, shall, except as herein otherwise specifically provided, receive such reasonable compensation as may be allowed by the township board of any township, ...

MCLA 168.683   Election inspectors, instruction, compensation, vacancies. ⟦MSA 6.1683⟧

Sec. 683. Each county clerk prior to each primary and election shall, by some reliable means, notify the clerk of each township ... in the county of a training school for election inspectors to be held at a place designated by the county clerk within 20 days prior to each primary, general and special election.   The township ... clerks shall notify each election inspector appointed to serve at that election of the time and place of such training school.   At such meeting, the county clerk shall instruct and demonstrate the manner in which the duties of election inspectors are required by law to be performed.   It shall be the duty of the inspectors, so notified, to attend such meeting unless excused by the county

262

clerk for good cause. Compensation may be paid them therefor by their respective municipalities at such rate as may be determined by the governing bodies. No inspector of election shall serve in any election unless he shall have within the last preceding 2 years either attended an election school or shall have passed satisfactorily an examination given by the election commission of the ... township ... in which appointed. The examination shall be subject to the approval of the secretary of state. This section shall not prevent the appointment of an inspector of election to fill a vacancy. This section shall not prohibit any ... township having a population of 10,000 or more from conducting its own training school for election inspectors of that ... township in which case election inspectors who have attended such school shall not be required to attend the county training school.

PREPARATION, PRINTING AND DELIVERY OF OFFICIAL BALLOTS

MCLA 168.684   Vignette; preparation, adoption, size; notice of change; provision of cuts.   [MSA 6.1684]

MCLA 168.685   New political party, requirements for placing on ballot; petition, form.   [MSA 6.1685]

MCLA 168.686   Certification of nominees; state convention; president and vice-president.   [MSA 6.1686]

MCLA 168.686a   Small parties; nomination of candidates, procedure.   County caucuses; nominees, certificate of acceptance, affidavit of identity, withdrawal.   Same; delegates to state convention.   State convention; nominees, certificate of acceptance, affidavit of identity, withdrawal.   [MSA 6.1686(1)]

MCLA 168.687   Certification of nominees; board of canvassers at primary election.   State at large.   District office.   County office. City or ward office.   Contents of certificate.   [MSA 6.1687]

MCLA 168.688   Certificates of nomination; delivery.   [MSA 6.1688]

Sec. 688. All certificates of nomination required to be made to the board of election commissioners of any county shall be delivered to the county clerk, or forwarded to him by registered or certified mail with return receipt demanded, ...

MCLA 168.689   Election ballots; preparation, number printed.
[MSA 6.1689]

Note: By board of election commissioners of county.

MCLA 168.690   Same; township, ... , delivery to clerks, time; duties enjoined upon county election commissioners, etc.
[MSA 6.1690]

Sec. 690. The township ... board of election commissioners ... shall cause the ballots required for any regular or special township ... or official primary election for the nomination of candidates for township ... offices, to be printed and delivered to the township ... clerk ... at least 10 days before any such election, and like duties as are hereinbefore enjoined upon county boards of election commissioners and upon county, township ... clerks relative to the printing, counting, packaging, sealing and delivery of official ballots, are hereby enjoined upon the several township ... boards of election commissioners and upon the several township ... clerks relative to the printing, counting, packaging, sealing and delivery of official ballots for use in each precinct of such township ... at any such ... township election.

MCLA 168.691   Same; names; identification numeral; married woman candidate. [MSA 6.1691]

MCLA 168.692   Persons nominated for same office by 2 parties; choice; same person nominated for 2 offices, choice. [MSA 6.1692]

MCLA 168.693   Same; effect of failure of candidate to make choice; method of determination. [MSA 6.1693]

MCLA 168.694   Application of certain sections.   [MSA 6.1694]

Sec. 694. All the provisions of sections 691, 692, 693 and 695 of this act shall also apply to all ... township elections held in this state under the provisions of this act, except that the notice herein required to be given by a candidate shall, in case of a ... township office be given by him to the proper ... township board of election commissioners within 2 days after his name has been so certified as nominated by 2 or more political parties for the same office.

MCLA 168.695   Ineligibility of candidate at subsequent election.
[MSA 6.1695]

MCLA 168.696   Printing of ballots; candidates with similar surnames; occupation. [MSA 6.1696]

Sec. 696.   The board of election commissioners in each county shall cause the names of all candidates for federal, state, district, county and township offices at any election to be printed on 1 ballot, separate from any other ballot. ...

MCLA 168.697   Order of offices; general November election; qualification to have party appear on ballot, form. [MSA 6.1697]

MCLA 168.699 Separate judicial ballot; order of offices. [MSA 6.1699]

MCLA 168.702   Placing of name to fill vacancy. [MSA 6.1702]

MCLA 168.703   Position of parties on ballot. [MSA 6.1703]

MCLA 168.703a   Position of candidates on ballot; incumbents, others. [MSA 6.1703(1)]

MCLA 168.704   Size of voting squares or circles. [MSA 6.1704]

MCLA 168.705 Ballots; paper; printing; numbering; color of paper. [MSA 6.1705]

MCLA 168.706 Election ballots; form. [MSA 6.1706]

MCLA 168.707 Constitutional amendment or question; certification, form; statement, separate ballot; submission of local amendment or question. [MSA 6.1707]

Sec. 707.   Whenever a proposed constitutional amendment or other proposition is to be submitted to the electors of the state for popular vote, the secretary of state shall, ... Any city ordinance ...

MCLA 168.708   Same; statement, publication. [MSA 6.1708]

MCLA 168.709 Same; secretary of state to furnish copies, distribution, publication. [MSA 6.1709]

Sec. 709.   The secretary of state shall also furnish the several county clerks in the state at least 2 copies of each such statement

on paper suitable for posting for each voting precinct in their respective counties. The county clerk shall furnish the said copies of
such statement to the several ... township clerks in his county at
the time other supplies for the election are furnished, and said ...
township clerks shall, before the opening of the polls on election
day, deliver 2 copies of such statement to each voting precinct in
his... township, to the board of election inspectors of said precinct,
who shall post the same in conspicuous places in the room where
such election is held.

**MCLA 168.710 Proof copies of ballots; placed on file; open for
public inspection.** MSA 6.1710

MCLA 168.711 Same; filing; public inspection. MSA 6.1711

Sec. 711. ...(county board of election commissioners to send
copy to each candidate, make any corrections requested within 2
days) ...

MCLA 168.712 Mistakes and omissions in printing; posters.
MSA 6.1712

**MCLA 168.713 Ballots, delivery to county clerk after approval of
proof, time, other supplies.** MSA 6.1713

**MCLA 168.714 Ballots and supplies delivered by county clerk,
time, receipt.** MSA 6.1714

**MCLA 168.715 Safeguarding absent voters' ballots; opening of
packages; delivery of ballots to election boards, receipt.**
MSA 6.1715

MCLA 168.716 Ballots; wrapping, sealing. MSA 6.1716

**MCLA 168.717 Absent voters' ballots; numbering, marking pack-
ages.** MSA 6.1717

**MCLA 168.717a Absent voter ballots where voting machines used
exclusively; form, contents, discontinuance.** MSA 6.1717(1)

MCLA 168.718 Printer; duty, unlawful acts; instruction ballots.
MSA 6.1718

MCLA 168.719 Election commission, party committees, duties, privileges; inspection of proof copy of ballot. MSA 6.1719

Sec. 719. *The election commission of each ... township ... shall perform such duties relative to the preparation, printing and delivery of ballots as are required by law of the boards of election commissioners of counties. Like duties and privileges as are enjoined and granted by this act upon and to the various committees of the different political organizations are hereby prescribed for ... township committees in matters pertaining to any ... township election, except that it shall not be necessary for a ... township ... committee of a political party or organization to furnish a vignette or heading for the ballots other than to designate the name of the party or political organization which they represent. In ... townships the names of candidates for ... township offices ... shall be given by the committees of the various political organizations to the board of election commissioners of such ... township not less than 18 days before each election, but it shall not be necessary for any party committee to give to the board of election commissioners the name of any candidate nominated at an official primary election. The proof of the ballot shall be open to public inspection at the office of the township ... clerk, not less than 15 days before such election.*

CONDUCT OF ELECTIONS AND MANNER OF VOTING

MCLA 168.720 Polls; opening and closing; hours. MSA 6.1720

Sec. 720. *On the day of any election, the polls shall be opened at 7 o'clock in the forenoon, and shall be continuously open until 8 o'clock in the afternoon and no longer. Every qualified elector present and in line at the polls at the hour prescribed for the closing thereof shall be allowed to vote.*

MCLA 168.721 Same; time to govern. MSA 6.1721

Sec. 721. *Unless otherwise specified, the hours for the opening and closing of polls and for the conducting of elections shall be governed by eastern standard time: Provided, however, That in the counties where central standard time is the observed time of any such county, the opening and closing of the polls and the conducting of elections may be governed by central standard time,* upon resolution to such effect adopted by the county board of supervisors.

MCLA 168.722   Same; announcement of opening and closing. [MSA 6.1722]

MCLA 168.723   Ballot boxes; examination, locking. [MSA 6.1723]

MCLA 168.724   Opening packages of ballots; distribution of pencils; unused absent voters' ballots. [MSA 6.1724]

MCLA 168.726   Ballots; delivery to elector. [MSA 6.1726]

MCLA 168.727   Challenges; duty of inspector; annoyance of voters, penalty. [MSA 6.1727]

Note: Right to vote may be challenged by election inspector or or a qualified elector, but not indiscriminately and without good cause.

MCLA 168.728   Same; challenged person to stand aside. . [MSA 6.1728]

MCLA 168.729   Same; oath to electors, questions, false statements. [MSA 6.1729]

Note: Election inspector may examine challenged person under oath.

MCLA 168.730   Challengers; right of designation; qualification; number. [MSA 6.1730]

Sec. 730.   At every election, each of the political parties and any incorporated organization or organized committee of citizens interested in the adoption or defeat of any measure to be voted for or upon at such election, or interested in preserving the purity of elections and in guarding against the abuse of the elective franchise, may designate challengers as herein provided.   Challengers shall be registered and qualified electors of the city or township in which they serve.   A candidate for nomination or election to any office shall not serve as a challenger at the primary or election in which he is a candidate except that a candidate for delegate to a county convention may serve as a challenger in a precinct other than the one in which he is a candidate.   A person who is appointed

268

as an election inspector at any primary election may not act as a challenger at any time during the primary or election day. Political parties, organizations or committees may designate not to exceed 1 challenger to serve in a precinct at any one time. ...

MCLA 168.731 Same; notice of appointment by organization; penalty for violation. [MSA 6.1731]

Sec. 731. Not less than 10 nor more than 20 days prior to any election, any organization or committee of citizens other than political party committees authorized by the provisions of this act intending to appoint challengers at such election shall file with the clerk of the ... township in which such election is to be held, a statement setting forth the intention of such organization or committee to appoint such challengers. Such statement shall set forth the reason why such organization or committee claims the right to appoint such challengers, with a facsimile of the card to be used, and shall be signed and sworn to by the chief presiding officer, the secretary or some other officer of such organization or committee. Prior to the opening of the polls, such clerk shall certify in writing to the inspectors of election in such ... township the names of any organization or committee authorized to appoint and keep challengers at the places of voting in such ... township. Any person who shall file such statement in behalf of any organization or committee not authorized by the provisions of this act to appoint such challengers, or any ... township clerk who shall wilfully and intentionally fail to perform the duties required of him by the provisions of this section shall, upon conviction, be punished by a fine not exceeding $1,000.00 or by imprisonment in the state prison not exceeding 2 years, or by both such fine and imprisonment in the discretion of the court.

MCLA 168.732; Same; evidence of the right to be present. [MSA 6.1732]

MCLA 168.733 Same; space, rights; expulsion for cause, protection. [MSA 6.1733]

MCLA 168.734 Same; penalty for preventing presence. [MSA 6.1734]

MCLA 168.735 Poll book; poll list; contents, names of absent voters. [MSA 6.1735]

MCLA 168.736 Persons permitted to vote; ballot numbers; inspector's explanation to voter. [MSA 6.1736]

MCLA 168.737 Ballot; marking. [MSA 6.1737]

MCLA 168.738 Same; folding; duty of election inspector; rejected for exposure. [MSA 6.1738]

MCLA 168.739 Same; general election, separate boxes; label on box. [MSA 6.1739]

MCLA 168.740 Same; spoiling. [MSA 6.1740]

MCLA 168.741 Same; unused and spoiled, preservation. [MSA 6.1741]

MCLA 168.742 Time elector may remain in booth. [MSA 6.1742]

MCLA 168.743 Return of ballots by elector. [MSA 6.1743]

MCLA 168.744 Persuading electors at polling places and soliciting contributions or signatures near polling places, prohibition. [MSA 6.1744]

Sec. 744. It shall be unlawful for any inspector of election, or any person in the polling room or any compartment therewith connected, to persuade or endeavor to persuade any person to vote for or against any particular candidate or party ticket, or for or against any proposition which is being voted on at such election. It shall be unlawful for any person to place or distribute stickers, other than stickers provided by the election officials pursuant to law, in the polling room or any compartment therewith connected or within 100 feet from any entrance to the building in which said polling place is located.

It shall be unlawful for any person to solicit donations, gifts, contributions, purchase of tickets, or similar demands or to request or obtain signatures on petitions in the polling room or any compartment therewith connected or within 100 feet from any entrance to the building in which the polling place is located.

MCLA 168.745 Ballot of challenged voter; endorsement, rejection. [MSA 6.1745]

MCLA 168.746 Same; endorsement and identification concealed. [MSA 6.1746]

MCLA 168.747 Contested election; challenged voters' ballots, identification. [MSA 6.1747]

MCLA 168.748 Same; petition to determine qualifications of electors. [MSA 6.1748]

MCLA 168.749 Same; removal of slips concealing endorsements, replacement. [MSA 6.1749]

MCLA 168.750 Elector; exemption from civil process. [MSA 6.1750]

Sec. 750. During the day on which any election or primary election shall be held, pursuant to the provisions of law, no civil process shall be served on any elector entitled to vote at such election or primary election.

ASSISTED VOTERS

MCLA 168.751 Assisting elector. [MSA 6.1751]

Sec. 751. When at any election an elector shall state under oath, duly administered by some member of the election board, that because of physical disability he cannot mark his ballot, and the disability shall be made manifest to the inspectors, he shall be assisted in the marking of his ballot by 2 inspectors of election. If an elector is so disabled on account of blindness, he may be assisted in the marking of his ballot by a member of his immediate family or by any person over 18 years of age designated by the blind person.

MCLA 168.752 Oath of assisted elector, form. [MSA 6.1752]

MCLA 168.753 Assisted voters' ballots, marking for identification. [MSA 6.1753]

MCLA 168.754 Assistance by inspectors. [MSA 6.1754]

MCLA 168.755 Record and report. [MSA 6.1755]

MCLA 168.756 False swearing; perjury. [MSA 6.1756]

MCLA 168.757 Unlawful acts; felony. [MSA 6.1757]

MCLA 168.758 Absent voter; definition. [MSA 6.1758]

271

MCLA 168.758a Absent voter ballot for president and vice president; qualifications. [MSA 6.1758(1)]

MCLA 168.759 Same; application, time, form; false statements. [MSA 6.1759]

MCLA 168.759a Armed services members, employees, and their immediate families and United States citizens and their spouses and dependents outside the United States and District of Columbia; absentee ballots, registration, application, disposition, size of precincts. [MSA 6.1759(1)]

MCLA 168.759b Emergency absent voter ballots; application. [MSA 6.1759(2)]

MCLA 168.760 Absent voter; filing; records; inspection. [MSA 6.1760]

MCLA 168.761 Same; mailing, numbering; statement of voter and person assisting voter, form. [MSA 6.1761]

MCLA 168.761a Absent voter balloting; precinct delegate ballots. [MSA 6.1761(1)]

MCLA 168.762 Absent voter ballots, no applications. [MSA 6.1762]

MCLA 168.764 Absent voter ballots; instructions. [MSA 6.1764]

MCLA 168.765 Same; safekeeping; public inspection; delivery to election inspectors; applications not received after opening of polls. [MSA 6.1765]

MCLA 168.766 Same; duty of inspectors. [MSA 6.1766]

MCLA 168.767 Same; illegal vote; rejection of ballot, initialing, preservation. [MSA 6.1767]

MCLA 168.768 Same; legal vote; deposit of ballot in box, record. [MSA 6.1768]

MCLA 168.769 Same; voting in person; return of ballot; double voting. [MSA 6.1769]

MCLA 168.770 **Voting machines authorized; contracts for use between governmental units.** [MSA 6.1770]

Sec. 770. At all elections hereafter held in this state, ballots or votes may be cast, registered, recorded and counted by means of voting machines, as provided in this chapter.

The governing body of any governmental unit in this state may contract with the governing body of any other governmental unit in this state with regard to the use of voting machines owned by either of the contracting units

MCLA 168.770a **Same; authorization of use by secretary of state; petition for use; rules when used.** [MSA 6.1770(1)]

Sec. 770a. The secretary of state may permit the use of any type of voting device for election purposes in any election upon petition for use of the device by the legislative body of the political subdivision desiring to use any new device. Permission granted by the secretary of state shall be valid for 1 election only. Local legislative body includes school boards. Upon authorizing the use of the device, the secretary of state shall prepare detailed rules as to election procedures when the device is used. The rules may include prescribing the counting of votes and the making of returns by persons other than precinct election inspectors. No rule shall be made which provides for reducing the secrecy of the ballot. In partisan general elections, candidates shall be listed under a party heading. Rules so promulgated shall be consistent with the election law.

MCLA 168.771 **Same; purchase.** [MSA 6.1771]

Sec. 771. Hereafter, the board of supervisors of any county, ..., the township board of any township in the state of Michigan, may, by a majority vote, authorize, purchase and order the use of any thoroughly tested or reliable voting machine in any 1 or more voting precincts within said county, ... township until otherwise ordered by the officers adopting the same.

MCLA 168.772 **Same; construction and operation.** [MSA 6.1772]

MCLA 168.773 **Same; maintenance, custody.** [MSA 6.1773]

MCLA 168.774 Same; contracts for purchase, terms. MSA 6.1774

Sec. 774.   The ... township board of any township, on the adoption and purchase of voting machines, may provide for the payment thereof in such manner as they deem for the best interest of the ... township, and may enter into a contract for the purchase of said machines with provision for payment thereof in annual installments not exceeding in all 10 years, and of such amounts and payable at such times as said local authorities shall determine, and said officials shall further have the right to acquire title to said machines at the time of installation or at any time thereafter by payment of the full amount of the purchase price or the balance thereof either in case or by the issuance and delivery in payment therefor of certificates of indebtedness drawn for the amounts of said annual installments; said certificates shall be valid negotiable obligations of said ... township and may be issued with or without interest, but in no case shall the interest exceed 6%. It is further provided that in case any ... township of a county in which the use of voting machines shall have been determined upon by the board of supervisors shall have previously purchased voting machines, such ... township ... shall have returned to it from the general fund of said county such pro rata amount of the whole cost for the county as the number of voting precincts so previously provided by any such ... township ... bears to the whole number in the county, but not exceeding the amount previously paid by any such ... township ...

MCLA 168.775 Same; ballot labels, printing arrangement, contents; amendments or questions; vignettes; printed ballots. MSA 6.1775

MCLA 168.776 Same; supplies and equipment; delivery and return of keys. MSA 6.1776

MCLA 168.777 Same; model machine and instructions. MSA 6.1777

MCLA 168.778 Same; control; officers of election, compensation, duties; lighting of machines; police protection. MSA 6.1778

Sec. 778. ... Provided, That police protection shall be furnished by the local authorities whenever the officers charged with the duty of preparing such machines shall deem such protection necessary to prevent possible injury of any 1 or more voting machines, but such machines shall at all times be under the supervision of such officer, except during the hours prescribed by law for voting on election day.

MCLA 168.779   Same; voting machine, instruction; vacancies. [MSA 6.1779]

MCLA 168.781   Voting machines; inspectors and clerks; opening polls, examination of machine seals and counter, delivery of keys, other duties. [MSA 6.1781]

MCLA 168.782a   Voting machines; vote for more write-in candidates than space upon machine; procedure to be followed. [MSA 6.1782(1)]

MCLA 168.782b   Same; no reserve machine available; emergency ballots. [MSA 6.1782(2)]

MCLA 168.783   Same; challenged voter's ballot. [MSA 6.1783]

MCLA 168.784   Same; irregular ballots, unlawful use. [MSA 6.1784].

MCLA 168.785   Same; location. [MSA 6.1785]

MCLA 168.786   Same, voting; secrecy; time limit. [MSA 6.1786]

MCLA 168.787   Same; keyboard concealed. [MSA 6.1787]

MCLA 168.788   Same; locking. [MSA 6.1788]

MCLA 168.789   Same; inspectors, instructions to voter, assistance to incapacitated voter. [MSA 6.1789]

MCLA 168.790   Same; defacing, altering or injuring machine or labels. [MSA 6.1790]

MCLA 168.791   Same; sealing against voting; reading and announcing of vote; tally of absent voters' ballots; locking of machines. [MSA 6.1791]

MCLA 168.791a   Printer type voting machine, definition, operation. [MSA 6.1791(1)]

MCLA 168.792   Voting machines; discrepancy in return; investigation, re-canvass procedure, petition. [MSA 6.1792]

MCLA 168.792a Absent voters' counting boards; establishment, number. [MSA 6.1792(1)]

Sec. 792a. (1) In any community using voting machines, the absent voters' ballots shall be counted by absent voters' counting boards except that in communities with 2 precincts or less ... the election commission may determine if the absent voter ballots shall be counted by absent voter counting boards in the manner provided in section 791. Such boards shall be established by the election commission. The number of such boards established, the number of voting machines or the number of ballot boxes and the number of inspectors of election to be used in each of said boards shall be determined and the inspectors appointed by the election commission at least 10 days prior to the primary or election at which they shall be used. In no case shall more than 1,000 ballots be counted by a single counting board. Combined ballots shall be regarded as the number of ballots as there are sections to the ballot. If more than 1 counting board is to be used the election commission shall also determine to which counting board the absent voters' ballots for the several precincts shall be assigned for counting. In any governmental unit using counting boards as herein provided, all absent voters' ballots shall be counted in the manner provided in this section and no absent voters' ballots shall be delivered to the polling places.

(2) In any governmental unit where absent voters' ballots are counted by absent voters' counting boards, the election commission shall provide places where the boards shall count the absent voters' ballots. ... No limit shall exist as to the number of such boards which may be located in 1 building.

(3) The clerk of any governmental unit using ... counting boards shall supply each board with such supplies as are necessary ...

(4) All ... ballots received by the clerk prior to election day shall be delivered to the ... counting board by the clerk ... (5, 6)

(7) ... Every person including election inspectors in attendance at any absent voter counting place at any time after the processing of ballots has been started shall take and sign the following oath which may be administered by the chairman or a member of the absent voters' counting board:

"I (name of person taking oath) do solemnly swear (or affirm) that I shall not communicate in any way any information relative to the processing or tallying of votes that may come to me while in in this counting place until after the polls are closed." ...

(8) ... (method of handling challenged voters' ballots)...

276

**MCLA 168.792b   Presidential primary elections, absent voters'
counting boards.** [MSA 6.1792(2)]

*Sec. 792b. The provisions of section 792a of this act shall
not apply in presidential primary elections.*

MCLA 168.793   Voting machines; inspectors' statement forms.
[MSA 6.1793]

ELECTRONIC VOTING SYSTEMS

MCLA   168.794   Definitions.   [MSA 6.1794]

*Sec. 794. As used in sections 794 to 799: (a) "Automatic
tabulating equipment" ... (b) "Ballot" ... (c) "Ballot label" ...
(d) "Counting center" ... (e) "Electronic voting system" ...
(f) "Voting device" ...*

**MCLA 168.794a   Use of systems, authorization; purchase or lease,
experiment, abandonment.** [MSA 6.1794(1)]

*Sec. 794a. The ... township board of a township in this state
by a majority vote, may authorize, acquire by purchase, lease or
otherwise, adopt, experiment with or abandon any electronic voting
system approved for use in the state, in any election or primary or
combination thereof, and may use such system in all or a part of the
precincts within its boundaries, or in combination with paper ballots
or voting machines.*

MCLA 168.794b   Payment for systems, manner.   [MSA 6.1794(2)]

*Sec. 794b. The ... township board of a township, on the adop-
tion and acquisition of an electronic voting system, shall provide
for payment therefor in the same manner as is provided for the
purchase and payment of voting machines in section 774 of this act.*

**MCLA 168.794c   Applicability of provisions; liberal construction;
rules, promulgation by secretary of state.**   [MSA   6.1794(3)]

MCLA 168.795 Specifications for systems. [MSA 6.1795]

**MCLA 168.795a Approval of systems, board of state canvassers;
improvement and changes, reapproval.**   [MSA   6.1795(1)]

MCLA 168.795b Ballot labels, materials, form, contents. [MSA 6.1795(2)]

MCLA 168.795c Parts of ballots, differentiation; voting straight party ticket or split ticket. [MSA 6.1795(3)]

MCLA 168.796 Sample ballots, contents, make up, posting copies; write-in votes. [MSA 6.1796]

MCLA 168.796a Voting equipment and supplies. [MSA 6.1796(1)]

MCLA 168.796b Election inspectors, instructions, qualifications, emergencies. [MSA 6.1796(2)]

MCLA 168.797 Duties of inspectors. [MSA 6.1797]

MCLA 168.797a Instructions for electors; marked ballots, removal of stub, deposit; spoiled ballots. [MSA 6.1797(1)]

MCLA 168.797b Unused ballots; opening ballot box; counting write-in votes; excessive votes for an office; voted ballots and voting devices, disposition. [MSA 6.1797(2)]

MCLA 168.797c Precinct election inspectors; report of votes cast and ballot container, disposition. [MSA 6.1797(3)]

MCLA 168.798 Automatic tabulating equipment; testing, notice, method. [MSA 6.1798]

MCLA 168.798a Counting center proceedings, direction, method. [MSA 6.1798(1)]

MCLA 168.798b Official and unofficial counts and returns; manual and mechanical counting. [MSA 6.1798(2)]

MCLA 168.798c Absentee votes, casting; absent voter ballots, counting, recounting, voting, processing. [MSA 6.1798(3)]

MCLA 168.799 Wilful injuries to voting devices or records, prohibition; enforcement; examination and repair of voting devices. [MSA 6.1799]

CHAPTER XXIX. CANVASS BY THE PRECINCT INSPECTORS

MCLA 168.825 Same; contents, certification, filing. [MSA 6.1825]

MCLA 168.826 Same; determination, exception, publication, certificate of election. [MSA 6.1826]

MCLA 168.827 Same; certificate of determination mailed to secretary of state and postoffice address of persons elected. [MSA 6.1827]

MCLA 168.828 Same; certified copy of statements to secretary of state. [MSA 6.1828]

MCLA 168.829 Canvass of special election. [MSA 6.1829]

MCLA 168.830 Canvassers and clerk, compensation. [MSA 6.1830]

CHAPTER XXXI. THE STATE CANVASS

MCLA 168.841 Board of state canvassers; duty to canvass returns. [MSA 6.1841]

MCLA 168.842 Same; meeting ; time, place, notice, adjournment. [MSA 6.1842]

MCLA 168.843 Same; secretary of state; duties. [MSA 6.1843]

MCLA 168.844 Same; statement, contents. [MSA 6.1844]

MCLA 168.845 Same; statement, determination and certificates of election, publication of constitutional amendments. [MSA 6.1845]

MCLA 168.846 Same; tie vote; certification to legislature, determination. [MSA 6.1846]

CHAPTER XXXII. DETERMINATION OF ELECTION BY LOT

MCLA 168.851 Determination by lot, procedure. [MSA 6.1851]

MCLA 168.852 Procedure; other officers; right to a recount. [MSA 6.1852]

CHAPTER XXXIII. RECOUNTS
COUNTY, CITY, TOWNSHIP AND VILLAGE
BOARDS OF CANVASSERS

MCLA 168.861 Fraudulent or illegal voting, tampering with ballots or ballot boxes before recount; quo warranto. [MSA 6.1861]

MCLA 168.862 Recount of votes; petition. [MSA 6.1862]

Sec. 862. Any candidate for any office, at any primary or election, conceiving himself aggrieved on account of any fraud or mistake in the canvass of the votes by the inspectors of election, or in the returns made thereon by the inspectors, may petition for a recount of the votes cast for such office in any precinct or precincts as in this chapter provided.

MCLA 168.863 Same; local amendments or propositions. [MSA 6.1863]

Sec. 863. Any qualified or registered elector voting in any ... township ... at the last preceding election who believes there has been fraud or error committed by the inspectors of election in their canvass or returns of the votes cast at said election, ... or any other proposition which shall be submitted to the voters of any ... township ..., may petition for a recount of the votes cast in any precinct or precincts of said ... township ... upon such proposed amendment or other proposition.

MCLA 168.864 Same; candidate for legislature, deposit, petition; nonlegislative recount in same precinct. Same; primary election for legislative office, board of canvassers. [MSA 6.1864]

MCLA 168.865 Same; contents. [MSA 6.1865]

MCLA 168.866 Recount; petition filed with board originally conducting canvass, time, copy, filing. [MSA 6.1866]

Sec. 866. ... In all cases, such petitions shall be filed within 6 days after the original canvass has been completed by the ... township ... board of canvassers. A copy of any such petition shall also be filed with the secretary of state within 2 days after the time the original petition is filed with the board of county canvassers as provided in this section. In case the office or proposition in question be a ... township ... office or proposition, a copy of such petition shall not be filed with the secretary of state, but a copy shall be transmitted within 24 hours to the clerk of the board of county canvassers by the appropriate local clerk if the recount fee has been paid.

MCLA 168.867 Same; deposit, amount, disposition. MSA 6.1867

MCLA 168.868 Same; notice to opposing candidates; counter petition, filing, time, deposit, copy. MSA 6.1868

Sec. 868. The clerk of the board of canvassers after a candidate has filed a petition and made the deposit herein required shall give notice thereof to the opposing candidate within 24 hours after filing same by delivering to such candidate a copy of such petition, or, if such candidate cannot be found, by leaving such copy at his last known place of residence with some member of his immediate family of suitable age, or, ... Any counter petition shall be filed within 48 hours after the original recount petition was filed and at the same time a deposit of money shall be made as hereinbefore stipulated for the original petitioner. ... In case the office or proposition in question be a ... township ... office or proposition, a copy of such petition shall not be filed with the secretary of state. In case the time designated for filing such petitions shall fall on a Saturday, Sunday or holiday, such petitions may be filed on the next succeeding business day. Failure of the clerk of the board of canvassers or the secretary of state to give notice to the opposing candidate shall not affect the results of the recount.

MCLA 168.869 Same; investigation; petition filed with the secretary of state, expenses of local recount (charged to the local unit). MSA 6.1869

MCLA 168.870 Same; meeting of board of canvassers, clerk to call; guarding ballots, poll lists, etc.; subpoena; fees and mileage to persons appearing. MSA 6.1870

MCLA 168.871 Same; counting of ballots. MSA 6.1871

MCLA 168.872 Same; investigation by canvassers, report to prosecutor and circuit judge. MSA 6.1872

MCLA 168.873 Same; misconduct of employees, guilty of felony. MSA 6.1873

MCLA 168.874 Same; return of ballots; manner of counting votes. MSA 6.1874

MCLA 168.875 Same; completion. MSA 6.1875

282

MCLA 168.876 Same; return by board of canvassers; deemed correct; withdrawal of petition; final report open to inspection by public. [MSA 6.1876]

MCLA 168.877 Same; review of error apparent on face. [MSA 6.1877]

STATE CANVASSERS

MCLA 168.878 State canvassers; action instituted against board of state canvassers, certain sections not construed to repeal. [MSA 6.1878]

MCLA 168.879 Recount of votes; petition, time, filing; seat in legislature, deposit, additional copies, filing, preservation of ballots. [MSA 6.1879]

MCLA 168.880 Same; votes on constitutional amendment or other proposition. [MSA 6.1880]

MCLA 168.880a Same; grounds for recount; notice to candidates; elections involving propositions, procedure. [MSA 6.1880(1)]

MCLA 168.881 Same; deposit; amount, disposition. [MSA 6.1881]

MCLA 168.882 Same; state election, notice to opposing candidate; counter petitions, filing, time, deposit. [MSA 6.1882]

MCLA 168.883 Same; notice to county clerk; preservation of ballots; investigation and recount by state canvassers. [MSA 6.1883]

MCLA 168.884 Same; clerks and assistants. [MSA 6.1884]

MCLA 168.885 Same; witnesses; right to subpoena, penalty. [MSA 6.1885]

MCLA 168.886 Same; compensation and mileage. [MSA 6.1886]

MCLA 168.887 Same; misconduct of employees, guilty of felony. [MSA 6.1887]

MCLA 168.888 Same; demand for ballot boxes, poll books, tally sheets and statements; concurrent recount; guarding ballots, etc. [MSA 6.1888]

MCLA 168.889 Same; conduct by county canvassers under direction of state canvassers; time, place, rules. [MSA 6.1889]

MCLA 168.890 Same; persons to conduct. [MSA 6.1890]

MCLA 168.891 Recount under direction of state canvassers, conduct. [MSA 6.1891]

MCLA 168.892 Report of recount by county board of canvassers to state board of canvassers deemed correct. [MSA 6.1892]

MCLA 168.893 Discontinuance of recount, original return deemed correct. [MSA 6.1893]

MCLA 168.894 Expenses of recount, payment. [MSA 6.1894]

CHAPTER XXXIV. CAMPAIGN EXPENSES

MCLA 168.901 Definitions. [MSA 6.1901]

Sec. 901. Terms used in this chapter shall be used as follows, unless other meaning is clearly apparent from the language or context, or unless such construction is inconsistent with the manifest intent of the law:

1. "Candidate" shall apply to any person whose name is printed on an official ballot for public office or whose name has been presented for public office, with his consent, for nomination or election;

2. "Political committee" or "committee" shall apply to every combination of 2 or more persons who shall aid or promote the success or defeat of a candidate, or a political party or principle or measure; and

3. "Public office" shall apply to any national, state, county or city ward, village or township office which is filled by the voters of this state, as well as to the office of presidential elector and United States senator.

MCLA 168.902 Campaign expenses of candidates, limit. [MSA 6.1902]

MCLA 168.903 Treasurer of political committee; appointment, duties. [MSA 6.1903]

MCLA 168.904 Lawful items of expense. [MSA 6.1904]

284

MCLA 168.905 Contributions payable only to candidates or committee. $\boxed{\text{MSA 6.1905}}$

Sec. 905. No person who is not a candidate or the treasurer of a political committee shall pay, give or lend, or agree to pay, give or lend, any money whether contributed by himself or by any other person for any election expenses whatever, except to a candidate or to a political committee.

MCLA 168.906 Nomination and election expense statements, requirement, form, contents, exemptions; candidates' names and addresses and ballot, filing. $\boxed{\text{MSA 6.1906}}$

MCLA 168.907 Same; inspection, preservation. $\boxed{\text{MSA 6.1907}}$

Sec. 907. All such accounts shall be open to public inspection in the offices where they are filed and shall be carefully preserved there for a period of 1 year, and it shall be the duty of the officers having custody of the same to give certified copies in like manner as of other public records.

MCLA 168.908 Same; official inspection, notice to delinquents. $\boxed{\text{MSA 6.1908}}$

MCLA 168.909 Same; failure to file, report to prosecuting attorney or attorney general. $\boxed{\text{MSA 6.1909}}$

MCLA 168.910 Witness not exempt from testifying. $\boxed{\text{MSA 6.1910}}$

MCLA 168.911 State to furnish blanks (at its expense to township clerks). $\boxed{\text{MSA 6.1911}}$

MCLA 168.912 Unlawful to threaten or intimidate employees. $\boxed{\text{MSA 6.1912}}$

MCLA 168.913 Solicitation of donations from candidate, demands in certain places for donations; unlawfulness. $\boxed{\text{MSA 6.1913}}$

MCLA 168.914 Newspaper advertising marked; payment for editorials. $\boxed{\text{MSA 6.1914}}$

Sec. 914. No publisher of a newspaper or other periodical and no director or person responsible for the operation of any other advertising medium shall insert, either in its advertising or reading columns or cause or permit to be disseminated any paid matter which is designed or tends to aid, injure or defeat any candidate or political party or organization, or proposition before the people, unless it is stated therein that it is a paid advertisement. No person shall pay the owner, editor, publisher or agent of any newspaper, periodical or other advertising medium to induce him to editorially advocate or oppose any candidate for nomination or election, and no such owner, editor, publisher or agent shall accept such payment.

MCLA 168.914a Paid advertisements as to proposals, naming of sponsors. [MSA 6.1914(1)]

Sec. 914a. No publisher of a newspaper or other periodical and no director or person responsible for the operation of any other advertising medium shall insert, either in his advertising or reading columns, or cause or permit to be disseminated, any paid matter which is designed or tends to support or oppose any proposed amendment or amendments to the constitution of this state, or before the people, unless it is stated therein that it is a paid advertisement, and stating the name or names of the persons, organization or organizations paying for such advertisement.

MCLA 168.915 False statement, penalty for publication or circulation. [MSA 6.1915]

MCLA 168.916 Accounts; unlawful to administer oath of office before filing. [MSA 6.1916]

Sec. 916. It shall be unlawful to administer the oath of office or to issue a commission or certificate of nomination or election to any person nominated or elected to any public office until he has filed an account as required by this act, which account shall upon its face be complete and show a lawful compliance with this chapter, and no such person shall enter upon the duties of his office until he has filed such account, nor shall he receive any salary or fees for any period prior to the filing of the same.

MCLA 168.917 Anonymous contributions; unlawfulness. [MSA 6.1917]

MCLA 168.918 Same; unlawful disbursement. [MSA 6.1918]

MCLA 168.919 Corporations not to contribute. [MSA 6.1919]

MCLA 168.920 Penalty for violation of chapter. [MSA 6.1920]

Sec. 920. Any person who shall incur any illegal election expenses or otherwise violate any of the provisions of this chapter shall, upon conviction thereof, be punished by a fine of not more than $1,000.00 or by imprisonment for not more than 2 years, or by both such fine and imprisonment in the discretion of the court.

CHAPTER XXXV. OFFENSES AND PENALTIES

MCLA 168.931 Penalty for violation of statutory provisions; enumeration. [MSA 6.1931]

Sec. 931. Any person who violates any of the following statutory provisions shall, on conviction, be deemed guilty of a misdemeanor: ...

MCLA 168.932 Violation of statute; felony. [MSA 6.1932]

Sec. 932. Any person who violates any of the following statutory provisions shall, on conviction, be guilty of a felony:
(a) **Corrupt influence of elector.** *No person shall, by means of bribery, menace or other corrupt means or device whatever, either directly or indirectly, attempt to influence any elector in giving his vote, or to deter him from, or interrupt him in giving the same at any election or primary election held pursuant to law.*
Unauthorized breaking open of seal or locks on ballot boxes or voting machines. ... Destruction, mutilation, fraud or concealment as to election records by custodian. ... Disclosure of contents of ballots; obstruction of electors. ...

MCLA 168.933 False affidavit, swearing falsely while under oath, penalty. [MSA 6.1933]

MCLA 168.934 Misdemeanor, penalty. [MSA 6.1934]

MCLA 168.935 Felony, penalty. [MSA 6.1935]

MCLA 168.936 Perjury, penalty. [MSA 6.1936]

MCLA 168.937 Forgery, penalty. [MSA 6.1937]

MCLA 168.938 Candidate convicted of felony, election void, quo warranto. [MSA 6.1938]

MCLA 168.939 Inspector, duty to furnish information to prosecutor. MSA 6.1939

MCLA 168.940 Prosecutor, duty. MSA 6.1940

MCLA 168.941 Peace officers, duty. MSA 6.1941

MCLA 168.942 Prosecution; time limitations; fraudulent registrations; immunity of witnesses. MSA 6.1942

MCLA 168.943 Jurisdiction of recorder's court. MSA 6.1943

Sec. 943. ...(circuit court for county involved) ...

MCLA 168.944 Incumbency designation; penalty for wrongful use. MSA 6.1944

MCLA 168.945 Absentee voters; inducing improper applications to vote, penalty. MSA 6.1945

MCLA 169.947 Voting machines, master keys, definition and penalty for possession. MSA 6.1947

CHAPTER XXXVI. RECALL

MCLA 168.951 Officers subject to recall; petition, circulation, time. MSA 6.1951

Sec. 951. Every elective officer in the state of Michigan, except (courts) ... *is subject to recall by the legal voters of the state or of the electoral district in which he is elected as hereinafter provided: Provided, That no petition shall be circulated against any officer until he has actually performed the duties of his office for a period of 45 days for a legislative office and 3 months for any other office: Provided further, That any officer sought to be recalled shall continue to perform duties of his office until the result of said election is declared.*

MCLA 168.952 Petitions; form, contents. MSA 6.1952

Sec. 952. All petitions for the recall of an officer shall be in substantially the following form, shall be printed or typewritten and shall state clearly the reason or reasons for said demand:
We, the undersigned qualified and registered electors of the

288

... township of ......, in the county of ...... and state of Michigan, hereby petition for the calling of an election to recall (name person sought to be recalled) from the office of (name office) for the following reason or reasons: ....
Name, residence (street and house number in cities having same, otherwise postoffice address). Date of signing.

MCLA 168.953 Same; modification. [MSA 6.1953]

Sec. 953. ... In case the electoral district of the official sought to be recalled includes a part only of any ... township, then the petitions circulated in such ... township shall recite that the persons signing the same are qualified and registered electors of that portion of such city or township lying within such electoral district.

MCLA 168.954 Same; signatures; school districts; qualifications of persons signing. [MSA 6.1954]

Sec. 954. The petitions shall be signed by registered and qualified electors of the electoral district of the official whose recall is sought: Provided, That in any school district where school electors are not required to be registered, then in such case the signers of such petition shall not be required to be such registered electors and the term "registered and qualified electors" shall be considered to mean "qualified electors". Each signer of the petition shall affix his signature, place of residence, which shall be his street address and house number in locations having same, otherwise his postoffice address, and the date of signing. The persons signing said petitions shall be registered and qualified electors of the governmental subdivision designated in the heading of the petitions.

MCLA 168.955 Same; signatures, persons entitled to sign, number, time limit. [MSA 6.1955]

Sec. 955. The petitions shall be signed by registered and qualified electors equal to at least 25% of the number of votes cast for candidates for the office of governor at the last preceding general election in the electoral district of the official sought to be recalled. Any signatures obtained more than 90 days before the filing of such petition shall not be counted.

MCLA 168.956 Same; village president. [MSA 6.1956]

MCLA 168.957 Same; circulator, qualifications; affidavit, contents, false statement, perjury. [MSA 6.1957]

Sec. 957. Each person actually circulating a petition shall be a qualified and registered elector in the electoral district of the official sought to be recalled and shall attach thereto his affidavit stating that he is such a qualified and registered elector and shall state the city or village in which he resides, together with his street address, if any, and, if not a resident of a city or village, the township wherein he resides and his postoffice address; further, that signatures appearing upon said petitions were not obtained through fraud, deceit or misrepresentation and that he has neither caused nor permitted any person to sign said petition more than once and has no knowledge of any person signing said petition more than once; that all signatures to said petition were affixed in his presence; and further, that to the best of his knowledge, information and belief, the signers of said petition are qualified and registered electors and the signatures appearing thereon are the genuine signatures of the persons of whom they purport to be. Any person knowingly making any false statement in the affidavit hereby required shall be deemed guilty of perjury and upon conviction thereof shall suffer the pains and penalties provided therefor by law.

MCLA 168.958 Same; separate circulation in city and township. [MSA 6.1958]

Sec. 958. Separate petitions shall be circulated in each city and township in the electoral district.

MCLA 168.959 Same; United States senator, congressmen, state senators and representatives, elective state officers; exception, filing; secretary of state. [MSA 6.1959]

MCLA 168.960 Same; elective county, township, city, village or school officials, filing; clerk or corresponding official. [MSA 6.1960]

Sec. 960. Petitions demanding the recall of any elective county, township, city or village or school official shall be filed with the clerk thereof, or, if there is no such officer in such governmental unit, then with the officer whose duties correspond to those of the clerk; petitions demanding the recall of the clerk or corresponding official shall be filed with the chief executive officer of such unit of government, except that in case it is sought to recall the county clerk, the petitions shall be filed with the presiding or senior judge of probate.

MCLA 168.961 Recall petitions; checking with registration lists, access, certificate, striking of names of unregistered electors. MSA 6.1961

MCLA 168.962 Same; insufficient number of signatures, notice to person or organization. MSA 6.1962

MCLA 168.963 Same; special election, time; additional filing. MSA 6.1963

Sec. 963. Immediately upon ascertaining that the petitions are sufficient, but in no case later than 30 days from the date of filing of such petitions, the officer with whom such petitions are filed shall call a special election to be held within 35 days after the calling thereof to determine whether the electors will recall the officer whose recall is sought: Provided, That if any general, special or primary election is to be held in the electoral district within 90 days and within such time that the clerk may check the petitions as herein provided, and preparation may be made for the election by election officials as provided by law after the filing of the petitions, then such recall election shall be held on the same date as such general, special or primary election. In the event of filing of additional petitions containing sufficient additional signatures of registered and qualified electors as above provided, then such election shall be called within 10 days after such additional petitions are filed as hereinbefore provided.

MCLA 168.964 Election; procedure, notice, ballots, supplies. MSA 6.1964

Sec. 964. The procedure governing the election on the question of the recall of any officer shall be the same, so far as possible and unless otherwise provided in this act, as that by which the officer is elected to office. If the official with whom the petition is filed be not an officer charged with the duty of giving notice of an election concerning the office in question, he shall notify the official or officials upon whom the duty rests under the general election laws or the school laws of the state or any city charter, and such official or officials shall proceed to give notice of the election, cause the ballots to be printed, provide election supplies and do all things necessary to conduct the election in the manner herein provided. Fewer precinct election officials than the number required under the general election laws of the state may be assigned to duty if it should appear that the votes to be cast will not necessitate the usual complement thereof.

MCLA 168.965; Same; recall of officer having duties in connection with election, appointment of impartial public official. MSA 6.1965

Sec. 965. In the event that a petition for the recall of an officer having duties to perform in connection with the election on such question is filed, the official with whom the petition is filed shall appoint some other impartial public officer having knowledge of the election laws involved and such officer thereupon shall discharge the election duties only of the officer sought to be recalled until the result on the question of the recall is finally determined; The public officer so appointed to act shall receive no additional compensation for his services.

MCLA 168.966 Ballot, contents; condensed statement; question printed on ballot. MSA 6.1966

MCLA 168.967 Expenses. MSA 6.1967

MCLA 168.968 Certification of result of election. MSA 6.1968

Sec. 968. If, upon a canvass of the votes cast upon the question of the recall of such officer, a majority of such votes shall be in favor of such recall, the board of canvassers shall certify such result as soon as may be to the officer with whom the recall petition was filed, and upon said certification said office shall be deemed to be vacant.

MCLA 168.969 Further recall petition, filing. MSA 6.1969

Sec. 969. After filing such recall petition and after such special election, no further recall petition shall be filed against the same incumbent of such office during the term for which he is elected unless such further petitioners shall first pay into the public treasury, which has paid such election expenses, the whole amount of election expenses for the preceding special election held for the recall of said incumbent.

MCLA 168.970 Vacancy. MSA 6.1970

Sec. 970. Upon the filing of the certificate of the canvassing board showing the recall of the officer as herein provided, the officer empowered by law to perform the duties of such recalled official, in the event of such officer's absence, death, illness or inability to act, shall perform and discharge the duties of the office so vacated until the successor to fill such vacancy is duly elected and qualified as herein provided or until the vacancy is temporarily filled. Where power to fill a vacancy by appointment exists, then in such case such office shall be filled in the same manner by temporary appointment effective until a successor shall be duly elected and qualified as herein provided, otherwise, the governor of the state may fill such vacancy until said recalled officer's successor is elected and qualified.

MCLA 168.971 Special election to fill vacancy. [MSA 6,1971]

Sec. 971. If the recall was successful, the officer with whom the recall petition shall have been filed, shall, within 5 days after receiving such certification, call a special election to be held within 45 days for the filling of such vacancy: Provided, That if any primary or election is to be held in such electoral district within 4 months of such certification and at such a time as will permit preparation for the election by election officials as provided by law, the election to fill the vacancy shall be held concurrently therewith. The same provisions made in section 964 for calling and conducting of the special recall election shall govern in the calling and conducting of such second special election, except as otherwise provided in this section.

MCLA 168.972 Same; candidates, nomination, petition. [MSA 6.1972]

Sec. 972. Candidates for the office may be nominated and voted for in such special elections by filing with the officer with whom the recall petition has been filed a petition, within 15 days after said special election is called, signed by not less than 3% of the registered and qualified electors of the electoral district, and said candidate so filing said petition shall be considered nominated for said office.

MCLA 168.973 Same; nominations, method. [MSA 6.1973]

Sec. 973. Party candidates shall be nominated as follows: In case the vacancy to be filled be in a state office ... and if such vacancy be in a ward or township office, the committee of each political party thereof shall nominate a candidate for such office. All nominations by such committee shall be certified to the officer with whom the recall petitions were filed within 15 days after the calling of the special election.

MCLA 168.974   Recalled officer, ineligibility.   [MSA 6.1974]

Sec. 974.   No recalled officer shall be a candidate to fill the vacancy created by his recall nor shall he be appointed to fill such vacancy pending the election of his successor.

MCLA 168.975   Candidate deemed elected.   [MSA 6.1975]

MCLA 168.976 Laws governing. [MSA 6.1976]

Sec. 976.   The laws relating to nominations and elections shall govern all nominations and elections under this act insofar as is not in conflict herewith.

Chapter IV

SERVICES, UTILITIES, CONTRACTS AND ORDINANCES

Provision for services and utilities is one of today's greatest challenges for local government officials, particularly in townships. Decisions as to need may be based on growth and development or density of population or when people, regardless of present use of land or of a particular right of way or without regard to local ordinances, feel that the time has come to demand such things as water, sanitary sewers, storm sewers or drains, street lights, curbing, sidewalk, pavement or other improvements or services such as fire and police protection.

The township board may install water mains, sewers or sidewalks on its own accord. If no objecting petition is filed following publication of a certificate of public necessity and notice of hearing, the township board has authority to create the district by holding public hearings and proceeding in accordance with other statutory provisions.

On the other hand, many statutes provide for local governing bodies such as township boards to render services and utilities upon demand of the people, by initiatory petition only. If a petition is found to be legally sufficient, the board has no discretionary power but must proceed according to the applicable statute. Regardless of either positive or negative feelings on the part of board members, immediate action should be taken. The quickest way is for the board to lay the general groundwork and then turn the matter over to the township engineer and township attorney for professional advice and information to guide them in arranging for financing, installation, maintenance and operation of the project if it is determined feasible.

Depending upon the controlling statutes, township residents may utilize several methods of financing. The most popular is that of special assessment, followed by revenue bonds, general obligation bonds, one-time payments of a special nature and/or payment out of the general fund or specially designated funds of the township. In addition, funding may be provided by extra millage under the general property tax act through the county tax allocation board, by general vote or through the department of county public works. One or more of the methods may be combined -- for instance, a service may be supported by a combination of general obligation and revenue bonds, along with special assessments and millage.

Township boards sometimes fail to take the initiative in these matters because they are reluctant to spend money or tax their constituents, or conceivably because they lack knowledge of procedure. One of the best ways to get started is to become involved in continuing studies of area needs with other units of government. Townships may do this by utilizing provisions of the second and third citations following -- increasing numbers of them are taking advantage of this method. Also, citizen committees may be appointed to assist the board in gaining a broad base of knowledge from which it may either project further studies or actually accomplish the installation, operation and maintenance of various public improvements.

Some of the smaller governmental units find it impossible to accomplish delivery of needed services and utilities without outside help. Many of the larger governments may find it less expensive and actually easier to provide better services through joint effort with other governmental units or agencies. Recognizing this, the legislature (particularly during the last twenty years) has passed numerous statutes which permit two or more political subdivisions to join together to study, plan, install, operate and maintain any kind of service or utility. In fact, there are over eighty such laws on the books. In view of this, any citation from this point on which permits some type of joint action between one or more political subdivisions is indicated by the use of the words **JOINT ACTION** above the title.

One of the most important considerations in retaining purity in government evolves around the methods used in spending public funds. There is no greater safeguard to protect monies entrusted to public officials and to guarantee integrity in government than the use of public bidding for purchase and sale of equipment and material or letting of contracts for construction, maintenance or repair of public works. It has long been established by the courts that a municipality has the right to do this. Some statutes specify bidding methods; otherwise it is up to the board to establish its own rules. Many township boards set a minimum figure of perhaps $200 or $500 as the point at which public bids will be called for.

It is imperative that local government officials realize that the township board may reject any or all bids which they deem to be improper, inconclusive, or indicative that a project may not succeed. If necessary, the board simply announces that all bids are rejected and that new ones will be taken at a subsequent date and then advertises on a wider basis. It is perfectly legal for a township board to go beyond the limits of its own county, or for that matter of the state, to inform more contractors about the provisions of the bid. As a result of this expanded notification of potential bidders, chances for receiving a successful bid are greatly improved.

Basic information regarding bidders on public works is to be found in Act No. 170, P.A. 1933, the first citation in this chapter. Since joint authorities are governmental agencies, even though not listed in section 1 of this act, they may also use public bids for their purposes.

Special attention is directed to Act No. 35, P.A. 1951, and section 18 of Act No. 359, P.A. 1947, which provide that general law and charter townships, respectively, may join with other governmental units or agencies for any service or utility which a township has a right to provide by itself. It should also be noted that the governing body of any municipality, including a township, may transfer a function or responsibility duly assigned to it by law -- this is covered in Act No. 8, P.A. 1967.

Act No. 217, P.A. 1957, and Act No. 342, P.A. 1939, are enabling acts for county government. They are included in this textbook because both the citizens and public officials of our townships should be aware of the fact that in the event a local unit of government cannot provide services or utilities, there are provisions made at the county level to take care of their needs.

Following World War II, townships were literally flooded with requests for expansion of services. Most of the statutes then in force were vague, ambiguous and in some instances practically impossible to utilize to attain the benefits they were supposed to provide. Something had to be done to help townships finance public improvements by special assessment and to allow a more liberal means of issuing township bonds in anticipation of collections. Through the efforts of The Honorable Roy H. Brigham and The Honorable William H. Thorne (both now deceased), Act No. 188, P.A. 1954, was introduced and passed by the legislature. These men were longtime township officials who also served in the House of Representatives and as President of the Michigan Townships Association. Mr. Brigham died in 1955 and Mr. Thorne in 1957.

After the first twelve citations, we have attempted to group the enabling acts according to general subject. However, since many provide for a variety of services, buildings and utilities, this was not always possible. Leading in importance are those having to do with the provision of water, followed closely by the related areas of sanitary sewers and garbage disposal. Generally the title and first section are given, with the rest of the act by section headings only.

Attention is also directed to the chapters on Environmental Protection and Control and Planning and Zoning for additional citations. The chapters on Elections and Finance and Taxation are also of related interest. The latter chapter includes reference to the Revenue Bond Act, which is particularly useful in implementing improvement projects.

BASIC JOINT ACTION STATUTES

Act No. 170, P.A. 1933 - Bidders on Public Works

AN ACT to regulate the practice of taking bids and awarding contracts on public work construction, maintenance or repair work, except public buildings, and to provide a means of prohibiting those not qualified by experience, financial resources or any other valid reason from undertaking such public construction work.

MCLA 123.501 Bidders on public works; statement as to qualifications, notice of rejection. [MSA 5.2311]

MCLA 123.502 Bidders on public works; failure to file statement; rejection of bid. [MSA 5.2312]

MCLA 123.503 Allotment of work by public officers. [MSA 5.2313]

298

MCLA 123.504 Questionnaire and statement; confidential treatment. [MSA 5.2314]

MCLA 123.505 Refusal to furnish data to bidder; discretion of public officers. [MSA 5.2315]

MCLA 123.506 Review of decision of public officers. [MSA 5.2316]

MCLA 123.507 False statements, penalty. [MSA 5.2317]

MCLA 123.508 Definition of person. [MSA 5.2318]

Sec. 8. The word "person" as used herein, shall mean and include any individual, corporation, co-partnership, association or their lessees, trustees or receivers.

JOINT ACTION
Act No. 200, P.A. 1957 - Intermunicipality Committees

AN ACT to provide for the creation by 2 or more municipalities of an intermunicipality committee for the purpose of studying area problems; and to provide authority for the committee to receive gifts and grants.

MCLA 123.631 Intermunicipality area problem study committee; definition of municipalities. [MSA 5.2450(1)]

MCLA 123.632 Same; organization; purposes. [MSA 5.2450(2)]

MCLA 123.633 Same; surveys, recommendations, reports. [MSA 5.2450(3)]

MCLA 123.634 Same; funds. [MSA 5.2450(4)]

MCLA 123.635 Same; contributions of service of personnel, equipment, office space. [MSA 5.2450(5)]

MCLA 123.636 Same; gifts and grants from governmental units and from private sources. [MSA 5.2450(6)]

JOINT ACTION
Act No. 217, P.A. 1957 - Supervisors' Intercounty Committees

AN ACT to provide for the creation by 2 or more counties of an intercounty committee for the purpose of studying area problems; and to provide authority for the committee to receive gifts and grants.

MCLA 123.641 Intercounty area problem study committees; establishment, recommendations. [MSA 5.400(1)]

MCLA 123.642 Same; surveys, findings, reports. [MSA 5.400(2)]

MCLA 123.643 Same; expenses. [MSA 5.400(3)]

MCLA 123.644 Same; contributions of service of personnel, equipment, office space. [MSA 5.400(4)]

MCLA 123.645 Same; gifts and grants from governmental units and from private sources; approval. [MSA 5.400(5)]

JOINT ACTION
Act No. 7, P.A. 1967, Ex. Sess. - Urban Cooperation Act of 1967

AN ACT to provide for interlocal public agency agreements; to provide standards for such agreements and for the filing and status thereof; and to provide for additional approval for such agreements.

MCLA 124.501 Short title. [MSA 5.4088(1)]

MCLA 124.502 Definitions. [MSA 5.4088(2)]

Sec. 2. As used in this act:
(a) "Interlocal agreement" means an agreement entered into pursuant to this act.
(b) "Province" means a province of the Dominion of Canada.
(c) "Public agency" means a political subdivision of this state or of any state of the United States or the Dominion of Canada, including, but not limited to, state government, a county, city,

300

village, township, charter township, school district, single and multipurpose special district, single and multipurpose public authority; provincial government, metropolitan government, borough, and any other political subdivision of the Dominion of Canada; any agency of the United States government; and any similar entity of any other states of the United States and of the Dominion of Canada.

(d) "State" means a state of the United States.

MCLA 124.503 Conflicting statutory provisions. ⌈MSA 5.4088(3)⌉

MCLA 124.504 Joint exercise of powers. ⌈MSA 5.4088(4)⌉

MCLA 124.505 Contracts for joint exercise of powers; Interlocal agreements; provisions. ⌈MSA 5.4088(5)⌉

MCLA 124.506 Execution of agreement; provision of services; exchange of services. ⌈MSA 5.4088(6)⌉

Sec. 6. An interlocal agreement may provide for 1 or more parties to the agreement to administer or execute the agreement. One or more parties to the agreement may agree to provide all or a part of the services set forth in the agreement in the manner provided in the agreement. The parties may provide for the mutual exchange of services without payment of any contribution other than such services.

MCLA 124.507 Administrative commission, board or council; public body, corporate or politic; powers. ⌈MSA 5.4088(7)⌉

MCLA 124.508 Payments, repayments or returns to parties from operation of revenue-producing facilities. ⌈MSA 5.4088(8)⌉

MCLA 124.509 Privileges, immunities, and benefits of officers, agents or employees; obligations and responsibilities of public agencies. ⌈MSA 5.4088(9)⌉

MCLA 124.510 Approval of certain agreements by governor; filing. ⌈MSA 5.4088(10)⌉

MCLA 124.511 Provision of services or facilities by state officer or agency; submission of agreement for approval. ⌈MSA 5.4088(11)⌉

MCLA 124.512 Appropriation of funds by public agency; sale, lease or gift of personnel, services, facilities, etc.; receipt of grants-in-aid. [MSA 5.4088(12)]

JOINT ACTION
Act No. 35, P.A. 1951 - Inter-governmental Contracts Between Municipalities

AN ACT to authorize inter-governmental contracts between municipal corporations; and to authorize any municipal corporation to contract with any person or any municipal corporation to furnish any lawful municipal service to property outside the corporate limits of the first municipal corporation for a consideration.

MCLA 124.1 Municipal corporation; definition. [MSA 5.4081]

MCLA 124.2 Inter-governmental contracts between municipal corporations authorized. [MSA 5.4082]

Sec. 2. Any municipal corporation shall have power to join with any other municipal corporation, or with any number or combination thereof by contract, or otherwise as may be permitted by law, for the ownership, operation, or performance, jointly, or by any 1 or more on behalf of all, of any property, facility or service which each would have the power to own, operate or perform separately.

MCLA 124.3 Municipal service outside corporate limits of municipality, contracts. [MSA 5.4083]

MCLA 124.4 Public utility. [MSA 5.4084]

Sec. 4. Nothing contained in this act shall be construed to grant the right to jointly own or operate a public utility for supplying transportation, gas, light, telephone service, or electric power except as may be provided by the statutes or constitution of the state of Michigan, nor to contract to furnish municipal services outside corporate limits except in accordance with the constitutional limitations on such sales. Nothing contained in this act shall be construed as to grant to municipal corporations acting jointly any power or authority which they do not have acting singly.

JOINT ACTION
Act No. 359, P.A. 1947 - Charter Townships

MCLA 42.18 Joining with other governmental agency. $\boxed{\text{MSA } 5.46(18)}$

Sec. 18. Each charter township may join with any governmental unit or agency, or with any number or combination thereof, by contract or otherwise as may be permitted by law, to perform jointly, or by one or more, for or on behalf of the other or others, any power or duty which is permitted to be so performed by law or which is possessed or imposed upon each such governmental unit or agency.

JOINT ACTION
Act No. 342, P.A. 1939 - County Public Improvements

AN ACT to authorize counties to establish and provide connecting water, sewer and/or sewage disposal improvements and services within or between cities, villages, townships and township improvement districts, or any duly authorized and established combinations thereof, within or without the county, and to establish and provide garbage and/or rubbish collection and disposal facilities and services for such units of government or combinations thereof, and for such purposes to acquire, purchase, construct, own, maintain and/or operate water mains and trunk and connecting lines, water pumping and purification plants, sewers, sewage interceptors, sewage disposal plants, settling basins, screens and meters, and incinerators and disposal grounds; to authorize counties to establish, administer, coordinate and regulate a system or systems of water, sewer and/or sewage disposal improvements and services, and garbage and rubbish collection and disposal facilities and services, within or between such units of government; to provide methods for obtaining money for the aforesaid purposes; to authorize counties to extend by laterals and connections, and to construct, improve, repair, manage and/or operate water, sewer and/or sewage disposal improvements and garbage and rubbish collection and disposal facilities and services of and situated within such cities, villages, townships and township improvement districts or any duly authorized and established combination thereof, and provide for the loan of money to such units of government for said purposes and the repayment thereof by agreements therefor; to provide methods for collection of rates, charges and/or assessments.

MCLA 46.171 County water and sewage disposal systems, garbage and rubbish collection; establishment; definitions. [MSA 5.2767(1)]

Sec. 1. The board of supervisors of any county may, by resolution adopted by a majority vote of its members-elect at any regular or special session of said board, authorize and direct that there be established a system or systems of water, sewer and/or sewage disposal improvements and services and garbage and/or rubbish collection and disposal facilities and services within or between cities, villages, townships and township improvement districts, or any duly authorized and established combinations thereof, within or without the county, and mains, trunks, connecting lines and disposal facilities therefor. For such purposes the agency of the county hereinafter designated shall locate, acquire, purchase, construct, own, maintain and/or operate water mains and trunks and connecting lines, water pumping and purification plants, sewers, sewage interceptors, sewage disposal plants, settling basins, screens and meters, and incinerators and disposal grounds and facilities, as shall be described in maps, plans and specifications therefor and be approved by the board of supervisors and/or contract with any such units of government, or any duly authorized and established combinations thereof for the purchase of water and for the use of their sewers and sewage disposal plants and garbage and/or rubbish collection and disposal facilities and services. Any county is authorized to establish, construct, administer, coordinate and regulate systems for water, sewer and sewage disposal improvements and services within or between, and garbage and rubbish collection and disposal facilities and services for, such units of government.

The term "sewers" as used in this act shall be defined as including interceptor sewers for the transportation of either sewage or storm water or both sewage and storm water, storm sewers, sanitary sewers, combined sanitary and storm sewers and all instrumentalities, facilities and properties used or useful in connection with the collection of sewage and/or storm water.

The term "garbage and/or rubbish collection and disposal facilities" as used in this act shall be defined as including incinerators, disposal grounds and all instrumentalities, facilities and properties used or useful in connection with the collection and disposal of garbage and rubbish.

The term "unit of government" or "units of government" as used in this act, shall be defined as including cities, villages, townships, township improvement districts and any duly authorized and established combinations thereof within or without the county establishing any of the improvements, facilities or services authorized under this act.

The terms "improvements", "facilities" and "services" as used in this act shall mean any of the improvements, facilities and services authorized under the provisions of this section.

MCLA 46.171a Same; short title of act. [MSA 5.2767(1.1)]

MCLA 46.172 Same; contracts with and loans to governmental units. [MSA 5.2767(2)]

MCLA 46.173 County water, sewage disposal, garbage and rubbish collection service; county agency, designation, duties. [MSA 5.2767(3)]

MCLA 46.174 Rates, charges or assessments; determination; repair and replacement. [MSA 5.2767(4)]

MCLA 46.175 Agreements with governmental units for service; levy and collection of charges or assessments; lien, enforcement as tax. [MSA 5.2767(5)]

Sec. 5. The county agency and any unit of government may enter into agreements for a term up to but not exceeding 40 years whereby ...

MCLA 46.175a Alternative method of financing; contracts; taxation. [MSA 5.2767(5.1)]

Sec. 5a. As an additional or alternative method of acquiring and constructing any of the improvements or facilities authorized by this act, the county agency and any city, village or township are authorized to enter into contracts providing for the acquisition, construction and financing of improvements or facilities in the manner herein authorized. The contracts shall provide for the allocation *and payment of the share of the total cost thereof to be borne by each city, village or township in annual installments for a period of not exceeding 40 years, and each contracting city, village or township is authorized to pledge its full faith and credit for the payment of the obligation ...*

MCLA 46.175b Same; resolution, publication; petition, qualifications of signers; election; verification of signatures on petition; refunding of bonds, issuance and sale. [MSA 5.2767(5.2)]

MCLA 46.175c Same; bonds, issuance; advancement by county, reimbursement; terms; financing; validation of former drain orders or bonds. [MSA 5.2767(5.3)]

Sec. 5c. For the purpose of obtaining funds for the acquisition and construction of the improvements or facilities authorized by this act, the county after the execution of the contract or contracts authorized by sections 5a and 5b of this act, upon ordinance or resolution adopted by its board of supervisors, may issue its negotiable bonds secured by the full faith and credit pledges made by each contracting city, village and township pursuant to authorization contained in this act ...

MCLA 46.176 Board of review; hearing on charges; adjustment; meetings. [MSA 5.2767(6)]

MCLA 46.177 Self-liquidating revenue bonds; issuance; pledge of full faith and credit, referendum; permission of municipal finance commission. Sale of bonds; trust agreement. [MSA 5.2767(7)]

MCLA 46.178 Appropriations for expense; vote; revolving fund. [MSA 5.2767(8)]

MCLA 46.179 Loans to governmental units; provision for payment. [MSA 5.2767(9)]

MCLA 46.180 Approval of loans and expenditures by board of auditors. [MSA 5.2767(10)]

MCLA 46.181 Enforcement of collection of charges and loans. [MSA 5.2767(11)]

MCLA 46.182 Permit from legislative body of city or village not required. [MSA 5.2767(12)]

MCLA 46.183 Construction of act. [MSA 5.2767(13)]

Sec. 13. This act being necessary for and to secure the public health, safety and welfare of the counties, cities, villages, townships and township improvement districts of the state of Michigan, shall be liberally construed to effect the provisions hereof.

MCLA 46.184 Purchase or condemnation of property by county agency. [MSA 5.2767(14)]

MCLA 46.185 Act cumulative. [MSA 5.2767(15)]

Sec. 15. The authority hereby given shall be in addition to and not in derogation of any power existing in any of the counties, cities, villages and townships under any statutory or charter provisions which they may now have or may hereafter adopt.

MCLA 46.186 County water and sewage disposal systems; action on behalf of partially incorporated city; binding effect upon township. [MSA 5.2767(17)]

Sec. 16. Whenever all or any part of a township has been incorporated as a city and the incorporation of such city has not been completed by the adoption of a charter therefor, then the township board may act hereunder on behalf of both the city and the remainder of the township, either jointly or severally, and for the purposes of this act shall be deemed to be the governing body of such city as well as that of the township. ...

MCLA 46.187 Joint action by 2 adjoining counties; administrative agency; bonds. [MSA 4.2767(18)]

JOINT ACTION
Act No. 185, P.A. 1957 - County Department and Board of Public Works, Ch. 1 - General Provisions

AN ACT to authorize the establishing of a department and board of public works in counties; to prescribe the powers and duties of any county subject to the provisions of this act; to authorize the issuance and payment of bonds; and to prescribe a procedure for special assessments and condemnation.

MCLA 123.731 County public works; definitions. [MSA 5.570(1)]

MCLA 123.732 Department of public works; board of public works, powers, membership, tenure, appointment, vacancies, compensation. [MSA 5.570(2)]

MCLA 123.733 Same; officers. [MSA 5.570(3)]

MCLA 123.734 Same; meetings, record, quorum. [MSA 5.570(4)]

MCLA 123.735 Same; expenses, appropriation. [MSA 5.570(5)]

MCLA 123.736 Same; director; project costs; civil service. [MSA 5.570(6)]

MCLA 123.737 Same; powers. [MSA 5.570(7)]

Sec. 7. Any county establishing a department of public works shall have the following powers to be administered by the board of public works subject to any limitations thereon:
(a) To acquire a water supply system within any 1 or more areas in the county and to improve, enlarge, extend, operate and maintain such system.
(b) To acquire a sewage disposal system within any 1 or more areas in the county and to improve, enlarge, extend, operate and maintain such system.
(c) To acquire a refuse system within any 1 or more areas in the county and to improve, enlarge, extend, operate and maintain such system.
(d) To make lake improvements within any 1 or more areas in the county and to improve, enlarge, extend, operate and maintain such improvements.

MCLA 123.738 Water supply, sewage disposal, and refuse systems and lake improvements, outside county. [MSA 5.570(8)]

MCLA 123.739 Same; service to municipalities and individual users. [MSA 5.570(9)]

Sec. 9. No county shall have the power to furnish water service, sewage disposal service or refuse service to the individual users within any municipality without its consent. ...

MCLA 123.740 Approval of establishment of systems and of making of improvements, procedure, effect; merger of systems.
MSA 5.570(10)

MCLA 123.741 Same; methods of financing. Bonds, revenue, secured, special assessment; county advances. Bonds, authorization, full faith and credit, issuance, maturity, tax exemption, sale.
MSA 5.570(11)

MCLA 123.742 Contracts to acquire, improve, or enlarge systems or make lake improvements; payment. MSA 5.570(12)

MCLA 123.743 Project special assessment district; municipal special assessments. MSA 5.570(13)

MCLA 123.744 Acquisition of property for water supply, sewage disposal, and refuse systems and for lake improvements; disposal of property. MSA 5.570(14)

MCLA 123.745 Municipality service contract with county; county contracts. MSA 5.570(15)

MCLA 123.746 Project costs. MSA 5.570(16)

MCLA 123.747 Delinquency in payment by municipality; authorized deductions. MSA 5.570(17)

Ch. 2 - Special Assessment Procedure

MCLA 123.751 Special assessments for project. MSA 5.570(21)

MCLA 123.752 Same; plans, estimate of cost, designation of district, hearing on objections, notice, additions. MSA 5.570(22)

MCLA 123.753 Same; final determination of district; special assessment roll. MSA 5.570(23)

MCLA 123.754 Special assessments; confirmation of roll.

MCLA 123.755 Same; installment payment. MSA 5.570(25)

MCLA 123.756 Same; certification of amounts to be spread. MSA 5.570(26)

MCLA 123.757 Same; collection. MSA 5.570(27)

MCLA 123.758 Same; lien. MSA 5.570(28)

MCLA 123.759 Same; apportionment on division of parcels. MSA 5.570(29)

MCLA 123.760 Same; prorated deficiency or surplus of collection. MSA 5.570(30)

MCLA 123.761 Same; curative proceedings. MSA 5.570(31)

MCLA 123.762 Same; exempted lands; agreement to pay assessment. MSA 5.570(32)

Sec. 32. Any person, firm or corporation, public or private, whose lands are exempt by law from the payment of special assessments, may agree in writing to pay any special assessments against such lands, and in such case the assessment, including all the installments thereof, shall be a valid claim against such corporation.

MCLA 123.763 Delinquent special assessments; advancement by municipality; reimbursement; reassessment. MSA 5.570(33)

Ch. 3 - Condemnation Procedure

MCLA 123.771 Condemnation; authority. MSA 5.570(41)

MCLA 123.772 Same; declaration of necessity. MSA 5.570(42)

MCLA 123.773 Petition; contents. MSA 5.570(43)

MCLA 123.774 Same; court order for hearing. MSA 5.570(44)

MCLA 123.775 Same; publication of order; service on named defendants. [MSA 5.570(45)]

MCLA 123.776 Court commissioners; appointment; discontinuance of proceedings. [MSA 5.570(46)]

MCLA 123.777 Same; meeting, adjournments; view of premises. [MSA 5.570(47)]

MCLA 123.778 Same; determination of necessity, damages, report. [MSA 5.570(48)]

MCLA 123.779 Multiple petitions; descriptions. [MSA 5.570(49)]

MCLA 123.780 Report of court commissioners; court orders. [MSA 5.570(50)]

MCLA 123.781 Same; confirmation, orders for payment of witness fees, attorney fees, damages. [MSA 5.570(51)]

MCLA 123.782 Compensation of court commissioners, expenses. [MSA 5.570(52)]

MCLA 123.783 Review by certiorari; procedure; time limitation. [MSA 5.570(53)]

MCLA 123.784 Court orders, service. [MSA 5.570(54)]

MCLA 123.785 Prima facie evidence of ownership. [MSA 5.570(55)]

MCLA 123.786 Lis pendens, filing. [MSA 5.570(56)]

JOINT ACTION
Act No. 116, P.A. 1923 - Township and Village Public Improvement Act

AN ACT to authorize improvements in and for lands in townships or waters, adjacent or contiguous thereto, by constructing bridges over natural or artificial waterways, grading, paving, curbing, stoning, graveling, macadamizing or cinderizing streets, laying storm sewers to care for surface water in such streets, destroying weeds, pro-

viding street markers and lighting, contracting for public transportation facilities, providing police protection or contracting therefor, establishing and maintaining garbage systems or plants for the collection and disposal of garbage or contracting therefor, constructing or acquiring and maintaining sanitary sewers and sewage disposal plants, constructing filtration plants, constructing sidewalks, purchasing or constructing waterworks, purchasing or contracting for fire apparatus and equipment, constructing and maintaining housing facilities for fire apparatus and equipment, making extension of water mains to provide water for fire protection and domestic uses, for the trimming and spraying of trees and shrubbery, and constructing breakwaters, retaining walls or sea walls, or any combination of the foregoing for beach and soil erosion control, providing for the suppression of swimmers' itch and other aquatic nuisance-producing organisms; to provide for making, levying and collecting of special assessments to pay the cost thereof, and to issue special assessment bonds in anticipation of the collection of such special assessment taxes to provide the money with which to pay the cost of such improvements, and advance the amount necessary to pay such bonds and reimburse the township for such advances, and if necessary thereto to reassess the district.

MCLA 41.411   Public improvements in townships and villages; authority of board of council; special assessments, bonds. [MSA 5.2411]

Sec. 1. In any township lands, the township board or common council or board of trustees of an incorporated village shall have the authority to make improvements and provide public service by constructing bridges over natural or artificial waterways, grading, paving, curbing, stoning, graveling, macadamizing or cinderizing streets, or to treat the streets with chloride or other suitable dust laying process or material, laying storm sewers to care for surface water in such streets, destroying weeds, providing street markers and lighting, contracting for public transportation facilities, providing police protection or contracting therefor, establishing and maintaining garbage and mixed refuse systems or plants for the collection and disposal of garbage and mixed refuse or contracting for such collection and disposal for not to exceed 30 years, construct-

ing or acquiring and maintaining sanitary sewers and sewerage disposal plants or equipment, constructing filtration plants, constructing sidewalks, purchasing or constructing waterworks, purchasing fire apparatus and equipment, constructing and maintaining housing facilities for fire apparatus and equipment, making extension of water mains to provide water for fire protection and domestic uses, for the trimming and spraying of trees and shrubbery, to provide and maintain soil and beach erosion control measures including, but not limited to, the construction of breakwaters, retaining walls or sea walls, or any combination of the foregoing, in or for any such lands or waters adjacent or contiguous thereto, to establish and conduct chemical beach treatment service necessary to the control of aquatic nuisances such as swimmers' itch or to contract with others to provide said services; to levy and collect special assessments to pay the cost thereof and to issue bonds in anticipation of the collection of said special assessments, upon filing the petition and subject to the terms and conditions hereinafter provided. In incorporated villages, the common council or board of trustees thereof shall be vested with and shall perform the powers and duties vested in the township board in areas outside incorporated villages.

Condemnation proceedings. *The township board or common council or board of trustees of any incorporated village may purchase, accept by gift or device (devise), or condemn private property. If by condemnation, the provisions of Act No. 149 of the Public Acts of 1911, as amended, being sections 213.21 to 213.41* **(MCLA 213.21 to 213.41 -** MSA 8.11 TO 8.31) *of the Compiled Laws of 1948, or such other appropriate provisions thereof as exist or shall be made by law, may be adopted and used for the purpose of instituting and prosecuting such condemnation proceedings.*

Short title. *This act shall be known and may be cited as the "township and village public improvement act."*

MCLA 41.412 Special assessment district, procedure for establishment or enlargement; petitions, signers. MSA 5.2412

MCLA 41.413 Improvement of platted lands; conditions precedent; issuance of bonds; assessment proceedings; deficiency; full faith and credit of township may be pledged. MSA 5.2413

MCLA 41.413a Waterworks; board of commissioners; election; terms. MSA 5.2413A

Sec. 3a. Any waterworks established under the provisions of this act, and any other service provided hereunder for a district having a waterworks, shall be under the control of and operated by a board of public service commissioners: Provided, That in incorporated villages such improvements or service shall be under the control of and operated by the common council or board of trustees of any said incorporated village. Said district board shall consist of 5 commissioners to be elected at the annual township election by the qualified electors residing in the district. ...

MCLA 41.413b Lighting special assessments, basis. [MSA 5.2413B]

MCLA 41.414 Special assessment installments; limitations, collection; appeal; district or village maintaining waterworks. [MSA 5.2414]

MCLA 41.415 Improvements in platted lands in townships and villages; special assessments on corner lots, portion payable by township. [MSA 5.2415]

Sec. 5. The governing body of any township, by resolution, may agree to pay up to 1/3 of the cost of the special assessments levied against any platted corner lot for the payment of public improvements authorized under the provisions of this act.

JOINT ACTION
Act No. 8, P.A. 1967, Ex. Sess. - Transfers of Functions and Responsibilities

AN ACT to provide for intergovernmental transfers of functions and responsibilities.

MCLA 124.531 Definitions. [MSA 5.4087(1)]

MCLA 124.532 Authority to contract for transfer of functions or responsibilities. [MSA 5.4087(2)]

Sec. 2. Two or more political subdivisions are authorized to enter into a contract with each other providing for the transfer of functions or responsibilities to one another or any combination thereof upon the consent of each political subdivision involved.

MCLA 124.533 Prerequisites to valid contract. MSA 5.4087(3)

MCLA 124.534 Contents of contract. MSA 5.4087(4)

MCLA 124.535 Joint board or commission; establishment; duty; membership. MSA 5.4087(5)

Sec. 5. A joint board or commission may be established by the political subdivisions involved to supervise the execution of a contract. An officer or employee of the state or a political subdivision or agency thereof, except a member of the legislature, may serve on or with any joint board or commission created by the contract and shall not be required to relinquish his office or employment by reason of such service.

MCLA 124.536 Amendment or termination of contract. MSA 5.4087(6)

JOINT ACTION
Act No. 188, P.A. 1954 - Public Improvements

AN ACT to provide for the making of certain public improvements by townships; to provide for assessing the whole or a part of the cost thereof against property benefited; and to provide for the issuance of bonds in anticipation of the collection of such special assessments, and for the obligation of the township thereon.

MCLA 41.721 Public improvements by townships; special assessment; cost. MSA 5.2770(51)

Sec. 1. The township board shall have the power to make the hereinafter named improvements and to determine that the whole or any part of the cost thereof shall be defrayed by special assessments against the property especially benefited thereby. The cost of engineering services, all expenses incident to the proceedings for the making of the improvement and the financing thereof, and not to exceed 1 year's interest on any bonds to be issued hereunder, shall be deemed to be a part of the cost of the improvement.

315

MCLA 41.722 Same; sewers, water mains, highways, sidewalks, parks, trees, elevated structures for foot travel, collection of garbage and rubbish; costs. [MSA 5.2770(52)]

Sec. 2. *The following improvements may be made under this act: (1) The construction and maintenance of sewers; (2) the construction of water mains; (3) the improvements of public highways by grading, graveling, paving, curbing or draining the same or constructing driveway approaches or sidewalks thereon; (4) the maintenance and improvement of parks or the trimming and spraying of trees; (5) the installation of elevated structures for foot travel over highways in the township; and (6) the collection of garbage and rubbish. No highway under the jurisdiction of either the state highway commissioner or the board of county road commissioners shall be improved under the provisions of this act without the written approval of the state highway commissioner or the board of county road commissioners. As a condition to the granting of such approval, the state highway commissioner or the board of county road commissioners may require that all engineering with respect to such improvement be performed by, and that all construction including the awarding of contracts therefor in connection with such improvement be under the supervision of and in accordance with the specifications of, the state highway commissioner or the board of county road commissioners and that the cost of such engineering and supervision be paid to the state highway commissioner or the board of county road commissioners from the funds of the special assessment district.*

MCLA 41.723 Same; petition, filing, names, qualifications; powers of township board. [MSA 5.2770(53)]

Sec. 3. *No improvement shall be made hereunder unless a petition shall be filed with the township board, signed as follows: (a) In case of highway improvements, by the record owners of lands whose frontage constitutes at least 65% of the total frontage upon the highway improvements; and (b) in case of water mains or sewers, by record owners of lands constituting at least 51% of the total land area in the special assessment district as finally thereafter established by the township board. In any township with a population in excess of 5,000, after notification by mail to the owners of lands whose names appear on the latest tax roll, no petition shall be required for water mains or sewers and the township*

316

board may exercise the powers granted by this act on its own initiative in accordance with the provisions of this act, except as they relate to a petition or action with reference thereto, but no such improvement shall be made without petition if the record owners of land constituting more than 20% of the total land area in the special assessment district file their written objections thereto with the township board at or prior to the hearing described in section 4 of this act. Record owners shall be determined as of the records in the register of deeds' office on the day of the filing of the petition, or in case written objections are filed as above provided, then on the day of the hearing. In determining the sufficiency of the petition, lands not subject to special assessment and lands within public highway and alleys shall not be included in computing frontage or assessment district area. Any filed petition may be supplemented as to signatures by the filing of an additional signed copy or copies thereof, and in such case the validity of the signatures thereon shall be determined by said records on the day of filing the supplemental petition.

MCLA 41.724 Same; plans, estimate of cost, filing; hearing, notice, place; increase in cost; supplemental petition; railroad companies, filing paper with secretary of state, contents. MSA 5.2770(54)

Sec. 4. Upon receipt of such a petition, the township board, if it desires to proceed on the petition, shall cause to be prepared by a registered engineer, plans showing the improvement and the location thereof and an estimate of the cost thereof. Upon receipt of such plans and estimate, the township board shall order the same to be filed with the township clerk, and if it shall desire to proceed further with the improvement it shall by resolution tentatively declare its intention to make such improvement and tentatively designate the special assessment district against which the cost of said improvement is to be assessed. The township board shall then fix a time and place when and where it will meet and hear any objections to the petition, to the improvement and to the special assessment district therefor, and shall cause notice of such hearing to be given by the publication thereof twice prior to such hearing in a newspaper circulating in the township, the first publication to be at least 10 days prior to the time of the hearing. Such notice shall state that the plans and estimates are on file with the township clerk for public examination and shall contain a description of the proposed special assessment district. At the time of such hearing, or any adjournment thereof which may be without further notice, the township board shall hear any objections to the petition, to the improvement, and to the special assessment district, and may revise, correct, amend or change the plans, estimate of cost and/or special assessment district: Provided, That no property shall be added to the district nor any increase in the estimate of cost in excess of 10% of the original estimate of cost be made unless notice be given as above provided, or by personal service upon the owners of the property in the entire proposed special assessment district and a hearing afforded to such owners. If property shall be added to the special assessment district and the original petition be insufficient because of said added property, then a supplemental petition shall be filed containing additional names. Railroad companies shall file with the secretary of state a paper stating the name and post-office address of the person upon whom may be served notice of any proceedings under this act, and when such paper has been so filed, notice in addition to the notice by publication shall be given to such person by registered mail, or personally, within 5 days after the first publication of such notice. An affidavit of such service shall be filed by the township board with the proof of publication of such notice.

MCLA 41.725 Same; resolution of board; approval of plans and estimate; special assessment roll, contents, certificate affixed.
MSA 4.2770(55)

Sec. 5. After the hearing provided for in the preceding section, if the township board then desires to proceed with the improvement, it shall by resolution determine to make the same and shall approve the plans and estimate of cost as originally presented or as revised, corrected, amended or changed, and shall also determine the sufficiency of the petition for the improvement. After such determination, the sufficiency of the petition shall not thereafter be subject to attack except in an action brought in a court of competent jurisdiction within 30 days after the adoption of the resolution determining such sufficiency. The township board after finally determining the special assessment district shall direct the supervisor to make a special assessment roll in which shall be entered and described all the parcels of land to be assessed, with the names of the respective owners thereof, if known, and the total amount to be assessed against each parcel of land, which amount shall be such relative portion of the whole sum to be levied against all parcels of

318

land in the special assessment district as the benefit to such parcel of land bears to the total benefit to all parcels of land in the special assessment district. When the supervisor shall have completed the assessment roll, he shall affix thereto his certificate stating that it was made pursuant to a resolution of the township board adopted on a specified date, and that in making such assessment roll he has according to his best judgment conformed in all respects to the directions contained in such resolution and the statutes of the state of Michigan.

MCLA 41.726 Same; assessment roll, filing, review, notice, publication; adjournment of hearing; confirmation. [MSA 5.2770(56)]

MCLA 41.727 Same; payment, installments, delinquency. [MSA 5.2770(57)]

MCLA 41.728 Same; assessment to constitute lien upon parcels of land. [MSA 5.2770(58)]

MCLA 41.729 Same; collection of assessments, warrant, statement of persons delinquent. [MSA 5.2770(59)]

MCLA 41.730 Same; reassessments. [MSA 5.2770(60)]

MCLA 41.731 Same; parcels, division; apportionment of uncollected amounts. [MSA 5.2770(61)]

MCLA 41.732 Same; additional assessment; refunds. [MSA 5.2770(62)]

MCLA 41.733 Same; illegal assessment, procedure in case of. [MSA 5.2770(63)]

MCLA 41.734 Same; corporations, agreement to pay assessment. [MSA 5.2770(64)]

Sec. 14. The governing body of any public or private corporation whose lands are exempt by law may, by resolution, agree to pay the special assessments against such lands, and in such case the assessment, including all the installments thereof, shall be a valid claim against such corporation.

MCLA 41.734a   Same; assessments against platted corner lots.
MSA 5.2770(64A)

Sec. 14a. The governing body of any township, by resolution, may agree to pay up to 1/3 of the cost of the special assessment levied against any platted corner lot for the payment of public improvements authorized under the provisions of this act.

MCLA 41.735   Same; bonds, issuance, interest, execution.   MSA 5.2770(65)

Sec. 15. The township board may borrow money and issue the bonds of the township therefor in anticipation of the collection of special assessments to defray the cost of any improvement made under this act after the special assessment roll therefor shall have been confirmed.   Such bonds shall not exceed the amount of the special assessments in anticipation of the collection of which they are issued, and shall bear interest at a rate not exceeding 5% per annum.   Collections on special assessments to the extent the same are pledged for the payment of bonds shall be set aside in a special fund for the payment of such bonds.   The issuance of special assessment bonds shall be governed by the provisions of the general laws of the state applicable thereto.   Bonds may be issued in anticipation of the collection of special assessments levied in respect to 2 or more public improvements, but no special assessment district shall be compelled to pay the obligation of any other special assessment district.   The township board may pledge the full faith and credit of the township for the prompt payment of the principal of and interest on the bonds authorized herein, as the same shall become due.   Bonds issued hereunder shall be executed by the supervisor and township clerk and the interest coupons to be attached thereto shall be executed by said officials causing their facsimile signatures to be affixed thereto.

MCLA 41.735a   Same; revolving fund, advancements, interest.
MSA 5.2770(65A)

Sec. 15a. The township board as an alternate method of defraying the cost of any improvement made under the provisions of this act, after the special assessment roll therefor shall have been confirmed, may pay the cost of the improvement from the township improvement revolving fund. The amount shall not exceed the amount the board anticipates will be collected by the special assessments. *The amount so advanced by the township shall bear interest at a rate not exceeding 5% per annum.*

MCLA 41.735b Township improvement revolving fund; creation; transfers of funds. [MSA 5.2770(65B)]

Sec. 15b. The township board of any township by resolution may create and designate a fund to be known as the township improvement revolving fund and thereafter may transfer to such fund from the general fund of the township in any one year an amount not exceeding 2 mills of the state equalized valuation of the real and personal property in the township and thereafter may each year transfer from the general fund to the township improvement revolving fund until such fund shall be equal to 5 mills of the state equalized valuation of the real and personal property in the township. All interest charges collected shall become a part of such fund and the township board may transfer from the township improvement revolving fund to the general fund such sum or sums and at such time or times as in the judgment of the board should be transferred.

MCLA 41.736 Public improvements by townships; powers granted. [MSA 5.2770(66)]

Sec. 16. The powers herein granted may be exercised by any township and shall be in addition to the powers granted by any other statute.

MCLA 41.737 Same; scope of act. [MSA 5.2770(67)]

Sec. 17. The provisions of this act shall not apply to any obligations issued or assessments levied except in accordance with the provisions of this act after the effective date thereof, and shall not validate any proceedings or action taken by any township prior to the effective date of this act.

JOINT ACTION
Act No. 312, P.A. 1929 - Metropolitan Districts

AN ACT to provide for the incorporation by any 2 or more cities, villages or townships, or any combination or parts of same, of a metropolitan district or districts comprising territory within their limits for the purpose of acquiring, owning and operating, either within or without their limits as may be prescribed herein, parks or public utilities for supplying sewage disposal, drainage, water, or transportation, or any combination thereof; to provide that any such district may sell or purchase, either within or without its limits as provided herein, sewage disposal, drainage rights, water, or transportation facilities; to provide that any such district shall have power to acquire and succeed to any or all of the rights, obligations and property of such cities, villages and townships respecting or connected with such functions or public utilities but subject to the approval thereof by a majority vote of the electors thereof voting thereon; to limit the rate of taxation of such districts for their municipal purposes and restrict their powers of borrowing money and contracting debts; to provide the method and vote by which charters may be framed, adopted and amended and laws and ordinances relating to its municipal concerns may be enacted and to define the powers, rights and liabilities of any such district.

MCLA 119.1 Metropolitan districts; purposes; body corporate.
[MSA 5.2131]

Sec. 1. Any 2 or more cities, villages or townships or any combination or parts thereof, may incorporate into a metropolitan district or districts comprising territory within their respective limits for the purpose of acquiring, owning, operating and maintaining either within or without their limits, as may be established hereunder, parks or public utilities for supplying sewage disposal, drainage, water or transportation or any combination thereof. Each organized district hereunder shall be a body corporate.

MCLA 119.1a "Metropolitan district act"; short title.
[MSA 5.2131(1)]

MCLA 119.2 Same; powers; referendum. [MSA 5.2132]

MCLA 119.3 Mandatory charter provisions. District officers. Offi-

322

cers; records; taxation. Sinking fund. Taxation subjects.
[MSA 5.2133]

MCLA 119.4 Permissive charter provisions. Taxes. Borrowing power; bonds; sinking fund. Improvements. Rents, tolls, excises. Public utility, cost. Franchises, public utility, acquisition; contract; referendum; sinking fund. Condemnation. Initiative, referendum, recall. Charter changes. Regulations, enforcement. Civil service. Business powers; acquisition of rapid transit company. [MSA 5.2134]

MCLA 119.5 Restrictions. Salary, term of office, change in. Referendum, failure. Contract with defaulter. Bonds. Debts. [MSA 5.2135]

MCLA 119.6 Proceedings for incorporation; commission to prepare budget. [MSA 5.2136]

Sec. 6. Proceedings for the incorporation of metropolitan districts shall be originated as follows: Any city, village or township may, by a resolution adopted by its legislative body, have prepared a description in general terms of the district proposed to be included in a metropolitan district. Each city, village or township desiring to become a part of said district shall thereupon by appropriate resolution of its legislative body indicate its desire to become a part of same. ...

MCLA 119.7 Charter commission, powers, duties; election. [MSA 5.2137]

MCLA 119.8 Charter rejected; unfavorable vote, charter provision; resubmission proceedings. [MSA 5.2138]

MCLA 119.9 Charter amendment; proceedings, form. [MSA 5.2139]

MCLA 119.10 Same; submission to governor. [MSA 5.2140]

MCLA 119.11 Charter or amendment; publication; independent propositions, authorizing vote. [MSA 5.2141]

MCLA 119.12 Same; copies, filing. [MSA 5.2142]

MCLA 119.13 Initiatory petition, filing; checking; submission to voters; insufficiency. [MSA 5.2143]

MCLA 119.15 Short title. [MSA 5.2145]

ACQUIRING PROPERTY FOR PUBLIC USE

Townships are included in a number of statutes which permit units of government to acquire property for public use. Some of the citations which follow also permit the acquisition to be accomplished for a joint purpose, such as land for hospitals, colleges, universities, etc., to be owned and operated by a number of municipalities, agencies, boards and/or commissions.

JOINT ACTION
Act No. 295, P.A. 1966 — Property for Public Highway Purposes

AN ACT to provide for the purchase and condemnation of property for public purposes by cities, villages, townships, counties, boards of county road commissions and the state highway commission.

MCLA 213.361 Cities, villages, townships, counties, boards of county road commissions, and state highway commission; property subject to acquisition. [MSA 8.261(1)]

MCLA 213.362 Taking of street or highway as prerequisite to proceedings under act; consent of village or city council. [MSA 8.261(2)]

MCLA 213.363 Manner of securing property; fluid mineral and gas rights; recordation of instruments. [MSA 8.261(3)]

MCLA 213.364 Manner of payment for property. [MSA 8.261(4)]

MCLA 213.365 Scope and extent of right to acquire property. [MSA 8.261(5)]

324

MCLA 213.366 Petition for acquisition of property; time and place of filing; contents; statement of estimated compensation; service. [MSA 8.261(6)]

MCLA 213.367 Declaration of taking. [MSA 8.261(7)]

MCLA 213.368 Motion to review necessity of taking; notice; hearing; appeal. [MSA 8.261(8)]

MCLA 213.369 Vesting of title in petitioner; recordation of copy of declaration of taking; securing compensation. [MSA 8.261(9)]

MCLA 213.370 Order to pay money deposited. [MSA 8.261(10)]

MCLA 213.371 Time and terms for surrender of property to petitioner; enforcement. [MSA 8.261(11)]

MCLA 213.372 Appointment of guardian ad litem for minor, insane or incompetent respondents. [MSA 8.261(12)]

MCLA 213.373 Order for hearing; contents; publication; service and mailing; proof by affidavit. [MSA 8.261(13)]

MCLA 213.374 Default judgment. [MSA 8.261(14)]

MCLA 213.375 Impanelling of jury; waiver of jury trial. [MSA 8.261(15)]

MCLA 213.376 Peremptory challenges; practice and procedure relating to impanelling, summoning and excusing jurors, etc. [MSA 8.261(16)]

MCLA 213.377 Oath or affirmance of jurors; duty, instructions, verdict. [MSA 8.261(17)]

MCLA 213.378 Award; division among respective parties in interest. [MSA 8.261(18)]

MCLA 213.379 Use of exhibits by jury; submission of blank verdict. [MSA 8.261(19)]

MCLA 213.380 Amendments in pleadings and proceedings.
[MSA 8.261(20)]

MCLA 213.381 Judgment of court; motion for new trial or appeal; interest. [MSA 8.261(21)]

MCLA 213.382 Transmittal of certified copies of verdict, judgment of confirmation and orders confirming judgment to petitioner; resolution directing payment; entry into possession. [MSA 8.261(22)]

MCLA 213.383 Witness fees; attorney fees. [MSA 8.261(23)]

MCLA 213.384 Evidence of ownership and interest in property. [MSA 8.261(24)]

MCLA 213.385 Notice of filing petition; recordation; constructive notice to purchaser of real estate. [MSA 8.261(25)]

MCLA 213.386 Constructive notice to purchaser of personalty; filing of statement. [MSA 8.261(26)]

MCLA 213.387 Lease or sale of property acquired; record. [MSA 8.261(27)]

MCLA 213.388 Enhancement in value of remainder of parcel; benefits; deduction in determining compensation. [MSA 8.261(28)]

MCLA 213.389 Date of valuation. [MSA 8.261(29)]

MCLA 213.390 Discontinuance of proceedings. [MSA 8.261(30)]

MCLA 213.391 Savings clause. [MSA 8.261(31)]

Sec. 31. This act does not directly or by implication repeal or amend any other condemnation act or part thereof.

Act No. 140, P.A. 1945 — Overhead and Underground Rights

AN ACT to provide for the acquisition of overhead and underground rights, and rights of access, air, view and light by public corporations, authorities or agencies of this state for the laying out, establishment or development of public streets and highways.

MCLA 213.251 Overhead and underground rights, acquisition; purposes. [MSA 8.251]

Act No. 190, P.A. 1929 – Boulevard, Street or Alley

AN ACT to authorize municipalities to purchase or condemn the fee to real estate to be used for acquiring, opening or widening of any boulevard, street or alley within such municipality and authorizing such municipalities to purchase or condemn the fee to private property adjacent to such proposed improvement whenever it is necessary to take such adjacent private property in order to carry out such proposed improvement most advantageously, and authorizing such municipalities to lease or sell any such real estate so taken after the proposed improvement is completed and which is not needed directly for such boulevards, streets or alleys.

MCLA 213.221 Boulevard, street, alley; acquisition of fee of adjacent property. [MSA 8.211]

MCLA 213.222 Condemnation proceedings. [MSA 8.212]

MCLA 213.223 Sale of unused portion. [MSA 8.213]

Act No. 352, P.A. 1925 – Private Property for Highway Purposes

AN ACT to provide for the purchase and condemnation of private property for public highway purposes.

MCLA 213.171 Acquisition of property by county road commissioners or state highway commissioner; approval of required officials. [MSA 8.171]

Note: This section spells out the types of property and various uses to which it may be put.

MCLA 213.172 County and trunk line highway land; conveyances, name, fluid mineral and gas rights, recording. [MSA 8.172]

MCLA 213.173 — 213.192 [MSA 8.173 — 8.193]

Note: These sections cover procedures.

MCLA 213.193 Right to acquire property of municipalities and cemetery associations; exchange. [MSA 8.194]

MCLA 213.194 Sale of excess land; conveyance; record. [MSA 8.195]

MCLA 213.197 — 213.199 [MSA 8.198 — 8.200]

Note: More procedures.

Act No. 288, P.A. 1957 — Taking Property of Public Hospital, College, or University

AN ACT to prescribe procedure for taking property of a public hospital or public college or public university for public use.

MCLA 213.301 Condemnation of property of public hospital, college or university for public use; definitions. [MSA 8.40(1)]

MCLA 213.302 Same; determination of relative necessity. [MSA 8.40(2)]

MCLA 213.303 Same; judicial determination. [MSA 8.40(3)]

MCLA 213.304 Same; abatement of pending proceedings. [MSA 8.40(4)]

Act No. 119, P.A. 1919 — Water, Light, Heat, Power or Transportation in Cities

AN ACT to authorize any city having a population of 25,000 or more to take for public use the absolute title in fee to any public utility for supplying water, light, heat, power or transportation to the municipality and the inhabitants thereof within or **without its corporate limits.**

MCLA 213.111 Cities, authority to take over public utilities. [MSA 8.71]

MCLA 213.112 — 213.134 [MSA 8.72 — 8.94]

Act No. 379, P.A. 1927 — Service on Unknown Owners or Claimants

AN ACT to provide for service of process or notice on unknown owners or claimants to land in condemnation proceedings.

MCLA 213.261 Condemnation; service of process on unknown claimants. [MSA 8.221]

Act No. 207, P.A. 1965 — Proration of General Taxes on Property Acquired for Public Purposes

AN ACT to provide for the proration of general taxes on real property acquired for public purposes.

MCLA 213.311 Dates of proration. [MSA 7.679(1)]

MCLA 213.312 Taxes to be prorated. [MSA 7.679(2)]

Note: Act No. 288, P.A. 1966, section 1, amends section 211.2 [MSA 7.2] of the Compiled Laws by adding a paragraph relating to the proration of taxes. The 1966 Act does not refer specifically to sections 213.311 and 213.312 but the added paragraph provides that taxes shall be prorated in accordance therewith "Notwithstanding any provision to the contrary in any law".

Act No. 270, P.A. 1931 — Condemnation Awards, Delinquent Taxes

AN ACT to provide for the application of awards in condemnation proceedings against taxes and/or special assessments, and to prescribe the effect thereof.

MCLA 213.291 Condemnation awards; application to payment of taxes and special assessments. [MSA 8.231]

Act No. 260, P.A. 1931 — Governmental Unit Purchases, Delinquent Tax Lands

AN ACT to authorize counties, cities, villages, townships, school districts and drainage districts to purchase land sold for delinquent taxes and drain assessments.

MCLA 211.421 Lands sold for delinquent taxes and drain assessments, purchase by governmental units. [MSA 7.941]

Sec. 1. The governing body of a ... township, school district or drainage district may appropriate money and purchase lands at the statutory sale of lands for delinquent tax assessments. In case of the purchase of such lands such governing body may also appropriate money and purchase the same lands, if they are tax delinquent, at the statutory sale of lands by county treasurers for delinquent general property taxes, it being the intent of this act to afford protection to the investment that any such local governmental unit may have in drains.

JOINT ACTION
Act No. 227, P.A. 1972 — Persons Displaced From Realty by State Agencies, Financial Assistance, Advisory Services, Expense Reimbursement

AN ACT to provide financial assistance, advisory services and reimbursement of certain expenses to persons displaced from real property or deprived of certain rights in real property; and to repeal certain acts and parts of acts.

MCLA 213.321 Definitions. [MSA 8.215(61)]

MCLA 213.322 Relocation assistance advisory services for displaced persons and occupants of land adjoining acquired land. [MSA 8.215(62)]

MCLA 213.323 Contents of relocation assistance advisory services programs; replacement dwellings, existence as prerequisite to required relocation; notice to vacate. [MSA 8.215(63)]

MCLA 213.324 Matching federal funds; financial assistance; expense reimbursement. [MSA 8.215(64)]

MCLA 213.325 Payment of cost, financial assistance, and expense reimbursement in absence of federal funds (by state). [MSA 8.215(65)]

MCLA 213.326 Displaced persons, definition, financial assistance. [MSA 8.215(66)]

MCLA 213.327 Ordinances or rules of state agencies, necessity, objectives. [MSA 8.215(67)]

MCLA 213.328 Financial assistance and reimbursements additional to compensation for property; payments to displaced persons, income, resources (not taxable). [MSA 8.215(68)]

MCLA 213.329 Review (by circuit court). [MSA 8.215(69)]

MCLA 213.330 Contracts, state agencies. [MSA 8.215(70)]

MCLA 213.331 Repeals. [MSA 8.215(71)]

MCLA 213.332 Effective date. [MSA 8.215(72)]

AFFECTS JOINT ACTION
Act No. 40, P.A. 1965 — Allowances for Expense of Moving Personalty from Condemned Realty

AN ACT to authorize and require public agencies to pay allowances for the expense of moving personal property from real property acquired for public purposes.

MCLA 213.351 Definitions. [MSA 8.214(1)]

MCLA 213.352 Conditions. [MSA 8.214(2)]

MCLA 213.353 Payments in accordance with applicable regulations for federal reimbursement. [MSA 8.214(3)]

MCLA 213.354 Highway projects. [MSA 8.214(4)]

MCLA 213.355 Moving allowances; independent of compensation for realty. [MSA 8.214(5)]

JOINT ACTION
Act No. 270, P.A. 1968 — Base Closure Committee

AN ACT to authorize counties in which are located military installations declared surplus by the United States to create a base closure committee; and to prescribe the membership, powers and duties of a base closure committee.

MCLA 46.271 Base closure committee; appointment; purpose. [MSA 5.1193(51)]

Sec. 1. ... committee to effect an orderly and expedient transition of the military installation from military operations to civilian activities and to establish criteria of use and employment, liaison, coordination of effort and implementation of procedures and fiscal matters by and between local units, federal and state agencies, civic organizations and the public as provided in this act.

MCLA 46.272 — 46.274 [MSA 5.1193(52) — 5.1193(54)]

MCLA 46.275 Base closure committee; duties. [MSA 5.1193(55)]

MCLA 46.276 Base closure committee; maintenance contracts with department of defense. [MSA 5.1193(56)]

MCLA 46.277 Base closure committee; recommendations to board of supervisors, acquisition of property, actions to expedite development or utilization of properties, matters incident to disposition of properties. [MSA 5.1193(57)]

MCLA 46.278 Base closure committee; report. [MSA 5.1193(58)]

MCLA 46.279 Base closure committee; actions by board of supervisors not in conflict with act validated. [MSA 5.1193(59)]

MCLA 46.280 Base closure committee; function until conversion of

military installation to civilian use or reactivation; dissolution. [MSA 5.1193(60)]

MCLA 46.281 Counties not affected by this act. [MSA 5.1193(61)]

JOINT ACTION
Act No. 150, P.A. 1967 — Michigan Military Act

CHAPTER 6. MILITARY FACILITIES

MCLA 32.750 Armories. [MSA 4.678(350)]

MCLA 32.752 Acquisition, construction, operation, control of military facilities, funds, operation and control policies. [MSA 4.678(352)]

Sec. 352. ... the adjutant general ... shall apply to the legislature, local units of government or the federal government for funds to acquire, construct, lease and equip armories and other military facilities.

MCLA 32.754 — 32.766 [MSA 4.678(354) — 4.678(366)]

MCLA 32.768 Gifts to provide for armories and training areas, acceptance; execution of deeds. [MSA 4.678(368)]

MCLA 21.772 Title to realty used for military purposes. [MSA 4.678(372)]

MCLA 21.774 Condemnation of property, armory building sites, military training areas. [MSA 4.678(374)]

MCLA 32.776 Easements, realty controlled by state military establishments; public utilities. [MSA 4.678(376)]

MCLA 32.778 Exchange of proposed armory erection sites. [MSA 4.678(378)]

MCLA 32.780 Local zoning and building ordinances, applicability. [MSA 4.678(380)]

Sec. 380. State-owned or leased armories and accessory buildings, military warehouses, arsenals and storage facilities for military equipment, and lands and appurtenances required for the construction of armories or buildings, are not subject to zoning or building ordinances of any local government. The state military board shall take cognizance of local zoning ordinances and restrictions in the selection and acceptance of lands for armory or other military buildings and shall conform as nearly as possible to master plans of the local governments where it may be done without impairing the convenience and usefulness of the armories and buildings.

MCLA 32.782 — 32.790 [MSA 4.678(382) — 4.678(390)]

WATER, SEWAGE, GARBAGE AND SOLID WASTE COLLECTION AND DISPOSAL

In the development of services and utilities, almost inevitably the number one priority is assigned to water and sanitary and storm sewers, with collection and disposal of garbage and solid waste closely related. Thus it is that this group of citations has been given number one place in this chapter.

Without water all life would come to an end. In the seventeenth, eighteenth and nineteenth centuries Americans found clear, unpolluted water in great abundance in every part of the nation. Except for the deserts in the southwestern part of the United States and some other arid or dry areas, water could be found in unlimited amounts through a number of delivery systems, starting with the simple use of a bucket to draw it from a stream or river to the more sophisticated, generally shallow hand pump well.

As the population increased, society became more complex. Industry developed to meet demands of the people for supplies and services. This, along with the increase in human wastes, polluted much of the surface water of the nation, making it necessary to obtain water through use of deep well systems, reservoirs and filtration plants, where sophisticated machinery purifies polluted water into reasonably acceptable condition for human consumption.

The statutes following present township boards with unlimited authority and capability to provide water for township citizens. Each should be carefully weighed to determine which will give the most efficient and economical delivery system. Note that many of

334

them permit the township board to negotiate contracts with other units of government or participate in joint authorities to bring water to a number of municipalities. It is strongly recommended that the board encourage citizens to become involved in study and advisory committees for the choice of a system which will be readily acceptable to all of the people in the township.

JOINT ACTION
Act No. 6, P.A. 1956, Ex. Sess. - Township Water Systems

AN ACT authorizing the formation of corporations for the purpose of supplying to, distributing and selling water to a township or townships and giving to such corporations rights to take water from the Great Lakes, Lake St. Clair, and the bays thereof; authorizing a township or townships to contract with such corporations for the purchase of water by said township or townships and authorizing any township to purchase waterworks, systems, installations and real or personal property of such corporations, and authorizing such township or townships to pass ordinances with respect thereto.

MCLA 486.501 Corporations to supply water to townships; incorporation. [MSA 5.2535(1)]

MCLA 486.502 Same; contracts; use of highways for mains, consent. [MSA 5.2535(2)]

MCLA 486.503 Great Lakes waters; intakes. [MSA 5.2535(3)]

MCLA 486.504 Townships; contracts, ordinances, (public) hearing. [MSA 5.2535(4)]

MCLA 486.505 Same; execution of contract. [MSA 5.2535(5)]

MCLA 486.506 Same; renewal, extension or amendment of contract. [MSA 5.2535(6)]

MCLA 486.507 Purchase of waterworks. [MSA 5.2535(7)]

MCLA 486.508 Short title. [MSA 5.2535(8)]

JOINT ACTION

Act No. 113, P.A. 1869 - Introduction of Water into Towns, Cities and Villages

AN ACT to authorize the formation of companies for the introduction of water into towns (townships), cities and villages, in the state of Michigan.

MCLA 486.301 Water-works in municipalities; incorporators; powers of corporation. [MSA 22.1681]

MCLA 486.302 Certificate, acknowledgment, contents, filing and recording; body corporate, name. [MSA 22.1682]

MCLA 486.303 Property; holding. [MSA 22.1683]

MCLA 486.304 Capital stock. [MSA 22.1684]

MCLA 486.305 Officers, election, term, powers; quorum of stockholders; right to vote. [MSA 22.1685]

MCLA 486.306 Powers of corporation. [MSA 22.1686]

MCLA 486.307 Survey and map, signing, filing; right of entry. [MSA 22.1687]

MCLA 486.308 Condemnation proceedings. [MSA 22.1688]

MCLA 486.309 Stock deemed personalty; certificates, transfer; report to assessing officer. [MSA 22.1689]

MCLA 486.310 Subscriptions, calling in; sale of stock; proceeds disposition; rights of purchaser. [MSA 22.1690]

MCLA 486.311 Stockholder's liability; recovery prerequisites; contribution. [MSA 22.1691]

MCLA 486.312 Contract between municipality and company; municipal obligations. [MSA 22.1692]

MCLA 486.313 Annual and special meetings of stockholders. [MSA 22.1693]

336

MCLA 486.314 Officers; designation, election, bonding.
MSA 22.1694

MCLA 486.315 Ordinances; use of streets, etc.; rates.
MSA 22.1695

MCLA 486.316 Purchase of corporate rights and property by municipality; arbitration. MSA 22.1696

MCLA 486.317 Municipality as stockholder; issuance of bonds, tax levy; certain corporations as stockholders. MSA 22.1697

MCLA 486.318 Company fully organized; construction, financial arrangements. MSA 22.1698

JOINT ACTION
Act No. 107, P.A. 1941 - Township Water Supply and Sewage Disposal System

AN ACT to authorize township boards to contract with cities or villages for the furnishing of water to township water supply districts for fire protection and other purposes; to provide for installation of water mains and financing of same on voluntary payment basis; to authorize township boards to promulgate and adopt plans for financing, installation, maintenance and control of township water mains; to prescribe the powers and duties of township boards in such cases; to provide for exclusive control of such water mains and use thereof by the township board, and to bring within the provisions of this act certain existing township water mains; and to authorize township water supply and sewage disposal systems, and the issuance of revenue bonds or notes therefor, and to authorize purchases thereof.

MCLA 41.331 Township water supply district; contract with city or village. MSA 5.2599(1)

Sec. 1. Upon filing with the township clerk of petitions verified both as to signature and ownership, signed by 60 per centum of the record owners of the land to be made into a township water supply district, the township board in such township shall have the

337

power to contract with any city or village for the furnishing of water for fire protection and domestic purposes to such water supply district under such terms and conditions as may be agreed upon between said township board and the common council or other representative body of the city or village.

MCLA 41.332 Water mains and fittings, purchase and laying.
[MSA 5.2599(2)]

MCLA 41.333 Same; payment of cost; share of township; tax exemption; amount set apart, ratio; map. [MSA 5.2599(3)]

MCLA 41.334 Cost, balance of, to be raised by popular subscription. [MSA 5.2599(4)]

MCLA 42.335 Financing of improvement, plan; connections, amount payable to township for making; rules and regulations.
[MSA 5.2599(5)]

MCLA 41.335a Township water board; loans; powers.
[MSA 5.2599(5A)]

MCLA 41.336 Publication of plan of financing. [MSA 5.2599(6)]

MCLA 41.337 Failure to raise balance in accordance with terms of plan; refund of prior payments. [MSA 5.2599(7)]

MCLA 41.338 Installation of improvement, duty of township board; authority to borrow funds. [MSA 5.2599(8)]

MCLA 41.339 Excess payments of connection fees over required amounts, disposition of; section retroactive to apply to previous installations. [MSA 5.2599(9)]

MCLA 41.340 Control over mains and fittings; authority of township board; amendment of rules and regulations. [MSA 5.2599(10)]

MCLA 41.341 Same; previously installed or extended; rules, publication, amendment. [MSA 5.2599(11)]

MCLA 41.342 Definitions. [MSA 5.2599(12)] (''Township water supply district'' and ''private connection.'')

338

MCLA 41.343 Township water supply and sewage disposal system; loan from corporation, bonds. [MSA 5.2599(14)]

MCLA 41.344 Same; contract for issuance of revenue bonds; interest, terms and conditions. [MSA 5.2599(15)]

MCLA 41.345 Same; ordinance. [MSA 5.2599(16)]

MCLA 41.346 Same; statutory lien upon net revenues; trust funds. [MSA 5.2599(17)]

MCLA 41.347 Same; duration of lien. [MSA 5.2599(18)]

MCLA 41.348 Default in payment; appointment of receiver. [MSA 5.2599(19)]

MCLA 41.349 Principal and interest, payment. [MSA 5.2599(20)]

MCLA 41.350 Borrower may use other revenue for operation and maintenance. [MSA 5.2599(21)]

MCLA 41.351 Powers conferred; ''corporation'' defined. [MSA 5.2599(22)]

JOINT ACTION
Act No. 76, P.A. 1965 - Joint Water Supply and Waste Disposal Systems

AN ACT to authorize counties, townships, villages, cities and any other governmental unit or entity to construct or build water supply systems and waste disposal systems by agreements or contracts with governmental units, entities or agencies of another state; or to enter into contracts or agreements with such governmental units or entities of another state for the use of such facilities.

MCLA 123.381 Definitions. [MSA 5.2769(101)]

MCLA 123.382 Local governmental units; power to construct and operate with units in another state. [MSA 5.2769(102)]

MCLA 123.383 Same; agreements with units of another state for waste disposal or water supply services. [MSA 5.2769(103)]

MCLA 123.384 Financing; law governing. [MSA 5.2769(104)]

AFFECTING JOINT ACTION
Act No. 19, P.A. 1967 - Water Companies

AN ACT to regulate water companies and the sale and distribution of water within the state; to provide a method of review of public service commission orders relating thereto; and to prescribe penalties for the violation hereof.

MCLA 486.551 Definitions. [MSA 22.1730(1)]

MCLA 486.552 Public service commission, powers and jurisdiction. [MSA 22.1730(2)]

Sec. 2. The commission is vested with power and jurisdiction to supervise and regulate every water company within the state and to do all things necessary and convenient in the exercise of such power and jurisdiction.

MCLA 486.553 Certificate of public convenience and necessity; construction of system; commencement, discontinuance, or abandonment of operations. [MSA 22.1730(3)]

MCLA 486.554 Service, facilities, rates; regulation by commission. [MSA 22.1730(4)]

MCLA 486.555 Schedule of rates, charges and rules; filing; changes; application, notice (to the affected municipalities), and approval (of the commission). [MSA 22.1730(5)]

MCLA 486.556 Rate or charge increases, (public) hearings. [MSA 22.1730(6)]

MCLA 486.577 Preferences. [MSA 22.1730(7)]

MCLA 486.558 Variance from filed schedules. [MSA 22.1730(8)]

340

MCLA 486.559 Commission; investigations, hearings, findings, and orders. [MSA 22.1730(9)]

MCLA 486.560 Burden of proof. [MSA 22.1730(10)]

MCLA 486.561 Interim rate or charge changes, bonds. [MSA 22.1730(11)]

MCLA 486.562 Orders of commission, effective date. [MSA 22.1730(12)]

MCLA 486.563 Legality and enforceability of commission's orders; penalty for violation. [MSA 22.1730(13)]

MCLA 486.564 Violations of laws or commission's rules or orders; inquiries, cease and desist orders. [MSA 22.1730(14)]

MCLA 486.565 Rehearings, reopenings, and reconsiderations; notice, application, review. [MSA 22.1730(15)]

MCLA 486.566 Amendment, modification, or revocation of commission's orders. [MSA 22.1730(16)]

MCLA 486.567 Rules and regulations, business of water companies and procedure before commission. [MSA 22.1730(17)]

MCLA 486.568 Ratification and confirmation of existing rules and regulations. [MSA 22.1730(18)]

MCLA 486.569 Audits and investigations of companies' records and facilities, number and expense. [MSA 22.1730(19)]

MCLA 486.570 Actions to vacate commission's orders; time, grounds, procedure; injunctions; evidence; judgments; burden of proof. [MSA 22.1730(20)]

MCLA 486.571 Department of public health, authority and duties. [MSA 22.1730(21)]

JOINT ACTION
Act No. 4, P.A. 1957 - Charter Water Authorities

341

AN ACT to provide for the incorporation of municipal authorities to acquire, own and operate water supply and transmission systems; to provide a municipal charter therefor; and to prescribe the powers and functions thereof.

MCLA 121.14 Same; terms, interest, redemption, payment. [MSA 5.2533(44)]

MCLA 121.14a Same; resolution, publication, referendum, petition, special election. [MSA 5.2533(44A)]

MCLA 121.15 Same; issuance, approval, sale, refunding. [MSA 5.2533(45)]

MCLA 121.16 Taxes; rates, assessment, levy, collection, subjects. [MSA 5.2533(46)]

MCLA 121.17 Same; deposit in debt retirement fund depositary. [MSA 5.2533(47)]

MCLA 121.18 Same; administration expenses. [MSA 5.2533(48)]

MCLA 121.19 Same; payment by constituent municipality. [MSA 5.2533(49)]

MCLA 121.20 Contract payments; powers of municipal legislative body. [MSA 5.2533(50)]

MCLA 121.21 Authority; body corporate; charter, powers. [MSA 5.2533(51)]

MCLA 121.22 Same; acquisition of water supply and transmission system, condemnation. [MSA 5.2533(52)]

MCLA 121.23 Change in municipal jurisdiction. [MSA 5.2533(53)]

MCLA 121.24 Advancements to authority for administrative expenses. [MSA 5.2533(54)]

MCLA 121.25 Contracts for water to nonconstituent municipalities, duration. [MSA 5.2533(55)]

MCLA 121.26 Joinder of municipality after incorporation of authority, procedure. [MSA 5.2533(56)]

MCLA 121.27 Additional powers. [MSA 5.2533(57)]

Sec. 27. The powers herein granted shall be in addition to those granted by any charter or other statute.

MCLA 121.28 Construction of act. [MSA 5.2533(58)]

Sec. 28. The provisions of this act shall be liberally construed in the interest of public health and welfare and the safety of persons and property within the authority incorporated under the provisions of this act.

MCLA 121.29 Short title. [MSA 5.2533(59)]

Act No. 5, P.A. 1870, Ex. Sess. - Water Supply

AN ACT to authorize the introduction of water into, and the construction or purchase of hydraulic works, in the cities and villages in the state of Michigan.

MCLA 123.111 Water supply; borrowing power of municipality. [MSA 5.2511]

MCLA 123.112 Bonds, issuance; payment principal, interest; referendum on borrowing. [MSA 5.2512]

MCLA 123.113 Acquisition of rights of water company; resolution of council affecting bonds. [MSA 5.2513]

MCLA 123.114 Management of waterworks; rates; regulations. [MSA 5.2514]

MCLA 123.115 Act construed. [MSA 5.2515]

MCLA 123.116 Levy to pay principal and interest of bonds. [MSA 5.2516]

MCLA 123.117 Acquisition of property rights. [MSA 5.2517]

MCLA 123.118 Same; notice of proceedings, contents. [MSA 5.2518]

MCLA 123.119 Notice, service; guardian ad litem. [MSA 5.2519]

MCLA 123.120 Report to officer mentioned in notice, contents; jury, summoning, empaneling, duties, compensation; procedure; fees; adjournments. [MSA 5.2520]

MCLA 123.121 Appeal procedure; bond. [MSA 5.2521]

MCLA 123.122 Return of proceedings, filing with clerk; evidence. [MSA 5.2522]

MCLA 123.123 Amount awarded, provisions for payment. [MSA 5.2523]

MCLA 123.124 Recording of copy of proceedings with register of deeds. [MSA 5.2524]

MCLA 123.125 Title vested in municipality; right of entry; user. [MSA 5.2525]

MCLA 123.126 Construction, operation, maintenance of works; rights pending appeal. [MSA 5.2526]

MCLA 123.127 Use of highways, limitation. [MSA 5.2527]

MCLA 123.128 Juror, incompetency on account of interest. [MSA 5.2528]

MCLA 123.129 Injury to waterworks; penalty. [MSA 5.2529]

MCLA 123.130 Scope. [MSA 5.2530]

Act No. 82, P.A. 1901 - Continuance of Corporate Life

AN ACT to provide for renewing the incorporation of companies organized for the purpose of the introduction of water into towns (townships), cities and villages.

MCLA 486.401 Continuance of corporate life of companies to supply water to municipalities; procedure, evidence. [MSA 22.1721]

MCLA 486.402 Renewed corporation; rights and duties.
MSA 22.1722

Note: Although all of the above acts are not listed as "joint action", nevertheless they are included in this text because townships may be involved in some way with a corporation or some unit of government organized under one of these acts.

Furthermore, Act No. 82 gives the corporation power to acquire and hold real estate, not only within the municipality, but "contiguous thereto," that it "may take water from any springs, ponds, rivers, fountains or streams, and divert and conduct the same to said city, and may lay and construct any pipes, conduits, aqueducts, wells, reservoirs or other works or machinery necessary or proper, and authorized for said purposes, upon any lands or property entered upon, purchased, taken or held." Also that it "may enter upon any lands, streets, highways, lanes, alleys, public squares, through which they deem it proper to carry water from said springs, ponds, rivers, fountains, streams, and reservoirs, and lay and construct any pipes, conduits, aqueducts, and other works for said purposes, leaving said lands, streets, highways, lanes or public squares in the same condition, as nearly as may be, as they were before said entry."

Several of the other acts make similar provisions.

JOINT ACTION
Act No. 196, P.A. 1952 - Municipal Water Supply and Sewage Disposal Systems

AN ACT to provide for the incorporation of municipal authorities to acquire, own and operate water supply systems; to prescribe the rights, powers and duties thereof; and to authorize contracts between such authorities and other public corporations.

MCLA 124.251 Water supply system; definition. MSA 5.2533(1)

MCLA 124.252 Same; authority, articles of incorporation, adoption, endorsement, form, publication, filing; validity. MSA 5.2533(2)

Sec. 2. Any 2 or more cities, villages or townships (hereinafter sometimes referred to as "municipalities") or any combination thereof, may incorporate an authority for the purpose of acquiring, owning, and/or operating a water supply system or systems, by the adoption of articles of incorporation by the legislative body of each municipality. ...

MCLA 124.253 Same; articles, contents. [MSA 5.2533(3)]

MCLA 124.254 Same; authority body corporate; powers. [MSA 5.2533(4)]

MCLA 124.255 Same; acquire, etc., property. [MSA 5.2533(5)]

MCLA 124.256 Same; sale and purchase of water; contracts. [MSA 5.2533(6)]

MCLA 124.257 Same; city, village or township may become constituent part; amendment of articles. [MSA 5.2533(7)]

MCLA 124.258 Same; tax. [MSA 5.2533(8)]

MCLA 124.259 Same; bonds, issuance, payment. [MSA 5.2533(9)]

MCLA 124.260 Same; services. [MSA 5.2533(10)]

MCLA 124.261 Same; jurisdiction; amendment of articles. [MSA 5.2533(11)]

MCLA 124.262 Same; powers. [MSA 5.2533(12)]

AFFECTS JOINT ACTION
Act No. 178, P.A. 1939 - Municipal Water Liens

AN ACT to provide for the collection of water rates, assessments, charges or rentals for water, and to provide a lien for water furnished by municipalities as herein defined.

MCLA 123.161 Definitions. [MSA 5.2531(1)]

MCLA 123.162 Municipal water lien; creation; accrual. [MSA 5.2531(2)]

MCLA 123.163 Same; enforcement; inapplicable in absence of ordinance. [MSA 5.2531(3)]

MCLA 123.164 Same; notice, records constitute. [MSA 5.2531(4)]

MCLA 123.165 Same; priority; affidavit, notice of termination of lease. [MSA 5.2531(5)]

MCLA 123.166 Discontinuance of service; institution of suit; no effect upon lien. [MSA 5.2531(6)]

MCLA 123.167 Cumulative of other remedies; enabling act. [MSA 5.2531(7)]

JOINT ACTION
Act No. 130, P.A. 1945 . Water Supply, Joint Source

AN ACT to authorize cities to extend and improve their municipally owned water systems through the acquisition and operation of a joint source of water supply, to finance the cost thereof through the issuance of water revenue bonds; providing for methods for the operation of such joint source of water; authorizing the purchase and condemnation of necessary property; and providing the procedure for such acquisition and financing.

MCLA 123.151 Water supply; joint source; bonds; agreements; expense. [MSA 5.2532(1)]

MCLA 123.152 Cities having outstanding water revenue bonds. [MSA 5.2532(2)]

MCLA 123.153 Acquisition of property; construction contracts. [MSA 5.2532(3)]

MCLA 123.154 Sale or delivery outside of corporate limits. [MSA 5.2532(4)]

MCLA 123.155 Certain limitations and procedural requirements removed. [MSA 5.2532(5)]

348

JOINT ACTION
Act No. 34, P.A. 1917 - Water Furnished Outside Territorial Limits

AN ACT to authorize municipal corporations having authority by law to furnish water outside their territorial limits, to sell water to other municipal corporations and contract regarding such sale; to contract with individuals, firms, or corporations regarding the construction of water mains, and the sale of water in such outside territory; to construct water mains through the highways outside their territorial limits, with the consent of the proper local authorities; to furnish water to individual consumers, fix rates thereof, and enforce collection thereof.

MCLA 123.141 Sale of water; authority to contract with cities, villages or townships; rates. MSA 5.2581

MCLA 123.142 Same; authority to contract with persons; construction of mains, payment. MSA 5.2582

MCLA 123.143 Same; rights, powers, when contract with persons. MSA 5.2583

MCLA 123.144 Enforcement of contracts; prerequisites. MSA 5.2584

Sec. 4. No contract relating to water service in such outside territory except in cases provided for in section 1 hereof, shall be enforceable against such corporation until the consent of the proper local authorities to the construction and maintenance of water mains in the highways of such territory has been obtained, and the burden of securing such consent **shall not be upon such corporation.***

---

*Because of conditions in this section, it is absolutely essential that sections twenty-nine and thirty of article seven of the Michigan constitution be thoroughly understood in dealing with other municipalities which render services necessitating the laying of wires, poles, pipes, tracks, conduits or other utility facilities without the consent of the duly constituted authority of the township when such are to be constructed leading to or through the township.

JOINT ACTION
Act No. 301, P.A. 1969 - Gifts by Municipalities
Owning or Operating Public Utilities

AN ACT authorizing municipalities owning or operating public utilities to make contributions and gifts as determined by its governing body.

MCLA 123.391 Authorization, source, legislative approval.
MSA 5.3422(1)

JOINT ACTION
Act No. 320, P.A. 1927 - Garbage, Sewage, Night
Soil, and Storm Water

AN ACT authorizing counties, cities, villages and townships, either individually or jointly by agreement, to provide a sanitary means of disposing of the garbage, sewage, night soil and storm water thereof; to charge owners or occupants of premises therefor; and to borrow money and issue bonds to own, acquire, construct, equip, operate and maintain intercepting sewers, other sanitary and storm sewers, sewage disposal plants, and garbage disposal plants.

MCLA 123.241 Disposal plants; construction; property powers, rights. MSA 5.2661

MCLA 123.242 Same; considered public utility; mortgage bonds, referendum. MSA 5.2662

MCLA 123.243 Same; supervising body; regulations; rates, collection. MSA 5.2663

MCLA 123.244 Mortgage bonds, manner of payment; sinking fund. MSA 5.2664

MCLA 123.245 Granting of franchise to private corporation, contents; referendum. MSA 5.2665

MCLA 123.246 Power to contract with private corporation, terms. MSA 5.2666

MCLA 123.247 Bonds, issuance, sale, interest, term, denomination, payment, taxation. MSA 5.2667

MCLA 123.248 Installation order, record by legislative body; plans submitted to commissioner of health; bonds. MSA 5.2668

MCLA 123.249 Act construed. MSA 5.2669

MCLA 123.250 Institution of proceedings. MSA 5.2670

MCLA 123.252 Inter-municipality contract power. MSA 5.2672

MCLA 123.253 Same; approval. MSA 5.2673

JOINT ACTION
Act No. 96, P.A. 1951 - Water Service for Fire Protection.

AN ACT to authorize the township board of any township where there are lands serviced by a revenue bond water system to provide by special assessment for the payment of the reasonable cost and value of such water service for fire protection within the district served by said water system through fire hydrants and water mains.

MCLA 41.831 Township water service for fire protection; assessment for cost and value. MSA 5.2770(31)

MCLA 41.832 Same; boundaries; estimate of cost and value; payment. MSA 5.2770(32)

MCLA 41.833 Same; funds for which may be used. MSA 5.2770(33)

MCLA 41.834 Public hearing. MSA 5.2770(34)

MCLA 41.835 Assessment levy. MSA 5.2770(35)

MCLA 41.836 Same; method, collection. MSA 5.2770(36)

351

MCLA 41.837 Notice of hearing; publication, posting.
MSA 5.2770(37)

MCLA 41.838 Hearing of objections; changes, corrections or modifications. MSA 5.2770(38)

MCLA 41.839 Review, etc., of assessment roll. MSA 5.2770(39)

MCLA 41.840 Annual assessment, levy; further hearings.
MSA 5.2770(40)

MCLA 41.841 Special assessment limitation. MSA 5.2770(41)

JOINT ACTION
Act No. 47, P.A. 1941 - Township Water Supply Contracts

AN ACT to authorize the township board of any township to provide water mains and/or water service for domestic uses and/or fire protection throughout certain areas of such township; to authorize the township board of any township to contract with municipalities or with organized water departments or districts through their authorized governing bodies for the construction of, and supplying water through, water mains and the extensions thereof throughout certain areas of such township for domestic or fire protection purposes; to provide for making, levying and collecting special assessments to pay the cost thereof; to issue special assessment bonds in anticipation of the collection of such special assessment taxes; and to advance amounts necessary to pay such bonds and to reimburse the township for such advances; to remit certain funds to property owners for taxes paid.

MCLA 41.351 Water service; authority of township board to contract with municipalities for; special assessments; issuance of bonds. MSA 5.2585(1)

MCLA 41.352 Special assessment district; procedure to establish; petition. MSA 5.2585(2)

352

MCLA 41.353 Contract, hearing on; levy of special assessment; issuance of bonds; township may advance funds to meet installments. [MSA 5.2585(3)]

MCLA 41.354 Water service in townships; cost, collection, maximum amount; annual installments. [MSA 5.2585(4)]

MCLA 41.355 Credit for connections by water users; limitations; payment. [MSA 5.2585(5)]

MCLA 41.356 Annual assessment for maintenance, determination and levy. [MSA 5.2585(6)]

JOINT ACTION
Act No. 88, P.A. 1919 - Township Water Supply Contracts

AN ACT to authorize township boards to contract with cities or villages for the furnishing of water for fire protection and other purposes; to authorize the issuing of bonds in connection therewith and to provide for the making, levying and collecting of special assessments to partially defray the cost thereof.

MCLA 41.391 Contract power of township board for water supply on filing petition. [MSA 5.2591]

MCLA 41.392 Necessary pipes; installation, maintenance. [MSA 5.2592]

MCLA 41.393 Cost, payment. [MSA 5.2593] (Contingent fund plus tax levy)

MCLA 41.394 Certification of tax. [MSA 5.2594]

MCLA 41.395 Bonds; terms, limit. [MSA 5.2595]

MCLA 41.396 Tax levy. [MSA 5.2596]

MCLA 41.397 Special assessments; bonds. [MSA 5.2597]

MCLA 41.398 Prerequisites to construction; bonds, issuance; proceedings. MSA 5.2598

JOINT ACTION
Act No. 207, P.A. 1953 - Water Contracts

AN ACT to authorize township boards of certain defined townships to contract with cities or villages for the furnishing of water to such townships for fire protection and other purposes; to authorize such township boards to borrow funds necessary to acquire and install township water supply facilities required by such water supply contracts; to authorize persons, firms, corporations, banks and trust companies to loan funds for such purposes; to authorize such township boards to pledge sales tax diversion funds accruing to such townships for the purpose of securing payment of funds so borrowed; and to authorize township boards of such defined townships to enact such ordinances as may be necessary to effectuate the foregoing.

MCLA 41.871 Water for fire protection, etc.; township authorized to contract for. MSA 5.2600(1)

Sec. 1. The township board of any township now or hereafter having a population of 5,000 or over, according to the latest or each succeeding federal decennial census, is hereby authorized to contract with any city or village for the supplying to such township of water for fire protection and domestic purposes, under such terms and conditions as may be agreed upon between said township board and the legislative body of such city or village.

MCLA 41.872 Same; borrow money, permission, limitation. MSA 5.2600(2)

MCLA 41.873 Notes; installments, interest, redemption, computation, appropriation, separate fund. MSA 5.2600(3)

MCLA 41.873a Same; approval, sale. MSA 5.2600(3A)

MCLA 41.874 Same; pledging sales tax funds, ordinance. MSA 5.2600(4)

MCLA 41.875 Ordinance; provisions. [MSA 5.2600(5)]

MCLA 41.876 Same; adoption, effective date, recording, publication. [MSA 5.2600(6)]

MCLA 41.877 Same; petition for referendum, signatures, verification. [MSA 5.2600(7)]

MCLA 41.878 Powers granted. [MSA 5.2600(8)]

JOINT ACTION
Act No. 202, P.A. 1887 - Water Power and Supply Corporations

AN ACT to authorize the formation of corporations for the purpose of damming, excavating, constructing and maintaining water courses with water power appurtenant thereto, for accumulating, storing, conducting, selling, furnishing and supplying upon an agreed rental, water and water power for mining, milling, manufacturing, domestic, municipal and agricultural purposes and for purposes of navigation.

MCLA 486.101 Water power and supply corporations; incorporators, powers. [MSA 22.1631]

MCLA 486.102 Same; certificate, acknowledgment, contents, recording, filing. [MSA 22.1632]

MCLA 486.103 Same; body corporate; governing law. [MSA 22.1633]

MCLA 486.104 Directors; powers, election, term, qualifications. [MSA 22.1634]

MCLA 486.105 Same; calling of election. [MSA 22.1635]

MCLA 486.106 Same; majority control. [MSA 22.1636]

MCLA 486.107 Subscriptions; increase in capital, procedure. [MSA 22.1637]

MCLA 486.108 Same; calling in; sale, procedure; proceeds, disposition; purchaser's rights. [MSA 22.1638]

MCLA 486.109 Corporate powers. [MSA 22.1639]

MCLA 486.110 Power to construct railroad, telephone and telegraph lines; holding of realty. [MSA 22.1640]

MCLA 486.111 Furnishing and use of water; rent, collection. [MSA 22.1641]

MCLA 486.112 Injury to stream or property; penalty. [MSA 22.1642]

MCLA 486.113 Annual report; contents. [MSA 22.1643]

MCLA 486.114 Real property; purchase, holding, disposal; personal property, disposal. [MSA 22.1644]

MCLA 486.115 Stockholder's liability; recovery prerequisites. [MSA 22.1645]

MCLA 486.116 Shares deemed personalty; transfer. [MSA 22.1646]

JOINT ACTION
Act No. 39, P.A. 1883 - Water Power and Supply Corporations

AN ACT to authorize the formation of corporations for the purpose of excavating, constructing and maintaining water courses with water power appurtenant thereto, for accumulating, storing, conducting, selling, furnishing and supplying, upon an agreed rental, water and water power for mining, milling, manufacturing, domestic, municipal and agricultural purposes.

MCLA 486.51 Water power and supply corporations; incorporators, powers. [MSA 22.1611]

MCLA 486.52 Same; certificate, acknowledgment, contents, recording, filing. [MSA 22.1612]

MCLA 486.53 Same; body corporate; governing law. [MSA 22.1613]

356

MCLA 486.54 Directors; powers, election, term, qualifications. MSA 22.1614

MCLA 486.55 Same; calling of election. MSA 22.1615

MCLA 486.56 Same; majority control. MSA 22.1616

MCLA 486.57 Subscriptions; increase in capital stock, procedure. MSA 22.1617

MCLA 486.58 Same; calling in; sale, procedure; proceeds, disposition; purchaser's rights. MSA 22.1618

MCLA 486.59 Corporate powers. MSA 22.1619

MCLA 486.60 Power to construct railroads, telegraph and telephone lines; holding of realty. MSA 22.1620

MCLA 486.61 Furnishing and use of water; rent, collection. MSA 22.1621

MCLA 486.62 Injury to stream or property; penalty. MSA 22.1622

MCLA 486.63 Annual report; contents. MSA 22.1623

MCLA 486.65 Stockholder's liability; recovery prerequisites. MSA 22.1624

MCLA 486.66 Shares deemed personalty; transfer. MSA 22.1625

JOINT ACTION
Act No. 232, P.A. 1863 - Water and Water Power Companies

AN ACT to provide for the incorporation of water power companies.

MCLA 486.1 Water power companies; incorporators, notice; articles, contents. MSA 22.1581

MCLA 486.2 Same; articles, signing, filing; body corporate, powers; evidence. MSA 22.1582

MCLA 486.3 Directors; powers, election, term, vacancy; officers, selection; bond of treasurer. [MSA 22.1583]

MCLA 486.4 Membership. [MSA 22.1584]

MCLA 486.5 Repairs; permanent improvements. [MSA 22.1585]

MCLA 486.6 Same; statement, contents. [MSA 22.1586]

MCLA 486.7 Assessment for repairs or improvements. [MSA 22.1587]

MCLA 486.8 Same; collection; user of water barred. [MSA 22.1588]

MCLA 486.9 Same; notice to non-resident. [MSA 22.1589]

MCLA 486.10 Mortgage lien; preference. [MSA 22.1590]

MCLA 486.11 Same; certificate, contents; recording; evidence. [MSA 22.1591]

MCLA 486.12 Same; foreclosure. [MSA 22.1592]

MCLA 486.13 Same; commencement of suit. [MSA 22.1593]

MCLA 486.14 Meetings, calling; notice, proof of service, filing. [MSA 22.1594]

MCLA 486.15 Watchman; appointment, duties, compensation. [MSA 22.1595]

MCLA 486.16 Contracts. [MSA 22.1596]

MCLA 486.17 Treasurer, duties. [MSA 22.1597]

MCLA 486.18 Assessment, recovery. [MSA 22.1598]

MCLA 486.19 Disposition of funds at annual meeting. [MSA 22.1599]

MCLA 486.20 By-laws. [MSA 22.1600]

358

MCLA 486.21 Stockholder's liability. $\boxed{\text{MSA 22.1601}}$

MCLA 486.22 Tenants in common, liabilities. $\boxed{\text{MSA 22.1602}}$

AFFECTS JOINT ACTION
Act No. 87, P.A. 1965 - Garbage and Refuse Disposal

AN ACT to protect the public health; to provide for planning and conducting refuse management systems; to license and regulate garbage and refuse disposal facilities and transporting units; to regulate collection centers; and to provide a penalty for violation of this act.

MCLA 325.291 Definitions. $\boxed{\text{MSA 14.435(1)}}$

Sec. 1. As used in this act:

(a) "Refuse" means solid wastes, except body wastes, and includes garbage, rubbish, ashes, incinerator ash, incinerator residue, street cleanings and solid market and solid industrial wastes.

(b) "Garbage" means rejected food wastes including waste accumulation of animal, fruit or vegetable matter used or intended for food or that attend the preparation, use, cooking, dealing in or storing of meat, fish, fowl, fruit or vegetable.

(c) "Rubbish" means nonputrescible solid wastes, excluding ashes, consisting of both combustible and noncombustible wastes, such as paper, cardboard, metal containers, yard clippings, wood, glass, bedding, crockery, demolished building materials or litter of any kind that will be a detriment to the public health and safety.

(d) "Ashes" means the residue from the burning of wood, coal, coke or other combustible materials.

(e) "Commissioner" means the state department of public health.

(f) "Health officer" means a full-time administrative officer of an approved city, county or district department of health.

(g) "Applicant" means any individuals, firms, corporations or any political subdivisions of the state including any governmental authority created by statute.

(h) "Refuse transfer facility" means a tract of land, building, unit or appurtenance or combination thereof that is used or intended for use in the rehandling or storage of refuse incidental to the transportation of the refuse.

(i) *"Refuse processing plant"* *means a tract of land, building, unit or appurtenance or combination thereof that is used or intended for use for the processing of refuse or the separation of materials for salvage or disposal or both.*

(j) *"Disposal area"* *means a refuse transfer facility, incinerator, sanitary landfill, processing plant or any other refuse handling or disposal facility utilized in the disposal of refuse.*

(k) *"Refuse transporting unit"* *means a container which may be an integral part of a truck or any other piece of equipment used for the transportation of refuse on or by a motor vehicle or by rail.*

(l) *"Collection center"* *means a tract of land, building, unit or appurtenance or combination thereof that is used to collect junk motor vehicles and farm implements pursuant to section 9 of this act.*

MCLA 325.292 Disposal of refuse, licensed areas. [MSA 14.435(2)]

Sec. 2. No person shall dispose of any refuse at any place except a disposal area licensed as provided in this act. Nothing in this act nor any act of the commissioner's shall usurp the legal right of a local governing body from developing and enforcing local ordinances, codes, or rules and regulations on solid waste disposal equal to or more stringent than the provisions of this act, nor will this act relieve the applicant for license to operate a disposal area from obtaining a license from a local governing body when required or relieve the person owning or operating a disposal area from responsibility for securing proper zoning permits or complying with all applicable local ordinances, codes, or rules and regulations not in conflict with this act.

MCLA 325.293 Disposal area licenses; necessity; application, contents, fees. [MSA 14.435(3)]

MCLA 325.294 Inspection, bonds; license expiration and renewal. [MSA 14.435(4)]

MCLA 325.295 License revocation. [MSA 14.435(5)]

MCLA 325.296 Standards for refuse transporting units and disposal areas: inspections; enforcement. [MSA 14.435(6)]

360

MCLA 325.296a Refuse transporting unit licenses, necessity, exemptions, applications, fee, issuance, transferability; sufficiency of unit. [MSA 14.435(6A)]

MCLA 325.297 Disposal of refuse on disposer's land; improvement of planting of farmland, disposal of rubbish accumulated. [MSA 14.435(7)]

MCLA 325.297a Actions to restrain unlicensed establishments or operations or other violations. [MSA 14.435(7A)]

MCLA 325.297b Municipal reports and proposals as to refuse disposal needs, requirements, guidelines, standards, assistance, regional reports. [MSA 14.435(7B)]

Note: It is **expected** that by the time this text comes off the press, the deadline set in this section will have been extended for one year to July 1, 1974.

MCLA 325.298 Penalty. [MSA 14.435(8)]

MCLA 325.299 Local governmental junk motor vehicle and farm implement collection centers, establishment, operation, definitions. [MSA 14.435(9)]

MCLA 325.300 Financing collection and disposal of junk motor vehicles and farm implements. [MSA 14.435(10)]

JOINT ACTION
Act No. 235, P.A. 1947 - Joint Water and Sewage Disposal System

AN ACT to regulate the ownership, extension, improvement and operation of public water and sewage disposal systems lying within 2 or more public corporations; to authorize the acquisition, by any public corporation, of that part of a public water or sewage disposal system lying within its boundaries; and to provide for the payment and security of revenue bonds issued for the construction, acquisition, extension and improvement of such systems.

MCLA 123.331 Definition. [MSA 5.2769(21)]

MCLA 123.332 Water or sewage disposal system, acquisition of part on change of boundaries; referendum. [MSA 5.2769(22)]

Sec. 2. When any public corporation shall have acquired any water or sewage disposal system, and, by subsequent incorporation, annexation or other change of boundaries, the land in which any part of such system lies shall have been placed within the boundaries of any other public corporation, the legislative or governing body of such other corporation, if it desires to acquire that part of such system lying within its boundaries, shall submit the question of acquiring the same to vote of its qualified electors at a regular or special election.

MCLA 123.333 Same; electors' approval; ordinance.
[MSA 5.2769(23)]

MCLA 123.334 Same; joint board or commission, control; members, election. [MSA 5.2769(24)]

MCLA 123.335 Same; alternative plans for division or operation [MSA 5.2769(25)]

MCLA 123.336 Same; retirement of bonds; non-callable bonds; bond and interest redemption fund, payment priority.
[MSA 5.2769(26)]

MCLA 123.337 Same; operation as a single unit; segregation and disposition of revenues, retirement of bonds. [MSA 5.2769(27)]

MCLA 123.338 Same; operation as separate unit after retirement of bonds; collection and disposition of revenues. [MSA 5.2769(28)]

MCLA 123.339 Same; division between public corporations; proportionate share of expenses or indebtedness. [MSA 5.2769(29)]

MCLA 123.340 Same; operation by joint board or agency as unit; fund payments; depreciation, contingent and surplus funds.
[MSA 5.2769(30)]

MCLA 123.341 Same; apportionment of revenues, debts, properties; realty, purchase, use. [MSA 5.2769(31)]

MCLA 123.342 Same; provisions applicable. [MSA 5.2769(32)]

MCLA 123.343 Same; cumulative effect of act; repeal of authority granted by other law. [MSA 5.2769(33)]

MCLA 123.344 Same; jointly acquired by public corporations under other statutes; contracts. [MSA 5.2769(34)]

MCLA 123.345 Same; contracts for division of systems existing or to be acquired. [MSA 5.2769(35)]

MCLA 123.346 Validation of public corporation's vote or proceedings before effective date of act. [MSA 5.2769(36)]

MCLA 123.347 Act not deemed part of bondholders' contract; proceedings impairing contracts prohibited. [MSA 5.2769(37)]

JOINT ACTION
Act No. 82, P.A. 1955 - Acquisition of Water or Sewage System

AN ACT to provide for the acquirement by a city of the water supply system and/or sewage disposal system of a metropolitan district and to permit such a city to own, maintain, operate, improve, enlarge and extend such system or systems either within or without its limits, and to provide for the transfer to such city of the rights, obligations, property and functions of the metropolitan district.

MCLA 123.351 Definitions. [MSA 5.2534(1)]

MCLA 123.352 Purchase of water supply system and/or sewage disposal system by city from adjoining metropolitan district, contract, approval. [MSA 5.2534(2)]

MCLA 123.353 Succession of rights, obligations and property, contract. [MSA 5.2534(3)]

MCLA 123.354 Services, continuance, extension. [MSA 5.2534(4)]

MCLA 123.355 Readjustment of service rates; adoption of ordinances, property outside limits. [MSA 5.2534(5)]

MCLA 123.356 Construction of act. [MSA 5.2534(6)]

JOINT ACTION
Act No. 233, P.A. 1955 - Municipal Water Supply and Sewage Disposal Systems

AN ACT to provide for the incorporation of certain municipal authorities to acquire, own, extend, improve and operate sewage disposal systems and water supply systems; to prescribe the rights, powers and duties thereof; to authorize contracts between such authorities and public corporations; and to provide for the issuance of bonds to acquire, construct, extend or improve sewage disposal systems or water supply systems.

MCLA 124.281 Joint authority for acquiring sewage disposal and water supply systems; definitions. [MSA 5.2769(51)]

MCLA 124.282 Same; incorporation, procedure. [MSA 5.2769(52)]

MCLA 124.283 Same; articles of incorporation, contents. [MSA 5.2769(53)]

MCLA 124.284 Same; body corporate, powers. [MSA 5.2769(54)]

MCLA 124.285 Same; acquisition of property, condemnation. [MSA 5.2769(55)]

MCLA 124.286 Same; subsequent addition of other municipalities; amendment of articles. [MSA 5.2769(56)]

MCLA 124.287 Same; contracts to acquire system; financing. [MSA 5.2769(57)]

MCLA 124.288 Same; contract with a constituent municipality, execution; referendum, petitions. [MSA 5.2769(58)]

MCLA 124.289 Same; bonds, contracts. [MSA 5.2769(59)]

MCLA 124.290 Same; contracts with other municipalities for service, income, duration. [MSA 5.2769(60)]

MCLA 124.291 Same; change in municipal jurisdiction of territory. [MSA 5.2769(61)]

MCLA 124.292 Same; revenue bonds; partly other methods of financing. [MSA 5.2769(62)]

MCLA 124.292a Same; pledge of municipal share of sales tax revenues. [MSA 5.2769(62A)]

MCLA 124.292b Same; projects costing over $50,000,000, financing, definition of cost. [MSA 5.2769(62B)]

MCLA 124.292c Trust indenture; terms, engineering supervision. Annual audit. Trustee's collateral security; expenses, default. Restriction to revenue bonds. Municipal finance commission approval. [MSA 5.2769(62C)]

MCLA 124.293 Taxing power of constituent municipalities. [MSA 5.2769(63)]

MCLA 124.294 Additional powers. [MSA 5.2769(64)]

JOINT ACTION
Act No. 119, P.A. 1919 — Water, Light, Heat, Power or Transportation in Cities

AN ACT to authorize any city having a population of 25,000 or more to take for public use the absolute title in fee to any public utility for supplying water, light, heat, power or transportation to the municipality and the inhabitants thereof within or without its corporate limits.

MCLA 213.111 Cities, authority to take over public utilities. [MSA 8.71]

Sec. 1. Any city in this state having a population of 25,000 or more is hereby authorized to take for public use the absolute title in fee to any public utility for supplying water, light, heat, power and transportation to the municipality and the inhabitants thereof **within or without its corporate limits,** *the same being then and there the private property of any person or of any corporation,* *within the limits of the state constitution, and to institute and prosecute proceedings for that purpose.*

JOINT ACTION
Act No. 288, P.A. 1972 - Sewage Disposal through Public System

AN ACT to protect the surface and subsurface waters of the state; to protect the health, safety and welfare of the people; to provide for connection of structures in which sanitary sewage originates to available public sanitary sewer systems; to define structures affected by the act; to give powers to certain local units of government; and to establish remedies.

MCLA 123.281 Legislative findings. [MSA 5.2769(151)]

MCLA 123.282 Definitions. [MSA 5.2769(152)]

MCLA 123.283 Connection of structures in which sanitary sewage originates to public sanitary sewers, necessity, municipal approval, time. [MSA 5.2769(153)]

MCLA 123.284 Notice to owner, necessity of connection to public sanitary sewer system, mode, contents, prerequisite to requiring connection. [MSA 5.2769(154)]

MCLA 123.285 Compelling connection, grounds for action, parties. [MSA 5.2769(155)]

MCLA 123.286 Voluntary connection with public sanitary sewer system. [MSA 5.2769(156)]

MCLA 123.287 Ordinances relating to connections with public sanitary sewer systems. [MSA 5.2769(157)]

Sec. 7. This act is in addition to and not in limitation of the power of a governmental agency to adopt, amend and enforce ordinances relating to the connection of a structure in which sanitary sewage originates to its public sanitary sewer system.

366

Act No. 129, P.A. 1943 - Sewers and Sewage Disposal, Contracts, Bonds

AN ACT to provide for contracts between political subdivisions relative to systems of sewers and sewage disposal, and to validate existing contracts of such nature; to authorize the issue of joint revenue bonds to construct, acquire, extend or improve such systems and to regulate the use of the revenues thereof.

MCLA 123.231 Definitions. [MSA 5.2769(1)]

MCLA 123.232 Sewers and sewage disposal; joint contracts. [MSA 5.2769(2)]

Sec. 2. Any 2 or more political subdivisions may contract for the joint ownership, use and/or operation of sewers and/or sewage disposal facilities. Any 2 or more political subdivisions may contract relative to the furnishing of sewage disposal services by 1 or more of such political subdivisions to the other political subdivision or subdivisions. Any such contract shall be authorized or approved by the legislative body of each contracting political subdivision and shall be effective for such term as shall be prescribed therein not exceeding 50 years.

MCLA 123.233 Contracts validated. [MSA 5.2769(3)]

MCLA 123.234 Same; joint revenue bonds, authorization. [MSA 5.2769(4)]

MCLA 123.235 Same; contract; of revenues. [MSA 5.2769(5)]

JOINT ACTION
Act No. 316, P.A. 1931 - Sewage Disposal Plants, Cities, Villages

AN ACT to authorize cities and villages to construct, own, equip, operate, maintain and improve works for the disposal of sewage; to authorize charges against owners of premises for the use of such works and to provide for the

367

collection of the same; to authorize cities and villages to issue revenue bonds payable solely from the revenues of such works; and to make such bonds exempt from taxation and to make them lawful investments of sinking funds; to authorize contracts for the use of such works by private corporations and by other cities and villages and political subdivisions and charges against owners of premises therein served thereby.

MCLA 123.201 Sewage disposal plants, cities and villages.
MSA 5.2701

MCLA 123.201a Cities or villages on boundary line may contract with city or village in another state for sewage disposal.
MSA 5.2701(1)

MCLA 123.202 Ordinance required. MSA 5.2702

MCLA 123.203 Control of works. MSA 5.2703

MCLA 123.204 Powers. MSA 5.2704

MCLA 123.205 Cost of works, what included in. MSA 5.2705

MCLA 123.206 Revenue bonds. MSA 5.2706

MCLA 123.207 Same; details of. MSA 5.2707

MCLA 123.208 Additional bonds of a same standing. MSA 5.2708

MCLA 123.209 Lien upon bond proceeds. MSA 5.2709

MCLA 123.210 Terms, conditions, covenants and trust indenture.
MSA 5.2710

MCLA 123.211 Application of revenues. MSA 5.2711

MCLA 123.212 Rates or charges; assumpsit. MSA 5.2712

MCLA 123.213 Municipality liable to payment of charges.
MSA 5.2713

MCLA 123.214 Services to other municipalities and political subdivisions and to private corporations. [MSA 5.2714]

Sec. 14. ... Any municipality operating or proposing to operate sewage disposal works under this act (in this section called the owner) is hereby authorized to contract with 1 or more other cities, villages or political subdivisions within the state, and with profit and non-profit corporations (in this section called the lessee), and such lessees are hereby authorized to enter into such contracts with such owners, for ...

MCLA 123.215 Acquisition of encumbered property. [MSA 5.2715]

MCLA 123.216 Additional bonds constituting a junior charge. [MSA 5.2716]

MCLA 123.217 Action by trustee and bondholders. [MSA 5.2717]

MCLA 123.218 Authority in addition and not in derogation of other powers. [MSA 5.2718]

MCLA 123.219 No additional proceedings required. [MSA 5.2719]

MCLA 123.220 Liberal construction. [MSA 5.2720]

JOINT ACTION
Act No. 151, P.A. 1961 - Sanitary Sewage Collection Facilities

AN ACT to protect the health, safety and welfare of the people in counties by requiring properties from which sanitary sewage emanates to be connected to available public sanitary sewage collection facilities; to define properties affected by the act; to establish remedies and to fix penalties for the violation thereof.

MCLA 123.191 Sanitary sewage collection facility; definitions. [MSA 5.2767(101)]

MCLA 123.192 Same; connection, time for completion. [MSA 5.2767(102)]

MCLA 123.193 Same; demand, posting, contents. [MSA 5.2767(103)]

MCLA 123.194 Same; connection by facility operator, penalty, costs, collection. [MSA 5.2767(104)]

MCLA 123.195 Same; enforced connection. [MSA 5.2767(105)]

JOINT ACTION
Act No. 261, P.A. 1927 - Disposal Plants

AN ACT to prevent the acquisition, construction, operation, maintenance or building of garbage disposal plants, garbage reduction plants, sewage disposal tanks, settling basins, apparatus or screens for the treatment of sewage matter in certain cities and villages without having first procured permission from said cities or villages; to provide for the enforcement of this act; to declare such acquisition, construction, operation, maintenance, or building, a nuisance, in certain cases; to provide a manner in which the consent of said cities and villages may be granted, and to provide a penalty for the violation of this act.

MCLA 123.271 Disposal plants; power to prevent construction. [MSA 5.2691]

MCLA 123.272 Required permit. [MSA 5.2692]

MCLA 123.273 Same; procedure to secure; disposal of sewage by municipality; members of municipal authority. [MSA 5.2693]

Sec. 3. Any public or municipal corporation desiring such permit shall make application for the granting thereof unto the legislative body of any city or village in which said work or plant is proposed to be located. ....

MCLA 123.274 Declaration of nuisance; action. [MSA 5.2694]

MCLA 123.275 Application of act. [MSA 5.2695]

JOINT ACTION

Act No. 179, P.A. 1947 - Garbage or Rubbish Disposal and Dog Pound Authority

AN ACT to provide for the incorporation of certain municipal authorities for the collection or disposal, or both, of garbage or rubbish, or both, and for the operation of a dog pound; and to prescribe the powers, rights and duties thereof.

MCLA 123.301 Garbage and rubbish disposal and dog pound authority; incorporation by municipalities. [MSA 5.2725(1)]

Sec. 1. Any 2 or more cities, villages or townships, hereinafter referred to as "municipalities", or any combination thereof, may incorporate an authority ...

MCLA 123.302 Same; articles of incorporation, contents. [MSA 5.2725(2)]

MCLA 123.303 Same; corporate powers; construction of act. [MSA 5.2725(3)]

MCLA 123.304 Same; acquisition, management, sale or lease of land; condemnation. [MSA 5.2725(4)]

MCLA 123.305 Same; contracts, time limitations, charges. [MSA 5.2725(5)]

MCLA 123.306 Same; right to make subcontracts. [MSA 5.2725(6)]

MCLA 123.307 Same; amendments of articles of incorporation. [MSA 5.2725(7)]

Sec. 7. ...(Provides for subsequent inclusion of additional city, village or township)...

MCLA 123.308 Power to raise and expend moneys; payment of contracts; taxing power denied authority. [MSA 5.2725(8)]

MCLA 123.309 Bonds; issuance; payment. [MSA 5.2725(9)]

MCLA 123.310 Powers additional. [MSA 5.2725(10)]

AFFECTS JOINT ACTION
Act No. 159, P.A. 1969 - Sewer Construction

AN ACT to provide financial assistance to local agencies for the construction of collecting sewers to prevent the discharge of untreated or inadequately treated sewage or other liquid wastes into the waters of the state and to abate and prevent pollution of the waters in and adjoining the state; and to implement Act No. 76 of the Public Acts of 1968.

MCLA 323.401 Definitions. [MSA 5.2769(401)]

MCLA 323.402 Funding of collecting sewers, establishment of priority. [MSA 5.2769(402)]

MCLA 323.403 State sewer construction fund; establishment; use; grants, eligible sewer projects. [MSA 5.2769(403)]

Sec. 3. A fund to be known as the state sewer construction fund is established to be used for state grants to local agencies for their construction of collecting sewers. Grants shall be made only for collecting sewers on which contracts for construction were awarded by local agencies **after June 30, 1968 and before July 1, 1975, or until the fund is exhausted, whichever occurs first.**

MCLA 323.404 Source of moneys in fund; disbursements.
[MSA 5.2769(404)]

MCLA 323.405 Grants; applications; eligible parties; amount; limitations. [MSA 5.2769(405)]

MCLA 323.406 Disbursements, purposes, procedure.
[MSA 5.2769(406)]

MCLA 323.407 Rules, promulgation. [MSA 5.2769(407)]

MCLA 323.408 Officers and employees of other state agencies, use; grant recipients, records; access to records. [MSA 5.2769(408)]

MCLA 323.409 Priority establishment and project certification procedures, compliance as prerequisite to grant. [MSA 5.2769(409)]

MCLA 323.410 Pollution control needs, point system of measurement. [MSA 5.2769(410)]

MCLA 323.411 Total priority points; tied projects, additional considerations. [MSA 5.2769(411)]

MCLA 323.412 Fiscal year; applications for grants, filing, time, life; pollution control plan, filing, time; point totals, assignment; certification of projects, time, conditions; reports to legislature; legislative approval or rejection. [MSA 5.2769(412)]

FIRE AND POLICE PROTECTION

Modern man has come a long way from the bucket brigade fire-fighting techniques of our forefathers to the modern miracle-performing equipment of today. And we have come a long way from the days when a single constable was able to protect the thirty-six square miles of the average township to the sophisticated police departments now operated by a number of Michigan townships.

Here again it is essential to weigh the benefits of any one statute against the others. We especially direct your attention to Act No. 33, P.A. 1951, covering fire protection and Act No. 181, P.A. 1951, dealing with police departments. They provide the governing body of a township with a genuine opportunity to establish a benefit for the whole township which can be financially supported on a township-wide basis. Both allow the board to provide these services within the township's own capabilities, or to join with other units of government if it is determined that such joint effort will give better protection to the residents. Water for fire protection may be obtained through the use of an appropriate statute listed in the section immediately preceding.

Care should be exercised in the selection of police and fire personnel. They must be mentally alert, physically capable and possessed of qualities of tolerance, understanding and deep appreciation for the problems of others. Michigan has pioneered in providing adequate instruction and training for firemen and police officers, and all such personnel are required to undergo that training, with few exceptions.

The Michigan State Police is available to township boards to provide a great deal of advisory assistance in police matters, as well as many aspects of organizing fire inspection techniques and prevention measures.

The Michigan Inspection Service, operated by the private insurance companies, has long been available to advise and assist local government in the field of fire protection in such matters as selection of the proper type equipment, spacing of fire hydrants, number of fire-fighting personnel and specialty training.

The National Safety Council and the Michigan Safety Council are additional sources for advice and information in these areas.

Of particular importance to township officials, these advisory services may be obtained at no cost to the township.

The Motor Vehicle Code, Act No. 300, P.A. 1939, cited in the Motor Vehicle and Snowmobile section of this chapter, should be carefully reviewed for references to emergency vehicles. If a township has a police department or traffic officers, the officers of course must be thoroughly familiar with the whole Motor Vehicle Code.

JOINT ACTION
Act No. 33, P.A. 1951 - Fire Protection

AN ACT to provide fire protection for townships, and for certain areas in townships and incorporated villages and for cities under 15,000 population; to authorize contracting for fire protection; to authorize the purchase of fire extinguishing apparatus and equipment, and the maintenance and operation thereof; to provide for defraying the cost thereof; to authorize the creation of special assessment districts, and for the levying and collecting of special assessments; to authorize the issuance of special assessment bonds in anticipation of the collection of special assessment taxes, to advance the amount necessary to pay such bonds, and providing for reimbursement for such advances by reassessment if necessary; and to repeal certain acts and parts of acts.

MCLA 41.801 Fire protection for townships; purchase of apparatus and equipment, limitation. [MSA 5.2640(1)]

Sec. 1. The township board of any township, or adjoining townships, acting jointly, whether or not such townships are located in the same county, may purchase fire extinguishing apparatus and equipment and housing for the same, and for that purpose may provide by resolution for the appropriation of general or contingent funds in an amount which in any one year shall not exceed 10 mills of the assessed valuation of the area in their respective townships for which fire protection is to be furnished.

Maintenance and operation. The township board of any township, or adjoining townships, acting jointly, whether or not such townships are located in the same county, may also provide annually by resolution for the appropriation of general or contingent funds for the purpose of maintenance and operation of a fire department, or for the providing of fire protection by contract.

Special assessment; bonds. The township board or boards acting jointly may provide that all or any part of the aforesaid sums for purchasing and housing of equipment or the operation thereof or contracting for protection may be defrayed by special assessment on all of the lands and premises in said township or townships to be benefited thereby, and may issue bonds in anticipation of the collection of said special assessments.

Same; referendum, creation of district. The question of raising money by special assessment may be submitted to the electors of the affected area in the township or townships by the township board, or township boards acting jointly, and shall be submitted by the township board or township boards acting jointly on the filing of a petition so requesting, signed by at least 10% of the owners of the land in each of the affected townships, to be made into such a special assessment district, at any general election or special election called for that purpose by the township board or township boards acting jointly. No such special assessment district shall be created unless approved by a majority vote of the electors voting on the question at such an election.

Estimate of cost, hearing, notice; levy, hearing of objections, collection of assessments...

MCLA 41.802 Same; annual appropriation for maintenance and operation. [MSA 5.2640(2)]

MCLA 41.803 Same; special assessments, levy, bonds, advancements. [MSA 5.2640(3)]

MCLA 41.804 Same; special election; laws governing. MSA 5.2640(4)

MCLA 41.805 Same; standard fire prevention code, adoption by publication by reference, inspection of copies. MSA 5.2640(5)

MCLA 41.806 Same; department; rules and regulations; care of equipment; administrative board. MSA 5.2640(6)

MCLA 41.807 Acts repealed. MSA 5.2640(7)

MCLA 41.808 Rights or obligations safeguarded. MSA 5.2640(8)

MCLA 41.809 Joint meetings of township boards. MSA 5.2640(9)

MCLA 41.810 Fire protection for townships, villages, and cities under 15,000; joint action. MSA 5.2640(10)

Sec. 10. ... No township, incorporated village or city under 15,000 inhabitants shall in any way use this act to lessen the number of paid full time firemen in their respective communities.

AFFECTS JOINT ACTION
Act No. 205, P.A. 1964 - Fire Fighting Equipment, Purchase by Municipalities

AN ACT authorizing the purchase by municipalities of fire trucks, fire fighting apparatus and equipment on executory title retaining contracts and under chattel mortgage financing.

MCLA 141.451 Fire trucks, fire fighting apparatus and equipment; purchase by municipalities; title-retaining contract, chattel mortgage. MSA 5.2586(11)

Sec. 1. The legislative body of any county, city, village, township or other local unit of government may purchase on executory title retaining contracts, or finance purchases by chattel mortgages as security for the purchase price, any fire trucks, fire fighting apparatus and equipment and pay for the same out of the general fund of such municipality, but such contracts or chattel mortgages

376

shall not provide for payments for longer than the estimated period of usefulness of the property being purchased, and in no event for longer than 6 years. Such contracts or chattel mortgages, and the purchase of such property thereunder, shall not be subject to the provisions of Act No. 202 of the Public Acts of 1943, as amended, being sections 131.1 [MSA 5.3188(1)] *to 138.2* [MSA 5.3188(49)] *of the Compiled Laws of 1948.*

JOINT ACTION
Act No. 15, P.A. 1942, 2nd Ex. Sess. - County Fire Protection

AN ACT to authorize county boards of supervisors to provide fire protection for certain areas in counties now or hereafter having a population of not less than 5,000 inhabitants; to authorize the contracting for fire protection or the purchase of fire extinguishing apparatus and equipment, and maintenance and operation thereof; and to authorize such counties to make appropriations to pay the cost thereof.

MCLA 46.301 Fire protection for certain counties; contracts with townships. [MSA 5.2586(1)]

MCLA 46.302 Same; appropriation; board of supervisors may make. [MSA 5.2586(2)]

MCLA 46.303 Declaration of emergency. [MSA 5.2586(3)]

AFFECTS JOINT ACTION
Act No. 57, P.A. 1951 - Police and/or Fire Administrative Board

AN ACT to provide for townships having an organized police or fire department, or both, for the creation of an administrative board; and to prescribe the powers and duties of such administrative board.

MCLA 41.751 Police and/or fire administrative board; members, terms, expenses, vacancies. [MSA 5.2640(21)]

MCLA 41.752 Same; budget, review, adoption. [MSA 5.2640(22)]

MCLA 41.753 Act supplemental. [MSA 5.2640(23)]

AFFECTS JOINT ACTION
Act No. 78, P.A. 1935 - Firemen and Policemen Civil Service

AN ACT to establish and provide a board of civil service commissioners in cities, villages and municipalities having full paid members in the fire and/or police departments; to provide a civil service system based upon examination and investigation as to merit, efficiency and fitness for appointment, employment and promotion of all officers and men appointed in said fire and police departments and respective cities, villages and municipalities; to regulate the transfer, reinstatement, suspension and discharge of said officers, firemen and policemen; and to repeal all acts and parts of acts inconsistent therewith.

MCLA 38.501 Civil service system for fire and police departments, commission created. [MSA 5.3351]

MCLA 38.502 Same; commission members, appointment, terms; president. [MSA 5.3352]

MCLA 38.503 Same; commissions, members, qualifications.
[MSA 5.3353]

MCLA 38.504 Same; vacancies, removal. [MSA 5.3354]

MCLA 38.505 Same; clerk. [MSA 5.3355]

MCLA 38.506 Eligibility for permanent appointment (of employees).
[MSA 5.3356]

MCLA 38.507 New appointments (of employees). [MSA 5.3357]

MCLA 38.508 Assistance by executive officers, supplies and printing (of governing body of municipality). [MSA 5.3358]

MCLA 38.509 Powers and duties of commission. [MSA 4.3359]

378

MCLA 38.510 Application for examination; eligibility; physical examination; reinstatement. [MSA 5.3360]

MCLA 38.510a Applications; municipalities of 10,000 or less in population. [MSA 5.3360(1)]

MCLA 38.511 Examinations; probationary appointments; filling positions; non-competitive examinations; temporary appointments; special examinations for electricians, mechanics, radio engineers, fire inspectors or fire alarm operators. [MSA 5.3361]

MCLA 38.512 Same; nature, notice; vacancies filled by promotions. [MSA 5.3362]

MCLA 38.513 Reduction in pay; suspensions and discharges; hearing. [MSA 5.3363]

MCLA 38.514 Removal or suspension; charges; hearing; appeal; reductions in force. [MSA 5.3364]

MCLA 38.515 Violations of act. [MSA 5.3365]

MCLA 38.516 Same; penalty. [MSA 5.3366]

MCLA 38.517 Same; definitions. [MSA 5.3367]

MCLA 38.517a Referendum. [MSA 5.3368]

MCLA 38.518 Referendum on rescission and repeal. [MSA 5.3369(1)]

Act No. 327, P.A. 1965 - Fire Department Standards

AN ACT to set certain minimum standards for fire departments in certain municipalities; and to provide a time within which they must comply.

MCLA 123.831 Fire departments in cities of 70,000 or more; minimum standards. [MSA 5.2585(101)]

Sec. 1. In each city, township or village which has or shall hereafter attain a population of 70,000 or more according to the last decennial census, the fire department shall meet the minimum stan-

dards set by the Michigan inspection bureau to qualify for class 6 fire classification.

MCLA 123.832 Time within which standards must be met.
[MSA 5.2585(102)]

Sec. 2. These minimum standards shall be met within 1 year from the effective date of this act or within 1 year from the date the municipality attains a population of 70,000 or more.

AFFECTS JOINT ACTION
Act No. 125, P.A. 1925 - Fire Department Hours of Labor

AN ACT to regulate the hours of labor of employes in the fire departments of municipalities, and providing penalties for the violation thereof.

MCLA 123.841 Fire department employees; period of duty; days off duty; work hours per week. [MSA 5.3331]

MCLA 123.842 Persons exempt. [MSA 5.3332]

MCLA 123.843 Penalty. [MSA 5.3333]

AFFECTS JOINT ACTION
Act No. 201, P.A. 1970 - Police Cadet Training Programs

AN ACT to authorize police cadets programs in cities, villages and townships operating under the provisions of Act No. 78 of the Public Acts of 1935, as amended.

MCLA 38.521 Program authorized; applicants for enrollment, qualifications; cadets, functions, advancement, term of service.
[MSA 5.3372(1)]

JOINT ACTION
Act No. 181, P.A. 1951 - Police Protection

AN ACT to provide police protection for townships and for certain areas in townships; to authorize the pur-

chase of police motor vehicles, apparatus and equipment, and the maintenance and operation thereof; to provide for defraying the cost thereof; to authorize the creation of special assessment districts, and for the levying and collection of special assessments.

MCLA 41.851 Police protection for townships; purchase of police motor vehicles, etc.; appropriation; special assessment; referendum; estimate of cost; hearing, notice; hearing objections; assessment, levy and collection. [MSA 5.2640(31)]

Sec. 1. The township board of any township, or adjoining townships, acting jointly, whether or not such townships are located in the same county, may purchase police motor vehicles, apparatus and equipment and housing for the same, and for that purpose may provide by resolution for the appropriation of general or contingent funds in an amount which in any 1 year shall not exceed 10 mills of the assessed valuation of the area in their respective townships for which police protection is to be furnished.

The township board of any township, or adjoining townships, acting jointly, whether or not such townships are located in the same county, may also provide annually by resolution for the appropriation of general or contingent funds in an amount which shall not exceed 2 1/2 mills of the assessed valuation of the area for which police protection is to be furnished for the purpose of maintenance and operation of a police department.

The said township board or boards, acting jointly, may provide that all or any part of the aforesaid sums for purchasing and housing of equipment and/or the operation thereof may be defrayed by special assessment on all of the lands and premises in said township or townships to be benefited thereby.

The question of raising money by special assessment may be submitted to the electors of the township or townships by the township board or township boards acting jointly, on the filing of a petition so requesting, signed by at least 10 per centum of the owners of the land in each of the affected townships, to be made into such a special assessment district, at any general election or special election called for that purpose by the township board or township boards acting jointly.

In the case of the creation of a special assessment district, the township board, or township boards acting jointly, shall estimate the cost and expenses of such police motor vehicles, apparatus and equipment and housing and/or police protection, and fix a day for a hearing on said estimate and on the question of creating a special assessment district and defraying any or all expenses thereof by special assessment upon the property to be especially benefited thereby. A notice ...: Provided, however, That in the event that the collections received from such special assessment so levied to defray the cost or portion intended to be defrayed thereby of said police protection shall be, at any time, insufficient to meet the obligations or expenses incurred for the maintenance and operation of said police department, the township board of said township, or townships acting jointly, may, by resolution, authorize the transfer or loan of sufficient money therefor from the general fund of said township or townships, to said special assessment police department fund, the same to be repaid to the general fund of the township or townships out of special assessment funds when collected.

MCLA 41.852 Same; annual appropriation. MSA 5.2640(32)

MCLA 41.853 Same; special assessments, provisions governing. MSA 5.2640(33)

MCLA 41.854 Same; special election, laws governing. MSA 5.2640(34)

MCLA 41.855 Police department, establishment and maintenance; administrative board. MSA 5.2640(35)

MCLA 41.856 Joint meetings of township boards. MSA 5.2640(36)

JOINT ACTION
Act No. 236, P.A. 1967 - Police, Municipal Mutual Assistance Agreements

AN ACT to authorize cities, villages and townships to enter into mutual police assistance agreements; to define the terms of the agreement; and to provide for the compensating of the cities, villages and townships entering into such agreements.

MCLA 123.811 Cities, villages, townships; authority to enter into agreements. MSA 5.3323(1)

382

MCLA 123.812 Agreements; nature and declaration of emergency; grounds for requests; officials entitled to request; payment for services; powers and duties; authority being served. [MSA 5.3323(2)]

MCLA 123.813 Compensation, disability, retirement, and furlough payments; equipment and supplies charges. [MSA 5.3323(3)]

MCLA 123.814 Adjacent cities, villages, or townships, contracts or establishment of inter-municipal police authorities; approval; administration, apportionment of costs. [MSA 5.3323(4)]

JOINT ACTION
Act No. 222, P.A. 1970 — Northern Michigan University

AN ACT to authorize the board of control of northern Michigan university to adopt ordinances respecting persons and property and to provide for the enforcement of the ordinances.

MCLA 390.591 - 390.594 [MSA 15.1120(101) - 15.1120(104)]

JOINT ACTION
Act No. 291, P.A. 1967 — Parking, Traffic and Pedestrian Ordinances

AN ACT to authorize state universities and colleges to enact parking, traffic and pedestrian ordinances and to provide for the enforcement of the ordinances; and to dispose of fines collected.

MCLA 390.891 Enactment of ordinances, governing boards; penalties; enforcement; uniform traffic code, conformance.
[MSA 15.1120(51)]

Sec. 1. The governing boards ... may each enact parking, traffic and pedestrian ordinances for the government and control of their respective campuses and may provide that violation of such ordinance is a misdemeanor punishable by a fine of not to exceed $25.00 for each violation: Provided, That enforcement of such ordinances shall be by law enforcement officers of the state of

Michigan, county, township or city wherein the violation ... occurs. Such ordinance shall be ...

MCLA 390.892 Enforcement of ordinances; jurisdiction; procedure; appeals; fines, disposition, costs. [MSA 15.1120(52)]

Sec. 2. Violation ... may be enforced in any court having jurisdiction over misdemeanors in the political subdivision where the violation occurs. ... Fines collected shall be paid to the treasurer of the political subdivision in which the offense is tried within 30 days after collection, and costs ...

MCLA 390.893 Parking violations bureau for state university or college, establishment, jurisdiction, duties, expenses, personnel. [MSA 15.1120(53)]

Sec. 3. The governing board ... may establish a parking violations bureau as an exclusive agency to accept pleas of guilty in cases of violation of ... ordinance and to collect and retain fines and costs as prescribed in such ordinance. ...

JOINT ACTION
Act No. 68, P.A. 1913 — Drunkenness on Train

AN ACT relating to drunkenness on railway trains or interurban cars, and prohibiting the drinking of intoxicating liquor thereon as a beverage, and providing for the arrest of offenders, and penalties for violation of this act.

MCLA 436.201 - 436.205 [MSA 1241 - 1245]

JOINT ACTION
Act No. 288, P.A. 1965 — Transportation of Migrant Agricultural Workers

AN ACT to require the department of commerce, public service commission division, to adopt rules and regulations for the minimum safety requirements for motor vehicles, and the operators thereof, used to transport migrant agricultural workers; and to provide a penalty for the violation of such rules.

MCLA 286.601 Transportation of migrant agricultural workers, department to adopt rules. MSA 17.425(1)

MCLA 286.602 Department to encourage compliance. MSA 17.425(2)

JOINT ACTION
Act No. 150, P.A. 1967 — Michigan Military Act

CHAPTER 2. COMMAND AND EMPLOYMENT OF FORCES

MCLA 32.551 Governor, commander-in-chief; adjutant general; power to order out organized militia. MSA 4.678(151)

MCLA 32.575 Martial law, declaration. MSA 4.678(175)

CHAPTER 5. DEFENSE FORCE

MCLA 32.736 Armories, air bases, naval installations; use, organized militia, veterans' organizations; intoxicating liquors. MSA 4.678(336)

Sec. 336. ... The use ... of intoxicating liquors ... is authorized. ... With the approval of the legislative body of the political subdivision in which an ... installation is located, outside parties of a non-military or state governmental nature may use or serve intoxicating liquors in conformity with rules and regulations of the liquor control commission, if not in violation of any other local ordinance, state or federal law or regulation.

JOINT ACTION
Act No. 139, P.A. 1947 - Recovery of Drowned Bodies

AN ACT to prescribe the powers and duties of certain public officers with respect to the recovery of the bodies of persons drowned in the waters over which the state of Michigan has jurisdiction.

MCLA 51.301 Drowned bodies; chiefs of police or sheriffs, duty to recover, expenses. MSA 18.1221

MCLA 51.302 Same; aid from other public agencies; jurisdiction. MSA 18.1222

JOINT ACTION
Act No. 62, P.A. 1941 - State Crime Detection Laboratory

AN ACT to establish a state crime detection laboratory; to provide for the coordination of state laboratory facilities; to prescribe the powers and duties of the state department of health and the Michigan state police with respect thereto; and to cooperate with law enforcement officers.

MCLA 325.101 State crime detection laboratory; rules and regulations. MSA 14.54

MCLA 325.102 Same; commissioner of health to organize; equipment; use; expenses. MSA 14.55

MCLA 325.103 State laboratories to cooperate regarding violations of law. MSA 14.56

JOINT ACTION
Act No. 295, P.A. 1972 - Forensic Polygraph Examaminers Act

AN ACT to license and regulate persons who purport to be able to detect deception, verify truthfulness, or provide a diagnostic opinion of either through the use of any device or instrumentation as lie detectors, forensic polygraphs, deceptographs, emotional stress meters or similar or related devices and instruments; to create a state board of forensic polygraph examiners with licensing and regulatory powers over all such persons and instruments; to provide for administrative proceedings and court review; to establish minimum standards and requirements for all such instrumentation or devices and to prohibit the use of instruments or devices which do not meet minimum standards and requirements; and to provide for injunctions and penalties.

386

MCLA 338.1701 Short title. [MSA 18.186(1)]

MCLA 338.1702 Persons subject to act. [MSA 18.186(2)]

MCLA 338.1703 Definitions. [MSA 18.186(3)]

MCLA 338.1704 Minimum standards for instruments or devices. [MSA 18.186(4)]

MCLA 338.1705 State board of forensic polygraph examiners, creation, membership. [MSA 18.186(5)]

MCLA 338.1706 Board officers and meetings; quorum; vote required for action by board; expenses; reimbursement; annual report. [MSA 18.186(6)]

MCLA 338.1707 Rules; filing of applications; order or certified copy, prima facie proof; disposition of fees collected; funds, source. [MSA 18.186(7)]

MCLA 338.1708 Licenses, necessity. [MSA 18.186(8)]

MCLA 338.1709 Issuance of examiner's license without examination, grounds; issuance of temporary examiner's license, grounds. [MSA 18.186(9)]

MCLA 338.1710 Issuance of examiner's license with examination, grounds. [MSA 18.186(10)]

MCLA 338.1711 Intern's licenses, qualifications of licensees. [MSA 18.186(11)]

MCLA 338.1712 Temporary examiner's license, qualifications of licensees. [MSA 18.186(12)]

MCLA 338.1713 Nonresident applicants for intern's license or temporary examiner's license, consent as to filing of actions and service of process; copy of process to applicants. [MSA 18.186(13)]

MCLA 338.1714 Persons licensed in other states or territories, issuance of licenses without examination, grounds. [MSA 18.186(14)]

MCLA 338.1715 Nonrefundable fees accompanying applications. [MSA 18.186(15)]

MCLA 338.1716 Terms of licenses; renewal of licenses. [MSA 18.186(16)]

MCLA 338.1717 Form, issuance, display, change of address notification, surrender, and evidence of licenses. [MSA 18.186(17)]

MCLA 338.1718 Renewal of licenses. [MSA 18.186(18)]

MCLA 338.1719 Suspension or revocation of licenses, grounds. [MSA 18.186(19)]

MCLA 338.1720 Investigation of applicant's or licensees' actions; notice and hearings; denial, suspension, or revocation of licenses. [MSA 18.186(20)]

MCLA 338.1721 Surrender or seizure of revoked or suspended licenses. [MSA 18.186(21)]

MCLA 338.1722 Reinstatement of suspended or revoked licenses. [MSA 18.186(22)]

MCLA 338.1723 Board proceedings, transcript of record; board's report, service; rehearing, motion; order. [MSA 18.186(23)]

MCLA 338.1724 Review of board's administrative decisions. [MSA 18.186(24)]

MCLA 338.1725 Witnesses, attendance, testimony; production of documents; contempt. [MSA 18.186(25)]

MCLA 338.1726 Discharge of employees, refusal of polygraph examination or lie detector or similar test, untruthfulness during examination or test; admissibility of examination or test results. [MSA 18.186(26)]

MCLA 338.1727 Orders enjoining violations or enforcing compliance; temporary injunctions; contempt proceedings; other remedies and penalties. [MSA 18.186(27)]

MCLA 338.1728 Divulging information, prohibition, offenses, suspension or revocation of licenses; confidential information. [MSA 18.186(28)]

MCLA 338.1729 Violations or falsely representing status as examiner or intern, offenses. [MSA 18.186(29)]

JOINT ACTION
Act No. 50, P. A. 1919 — Traffic Officers

AN ACT to provide for the appointment of traffic officers in townships and defining their powers and duties, and providing for their compensation.

MCLA 41.201   Traffic officers; compensation. [MSA 5.191]

Sec. 1. The township board of any township may, by a majority vote of the township board at any regular meeting or any special meeting called for that purpose, provide for the employment of a traffic officer or officers in such township, the compensation of such officer or officers to be paid from the general fund of such township: Provided, That 2 or more townships may, by a majority vote of all the township boards, appoint such officer at a joint meeting of such township boards held for that purpose, and the proportion of the compensation of such traffic officer or officers to be paid by each of such townships shall be determined at such joint meeting.

MCLA 41.202 Same; powers. [MSA 5.192]

Sec. 2. Whenever any traffic officer shall be appointed under the provisions of this act, such traffic officer shall be vested with all powers of arrest, and other powers, now vested by law in deputy sheriffs. The compensation and service of such officers shall be determined by the township board or boards.

AFFECTS JOINT ACTION
Act No. 345, P. A. 1937 — Firemen and Policemen Pensions

AN ACT to provide for the establishment, maintenance and administration of a system of pensions and retirements for the benefit of the personnel of fire and/or police departments, employed by cities, villages or municipalities having full paid members in such departments, and for the widows and children of such members, and to provide for the creation of a board of trustees to manage and operate same; to authorize appropriations and deductions from salaries; and to repeal all acts and parts of acts inconsistent therewith.

MCLA 38.551 Fire and police department pension system; retirement board, members, qualifications, election, appointment, term. MSA 5.3375(1)

MCLA 38.552 Powers and duties of board. MSA 5.3375(2)

MCLA 38.553 Custodian of funds; bond; disbursements, authorization by board. MSA 5.3375(3)

Sec. 3.   The treasurer of the ... municipality shall be the custodian of all funds of the retirement system and shall be required to give a good and sufficient bond to said board ... to be paid by said ... municipality, and ...

MCLA 38.554   Credit for prior service. MSA 5.3375(4)

MCLA 38.555 Actions of board reviewable by writ of certiorari. MSA 5.3375(5)

MCLA 38.556 Pensions and benefits payable. Age and service retirement. Retirement at age 55 with 25 years of service. Retirement at age 60 on application of head of department. Compulsory retirement at age 65. Regular retirement pension; amount; return of contributions. Average final compensation. Service credit, computation. Optional retirement pensions. Death after 20 years of service without election of option; payment to widow. Service of 45 years; election of option I. Disability and service-connected death benefits. Widow's duty death pension. Children's duty death pension. Other dependents duty death pension. Duty disability pension; medical examination. Nonduty disability pension; medical examination. Periodic medical examination; workmen's compensation, effect. Disability retirant; election to continue disability pension after age 55. MSA 5.3375(6)

MCLA 38.556a Same; death of member without election of option, duration of service in certain cities (municipalities over 80,000). [MSA 5.3375(6.1)]

MCLA 38.556b Vested rights, pensions and benefits other than disability benefits; subsequent disciplinary actions, charges, complaints. [MSA 5.3375(6.2)]

MCLA 38.557 Act of duty defined; municipality, definition. [MSA 5.3375(7)]

MCLA 38.558 Refunds of salary contributions. [MSA 5.3375(8)]

MCLA 38.559 Revenues and accumulations of an adequate reserve. [MSA 5.3375(9)]

MCLA 38.560 Investment of cash assets and funds on hand. [MSA 5.3375(10)]

MCLA 38.561 Referendum; township or charter township. [MSA 5.3375(11)]

Sec. 11. At any time after this act shall become effective, any ... municipality having a paid or part paid fire or police department, may come under the provisions of this act and create a pension board hereunder by submitting the same to the electors of any such ... municipality at any regular or special election for adoption, in the manner provided by law for amending charters: Provided, That this act shall not become effective until the beginning of the next succeeding fiscal year after such adoption of the provisions of this act by any ... municipality: Provided further, That where no provision is made in the charter of the ... municipality for amending said charters, this act may be submitted for adoption in accordance with any law authorizing the amending of the charters of cities: Provided further, That in case of a township or charter township, this act shall be submitted to the qualified electors of such township or townships by the township board on the filing of a petition requesting the submission, signed by 10 per cent of the registered and qualified electors in such township or charter township, at any general election or special election called for that purpose by the township board, in accordance with the laws of this state, and this act shall be in force and effect in any such township or charter township if a majority of electors voting on such proposition, as determined by the canvass of votes cast, shall vote in favor thereof.

MCLA 38.562 Membership of retirement system; inclusions, exclusions. [MSA 5.3375(12)]

AFFECTS JOINT ACTION
Act No. 329, P.A. 1937 — Peace Officers Injured in Active Duty

AN ACT providing for compensation to certain peace officers injured in active duty, and payment to dependents in case of death arising from active duty; and to make an appropriation therefor.

MCLA 419.101 Peace officer (elective or appointive); **disability, total, partial, compensation, medical care.** [MSA 4.456]

MCLA 419.102 Same; dependents, compensation; medical and burial expense. [MSA 4.457]

MCLA 419.103 Same; payment; appropriation; review of claims by attorney general. [MSA 4.458]

MCLA 419.104 Peace officer suffering disability as result of active duty; application of act; definition. [MSA 4.459]

AFFECTS JOINT ACTION
Act No. 9, P.A. 1942, 1st Ex. Sess. — Firemen Injured in Duty

AN ACT providing for compensation to certain firemen injured in the safeguarding of life and property, and payment to dependents in case of death; and to make an appropriation therefor.

MCLA 419.201 Co-operation between fire departments and state fire marshal; authority of departments outside of their municipality in emergencies. [MSA 4.584(1)]

MCLA 419.202 Firemen (volunteer, part-paid, full-paid) **injured outside of jurisdiction; compensation.** [MSA 4.584(2)]

MCLA 419.203 Same; death, compensation payable to dependents. [MSA 4.584(3)]

MCLA 419.204 Same; payment of compensation from general fund; appropriation. [MSA 4.584(4)]

MCLA 419.205 Application of act; provisions of local charter. [MSA 4.584(5)]

Sec. 5. ... The ... municipality may, in accordance with its charter provisions, pay to said employee, his dependent or dependents, the difference between the benefits provided by this act and the benefits provided for by the municipalities ..., but shall pay no more than said difference. Any contributions made by said employee to any benefit fund or protective association independent of the charter of the municipality shall be taken into consideration in determining the compensation to be paid hereunder.

AFFECTS JOINT ACTION
Act No. 312, P. A. 1969 — Compulsory Arbitration of Labor Disputes, Policemen and Firemen

AN ACT to provide for compulsory arbitration of labor disputes in municipal police and fire departments; to define such public departments; to provide for the selection of members of arbitration panels; to prescribe the procedures and authority thereof; and to provide for the enforcement and review of awards thereof.

MCLA 423.231 Public policy. [MSA 17.455(31)]

Sec. 1. It is the public policy of this state that in public police and fire departments, where the right of employees to strike is by law prohibited, it is requisite to the high morale of such employees and the efficient operation of such departments to afford an alternate, expeditious, effective and binding procedure for the resolution of disputes, and to that end the provisions of this act, providing for compulsory arbitration, shall be liberally construed.

MCLA 423.232 Public police and fire departments, definitions. [MSA 17.455(32)]

Sec. 2. Public police and fire departments means any department of a ... township having employees engaged as policemen or in fire fighting or subject to the hazards thereof.

MCLA 423.233 Grounds for initiation of arbitration proceedings. [MSA 17.455(33)]

MCLA 423.234 Arbitration panel, selection of delegates. [MSA 17.455(34)]

MCLA 423.235 Arbitrator or chairman of panel, appointment. [MSA 17.455(35)]

MCLA 423.236 Hearing; notice of time and place; evidence; parties; record, transcripts; expenses; time limit; majority rule. [MSA 17.455(36)]

MCLA 423.237 Oaths; attendance of witnesses; production of documents; contempt. [MSA 17.455(37)]

MCLA 423.237a Remanding dispute to parties for further collective bargaining. [MSA 17.455(37A)]

MCLA 423.238 Disputed economic issues, identification; submissions of settlement offers, adoption; findings, opinion, and order, delivery of copies, basis. [MSA 17.455(38)]

MCLA 423.239 Basis for findings, opinions, and orders. [MSA 17.455(39)]

MCLA 423.240 Majority decision, finality, binding effect, enforcement; commencement of new fiscal year, effect; compensation increases, effective date; stipulations, effect. [MSA 17.455(40)]

MCLA 423.241 Disobedience of lawful enforcement order, unlawful strike; penalty. [MSA 17.455(41)]

MCLA 423.242 Review, venue, scope, stay of order. [MSA 17.455(42)]

MCLA 423.243 Change of employment conditions during pendency of arbitration proceedings. [MSA 17.455(43)]

MCLA 423.244 Supplementary to act forbidding strikes by public employees; fact finding requirements, applicability. [MSA 17.455(44)]

MCLA 423.245 Expiration date; pending cases, disposition. [MSA 17.455(45)]

Sec. 15. This act shall expire June 30, 1975. Cases pending under negotiations on June 30, 1975 shall be completed under the provisions of this act.

MCLA 423.246 Imprisonment for violations, prohibition. [MSA 17.455(46)]

MCLA 423.247 Effective date. [MSA 17.455(47)]

JOINT ACTION
Act No. 203, P.A. 1965 -- Law Enforcement Officers Training Council Act

AN ACT to provide for the creation of a law enforcement officers training council; to provide for additional costs in criminal cases and the establishment of the law enforcement officers training fund and a locations therefrom to local agencies of government participating in a police training program.

MCLA 28.601 Short title. [MSA 4.450(1)]

MCLA 28.602 Definitions. [MSA 4.450 (2)]

Sec. 2. ... "Police officer" or "law enforcement officer" means a member of a police force or other organization of a ... township ... regularly employed as such and who is responsible for the prevention and detection of crime and the enforcement of the general criminal laws of this state, but shall not include any person serving as such solely by virtue of his occupying any other office or position.

MCLA 28.603 - 28.604 [MSA 4.450(3) - 4.450(4)]

MCLA 28.605 Same; designation of chairman, powers.
[MSA 4.450(5)]

MCLA 28.606 - 28.608 [MSA 4.450(6) - 4.450(8)]

MCLA 28.609 Minimum employment standards, preparation, publication, subject matter, waiver of requirements. [MSA 4.450 (9)]

Sec. 9. (1) The council shall prepare and publish minimum employment standards with due consideration to varying factors and special requirements of local police agencies relative to: ...

(2) Notwithstanding any other provision of this, or any statute, a regularly employed person employed on or after January 1, 1971, as a member of a police force having 3 or more full-time officers shall not be empowered to exercise all the authority of a peace officer in this state, nor employed in a position which is granted (such) authority by statute, unless the person has complied with the minimum employment standards prepared and published by the council pursuant to this section. Law enforcement officers employed on or before January 1, 1971, may continue their employment and participate in training programs on a voluntary or assigned basis but failure to meet standards shall not be grounds for dismissal of or termination of employment.

MCLA 28.610 Same; agreements with other agencies.
[MSA 4.450(10)]

MCLA 28.611 - 28.613 [MSA 4.450 (11) - 4.450(13)]

MCLA 28.614 Payments to police officers meeting standards and participating in training. [MSA 4.450(14)]

MCLA 28.615 Applications for aid. [MSA 4.450(15)]

Sec. 15. Any ... township ... which desires to receive aid pursuant to this act shall make application to the council for such aid. The application must be accompanied by a certified copy of an ordinance or resolution adopted by its governing body providing that while receiving ...(such)... aid ..., the ... township ... will adhere

396

to the standards established by the council. The application shall contain such information as the council may request.

MCLA 28.616 Effective date. [MSA 4.450(16)]

JOINT ACTION
Act No. 246, P.A. 1945 - Township Ordinances

AN ACT to authorize township boards to adopt ordinances and regulations to secure the public health, safety and general welfare; to provide for the establishment of a township police department; to provide for the policing of townships by the county sheriff; to provide penalties; and to repeal all acts and parts of acts in conflict therewith.

MCLA 41.181 - 41.183 [MSA 5.45(1) - 5.45(3)]

Note: This act makes provision for policing of the township by a township police department or by contract with the county sheriff for ordinance enforcement. See the full citation in the section on Ordinances at the end of this chapter.

AMBULANCE, INHALATOR AND FIRST AID SERVICES

People, in a hurry to get themselves and their goods from one place to another in high speed trucks and other motor vehicles, have brought about the construction of a proliferation of interstate four-lane highways throughout the country in the past thirty years. The attendant automobile accidents occurring with clocklike regularity, day after day, year after year, have created more and more demands upon local governments by various organizations, including the state, to provide ambulance, inhalator and first aid services to take care of emergencies.

Since this can be a very costly operation, township officials are urged to thoroughly study all facilities already available within a given area -- the number of ambulances and the amount of equipment and trained personnel -- and then determine the best way of providing what is needed. The service may be operated within the framework of the fire or police department, or through contract with another municipality or a private agency. A great deal of advice, suggestions and recommendations may be obtained from representatives of insurance agencies. Again, care should be taken to select the proper statute to organize the system which can best serve the township.

The Motor Vehicle Code, Act No. 30, P.A. 1949, cited in the Motor Vehicle and Snowmobile section of this chapter, should be carefully reviewed for references to ambulances and emergency vehicles.

JOINT ACTION
Act No. 50, P.A. 1960 - Ambulance and Inhalator Service

AN ACT to permit townships and counties to operate or to contract for ambulance and inhalator service.

MCLA 41.711 Ambulance and inhalator services, counties, townships. [MSA 5.160]

MCLA 41.711a Civil liability; municipal or private ambulance driver or attendant, policemen, fireman. [MSA 5.160(1)]

MCLA 41.711b Red cross first aid course. [MSA 5.160(2)]

JOINT ACTION
Act No. 258, P.A. 1968 - Ambulances

AN ACT to regulate the licensing and operation of ambulances; to provide for renewal of licenses; to regulate the licensing and qualifications of drivers and attendants; to regulate the operation of ambulances; to authorize counties, cities, villages, charter townships and townships to contract for ambulance and inhalator services; and to provide procedures for the payment for services.

MCLA 257.1201 Definitions. [MSA 14.528(51)]

MCLA 257.1202 Director of state department of public health; promulgation of rules. [MSA 14.528(52)]

MCLA 257.1203 Transportation of patients upon public ways prohibited; exception. [MSA 14.528(53)]

MCLA 257.1204 Necessity of supervision and direction of qualified attendant or attendant-driver; exceptions. [MSA 14.528(54)]

MCLA 257.1205 Ambulance licenses; applications, forms, preparation, contents. MSA 14.528(55)

MCLA 257.1206 Ambulance licenses; term. MSA 14.528(56)

MCLA 257.1207 Ambulance licenses; requirements.
MSA 14.528(57)

MCLA 257.1208 Privileges of ambulance driver responding to emergency call or transporting patient; conditions; duty.
MSA 14.528(58)

MCLA 257.1209 Driver, attendant or attendant-driver license; applications, forms, preparation, contents. MSA 14.528(59)

MCLA 257.1210 Driver, attendant or attendant-driver license; term.
MSA 14.528(60)

MCLA 257.1211 Investigation of applicant; issuance of license, grounds; necessity for license, exceptions. MSA 14.528(61)

MCLA 257.1212 Repealed. MSA 14.528(62)

MCLA 257.1213 Contracts for ambulance and inhalator services, cities, townships, villages, counties. MSA 14.528(63)

MCLA 257.1214 Municipal ordinances. MSA 14.528(64)

Sec. 14. Any city, township, village or county may establish ordinances regulating ambulances, attendants, drivers and attendant-drivers meeting not less than the minimum requirements of this act and the rules of the director promulgated hereunder.

MCLA 257.1215 Suspension, revocation or termination of licenses.
MSA 14.528(65)

MCLA 257.1216 Penalty. MSA 14.528(66)

STREET AND HIGHWAY LIGHTING

The Federal Bureau of Investigation, the Michigan State Police and various local law enforcement agencies urge homeowners to light their property in order to lessen burglaries and robberies. Insurance agencies take lighting into consideration when establishing premium rates for theft insurance. It follows, then, that adequate lighting of streets will also lessen crimes against persons and property, resulting in lowered insurance rates for the entire community.

In addition, reports emanating from organizations such as the National Safety Council indicate that fifty per cent of all accidents occur on highways and streets in rural or suburban areas where there is inadequate lighting.

These two factors make it imperative that townships initiate studies which may lead to appropriate street lighting systems, choosing the statute which will do the best job under local conditions.

JOINT ACTION
Act No. 264, P.A. 1917 - Lighting of Highways and Bridges

AN ACT to authorize township boards to provide for the lighting of highways and bridges outside of the limits of incorporated cities and villages by artificial means, and to provide for the payment of the expense so incurred.

MCLA 41.251 Lighting of highways and bridges in township; expense, limitations, apportionment. [MSA 5.2481]

Sec. 1. The township board of any township may vote a sum to provide for the lighting by artificial means of any of the highways and bridges in such township, located outside of the limits of incorporated villages, the expense of such lighting to be paid out of the contingent fund of the township. Where any highway or bridge is situated in or between 2 or more townships, such provision shall be made by a majority vote of all of the township boards in which the highway is situated, at a joint meeting of the township boards, held for that purpose, and the proportion of the expense to be paid by each of the townships shall be determined at the joint meeting.

400

This act for reasons of public safety shall be construed to authorize the lighting of any state trunk line highway, county road or any platted road or street outside the limits of incorporated villages whether such road or street has been dedicated to the public use or not.

MCLA 41.252 Same; supervision; power of board to contract for service. [MSA 5.2482]

MCLA 41.253 Same; expense; assessment district, hearing, notice. [MSA 5.2483]

MCLA 41.254 Same; special assessment. [MSA 5.2484]

MCLA 41.255 Rescinding action. [MSA 5.2485]

MCLA 41.256 Saving clause. [MSA 5.2586]

MCLA 41.257 Maintenance of private roads, special assessment districts, establishment. [MSA 5.2487]

JOINT ACTION
Act No. 221, P.A. 1931 - Lighting of Highways and Bridges

AN ACT to provide for the lighting, by artificial means, of certain roads, highways and bridges outside of the limits of incorporated cities and villages, and to provide for the payment of the expense so incurred.

MCLA 41.261 Lighting of highways in townships, contracts, appropriation. [MSA 5.2491]

MCLA 41.262 Same; state trunk line highways, payment of expense; effect of act. [MSA 5.2492]

HOSPITALS

Fifty years ago it was unheard of for a township in Michigan to consider operating a hospital with another unit of government, let alone by itself. However, township hospital facilities have become quite commonplace. The private sector has been unable to keep pace with the tremendous demands for hospital rooms because of increased population, more sophisticated treatment of illnesses and the high incidence of accidents and other emergencies.

Legislators, in the past decade, have given local units of government more authority to provide needed hospital rooms as well as emergency care facilities. Township officials should take a close look at this modern day need which has taken its place alongside other vitally needed services and utilities. Careful studies must include a look, not only at need, but at whether adequate staff is available to operate a hospital. It is saddening to erect a hospital and then find there is little or no staff for it. In fact, the legislature, recognizing this problem, has provided that all hospitals must be licensed, with proper staffing as one of the criteria.

A study and advisory committee should be carefully selected to include among its members representatives from the various medical professions, who will be happy to work with townships to provide the best possible medical services to the citizens. An ideal committee would be composed of two medical doctors (perhaps a surgeon and a general practitioner), an osteopath, a nurse, an engineer, an architect, a successful businessman, the township attorney and, serving ex-officio, the township supervisor or such other officer as may be determined by the township board.

A township study committee should of course consult and cooperate with any local or regional areawide comprehensive health planning agency which may be organized in the area. Recommendation from such agency is an additional criteria for licensing of a hospital.

Local health and fire departments may be called upon by a state official to act as agent for inspection of facilities.

The tuberculosis sanatorium commission was abolished in 1960 and its powers and duties transferred to the state health commissioner. The office of the state health commissioner was transferred intact to the department of public health. Although care of tuberculosis patients is a county responsibility, we are giving brief citations for four statutes which deal with tuberculosis sanatoria, in addition to those which include tuberculosis care among other hospital care provisions.

JOINT ACTION
Act No. 144, P.A. 1949 — Hospitals

AN ACT to permit townships to pay part of the cost of maintaining and supporting hospitals whose facilities are made available to residents of such townships.

MCLA 41.701 Townships permitted to furnish funds for part of cost of maintenance and support of hospitals. [MSA 14.1181]

JOINT ACTION
Act No. 47, P.A. 1945 — Joint Municipal Hospitals

AN ACT to authorize 2 or more cities, townships and incorporated villages, or any combination thereof, to incorporate a hospital authority for planning, promoting, acquiring, constructing, improving, enlarging, extending, owning, maintaining and operating 1 or more community hospitals and related facilities; to provide for changes in the membership therein; to authorize such cities, townships and incorporated villages to levy taxes for such purpose; to provide for the issuance of revenue bonds; to provide for borrowing money for operation and maintenance and issuing notes therefor; to validate elections heretofore held and notes heretofore issued; to provide for the issuance of bonds; to authorize condemnation proceedings; and to grant certain powers of a body corporate.

MCLA 331.1 Cities, villages and townships, joint hospital authority; bonds, purposes, limitation. [MSA 5.2456(1)]

MCLA 331.2 Same; body corporate; powers and authority. [MSA 5.2456(2)]

MCLA 331.3 Same; resolution, contents; tax, limitation; payment of bonds; contracts; release from membership; prior actions and proceedings validated. [MSA 5.2456(3)]

MCLA 331.4 Same; tax, limitation. [MSA 5.2456(4)]

MCLA 331.5 Same; hospital board; medical advisory committee. [MSA 5.2456(5)]

MCLA 331.6 Hospital board meetings, times, notice, quorum, record; accounts; audits; treasurer's bond; operation of hospital; staff qualifications; professional work. [MSA 5.2456(6)]

MCLA 331.7 Budget, preparation, contents, notice of hearing, hearing, adoption; tax levy, equalization, payment; operation reports. [MSA 5.2456(7)]

MCLA 331.8 Joint hospital authority board; bonds, referendum; validation of previous acts. [MSA 5.2456(8)]

MCLA 331.8a Same; notes, issuance; interest rate; sinking fund; not subject to municipal finance act; notes previously issued, validation. [MSA 5.2456(8A)]

MCLA 331.8b Same; bonds for capital improvements, limitations. [MSA 5.2456(8B)]

MCLA 331.9 Acquisition, holding, management, and disposition of private property; sales at market value; retention of proceeds. [MSA 5.2456(9)]

MCLA 331.11 Necessity. [MSA 5.2456(11)]

JOINT ACTION
Act No. 38, P.A. 1969 - Hospital Finance Authority Act

AN ACT to create a state hospital finance authority to lend money to nonprofit hospitals for capital improvements; to provide for the incorporation of local hospital authorities with power to construct, acquire, reconstruct, remodel, improve, add to, enlarge, repair, own, lease and sell hospital facilities; to authorize the authorities to borrow money and issue obligations and to enter into loans, contracts, leases, mortgages and security agreements which may include provisions for the appointment of receivers; to exempt obligations and property of the authorities from taxation; and to provide other rights, powers and duties of the authorities.

CHAPTER 1. IN GENERAL

MCLA 331.31 Short title. MSA 14.1220(1)

MCLA 331.32 Legislative purpose. MSA 14.1220(2)

MCLA 331.33 Definitions. MSA 14.1220(3)

CHAPTER 2. STATE HOSPITAL FINANCE AUTHORITY

MCLA 331.41 Creation of authority; state public body and politic; membership, terms, vacancies; deputies; quorum; action by majority; compensation, expenses; exercise of powers. MSA 14.1220(11)

MCLA 331.42 Powers of authority. MSA 14.1220(12)

MCLA 331.43 Hospital loans, purposes, sufficiency of sources for repayment of funds, security, receivership, amount, loan period, interest. MSA 14.1220(13)

MCLA 331.44 Bonds and notes, issuance, obligations, contract provisions. MSA 14.1220(14)

MCLA 331.45 Special funds, purpose; bond reserve funds, deposits, use, withdrawals, income, loan provisions. MSA 14.1220(15)

MCLA 331.46 State treasurer, agent for authority; deposits; payments; security; custody, collection, security, investment, and payment agreements; system of accounts. MSA 14.1220(16)

CHAPTER 3. LOCAL HOSPITAL AUTHORITIES

MCLA 331.51 Incorporation; purpose. MSA 14.1220(21)

MCLA 331.52 Articles of incorporation, adoption. MSA 14.1220(22)

MCLA 331.53 Contents of articles. MSA 14.1220(23)

MCLA 331.54 Execution, delivery, publication and filing of articles; time of establishment of local authority; validity of incorporation, presumption. MSA 14.1220(24)

CHAPTER 4. PROVISIONS APPLICABLE
TO STATE AND LOCAL AUTHORITIES AND OTHERS

MCLA 331.76 Municipal finance commissions, approval of bonds and notes. [MSA 14.1220(46)]

MCLA 331.77 Approval of health facilities to be financed as prerequisite to issuance of bonds and notes; findings; proofs, testimony. [MSA 14.1220(47)]

MCLA 331.78 Negotiability of notes and bonds. [MSA 14.1220(48)]

MCLA 331.79 Legal investments, notes and bonds. [MSA 14.1220(49)]

MCLA 331.80 Tax exemption, property, income, and operation of any authority. [MSA 14.1220(50)]

MCLA 331.81 Covenants as to tax exemptions, notes and bonds; exceptions, estate, inheritance, gift, and transfer taxes. [MSA 14.1220(51)]

MCLA 331.82 Nondiscrimination, hospital facilities, construction or alteration operations. [MSA 14.1220(52)]

Sec. 52. The authority shall require that use of hospital facilities assisted under this act shall be open to all regardless of race, religion or creed and that contractors and subcontractors engaged in the construction or alteration of such facilities shall provide an equal opportunity for employment, without discrimination as to race, religion or creed. The hospital to which any hospital loan is made shall covenant with the authority that the nondiscrimination provision shall be enforced.

MCLA 331.83 Cumulative authority as to powers conferred; applicability of other statutes and charters. [MSA 14.1220(53)]

MCLA 331.84 Liberal construction. [MSA 14.1220(54)]

JOINT ACTION
Act No. 350, P. A. 1913—County Hospitals and Sanatoria

AN ACT to enable counties to establish and maintain public hospitals, levy a tax and issue bonds therefor, borrow money and issue bonds and notes therefor, elect hospital trustees, maintain training schools for nurses, maintain nursing home facilities, provide suitable means for the care of tuberculous persons, and to make possible the ultimate establishment of an adequate supply of hospitals.

MCLA 331.151 County public hospital; contagious diseases; establishment, referendum. [MSA 14.1131]

MCLA 331.152 Election procedure, ballots. [MSA 14.1132]

MCLA 331.153 County public hospital board of trustees, number, appointment, qualifications, vacancies. [MSA 14.1133]

MCLA 331.154 Same; oath, organization, compensation, mileage, powers, interest in contracts. [MSA 14.1134]

MCLA 331.154a Retirement and pensions, county plan membership. [MSA 14.1134(1)]

MCLA 331.156 Bonds; issuance, referendum. [MSA 14.1136]

MCLA 331.158 Approval of building plans; bids, advertisement. [MSA 14.1132]

MCLA 331.159 Annual appropriation for improvement and maintenance. [MSA 14.1138]

MCLA 331.160 Admission to hospital; payment of compensation for care; regulations; non-residents. [MSA 14.1139]

MCLA 331.161 Rules as to operation of hospital, records; denial of privileges to physicians. [MSA 14.1140]

MCLA 331.162 Donations. [MSA 14.1141]

MCLA 331.163 Physician's right to treat patients; right of patient to employ physician or nurse. [MSA 14.1142]

MCLA 331.164 Nurses training school. [MSA 14.1143]

408

MCLA 331.164a Nursing home facilities. [MSA 14.1143(1)]

MCLA 331.165 Insanity; examination room. [MSA 14.1144]

MCLA 331.166 Tubercular cases; accommodations, rules, head nurse. [MSA 14.1145]

MCLA 331.167 Compensation for patient's care; charity patient. [MSA 14.146]

MCLA 331.168 Tubercular patient; contract power of commissioners. [MSA 14.1147]

MCLA 331.169 Dependent children. [MSA 14.1148]

JOINT ACTION
Act No. 109, P. A. 1945 — County Hospitals and Sanatoria

AN ACT to protect and promote the public health and welfare and to enable boards of commissioners of certain counties to acquire, own, construct, establish, maintain and operate hospitals, county general hospitals, sanatoria and other institutions for the treatment of persons suffering from contagious and infectious diseases and for the treatment of indigent persons suffering from any physical ailment or impairment, and for temporary detention of mentally ill patients, both non-indigent and indigent, to authorize emergency treatment for emergency cases, to levy a tax therefor, appoint hospital trustees, authorize operation of hospitals by boards of county institutions, provide suitable means for the care of such afflicted persons, to limit the liability of counties maintaining such hospitals in respect to such cases, and to repeal acts inconsistent herewith.

MCLA 331.201 Hospitals defined. [MSA 14.1150(1)]

MCLA 331.202 Contagious disease hospitals; psychiatric wards; boards of commissioners, appropriations. [MSA 14.1150(2)]

MCLA 331.203 Same; (1 mill) **tax limitation; special fund.**
[MSA 14.1150(3)]

MCLA 331.204 Same; **board of trustees, number, terms; cooperation with state health commissioner; control vested in board.**
[MSA 14.1150(4)]

Note: Appointed by county board of commissioners from among residents and freeholders of the county.

MCLA 331.205 Same; **advertising for bids and letting of contracts.**
[MSA 14.1150(5)]

MCLA 331.206 **Board of trustees; medical staff, employment, rules; qualification standards.** [MSA 14.1150(6)]

MCLA 331.207 **Admittance of patients upon certificate of county health officer. Indigents, admittance upon order of social welfare board. Admittance of others; temporary detention of mentally ill, terms. Regulations.** [MSA 14.1150(7)]

MCLA 331.208 **Board of trustees not to receive compensation; claims submitted to board; vacancies; body corporate.**
[MSA 14.1150(8)]

MCLA 331.209 **Gifts, devises, bequests and donations.**
[MSA 14.1150(9)]

MCLA 331.210 **Board to make report to board of commissioners; estimate of funds necessary; referendum.** [MSA 14.1150(10)]

MCLA 331.211 **Tuberculosis patients; care, etc., of, not affected by act.** [MSA 14.1150(11)]

MCLA 331.212 **Transfer of control of hospitals to board of trustees.**
[MSA 14.1150(12)]

MCLA 331.212a **County general hospital; patients admissible; site; out-patient facilities; estimate of funds.** [MSA 14.1150(12A)]

MCLA 331.213 **Repeal.** [MSA 14.1150(13)]

410

AFFECTS JOINT ACTION
Act No. 17, P.A. 1968 - Hospital Licensing and Operation

AN ACT to protect the public health; to provide for the licensing of hospitals; to create the state health facilities council and prescribe its duties; to provide for standards, rules and regulations for the maintenance and operation of hospitals; to prescribe the powers and duties of the state director of public health and other state officials; to prescribe certain duties of hospital governing bodies; and to provide penalties for violations.

MCLA 331.411 Scope of act. [MSA 14.1179(1)]

MCLA 331.412 Hospital; definition. [MSA 14.1179(2)]

MCLA 331.413 State health facilities council; establishment, members, duties. [MSA 14.1179(3)]

Note: Although it did not officially repeal this section, MCLA 331.460 [MSA 14.1179(60)] of Act No. 256, P.A. 1972 abolished the state health facilities council and transferred its functions, powers and duties to the state health facilities commission.

MCLA 331.414 Director's responsibilities. [MSA 14.1179(4)]

MCLA 331.415 Adoption and enforcement of standards, rules and regulations. [MSA 41.1179(5)]

MCLA 331.416 License; term. [MSA 14.1179(6)]

MCLA 331.417 License; inspection by fire marshal. [MSA 14.1179(7)]

MCLA 331.418 License; fees. [MSA 14.1179(8)]

MCLA 331.419 Periodic inspections of premises. [MSA 14.1179(9)]

MCLA 331.420 Inspection and reports; records; confidentiality of records. [MSA 14.1179(10)]

MCLA 331.421 Certification of non-discriminatory practice. [MSA 14.1179(11)]

MCLA 331.422 Responsibility for operation of hospital, selection of medical staff, quality of care rendered; records and data, use, confidentiality. [MSA 14.1179(12)]

MCLA 331.423 Noncompliance; notice; hearing; suspension, denial or revocation of license. [MSA 14.1179(13)]

MCLA 331.424 Appeal of decision of director or fire marshal. [MSA 14.1179(14)]

MCLA 331.425 Exempt institutions. [MSA 14.1179(15)]

MCLA 331.426 Limitation on use of term "hospital"; exceptions. [MSA 14.1179(16)]

MCLA 331.427 Construction of act. [MSA 14.1179(17)]

MCLA 331.428 Interference with authority of director. [MSA 14.1179(18)]

MCLA 331.429 Director's authority to maintain action. [MSA 14.1179(19)]

MCLA 331.430 Violation. [MSA 14.1179(20)]

AFFECTS JOINT ACTION
Act No. 256, P.A. 1972 - Construction, Conversion, or Modernization of Health Facilities

AN ACT to require certificates of need for new construction or conversion of, addition to or modernization of health facilities; to provide for the issuing of certificates of need; to establish a state health facilities commission; to provide fees and penalties; and to make appropriations.

MCLA 331.451 Definitions. [MSA 14.1179(51)]

MCLA 331.452 State health facilities commission, creation; membership, number, qualifications, appointment, terms, vacancies, compensation; quorum; chairman; meetings. [MSA 14.1179(52)]

MCLA 331.453 Implementation of act; review of applications for certificate of need; hearings; decisions of commission. [MSA 14.1179(53)]

MCLA 331.454 Certificates of need; necessity; issuance, rules; reports; state plans; federal grant-in-aid or loan guarantee programs; waiver. [MSA 14.1179(54)]

MCLA 331.455 Applications for certificates of need, forms. [MSA 14.1179(55)]

MCLA 331.455a Evaluation of certificates of need; criteria. [MSA 14.1179(55A)]

MCLA 331.456 Evidence of ability to finance construction and operation of facility; recommendations of local or regional health planning agencies, decisions, review; advice from commission. [MSA 14.1179(56)]

MCLA 331.457 Fee for certificate of need. [MSA 14.1179(57)]

MCLA 331.458 Hearings before commission on applications for certificates of need; review by circuit court. [MSA 14.1179(58)]

MCLA 331.459 Injunction or other process to prevent construction. [MSA 14.1179(59)]

MCLA 331.460 State health facilities council; abolishment; transfer of functions, powers, and duties. [MSA 14.1179(60)]

MCLA 331.461 Appropriation. [MSA 14.1179(61)]

MCLA 331.462 Effective date. [MSA 14.1179(62)]

JOINT ACTION
Act No. 299, P. A. 1947 — Hospital Inventory

AN ACT to provide for an inventory of existing hospitals, for a survey of the need for additional hospital facilities, and for the development and administration of a hospital construction program which will, in conjunction with existing facilities, afford hospitals adequate to serve all the people of the state; to provide for compliance with the requirements of the federal hospital survey and regulations thereunder; to create an office of hospital survey and construction, and to prescribe its powers and duties; to create the Michigan advisory hospital council, and to prescribe its powers and duties; to prescribe penalties; and to make appropriations to carry out the provisions of this act.

PART A – GENERAL

MCLA 331.501 Short title. [MSA 14.1201]

MCLA 331.502 Definitions. [MSA 14.1202]

MCLA 331.503 Office of hospital survey and construction, establishment; director, appointment, salary; state agency, purposes. [MSA 14.1203]

MCLA 331.504 Same; authority of director. [MSA 14.1204]

MCLA 331.505 Same; application for federal funds, deposit, expenditure, repayment of unexpended fund; gifts or grants. [MSA 14.1205]

MCLA 331.506 Michigan advisory hospital council; creation, duties, members, appointment, qualifications, terms, expenses, quorum. [MSA 14.1206]

MCLA 331.507 State appropriation and grant of federal funds. [MSA 14.1207]

PART B – SURVEY AND PLANNING

MCLA 331.508 Inventory and survey of hospitals; construction program. [MSA 14.1208]

414

MCLA 331.509 Hospital construction program; facilities, state residents. [MSA 14.1209]

PART C – HOSPITAL CONSTRUCTION PROGRAM

MCLA 331.510 State plan; contents, submission to surgeon general, hearing, approval, publication, review, modification. [MSA 14.1210]

MCLA 331.511 Same; minimum standards for maintenance and operation of hospitals receiving federal aid; medical personnel. [MSA 14.1211]

MCLA 331.512 Same; relative need of projects, federal regulations, priority. [MSA 14.1212]

MCLA 331.513 Application for construction projects; submittance to director; conformity with federal or state requirements. [MSA 14.1213]

MCLA 331.514 Same; hearing prior to approval, recommending and forwarding to surgeon general. [MSA 14.1214]

MCLA 331.515 Inspection of approval (approved) **projects; certification of conformity, federal installment due.** [MSA 14.1215]

MCLA 331.516 Federal funds; power of budget director to receive; hospital construction planning fund, deposit, disbursement. [MSA 14.1216]

Act No. 270, P. A. 1967 – Release of Information for Medical Research and Education

AN ACT to provide for the release of information for medical research and medical education purposes; to limit the liability with respect thereto; and to safeguard the confidential character thereof.

MCLA 331.531 Data relating to medical condition and treatment, use, liability. [MSA 14.57(21)]

MCLA 331.532 Limitation, use or publication by committee, exception. [MSA 14.57(22)]

MCLA 331.533 Identity of person, confidential, exceptions.
MSA 14.57(23)

JOINT ACTION
Act No. 139, P.A. 1956 - Nursing Homes, or Homes for the Aged

AN ACT to protect the public health and the welfare of the people of this state while receiving care in nursing homes, or in homes for the aged; to define a nursing home; to define a home for the aged; and to provide for licenses and permits for nursing homes and homes for the aged.

MCLA 331.651 Nursing homes, homes for the aged; licenses.
MSA 14.1281

MCLA 331.652 Same; definitions. MSA 14.1282

MCLA 331.653 Same; state health commissioner, licenses, rules and regulations, hearings, reports, inspections. MSA 14.1283

MCLA 331.654 Licenses, necessity, term, provisional.
MSA 14.1284

MCLA 331.655 Same; licenses, application, fees, exceptions; inspection by health commissioner, fire marshal; books and records.
MSA 14.1285

MCLA 331.656 Same; state health commissioner, suspension and revocation of license. MSA 14.1286

MCLA 331.657 Same; penalty for operating home without license.
MSA 14.1287

MCLA 331.658 Same; injunction. MSA 14.1288

MCLA 331.659 Same; practice of healing; communicable diseases; faith healing; examination of food handlers. MSA 14.1289

MCLA 331.659a Same; licensees as consumers of tangible personal property. MSA 14.1289(1)

416

MCLA 331.660 Transfer of powers to state health commissioner. [MSA 14.1290]

JOINT ACTION
Act No. 287, P.A. 1972 - Adult Foster Care Facility Licensing Act

AN ACT to provide for the licensing and regulation of adult foster care facilities providing alternate care services including room and board, supervision, assistance, protection and personal care to adults not requiring organized institutional medical or nursing care; and to provide penalties for violations of this act.

MCLA 331.681 Short title. [MSA 16.610(1)]

MCLA 331.682 Definitions [MSA 16.610(2)]

MCLA 331.683 Administration, direction; licenses, issuance, review, suspension, revocation; rules, promulgation, contents; reports; standards; procedures; inspections; consultation. [MSA 16.610(3)]

MCLA 331.684 Advisory council, creation, membership, compensation, meetings, duties. [MSA 16.610(4)]

MCLA 331.685 Licenses necessity; maximum number of persons receiving care; terms; provisional; temporary, terms, grounds for issuance, renewals, extensions; fire safety inspections. [MSA 16.610(5)]

MCLA 331.686 Applications for license, form, contents; license fee; issuance of licenses, grounds; qualifications of licensees; contents of licenses. [MSA 16.610(6)]

MCLA 331.687 Inspections, entry, purpose, time, standards, confidentiality. [MSA 16.610(7)]

Sec. 7. ... The state fire marshal or **organized local fire department,** *at the request of the director, may inspect any facility for fire safety. All inspections shall be conducted in accordance with the standards established in rules promulgated pursuant to this act. ...*

MCLA 331.688 Denial, suspension, and revocation of licenses and refusal to renew licenses, grounds, protest, notice, hearing, decision; failure to protest. [MSA 16.610(8)]

MCLA 331.689 Review. [MSA 16.610(9)]

MCLA 331.690 Violations, penalty. [MSA 16.510(10)]

MCLA 331.691 Injunction or other process. [MSA 16.610(11)]

MCLA 331.692 Administrative division, establishment; reports. [MSA 16.610(12)]

MCLA 331.693 Local regulations, supersedence. [MSA 16.610(13)]

Sec. 13. This act supersedes all local regulations licensing and regulating adult foster care facilities.

MCLA 331.694 Effective date. [MSA 16.6101(14)]

JOINT ACTION
Act No. 13, P.A. 1944, 1st Ex. Sess. - Children's Clinic

AN ACT to authorize county boards of supervisors and local governing bodies to appropriate moneys to child guidance clinics and community mental health clinics providing service for children and/or adults.

MCLA 722.481 Child guidance and community mental health clinics, financing. [MSA 25.265]

Sec. 1. The board of supervisors of any county or the governing body of any city, village, school district or township in this state may, except as otherwise specifically provided, furnish and appropriate moneys for the operation of child guidance clinics and community mental health clinics providing service for children or adults established by state authority and the governing body of any school district may appropriate money for land and buildings to be used by the clinics although title thereto is not vested in the appropriating body.

418

JOINT ACTION
Act No. 137, P.A. 1921 - Contract Powers of Counties

AN ACT authorizing and empowering counties of this state to contract with agencies, institutions and hospitals licensed by the state board of corrections and charities for the aid, care, support, maintenance, treatment, cure or relief of children.

MCLA 722.501 Care of children; contracts by boards of supervisors, expenses, tax. [MSA 25.361]

MCLA 722.502 Approval of contracts. [MSA 25.362]

MCLA 722.503 Probate judge, duties. [MSA 25.363]

MCLA 722.504 Forfeiture of license, effect on contracts. [MSA 25.364]

MCLA 722.505 Construction of act. [MSA 25.365]

Act No. 115, P.A. 1929 - Tuberculosis Sanatorium Commission

AN ACT to create a tuberculosis sanatorium commission to have supervision and control of all state tuberculosis sanatoria; to transfer all of the powers and duties of the present board of trustees of the state tuberculosis sanatorium to such commission; to fix the compensation for such hospitalization, care and treatment; and to give general powers and duties to such commission and the state administrative board.

MCLA 332.1-332.7 [MSA 14.1001-14.1007]

Act No. 254, P.A. 1905 - State Sanatorium

AN ACT to establish a state sanatorium in some suitable locality in Michigan, for the care and treatment of persons having tuberculosis, and making appropriations therefor, and to provide a tax to meet the same.

419

MCLA 332.51-332.70 [MSA 14.1011-14.1030]

Act No. 343, P.A. 1917 - Joint County Sanatoriums

AN ACT to provide for the establishment, enlargement, extension and maintenance of joint county sanatoriums for the treatment of tuberculosis.

MCLA 332.101-332.118 [MSA 14.1061-14.1078]

Act No. 177, P.A. 1925 - County Sanatoriums

AN ACT to protect and promote the public health and welfare, and to provide for the construction, maintenance and operation of hospitals and sanatoriums for the treatment of tuberculosis; and to make an appropriation therefor.

MCLA 332.151-332.164 [MSA 14.1091-14.1104]

JOINT ACTION
Act No. 108, P.A. 1939 — Medical Care Corporations

AN ACT to provide for and to regulate the incorporation of non-profit medical care corporations; to provide for the supervision and regulation of such corporations by the state commissioner of insurance; and to prescribe penalties for the violation of the provisions of this act.

MCLA 550.301 — 550.312 [MSA 24.591 — 24.602]

MCLA 550.313 Needy persons and others, medical care for; subscriptions from governmental and private agencies and corporations. [MSA 24.603]

MCLA 550.314 Immunity of corporation from certain suits. [MSA 24.604]

MCLA 550.315 Taxation, assets of corporation exempt from; benevolent character. [MSA 24.605]

MCLA 550.316 Violations of act, penalty. [MSA 24.606]

Act No. 109, P.A. 1939 - Hospital Service Corporations

AN ACT to provide for and to regulate the incorporation of non-profit hospital service corporations; to provide for the supervision and regulation of such corporations by the state commissioner of insurance; and to prescribe penalties for the violation of the provisions of this act.

MCLA 550.501 - 550.514 MSA 24.621 - 24.634

MCLA 550.515 **Taxation, assets of corporation exempt from; benevolent character.** MSA 24.635

MCLA 550.516 - 550.517 MSA 24.636 - 24.637

POWER, ELECTRIC, TELEGRAPH AND TELEPHONE COMPANIES.

The Michigan Public Service Commission has performed fairly adequately in fulfilling its mission of insuring sufficient capacity plus fair and adequate rates by public power companies. The companies themselves have advanced technologically in providing energy. However, there is still sufficient interest in municipally owned utilities to warrant the inclusion in this textbook of statutes governing their establishment and operation. Although townships are not directly concerned with installation and operation of telegraph and telephone companies, there is enough indirect involvement of township authority to include references regarding them as well.

Section twenty-nine of article seven of the Michigan constitution stipulates that "no person, partnership, association or corporation, public or private, operating a public utility" has the right to the use of any highways, streets, alleys or other public places of any township without first **obtaining consent of the township board,** or to transact business in the township without first **obtaining a franchise from the township.** In addition, fence viewers need to be aware of the rights of corporations vs. private landowners.

The right of a township board to negotiate with power companies for township power requirements is well established by Michigan law. Generally this is accomplished by a resolution of the township board directing that the township supervisor negotiate with the local power company for whatever services are desired. These would include power for such things as street lighting and operation of well sites, filtration plants and sanitary sewer treatment plants located within or without the township.

The Michigan Railroad Commission was abolished and its functions transferred to the Michigan Public Utilities Commission. The commission was in turn abolished and its functions transferred to the Michigan Public Service Commission, which was then transferred intact to the Department of Commerce.

JOINT ACTION
Act No. 86, P.A. 1893 - Operation of Electrical Plants by Water Supply Companies

AN ACT to authorize certain water supply companies, now or hereafter organized, to also operate electrical plants in connection with their waterworks systems.

MCLA 486.351 Water supply companies; right to purchase and operate electrical plants. [MSA 22.1711]

Sec. 1. That any company or corporation hereafter organized for the purpose of supplying water to any city, town (township) or village in this state, the population whereof does not exceed 25,000 inhabitants according to the last official census thereof preceding the organization of such company or corporation, shall, by specifying the same in its articles of association, have the right to also produce and supply any such city, town (township) or village, and the inhabitants thereof, with electricity for lighting, heating and motive purposes and any other purpose for which the same is, or may become, of practical use. And to that end shall also have the right to purchase from any individual, copartnership or corporation owning or operating any electricity producing plant, its said plant, together with any or all of the property franchises and rights connected therewith, to be operated in the city, town (township) or village in which such company is to be located and operating.

MCLA 486.352 Same; amendment of articles to show right.
[MSA 22.1712]

422

MCLA 486.353 Powers of company. MSA 22.1713

Sec. 3. ... And such company or corporation shall have the power to lay, construct and maintain conductors and poles, and stretch wires for the conducting of electricity through the streets, alleys, lands and squares of any such city, town (township) or village, with the consent of the municipal authorities thereof, under such reasonable regulations as they may prescribe; and such company or corporation may make and enforce all such contracts, by-laws and rules as may be deemed necessary and proper to carry into effect the foregoing powers.

JOINT ACTION
Act No. 106, P.A. 1909 - Transmission of Electricity

AN ACT to regulate the transmission of electricity through the public highways, streets and places of this, state, where the source of supply and place of use are in the same or different counties; to regulate the charges to be made for electricity so transmitted; to regulate the rules and conditions of service under which said electricity shall be furnished and to confer upon the Michigan public utilities commission certain powers and duties in regard thereto.

MCLA 460.551 Transmission of electricity in or between counties; control. MSA 22.151

MCLA 460.552 Same; rate regulation by commission. MSA 22.152

MCLA 460.553 Same; user of streets, regulation. MSA 22.153

Sec. 3. Any person, firm or corporation engaged or organized to engage in any such business of transmitting and supplying electricity in 1 or more counties of this state shall, with the consent of the duly constituted city, village and township authorities of the cities, villages and townships in or through which it operates or may hereafter ...

MCLA 460.554 Data and information, specifications of construction, filing; height of lines; stenciling of poles. MSA 22.154

MCLA 460.555 Commission; inspection; order for improvements. [MSA 22.155]

MCLA 460.556 Same; discretionary powers; annual report of utilities; audit, expense. [MSA 22.156]

MCLA 460.557 Same; investigation of complaints; rules; fixing of rates, restrictions; discrimination; laws governing. [MSA 22.157]

MCLA 460.558 Same; order mandatory; failure to comply, penalty. [MSA 22.158]

MCLA 460.599 Scope, limitation. [MSA 22.159]

Sec. 9. This act shall not apply to the transmission or use of electricity for the purpose of conveying intelligence by telegraph, telephone or by other methods now or hereafter adopted therefor.

AFFECTS JOINT ACTION
Act No. 3, P.A. 1939 - Public Service Commission

AN ACT to provide for the regulation and control of public utilities and other services affected with a public interest within this state; to create a public service commission and to prescribe and define the powers and duties thereof; to abolish the Michigan public utilities commission, and to confer the powers and duties now vested by law therein, on the public service commission hereby created; to provide for the continuance, transfer and completion of matters and proceedings now pending; to provide for appeals; to provide appropriations therefor; to declare the effect of this act and prescribe penalties for the violations of the provisions thereof; and to repeal all acts contrary to the provisions of this act.

MCLA 460.1 Public service commission, creation; members, appointment, qualifications, terms, vacancies. [MSA 22.13(1)]

MCLA 460.2 Same; oath, chairman, removal, quorum, seal, offices. [MSA 22.13(2)]

424

MCLA 460.3 Same; compensation, employees, experts, appointment; expenses. [MSA 22.13(3)]

MCLA 460.4 Abolishment of public utilities commission; transfer of rights, powers, and duties to public service commission; references to mean public service commission; review; injunctions.
[MSA 22.13(4)]

MCLA 460.5 Same; books, records, files. [MSA 22.13(5)]

MCLA 460.6 Same; powers and jurisdiction; rates, rules, service of public utilities. Powers and jurisdiction. Railroads. [MSA 22.13(6)]

MCLA 460.6a Gas, telephone and electric utilities, rate changes. Notice; orders; hearings. Filing, investigation, and hearing of petitions or applications; fuel or purchase gas adjustment clauses. Final decisions, expediting, reports. [MSA 22.13(6A)]

MCLA 460.6b Gas utility rates, authority of public service commission; rates, etc., on file with federal power commission received in evidence; proceedings; appeal; refund. [MSA 22.13(6B)]

MCLA 460.7 Railroad unions, parties in interest in commission proceedings. [MSA 22.13(7)]

MCLA 460.8 Voluntary associations; parties in interest in commission proceedings. [MSA 22.13(8)]

JOINT ACTION
Act No. 419, P.A. 1919 - Public Utilities Commission

AN ACT to provide for the regulation and control of certain public utilities operated within this state; to create a public utilities commission and to define the powers and duties thereof; to abolish the Michigan railroad commission and to confer the powers and duties thereof on the commission hereby created; to provide for the transfer and completion of matters and proceedings now pending before said railroad commission; and to prescribe penalties for violations of the provisions hereof.

MCLA 460.51 Public utilities commission; creation; members, appointment, term, vacancy, interest in utilities; seal, offices, equipment. [MSA 22.1]

MCLA 460.52 Same; officers, employes, engineers and experts; appointment, compensation, expenses. [MSA 22.2]

MCLA 460.53 Railroad commission; abolition, transfer; regulations relating to sanitation and adequate shelter for railroad employees. [MSA 22.3]

MCLA 460.53a Railroads; equipment of vehicles for transporting employees. [MSA 22.3(1)]

MCLA 460.54 Commission, powers and duties respecting rates; franchise rights; municipally owned utility. [MSA 22.4]

MCLA 460.55 Reports, verification; rules of commission; penalties. [MSA 22.5]

MCLA 460.56 Examination by commission, powers; failure to obey order, penalty; compulsory process. [MSA 22.6]

MCLA 460.57 Location of office of utility; records; rate schedules, filing and posting, approval; rules. [MSA 22.7]

MCLA 460.58 Investigation of rates on complaint, procedure; contempt; order of commission; witness fees. [MSA 22.8]

MCLA 460.59 Review of orders; opportunity to be heard. [MSA 22.9]

MCLA 460.60 Rights not conferred. [MSA 22.10]

MCLA 460.61 Public utilities commission; securities, issuance, fee. [MSA 22.11]

MCLA 460.61a Disposition of funds paid into state treasury. [MSA 22.11A]

MCLA 460.62 Declaration of necessity. [MSA 22.12]

AFFECTS JOINT ACTION
Act No. 299, P.A. 1972 - Costs of Regulating Public Utilities

AN ACT to provide for the assessment, collection and disposition of the costs of regulation of public utilities.

MCLA 460.111 Definitions. [MSA 22.84(1)]

Sec. 1. As used in this act:
(a) "Commission" means the public service commission.
(b) "Department" means the department of commerce.
(c) "Public utility" means a steam, heat, electric, power, gas, water, telephone, telegraph, communications, pipeline or gas producing company regulated by the commission, whether private, corporate or cooperative, **except a municipally owned utility.**

MCLA 460.112 Assessments against public utilities, amount, apportionment, minimum assessments. [MSA 22.84(2)]

MCLA 460.113 Deductions for prior overassessments. [MSA 22.84(3)]

MCLA 460.114 Credits for fees paid by public utilities during previous fiscal year. [MSA 22.84(4)]

MCLA 460.115 Disposition of moneys paid by public utilities. [MSA 22.84(5)]

MCLA 460.116 Objection to assessments, time for filing, contents, hearing, disposition; payment of assessments, time, interest, collection of assessments. [MSA 22.84(6)]

MCLA 460.117 Restraining or delaying collection or payment of assessments; statements of claims; actions for recovery of payments, issues, review, exclusiveness of remedy. [MSA 22.84(7)]

MCLA 460.118 Exemption of a public utility, grounds, procedure, alternative assessment. [MSA 22.84(8)]

MCLA 460.119 Fees in lieu of assessments. [MSA 22.84(9)]

MCLA 460.120 Effective date. [MSA 22.84(10)]

AFFECTS JOINT ACTION
Act No. 144, P.A. 1909 - Issuance of Securities

AN ACT to regulate the issuance of stocks, bonds and other evidences of indebtedness by persons, corporations and associations owning, conducting or operating certain public utilities, and to provide a penalty for the violation thereof.

MCLA 460.301 Public utilities securities; approval by commission; appraisal of property, expense; review of order. [MSA 22.101]

Sec. 1. Any corporation or association **except municipal corporations, ...**

MCLA 460.302 Penalty; recovery, disposition. [MSA 22.102]

MCLA 460.303 Unauthorized issuance of securities; penalty. [MSA 22.103]

AFFECTS JOINT ACTION
Act No. 94, P.A. 1923 - Rehearings and Amendment of Findings

AN ACT to authorize the Michigan public utilities commission to grant rehearings and to alter, modify or amend its findings and orders.

MCLA 460.351 Rehearings; amendment of orders. [MSA 22.111]

MCLA 460.352 Suit to review order, time. [MSA 22.112]

AFFECTS JOINT ACTION
Act No. 47, P.A. 1921 - Expense for Audit and Appraisal

AN ACT to provide for the payment to the state by certain public utilities of the expense incurred by the Michigan public utilities commission in auditing the books and records and appraising the plants, properties and facilities of said public utilities; and to appropriate said moneys toward the maintenance of said commission.

MCLA 460.401 Expenses of audit or appraisal by utilities commission; account. MSA 22.121

MCLA 460.402 Same; payment. MSA 22.122

MCLA 460.403 Moneys paid into state treasury, disposition. MSA 22.123

AFFECTS JOINT ACTION
Act No. 38, P.A. 1925 - Municipal Utilities, Accounts

AN ACT to require municipalities owning or operating public utilities to adopt and keep a uniform system of accounts, and to make and publish annual reports relating to the operation of each such utility, and to require the Michigan public utilities commission to prescribe the forms thereof.

MCLA 460.451 Municipal public utilities; system of accounts; annual report, publication; forms. MSA 22.131

AFFECTS JOINT ACTION
Act No. 182, P.A. 1971 - Short-Term Loans

AN ACT to permit a city or village owning and operating a public utility to borrow money for a term not to exceed 5 years for the purpose of purchasing, acquiring, constructing, improving, enlarging, extending or repairing the facilities of the public utility; to issue notes or other evidences of indebtedness therefor; to repay such borrowing from the revenues of the utility; to permit the pledging or assignment of bonds or other securities or evidences of debt held as investments for said public utility to secure such borrowings; and to provide other powers, rights and duties.

MCLA 460.461 Public utilities owned and operated by cities or villages, financing, 5 year limitation. MSA 22.135(1)

Note: This act was amended in 1972 to specify cities and villages; originally it stated "municipally-owned public utility."

MCLA 460.462 Interim financing, approval of long term financing, notice of intention to issue obligation. [MSA 22.135(2)]

MCLA 460.463 Forfeiture of security. [MSA 22.135(3)]

AFFECTS JOINT ACTION
Act No. 69, P.A. 1929 - Certificates of Convenience and Necessity

AN ACT to define and regulate certain public utilities and to require them to secure a certificate of convenience and necessity in certain cases.

MCLA 460.501 Definitions. [MSA 22.141]

MCLA 460.502 Certificate of convenience; necessity for gas or electric utilities. [MSA 22.142]

MCLA 460.503 Petition, contents. [MSA 22.143]

MCLA 460.504 Hearing; notices. [MSA 22.144]

MCLA 460.505 Same; matters for consideration; certificate, contents. [MSA 22.145]

MCLA 460.506 Review of order. [MSA 22.146]

AFFECTS JOINT ACTION
Act No. 347, P.A. 1921 - Interest on Guaranty Deposits

AN ACT to require public utilities to pay interest on guaranty deposits.

MCLA 460.651 Interest on guaranty deposits. [MSA 22.181]

Sec. 1. Whenever any public utility in this state requires a deposit of money exceeding 50 dollars as a guaranty for the payment of charges of any kind whatsoever, such public utility shall

430

pay to the person, firm or corporation depositing such money, interest at the rate of 4 per centum per annum, said interest to be computed annually on all sums that have remained on deposit for 6 months.

MCLA 460.652   Same; semi-annual payment; enforcement of claim.
[MSA 22.182]

AFFECTS JOINT ACTION
Act No. 283, P.A. 1905 - Power Companies

AN ACT to authorize the formation of corporations for the purpose of damming, excavating, constructing and maintaining water courses with water power appurtenant thereto, for accumulating, storing, manufacturing, conducting, using, selling, furnishing and supplying water and water power, electricity and electric power, and all and every kind of power for mining, milling, manufacturing, domestic, municipal and agricultural purposes, and for the purpose of transportation and for all other purposes in the upper peninsula of Michigan.

MCLA 486.201   Power corporations in upper peninsula; incorporators, powers. [MSA 22.1651]

MCLA 486.202   Same; certificate, acknowledgment, contents, recording, filing. [MSA 22.1652]

MCLA 486.203   Same; body corporate; governing law. [MSA 22.1653]

MCLA 486.204   Directors; powers, election, term, qualification. [MSA 22.1654]

MCLA 486.205   Same; calling of election. [MSA 22.1655]

MCLA 486.206   Same; majority control. [MSA 22.1656]

MCLA 486.207   Subscriptions; increase in capital, procedure. [MSA 22.1657]

MCLA 486.208   Same; calling in; sale, procedure; proceeds, disposition; purchaser's rights. [MSA 22.1658]

431

MCLA 486.209 Corporate powers. [MSA 22.1659]

MCLA 486.210 Power to construct railroad, telegraph or telephone lines; holding of realty. [MSA 22.1660]

MCLA 486.211 Furnishing and use of water or power; compensation; right to sue and be sued. [MSA 22.1661]

MCLA 486.212 Injury to stream or property; penalty. [MSA 22.1662]

MCLA 486.213 Annual report; contents. [MSA 22.1663]

MCLA 486.214 Real property; purchase, holding, disposal; personal property, disposal. [MSA 22.1664]

MCLA 486.215 Stockholder's liability; recovery prerequisites. [MSA 22.1665]

MCLA 486.216 Shares deemed personalty; transfer. [MSA 22.1666]

AFFECTS JOINT ACTION
Act No. 238, P.A. 1923 - Power Companies

AN ACT authorizing the formation of corporations for the purpose of generating, manufacturing, producing, gathering, storing, transmitting, distributing, transforming, selling and supplying electric energy or gas, either artificial or natural, or both electric energy and gas, to the public generally, or to public utilities or natural gas companies, and providing for and giving to such corporations and also to corporations heretofore lawfully organized, among other things, for such purposes; to corporations heretofore lawfully organized, or that may hereafter be lawfully organized and duly authorized to carry on the electric or gas business as a public utility in the state of Michigan; and to foreign corporations heretofore lawfully organized or that may hereafter be lawfully organized, among other things, for such purposes, and duly authorized to carry on business in the state of Michigan, the right to condemn private property for the uses provided for herein.

MCLA 486.251 Electric or gas corporations, incorporators; powers. [MSA 22.1671]

MCLA 486.252 Corporate powers. Examination and survey for improvements. Property. Dams; improvement of stream or canal. Flooding. Condemnation; exception as to certain mineral rights; generating, transmitting or transforming electric energy. Same; gas pipe line rights of way, underground natural gas storage field; procedure; drilling through formation used for storage. [MSA 22.1672]

MCLA 486.252a Condemnation proceedings; order for hearing, time, contents, service; guardian ad litem. [MSA 22.1672(1)]

MCLA 486.252b Same; order for appearance, affidavit, publication, proof, service or mailing; jurisdiction. [MSA 22.1672(2)]

MCLA 486.252c Same; commissioners, appointment, qualifications, duties, meeting, report. [MSA 22.1672(3)]

MCLA 486.252d Same; commissioners' meetings, oath, adjournments, view of premises, determination, reports; witnesses. [MSA 22.1672(4)]

MCLA 486.252e Same; commissioners' report, setting aside, retrial, confirmation; vesting title, deposit of award, time, notice. [MSA 22.1672(5)]

MCLA 486.252f Same; amendments; commissioners, vacancies, removal; setting aside defective proceedings; division of award; adjournments. [MSA 22.1672(6)]

MCLA 486.252g Same; owner's application for award, payment, receipt; failure to deposit award; expenses, attorney fees; evidence. [MSA 22.1672(7)]

MCLA 486.252h Same; entry for survey, liability for damages; petitioner's occupancy pending proceedings, requisites, hearing. [MSA 22.1672(8)]

MCLA 486.252i Same; appeals; petitioner's possession pending appeal, bond; perfected appeal, effect of withdrawal of final award. [MSA 22.1672(9)]

MCLA 486.252j Same; service of notices and orders.
MSA 22.1672(10)

MCLA 486.253 Electricity or gas furnished public; rates, conditions; books, examination; order of commission, review; certificate of necessity. MSA 22.1673

MCLA 486.254 Existing corporations; right of condemnation.
MSA 22.1674

Act No. 123, P.A. 1867 - Telegraph Companies, Licenses, Reports

AN ACT to regulate telegraph companies and their agents, and individuals doing telegraph business, not incorporated by the state of Michigan.

MCLA 484.201 License and reports. MSA 22.1391

MCLA 484.202 Taxation. MSA 22.1392

MCLA 484.203 Permission to do business. MSA 22.1393

MCLA 484.204 Penalty. MSA 22.1394

Act No. 59, P.A. 1851 - Telegraph Companies

AN ACT to authorize the formation of telegraph companies.

MCLA 484.151 Telegraph companies; incorporators. MSA 22.1361

MCLA 484.152 Same; certificate of organization, contents, filing.
MSA 22.1362

MCLA 484.153 Body corporate; certified copy of certificate as evidence. MSA 22.1363

MCLA 484.154 Power to hold realty; officers and agents; rules and by-laws. MSA 22.1364

MCLA 484.155 Telegraph lines; construction, restrictions.
MSA 22.1365

434

MCLA 484.156 Aggrieved property owner; remedy, procedure. [MSA 22.1366]

MCLA 484.157 Injury to line; penalty. [MSA 22.1367]

MCLA 484.158 Stockholder's liability for corporate debts; contribution. [MSA 22.1368]

MCLA 484.159 Annual report; contents; failure to make, liability of directors. [MSA 22.1369]

MCLA 484.160 Annual tax; in lieu of other state taxes. [MSA 22.1370]

MCLA 484.161 Shares of stock; status as personalty, transfer, purchase in other corporations. [MSA 22.1371]

MCLA 484.163 Books, inspection, use as evidence; penalty, forfeiture. [MSA 22.1372]

MCLA 484.164 Transmission of dispatches; penalty. [MSA 22.1373]

MCLA 484.165 Same; order of transmission; penalty. [MSA 22.1374]

MCLA 484.166 Divulging contents, willful failure to transmit; penalty, civil liability. [MSA 22.1375]

MCLA 484.167 State's lien for taxes; sale; surplus. [MSA 22.1376]

MCLA 484.168 Amendment or repeal of act, effect. [MSA 22.1377]

MCLA 484.169 Immediate effect. [MSA 22.1378]

MCLA 484.170 Appraisal of damages; lands in more than 1 county. [MSA 22.1379]

MCLA 484.171 Same; contiguous lands of same person. [MSA 22.1380]

MCLA 484.172 Amendment to articles; filing, recording, use of certified copy as evidence. [MSA 22.138ᵀ]

Act No. 129, P.A. 1883 - Telephone and Messenger Service Companies

AN ACT for the organization of telephone and messenger service companies.

MCLA 484.1 Incorporators; articles, contents, recording, filing. [MSA 22.141ᵀ]

MCLA 484.2 Directors; powers, election, term, qualifications. [MSA 22.1412]

MCLA 484.3 Shares of stock; par value, status as personalty. [MSA 22.1413]

MCLA 484.4 Construction of line, restrictions; condemnation; purchase of stock; holding of realty (includes special provisions for upper peninsula). [MSA 22.1414]

MCLA 484.6 Injury to property; penalty. [MSA 22.1415]

MCLA 484.7 Stockholder's liability for corporate debts; contribution. [MSA 22.1416]

MCLA 484.8 Governing laws (including taxation of corporation). [MSA 22.1417]

MCLA 484.9 Lines in lower peninsula; location. [MSA 22.1418]

MCLA 484.10 Condemnation; procedure, restrictions. [MSA 22.1419]

Act 206, P.A. 1913 - Telephone Company as Common Carrier

AN ACT to declare telephone lines and telephone companies within the state of Michigan to be common carriers, to regulate the business of the same, provide for the consolidation thereof and prescribe a penalty for the violation of this act.

436

MCLA 484.101 Telephone companies, status as common carriers; governing laws. [MSA 22.1441]

MCLA 484.102 Powers of commission (Michigan railroad commission). [MSA 22.1442]

MCLA 484.103 Duty to serve; reasonable rates; commission, powers. [MSA 22.1443]

MCLA 484.104 Discrimination; rebates. [MSA 22.1444]

MCLA 484.105 Preferences. [MSA 22.1445]

MCLA 484.106 Physical connection, joint rates, power of commission to order; division of cost. [MSA 22.1446]

MCLA 484.107 Switching service. [MSA 22.1447]

MCLA 484.108 Sale or lease of lines; procedure. [MSA 22.1448]

MCLA 484.109 Construction of lines; procedure. [MSA 22.1449]

Sec. 9. Any person, copartnership or corporation desiring to obtain a franchise to construct a telephone system in any municipality in the state of Michigan, shall apply to the commission for a certificate of public convenience and necessity, and the commission may grant or withhold said certificate after a public hearing and investigation upon the merits of the application in the manner provided herein for holding of public hearings and investigations on complaint, and no such person, copartnership or corporation **shall be granted a franchise in any municipality** *in the state of Michigan to construct a telephone system until they have received a certificate of public convenience and necessity herein provided for. ...*

MCLA 484.110 Increase of rates; application, finding, notice, proof of publication. [MSA 22.1450]

MCLA 484.111 Hearing and determination of complaints; authority of commission. [MSA 22.1451]

MCLA 484.112 Same; procedure. [MSA 22.1452]

MCLA 484.113 Rules of procedure. [MSA 22.1453]

MCLA 484.114 Judicial review of orders; procedure. [MSA 22.1454]

MCLA 484.115 Same; injunction. [MSA 22.1455]

MCLA 484.116 Same; procedure when new evidence is introduced. [MSA 22.1456]

MCLA 484.117 Same; procedure on appeal. [MSA 22.1457]

MCLA 484.118 Same; burden of proof. [MSA 22.1458]

MCLA 484.119 Annual report; contents. [MSA 22.1459]

MCLA 484.120 Records; form. [MSA 22.1460]

MCLA 484.121 Schedules of rates; filing, public inspection. [MSA 22.1461]

MCLA 484.122 Penalty. [MSA 22.1462]

MCLA 484.123 Saving clause. [MSA 22.1463]

MCLA 484.124 Employes of commission. [MSA 22.1464]

WHARFS, PIERS, DOCKS AND PORT FACILITIES

Of Michigan's 1,245 townships, 219 border on one of four of the Great Lakes -- Michigan, Superior, Huron and Erie -- or Lake St. Clair. Of the balance, 401 have shorelines on large inland lakes such as Houghton, Higgins, Burt and Gull Lakes. The rest are involved in some way with one or more of the 11,000 lakes and scores of streams and rivers in Michigan. Rivers account for thousands of miles of shoreline, some major ones being the Tahquamenon, Detroit, Grand and Kalamazoo. One of national acclaim is the Au Sable which traverses the northern part of central Michigan. Michigan is truly a water wonderland.

More and more demands will be made upon local government in general and township government in particular as the need for conservation of natural resources and energy grows. Recreation needs

438

of our own residents and increasing demands for additional facilities to meet the needs of our tourist industry are of vital concern to townships. According to figures released by the Michigan Department of Commerce, it is estimated that Great Lakes shipping will double by the year 2000, one of the reasons being that it costs far less per ton and is more efficient to ship by water than by any other means.

There is already great demand in many townships for activities leading to the construction, operation and maintenance of such things as wharfs, piers, docks and port facilities, both for recreation and commercial purposes. Township boards should be fully aware of those things which they can or cannot do in meeting the challenge in this area of concern which has such a profound effect on the economy of the state.

Act No. 286, P.A. 1923 - Wharfs, Piers and Docks

AN ACT to enable townships to construct and maintain wharfs, piers, docks and landing places for the use and benefit of the public.

MCLA 41.481 Public docks, township ownership; authorizing vote. [MSA 5.2391]

Sec. 1. Any township in this state abutting upon any navigable waters may acquire, construct and maintain wharfs, piers, docks and landing places for the use and benefit of the public, and may lease and control the same, and the township board shall act for said township in acquiring, constructing and maintaining the same when authorized so to do by the affirmative vote of 3/5 of the qualified electors of said township voting thereon at any general election or at any special election, at which the same shall be submitted.

MCLA 41.482 Same; powers; proceedings. [MSA 5.2392]

Sec. 2. Any and all proceedings had or taken under this act shall be had and taken by said township board who are hereby vested with all the power and ...

Act No. 234, P.A. 1925 - Port Districts

AN ACT to provide for the creation and establishment of port districts; to prescribe their rights, powers, duties and privileges; to prescribe their powers of regulation in certain cases; to prescribe their powers in respect to acquiring, improving, enlarging, extending, operating, maintaining and financing various projects and the conditions upon which certain of said projects may extend into another state or county.

MCLA 120.1 Port districts; incorporation, exercise of powers. [MSA 5.2151]

MCLA 120.2 Referendum petition; filing, examination, certification; resolution of board of (county) **supervisors.** [MSA 5.2152]

MCLA 120.3 Establishment of port district; petitions, election. [MSA 5.2153]

MCLA 120.4 Election, notice; form of ballot. [MSA 5.2154]

MCLA 120.5 Formation, procedure, referendum, effective date of creation. [MSA 5.2155]

MCLA 120.6 District comprising more than 1 county, limitation; lesser port districts. [MSA 5.2156]

MCLA 120.7 Canvass and declaration of election results; three-fifths vote. [MSA 5.2157]

MCLA 120.8 Election and survey expenses. [MSA 5.2158]

MCLA 120.9 Port commission; appointment, term, vacancies. [MSA 5.2159]

MCLA 120.10 Same; quorum, member, term, eligibility, vacancy, removal, oath. [MSA 5.2160]

MCLA 120.11 Same; submission of propositions at elections, canvass of votes. [MSA 5.2161]

MCLA 120.12 Same; compensation of commissioners, mileage, expenses. [MSA 5.2162]

MCLA 120.13 Same; acquisition of property. [MSA 5.2163]

MCLA 120.13a Acceptance of grants, approval. [MSA 5.2163(1)]

Sec. 13a. Each port commission may accept gifts, grants, loans or contributions from the United States of America, this state, local municipalities, foundations, any public or private agency or any individual. ...

MCLA 120.14 Port district public improvements; commodity handling; advertising; acquisition. Construction in navigable waters; harbor, pierhead and bulkhead lines. Private marine facilities. Rules and regulations of board of supervisors. Representation for port district. Cooperation with other agencies, industry and business. Planned industrial districts. [MSA 5.2164]

MCLA 120.15 Same; issue of evidence of indebtedness. [MSA 5.2165]

MCLA 120.16 Same; bonds for public improvement, revenue, full faith and credit, approvals. [MSA 5.2166]

MCLA 120.17 Same; lands, leases and easements. [MSA 5.2167]

MCLA 120.18 Same; streams, improvement. [MSA 5.2168]

MCLA 120.19 Same; waterways, creation and improvement. [MSA 5.2169]

MCLA 120.20 Payments in lieu of taxes on income-producing public improvement. [MSA 5.2170]

MCLA 120.21 Rates, approval. [MSA 5.2171]

MCLA 120.22 Lease of property, maximum term, bond. [MSA 5.2172]

MCLA 120.23 Sale of property, approval. [MSA 5.2173]

MCLA 120.24 Port commission; taxes, special assessments; allocation of millage. [MSA 5.2174]

MCLA 120.25 Port commission; bond issues, limit, approval by governing bodies or electors. [MSA 5.2177]

MCLA 120.26 Same; assistants and employes. [MSA 5.2178]

MCLA 120.27 Same; expenditures, authority, bids. [MSA 5.2179]

MCLA 120.28 Same; lease of harbor area, rents. [MSA 5.2180]

MCLA 120.29 Same; officers, election, power; seal; proceedings; funds; office; maps, charts, plans and documents. [MSA 5.2181]

MCLA 120.30 Comprehensive port plan of harbor improvements; notice, hearing; approval by municipalities; restrictions. [MSA 5.2182]

MCLA 120.31 Property rights in improvements; cooperation between port district and certain other public bodies. [MSA 5.2183]

MCLA 120.32 Power to borrow in anticipation of tax. [MSA 5.2184]

MCLA 120.33 Fund created; special funds; disbursement. [MSA 5.2185]

MCLA 120.34 Annual reports, budgets; budget committee. [MSA 5.2186]

MCLA 120.34a Port districts coterminous with cities and townships; powers of local governing bodies. [MSA 5.2186(1)]

MCLA 120.35 Act construed. [MSA 5.2187]

Sec. 35. This act shall not be construed to repeal, amend, or modify any law heretofore enacted, providing a method of harbor improvement, regulation or control in this state, but shall be held to be an additional and concurrent method providing for such purpose and except by agreement between the port commission and the parties at interest, shall not be construed to include within its terms any property now or hereafter devoted to public use, owned, operated or controlled by any person, municipality or private corporation.

JOINT ACTION
Act No. 251, P.A. 1966 - Port Districts

AN ACT relating to declare certain policies of the state of Michigan; to designate the department of commerce as the agency of this state to cooperate and negotiate with port districts and others; to provide for the making of grants to port districts and the administration thereof; to authorize studies to assist in stimulating port traffic; to authorize the department to represent the state before other governmental units; to direct the establishment of port promotional programs; and to provide other powers, rights and duties of the department.

MCLA 120.51 Department of commerce designated state agency to cooperate and negotiate with port districts, etc. [MSA 5.2195(1)]

MCLA 120.52 Request for matching grants by port districts; disbursement of funds. [MSA 5.2195(2)]

MCLA 120.53 Cooperation and agreements with United States; conduct of studies, research programs, etc. [MSA 5.2195(3)]

MCLA 120.54 Investigation of transportation rates; representation of state and port districts. [MSA 5.2195(4)]

MCLA 120.55 Budget requests. [MSA 5.2195(5)]

MCLA 120.56 Construction of act. [MSA 5.2195(6)]

Sec. 6. In construing this act, port districts coterminous with a city or township shall follow the same procedure as is prescribed for counties, substituting the local governing body and officers where applicable for the board of supervisors and county officials. Whenever in this act any power is granted to a port district, it shall be exercised by the port commission unless otherwise provided herein. Whenever in this act any power is granted to a port com-

443

mission it shall be deemed to be granted to the port district but to be exercised by such port commission.

SIDEWALKS AND PAVEMENT

Statistics from the National Safety Council indicate that many pedestrian-automobile accidents occur because of people walking in the roadway either for lack of sidewalks or because they are poorly constructed or maintained. This is particularly true where there is heavy use of streets by children on their way to school. In the past, townships have made few attempts to create sidewalk special assessment districts near schools since most of the lands surrounding schools are owned by the school districts. However, recent legislation has made it possible for townships to join with a school district to construct and maintain not only necessary sidewalks, but also overhead walkways for the safety of children crossing highly traveled highways. Paving of streets is also often a safety measure.

Act No. 188, P.A. 1954, which appears at the beginning of this chapter, as well as the statutes which follow, provide several methods of meeting township sidewalk and pavement needs.

As it is considering what delivery system(s) it will use for sidewalks, the board should carefully study needed minimum standards of construction. These do not necessarily have to be uniform for all walks. Width and thickness of concrete (or conceivably, even blacktopping) in a heavily traveled public area might very well be greater than those in a residential area. Also, if a walk is part of a heavily used driveway, standards might have to be higher. This is a matter of great importance since many property owners, for one reason or another, wish to construct their own sidewalks. This privilege cannot be denied them so long as they guarantee through a building permit or some other performance agreement that they will meet minimum standards established by the township.

Township boards may also include in their sidewalk ordinance conditions that walks shall be cleared of all ice and snow and other materials that might in any way interfere with normal public use, as well as standards on repair and replacement of sidewalks.

444

JOINT ACTION

Act No. 246, P.A. 1931 - Sidewalks and Pavements in Townships

AN ACT to provide for the construction and maintenance of pavements and/or sidewalks on or along public highways in certain cases.

MCLA 41.271 Pavements or sidewalks in townships; application, eligibility of signers; certificate of tax status; authority of county road commissioners. MSA 9.571

Sec. 1. Whenever the owners of more than 51% of the lineal frontage of lands outside of the corporate limits of any city or village fronting or touching upon any public highway or portion thereof, desire a pavement or sidewalks built thereon, they may file an application for such improvement with the county road commissioners of the county in which such pavement or sidewalk is proposed to be built. No application for the paving of any highway, or portion thereof, shall be considered unless at least 75% of the lands fronting thereon have been subdivided into parcels having a frontage of not more than 300 feet each on such highway or there shall be an average of at least 1 building, including buildings under construction, located along the portion of such highway proposed to be paved for every 300 lineal feet thereof, according to a survey thereof to be made by the commissioners. The eligibility of signers to any application hereby authorized may be determined by their interest of record in the office of the register of deeds or in the probate court of the county in which such lands are situated at the time the petition is presented or by other satisfactory proof of interest presented to the commissioners. Such petition shall be accompanied by a description of the land fronting or touching on the highway owned by each signer and by a certificate of the county treasurer, showing the taxes or special assessments, if any, against such lands which appear delinquent on his books; no name of any signer on the petition shall be considered valid whose land fronting or touching on the highways shows delinquent assessments or taxes on such certificate. Any petition so received by the commissioners or presented to them under the provisions of this act, shall be deemed to confer full authority to cause such work to be done in order that the proper proportion of the expense thereof may be met accordingly. The commissioners shall have all the power of laying

445

out and establishing all such pavements or sidewalks. The words "highway" or "public highway" as used in this act mean any road, street or alley taken over by and under the jurisdiction of the board of county road commissioners.

MCLA 41.271a Same; application for improvement; compliance to subdivision and building requirements; declaration of necessity; public hearing; petition. [MSA 9.571(1)]

Sec. 1a. Any township board, by resolution, may make application to the board of county road commissioners for the improvement of a county road or portion thereof located within the township. The resolution when received and accepted by the county road commissioners shall confer the same authority to cause an improvement to be made and benefits assessed as if a petition were filed in accordance with the provisions of section 1. The petition shall not be considered unless it complies with the subdivision and building requirements set forth in section 1 relating to applications by property owners.

A declaration of necessity shall be made by resolution of the board of county road commissioners who shall thereafter hold a public hearing at the township hall upon the declaration of necessity in the same manner as if an application had been filed by property owners as set forth in section 1. After the date of the public hearing on the declaration of necessity, the property owners of 51% or more of the lineal frontage along the proposed improvement may submit within 45 days a petition to the board of county road commissioners requesting that the project be discontinued. The project shall be discontinued if, upon examination, the owners of 51% or more of the lineal frontage along the improvement have signed the petition. If no petition is filed within 45 days, the project shall proceed in the same manner as if inaugurated by property owners.

MCLA 41.272 Same; examination; survey; plat; construction; inspection. [MSA 9.572]

MCLA 41.273 Same; bridges, drains, curbing, culverts, right of way. [MSA 9.573]

446

MCLA 41.274 Same; first order of determination, description of assessment district; along state trunk line highway, approval by state highway commissioner. [MSA 9.574]

MCLA 41.275 Same; hearing, notice, contents; change in specifications or district; new hearing. [MSA 9.575].

MCLA 41.276 Same; liability of petitioners; dismissal of proceedings. [MSA 9.576]

MCLA 41.277 Final order of determination within 30 days; attachment of specifications. [MSA 9.577]

MCLA 41.278 Contracts for construction; effect of delinquent taxes; bids, procedure for letting; when commenced. [MSA 9.578]

MCLA 41.279 Assessment district; determination, addition of lands; installments. [MSA 9.579]

MCLA 41.280 Same; assessment of benefits against township and parcels of land; review; assessment on state lands; numbering of assessment districts. [MSA 9.580]

MCLA 41.281 Indebtedness; approval by board of supervisors and township boards, limit on township bonds. [MSA 9.581]

MCLA 41.282 Maintenance and repair, proration of expense of joint improvement. [MSA 9.582]

MCLA 41.283 Application of Covert act; interest chargeable. [MSA 9.583]

MCLA 41.283a Issue and sale of bonds, interest rate; assessment district sinking fund. [MSA 9.583(1)]

MCLA 41.284 Advancement of money from county road funds; full faith and credit of township pledged; reimbursement; delinquent special assessments turned over to township. [MSA 9.584]

MCLA 41.285 Same; (board of) supervisors, powers. [MSA 9.585]

MCLA 41.286 Pavements or sidewalks in townships; hearing examiners; determination of board of county road commissioners; reconsideration. [MSA 9.585(1)]

JOINT ACTION
Act No. 251, P.A. 1957 - Sidewalks along Highways

AN ACT to provide for the making of certain public improvements by townships and to permit the expenditure of public moneys with respect thereto independently of or in conjunction with proceedings under laws providing for special assessments.

MCLA 41.401 Sidewalks along and footwalks over highways; approval. [MSA 9.570(1)]

Sec. 1. The township board of any township may make a public improvement by the installation of sidewalks along the sides of any highway and elevated structures for foot travel over highways in the township, and pay for the elevated structures out of the funds of the township, or may purchase the same on title retaining contracts. Such contracts shall not be entered into or issued for a longer period than 10 years. No highway under the jurisdiction of the state highway commissioner or the board of county road commissioners shall be improved under the provisions of this act without the written approval of the state highway commissioner or the board of county road commissioners.

MCLA 41.402 Same; payment from township contingent or general funds. [MSA 9.570(2)]

Act No. 67, P.A. 1961 - Sidewalks Outside Cities and Villages

AN ACT to authorize township boards to provide for the repair and maintenance of sidewalks outside of the limits of incorporated cities and villages; and to provide for the payment of the expenses so incurred.

MCLA 41.921 Township sidewalks; maximum annual expenditure. [MSA 9.586(1)]

Sec. 1. The township board of any township, at any regular meeting or at any special meeting called for that purpose, may vote a sum not exceeding $6,000.00 for any one year to provide for the repair and maintenance of sidewalks in the township, located outside of the limits of incorporated cities and villages, the expenses of such repairs and maintenance to be paid out of the contingent fund of the township. In townships having an assessed valuation of less than $1,000,000.00, the township board shall not vote a sum exceeding $1,000.00 for any one year for such purpose. In townships having an assessed valuation of more than $1,000,000.00 but less than $7,000,000.00, the township board shall not vote a sum exceeding $2,500.00 for any one year for such purpose. In townships having an assessed valuation of more than $7,000,000.00 but less than $15,000,000.00, the township board shall not vote a sum exceeding $5,000.00 for any one year for any such purpose.

MCLA 41.922   Same; special assessment district; establishment, notice. [MSA 9.586(2)]

Sec. 2. The township board, at any regular meeting, either on its own motion or upon petitions signed by not less than 10 freeholders in the district described in the petitions for repair and maintenance of sidewalks, after 60 days' notice by certified mail, may order the expenses for the repair and maintenance of such sidewalks to be defrayed by a special assessment on all the taxable lands and premises in the territory described in the petitions or in the order of the township board. ...

MCLA 41.923   Same; special assessments, collection. [MSA 9.586(3)]

MCLA 41.924   Same; transfer of cost from district to township. [MSA 9.586(4)]

MCLA 41.925   Same; act not affected. [MSA 9.586(5)]

Act No. 35, P.A. 1966 - Sidewalks in Townships

AN ACT to provide for the construction of sidewalks in townships; to authorize township boards to construct or order the construction of sidewalks; and to provide for the payment thereof.

MCLA 41.931 Construction of township sidewalks; power of board. MSA 9.587(1)

Sec. 1. *The township board of any township may order the construction or construct sidewalks in any designated area within the township because of the health, safety or welfare of the residents of the township.*

MCLA 41.932 Public meeting; notice. MSA 9.587(2)

MCLA 41.933 Assessment for sidewalk construction; approval where constructed on state highways or county roads. MSA 9.587(3)

MCLA 41.934 Main or arterial road walkways or sidewalks, construction, maintenance, financing. MSA 9.587(4)

MOTOR VEHICLES AND SNOWMOBILES

Safe movement of motor vehicles has become one of the great concerns of the nation, the state and local government. In addition to the problems caused by motor vehicles, township officials should be fully cognizant of those created in the past four or five years by snowmobiles.

The next grouping of services through ordinances available to township government include, but are not limited to the motor vehicle code, the uniform traffic code, the registration and regulation of snowmobiles, the operation of parking lots on school property, authorization for local units of government to regulate and control traffic in parking lots of shopping centers, garage keeper's liability and a brief mention of the Michigan State Safety Commission. These are all a necessary and integral part of the safety programs of townships.

Township boards need not be overly concerned about being unable to enforce their ordinances or codes in this area because of lack of economic capability. In such cases, the statutes provide that Township A and Township B each may adopt its own ordinance and then both share in the cost of enforcement through a jointly operated police organization.

When adopting ordinances, it is important to achieve a good balance. A free flow of motor vehicle traffic can be provided that is consistent with safety standards. Property can be protected while allowing the snowmobile operator to enjoy this type of recreation. When local government officials take time to thoroughly study and analyze conditions, they will generally be able to establish good ordinances.

In reviewing the statutes, it should be kept in mind that the office of state highway commissioner was abolished and his powers and duties transferred to the state highway commission. Powers and duties of the commissioner of state highways were then transferred to the department of state highways.

JOINT ACTION
Act No. 188, P.A. 1941 - Michigan State Safety Commission

AN ACT to create the Michigan state safety commission for the promotion of greater safety on the public highways and other places within the state of Michigan; to study traffic conditions; to investigate and eliminate menaces to public safety; to form the Michigan state safety council and appropriate moneys therefor.

MCLA 256.561 Michigan state safety commission, members.
[MSA 9.1704]

MCLA 256.562 Same; meetings, purpose. [MSA 9.1705]

Sec. 2. It shall be the duty of said commission to hold meetings at least once during each calendar month hereafter, at such places as it may determine, to consult and cooperate with all departments of state government in regard to traffic safety, to promote uniform and effective programs of safety on streets and highways; to interchange information among the several departments of the state government for more effective safety conditions; to cooperate with officials of the United States Government and with local governments in regulating highway traffic, and to encourage safety education in the state of Michigan.

MCLA 256.563 Same; employes, offices and equipment.
MSA 9.1706

Act No. 391, P.A. 1919 - Garage Keeper's Liability

AN ACT to protect the owners of motor vehicles, entrusting the same for any purpose, to the care, custody or control of the owner or keeper of a public garage or other establishment where such motor vehicles are so accepted for hire or gain.

MCLA 256.541 Garage keeper; prima facie evidence of negligence.
MSA 9.1721

MCLA 256.542 Same; prima facie evidence of conversion.
MSA 9.1722

MCLA 256.543 Examination of vehicle and notice of loss.
MSA 9.1723

MCLA 256.544 Forms for statement of condition, owner's refusal to sign bar to recovery of damages. MSA 9.1724

MCLA 256.545 Contract nullifying act, validity. MSA 9.1725

Act No. 235, P.A. 1969 - Shopping Center Parking Lots

AN ACT authorizing local units of government to regulate and control traffic in parking lots of shopping centers; and to provide a penalty for violations thereof.

MCLA 257.941 Definitions. MSA 9.2641

MCLA 257.942 Traffic regulation, signs, signals, turning, crossings, one way traffic, parking, safety and loading zones, removal of vehicles. MSA 9.2642

MCLA 257.943 Violations, penalty. MSA 9.2643

JOINT ACTION
Act No. 175, P.A. 1958 - School Property

AN ACT to authorize municipalities to adopt ordinances governing the operation, parking without fees and the speed of motor vehicles upon properties of boards of education, school districts or community college districts lying within such municipalities; to require the boards of education, school districts or community college districts to request such ordinances; and to impose penalties for the violation thereof.

MCLA 257.961 School property; municipal regulation of operation, parking and speed of vehicles. [MSA 9.2660]

Sec. 1. ... No municipal legislative authority shall adopt such ordinances without first receiving a resolution from the board of education, school district or board of trustees of the community college district over whose property the ordinances shall apply requesting the adoption of such ordinances.

Act No. 198, P.A. 1965 - Motor Vehicle Accident Claims Act

AN ACT providing for the establishment, maintenance and administration of a motor vehicle accident claims fund for the payment of damages for injury to or death of certain persons or property damage arising out of the ownership, maintenance or use of motor vehicles in the state in certain cases; and to provide penalties for violation of this act.

MCLA 257.1101 Title. [MSA 9.2801]

MCLA 257.1102 Definitions. [MSA 9.2802]

Sec. 2. As used in this act:
(a, b, c, d) ...
(e) "Person" includes natural persons, firms, copartnerships, associations and corporations, except the state or any agency or political subdivision thereof. The word "person" shall not include

453

any municipal corporation or any corporation owned or operated by the state or any political subdivision thereof.

MCLA 257.1103 to 257.1131 ⎡MSA 9.2803 TO 9.2831⎤

JOINT ACTION (ENFORCEMENT)
Act No. 74, P.A. 1968 - Registration and Regulation of Snowmobiles

AN ACT to register and regulate snowmobiles.

MCLA 257.1501 Definitions. ⎡MSA 9.3200(1)⎤

Sec. 1. As used in this act:

(a) "Operator" means any person who operates or is in actual physical control of a snowmobile.

(b) "Owner" means any of the following:

(i) A person who holds the legal title to a snowmobile.

(ii) A vendee or lessee of a snowmobile which is the subject of an agreement for the conditional sale or lease thereof with the right of purchase upon performance of the conditions stated in the agreement and with an immediate right of possession vested in the conditional vendee or lessee.

(iii) A person renting a snowmobile or having the exclusive use of a snowmobile for more than 30 days.

(c) "Operate" means to ride in or on and be in actual physical control of the operation of a snowmobile.

(d) "Person" means an individual, partnership, corporation, the state and any of its agencies or subdivisions, and any body of persons whether incorporated or not.

(e) "Snowmobile" means any motor driven vehicle designed for travel primarily on snow or ice of a type which utilizes sled type runners or skis, or an endless belt tread or any combination of these or other similar means of contact with the surface upon which it is operated. It is not a vehicle which must be registered under Act No. 300 of the Public Acts of 1949, as amended, being sections 257.1 ⎡MSA 9.1801⎤ *to 257.923* ⎡MSA 9.2623⎤ *of the Compiled Laws of 1948.*

(f) "Dealer" means any person engaged in the sale, lease or rental of snowmobiles as a regular business.

(g) "Highway or street" means the entire width between the boundary lines of every way publicly maintained when any part

thereof is open to the use of the public for purposes of vehicular travel.

(h) "Roadway" means that portion of a highway improved, designated, or ordinarily used for vehicular travel. If a highway includes 2 or more separate roadways the term roadway refers to any such roadway separately, but not to all such roadways collectively.

(i) "Department" means department of state.

(j) "Right of way" means that portion of a highway less the roadway and any shoulder.

(k) "Shoulder" means that portion of a highway on either side of the roadway which is normally snowplowed for the safety and convenience of vehicular traffic.

(l) "Zone 1" means all of the upper peninsula.

(m) "Zone 2" means all of that part of the lower peninsula north of a line beginning at and drawn from a point on the Michigan-Wisconsin boundary line due west of the westerly terminus of river road in Muskegon county; ...

(n) "Zone 3" means all that part of the lower peninsula south of the line described in zone 2.

MCLA 257.1502 Exemption from taxes and fees. [MSA 9.3200(2)]

MCLA 257.1503 Registration, necessity, exception. [MSA 9.3200(3)]

MCLA 257.1503a Special events, registration exemption. [MSA 9.3200(3A)]

MCLA 257.1504 Application for registration, time, form, fees; registration year; certificate of registration, issuance, contents, form, inspection. [MSA 9.3200(4)]

MCLA 257.1504a Disposition of revenue; trail programs. [MSA 9.3200(4A)]

MCLA 257.1504b Enforcement of act and safety programs. State budget requests; allocation between state and county programs. County programs, submission of expenditure estimates and other information; allocations of state aid. Expenditure statements, time, form, state aid allocation procedure. Audits by state; refunds to

state. State and county cooperation, sheriffs, records, reports. Rules. [MSA 9.3200(4B)]

MCLA 257.1504c Snowmobile information, safety education, and training program. [MSA 9.3200(4C)]

Sec. 4c. (1) The department may implement a comprehensive snowmobile information, safety education and training program which shall include the preparation and dissemination of snowmobile information and safety advice to the public and training of operators. The program shall provide for the training of youthful operators and for the issuance of snowmobile safety certificates to those who successfully complete the training provided under the program.

(2) In implementing a program which is established pursuant to this section, the department shall cooperate with private organizations and associations, private and public corporations, schools and local governmental units. The department shall consult with the department of state police and county sheriffs in regard to subject matter of a training program and performance testing that leads to certification of snowmobile operators.

(3) The department may designate any person it deems qualified to provide course instruction and to award snowmobile safety certificates.

MCLA 257.1505 Registration and identification number; display; decal; term; awarding certificate; records. [MSA 9.3200(5)]

MCLA 257.1506 Notice of surrender of certificate, destruction or abandonment; change of address, transfer, fee; duplicate, fee. [MSA 9.3200(6)]

MCLA 257.1507 Dealer's and manufacturer's certificates of registration, use, applications, fees, temporary placement of numbers. [MSA 9.3200(7)]

MCLA 257.1508 Identifying number stamped on frame, necessity, location, registration certificate, penalty for possession of snowmobile with altered or defaced number. [MSA 9.3200(8)]

MCLA 257.1509 Dealers; duty in renting, leasing and furnishing; liability, insurance. [MSA 9.3200(9)]

456

MCLA 257.1510 Foreign registry; limited operation.
MSA 9.3200(10)

MCLA 257.1511 Repealed.

MCLA 257.1512 Regulation of snowmobile operations.
MSA 9.3200(12)

Note: This section stipulates when a snowmobile may or may not be operated on or near public highways.

MCLA 257.1512a Age restrictions, operators, violations.
MSA 9.3200(12A)

MCLA 257.1512b Hunting or pursuing birds or animals, prohibition.
MSA 9.3200(12B)

MCLA 257.1513 Lights and brakes. MSA 9.3200(13)

MCLA 257.1514 Ordinances regulating operations. MSA 9.3200(14)

Sec. 14. Any city, village or township may pass an ordinance regulating the operation of snowmobiles if the ordinance meets substantially the minimum requirements of this act. A city, village, township or county may not adopt an ordinance which:

(a) Imposes a fee for a license.

(b) Specifies accessory equipment to be carried on the snowmobile.

(c) Requires a snowmobile operator to possess a motor vehicle driver's license.

(d) Restricts operation of a snowmobile on the frozen surface of public waters or on lands owned by or under the control of the state except pursuant to section 14a.

MCLA 257.1514a Rules and ordinances regulating operations.
MSA 9.3200(14A)

Sec. 14a. (1) **Commission defined** (natural resources commission). ... *(2)* **Speed limits, times of use, use on frozen waters.** ... *(3)* **Investigations; hearings, notice.** ...

(4) **Approval by governing body of political subdivision containing the frozen waters; ordinance.** *After a hearing is held pursuant to subsection (3) the proposed rule shall be submitted to the governing body of the political subdivision in which the affected frozen waters lie. The governing body shall inform the department that it approves or disapproves of the proposed rule within 30 days after receiving the rule from the department of natural resources. If the governing body disapproves the proposed rule, further action shall not be taken. If the governing body approves the proposed rule, it may enact an ordinance which shall be identical to the proposed rule and the commission shall promulgate the rule. An ordinance enacted pursuant to this subsection shall not be effective until the proposed rule is promulgated and effective in accordance with Act No. 306 of the Public Acts of 1969, as amended.*

(5) **Suspension, amendment, and repeal of ordinances.** *An ordinance which is the same as a rule which is suspended by the legislature, or amended or repealed by the commission, shall likewise be suspended, amended or repealed. The governing body, by majority vote, may repeal the ordinance at any time.*

(6) **Enforcement.** *Local law enforcement officers may enforce ordinances enacted pursuant to this section and state and county enforcement officers shall enforce rules which are promulgated pursuant to this section.*

MCLA 257.1515 Prohibited operations. Speed. Liquor and drugs. Lights. Forest nurseries, planting areas, forest reproduction areas, and natural dedicated areas. Frozen public waters, proximity to persons or shelters, skating areas, reduced speed. Mufflers. Proximity to dwellings, time. Fenced or enclosed premises, posting, personal notice, farmlands, farm woodlots, platted property. Public hunting areas, exceptions: access to residences, hunting camps, transmission lines, and timber for harvesting, owner or possessor of land, invitees. Bows and firearms. Cemeteries. Slide, ski, or skating areas. Railroads and right of way. [MSA 9.3200(15)]

MCLA 257.1516 Accidents, notification of authorities, report. [MSA 9.3200(16)]

MCLA 257.1517 Penalty. [MSA 9.3200(17)]

MCLA 257.1517a Violations; appearance tickets, issuance; owner as operator, prima facie evidence. [MSA 9.3200(17A)]

458

MCLA 257.1518 Effective date. [MSA 9.3200(18)]

Act No. 62, P.A. 1956 - Uniform Traffic Code

AN ACT to authorize the commissioner of the state police to promulgate a uniform traffic code; to authorize any city, township or village to adopt such uniform traffic code by reference without publication in full.

MCLA 257.951 Uniform traffic code for cities, townships and villages; promulgation by commissioner of the state police. [MSA 9.2651]

MCLA 257.952 Same; publication of adopting ordinance. [MSA 9.2652]

MCLA 257.953 Same; amendment. [MSA 9.2653]

MCLA 257.954 Same; copies for inspection by and distribution to public. [MSA 9.2654]

Sec. 4. Upon adoption of any such code by reference, the city, township or village **clerk shall maintain in his office a supply of copies of the code** *for inspection by and distribution to the public without charge.*

JOINT ACTION (ENFORCEMENT)
Act No. 300, P.A. 1949 - Michigan Vehicle Code

AN ACT to provide for the registration, titling, sale and transfer, and regulation of vehicles operated upon the public highways of this state; to provide for the licensing of vehicle dealers and wreckers; to provide for the examination, licensing and control of operators and chauffeurs; to provide for the giving of proof of financial responsibility and security by the owners and operators of vehicles; to provide for the imposition, levy and collection of specific taxes on vehicles, and the levy and collection of sales and use taxes, license fees and permit fees; to provide for the regulation and use of streets and highways; to provide penalties for violation of any of the provisions of this act;

*to provide for civil liability of owners and operators of
vehicles and service of process on nonresidents; and to
repeal all other acts or parts of acts inconsistent herewith
or contrary hereto.*

CHAPTER I. WORDS AND PHRASES DEFINED

Note: There are numerous definitions included in this chapter
with which township officials should be concerned regarding traffic
signs and other Michigan Vehicle Code regulations.

MCLA 257.1 Words and phrases. [MSA 9.1801]

MCLA 257.1a Accessory. [MSA 9.1801(1)]

MCLA 257.2 Authorized emergency vehicle. [MSA 9.1802]

*Sec. 2. "Authorized emergency vehicle" means vehicles of
the fire department, police vehicles, ambulances, emergency vehicles of governmental departments, or such vehicles of public
service corporations and privately owned motor vehicles of volunteer and paid firemen as are authorized by the commissioner.*

MCLA 257.3 - 257.26 [MSA 9.1803 - 9.1826]

MCLA 257.27 Local authorities. [MSA 9.1827]

*Sec. 27. "Local authorities" means every municipal and other
local board or body having authority to enact laws relating to traffic
under the constitution and laws of this state.*

MCLA 257.28 - 257.30 [MSA 9.1828 - 9.1830]

MCLA 257.30a Mobile home. [MSA 9.1830(1)]

*Sec. 30a. "Mobile home" means a vehicle which can be drawn
on a highway and is used exclusively for residential or camping
purposes.*

MCLA 257.31 - 257.41 [MSA 9.1831 - 9.1841]

460

MCLA 257.42 Police officer. MSA 9.1842

Sec. 42. "Police officer" means every sheriff or his deputies, village marshal, officer of the police department of any incorporated city or village, and officer of the Michigan state police.

MCLA 257.43 - 257.59 MSA 9.1843 - 9.1859

MCLA 257.60 Sidewalk. MSA 9.1860

Sec. 60. "Sidewalk" means that portion of a street between the curb lines, or the lateral lines of roadway, and the adjacent property lines intended for the use of pedestrians.

MCLA 257.61 - 257.69 MSA 9.1861 - 9.1869

MCLA 257.70 Traffic control devices. MSA 9.1870

Sec. 70. "Traffic control devices" means all signs, signals, markings, and devices not inconsistent with this act placed or erected by authority of a public body or official having jurisdiction, for the purpose of regulating, warning or guiding traffic.

MCLA 257.71 Traffic control order. MSA 9.1871

Sec. 71. "Traffic control order" means an order officially establishing the location of traffic control devices and traffic control signals on the highways of this state by the authority having jurisdiction over such highway and filed with the county clerk of the county traversed by such highway. A certified copy thereof shall be prima facie evidence in all courts of the issuance of such order.

MCLA 257.72 Traffic control signal. MSA 9.1872

MCLA 257.73 Trailer. MSA 9.1873

MCLA 257.74 Trailer coach. MSA 9.1874

Sec. 74. "Trailer coach" means every vehicle designed or used for dwelling or camping purposes or exclusively for camp living and drawn behind a motor vehicle.

MCLA 257.75 - 257.82 ⎡MSA 9.1875 - 9.1882⎤

MCLA 257.602a Failure to stop in obedience to direction of police or conservation department officer; misdemeanor. [MSA 9.2302(1)]

MCLA 257.603 Government vehicles, authorized emergency vehicles, workers upon surface of highways. [MSA 9.2303]

MCLA 257.604 Riders of animals and drivers of animal-drawn vehicles, application of act. [MSA 9.2304]

MCLA 257.605 Uniformity of application throughout state. [MSA 9.2305]

Sec. 605. The provisions of this chapter shall be applicable and uniform throughout this state and in all political subdivisions and municipalities therein and no local authority shall enact or enforce any ordinance, rule or regulation in conflict with the provisions of this chapter.

MCLA 257.606 Local authorities; powers as to traffic; impounding of vehicles. [MSA 9.2306]

MCLA 257.607 Realty owner's regulation of traffic on private property. [MSA 9.2307]

MCLA 257.608 Uniform system of traffic-control devices; manual. [MSA 9.2308]

MCLA 257.609 Same; placement and maintenance; restriction of local authorities; county road commissioners, permission, cost. [MSA 9.2309]

MCLA 257.610 - 257.614 [MSA 9.2310 - 9.2314]

Note: The above sections deal with traffic signal placement and control (including local government).

MCLA 257.615 Signs or lights resembling traffic control devices; commercial advertising prohibited on traffic signs. Imitation of traffic control devices. Emergency vehicles; distinguishing lights; prohibited lights. Prohibited signs; public nuisance, removal.

Placement of street decorations and banners; obstruction of traffic lights and signals. ⌐MSA 9.2315⌐

MCLA 257.616 Interference with traffic-control devices or railroad signs or signals. ⌐MSA 9.2316⌐

MCLA 257.617 - 257.623 ⌐MSA 9.2317 - 9.2324⌐

Note: The above sections deal with accidents and accident reports on both private and public property.

MCLA 257.624 Same; use of reports. ⌐MSA 9.2324⌐

MCLA 257.625 - 257.625g ⌐MSA 9.2325 - 9.2325(7)⌐

Note: The above sections deal with driving under the influence of drugs or intoxicating liquor.

MCLA 257.626 Reckless driving upon highway, frozen public lake, parking place. Reckless driving. Penalty. ⌐MSA 9.2326⌐

MCLA 257.626a Drag races; prohibition upon any highway or other place open to public. ⌐MSA 9.2326(1)⌐

MCLA 257.626b Driving upon highway, frozen public lake or parking place in negligent manner. ⌐MSA 9.2326(2)⌐

MCLA 257.627 Speed restrictions; assured clear distance ahead. Speed and distance ahead. Business or residence districts; public parks, posted speed limits. Vehicles with trailers. Trucks and combinations weighing over 5,000 pounds. School buses. ⌐MSA 9.2327⌐

MCLA 257.628 Speed limits; maximum, minimum, day and night. ⌐MSA 9.2328⌐

Sec. 628. **Determination and declaration.** ... *(b)* **Speed control signs.** *If upon investigation* ... (it is found) ... *in the interest of public safety, they* (state highway commissioner, state police commissioner, county road commissioner) *may order the township board* ... *to erect and maintain, take down or regulate such speed*

464

control signs, signals or devices as ... (they) ... shall direct, and in default thereof ... (they) ... shall be authorized to cause such designated signs, signals and devices to be erected and maintained, taken down, regulated or controlled, in the manner previously directed, and pay for same out of the highway fund designated. **Public record in office of county clerk; temporary construction or repair signs, authorization; evidence. ... Failure to observe speed or traffic control signs. ...**

MCLA 257.628a - 257.629a [MSA 9.2328(1) - 9.2329(1)]

Note: The above sections deal with speed limits and county traffic safety organization.

MCLA 257.630 Motor-driven cycles; lights, speed. [MSA 9.2330]

MCLA 257.631 Speed and load limitations on signposted bridges, causeways, and viaducts. [MSA 9.2331]

Sec. 631. (a) ...
(b) The state highway commissioner, county road commission, or other authority having jurisdiction of any public bridge, causeway or viaduct may conduct an investigation of any public bridge, causeway or viaduct, and if it is thereupon found that such structure cannot with safety to itself withstand vehicles traveling at the speed or carrying a load otherwise permissible under this chapter, the commissioner, commission or other authority shall determine and declare the maximum speed of vehicles or load which such structure can withstand, and shall cause or permit suitable signs stating such maximum speed and load limitations to be erected and maintained not more than 50 feet from each end of the structure, and also at a suitable distance from each end of the bridge to enable vehicles to take a different route.
(c) ...

MCLA 257.632 Vehicles in pursuit of criminals, fire patrols, ambulances. [MSA 9.2332]

MCLA 257.633 - 257.652 [MSA 9.2333 - 9.2352]

Note: The above sections deal with rules for proper operation of vehicles (Sec. 647 permits local jurisdiction regarding turning at intersections).

MCLA 257.653 Authorized emergency vehicle; right of way yielded by other vehicles. [MSA 9.2353]

MCLA 257.654 Funeral procession; right of way. [MSA 9.2354]

MCLA 257.655 Pedestrians on highways. [MSA 9.2355] (Also where there are no sidewalks.)

MCLA 257.656 Bicycles, motorcycles, regulations applicable, penalty. [MSA 9.2356]

MCLA 257.657 Bicyclists; regulations applicable. [MSA 9.2357]

MCLA 257.658 Bicycles, motorcycles, motor driven cycles; operators and riders, seating, number, crash helmets, rules. [MSA 9.2358]

MCLA 257.659 Clinging to other vehicles. [MSA 9.2359]

MCLA 257.660 Bicycles, motorcycles, and motor driven cycles; lane of travel, special paths, passing, police officers. [MSA 9.2360]

MCLA 257.660a Pedal bicycles with helper motors, operators, age. [MSA 9.2360(1)]

MCLA 257.661 Same; carrying articles, hands on handle bars. [MSA 9.2361]

MCLA 257.661a Handlebars of motorcycles or motor driven cycles, heighth. [MSA 9.2361(1)]

MCLA 257.662 Bicycles; lights, bells, brakes. [MSA 9.2362]

MCLA 257.663 Street cars; passage to left. [MSA 9.2363]

MCLA 257.664 Same; stopping. [MSA 9.2364]

MCLA 257.665 Street car tracks; removal of vehicle after signal. [MSA 9.2365]

466

MCLA 257.666 Safety zones occupied by persons. [MSA 9.2366]

MCLA 257.667 Railroad grade crossings. [MSA 9.2367]

MCLA 257.668 Same; stop signs, erection; obedience by drivers; failure to replace or maintain; action of negligence against governmental officers (by local authorities). [MSA 9.2368]

MCLA 257.669 Same; duty to stop, carriers of passengers for hire, school busses, carriers of explosives or flammable liquids. [MSA 9.2369]

MCLA 257.670 Same; slow-moving or heavy equipment, notice to railroad agent. [MSA 9.2370]

MCLA 257.671 Through highways, designation, stop signs (by local authorities). [MSA 9.2371]

MCLA 257.672 Stopping, parking, standing on pavement outside cities, villages; limited access highways, emergencies. [MSA 9.2372]

MCLA 257.673 Removal of illegally stopped vehicles, costs. [MSA 9.2373]

MCLA 257.674 Prohibited parking. [MSA 9.2374]

MCLA 257.674a Clear vision area; parking, commercial enterprises. [MSA 9.2374(1)]

MCLA 257.675 Parking regulations. Highways. One-way roadway. Angle parking. Signs, placing; traffic order, filing, hearing. Physically handicapped; certificate, display; evidence of qualification. [MSA 9.2375]

MCLA 257.676 Unattended motor vehicle, brakes, grade. [MSA 9.2376]

MCLA 257.676a Highways outside of cities and villages; display of goods, produce, merchandise within right of way, penalty. [MSA 9.2376(1)]

MCLA 257.676b Interference with flow of traffic. [MSA 9.2376(2)]

MCLA 257.677 Interference with driver's view or control. [MSA 9.2377]

MCLA 257.678 Coasting prohibited. [MSA 9.2378]

MCLA 257.679 Following fire apparatus prohibited. [MSA 9.2379]

MCLA 257.679a Limited access highway; pedestrians and certain vehicles prohibited. [MSA 9.2379(1)]

MCLA 257.680 Crossing fire hose. [MSA 9.2380]

MCLA 257.682 School buses. Painting, signs. Flashing lights, overtaking or oncoming vehicles; bus passengers, crossing road; traffic controlled intersections (local ordinance enforcement). **Visibility of bus in stopped position. Divided highway, vehicle on opposite section from school bus. Flashing lights, color, location, intensity, use in incorporated cities and villages. Front end mirror for driver's view of road from front bumper forward. Presumption, registered owner as driver; sufficiency of evidence.** [MSA 9.2382]

MCLA 257.682a - 257.693 [MSA 9.2382(1) - 9.2393]

Note: The above sections deal with safety equipment (lights, reflectors, flags, etc.) on all types of vehicles.

MCLA 257.694 Parked vehicles, lighting (local ordinance control). [MSA 9.2394]

MCLA 257.695 - 257.697b [MSA 9.2395 - 9.2397(2)]

Note: These sections provide additional control regarding lights.

MCLA 257.698 Permissible additional lights; flashing, oscillating or rotating lights. [MSA 9.2398]

Sec. 698. (a, b, c, d) ... Flashing, oscillating or rotating red lights may be used only as follows:

468

1. By authorized emergency vehicles as provided by section 603 of this chapter. State, county or municipal vehicles engaged in snow removal or ice control operations shall be equipped with flashing, oscillating or rotating amber lights placed in such position on the vehicle as to be visible throughout an arc of 360 degrees.

2. By public utility service vehicles, ambulances, authorized emergency vehicles, automobile service cars and wreckers engaged in removing or assisting vehicles at the site of traffic accidents and state, municipal and county vehicles actually engaged in the maintenance or repair of the highway. ...

MCLA 257.698a - 257.705a [MSA 9.2398(1) - 9.2405(1)]

Note: The above sections provide additional vehicle specifications (lights, brakes).

MCLA 257.706 Horns and other warning devices (any authorized emergency vehicle). [MSA 9.2406]

MCLA 257.707 - 257.715 [MSA 9.2407 - 9.2415]

Note: The above sections provide additional vehicle specifications (safety devices, inspection, etc.). Sec. 714: Explosive transportation controls.

MCLA 257.716 Size, weight and load restrictions (fire apparatus, other exceptions). [MSA 9.2416]

MCLA 257.717 Maximum width of vehicles; exceptions; operation of certain buses (local ordinance jurisdiction). [MSA 9.2417]

MCLA 257.718 - 257.719 [MSA 9.2418 - 9.2419]

Note: Above sections deal with size and load limitations on all types of vehicles.

MCLA 257.719a Mobile homes; length, width, height; permits, over-length and over-width; exclusion from highways, periods; lights, signs, escorts, axles, tires; definition. [MSA 9.2419(1)]

Note: Provides for permits by local authorities. Defines "mobile home" as: *... a prebuilt housing module or a home which* is designed to be transported by any motor vehicle upon a public highway and designed, equipped and used for sleeping, eating and living quarters, or is intended to be so used.

MCLA 257.720 - 257.726 [MSA 9.2420 - 9.2426]

Note: Above sections deal with size, weight, other limitations and controls, including local authority over springtime restrictions and non-conforming vehicles.

MCLA 257.726a Peace officers' authority to enforce act on boundary streets and highways. [MSA 9.2426(1)]

MCLA 257.727 - 257.732 [MSA 9.2427 - 9.2432]

Note: The above citations deal with traffic offense arrest procedures, with audit of citations provided for in Sec. 728c.

CHAPTER VII. REGISTRATION FEES

MCLA 257.801 Motor vehicle registration fees. Motor vehicles not excepted. Trailer coaches; habitations not exempt from real property taxes. Road tractor, truck or truck tractor for farms. Hearses and ambulances. State and municipally-owned vehicles; municipal franchise operation. School buses. Vehicle owned by charitable corporation, Red Cross, girl scouts, boy scouts. Trucks. Trailers or semi-trailers for farms. Farm wagons. Road tractors, truck tractors. Poletrailers, semitrailers, or trailers. Commercial passenger vehicles. Motor cycles and motor driven cycles. Trucks, road or truck tractors transporting household furniture and effects or carnival equipment. Pick-up trucks. Computation of tax; sale weight receipt for trucks, trailers, tractors, buses, certificate of no structural change. Ad valorem taxes on manufacturer's vehicles in stock or bond; exemption of dealers. Minimum specific tax. [MSA 9.2501]

MCLA 257.801a - 257.815 [MSA 9.2501(1) - 9.2515]

Note: The above sections make additional provisions for licensing and fees for operators of various types of vehicles, including use and sales taxes.

CHAPTER VIII. PENALTIES

MCLA 257.901 - 257.904a [MSA 9.2601 - 9.2604(1)]

MCLA 257.904b Impounding of motor vehicles; time; impoundment order, execution; expenses, insurance, removal, storage; disposal upon abandonment, third persons' rights. [MSA 9.2604(2)]

MCLA 257.905 Financial responsibility ... [MSA 9.2605]

CHAPTER IX. MISCELLANEOUS

MCLA 257.921 - 257.923 [MSA 9.2621 - 9.2623]

JOINT ACTION
Act No. 219, P.A. 1952 - Municipal Parking Facilities

AN ACT to authorize townships to acquire and operate automobile parking facilities for the use of the public; to provide the manner of acquiring and financing the same; and to authorize the leasing of space therein for other uses.

MCLA 141.171 Automobile parking facilities; (taxation of) **leasing space, limitation.** [MSA 5.280(1)]

MCLA 141.172 Same; townships may acquire, etc.; referendum (income). [MSA 5.280(2)]

MCLA 141.173 Scope of act. [MSA 5.280(3)]

HOUSING AND HOUSING AUTHORITIES

Such expressions as Planned Unit Development (PUD), Housing and Urban Development (HUD) and Rural and Urban Development were practically unknown less than three decades ago. However, increased demands created by population growth, deterioration of buildings and in some cases a whole new way of life, have made it increasingly evident that Michigan townships cannot avoid involvement in the great effort to provide decent standards of housing to every citizen regardless of race, color, creed, nationality or economic level. According to information released in 1972 by the United States Department of Labor, it is anticipated that 30,000 housing units, either new ones or old ones repaired and maintained in good condition, will be needed annually in Michigan in the next twenty-eight years.

Federal and state laws have provided for the establishment of all kinds of housing and building authorities to meet these needs, but they also provide rather stringent controls in order to assure nondiscrimination and availability. Therefore, it behooves a township board to give careful study to both housing requirements and alternate methods which may be selected to meet the challenge in this area of their responsibility. Care must be taken to avoid either overbuilding or underbuilding and to make sure that there are satisfactory supportive facilities such as sewers and drains, water supply, shopping areas, schools, recreation facilities and a myriad of other considerations involved in proper land use. A township board may also want to take advantage of the statute which provides for the establishment, by itself or jointly with another subdivision, of a fair housing commission.

Every township must develop a well thought out master plan supported by careful analysis and study if we are to avoid the mistakes made in the years immediately following World War II. Development of such a master plan (discussed in detail in the chapter on Planning and Zoning), will enable the township board to select the proper procedure to provide adequate housing at all levels.

JOINT ACTION
Act No. 183, P.A. 1964 - State Building Authority

AN ACT creating the state building authority with power to acquire, furnish, equip, own, improve, enlarge, operate and maintain buildings, necessary parking structures and facilities, and sites therefor, for the use of the state or any of its agencies; to authorize the execution of leases pertaining to such properties and facilities by said building authority with the state of Michigan or any of its agencies; to provide for the issuance of revenue bonds by such building authority; to authorize the conveyance of lands by the state or any of its agencies for the purposes herein authorized; and to provide for other matters in relation thereto.

MCLA 830.411 State building authority; definitions.
[MSA 3.447(101)]

MCLA 830.412 Same; creation; board of trustees, general grant of powers; appointment, term, vacancies; oath; officers; quorum.
[MSA 3.447(102)]

MCLA 830.413 Same; specific powers; records; audit.
[MSA 3.447(103)]

MCLA 830.414 Same; acquisition of property, condemnation.
[MSA 3.447(104)]

MCLA 830.415 Same; conveyance by state. [MSA 3.447(105)]

MCLA 830.416 Same; lease of facilities to state, approval.
[MSA 3.447(106)]

MCLA 830.417 Same; authority to state to execute lease, approval.
[MSA 3.447(107)]

MCLA 830.418 Same; revenue bonds, terms, exemption from taxation; approval; sale. [MSA 3.447(108)]

MCLA 830.419 Same; lien of bonds. [MSA 3.447(109)]

MCLA 830.420 Compliance with constitution. [MSA 3.447(110)]

MCLA 830.421 Buildings exempt from taxation or assessments, income. [MSA 3.447(111)]

MCLA 830.422 Bonds, investments for banks, trust companies, insurers, fiduciaries. [MSA 3.447(112)]

MCLA 830.423 Construction of act; governmental function.
[MSA 3.447(113)]

MCLA 830.424 Additional or alternative method. [MSA 3.447(114)]

JOINT ACTION
Act No. 293, P.A. 1937 - Housing Cooperation Law

AN ACT to authorize cities, incorporated villages, metropolitan districts, counties, and other public bodies to aid housing projects of housing authorities, housing commissions and the federal government by furnishing parks, playgrounds, streets, and other improvements and facilities, by exercising certain other powers and by making agreements relating to such aid; to authorize cities, incorporated villages, metropolitan districts, counties and other political subdivisions to contract with respect to the sums to be paid them for improvements, services and facilities to be provided for the benefit of housing projects and the occupants thereof, to make agreements respecting the exercise of the powers of such public bodies relating to the remedying or elimination of unfit dwellings, and to make other agreements with respect to housing projects; to prescribe the form and nature of agreements by a city, incorporated village or county with respect to a housing project of the housing commission created for such city, incorporated village or county; to require cities, incorporated villages, metropolitan districts, and counties to make an appropriation for the first year's administrative expenses of housing commissions or housing authorities; to authorize certain cities, incorporated villages, metropolitan districts and counties to pay moneys to housing commissions or housing authorities; to regulate the selection and payment of the personnel of housing commissions; and to declare an emergency requiring that this act take effect immediately.

MCLA 125.601 Short title. [MSA 5.3057(1)]

MCLA 125.602 Declaration of necessity. [MSA 5.3057(2)]

MCLA 125.603 Definitions. [MSA 5.3057(3)]

MCLA 125.604 Cooperation in undertaking housing projects; powers. [MSA 5.3057(4)]

474

MCLA 125.605 Contract powers for payment for services. [MSA 5.3057(5)]

MCLA 125.606 Advances to housing authority. [MSA 5.3057(6)]

MCLA 125.607 Procedure for exercising powers. [MSA 5.3057(7)]

MCLA 125.608 Supplemental nature of act. [MSA 5.3057(8)]

MCLA 125.610 Emergency clause. [MSA 5.3057(10)]

JOINT ACTION
Act No. 18, P.A. 1933, Ex. Sess. - Municipal Housing Facilities

AN ACT to authorize any city, village, township or county to purchase, acquire, construct, maintain, operate, improve, extend and repair housing facilities; to eliminate housing conditions which are detrimental to the public peace, health, safety, morals or welfare; and for any such purposes to authorize any such city, village, township or county to create a commission with power to effectuate said purposes, and to prescribe the powers and duties of such commission and of such city, village, township or county; and for any such purposes to authorize any such city, village, township or county to issue notes and revenue bonds; to regulate the issuance, sale, retirement and refunding of such notes and bonds; to regulate the rentals of such projects and the use of the revenues of the projects; to prescribe the manner of selecting tenants for such projects; to provide for the condemnation of private property for such projects; to confer certain powers upon such cities, villages, townships and counties in relation to such projects, including the power to receive aid and cooperation of the federal government; to provide for a referendum thereon; to create a board of tenant affairs in any city of 1,000,000 or over having a housing commission and operating 1 or more housing projects; to define the powers and duties of such board; to provide for the right of appeal from its determinations; to provide for cooperative financing by 2 or more cities, villages, townships or counties or any combination thereof; to provide for the issuance, sale and retirement of revenue bonds and special obligation notes for such purposes; to provide for financing agreements between cooperating borrowers; to provide for other matters relative to the bonds and notes and methods of cooperative financing; and for other purposes.

MCLA 125.651 Definitions. [MSA 5.3011]

MCLA 125.652 Cities, villages, townships, counties; housing facilities and conditions, powers. [MSA 5.3012]

MCLA 125.653 Municipal housing commission. Creation, referendum. Rejection, effect. Township commission, powers, duties, liabilities. County commission, powers, duties, liabilities. [MSA 5.3013]

MCLA 125.654 Same; membership, appointment, term, compensation, vacancies. [MSA 5.3014]

MCLA 125.655 Same; meetings, rules, record, quorum, officers, employes. [MSA 5.3015]

MCLA 125.656 Same; funds for operation. [MSA 5.3016]

MCLA 125.657 Same; powers and duties. [MSA 5.3017]

MCLA 125.658 Same; interest of members, officers, employes in contracts. [MSA 5.3018]

MCLA 125.659 Same; report to governing body. [MSA 5.3019]

MCLA 125.660 Same; eminent domain, procedure, public purposes, counties. [MSA 5.3020]

MCLA 125.661 Same; deeds, contracts, leases, purchases. [MSA 5.3021]

MCLA 125.662 Same; control of projects. [MSA 5.3022]

MCLA 125.663 Claims against project; damages. [MSA 5.3023]

MCLA 125.664 Same; contractual. [MSA 5.3024]

MCLA 125.665 Preliminary estimate of cost. [MSA 5.3025]

MCLA 125.666 Enabling ordinances. [MSA 5.3026]

MCLA 125.667 Revenue bonds, terms, tax exemption, negotiability. [MSA 5.3027]

MCLA 125.668 Bondholders' lien, creation, priority; additional security, annual contributions contract. [MSA 5.3028]

MCLA 125.669 Extent and enforcement of lien. [MSA 5.3029]

MCLA 125.670 Receivers, appointment, powers. [MSA 5.3030]

MCLA 125.671 Bonds; inapplicability of other laws. [MSA 5.3031]

MCLA 125.672 Same; depository; segregation of funds. [MSA 5.3032]

MCLA 125.674 Same; signatures. [MSA 5.3034]

MCLA 125.675 Free services (prohibited). [MSA 5.3035]

MCLA 125.676 Additional bonds. [MSA 5.3036]

MCLA 125.677 Rent schedule; policy of the state, basis. [MSA 5.3037]

MCLA 125.681 Income from other sources than operation, use. [MSA 5.3041]

MCLA 125.683 Operating year. [MSA 5.3043]

MCLA 125.684 Rents; supervision; state department of health. [MSA 5.3044]

MCLA 125.685 Records, accounts, inspection. [MSA 5.3045]

MCLA 125.687 Construction of act. [MSA 5.3047]

MCLA 125.689 Authority conferred. [MSA 5.3049]

MCLA 125.690 Declaration of necessity, liberal construction. [MSA 5.3050]

MCLA 125.692 Slum clearance and housing projects as public purposes. [MSA 5.3052]

MCLA 125.693 Immediate necessity. [MSA 5.3053]

MCLA 125.694 Duties of operation and management; rentals and selection of tenants. Receivers; freedom from restrictions. [MSA 5.3054]

MCLA 125.694a Tenancy or contract right to occupy housing; termination; just cause. [MSA 5.3054(1)]

MCLA 125.694b Housing commission; rules, adoption, promulgation, publication. [MSA 5.3054(2)]

MCLA 125.695 Contract provisions relative to minimum wages and maximum hours. [MSA 5.3055]

MCLA 125.696 Additional powers; intent of act. [MSA 5.3056]

MCLA 125.697 Promissory notes; authorization, interest rate; obligation of commission. [MSA 5.3056(1)]

MCLA 125.698 Bonds; powers of borrower. [MSA 5.3056(2)]

MCLA 125.699 Board of tenant affairs; creation. [MSA 5.3056(3)]

Sec. 49. There is created a board of tenant affairs for each city, village or township having a housing commission and operating 1 or more housing projects as provided by this act.

MCLA 125.700 Board of tenant affairs; members; size; composition; terms; qualifications; nomination. [MSA 5.3056(4)]

MCLA 125.701 Board of tenant affairs; members, meeting, rules of procedure, record, quorum, staff. [MSA 5.3056(5)]

MCLA 125.702 Board of tenant affairs; powers and duties. [MSA 5.3056(6)]

MCLA 125.703 Hearing and review; notice; petition; waiver; right to be represented by counsel. [MSA 5.3056(7)]

MCLA 125.704 Hearing and review; termination of right to use and occupation; action to regain possession of premises. [MSA 5.3056(8)]

MCLA 125.705 Application of act. [MSA 5.3056(9)]

MCLA 125.706 Federal grants or assistance, cooperation between borrowers. [MSA 5.3056(10)]

MCLA 125.707 Cooperating financing arrangements, procedure; agent borrowers; financing agreements, preparation. [MSA 5.3056(11)]

MCLA 125.708 Financing agreements, preparation, execution, contents; notes and revenue bonds, issuance, sale, proceeds, payment. [MSA 5.3056(12)]

MCLA 125.709 Borrowing money and issuance of notes or revenue bonds; form of bonds. [MSA 5.3056(13)]

MCLA 125.709a Fiscal agents and their successors and alternate paying agents, appointment; removal and duties of fiscal agent; authorizing ordinance as contract. [MSA 5.3056(13A)]

MCLA 125.709b Disposition of bond proceeds. [MSA 5.3056(13B)]

MCLA 125.709c Revenues from cooperatively financed projects, disposition. [MSA 5.3056(13C)]

MCLA 125.709d Additional bonds of equal standing, issuance. [MSA 5.3056(13D)]

MCLA 125.709e Notice of sale of bonds; ratification of sale by cooperating borrowers. [MSA 5.3056(13E)]

Act No. 268, P.A. 1941 - Defense Housing Facilities

AN ACT to authorize cities and incorporated villages to undertake the development or administration of projects to assure the availability of safe and sanitary dwellings for persons engaged in national defense activities who would not otherwise be able to secure such dwellings within the vicinity thereof; to authorize cities and incorporated villages to cooperate with or act as agents of the federal government in the development and administration of such projects of the federal government, to acquire or lease such projects and to sell certain projects to the federal government; to authorize public bodies to assist such projects of cities and incorporated villages and of the federal government; to confer certain powers on housing commissions and to authorize cities and incorporated villages to confer certain powers on such commissions; and to declare valid all bonds, notes and obligations of cities and incorporated villages issued for projects heretofore undertaken to assure the availability of safe and sanitary dwellings for persons engaged in national defense activities.

MCLA 125.711 Housing shortage; legislative finding. [MSA 5.3059(1)]

MCLA 125.712 Housing projects; powers of cities and villages and housing commission; unlawful to initiate after termination of present war. [MSA 5.3059(2)]

MCLA 125.713 Same; co-operation with federal projects; sale to United States. [MSA 5.3059(3)]

MCLA 125.714 State public bodies; authority to co-operate in housing projects. [MSA 5.3059(4)]

MCLA 125.715 Validation of bonds, notes, etc., heretofore issued. [MSA 5.3059(5)]

MCLA 125.716 Restrictions imposed by other acts inapplicable. [MSA 5.3059(6)]

MCLA 125.717 Definitions. [MSA 5.3059(7)]

MCLA 125.718 Act supplemental and not restrictive of other powers. [MSA 5.3059(8)]

JOINT ACTION
Act No. 162, P.A. 1953 - Acquisition and Maintenance of Housing Projects

AN ACT to authorize cities and incorporated villages or townships to acquire, own, operate, maintain and dispose of housing projects of the United States government or any agency thereof, and in so doing to comply with all conditions imposed pursuant to the applicable laws of the United States; and to authorize payments in lieu of taxes.

MCLA 125.731 Housing projects; acquisition and maintenance by municipality; operating agent; public functions; inapplicable act; time limits. [MSA 5.4091]

MCLA 125.732 Same; payments in lieu of taxes, rate. [MSA 5.4092]

JOINT ACTION
Act No. 14, P.A. 1946, 1st Ex. Sess. - Servicemen Housing Projects

AN ACT to authorize counties, cities, incorporated villages and townships of this state to undertake the development and administration of housing projects to assure the availability of safe and sanitary dwellings for servicemen and veterans, and their families.

MCLA 125.871 Municipal housing projects for servicemen authorized. [MSA 4.1484(1)]

MCLA 125.872 Authority exercised by resolution. [MSA 4.1484(2)]

AFFECTS JOINT ACTION
Act No. 323, P.A. 1966 - Urban Renewal, Housing for Displaced Persons

AN ACT relative to housing for persons displaced by urban renewal.

MCLA 125.961   Assurance of relocation of occupants under urban renewal by condemning unit of government. [MSA 5.3535(1)]

MCLA 125.962   Renewal of substandard residential area with new housing; assurance of available land or housing for rental or purchase. [MSA 5.3535(2)]

MCLA 125.963   Neighborhood advisory council; consultations with local government agency; records. [MSA 5.3535(3)]

JOINT ACTION
Act No. 346, P.A. 1966 - State Housing Development Authority

AN ACT to create a state housing development authority; to define the powers and duties of the authority; to establish a housing development revolving fund; to establish a land acquisition and development fund; to authorize loans and grants to qualified sponsors, individuals and municipalities; to provide tax exemption; and to authorize payments in lieu of taxes by nonprofit housing corporations, consumer housing cooperatives and limited dividend housing corporations.

PURPOSE AND POLICY

MCLA 125.1401   Legislative declaration. [MSA 16.114(1)]

CHAPTER 1.   DEFINITIONS AND GENERAL PROVISIONS

MCLA 125.1411   Definitions. [MSA 16.114(11)]

MCLA 125.1415a   Housing project; tax exemption; service charge for public services. [MSA 16.114(15A)]

Sec. 15a. ... (8) The state shall not reimburse any unit of government for tax exemption granted to any housing project under this section.

MCLA 125.1417 Advisory, consultative, technical, training, and educational services. [MSA 16.114(17)]

CHAPTER 2. STATE HOUSING DEVELOPMENT AUTHORITY

MCLA 125.1421 State housing development authority; creation; membership; appointment and tenure; meetings; chairman and vice-chairman. [MSA 16.114(21)]

MCLA 125.1422 Powers of authority. [MSA 16.114(22)]

Sec. 22. (a, b, c, d, e, f, g, h, i, j, k) (l) ... Nothing in this act shall be deemed to impede the operation and effect of local zoning, building and housing ordinances or ordinances relating to subdivision control, land development, fire prevention or other ordinances having to do with housing or the development thereof. (m, n, o, p, q, r, s, t) ...

MCLA 125.1423 Housing development fund; creation; payments into fund. [MSA 16.114(23)]

MCLA 125.1424 Use of moneys held in fund; advances. [MSA 16.114(24)]

MCLA 125.1424a Land acquisition and development fund, creation, contents. [MSA 16.114(24A)]

MCLA 125.1424b Use of fund; land acquired, disposition. [MSA 16.114(24B)]

MCLA 125.1425 Notes and bonds; issuance; status; approval. [MSA 16.114(25)]

MCLA 125.1426 Same; authorization; terms. [MSA 16.114(26)]

MCLA 125.1427 Same; resolution authorizing issuance, contents. [MSA 16.114(27)]

MCLA 125.1428 Same; validity and effect of pledge.
MSA 16.114(28)

MCLA 125.1429 Same; personal liability of members of authority.
MSA 16.114(29)

MCLA 125.1430 Same; purchase for cancellation. MSA 16.114(30)

MCLA 125.1431 Same; liability of state. MSA 16.114(31)

MCLA 125.1432 Capital Reserve fund; bonds; federal programs. Fund, establishment, source, use, transfers. Issuance of bonds, amount in fund. Outstanding bonds and notes, limitation. Principal and interest accumulations in fund. Amount of fund, computation. Interest rate, changes. Federal housing subsidy programs. Recipients of low income multifamily dwelling units, priority. Rules. MSA 16.114(32)

MCLA 125.1433 General reserve fund. MSA 16.114(33)

MCLA 125.1434 Notes and bonds; pledge and agreement of state.
MSA 16.114(34)

MCLA 125.1435 Default; trustee. MSA 116.114(35)

MCLA 125.1436 Trustee; additional powers. MSA 16.114(36)

MCLA 125.1437 Venue. MSA 16.114(37)

MCLA 125.1438 Notice before declaration that notes or bonds are due and payable. MSA 16.114(38)

MCLA 125.1439 Moneys of authority; deposit; agreement with noteholders and bondholders; system of accounts; expenditures for operating purposes. MSA 16.114(39)

MCLA 125.1440 Notes and bonds as legal investments.
MSA 16.114(40)

MCLA 125.1441 Faith and credit bonds. MSA 16.114(41)

MCLA 125.1442 Property of authority; exemption from taxation.
[MSA 16.114(42)]

MCLA 125.1443 Notes and bonds; exemption from taxation.
[MSA 16.114(43)]

MCLA 125.1444 Loans, authorization, purpose, restrictions; sales of housing units, mortgage changes, employment of labor, purchasers as laborers; term of loan; interest. [MSA 16.114(44)]

MCLA 125.1445 Preference to the elderly and displaced persons.
[MSA 16.114(45)]

MCLA 125.1446 Equality of occupancy and employment.
[MSA 16.114(46)]

CHAPTER 3. LOW AND MODERATE INCOME HOUSING ·

MCLA 125.1451 Low and moderate income housing; definitions.
[MSA 16.114(51)]

MCLA 125.1452 Same; dwelling units to certain low income persons and families. [MSA 16.114(52)]

MCLA 125.1453 Same; criteria and procedures for determination of eligibility of occupants and rental charges. [MSA 16.114(53)]

MCLA 125.1454 Same; agreements for services of selection of eligible families and individuals. [MSA 16.114(54)]

MCLA 125.1455 Same; rights of persons or families benefited.
[MSA 16.114(55)]

MCLA 125.1456 Same; financing for small scale housing developments. [MSA 16.114(56)]

MCLA 125.1457 Appropriation. [MSA 16.114(57)]

CHAPTER 4. QUALIFIED NONPROFIT HOUSING PROGRAM

MCLA 125.1461 Incorporation. [MSA 16.114(61)]

MCLA 125.1462 Name. [MSA 16.114(62)]

MCLA 125.1463 Articles of incorporation, provisions.
[MSA 16.114(63)]

MCLA 125.1464 Power of authority to appoint majority of directors
on board. [MSA 16.114(64)]

MCLA 125.1465 Articles of incorporation; filing with approval of
authority. [MSA 16.114(65)]

CHAPTER 5. CONSUMER HOUSING COOPERATIVES

MCLA 125.1471 Incorporation. [MSA 16.114(71)]

MCLA 125.1472 Name. [MSA 16.114(72)]

MCLA 125.1473 Articles of incorporation; provisions.
[MSA 16.114(73)]

MCLA 125.1474 Power of authority to appoint majority of directors
on board. [MSA 16.114(74)]

MCLA 125.1475 Articles of incorporation; filing with approval of
authority. [MSA 16.114(75)]

CHAPTER 6. LIMITED DIVIDEND HOUSING CORPORATIONS

MCLA 125.1481 Incorporation or qualification. [MSA 16.114(81)]

MCLA 125.1482 Corporate name. [MSA 16.114(82)]

MCLA 125.1483 Purpose; repayment of stockholders' investments;
supervision by authority. [MSA 16.114(83)]

MCLA 125.1484 Surplus. [MSA 16.114(84)]

MCLA 125.1485 Directors, power of authority to appoint a majority.
[MSA 16.114(85)]

MCLA 125.1486 Authority's consent to or approval of articles of
incorporation. [MSA 16.114(86)]

486

JOINT ACTION
Act No. 112, P.A. 1968 - Fair Housing

AN ACT to prevent discrimination in real property transactions on the basis of race, color, religion or national origin; to prescribe the functions of the civil rights commission; to authorize the creation and prescribe the functions of local commissions; and to provide remedies for violations of the act.

CHAPTER 1. GENERAL PROVISIONS

CHAPTER 2. UNFAIR HOUSING PRACTICES

MCLA 564.201 Unfair housing practice; owner, real estate broker or salesman, or any other person as defined in act. [MSA 26.1300(201)]

MCLA 564.202 Unfair housing practice; financial assistance. [MSA 26.1300(202)]

MCLA 564.203 Unfair housing practice; promoting real estate transaction by representations, advertisements or contracts. [MSA 26.1300(203)]

MCLA 564.204 Unfair housing practice; retaliation, coercion, interference and obstruction. [MSA 26.1300(204)]

MCLA 564.205 Unfair housing practice; personal information. [MSA 26.1300(205)]

CHAPTER 3. EXCLUSIONS

MCLA 564.301 Two families or less, lessor or family member as a resident, no public listing or advertising for sale or rental; room rentals; temporary vacation by owner or lessor. [MSA 26.1300(301)]

CHAPTER 4. ENFORCEMENT BY CIVIL RIGHTS COMMISSION

MCLA 564.401 Complaint; contents; determination of good faith; time of filing; amendments; copy to respondents; investigation by commission. [MSA 26.1300(401)]

MCLA 564.401a Removal of proceedings to circuit court; time to file petition; order of removal; jurisdiction; determination; costs. [MSA 26.1300(401A)]

MCLA 564.402 Investigation of complaint; order requiring production of books, papers, etc. [MSA 26.1300(402)]

MCLA 564.403 Investigation of complaint; dismissal; application for reconsideration. [MSA 26.1300(403)]

MCLA 564.404 Investigation of complaint; conciliation agreement, contents. [MSA 26.1300(404)]

MCLA 564.405 Temporary relief or restraining order; motion to hear case on its merits; notice of pendency. [MSA 26.1300(405)]

MCLA 564.406 Service of formal charge; notice of hearing; filing of answer; amendments. [MSA 26.1300(406)]

MCLA 564.407 Hearings; disqualified commissioner or staff member; representation; evidence; examination of witnesses. [MSA 26.1300(407)]

MCLA 564.408 Hearing; subpoena; witness and mileage fees; failure to comply with subpoena. [MSA 26.1300(408)]

MCLA 564.409 Hearing; burden of proof; testimony, record, further evidence or argument. [MSA 26.1300(409)]

MCLA 564.410 Hearing; dismissal; cease and desist. [MSA 26.1300(410)]

MCLA 564.411 Remedies. [MSA 26.1300(411)]

MCLA 564.412 Fines; nature of fines; multiple discrimination. [MSA 26.1300(412)]

MCLA 564.413 Motion for reconsideration. [MSA 26.1300(413)]

MCLA 564.414 Certification of violation to licensing agency; finality of certification. [MSA 26.1300(414)]

MCLA 564.415 Appeal; procedure, time. [MSA 26.1300(415)]

MCLA 564.416 Actual costs and attorney fees on dismissal of complaint. [MSA 26.1300(416)]

MCLA 564.417 Perjury. [MSA 26.1300(417)]

MCLA 564.418 Constitutional and statutory guarantees. [MSA 26.1300(418)]

CHAPTER 5. ENFORCEMENT BY DEPARTMENT OF LICENSING AND REGULATION

MCLA 564.501 Licensing; suspension or revocation.
[MSA 26.1300(501)]

CHAPTER 6. LOCAL COMMISSIONS

MCLA 564.601 Local ordinances. [MSA 26.1300(601)]

Sec. 601. A political subdivision may adopt and enforce an ordinance prohibiting discrimination in real estate transactions because of race, color, religion or national origin which is not in conflict with the provisions of this act.

MCLA 564.602 Local commission; joint actions of 2 or more political subdivisions; expenses. [MSA 26.1300(602)]

Sec. 602. A political subdivision, or 2 or more political subdivisions acting jointly, may create a local commission to promote the purposes of this act and to secure for all individuals within the jurisdiction of the political subdivision or subdivisions freedom from discrimination in real estate transactions because of race, color, religion or national origin, and may appropriate funds for the expenses of the local commission.

MCLA 564.603 Local commission; powers, limitations; records; orders. [MSA 26.1300(603)]

MCLA 564.604 Transfer of jurisdiction; state commission.
[MSA 26.1300(604)]

MCLA 564.605 Transfer of jurisdiction; local commission.
[MSA 26.1300(605)]

MCLA 564.606 Power of political subdivision; criminal sanctions in ordinances. [MSA 26.1300(606)]

Sec. 606. This chapter shall not be construed to imply the absence of power in a political subdivision to provide criminal sanctions in an ordinance passed pursuant to the police power or other power inherent in the political subdivision.

MCLA 564.701 **Injunction; remedies; rescission or revocation of instrument transferring real property.** [MSA 26.1300(701)]

MCLA 564.702 **Complaints previously filed in court; defense.** [MSA 26.1300(702)]

MCLA 564.703 **Trial by jury.** [MSA 26.1300(703)]

MCLA 564.704 **Right to legal or equitable remedies in the courts.** [MSA 26.1300(704)]

TOWNSHIP BUILDINGS

In addition to the statutes quoted at the beginning of this chapter which provide for the erection of township buildings without the necessity of levying any local tax, following are six additional statutes which provide alternate means for erecting township halls, fire stations, police stations and other public utility buildings.

Certain limitations are established regarding bonding capability and other means of financing township buildings. Provision is also made for townships to participate with other units of government, including a school district, to construct, operate and maintain public buildings.

The section on Township Property - Purchase, Rental, Use should also be studied along with these citations, particularly with regard to Act 31 of 1948.

Act No. 50, P.A. 1921 - Memorials, Township Lands

AN ACT to authorize and empower townships to own and acquire land by gift or purchase for the erection of memorials to soldiers and sailors; to authorize the erection of such memorials; to provide for the assessment, levy and collection of taxes therefor, for the custody, control and management of such memorials and providing for a referendum by the electors thereof.

MCLA   35.861   Lands, acquisition by township for soldiers' memorial; use.   [MSA   4.1371]

Sec. 1.   It shall be lawful for, and the several townships in the state of Michigan are hereby authorized and empowered to own and acquire by gift or purchase, land for the purpose of erecting thereon a suitable memorial to soldiers and sailors of any 1 or more of the wars in which the United States of America has been a participant, and to erect and own such memorial or receive the same, or money or property for the same, as a gift.   Said memorial may be of such a nature as to be used, maintained and enjoyed in whole or in part as a museum, library, auditorium or for any other public use or purpose, and such land may be used, enjoyed and improved, in whole or in part, as a park, or the memorial may take such shape or form or be of such a nature as the township board shall adopt.

MCLA   35.862   Same; tax levy.   [MSA   4.1372]

MCLA   35.863   Same; custody.   [MSA   4.1373]

MCLA   35.864   Referendum; petition; proceedings; ballot, form.   [MSA   4.1374]

JOINT ACTION
Act No. 130, P.A. 1889 - Monumental Buildings

AN ACT to provide for the joint erection of veterans' memorial or monumental buildings or structures by counties, townships, incorporated villages and cities; to provide for the maintenance of soldiers' monumental buildings erected jointly by municipalities and the grand army of the republic, and the care of property of the grand army of the republic deposited therein.

MCLA   35.851   Veterans' memorial; joint municipal aid.   [MSA   4.1361]

MCLA   35.852   Same; building committee; powers.   [MSA 4.1362]

MCLA   35.853   Same; raising funds.   [MSA 4.1363]

MCLA 35.854 Same; uses, post contributions to be maintenance fund. [MSA 4.1364]

AFFECTS JOINT ACTION
Act No. 381, P.A. 1927 - Town Hall and Other Buildings

AN ACT to authorize the issue of bonds to provide sites for and for the erection thereon of town halls, fire stations, libraries or other buildings required for the public use in whole or in part, for township purposes or for the purpose of acquiring a site with buildings thereon and furnishing a town hall, fire station, library or other building or buildings required for the public use of such inhabitants in whole or in part for township purposes or for additions to and improvements of such sites and the buildings thereon, whether now existing or hereafter acquired, in any township in this state, and for the raising by townships of money for the maintenance, upkeep or repairs of the township hall, fire station, library or other public buildings of the township, and for the repeal of Act No. 397 of the Public Acts of 1921.

MCLA 41.241 Town hall, fire station, library; borrowing power of township board. [MSA 5.2371]

Sec. 1. The township board of any organized township in this state, upon application being first filed with such township board, signed by at least 12 freeholders of such township, may borrow a sum of money, not exceeding 2-1/2% of the assessed valuation of such township according to the assessed valuation of all the real and personal property of said township for the preceding year, on the faith and credit of such township, and to issue the bonds of such township therefor, the moneys so borrowed to be used for the purpose of acquiring a site for and erecting and furnishing a town hall, fire station or library or for the purpose of making additions and improvements to such sites and town halls, fire stations or libraries whether now existing or hereafter acquired, or for the purpose of purchasing a building or site to be used for a town hall, fire station or library and furnishing and equipping the same.

MCLA 41.241a Acquisition of real estate, referendum.
[MSA 5.2371(1)]

MCLA 41.242 Referendum proceedings; ballot, form. [MSA 5.2372]

MCLA 41.243 Conduct of election. [MSA 5.2373]

MCLA 41.244 Bonds, issuance. [MSA 5.2374]

MCLA 41.245 Tax levy. [MSA 5.2375]

MCLA 41.246 Tax for maintenance, upkeep, or repairs. [MSA 5.2376]

MCLA 41.246a Libraries, sites, buildings, maintenance. [MSA 5.2376(1)]

MCLA 41.247 Repeal; saving clause. [MSA 5.2377]

JOINT ACTION
Act No. 31, P.A. 1948, 1st Ex. Sess. - Authorities for Joint Public Buildings

AN ACT to provide for the incorporation of authorities to acquire, furnish, equip, own, improve, enlarge, operate and maintain buildings, automobile parking lots or structures, recreational facilities, stadiums, and the necessary site or sites therefor, together with appurtenant properties and facilities necessary or convenient for the effective use thereof, for the use or benefit of any county or for the use or benefit of any county and any city or village therein, or for the use or benefit of any city, village or township or for the use of any school district and any city, village or township wholly or partially within the district's boundaries; or for the use of any intermediate school district and any constituent school district or any city, village or township, wholly or partially within the intermediate school district's boundaries; to provide for compensation of authority commissioners; to permit transfers of property to authorities; to authorize the execution of contracts, leases and subleases pertaining to authority property and the use thereof; to provide for the issuance of revenue bonds by such authorities; to validate action taken and bonds issued; and to provide other powers, rights and duties of authorities and incorporating units, including those for the disposal of authority property.

MCLA 123.951 County, city, village, or township authorities; incorporation, purposes. [MSA 5.301(1)]

MCLA 123.952 County and city, township, or village authorities; incorporation, purposes. [MSA 5.301(2)]

MCLA 123.952a Same; school district and municipalities; authorities, incorporation, acquisition, operation, maintenance; use. [MSA 5.301(2A)]

MCLA 123.952b Constituent school districts with intermediate school district; authority, purpose. [MSA 5.301(2B)]

MCLA 123.953 Incorporating unit defined. [MSA 5.301(3)]

MCLA 123.954 Incorporation of authority, procedure. [MSA 5.301(4)]

MCLA 123.955 County or municipal building authority; articles of incorporation, contents; legislative body members ineligible for authority commission. [MSA 5.301(5)]

MCLA 123.955a Board of commissioners. [MSA 5.301(5A)]

MCLA 123.955b Board of commissioners; compensation, per diem, mileage. [MSA 5.301(5B)]

MCLA 123.956 Articles of incorporation; execution, filing, time effective. [MSA 5.301(6)]

MCLA 123.957 Body corporate; powers. [MSA 5.301(7)]

MCLA 123.958 Contracts to acquire property; leases to incorporating units, terms, consideration; subleases, conditions, terms; stadiums. [MSA 5.301(8)]

MCLA 123.959 Acquisition of property, condemnation. Transfer of property. [MSA 5.301(9)]

MCLA 123.960 Amendment of articles. [MSA 5.301(10)]

MCLA 123.961 Revenue bonds; referendum. [MSA 5.301(11)]

MCLA 123.962 Tax exemption. [MSA 5.301(12)]

MCLA 123.963 Bonds retired; conveyance of property. [MSA 5.301(13)]

MCLA 123.964 Construction of act. [MSA 5.301(14)]

MCLA 123.965 Validation of actions heretofore taken. [MSA 5.301(15)]

JOINT ACTION
Act No. 150, P.A. 1923 - Joint Public Buildings

AN ACT to authorize and empower counties, cities, villages and townships or any combination of them, to singly or jointly acquire by gift, devise or public condemnation a site or sites and/or construct, erect, lease, sublease and maintain public buildings for the purpose of housing within the same building or buildings city, county, village or township offices, and/or for any other public uses and purposes, which may include a memorial hall for war veterans of the United States of America and for public assemblage.

MCLA 123.921 Public buildings, joint maintenance and acquisition. [MSA 5.2351]

MCLA 123.922 Same; contracts. [MSA 5.2352]

MCLA 123.923 Same; raising of moneys; joint ventures. [MSA 9.2353]

MCLA 123.924 Same; approval of contracts. [MSA 5.2354]

MCLA 123.925 Same; veterans' memorial hall; bonds, referendum, issuance. [MSA 5.2355]

Act No. 157, P.A. 1867 - Township Buildings

AN ACT to define and limit the amount of money which may be granted and voted by the qualified electors of townships, for the purpose of erecting town halls or other buildings for the public use of the inhabitants thereof.

MCLA 41.231 Township buildings, appropriation; meeting, notice, vote. [MSA 5.2361]

MCLA 41.232 Rescinding action; tax levy allocation. [MSA 5.2362]

Note: This act permits electors at a township meeting to vote a tax for erecting public buildings in the township, and then to later decide to use the money instead for township highway construction or redemption of township highway bonds.

It should be pointed out that no such tax can be levied unless there is room within the fifteen mill tax limitation, or the people have voted to increase the limitation at a general or special election, as set forth in the 1963 Michigan constitution. Also, although this particular act has never been repealed, precedent has been established by many more recent statutes vesting such authority in the electors only through the referendum process.

In view of these facts, the township attorney **must** be consulted if the township board contemplates use of the provisions of this statute.

AIRPORTS

The automobile plays a dominant role in mass transportation and communication in the nation. However, the airplane is becoming highly competitive, even though many still consider it somewhat inconvenient and beyond the economic reach of the general public. Since air travel is one of the fastest and most comfortable means of getting from one place to another, it has created the need for more and larger planes and consequently larger airports, thus bringing about problems of vital concern to townships.

No longer is it possible for an official to put a finger down on the map and say, "Here will be an airport." Airport planning calls for considerable study and research, as well as consultation and advice from experts. It generally requires a regional approach, with several units of government joining together. Even though there may be no real interest on the part of township residents in having an airport, they may very well be drawn into helping develop one. Cities do not have the necessary land -- townships do.

Therefore, township boards in more populous areas should thoroughly study and analyze the following group of statutes (as well as the Airport Zoning Act and the Tall Structures Act in the chapter on Planning and Zoning) so they can be prepared to deal with the situation if a city or county should decide it wants an airport. Some of the things that have to be considered are:

(a) The large amount of land required for present and future needs.

(b) Industrial and commercial facilities, often located near airports.

(c) Problems with regard to sanitary sewers and drains and other public service facilities.

(d) The need for adequate public transportation between the airport and surrounding communities. (Such travel now often takes more time than is spent in cross-country flight.)

(e) If it is to be a national or international airport, there are attendant noise and pollution problems.

(f) The larger airports in particular call for attainment of a reasonable degree of safety for both those who use the airport and those who live in adjacent areas.

Once the township board has determined need for further study, a representative citizen committee should be appointed to work with the planning commission or zoning board. The Michigan Aeronautics Commission and the Federal Aviation Administration in Washington should also be consulted.

JOINT ACTION
Act No. 327, P.A. 1945 - Aeronautics Code

AN ACT relating to aeronautics in this state; providing for the development and regulation thereof; creating a department of aeronautics consisting of a state aeronautics commission and a director of aeronautics; prescribing their respective powers and duties; providing for the licensing, supervision and control of all airports and landing fields, schools of aviation, flying clubs, aviation instructors and airport managers; providing for rules and regulations pertaining thereto; providing for the registration of aircraft; prescribing a privilege tax for the use of the aeronautical facilities on the lands and waters of this state; providing for the acquisition, development and operation of airports, landing fields and other aeronautical facilities by the state and the political subdivisions of this state; providing jurisdiction of crimes, torts and contracts; providing for civil liability of owners, operators and others; making hunting from aircraft unlawful; providing for repair station operators lien; providing for appeals from any rules, regulations or orders issued by the commission; providing for the transfer from the Michigan board of aeronautics to the department of aeronautics all properties and funds held by said board of aeronautics; providing for a state aeronautics fund and making an appropriation therefor; prescribing penalties; and making uniform the law with reference to state development and regulation of aeronautics.

CHAPTER I. DECLARATION OF INTENT

MCLA 259.1 Aeronautics code; declaration of intent. [MSA 10.101]

Sec. 1. It is hereby declared that the purpose of this act is to further the public interest and aeronautical progress by providing for the protection and promotion of safety in aeronautics; by cooperating in effecting a uniformity of the laws relating to the development and regulation of aeronautics in the several states; by revising existing statutes relative to the development and regulation of aeronautics so as to grant to a state agency such power and impose upon it such duties that the state may properly perform its functions relative to aeronautics and effectively exercise its jurisdiction over persons and property within such jurisdiction, may develop a statewide system of airports, may cooperate with and assist the political subdivisions of this state and others engaged in aeronautics, and may encourage and develop aeronautics; by establishing uniform regulations, consistent with federal regulations and those of other states, in order that those engaged in aeronautics of every character may so engage with the least possible restriction, consistent with the safety and the rights of others; and by providing for cooperation with the federal authorities and the authorities of this state to eliminate costly and unnecessary duplication of functions.

CHAPTER II. DEFINITIONS

MCLA 259.2 through 259.23 [MSA 10.102 THROUGH 10.123]

Note: These sections provide definitions of aeronautics; aeronautical facilities; aircraft; aircraft, civil; aircraft, public; airman; air navigation; airport; airport managers; airspace, navigable; airspace reservations; aviation instructor; aviation school; commission; department; director; flying club; fuel; hazards to air navigation; landing field; landing area; operation of aircraft or operate aircraft; person.

MCLA 259.24 Definition; political subdivision. [MSA 10.124]

Sec. 24. ... Any county, city, village or township of this state, and any other political subdivision, public corporation, authority, or district in this state which is or may be authorized by law to acquire, establish, construct, maintain, improve, and operate airports, landing fields and other aeronautical facilities.

MCLA 259.25 Same; rules and regulations. [MSA 10.125]

*CHAPTER III. AERONAUTICS DEPARTMENT --
CREATION -- MEMBERSHIP -- FUNDS*

MCLA 259.26 Aeronautics commission and department of aeronautics, membership, terms of commission. [MSA 10.126]

MCLA 259.27 Director of aeronautics. [MSA 10.127]

MCLA 259.28 Commissioners; qualifications. [MSA 10.128]

MCLA 259.29 Same; reimbursement for expenses. [MSA 10.129]

MCLA 259.30 Same; removal. [MSA 10.130]

MCLA 259.31 Organization, meetings and reports of commission. [MSA 10.131]

MCLA 259.32 Aeronautics commission; biennial reports to governor, contents. [MSA 10.132]

MCLA 259.33 Assistants and expenses. [MSA 10.133]

MCLA 259.34 Aeronautics fund. [MSA 10.134]

MCLA 259.35 Appropriation. MSA 10.135

MCLA 259.36 Properties, etc., transferred to department of aeronautics. MSA 10.136

CHAPTER IV. GENERAL POWERS AND DUTIES OF
AERONAUTICS COMMISSION AND DIRECTOR OF AERONAUTICS

MCLA 259.51 General supervisory powers; rules and regulations. Powers and duties of commission. Cooperation with federal and state governments, political subdivisions and others; joint hearings. General public interest, health, welfare and safety. State airways system; maps, charts, information, distribution. Enforcement of act and rules and regulations; injunction. Investigations. Same; restrictions on use of reports. Contracts. MSA 10.151

MCLA 259.52 Powers and duties of director. MSA 10.152

MCLA 259.53 Delegation of powers to director. MSA 10.153

MCLA 259.54 Cooperation with federal government; federal moneys; state agent; powers of commission. MSA 10.154

CHAPTER V. REGULATION OF AIRCRAFT, AIRMEN,
AIRPORTS AND AIR INSTRUCTION

MCLA 259.76 Registration of aircraft. MSA 10.176

MCLA 259.77 Same; application; fees. MSA 10.177

MCLA 259.78 Same; transfer. MSA 10.178

MCLA 259.79 Same; display of certificate. MSA 10.179

MCLA 259.80 Airworthiness certificate. MSA 10.180

MCLA 259.81 Inspection of aircraft. MSA 10.181

MCLA 259.82 Manufacturers and dealers; registration numbers for aircraft. MSA 10.182

MCLA 259.83 Airman, certificate of competency. MSA 10.183

MCLA 259.84 Exemptions; registration and certificate requirements. Aircraft and airmen; public aircraft. Aircraft and airmen; non-resident. Aircraft and airmen; military and foreign. Aircraft and airmen; interstate commerce. [MSA 10.184]

MCLA 259.85 Aviation schools and instructors. [MSA 10.185]

MCLA 259.86 Airports, landing fields, other aeronautical facilities; managers, licenses; certificate of approval, fee, necessity; temporary field permits. [MSA 10.186]

MCLA 259.87 Same; rejection of application for permission to operate. [MSA 10.187]

MCLA 259.88 Same; annual registration. [MSA 10.188]

MCLA 259.89 Exemptions, landing areas limited to personal use, proximity to public use facility. [MSA 10.189]

MCLA 259.90 Substandard noncommercial landing areas for emergency public use, approval, civil liability. [MSA 10.190]

CHAPTER VI. ACQUISITION AND OPERATION OF STATE AIRPORTS

MCLA 259.101 State airport and landing fields authorized. [MSA 10.201]

MCLA 259.102 Airport protection privileges. [MSA 10.202]

Sec. 102. ... Where necessary ... **This authority shall not be so construed as to limit the right, power, or authority of the state or any political subdivision to zone property adjacent to any airport or restricted landing area pursuant to laws of this state.**

MCLA 259.103 Joint operations. [MSA 10.203]

MCLA 259.104 Condemnation. [MSA 10.204]

MCLA 259.105 Aeronautics commission; leases and sales; capital city airport leases. [MSA 10.205]

MCLA 259.106 Charges and rentals. MSA 10.206

MCLA 259.107 Aeronautics commission; traffic code for state-owned facilities; enforcement, penalty. MSA 10.207

CHAPTER VII. ACQUISITION AND OPERATION OF AIRPORTS, LANDING FIELDS AND OTHER AERONAUTICAL FACILITIES BY POLITICAL SUBDIVISIONS OF THIS STATE

MCLA 259.126 Airports, etc., operation, etc., by political subdivisions; condemnation; approval by board of supervisors. MSA 10.226

MCLA 259.126a Airports of political subdivisions; location outside of state, reciprocity. MSA 10.226(1)

MCLA 259.127 Air space rights, acquisition. MSA 10.227

MCLA 259.128 Encroachments on airport protection privileges declared public nuisance, abatement. MSA 10.228

MCLA 259.129 Prior acquisitions validated. MSA 10.229

MCLA 259.130 Political subdivisions may appropriate funds. MSA 10.230

MCLA 259.131 Aeronautical facilities; general obligation bonds; revenue bonds, additional security. MSA 10.231

MCLA 259.131a Aeronautics commission; capital city airport revenue bonds. MSA 10.231(1)

MCLA 259.132 Declaration of public purpose and necessity. MSA 10.232

MCLA 259.133 Aeronautical facilities; specific powers of political subdivisions. Construction, enlargement, improvement, maintenance, equipment, operation and regulation; Wayne county. Airport manager, employment. Management, government, use of properties, rules, guards, penalties. Public safety, rules. Property; lease, donation, sale; concessions; bond security. Same; sale, donation or lease of property not required. Charges, rentals, fees; bond, security; liens for repairs, improvements, storage or care of personalty. Incidental powers. [MSA 10.233]

MCLA 259.134 Joint operation. [MSA 10.234]

MCLA 259.135 Federal aid to political subdivisions; commission as agent. [MSA 10.235]

MCLA 259.136 Board of commissioners may vote aid. [MSA 10.236]

CHAPTER VIII. APPROACH PROTECTION FOR AIRPORTS, LANDING FIELDS AND OTHER AERONAUTICAL FACILITIES

MCLA 259.151 State plan for approach protection areas. [MSA 10.251]

Note: Michigan aeronautics commission empowered to establish standards of height for structures or obstructions within safe distance of airport boundaries.

MCLA 259.152 Determination of hazard, notice to owner. [MSA 10.252]

MCLA 259.153 Execution of order to abate hazard; failure to comply. [MSA 10.253]

MCLA 259.154 Same; privately-owned. [MSA 10.254]

MCLA 259.155 Hazards surrounding state-owned airports, fields and facilities. [MSA 10.255]

MCLA 259.156 Encroachments upon approach protection areas declared public nuisance. [MSA 10.256]

*CHAPTER IX. PENAL PROVISIONS --
JURISDICTION OF CRIMES, TORTS, CONTRACTS*

MCLA 259.176 Misdemeanor; penalty. [MSA 10.276]

MCLA 259.177 Jurisdiction of crimes and torts. [MSA 10.277]

MCLA 259.178 Contracts made during flight. [MSA 10.278]

CHAPTER X. MISCELLANEOUS PROVISIONS

JOINT ACTION
Act No. 206, P.A. 1957 - Community Airports

AN ACT to authorize 2 or more counties, cities, townships and incorporated villages, or any combination thereof, to incorporate an airport authority for the planning, promoting, acquiring, constructing, improving, enlarging, extending, owning, maintaining and operating the landing,

*navigational and building facilities necessary thereto of
1 or more community airports; to provide for changes in the
membership therein; to authorize such counties, cities,
townships and incorporated villages to levy taxes for such
purpose; to provide for the operation and maintenance and
issuing notes therefor; and to authorize condemnation
proceedings.*

MCLA 259.621 Community airport authority; revenue bonds; location of site. [MSA 10.311]

MCLA 259.622 Same; body corporate, powers. [MSA 10.312]

MCLA 259.623 Procedure for creating authority; membership. Resolution, contents; charter authority; taxation. Admission to and release from membership, obligations. [MSA 10.313]

MCLA 259.624 Taxing power, limitation. [MSA 10.314]

MCLA 259.625 Airport board, purpose, membership, officers and employees, meetings, executive and advisory committees, compensation, expenses. [MSA 10.315]

MCLA 259.626 Same; meetings, quorum, records, accounting, bond, rules, regulations, policies. [MSA 10.316]

MCLA 259.627 Same; budget, payments by municipalities, financial report. [MSA 10.317]

MCLA 259.628 Same; revenue bonds; referendum. [MSA 10.318]

MCLA 259.629 Same; loans for current expenses. [MSA 10.319]

MCLA 259.630 Same; control of property; condemnation proceedings; taxation. [MSA 10.320]

MCLA 259.631 Community airport; definition. [MSA 10.321]

JOINT ACTION
Act No. 107, P.A. 1969 - Airport Development

506

AN ACT to authorize the department of commerce, through the aeronautics commission, to make loans to counties, cities, townships and incorporated villages, or any combination thereof, and to establish a revolving fund for the purpose of airport development; and to authorize the commission to prescribe rules for granting loans and repayment of loans.

MCLA 259.251 Airport loan program, creation, administration, purpose. [MSA 10.379(1)]

MCLA 259.252 Revolving loan account, appropriation, administration. [MSA 10.379(2)]

MCLA 259.253 Loans, promulgation of rules, limits, security, payment, interest. [MSA 10.379(3)]

MCLA 259.254 Report to legislature, time, contents. [MSA 10.379(4)]

MCLA 259.255 Construction of act. [MSA 10.379(5)]

JOINT ACTION
Act No. 90, P.A. 1913 - Parks, Zoological Gardens and Airports

AN ACT authorizing and empowering the boards of supervisors of counties to purchase, acquire by condemnation, accept gifts and devises of real estate for, and to improve and maintain public parks and zoological gardens, airports and landing fields, and to contribute to the improvement and maintenance of public parks and public zoological gardens, airports and landing fields, owned or held in trust by cities, villages or townships or used for the benefit of the public; to authorize the making of reasonable rules and regulations relative to the public use of park property; and to provide penalties for violations of such rules and regulations.

MCLA 123.61 County park, zoological garden or airport; land, acquisition, appropriation. [MSA 5.2431]

MCLA 123.62 Same; appropriation for improvement and maintenance. [MSA 5.2432]

MCLA 123.63 Same; owned or held in trust. [MSA 5.2433]

MCLA 123.64 Same; county tax. [MSA 5.2434]

MCLA 123.65 Powers construed; boulevards. [MSA 5.2435]

MCLA 123.66 County park trustees; board of county road commissioners; rules and regulations, resolution, publication; report to board of supervisors. [MSA 5.2436]

MCLA 123.66a County airport committee; appointment, powers, organization. [MSA 5.2436(1)]

MCLA 123.67 Funds, payment to local treasurer; misapplication penalty. [MSA 5.2437]

MCLA 123.68 Penalty for violation of rules and regulations. [MSA 5.2437(1)]

TRANSPORTATION

Dating back to the saddle horse and stagecoach days, the need for public transportation in and between communities was met by private companies such as Wells Fargo and local stables, and later by railroads, buses, trolleys and steamship lines. However, in the past thirty years, the airlines have cut into the traffic volume and one by one most of the private companies disappeared. A few have hung on with government subsidies, but even they can no longer provide adequate service. Now the order of the day is publicly supported mass transit.

Areas such as Wayne, Oakland and Macomb Counties; Genesee and Saginaw Counties; Kent County; and Kalamazoo and Calhoun Counties are at various stages of organization of metropolitan transit authorities to help solve this acute problem. Residents of the Ann Arbor metropolitan area recently did something which astonished local government officials throughout the state by voting substantial extra millage on their real and personal property to provide funds to operate a "demand bus" system. Many are saying that this will be the normal procedure in the years ahead.

At the time of this writing, there is much controversy in Michigan regarding the feasibility (even legality) of using monies from the gasoline and weight tax for public transportation. The very mention of mass transit coupled with an increase in that tax immediately elicits heated argument.

There is no question, however, of the legality of any township joining with other units of government to provide mass transit. The following statute should prove useful to those officials in metropolitan townships seeking to solve their public transportation problems.

JOINT ACTION
Act No. 204, P.A. 1967 - Metropolitan Transportation Authorities

AN ACT to create metropolitan transportation authorities and to define their powers and duties.

MCLA 124.401 Short title. [MSA 5.3475(101)]

MCLA 124.402 Definitions. [MSA 5.3475(102)]

MCLA 124.403 Powers of authorities. [MSA 5.3475(103)]

MCLA 124.404 Establishment of authorities. [MSA 5.3475(104)]

MCLA 124.405 Southeastern Michigan transportation authority, establishment, withdrawal of counties. [MSA 5.3475(105)]

MCLA 124.406 Additional powers and duties. [MSA 5.3475(106)]

MCLA 124.407 Rates and charges; services; public service commission, jurisdiction; appeals; injunctions. [MSA 5.3475(107)]

MCLA 124.408 Southeastern Michigan transportation authority. powers and duties. [MSA 5.3475(108)]

MCLA 124.409 Motor carrier and public service acts, applicability. [MSA 5.3475(109)]

MCLA 124.410 Governing boards; members, residence, terms, appointments, vacancies, compensation; meetings; rules; records; quorum; enlargement of southeastern Michigan transportation authority. [MSA 5.3475(110)]

MCLA 124.411 General manager; policies; annual audits. [MSA 5.3475(111)]

MCLA 124.412 Same; appointment, powers, duties, term. [MSA 5.3475(112)]

MCLA 124.413 Officers, employees, agents; appointment, classification, merit rating; collective bargaining; assumed wage, hour, and other benefit obligations; returning servicemen. [MSA 5.3475(113)]

MCLA 124.414 Taxation; financing. [MSA 5.3475(114)]

MCLA 124.415 Annual operating and capital budget, review, approval; quinquennial capital program budgets, annual revision; financial audits; construction programs. [MSA 5.3475(115)]

MCLA 124.416 Bonds, issuance, payment, form, term, sale; advancements, receipt, repayment, evidence of indebtedness. [MSA 5.3475(116)]

MCLA 124.417 Competitive bids, necessity, procedure; written price quotations; procurement procedures; waiver. [MSA 5.3475(117)]

MCLA 124.418 Concessions; award, procedure. [MSA 5.3475(118)]

MCLA 124.419 Claims; notice, allowance, jurisdiction over actions against authority. [MSA 5.3475(119)]

MCLA 124.420 Assistance from political subdivisions and public and private agencies. [MSA 5.3475(120)]

MCLA 124.421 Liberal construction. [MSA 5.3475(121)]

MCLA 124.422 Tax exemption. [MSA 5.3475(122)]

MCLA 124.423 Annual public report and financial statement.
[MSA 5.3475(123)]

MCLA 124.424 Acquisition of transportation systems, negotiation, condemnation, arbitration; competitive service. [MSA 5.3475(124)]

MCLA 124.425 Records, public inspection; meetings, open to public, notice to public. [MSA 5.3475(125)]

Act No. 51, P.A. 1951 – State Trunk Line Highways System

MCLA 247.660 – 247.660k [MSA 9.1097(10) – 9.1097(10K)]

Note: Please see the chapter on Highways, Roads, Bridges and Culverts. This portion of the statute, added in 1972, deals with state funds for public transportation programs and facilities for nonmotorized transportation.

LIBRARIES

Free libraries, whether public or private, are one of the greatest services which may be rendered to mankind. Historical evidence stands unchallenged that many outstanding leaders of this nation in most fields of endeavor, including government, business, education, industry and commerce, reached the pinnacle of success through self-education, with the cornerstone being the availability and use of books. As a matter of fact, probably one of the greatest leaders of all time, Abraham Lincoln, "self-read" himself into the right to practice law and later to become perhaps the greatest president in the history of the United States.

Eminently qualified psychologists and criminologists have attested to the fact that reading is not only a healthy exercise of the mind, but is also an effective tool in the reduction of crime and other social ills of the nation.

Township officials, like their counterparts in other areas of government, should never miss an opportunity to provide library services to their constituents. There are many statutes providing opportunity to join with other units of government to do so.

The community room, which more and more has become a part of libraries, provides a meeting place for study committees close to the source of many needed resources and reference material. A number of townships have also attained greater efficiency at less cost in the operation of services by constructing one building to house the township business offices, public meeting rooms, library and fire and/or police departments.

AFFECTS JOINT ACTION
Act No. 381, P.A. 1927 - Town Hall and Other Buildings

AN ACT to authorize the issue of bonds to provide sites for and for the erection thereon of town halls, fire stations, libraries or other buildings required for the public use in whole or in part, for township purposes or for the purpose of acquiring a site with buildings thereon and furnishing a town hall, fire station, library or other building or buildings required for the public use of such inhabitants in whole or in part for township purposes or for additions to and improvements of such sites and the buildings thereon, whether now existing or hereafter acquired, in any township in this state, and for the raising by townships of money for the maintenance, upkeep or repairs of the township hall, fire station, library or other public buildings of the township, and for the repeal of Act No. 397 of the Public Acts of 1921.

MCLA 41.241 Town hall, fire station, library; borrowing power of township board. MSA 5.2371

Sec. 1. The township board of any organized township in this state, upon application being first filed with such township board, signed by at least 12 freeholders of such township, may borrow a sum of money, not exceeding 2-1/2% of the assessed valuation of such township according to the assessed valuation of all the real and personal property of said township for the preceding year, on the faith and credit of such township, and to issue the bonds of such township therefor, the moneys so borrowed to be used for the purpose of acquiring a site for and erecting and furnishing a town hall, fire station or library or for the purpose of making additions and improvements to such sites and town halls, fire stations or libraries whether now existing or hereafter acquired, or for the

*purpose of purchasing a building or site to be used for a town hall,
fire station or library and furnishing and equipping the same.*

MCLA 41.241a Acquisition of real estate, referendum.
MSA 5.2371(1)

MCLA 41.242 Referendum proceedings; ballot, form. MSA 5.2372

MCLA 41.243 Conduct of election. MSA 5.2373

MCLA 41.244 Bonds, issuance. MSA 5.2374

MCLA 41.245 Tax levy. MSA 5.2375

MCLA 41.246 Tax for maintenance, upkeep, or repairs.
MSA 5.2376

*Sec. 6. Any township of this state may at any annual township
meeting* vote a tax upon the property of such township of not to*

----

*See MCLA 41.242 which requires a referendum election.

----

*exceed 1/20 of 1% of the assessed valuation of such township ac-
cording to the assessed valuation of all the real or personal property of said township of the preceding year and the money so raised
shall be used by the township board for the maintenance, upkeep
or repairs of the township hall, fire station, library or other public
buildings of the township.*

MCLA 41.246a Libraries, sites, buildings, maintenance.
MSA 5.2376(1)

*Sec. 6a. The **township board** of any organized township may
purchase sites and buildings for libraries, or lease, construct, and
remodel, add to and maintain building or space for libraries.*

MCLA 41.247 Repeal; saving clause. MSA 5.2377

JOINT ACTION
Act No. 92, P.A. 1952 - Public Libraries, Cooperation in Maintenance and Operation

AN ACT to provide for cooperation and coordination in the maintenance and operation of libraries open for use by the public generally; to authorize certain contracts or arrangements for extension of library services; and to authorize the legislative body of political subdivisions to contract and pay therefor.

MCLA 397.471 Public libraries; cooperation and coordination in maintenance and operation, contracts. MSA 15.1792(1)

MCLA 397.472 Same; contracts and arrangements; rights and privileges of residents; expenditures; political subdivisions. MSA 15.1792(2)

AFFECTS JOINT ACTION
Act No. 305, P.A. 1919 - Sites, Bond Issue and Sinking Fund

AN ACT to authorize the issue of bonds; to provide sites for and for the erection thereon of public libraries and for additions to and improvements of such sites and the buildings thereon, whether now existing or hereafter acquired, in cities, villages and school districts where free public libraries have or may hereafter be established.

MCLA 397.241 Legislative bodies to provide sites and buildings; improvement of existing property; bonds, limitation. MSA 15.1681

MCLA 397.242 Bonds; form, issuance, negotiation. MSA 15.1682

MCLA 397.243 Same; approval of issue. MSA 15.1683

MCLA 397.244 Same; sinking fund for redemption; receipts from sale, disposition. MSA 15.1684

MCLA 397.245 Same; budget items for sinking fund and interest. MSA 15.1685

MCLA 397.246 City or village may borrow for library buildings. MSA 15.1686

AFFECTS JOINT ACTION
Act No. 261, P.A. 1913 - Libraries under Boards of Education

AN ACT to authorize boards of education to provide for the maintenance of free public libraries existing under the control of boards of education of the cities; to authorize and empower said boards of education to raise or borrow money and issue bonds in sufficient sum to purchase property or site, erect and maintain buildings for use as a free public library and other educational purposes.

MCLA 397.261 Boards of education; library, annual expense estimate. [MSA 15.1691]

MCLA 397.262 Same; issuance of bonds, maturity, approval by electors. [MSA 15.1692]

Note: Must be approved by majority of electors of the district affected, voting thereon.

JOINT ACTION
Act No. 136, P.A. 1921 - Donations

AN ACT to authorize and facilitate the acquisition and disposal of public library property by public corporations empowered to maintain public libraries.

MCLA 397.381 Donations. [MSA 15.1751]

Sec. 1. Any board of education, library commission or other public corporation empowered to maintain a public library may receive and accept gifts and donations of property, real or personal, for the purpose of such library and shall hold, use and apply the property so received for the purposes set forth in the instrument of gift and in accordance with the provisions of such instrument and subject to the conditions and limitations, if any, therein expressed.

MCLA 397.382 Disposal of property not needed. [MSA 15.1752]

Act No. 5, P.A. 1917 - Township and Village
Libraries

AN ACT authorizing organized townships and incorporated villages in the state of Michigan to borrow money and to issue bonds therefor for the purpose of establishing free public libraries, purchasing sites and constructing buildings thereon.

MCLA 397.321 Issuance of library bonds by townships or villages; approval by electors. [MSA 15.1711]

MCLA 397.322 Same; referendum notice. [MSA 15.1712]

Note: The above two sections refer to "legal voters" and an "election." Accordingly the statute is ambiguous and consultation should be had with an attorney on the same if proceedings are planned at a "meeting."

MCLA 397.323 Same; form of ballot; conduct of election. [MSA 15.1713]

MCLA 397.324 Same; terms, signature, negotiation; tax. [MSA 15.1714]

MCLA 397.325 Same; negotiation at less than par. [MSA 15.1715]

MCLA 397.326 Declaration of necessity. [MSA 15.1716]

JOINT ACTION
Act No. 165, P.A. 1927 - Consolidation of Township
Libraries

AN ACT to authorize the consolidation of township libraries in adjoining townships in certain cases, and to provide for their joint maintenance.

MCLA 397.351 Consolidation of township libraries. [MSA 15.1721]

MCLA 397.352 Referendum; petition. [MSA 15.1722]

MCLA 397.353 Same; form of ballot; conduct of election.
MSA 15.1723

MCLA 397.354 Same; joint resolution of township boards canvassing returns. MSA 15.1724

MCLA 397.355 Site, designation. MSA 15.1725

MCLA 397.356 Maintenance. MSA 15.1726

MCLA 397.357 Control. MSA 15.1727

MCLA 397.358 Free public library. MSA 15.1728

JOINT ACTION
Act No. 164, P.A. 1877 - City Libraries

AN ACT to authorize cities, incorporated villages, and townships, to establish and maintain free public libraries and reading rooms.

MCLA 397.201 City library; establishment, maintenance; library fund. MSA 15.1661

MCLA 397.202 Board of directors of city library; number, appointment, qualifications. MSA 15.1662

MCLA 397.203 Same; vacancy, term, removal. MSA 15.1663

MCLA 397.204 Same; vacancies, compensation. MSA 15.1664

MCLA 397.205 Same; officers; powers and duties; library fund, accounting. MSA 15.1665

MCLA 397.206 Free use of library; regulations. MSA 15.1666

MCLA 397.207 Board of directors; annual report, contents.
MSA 15.1667

MCLA 397.208 City library; injury, ordinances. MSA 15.1668

MCLA 397.209 Same; donations. MSA 15.1669

MCLA 397.210 Village or township library; petition for tax; referendum; estimate of cost of maintenance; assessment. [MSA 15.1670]

MCLA 397.210a City library; referendum on tax for establishment, tax for maintenance. [MSA 15.1671]

MCLA 397.211 City, village or township library board; temporary appointment, election, term, powers, vacancy. [MSA 15.1672]

MCLA 397.212 Application of act. [MSA 15.1673]

MCLA 397.213 Joint municipal libraries; townships. [MSA 15.1674]

MCLA 397.214 Same; contract for use of municipal library by township, vote, term; tax. [MSA 15.1675]

MCLA 397.216 Same; right to user under contract. [MSA 15.1676]

MCLA 397.217 Same; villages and cities. [MSA 15.1677]

JOINT ACTION
Act No. 269, P.A. 1955 - School Code, Chapter 27 - Libraries

MCLA 340.901 Libraries; township, school and free public libraries; maintenance; legal actions; persons entitled to privileges. [MSA 15.3901]

MCLA 340.902 Township library; control; township treasurer, duties; books; buildings, hearing, notice. [MSA 15.3902]

MCLA 340.903 Same; care and preservation, rules. [MSA 15.3903]

MCLA 340.904 Same; location; librarian. [MSA 15.3904]

Sec. 904. The township board shall cause the township library to be kept at some central and suitable place in the township, which it shall determine. Said board shall also, within 10 days after the annual township meeting, appoint a librarian for the term of 1 year to have the care and superintendence of said library, and such librarian shall be responsible to the township board for the *impartial enforcement of all rules and regulations lawfully established in relation to said library.*

MCLA 340.905 Same; tax for support. MSA 15.3905

Note: Subsequent statutes make it mandatory that any millage proposed shall be approved at a referendum election.

MCLA 340.907 School district libraries; establishment.
MSA 15.3907

MCLA 340.908 Same; control; persons entitled to privileges.
MSA 15.3908

MCLA 340.909 Same; tax for support. MSA 15.3909

MCLA 340.914 School district library books; sale or donation to other libraries. MSA 15.3914

JOINT ACTION
Act No. 106, P.A. 1937 - State Board for Libraries

AN ACT to create a state board for libraries, and to prescribe its powers and duties; to provide for the transfer to said board of the powers and duties now vested by law in the state librarian and in the state board of library commissioners; to provide for the management and control of the state library; to declare the effect of this act; and to repeal certain acts and parts of acts.

Note: Powers and duties of the state board of library commissioners and the state librarian were transferred to the state board for libraries, which, in turn, were transferred to the department of education (see **MCLA 16.409** MSA 3.29(309) and **MCLA 397.8** MSA 15.1565(8)).

MCLA 397.1 State board for libraries; members, term, appointment, vacancy, secretary, meetings, compensation and expenses, employes. MSA 15.1565(1)

MCLA 397.2 Same; powers and duties. MSA 15.1565(2)

MCLA 397.3 Same; control and direction of Michigan traveling libraries. [MSA 15.1565(3)]

MCLA 397.4 Same; rules and regulations. [MSA 15.1565(4)]

MCLA 397.5 State librarian; appointment, qualifications, term, compensation. [MSA 15.1565(5)]

MCLA 397.6 Assistant state librarian; appointment, title, bond; general assistants and employes; compensation. [MSA 15.1565(6)]

MCLA 397.7 Annual report. [MSA 15.1565(7)]

MCLA 397.8 Transfer of powers and duties of state board of library commissioners and state librarian. [MSA 15.1565(8)]

AFFECTS JOINT ACTION
Act No. 115, P.A. 1899 - Free Libraries

AN ACT to create a state board of library commissioners, to promote the establishment and efficiency of free public libraries, and to provide an appropriation therefor.

MCLA 397.453 Free libraries; annual report. [MSA 15.1632]

JOINT ACTION
Act No. 286, P.A. 1965 - State Aid to Public Libraries Act

AN ACT to authorize the establishment of library systems; to provide state aid for the support of libraries and library systems; to prescribe the powers and duties of library boards; and to repeal certain acts and parts of acts.

MCLA 397.501 Short title. [MSA 15.1791(101)]

MCLA 397.502 Definitions. [MSA 15.1791(102)]

MCLA 397.503 Minimum local support. [MSA 15.1791(103)]

Sec. 3. A public library or local government shall be eligible to become a library system or to remain a member of a library system if in the fiscal year prior to July 1 of the year of distribution the library received local support or the local government provided local support equal to not less than 3/10 mill on the state equalized valuation of its governmental unit or units.

MCLA 397.504 Plan of library service; submission, approval, designation. [MSA 15.1791(104)]

MCLA 397.505 Library groups; eligibility to submit plan, approval, designation. [MSA 15.1791(105)]

MCLA 397.506 Local boards; eligibility to submit plan, approval, designation. [MSA 15.1791(106)]

MCLA 397.507 Libraries serving certain population areas, eligibility to seek approval. [MSA 15.1791(107)]

MCLA 397.508 System board; notice of meeting, election of members. [MSA 15.1791(108)]

MCLA 397.509 System board, duties. [MSA 15.1791(109)]

MCLA 397.510 Fiscal year of system. [MSA 15.1791(110)]

MCLA 397.511 Use of facilities; availability. [MSA 15.1791(111)]

MCLA 397.512 Local board; request to become participating library, approval. [MSA 15.1791(112)]

MCLA 397.513 Withdrawal from membership, notice.
[MSA 15.1791(113)]

MCLA 397.514 Continuing state aid; grants per capita.
[MSA 15.1791(114)]

MCLA 397.515 Annual contribution amount, payment and use.
[MSA 15.1791(115)]

MCLA 397.516 Public libraries; grants per capita from state aid; certification of salary. [MSA 15.1791(116)]

MCLA 397.517 Certification requirements for state aid.
[MSA 15.1791(117)]

MCLA 397.518 Certification of amounts received.
[MSA 15.1791(118)]

MCLA 397.519 Allocation of available funds. [MSA 15.1791(119)]

MCLA 397.520 Statement of amounts to be distributed; vouchers.
[MSA 15.1791(120)]

MCLA 397.521 State aid; deposit in separate library fund.
[MSA 15.1791(121)]

MCLA 397.522 State aid; permitted uses. [MSA 15.1791(122)]

MCLA 397.523 Eligibility of proposed members; determination, approval or rejection of plan. [MSA 15.1791(123)]

MCLA 397.524 Needs to be considered by board in carrying out its duties. [MSA 15.1791(124)]

MCLA 397.525 State board; adoption of rules and regulations.
[MSA 15.1791(125)]

MCLA 397.527 Effective date. [MSA 15.1791(127)]

JOINT ACTION
Act No. 138, P.A. 1917 - County Libraries

AN ACT to authorize the creation of county libraries; to authorize the contracting by the board of supervisors of any county for library service; to authorize the contracting by the board of supervisors of any county or the board of trustees of any regional library with any other municipality for the furnishing of such service; and to provide for a tax for the purposes of this act.

MCLA 397.301 County library, establishment; contract for service; tax. [MSA 15.1701]

MCLA 397.302 Library board, members, term; body corporate; powers. [MSA 15.1702]

MCLA 397.303 Contract for use of existing library; county library fund administered by library board. [MSA 15.1703]

MCLA 397.304 County library fund, disbursement. [MSA 15.1704]

MCLA 397.305 County or regional library, contract for service to municipality; tax; effect of establishment of municipal library. [MSA 15.1705]

JOINT ACTION
Act No. 371, P.A. 1972 - Library Network Act of 1971

AN ACT to establish a library network and to prescribe the duties and qualifications of libraries in networks.

MCLA 397.131 Short title. [MSA 15.1780(21)]

MCLA 397.132 Definitions. [MSA 15.1780(22)]

MCLA 397.133 Membership network, prerequisites. [MSA 15.1780(23)]

MCLA 397.134 Interlibrary loan service, administration. [MSA 15.1780(24)]

MCLA 397.135 Application for inclusion in network. [MSA 15.1780(25)]

MCLA 397.136 Rules, promulgation. [MSA 15.1780(26)]

JOINT ACTION
Act No. 164, P.A. 1955 - District Libraries

AN ACT to authorize boards of education to provide for the maintenance of free public libraries existing under the control of boards of education of the cities; to authorize and empower said boards of education to raise or

523

*borrow money and issue bonds in sufficient sum to pur-
chase property or site, erect and maintain buildings for
use as a free public library and other educational purposes.*

MCLA 397.271 District libraries; establishment. [MSA 15.1780(1)]

MCLA 397.272 Same; proposal to unite, approval. [MSA 15.1780(2)]

**MCLA 397.273 Library board of trustees; appointment, term, va-
cancies, expenses, officers.** [MSA 15.1780(3)]

MCLA 397.274 Same; powers (includes contracting authority).
[MSA 15.1780(4)]

**MCLA 397.275 Financing establishment and operation, appropria-
tions, tax levy.** [MSA 15.1780(5)]

*Sec. 5. The sums necessary for the establishment and opera-
tion of said district library shall be appropriated by the governing
or legislative boards of the municipalities entering into the formation of the district library, or by a tax levy for this purpose authorized by a vote of the qualified electors in any participating municipality.* **If any municipality withdraws from the district library, any
previously voted tax levy shall be continued for provision of public
library support.**

**MCLA 397.276 Inter-municipal district libraries, withdrawal of
participating municipality, procedure.** [MSA 15.1780(6)]

JOINT ACTION
Act No. 250, P.A. 1931 - Regional Libraries

*AN ACT to provide for the establishment and main-
tenance of regional libraries; to provide for boards of
trustees to have control of such libraries; to provide for
the powers and duties of the state board for libraries in
connection with such libraries; and to provide for the
support of such libraries by counties.*

**MCLA 397.151 Regional libraries; plan for establishment and loca-
tion.** [MSA 15.1781]

MCLA 397.152 Same; action by boards of supervisors, alteration of plan. [MSA 15.1782]

MCLA 397.153 Board of trustees; number, appointment, term, vacancies, expenses. [MSA 15.1783]

MCLA 397.155 Board of trustees; powers. [MSA 15.1785]

MCLA 397.156 Appropriations; budget, disbursement. [MSA 15.1786]

MCLA 397.157 Same; exemptions. [MSA 15.1787]

MCLA 397.158 Municipal libraries, transfer to regional libraries. [MSA 15.1788]

JOINT ACTION
Act No. 213, P.A. 1925 - Privately Owned Library

AN ACT to provide for the maintenance and operation of libraries for public use, owned or controlled by associations or individuals.

MCLA 397.371 Privately owned library; conditions of support by public, limitation. [MSA 15.1741]

AFFECTS JOINT ACTION
R.S. 1846, c. 53 - Libraries and Lyceums

MCLA 450.691 Incorporation of library; meeting, calling. [MSA 21.321]

MCLA 450.692 Same; proprietors, powers; certificate of proceedings, recording. [MSA 21.322]

MCLA 450.693 Powers of corporation; governing law. [MSA 21.323]

MCLA 450.694 Bond of collector and treasurer. [MSA 21.324]

MCLA 450.695 Shares, assessment, transfer; holding of property (may accept gifts, etc.). [MSA 21.325]

MCLA 450.696 Organization; powers. ⌈MSA 21.326⌉

Note: Since there are no longer justice courts in Michigan, anyone interested in utilizing this particular act should also refer to **Act 236, P.A. 1961 - Revised Judicature Act of 1961,** at **MCLA 600.9928** ⌈MSA 27A.9928⌉, **Municipal or Police Courts,** second and third paragraphs.

JOINT ACTION
Act No. 59, P.A. 1964 - Penal Fines

AN ACT to provide for the distribution of penal fines and their application to the support of public libraries; to provide for the appointment of a county library board to receive penal fines; to define its powers and duties; and to repeal certain acts and parts of acts.

MCLA 397.31 Libraries; definitions. ⌈MSA 15.1793(1)⌉

MCLA 397.32 Same; apportionment of penal fine moneys.
⌈MSA 15.1793(2)⌉

MCLA 397.33 Same; county library board, contracts for service.
⌈MSA 15.1793(3)⌉

MCLA 397.34 Same; new library; powers of board. ⌈MSA 15.1793(4)⌉

MCLA 397.35 Apportionment of funds; contract for service. Apportionment of penal funds. Same; more than 1 public library.
⌈MSA 15.1793(5)⌉

MCLA 397.36 Use of penal fine moneys; report. ⌈MSA 15.1793(6)⌉

MCLA 397.37 County law libraries. ⌈MSA 15.1793(7)⌉

MCLA 397.38 Statement of eligible libraries. ⌈MSA 15.1793(8)⌉

MCLA 397.39 Rules and regulations. ⌈MSA 15.1793(9)⌉

Opinion 3-20-59: Use of Township Hall and Township Owned Library Can be Reserved Exclusively for Township Purposes.

Opinion 6-12-67: Procedures to Establish Township Library (Organization and financing)

PRESERVATION OF TOWNSHIP RECORDS, FORMS AND HISTORY

Dating back as far as 1913, the legislature recognized the need and provided the means for township government to become involved in the preservation of material and places significant in the development of our great country. We owe it to future generations to record all facts concisely and accurately and keep them safe, as well as to seek out and preserve places and items of historical interest. Since township government stands as the grass roots of democracy, township boards have an extra degree of responsibility to make sure that our descendants have access to as much as we can leave them.

There are citations in some enabling statutes which are not included among the more general references in this section regarding record keeping. Any public official, elected or appointed, must be careful to keep records according to appropriate statutory provisions. Furthermore, since all records maintained in the discharge of his/her duties are the property of the people of the state, they may not be disposed of, mutilated or destroyed except as provided by law.

Some might wonder why an assessment roll would be considered useful a hundred years from now. Among other things, such records provide invaluable assistance to genealogists in their search for family history. Further, since they reflect the growth and development of a community, the rolls are often used by planning consultants and others involved in the zoning process.

Many groups such as the Grand Army of the Republic, Daughters of the American Revolution, veterans' organizations and various others have had their headquarters in township halls. Quite often their records have been stored in the buildings and do not come to light, perhaps, until the building is being vacated, renovated or torn down. If these or any other records of historical interest should be found, the law specifically requires that they be turned over to the Michigan Historical Commission.

Note the possibilities of joining with other units of government for the purpose of collecting, arranging and housing all kinds of documents and artifacts, as well as preservation of historical sites and monuments. Of special significance is the fact that the state, through the Michigan Historical Commission, is most eager to provide highly qualified historians and other specialists for advice, counsel and assistance to local government officials. Universities also have specialists available for consultation. Local historical and archeological societies should be developed and encouraged in their efforts.

Since records begin with forms, we are including a subsection on forms which have been developed for use of township government. They will be found at the end of this section after the law citations.

JOINT ACTION
Act No. 254, P.A. 1919 - County Historical Material

AN ACT to authorize boards of supervisors to raise money for the collection, publication, housing or displaying of historical material, bearing upon their county and to foster the historical interest thereof.

MCLA 46.231 County historical interests; power to appropriate. MSA 5.491

JOINT ACTION
Act No. 271, P.A. 1913 - Historical Commission

AN ACT to create the Michigan historical commission; to provide for the appointment of members of such commission; to fix their term of office, prescribe their powers and duties, make an appropriation to carry out the provisions of this act; to provide for the listing and destruction of useless documents, books and papers; and to repeal all acts and parts of acts inconsistent herewith.

MCLA 399.1 Historical commission; members, appointment, expenses. MSA 15.1801

MCLA 339.2 Same; terms of office. [MSA 15.1802]

MCLA 399.3 Same; meetings; organization; acceptance of property. [MSA 15.1803]

MCLA 399.4 Same; duties. [MSA 15.1804]

MCLA 399.5 Historical records; collection; preservation; copies as evidence; property of state; exceptions; inspection; disposal schedule. [MSA 15.1805]

Sec. 5. ... Any record that is required to be kept by a public officer in the discharge of the duties imposed on him by law, or that is a writing required to be filed in a public office, or is a written memorial of a transaction of a public officer made in the discharge of his duty, shall be the property of the people of the state, and may not be disposed of, mutilated or destroyed except as provided by law. ...

MCLA 399.6 Publication of material; payment of expenses. [MSA 15.1806]

MCLA 399.7 Custodian of publications of historical commission, museum; distribution, exchange and/or sale of publications. [MSA 15.1807]

MCLA 399.8 Secretary, employees; authority delegated to secretary; salaries and expenses. [MSA 15.1808]

MCLA 399.8a Rules and regulations. [MSA 15.1808(1)]

MCLA 399.9 Annual report; contents. [MSA 15.1809]

Act No. 212, P.A. 1957 - Historical Activities and Projects

AN ACT to authorize townships to appropriate money for historical activities and projects.

MCLA 399.161 Historical activities and projects; townships, appropriation. [MSA 5.267(1)]

JOINT ACTION
Act No. 10, P.A. 1955 - Registration of Historic Sites

AN ACT to provide for the registration of historic sites.

MCLA 399.151 Historical sites; listing. [MSA 15.1815(1)]

MCLA 399.152 Same; register, marker. Registered marker. Protar property, Beaver Island, restoration, appropriation. [MSA 15.1815(2)]

JOINT ACTION
Act No. 327, P.A. 1931 - General Corporation Act

MCLA 450.163 Foundations; incorporators; expenditure of funds. [MSA 21.164]

Act No. 51, P.A. 1948, 1st Ex. Sess. - Department of Administration

MCLA 18.13a Office services division, duty as to state records. [MSA 3.516(13A)]

MCLA 18.13b Records; definition; preservation, delivery to successors in office. [MSA 3.516(13B)]

MCLA 18.13c Same; making and filing, procedure as to transfer, destruction. [MSA 3.516(13C)]

Act No. 328, P.A. 1931 - Penal Code

Chapter LXXI. Public Records

MCLA 750.491 Removal, mutilation, or destruction of public records, penalty. [MSA 28.759]

Sec. 491. All official books, papers or records created by or received in any office or agency of the state of Michigan or its political subdivisions, are declared to be public property, belonging to the people of the state of Michigan. All books, papers or records shall be disposed of only as provided in section 13c of Act No. 51 of the Public Acts of the First Extra Session of 1948, as added, being section 18.13c [MSA 3.516(13C)] *of the Compiled Laws of 1948, section 5 of Act No. 271 of the Public Acts of 1913, as amended, being section 399.5* [MSA 15.1805] *of the Compiled Laws of 1948 and sections 2137 and 2138 of Act No. 236 of the Public Acts of 1961, being sections 600.2137* [MSA 27A.2137] *and 600.2138* [MSA 27A.2138] *of the Compiled Laws of 1948.*

Any person who shall wilfully carry away, mutilate or destroy any of such books, papers, records or any part of the same, and any person who shall retain and continue to hold the possession of any books, papers or records, or parts thereof, belonging to the afore-said offices and shall refuse to deliver up such books, papers, records, or parts thereof to the proper officer having charge of the office to which such books, papers, or records belong, upon demand being made by such officer or, in cases of a defunct office, the Michigan historical commission, shall be guilty of a misdemeanor, punishable by imprisonment in the state prison not more than 2 years or by a fine of not more than $1,000.00.

MCLA 750.492 Inspection and use of public records. [MSA 28.760]

Sec. 492. Any officer having the custody of any county, city or township records in this state who shall when requested fail or neglect to **furnish proper and reasonable facilities for the inspection and examination of the records and files in his office and for making memoranda of transcripts therefrom during the usual business hours, which shall not be less than 4 hours per day,** *to any person having occasion to make examination of them for any lawful purpose shall be guilty of a misdemeanor, punishable by imprisonment in the county jail not more than 1 year, or by a fine of not more than $500.00.* **The custodian of said records and files may make such reasonable rules with reference to the inspection and examination of them as shall be necessary for the protection of said records and files, and to prevent interference with the regular discharge of the duties of such officer.** *The officer shall* **prohibit the use of pen and ink** *in making copies or notes of records and files in his office.* **No books, records and files shall be removed from the office of the custodian thereof, except by the order of the judge of any court of competent jurisdiction,** *or in response to a subpoena duces tecum issued therefrom, or for audit purposes conducted pursuant to ...(several statutes)... with the permission of the official* *having custody of the records if the official is given a receipt listing the records being removed.*

Note: In chapter two it was indicated that no township official can be forced to remain at his/her post for any specified hours, except in a few instances where the statutes direct that an officer must be available at certain times for certain purposes. However, the above statute does require that official records must be available to the public during certain periods. Your attention is directed particularly to the emphasized portions of the second section.

If there is a need for logic and common sense in complying with a statute, this is a classic example. It is not to be interpreted as meaning that the official himself must be present with the records. A deputy or some other responsible person may be designated by the officer to act in his behalf for this purpose. Whatever arrangements are made, however, should be thoroughly publicized so township residents know when and where they may have access to the records.

The next two citations specify that township records may not be kept where "gaming and plays of chance of any kind are carried on." The reader is directed to the editorial notes following Act No. 239, P.A. 1972 - Lotteries and Act No. 382, P.A. 1972 - Bingo in the section on Parks and Recreation in the chapter on Environmental Protection and Control.

R.S. 1846, c. 16 - Township Supervisor

MCLA 41.62 Records, preservation, turning over; certified copies, fees, evidence. MSA 5.53

Sec. 62. The supervisor shall preserve and keep all books, assessment rolls, and other papers belonging to his office, in a safe and suitable place, but not in any saloon, restaurant, public inn, hotel, place of public amusement, nor in any place where intoxicating drinks of any kind are kept or sold, or where **gaming or plays of chance of any kind are carried on,** *or where they will be exposed to unusual hazard from fire or theft, and he shall deliver the same on demand to his successor in office, and on application of any person he shall give certified copies of any such papers, or abstracts from any assessment roll or books in his office; and for making any such copies or abstracts he shall be entitled to receive from the person applying therefor 6 cents for each folio; but no such* copy or abstract and certificate shall be required for less than 12 1/2 cents; and such certified copies or abstracts shall be presumptive evidence of the facts therein contained.

R.S. 1846, c. 16 - Township Clerk

MCLA 41.65 Township records; contents, preservation, turning over. [MSA 5.57]

Sec. 65. The township clerk of each township shall have the custody of all the records, books, and papers of the township, when no other provision is made by law; and he shall duly file and safely keep all certificates of oaths and other papers required by law to be filed in his office, and record such as are required by law to be recorded therein; such records, books, and papers shall not be kept in any saloon, restaurant, public inn, hotel, place of public amusement, nor in any place where intoxicating drinks of any kind are kept or sold, or where **gaming or plays of chance of any kind are carried on,** *nor where they will be exposed to unusual hazard of fire or theft, and he shall deliver the same on demand to his successor in office; he shall also open and keep an account with the treasurer ...*

R.S. 1846, c. 16 - Township Treasurer

MCLA 41.78 Accounts. [MSA 5.70]

Sec. 78. Each township treasurer shall keep a just and true account of the receipts and expenditures of all moneys which shall come into his hands by virtue of his office, in a book to be provided for that purpose, at the expense of the township, and to be delivered to his successor in office.

Act No. 105, P.A. 1964 - Reproduction of Records

AN ACT to provide for photostating, photographing, microphotographing or filming of records of the state, political subdivisions thereof and municipal courts of record; and to provide for the use thereof as evidence.

MCLA 691.1101 Public records, municipal court of record records; photograph; destruction. [MSA 3.993(1)]

MCLA 691.1102 Register of deeds; microphotograph, duplicates; display equipment. [MSA 3.993(2)]

MCLA 691.1103 Photographs, microphotographs, admissibility in evidence. [MSA 3.993(3)]

Act No. 173, P.A. 1929 - Aboriginal Records and Antiquities

AN ACT to protect and preserve, and to regulate the taking of aboriginal records and antiquities within the state of Michigan, and to provide penalties for the violation of this act.

MCLA 299.51 Aboriginal records and antiquities; exclusive right in state, exceptions. [MSA 13.21]

MCLA 299.52 Same; property right of state; exceptions. [MSA 13.22]

MCLA 299.53 Same; permit for exploration on state land. [MSA 13.23]

MCLA 299.54 Same; consent of landowner to removal. [MSA 13.24]

MCLA 299.55 Penalty. [MSA 13.25]

Act No. 190, P.A. 1867 - Mutilated Archives

AN ACT to provide for copying and binding mutilated assessment rolls and other papers.

MCLA 46.241 Mutilated archives, preservation. [MSA 5.501]

MCLA 46.242 Same; supervision; copyist; certificate. [MSA 5.502]

MCLA 46.243 Same; evidence, copies. [MSA 5.503]

Act No. 8, P.A. 1897 - Veterans' Headquarters

MCLA 35.232 Michigan veterans' headquarters room; ... [MSA 4.1162]

*Sec. 2. ... All the records, files and documents of the depart-
ment of the Michigan Grand Army of the Republic shall be turned
over to the Michigan historical commission, ... and shall be preserved by the Michigan historical commission.*

**Act No. 281, P.A. 1927 - Name and Insignia of Cer-
tain Organizations**

*AN ACT to provide for the registration and protection
of the names, badges, buttons, decorations, charms, em-
blems, rosettes and other insignia of associations, lodges,
orders, fraternal societies, beneficial societies, or fraternal and beneficial societies or associations, historical,
military or veterans' organizations, labor union, foundation, federation, or any other society, organization or
association, degree, branch, subordinate lodge or auxiliary
thereof; to prohibit the wearing, exhibition, display or use
of the same by any person not entitled to wear, exhibit,
display or use the same, and fixing a penalty for the violation of this act.*

**MCLA 430.1 Registration of name and insignia of certain organiza-
tions.** [MSA 18.641]

MCLA 430.2 Same; application. [MSA 18.642]

MCLA 430.3 Same; record. [MSA 18.643]

MCLA 430.4 Same; disallowance. [MSA 18.644]

MCLA 430.5 Same; certificate. [MSA 18.645]

MCLA 430.6 Wilful unauthorized use of insignia; penalty.
[MSA 18.646]

MCLA 430.7 Fee; disposition. [MSA 18.647]

RETENTION SCHEDULE FOR RECORDS

This information was compiled from General Schedule 10, Michigan State Administrative Board, dated February 18, 1964 and from the statutes.

RECORD TITLE	OFFICE RETENTION PERIOD
Account Journals	10 years
Bills and/or Invoices	7 years after audit
Bonds and Oaths of Officials	Permanent
Cancelled Checks and/or Stubs	7 years after audit

Correspondence

(a) General – routine nature	Current year
(b) General – fiscal in nature	Current year plus 6 years
(c) Policy in nature	Permanent

Election Materials

(a) Applications to Vote	2 years after date of election
(b) Application for Absent-Voter Ballot	2 years after date of election
(c) Determinations by Board of Canvassers	Permanent
(d) Petitions	May be destroyed January 1 after Primary election providing permanent record is maintained
(e) Poll Books	2 years after date of election
(f) Registration Forms Duplicates	2 years after registration is cancelled
Originals	10 years after registration is cancelled or 2 years if original has been reproduced on film and the film is on file in office of clerk. The film may be destroyed 10 years after registration is cancelled.

(g) Return Absent-Voter Envelopes	2 years after date of election
(h) Statement Books	2 years after date of election
General Ledger	20 years
Minute Books — Township Board	Permanent*
Purchase Orders	7 years after audit
Tax Bills or Receipts	7 years after audit
Tax Rolls	10 years**
Vouchers	7 years after audit

_____

*May be transferred to the Michigan Historical Commission, Division of Archives, after 25 or more years old.

**Any township tax rolls prior to 1880 shall be transferred to the Michigan Historical Commission, Division of Archives.
_____

FORMS

The following forms are, in the opinion of the author, used most frequently by township officials. The great majority are required by law, with style and content actually specified in some cases. Although the titles are statutory, the numbers are catalog numbers assigned by Doubleday Bros. & Company of Kalamazoo, noted authorities on the printing and publishing of forms of all kinds for local governments. They are separated into six categories plus one miscellaneous section. Also included are five types of minute books required by township government.

Not to be overlooked are the three volumes of **Municipal Legal Forms,** a comprehensive library of working municipal forms. Although designed primarily for city attorneys, they provide practical help and guidance for any local government official. They may be ordered from Callaghan & Company, Law Publishers, Chicago, Illinois 60646.

ACCOUNTING FORMS

M78B	Order on Township Treasurer
M78C	Order on Township Treasurer
TUA1	Record of Tax Collections
TUA3	Receipt Journal
TUA5	Disbursement Journal
TUA5A	Trust & Agency Disbursement Journal
TUA5B	Current Tax Disbursement Journal
TUA5C	Check Register Disbursement Journal
TUA7	General Ledger Sheet
TUA10	Transmittal Advice
TUA12	Receipts
S798½	Binder for Receipts
TUA19	Journal Entry
SFA18C	Voucher Check - w/payroll deduction
SFA18NCR	Voucher Check - NCR paper
S792½	Binder for Voucher Check
M201	Journal Summary Sheets
M202	Fund Book Sheet

BUILDING DEPARTMENT FORMS

M298	Building Permit
M298A	Building Permit Application
M298C	Building Permit Card
M298D	Condemned Sign
M298R	Record of Building Permits
M749	Special Assessment Roll Sheets
M750	Special Assessment Roll Sheet
M751	Notice of Special Assessment Tax Forms
M752	Special Assessment Roll Sheets
M745	Change on Tax Roll

CEMETERY FORMS

M206	Cemetery Deeds
M350	Cemetery Record Sheets
M351	Burial Journal Sheets
M352	Cemetery Index Sheets
M1933	Cemetery Record Sheet

ELECTION FORMS

E3	Receipt for Ballots
E4	Ballot Bags
E4C	Ballot Bag Certificate
E4H	Ballot Bag Certificate Holder
E5	Election Inspectors Certificate
E7	Absent Voter Ballot Envelope (Outgoing)
E8	Absent Voter Ballot Envelope (Incoming)
E9	Receipt from Chairman of Inspectors
E10	Instruction to Absent Voter
ET10	Certificate of Nomination
ES19	Poll Book
ES19VM	Poll Book
EX19	Poll Book
EX19VM	Poll Book
E20X	Tally Books
E20	Tally Sheet
E20R	Recount Tally Sheet
E20VM	Statement Sheet
E20VMS	Statement Sheet Shoup
E20VMR	Recount Statement Sheet
E21X	Statement Book
E21	Statement Sheets
E21R	Recount Statement Sheet
E24	Election Inspector Application Blank
E26	List of Absent Voters
E30	Custodian's Certificate
E40	Absent Voters Ballot Envelope
E52	Notice of Annual Township Meeting
E55	Red paper Election Seals
E60	Absent Voter Envelope & List of Absent Voters
E84	Challenger Badges
E85	Election Badges
E86	Vote Here Signs
E87	Election Pencils - paper ballot
E87VM	Election Pencils - voting machine
E88	Election seals metal
E94	Ballot Box Tag
E95	Lead & Wire Seals
E107	Absent Voter "Free Air Mail" envelopes (outgoing)
E108	Absent Voter "Free Air Mail" envelopes (incoming)

E114	Voting Machine Key Envelope
E115	Voting Machine Key Return Envelope
E116	Tag "Do Not Break this Seal until Polls Close"
E117	Tag "Do Not Break this Seal at any Time"
E119	Voting Machine Key Envelope (Shoup)
E120	Tally Sheet for Absent Voter Ballots
E121	Emergency Absent Voters Applications
E122	Absent Voters Ballot Application Binder
E123	Absent Voter Ballot Application
E124	Absent Voter Ballot Application - Property Owner
E135	Certificate of Attendance at V.M. Instruction Meeting
E136	Voting Machine Write-In Instructions
E137	Examiners Certificate
E143	Transfer of Registration on Election Day
E197	Absent Voters Counting Board Affidavit
E198	Application & Affidavit for Members of Board of Canvassers
M396	Record of Petitions
M397	Canvass of Votes Cast
M398	Canvass of Votes Cast - General Election
M398PC	Canvass of Votes Cast - Primary
M398R	Precinct Record Sheets
M399	Record of Nominating Petitions Filed
MV400	Sheet Shifter
MV401	Registration Sheets
MV402	Registration Sheet
MV403	Registration Sheet
MV404	Registration Sheet
MV406	Registration Sheet
MV406-10	Registration Form - set of MV406 & SV10
MV406-13	Registration Form - set of MV406 & MV413
M410	Work Sheet (Registration)
MV411	Registration Card
MV413	Registration Master Card
MV414	Registration Master Card
MV418	Registration Form - set of MV406, SV10, MV413
M419	Notice of Division of Precinct
M420	Notice of Division of Voting Precinct
M420E	Envelope for M420
M421	Removal of Elector
M422	Transfer of Registration
M424	Notice of Registration - after 5th Friday

540

M425	Change of Polling Place Notice
M427	Cancellation of Previous Registration
M431	Transfer of Registration on Election Day
MV433-2	Notice of Suspension of Registration
M435C	Blank Certificate
M434	Township Officer Certificate
M440	Transfer of Registration on Election Day
MV441	Corrected Information for Clerks Office
M443	Application for Election Inspectors
M445	Applications for Ballot
M446	Application for Ballot
M448	Ballot Application Binder
M450	Change of Address Affidavit
M453	Registration Record Card
M1200	Alum. Case for Style A registration binder
M1201	Black Imit. Leather Case for Style A registration binder
M1917	Township Certificate of Determination
M1920	Certificate Holders

MINUTE BOOKS

KM215	Minute Book - hand written
B2511	Minute book - 11'' x 8½'' typewriter style black
R2511	Minute book - 11'' x 8½'' typewriter style red
B2514	Minute book - 14'' x 8½'' typewriter style black
R2514	Minute book - 14'' x 8½'' typewriter style red

MISCELLANEOUS FORMS

M98	Permit
M98A	Application for License
M99	General License Forms
M110	Application for Sale
M111	Principal Inventory
M112	Inventory
M200	Minute Book Record Sheets
M201	Journal Summary Sheet
M202	Fund Book Sheets
M203	Annual Settlement Sheet
M205L	Annual Itemized Statement Book
M210	Notice of Meeting of Board of Review

M212	Register of Officers Elected or Appointed
M280	Petition to Board of Review
M283-1	Real Property Analysis
M283-2	Personal Property Analysis
M284	Classification Work Sheets
M284A	Equalization Analysis Sheets
M285	Classification Work Sheets
M286	Assessment Roll Change Work Sheets
M287	Notice of Township Board Meeting
M288	Notice of Assessment
M288C	Notice of Assessment
M290	Business Personal Property Statement
M290A	Business Personal Property Statement Sheets
M292	Real Property Statement Sheets
M293	Residential Assessment Record
M294	Commercial Assessment Record
M294FI	Industrial Assessment Record
M294FF	Farm Assessment Record
M293B	Residential Assessment Record
M294B	Commercial Assessment Record
M294FFB	Farm Assessment Record
M321	Notice to Taxpayer
M322	Board of Review Record
M323	Minutes of Board of Review
M582	Bond Register
M583	Insurance Policy Record
M584	Employee Earnings Ledger
M585	Surety Bond Register
M728A	Assessment Roll
M728L	Assessment Roll
M733	Notice of Increase in Assessment
M1000	Cancelled Coupon Sheets
MV1001	Insurance Records

POLICE FORMS

M64	Complaint Forms
M65	Recording Jail Inmates & Arrests File Card
M66	Violation File Cards
M67	Traffic Violations Summons
M70	Arrest Record Card
M71	Jail Inmate Medical Record

| M72 | Analysis of Inmate Funds |
| M80 | Bad Check Notice |

WATER DEPARTMENT FORMS

| M153 | Water Meter Sheets |
| M154 | Water Ledger Sheets |

PARKS AND RECREATION

Although parks and recreation facilities are a service to township residents, it is felt that it more properly belongs in the chapter on Environmental Protection and Control. Therefore no citations are listed in this chapter.

COUNTY FAIRS

The county fair, which is still considered to be the big event of the year in many communities, must have the total effort of the whole county if it is to be successful. Adequate facilities must be provided, maintained and continually improved. The county board of commissioners may appropriate or borrow money and levy taxes for this purpose. Townships are permitted to make donations of money, material or labor for the purpose of improving fairground property.

Note: See the section on Agricultural, Industrial and Other Interests in chapter ten for additional citations in this area of concern.

JOINT ACTION
Act No. 228, P.A. 1911 - Fairs and Exhibitions

AN ACT to authorize the boards of supervisors of the several counties in this state to borrow money, and issue bonds therefor, for the purchase of land and improve the same by the erection of buildings and other improvements thereon or for the purpose of improving and erecting buildings upon lands already purchased and held by said county to be used for the purpose of holding thereon fairs and exhibitions of an agricultural character.

MCLA 46.111 Fairs; borrowing, land improvements; donations; referendum. [MSA 5.411]

Sec. 1. The boards of supervisors of the several counties in this state are hereby authorized ... **for the purpose of improving such lands the said boards may receive donations of money, material or labor from any person, township, city or village within the county: ...**

AFFECTS JOINT ACTION
Act No. 12, P.A. 1921, 1st Ex. Sess. - Fair Property
Held in Trust, Mortgage

AN ACT to authorize and empower the board of supervisors of any county holding in trust the property of any agricultural society organized under any law of this state, to execute and deliver in conjunction with such society, a mortgage or mortgages covering all or any of the real estate of such society in order to provide means for the payment of its obligations contracted for or arising from, the maintenance of such fair.

MCLA 46.121 Mortgage of fair property held by board in trust. [MSA 5.421]

AFFECTS JOINT ACTION
Act No. 13, P.A. 1927 - Fair Property Held in Trust,
Purchase

AN ACT to authorize and empower the board of supervisors of any county holding in trust the property of any agricultural society organized under any law of this state, to purchase and acquire all or any part of the beneficial interest of such agricultural society in such property or any part thereof so held in trust, and to have and hold such property in fee.

MCLA 46.131 Purchase of fair property held in trust. [MSA 5.431]

AFFECTS JOINT ACTION
Act No. 36, P.A. 1917 - County Owned Fairgrounds

AN ACT authorizing the board of supervisors in a county owning its own fair grounds to make appropriations for the construction and maintenance of buildings, fences and driveways on said fair grounds.

MCLA 46.141 Fairgrounds; appropriation. [MSA 5.441]

AFFECTS JOINT ACTION
Act No. 11, P.A. 1929 - County Owned Fairgrounds

AN ACT authorizing boards of supervisors, in counties where the title to fairgrounds is held by the county, to take over the management and control for the purpose of conducting agricultural fairs thereon, and to provide for the spreading of a tax for same.

MCLA 46.151 Fair; management by supervisors. [MSA 5.451]

MCLA 46.152 Fair board. [MSA 5.452]

MCLA 46.153 Management regulations; admission; power to tax. [MSA 5.453]

AFFECTS JOINT ACTION
Act No. 188, P.A. 1921 — Societies Receiving Public Funds

AN ACT to require the secretary of agricultural or other fair associations receiving aid from public funds to make, publish and file fiscal reports.

MCLA 453.341 Report of fair association receiving public funds; contents. [MSA 21.511]

MCLA 453.342 Same; publication; filing. [MSA 21.512]

MCLA 453.343 Same; failure to make, false statements; penalties. [MSA 21.513]

MARKETS, EXHIBITION AREAS, TOWNSHIP SCALES

Although there is no statutory provision for a township to create a market authority, nonetheless a township may appropriate money for the establishment, maintenance, management and control of township scales for the weighing of farm produce and other purposes.

Township residents are permitted by law to sell their produce in any public market which may be established by a city. Such markets, as well as exhibition areas for commercial, industrial and agricultural products, may be constructed within or without a city's limits. The statute governing markets specifically requires adherence to local zoning and other police ordinances and stipulates that the property is not exempt from taxation.

Note: See the section on Agricultural, Industrial and Other Interests in chapter ten for additional citations in this area of concern.

Act No. 123, P.A. 1917 - Township Scales

AN ACT to authorize townships to appropriate money for the establishment of township scales, for the weighing of farm produce and other purposes; and to provide for the maintenance, management and control of such scales when established.

MCLA 41.491 Scales, control; tax levy. [MSA 5.2401]

Act No. 185, P.A. 1956 - Market Authority Act

AN ACT to authorize cities to establish market authorities; to provide the powers and duties of such authorities; to provide that such authorities are not tax exempt; to authorize agreements with the United States; and to provide penalties for violations.

MCLA 123.671 Market authority act; short title. [MSA 5.2770(101)]

MCLA 123.672 Same; construction of act. [MSA 5.2770(102)]

MCLA 123.673 Market authority; establishment, powers, areas. Definitions. Site; board of directors; financing; profits; construction, repair, ornamentation. [MSA 5.2770(103)]

MCLA 123.674 Same; board of directors, powers. [MSA 5.2770(104)]

MCLA 123.675 Same; limitations on operations. [MSA 5.2770(105)]

Sec. 5. The following limitations shall govern the operations of the authority and its board of directors:
(1) The authority shall be subject to all the zoning, building, fire, sanitary, health and other police ordinances and regulations of the state and political subdivisions in which it is established. ...

MCLA 123.676 Same; (bonding) powers. [MSA 5.2770(106)]

MCLA 123.677 Same; acquisition of property, market deemed public improvement. [MSA 5.2770(107)]

MCLA 123.678 Same; property subject to taxation. [MSA 5.2770(108)]

MCLA 123.679 - 123.680 [MSA 5.2770(109) - 5.2770(110)]

JOINT ACTION
Act No. 70, P.A. 1955 - City Exhibition Areas

AN ACT to authorize cities to acquire and operate exhibition areas for commercial, industrial and agricultural products; ...

MCLA 123.651 Exhibition areas for display of commercial, industrial and agricultural products; locations, gifts. [MSA 5.2770(81)]

MCLA 123.652 - 123.655 [MSA 5.2770(82) - 5.2770(85)]

TOWNSHIP OBLIGATIONS WITH REGARD TO SOCIAL SERVICES

It may be surprising to some how many areas a township may become involved in with regard to social services. However, we would caution that great care be taken that no public monies be contributed to private charitable or service organizations, no matter how worthy they may be, since this is specifically prohibited by law.

Mental and emotional problems have more and more become recognized as a local responsibility. Although children are the most important asset of a community, they are also the source of many problems. Psychological and criminal research indicates that a young person who is involved in wholesome activities is less likely to run afoul of the rules of society and family. Thus it has been made possible for townships to provide financial support to child guidance and community mental health clinics, participate in rehabilitation work camps for juveniles and operate their own youth activity centers. Also, since fire safety standards in child care institutions are of utmost importance, townships may either establish their own fire safety ordinance or enforce state standards. The state curfew law or a local curfew ordinance is another tool which local government may use when necessary to curb juvenile delinquency. State law also provides for reporting and care of battered children.

Act No. 116, P.A. 1903 - Rabies Treatment

AN ACT to provide for the prevention of rabies in indigent persons.

MCLA 329.121 Poor persons; treatment, expenses. [MSA 14.331]

JOINT ACTION
Act No. 13, P.A. 1944, 1st Ex. Sess. - Children's Clinic

AN ACT to authorize county boards of supervisors and local governing bodies to appropriate moneys to child guidance clinics and community mental health clinics providing service for children and/or adults.

MCLA 722.481 Child guidance and community mental health clinics, financing. [MSA 25.265]

JOINT ACTION
Act No. 137, P.A. 1921 - Contract Power of Counties

AN ACT authorizing and empowering counties of this state to contract with agencies, institutions and hospitals licensed by the state board of corrections and charities for the aid, care, support, maintenance, treatment, cure or relief of children.

MCLA 722.501 Care of children; contracts by board of supervisors, expenses, tax. [MSA 25.361]

MCLA 722.502 Approval of contracts. [MSA 25.362]

MCLA 722.503 Probate judge, duties. [MSA 25.363]

MCLA 722.504 Forfeiture of license, effect on contracts. [MSA 25.364]

MCLA 722.505 Construction of act. [MSA 25.365]

JOINT ACTION
Act No. 47, P.A. 1944, 1st Ex. Sess. - Child Welfare Agencies and Homes

AN ACT to provide for the licensing of child welfare agencies and for the regulation and supervision of the care and placement of minor children in the private homes of persons unrelated to them; and to provide penalties for the violation of the provisions of this act.

MCLA 722.101 Definitions. [MSA 25.358(1)]

MCLA 722.102 Standards of child care. Rules; enforcement. Educational programs, teachers, equipment, special services. Cooperation with other agencies. [MSA 25.355(2)]

MCLA 722.103 Licenses; application, form; issuance; provisional licenses. [MSA 25.358(3)]

MCLA 722.104 Examination; inspection of buildings; records; reports; children not placed by court or agency; notice of termination of care; records confidential. [MSA 25.358(4)]

MCLA 722.105 Revocation or denial of renewal of license; notice, hearing. [MSA 25.358(5)]

MCLA 722.106 Appeal; transcript, stay of action. [MSA 25.358(6)]

MCLA 722.107 Placement of children in family homes. [MSA 25.358(7)]

MCLA 722.108 Misdemeanor; penalty. [MSA 25.358(8)]

Act No. 98, P.A. 1964 - Physical Injuries to Children, Reports.

AN ACT to require the reporting of certain injuries to certain minors; to provide immunity for certain persons making such reports; to provide rules of evidence in certain cases and to provide a penalty for violation of this act.

Note: Provisions superseded as to persons over 18, see **MCLA 722.53** [MSA 25.244(53)] .

MCLA 722.571 Physician's examination of injured child under 17; report; release from hospital as endangering child's health or welfare, physician's report, procedure. [MSA 14.564(1)]

Note: This will apply to any township hospital and police officer.

Act No. 41, P.A. 1960 - Curfew

AN ACT to regulate the hours that children under the age of 16 years may be in or on the public streets, highways, alleys and parks; and to prescribe penalties for violations of the provisions of this act.

MCLA 722.751 Curfew for 12 year old children. [MSA 28.342(1)]

MCLA 722.752 Curfew for 16 year old children. [MSA 28.342(2)]

MCLA 722.753 Aiding underage children to violate law, misdemeanor. [MSA 28.342(3)]

MCLA 722.754 Local regulation as to curfew. [MSA 28.342(4)]

Sec. 4. Nothing in this act shall be deemed to limit any powers now or hereafter possessed by law by any township, charter township, city or village to regulate by ordinance a curfew of minors.

Act No. 288, P.A. 1939 - Probate Code, Ch. XII A - Juveniles and Juvenile Division

MCLA 712A.14 Juvenile taken into custody; release to parents, guardian, or custodian; hearing; order of court; placement. [MSA 27.3178(598.14)]

Note: Next sections continue regarding terms of confinement, methods, limitations, etc.

JOINT ACTION
Act No. 179, P.A. 1967 - Youth Centers

AN ACT to authorize a county, city, village or township to levy taxes and expend funds for youth centers.

MCLA 123.461 Municipal, financing operations. [MSA 5.3440(1)]

JOINT ACTION
Act No. 17, P.A. 1965 - Rehabilitation Work Camps

AN ACT authorizing the establishing of county rehabilitation work camps for the custody of juvenile offenders and the powers and duties of the board of supervisors.

MCLA 722.761 Board of supervisors; power to operate camps. [MSA 25.399(11)]

MCLA 722.762 Agreements with a county maintaining work camps. [MSA 25.399(12)]

JOINT ACTION
Act No. 11, P.A. 1960 - Old Age Assistance

AN ACT to establish a state commission on aging; to provide for the appointment of a director and such advisory committees as the commission deems necessary; to prescribe the powers and duties of the commission and its director; to provide for the administration and financing of demonstration programs for the aging; and to repeal certain acts and parts of acts.

MCLA 400.501 - 400.507 [MSA 2.624 - 2.630]

MCLA 400.508 Commission on aging; duties, recommendations. [MSA 2.631]

MCLA 400.509 Same; demonstration programs. [MSA 2.632]

MCLA 400.510 Same; cooperation with federal government. [MSA 2.633]

MCLA 400.511 Same; gifts (to state); **acceptance, reversion.** [MSA 2.634]

MCLA 400.512 Same; appropriations, demonstration programs (money from townships). [MSA 2.635]

MCLA 400.513 Repeal; transfer of records of legislative advisory council on problems of the aging. [MSA 2.636]

JOINT ACTION
Act No. 238, P.A. 1939 — Township Contingent Fund

AN ACT to authorize the use of surplus moneys in the contingent fund of townships for school purposes in certain cases.

MCLA 388.321 Township contingent fund, use for lunches to pupils, retiring indebtedness, etc.; election; petition. [MSA 15.91(4)]

552

MCLA 388.322 Same; vote at election; ballots; transfer of moneys.
MSA 15.91(5)

JOINT ACTION
Act No. 238, P.A. 1964 — Demonstration Education

AN ACT to authorize the state of Michigan, boards of supervisors, local governing boards and school districts to appropriate moneys to foster and maintain demonstration educational and work experience programs through a special job upgrading program for unemployed, out of work school dropouts; define the powers and duties of the superintendent of public instruction; and to provide for appropriations.

MCLA 395.171 Demonstration education and work experience programs; subsidized work for school drop outs. MSA 15.833(1)

MCLA 395.172 Same; rules and regulations; approval for state grants; eligibility of applicants. MSA 15.833(2)

MCLA 395.173 Same; participation by local school district. MSA 15.833(3)

MCLA 395.174 Same; job upgrading program; local community, subsidizing. MSA 15.833(4)

MCLA 395.175 Same; appropriation, report. MSA 15.833(5)

JOINT ACTION
Act No. 195, P.A. 1972 — Commission on Indian Affairs

AN ACT to provide for the creation and functions of the commission on Indian affairs; and to repeal certain acts and parts of acts.

MCLA 16.711 — 16.714 MSA 3.547(101) — 3.547(104)

MCLA 16.715 Executive Director; employees; access to decision making bodies; consultations and cooperation with other agencies; legislative recommendations; grants and gifts; reports.
MSA 3.547(105)

MCLA 16.719 – 16.720 [MSA 3.547(109) – 3.547(110)]

Act No. 22, P. A. 1968 – Alcoholism Program

AN ACT to protect the public health; to define alcoholism; to authorize educational and preventive programs concerned with alcoholism and programs for the treatment and rehabilitation of alcoholics; to define the duties of the department of public health; to establish a state advisory board of alcoholism and define its powers and duties; and to repeal certain acts and parts of acts.

MCLA 325.701 Definitions. [MSA 18.1031(1)]

MCLA 325.702 Alcoholism program; duty and power of director. [MSA 18.1031(2)]

MCLA 325.703 State advisory board of alcoholism; appointment, term, qualifications, compensation, duties. [MSA 18.1031(3)]

MCLA 325.704 Cooperation with federal agencies; use of federal funds. [MSA 18.1031(4)]

MCLA 325.705 Gifts or grants; disposition. [MSA 18.1031(5)]

MCLA 325.706 Repeal. [MSA 18.1031(6)]

MCLA 325.707 Effective date. [MSA 18.1031(7)]

JOINT ACTION
Act No. 3, P.A. 1971 - Drug Abuse and Alcoholism

AN ACT to authorize the state of Michigan and the governing bodies of counties, cities, villages and townships to contract for and expend funds for the curbing of drug abuse.

MCLA 335.21 Prevention; treatment. [MSA 18.1065(1)]

Sec. 1. The state of Michigan and the governing bodies of any ... township may contract for and expend funds for the prevention of drug abuse and for the counseling and treatment of drug abusers. The state of Michigan and any such ... township may contract on its own behalf or may enter into such contracts with the governing body of a county or the governing bodies of other cities, villages and townships to accomplish such purposes.

JOINT ACTION
Act No. 197, P.A. 1971 - Drug Abuse and Alcoholism

AN ACT to create an agency on drug abuse and alcoholism problems; to prescribe powers and duties; to establish an advisory commission; to abolish certain boards and offices; and to provide appropriations and reversion of appropriations.

MCLA 335.31 Definitions. [MSA 15.467(1)]

MCLA 335.32 Office of drug abuse and alcoholism, creation, term; director of office, appointment, commission chairman, compensation. [MSA 15.467(2)]

MCLA 335.33 Purpose and duties of office. [MSA 15.467(3)]

MCLA 335.34 Proposed program, review, approval. [MSA 15.467(4)]

MCLA 335.35 Intervention in state police criminal investigations or law enforcement activities (not permitted). [MSA 15.467(5)]

MCLA 335.36 Annual report to legislature. [MSA 15.467(6)]

MCLA 335.37 Advisory commission on drug abuse and alcoholism, establishment, membership, officers, vacancies, compensation. [MSA 15.467(7)]

MCLA 335.38 Duties of commission. [MSA 15.467(8)]

MCLA 335.39 Duties of departments and agencies of executive branch of government. [MSA 15.467(9)]

MCLA 335.40 State advisory board of alcoholism, transfer of duties and functions. [MSA 15.467(10)]

MCLA 335.41 Office of drug abuse in department of mental health abolished; equipment, records, and supplies transferred; appropriation, disposition. [MSA 15.467(11)]

MCLA 335.42 - 335.45 [MSA 15.467(12) - 15.467(15)]

Meeting the needs of the handicapped requires a great deal of compassion and understanding. The state government has established a commission on the employment of the handicapped, with special emphasis upon promoting increased public and private interest and support and the formulation of local committees for that purpose.

JOINT ACTION
Act No. 11, P.A. 1968 - Commission on Employment of the Handicapped

AN ACT to establish a commission on employment of the handicapped; and to prescribe its powers and duties.

MCLA 395.301 Establishment of commission. [MSA 15.1026(1)]

MCLA 395.302 Members; terms; vacancies; expenses. [MSA 15.1026(2)]

MCLA 395.303 Duties. [MSA 15.1026(3)]

MCLA 395.304 Funds; grants, gifts, acceptance. [MSA 15.1026(4)]

MCLA 395.305 Cooperation of departments and agencies. [MSA 15.1026(5)]

MCLA 395.306 Annual report, recommendations. [MSA 15.1026(6)]

MCLA 395.307 Rules and regulations. [MSA 15.1026(7)]

JOINT ACTION
Act No. 280, P.A. 1939 - Social Welfare Act

AN ACT to protect the welfare of the people of this state; to provide general relief, hospitalization, infirmary and medical care to poor or unfortunate persons; to provide for compliance by this state with the provisions of the social security act; to provide protection, welfare and services to aged persons, dependent children, the blind, and the permanently and totally disabled; to administer programs and services for the prevention and treatment of delinquency, dependency and neglect of children; to create a state department of social services; to prescribe the powers and duties of the department; to provide for the interstate and intercounty transfer of dependents; to create county and district departments of social services; to create within certain county departments, bureaus of social aid and certain divisions and offices thereunder; to prescribe the powers and duties of the departments, bureaus and officers; to provide for appeals in certain cases; to prescribe the powers and duties of the state department with respect to county and district departments; to make an appropriation; and to prescribe penalties for the violation of the provisions of this act.

MCLA 400.10 Cooperation with federal government under social security act; powers and duties of social welfare commission. MSA 16.410

Sec. 10. ... The commission is hereby authorized to cooperate with the proper departments or agencies of the federal government and with all other departments or agencies of the state and local governments, and to supervise ... The commission shall be authorized and empowered to adopt any rules and regulations and enter into any agreement or agreements with local units of government as may be necessary to ...

MCLA 400.14 State department of social welfare; additional powers and duties. Allocation of state and federal aid. Distribution of social security aid. Juvenile detention facilities; child welfare programs. Placement of children. Blind. Assistance to other agencies; rules for eligibility for aid or service. Statistics; fact-finding studies; reports. Contested claims against counties; determination of settlement or domicile. General powers; codification of laws. County infirmaries, juvenile detention places, inspection orders (sanitation, fire protection, enforcement). **Schedule of payment for care and maintenance, rules and regulations. Cruelty to children; study; action; rules and regulations** (other governmental units; participation, contracts). MSA 16.476

MCLA 400.14c Juvenile detention facilities; child welfare programs. MSA 16.414(3)

MCLA 400.71 Distinction between township, city, and county poor; abolition. MSA 16.471

MCLA 400.76 Liability of relatives for support; act not to relieve. Construction of act. Action for reimbursement of county granting aid. Prosecuting attorney; duties; legally responsible relative in another state; reciprocal enforcement of support. MSA 16.476

The national government, seeking to honor the men and women who have served in the armed forces, has from time to time brought about the necessity for states through legislation and local units through ordinance to adopt provisions to create, operate and maintain local councils of veterans' affairs. The township board may financially support such endeavors.

JOINT ACTION
Act No. 77, P.A. 1945 - Local Councils of Veterans' Affairs

AN ACT to provide for local councils of veterans' affairs; and to authorize appropriations by counties, cities, villages and townships.

MCLA 35.11 Appropriation for local councils of veterans' affairs. MSA 4.1471

Act No. 214, P.A. 1899 — Veterans' Relief Fund

AN ACT to provide relief outside of the soldiers' home for honorably discharged indigent soldiers, sailors, marines, nurses and members of women's auxiliaries and the indigent wives, widows and minor children of such indigent or deceased soldiers, sailors, marines, nurses and members of women's auxiliaries, and to repeal certain acts and parts of acts.

MCLA 35.21 Veterans' relief fund; county tax; disbursement. MSA 4.1051

MCLA 35.22 Soldiers' relief commission; membership, term, appointment, compensation, removal. [MSA 4.1052]

MCLA 35.23 Same; determination of relief to be granted; judicial review. [MSA 4.1053]

Sec. 3. The supervisor of each township ... shall, on or before the last Monday in September in each year, make and place in the hands of the soldiers' relief commission of the county, a list of all the persons entitled to relief under the provisions of this act, and the ...

MCLA 35.24 Provision for emergency relief, limit. [MSA 4.1054]

Sec. 4. Whenever any emergency shall arise in case of sickness, accident or death, which, in the opinion of any (township) supervisor, needs relief, such supervisor ...

MCLA 35.25 Annual report of commission; contents. [MSA 4.1055]

MCLA 35.26 Unexpended moneys, transfer to general fund. [MSA 4.1056]

Note: This section outdated as of April, 1900.

MCLA 35.27 Administration of oaths (by commissioners). [MSA 4.1057]

One of the holdovers from the past is the publicly supported township band. The question of having a band must be submitted to the qualified electors through a referendum. Although the township board may levy up to two mills for the maintenance and employment of such band, referendum is required if the levy exceeds the fifteen mill limitation.

Act No. 230, P.A. 1923 - Band, Village or Township

AN ACT to authorize and empower villages and townships of this state, also cities having a population not exceeding 50,000 inhabitants, to levy a tax for the maintenance and employment of a band for musical purposes for the benefit of the public, provided said special ques-

*tion is submitted to the duly qualified voters of such vil-
lages, townships or cities and adopted or agreed to by a
majority vote of those participating in said election.*

MCLA 123.861 Referendum. [MSA 5.3391]

MCLA 123.862 Band maintenance; annual tax, limit. [MSA 5.3392]

MCLA 123.863 Existing bands (relinquishment of authority); **adoption of provisions of act, procedure.** [MSA 5.3393]

TOWNSHIP PROPERTY - PURCHASE, RENTAL, USE

The legislature has long recognized the economical advantages
of governmental cooperation in establishing all kinds of services,
including buildings. The following statutes provide various methods for funding the acquisition of lands and buildings, and should
be carefully studied with regard to their effect on other statutes
included in this chapter, particularly the section on Township
Buildings, and especially regarding **Act No. 31, P.A. 1948 - Authorization for Joint Public Buildings (MCLA 123.951 through 123.965)**
[MSA 5.301(1) THROUGH 5.301(15)], which provides for a township
building authority.

Private corporations, when they construct buildings, often
charge back into the cost of production reasonable amounts for
rental or lease of its facilities to its various agencies. Many Michigan townships have elected to take advantage of this modern
method and now have beautiful up-to-date accommodations for their
administrative and operational services, including various departments such as water and sewer, fire and police, public works,
planning and zoning, libraries, etc. Under certain conditions,
facilities in a township building may be rented to other governmental entities. Within forty years, sometimes less, the mortgage
can be burned and the property will belong to the people free and
clear. The great thing about it is that there is no cost to the residents through tax levy.

When township facilities are leased or rented, however, care
must be exercised that funds received are not commingled with
other township monies. Fees should be established that will adequately cover costs, including maintenance, repairs, utilities, etc.,

and a reasonable return upon the investment for purposes of recapitalization.

Township officials who are interested in serving the best interests of their constituents should take a long hard look at the alternatives open to them in this area. A good way to get started after that is to appoint a citizen committee to study township needs and how they can best be met through the opportunities which have been made available by the legislature.

AFFECTS JOINT ACTION
Act No. 177, P.A. 1943 - Public Improvement Funds

AN ACT to provide for the creation of a fund or funds in political subdivisions for acquiring, constructing, extending, altering, repairing or equipping public improvements or public buildings; to provide for appropriations, credits and transfers to said fund or funds; and to provide for the disbursement thereof.

MCLA 141.261 Funds for public improvements or buildings.
MSA 5.2770(1)

MCLA 141.262 Same; transfer or encumbrance. MSA 5.2770(2)

MCLA 141.263 Same; allocation of miscellaneous revenues; sale of lands. MSA 5.2770(3)

MCLA 141.264 Tax limitation. MSA 5.2770(4)

MCLA 141.265 Powers additional; "political subdivision" construed. MSA 5.2770(5)

JOINT ACTION
Act No. 99, P.A. 1933 - Municipal Property, Purchase on Installments

AN ACT to authorize contracts and agreements of incorporated villages, townships and cities for the purchase of lands and property for public purposes; to validate such contracts or agreements heretofore entered into; to provide for the payment of the purchase price thereof; and to prescribe the use of such lands and property.

MCLA 123.721 Village, township, and city property purchased on installment plan; validation of contracts, taxes, surplus lands. MSA 5.3461

MCLA 123.722 Same; use and leasing. MSA 5.3462

MCLA 123.723 Same; control and maintenance. MSA 5.3463

Sec. 3. The legislative body of any such village and/or township and/or city shall at all times have control of said property and shall maintain the same for public use and purposes.

JOINT ACTION
Act No. 179, P.A. 1962 - Municipal Rental Property

AN ACT to authorize the erection of municipal buildings which contain facilities for rental.

MCLA 124.51 Municipal buildings; rental of facilities to other governmental entities. MSA 5.2350

Sec. 1. When any municipality erects any building, whether financed by a sinking fund or by issuance of bonds, it may include in the building facilities for rental to any other governmental entity.

Note: An area annexed to a village or city quite often includes property on which township buildings are located. The following statute permits continued use of the buildings by the township. Although it does not specifically express the need for it, caution dictates that there should be continuity of use. The annexing government should not be provided with any technical advantage which could materialize as a result of the township either temporarily or permanently abandoning use of the building(s).

AFFECTS JOINT ACTION
Act No. 45, P.A. 1941 - Township Buildings in Cities

AN ACT to provide for the use by the township, for township purposes, of any building or buildings owned by said township, but located at the present time within the corporate limits of any incorporated village or city, which includes within its limits, lands upon which said building or buildings are located and forming a part of said township.

MCLA 41.221 Township buildings in cities; use by township. MSA 5.2378

Sec. 1. Whenever a township in this state shall be the owner of lands within said township upon which are located building or buildings used for township purposes, which lands subsequent to the erection of said building or buildings were included within the limits of any incorporated village or city, the said township is hereby authorized and empowered to use said building or buildings for any and all township purposes, including elections, and any and all resolutions or actions by the said township, or any of its officers, in said building or buildings shall be as legal in all respects as though said building or buildings were located within the corporate limits of said township.

ORDINANCES

The ordinance is to the township what a statute is to the state -- in other words, it is the law. Although the township receives one third of fines and costs levied and collected, these usually are insufficient to cover costs of prosecution and a police department.

Township ordinances are the usual "gateway" for establishing delivery systems for services and utilities, as well as providing for the safety and welfare of the residents. It is therefore of utmost importance that much study, research and consultation go into preparation of the content of any ordinance or amendment to an ordinance to make sure that it does what is intended and still meets all requirements of the law. Equally important are the adoption, recording and filing procedures which must be followed.

Many statutes call for ordinances to implement and enforce their terms, thus requiring careful study of the procedures stipulated in each instance. Also, we are including next several citations which deal specifically with ordinances in general, along with procedure for adopting a zoning ordinance which may be used as a model.

One of the most vital steps in the zoning ordinance procedure is the public hearing. There must be at least one such hearing, but

563

this does not mean additional sessions cannot be held -- in fact, it may be to the township board's advantage to hold several additional informal public meetings, either before or after the legal hearing. This is particularly true in the area of land use planning and zoning.

Logic and common sense must guide the conduct of public hearings. This is the place where the citizen can let the public official know how he feels about something. He should not be cut off or his opinions ignored, although on the other hand, care must be taken not to let an unruly person or group disrupt the meeting. There must be absolute honesty and sincerity evidenced by the leadership. Citizens must be assured that their opinions will be considered and incorporated whenever possible. And when this is not possible, they must understand why. In view of this, it is imperative that public hearing proceedings be carefully and fully recorded.

If township officials have done their homework, they will be able to answer most questions that arise. If something cannot be answered, however, then perhaps another hearing is in order to allow time to obtain additional facts. Officials responsive to their constituents will realize that if the project under discussion creates much dissension at the meeting, it is either because there is misunderstanding of the purpose, that it does not properly meet the need, or it is something that is not desired at all. Thus the public hearing provides a forum for clearing up misunderstandings, making any necessary changes, or deciding to drop the project.

Once over the hurdle of determination of need and of proper content of an ordinance or amendment, equal care must be given to the procedure for final adoption, recording and filing. Too often a case has been thrown out of court because the lawful procedure was not followed in every minute detail. One of these steps is that the township clerk "shall record the ordinance in a book of ordinances kept by him (her) for that purpose ..." Thus a separate, special ordinance book is an absolute requirement, and every ordinance or amendment to an ordinance must be recorded in it. **Those townships which do not have such a book should immediately review all of their past minutes and prepare an ordinance book which will meet statutory requirements. It is too late to do anything about this on the day that a township clerk is subpoenaed to appear in court with the township ordinance book!**

JOINT ACTION
Act No. 246, P.A. 1945 - Township Ordinances

AN ACT to authorize township boards to adopt ordinances and regulations to secure the public health, safety and general welfare; to provide for the establishment of a township police department; to provide for the policing of townships by the county sheriff; to provide penalties; and to repeal all acts and parts of acts in conflict therewith.

MCLA 41.181 Adoption of ordinances; subjects of ordinances; enforcement, police, sheriff, deputies; application of ordinances; costs. MSA 5.45(1)

Sec. 1. The township board of a township may, at a regular or special meeting by a majority of the members elect of the township board, adopt ordinances regulating the public health, safety and general welfare of persons and property, fire protection, the licensing or use of bicycles, traffic and parking of vehicles, sidewalk maintenance and repairs, the licensing and regulating of hawkers, vendors, peddlers, solicitors, circuses, carnivals and public amusements, and provide penalties for the violation thereof, and shall enforce the same and may for that purpose employ and establish a police department with full power and authority to enforce all local township ordinances and state laws, provided that in the event state laws are to be enforced, such townships shall have a law enforcement unit composed of at least 1 full time person, all members of which shall have at least 2 weeks prior police work experience or its equivalent as approved by the township board or may by resolution appropriate funds and call upon the sheriff of the county in which the township is located to provide special police protection for the township. It shall be the duty of the sheriff, when so called upon, to provide special police protection for the township and to enforce all local township ordinances, to the extent that township funds are appropriated therefor. Special township deputies appointed by the sheriff shall be under the jurisdiction of and solely responsible to the sheriff. Ordinances regulating traffic and parking of vehicles shall not be in contravention of the provisions of Act No. 300 of the Public Acts of 1949, as amended, being sections 257.1 to 257.923 MSA 9.1801 TO 9.2623 *of the Compiled Laws of 1948.*

Ordinances so enacted may apply to the streets, roads, highways, or portions of the township as shall be determined by the board, or may be limited to specified platted lands within the township, and with respect thereto shall be valid and enforceable whether the roads and streets therein have been dedicated to public use or not. Township boards of townships enacting ordinances hereunder may accept contributions from duly constituted representatives of the platted lands benefited by such ordinances, to defray all administrative and enforcement costs incident thereto.

MCLA 41.182 Publication of ordinances. [MSA 5.45(2)]

Sec. 2. Said ordinances shall be published as provided in Act No. 191 of the Public Acts of 1939 (**MCLA 41.191, 41.192**) [MSA 5.6(1), 5.6(2)] .

MCLA 41.183 Penalties, fines or imprisonments; courts, institution of prosecution; review; costs. [MSA 5.45(3)]

Sec. 3. (1) The township board may in such ordinances provide a penalty for violation thereof, of a fine not exceeding $500.00, or by imprisonment in the county jail not to exceed 90 days, or by both such fine and imprisonment.

(2) If the township lies within a district served by 1 or more municipal courts, prosecutions for the violation of such ordinances shall be instituted in any one of the municipal courts of the district, and in such cases the same right to appeal to the circuit courts shall exist as in cases of violations of the state law cognizable by the municipal court in which the prosecution is instituted. Fines, penalties and forfeitures shall be payable in the same manner and to the same fund as fines for the violation of the laws of the state. Costs shall be paid and reported by such municipal courts in the same manner as is provided for offenses under state law where the prosecution is instituted in a municipal court.

(3) If the township lies within a district served by the district court, prosecutions for the violation of such ordinances shall be instituted in the district court, unless the person accused of violating such an ordinance enters a plea of guilty before a magistrate or a traffic bureau as otherwise provided and authorized by law. Fines and costs imposed or assessed in such an action shall be distributed in accordance with section 8379 of Act No. 236 of the

Public Acts of 1961, as added, being section 600.8379 MSA 27A.8379 *of the Compiled Laws of 1948.*

AFFECTS JOINT ACTION
Act No. 191, P.A. 1939 - Township Ordinances, Publication

AN ACT to provide for the publication of all ordinances passed by any township, to fix the limits of the penalty imposed by such ordinance and for the record thereof.

MCLA 41.191 Township ordinances; publication, effective date, penalty. MSA 5.6(1)

Sec. 1. In all cases where it shall be lawful for any township to pass an ordinance, such ordinance shall contain a provision stating when such ordinance shall take effect. And if an ordinance shall impose a penalty for the violation of any provision thereof, such ordinance shall not take effect until 30 days shall have elapsed after the first publication of such ordinance.

Publication of such ordinance shall be made by causing a true copy thereof to be inserted once in some newspaper circulating within said township, which insertion shall be made within 10 days after the passage thereof.

No penalty imposed shall exceed that imposed by the general law for misdemeanors.

Any ordinance not imposing a penalty for the violation thereof shall take effect immediately after the date of the publication thereof.

MCLA 41.192 Passage, publication, and filing of ordinances, records, time; copies of ordinances, fees. MSA 5.6(2)

Sec. 2. (1) Within 1 week after the first publication of any ordinance as herein provided, the township clerk shall record the ordinance in a book of ordinances kept by him for that purpose and record the date of the passage thereof, the names of the members voting thereon and how each member voted, and file an attested copy of the ordinance with the county clerk. The township clerk shall certify under the ordinance in a blank space provided therefor the date or dates of publication thereof and the name of the news-

paper in which publication was made and the date of filing with the county clerk. ...

AFFECTS JOINT ACTION
Act No. 144, P.A. 1969 - Codification and Publication of Ordinances

AN ACT to provide for the codification and publication of all township ordinances.

MCLA 41.641   Authority to codify; mode of publication; repeals; revision. [MSA 5.45(51)]

Sec. 1. Each township may codify, recodify and continue in code its ordinances in whole or in part, without the necessity of publishing the entire code in full. The ordinance adopting the code, as well as subsequent ordinances repealing, amending, continuing or adding to the code, shall be published as required by law. The ordinance adopting the code may amend, repeal, revise or rearrange ordinances or parts of ordinances by reference by title only.

PROCEDURE FOR ADOPTION OF AN ORDINANCE

The following is adapted from a legal opinion provided by John H. Bauckham of Bauckham, Reed, Lang and Schaefer (MTA Legal Counsel).

In our travels around the state representing various member townships, it has been brought to our attention that a great laxity exists in many townships in the maintenance of zoning ordinance proceedings in sufficient form to support the validity of the ordinance in Circuit Court when the same is being contested or enforced. The same laxity also appears with respect to general police ordinances adopted by townships.

If the rather technical procedure taken to adopt a zoning ordinance cannot be proven, the ordinance will more than likely be set aside by the Circuit Court as invalid. In many cases, the proceedings may have been accurately taken but the documents to prove the same are missing as a result of change of officials, improper record keeping or other reasons. We further believe that in many cases, although the township has retained an attorney to assist them in conducting the proceedings, they have only employed him on an infrequent basis and have attempted to conduct some of the proceedings themselves without the benefit of legal advice. It may also be that in some instances the advice has not been sufficient to fully comply with the statute. In any case, a considerable amount of money has been expended to adopt an ordinance which later appears useless and unenforceable as a result of the foregoing. We believe that no township should attempt the adoption of a zoning ordinance or a zoning ordinance amendment without the benefit of legal counsel throughout the proceedings. The procedure is technical in nature and should not be attempted to be construed by officials not trained in the law.

Michigan statutes, for example, require the township to maintain an official ordinance book, containing all the ordinances of the township, including the zoning ordinance. Each ordinance must be followed by a certificate of the clerk certifying the date of adoption, how each member voted, which should be by roll call vote, and the date and newspaper in which the same was published. We further believe that such ordinance book should also contain, for ease of reference and presentation in evidence in court, the total proceedings employed to adopt a zoning ordinance or a zoning ordinance amendment.

We urge every township that is enforcing a zoning ordinance to take an inventory of its procedure as outlined, and documentation of each step for insertion in the official ordinance book. If it finds that it cannot document such procedure for lack of proper records or other reasons, it should redo the entire proceedings with the guidance of its local attorney, following the steps herein outlined. We cannot emphasize enough the importance of this advice.

OUTLINE OF PROCEDURE TO ENACT A ZONING ORDINANCE BY A GENERAL TOWNSHIP

This procedure is according to Act No. 184, P.A. 1943, as amended – Township Rural Zoning Act. (See the chapter on Planning and Zoning.)

1. The township board adopts a resolution declaring its intent to proceed under the provisions of Act No. 184, P.A. 1943, as amended, and publishes notice of this resolution within ten

569

days after its passage in a newspaper of general circulation in the township.

2. (a) The township must take the aforesaid action if a petition signed by eight percent of the persons who are residents and property owners in the township is filed with it requesting such action to be taken.

   (b) Proof of publication should be preserved by an affidavit of the publisher, filed with the township ordinance book.

3. The township board then appoints a zoning board, consisting of between four and seven members, for initial terms of two and four years each to effect staggered terms.

   (a) No elected officer of the township, nor any employee of the township, shall be a member of the zoning board.

   (b) At least two-thirds of the members shall be electors who reside in and have property assessed for taxes in the township.

   (c) The members may receive up to $25 per diem compensation and not to exceed $5,000 for the entire board expense for each year.

4. The zoning board meets and elects a chairman and secretary and adopts a tentative zoning map and zoning ordinance text.

   (a) A township zoning plan can first be developed but this generally takes considerable time and most townships wish to work on the adoption of a zoning ordinance first.

   (b) The board must meet at least twice annually and precede such meeting by newspaper notice, not more than fifteen days nor less than eight days prior to the meeting.

   (c) The zoning board may engage the services of a township planning expert with the consent of the township board.

5. At least one public hearing preceded by notice in the newspaper at least twice: the first, between twenty and thirty

days prior to the hearing and the second between one and eight days prior thereto; must be held by the zoning board before it submits any recommendations concerning a zoning ordinance and map. In addition, notice of the hearing must be given by certified mail to each electric, gas pipeline and telephone public utility company that registers with the township and to each railroad operating within the township, at least twenty days prior to the hearing. These notices must indicate where the tentative text and maps may be examined.

6. After the hearing (at which everyone must be given an opportunity to be heard), and after the zoning board has determined upon its recommendation, it must submit the proposed ordinance and zoning map to the appropriate county zoning agency for consideration and recommendation.

   (a) This may be a county coordinating committee or a county planning commission.

   (b) Approval of the county is presumed unless, within thirty days of receipt, the county agency has notified the township clerk of its disapproval.

   (c) The action of the county is advisory only and not binding upon the township.

7. The township zoning board, following action by the county, then transmits its proposed ordinance and map to the township board for consideration.

   (a) If the township board desires to make any changes in the recommendations, it must refer the matter back to the zoning board for a second report within a time specified.

   (b) If any property owners file certified mail notice with the township clerk of a desire to be heard in the matter, the township board must grant a hearing to such person or persons and shall request the zoning board to attend the same.

   (c) Thereafter, at any regular or special meeting, the township board may adopt the zoning ordinance and map, with or without any amendments, that have previously been considered by the zoning board and may give the ordinance immediate effect.

(d) We prefer to have townships also hold a hearing before the township board, preceded by informal newspaper notice prior to adoption of the ordinance, to avoid any claim of lack of opportunity to be heard. This, however, is not required by statute.

8. Following the adoption of the ordinance by the township board, it must be published in full, together with the map, within ten days after adoption in a newspaper of general circulation in the township. The published notice should include an opening brief paragraph that the following ordinance was adopted at a regular or special meeting of the township board held on a particular date, to become effective immediately.

9. Within seven days after the publication, the township clerk must record the ordinance and map in a book of ordinances kept for that purpose.

(a) We prefer to also file with such ordinance in such book the various affidavits of publication of notice, together with the affidavits of mailing of notices. This provides for easier proof in court when enforcing the ordinance.

(b) The ordinance must also be followed by a certificate of the township clerk, stating the date of the passage of the ordinance, the names of the township board members voting on the same and how each member voted, the date of the publication of the notice, and the name of the newspaper in which the same was published.

(c) We have also adopted a policy of filing with the ordinance the approval or recommendations of the county concerning the ordinance. In this regard, it is sometimes necessary to furnish such a form of approval to the county to obtain such evidence.

10. The statute provides for a right of referendum on the ordinance if a petition signed by a number of qualified and registered

voters equal to eight percent of the total vote cast for Governor at the last election in the township is filed with the township clerk within thirty days following the passage of the ordinance. The ordinance shall continue in effect until rejected by the electors at the polls. In the event of such a petition being filed, the township board shall provide the manner of submitting the ordinance to the voters for their approval or rejection.

11. Amendments or supplements to the zoning ordinance may be made in the same manner provided for the adoption of the original ordinance except as follows:

    (a) Any property proposed for rezoning must be conspicuously posted with a notice of the hearing before the zoning board at least eight days prior to the hearing.

    (b) The zoning board must also give notice by mail or by personal delivery, to the owner of each property proposed to be rezoned, to all persons to whom any real property within 300 feet of such premises is assessed and to the occupants of all single and two family dwellings within such 300 feet. Addresses are sufficient if taken from the last assessment roll. If the tenant's name is not known, the term "occupant" may be used. An affidavit of mailing or personal delivery should be filed with the zoning board prior to the hearing. The notice must state the time, place, date and purpose of the hearing and should be given at least eight days prior to the hearing date.

    (c) It is only necessary to publish the section or sections to be amended and not the entire ordinance.

    (d) It is not necessary to publish the zoning map but only the legal descriptions of the properties being rezoned.

    (e) Any amendment necessary to conform to a decree of a court may be adopted by the township board and published without referring the same to any other board or agency.

12. A board of appeals should be established by the township board selecting one of its members to serve upon the same. The

chairman of the zoning board is the second member and a third member of the board of appeals is selected by the first two.

PROCEDURE FOR A CHARTER TOWNSHIP

Although there is no specific reference to zoning in the Charter Township Act, it is our opinion that the same proceedings should be followed, as hereinbefore outlined for a regular township, with the exception that under Section 20 of the Charter Township Act, no ordinance can be passed by the township board at the same meeting at which it is introduced. Accordingly, the township board should have at least one additional reading of the ordinance before the meeting at which it is adopted. Section 20 of the Charter Township Act also seems to require that an ordinance be published at least once prior to its passage. This would appear to be a burden but the safer course to follow until clarification is made in the Charter Township Act.

LEGAL ASSISTANCE

Every township may, and should, employ a township attorney to insure that township business is taken care of in accordance with applicable laws. It is advisable that the attorney attend board meetings and that he/she be consulted frequently regarding legal implications of actions which the board takes or contemplates taking. His/her guidance should be accepted and followed implicitly unless there is good reason to believe he/she may be in error. In that case, however, other expert advice should always be obtained. It is safer to spend money in this manner than to pay the cost involved in correcting mistakes -- or even having a whole project negated because it was not done in accordance with the law. This is especially true in the crucial matters of planning and zoning and bond issues.

A day-long lawyers' institute is held each year during the MTA Annual Convention, which is designed specifically around legal problems involving township government. Any township attorney should find these sessions most beneficial in providing them with information to enable them to better serve the needs of their townships.

Legal assistance is also available to member townships through the office of the Michigan Townships Association -- by telephone in emergency situations, but preferably by letter request. Questions may be asked about such things as the proper procedure for developing land use plans, methods for implementation of such plans, and necessary legal procedures to adopt and amend zoning ordinances. Other subjects might be bond issues, riparian rights, division of assets following annexation, or consolidation or incorporation. Some might hinge upon whether or not certain actions taken at township board meetings or meetings of the electorate are legal, or what action must be taken to correct former errors.

So that accurate answers may be assured, it is absolutely essential that each question posed be supported by a clear, concise description of every detail surrounding it. Included should be dates and documentation of all kinds, i.e. copies of deeds, filing documents, plat maps, legal descriptions, prior legal action taken, the statutes involved, the result of public hearings which have been held, minutes of meetings (or at least the pertinent motions and resolutions passed), status of any pending litigation, etc. Of equal importance are any opinions which have been given by local attorneys, decisions of local courts, opinions of professional consultants who may have been involved, and any other documents which may be perused by MTA legal counsel before formulating an opinion.

Such information contributes immeasurably to cutting down research time, thus bringing about quicker replies. Too often an answer has to be couched in an "iffy" manner: "If you did so and so, then you have to do this; however, if you did it another way, then you will have to take this kind of action." This can be avoided by compliance with the paragraph immediately above.

The MTA staff will review each request and if necessary will refer it to MTA legal counsel. Opinions so referred, if determined to be of benefit to townships in general, will be billed to MTA and published in the Michigan Township News; others will be billed directly to the township involved. Individual townships may also directly retain the services of MTA legal counsel. In such case, it becomes an attorney-client relationship and need not include the MTA.

In certain situations, by prior appointment, township officials (including the township attorney whenever possible) may take advantage of bimonthly sessions which MTA legal counsel conducts at MTA headquarters in Lansing. Normally restricted to thirty minutes, in a few cases this may be extended to an hour. In order to provide the best service, the background information described above should be submitted a few days prior to the appointment.

Proper documentation and prestudy of the facts will reduce the time required to render an opinion. If for some reason the information cannot be provided ahead of time, it should at least accompany the officials.

Occasionally an irate township official calls the MTA office asking that an opinion be obtained from the attorney general's office. This is incorrect procedure. That office operates with approximately 150 assistant attorneys representing all state agencies, and is one of the busiest offices in state government. Because of this, one of the rules established by the attorney general is that requests for legal opinions from that office come only from the following persons, in priority as listed: members of the legislature; directors of state agencies, boards and commissions; and prosecuting attorneys. Therefore, if a township official feels there is a need for an attorney general's opinion, his/her best course is to go either to the local prosecutor or to his/her state senator or representative.

A township treasurer may call upon the county prosecuting attorney for advice and counsel regarding duties having to do with taxation matters, and receive such service free of charge. This is the only statute providing for township government to receive free legal assistance.

Act No. 97, P.A. 1954 - Township Attorney

AN ACT to authorize the township board in certain townships to employ an attorney to represent the township in civil matters and in the prosecution of violations of township ordinances.

MCLA 41.661 Township attorney; employment by board; compensation; counter signature of certificates of jurors and witnesses. MSA 5.47

Sec. 1. The township board of any township may employ an attorney to represent the township in civil matters and in the prosecution of violations of township ordinances. Such attorney shall receive such compensation as shall be determined by the township board. In all prosecutions of violations of township ordinances, the township attorney shall countersign the certificates of jurors and witnesses in the same manner as is provided for the countersigning by the prosecuting attorney of the county.

Act No. 206, P.A. 1893 - Assessment, Levy and Collection of Taxes - Miscellaneous Provisions

MCLA 211.100 Prosecuting attorney; duties. [MSA 7.154]

Sec. 100. It shall be the duty of the prosecuting attorney of each county to give his counsel and advice to the county treasurer, the township treasurers, and the supervisors of the county whenever they or any of them deem it necessary for the proper discharge of the duties imposed upon them in this act free of charge.

Chapter V

HEALTH

Township board members also comprise the township board of health and the officers serve in the same capacity as they serve on the township board. One exception is that the clerk is treasurer for perpetual care trust funds for cemeteries. **No township board of health business may be conducted during a regular township board meeting.** The minutes are never, under any circumstances, to be mixed with the township board minutes--**the clerk must keep a separate book for the board of health minutes.**

There are three areas of responsibility for the township board of health--matters regarding people, animal control and cemeteries. Many statutes have been enacted to protect the health of Michigan's citizens. In fact, the first joint-action statute in Michigan was one to allow local governments to cooperate in providing quarantine grounds for persons afflicted with contagious diseases. We found references to it in the Compiled Laws of 1857, and it is still operative.

Contagious diseases in epidemic form used to infect and kill or cripple great numbers of people. Today's alarm is over what has been termed by many as a crisis in the incidence of venereal diseases. True, there is much more than there used to be, but consideration must be given to the fact that there is a greater population involved. Percentage-wise the increase is not so great. We do not mean to imply, however, that there is not a need for great effort to be extended to control and hopefully eventually eliminate its incidence.

578

The proliferation of botulism and other food poisonings is another, perhaps even more serious problem in today's society, calling for strict regulation of food processing and distribution. Related to the health and safety of persons, of course, is the need for regulation and control of birds, fowl, cats, dogs and animals of all kinds. This too is a responsibility of the township board of health, and in some instances of the township board as well.

Tremendous advances in medical science through research and development and enforcement of strict health laws have pretty much eliminated epidemics. However, the potential is always present, and it would be tragic if one were to occur because someone responsible for containing the dangers failed to do his/her job. Each local unit of government must strive to provide the very best health services to its citizens. It takes many people of diversified degrees and professions to make the medical and health impact of a community really effective--a township health officer, township nurse, medical inspectors, bacteriologists and county medical examiners, to name a few. Accessibility of adequate health care facilities is equally important. For additional citations in this area, refer to the section on Hospitals in the chapter on Services, Utilities, Contracts and Ordinances.

The legislature has provided in recent years for county, or even regional or district boards of health, to provide health controls and services, relieving townships of many of their original responsibilities. However, there are still a few townships who must be active across the full range of health activities because there is no county health department available.

Although a number of the citations may at first seem not to affect township government, they are provided for information and guidance of township officials who might be called upon from time to time by the state health commissioner to deal with the administration or enforcement of state health laws.

Note: The State Board of Health was abolished and its duties transferred to the State Health Commissioner. Then the powers and duties of the Department of Health and the State Health Commissioner were transferred to the Department of Public Health.

STATUTES REGARDING PEOPLE

JOINT ACTION
R.S. 1846, c. 35 — Of the Preservation of Public Health: Quarantine, Nuisances and Offensive Trades

GENERAL PROVISIONS

MCLA 327.1 Township board of health; record of proceedings. [MSA 14.61]

Sec. 1. *In every township the township board shall be the board of health. The supervisor shall be the president, and the township clerk shall be the clerk of said board. The clerk shall keep a record of the proceedings of the board in a book to be provided for that purpose at the expense of the township.*

MCLA 327.2 Health officer; appointment, notice to state board; township board, meetings, duties. [MSA 14.62]

Sec. 2. *Every board of health shall appoint and constantly have a health officer, who shall be a well educated physician, and act as the sanitary adviser and executive officer of the board: Provided, That in townships where it is not practicable to secure the services of a well educated and suitable physician, the board may appoint the supervisor or some other person as such health officer. The board of health shall establish his salary or other compensation, and shall regulate and audit all fees and charges of persons employed by them in the execution of the health laws and of their own regulations, except as hereinafter provided in section 15 ... with regard to dangerous communicable diseases. Within 30 days after the annual township meeting in each year, the board of health shall meet for the transaction of business, and shall appoint or reappoint a health officer, and shall immediately cause to be transmitted to the secretary of the state board of health, at Lansing, the full name and postoffice address of such health officer, and a statement whether he is a physician, the supervisor, or some other person not a physician. A special meeting of the board may be called by the order of the president or of any 2 members of said board.*

MCLA 327.3 Rules of local boards; nuisances, sources of infection; violation, penalty. [MSA 14.63]

Sec. 3. The board of health shall make such regulations and by-laws respecting nuisances, sources of filth and causes of sickness, within their respective townships, and on board of any vessels in their ports or harbors, as they shall ...

MCLA 327.4 Same; articles conveying infection; violation, penalty. [MSA 14.64]

MCLA 327.5 — 327.6 [MSA 14.65 — 14.66]

Note: See the citations under heading of Cemeteries at the end of this chapter.

MCLA 327.7 Notice of regulations. [MSA 14.67]

Sec. 7. Notice shall be given by the board of health, of all regulations made by them, by publishing the same in some news - paper of the township, ... (or) by posting them up in 5 public places in such township; and such notice of said regulations shall be deemed legal notice to all persons.

MCLA 327.8 Nuisances and sources of infection; examination by board, eradication. [MSA 14.68]

MCLA 327.9 Same; order to remove; penalty. [MSA 14.69]

MCLA 327.10 Same; failure to remove; removal by board; expenses, assessment; civil liability. [MSA 14.70]

MCLA 327.11 Same; court order to remove. [MSA 14.71]

MCLA 327.12 Refusal of entry for examination of building; complaint. [MSA 14.72]

MCLA 327.13 Same; warrant to sheriff. [MSA 14.73]

MCLA 327.14 Removal permits. [MSA 14.74]

Sec. 14. The board of health may grant permits for the removal of any nuisance, infected article or sick person, within the limits of their township, when they shall think it safe and proper so to do.

MCLA 327.15 Quarantine; removal of person, provisions for care; indigents, payment by county; fees; district boards of health; cases reported. [MSA 14.75]

MCLA 327.16 Same; infected persons not able to be removed. [MSA 14.76]

MCLA 327.17 Travelers from infected districts (in neighboring states), restraint by board; penalty. [MSA 14.77]

MCLA 327.18 Infected persons; warrant for removal and care. [MSA 14.78]

MCLA 327.19 Control of infected goods; issuance of warrant. [MSA 14.79]

MCLA 327.20 Same; storage in impressed houses. [MSA 14.80]

MCLA 327.21 Same; execution of warrant. [MSA 14.81]

MCLA 327.22 Same; owner to pay charges. [MSA 14.82]

MCLA 327.23 Rental, nurse hire, necessaries; county to pay. [MSA 14.83]

MCLA 327.24 Infected persons in jails; removal and care, return on recovery. [MSA 14.84]

MCLA 327.25 Same; order for removal, filing; act not deemed an escape. [MSA 14.85]

MCLA 327.26 Infected persons in poor-houses; removal and care. [MSA 14.86]

QUARANTINE

MCLA 327.27 Quarantine ground; single township. [MSA 14.87]

MCLA 327.28 Same; 2 or more townships. [MSA 14.88]

MCLA 327.29 Quarantine of vessels. [MSA 14.89]

MCLA 327.30 - 327.34 [MSA 14.90 - 14.94]

SMALL POX, AND OTHER DANGEROUS DISEASES

MCLA 327.35 Township communicable disease hospitals.
[MSA 14.95]

MCLA 327.36 Same; rules; consent of adjoining township.
[MSA 14.96]

MCLA 327.37 - 327.45 [MSA 14.97 - 14.106]

Note: The above sections deal with smallpox inoculation, other communicable disease regulations, care of sick persons, public notices.

OFFENSIVE TRADES

MCLA 327.46 Designated places; records; supervision. [MSA 14.107]

Sec. 46. The township board of every township, ... shall ... assign certain places for the exercising of any trade or employment, offensive to the inhabitants, or dangerous to the public health; and they shall forbid the exercise thereof in places not so assigned; and all such assignments shall be entered in the records of the township ... and they may be revoked when ... officers may think proper.

MCLA 327.47 Same; revocation, removal, conditions authorizing (complaint; board of health, other person). [MSA 14.108]

MCLA 327.48 Civil damage suit. [MSA 14.109]

Act No. 137, P. A. 1883 — Isolation of Infected Persons

AN ACT to specify certain duties of health officers and provide for compensation therefor in townships, cities and villages where the health officer is not otherwise instructed by the local board of health.

MCLA 327.151 Isolation of infected persons; health officer, duties. [MSA 14.141]

MCLA 327.152 Health officers; orders, effect; penalty. [MSA 14.142]

MCLA 327.153 Same; compensation. [MSA 14.143]

Act No. 230, P. A. 1885 — Quarantine Regulations

AN ACT to provide for the prevention of the introduction and spread of cholera and other dangerous communicable diseases.

MCLA 329.1 - 329.7 [MSA 14.281 - 14.287]

JOINT ACTION
Act No. 105, P. A. 1927 — Biological Products

AN ACT to protect the public health; to provide for the manufacture and distribution by the state commissioner of health of antitoxin and other biological products for use in the control of communicable diseases; and to repeal Act 370 of Public Acts of 1921.

MCLA 325.41 Biological products, sulphonamides, etc., distribution by state. [MSA 14.41]

Sec. 1. *The state commissioner of health may ... distribute ... (biological products) ... for use in the control of communicable diseases ... health officers and health boards, ... municipal hospitals of the various ... townships of the state may from time to time make requisition on the state ...*

MCLA 325.42 Supplies and labor. [MSA 14.42]

Act No. 146, P. A. 1879 — Vaccination

AN ACT to authorize boards of health of cities, villages and townships, to furnish vaccination to the inhabitants thereof.

MCLA 329.81 Vaccination; public expense. [MSA 14.301]

Act No. 164, P. A. 1949 — Immunization of Children

AN ACT to provide free immunization treatments of children for protection against diphtheria, whooping cough, poliomyelitis, tetanus and smallpox; and to provide free immunization treatments of the public at large for protection against smallpox, poliomyelitis and typhoid in the event of an epidemic or threatened epidemic of said diseases.

MCLA 329.501 Immunization treatments to children against certain diseases; consent. [MSA 14.378(1)]

Sec. 1. ... every ... township ... employing a full-time health officer, shall ...

MCLA 329.502 Free (county) clinics; notice of service, time and place; approval of immunization. [MSA 14.378(2)]

MCLA 329.503 Free treatment to public for protection against smallpox, poliomyelitis and typhoid. [MSA 14.378(3)]

MCLA 329.504 Treatments by public health nurses. [MSA 14.378(4)]

MCLA 329.505 Certificate, contents. [MSA 14.378(5)]

Act No. 314, P. A. 1927 — Tuberculosis

AN ACT to protect the people from tuberculosis, to provide for the care, treatment, isolation and hospitalization of persons afflicted therewith, to provide for the commitment of certain persons afflicted with tuberculosis, to provide for their care, custody and discharge, and to prescribe penalties for the violation of this act.

MCLA 329.401 – 329.405 [MSA 14.361 – 14.365]

Note: A local health officer has responsibility to report any knowledge of individuals having tuberculosis.

Act No. 272, P. A. 1919 — Venereal Diseases

AN ACT to protect the public health; to prevent the spreading of venereal diseases, to prescribe the duties and powers of the state department of health and of local health officers and health boards, and physicians, with reference thereto.

MCLA 329.151 - 329.158 [MSA 14.341 - 14.344]

Act No. 6, P. A. 1942, 2nd Ex. Sess. — Venereal Diseases

AN ACT to protect the people from venereal disease, to provide for the care, treatment, isolation and hospitalization of persons afflicted therewith, to provide for the commitment of certain persons afflicted with venereal disease, to provide for their care, custody and discharge, and to prescribe penalties for the violation of this act.

MCLA 329.201 - 329.208 [MSA 14.345(1) - 14.345(8)]

Act. No. 276, P. A. 1941 — Venereal Prophylactics

AN ACT to safeguard the public health by regulating the sale or the giving away of any articles, devices, appliances, drugs, or other medicinal preparations designed or intended for the purpose of preventing syphilis, gonorrhea, chancroid, or such other diseases as may be defined as genito-infectious or venereal diseases by regulations of the Michigan department of health; and to prescribe penalties for the violation of the provisions of this act.

MCLA 329.251 - 329.255 [MSA 14.353(1) - 14.353(5)]

586

Act No. 238, P. A. 1969 — Venereal Diseases

AN ACT concerning consent by minors to treatment for venereal disease.

MCLA 329.221 Minors' consent to treatment, effect, disaffirmance; liability of parents, guardians, custodians; consent of others, necessity; informing spouse, parents, custodians, guardians. [MSA 14.346(1)]

Act No. 353, P. A. 1919 — Venereal Diseases, Cigar Workers

AN ACT to prohibit the employment of persons affected with infectious or venereal disease in places where cigars are manufactured.

MCLA 329.271 - 329.272 [MSA 14.351 - 14.352]

Act No. 138, P. A. 1958 — Scientific Use of Dead Bodies

AN ACT to create within the state department of health an anatomy committee; to prescribe the powers and duties of the committee in relation to dead human bodies for scientific use; to provide penalties; and to repeal certain acts and parts of acts.

MCLA 328.11 — 328.14 [MSA 14.513(1) — 14.513(4)]

MCLA 328.15 Unclaimed body; availability to anatomy committee; surrender to religious benevolent association. [MSA 14.513(5)]

Sec. 5. Every official of a public institution or ... township officer having charge or control of remains of a person who died leaving no property and would have to be interred at public expense shall ...

MCLA 328.16 — 328.23 [MSA 14.513(6) — 14.513(13)]

Act No. 189, P. A. 1969 — Uniform Anatomical Gift Act

AN ACT authorizing the gift of all or part of a human body after death for specified purposes; and to repeal certain acts and parts of acts.

MCLA 328.261 — 328.269 [MSA 14.523(51) — 14.523(59)]

Note: This act will have special interest to townships where there are community hospitals.

Act No. 95, P. A. 1953 — Consent to Autopsies, Post-Mortems and Dissections

AN ACT to regulate the obtaining of consent to the performance of autopsies, post-mortems and dissections of bodies of deceased persons.

MCLA 328.151 Autopsy, post-mortem or dissection; consent, custody; exceptions. [MSA 14.524]

Act No. 70, P. A. 1954 — Agreements for Disposition of Dead Human Bodies

AN ACT relative to agreements providing for the final disposition of a dead human body; and to prescribe penalties for violations of the provisions of this act.

MCLA 328.201 — 328.203 [MSA 14.527(1) — 14.527(3)]

Act No. 95, P. A. 1970 — Disinterment of Human Remains

AN ACT to provide for lawful authorization for disinterment of human remains; to provide for supervision, permits, court action, records and fees.

MCLA 328.281 Permit for disinterment or removal, necessity, issuance. [MSA 14.523(71)]

Sec. 1. A cemetery authority shall not remove or permit the removal of interred remains unless a permit for the removal has been issued by the local health officer in whose jurisdiction the cemetery is located.

MCLA 328.282 Uniform procedure for issuance of permit.
[MSA 14.523(72)]

MCLA 328.283 Requests for disinterment, affidavit forms, petitioners, recipient of request. [MSA 14.523(73)]

MCLA 328.284 Contents of affidavits. [MSA 14.523(74)]

MCLA 328.285 Failure to obtain consent. [MSA 14.523(75)]

MCLA 328.286 Disinterment order, petition. [MSA 14.523(76)]

MCLA 328.287 Records of affidavits for disinterment.
[MSA 14.523(77)]

Sec. 7.   The affidavit ... retained by the local health officer for ... 5 years.   A duplicate copy of the permit shall be maintained as part of the permanent records of the cemetery from which the deceased was removed.

MCLA 328.288 Fee for issuing permit. [MSA 14.523(78)]

MCLA 328.289 Delayed interment; authorization, necessity, signers, contents. [MSA 14.523(79)]

Sec. 9.   When weather conditions prevent an immediate interment and a period of storage is necessary, the cemetery shall ...

Act No. 248, P. A. 1929 — Disinterment of Remains of War Veterans

AN ACT to authorize the disinterment and removal of remains of war veterans in certain cases, and to prescribe the proceedings to be taken.

MCLA 35.841 - 35.844 [MSA 4.1341 - 4.1344]

Act No. 37, P. A. 1917 — Registration of Cremations

AN ACT to provide for the registration of cremations in Michigan.

MCLA 327.311 Report of cremations; time. [MSA 14.211]

Sec. 1. It shall be the duty of the health officer of each township ... to make a report of the cremations of the dead in their respective localities, or of the dead bodies removed from such township ... for the purpose of incineration in other states, said report to be rendered to the state board of health at the end of each calendar year.

MCLA 327.312 Same; contents. [MSA 14.212]

MCLA 327.313 Separate record. [MSA 14.213]

Sec. 3. ... health officers ... are required ...

MCLA 327.314 Incorporation into state statistics. [MSA 14.214]

MCLA 327.315 Local boards, duties; penalty. [MSA 14.215]

Act No. 268, P. A. 1949 – Mortuary Science

AN ACT to revise and codify the laws relating to the profession of embalming and funeral directing; to create a state board of examiners in mortuary science; to define the powers and duties thereof; to provide for the examination of applicants for embalmers', funeral directors' and mortuary science licenses; to provide for the registration of resident trainees and licensing of embalmers, funeral directors and practitioners in mortuary science to practice their profession in the state of Michigan; to regulate the practice of licensees and the sale of funeral services and funeral merchandise by licensees; to provide for licensing of establishments; to provide regulations for revoking such licenses and resident trainees' certificates; to prohibit participation by licensees in any group plan for giving reduced rates in the purchase of a funeral or funeral merchandise; to prohibit solicitation of funerals by all persons; to prohibit purchase of a vault from a particular person as a condition of burial in a cemetery; to prohibit any owner or operator of a cemetery from owning or operating a funeral establishment and from allowing a funeral establishment to be owned or conducted on cemetery premises; to prescribe civil remedies and criminal penalties against all persons for the violation of this act; and to repeal Act No. 229 of the Public Acts of 1939, as amended, and other acts and parts of acts inconsistent with the provisions of this act.

MCLA 338.861 – 338.866 [MSA 14.509(1) – 14.509(6)]

MCLA 338.867 Registration in local municipalities; transportation permit. [MSA 14.509(7)]

Sec. 7. The owner of any funeral director's or mortuary science license or renewal provided for in this act shall cause a registration card to be filed in ... (the community) *... wherein he intends to practice ... and no transportation permit shall be issued ... to any person who has not filed a registration card: Provided, That any local registrar is hereby authorized to ...*

MCLA 338.868 – 338.869 [MSA 14.509(8) – 14.509(9)]

MCLA 338.870 Violations; hearing, notice; revocation or suspension of license; appeal; non-renewal of license; cooperative plan, scope; removal of dead body, permission; rights of next of kin, insurance. [MSA 14.509(10)]

Sec. 10. ... No public officer or employee, or the official of any public institution, ... public or private hospital, or physician or surgeon, or any other person having a professional relationship with any decedent or coroner or other public official having temporary custody thereof, shall ...

MCLA 338.871 Act repealed. [MSA 14.509(11)]

MCLA 338.872 Cooperative plan; sponsoring, etc., unlawful; capper, steerer or solicitor; vault, purchase, discrimination. [MSA 14.509(12)]

MCLA 338.873 Cemetery associations not to operate mortuary or funeral establishment. [MSA 14.509(13)]

MCLA 338.874 – 338.875 [MSA 14.509(14) – 14.509(15)]

JOINT ACTION
Act No. 248, P. A. 1911 – Medical Milk Commission

AN ACT providing for the incorporation of medical milk commissions, and certification of milk produced under their supervision.

MCLA 327.251 Medical milk commission; members, appointment, powers, term, removal, certificate. [MSA 14.181]

Sec. 1. Authority is hereby given the board of health of any ... township ..., so constituted as to have in its membership 2 or more physicians duly authorized to practice medicine under the laws of this state, to appoint 5 physicians ... a medical milk commission for the purpose of ...

MCLA 327.252 Certificates; contents. [MSA 14.182]

MCLA 327.258 [MSA 14.183 - 14.188]

MCLA 327.259 State investigation; ex-officio membership. [MSA 14.189]

Sec. 9. The work and methods ... shall at all times be subject to investigation and scrutiny by the local board of health ...

MCLA 327.260 Certified milk standard. [MSA 14.190]

Sec. 10. No person, firm or corporation shall sell or exchange or offer or expose for sale or exchange in any ... township as and for certified milk, any milk which is not certified by the medical milk commission of that ... township, and which ...

MCLA 327.261 Penalty. [MSA 14.191]

Act No. 269, P. A. 1968 – Food Service Establishment

AN ACT to protect the public health; to provide for the licensing of food service establishments and vending machine locations; to provide for the payment of license fees; to provide for standards of sanitation and public health; to provide for enforcement procedures; to prescribe the powers and duties of the director, department of public health and local health departments; and to provide penalties for the violation of the provisions of this act.

MCLA 325.801 Definitions. [MSA 14.529(1)]

MCLA 325.802 Licenses; application, term, display, transferability. [MSA 14.529(2)]

MCLA 325.803 Licenses; applications not within jurisdiction of certified health departments. [MSA 14.529(3)]

MCLA 325.804 Licenses; sanitation service fees; exempt organizations. [MSA 14.529(4)]

MCLA 325.805 Licenses; defective applications and noncompliance; denial; suspension, revocation; discontinuance of operation. [MSA 14.529(5)]

MCLA 325.806 Director; delegation of authority and responsibility for enforcement of act. [MSA 14.529(6)]

MCLA 325.807 Director; responsibility for administration and enforcement of act; promulgation of rules; adoption of federal code; enforcement procedures; definitions. [MSA 14.529(7)]

MCLA 325.808 Investigation of food-borne diseases and poisonings; report. [MSA 14.529(8)]

MCLA 325.809 Certified health department; criteria for determination. [MSA 14.529(9)]

MCLA 325.810 Certified health department; departments established under sections 327.201 to 327.208b; failure to maintain criteria. [MSA 14.529(10)]

MCLA 325.811 Penalty. [MSA 14.529(11)]

MCLA 325.812 Local authority; codes, regulations or ordinances. MSA 14.529(12)

Sec. 12. Nothing in this act limits the authority of any ... township to regulate food service establishments or vending machines. Nothing in this act shall relieve the applicant for a license or a licensee from responsibility for securing any local permits or complying with all applicable local codes, regulations or ordinances not in conflict with this act.

MCLA 324.813 Other remedies to prevent operation of business without a valid license. MSA 14.529(13)

JOINT ACTION
Act No. 193, P. A. 1895 — Adulteration, Fraud and Deception

AN ACT to prohibit and prevent adulteration, fraud and deception in the manufacture and sale of articles of food and drink.

MCLA 289.81 - 289.99 MSA 12.871 - 12.886

Note: The above sections deal with definitions, regulations, inspections, penalty, etc.

MCLA 289.100 Duties of various officers. MSA 12.887

Sec. 20. ... It shall also be the duty of all ... health officers in townships to take cognizance of and report or prosecute all violations of this act that may be brought to their notice or they may have cognizance of, within their jurisdiction.

JOINT ACTION
Act No. 263, P. A. 1917 — Food and Drug Commissioner

AN ACT to create the office of food and drug commissioner; to prescribe his powers, duties and compensation; to provide for the enforcement of drug and liquor, dairy and food, and weights and measures laws; to abolish

594

the office of dairy and food commissioner; and to provide for expenditures in connection therewith.

MCLA 289.2 — 289.6 [MSA 12.811 — 289.813]

MCLA 289.7 **Aid and assistance, rendering to commissioner.** [MSA 12.814]

MCLA 289.9 Refusal to give assistance, effect; duties of officers. [MSA 12.816]

MCLA 289.11 — 289.12 [MSA 12.817 — 12.818]

JOINT ACTION
Act No. 293, P. A. 1909 — Medical Inspector

AN ACT in relation to the public health in this state.

MCLA 329.51 Medical inspector; powers; communicable diseases, designation; local health authorities, duties. [MSA 14.291]

MCLA 329.52 Same; duties. [MSA 14.292]

Sec. 2. Every person selected to act as (a state) medical inspector shall ... make a thorough and complete investigation of all nuisances, sources of sickness, epidemics of infectious or contagious diseases, water supplies, the sewerage disposal systems, the sanitary conditions of public vaults, jails, school houses and school grounds, and such other work as is found necessary to improve the general sanitary and hygenic condition of the state.

MCLA 329.53 — 329.55 [MSA 14.293 — 14.295]

JOINT ACTION
Act No. 277, P. A. 1921 — Township Nurse

AN ACT to authorize townships to employ nurses and to provide for their compensation.

MCLA 338.391 **Township nurse; employment; appropriation.** [MSA 14.711]

Sec. 1. The inhabitants of any township shall have the power at any legal meeting, by a vote of the qualified electors thereof, to grant and vote money for the purpose of employing a public nurse or nurses for said township.

MCLA 338.392 Same; contract; limited powers; duties; misdemeanor, penalty. [MSA 14.712]

Sec. 2. Whenever the qualified electors of any township have voted any money for the employment of a public nurse or nurses for said township, the township board may ..., or said board may ...join with any other ... (local unit of government) ...in procuring and paying for the services of a nurse or nurses for the common benefit of such organizations: Provided, ... Any person employed and serving as nurses under this act who shall violate any of the provisions thereof shall be deemed guilty of a misdemeanor, and on conviction thereof shall be punished by a fine not exceeding 100 dollars or by imprisonment in the county jail not exceeding 60 days, or by both such fine and imprisonment in the discretion of the court.

MCLA 338.393 Declaration of necessity. [MSA 14.713]

Act No. 181, P.A. 1953 — County Medical Examiners

AN ACT relative to investigations in certain instances of the causes of death within this state due to violence, negligence or other act or omission of a criminal nature or to protect public health; to provide for the taking of statements from injured persons under certain circumstances; to abolish the office of coroner and to create the office of county medical examiner in certain counties; to prescribe the powers and duties of county medical examiners; to prescribe penalties for violations of the provisions of this act; and to prescribe a referendum thereon.

MCLA 52.201 - 52.216 [MSA 5.953(1) - 5.953(16)]

JOINT ACTION
Act No. 146, P.A. 1919 — State Department of Health

AN ACT to protect the public health; to provide for the appointment of a state health commissioner, deputy *state health commissioner and state advisory council of health; to prescribe the compensation, powers and duties thereof; to provide immunity from liability for personnel of the department of public health; the powers and duties of the township, village and city health officers and health boards; and to abolish the state board of health.*

MCLA 325.1 State health commissioner; appointment, term, qualifications. [MSA 14.1]

MCLA 325.2 - 325.6 [MSA 14.2 - 14.6]

Note: The above sections deal with matters regarding the commissioner, deputy, abolition of state board of health, agreements for use of copper country tuberculosis sanatorium, and the state council of health.

MCLA 325.7 State health commissioner; rules and regulations, conformity to federal requirements; hospitals, standards of maintenance, inspection, limitations; publication of rules and regulations. [MSA 14.7]

MCLA 325.7a Family planning services; notice of availability to medically indigent women. [MSA 14.7(1)]

Sec. 7a. The state health commissioner, and under his supervision, health departments or boards of ... (local communities) ... may provide written or oral notice to medically indigent women of the availability of family planning services. Such notice shall ...

MCLA 325.8 Administration by commissioner in municipalities of health laws and regulations; exception as to certain cities. [MSA 14.8]

Sec. 8. Whenever in the opinion of the state health commissioner, conditions found by him to exist in any township ... are such as to constitute a menace to the public health, either within or without the limits of such municipality, such commissioner may by himself, or by his deputy, or medical inspector, enter such township ... and take full charge of the administration of the health laws, rules, regulations and ordinances applicable thereto: ...

MCLA 325.9 Epidemic; order regulating public meetings. [MSA 14.9]

MCLA 325.10 Assistants; offices; expenses. [MSA 14.10]

MCLA 325.11 Local health officers; powers and duties, co-operation. [MSA 14.11]

Sec. 11. Subject to the provisions of this act, all ... township health officers, health board and health departments shall respectively perform the duties and exercise the powers not imposed and granted by law. It shall be the duty of all local health officials to co-operate in every way possible with the state health commissioner and the state advisory council of health. Wilful failure to do so shall be deemed to be misfeasance in office.

MCLA 325.12 Misdemeanor, penalty; right of individual to select physician. [MSA 14.12]

MCLA 325.13 Branch laboratories; establishment, limit. [MSA 14.13]

MCLA 325.14 Director of department, representative and employees not personally liable for damages; exception for negligence. [MSA 14.13(1)]

Act No. 147, P.A. 1963 — Sanitarians

AN ACT to require the state health commissioner to register sanitarians and provide for issuance, renewal and revocation of certificates of registrations of sanitarians; to create a board of examiners for sanitarians; to provide for fixing of fees; to provide for payment of actual and necessary expenses of board members; to delegate authority for making rules and regulations; to provide a method for reciprocity between states for registered sanitarians; and to provide remedies and penalties for the violation of this act.

MCLA 338.1301 Sanitarian's registration act; short title. [MSA 14.425(1)]

MCLA 338.1302 Same; definitions. [MSA 14.425(2)]

MCLA 338.1303 Registration of qualified sanitarians. [MSA 14.425(3)]

MCLA 338.1304 — 338.1312 [MSA 14.425(4) — 14.425(12)]

MCLA 338.1313   Registered sanitarians; conflict of interest. [MSA 14.425(13)]

Sec. 13.   No registered sanitarian shall be engaged in or have any interest in any work, project or operation prejudicial to his professional interest therein, nor be in conflict with Act No. 240 of the Public Acts of 1937, as amended, being sections 338.551 to 338.576 [MSA 18.84(1) — 18.84(26)] *of the Compiled Laws of 1948.*

MCLA 338.1314 Same; title. [MSA 14.425(14)]

MCLA 338.1315 Violation of act; penalty. [MSA 14.425(15)]

JOINT ACTION
Act No. 43, P. A. 1897 — Analysis of Water

AN ACT to provide for the analysis of water in use by the public in certain cases.

MCLA 390.81   Water analysis by university; submission of sample. [MSA 15.991]

Sec. 1.   That in any case where any ... township ... shall be supplied with water for domestic uses by any individual, company or corporation, city or village, or where there is within such ... township, any water in swales, wells, rivers or other places, which might be the cause of disease or epidemic, a sample of such water may be sent to the university of Michigan for analysis by the ... supervisor of any such township, upon the resolution of the ... township board ... for that purpose duly passed.

MCLA 390.82 Same; statement; cost. [MSA 15.992]

Sec. 2.   ... free of charge except the actual cost of materials and animals used in making such analysis and experiment.

MCLA 390.83 Same; record; second analysis. [MSA 15.993]

Sec. 3.   ... in no case shall a second analysis be required of the same water within 1 year except ...

JOINT ACTION
Act No. 109, P. A. 1907 — Bacteriologist and Supplies

AN ACT to provide for the appointment of a bacteriologist by the state board of health; to provide for the purchase of the necessary appliances and apparatus for bacteriological examinations, and providing an appropriation therefor.

MCLA 325.21 Bacteriologist, assistants; appointment, salaries. [MSA 14.21]

MCLA 325.22 Same; duties. [MSA 14.22]

MCLA 325.23 Bacteriological examinations and water analyses, upon request. [MSA 14.23]

MCLA 325.24 Apparatus, purchase; expenses, limitation, apportionment. [MSA 14.24]

JOINT ACTION
Act No. 164, P. A. 1915 — Laboratory in Upper Peninsula

AN ACT to provide for the establishment of a branch bacteriological laboratory in the upper peninsula of the state and authorizing the employment of a bacteriologist to take charge thereof; to authorize the purchase of the necessary appliances and apparatus for such laboratory, and providing an appropriation therefor.

MCLA 325.31 — 325.33 [MSA 14.31 — 14.33]

Note: Duties and costs of services same as those in Act 109, P. A. 1907, being MCLA 325.21 — 325.24 [MSA 14.21 — 14.24]

JOINT ACTION
Act No. 328, P. A. 1931 — Michigan Penal Code

CHAPTER LXIX. PUBLIC HEALTH

MCLA 750.466 - 750.477a [MSA 28.734 - 28.745(1)]

Note: The above sections provide health regulations regarding care, sale and control of people, food, animals, instruments, fountains, establishments, and free distribution of medicines.

STATUTES REGARDING ANIMALS

Act No. 70, P. A. 1877 — Cruelty to Animals

AN ACT for the more effectual prevention of cruelty to animals.

MCLA 752.21 - 752.30 [MSA 28.161 - 28.167]

Note: The above sections deal with arrest procedures, impoundment of animals and definitions.

JOINT ACTION
Act No. 339, P. A. 1919 — Dog Law

AN ACT relating to dogs and the protection of livestock and poultry from damage by dogs; providing for the licensing of dogs; regulating the keeping of dogs, and authorizing their destruction in certain cases; providing for the determination and payment of damages done by dogs to live stock and poultry; imposing powers and duties on certain ... township officers and employes, and to repeal Act No. 347 of the Public Acts of 1917, and providing penalties for the violation of this act.

MCLA 287.261 Short title; definitions. [MSA 12.511]

MCLA 287.262 Licensing and control of dogs; hunting dogs; female dogs in heat; straying dogs. [MSA 12.512]

MCLA 287.264 Supervision and enforcement. [MSA 12.514]

Sec. 4. The state livestock sanitary commission shall have the general supervision ... and all police officers of the ... township shall be at its disposal for that purpose. An animal control officer or a law enforcement officer of the state shall issue a citation, summons or appearance ticket for a violation of this act.

MCLA 287.265 Tags, blanks and license forms (issued to county treasurers). [MSA 12.515]

MCLA 287.266 Dog license; application, contents, proof of vaccination of dog; fee, powers of supervisors; increase of fees. [MSA 12.516]

MCLA 287.267 Dog license; tag, approval; kept on dog. [MSA 12.517]

MCLA 287.268 Same; unlicensed and young dogs; application, half fee after certain date. [MSA 12.518]

MCLA 287.269 Same; contents. [MSA 12.519]

MCLA 287.270 Kennel facility; license, issuance, form, fee, metal tags; inspection certificate, contents; rules; inspection; exception. [MSA 12.520]

MCLA 287.270b Kennel licenses, issuance; effect of adoption of kennel licensing ordinance. [MSA 12.520(1)]

Sec. 10b. Any ... township ... having in its employment a full-time animal control officer may adopt an ordinance providing for the issuance of kennel licenses by the animal control officer on the same terms, conditions and fees as is provided in section 10. Upon the adoption of the ordinance, the ... township ... shall be excepted from the provisions of sections 10 and 11 of this act.

MCLA 287.271 Rules governing kennel dogs. [MSA 12.521]

MCLA 287.272 Tag lost. [MSA 12.522]

MCLA 287.273 License and tag, transferability. [MSA 12.523]

MCLA 287.274 Township ... treasurer, duties; fees; ... [MSA 12.524]

MCLA 287.275 County treasurer's record; inspection. [MSA 12.525]

MCLA 287.276 Listing of dogs; reports; compensation; animal control officers, appointment, duties. [MSA 12.526]

Sec. 16. The supervisor of each township ... may ..., and on or before June 1, make a complete report to ...

MCLA 287.277 Comparison of dog lists and license records; killing of unlicensed dogs. [MSA 12.527]

MCLA 287.278 Killing of dogs; duty of officer; fee. [MSA 12.528]

MCLA 287.279 Same; justification. [MSA 12.529]

MCLA 287.280 Damage to livestock or poultry by dogs, remedy; complaint, proceedings; liability for damages and costs. [MSA 12.530]

Sec. 20. Whenever any person sustains any loss or damage to ... such person or his agent or attorney, may complain to the township supervisor or appointed trustee of the township ... The complaint shall ... The township supervisor or a township trustee ... shall ...

MCLA 287.281 - 287.288 [MSA 12.531 - 12.539]

Note: The above sections deal with court procedures, costs, accounting, penalties and fines, illegal killing, common law liability.

MCLA 287.289 Dogs imported temporarily. [MSA 12.540]

MCLA 287.289a Animal control agency, establishment, employees, jurisdiction; county animal control ordinances, contests. [MSA 12.540(1)]

Sec. 29 a. The board of county commissioners by ordinance may establish an animal control agency ... (which) ... shall have jurisdiction to enforce this act in any ... township which does not have an animal control ordinance. ...

MCLA 287.289b County animal control officer, minimum employment standards. [MSA 12.540(2)]

MCLA 287.289c City, village, or township animal control officers, minimum employment standards. [MSA 12.540(3)]

MCLA 287.290 City, village, or township animal control ordinances, authorization, contents; proof of vaccination for rabies. MSA 12.541

Sec. 30. A ... township by action of its governing body may adopt an animal control ordinance to regulate the licensing, payment of claims and providing for the enforcement thereof. A ... township adopting a dog licensing ordinance or ordinances shall also ...

JOINT ACTION
Act No. 306, P. A. 1909 — Rabies

AN ACT in relation to the disease of rabies among dogs, to provide for the treatment of persons infected with the virus of rabies, and for the payment of certain damages for domestic animals infected with rabies by dogs and to provide penalties for the violation of this act.

MCLA 329.101 Rabid dog, quarantine; complaint by township board. MSA 14.311

Sec. 1. It is hereby made the duty of all township boards of health ...

MCLA 329.102 - 329.108 MSA 14.312 - 14.318

Act No. 309, P. A. 1939 — Registration and Identification of Dogs

AN ACT to provide for the regulation, registration, identification and licensing of dogs; to prescribe the powers and duties of the commissioner of agriculture with respect thereto; to prescribe penalties for violation of the provisions of this act; and to declare the effect of this act.

MCLA 287.301 — 287.308 MSA 12.545(1) — 12.545(8)

Note: This act delineates state responsibility, but local officials should know about the process.

Act No. 207, P. A. 1970 — Leader Dogs for Blind Persons

604

AN ACT to exempt certain dogs from licenses.

MCLA 287.291   Licensing fee, exemption.   [MSA 12.543(11)]

Sec. 1. *Notwithstanding any other provisions to the contrary, a dog which is used as a leader dog for a blind person shall not be subject to any fee for licensing.*

Act No. 287, P. A. 1969 — Pet Shops, Dog Pounds, and Animal Shelters

AN ACT to regulate pet shops, dog pounds and animal shelters.

MCLA 287.331   Definitions.   [MSA 12.481(101)]

MCLA 287.332   Rules, promulgation, purpose.   [MSA 12.481(102)]

MCLA 287.333   Licensing of pet shops, necessity.   [MSA 12.481(103)]

MCLA 287.334   Applications for licenses, forms, fees.   [MSA 12.481(104)]

MCLA 287.335   Inspection of pet shop premises.   [MSA 12.481(105)]

MCLA 287.336   Registration of dog pounds and animal shelters, necessity.   [MSA 12.481(106)]

Sec. 6. *No ... township shall operate a dog pound unless they first register the dog pound with the department of agriculture.   ...*

MCLA 287.337   Applications for registration, forms.   [MSA 12.481(107)]

MCLA 287.338   Inspection of dog pounds and animal shelters.   [MSA 12.481(108)]

MCLA 287.339   Animal breeders and persons subject to research use licensing, applicability.   [MSA 12.481(109)]

MCLA 287.340   Violations, penalty.   [MSA 12.481(110)]

Act No. 224, P. A. 1969 — Research Using Dogs

and Cats, Regulation of Dealers and Research Facilities

AN ACT to license and regulate dealers in and research facilities using dogs and cats for research purposes; and to repeal certain acts and parts of acts.

MCLA 287.381 — 287.387 [MSA 12.580(21) — 12.580(27)]

MCLA 287.388 Holding period (five days). [MSA 12.580(28)]

MCLA 287.389 Sales by public auction or weight, prohibition; purchases, restrictions; unclaimed dogs and cats, disposal, maximum price. [MSA 12.580(29)]

MCLA 287.390 — 287.393 [MSA 12.580(30) — 12.580(33)]

MCLA 287.394 Application of dog law of 1919. [MSA 12.580(34)]

Sec. 14. The provisions of this act shall be in addition to and not in contravention of the provisions of Act No. 339 of the Public Acts of 1919, as amended, being sections **287.261 to 287.290** [MSA 12.511 — 12.541] *of the Compiled Laws of 1948.*

Act No. 226, P. A. 1929 — Bodies of Dead Animals

AN ACT to promote the health, safety and welfare of the people by regulating the business of disposing of the bodies of dead animals or parts of bodies thereof by burying, burning or cooking; and to provide penalties for the violation of the terms hereof.

MCLA 287.231 — 287.232a [MSA 12.581 — 12.582(1)]

MCLA 287.233 Disposal plant, specifications, drainage, sanitation; burial, burning; vehicles; transfer stations. [MSA 12.583]

MCLA 287.234 — 287.241 [MSA 12.584 — 12.592]

Note: A township where there is an animal shelter or business for the purpose of disposing of dead animals, would have interest in the above act.

Act No. 181, P. A. 1919 — Animal Industry

AN ACT to provide for the prevention and suppression of contagious, infectious and communicable diseases of livestock; to prohibit the importation into or release within this state of certain rabbits; to provide for the creation of a department of animal industry of the state of Michigan, to authorize and require the appointment of a state commissioner of animal industry, of 2 advisory commissioners and of a state veterinarian; to prescribe the powers and duties of said officers; to make an appropriation therefor; and to repeal all acts or parts of acts contravening the provisions of this act.

MCLA 287.2 — 287.3 [MSA 12.371 — 12.372]

MCLA 287.4 Domestic animals, contagious or infectious diseases and noxious materials, regulations. [MSA 12.373]

MCLA 287.5 Domestic animals affected with disease; report; duty of local health boards, quarantine; expense. [MSA 12.374]

MCLA 287.6 Quarantine; examination of animals; preventive rules; quarantine; right of entry; dogs; killing of animals; enforcement. [MSA 12.375]

MCLA 287.7 — 287.11a [MSA 12.376 — 12.380(1)]

MCLA 287.12 Execution of orders; arrest; notice to prosecutor, duty. [MSA 12.381]

MCLA 287.13 — 287.17 [MSA 12.382 — 12.387]

MCLA 287.18 Hog cholera serum; living virus, source of supply, use, sale permit, expense, local appropriations. [MSA 12.388]

Sec. 18. ... the township board ... shall have the power to appropriate money to be expended for hog cholera serum for use within their respective ... townships.

MCLA 287.19 — 287.26 [MSA 12.389 — 12.399]

Act No. 185, P. A. 1867 — Animals Running at Large

AN ACT to prevent animals from running at large in the public highways.

MCLA 433.1 Livestock, running at large in highway, unlawfulness; powers reserved to townships. [MSA 18.781]

MCLA 433.2 Inapplicability of act. [MSA 18.782]

MCLA 433.3 - 433.6 [MSA 18.783 - 18.786]

Note: The above sections deal with rights and responsibilities of seizors and owners of the animals.

R.S. 1846, c. 47 — Lost Goods and Stray Beasts

MCLA 434.1 Lost money or goods; notice of finding. [MSA 18.701]

Sec. 1. When any person shall find any lost money, or lost goods, if the owner thereof be known, he shall immediately give notice thereof to such owner; if the owner thereof be unknown, and such money or goods be of the value of 3 dollars or more, the finder shall, within 2 days, cause notice thereof to be posted in 2 public places within the township where the same were found; and shall also, within 7 days, give notice thereof in writing to the township clerk of such township, and pay him 25 cents for making an entry thereof in a book to be kept for that purpose.

MCLA 434.2 Same; notice by publication. [MSA 18.702]

MCLA 434.3 Taking up of animal running at large. [MSA 18.703]

MCLA 434.4 Same; notice to owner, to township clerk, to county clerk; entry, fees. [MSA 18.704]

MCLA 434.5 Same; publication of notice. [MSA 18.705]

MCLA 434.6 Appraisal of lost goods or stray animals; filing, fees. [MSA 18.706]

MCLA 434.7 Lost money or goods; restitution to owner. [MSA 18.707]

MCLA 434.8 Same; remaining in finder; township entitled to one-half of value. [MSA 18.708]

MCLA 434.9 Stray beasts; restitution to owner. [MSA 18.709]

MCLA 434.10 Same; sale; notice, finder as bidder, proceeds. [MSA 18.710]

MCLA 434.11 Same; proceeds of sale, receipt by owner or township. [MSA 18.711]

MCLA 434.12 Finder; preclusion from certain benefits; wilful neglect to comply, penalty. [MSA 18.712]

MCLA 434.13 Unlawful taking of animal taken up as stray, liability. [MSA 18.713]

MCLA 434.14 Moderate working of horses, etc., taken up, value of labor deducted from charges. [MSA 18.714]

Act No. 71, P.A. 1867 - Bulls, Stallions, Boars and Rams

AN ACT to prevent the running at large of bulls, stallions, boars and rams.

MCLA 433.81 Allowing male animals to run at large; forfeiture, time of prosecution. [MSA 18.821]

MCLA 433.82 Same; civil liability. [MSA 18.822]

R. S. 1846, c. 125 — Distraining and Replevying Beasts

MCLA 433.101 Beasts distrained; impounding. [MSA 18.831]

MCLA 433.102 Fees; distraining and impounding. [MSA 18.832]

MCLA 433.103 Same; payment prerequisite to delivery of beast. [MSA 18.833]

MCLA 433.104 Recovery for damages caused by beasts. [MSA 18.834]

MCLA 433.105 Impounding beasts doing damage. [MSA 18.835]

MCLA 433.106 Delivery of beasts by poundmaster. [MSA 18.836]

MCLA 433.107 Care of beasts by person distraining. [MSA 18.837]

MCLA 433.108 Notice of beasts distrained; to owner. [MSA 18.838]

MCLA 433.109 Same; posting in certain cases. [MSA 18.839]

MCLA 433.110 Same; publication in newspaper. [MSA 18.840]

MCLA 433.111 Determination of damage; application by owner of animals. [MSA 18.841]

MCLA 433.112 Same; application by person impounding animals. [MSA 18.842]

MCLA 433.113 Sale of beasts; notice. [MSA 18.843]

MCLA 433.114 Same; proceeds. [MSA 18.844]

MCLA 433.115 Beasts escaped or rescued; retaking. [MSA 18.845]

MCLA 433.116 Rescuing beasts distrained; penalty. [MSA 18.846]

MCLA 433.117 Legality of distress determined in replevin action. [MSA 18.847]

R. S. 1846, c. 18 — Pounds and Impounding Cattle

MCLA 43.122 Pounds (for farm animals), maintenance by township. [MSA 5.232]

MCLA 43.123 Same; injury, penalty. [MSA 5.233]

Act No. 109, P. A. 1847 - Damages by Beasts

AN ACT to provide against the recovery of damages done by beasts on lands which are not enclosed by a lawful fence.

MCLA 433.151 Damages upon lands by beasts; barred unless enclosed. [MSA 5.241]

Note: Provides specification regarding fencing.

Act No. 50, P.A. 1915 — Rats

AN ACT to provide for the payment of bounties for the killing of common rats.

MCLA 433.251   Rat bounty (payable by county). [MSA 18.761]

MCLA 433.252   Same; applicant, duty; certificate; destruction of heads. [MSA 18.762]

Sec. 2. Every person applying for such bounty shall take the heads of such rats, in lots of not less than 5, to the clerk of the township ... in a state of good preservation, and if satisfied with the correctness of such claim, said township ... clerk shall issue a certificate stating the amount of bounty to which such applicant is entitled and deliver the same to said applicant, and shall destroy the heads of such rats by burning.

MCLA 433.253   Payment of certificate; nonliability of county. [MSA 18.763]

Note: Act may be declared inoperative by county board of commissioners.

Act No. 4, P.A. 1885 — English Sparrows

AN ACT to authorize the killing of "English sparrows."

MCLA 433.271   English sparrows, lawful to kill. [MSA 18.741]

Act No. 226, P.A. 1907 — English Sparrows

AN ACT to provide for the payment of bounties for the killing of English sparrows.

MCLA 433.281   English sparrow bounty; power of board of supervisors. [MSA 18.751]

MCLA 433.282   Same; applicant, duty; certificate; destruction of sparrows. [MSA 18.752]

Sec. 2. Every person applying for such bounty shall take such

sparrows, in lots of not less than 10, to the clerk of the township,
... (who) *shall ...*

MCLA 433.283 — 433.284 [MSA 18.753 — 18.754]

Note: Act must be adopted by resolution of county board of commissioners.

Act No. 152, P.A. 1941 — Starlings and Crows

AN ACT to provide for the payment of bounties for the killing of starlings and crows; and to prescribe penalties for the violation of the provisions of this act.

MCLA 433.301 Starlings and crows; bounty for killing; resolution of board of supervisors (if to be operative in county). [MSA 18.755(1)]

MCLA 433.302 Same; delivery to local (township) **clerk; certificat e.** [MSA 18.755(2)]

MCLA 433.303 — 433.304 [MSA 18.755(3) — 18.755(4)]

JOINT ACTION
Act No. 280, P.A. 1965 — Slaughterhouses and Edible Rendering, Wholesale Fabricating, Processing, and Storage Establishments

AN ACT to provide for licensing and regulating of slaughterhouses, edible rendering establishments and wholesale fabricating, processing or storage establish-ments of meat; to provide for the antemortem and post-mortem inspection and reinspection of slaughtered meat animals; to prescribe the duties and powers of the depart-,ment of agriculture to prescribe license fees; to provide for the transfer of personnel and the rights of employees affected by this act; to provide for inspection of large wild game animals; and to provide penalties for violation of the provisions of this act.

MCLA 287.571 - 287.582 [MSA 18.844(1) - 18.844(12)]

Note: The above sections provide for licensing of establish-ments (no local permit required), for state approval and payment of

612

costs of all meat inspection programs of local (including township) health departments and for inspection procedures.

Act No. 173, P.A. 1953 — Regulation and Feeding of Garbage to Swine

AN ACT to provide for the regulation of garbage and the feeding of garbage to swine; to provide for the powers and duties of the Michigan department of agriculture with respect thereto; and to prescribe penalties for the violations of the provisions of this act.

MCLA 287.401 - 287.409 [MSA 12.483(1) - 12.483(9)]

CEMETERIES

Population increases have brought about the necessity, particularly in metropolitan areas, to add to established cemeteries or create new ones. However, less and less land is available for the purpose, and the cost is becoming prohibitive as well. It seems almost ironic that in the United States--a land of plenty, a land of millions of acres--the problem of burying the dead has become so acute.

Government officials are being forced to consider alternatives to the traditional horizontal burial in local cemeteries. Some alternatives are required: cremation, vertical burial, above-ground burial in high rise mausoleums and transportation of bodies for burial in central locations throughout the United States in areas which are undesirable for other uses--slopes of mountains, deserts and other areas not conducive to the good and welfare of the living. Some European countries already require vertical burial, especially in areas where there are large concentrations of people.

Apparently a township is required to make adequate provisions for burial of its deceased citizens, and may join with other units of government for this purpose. There are also methods of cooperating, through contractual agreements with private cemetery associations or corporations, although it is illegal to contribute public funds to such organizations, without such contract. Any township board which has been doing so should consult its township attorney immediately and take steps to rectify the situation.

The citations which follow are for the most part presented with title and section headings only. They should be carefully studied and the township attorney consulted regarding implementation.

R.S. 1846, c. 35 — Of the Preservation of Public Health: Quarantine, Nuisances and Offensive Trades

GENERAL PROVISIONS

MCLA 327.5 Rules of local boards (of health); **cemeteries; purchase of necessary grounds.** [MSA 14.65]

Sec. 5. *The said board shall also make all regulations which they may deem necessary for the interment of the dead, and respecting burying grounds, for their township; and it shall also be the duty of said board to purchase in each surveyed township so much land for burying grounds as shall be necessary for burying the dead of such township, provided suitable grounds therefor can be found and procured within the township, and if not, they shall then provide such grounds in the nearest adjoining township where such suitable grounds can be procured.*

MCLA 327.6 Township cemeteries; fee in trust; fences; separate funds for cemeteries in same township; sale of lots; expenses; maps, filing. [MSA 14.66]

Sec. 6. *The board of health of the township for which such burying ground shall be procured, and their successors in office, shall hold the fee of such land in trust for said township; and they shall ...*

Act No. 215, P.A. 1861 — Disposal of Burial Grounds

AN ACT to authorize boards of health to dispose of real estate.

MCLA 327.301 Fee in board, sale; cemetery ground, sale by court order. [MSA 14.201]

Act No. 215, P. A. 1937 — Municipal Cemeteries

AN ACT to authorize cities, villages, townships and municipal subdivisions of the state to own or control cemetery or burial grounds; to provide for perpetual care and maintenance; and to declare the effect of this act.

MCLA 128.1 Cemetery or burial grounds; authority to own or control; transfer of certain trust funds. [MSA 5.3165]

Act No. 46, P.A. 1931 — City (and Township) Cemeteries

AN ACT to supplement the laws providing for the establishment, control, maintenance and care of public cemeteries by cities and townships within this state; to define the powers and duties of cemetery boards and other public officials invested by law with the management thereof; to provide for the termination and forfeiture of rights in certain unused burial spaces in such cemeteries; to prescribe and regulate the procedure with reference thereto; to authorize the resale of such spaces and to direct the investment and use of the funds received therefrom; and to repeal all acts or parts of acts inconsistent with the provisions hereof.

MCLA 128.11 Definitions. [MSA 5.3101]

MCLA 128.12 Burial space, proceedings for termination of rights; copy of resolution served on owner; petition, hearing; service on owner. [MSA 5.3102]

MCLA 128.13 Burial space, proceedings for termination of rights; forfeiture; city, village or township may˙re-sell; copy of order served on owner; redemption. [MSA 5.3103]

MCLA 128.14 Duty of board. [MSA 5.3104]

MCLA 128.15 Reconveyance; perpetual care trust fund. [MSA 5.3105]

MCLA 128.16 Rights not forfeited, when. [MSA 5.3106]

Act No. 272, P.A. 1909 — Township Cemeteries

AN ACT to authorize the boards of health of the several townships of this state to acquire and enlarge burying grounds and approaches thereto in their respective townships and to provide the manner of acquiring private property for such purpose.

MCLA 128.151 Cemeteries, provided by township health board; compensation, determination. [MSA 8.141]

MCLA 128.152 Compensation, jury determination; summoning of jurors; notice. [MSA 8.142]

MCLA 128.153 Previous notice by board; contents, service. [MSA 8.143]

MCLA 128.154 Judge, duties; jury summons, return, contents; empaneling. [MSA 8.144]

MCLA 128.155 Jury sworn; subpoena power; determination of necessity, compensation; certificates by judge and jury, contents. [MSA 8.145]

MCLA 128.156 Judgement; collection. [MSA 8.146]

MCLA 128.157 Incompetent or unknown owner; county treasurer, duties; funds subject to court order. [MSA 8.147]

MCLA 128.158 Vesting of fee, conditions; writ of possession. [MSA 8.148]

MCLA 128.159 Possession by township; writ of possession. [MSA 8.149]

MCLA 128.160 Jury disagreement; adjournment, limit. [MSA 8.150]

MCLA 128.161 Parties to suit; proof of claims; settlement. [MSA 8.151]

MCLA 128.162 Payment order, issuance; receipt; evidence. [MSA 8.152]

MCLA 128.163 Subsequent proceedings. [MSA 8.153]

MCLA 128.164 Fees; compensation. [MSA 8.154]

JOINT ACTION
Act No. 113, P.A. 1915 — Care of Cemeteries by Municipalities

AN ACT prescribing the powers and duties of township boards and legislative bodies of cities and villages with relation to the care of cemeteries; and to provide for the perpetual care deposits, and the disbursement thereof.

MCLA 128.61 Cemeteries; joint maintenance by municipalities; money deposited in trust, limitation, expenditure. [MSA 5.3121]

MCLA 128.62 Cemetery day. [MSA 5.3122]

Sec. 2. The third Wednesday in August of each year is hereby designated as "cemetery day" and is set aside as a day upon which the people in townships may devote a portion of their time to the improvement of their cemeteries. The township boards shall direct the manner of making such improvements.

Act No. 22, P.A. 1905 – Memory Days

AN ACT to provide for the better care of cemeteries and of the graves therein.

MCLA 128.121 Memory days, purpose. [MSA 5.3111]

Sec. 1. That the twenty-fifth day of May and the thirtieth day of September in each year be and hereby are set apart and designated as "Memory Days"; said days to be used for the purpose of improving and beautifying the various cemeteries throughout the state and of the graves therein; that all may thus show forth on these days by these appropriate acts a loving and tender remembrance for the dead: Provided, however, That if either of the days herein designated shall fall on Sunday, the next Monday following shall be deemed "Memory Day" for all or any of the purposes of this act.

Act No. 251, P.A. 1968 - Cemetery Regulation Act

AN ACT to regulate the creation, management and maintenance of cemeteries; to regulate the sale of cemetery services and merchandise; to create a cemetery commission and to prescribe its powers and duties; to require the registration, regulation and inspection of cemeteries; to license and regulate persons selling burial, entombment or columbarian rights, cemetery services or cemetery merchandise; and to prescribe penalties.

MCLA 456.521 — 456.529 [MSA 21.820(21) — 21.820(29)]

MCLA 456.530 State cemetery commission; registration and inspection of cemeteries authorized to be created, maintained and operated; exemptions. [MSA 21.820(30)]

Sec. 10. ... *Cemeteries owned and operated by a municipality, church or religious institution shall be exempt from the provisions of this act.* ...

MCLA 456.531 — 456.543 [MSA 21.820(31) — 21.820(43)]

Act No. 55, P.A. 1915 — Establishment Requirements

AN ACT to regulate the establishment of cemeteries and to define the duties of local boards of health and of the state board of health in relation thereto.

MCLA 128.21 Cemeteries, establishment; local board, duties; additions. [MSA 5.3061]

Sec. 1. *No person or incorporated cemetery association shall establish a cemetery at any place in this state until a description of the premises and a plat showing the division thereof shall have been filed in duplicate with the local board of health having jurisdiction of the premises and approved as hereinafter provided. The local board of health shall determine as soon as may be thereafter whether or not it is necessary or desirable for a cemetery to be established in the proposed location and if it approves of such location and the plat of said premises, it shall endorse such approval on both plats. When the establishment of any such cemetery has been approved as aforesaid 1 of said plats shall be returned to the proprietor thereof and the other shall be retained and preserved by the local board of health: Provided, That this act shall not apply to the acquiring of contiguous additions to existing cemeteries.*

Act No. 201, P.A. 1911 — Fencing of Private Cemeteries

AN ACT to compel owners of private cemeteries to keep the same enclosed with a suitable fence to prevent encroachment of live stock.

618

MCLA 128.91 Private cemeteries, fencing (under direction of township board of health). MSA 5.3141

MCLA 128.92 Same; notice to build or repair. MSA 5.3142

MCLA 128.93 Non-compliance, erection by township health board; expense. MSA 5.3143

R.S. 1846, c. 158 — Way Through Cemetery

MCLA 752.73 Unauthorized construction of way through cemetery; penalty. MSA 28.132

Sec. 23. If any person shall open or make any highway, or shall construct any railroad, turnpike or canal, or any other thing in the nature of a public easement, over, through, in or upon, such part of any enclosure, being the property of a township, city, religious society, or of any other body corporate, or of private proprietors, as may be used or appropriated for the burial of the dead, unless an authority for that purpose shall be especially granted by law, or unless the consent of such ... (owner) ... shall be first obtained, he shall be punished by fine not exceeding 2,000 dollars, or imprisonment in the county jail not more than 1 year.

Act No. 88, P.A. 1875 — Exemption from Taxation on Attachment

AN ACT to exempt private burial grounds and places of interment for the dead from taxation and levy on execution or attachment.

MCLA 128.111 Private burial grounds; laying out; deed. MSA 5.3161

MCLA 128.112 Same; exemptions. MSA 5.3162

JOINT ACTION
Act No. 174, P.A. 1931 — United Spanish War Veterans

AN ACT to incorporate the United Spanish War Veterans, Department of Michigan, and subordinate camps of the United Spanish War Veterans.

MCLA 35.271 — 35.276 [MSA 21.1031 – 21.1036]

MCLA 35.277 Articles of association; joint erection of buildings; cemeteries. [MSA 21.1037]

MCLA 35.278 Same; application of general corporation act. [MSA 21.1038]

Act No. 63, P.A. 1915 — Markers for Veterans' Graves

AN ACT to provide for the furnishing, at public expense, suitable markers for graves of honorably discharged soldiers, sailors and marines, who served in the army of the United States, to provide for the marking and designation of such graves for memorial purposes, to provide a penalty for the removal or destruction of such markers or designs when placed, and to repeal Act No. 136 of the Public Acts of 1907, approved June 12, 1907.

MCLA 35.831 Markers for graves of veterans; furnished by municipality. [MSA 4.1351]

MCLA 35.832 Same; petition, contents. [MSA 4.1352]

MCLA 35.833 Same; destruction, etc., penalty. [MSA 4.1353]

Note: The above act provides for the township to place markers on veterans' graves in all cemeteries in the township, whether controlled by the township or not.

JOINT ACTION
Act No. 95, P.A. 1909 — Property Held by Township Boards

AN ACT to authorize township boards of health to receive and hold any property, real or personal, left to said board in trust for the upkeep of any cemetery or lots therein, and permitting said board to expend such funds in accordance with the provisions of such trust.

MCLA 128.71 Township board, realty trusteeship duties. [MSA 5.3131]

MCLA 128.72 Trust fund; investment. [MSA 5.3132]

*Sec. 2.   All moneys and property ... (to be held in trust) ...,
and no part of such income shall be used or appropriated for other
than the purposes expressed in said trust, except the paying of the
clerk of said board for his services in carrying out the provisions
of said trust, which amount shall be determined by the board.*

MCLA 128.73 Same; not transferable. [MSA 5.3133]

MCLA 128.74 Treasurer and custodian; bond. [MSA 5.3134]

*Sec. 4.   The clerk of said board shall be the treasurer of said
board and custodian of such trust fund, and said board shall take
into consideration this duty of the clerk in fixing the amount of
his official bond, which in all cases shall be adequate to cover
the moneys or property under his control for the purposes of this
act.*

JOINT ACTION
Act No. 81, P.A. 1903 — Cemetery Lots, Care Deposits

*AN ACT to provide for the care and preservation of
cemetery lots.*

MCLA 128.81 Cemetery lots, deposit for care with county treasurer.
[MSA 5.731]

MCLA 128.82   Same; investment; county may borrow. [MSA 5.732]

MCLA 128.83   Interest; payment sexton's claims.   [MSA 5.733]

MCLA 128.84   Treasurer's receipts, contents; duplicate, filing.
[MSA 5.734]

MCLA 128.85 Treasurer's bond, increase. [MSA 5.735]

MCLA 128.86 Annual report. [MSA 5.736]

MCLA 128.87 Deposits; county liability. [MSA 5.737]

MCLA 128.88 Same; tax exempt. [MSA 5.738]

Note: The above act provides for care when a local municipality has no plan of its own.

Act No. 49, P.A. 1895 — Private Cemetery in Township, Vacation

AN ACT to provide for vacating cemeteries in townships.

MCLA 128.31   Private township cemetery, proceedings to vacate.
[MSA 5.3071]

MCLA 128.32   Petition by local health board, contents; notice; failure to act; costs. [MSA 5.3072]

Note: If health board fails to act, a freeholder may.

MCLA 128.33   Hearing; burden of proof; order, recording. [MSA 5.3073]

MCLA 128.34   Reinterment; expenses. [MSA 5.3074]

MCLA 128.35   Lot owner; reimbursement. [MSA 5.3075]

MCLA 128.36   Reversion to original owner, conditions. [MSA 5.3076]

JOINT ACTION
Act No. 164, P.A. 1871 — Cemetery in City or Village, Vacation

AN ACT to provide for vacating cemetery plats and cemetery grounds in the limits of incorporated cities and villages.

MCLA 128.41   Vacation of cemetery; jurisdiction of chancery court.
[MSA 5.3081]

MCLA 128.42   Petition of trustees or council to vacate; notice.
[MSA 5.3082]

MCLA 128.43   Court proceedings; order to vacate; recording.
[MSA 5.3083]

MCLA 128.44   Reinterment; time of year; expenses, payment.
[MSA 5.3084]

Note: May be in cemetery within six miles of city or village limits.

MCLA 128.45 Price of lots repaid. [MSA 5.3085]

Act No. 297, P.A. 1929 — Cemetery in City or Village, Vacation

AN ACT to provide for vacating private and public cemetery plats and cemetery grounds in the limits of incorporated cities and villages and to provide for the acquisition by said cities and villages of the cemetery grounds and plats vacated hereunder.

MCLA 128.51 — 128.57 [MSA 5.3091 — 5.3097]

Note: The following several citations refer to corporations and/or associations with which a township may cooperate with regard to cemeteries.

JOINT ACTION
Act No. 284, P.A. 1972 — Business Corporation Act

AN ACT to provide for the organization and regulation of corporations; to prescribe their duties, rights, powers, immunities and liabilities; to provide for the authorization of foreign corporations within this state; to prescribe the functions of the administrator of this act; to prescribe penalties for violations of this act; and to repeal certain acts and parts of acts.

MCLA 450.1123 Applicability to listed types of corporations. [MSA 21.200(123)]

Sec. 123. (1) Unless otherwise provided in, or inconsistent with, the act under which such corporation is or has been formed, this act applies to ... cemetery, burial and cremation associations, ...

JOINT ACTION
Act No. 87, P.A. 1855 — Cemetery Corporations

AN ACT relative to burying grounds.

MCLA 456.1 Cemetery corporation; incorporators. [MSA 21.821]

MCLA 456.2 Land; acquisition, encumbrance, payment; lease, restriction. [MSA 21.822]

MCLA 456.3 Right of burial; definition. [MSA 21.823]

MCLA 456.3a Same; granting of, in tax delinquent lands prohibited. [MSA 21.823(1)]

MCLA 456.4 - 456.16 [MSA 21.824 - 21.836]

Note: The above sections deal with rights and responsibilities of members, officers, corporation; by-laws and rules, elections, compensation, bonding, etc.

MCLA 456.17 Laying out of burial ground; maps and certificate, filing. [MSA 21.837]

MCLA 456.18 Actions and suits; common seal. [MSA 21.838]

MCLA 456.19 Reincorporation under act; lot owners in public burying ground, incorporation; transfer of rights from municipalities. [MSA 21.839]

MCLA 456.20 Saving clause. [MSA 21.840]

MCLA 456.21 Vacation of burying ground; procedure. [MSA 21.841]

MCLA 456.22 - 456.34 [MSA 21.842 - 21.854]

Note: The above sections deal with burial rights, assessments, voting, records and record-keeping, prices and payments, by-laws, treasurer's duties, potter's field, etc.

MCLA 456.35 Memorial fund, use; contributions, etc., investment, use; gifts, etc., in trust. [MSA 21.855]

MCLA 456.35a Endowment care fund; creation; deposits; administration; investment; use; remedies. [MSA 21.855(1)]

MCLA 456.35b Endowment care fund; exemption. [MSA 21.855(2)]

MCLA 456.36 Additional land; taxation; conveyance. [MSA 21.856]

Act No. 185, P.A. 1929 — Extension of Corporate Life

AN ACT to provide for the extension in perpetuity or for a term of years, of the term of existence of corporations or associations, organized under Act No. 87 of acts of the legislature of the state of Michigan of 1855, approved February twelfth, 1855, entitled "An act relating to burying grounds," or under said act as amended, the corporate term of existence of which has heretofore expired, or may hereafter expire by limitation, and to fix the duties and liabilities of such renewed corporations or associations, and to repeal Act No. 154 of the Public Acts of 1893, ...

MCLA 456.51 - 456.52 [MSA 21.861 - 21.862]

JOINT ACTION
Act No. 12, P.A. 1869 — Rural Cemeteries

AN ACT to authorize and encourage the formation of corporations to establish rural cemeteries, and to provide for the care and maintenance thereof, and to provide for the revision and codification of the laws relating to cemeteries, mausoleums, crypts, vaults, crematoriums, and other means of disposing of the dead, and to make an appropriation therefor.

MCLA 456.101 Cemetery corporations; incorporators, name. [MSA 21.871]

MCLA 456.102 - 456.106 [MSA 21.872 - 21.876]

MCLA 456.106a Conveyance of land. [MSA 21.876(1)]

MCLA 456.107 Board of directors, duties, reports, accounting. [MSA 21.877]

MCLA 456.107a Endowment care funds, minimum, administration investment, supervision. [MSA 21.877(1)]

MCLA 456.108 Tax exemption. [MSA 21.878]

MCLA 456.109 Burial rights, granting of, in lands subject to lien or tax delinquent prohibited. [MSA 21.879]

MCLA 456.110 Highways, etc., through grounds; right to purchase additional property. [MSA 21.880]

MCLA 456.111 Saloons and amusements prohibited. [MSA 21.881]

MCLA 456.112 Burial rights, transfer, rights of surviving spouse, next of kin. [MSA 21.882]

MCLA 456.113 Arrests, power of employes to make; offender brought before justice and tried or bound over. [MSA 21.883]

MCLA 456.114 Use of firearms in cemetery; entering over fence; penalty. [MSA 21.884]

MCLA 456.115 Perpetual care fund; receipts; investment; bond; account. [MSA 21.886]

MCLA 456.116 Non-profit corporation. [MSA 21.887(1)]

MCLA 456.117 Charter not deemed forfeited; filing articles; affidavit, report. [MSA 21.887(2)]

MCLA 456.118 Corporate name. [MSA 21.887(3)]

MCLA 456.119 List of corporations, compilation; forwarding to corporation and securities commission. [MSA 21.887(4)]

JOINT ACTION
Act No. 14, P.A. 1903 — Extension of Corporate Life

AN ACT to provide for the extension of the term of existence of corporations or associations organized under Act No. 12 of the Public Acts of 1869, entitled "An act to authorize and encourage the formation of corporations to establish rural cemeteries and to provide for the care and maintenance thereof," as amended, ... the corporate term of which has heretofore expired or which (may) hereafter expire by limitation, and to fix the duties and liabilities of such renewed corporations or associations.

MCLA 456.151 Extension of corporate life; reorganization or incorporation; procedure; articles or certified copy as evidence; rights and duties. [MSA 21.891]

JOINT ACTION
Act No. 138, P.A. 1941 – Reinstatement of Charters; Cemetery Associations

AN ACT to provide the terms and conditions upon which nonprofit cemetery associations, the charters of which have become void through operation of law, may be reinstated and the filing of delinquent reports and fees and avoidance of charter waived; and to direct the county clerk to furnish a written list to the Michigan corporation and securities commission of all nonprofit cemetery associations located within the counties.

MCLA 450.471 Nonprofit cemetery associations; reinstatement of charters, reports, penalties. [MSA 21.934]

MCLA 450.472 Same; restoration of rights; validation of contracts. [MSA 21.935]

MCLA 450.473 Duty of county clerk to forward list of associations to commission. [MSA 21.936]

JOINT ACTION
Act No. 10, P.A. 1927 – Transfer of Rights to Municipal Corporation

AN ACT to authorize cemetery corporations to sell or convey property rights, franchises and liabilities to a municipal corporation.

MCLA 456.181 Cemetery corporations; sale to municipal corporation, defined. [MSA 21.901]

MCLA 456.182 Resolution of directors; special meeting of stockholders. [MSA 21.902]

MCLA 456.183 Notice of special meeting; publication. [MSA 21.903]

MCLA 456.184 Rights, not affected by sale; duties of municipal corporation. [MSA 21.904]

JOINT ACTION
Act No. 58, P.A. 1915 — Cremation Companies

AN ACT to provide for the incorporation of cremation companies and associations.

MCLA 456.201 Cremation companies; incorporators, purposes. [MSA 21.911]

MCLA 456.202 Articles; signing, acknowledgment, contents. [MSA 21.912]

MCLA 456.203 Certificate of organization; signing, recording, fee. [MSA 21.913]

MCLA 456.204 Holding of land. [MSA 21.914]

MCLA 456.205 Tax exemption; exception. [MSA 21.915]

MCLA 456.206 Encumbrance of certain property prohibited. [MSA 21.916]

MCLA 456.207 - 456.209 [MSA 21.917 - 21.919]

MCLA 456.210 Records; cremations. [MSA 21.920]

MCLA 456.211 Same; niches. [MSA 21.921]

MCLA 456.212 Grounds; laying out, improvement. [MSA 21.922]

MCLA 456.213 Sale of niches; trust fund, investment and use. [MSA 21.923]

JOINT ACTION
Act No. 13, P.A. 1882 — Vault Associations

AN ACT to authorize the formation of vault associations in the state of Michigan for the purpose of preserving and protecting bodies of deceased persons before burial.

MCLA 456.251 Vault associations; incorporators; articles, execution, filing; body corporate. [MSA 21.931]

MCLA 456.252 Articles; contents. [MSA 21.932]

MCLA 456.253 Powers of corporation. [MSA 21.933]

Note: The following fraternal and ecclesiastical associations are included since a township official may at some time or another have to deal with problems which may arise regarding operation of a cemetery within the township limits by one of these organizations.

JOINT ACTION
Act No. 207, P.A. 1867 — Roman Catholic Bishops

MCLA 458.1 — 458.2 [MSA 21.1691 — 21.1692]

JOINT ACTION
Act No. 54, P.A. 1899 — Baptist Churches

MCLA 458.101 — 458.112 [MSA 21.1781 — 21.1792]

JOINT ACTION
Act No. 53, P.A. 1901 — Congregational Churches

MCLA 458.301 - 458.310 [MSA 21.1881 - 21.1890]

JOINT ACTION
Act No. 54, P.A. 1899 - Baptist Churches

MCLA 458.101 - 458.112 [MSA 21.1781 - 21.1892]

JOINT ACTION
Act No. 82, P.A. 1899 — Reformed Protestant Dutch Churches

MCLA 458.401 — 458.408 [MSA 21.1921 — 21.1928]

JOINT ACTION
Act No. 134, P.A. 1871 — St. George's Societies

MCLA 457.1 — 457.7 [MSA 21.1051 — 21.1057]

JOINT ACTION
Act No. 173, P.A. 1891 — Sons of St. George

MCLA 457.11 — 457.19 [MSA 21.1061 — 21.1069]

JOINT ACTION
Act No. 53, P.A. 1875 — St. Patrick Societies

MCLA 457.31 — 457.37 [MSA 21.1091 — 21.1096]

JOINT ACTION
Act No. 55, P.A. 1895 — Loyal Orange Institution

MCLA 457.51 — 457.58 [MSA 21.1121 — 21.1128]

JOINT ACTION
Act No. 145, P.A. 1865 — Masonic Lodges

MCLA 457.201 — 457.210 [MSA 21.1201 — 21.1210]

JOINT ACTION
Act No. 256, P.A. 1897 — White Shrine of Jerusalem

MCLA 457.291 — 457.297 [MSA 21.1281 — 21.1287]

JOINT ACTION
Act No. 90, P.A. 1905 — Independent Order of Odd Fellows

MCLA 457.321 — 457.332 [MSA 21.1301 — 21.1312]

JOINT ACTION
Act No. 17, P.A. 1877 — Knights of Pythias Lodges

MCLA 457.351 — 457.359 [MSA 21.1321 — 21.1329]

JOINT ACTION
Act No. 16, P.A. 1875 — Improved Order of Red Men

MCLA 457.481 — 457.488 [MSA 21.1431 — 21.1438]

JOINT ACTION
Act No. 78, P.A. 1891 — Knights of the Golden Eagle

630

MCLA 457.581 — 457.590 [MSA 21.1531 — 21.1540]

JOINT ACTION
Act No. 39, P.A. 1893 — Knights of the Ancient Essenic Order

MCLA 457.621 — 457.629 [MSA 21.1571 — 21.1579]

JOINT ACTION
Act No. 208, P.A. 1895 — Rathbone Sisters

MCLA 457.651 — 457.657 [MSA 21.1611 — 21.1617]

Robert Fitzke in His People Powered Vehicle

It's Called PPV

Three-Wheeler As Easy to Ride As a Bike

By SUE STEPHENSON
Staff Writer

It has adjustable bucket seats, three-on-the-floor and a low-slung, smartly painted, polyethylene body.

A snazzy little sports car? Wrong. Its retail price is only $380.

BESIDES, IT has three wheels, runs on pedal power and is steered with a handlebar.

An adult tricycle? Wrong again.

This snazzy, sports-car-appearing, pedal-powered-thing is a People Powered Vehicle (PPV), developed and manufactured by the EVI Co.

PPVS HAVE only been mass produced in Sterling Heights since January 1973, and Robert Fitzke, 1111 Elmwood, is the proud owner of one.

Fitzke, 47, is a lobbyist for the Hazel Park Race Track, consultant for the Michigan Bar Association and vice president of Capitol Associates.

A "bike nut" since 1957, his left side was partly paralyzed two years ago after an operation for a blood clot on his brain.

THIS ENDED his normal practice of riding a ten-speed bike to work four to five days a week, so he started looking for alternatives.

The first was an adult tricycle. But after a few spills, he became a believer in Ralph Nader's report on the instability of tricycles and looked for another alternative.

"Then I read about the PPV in a Popular Science magazine article," Fitzke said, said, "so I called up the distributor in Saranac and checked with him on the possibility of a handicapped person using a PPV.

"I WAS convinced to go there and try one out and I ended up buying it on the spot. The PPV is as easy to ride as a bike, but it's more stable."

The sporty three-wheeler can go as fast as 20 miles an hour in high gear if the driver's legs hold out. Since pedaling is in front, rather than beneath, weight can't be used to replace muscle-power.

It stands on end and locks to a post for parking, and carries 400 pounds easily.

"THE PPV abides by the same rules of the.road as a bicycle," said Fitzke.

Fitzke is hesitant to use the PPV around a lot of people and traffic, so he usually only goes shopping at the nearby Lansing Mall or for casual drives.

"About 15 per cent of the customers buy PPVs for medically prescribed exercise," said Wynell Whitmore, manager of marketing services for EVI. "A few buy PPVs to commute to and from work, but many buy them for neighborhood recreation.

"WE HAVE forcused on short-ranged, leisurely, fun transportation," he said, "a market which is missed by everybody."

"The cost of two years insurance on a second automobile could buy a PPV," Whitmore said, and "you'd never have to say 'fill it up.' "

"Besides," he said, "our researchers predict that in the near future gasoline may cost as much as $2 a gallon."

As a safety feature, EVI "developed a super strong fork in the PPV," said Whitmore. "This is the weakest point on any bike," he says.

ANOTHER FIRM of EVI is developing an Electric Powered Vehicle (EPV), complete with an FM stereo radio.

"Anybody can build an internal combustion engine to pump out dirt and smog," Whitmor says, "but it takes a little effort to create an alternative. And the PPV is even healthful."

Chapter VI

ROADS, HIGHWAYS, BRIDGES AND CULVERTS

After viewing the picture and article on the opposite page, the temptation was great to fold up the material on highways, roads and bridges and forget the whole thing. However, reason prevailed. There will always be need for adequate highways to take care of emergency vehicles, public transportation and large construction vehicles, even if the passenger motor vehicle as we know it should some day pass from the scene.

Michigan pioneers traveled about mainly by foot and horseback and sometimes by water transportation. Then came wagons and the stage coach, and in the towns those awkward high-wheeled bicycles made their appearance. Trails through the woods developed into dirt roads, with the more heavily traveled ones being supported by log roadbeds, creating what became known as corduroy roads. Railroads provided the solution to wider travel needs. Then at the turn of the century the first statute was passed in Michigan taking into account the automobile. Today there is a vast network of federal interstate and state expressways and highways, laced with many local connecting roads and streets to take care of millions of motor vehicles of all kinds. Passenger train service has given way to the more convenient and faster plane travel, as well as buses and private motor vehicles. Trucks compete with railroads for long-haul transportation of goods.

We have become a motorized generation, calling for bigger and better highways. When that first highway act was passed in 1909, there were one or two cars per day using a right of way fifteen feet wide; today's modern freeway has a right of way often measuring more than 200 feet in width, with interchanges consuming anywhere from a half dozen to more than 1,200 acres. Few people realize, as they drive over the average freeway or interstate highway, that each time their wheels turn the odometer another mile, they have traveled over twenty-four and a half acres of land. Much of it has been cut out of prime agricultural land, making serious inroads on Michigan's historical agricultural economy. Furthermore, there is alarm that although highways have opened up much new recreational area in the state, the delicate balance of nature and wildlife is being disrupted. Michigan's economy is based mainly on agriculture, recreation and the automobile industry. Somehow a balance must be created so that the latter does not eliminate the others. Highways and roads are just one phase of the problem--the reader is also urged to consider the chapters on Environmental Protection and Control, and Planning and Zoning.

Reckless waste of land resources must be stopped. Highway engineers, environmentalists, ecologists and safety experts predict that in the future, if there is not some miraculous transition in highway design and form of vehicle power, highway construction will cost more. Land which is not suitable for agriculture is generally hilly and/or swampy. Highways in these areas will call for more bridges, curves, grades and safety devices. All this along with shortages of gasoline and diesel fuel, is bringing us almost full circle back to the need for providing overland mass transit, along with provisions for slow-moving people-powered vehicles such as bicycles, adult tricycles and the modern contraption illustrated at the beginning of this chapter. Such vehicles, of course, have no place on heavily traveled highways and roads--in fact, they are prohibited on interstate highways, freeways and many of the more heavily traveled streets and roads.

The District of Columbia, working with the city of Washington, has provided bicycle paths and bus-only routes paralleling several of the main thoroughfares in and around the city. Recent estimates indicate that more than 20,000 people there are using pedal power to go to and from work. In Michigan, automobile plant parking lots show that many employees are choosing motorcycles as a cheaper and more convenient way of getting to and from work. Employers of large numbers of people, with state government leading the way in Lansing, are encouraging their employees to use car pools, public transportation, motorcycles and bicycles. A recent mass transit package passed by the Michigan legislature has diverted from highway use $100.000 of Michigan's gas and weight taxes (which were increased at the same time) for laying out and constructing bicycle paths, and additional funds are to be utilized for improving mass transit. Congress has included both of these uses among those which may be funded through federal revenue sharing moneys.

GENERAL HIGHWAY LAWS

Prior to 1932 townships were responsible, with some assistance from the state, for laying out, constructing and maintaining township roads and bridges. However, during the depression years of the thirties, circumstances required that that responsibility be vested in the county boards of supervisors. There was a transitional period of five years during which the title and all activities regarding township roads were integrated with the county road networks. Since township supervisors were members of the county boards of supervisors, townships still had a measure of assurance that their needs would be met. However, subsequent elimination of the township supervisor from the county governing body and the establishment of the county road commissions brought about a situation that leaves much to be desired.

County officials now generally seem to think that since the roads and bridges serve people living in the townships, then the townships should pay a considerable portion of construction and maintenance costs. They point to the fact that federal and state revenue sharing funds will build roads, and build them now. Furthermore, they say that the state statutes permit township boards to levy up to three mills for road maintenance and improvement without a vote of the people. (See MCLA 247.670, [MSA 9.1019])

First of all, it should be made clear that 44.5 percent of the state's gas and weight tax funds go to the state, 35.7 per cent to the counties and 19.8 per cent to cities and villages--**not one cent goes to any township.** As little as 4 per cent would enable townships to do a creditable job of taking care of their needs, but it has not been forthcoming. As for the three mills for township roads, the courts and the attorney general have in effect ruled that the constitution has eliminated that as a source of funding since it may be levied **only** within the fifteen mill constitutional limitation. **Since each of the eighty-three counties in the state are at or have exceeded the fifteen mill limitation, this means that no township can raise road funds in this way.** It is a sad situation that the legislature permits a law to remain on the books with a provision which is not only meaningless, but actually harmful to the relationship between township boards, county road commissions and others who read the citation as a legal fact rather than as an unenforceable provision of the law.

As for the six mills which may be authorized by vote of the of the electorate and other state federal revenue sharing funds, township residents are arguing that providing services and utilities such as fire and police protection, sanitary and storm sewers, street lights, sidewalks, tree trimming, libraries and myriads of other things are equally as important as roads and their tax dollars should go for these things. Since counties receive gas and weight tax funds for road use and since township roads are almost entirely under county control, township citizens feel the counties should take basic financial responsibility for them.

BRIDGES AND CULVERTS

This introduction would not be complete without some specific discussion of the problems created by the high cost of bridge construction. Costs far exceed an average mile-per-car use. Present laws provide for inter-community participation, with cost apportioned according to general road-use requirements and/or the watercourse to be bridged. A number of counties have found it necessary to levy a special county-wide tax for bridges and may also require certain communities, including townships, to pay an additional proportion. There must be a great deal of cooperation between governmental units and realization on the part of the citizens that bridges are necessary even if they are expensive.

Compounding the problem right now is the fact that so many of the older bridges are becoming obsolete or unsafe for modern traffic and too often have actually reached the stage of deterioration where they are breaking down completely. County road commissions, which usually have the final say on safety of a bridge, frequently close a bridge or establish load restrictions. It is not uncommon for a driver with a heavy load to ignore the weight restrictions and the bridge goes out. The structure may be seriously damaged or even destroyed because a driver loses control of the vehicle on rain-slick or icy bridge approaches, striking a weakened portion of an old bridge. Thus communities are often almost completely isolated, with citizens having to drive many miles to reach a destination

636

which may be only a few miles away. School bus drivers very often have to escort their passengers across a bridge on foot, then go back and bring the bus very slowly across.

Plans have long been under way to restudy the entire system of financing bridge replacements. It is time for action in this respect. This might again be a matter for some regional planning to occur, with representatives of the state and federal governments involved as well.

Act No. 283, P.A. 1909 — General Highway Law

AN ACT to revise, consolidate and add to the laws relating to the establishment, opening, discontinuing, vacating, closing, altering, improvement, maintenance and use of the public highways and private roads, the condemnation of property and gravel therefor; the building, repairing and preservation of bridges; setting and protecting shade trees, drainage, cutting weeds and brush within this state, and providing for the election or appointment and defining the powers, duties and compensation of state, county, township and district highway officials.

GENERAL PURPOSE OF ACT

MCLA 220.1 Establishment and maintenance of highways and private roads; authority of municipalities; duties of highway officials. [MSA 9.1]

CHAPTER I. LAYING OUT, ALTERING AND DISCONTINUING HIGHWAYS

MCLA 221.20 Public highway; definition, width. [MSA 9.21]

MCLA 221.22 Discontinued highway. [MSA 9.23]

MCLA 221.27 Highway across railroads; permission; right of way; public utilities commission, powers; construction, maintenance; cost, allocation; penalties. [MSA 9.28]

CHAPTER IV. COUNTY ROAD LAW

MCLA 224.1 Adoption of county road system; referendum, form of resolution; special election. [MSA 9.101]

Sec. 1.   On petition of not less than 10 per centum of the resident freeholders residing in each of the several organized townships, ...

MCLA 224.2 – 224.5 [MSA 9.102 – 9.105] (Regarding the election procedure)

MCLA 224.6 County road commissioners; appointment or election, procedure; term of office; removal of appointed commissioner; complete board. [MSA 9.106]

MCLA 224.7 – 224.10a [MSA 9.107 – 9.110(1)] (Regarding the commission)

MCLA 224.11 Same; authority to lay out, widen or change (any) **road** (over which authority is assumed); **purchase of private property.** [MSA 9.111]

MCLA 224.12 – 224.16 [MSA 9.112 – 9.116] (Regarding condemnation procedures)

MCLA 224.17 County line road; disagreement, arbitration; neglect of county commissioners; authority of state highway commissioner, deduction from county tax refunds. [MSA 9.1117]

MCLA 224.18 State reward for county roads; map; conversion to county roads; determination, notice; name; intercounty roads; abandonment; discontinuance of jurisdiction; petition, list of occupants on abutting lands. Procedure; conversion; abandonment; discontinuance. Abandonment, notice of hearing, service. Affidavit of service; hearing examiner, report of findings. View of premises; necessity for abandonment. Record of determination, filing with state highway commissioner. Reservation of easement, extinguishment. [MSA 9.1118]

MCLA 224.19 County road commissioner; roads and bridges; borrowing power; validation of bonds; county highway engineer, duties; gravel; actions for injuries to road; bids; review of plans by state highway commissioner. [MSA 9.119]

MCLA 224.20 Same; surveys; tax, determination, maximum; submission to supervisors, revision, apportionment; tax levy, collection, disbursement. [MSA 9.120]

MCLA 224.20a Same; nonapplication of tax rate limitations, use of revenues. [MSA 9.120(1)]

MCLA 224.20b Highway, road, or street tax levy, submission to electorate; allocation of revenues. [MSA 9.120(2)]

MCLA 224.21 Same; authority to obligate county, limitation; roads under construction; duty of county to keep roads in repair; actions brought against board; liability for damages. [MSA 9.121]

MCLA 224.22 Bond issue; submission to electors, notice, vote; disbursement of proceeds. [MSA 9.122]

MCLA 224.25 Board of county road commissioners, statement of accounts made to board of supervisors, audit, proof of filing, publication, statement of county clerk, filing with state highway commissioner. [MSA 9.125]

CHAPTER V. STATE REWARD FOR ROADS

MCLA 225.1 State highway department; duties. [MSA 9.201]

MCLA 225.2b Commissioner to control state roads; condemnation, construction and improvement of drains. [MSA 9.204]

Sec. 2b. ... Such right of purchase or condemnation shall be deemed to exist in the case of the construction or maintenance of any road built ... in conjunction with any of the municipalities of the state. ...

MCLA 225.3 Road institutes; purpose, compensation for attendance. [MSA 9.205]

MCLA 225.14 Office and equipment, state department. [MSA 9.213]

CHAPTER IX. OPENING OF PRIVATE ROADS AND TEMPORARY HIGHWAYS

MCLA 229.1 Private road; application; hearing, notice. [MSA 9.281]

Sec. 1. When an application is made to the township supervisor for a private road, he shall give notice in writing to the owner or occupant of the land over which the road is proposed to be laid out, to meet on a day and at a place certain, which shall not be more than 10 nor less than 5 days from the time of service of the notice, for the purpose of aiding in the striking of a jury to determine the necessity of the road. If the land over which it is proposed to lay the road is nonresident and the owner thereof does not reside in the county, the notice shall be served in the same manner as is provided in laying out public roads, and proof of service or posting shall be made in like manner.

MCLA 229.2   Jury; formation; citation to appear.   MSA 9.282

Sec. 2. At the time and place designated the township supervisor shall ...

MCLA 229.3 Same; oath, duty. MSA 9.283

MCLA 229.4   Same; certificate; laying out of road.   MSA 9.284

Sec. 4. If the jury determines ... shall deliver the same to the township supervisor who shall thereupon lay out the road, describing the same particularly by its bounds, courses and distances, and shall cause a record thereof to be made in the clerk's office of the proper township, which shall be recorded in the same manner as is required of public roads.

MCLA 229.5 Damages and costs; payment. MSA 9.285

Sec. 5. The damages (and expenses) awarded ... shall be paid to the township supervisor by the person applying for the road, which damages shall be paid or tendered by the supervisor to the owner or occupant, and when paid or tendered the supervisor shall proceed to open the road.

MCLA 229.6 Width of road; use, purpose. MSA 9.286

Sec. 6. Private roads shall not be less than 1 rod in width, ...

MCLA 229.7   Temporary highways; application.   MSA 9.287

Sec. 7. Whenever an owner of any timbered land, not less than 40 acres, shall wish to have a temporary highway laid out, ...

MCLA 229.8 Same; notice; determination of necessity, damages, duration; logging railroad. MSA 9.288

MCLA 229.9 Same; consent of owner; deemed private highway; damages and expense, payment. [MSA 9.289]

MCLA 229.10 Same; winter use. [MSA 9.290]

MCLA 229.11 Appeal; procedure, bond, fees; judgment, certification; costs. [MSA 9.291]

Sec. 11. Any party in interest may appeal ... within 30 days, by filing with the township clerk an affidavit ... The party shall file with the clerk within the time a bond running to the township supervisor for ... The appellant shall pay to the township clerk the sum of $1.00 for making his return on appeal, and a sum of $3.00 as clerk and entry fee to be paid by the township clerk to the clerk of the circuit court. The appeal shall be heard before ...

CHAPTER X. PENALTIES AND FORFEITURES

MCLA 230.4 Obstruction of navigable stream, highway drain or water course; forfeiture. [MSA 9.334]

MCLA 230.5 Wilful destruction or injury; mile-stone, guide-post, etc., forfeiture. [MSA 9.335]

MCLA 230.6 Same; trees or shrubs, civil liability. [MSA 9.336]

MCLA 230.7 Injury to bridges; treble damages. [MSA 9.337]

MCLA 230.8 Trees felled in highway; removal, forfeiture for failure. [MSA 9.338]

CHAPTER XIII. MISCELLANEOUS PROVISIONS

MCLA 233.14 Ferry landings. [MSA 9.390]

Sec. 14. Ferry landings shall be deemed public highways, and may be laid out, constructed, maintained, altered, or discontinued in the same manner, and shall in all respects be subject to the same regulations, so far as they may be applicable, as other public highways and bridges; ...

CHAPTER XV. DRAINS

MCLA 235.1 Drain in public highway; release of right of way, damages. [MSA 9.431]

MCLA 235.2 Same; bridges and culverts; construction strength, apportionment and payment of cost, maintenance by property owner. [MSA 9.432]

MCLA 235.3 Open drain in highway; consent of commissioner, location, disposition of earth. [MSA 9.433]

MCLA 235.4 Same; drain commissioner to apportion costs. [MSA 9.434]

Sec. 4. The county drain commissioner shall apportion the per centum of the cost of construction of such drain which any township traversed or benefited thereby shall be liable to pay by reason of the benefit to the public health, convenience or welfare,...

MCLA 235.5 Drain across adjacent land; acquisition of right of way, approval of board, deed. [MSA 9.435]

MCLA 235.6 Report to township electors, contents; highway drain fund, use of surplus. [MSA 9.436]

MCLA 235.7 Construction report, contents, filing; powers limited to highway drainage. [MSA 9.437]

MCLA 235.8 Failure to secure right of way; application to drain commissioner, procedure; jurisdiction. [MSA 9.438]

Note: The above sections all refer to duties of the township highway commissioner, which position no longer exists. No other officer is specifically charged with these duties in this act.

MCLA 235.8a Detour roads; expense. [MSA 9.439]

CHAPTER XIX. CULVERTS, OR CATTLE-PASSES AND HEDGES

MCLA 239.1 Culverts or cattle passes; construction, permission, cost. [MSA 9.521]

Sec. 1. It shall be lawful for all persons owning land on

opposite sides of any public highway to construct culverts or cattle-passes under such highways: ...

MCLA 239.2 Same; material of construction. MSA 9.522

MCLA 239.3 Same; failure to repair, removal, cost. MSA 9.523

MCLA 239.4 Same; record. MSA 9.524

MCLA 239.5 Hedges; trimming, removal of brush, ... MSA 9.525

Sec. 5. It shall be the duty of every owner, occupant or person having charge of lands in this state, to cut or trim, or cause to be cut or trimmed, to a height not exceeding 4½ feet and a width not exceeding 3 feet, all hedges or hedge rows along or on the public highway or adjacent thereto in each and every year, except such hedges as shall have been set out for the protection of fruit trees and nursery stock. Trimmings or brush from such hedge rows shall not be left lying within the limits of the highway, but shall be forthwith removed: ...

MCLA 239.6 Penalty for neglect. MSA 9.526

Act No. 40, P.A. 1956 — The Drain Code of 1956, Ch. 13 — Highways

MCLA 280.321 — 280.327 MSA 11.1321 – 11.1327

Act No. 156, P.A. 1851 — Boards of Supervisors (Commissioners)

AN ACT to define the powers and duties of the boards of supervisors of the several counties, and to confer upon them certain local, administrative and legislative powers; and to prescribe penalties for the violation of the provisions of this act.

MCLA 46.7 Boards of supervisors; repair, buildings, bridges; borrowing power; current county operating expenses, limitation (1/10 of 1 mill, 1 year). MSA 5.327

MCLA 46.11 Same; powers. MSA 5.331

Sec. 11. The said several boards of supervisors shall have power and they are hereby authorized at any meeting thereof lawfully held: ...

Purchase of realty; poor farm. Same; county building sites. Building site, location. Sale or lease of realty. **New** sites for county buildings. Erection of buildings. Borrowing power, taxation. Loans; time limit on payment. Salaries; claims. Raising money for current expenses. Township and county poor. New tax roll. Laws, regulations, and ordinances. County officers, reports, bonds, removal, vacancies.

Township roads and bridges, financing. ... *To authorize any township or townships in their respective counties, by a vote of the electors of said township or townships, to borrow or raise by tax upon such township any sum of money not exceeding $10,000.00 in any township in any one year, to build or repair any roads or bridges in such township or townships, or in the use of which such township or townships may be interested, and to prescribe the time for payment of any such loan, which shall be within 15 years, and for assessing the principal and interest thereof upon such township or townships; and if any road or bridge is situated partly in one township and partly in another, or on the line between townships, or in case any township has any particular local interest in the construction or repair of any bridge, such boards of supervisors may determine, under such regulations as they may establish, the relative proportion which each township shall contribute in the building and repairing thereof, and the amount so apportioned to the several townships shall be assessed and collected in the same manner as other township taxes are now assessed and collected by law; ...*

Property and business management. Proceedings before board; audit of claims, removal of officers, hearing. Exchange of lands.

JOINT ACTION
Act No. 354, P.A. 1925 — Bridges and Culverts

AN ACT to provide for the construction, improvement, repair and maintenance of bridges; to provide for intermunicipal and interstate bridges; to provide for bridges over navigable streams and for their operation; to provide for the construction, improvement and maintenance of bridges over mill races; and to regulate the altering of the stage of water, and the widening and deepening of the channel of watercourses.

MCLA 254.1 Bridges and culverts; construction, improvement and repair; part of road. MSA 9.1171

Sec. 1. Bridges and culverts shall be considered in all respects as a part of the road upon which they are, or are proposed to be located. ...

MCLA 254.5 Obstructions to navigation; powers of commissioner; costs of removal; failure to remove, penalty. MSA 9.1175

INTER-MUNICIPAL BRIDGES

MCLA 254.6 Inter-township bridge; construction, repair, expense, joint action. MSA 9.1176

Sec. 6. Whenever the ... township boards of any 2 adjoining townships in either the same or different counties shall determine that a bridge on or across the township line over any stream or sink-hole, either crossing or running along the boundary line between such townships, should be constructed, rebuilt or repaired, such bridge shall be constructed, rebuilt or repaired and maintained at the joint expense of such townships. ...

MCLA 254.8 "Townships", "commissioners" construed; authority to contract. MSA 9.1178

Sec. 8. The word "townships", as used in the 2 last preceding sections, shall be deemed to include cities and incorporated villages, both in their relation to each other and to townships, and when the word commissioner is used with reference to townships, it shall be deemed to include the corporate authorities of cities and incorporated villages. ...

MCLA 254.9 Failure to join; petition to state commissioner. MSA 9.1179

MCLA 254.10 Same; hearing on petition, notice. MSA 9.1180

MCLA 254.11 Same; duties of commissioner; approval of supervisors for navigable streams. MSA 9.1181

MCLA 254.12 Same; determination of quota, alteration. MSA 9.1182

MCLA 254.13 Same; copy of determination, filing; tax levy. [MSA 9.1183]

Sec. 13. A copy of the determination of the state highway commissioner shall be filed with the clerk of each township, city and village affected, and thereupon such bridge shall be constructed, ... Each such township, ... shall cause to be levied and assessed upon the taxable property therein an amount sufficient to pay for its quota of costs as above determined, which shall be disbursed by the treasurers of the respective townships, ...

MCLA 254.14 Inter-county bridge; failure of boards of commissioners to agree on apportionment, petition to state commissioner. [MSA 9.1184]

MCLA 254.15 Interstate bridge; commissioners' authority to contract; supervisors, raising of funds, special tax, limitation. [MSA 9.1185]

GENERAL PROVISIONS

MCLA 254.17 - 254.23 [MSA 9.1187 - 9.1193]

Note: The above sections deal with bridges; specifications, carrying capacity, annual inspection, narrow, movable, movable span, construction, maintenance, posting, etc.

ALTERATION OF WATERCOURSES

MCLA 254.25 Permit. [MSA 9.1195]

MCLA 254.26 Same; costs of alteration, payment, contract. [MSA 9.1196]

MILL RACES

MCLA 254.27 - 254.29 [MSA 9.1197 - 9.1199] (Bridging race, duty of commissioner, financing)

MCLA 254.30 "Bridge", "culvert", synonymous. [MSA 9.1200]

MCLA 254.32 Bridges excepted. [MSA 9.1202]

Act No. 398, P.A. 1919 — Bridges over Navigable Streams

AN ACT to authorize the construction of bridges over navigable streams and waters in certain cases, for the continuance of public highways over such water as avenues of public travel; to authorize the levying, spreading and collecting of special taxes and assessments for any such bridge; to authorize the borrowing of money and issuance of bonds under certain restrictions, regulations and limitations; to provide for the recovery by the owners of property or property rights abutting upon or adjoining any such highway of their damages resulting by reason of the construction of such bridge and providing the procedure for recovery of such damages; and to prescribe the powers and duties of certain officers with reference thereto.

MCLA 254.51 Bridge over navigable waters in certain counties: petition. [MSA 9.1211]

Sec. 1. Whenever in any county ... there are any 2 or more organized townships, or any 1 or more townships and 1 or more villages, or 1 or more townships and 1 or more cities, or any combination of townships, villages and cities, or any combination of any of them, ... by its or their respective legislative bodies, petition the board of supervisors of said county for the construction or reconstruction of a bridge ... Such petition may be presented at any regular meeting of the said board of supervisors or at any special meeting thereof duly called for the presentation of such petition: Provided, That the provisions of this act shall apply only to counties having a population of 400,000 or more.

MCLA 254.52 Same; meeting of supervisors, notice; plans and specifications. [MSA 9.1212]

MCLA 254.53 Same; authority of board of supervisors, type of bridge. [MSA 9.1213]

MCLA 254.54 County under road system; authority of commissioners; specifications; type of bridge not to be changed. [MSA 9.1214]

MCLA 254.55 Same; special assessment district; hearing of objections, notice; change in specifications, new hearing; district, change in boundaries. [MSA 9.1215]

MCLA 254.56 Same; final order of commissioners. [MSA 9.1216]

MCLA 254.57 Same; powers and duties of commissioners. [MSA 9.1217]

MCLA 254.58 Same; rights, duties, remedies and limitations; legislative intent. [MSA 9.1218]

MCLA 254.59 Same; annual installments; apportionment of cost; announcement of decision; exemption. [MSA 9.1219]

MCLA 254.60 County not under road system; authority of supervisors, delegation. [MSA 9.1220]

MCLA 254.61 Same; powers and duties; legislative intent. [MSA 9.1221]

MCLA 254.62 Bridge deemed public highway; maintenance by county. [MSA 9.1222]

MCLA 254.63 Tax limit; referendum; application to other acts. [MSA 9.1223]

MCLA 254.64 Recovery of damages; plaintiff; bringing of action within year. [MSA 9.1224]

MCLA 254.65 Same; action commenced by summons, service; alias and pluries summons; return, filing. [MSA 9.1225]

MCLA 254.66 Same; pleadings, proceedings. [MSA 9.1226]

MCLA 254.67 Same; tax levy. [MSA 9.1227]

Act No. 59, P.A. 1915 - Assessment Districts - Covert Act

AN ACT to provide for the construction, improvement and maintenance of highways; for the levying, spreading and collecting of taxes and of special assessments there-

for; to authorize the borrowing of money and the issuance of bonds under certain restrictions, regulations and limitations; to prescribe the powers and duties of certain officers with reference thereto; and to validate certain proceedings heretofore taken.

MCLA 247.418 - 247.481 [MSA 9.714 - 9.775]

Note: The Covert Act has been substantially repealed. The only portion that remains effective pertains to special assessment proceedings which, unless referred to by other statutes, are of no particular significance at this time.

Act No. 359, P.A. 1947 — Charter Townships

MCLA 42.16 Streets, alleys, bridges and other public places, use and licensing; ordinance records, filing. [MSA 5.46(16)]

JOINT ACTION
Act No. 111, P.A. 1956 — Highways within Townships

AN ACT to provide for the acquisition, construction, establishment, opening, altering, improving and maintaining of highways; authorizing contracts between townships and boards of county road commissioners for the same; authorizing townships to finance their share of the cost of the same from its contingent fund, special assessments, and bonds or short term notes issued in anticipation of the receipt of sales tax moneys or general obligation bonds; and to prescribe procedures and conditions relative to the issuance of said bonds or short term notes.

MCLA 247.351 Highways within townships; contracts, included structures. [MSA 9.195(1)]

Sec. 1. The township board of any township and the board of county road commissioners in which said township is located are hereby authorized and shall have power to enter into a contract to provide for the acquisition, construction, establishment, opening, altering, improving and maintaining of any highways within the township. ...

MCLA 247.352 Same; contracts, contents; approval by electors, board of county road commissioners; execution. [MSA 9.195(2)]

649

MCLA 247.353 Same; funds. [MSA 9.195(3)]

Sec. 3. *For the purpose of obtaining funds to carry out the provisions of this act the township board ... is hereby authorized to pay its allocable share of the cost of any such highway improvements from any, all, or any combination of, the following methods of raising money therefor: ...*

MCLA 247.354 Same; bonds, short term notes, terms, interest, limitations. [MSA 9.195(4)]

MCLA 247.355 Same; general obligation bonds. [MSA 9.195(5)]

MCLA 247.356 Enlargement of powers. [MSA 9.195(6)]

Sec. 6. *The powers herein granted shall be deemed an enlargement of any power granted to townships and boards of county road commissioners.*

Act No. 381, P.A. 1925 — Inter-County, Super and Limited Access Highways

AN ACT to authorize certain counties to combine for the purpose of planning systems of inter-county highways, super-highways and limited access highways; to define the terms "super-highways" and "limited access highways"; to authorize the establishment of inter-county highway commissions; to prescribe their powers and duties; to provide for the appropriation of funds therefor; and to empower counties to legislate with respect thereto.

MCLA 252.1 - 252.3 [MSA 9.1081 - 9.1083]

MCLA 252.4 Same; plan, recording; plats, buildings, rules. [MSA 9.1084]

MCLA 252.5 - 252.12 [MSA 9.1085 - 9.1092]

Act No. 334, P.A. 1913 — State Reward Trunk Line Highways

AN ACT to provide for the establishment, survey, improvement and maintenance of state reward trunk line

650

highways to provide for the payment of triple state reward thereon, to define the duties of state, county, good roads district and township officers in regard thereto, and to appropriate funds to carry out the provisions thereof.

MCLA 250.2 State reward trunk lines; divisions; new highways, laying out, surveying, maps, routes; triple reward, computation. [MSA 9.862]

MCLA 250.9 Preliminary surveys; employment of engineers and employes. [MSA 9.869]

JOINT ACTION
Act No. 17, P.A. 1925 - Trunk Line Highways

AN ACT to provide for the construction, improvement and maintenance of trunk line highways.

MCLA 250.61 State trunk line highway expense, relief of local units. [MSA 9.901]

MCLA 250.62 Construction, improvement, and maintenance; contracts, work on state account. [MSA 9.902]

Sec. 2. The state highway commission is authorized to contract with ... township boards ... for the construction, improvement and maintenance of trunk line highways, or ... for an amount not exceeding $250,000.00 under any such contract with ... township boards ... The highway commission ... is authorized to contract, for an amount not exceeding $5,000.00 for each contract, for toilet vault cleaning, use of licensed sanitary landfills, rental of equipment for emergency repairs and maintenance operations, curb replacement, maintenance of office equipment, installation of utility services and installation of traffic control devices and ... may authorize ... township boards ... under contracts for the maintenance of trunk line highways, to subcontract in amounts not to exceed $5,000.00 for each subcontract.

Act No. 51, P.A. 1951 — State Trunk Line Highway System

AN ACT to provide for the classification of all public roads, streets and highways in the state of Michigan, and for the revision of such classification and for additions to and deletions from each classification; to set up and establish the motor vehicle highway fund and to provide for the deposits therein of specific taxes on motor vehicles and motor vehicle fuels; to provide for the allocation of funds therefrom and the use and administration thereof for highway purposes; to provide for the continuing review of highway needs within the state; to authorize the state highway commissioner, counties and incorporated cities and villages to borrow money, issue bonds and make pledges of funds for highway construction purposes; to authorize counties to advance funds for the payment of deficiencies necessary for the payment of bonds issued under the provisions of this act; to provide for the limitations, payment, retirement and security of such bonds and pledges; and to provide for appropriations and tax levies by counties and townships for county roads and to authorize contributions by townships therefor; and to repeal certain acts and parts of acts.

MCLA 247.651 - 247.651f [MSA 9.1097(1) - 9.1097(1F)]

MCLA 247.652 Tentative system of county primary roads; selection and certification, approval; official name. [MSA 9.1097(2)]

MCLA 247.653 Same; roads included or deleted. [MSA 9.1097(3)]

MCLA 247.654 Same; roads under jurisdiction of county road commissioners; certification and review. [MSA 9.1097(4)]

MCLA 247.655 Same; official name; establishment, certification and approval. [MSA 9.1097(5)]

Sec. 5. *All roads, streets and highways included in the county primary road system of any county shall be officially known as county primary roads, and all roads, streets and highways included in the county local road system of any county shall be officially known as county local roads. ...*

MCLA 247.656 Tentative system of streets; selection and certification; approval. [MSA 9.1097(6)]

MCLA 247.657 Same; included or deleted streets. [MSA 9.1097(7)]

MCLA 247.658 Same; streets not included, certification and approval. [MSA 9.1097(8)]

MCLA 247.659 Same; official name; establishment and certification. [MSA 9.1097(9)]

MCLA 247.659a Transportation needs, study and reports. [MSA 9.1097(9A)]

Sec. 9a. (1) The department of state highways in cooperation with the various county road commissions, cities and villages shall maintain a continuing study of the transportation needs of the state and shall report the results to the governor and the legislature by January 1, 1975, and every 2 years thereafter. ...

(2) The continuing study shall include an annual review and report of the functional classification of the highways, roads and streets of the state.

MCLA 247.660 Motor vehicle highway fund; establishment, deposits; apportionment, distribution. [MSA 9.1097(10)]

Sec. 10. ... all moneys in the motor vehicle highway fund are apportioned and appropriated for each fiscal year as follows: (a) 44.5% thereof to the department of state highways, (b) 35.7% thereof to the several county road commissions of the state, and (c) 19.8% thereof to the incorporated cities and villages of the state, to be distributed and used for highway purposes as hereinafter provided in this act. (Author's note: **Nothing** for townships)

MCLA 247.660a Highway, road, and street mileage, determination, transfers; current average revenue worth per mile; money transfers. [MSA 9.1097(10A)]

MCLA 247.660b General transportation fund, creation, appropriation, administration; department of state highways, general functions. [MSA 9.1097(10B)]

MCLA 247.660c Definitions. [MSA 9.1097(10C)]

MCLA 247.660d Use and objective of general transportation fund. [MSA 9.1097(10D)]

MCLA 247.660e Priorities (and amounts) in use of general transportation fund. [MSA 9.1097(10E)]

MCLA 247.660f Urban public transportation plans, development, review, acceptance, notice (to affected townships), comments. [MSA 9.1097(10F)]

MCLA 247.660g Rules, implementation and administration of general transportation fund. [MSA 9.1097(10G)]

MCLA 247.660h Reports as to projects and eligible authorities and governmental agencies; approval or rejection of projects; financial reports; audits. [MSA 5.1097(10H)]

MCLA 247.660i Public transportation council, creation, membership, advisory functions. [MSA 9.1097(10 - I)]

MCLA 247.660j Eligible authorities ineligible to receive grants, grounds. [MSA 9.1097(10J)]

MCLA 247.660k Facilities (lanes, paths, roads) for nonmotorized transportation (including bicycles). [MSA 9.1097(10K)]

MCLA 247.661 Same; transfer to state trunk line fund; priority of purpose. Limited access highways. Highway construction bonds; series. Same; future issues. State highway department operating expenses. State trunk line highways and bridges; maintenance. Same; opening, widening, improving, construction, reconstruction, interstate highway system. Contracts with boards of county road commissioners, cities and villages, joint participation in costs. [MSA 9.1097(11)]

MCLA 247.661a State trunk line fund, use of additional moneys from motor fuel tax increase. [MSA 9.1097(11A)] (Specific locations)

MCLA 247.661b Critical bridge program, appropriation, rules. [MSA 9.1097(11B)]

MCLA 247.662 Same; uses of county allocation. Registered professional engineers. Snow removal. County primary or local roads in urban areas. County primary road systems, in general. County local road systems, in general. Bond payments. County primary and local road system funds, matching funds, emergency uses. Highway construction and reconstruction; snow removal. Roadside parks and motor parkways. Deposits; administration expenses. Board of county road commissioners, duties. Contracts with state highway commission, cities, villages, and other counties. County local roads and bridges, matched moneys, expenditure limitation. [MSA 9.1097(12)]

Note: The township budget may include an item for maintenance or improvement of county roads within township boundaries, including an item for matching county funds.

MCLA 247.662a Snow removal; distribution of funds.
[MSA 9.1097(12A)]

MCLA 247.662b Funds returned to counties from motor vehicle highway fund, distribution; urban area boundaries. [MSA 9.1097(12B)]

MCLA 247.663 Same; uses of city and village allocation, population, determination of mileage. Major street system, roadside parks and motor parkways. Local street systems. Same; matched funds. Transferrable amounts from and to major street system uses; administrative expenses. Street administrator. Contracts with county and state highway commission. [MSA 9.1097(13)]

MCLA 247.663a Right-of-way; acquisition. [MSA 9.1097(13A)]

MCLA 247.664 Motor vehicle highway fund; administration and use; programs submitted to state highway commissioner; separate accounts; records; annual report to governor, contents.
[MSA 9.1097(14)]

MCLA 247.664a Expenditure of allocated funds, prerequisites; rules, engineering determination of benefits; payment of drain assessments. [MSA 9.1097(14A)]

MCLA 247.665 Reports to state highway commissioner, contents.
[MSA 9.1097(15)]

MCLA 247.666 Forfeiture of funds. [MSA 9.1097(16)]

MCLA 247.667 Motor vehicle and gasoline taxes; deposits to motor vehicle highway fund; distribution; advances to local units.

State highway commissioner's report to legislature and governor as to revenues and disbursements. [MSA 9.1097(17)]

MCLA 247.668a Motor vehicle highway fund; use of moneys distributed. [MSA 9.1097(18A)]

MCLA 247.668b State highway commissioner bonds; issuance, pledge of motor vehicle highway fund receipts. [MSA 9.1097(18B)]

MCLA 247.668c County highway bonds, issuance, pledge of motor vehicle highway fund receipts. [MSA 9.1097(18C)]

MCLA 247.668d Joint contract bonds; approval, issuance, bids. Limitation on pledge. [MSA 9.1097(18D)]

MCLA 247.668e Bonds; maturities, interest, redemption, registration. [MSA 9.1097(18E)]

MCLA 247.668f Same: county, approval; public sale. [MSA 9.1097(18F)]

MCLA 247.668g Same; protection of outstanding bonds. [MSA 9.1097(18G)]

MCLA 247.668h Same; negotiability; payment, exemption from taxation. [MSA 9.1097(18H)]

MCLA 247.668i Cumulative authority of act. [MSA 9.1097(18 - I)]

MCLA 247.668j Revenues subject to pledge; successive borrowings. [MSA 9.1097(18J)]

MCLA 247.669 Roads, streets and alleys taken over as county roads. [MSA 9.1097(19)]

MCLA 247.670 Unexpended balances of township funds; appropriation for local road maintenance or improvement; additional powers; snow removal in Marquette county townships. [MSA 9.1097(20)]

Sec. 20. Notwithstanding any other provisions of this act the township board of any township may appropriate any unexpended balances in the contingent or general fund of the township without submitting the question to the electors of said township, or raise

656

money by the issuance of bonds of the township, ... and to pay any sum so appropriated or raised into the county road fund of the county for the maintenance and/or improvement of county roads within the townships, or for the widening of state trunk line highways beyond the width required for state trunk line traffic in unincorporated areas of such township, pursuant to an agreement between the township and the county road commission. Where funds are to be used for the widening of a state trunk line highway, the county road commission shall enter into agreement with the state highway commissioner for the work. Notwithstanding any other provisions of this act the township board of any township may also levy a property tax of not to exceed 3 mills* on each dollar of

----

*Since every county has reached or surpassed the constitutional fifteen mill limitation, this tax provision is no longer operative in any township.

----

assessed valuation of the township in any year for the maintenance or improvement of county roads within the township or for the widening of state trunk line highways, as aforesaid, without submitting the question to the electors of said township, and pay any sum so raised into the county road fund of the county for the aforesaid purposes pursuant to an agreement with the county road commission: Provided, That in addition to the foregoing powers any township may, when authorized by a vote of the electorate, levy a property tax of not to exceed 6 mills on each dollar of assessed valuation of the township in any year for the maintenance or improvement of county roads or for the widening of state trunk line highways beyond the width required for state trunk line traffic in unincorporated areas of the township and pay any sum so raised into the county road fund of the county for the maintenance and/or improvement of county roads within such township or the widening of state trunk line highways, as aforesaid, pursuant to an agreement between the township and the county road commission. Where funds are to be used for the widening of a state trunk line highway, the county road commission shall enter into agreement with the state highway commissioner for such work. Notwithstanding any other provisions of this act the township board of any township in the county of Marquette, out of any unexpended balances in the contingent or general fund of the township, after first submitting the question to the electors of the township, and a majority of those voting thereon approve of such expenditure, *may purchase and operate snow removal equipment.*

MCLA 247.671 Acts repealed. [MSA 9.1097(21)]

MCLA 247.672 Effective date of act. [MSA 9.1097(22)]

MCLA 247.673 Effective upon passage of certain act.
[MSA 9.1097(23)]

Act No. 19, P.A. 1919, 1st Ex. Sess. — Additional Trunk Line Mileage

AN ACT to provide for the laying out and establishing of additional trunk line mileage, the same to be added to and connected with the state trunk line highways heretofore established, under the provisions of Act No. 334 of the Public Acts of 1913, as amended. ...

MCLA 250.101 Additional trunk line highways; preliminary investigation. [MSA 9.921]

Sec. 1.   The state highway commissioner ... may solicit the co-operation of the ... township boards, ...

Act No. 12, P.A. 1925 — Additional Trunk Line Mileage

AN ACT to provide for the laying out and establishing of additional trunk line mileage; to make all roads that have been improved as federal aid projects, and all roads that have been, or that may hereafter be, approved for federal aid, trunk line highways; to provide for the widening, altering or straightening of trunk line highways; to provide for the abandonment, alteration or change of any portion of the trunk line highway; and to repeal all acts and parts of acts inconsistent herewith.

MCLA 250.111 Additional trunk line highways; federal aid projects declared trunk line highways. [MSA 9.931]

MCLA 250.112 Widening or altering of trunk line highway; approval.
[MSA 9.932]

MCLA 250.114 Trunk line highway route; alteration, abandonment, hearing of objections; new lines, approval. $\boxed{\text{MSA } 9.934}$

MCLA 250.115 Trunk line highway, abandonment of part of right of way; easement for public utilities. $\boxed{\text{MSA } 9.935}$

Act No. 274, P.A. 1929 — Vacation and Alteration of State Highways

AN ACT to prohibit counties, townships, cities and villages from vacating and altering state highways and to repeal certain acts and parts of acts inconsistent with the provisions of this act.

MCLA 250.231 State highway; prohibited vacation or alteration (by township). $\boxed{\text{MSA } 9.541}$

Sec. 6. The term "adjacent" as used herein, shall be construed to include any highway, or portion thereof, lying within 5 rods of the shore of any lake or the general course of any stream.

Act No. 341, P.A. 1927 — Highway Bordering Lake or Stream, Discontinuance

AN ACT to prevent the abandonment, discontinuation or alteration of the course of any public highway which borders upon, or is adjacent to any lake, or to the general course of any stream, or the course of any portion of such a highway, or bordering upon a lake or general course of any stream, by the public authorities of any township, village or city, until after the approval thereof by the circuit court of the county in which said highway is situated; and to provide for a notice of application therefor, and a method of hearing in such court, and the method for review of orders made thereon.

MCLA 247.41 Highway bordering on lake or stream, discontinuance. $\boxed{\text{MSA } 9.51}$

MCLA 247.42 Same; application signed by (seven) freeholders. $\boxed{\text{MSA } 9.52}$

MCLA 247.43 Same; hearing; notice, publication, posting, personal service. [MSA 9.53]

Sec. 3. ... a copy ... (of the public notice) ... shall be personally served upon the supervisor of the township ... in which such highway is situated and upon the state highway commissioner at least 20 days before the date fixed for hearing thereon. ...

MCLA 247.44 Same; court order. [MSA 9.54]

MCLA 247.45 Same; review by certiorari. [MSA 9.55]

Sec. 5. The proceedings ... subject to review ... upon application of any taxpayer of such township ... Notice of such application for review shall be served upon ... the supervisor of the township ... within 10 days ...

MCLA 247.46 Adjacent defined. [MSA 9.56]

Act No. 205, P.A. 1941 — Limited Access Highways

AN ACT to provide for the construction, establishment, opening, use, discontinuing, vacating, closing, altering, improvement, and maintenance of limited access highways; the acquiring of property and property rights therefor; closing or other treatment of intersecting roads; the borrowing of money and issuing bonds or notes payable from special funds for the acquisition, construction or improvement of such highways.

MCLA 252.51 Limited access highways; definition. [MSA 9.1094(1)]

MCLA 252.52 Same; establishment, improvement, discontinuance; commercial enterprises prohibited. [MSA 9.1094(2)]

Sec. 2. The state highway commissioner, boards of county road commissioners, and cities and villages, either acting alone or in cooperation with each other or with any federal, state or local agency having authority to participate in the construction and maintenance of highways, are hereby authorized to establish, open, discontinue,

*vacate, close, alter, improve, maintain and provide for the public
use of limited access highways: Provided ... No commercial enterprise shall be authorized or conducted within or on property acquired
for or designated as a limited access highway.*

**MCLA 252.53 Authority to acquire property by purchase, condemna-
tion, etc.** [MSA 9.1094(3)]

MCLA 252.54 Authority to acquire entire lot, block or plat of land.
[MSA 9.1094(4)]

**MCLA 252.55 Intersections; elimination; establishment in future
prohibited.** [MSA 9.1094(5)]

**MCLA 252.56 Limited access highway or highways; plans and
specifications, approval.** [MSA 9.1094(6)]

**MCLA 252.57 Same; contracts for construction, etc.; allocation of
cost, approval.** [MSA 9.1094(7)]

**MCLA 252.58 Same; contributions and pledges of funds; payment;
limitation.** [MSA 9.1094(8)]

MCLA 252.59 Same; county, city or village contributions.
[MSA 9.1094(9)]

MCLA 252.60 Same; federal aid. [MSA 9.1094(10)]

**MCLA 252.61 Same; bonds, issuance, approval, resolution; lien;
maximum.** [MSA 9.1094(11)]

MCLA 252.62 Dedicated tax bonds, issuance, payment.
[MSA 9.1094(12)]

MCLA 252.63 Registration of bonds or notes; exchange.
[MSA 9.1094(13)]

MCLA 252.64 Scope of act. [MSA 9.1094(14)]

**Act No. 253, P.A. 1917 — Transfer from General
Fund**

AN ACT to authorize the transfer of moneys from the general fund of counties, in certain instances, to the county road fund of said counties, to be used in the construction, maintenance and repair of highways.

MCLA 247.121 Transfer of funds. [MSA 9.171]

JOINT ACTION
Act No. 99, P.A. 1917 — Federal Aid Roads

AN ACT to provide for the construction, maintenance and improvement of federal aided roads; to authorize townships, good roads districts and counties to raise money by taxation and by loan for the purpose of contributing thereto; to validate and legalize proceedings heretofore taken to raise money for the purpose contemplated by this act; and to provide an appropriation for paying the state's portion of the expense incurred hereunder.

MCLA 249.1 Assent to federal aid; authority to survey, contract, receive and disburse money. [MSA 9.831]

MCLA 249.2 Authority to raise funds; bonds; estimates, plans; separate account. [MSA 9.832]

Sec. 2. Townships, ... are hereby authorized to raise funds, either by general taxation or bond issues, for the building of federal aided roads and to deposit their portion of the cost of such roads with the state treasurer to be credited to the specific federal aid road project ... Taxes for such purpose may be authorized, spread and collected, and bonds may be issued and sold, ... the state highway commissioner shall upon written request by a ... township board, or at his own option, furnish estimates, plans and specifications for any such improvement. ...

Act No. 296, P.A. 1969 - Transfer of Jurisdiction over Highways

AN ACT to provide for the transfer of jurisdiction over highways; to provide for the final determination of disputes involving transfers of highway jurisdiction; and to supersede certain acts and parts of acts.

MCLA 247.851 Definitions. [MSA 9.393(31)]

MCLA 247.852 – 247.859 [MSA 9.393(32) – 9.393(39)]

MCLA 247.860 County roads in areas becoming incorporated through annexation, incorporation, or consolidation, applicability.
[MSA 9.393(40)]

MCLA 247.861 Superseding other statutes. [MSA 9.393(41)]

Act No. 12, P.A. 1967, Ex. Sess. – Arbitration of Disputes

AN ACT to provide for arbitration of disputes involving the determination of routes for interstate highways through municipalities and to authorize the acquisition of property therefor.

MCLA 252.151 Definitions. [MSA 9.1095(51)]

MCLA 252.152 Notice of proposed route location and proceedings; final determination. [MSA 9.1095(52)]

MCLA 252.153 Highway location arbitration board. [MSA 9.1095(53)]

MCLA 252.154 Time and place for convening; notice.
[MSA 9.1095(54)]

MCLA 252.155 Submission of maps of proposed locations.
[MSA 9.1095(55)]

MCLA 252.156 Hearing; final approval; notice of approval.
[MSA 9.1095(56)]

MCLA 252.157 Effect of approval by board; acquisition of property.
[MSA 9.1095(57)]

MCLA 252.158 Appropriation. [MSA 9.1095(58)]

FRANCHISES FOR USE OF HIGHWAYS

Railroads, buses, various motor and water carriers, natural gas companies and various other public utilities, as well as regulation of ferries (since ferry landings are deemed to be public highways), are all factors of consideration in maintaining an adequate road network in the townships of the state. There are also some other considerations which must be taken into account with regard to townships in their relationship with various commercial interests which have a direct affect on township thoroughfares.

Michigan Constitution – Article 7 – Local Government

Section 29. Highways, streets, alleys, public places; control, use by public utilities.

Sec. 29. No person, partnership, association or corporation, public or private, operating a public utility shall have the right to the use of the highways, streets, alleys or other public places of any county, township, city or village for wires, poles, pipes, tracks, conduits or other utility facilities, without the consent of the duly authorized authority of the ... township; or to transact local business therein without first obtaining a franchise from the township ... Except as otherwise provided in this constitution the right of all ... townships ... to the reasonable control of their highways, streets, alleys and public places is hereby reserved to such local units of government.

Section 30. Franchises and licenses, duration.

Sec. 30. No franchise or license shall be granted by any township ... for a period longer than 30 years.

Act No. 266, P.A. 1909 - Franchise for Use of Highways

AN ACT to authorize township boards to grant the right to use the highways, streets, alleys and other public places of any township for poles, wires, pipes or conduits, or tracks for railways, and to operate and maintain the same, and to authorize townships to grant public utility franchises, and to provide for the submission of such public utility franchise grants to the electors for confirmation.

MCLA 460.601 Franchise to use streets and public places, grant by township board. [MSA 22.171]

MCLA 460.602 Confirmation by electors of grant; time. [MSA 22.172]

Sec. 2. ... the action of the board in granting the franchise shall be submitted to a vote of the electors of such township for confirmation at the next regular election.

MCLA 460.603 Same; notice to electors; form of ballot. [MSA 22.173]

MCLA 460.604 Same; special election at instance of grantee; costs. [MSA 22.174]

MCLA 460.605 Same; majority vote, effect. [MSA 22.175]

Act No. 300, P.A. 1909 — Railroads

AN ACT to define and regulate common carriers and the receiving, transportation and delivery of persons and property, prevent the imposition of unreasonable rates, prevent unjust discrimination, insure adequate service, create the Michigan railroad commission, define the powers and duties thereof, and to prescribe penalties for violations hereof.

MCLA 462.2 Commissioners. Qualifications. Removal. Pecuniary interest. Oath. Salary. Organization; quorum; hearings; adjournment; rehearing. Secretary and employes, salary; inspector, powers and duties. Secretary; duties, oath. Chief inspecting engineer; duties, salary. Michigan railroad commission; name, seal. Offices, equipment; meetings; expenses; free transportation. Rules. Conferences. [MSA 22.21]

MCLA 462.3 Definitions and scope. Common carrier. Transportation. Railroad, construed; scope, limitations. Scope. Express and sleeping car companies. [MSA 22.22]

MCLA 462.4 — 462.50 [MSA 22.23 — 22.68]

Act No. 198, P.A. 1873 — Railroad, Bridge and Tunnel Companies

AN ACT to revise the laws providing for the incorporation of the railroad bridge and tunnel companies and to regulate the running and management and to fix the duties and liabilities of all railroad, bridge, tunnel and other corporation owning or operating any railroad, bridge, or tunnel within this state, and to authorize the use of certain provisions of this act having to do with the exercise of the power of eminent domain by the state highway commissioner in certain cases, and to provide certain changes in such procedure when used by the state highway commissioner, and to confer certain rights and powers upon everyone coming under the provisions of this act.

ARTICLE I. ORGANIZATION

MCLA 463.1 – 463.4 [MSA 22.201 – 22.203(1)]

ARTICLE II. CORPORATE POWERS AND DUTIES OF DIRECTORS

MCLA 464.1 – 464.6 [MSA 22.204 – 22.209]

MCLA 464.7 Map of route, approval, filing; crossings, unlawful construction, penalty; change in route, procedure; expenses; condemnation. [MSA 22.210]

MCLA 464.8 Change in line; procedure. [MSA 22.211]

MCLA 464.9 Powers; liabilities; restrictions. Surveys; bond. Property; voluntary grants and donations. Same; purchase; voluntary grants and donations; use; payment of compensation. Width of road; material for road, taking. Right of way; crossings; local assessment; damages. Connections, intersections (with other railroads). **Transportation; tolls. Equipment; lands. Transportation, time and manner.** [MSA 22.212]

MCLA 464.10 – 464.12 [MSA 22.213 – 22.215]

MCLA 464.13 Unclaimed property; sale, notice; surplus. [MSA 22.216]

MCLA 464.14 Rights and liabilities; agreement. [MSA 22.217]

666

MCLA 464.15 — 464.23 [MSA 22.218 — 22.226]

MCLA 464.23a Condemnation proceedings; acquisition of railroad right of way for highway purposes, procedure; pending proceedings. [MSA 22.227]

MCLA 464.24 — 464.26 [MSA 22.228 — 22.230]

MCLA 464.27 Public lands, acquisition, execution of grant; service of process. [MSA 22.231]

MCLA 464.28 — 464.30 [MSA 22.232 — 22.234]

MCLA 464.31 Bridge or tunnel company; rights. [MSA 22.235]

MCLA 464.32 — 464.41 [MSA 22.236 — 22.245]

MCLA 464.42 Land for yards, terminals and depots; acquisition. [MSA 22.246]

MCLA 464.44 — 464.48 [MSA 22.247 — 22.251]

MCLA 464.49 Railroads subject to general railroad law. [MSA 22.252]

MCLA 464.50 Taxation. [MSA 22.254]

ARTICLE III. TAXATION

MCLA 465.1 — 465.2 [MSA 22.255 — 22.256]

MCLA 465.3 Specific tax; rate, payment in lieu of other taxes, exception. [MSA 22.257]

MCLA 465.4 Leased road; tax assessment. [MSA 22.258]

MCLA 465.5 Lien of state and citizen. [MSA 22.259]

ARTICLE IV. POLICE REGULATIONS

MCLA 466.1 Brakes for passenger trains, locomotives and tenders; penalty, civil liability. [MSA 22.260]

MCLA 466.2 Crossing protection; penalty for neglect to maintain. [MSA 22.261]

667

MCLA 466.3 Same; notice of requirement, duty of railroad. [MSA 22.262]

MCLA 466.4 Same; construction requirements; flagman, duties; expense; penalties. [MSA 22.263]

MCLA 466.5 — 466.12 [MSA 22.264 — 22.271]

MCLA 466.13 Bells, whistles or sirens on locomotives; equipping and use; penalty; civil liability; signal boards; crossing markers. [MSA 22.272]

MCLA 466.14 Crossing other railroads; stopping, precedence; penalty. [MSA 22.273]

MCLA 466.15 Fences, cattleguards and crossings; erection; injury to animals; destruction; penalties and civil liability. [MSA 22.274]

Sec. 15. ... shall erect and maintain in effective condition of repair, fences on each side of the right of way to their respective roads, as hereinafter provided. A legal railroad fence shall not be ... (very extensive and restrictive regulations) ...

MCLA 466.16 Loss by fire; liability, exceptions. [MSA 22.275]

MCLA 466.17 Unfenced railroad, permission of land-owner or occupant to operate; complaint, injunction. [MSA 22.276]

MCLA 466.18 — 466.21 [MSA 22.277 — 22.280]

MCLA 466.22 Restoration of stream, road, etc., penalty; culverts and openings, construction; actions for penalties. [MSA 22.281]

MCLA 466.23 Obstruction of vehicular traffic for more than 5 minutes; unlawful. [MSA 22.281(1)]

MCLA 466.24 Same; clearing of delayed traffic, (five minute) delay between train movements. [MSA 22.281(2)]

MCLA 466.25 Violation; penalty. [MSA 22.281(3)]

ARTICLE V. MISCELLANEOUS PROVISIONS

MCLA 467.1 — 467.36 [MSA 22.282 — 22.309]

Act No. 64, P.A. 1885 — Cable Railway

AN ACT supplementary to ... (Act 198, P.A. 1873) ...

MCLA 467.101 - 467.103 [MSA 22.311 - 22.313]

Act No. 124, P.A. 1867 — Liability as Common Carrier

AN ACT to fix the liability of railroad companies, as common carriers, in certain cases.

MCLA 467.151 — 467.152 [MSA 22.1181 — 22.1182]

Act No. 156, P.A. 1905 — Ownership and Operation of Vessels

AN ACT authorizing street railway companies or any railroad company organized under the laws of this state to own, maintain and operate steamboats, barges or vessels.

MCLA 467.201 - 467.202 [MSA 22.1041 - 22.1042]

Act No. 193, P.A. 1929 — Motor Vehicle and Aerial Transportation

AN ACT to authorize railroad corporations to engage in the business of transporting persons and property for hire upon the public highways and the business of aerial transportation; to own capital stock and securities of corporations organized for or engaged in such transportation; to operate the property or any part or parts thereof of such corporations and to enter into working arrangements with them.

MCLA 467.251 Railroad; operation of motor vehicles; aerial trans-

portation; purchase of stock; leases and agreements. [MSA 22.1061]

Act No. 137, P.A. 1956 – Investments and Activities of Railroad Corporations

AN ACT to authorize railroad corporations organized under the laws of this state to diversify their investments and business activities by permitting such corporations to organize and hold an interest in noncommon carrier subsidiary corporations and to invest in the stock of other corporations.

MCLA 467.301 – 467.302 [MSA 22.1065 – 22.1066]

Act No. 115, P.A. 1921 – (Railroad) Passenger Rates

AN ACT to fix the rates of fare for the transportation of passengers, within this state, which may be charged by any interurban railroad, and to provide for the regulation of such rates of fare by the Michigan public utilities commission.

MCLA 468.31 – 468.35 [MSA 22.981 – 11.985]

MCLA 468.36 Municipal rights not impaired. [MSA 22.986]

MCLA 468.37 Failure to comply; penalty, disposition; other remedies. [MSA 22.987]

Act No. 138, P.A. 1863 – Acquisition of Right of Way

AN ACT relative to tender of damages by railroad companies.

MCLA 468.301 Acquisition of right of way; tender of damages, effect. [MSA 22.741]

Act No. 96, P.A. 1859 – Foreclosure Sale, Preferred Stock and Delivery of Goods

AN ACT in relation to mortgages against preferred stock in, and the delivery of goods by railway companies.

MCLA 468.371 — 468.372 [MSA 22.1211 — 22.1212]

MCLA 468.373 Personal delivery of goods; rights of consignor and consignee; draymen's municipal licenses. [MSA 22.1213]

JOINT ACTION
Act No. 270, P.A. 1921 — Railroad Grade Crossings

AN ACT to promote the public safety and make more safe crossings of streets and highways with railroads and railways.

MCLA 469.1 Railroad grade crossings at highways; improvement, maintenance, alteration, apportionment of cost. [MSA 22.761]

MCLA 469.2 - 469.7 [MSA 22.762 - 22.767]

Note: Above sections deal with cost, type, location and placement of warning signs and regulation regarding control of weeds, etc., for clear vision.

MCLA 469.8 Flashing light protection, standards; cost. [MSA 22.768]

Sec. 8. ... The cost of all flashing light installations and alterations or relocations of same shall be borne equally by the railway and highway authorities, and thereafter they shall be maintained by the railway authorities at their own expense except that the highway authorities shall pay $10.00 per month to the railroad authorities for each crossing protected by flash light signals. ... (Author's Note: Townships have no financial obligations.)

MCLA 469.9 Failure of railroad or highway authorities to comply; penalty. [MSA 22.769]

MCLA 469.10 Molesting warning sign; penalty. [MSA 22.770]

MCLA 469.11 Enforcement; notice to parties in charge of tracks and highways. [MSA 22.771]

Sec. 11. The Michigan public utilities commission is hereby charged with the duty of carrying out the provisions of this act and investigating complaints of violations of this act. ...

MCLA 469.12 Maintenance of crossing signs; notice of omissions. [MSA 22.772]

Sec. 12. ... All railway authorities shall advise the Michigan public utilities commission of failure on the part of the highway authorities to provide the crossing signs in this act provided, when such failure shall come to their notice.

MCLA 469.13 Crossings (at grade only) **affected.** [MSA 22.773]

Act No. 171, P.A. 1893 — Tracks of Intersecting Railroads

AN ACT to regulate the construction of the tracks of railroads and street railroads across each other, and the stringing of wires, electric or other, over railroad tracks, and relative to the maintenance of such tracks heretofore so constructed and wires heretofore strung and providing for the construction of tracks of municipally owned or operated street railways and privately owned railroads and street railways across each other and the stringing of wires, electric or other, over railroad tracks, and relative to the maintenance of such tracks so constructed and wires so strung.

MCLA 469.31 Intersecting railroad tracks; approval of construction. [MSA 22.781]

Note: Permission for crossing may not be denied to a municipally owned railway.

MCLA 469.32 - 469.37 [MSA 22.782 - 22.787]

Act No. 27, P.A. 1875 — Trees Along Tracks

672

AN ACT to authorize railroad companies to cut decayed or dangerous trees standing within a certain distance of either side of their track.

MCLA 469.51 Dangerous trees along tracks, cutting. MSA 22.811

Act No. 275, P.A. 1887 — Abandonment of Subsidized Roads

AN ACT to prohibit railroad companies from taking up their tracks, abandoning their stations, and failing to operate their roads in certain cases.

MCLA 469.221 — 469.222 MSA 22.591 — 22.592

Act No. 56, P.A. 1919 — Abandonment of Tracks

AN ACT to regulate the discontinuance of service by certain common carriers, the abandonment of facilities thereof and the dismantling of railroad tracks and stations, and to provide a penalty for the violation hereof.

MCLA 469.241 — 469.246 MSA 22.611 — 22.616

Act No. 114, P.A. 1941 — Railroad Policemen

AN ACT to provide for the appointment and commissioning of railroad policemen, to prescribe their qualifications, rights, powers and duties, and to define the duties of the keepers of jails, lockups and station houses in respect of persons arrested by such railroad policemen.

MCLA 470.51 — 470.54 MSA 22.1260(1) — 22.1260(4)

MCLA 470.55 Railroad policemen; police powers of; duty to enforce laws. MSA 22.1260(5)

MCLA 470.56 — 470.61 MSA 22.1260(6) — 22.1260(11)

Act No. 156, P.A. 1941 — Clearance Space

AN ACT to provide for the safety of brakemen and

other employees on railroads by prescribing the minimum clearances at which bridges, structures or other obstructions, with certain exceptions, may be constructed or placed over or adjacent to the tracks of railroads; by requiring bridge guards or telltales or warning signs where clearances are less than those prescribed; by prescribing the minimum spacing between adjacent railroad tracks; to prohibit scrap iron, lumber, debris or other material in certain locations; and to authorize the Michigan public service commission to make exceptions in certain cases; and to prescribe penalties for the violation of the provisions of this act.

MCLA 470.101 – 470.109 [MSA 22.804(1) – 22.804(9)]

Act No. 26, P.A. 1968 – Safe Space

AN ACT to regulate safe space in regard to railroad rights of way; to prescribe the powers and duties of the public service commission; and to provide for the enforcement hereof.

MCLA 470.121 – 470.126 [MSA 22.805(1) – 22.805(6)]

Act No. 244, P.A. 1881 – Union Depot Companies

AN ACT to authorize the incorporation of companies for the construction of union railroad stations and depots, with the necessary connecting tracks, and the management of the same.

MCLA 471.1 – 471.3 [MSA 22.321 – 22.323]

MCLA 471.4 Powers; liabilities; restrictions. Examination and survey. Property. Tracks (in townships). **Same; connections. Station facilities.** [MSA 22.324]

MCLA 471.5 – 471.20 [MSA 22.325 – 22.340]

MCLA 471.21 Specific tax; rate, payment in lieu of other taxes, exception. [MSA 22.341]

Sec. 21. ... but such real estate so excepted shall be liable to taxation ... as other real estate in the several townships ... within which the same may be situated.

MCLA 471.22 Lien of state and citizens. [MSA 22.342]

MCLA 471.23 Fences, cattle-guards and ditches; penalties; civil liability. [MSA 22.343]

MCLA 471.24 Loss by fire; liability, exceptions. [MSA 22.344]

Sec. 24. Any such company shall be liable for all loss or damage to property by fire originating either from engines passing over its tracks, fires set by company employes by order of its officers, or otherwise through the neglect of such company: Provided, That such company shall not be held so liable if it prove to the satisfaction of the court or jury that such fire originated from fire by engines whose machinery, smoke-stack, or fire-boxes were in good order and properly managed, or fires originating in building, operating, or repairing the same, and that all reasonable precautions had been taken to prevent their origin, and that proper efforts had been made to extinguish the same in case of their extending beyond the limits of such road, when the existence of such fire is communicated to any of the officers of such company.

MCLA 471.25 − 471.29 [MSA 22.345 − 22.349]

MCLA 471.30 Local and suburban passenger business, fares; power of commissioner. [MSA 22.350]

MCLA 471.31 − 471.47 [MSA 22.351 − 22.367]

Act No. 35, P.A. 1867 − Street Railway Companies

AN ACT to provide for the formation of street railway companies, defining their powers and duties and authorizing the construction, use, maintenance and ownership of street railways for the transportation of passengers, and for accumulating, storing, manufacturing, conducting, using, selling, furnishing and supplying electricity and electric power, by such companies.

MCLA 472.1 Street railway companies; organization [MSA 22.421]

MCLA 472.2 Same; incorporators, name. [MSA 22.422]

Sec. 2.   Any number of persons, not less than 3, desiring to form a corporation for the purpose of constructing, owning, maintaining, or using any street railway in any city, village or township in this state, may ...

MCLA 472.3 — 472.12 [MSA 22.423 — 22.432]

MCLA 472.13 Street railway, consent to construction and maintenance; condemnation, procedure, minerals; generation and sale of electric power. [MSA 22.433]

MCLA 472.14 Same; acceptance by company; revocation. [MSA 22.434]

Sec. 14.   After any ... township shall have consented as in this act provided, to the construction and maintenance of any street railways therein, or granted any rights and privileges to any such company, and such consent and grant have been accepted by the company, such township ... shall not revoke such consent, nor deprive the company of the rights and privileges so conferred.

MCLA 472.15 Property and franchises, power to purchase, sell, lease and convey; motor vehicles, operation, restrictions; acquisition of capital stock. [MSA 22.435]

MCLA 472.16 Borrowing power; bonds and mortgages, issuance. [MSA 22.436]

MCLA 472.17 Street grades; conformance by company; change. [MSA 22.437]

MCLA 472.18 Laying of track; repair of roadbed. [MSA 22.438]

MCLA 472.19 Municipalities; authority to establish street rules (by ordinance or otherwise). [MSA 22.439]

676

MCLA 472.20 Fares; agreement with municipality, increase. [MSA 22.440]

MCLA 472.22 — 472.31 [MSA 22.441 — 22.449]

MCLA 472.31a Elevated railways. [MSA 22.450]

MCLA 472.32 Cars to stop at railroad crossing, exception; penalty. [MSA 22.451]

MCLA 472.34 Express and light freight; carriage, time of operation. [MSA 22.452]

MCLA 472.35 — 472.36 [MSA 22.453 — 22.454]

Act No. 197, P.A. 1891 — Street Railway and Electric Light Companies

AN ACT to authorize the consolidation of street railway and electric light companies.

MCLA 473.1 Consolidation of street railway and electric light companies, procedure; powers and duties of new company; evidence. [MSA 22.471]

MCLA 473.2 New company; rights, franchises and liabilities. [MSA 22.472]

Act No. 128, P.A. 1899 — Street Railway, Electric Light and Gas Light Companies

AN ACT to authorize the consolidation of street railway, electric light and gas light companies, or any 2 thereof.

MCLA 473.41 Consolidation of street railway, electric and gas light companies, procedure; new company, rights and duties; evidence. [MSA 22.491]

MCLA 473.42 New company, rights and liabilities; scope, limitations. [MSA 22.492]

Act No. 54, P.A. 1903 — Gas Light, Consolidated and Foreign Companies

AN ACT to authorize any gas light company and any consolidated company formed by the union of a street railway and electric light company, being corporations organized under the laws of this state, and having their principal place of business in the same town (township), village or city, to unite and consolidate with any corporation organized under the laws of an adjoining state, and which, under and by virtue of the rights, powers and franchises possessed and enjoyed by it under the laws of such adjoining state, owns and operates a street railway therein and also manufactures, produces, generates, sells and furnishes gas and electricity for heating, lighting and power purposes, where the street railway lines of the 2 corporations last mentioned shall form a connecting and continuous line of railway between this state and such adjoining state.

MCLA 473.61 Consolidation of gas light, consolidated and foreign companies, restriction. [MSA 22.501]

MCLA 473.62 — 473.65 [MSA 22.502 — 22.505]

Act No. 246, P.A. 1921 — Carriers by Water

AN ACT to regulate the service, rates, fares and charges of carriers by water within this state.

MCLA 460.201 Carriers by water; rates; filing, fixing by commission, exception. [MSA 22.91]

Sec. 1. ... Provided, That any ferry company operating within any municipality under an agreement with such municipality shall not be affected either as to fares or operation by this act.

MCLA 460.202 — 460.206 [MSA 22.92 — 22.96]

Act No. 254, P.A. 1933 — Motor Carriers

*AN ACT to promote safety upon and conserve the
use of the public highways of the state; to provide for
the supervision, regulation and control of the use of such
highways by all motor vehicles operated by carriers of
passengers and property for hire upon or over such highways; to preserve, foster and regulate transportation and
permit the coordination of motor vehicle transportation
facilities; to provide for the supervision, regulation and
control of the use of such highways by all motor vehicles
for hire for such purposes, to classify and regulate
carriers of persons and property by motor vehicles for
hire upon such public highways for such purposes: ...*

ARTICLE I. GENERAL DEFINITIONS AND PURPOSE

MCLA 475.1 Motor carrier act; definitions. [MSA 22.531]

MCLA 475.1a Same; short title. [MSA 22.531(1)]

MCLA 475.2 Same; general purpose of act. [MSA 22.532]

**MCLA 475.3 Common motor carriers of passengers, temporary
authority for service urgently needed; temporary approval or consolidation or merger.** [MSA 22.533(1)]

ARTICLE II. COMMON MOTOR CARRIERS

MCLA 476.1 Certificate of public convenience and necessity.
[MSA 22.534]

MCLA 476.2 – 476.4 [MSA 22.535 – 22.537]

**MCLA 476.5 Same; classification, issuance; character of high-
ways, vehicles.** [MSA 22.538]

MCLA 476.6 – 476.14 [MSA 22.539 – 22.547]

ARTICLE III. CONTRACT MOTOR CARRIERS

MCLA 477.1 Permit. [MSA 22.548]

MCLA 477.2 Same; determination of commission. [MSA 22.549]

MCLA 477.3 Same; character of operation proposed. [MSA 22.550]

Note: Same conditions as in 476.5 above

MCLA 477.4 – 477.12 [MSA 22.551 – 22.559]

ARTICLE IV. FEES

MCLA 478.1 – 478.6 [MSA 22.560 – 22.565]

*ARTICLE V. POLICY OF STATE, EXEMPTIONS, LIMITATIONS,
GENERAL REGULATIONS AND PROCEDURE; PENALTIES;
MISCELLANEOUS*

MCLA 479.1 Declaration of public interest; purpose of regulation; participation by labor organizations. [MSA 22.566]

MCLA 479.2 Exemptions; reciprocity. [MSA 22.567]

MCLA 479.3 Control by cities and villages; local business. [MSA 22.568]

MCLA 479.4 Highway commissioner, duty to furnish information. [MSA 22.569]

MCLA 479.5 Certificates and permits (not construed franchise); construction, transfer. [MSA 22.570]

MCLA 479.6 Public service commission; rules and regulations, promulgation; bi-weekly bulletin or digest, fee. [MSA 22.571]

Sec. 6. ... Such bulletin or digest shall be furnished and mailed to the public upon payment by anyone subscribing therefor of ...

MCLA 479.6a – 479.11 [MSA 22.571(1) – 22.576]

MCLA 479.12 Impounding of motor vehicles (by any peace officer), release. [MSA 22.583]

MCLA 479.13 Enforcement of act, rules and regulations; assistance. MSA 22.578

MCLA 479.14 Complaints and investigations; notices; findings. MSA 22.579

MCLA 479.14a Orders of commission, determination, effective date. MSA 22.579(1)

MCLA 479.15 — 479.18 MSA 22.580 — 22.583

MCLA 479.19 Injunctive relief (upon application of any body politic or municipal organization). MSA 22.584

MCLA 479.20 Motor carrier act; appeal to circuit court; proceedings stayed; rescission of order; appeal to supreme court. MSA 22.585

ARTICLE VI. COMMERCIAL ZONE REGISTRATION

MCLA 479.41 Necessity of registration; ''commercial zone'' defined. MSA 22.587(101)

Sec. 1. ... For the purposes of this act, the term ''commercial zone'' means that area within an 8—mile radius of the boundary line of the city and includes all other municipalities any part of which may be located within that 8—mile radius.

MCLA 479.42 — 479.48 MSA 22.587(102) — 22.587(108)

MCLA 479.49 Inapplicability of article to dump trucks and dump trailers (or their commodities). MSA 22.587(109)

Act No. 181, P.A. 1963 — Motor Carrier Safety Act

AN ACT to promote safety upon the public highways by regulating the operation of motor trucks, tractors and trailers; to provide the number of persons necessary to the operation of such motor trucks and tractors; to limit the hours of service of persons engaged in operating such vehicles; to require the keeping of records of such opera-

tions; to provide penalties for the violation of this act; and to repeal certain acts and parts of acts.

MCLA 480.11 – 480.15 [MSA 9.1666(1) – 9.1666(5)]

MCLA 480.16 Exemptions from act. [MSA 9.1666(6)]

MCLA 480.17 Violation of act; penalty. [MSA 9.1666(7)]

MCLA 480.18 Venue. [MSA 9.1666(8)]

Sec. 8. Whenever any provision of this act has been violated, the offense may be prosecuted in any county, city or jurisdiction in or through which the motor vehicle implicated was situated or passed when the offense was committed.

MCLA 480.19 Repeal. [MSA 9.1666(9)]

Act No. 16, P.A. 1929 – Crude Oil and Petroleum

AN ACT to regulate the business of carrying or transporting, buying, selling or dealing in crude oil or petroleum or its products, through pipelines; to authorize the use of public highways and the condemnation of private property; to regulate the purchase and storage of crude oil or petroleum; to provide for the control and regulation of all corporations, associations and persons engaged in such business, by the Michigan public utilities commission; to define the powers and duties of the commission in relation thereto; and to prescribe penalties for violations of the provision hereof.

MCLA 483.1 Crude oil or petroleum; buying, selling or transporting. [MSA 22.1341]

MCLA 483.2 Condemnation; use of highways. [MSA 22.1342]

MCLA 483.3 – 483.5 [MSA 22.1343 – 22.1345]

MCLA 483.6 Acceptance of act, plat, filing. [MSA 22.1346]

682

MCLA 483.7 – 483.11 [MSA 22.1347 – 22.1351]

Act No. 9, P.A. 1929 – Natural Gas

AN ACT to regulate corporations, associations or persons engaged in the business of carrying and transporting natural gas through pipe lines and to regulate the production, purchase and sale of natural gas; to provide for the control and regulation of such corporations, associations and persons by the Michigan public utilities commission; to define the powers and duties of the commission relative thereto; to prescribe penalties for the violations of the provisions hereof; and to repeal Act No. 29 of the Public Acts of 1889.

MCLA 483.101   Natural gas; buying, selling or transporting. [MSA 22.1311]

MCLA 483.102   Condemnation, use of highways; limitation to intrastate transportation. [MSA 22.1312]

MCLA 483.103   Control vested in commission; scope, limitations.

MCLA 483.104 – 483.108 [MSA 22.1314 – 22.1318]

MCLA 483.109 Map or plat of proposed line, filing with commission, approval; existing carriers. [MSA 22.1319]

MCLA 483.110 – 483.116 [MSA 22.1320 – 22.1326]

MCLA 483.117   Municipal corporations excepted. [MSA 22.1327]

MCLA 483.120 Immediate effect. [MSA 22.1330]

Act No. 165, P.A. 1969 – Gas Safety Standards

AN ACT to authorize the public service commission to establish and enforce gas safety standards; and to provide penalties for violations thereof.

MCLA 483.151 Definitions. [MSA 22.1332(1)]

MCLA 483.152 Rules; considerations in prescribing standards; waiver of compliance with standards, application, notice, hearing, conditions, reasons. [MSA 22.1332(2)]

MCLA 483.153 - 483.162 [MSA 22.1332(3) - 22.1332(12)]

Act No. 182, P.A. 1881 — Brine Pipe Line Companies

AN ACT to provide for the incorporation of pipe line companies, and to define their powers and duties.

MCLA 483.102 Brine pipe line companies, purpose, incorporators; articles, contents, filing, recording; body corporate, powers. [MSA 22.1271]

MCLA 483.202 — 483.212 [MSA 22.1271 — 22.1282]

MCLA 483.213 Staking of pipe line; survey and map, filing. [MSA 22.1283]

MCLA 483.214 Pipe line; in highway, consent. [MSA 22.1284]
Sec. 14. No pipe line shall be constructed across, along or upon any public highway without the consent of the highway commissioner of the township in which such highway is located, upon such terms as may be agreed upon with such commissioner, or upon the order of the circuit court for the county in which such highway is located, made upon petition and notice to the commissioner of highways of such town (township) according to the practice or order of said court, or an order to show cause, and in such manner and upon such terms as shall be ordered by said court.

Note: Office of township highway commissioner has been abolished, so it would fall upon whatever officer may be responsible for supervision of township highways, such as the county road commissioner.

MCLA 483.215 Same; in village or city, consent; bond; suit. [MSA 22.1285]

MCLA 483.216 Public lands, grant. [MSA 22.1286]

684

Sec. 16. If any such company shall, for its purposes aforesaid, require any land belonging to the ... town (township), the ... town (township) officers ... having charge of the said lands, may grant such to such company for a compensation, which shall be agreed upon between them.

MCLA 483.217 General powers and restrictions. Examination and survey. Property; voluntary grants, use. Same; purchase. Laying out of route; additional width. Conveyance of brine. Same; compensation. Use; storage; rates; rules; penalty. [MSA 22.1287]

MCLA 483.218 Construction restrictions (across cemeteries, highways). [MSA 22.1288]

MCLA 483.219 Fencing of pipe lines; liability. [MSA 22.1289]

MCLA 483.220 – 483.228 [MSA 22.1290 – 22.1298]

Act No. 368, P.A. 1925 – Obstructions and Encroachments; Use of Highway by Public Utilities

AN ACT to prohibit obstructions and encroachments on public highways, to provide for the removal thereof, to prescribe the conditions under which telegraph, telephone power, and other public utility companies, cable television companies and municipalities may enter upon, construct and maintain telegraph, telephone, power or cable television lines, pipe lines, wires, cables, poles, conduits, sewers and like structures upon, over, across or under public roads, bridges, streets and waters and to provide penalties for the violation of this act.

MCLA 247.171 Encroachments; removal order, service; temporary permit. [MSA 9.251]

MCLA 247.172 Same; removal by commissioner; penalty, expense charged to occupant, collection by tax; limitation. [MSA 9.252]

MCLA 247.173 Same; denied, notice to commissioner; trespass action. [MSA 9.253]

686

MCLA 247.189   Same; left in roadway, penalty.   MSA 9.269

MCLA 247.190 Width of highway; encroachment does not give right to land. MSA 9.270

Note: The "commissioner" referred to in this act means the local commissioner or officer with supervision of the highways, roads or bridges involved, such as the county road commissioner.

Act No. 96, P.A. 1959 — Bus Passenger Shelters

AN ACT to prescribe the conditions under which persons, firms, corporations and municipalities may enter upon, construct and maintain bus passenger shelters upon public highways within the corporate limits of municipalities; to permit the posting of advertisements thereon; and to provide for the regulation thereof.

MCLA 247.331 — 247.336 MSA 9.391(1)— 9.391(6)

Note: The first section of this act defines a "municipality" as any city or incorporated village.

JOINT ACTION
Act No. 92, P.A. 1893 — Separate Grades for Highways and Railroads

AN ACT to provide separate grades for railroads and public highways and streets where railroads intersect such highways and streets.

MCLA 253.1   Agreement to separate grade crossing; parties, judicial proceedings; representative board or officer, construed. MSA 9.1101

MCLA 253.2   Same; map and plans, cost, damages, approval. MSA 9.1102

MCLA 253.3 - 253.26 MSA 9.1103 - 9.1126

Note: The above sections include assessment, compensation as general tax, etc.

MCLA 253.27 Same; in accordance with plan, plat and profile; grade change; duty of railroad, of municipality. [MSA 9.1127]

MCLA 253.28 Order of confirmation; payment of assessment and change in grade, within year; judgment, effect, enforcement. [MSA 9.1128]

MCLA 253.29 Compensation of officers, jurors and witnesses. [MSA 9.1129]

MCLA 253.30 Costs of proceedings, payment; attorney fee. [MSA 9.1130]

MCLA 253.31 Discontinuance of proceedings; new trial; appeal. [MSA 9.1131]

MCLA 253.32 Averments in petition true unless contradicted. [MSA 9.1132]

MCLA 253.33 Detroit; head of legal department, duties. [MSA 9.1133]

JOINT ACTION
Act No. 114, P.A. 1925 — Separate Grades for Highways and Railroads

AN ACT to regulate the separating of grades; the reconstruction of existing grade separations; and the alteration of existing grade separations for increased highway or railroad facilities at crossings of railroads with public streets and highways; to authorize the relocation of such crossings and the closing of certain highways; and to provide for apportioning the cost thereof against the railroad company and the state, county, township, city or village, or the board, commission or other agency interested therein; and to provide the procedure for the judicial determination of grade separation damages to abutting property.

688

MCLA 253.51 Grade separations; supervision of public service commission. [MSA 9.1141]

MCLA 253.52 Same; application, submission of plans and agreement. [MSA 9.1142]

MCLA 253.53 Same; hearing, notice, parties' right to appear, witnesses; agreement between municipal and railroad authorities. [MSA 9.1143]

MCLA 253.54 - 253.74 [MSA 9.1144 - 9.1151(14)]

Note: The above sections include costs, right of way, damages and compensation, court proceedings.

R.S. 1846, c. 29 — Regulation of Ferries

MCLA 255.1 Board of supervisors, ferries; grant of license, term. [MSA 9.1371]

Sec. 1. The board of supervisors of each of the counties ... may grant licenses for keeping ferries, in their respective counties, to as many suitable persons as they may think proper, which licenses shall continue in force for a time to be specified therein by said board, not exceeding 10 years.

MCLA 255.2 — 255.11 [MSA 9.1372 — 9.1379]

MCLA 255.12 Ferry landings deemed public highways. [MSA 9.1380]

Sec. 12. Ferry landings shall be deemed public highways, and may be laid out, constructed, maintained, altered, or discontinued in the same manner, ...

689

Chapter VII

ENVIRONMENTAL PROTECTION
AND CONTROL

*"The problem is to take the pollution out of the
environment while at the same time taking the hysteria out of the discussion."*
            --Bill Vaughan, Kansas City Star

Times have changed the environment "game." Residents no
longer resist governmental efforts -- they are in fact now demanding
controls. Any discussion about environmental protection and control invariably brings about a sharp division of opinion and expression. One group says such things as: "Calm down; let's take
enough time to do it right," "Man has been polluting the air ever
since he discovered he could cook his food and warm himself with
the heat of a flame," and "There has been water pollution from as
far back as the days of the Roman Empire." The opposition group
says: "We ran out of time long ago," "Commercial interests can't
be permitted to continue their dangerous practices any longer," and
"We've got to do something drastic, and do it right now, even if it
means closing down an industry."

The answer has to lie somewhere in the middle. If extreme
pollution control restrictions put hundreds of people out of work,
then consideration must be given to allowing more time. Science
and technology must be encouraged to work faster, and new ways
must be found for financing necessary installations. Industrial engineers have made great strides in this regard, but it is not some-

690

thing that can be done overnight -- there are too many facets to the problem.

Generally speaking, there are two broad categories of concern. First, the problems of ecology are mounting almost daily, especially in the threats to birds and wild animals as land development and pest control methods destroy their natural habitat. Inherent in this is the need for providing adequate parks and recreation areas and for the preservation of wild lands and forests. Secondly, there is the matter of air and water pollution.

Parks and recreation areas and centers, military reservations, trailer coach parks and summer resort and park associations, public beaches, swimming pools, hunting and fishing and other recreational activities; soil conservation and irrigation districts, water control devices, the drain code, river management, inland lake levels, surplus waters, flooding, beach erosion, municipal forests; insecticides and pesticides, wells, mining, industrial wastes and many other things affect the environment, and in many instances the ecological balance of nature itself.

Planning for any of them means regulation of the way we live and therefore we must take into consideration the vital concerns of an alarmed public. As Mr. Vaughan suggests, however, our real problem is to cure pollution, not to create hysteria. For every topic of discussion at meetings, whether of committees or formal sessions of a park commission or a township board, there will be both real and self-styled experts. It is imperative that government officials make sure that first there are in-depth studies, that everyone concerned has an opportunity to be heard and his or her ideas accepted if possible, that advice is sought from persons who have gained knowledge through actual and practical experience in their fields, and that professional consultants and advisors are employed to prepare and implement adequate programs. To do anything less in a field as vital as this is to ignore the responsibility vested in the governing body to do its part in dealing with the very real problems of pollution of our environment and waste of our natural resources.

Many federal and state statutes govern construction and maintenance of dams, reservoirs and other man-made water control devices, as well as recreation areas and other land use. However, the industrial capacity needed to meet even minimum requirements for today's standard of living, and the noise and fumes from planes, cars and trucks has become a major health hazard, not only in the metropolitan areas of the nation, but in the outlying countryside as well. It has also become the gateway to what appears to be a major

691

crisis in the United States -- the deterioration and rapid decline of our energy resources.

The effects of all this are probably felt more at the local level than anywhere else as efforts are made to provide adequate environmental protection and control. Communities must cooperate in planning and development if there is to be any real relief and success.

SOIL CONSERVATION AND IRRIGATION DISTRICTS AND DRAINS

Adoption of good soil conservation practices is an investment in the future, doing much to preserve land resources by preventing and controlling soil erosion. Therefore, townships are urged to cooperate with counties in the establishment of soil conservation districts -- Act No. 297, P.A. 1937 provides a good place to begin. Closely paralleling this is the establishment of irrigation districts and adequate drainage programs. When properly planned, these three areas of concern will not only provide means for dealing with many environmental programs, but will also do much to enhance the agricultural capabilities of land within the townships.

JOINT ACTION

Act No. 40, P.A. 1956 - Drain Code of 1956

AN ACT to codify the laws relating to the laying out of drainage districts, the consolidation of drainage districts, the construction and maintenance of drains, sewers, pumping equipment, bridges, culverts, fords and such structures and mechanical devices as will properly purify the flow of such drains; to provide for flood control projects; to provide for water management, water management districts and sub-districts, and for flood control and drainage projects within such districts; to provide for the assessment and collection of taxes; to provide for the investment of funds; and to prescribe penalties for violations of the provisions of this act.

CHAPTER 1. DRAINS

MCLA 280.1 Drain code of 1956, short title. [MSA 11.1001]

MCLA 280.2 Drains, location, establishment, consolidation, purification, improvement. [MSA 11.1002]

Sec. 2. Drains including branches may be located, established, constructed and maintained, and existing drains, creeks, rivers and watercourses and their branches, or tributaries whether located, established and constructed by a county drain commissioner or drainage board or by a ... township, may be cleaned out, straightened, widened, deepened, extended, consolidated, relocated, tiled, connected and relocated along a highway, or there may be provided for the same structures or mechanical devices that will properly purify or improve the flow of the drain or pumping equipment necessary to assist or relieve the flow of the drain, or 1 or more branches may be added thereto, by petition under the provisions of this act, whenever the same shall be conducive to the public health, convenience and welfare.

MCLA 280.3 Drain defined. [MSA 11.1003]

Sec. 3. The word "drain", whenever used in this act, shall include the main stream or trunk and all tributaries or branches of any creek or river, any watercourse or ditch, either open or closed, any covered drain, any sanitary or any combined sanitary and storm sewer or storm sewer or conduit composed of tile, brick, concrete, or other material, any structures or mechanical devices, that will properly purify the flow of such drains, any pumping equipment necessary to assist or relieve the flow of such drains and any levee, dike, barrier, or a combination of any or all of same constructed, or proposed to be constructed, for the purpose of drainage or for the purification of the flow of such drains, but shall not include any dam and flowage rights used in connection therewith which is used for the generation of power by a public utility subject to regulation by the public service commission.

MCLA 280.4 Commissioner defined (county drain commissioner). [MSA 11.1004]

MCLA 280.5 Drainage district a body corporate. [MSA 11.1005]

MCLA 280.6 Drains; public easements and rights of way, use; release, notice, protest. [MSA 11.1006]

MCLA 280.10 Drains, location.

Sec. 10. Drains may be laid or extended into or along or from any lake or other body of water surrounded wholly or in part by a swamp, marsh or other low lands for the general purpose of drainage contemplated by this act, but not so as to impair the navigation of any navigable river.

Meetings, adjournment by public announcement. Drains entirely within municipality; jurisdiction of commissioner, consent. Same; payment of bonds, drain orders, deficiency. [MSA 11.1010]

MCLA 280.11 Easement, right of way, release of damages, recording. [MSA 11.1011]

MCLA 280.12 Time, effect of specification in act, directory, mandatory. [MSA 11.1012]

CHAPTER 2. COUNTY DRAIN COMMISSIONER

MCLA 280.21 - 280.32 [MSA 11.1021 - 11.1032]

CHAPTER 3. COUNTY DRAINAGE DISTRICTS

MCLA 280.51 County drainage districts, application, signers, eligibility, sufficiency; deposit for costs. [MSA 11.1051]

Sec. 51. Before a commissioner takes any action on any application to locate, establish and construct any drain, there shall first be filed with him an application ... signed by not less than 10 freeholders of the township or townships ...

MCLA 280.52 Same; practicability of drainage; survey, determination; tax delinquency. [MSA 11.1052]

MCLA 280.53 Surveyor; duties as to county drain, delivery of papers to commissioner; route. [MSA 11.1053]

MCLA 280.54 Order designating county drainage district; contents, notice of filing, publication. Same; amendment of name or number of drain, procedure. [MSA 11.1054]

CHAPTER 4. COUNTY DRAINS

MCLA 280.71 Petition to establish, filing, signers, eligibility, certificate of county treasurer, form; municipally-signed petition. MSA 11.1071

Sec. 71. ... In lieu of a petition signed by freeholders ...(it)... may be signed solely by a city, village or township when duly authorized by its governing body, or by any combination of such municipalities, if such petitioning municipality or municipalities will be liable to assessments at large for at least a percentage of the total amount to be assessed for the cost of the proposed drain. ...

MCLA 280.72 County drain board of determination. Appointment, qualifications, meetings, compensation. Meeting, notice, expense. Chairman; secretary; determination of necessity; appearances; tax statements; apportionment of costs; notice; review. MSA 11.1072

MCLA 280.72a Action for determination of necessity, parties, time for filing. MSA 11.1072(1)

MCLA 280.73 Proposed drain; release of right of way and damages. MSA 11.1073

MCLA 280.74 Same; acknowledgments, oaths, form, area, signature of wife, resolution covering street or public place; open drain. MSA 11.1074

Sec. 74. ... Whenever a portion of a drain shall be located within any street, highway or public place, then a resolution adopted by a majority vote of the governing body ... shall be sufficient release of the right of way, and shall be deemed a sufficient conveyance under this act, and said governing body may permit the construction of an open drain if such consent be set forth in such resolution.

MCLA 280.75 Condemnation proceedings; special commissioners, application for appointment, contents. MSA 11.1075

MCLA 280.76 - 280.88 MSA 11.1076 - 11.1088

CHAPTER 5. INTERCOUNTY DRAINAGE DISTRICTS

MCLA 280.101 Intercounty drainage districts, application; signers, eligibility. [MSA 11.1101]

MCLA 280.102 Same; copies; joint drainage board, meeting, time, location, notice. [MSA 11.1102]

MCLA 280.103 - 280.105 [MSA 11.1103 - 11.1105]

MCLA 280.106 Review of apportionment; arbitration board, members, claim for review, filing, copies, meeting of board, notice, review. [MSA 11.1106]

Sec. 106. ... Notice of ... meeting (of board of review) shall be posted in 5 public places in each county affected and served on the county clerk of each county and the supervisor of each township in every county traversed by said drain personally or by registered mail at least 10 days before such meeting and ...

CHAPTER 6. INTERCOUNTY DRAINS

MCLA 280.121 Petition to establish; filing, signers, eligibility, certificate of county treasurer, form; effect petition signed by municipality. [MSA 11.1121]

Sec. 121. ... In lieu of a petition signed by freeholders, the petition may be signed solely by a city, village or township in each county involved, when duly authorized by its governing body, or by any combination of such municipalities, if each petitioning municipality will be liable to assessment at large for public health for any part of the cost of the proposed drain. ...

MCLA 280.122 Drainage board, notice of meeting; first order of determination; apportionment of costs; arbitration. [MSA 11.1122]

MCLA 280.122a Action for determination of necessity, parties, time for filing. [MSA 11.1122(1)]

MCLA 280.123 - 280.127 [MSA 11.1123 - 11.1127]

MCLA 280.128 Condemnation proceedings; appointment of special commissioners, qualifications. [MSA 11.1128]

MCLA 280.129 - 280.132 [MSA 11.1129 - 11.1132]

MCLA 280.133 Interstate drain, application and petition, drainage district, proceedings; release of right of way, obstruction agreement. [MSA 11.1133]

MCLA 280.134 Intercounty drain; venue of actions; appointment of outside circuit judge. [MSA 11.1134]

MCLA 280.135 Same; extension into county not in original district; procedure, apportionment of cost; addition of lands by expanded board. [MSA 11.1135]

CHAPTER 7. APPORTIONMENT AND REVIEW

MCLA 280.151 Final order of determination, filing; contracts for sections or whole; apportionment of costs, benefits; review, appeal. [MSA 11.1151]

MCLA 280.152 - 280.154 [MSA 11.1152 - 11.1154]

MCLA 280.155 Same; appeal; application for board of review, bond. [MSA 11.1155]

Sec. 155. ... appeal may be taken by the ... supervisor in behalf of any township, ... when authorized by the ... township board. ...

MCLA 280.156 Same; board of review, appointment, meeting, time, notice, duties. [MSA 11.1156]

MCLA 280.157 - 280.160 [MSA 11.1157 - 11.1160]

MCLA 280.161 Certiorari to review drain proceedings and taxes; issues of fact, costs, postponement of proceedings. [MSA 11.1161]

MCLA 280.162 Village or city, incorporation or annexation; reapportionment of cost of drain. [MSA 11.1162]

CHAPTER 8. CLEANING, WIDENING, DEEPENING, STRAIGHTENING AND EXTENDING DRAINS

MCLA 280.191 County drain; cleaning out, etc.; relief drain, tiling, petition, determination of necessity; apportionment of cost, review.

Sec. 191. ... Whenever it is necessary for the public health of 1 or more cities, villages and townships, such petition may be signed solely by a city, village or township when duly authorized by its governing body or by any combination of such municipalities, if such municipality or municipalities will be liable to assessments at large for a percentage of the total amount to be assessed for the cost of the proposed work. ...

MCLA 280.192 Intercounty drain; cleaning out, etc.; devices to purify flow; relief drains, petitions, drainage board, survey, procedure. [MSA 11.1192]

Note: Language similar to above section.

MCLA 280.193 Drains; apportionment for cleaning, widening, deepening, straightening, and extending; review, notice; consolidated districts. [MSA 11.1193]

MCLA 280.194 Petitions and proceedings; limitation on number, description of drain. [MSA 11.1194]

MCLA 280.195 Further right of way, damages. [MSA 11.1195]

MCLA 280.196 Inspection; maintenance and repair; expense, reassessment; emergency. [MSA 11.1196]

Sec. 196. (1) An annual inspection may be made of all drains laid out and constructed under this act. ... upon the request of the governing body of any public corporation ... served in whole or in part by the drain to be inspected. ...

MCLA 280.197 Survey of drain or district, filing of data; additions to district; new notice, service, expense. Hearing by reconvened board of determination; determination; construction. [MSA 11.1197]

MCLA 280.198 Drain taxes, subsequent assessment. [MSA 11.1198]

MCLA 280.199 Cleaning out drain; apportionment of cost; use of surplus in drain fund. [MSA 11.1199]

MCLA 280.200 Same; cost of maintenance and repair; public contracts. [MSA 11.1200]

CHAPTER 9. LETTING OF CONTRACTS

MCLA 280.221 Construction of drain; bids; contract; readvertisement, installment bonds. Abandonment of petition; litigation. Road commissioners, bid. [MSA 11.1221]

MCLA 280.222 - 280.223 [MSA 11.1222 - 11.1223]

CHAPTER 10. INSPECTION AND APPROVAL OF CONSTRUCTION AND PAYMENT FOR THE DRAIN

MCLA 280.241 Inspection of drain; order of approval, payments on contract. [MSA 11.1241]

MCLA 280.242 Extension of time on contract; forfeiture; reletting unfinished portion; recovery of excess cost. [MSA 11.1242]

MCLA 280.243 Deficiency; assessment, collection, review, appeal; embezzlement; payment from county general fund, conditions. [MSA 11.1243]

MCLA 280.244 - 280.248 [MSA 11.1244 - 11.1248]

CHAPTER 11. LEVY AND COLLECTION OF DRAIN TAXES

MCLA 280.261 Computation of cost, items included; contingent expenses. [MSA 11.1261]

MCLA 280.262 Special assessment rolls, filing.

Sec. 262. The commissioner shall ... make a special assessment roll for such drain for each ... township ..., which roll shall be designated ..., and ... Such rolls shall be dated and signed by said commissioner and filed on or before the last Wednesday in September in each year, in the office of the county clerk.

Current assessment roll; permanent assessment roll. Installment payments. [MSA 11.1262]

MCLA 280.263 Spread of drain taxes on rolls, time. [MSA 11.1263]

Sec. 263. It shall be the duty of the supervisor ... to spread on his roll the total amount of all drain taxes determined upon by the county drain commissioner to be assessed upon the ... township ... at large by adding to ...

MCLA 280.265 Drain taxes, general tax law applicable, payment under protest, action, lien, personal claim. [MSA 11.1265]

MCLA 280.266 Return of delinquent drain taxes; general tax law applicable. [MSA 11.1266]

MCLA 280.267 Injunction after assessment. [MSA 11.1267]

MCLA 280.268 Perpetual injunction not allowed for informalities; plaintiff may show injury. [MSA 11.1268]

MCLA 280.269 Invalidation proceedings; proofs, correction of damages or assessment, order, costs. [MSA 11.1269]

MCLA 280.270 Tax lien; proceeding to compel spread of tax; established drains. [MSA 11.1270]

MCLA 280.271 Tax collection suits; tax reassessment. [MSA 11.1271]

MCLA 280.272 Same; assumpsit, prima facie evidence, judgment based on benefits; authority to sue. [MSA 11.1272]

MCLA 280.273 New proceedings when tax set aside; report of defects to supervisors, reassessment. [MSA 11.1273]

MCLA 280.274 Invalidation proceedings, commissioner as party. [MSA 11.1274]

MCLA 280.275 Drainage district bonds; issuance, terms, sale, premium; application of act; limitation on payment from county general fund. [MSA 11.1275]

700

MCLA 280.276 Same; intracounty drains; advancement from county general fund, reassessment. [MSA 11.1276]

MCLA 280.277 Same; delinquent assessments, advancements by municipalities, reimbursement, reassessment, validation of drain orders or bonds. [MSA 11.1277]

MCLA 280.278 Same; interest on taxes; moneys, disposition; bank deposits. [MSA 11.1278]

MCLA 280.279 Special assessments, payment in full; notice to commissioner; deficiency assessment. [MSA 11.1279]

MCLA 280.280 Drainage district bonds; deficiency assessment, surplus. Lands exempted from deficiency assessments; invalid bonds or obligations. [MSA 11.1280]

MCLA 280.281 Special drain assessment; definition of municipal corporation. [MSA 11.1281]

Sec. 281. Any municipal corporation may contract to pay ...

MCLA 280.282 Surplus funds; investment; interest earnings, disposition. [MSA 11.1282]

MCLA 280.283 Construction fund surplus, disposition; public corporation defined. [MSA 11.1283]

CHAPTER 12. REVOLVING FUNDS FOR DRAINS

MCLA 280.301 Revolving drain fund; creation, use. [MSA 11.1301]

MCLA 280.302 - 280.305 [MSA 11.1302 - 11.1305]

MCLA 280.306 Same; expenditure before completion of improvement of drain, apportionment. [MSA 11.1306]

Sec. 306. ... If the sum involved is too small to justify spreading the same over the designated district above referred to, such board of supervisors may order the sum to be spread against the property of the original petitioners according to such percentage as the commissioners shall deem just and equitable, based on the same benefit theory as if the improvement had been completed. ...

MCLA 280.307 Same; intercounty drain, apportionment, recovery of moneys. [MSA 11.1307]

CHAPTER 13. HIGHWAYS

MCLA 280.321 Drains in public highways, permit; release of right of way. [MSA 11.1321]

Sec. 321. Drains may be laid within or across the right of way of any highway, provided it shall be necessary for the county drain commissioner to obtain first a permit from the highway authority having jurisdiction. ...

MCLA 280.322 Same; cost of construction; contract; maintenance, bridges or passageways to farms. [MSA 11.1322]

Sec. 322. ... As part of such drain ... connecting the highway ... with each farm entrance, and when a drain crosses a farm or any portion thereof there shall be constructed 1 bridge, culvert or ford across the drain ... charged ... as a part of the construction of such drain, after which ...(it)... shall be maintained by the owner of the land. ...

MCLA 280.322b Same; installation for agricultural benefits expense of material and labor; notification of necessity. [MSA 11.1322(2)]

MCLA 280.323 Drains along public highways. Consent of highway authorities, location, disposition of material; apportionments against state trunk line highways, assessments. Drains constructed prior to 1923. [MSA 11.1323]

MCLA 280.324 Drainage across lands adjacent to highways; right of way. Approval of purchase of right of way by township board. [MSA 11.1324]

MCLA 280.325 Cost to township for highway drainage, report by county road commission, drain fund. [MSA 11.1325]

MCLA 280.326 Construction report; restriction on county road commission. [MSA 11.1326]

MCLA 280.382 Same; appointment of disinterested commissioner, duties as to county drain. [MSA 11.1382]

MCLA 280.383 Same; appointment in case of intercounty drain. [MSA 11.1383]

MCLA 280.384 Disinterested commissioner; salary and expenses, assessment. [MSA 11.1384]

CHAPTER 17. ABANDONED AND VACATED DRAINS -- DISPOSAL OF FUNDS

MCLA 280.391 Abandoned or vacated drains, procedure; private rights; new drain. [MSA 11.1391]

MCLA 280.392 Same; notices; disposal of money in drain fund. [MSA 11.1392]

MCLA 280.393 Same; duties of township treasurer in distribution of funds. [MSA 11.1393]

Sec. 393. Upon receiving such money, and the accompanying statement, if required to be furnished hereby, the township treasurer shall give his receipt therefor to the county treasurer. He shall also ...

MCLA 280.394 Same; disposal of funds, payments by township treasurer. [MSA 11.1394]

MCLA 280.395 County drainage district wholly within township, city or village, transfer of jurisdiction, approval. [MSA 11.1395]

Sec. 395. The county drain commissioner may relinquish jurisdiction and control to a township ...

Distribution of drain fund. *Any money which shall be in the drain fund of any such drainage district at the time jurisdiction over it is transferred ... shall be distributed in the same manner as is provided ... in the case of abandoned or vacated drains.*

MCLA 280.396 Transfer of drain project to county department of public works. [MSA 11.1396]

CHAPTER 18. OBSTRUCTIONS IN DRAINS; SEWAGE; MISCELLANEOUS PROVISIONS

MCLA 280.421 Obstructions; removal; expenses, notice; livestock; criminal complaint. [MSA 11.1421]

MCLA 280.422 Same; public utility companies; removal, mandamus. [MSA 11.1422]

MCLA 280.423 Use of drain for sewage or wastes. [MSA 11.1423]

Sec. 423. **Prohibited and permitted discharges; purification devices, and drains, construction.** *A municipality, industry, public or private corporation, individual, partnership association, or any other entity shall not continue to discharge or permit to be discharged into any county drain or intercounty drain of the state any sewage or waste matter capable of producing in the drains detrimental ...*

Surveys, studies, and investigations; contracts. *The drain commissioner or drainage board may make and cause to be made, surveys, studies and investigations for the purpose of ...*

Penalty. *Failure to comply with any of the provisions of this section shall subject the offender to the penalties described in section 602.*

MCLA 280.424 Inadequate disposal or filtration plant; abatement of nuisance; estimate of annual cost, appeal, notice, posting. Review of apportionment; notice of appeal, board of review, appointment, meeting. Same; notice of meeting, service, return. Same; certiorari; roll of apportionments; payment by municipalities. Same; payment for services; costs; annual assessments; reapportionment. Municipal assessments added to water rates. [MSA 11.1424]

MCLA 280.425 Additional drains at expense of petitioner; construction, consent, supervision; open drain, tiling. [MSA 11.1425]

MCLA 280.426 Drain orders received for drain taxes. [MSA 11.1426]

Sec. 426. *The drain orders issued for each particular drain shall be received for drain taxes for benefits levied for the construction of such drain by the township treasurer or county treasurer, as the case may be.*

MCLA 280.427 Corporation or land contract vendee as freeholder; corporate agent or officer as signer of petition. [MSA 11.1427]

MCLA 280.428 Drainage district including state lands; assessment, payment. [MSA 11.1428]

MCLA 280.429 Flood control projects; easements to United States; approval. [MSA 11.1429]

MCLA 280.430 Sanitary sewage; contracts for use of drains, charges. Contracts for use. Lien for charges, collection, discontinuance of service. Costs includable in charges. [MSA 11.1430]

MCLA 280.431 Contracts for drain projects; federal government; public corporations; relief from assessments. Flood control projects; conservation and utilization of soil and water. Public corporation; definition (includes townships). [MSA 11.1431]

MCLA 280.432 Obstruction of drain commissioner, drainage board, or agents, misdemeanor. [MSA 11.1432]

MCLA 280.433 Enlargement of drains, agreements, certificates, drain facilities, rights of way, easements. [MSA 11.1433]

MCLA 280.434 Reimbursement for advancements, drain costs; contracts, notes, pledge of full faith and credit, source of payment. [MSA 11.1434]

CHAPTER 19. CONSOLIDATED DISTRICTS

MCLA 280.441 County drainage districts; consolidation; petition; board of determination, residence, meeting, compensation. Meeting, notice, expenses. Determination as to conduciveness to public health, convenience or welfare, filing of order. [MSA 11.1441]

MCLA 280.441a Intercounty drainage districts; consolidation; petition; drainage board. Meeting, notice, expenses. Determination as to conduciveness to public health, convenience or welfare; filing of order. [MSA 11.1441(1)]

MCLA 280.442 Drainage districts, consolidation; surveys. [MSA 11.1442]

MCLA 280.443 Same; existing drain, recognition and credit, exemption from special assessment. [MSA 11.1443]

MCLA 280.444 Same; indebtedness, retirement; special assessment. [MSA 11.1444]

MCLA 280.445 Same; bonds and contracts, assumption by consolidated district. [MSA 11.1445]

MCLA 280.446 Same; abandonment or vacation of included drain; proration of moneys. [MSA 11.1446]

MCLA 280.447 Same; rights and powers, validation of bonds. [MSA 11.1447]

MCLA 280.448 Same; consent of county auditors or comptroller. [MSA 11.1448]

CHAPTER 20. INTRACOUNTY DRAINS; PUBLIC CORPORATIONS

MCLA 280.461 Definitions. [MSA 11.1461]

MCLA 280.462 County drains; public health, assessment against public corporations. [MSA 11.1462]

Sec. 462. County drains which are necessary for the public health may be located, established and constructed under the provisions of this chapter where the cost thereof is to be assessed wholly against public corporations.

MCLA 280.463 Same; petition, filing, signatures, contents, certified copy of resolution. [MSA 11.1463]

Sec. 463. Whenever it shall be necessary for the public health to locate, establish and construct a county drain, then a petition therefor may be filed with the county drain commissioner signed by 2 or more public corporations which will be subject to assessments to pay the cost thereof. Such petition shall state ... The county drain commissioner shall notify all public corporations which may be subject to an assessment or are within 1 mile of the assessment district ... that a petition has been filed. ...

MCLA 280.464 Drainage board, creation, members, chairman; compensation, mileage and expenses; minutes; records. [MSA 11.1464]

MCLA 280.465 Same; meetings, notice, waiver, quorum, adjournment; orders. [MSA 11.1465]

MCLA 280.466 Same; first meeting, notice. [MSA 11.1466]

MCLA 280.467 Same; tentative determination; name; district assessed; hearing of objections, notice, form; final order of determination. [MSA 11.1467]

MCLA 280.468 Same; plans, specifications, estimates, approval of route, designation of area served; apportionments. [MSA 11.1468]

MCLA 280.469 Same; hearing of objections, notice, contents; confirmation or readjustment of apportionments; final order of apportionment. [MSA 11.1469]

MCLA 280.470 Same; lands and rights of way; condemnation; procedure, federal government participation; costs. [MSA 11.1470]

MCLA 280.471 Same; contracts with federal government or corporations; bids. [MSA 11.1471]

MCLA 280.472 Funds; county treasurer, deputies; bonds; expenditures. [MSA 11.1472]

MCLA 280.473 Special assessment roll; installments, payment, interest. [MSA 11.1473]

MCLA 280.474 Same; contents, approval; certification to public corporation assessed; annual notice; advancements. Deductions for advancements; assessments against state; spread of tax; corrections. [MSA 11.1474]

MCLA 280.475 Assessments and taxes not subject to statutory or charter debt and tax limitations. [MSA 11.1475]

Sec. 475. Assessments made under the terms of this chapter shall not constitute an indebtedness of a public corporation within any statutory or charter debt limitation, ...

MCLA 280.476 Bonds, issuance, maturity, signatures; collection of assessments. [MSA 11.1476]

MCLA 280.477 Additional assessment, apportionment. [MSA 11.1477]

MCLA 280.478 Drainage board; continuation, responsibility, expenses, assessments, relinquishment of jurisdiction, indebtedness, contract liability. [MSA 11.1478]

MCLA 280.479 Advancements by corporations, reimbursement. [MSA 11.1479]

MCLA 280.480 Costs, items. [MSA 11.1480]

MCLA 280 481 Assessments against townships and villages. [MSA 11.1481]

Sec. 481. Unless otherwise provided by the drainage board, assessments against a township shall be against the township as a whole, including any incorporated village, but the drainage board may determine to assess a village separately, in which case the assessment against the township shall be exclusive of the village and the tax levies to be made by the township to pay such assessment shall not include any property taxable in the village.

MCLA 280.482 Cleaning out and other improvements for public health; procedure; backfilling. [MSA 11.1482]

MCLA 280.483 Certiorari; time; legal establishment of drain. [MSA 11.1483]

MCLA 280.484 Procedures; incorporation of other chapters in drainage board orders. [MSA 11.1484]

MCLA 280.485 Relief drains. [MSA 11.1485]

MCLA 280.486 Drains entirely within or serving an area entirely within single municipality. [MSA 11.1486]

MCLA 280.487 Drainage board, absence of members, deputies, vice-chairmen. [MSA 11.1487]

MCLA 280.488 Additional grant of power; prior projects. [MSA 11.1488]

Sec. 488. ... Projects completed prior to November 21, 1951, shall not be financed under this chapter.

MCLA 280.489 New cities; service of notice on township clerks or defacto city officer. [MSA 11.1489]

MCLA 280.490 Special assessments; connection, readiness to serve, availability of service charges. [MSA 11.1490]

MCLA 280.491 River, creek or watercourse; petition for assumption of jurisdiction. [MSA 11.1491]

MCLA 280.492 Same; agreement to pay and deposit of estimated cost of planning. [MSA 11.1492]

MCLA 280.493 Same; board of determination, final order, recording. [MSA 11.1493]

MCLA 280.494 Same; recording of description; effect. [MSA 11.1494]

MCLA 280.495 Same; determination as to public corporations to be assessed. [MSA 11.1495]

MCLA 280.496 Surplus funds; investment; interest earnings, disposition. [MSA 11.1496]

MCLA 280.497 Construction fund surplus, disposition; public corporation defined. [MSA 11.1497]

Sec. 497. ... The drainage board shall contract with any public corporation, which ... includes ... township ... whenever they have been assessed for ...

CHAPTER 21. INTERCOUNTY DRAINS;
PUBLIC CORPORATIONS

MCLA 280.511 Definitions. [MSA 11.1511]

MCLA 280.512 Intercounty drains; public health, assessment against public corporations. [MSA 11.1512]

MCLA 280.513 Same; petition, filing, signatures, contents, certified copy of resolution. [MSA 11.1513]

MCLA 280.514 Drainage board; members, chairman. [MSA 11.1514]

MCLA 280.515 Augmented drainage board, members, chairman, secretary; compensation, mileage, expenses. [MSA 11.1515]

MCLA 280.516 - 280.518 [MSA 11.1516 - 11.1518]

MCLA 280.519 Augmented board; tentative determination; name of drain and district; hearing; notice, publication; final order of determination; corrections. [MSA 11.1519]

MCLA 280.520 Drainage board; plans, specifications, estimates, approval of route, designation of area served; apportionments. [MSA 11.1520]

MCLA 280.521 Hearing of objections, notice, contents; confirmation or readjustment of apportionments; final order of apportionment. [MSA 11.1521]

MCLA 280.522 Lands and rights of way; condemnation; procedure, federal government participation; prior agreement as to highways; costs. [MSA 11.1522]

MCLA 280.523 Contracts with federal government or corporations; bids. [MSA 11.1523]

MCLA 280.524 Designation of a county treasurer, deputy, bonds; expenditures. [MSA 11.1524]

MCLA 280.525 Special assessment roll, installments, payment, interest, city tax levy. [MSA 11.1525]

MCLA 280.526 Same; contents, approval; certification to public corporation assessed; annual notice; advancements. Deductions for advancements; assessments against state; spread of tax; corrections. [MSA 11.1526]

MCLA 280.527 Intercounty drain assessments and taxes not subject to statutory or charter debt and tax limitations. [MSA 11.1527]

Sec. 527. Assessments made under the terms of this chapter shall not constitute an indebtedness of a public corporation within any statutory or charter debt limitation, and taxes levied by a public corporation for the payment of such assessments shall not be deemed to be within any statutory or charter tax limitation. Nothing contained in this chapter shall be construed as requiring any county, township, metropolitan district or authority to levy a tax beyond its constitutional tax limitation or any lawful increase thereof.

MCLA 280.528 Bonds, issuance, maturity, signatures; collection of assessments. [MSA 11.1528]

MCLA 280.529 Additional assessment, apportionment.
[MSA 11.1529]

MCLA 280.530 Drainage board, continuation, responsibility, expenses, assessments, relinquishment of jurisdiction, indebtedness, contract liability. [MSA 11.1530]

MCLA 280.531 Advancements by corporations, reimbursement.
[MSA 11.1531]

MCLA 280.532 Venue of actions; appointment of circuit judge.
[MSA 11.1532]

MCLA 280.533 Costs, items. [MSA 11.1533]

MCLA 280.534 Deputy for director of agriculture, powers.
[MSA 11.1534]

MCLA 280.535 Cleaning out and other improvements for public health; procedure, backfilling. [MSA 11.1535]

MCLA 280.536 Certiorari; time; legal establishment of drain.
[MSA 11.1536]

MCLA 280.537 Procedures; incorporation of other chapters in drainage board orders. [MSA 11.1537]

MCLA 280.538 New cities; service of notice on township clerk or de facto city officer. [MSA 11.1538]

MCLA 280.539 Special assessments; connection, readiness to serve, availability of service charges. [MSA 11.1539]

MCLA 280.540 Relief drains. [MSA 11.1540]

MCLA 280.541 River, creek or watercourse; petition for assumption of jurisdiction. [MSA 11.1541]

MCLA 280.542 Same; agreement to pay and deposit of estimated cost of planning. [MSA 11.1542]

MCLA 280.543 Same; board of determination, final order, recording. [MSA 11.1543]

MCLA 280.544 Same; recording of description; effect. [MSA 11.1544]

MCLA 280.545 Same; determination as to public corporations to be assessed. [MSA 11.1545]

MCLA 280.546 Surplus funds; investment; interest earnings, disposition. [MSA 11.1546]

MCLA 280.547 Construction fund surplus, disposition; public corporation defined (includes township). [MSA 11.1547]

CHAPTER 22. WATER MANAGEMENT --
DISTRICTS AND SUBDISTRICTS

MCLA 280.551 Water management; definitions. [MSA 11.1551]

MCLA 280.552 Same; petition for flood control or drainage project, filing, signatures, contents, map. [MSA 11.1552]

MCLA 280.553 Water management commission; members, appointment, compensation, expenses, approval of official plans, orders and assessments. [MSA 11.1553]

MCLA 280.554 Water management board, members, term, vacancy, qualification, chairman, procedure. Composition of board. Employees; treasurer, bond; secretary; annual audit. [MSA 11.1554]

MCLA 280.555 Meetings, notice, quorum, adjournment; orders, signatures; minutes, filing, certified copies, meetings open to public; records, inspection. [MSA 11.1555]

MCLA 280.556 Petitions, review; notice of first meeting. [MSA 11.1556]

MCLA 280.557 Water management commission; temporary secretary, by-laws, tentative determination, amendment of petition, notice of adjourned meeting; dismissal of petition; name of district; board; tentative determination; preliminary plans. [MSA 11.1557]

MCLA 280.558 Water management board; hearing on objections to project, notice, publication, form; preliminary order of determination. [MSA 11.1558]

MCLA 280.559 Assessment, basis. [MSA 11.1559]

MCLA 280.560 Preliminary plans, approval; detailed plans, contents, approval; official plans, filing. [MSA 11.1560]

MCLA 280.561 Tentative percentage of cost for assessment, apportionment. [MSA 11.1561]

MCLA 280.562 Same; hearing on objections to apportionment, notice, publication; report of findings. [MSA 11.1562]

MCLA 280.563 Water management commission; review of board's apportionment; final order of apportionment; annual meeting; work plan, advisory committees. [MSA 11.1563]

MCLA 280.564 Lands and rights of way; condemnation, procedure, federal governmental participation; costs. [MSA 11.1564]

MCLA 280.565 Contracts with federal government or corporations; bids. [MSA 11.1565]

MCLA 280.566 Special assessment roll; installments, payment, interest. [MSA 11.1566]

MCLA 280.567 Same; contents, approval; certification to corporation assessed; annual notice of installment and interest; advancement by county; assessment against state; correction of assessment. [MSA 11.1567]

MCLA 280.568 Assessments and taxes not subject to statutory or charter debt or tax limitations. [MSA 11.1568]

MCLA 280.569 Bonds, issuance, maturity, signatures; collection of assessments. [MSA 11.1569]

MCLA 280.570 Additional assessment, apportionment. [MSA 11.1570]

MCLA 280.571 Water management board; continuation, responsibility; budget, hearing, adoption. [MSA 11.1571]

MCLA 280.572 Advancements by corporations, reimbursement. [MSA 11.1572]

MCLA 280.573 Costs; items, contingent expenses. [MSA 11.1573]

MCLA 280.574 Water management commission, powers. [MSA 11.1574]

MCLA 280.575 Subdistrict; petition; official plan, final order of apportionment of cost; assessment. [MSA 11.1575]

MCLA 280.576 Water management district in interstate river basin, powers of commission. [MSA 11.1576]

MCLA 280.577 Venue of actions; appointment of circuit judge. [MSA 11.1577]

MCLA 280.578 Deputy for director of agriculture, powers. [MSA 11.1578]

MCLA 280.579 Intercounty drain constructed or improved for public health as part of flood control project. [MSA 11.1579]

MCLA 280.580 Public and private construction in works owned by water management district, plans, approval. [MSA 11.1580]

MCLA 280.581 Certiorari; time; legal establishment of project. [MSA 11.1581]

MCLA 280.582 Provisions applicable. [MSA 11.1582]

Sec. 582. In operating under the terms of this chapter, the several boards and officials shall not be limited by the provisions contained in other chapters of this act and the procedures required under the terms of such other chapters shall not be deemed to be applicable.

MCLA 280.583 Validation of prior bonds. [MSA 11.1583]

CHAPTER 23. PENALTIES

MCLA 280.601 Signatures to petition for drain secured by commissioner; penalty. [MSA 11.1601]

MCLA 280.602 Removal of stakes, injury to drain; penalty. [MSA 11.1602]

CHAPTER 24. REPEALS AND SAVING CLAUSES

MCLA 280.621 - 280.623 [MSA 11.1621 - 11.1623]

JOINT ACTION
Act No. 297, P.A. 1937 - Soil Conservation Districts

AN ACT to declare the necessity of creating governmental subdivisions of the state, to be known as "soil conservation districts," to engage in conserving soil resources and preventing and controlling soil erosion; to establish the state soil conservation committee, and to define its powers and duties; to provide for the creation of soil conservation districts; to define the powers and duties of soil conservation districts, and to provide for the exercise of such powers, including the power to acquire property by purchase, gift, and otherwise; to em-

power such districts to adopt programs and regulations for the discontinuance of the land-use practices contributing to soil wastage and soil erosion, and the adoption and carrying out of soil-conserving land-use practices, and to provide for the enforcement of such programs and regulations; to provide for establishing boards of adjustment in connection with land-use regulations, and to define their functions and powers; to provide for financial assistance to such soil conservation districts, and making an appropriation for that purpose; to declare the effect of this act, and for other purposes.

MCLA 282.1 Short title. [MSA 13.1781]

MCLA 282.2 Declaration of policy. [MSA 13.1782]

MCLA 282.3 Definitions. [MSA 13.1783]

MCLA 282.4 Soil conservation committee; membership, terms; powers, duties. [MSA 13.1784]

MCLA 282.5 Soil conservation districts; creation, procedure. Petition. Hearing; notice; determination of soil conservation committee; subsequent petitions. Determination of practicability; referendum. Hearings and referenda, expenses; rules; informalities. Referendum, publication; determination of committee. Directors, governmental subdivision, body corporate; application filed with secretary of state, duties, certificate. Denial of petition; subsequent petitions. Additional territory; petitions; evidence. Boundary line change; petition, hearing, certificate. Municipalities, inclusion, land owners' rights. Name of district, change, procedure. [MSA 13.1785]

MCLA 282.6 Election of 3 directors for each district. [MSA 13.1786]

MCLA 282.7 Directors, appointment, qualifications, term; chairman; quorum; employees. [MSA 13.1787]

MCLA 282.8 Powers of districts and directors. [MSA 13.1788]

MCLA 282.13 Cooperation between districts. [MSA 13.1793]

MCLA 282.14 Cooperation with state agencies and subdivisions.
[MSA 13.1794]

Sec. 14. (a) Agencies ... of any ... governmental subdivision of the state which have jurisdiction over, or are charged with the administration of, any ... publicly owned lands, lying within the boundaries of any district, shall cooperate to the fullest extent with the directors of the districts in the effectuation of programs and operations undertaken by the directors under the provisions of this act. ...

(b) The board of directors of a soil conservation district may cooperate with and enter into agreement with a ... township ...

MCLA 282.15 Discontinuance of districts; procedure; referendum.
[MSA 13.1795]

MCLA 282.15a Consolidation of districts; petition, notice of hearing. Petition and hearing. Order of consolidation. Certificate of due organization. Board of directors, term. Transfer of assets, liabilities, records, documents, writings, property. [MSA 13.1795(1)]

MCLA 282.16 Appropriations. [MSA 13.1796]

JOINT ACTION
Act No. 205, P.A. 1967 - Irrigation Districts and Projects

AN ACT to provide for the establishment of irrigation districts in counties of 400,000 population or less; to provide for irrigation boards; to provide for irrigation projects in such districts; to provide for the assessment and collection of taxes in such districts; to provide for the issuance of bonds or irrigation orders by such districts and to provide for maintenance assessments in such districts; to prescribe the duties of various officials in such irrigation districts and authorize cooperation at (of) various governmental agencies and their officers with such districts.

MCLA 279.201 Applicability of act; Great Lakes, withdrawal of water; water resources commission, enforcement of act, assistance.
[MSA 11.302(1)]

Sec. 1. This act shall be applicable in counties of 400,000 population or less to the use of water from the Great Lakes only, ...

MCLA 279.202 Liberal construction; purpose. [MSA 11.302(2)]

Sec. 2. The provisions of this act shall be liberally construed to promote the public welfare by irrigating lands, improving the existing water supply for the lands or providing new means or methods of water supply, or constructing ...

MCLA 279.203 Previously organized districts; validity, rights, privileges, applicability of act, obligations. [MSA 11.302(3)]

MCLA 279.204 Districts, powers, term, state agencies. [MSA 11.302(4)]

MCLA 279.205 Contracts, federal, state, approval, invasion of state's public trust in its waters. [MSA 11.302(5)]

Sec. 5. ... The irrigation district may also contract with the state or any agency thereof or with any person, private corporation or with any public corporation in respect to any matter connected with the construction, operation or maintenance of any irrigation works or for the improvement or providing new means of water supply or the improvement of the existing water supply for the lands within the irrigation district. ...

MCLA 279.206 Easements and rights of way of drainage districts or counties, grant to United States or irrigation districts; private rights relating to drain. [MSA 11.302(6)]

MCLA 279.207 Dams, approval. [MSA 11.302(7)]

MCLA 279.208 Federal, state or private grants or aid. [MSA 11.302(8)]

Sec. 8. Any irrigation district may apply for and accept grants or any aid which the United States government or any agency thereof or the state or any of its political subdivisions or any private person, corporation or trust may authorize to be made or given in aid of any irrigation project.

MCLA 279.209 Petition for establishment of irrigation district; qualifications of petitioners, purpose, contents. [MSA 11.302(9)]

MCLA 279.210 Affidavit of signers, evidence of facts stated. [MSA 11.302(10)]

MCLA 279.211 Lands to be included in district. [MSA 11.302(11)]

Sec. 11. The lands proposed to be included in any irrigation district need not be contiguous if the benefit of the proposed work in each part will exceed the costs of the proposed work in each part; and lands within any ... township ...

MCLA 279.212 - 279.222 [MSA 11.302(12) - 11.302(22)]

Note: These sections have to do with creation of irrigation boards and procedures for establishing districts.

MCLA 279.223 Assessment roll, contents; basis for assessments; objections to roll. [MSA 11.302(23)]

MCLA 279.224 Hearing on objections to roll, notice. [MSA 11.302(24)]

MCLA 279.225 Proofs and allegations on hearing on objections to roll; review of descriptions and benefit apportionments, equalization. [MSA 11.302(25)]

MCLA 279.226 Final order of apportionment and order of confirmation of roll; indorsement upon roll; memorandum of installments; special assessments roll, confirmation, finality. [MSA 11.302(26)]

MCLA 279.227 Irrigation special assessments lien. [MSA 11.302(27)]

MCLA 279.228 Tax assessment roll, preparation, certification, contents; permanent roll. [MSA 11.302(28)]

MCLA 279.229 Spread of special assessments on local tax rolls. [MSA 11.302(29)]

Sec. 29. The board of supervisors of the counties involved shall order the spread of all irrigation special assessments on the local tax rolls by the local tax assessing officials ...

MCLA 279.230 Supervisor, village or city assessor, spreading special assessment taxes on local tax roll. [MSA 11.302(30)]

MCLA 279.231 Special assessment taxes, interest, charges, collection, disbursement; defense of collecting officer; limitation of actions; payment under protest; tax liens. [MSA 11.302(31)]

MCLA 279.232 Additional pro rata assessments, limitation. [MSA 11.302(32)]

MCLA 279.233 Invalid assessments, validation procedure; application of payments to reassessments. [MSA 11.302(33)]

MCLA 279.234 Irrigation orders for payment of charges. [MSA 11.302(34)]

MCLA 279.235 Pledge of full faith and credit of county for payment of interest. [MSA 11.302(35)]

MCLA 279.236 Irrigation board; operation and maintenance of district properties; water charges, fixing and collecting, lien, certification; service charges; future expenses, assessment. [MSA 11.302(36)]

Sec. 36. ... The time and manner of certification and the other details in respect to the collection of such charges and the enforcement of such lien shall be prescribed by the irrigation board in cooperation with the governing bodies of the public corporations in which the lands are located. ...

MCLA 279.237 Determination or apportionment of benefits or confirmation of special assessment roll; review, writ of superintending control, limitation. [MSA 11.302(37)]

MCLA 279.238 Suspension of water delivery, unpaid irrigation taxes; rights of way for laterals, condemnation, payment. [MSA 11.302(38)]

MCLA 279.239 - 279.246 $\overline{\text{MSA } 11.230(39)}$ - $11.230(46)]$

Note: These sections have to do with fiscal responsibilities of the board.

Act No. 157, P.A. 1953 - Deferred Drain Taxes

AN ACT to authorize the extension of time of payment of certain drain taxes; to provide for the assessment, levy and collection of such deferred drain taxes; to authorize the payment of drainage district bonds issued in anticipation of the collection thereof; and to provide for the disposition of such drain taxes when collected.

MCLA 279.31 Drain taxes; extending time of payment, maximum; drainage district bonds, payment. $\overline{\text{MSA } 11.170(1)]}$

MCLA 279.32 Same; resolution of board of supervisors. $\overline{\text{MSA } 11.170(2)]}$

MCLA 279.33 Same; unpaid interest and principal of outstanding drainage district bonds, payment; agreement. $\overline{\text{MSA } 11.170(3)]}$

MCLA 279.34 Same; assessment, levy and collection, procedure; duty of drain commissioner; new assessment. $\overline{\text{MSA } 11.170(4)]}$

MCLA 279.35 Money credited to general fund. $\overline{\text{MSA } 11.170(5)]}$

MCLA 279.36 Lien. $\overline{\text{MSA } 11.170(6)]}$

MCLA 279.37 Drain taxes assessed at large; defect in proceedings not legalized or waived. $\overline{\text{MSA } 11.170(7)]}$

MCLA 279.38 Scope of act. $\overline{\text{MSA } 11.170(8)]}$

Sec. 8.   The provisions of this act shall only apply to the property owned by such persons who request the extension authorized under the provisions of this act.

JOINT ACTION
Act No. 278, P.A. 1952 - Flood, Drainage or Beach Erosion Control

AN ACT to authorize the township boards of townships, the legislative bodies of incorporated cities and incorporated villages, or the board of county road commissioners of any county when directed by the board of supervisors of the county, to acquire interests in lands and to contract with the federal government, or any agency thereof, with respect to flood control, drainage control and beach erosion control; and to authorize participation of townships, incorporated cities and incorporated villages, and counties in such projects.

MCLA 281.621 Flood, drainage or beach erosion control; lands, acquisition; contract with federal government, terms. [MSA 13.1821]

MCLA 281.622 Relieved from assessment. [MSA 13.1822]

MCLA 281.623 Contract; provisions. [MSA 13.1823]

MCLA 281.624 Expenditures from municipal or county funds. [MSA 13.1824]

Sec. 4. The township board ... pursuant to a resolution adopted by a 2/3 vote of the members thereof, is hereby authorized in connection with any such contract to make expenditures from its general fund, contingent fund or from any special funds available therefor.

MCLA 281.625 Assurances to federal government. [MSA 13.1825]

MCLA 281.626 Joint contracts. [MSA 13.1826]

Sec. 6. The township board of any township, the legislative body of any incorporated city or incorporated village, or the board of county road commissioners of any county when directed by the board of supervisors of the county, may provide for joint participation and a joint contract or contracts in carrying out the purposes of this act.

MCLA 281.627 Contracts; approval by municipal finance commission; borrowings, debt and interest limitations. [MSA 13.1827]

Sec. 7. Such contracts as may be entered into under the provisions of this act must have prior approval of the municipal finance commission as to ...

MCLA 281.628 Interest in lands; easement for flood plain; acquisition; declared public purposes. [MSA 13.1828]

Sec. 8. ... Two or more adjoining cities, villages or townships are authorized to maintain such proceedings (acquisition of lands) in accordance with the procedure prescribed by ...

JOINT ACTION
Act No. 44, P.A. 1952 - Flood, Drainage or Beach Erosion Control

AN ACT to authorize political subdivisions to make expenditures for coastal beach erosion investigations and studies.

MCLA 281.601 Coastal beach erosion or protection, expenditures authorized. [MSA 13.1811]

Sec. 1. Any political subdivision of the state, by resolution of its legislative body adopted by a majority vote of its full membership, is hereby authorized to make expenditures from its general fund, contingent fund, or from any special funds available therefor, to undertake, either independently or in cooperation with any other political subdivision or with any agency of the state and/or federal government, investigative or study functions related to coastal beach erosion or protection.

Act No. 187, P.A. 1851 - Sale and Reclamation of Swamp Lands

AN ACT to provide for the sale and reclaiming of swamp lands granted to the state, and for the disposition of the proceeds.

MCLA 322.151 Swamp lands; receipt on basis of notes on file in surveyor general's office. [MSA 13.361]

MCLA 322.156 Same; sale in legal subdivisions; subject to private entry after public auction. [MSA 13.362]

MCLA 322.157 Same; procuring records for office of commissioner of land office. [MSA 13.363]

Act No. 101, P.A. 1869 - Swamp Land Patents

AN ACT to provide for the issuing, delivering or depositing patents to swamp lands, and to provide for the assessment and taxation of such lands.

MCLA 322.511 Swamp land patents; issuance for certain purposes. [MSA 13.951]

MCLA 322.512 Same; annual list furnished county treasurer; assessment and taxation of lands. [MSA 13.952]

MCLA 322.513 Same; issuance for alternate descriptions. [MSA 13.953]

JOINT ACTION
Act No. 247, P.A. 1955 - Great Lakes Submerged Lands Act

AN ACT to authorize the department of conservation of the state of Michigan to grant, convey or lease certain unpatented lake bottomlands and unpatented made lands in the Great Lakes, including the bays and harbors thereof, belonging to the state of Michigan or held in trust by it; to permit the private and public use of waters over submerged patented lands and the making of agreements limiting and regulating the use thereof; to provide for the disposition of revenue derived therefrom; and to provide penalties for violation of this act.

MCLA 322.701 Great Lakes submerged lands act; short title. [MSA 13.700(1)]

MCLA 322.702 Unpatented submerged lake bottom lands and un-

patented made lands in great lakes; construction of act.
MSA 13.700(2)

MCLA 322.703 Same; conveyances, leases and agreements; reservation of mineral rights. MSA 13.700(3)

MCLA 322.704 Same; application for conveyance, contents, qualifications of applicant; consent. Form of application. Approvals required; abstract of title and tax history of riparian land. Deposit with application. MSA 13.700(4)

MCLA 332.705 Same; consideration for conveyances. Artificial changes in land; standards for determining consideration. (Agreements for) Conveyances to local units of government. Flood control, shore erosion control, drainage and sanitation control. Leases for marina purposes; definition. Fraud, consideration; hearing on determination. MSA 13.700(5)

MCLA 322.706 Same; evaluation by department of conservation; appraisal by court-appointed appraisers. MSA 13.700(6)

MCLA 322.707 Moneys credited to general fund; accounting; employees. MSA 13.700(7)

MCLA 322.708 Taxation of lands conveyed. MSA 13.700(8)

Sec. 8. All lands conveyed or leased under this act shall be subject to taxation and the general property tax laws and other laws as other real estate used and taxed by the governmental unit or units within which the land is or may be included.

MCLA 322.709 Rules and regulations. MSA 13.700(9)

MCLA 322.710 Lands filled, excavated or altered without approval, penalty, consideration. MSA 13.700(10)

MCLA 322.711 Certificate of location of lakeward boundary, application by riparian owner, fee. MSA 13.700(11)

MCLA 322.712 Prohibitions; exceptions. MSA 13.700(12)

MCLA 322.713 Application for construction, etc.; fee.
MSA 13.700(13)

MCLA 322.714 Objections; public hearings; notice of public hearings. MSA 13.700(14)

Sec. 14. *Upon receipt of the application, the department shall mail copies to the state department of public health, clerks of the county, city, village and township, ...*

MCLA 322.715 Permit; conditions; maintenance of land fronting waterway. MSA 13.700(15)

INLAND LAKES AND RIVERS

JOINT ACTION
Act No. 253, P.A. 1964 - Local River Management

AN ACT to enable local units of government to co-operate in planning and carrying out a coordinated water management program in the watershed which they share.

MCLA 323.301 Local river management act; short title.
MSA 11.431

MCLA 323.302 Same; definitions. MSA 11.432

MCLA 323.303 Watershed council; creation, organizational meeting; notice. MSA 11.433

Sec. 3. *(1) To promote cooperation among local governments in river management, a watershed council shall be established by the commission upon a petition from 3 or more local governments lying wholly or partially in the watershed as defined ...*

(2) Upon finding that the petition is in conformance with this statute the commission shall adopt an order establishing the council, ...

MCLA 323.304 Same; membership, voting rights, term; river manage-

ment boards. [MSA 11.434]

MCLA 323.305 Same; bylaws, budget, annual meeting, officers.
[MSA 11.435]

MCLA 323.306 Same; permissive powers. [MSA 11.436]

MCLA 323.307 River management district; establishment, powers, consolidation, coordination. [MSA 11.437]

> *Sec. 7. The governing bodies of any two or more local governments may petition the water resources commission to establish a river management district ...*

MCLA 323.308 Same; organizational meeting, board, officers, membership, voting rights. [MSA 11.438]

> *Sec. 8. Within 60 days after the adoption of an order establishing a district the commission shall schedule an organizational meeting of the district board and shall ...*

MCLA 323.309 Same; powers of board. [MSA 11.439]

MCLA 323.310 Same; corporate powers; financing. [MSA 11.440]

> *Sec. 10. ... costs shall be payable from general funds or taxes raised by the local governments; ...*

MCLA 323.311 Same; board, duties, bylaws, budgets, assessments, annual meeting, records. [MSA 11.441]

MCLA 323.312 Executive secretary, additional staff. [MSA 11.442]

MCLA 323.313 Minimum level of stream flow; industrial use of water. [MSA 11.443]

MCLA 323.314 Same; order of determination, notice, review.
[MSA 11.444]

MCLA 323.315 Same; request to watershed council for determination. [MSA 11.445]

728

MCLA 323.316 Measurement of stream flow, lake levels, and water quality. [MSA 11.446]

MCLA 323.317 Water resources commission, approval of plan, supervision over functioning of district. [MSA 11.447]

Sec. 17. The commission may cooperate and negotiate with any government, unit of government, agency thereof, or with any person in establishing and maintaining gauges and sampling devices ... shall provide technical advice and assistance in the preparation of a ... plan ...

MCLA 323.318 Same; rules and regulations. [MSA 11.448]

MCLA 323.319 Same; powers under other acts not abridged. [MSA 11.449]

Sec. 19. Nothing in this act shall be construed so as to abridge the authority vested in the commission by Act No. 245 of the Public Acts of 1929, as amended, being sections 323.1 to 323.12 [MSA 3.521 TO 3.532] of the Compiled Laws of 1948. Permits granted by the commission in accordance with Act No. 143 of the Public Acts of 1959, being sections 323.251 to 323.258 [MSA 13.145(1) TO 13.145(8)] of the Compiled Laws of 1948 shall not be affected by this act. The granting of future permits under Act No. 143 of the Public Acts of 1959 shall proceed without regard to anything contained in this act.

MCLA 323.320 State health commissioner; powers unaffected. [MSA 11.450]

Townships are leading the way in Michigan to prove that rivers can be used by a reasonable amount of people while maintaining the wild and scenic values of these bodies of water. Four townships in Kent County, using the following statute and working with the Michigan Department of Natural Resources, the State Treasury Department and the Michigan Townships Association, are in the process of concluding a multi-unit ordinance to preserve the beauty of the Rogue River in Kent County.

The alternative to this kind of cooperation is inaction, leading to destruction, erosion, pollution and eventual death of the beautiful rivers in our state -- unless, of course, the state and federal governments take over. It is hard to believe that Michigan's townships are willing to let that happen.

JOINT ACTION
Act No. 231, P.A. 1970 - Natural River Act of 1970

AN ACT to authorize the establishment of a system of designated wild, scenic and recreational rivers; to prescribe the powers and duties of the natural resources commission with respect thereto; to fund necessary study and comprehensive planning for the establishment of the system; to provide for planning, zoning and cooperation with local units of government; to authorize the protection of designated river frontage by acquisition, lease, easement or other means; to authorize local units of government and the commission to establish zoning districts in which certain uses of rivers and related lands may be encouraged, regulated or prohibited; to provide for limitations on uses of land and their natural resources, and on the platting of land; and to provide that assessing officers shall take cognizance of the effect of zoning on true cash value.

MCLA 281.761 Short title. [MSA 11.501]

MCLA 281.762 Definitions. [MSA 11.502]

MCLA 281.763 Natural river area, designation, purposes, boundaries, planning, state land, federal programs. [MSA 11.503]

MCLA 281.764 Pre-requisites for designation; categories of natural rivers, definition, establishment. [MSA 11.504]

MCLA 281.765 Acquisition of lands or interests in lands. [MSA 11.505]

MCLA 281.766 Federal programs, administration; leases or agreements to administer; preservation and enhancement of area; facilities, construction, maintenance. [MSA 11.506]

MCLA 281.767 Hearings prior to designation, place, notice. [MSA 11.507]

730

MCLA 281.768 Zoning; ordinances, rules. [MSA 11.508]

Sec. 8. After designation of a river or portion of a river as a natural river area and following the preparation of the long range comprehensive plan, the commission may determine that the uses of land along the river except within the limits of an incorporated municipality, shall be controlled by zoning contributing to accomplishment of the purposes of this act and the natural river plan. County and township governments are encouraged to ...

MCLA 281.769 Purposes of ordinances or rules. [MSA 11.509]

Sec. 9. A zoning ordinance adopted by a local unit of government or a zoning rule promulgated by the commission shall provide for the protection of the river and its related land resources consistent with the preservation and enhancement of their values and the objectives set forth in section 3. ...

MCLA 281.770 Zoning districts; structures; subdivisions; roads; public utility lines; vegetation, cutting; mining; drilling for gas and oil. [MSA 11.510]

Sec. 10. The ordinance or rule shall establish zoning districts within which such uses of land as for agriculture, forestry, recreation, residence, industry, commerce and additional uses may be encouraged, regulated or prohibited. It may limit or prohibit ...

MCLA 281.771 County and township zoning. [MSA 11.511]

Sec. 11. A local unit of government in establishing a zoning ordinance, in addition to the authority and requirements of this act, shall conform to Act No. 184 of the Public Acts of 1943, as amended, being sections 125.271 to 125.301 [MSA 5.2963(1) TO 5.2963(31)] *of the Compiled Laws of 1948, or Act No. 183 of the Public Acts of 1943, as amended, being sections 125.201 to 125.232* [MSA 5.2961(1) TO 5.2961(32)] *of the Compiled Laws of 1948. Any conflict shall be resolved in favor of the provisions of this act. The powers herein granted shall be liberally construed ...*

MCLA 281.772 Maps of zoning districts, filing; property within districts, true cash value for assessments. [MSA 11.512]

Sec. 12. Upon adoption of a zoning ordinance or rule, certified copies of the maps, showing districts shall be filed with the local tax assessing officer and the state tax commission. In establishing true cash value of property within the districts zoned, the assessing officer shall take cognizance of the effect of limits on use established by the ordinance or rule.

MCLA 281.773 Administrative procedures and rules; personnel; violations; zoning rules, promulgation, procedure, review, nonconforming uses. ⌈MSA 11.513⌉

Sec. 13. (1) The commission shall prescribe such administrative procedures and rules and provide such personnel as it may deem necessary for the enforcement of a zoning ordinance or rule enacted in accordance herewith. ...

(2) A zoning rule of the commission shall be promulgated in accordance with and subject to the provisions of Act No. 306 of the Public Acts of 1969, as amended, being sections 24.201 to 24.315 ⌈MSA 3.560(101) TO 3.560(215)⌋ of the Compiled Laws of 1948. The rule shall include procedures for receiving and acting upon applications from local units of government or landowners for change of boundaries or change in permitted uses in accordance with sections 71 to 87 of Act No. 306 of the Public Acts of 1969 **(MCLA 24.271 to 24.287** ⌈MSA 3.560(271) TO 3.560(187)⌋ **).** *An aggrieved party may seek judicial review in accordance with and subject to the provisions of sections 101 to 106 of Act No. 306 of the Public Acts of 1969.* **(MCLA 24.301 to 24.306** ⌈MSA 3.560(201) TO 3.560(206)⌋**).**

(3) The lawful use of any building or structure and of any land or premise as existing and lawful at the time of enactment of a zoning ordinance or rule or of an amendment thereof may be continued although such use does not conform with the provisions of the ordinance, rule or amendment. ...

MCLA 281.774 Federal wild and scenic river systems, inclusion of natural river areas, cooperative agreements. ⌈MSA 11.514⌉

MCLA 281.775 Plans, approval; erosion or flow alteration, control; rules. ⌈MSA 11.515⌉

Sec. 15. The commission shall approve preliminary and final plans for site or route location, construction or enlargement of utility transmission lines, publicly provided recreation facilities, ...

MCLA 281.776 Use of natural resources. [MSA 11.516]

Sec. 16. This act may not be construed to prohibit a reasonable and lawful use of any other natural resource which will benefit the general welfare of the people of this state and which is not inconsistent with the purpose of this act.

Time and erosion have made eyesores of many shallow bodies of water in Michigan. The following statute permits the legislative bodies of local units of government to cooperate with the Department of Natural Resources to alleviate such problems by granting authorization to raise money by taxation and special assessments, including the acquisition of required lands and other property by gift, grant, purchase or condemnation.

JOINT ACTION
Act No. 345, P.A. 1966 - Inland Lake Improvement

AN ACT to provide for the improvement of certain inland lakes; to authorize the dredging and removal of undesirable materials from lakes; to authorize the acquisition of lands and other property by gift, grant, purchase or condemnation; to authorize the raising of money by taxation and special assessments for the purpose of this act; to provide for review and appeal; to prescribe the duties and powers of the legislative bodies of local units of government and the department of conservation; and to repeal certain acts and parts of acts.

MCLA 281.901 Short title. [MSA 11.419(1)]

MCLA 281.902 Definitions. [MSA 11.419(2)]

MCLA 281.903 Petition for improvement of lake. [MSA 11.419(3)]

Sec. 3. (1) The local governing body of any local unit in which the whole or any part of the waters of any public inland lake is situated, upon its own motion or by petition of 2/3 of the freeholders owning lands abutting the lake, ...

(2) Upon receipt of the petition or upon its own motion, the local governing body of a local unit within 60 days shall set up a lake board as provided in section 4 which shall proceed with the necessary steps for improving the lake or to void the proposed project.

MCLA 281.904   Lake board; membership; appointment; chairman; secretary; quorum; technical data; recommendations.
[MSA 11.419(4)]

MCLA 281.905 Number of petitioning freeholders required.
[MSA 11.419(5)]

MCLA 281.906 Preliminary costs; revolving fund. [MSA 11.419(6)]

MCLA 281.907 Institution of proceedings; resolution of local governing body. [MSA 11.419(7)]

Sec. 7. (1) Whenever a local governing body, in accordance with section 3, deems it expedient to have a lake improved, it, by resolution, shall direct the lake board to institute proceedings as prescribed in this act.

(2) When the waters of any inland lake are situated in 2 or more local units, the improvement of such lake may be determined jointly in the same manner ...

MCLA 281.908 Petition (from conservation department) **for improvement of lake by local governing body.** [MSA 11.419(8)]

MCLA 281.909 Determination of scope of project by lake board; establishment of special assessment district; other ministerial duties. [MSA 11.419(9)]

MCLA 281.910   Engineering report; economic study and estimate of cost; contents. [MSA 11.419(10)]

Sec. 10. (1) The lake board shall retain a registered professional engineer ...

MCLA 281.911 Review of reports by board; determination of practicability; public hearing; publication of notice. [MSA 11.419(11)]

MCLA 281.912 Contribution toward cost by county board of supervisors. ⌐MSA 11.419(12)⌐

Sec. 12. ... may provide up to 25% of the cost ... on any public inland lake.

MCLA 281.913 Approval of plans and estimate of costs; determination of sufficiency of petition; resolution; publication; assessment roll. ⌐MSA 11.419(13)⌐

MCLA 281.914 Report of assessment roll to board; review; notice and hearing; confirmation. ⌐MSA 11.419(14)⌐

MCLA 281.915 Special assessment installments. ⌐MSA 11.419(15)⌐

MCLA 281.916 Lien of special assessment. ⌐MSA 11.419(16)⌐

MCLA 281.917 Collection of assessments. ⌐MSA 11.419(17)⌐

MCLA 281.918 Delinquent assessments; reassessment.
⌐MSA 11.419(18)⌐

MCLA 281.919 Division of parcel of land; apportionment of uncollected assessment. ⌐MSA 11.419(19)⌐

MCLA 281.920 Additional assessments. ⌐MSA 11.419(20)⌐

MCLA 281.921 Invalidity of assessment; reassessment.
⌐MSA 11.419(21)⌐

MCLA 281.922 Exempt lands; payment of assessment by governing body. ⌐MSA 11.419(22)⌐

Sec. 22. The governing body of any ... townships ... whose lands are exempt by law, by resolution, may agree to pay the special assessments against such lands, in which case the assessment, including all the installments thereof, shall be a valid claim against the local unit.

MCLA 281.923 Borrowing money; lake level orders or bonds, issuance, purpose, amount, payment, execution, form; pledge of full faith and credit. ⌐MSA 11.419(23)⌐

Sec. 23. ... The local governing body may pledge the full faith and credit of a local unit for the prompt payment of the principal of and interest on the bonds or lake level orders as they become due. The pledge ... shall be included within the total (statutory) limitation ...

MCLA 281.924 Condemnation proceedings. [MSA 11.419(24)]

MCLA 281.925 Gifts or grants in aid; acceptance by lake board. [MSA 11.419(25)]

MCLA 281.926 Gifts or grants in aid; acceptance by conservation department. [MSA 11.419(26)]

MCLA 281.927 Advertisement for bids; letting of contracts. [MSA 11.419(27)]

MCLA 281.928 Computation of project cost. [MSA 11.419(28)]

MCLA 281.929 Intervention by conservation department. [MSA 11.419(29)]

MCLA 281.930 Repeals. [MSA 11.419(30)]

JOINT ACTION
Act No. 346, P.A. 1972 - Inland Lakes and Streams Act of 1972

AN ACT to regulate inland lakes and streams; to protect riparian rights and the public trust in inland lakes and streams; to prescribe powers and duties; to provide remedies and penalties; and to repeal certain acts and parts of acts.

MCLA 281.951 Short title. [MSA 11.475(1)]

MCLA 281.952 Definitions. [MSA 11.475(2)]

MCLA 281.953 Permits, necessity. [MSA 11.475(3)]

Sec. 3. Except as provided in this act, a person without a per-

mit from the department shall not:

(a) Dredge or fill bottomland.

(b) Construct, enlarge, extend, remove or place a structure on bottomland.

(c) Erect, maintain or operate a marina.

(d) Create, enlarge or diminish an inland lake or stream.

(e) Structurally interfere with the natural flow of an inland lake or stream.

(f) Construct, dredge, commence, extend or enlarge an artificial canal, channel, ditch, lagoon, pond, lake or similar waterway where the purpose is ultimate connection with an existing inland lake or stream, or where any part of the artificial waterway is located within 500 feet of the ordinary high water mark of an existing inland lake or stream.

(g) Connect any natural or artificially constructed waterway, canal, channel, ditch, lagoon, pond, lake or similar water with an existing inland lake or stream for navigation or any other purpose.

MCLA 281.954 Operations not requiring a permit. MSA 11.175(4)

MCLA 281.955 Application for permit, filing, form, contents, fee. MSA 11.175(5)

Sec. 5. (1) Before a project which is subject to this act is undertaken, a person shall file an application and receive a permit from the department. The application shall be ...

MCLA 281.956 Notification of pending applications; proceedings on applications. Requests for notification, form, fee; lists; hearings on applications. Review of applications; public hearings. Final inspection; certification of compliance with permit requirements. Notice of hearing. Grant or denial of permit; statement of reasons; modification of application; conditional permits. MSA 11.175(6)

MCLA 281.957 Issuance of permit, prerequisites; contents of permit. MSA 11.175(7)

MCLA 281.958 Term of permit; renewal; terms and conditions of work; revocation of permits, grounds, hearing. MSA 11.175(8)

MCLA 281.959 Bulk head lines, establishment, application, jurisdiction. MSA 11.475(9)

MCLA 281.960 Ordinary high water mark, agreements with riparian owners, prerequisites, effect. [MSA 11.475(10)]

MCLA 281.961 Rules; hearings; review; proceedings by riparian owners. [MSA 11.475(11)]

MCLA 281.962 Water frontage and exposed bottomland rights, riparian owners. [MSA 11.475(12)]

MCLA 281.963 Violations, injunctions, offenses. [MSA 11.475(13)]

MCLA 281.964 Repeals. [MSA 11.475(14)]

MCLA 281.965 Saving provision. [MSA 11.475(15)]

Sec. 15. All proceedings pending and all rights and liabilities existing, acquired or incurred at the time this act takes effect are saved and may be consummated according to the law in force when they were commenced. This act shall not be construed to affect any prosecution pending or begun before the effective date of this act. (January 9, 1973)

JOINT ACTION
Act No. 146, P.A. 1961 - Inland Lake Level Act of 1961

AN ACT to provide for the determination and maintenance of the normal height and level of the waters in inland lakes of this state, for the protection of the public health, safety and welfare and the conservation of the natural resources of this state; to authorize the building and maintenance of dams and embankments to accomplish such purposes; to authorize the acquisition of lands and other property by gift, grant, purchase or condemnation proceedings; to authorize the acceptance of gifts and grants of funds for the construction and maintenance of such dams and embankments; to authorize the raising of money by taxation and by special assessments for the purposes of this act; to prescribe the duties and powers of boards of supervisors, the conservation department of Michigan and county drain commissioners with reference hereto; and to repeal certain acts and parts of acts.

MCLA 281.61 Inland lake level; short title of act. [MSA 11.300(1)]

MCLA 281.62 Same; definitions. [MSA 11.300(2)]

MCLA 281.63 Same; petition; dams, wells, pumps. [MSA 11.300(3)]

MCLA 281.64 Same; deposit for preliminary costs. [MSA 11.300(4)]

MCLA 281.65 Same; financing initial costs and maintenance of project, expediency, method; special assessment districts. Lake in 2 or more counties. [MSA 11.300(5)]

MCLA 281.66 Same; special assessment bonds, lake level orders, procedure. [MSA 11.300(6)]

MCLA 281.67 Same; tax anticipation notes, issuance. [MSA 11.300(7)]

MCLA 281.68 Same; institution of proceedings by director of conservation. [MSA 11.300(8)]

MCLA 281.69 Same; establishment of special assessment districts, parcels includable. [MSA 11.300(9)]

Sec. 9. The department, ... shall establish a special assessment district including therein all parcels of land and political subdivisions ... which are benefited ...

MCLA 281.70 Same; hearing; notice, publication, service, mailing; lake level determination, departure; confirmation of special assessment district boundaries, time. [MSA 11.300(10)]

MCLA 281.71 Same; gifts, purchase, or condemnation by board of supervisors; dam in adjoining county. [MSA 11.300(11)]

MCLA 281.72 Same; gifts, purchase, or condemnation by department of conservation; construction of dam. [MSA 11.300(12)]

MCLA 281.73 Same; dams in navigable streams. [MSA 11.300(13)]

MCLA 281.74 Same; condemnation of private property. [MSA 11.300(14)]

MCLA 281.75 Same; condemnation procedure. [MSA 11.300(15)]

MCLA 281.76 Same; gifts, grants in aid to board of supervisors, apportionment. [MSA 11.300(16)]

Sec. 16. The board of supervisors ... may receive and accept ... gifts or grants in aid, for the purpose of carrying out the provisions of this act, from persons and from other governmental units....

MCLA 281.76a Same; federal participation contracts; private contracts; approval by conservation department. [MSA 11.300(16A)]

Sec. 16a. ... The board of supervisors of any county or counties may contract or make agreement with any private corporation or with any public corporation, or any agency thereof, ...

MCLA 281.77 Same; gifts, grants in aid to department of conservation. [MSA 11.300(17)]

Sec. 17. The conservation department ... may receive and accept, on behalf of the state, gifts and grants in aid from persons and other governmental units.

MCLA 281.78 Same; plans and specifications, bids, work relief project. [MSA 11.300(18)]

MCLA 281.79 Expenses, assessment, levying, collection. [MSA 11.300(19)]

Sec. 19. The expense ... may be assessed, levied and collected upon the taxable property within the special assessment district.

MCLA 281.80 Same; computation of entire cost, items included. [MSA 11.300(20)]

MCLA 281.81 Same; public lake; fish ladders. [MSA 11.300(21)]

Sec. 21. ... the department of natural resources may join with any board of supervisors in the proceedings ... and may intervene for the protection and conservation of the natural resources of the state. ...

740

MCLA 281.82 Same; unauthorized change of level, penalty. [MSA 11.300(22)]

MCLA 281.83 Same; artificial lakes. [MSA 11.300(23)]

Sec. 23. No normal water level shall be established under this act for an artificial lake created for the purpose of providing a reservoir for a municipal water supply system unless petitioned for by the governing body of the municipality.

MCLA 281.84 Same; inspection of control structures, time, inspectors, reports; dams, repair, removal; offense. [MSA 11.300(24)]

MCLA 281.86 Repeal. [MSA 11.300(26)]

Occasionally the trend toward diminishing water supplies is reversed by the God-given blessing of surplus water. Engineering technology has made it possible to conserve these surpluses for the protection of the public health, safety and welfare. However, experience has proven that too often local governing bodies practice the dangerous art of being "penny wise and pound foolish." Because there is an abundance, or even surplus of water in a number of areas of the state, little or no thought is being given there to the establishment of plans for preservation of water for the future.

The world's most abundant supply of water is found in the Great Lakes region. The governments of the bordering states have taken steps to establish and control adequate water levels in the Great Lakes. In order for this action to ultimately be effective, however, similar controls must be established for the inland lakes as well. Every township in Michigan should start the process at once. There are adequate statutory provisions to do so.

JOINT ACTION
Act No. 20, P.A. 1964 - Surplus Waters Act of 1964

AN ACT to regulate the impoundment and utilization of surplus water; to prescribe the powers and duties of the water resources commission and the several boards of supervisors; and to provide penalties for the violation of this act.

MCLA 281.301 Surplus waters act of 1964; short title.
[MSA 3.533(21)]

MCLA 281.302 Same; definitions. [MSA 3.533(22)]

MCLA 281.303 Request for surveys; reports. [MSA 3.533(23)]

Sec. 3. Any board or group of boards or local unit or units acting singly or in concert may request the commission to undertake a survey of the water in a river basin or watershed located or partially located in such county or counties or in local unit or units of government to determine whether there is surplus water which may be available and if so, how it may be best impounded, utilized and conserved. All studies, surveys and reports made by public and other competent authorities may be utilized by the commission in making such determinations.

MCLA 281.304 Same; involvement of other boards. [MSA 3.533(24)]

MCLA 281.305 Same; determination of optimum flow; plan for improvement, utilization, and conservation of surplus water; factors; limitations. [MSA 3.533(25)]

MCLA 281.306 Public hearing, determination of optimum flow; notices. Hearing. Order making determination of optimum flow; finality, review, parties. Public hearing, proposed plan, notices, review, order of approval. [MSA 3.533(26)]

MCLA 281.307 Transmission of plan to boards, adoption, dams, supervision. Transmission of plan. Contracts; responsibility for construction. [MSA 3.533(27)]

Sec. 7. ... the boards, either singly or jointly, may establish such governmental agency or commission as may be necessary. ...

MCLA 281.308 Gifts, exchange, condemnation by boards; restrictions on financing. [MSA 3.533(28)]

MCLA 281.309 Commission, gifts, grants in aid. [MSA 3.533(29)]

MCLA 281.310 Use of increased flowage; waste assimilation; rates for usage. [MSA 3.533(30)]

MCLA 281.311 Commission, authority; permits for iron ore benefication. [MSA 3.533(31)]

MCLA 281.312 Rules and regulations. [MSA 3.533(32)]

MCLA 281.313 Redetermination of optimum flow; modification of plan. [MSA 3.533(33)]

MCLA 281.314 Penalty. [MSA 3.533(34)]

MCLA 281.315 Nonapplication of act to river management districts. [MSA 3.533(35)]

Sec. 15. This act shall not apply within the boundaries of any river management district created under the local river management act.

Act No. 184, P.A. 1963 - Erection of Dams

AN ACT to require approval of the department of natural resources before erection of dams; to provide fees for granting approval; and to provide a penalty for failure to comply with the provisions of this act and the rules adopted thereunder.

MCLA 281.131 Construction plans, approval permit, necessity. [MSA 11.421]

Sec. 1. No person shall construct or permit construction of any dam on land owned by him impounding more than 5 acres or with a head of 5 or more feet without first obtaining a permit ..., except that ponds impounding less than 5 surface acres of water with a contributing drainage area of less than 1 square mile, designed and constructed under the provisions of federal or state soil conservation programs shall not require a permit ...

MCLA 281.132 Issuance of permit, pre-requisites; inspection; fees; underspill devices; repair or reconstruction permits; permit extensions. [MSA 11.422]

MCLA 281.132a Lake level, petition for establishment, special assessment district for maintenance, record. [MSA 11.422(1)]

MCLA 281.132b Fish, wildlife, or recreational values; effect of impoundment. [MSA 11.422(2)]

MCLA 281.132c Hazardous conditions; report, necessity, contents; inspection, repairs, removal. [MSA 11.422(3)]

MCLA 281.133 Rules as to construction; cancellation of permits. [MSA 11.423]

MCLA 281.134 Board of supervisors; rights as to construction of dams. [MSA 11.424]

MCLA 281.135 Violations, penalty. [MSA 11.425]

Michigan has more shoreline than any other state in the nation, or for that matter, the United States. It becomes incumbent upon Michigan, therefore, to provide adequate control of its waterways. It is important for township officials to maintain close liaison with the Michigan State Waterways Commission so that local governments may participate both in the benefits and the responsibilities inherent in maintaining an excellent waterways system.

JOINT ACTION
Act No. 320, P.A. 1947 - Michigan State Waterways Commission

AN ACT to create the Michigan state waterways commission, and to prescribe its powers and duties; to provide for the acquisition, construction and maintenance of harbors and channels, and to provide for the granting of concessions; to prescribe the powers and duties of the state and the several political subdivisions thereof; to impose a specific tax on fuel sold or used in producing or generating power for propelling vessels on the navigable waters lying within the boundaries of this state, and to provide for the disposition thereof; to provide for the regulation and control of boating within the boundaries of this state; to provide for state participation in certain federal programs; and to make an appropriation to carry out the provisions of this act.

MCLA 281.501 Definitions. [MSA 3.534(1)]

744

MCLA 281.502 Waterways commission; members, appointment, oath, expenses, removal; rules; chairman, term; quorum; reports; offices. [MSA 3.534(2)]

MCLA 281.503 Same; director, appointment, qualifications, term, compensation, duties, assistants, salaries, expenses. [MSA 3.534(3)]

MCLA 281.504 Same; powers and duties. [MSA 3.534(4)]

MCLA 281.505 Same; authority of local agencies to enter contracts with commission, inland waterways or channels. [MSA 3.534(5)]

Sec. 5. The several ... townships ... (may) enter into contracts and agreements with the commission in the accomplishment of the purposes herein set forth.

MCLA 281.506 Facilities in harbors and connecting waterways; use. [MSA 3.534(6)]

MCLA 281.507 Waterways commission; financing of local agencies to obtain United States participation; contracts with war department. [MSA 3.534(7)]

MCLA 281.508 Appropriation; state waterways fund, disbursement. [MSA 3.534(8)]

MCLA 281.509 Tax on marine gasoline, payment. Amount and payment. Gasoline, marine use; amount credited to waterways fund. Revenue division -- department of treasury, duties. Refunds, method of claiming. False statements, penalty. [MSA 3.534(9)]

MCLA 281.510 State appropriation deemed advancement, repayment from revenues; use of tax revenues to pay expenses. [MSA 3.534(10)]

MCLA 281.511 State acceptance of federal program for construction of harbors of refuge. [MSA 3.534(11)]

JOINT ACTION
Act No. 245, P.A. 1970 - Shorelands Protection and
Management Act of 1970

AN ACT to provide for the protection and management of shorelands; to provide for zoning and zoning ordinances; to provide certain powers and duties; to authorize certain studies; to provide for development of certain plans; to promulgate rules; and to provide for certain remedies for violations of rules.

MCLA 281.631 Short title. [MSA 13.1831]

MCLA 281.632 Definitions. [MSA 13.1832]

MCLA 281.633 Engineering study of shoreland, high risk areas, erosion, protection. [MSA 13.1833]

MCLA 281.634 Environmental study of shoreland; environmental areas; marshes; fish and wildlife habitat areas, protection. [MSA 13.1834]

MCLA 281.635 Regulation of use of high risk area. [MSA 13.1835]

Sec. 5. The commission ... shall determine if the use ... shall be regulated to prevent property loss or if suitable methods of protection shall be installed to prevent property loss. ...(and)... shall notify a local agency of its determinations and recommendations ...

MCLA 281.636 Notice and protection of environmental areas. [MSA 13.1836]

Sec. 6. The department ... shall notify a local agency of the existence of any environmental area which is in a local agency and shall recommend to the commission appropriate use regulations necessary to protect an environmental area.

MCLA 281.637 County zoning. [MSA 13.1837]

Sec. 7. Within 3 years ... a county ... may zone any shoreland and land to be zoned which is in the county.

MCLA 281.638 City or village zoning. [MSA 13.1838]

MCLA 281.639 Township zoning. [MSA 13.1839]

Sec. 9. Within 3 years after the effective date of this act a township, pursuant to rules ... may zone any shoreland and land to be zoned which is in the township.

MCLA 281.640 Approval or disapproval of zoning ordinance.
[MSA 13.1840]

Sec. 10. An existing zoning ordinance or a zoning ordinance or a modification or amendment thereto which regulates a high risk area or an environmental area shall be submitted to the commission for approval or disapproval. ...

MCLA 281.641 Rules, promulgation, enforcement. [MSA 13.1841]

MCLA 281.642 Shoreland use and management plan, preparation, contents, hearings. [MSA 13.1842]

Sec. 12. (1) Within 18 months after the effective date of this act (April 1, 1971) the commission shall in compliance with the purposes of this act, prepare a plan for the use and management of shoreland. The plan shall include but not be limited to: ...

MCLA 281.643 Agreements with federal government and state, local, and private agencies; use of studies, plans, and recommendations. [MSA 13.1843]

Sec. 13. The department and commission may enter into an agreement jointly or separately or to make contracts with the federal government, other state agencies, local agencies or private agencies for the purposes of making studies and plans for the efficient use, development, preservation or management of the state's shoreland resources. ...

MCLA 281.644 Moneys, grants, or grants-in-aid, acceptance.
[MSA 13.1844]

MCLA 281.645 Legislative intent. [MSA 13.1845]

Sec. 15. It is the intent of the legislature that any additional cost of the implementation of section 3 of this act shall only be financed from federal funds.

Municipalities, including townships, must determine the extent of need for public navigational facilities, boat liveries, etc., based on public demand. In addition to the following citations, the reader is referred to the section on Wharves, Piers, Docks and Port Facilities in the chapter on Services, Utilities, Contracts and Ordinances.

JOINT ACTION
Act No. 66, P.A. 1952 - Municipal Navigational Facilities

AN ACT to authorize political subdivisions of the state to acquire, establish, construct, maintain, improve and operate harbors, channels and other navigational facilities; and to authorize ordinances and resolutions.

MCLA 281.541 Definition. [MSA 5.2768(11)]

Sec. 1. The term "political subdivision" used herein is defined to mean any county, city, village, township or port district ...

MCLA 281.542 Waterways; harbor guards, ordinances, harbor masters. [MSA 5.2768(12)]

Sec. 2. A political subdivision is hereby authorized (a) to adopt and amend all needful rules, regulations and ordinances for the management, government and use of any waterways, harbors, channels or other navigational facilities under its control, either within or without its territorial limits; ...

MCLA 281.543 Same; jurisdiction, contents. [MSA 5.2768(13)]

Sec. 3. All powers, right and authority granted to any political subdivision in this act may be exercised and enjoyed by 2 or more of them, ...

Act No. 257, P.A. 1952 - Boat Liveries

AN ACT to provide for the registration of certain boat liveries; to provide for the adoption of certain minimum safety standards; to provide for the inspection of such boat liveries and their equipment and watercraft, and for

*the issuance of certificates and passenger capacity tags
by the sheriffs of the various counties; to provide for review of a denial of such certificate or finding of passenger
capacity; to establish fees to finance such inspection; to
define the duties of the Michigan state waterways commission concerning such boat liveries; and to prescribe penalties for violations of the provisions of this act.*

MCLA 281.561 Boat liveries; definitions. [MSA 18.1251]

MCLA 281.562 Same; registration (with sheriff), **forms.**
[MSA 18.1252]

MCLA 281.563 Same; safety standards. [MSA 18.1253]

**MCLA 281.564 Same; inspection, certificate, passenger capacity
tags.** [MSA 18.1254]

MCLA 281.565 Same; violations. [MSA 18.1255]

MCLA 281.566 Review of sheriff's and commission's orders.
[MSA 18.1256]

MCLA 281.567 Passenger capacity tags, fees. [MSA 18.1257]

MCLA 281.568 Penalty. [MSA 18.1258]

As with every other aspect of our way of life, a very complex
and on-the-go society has brought about the necessity for regulations to provide for marine safety. Because of the irresponsible
actions of a few, many must learn to live under sometimes highly
restrictive regulations such as those imposed by the following
statute.

JOINT ACTION
Act No. 303, P.A. 1967 - Marine Safety Act

*AN ACT to promote the safe use of the waters of this
state; to provide for the numbering of motorboats; to provide for regulations relative to the operation of vessels
and motorboats on such waters and to the use of waters of
this state for boating; to prescribe the duties and respon-*

sibilities of owners and operators of vessels and motorboats; to prescribe the powers and duties of certain state departments; to provide for the disposition of revenue; to provide for penalties; and to repeal certain acts and parts of acts.

MCLA 281.1001 **Short title.** [MSA 18.1287(1)]

MCLA 281.1002 **Waters of this state; commission; department; director; political subdivision.** [MSA 18.1287(2)]

MCLA 281.1004 **Marine safety program; state aid; authorized expenditures.** [MSA 18.1287(4)]

MCLA 281.1006 **Boating safety certificate; vessel; motorboat; lifeboat; person; owner.** [MSA 18.1287(6)]

MCLA 281.1008 **Operate; slow -- no wake speed; high speed boating; regatta; boat race; marine parade; tournament; exhibition; anchored rafts; starboard; port.** [MSA 18.1287(8)]

Note: Defines a number of craft operational controls.

MCLA 281.1011 **Administration of act by department of conservation; advisory representative to department; advisory council.** [MSA 18.1287(11)]

MCLA 281.1012 **Regulation of operation of contrivances on state waters; speed limits; use, prohibitions, restrictions; exclusive diving, fishing, swimming, or water skiing areas; special local regulations.** [MSA 18.1287(12)]

MCLA 281.1013 **Procedure for establishing rules.** [MSA 18.1287(13)]

MCLA 281.1014 **Special rules and regulations for use of contrivances on waters, preparation, presentation, notice of hearing, hearing.** [MSA 18.1287(14)]

MCLA 281.1015 **Submission of rules and regulations to governing body of political subdivision, approval, disapproval, adoption.** [MSA 18.1287(15)]

750

Sec. 15. The proposed rule shall then be submitted to the governing body of the political subdivision in which the controlled waters lie. Within 30 calendar days the governing body shall inform the department that it approves or disapproves ...

MCLA 281.1016 Request by political subdivisions for special rules, form, procedure by department. [MSA 18.1287(16)]

Sec. 16. Local political subdivisions which believe that special local rules of the type authorized by this act are needed on waters subject to their jurisdiction shall inform the department and request assistance. ...

MCLA 281.1017 Local ordinances; identity with state rule; changes, amendments, repeals; enforcement. [MSA 18.1287(17)]

Sec. 17. (1) Local political subdivisions within whose jurisdiction specially controlled waters lie shall enact a local ordinance identical in all respects to the established state rule. Whenever the department changes, amends or repeals an existing rule, the concerned local political subdivision shall change, amend or repeal the previously enacted ordinance to assure uniformity with state regulations.

(2) The sheriff or his authorized deputies shall enforce local ordinances enacted in accordance with the provisions of this act.

(3) Local political subdivisions may enact as an ordinance any or all of sections 2 to 8, 31 to 34, 36, 61, 62, 71 to 79, 91 to 98, 101, 111 to 113, 151, 152 and 161 to 168.

MCLA 281.1021 Disposition of revenue received; marine safety fund, source of funds, appropriations from funds. [MSA 18.1287(21)]

MCLA 281.1023 State aid to counties; county marine safety programs, estimates and statements of expenditures. [MSA 18.1287(23)]

MCLA 281.1024 Allocation of state aid to counties.
[MSA 18.1287(24)]

MCLA 281.1025 Audits of county marine safety programs; refunds to state. [MSA 18.1287(25)]

MCLA 281.1026 Cooperation between department and sheriffs; sheriffs' records and reports. [MSA 18.1287(26)]

MCLA 281.1027 Rules. [MSA 18.1287(27)]

MCLA 281.1031 Numbering of motorboats; requirement, numbering systems, exemptions; certificate of number. [MSA 18.1287(31)]

MCLA 281.1032 Certificate of number; application, necessity as to motorboat having certificate. [MSA 18.1287(32)]

MCLA 281.1033 Motorboats requiring Michigan numbering; application for numbering, filing, form, fee, exemptions as to fee; certificate of number, issuance, form, inspection by peace officer; numbering of motorboats; numbering system. [MSA 18.1287(33)]

MCLA 281.1034 Certificates of number; expiration of initial and renewal certificates. [MSA 18.1287(34)]

MCLA 281.1035 Notice of destruction, abandonment, or transfer of motorboat or change of address; form, fee; cancellations, and transfers of certificates of number; duplicate certificates. [MSA 18.1287(35)]

MCLA 281.1036 Testing and demonstrating motorboats, certificates of number for manufacturers and sellers, fees, temporary placement of numbers. [MSA 18.1287(36)]

MCLA 281.1037 Award of certificate of number by secretary of state or his agent. [MSA 18.1287(37)]

MCLA 281.1038 Records of secretary of state; public; annual compilation of numbers and owners, copies. [MSA 18.1287(38)]

MCLA 281.1051 Assistance required of vessel operator as to persons affected by casualty involving vessel. [MSA 18.1287(51)]

MCLA 281.1052 Stopping vessel and giving information as operator and owner in case of casualty involving vessel. [MSA 18.1287(52)]

MCLA 281.1053 Report of casualty resulting in death.
[MSA 18.1287(53)]

Sec. 53. ... report ... to the nearest peace officer, ... without delay and in any event, not later than 48 hours following ...

Any report ... made to any peace officer other than the sheriff of the county in which the ... casualty occurred shall be reported without delay by the peace officer to the sheriff ...

MCLA 281.1054 Report of property damage. [MSA 18.1287(54)]

MCLA 281.1055 Report of peace officer. [MSA 18.1287(55)]

Sec. 55. A peace officer receiving a report or investigating the collision, accident or other casualty involving a vessel shall prepare and submit within 15 days a complete report thereof to ...

MCLA 281.1056 Reports, purposes, copies, admissibility in evidence. [MSA 18.1287(56)]

MCLA 281.1057 Transmission of information to federal officers or agencies. [MSA 18.1287(57)]

MCLA 281.1061 Comprehensive educational programs; youthful boat operators training programs, boating safety certificates.
[MSA 18.1287(61)]

MCLA 281.1062 Motorboat operators; age restrictions, exemptions.
[MSA 18.1287(62)]

MCLA 281.1071 Passing and right of way rules; duty of due regard for others. [MSA 18.1287(71)]

MCLA 281.1072 Care in operating vessel; speed. [MSA 18.1287(72)]

MCLA 281.1073 Operating vessel while under influence of intoxicants or narcotics or while a habitual user of narcotics; owners' obligations. [MSA 18.1287(73)]

MCLA 281.1074 Reckless operation of vessels or other contrivances, definition, punishment. [MSA 18.1287(74)]

MCLA 281.1075 Operation, counter-clockwise, distance from other objects. [MSA 18.1287(75)]

MCLA 281.1076 Operating vessel within area prohibited to vessels, prohibition. [MSA 18.1287(76)]

MCLA 281.1077 Hours for water skiing or sledding, surfboarding, or similar operations, penalty. [MSA 18.1287(77)]

MCLA 281.1078 Observer in addition to operator and rear view mirror, vessels used in water skiing or sledding, aquaplaning, surfboarding, or similar operations; exceptions. [MSA 18.1287(78)]

MCLA 281.1079 Positions of occupants of vessels, restrictions, exceptions. [MSA 18.1287(79)]

MCLA 281.1080 Interference with operation of vessel, prohibition. [MSA 18.1287(80)]

MCLA 281.1091 Capacity plates, vessels; manufacture, definition. [MSA 18.1287(91)]

MCLA 281.1092 Form, content, and position of capacity plate. [MSA 18.1287(92)]

MCLA 281.1093 Information to be contained in capacity plates; procedure for determining, uniformity. [MSA 18.1287(93)]

MCLA 281.1094 Person other than manufacturer affixing capacity plate. [MSA 18.1287(94)]

MCLA 281.1095 Warranty as to information on capacity plate; horsepower limitations. [MSA 18.1287(95)]

MCLA 281.1096 Substitute for capacity plate, authorization. [MSA 18.1287(96)]

MCLA 281.1097 Vessels of unconventional design or construction, exemptions; effective date. [MSA 18.1287(97)]

MCLA 281.1098 Exceeding loading or horsepower limits as careless operation. [MSA 18.1287(98)]

MCLA 281.1101 Diving buoys or boats at point of submergence, requirement; flag size, design, time, operations within 100 feet. [MSA 18.1287(101)]

MCLA 281.1111 Life saving devices; requirement, description. [MSA 18.1287(111)]

MCLA 281.1112 Lights; time for use, types required. [MSA 18.1287(112)]

MCLA 281.1113 Mufflers; necessity, types. [MSA 18.1287(113)]

MCLA 281.1131 Liability for negligent operation, vessel owner; consent, presumption. [MSA 18.1287(131)]

MCLA 281.1132 Damage to life or property from wake, liability of vessel owner; consent. [MSA 18.1287(132)]

MCLA 281.1141 Buoys or beacons; issuance of revocable permits, navigation obstructions, bathing areas, anchorages; applications; removal and revocation procedure. [MSA 18.1287(141)]

MCLA 281.1142 Uniform waterway marking system; buoys, beacons. [MSA 18.1287(142)]

MCLA 281.1143 Federal laws or regulations; compliance, federal permits. [MSA 18.1287(143)]

MCLA 281.1144 Mooring vessel to buoy or beacon; moving, removal, or damaging buoy or beacon. [MSA 18.1287(144)]

MCLA 281.1145 Anchored rafts, relocation or removal as navigation hazard. [MSA 18.1287(145)]

MCLA 281.1151 Regattas, races, parades, tournaments, exhibitions, trials; authorization, rules, application for permission. [MSA 18.1287(151)]

Sec. 151. ... Whenever ...(the above)... is proposed to be held, the person in charge thereof, at least 30 days prior thereto, shall file an application with the department for permission to hold ... (it)... The application shall set forth ... and it shall not be conducted without authorization of the department in writing.

MCLA 281.1152 Federal laws or regulations, compliance; waiver of provisions of act by department. [MSA 18.1287(152)]

MCLA 281.1161 Peace officers; stopping vessel or permitting officer to come along side; information to be given; inspection; testing of equipment; arrests without warrant. [MSA 18.1287(161)]

MCLA 281.1162 Person arrested without warrant, taking before magistrate, applicable offenses. [MSA 18.1287(162)]

MCLA 281.1163 Notice to appear in court, contents; taking before magistrate in lieu of notice; appearance, plea, notice of day of appearance. [MSA 18.1287(163)]

MCLA 281.1164 Nonresidents arrested without warrant, taking before magistrate; recognizance, receipt, forfeiture, deposit with magistrate, embezzlement. [MSA 18.1287(164)]

MCLA 281.1165 Officers or magistrates; misconduct in office, removal; arrests, with and without warrants. [MSA 18.1287(165)]

MCLA 281.1166 Act, rules, or ordinances; violations, penalties; refusal of right to operate vessel, additional penalty. [MSA 18.1287(166)]

MCLA 281.1167 Negligent crippling or homicide, penalty. [MSA 18.1287(167)]

MCLA 281.1168 Crippling caused by careless operation of vessel in wanton disregard of others' rights and at speed or in manner likely to endanger another, penalty. [MSA 18.1287(168)]

MCLA 281.1169 Negligent homicide, inclusion in charge of manslaughter. [MSA 18.1287(169)]

MCLA 281.1170 Nonresidents; secretary of state as attorney for service of summons; service, procedure, sufficiency; death, appointment of secretary as attorney, abatement of actions; costs; application to all courts. [MSA 18.1287(170)]

MCLA 281.1191 Public dock, pier, wharf, or retaining wall, unsafe wind conditions. [MSA 18.1287(191)]

Sec. 191. (1) When wind conditions on the Great Lakes attain a magnitude whereby ...

(2) When such conditions exist any harbormaster, peace or police officer or other authorized official may rope off or barricade entry to these structures or post in a conspicuous manner ...

MCLA 281.1192 Public bathing beaches, buoys, swimming beyond buoys. [MSA 18.1287(192)]

Sec. 192. (1) The owner or person in charge of a bathing beach maintained primarily for public usage shall not knowingly permit a person to bathe or swim from the bathing beach unless buoys are established in accordance with section 141, outlining a safe bathing or swimming area. ...

MCLA 281.1197 Rights under federal laws. [MSA 18.1287(197)]

MCLA 281.1198 Repeal. [MSA 18.1287(198)]

MCLA 281.1199 Effective date, exceptions. [MSA 18.1287(199)]

JOINT ACTION
Act No. 245, P.A. 1929 - Water Resources Commission

AN ACT to create a water resources commission to protect and conserve the water resources of the state, to have control over the pollution of any waters of the state and the Great Lakes, to have control over the alteration of the watercourses and the flood plains of all rivers and streams, with powers to make rules governing the same, and to prescribe the powers and duties of such commission; to require the registration of manufacturing products, production materials and waste products where certain wastes are discharged; to provide for surveillance fees upon discharges to the waters of the state in order to provide for investigation, monitoring and surveillance necessary to prevent and abate water pollution; to require permits to regulate the discharge or storage of any substance which may affect the quality of the waters of the state and to establish restrictions to assure compliance with applicable state standards and to authorize the establish-

ment of permit restrictions and programs to assure compliance with applicable federal law and regulations; to prohibit the pollution of any waters of the state and the Great Lakes; to prohibit the obstruction of the floodways of the rivers and streams of the state; to designate the commission as the state agency to cooperate and negotiate with other governments and agencies in matters concerning the water resources of the state; and to provide penalties for the violation of this act.

MCLA 323.1 Water resources commission; members, terms, vacancies, expenses, representatives of state officers. [MSA 3.521]

Sec. 1. ... commission ...(shall include)... 1 (member) from groups representative of municipalities ...

MCLA 323.2 Organization, powers, and duties of commission. [MSA 3.522]

Sec. 2. The commission shall ... protect and conserve the water resources of the state and shall have control of the pollution of surface or underground waters of the state and the Great Lakes, which are or may be affected by waste disposal of municipalities, industries, public or private corporations, individuals, partnership associations, or any other entity. ...

MCLA 323.2a Cooperation and negotiation with other governmental units and agencies, scope; alteration of water courses and flood plains; water resources planning and pollution control; reports; recommendations. [MSA 3.522(1)]

MCLA 323.3 Same; suits, enforcement of laws. [MSA 3.523]

MCLA 323.4 Same; investigation powers. [MSA 3.524]

MCLA 323.5 Pollution standards, establishment, compliance through issuance of permits; water volume, ascertainment, recording; pollution restrictions and prevention. [MSA 3.525]

Sec. 5. ... It shall issue permits which will assure compliance with state standards to regulate municipal, industrial and commercial discharges or storage of any substance which may affect the quality of the waters of the state. ...

758

MCLA 323.5a **Same; interference with streams, regulations and orders.** [MSA 3.525(1)]

MCLA 323.5b **Unlawful occupation and use of flood plains, stream bed or channel of stream; permit.** [MSA 3.525(2)]

MCLA 323.6 **Unlawful discharge into waters.** [MSA 3.526]

Sec. 6. (a) It shall be unlawful for any persons directly or indirectly to discharge into the waters of the state any substance which is or may become injurious to the public health, safety or welfare; ...

(b) The discharge of any raw sewage of human origin, directly or indirectly into any of the waters of the state shall be considered prima facie evidence of the violation of this section ...

(c) Any violation of any provision of section 6 shall be prima facie evidence of the existence of a public nuisance and in addition to the remedies provided for in this act may be abated according to law in an action brought by the attorney general in a court of competent jurisdiction.

MCLA 323.6a **Waste treatment facilities of industrial or commercial entity; personnel having supervision and control of facilities, examination, certification; reports.** [MSA 3.526(1)]

MCLA 323.6b **Reports of discharges of waste other than sanitary sewage, necessity, annual, contents, use confidentiality, injunctions, rules.** [MSA 3.526(2)]

MCLA 323.7 **Permit for discharge of waste into state waters, necessity, conditions, revocation, time for compliance, reissuance; unlawful pollution, notice of determination, hearing, pleadings, disposition of case.** [MSA 3.527]

Sec. 7. (1) After the effective date of this ... amendatory act (April 15, 1973), a person shall not discharge any waste or waste effluent into the waters of this state unless he is in possession of a valid permit therefor from the commission. ...

(2) Whenever in the opinion of the commission any person is causing or is about to cause unlawful pollution of the waters of this state, the commission may notify the alleged offender of its determination. ...

MCLA 323.8 Petition for hearing; hearing, time, place, notice, procedure, determination; statements as to water use; permits, issuance; denial of proposed new use; hearing; review. [MSA 3.528]

MCLA 323.9 Criminal complaint; penalty. [MSA 3.529]

MCLA 323.10 Violations, penalties; injuries to natural resources and costs of surveillance and enforcement action, recovery; probation. [MSA 3.530]

MCLA 323.11 Definitions. [MSA 3.531]

MCLA 323.12 Act construed. [MSA 3.532]

Sec. 12. This act shall not be construed as repealing any of the provisions of the law governing the pollution of lakes and streams, but shall be held and construed as ancillary to and supplementing the same and in addition to the laws now in force, except as the same may be in direct conflict herewith. ...

MCLA 323.12a Provisions of act construed. [MSA 3.532(1)]

Sec. 12a. The provisions of this act shall be construed as supplemental to and in addition to the provisions of Act No. 316 of the Public Acts of 1923, as amended, being sections 261.1 to 277.10 [MSA 11.1 TO 11.142(1)], inclusive, of the Compiled Laws of 1948; and nothing in this act shall be construed to amend or repeal any law of the state of Michigan relating to the public service commission, the department of conservation and the department of health relating to waters and water structures, or any act or parts of acts not inconsistent with the provisions of this act.

MCLA 323.13 Surveillance fees, persons liable, use, notice, payment, disposition of proceeds, reports, basis, computation, rules. [MSA 3.533]

Sec. 13. (a) ... an annual surveillance fee is payable by a person, company, corporation, but not a municipality, ... The cost of necessary surveillance of municipal discharges shall not be financed from revenues so derived but may be provided otherwise by law. ... Discharges into a municipal sewerage system shall be assessed only the $50.00 administrative fee unless such discharge *after municipal treatment is or may become injurious to the waters of the state ... in which event the assessment will be based upon the same considerations as if the discharge after treatment were being discharged by the manufacturing facility or commercial establishment directly into the waters of the state. ...*

JOINT ACTION
Act No. 222, P.A. 1949 - Water Pollution

AN ACT to authorize public corporations to accept grants and other aid from the United States government or any agency thereof and from industries for the construction of public improvements the purpose of which is to aid in the prevention and abatement of water pollution and in furtherance of such purpose to authorize public corporations to enter into contracts with industries covering the use, operation and coordination of sewage collection, treatment and/or disposal facilities.

MCLA 323.101 Definitions. [MSA 5.2770(21)]

MCLA 323.102 Aid in prevention or abatement of water pollution; public corporation may accept, from federal government, etc. [MSA 5.2770(22)]

MCLA 323.103 Same; contracts and agreements. [MSA 5.2770(23)]

Sec. 3. Any public corporation is further authorized to accept contributions and other aid from industries ... and in furtherance of such purpose to enter into contracts and agreements with industries covering the following ...

Act No. 167, P.A. 1970 - Water Pollution Control Act of 1970

AN ACT to regulate the disposal of oil and sewage from watercraft; and to prohibit littering of waterways.

MCLA 323.331 Short title. [MSA 3.533(201)]

MCLA 323.332 Definitions. [MSA 3.533(202)]

MCLA 323.333 Litter, sewage, oil, garbage, or other materials rendering water unsightly, noxious, or unwholesome; prohibition. [MSA 3.533(203)]

MCLA 323.334 Watercraft, moored or registered in another jurisdiction, pollution control device approved by other jurisdiction; marine toilets, requirements. [MSA 3.533(204)]

MCLA 323.335 Marinas, operating on bottom lands under state lease or permit, pump-out facilities for marine toilets, necessity; noncompliance, effect, notice, hearing. [MSA 3.533(205)]

MCLA 323.335a Marinas of Michigan waterways commission, pump-out facilities. [MSA 3.533(205A)]

MCLA 323.335b Marinas or docks of state or local government, pumping station. [MSA 3.533(205B)]

MCLA 323.335c Exempt marinas and docks, pump-out facilities. [MSA 3.533(205C)]

MCLA 323.336 Marine toilets and pollution control devices, boat plate registration application, disclosure of existence; reports as to nonexistence. [MSA 3.533(206)]

MCLA 323.337 Oil or oily wastes, discharge, prohibition; removal; duty; cost of removal by state, persons liable, actions. [MSA 3.533(207)]

MCLA 323.338 Inspection of watercraft and waterside facilities; commercial docks and wharfs, facilities required to prevent pollution. [MSA 3.533(208)]

Sec. 8. All watercraft moored, operated or located upon the waters of this state are subject to inspection by the commission, any lawfully designated agent or inspector thereof or any peace, conservation or police officer ...

MCLA 323.339 Exclusive state regulation of disposal or discharge of watercraft sewage, litter, and oil. [MSA 3.533(209)]

Sec. 9. ... In order to assure statewide uniformity, the regulation by any political subdivision of the state of waste disposal from watercraft is prohibited.

MCLA 323.340 Rules. [MSA 3.533(210)]

MCLA 323.341 Violations, penalties; permitting compliance with other maritime, marine, and navigation requirements. [MSA 3.533(211)]

MCLA 323.342 Effective date. [MSA 3.533(212)]

Act No. 222, P.A. 1966 - Water Pollution Control Facilities, Tax Exemption

AN ACT to provide for the exemption of water pollution control facilities from certain taxes.

MCLA 323.351 Definitions. [MSA 7.793(51)]

MCLA 323.352 Application for tax exemption certificate; filing; manner and form; approval of water resources commission; hearing. [MSA 7.793(52)]

Sec. 2. (1) ... (2) ... the water resources commission and (shall) give notice in writing by certified mail to the ... assessor of the taxing unit in which the facility is located or to be located, and shall afford to the applicant and the assessor an opportunity for a hearing. Tax exemption granted under this act shall be reduced to the extent of any commercial or productive value derived from any materials captured or recovered by any facility.

MCLA 323.353 Grounds for issuance of certificate; effective date. [MSA 7.793(53)]

MCLA 323.354 Exemption from certain taxes. [MSA 7.793(54)]

MCLA 323.355 Transmission of certificate and copies to applicant and assessor of taxing unit. [MSA 7.793(55)]

MCLA 323.356 Grounds for modification or revocation of certificate. [MSA 7.793(56)]

MCLA 323.357 Appeal. [MSA 7.793(57)]

MCLA 323.358 Rules and regulations. [MSA 7.793(58)]

JOINT ACTION
Act No. 76, P.A. 1968 - Water Pollution Control Facilities, Issuance of Bonds

AN ACT to authorize the issuance of general obligation bonds of the state of Michigan and to pledge the full faith and credit of the state of Michigan for the payment of principal and interest thereon for the planning, acquisition and the construction of facilities for the prevention and abatement of water pollution and for the making of grants, loans and advances to municipalities of the state for such purposes; to provide for other matters relating to said bonds and the use of the proceeds of sale of said bonds; and to provide for the submission of the question of the issuance of said bonds to the electors of the state of Michigan.

MCLA 323.371 Municipality, defined. [MSA 5.2769(201)]

Sec. 1. The terms "municipality" or "municipalities" as herein used shall be construed to mean and include any county, city, village, township, school district, metropolitan district, port district, drainage district, authority or other governmental authority, agency or department within or of the state with power to acquire, construct, improve or operate facilities for the prevention or abatement of water pollution or any combination thereof.

MCLA 323.372 Legislative determination. [MSA 5.2769(202)]

MCLA 323.373 Bonds; authorization. [MSA 5.2769(203)]

MCLA 323.374 - 323.382 [MSA 5.2769(204) - 5.2769(212)]

AFFECTS JOINT ACTION
Act No. 98, P.A. 1913 - Waterworks and Sewage Disposal

AN ACT providing for the supervision and control by the state health commissioner over waterworks systems and sewerage systems, for the submission of plans and specifications for waterworks and/or sewerage systems and the issuance of construction permits therefor, for the supervision and control of such systems, for the classifying of water treatment plants, and sewage treatment works, for the examination, certification, and regulation of persons in charge of such water treatment plants and sewage treatment works, and providing penalties and defining liabilities for violations of this act.

MCLA 325.201 Control over waterworks and sewerage systems by state health commissioner; governmental agencies defined. MSA 14.411

Sec. 1. The state health commissioner is hereby given supervisory and visitorial power and control as limited in this act over all cities, villages, townships, counties and other governmental agencies, ...

MCLA 325.202 State health commissioner; inspection powers; waterworks, sewerage systems defined. MSA 14.412

MCLA 325.203 Waterworks, sewerage, and filtration plants; rules and regulations; examination, etc., of operators; orders to cleanse; classification of sewage treatment works; operators, examination. MSA 14.413

MCLA 325.204 Contaminated water; investigation, examination, evidence. MSA 14.414

Sec. 4. Whenever the ... supervisor of a township, health officer or representative of the state health commissioner has reason to believe that the water furnished by any governmental agency, corporation, ... is contaminated, then ...

MCLA 325.205 Same; expenses of investigation. MSA 14.415

Sec. 5. The expenses of the investigation and analysis ... shall be borne by the locality, and shall be paid for at the rate of ...

MCLA 325.206 Waterworks or sewerage systems; plans and specifications, contents, certification and filing; permit for construction; rules and regulations; misdemeanor. [MSA 14.416]

MCLA 325.207 Plans and specifications, definition. [MSA 14.417]

MCLA 325.208 Water or sewage treatment works, reports; perjury. [MSA 14.418]

MCLA 325.210 Inspection by state health commissioner; recommendations and orders. [MSA 14.420]

MCLA 325.211 Sewerage systems; planning, construction and operation; counsel with governmental agencies; agent for stream control commission; cooperation. [MSA 14.421]

MCLA 325.212 Engineers and other assistants; appointment. [MSA 14.422]

MCLA 325.213 Penalty; prosecutions. [MSA 14.423]

MCLA 325.214 Actions. [MSA 14.424]

JOINT ACTION
Act No. 159, P.A. 1969 - Sewer Construction

AN ACT to provide financial assistance to local agencies for the construction of collecting sewers to prevent the discharge of untreated or inadequately treated sewage or other liquid wastes into the waters of the state and to abate and prevent pollution of the waters in and adjoining the state; and to implement Act No. 76 of the Public Acts of 1968.

MCLA 323.401 Definitions. [MSA 5.2769(401)]

MCLA 323.402 Funding of collecting sewers, establishment of priority. [MSA 5.2769(402)]

MCLA 323.403 State sewer construction fund; establishment; use; grants, eligible sewer projects. [MSA 5.2769(403)]

Sec. 3. ... Grants shall be made only for collecting sewers on which contracts for construction were awarded by local agencies after June 30, 1968 and before July 1, 1975, or until the fund is exhausted, whichever occurs first.

MCLA 323.404 Source of moneys in fund; disbursements.
[MSA 5.2769(404)]

MCLA 323.405   Grants; applications, eligible parties; amount; limitations. [MSA 5.2769(405)]

Sec. 5. (1) A local agency may apply to the commission for a grant under this act.

(2) A grant shall be made in an amount equal to 1/2 that portion of the cost of construction of collecting sewers, computed upon the cost of the current year's project only, in excess of 10% of the state equalized value of all taxable property within the political boundaries of the unit of government served by the collecting sewers certified under subsection (2) of section 6 or $1,000,000.00, whichever is less.

(3) Grants are subject to the following limitations: ...

MCLA 323.406 Disbursements, purposes, procedure.
[MSA 5.2769(406)]

Sec. 6. (1) ... (2) ... (3) A disbursement from the fund to a local agency shall be made for projects on the priority list ... A local agency may request and receive disbursement of the state grant in not more than 5 installments:

(a) An installment of 50% of the reasonable cost for preparing completed final construction plans and specifications, ...

(b) An installment when not less than 25% of the cost of construction of the collecting sewers is completed.

(c) An installment when not less than 50% of the cost of construction of the collecting sewers is completed.

(d) An installment when not less than 75% of the cost of construction of the collecting sewers is completed.

(e) A final installment of the unpaid balance of the grant based upon the actual cost of the collecting sewers when construction is completed.

MCLA 323.407 Rules, promulgation. [MSA 5.2769(407)]

MCLA 323.408 Officers and employees of other state agencies, use; grant recipients, records; access to records. [MSA 5.2769(408)]

MCLA 323.409 Priority establishment and project certification procedures, compliance as prerequisite to grant. [MSA 5.2769(409)]

MCLA 323.410 Pollution control needs, point system of measurement. [MSA 5.2769(410)]

MCLA 323.411 Total priority points; tied projects, additional considerations. [MSA 5.2769(411)]

MCLA 323.412 Fiscal year; applications for grants, filing, time, life; pollution control plan, filing, time; point totals, assignment; certification of projects, time, conditions; reports to legislature; legislative approval or rejection. [MSA 5.2769(412)]

Sec. 12. (1) For the purposes of sections 9 to 12, the fiscal year is July 1 to June 30.

(2) Applications for collecting sewer construction grants ... For the fiscal year ending June 30, 1973 and for subsequent fiscal years, applications ... and official pollution control plans required by sections 7 and 8 of Act No. 329 of the Public Acts of 1966, as added and amended (**MCLA 323.117, 323.118** [MSA 3.533(57), MSA 3.533(58)]), shall be filed with the commission not later than September 15 preceding the period or fiscal year for which the application is filed. Applications postmarked not later than midnight of September 15 meet this requirement. ...

JOINT ACTION
Act No. 329, P.A. 1966 - Sewage Treatment Facilities, State Grants

AN ACT to prevent the discharge of untreated or inadequately treated sewage or other liquid wastes into any waters of the state; to provide financial assistance to local agencies for the construction of treatment works to prevent such discharge; and to abate and prevent pollution of the waters in and adjoining the state; and to implement Act No. 76 of the Public Acts of 1968 (**MCLA 373.371 to 373.382** [MSA 5.2769(201) TO 5.2769(212)]).

MCLA 323.111 State water pollution control fund, establishment, use; definitions. [MSA 3.533(51)]

MCLA 323.112 Deposits in state water pollution control fund; disbursements, use, procedure. [MSA 3.533(52)]

MCLA 323.113 Eligible projects; amount of grant; financial assistance to local agency. [MSA 3.533(53)]

MCLA 323.113a Disbursements, mode, certificates. [MSA 3.533(53A)]

MCLA 323.114 Rules, promulgation. [MSA 3.533(54)]

MCLA 323.115 Funding of grants and advances, priorities, limitations. [MSA 3.533(55)]

MCLA 323.116 Federal funds, reimbursements to local agencies and state. [MSA 3.533(56)]

MCLA 323.117 Official plan; adoption and submission as prerequisite to grant; joint submission. [MSA 3.533(57)]

Sec. 7. Effective July 1, 1968, a grant shall not be made until the local agency's governing body has adopted and submitted to the water resources commission a comprehensive long-range plan for the control of pollution in the area within its jurisdiction, hereinafter referred to as the official plan. If more than 1 local agency has authority to provide service for sewage collection in the same area, the required plan may be submitted jointly by the local agencies concerned or by 1 local agency with the concurrence of the others.

MCLA 323.118 Official plan; contents. [MSA 3.533(58)]

MCLA 323.119 Official plan; preparation; cost. [MSA 3.533(59)]

Sec. 9. The ... commission may administer grants to local agencies to assist them in preparing official plans. ...

MCLA 323.120 Official plan; approval; modification; assistance; cooperation with governmental and private organizations; submission of priority list. [MSA 3.533(60)]

MCLA 323.121 Assistance to state agencies; maintenance of records and audit. [MSA 3.533(61)]

MCLA 323.122 Grants or advances, prerequisites; point system, purpose. [MSA 3.533(62)]

MCLA 323.124 Pollution control needs, application of point system. [MSA 3.533(64)]

MCLA 323.125 Total priority points, computation, assignment of priorities in event of equal point totals. [MSA 3.533(65)]

MCLA 323.126 Fiscal year; treatment works construction applications and official plans, filing; point totals; certification of projects entitled to construction grants; priority certification; grant withdrawals; award deadlines; reports to legislature; priority lists. [MSA 3.533(66)]

Sec. 16. (1) For the purposes of sections 12 to 16 the fiscal year is July 1 to June 30. ...

MCLA 323.127 Abatement of unlawful water pollution. [MSA 3.533(67)]

Sec. 17. It is the intent of this act that the water resources commission encourage local agencies to use grants provided herein to assist in abatement of any unlawful pollution of waters of this state. ...

MCLA 323.128 Public corporations, petitioning to alleviate water pollution. [MSA 3.533(68)]

Sec. 18. Notwithstanding any other provision of law to the contrary a petition under chapters 20 or 21 of the drain code of 1956 may be filed by 1 public corporation when the purpose thereof is to alleviate pollution of the waters of the state.

Act No. 211, P.A. 1956 - Sewage Disposal and Water
Supply

*AN ACT to prescribe certain powers and duties of the
water resources commission; to authorize the commission
to make surveys, studies and investigations of the water
resources of the state and of the sewage disposal requirements of local units of government; to authorize the establishment of sewage disposal and water supply districts; to
define the powers and duties of the districts; to provide
for the exercise of such powers of the districts, including
the power to acquire property by condemnation, purchase,
gift or otherwise; to empower districts to adopt programs,
to acquire, construct, extend, improve and operate sewage
disposal systems and water supply systems; to provide for
the issuance of bonds by the districts, to authorize districts to make contracts and agreements with municipalities for said purposes; and to empower municipalities to
finance by taxes or issuance of bonds the carrying out of
the contracts.*

**MCLA 323.151   Sewage disposal and water supply district act;
definitions.** MSA 5.2769(81)

MCLA 323.152   Same; water resources commission, duties.
MSA 5.2769(82)

**MCLA 323.153   Same; joint municipal action to form district, peti-
tion.** MSA 5.2769(83)

*Sec. 3.   Any 2 or more municipalities, by resolution of their
legislative body, may file a petition ...(which)... shall set forth: ...
When more than 1 petition is filed covering parts of the same territory the agency may consolidate all or any such petitions.*

**MCLA 323.154   Same; hearing, notice, adjournment: determination
as to territory affected.** MSA 5.2769(84)

**MCLA 323.155   Determination of no necessity, recording. No neces-
sity; denial of petition.   Determination of necessity; referendum,
qualification of electors. Expenses of referendum. Creation of dis-**

trict. Temporary governing body of district. District; application for incorporation, contents. Same; certified statement, contents. Same; public body corporate, certificate of organization. Same; additional territory. Same; evidence of establishment. [MSA 5.2769(85)]

MCLA 323.156 Permanent governing body; election, term, vacancy; quorum, compensation, expenses. [MSA 5.2769(86)]

MCLA 323.157 Officers, employees, technical assistance, records, rules, municipal representatives. [MSA 5.2769(87)]

MCLA 323.158 Districts, powers. Construction of sewage disposal and water supply systems. Investigation as to new sources of supply of water. Investigation as to sewage disposal facilities. Acquisition of property, condemnation. Acceptance of appropriations from state. Acceptance of federal funds. [MSA 5.2769(88)]

MCLA 323.159 Districts; contracts with municipalities for construction and financing of systems. Contract provisions; full faith and credit; rebates; tax levies. Contracts by municipality, petition for referendum, special election. District bonds based on municipal pledges. [MSA 5.2769(89)]

MCLA 323.160 Contracts for sewage treatment; application of revenues. [MSA 5.2769(90)]

MCLA 323.161 Detachment of territory from participating municipality. [MSA 5.2769(91)]

MCLA 323.162 Existing systems, purchase, self-liquidating revenue bonds. [MSA 5.2769(92)]

JOINT ACTION
Act No. 13, P.A. 1956, Ex. Sess. - Water Pollution

AN ACT to authorize the state water resources commission to comply with the provisions of Public Law 660 of the 84th Congress; to appropriate funds therefor, and to provide for the disbursement thereof.

MCLA 323.201 Water pollution; water resources commission, expenditure of (federal) funds. [MSA 3.533(1)]

MCLA 323.202 Appropriation of available federal funds. [MSA 3.533(2)]

MCLA 323.203 Accounting, disbursement. [MSA 3.533(3)]

COMMERCIAL INTERESTS

Act No. 233, P.A. 1875 - Canal and Harbor Companies

AN ACT to re-enact and amend chapter 84 of the Compiled Laws of 1871, relative to the formation of corporations to construct canals or harbors and improve the same, by adding 2 new sections thereto, and by restricting its operations to the upper peninsula.

MCLA 485.1 Canal or harbor company; incorporators, procedure (public notice); **articles, contents.** [MSA 22.1481]

Sec. 1. Any number of persons, not less than 3, may be formed into a corporation for the purpose of constructing a canal or harbor, or improving the navigation of any river or stream in the upper peninsula and in Branch and Macomb counties by ...

MCLA 485.2 - 485.7 [MSA 22.1482 - 22.1487]

MCLA 485.8 Construction of route; restrictions. [MSA 22.1488]

MCLA 485.9 Real estate; power to hold. [MSA 22.1489]

MCLA 485.10 Condemnation, procedure; use of property. [MSA 22.1490]

MCLA 485.11 Tolls and charges; establishment, lien, evidence. [MSA 22.1491]

MCLA 485.12 Injury to property; violation of regulation; liability for damages, lien. [MSA 22.1492]

MCLA 485.13 Repair of bridges. [MSA 22.1493]

MCLA 485.14 Stockholder's liability, recovery prerequisites; subrogation; contribution. [MSA 22.1494]

MCLA 485.15 Avoidance of payment of toll, penalty. [MSA 22.1495]

MCLA 485.16 Amendment or repeal. [MSA 22.1496]

MCLA 485.17 Taxation. [MSA 22.1497]

MCLA 485.18 Existing corporation; organization under act, preference in subscription. [MSA 22.1498]

MCLA 485.19 Failure to furnish cargo statement; penalty. [MSA 22.1499]

MCLA 485.20 Bonds; issuance, restrictions. [MSA 22.1500]

MCLA 485.21 Canal or improvement, purchase by county, procedure; operation; sale to United States. [MSA 22.1501]

MCLA 485.22 Same; submission to electors; bonds, issuance. [MSA 22.1502]

MCLA 485.23 Re-instated corporations. [MSA 22.1503]

MCLA 485.24 Same; formation of companies to purchase and operate. [MSA 22.1504]

MCLA 485.25 Purchasing corporation, powers and duties; log interest; public rights. [MSA 22.1505]

Act No. 149, P.A. 1869 - River Improvement Companies

AN ACT to authorize the formation of corporations for the purpose of improving the navigation of rivers (St. Mary's River, etc.).

MCLA 485.101 Corporations to improve rivers; formation; tolls. [MSA 12.1511]

MCLA 485.102 Same; certificate, contents, acknowledgment, recording, filing. [MSA 12.1512]

MCLA 485.103 Body corporate, powers; governing law. [MSA 12.1513]

MCLA 485.104 Improvement of streams, consent of governor and attorney general. [MSA 12.1514]

MCLA 485.105 Map or plan, application for approval; hearing, procedure, approval; alteration of plan. [MSA 12.1515]

MCLA 485.106 - 485.112 [MSA 12.1516 - 12.1522]

MCLA 485.113 Corporate powers. [MSA 12.1523]

MCLA 485.114 Tolls; forfeiture of right to collect. [MSA 12.1524]

MCLA 485.115 Same; power of board to fix; jurisdiction of corporation; annual statement, contents. [MSA 12.1525]

MCLA 485.116 Same; improved streams open to all. [MSA 12.1526]

MCLA 485.117 Same; collection. [MSA 12.1527]

MCLA 485.118 Lien on floatables; sale, procedure. [MSA 12.1528]

MCLA 485.119 Stream to be kept in repair; forfeiture. [MSA 12.1529]

MCLA 485.120 Injury to stream or property; penalty. [MSA 12.1530]

MCLA 485.121 Log jam; power to break, lien for cost. [MSA 12.1531]

MCLA 485.122 Lien; enforcement. [MSA 12.1532]

MCLA 485.123 Lien on floatables; owner unknown or without jurisdiction of court. [MSA 12.1533]

MCLA 485.124 Annual report; contents. [MSA 12.1534]

MCLA 485.125 Taxation. [MSA 12.1535]

MCLA 485.126 Stockholder's liability; recovery prerequisites. [MSA 12.1536]

MCLA 485.127 Shares deemed personalty; transfer. [MSA 12.1537]

MCLA 485.129 Governing laws. [MSA 12.1538]

Act No. 91, P.A. 1887 - Improvement of State Boundary Rivers (by Corporations)

AN ACT to authorize the formation of corporations for the purpose of improving rivers which form, in whole or part, the boundary between this and any adjoining state, and their tributaries, and for driving, sorting, holding and delivering logs thereon.

MCLA 485.201 Corporations to improve state boundary rivers; incorporators. [MSA 22.1551]

Sec. 1. That any number of persons, not less than 5, may be formed into a corporation to improve any river and its tributaries which form, in whole or part, the boundary between this and any adjoining state, for the purpose of driving, sorting, holding and delivering logs thereon, and for such purpose only.

MCLA 485.202 - 485.208 [MSA 22.1552 - 22.1558]

MCLA 485.209 Property; holding. [MSA 22.1559]

Sec. 9. Every such corporation shall ... have powers to acquire, use and hold all such works and improvements, and all such real and personal property as may be necessary or suitable for the purposes of such corporation, and to take or flow lands or property in the construction of the works or improvements hereby authorized.

MCLA 485.210 Condemnation. [MSA 22.1560]

MCLA 485.211 Improvement powers; repair duty; driving of logs; tolls and expenses, lien. [MSA 22.1561]

MCLA 485.212 Lien; enforcement. [MSA 22.1562]

MCLA 485.213 Consolidation, procedure; powers of new corporation; articles or certified copy as evidence. [MSA 22.1563]

MCLA 485.214 Delivery duties; liability for damages. [MSA 22.1564]

Act No. 188, P.A. 1889 - Improvement of Rivers for Logging

AN ACT to provide for the organization and incorporation of companies for clearing out and improving rivers and streams in this state (St. Mary's River, etc.), for the purpose of driving, sorting, holding and delivering logs thereon.

MCLA 485.301 Corporations to improve rivers for logging; incorporation; control of stream. [MSA 22.1571]

MCLA 485.302 Procedure to come under act; forfeiture of rights. [MSA 22.1572]

MCLA 485.303 Corporation; vested rights, restrictions. [MSA 22.1573]

JOINT ACTION
Act No. 294, P.A. 1965 - Water Wells

AN ACT to protect the public health; to regulate the drilling of water wells and the installation of well pumps; to register and regulate water well drillers and well pump installers; to provide drilling records for the department of conservation; to prescribe the powers and duties of the state health commissioner; to create an advisory board; to prescribe penalties for violations of this act; and to provide an appropriation therefor.

MCLA 325.221 Definitions. [MSA 14.426(1)]

MCLA 325.222 Exemptions. [MSA 14.426(2)]

MCLA 325.223 Wells for single family house or for farming; exemption; drilling record. [MSA 14.426(3)]

MCLA 325.224 Master plumbers; exemption. [MSA 14.426(4)]

MCLA 325.225 Registration of well drilling contractors and pump installers, dewatering well construction; necessity for registration; fees, initial, renewal; drilling machine fees. [MSA 14.426(5)]

MCLA 325.226 Certificates of registration; issuance by commissioner, conditions. [MSA 14.426(6)]

MCLA 325.277 Registration; with and without examination. [MSA 14.426(7)]

MCLA 325.228 Certificate of registration; reciprocity. [MSA 14.426(8)]

MCLA 325.229 Governmental units; registration, exemption from fees. [MSA 14.426(9)]

Sec. 9. A ... township or other governmental unit engaged in well drilling or pump installing shall be registered under this act, but shall be exempt from paying the registration fees if the drilling or installing is done by regular employees of, and with equipment owned by, the governmental unit and the work is on wells or pumps intended for use by the governmental unit.

MCLA 325.230 Registration number; posting on drilling machine, seal. [MSA 14.426(10)]

MCLA 325.231 Completion of wells; records to be furnished, content. [MSA 14.426(11)]

MCLA 325.232 Entry and inspection; right of commissioner. [MSA 14.426(12)]

Sec. 12. The commissioner or health department may enter and inspect, at reasonable hours, on public or private property, any installation for the development or abandonment of ground water supplies.

MCLA 325.233 Investigation of violations; order for correction.
[MSA 14.426(13)]

MCLA 325.234 Violations; notice of suspension, hearing.
[MSA 14.426(14)]

MCLA 325.235 Advisory board; membership, qualifications, appointment. [MSA 14.426(15)]

MCLA 325.236 Advisory board; terms, vacancies. [MSA 14.426(16)]

MCLA 325.237 Advisory board; meetings, compensation, expenses.
[MSA 14.426(17)]

MCLA 325.238 Rules, promulgation, scope. [MSA 14.426(18)]

Sec. 18. The commissioner, ... shall make such rules and construction code as are reasonably necessary to carry out the intent of this act. ...(they) shall include, but are not limited to, provisions for qualifications and examination of well drilling contractors and pump installers, standards for the construction and installation of developments of ground water supplies, dewatering wells, abandonment of wells and dewatering wells, and for the administration of this act.

MCLA 325.239 Violation, penalty. [MSA 14.426(19)]

Act No. 61, P.A. 1939 - Supervisor of Wells (Oil and Gas)

AN ACT to provide for a supervisor of wells; to prescribe his powers and duties; to provide for an advisory board and an appeal board; to prescribe their powers and duties; to provide for the prevention of waste and for the control over certain matters, persons and things relating to the conservation of oil and gas, and for the making and promulgation of rules, regulations and orders relative

779

thereto; to provide for the plugging of wells and for the entry on private property for that purpose; to provide for the enforcement of such rules, regulations and orders and of the provisions of this act, and to provide penalties for the violations thereof; and to provide for the assessment and collection of certain fees.

MCLA 319.1   Declaration of policy; conservation of oil and gas. [MSA 13.139(1)]

MCLA 319.2   Definitions. [MSA 13.139(2)]

MCLA 319.3 - 319.5 [MSA 13.139(3) - 13.139(5)]

MCLA 319.6   Supervisor of wells; rules and regulations; prevention of waste; regulation of drilling; bonds. [MSA 13.139(6)]

Sec. 6. (a) ... (b) ... (c) To require the locating, drilling, deepening, redrilling or reopening, casing, sealing, operating and plugging of wells drilled for oil and gas or for geological information or as key wells in secondary recovery projects, or wells for the disposal of salt water, brine or other oil field wastes, to be done in such manner ...

MCLA 319.7   Prevention of waste; procedure; hearing by board; supervisor to promulgate rules and regulations. [MSA 13.139(7)]

MCLA 319.8 - 319.27 [MSA 13.139(8) - 13.139(27)]

Act No. 326, P.A. 1937 - Natural Dry Gas Wells

AN ACT to provide for a supervisor of natural dry gas wells; to prescribe his powers and duties; to provide regulations for the locating, sinking, drilling, casing, deepening, operating, abandonment and plugging of natural dry gas wells and test holes; to provide for the plugging of wells and for the entry on private property for that purpose; to provide for and regulate the payment of fees, issuance of permits and payment of money received under the provisions of this act; to provide for an appeal board; to prohibit waste in the development, production and handling of natural dry gas and to define waste and other terms used herein; to provide for public hearings and notice thereof, and procedure upon appeals; and to prescribe penalties for the violation of this act.

MCLA 319.51 Definitions. [MSA 13.138(1)]

MCLA 319.52 Director of conservation to act as supervisor of wells; assistants. [MSA 13.138(2)]

MCLA 319.53 Same; employees, compensation and expenses; offices. [MSA 13.138(3)]

MCLA 319.54 Same; duties; waste, definition. [MSA 13.138(4)]

MCLA 319.55 - 319.82 [MSA 13.138(5) - 13.138(72)]

Act No. 178, P.A. 1941 - Mineral Rights; Undivided Interests

AN ACT defining the rights of cotenants, joint owners, tenants in common and coparceners in lands; to provide for the development and operation of such lands for oil and gas mining purposes; to grant jurisdiction to the circuit court to authorize the exploration, development and operation of such lands for oil and gas mining purposes; to determine and quiet the title to said lands and to repeal all acts in conflict herewith.

MCLA 319.101 - 319.110 [MSA 13.140(1) - 13.140(10)]

Act No. 59, P.A. 1945 - Co-Tenants and Joint Land Ownership

AN ACT defining the rights of co-tenants, joint owners, tenants in common and co-parceners in lands; to provide for the development and operation of such lands for mining purposes other than oil and gas; to grant jurisdiction to the circuit court to authorize the exploration, development and operation of such lands for mining purposes except oil and gas; to determine and quiet the title to said lands; and to repeal all acts in conflict herewith.

MCLA 319.151 Exploration, etc., of certain lands for mining purposes. [MSA 26.1251]

MCLA 319.152 Definitions. [MSA 26.1252]

MCLA 319.153 - 319.156 [MSA 26.1253 - 26.1256]

Act No. 315, P.A. 1969 - Mineral Well Act

AN ACT to provide control of the drilling, operating and abandoning of mineral wells to prevent surface and underground waste; to provide for a supervisor of mineral wells and prescribe his powers and duties; to provide for an advisory board and prescribe its duties; to provide for inspecting, repairing and plugging of mineral wells and for entering on private property for that purpose; to provide for the assessing of certain fees; to provide for the promulgation of rules and orders to enforce this act; and to prescribe penalties.

MCLA 319.211 Short title. [MSA 13.141(1)]

MCLA 319.212 Definitions. [MSA 13.141(2)]

MCLA 319.213 Waste, prohibition. [MSA 13.141(3)]

MCLA 319.214 Supervisor of mineral wells, designation, assistants, salaries, expenses. [MSA 13.141(4)]

MCLA 319.215 - 319.235 [MSA 13.141(5) - 13.141(25)]

MCLA 319.236 Applicability, wells drilled under other acts, water resources commission act. [MSA 13.141(26)]

Act No. 197, P.A. 1959 - Michigan Unitization Law

AN ACT to provide for the unitized management, operation and development of common sources of supply of oil, gas, oil and gas, or gas distillate in this state; to prescribe the powers and duties of the supervisor of wells; to authorize the organization of units and prescribing the procedure therefor; to create an advisory board and an appeal board; to provide for the enforcement of this act; and to provide penalties for the violation thereof.

MCLA 319.351 - 319.394 [MSA 13.139(101) - 13.139(144)]

Act No. 163, P.A. 1911 - Copper and Iron Mine Inspectors

AN ACT to provide for the election of inspectors of mines in certain cases and the appointment of their deputies, for the appointment of such inspectors of mines and their deputies until the election and qualification of the first inspectors of mines, to prescribe their powers and duties and to provide for their compensation, and to repeal Act No. 213 of the Public Acts of 1887.

MCLA 425.101 Inspector of mines; election, term, qualifications, eligibility. [MSA 17.311]

Sec. 1. ... No person elected to any other public office shall be eligible for election as an inspector of mines, nor for appointment as a deputy director.

MCLA 425.102 - 425.107 [MSA 17.312 - 17.317]

MCLA 425.108 Powers and duties; abandoned mines, fencing; expenses, audit, payment, assessment. [MSA 17.318]

Sec. 8. ... The county clerk shall certify to the board of supervisors at its annual meeting in each year the amount of expense incurred under the provisions of this section during the preceding year and the amount belonging to each and every description of land on which any such mines are situated, and said amount shall be certified to the supervisors of the proper townships in the same manner as county taxes are certified to said supervisors, and the amount of the expense incurred as above on each description shall be assessed by said supervisors upon the said description upon their assessment rolls for that year in a separate column, and shall be collected in the same manner as county taxes, and when so collected paid into the general fund of the county.

MCLA 425.108a - 425.113 [MSA 17.318(1) - 17.323]

Act No. 92, P.A. 1970 - Metallic Mineral Mining Operations

AN ACT to provide for reclamation of lands subjected to the mining of minerals; to control possible adverse environmental effects of mining; to preserve the natural resources; to encourage the planning of future land use; and to promote the orderly development of mining, the encouragement of good mining practices, and the recognition and identification of the beneficial aspects of mining.

MCLA 425.181 Definitions. [MSA 18.594(1)]

MCLA 425.182 Study and survey. [MSA 18.594(2)]

Sec. 2. The supervisor (defined above) shall conduct a comprehensive study and survey in order to determine, consistent with the intent of this act, the extent and type of regulation of mining areas necessary in the public interest. The supervisor shall consider the effects of mining upon: (a) environment, (etc.)...

MCLA 425.183 Rules. [MSA 18.594(3)]

MCLA 425.184 Promulgation of rules; modifications, variances. [MSA 18.594(4)]

MCLA 425.185 Administration and enforcement of acts and rules; consultations, investigations, inspections, research, contracts, reclamation. [MSA 18.594(5)]

MCLA 425.186 Plan maps, filing, form, annual filing; long range environment plans. [MSA 18.594(6)]

MCLA 425.187 Performance bonds or other security or assurances; postponement. [MSA 18.594(7)]

MCLA 425.188 Violations of rules, restraining orders, injunctions, other remedies. [MSA 18.594(8)]

Act No. 314, P.A. 1968 - Acquisition of Surface Lands for Water Quality Control (re Iron Ore)

AN ACT to assist and encourage the acquisition of surface land areas and rights required for water quality control and other purposes in connection with mining and beneficiating low grade iron ore and the beneficiating and agglomerating of underground iron ore; and to provide adequate compensation therefor.

MCLA 425.171 Declaration of public interest and public purpose; condemnation of parcels of land; conveyance of land for purposes stated. [MSA 13.145(101)]

MCLA 425.172 Condemnation; adequate compensation. [MSA 13.145(102)]

MCLA 425.173 Lease or conveyance of land; conditions for issuance; provisions to protect materials deposited upon lands. [MSA 13.145(103)]

Act No. 143, P.A. 1959 - Use of Water in Mining Low Grade Iron Ore

AN ACT to authorize permits for the use of water for the operation of low grade iron ore mining property; to prescribe the terms and conditions of water use permits; and to prescribe the powers and duties of the state water resources commission.

MCLA 323.251 Low grade iron ore; mining and beneficiation, water permits (Upper Peninsula). [MSA 13.145(1)]

MCLA 323.252 Definitions. [MSA 13.145(2)]

MCLA 323.253 Water permits; application, contents, hearing, notice, publication; findings. [MSA 13.145(3)]

MCLA 323.254 Same; liability of state. [MSA 13.145(4)]

MCLA 323.255 Same; duration. [MSA 13.145(5)]

MCLA 323.256 Same; contents; modification, hearing; violation, revocation; emergency order for abatement. [MSA 13.145(6)]

MCLA 323.257 Administration of act; water resources commission, hearings. [MSA 13.145(7)]

MCLA 323.258 Rules and regulations; review of commission action. [MSA 13.145(8)]

REGULATORY CONTROLS - POLLUTION - GENERAL

JOINT ACTION
Act No. 127, P.A. 1970 - Anderson-Rockwell Environmental Protection Act of 1970

AN ACT to provide for actions for declaratory and equitable relief for protection of the air, water and other natural resources and the public trust therein; to prescribe the rights, duties and functions of the attorney general, any political subdivision of the state, any instrumentality or agency of the state or of a political subdivision thereof, any person, partnership, corporation, association, organization or other legal entity; and to provide for judicial proceedings relative thereto.

MCLA 691.1201 Short title. [MSA 14.528(201)]

MCLA 691.1202 Actions for declaratory and equitable relief; standards for pollution or anti-pollution devices or procedure. [MSA 14.528(202)]

MCLA 691.1202a Surety bonds or cash, posting to secure costs or judgments. [MSA 14.528(202A)]

MCLA 691.1203 Prima facie showing of pollution, rebuttal; affirmative defenses; burden of proof; weight of evidence; masters or referees; costs, apportionment. [MSA 14.528(203)]

MCLA 691.1204 Granting equitable relief; imposition of conditions; remitting parties to other proceedings; review. [MSA 14.528(204)]

MCLA 691.1205 Intervention; determination as to pollution; collateral estoppel; res judicata. [MSA 14.528(205)]

MCLA 691.1206 Supplementary to existing administrative and regulatory procedures. [MSA 14.528(206)]

MCLA 691.1207 Effective date. [MSA 14.528(207)]

JOINT ACTION
Act No. 106, P.A. 1963 - Littering of Property and Waters

AN ACT to define, control and prohibit the littering of public and private property and waters; to prescribe penalties for violation of this act; and to repeal certain acts and parts of acts.

MCLA 752.901 Litter; prohibition; construction of terms; removal of debris from highways. [MSA 28.603(1)]

Sec. 1. It is unlawful for any person knowingly, without the consent of the public authority having supervision of public property or the owner of private property, to dump, deposit, place, throw or cause or permit the dumping, depositing, placing, throwing or leaving of, litter on any public or private property or waters other than property designated and set aside for such purposes. The phrase "public or private property or waters" includes, ...

MCLA 752.901a Litter; causing to fall on or throwing into path of vehicle prohibited; penalty. [MSA 28.603(1A)]

MCLA 752.902 Same; definition. [MSA 28.603(2)]

MCLA 752.903 Penalty; sentence. [MSA 28.603(3)]

MCLA 752.904 Publication of act; receptacles for litter. [MSA 28.603(4)]

MCLA 752.905 Repeal. [MSA 28.603(5)]

MCLA 752.906 Municipal ordinances. [MSA 28.603(6)]

Sec. 6. This act shall not affect or in any way limit the powers of ... townships to enact and enforce ordinances for the control and elimination of litter.

The disastrous results of promiscuous use of insecticides, pesticides and economic poisons have been brought into sharp focus in the last few years. Private organizations and individual citizens have joined with the U.S. Food and Drug Administration, the U.S. Department of Agriculture and several state departments in research that has resulted in methods of control which are aiding improvement of the environment.

Another trend of the times is noted in the fact that municipalities all through the United States are establishing very restrictive permit controls over possible radiation emission. Local government officials are urged to consult with the Michigan Department of Agriculture and the Department of State Police with regard to motor vehicles, trains and planes carrying potentially dangerous radioactive materials into or through the jurisdiction of their political subdivisions.

JOINT ACTION
Act No. 313, P.A. 1929 - White Pine Blister Rust

AN ACT to provide for the control and eradication of white pine blister rust; to provide for the destruction of trees, plants and bushes infected with white pine blister rust; to authorize the commissioner of agriculture to remove, appraise and pay for healthy host plants necessarily destroyed; to declare certain plants and bushes a public nuisance; to authorize the commissioner to set aside fruiting currant and gooseberry and white pine growing districts as control areas; to provide for co-operation between state departments; to authorize the promulgation of rules and regulations; to provide funds for carrying out the purposes of this act; and to provide penalties for its violation.

MCLA 286.101 Definitions. [MSA 12.271]

MCLA 286.102 White pine blister rust declared dangerous pest; enforcement of act; rules; co-operation. [MSA 12.272]

MCLA 286.103 Destruction of plants. [MSA 12.273]

MCLA 286.104 Cultivated black currant declared public nuisance; destruction. [MSA 12.274]

788

MCLA 286.105 Blister rust control areas; fruiting currant and gooseberry control areas; destruction of plants, expense.
[MSA 12.275]

MCLA 286.106 Compensation to owner; noxious weeds.
[MSA 12.276]

Sec. 6. ... any and all wild currants and gooseberries are hereby declared noxious weeds and no compensation shall be paid therefor.

MCLA 286.107 Right of entry. [MSA 12.277]

MCLA 286.108 Co-operation; state lands. [MSA 12.278]

Sec. 8. The commissioner may co-operate with the United States department of agriculture, with the department of conservation, and with ... townships ... for the suppression and control of white pine blister rust ...

MCLA 286.109 Entry or movement of certain plants. [MSA 12.279]

MCLA 286.112 Penalty. [MSA 12.282]

JOINT ACTION
Act No. 6, P.A. 1919, Ex. Sess. - Grasshoppers and Similar Pests

AN ACT to authorize county boards of supervisors and township boards to appropriate money for the extermination of grasshoppers and other similar pests.

MCLA 286.121 Extermination of grasshoppers, similar pests; county appropriation. [MSA 12.291]

MCLA 286.122 Same; township appropriation. [MSA 12.292]

Sec. 2. Whenever any board of supervisors shall have purchased any such poison, as in this act provided, the township board ... is hereby authorized to appropriate money for the spreading of such poison as may be alloted to such township, or to use other means to exterminate such pests.

MCLA 286.123 Expense, payment. [MSA 12.293]

Sec. 3. Any expense incurred or money appropriated under this act shall be treated as a general ... township expense, ... and shall be payable as other general ... township expenses are now payable.

JOINT ACTION
Act No. 297, P.A. 1949 - Insecticides, Fungicides, Rodenticides and Other Economic Poisons

AN ACT to regulate the distribution, transportation or sale of insecticides, fungicides, rodenticides, defoliants, desiccants, plant regulators, nematocides, larvicides, ovicides, herbicides and other "economic poisons"; to prohibit adulterated and misbranded economic poisons; to provide for registration and fixing a fee therefor, guarantees, and labeling of all economic poisons; to authorize the expenditure of such fees; to authorize seizure of misbranded, adulterated or unregistered economic poisons; and to fix penalties for the violation of this act.

MCLA 286.161 The insecticide, fungicide, and rodenticide act of 1949; short title. [MSA 12.352(1)]

MCLA 286.162 Definitions. [MSA 12.352(2)]

MCLA 286.163 Unlawful distribution, sale or transportation of economic poisons; container; label contents, detaching, etc., unlawful. [MSA 12.352(3)]

MCLA 286.164 Economic poison registration fees, imposition, amount, payment, exemptions; registration, necessity, eligibility; records; distribution and sales licenses, necessity, fees, applications; reports, use of information. [MSA 12.352(4)]

MCLA 286.165 Cancellation of registration, grounds; change of guaranteed analysis or active ingredients; denial of registration, appeal; noncompliance as to claims, labeling or other submissions; restricted use pesticide dealer's license, denial, suspension, revocation. [MSA 12.352(5)]

MCLA 286.166 Powers and duties of director. [MSA 12.352(6)]

MCLA 286.167 Examination of poisons and devices; report of violations; notice of judgments. [MSA 12.352(7)]

MCLA 286.168 Penalties; exemptions. [MSA 12.352(8)]

Sec. 8. a. The penalties provided for violations of this act shall not apply to --
(1) ... (2) Public officials of this state and the federal government engaged in the performance of their official duties; ...

MCLA 286.169 Violations; penalty. [MSA 12.352(9)]

MCLA 286.170 Seizures, procedure; complaints; forfeiture; destruction or sale; proceeds from sale credited to general fund. [MSA 12.352(10)]

MCLA 286.171 Authority vested in employees of department of agriculture. [MSA 12.352(11)]

MCLA 286.172 Cooperation with state agencies, United States department of agriculture and other states. [MSA 12.352(12)]

MCLA 286.173 Jurisdiction vested in department of agriculture. [MSA 12.352(13)]

Act No. 189, P.A. 1931 - Insect Pest and Plant Disease Act

AN ACT to regulate the sale and distribution of nursery stock, plants and plant products; to prevent the introduction into and the dissemination within this state of insect pests and plant diseases and to provide for their repression and control; to provide for license and to provide for inspection; and imposing certain powers and duties on the director of agriculture; and providing penalties.

MCLA 286.201 Short title. [MSA 12.201]

MCLA 286.202 Definitions. [MSA 12.202]

MCLA 286.203 - 286.219 [MSA 12.203 - 12.219]

MCLA 286.220 Eradication of nuisances; prerequisite procedure, inspection, abatement of nuisance, expenses. [MSA 12.220]

Sec. 20. ... The director may employ the necessary aid in abating any nuisance under this section and he may render a bill against the owner for the expense incurred. If the owner refuses to pay the bill, it shall be certified to the local assessing officer and assessed against the property.

MCLA 286.221 Inspection of public grounds; application, payment of expense. [MSA 12.221]

Sec. 21. Any municipality, park board, or other board or person in control of public grounds may apply to the commissioner of agriculture for an inspection of the same with reference to the presence of insect pests or plant diseases; and upon receipt of such application, or as soon thereafter as may be conveniently practicable, the commissioner of agriculture shall comply with such request, and send to such applicant a statement as to the facts disclosed, with any recommendations which the commissioner ... may deem pertinent. The expense of the special inspection shall be paid by the applicant.

MCLA 286. 222 Inspection of plants and plant products before interstate shipment; expense, certificate. [MSA 12.222]

MCLA 286.223 Quarantine; enforcement, hearing, notice. [MSA 12.223]

MCLA 286.224 Violation of act, quarantine or rule, misdemeanor. [MSA 12.224]

MCLA 286.225 Review of rule or order; appeal to circuit court. [MSA 12.225]

MCLA 286.226 Violations, penalty. [MSA 12.226]

JOINT ACTION

Act No. 72, P.A. 1945 - Insect Pests and Plant Diseases

AN ACT to prevent the importation from other states, and the spread within this state, of all serious insect pests and contagious plant diseases and to provide for their repression and control, imposing certain powers and duties on the commissioner of agriculture; to prescribe penalties for the violation of the provisions of this act; and to repeal certain acts and parts of acts.

MCLA 286.251 Examinations for insects or infectious diseases; marking; notice to destroy, posting; appeals. [MSA 12.263(1)]

MCLA 286.252 Refusal to carry out orders of commissioner. [MSA 12.263(2)]

MCLA 286.253 Declared public nuisances. [MSA 12.263(3)]

MCLA 286.254 Report of inspections. [MSA 12.263(4)]

MCLA 286.255 Authority to enter upon premises; treatment to prevent spread of disease; owners recompensed for loss. [MSA 12.263(5)]

MCLA 286.256 Commissioner may make rules and regulations; quarantines. [MSA 12.263(6)]

MCLA 286.257 Liability of agent, etc. [MSA 12.263(7)]

MCLA 286.259 Misdemeanor; penalty; fines turned into state treasury. [MSA 12.263(9)]

JOINT ACTION
Act No. 233, P.A. 1959 - Economic Poisons, Licenses

AN ACT to prevent harm to man, contamination of food or feed or the destruction or damage of agricultural crops, growing plants, livestock or wildlife from the application of any economic poison, pesticide, insecticide, herbicide, fungicide, rodenticide; to provide for the licensing of persons engaged in the business of applying economic poisons and imposing penalties for violations;

to provide for the collection of licensing fees; and to pre-scribe the powers and duties of certain officers.

MCLA 286.411 Economic poisons; definitions. ⎡MSA 12.353(1)⎤

MCLA 286.412 Same; exemptions. ⎡MSA 12.353(2)⎤

Sec. 2. This act shall not apply to ... municipalities, road commissions, or state or federal agencies.

MCLA 286.413 - 286.420 ⎡MSA 12.353(3) - 12.353(10)⎤

JOINT ACTION (STATE)
Act No. 187, P.A. 1965 - Pest Control Compact

AN ACT providing for the joinder of this state in the pest control compact, and for related purposes.

MCLA 286.501 Pest control compact; findings, definitions, insurance fund, assistance, committees, relations, finance, entry and withdrawal, construction. ⎡MSA 4.149(1)⎤

MCLA 286.502 Departments of the state; cooperation with insurance fund. ⎡MSA 4.149(2)⎤

MCLA 286.503 Department of agriculture; filing of copies of by-laws and amendments. ⎡MSA 4.149(3)⎤

MCLA 286.504 Director of agriculture; compact administrator; duties. ⎡MSA 4.149(4)⎤

MCLA 286.505 Application for assistance from insurance fund. ⎡MSA 4.149(5)⎤

MCLA 286.506 Department liable for expenditure; credit to account. ⎡MSA 4.149(6)⎤

MCLA 286.507 Executive head; definition. ⎡MSA 4.149(7)⎤

JOINT ACTION
Act No. 195, P.A. 1959 - Dutch Elm Disease

AN ACT to authorize townships to spray trees to prevent infection of Dutch elm disease or any other diseases or insect pests destructive to trees or shrubs; and to provide for the manner of payment.

MCLA 41.681 Dutch elm disease, spraying; payment. [MSA 12.264]

Sec. 1.   The governing body of any township may provide for the spraying of trees within their jurisdiction for the prevention of Dutch elm disease or any other diseases or insect pests destructive to trees or shrubs.   The cost of the tree spraying may be paid from:
(a)   Funds created specially for this purpose.
(b)   Money appropriated from other funds of the political subdivision.

Act No. 32, P.A. 1962 - Female Box Elder Trees

AN ACT to authorize townships, villages and cities to adopt ordinances providing for the destruction of female box elder trees.

MCLA 124.151   Female box elder trees, destruction as nuisance. [MSA 12.270(1)]

Sec. 1.   Female box elder trees are hereby declared to be a public nuisance and the legislative body of any township ... may adopt an ordinance providing for the ordering by a designated authority of the destruction of female box elder trees.

JOINT ACTION
Act No. 68, P.A. 1957 - Houseboats, Sanitation and Location

AN ACT to provide for the regulation by county boards of supervisors of sanitation requirements and location of houseboats in the portion of the county outside incorporated cities and villages and to prescribe penalties for the violation of such regulations.

MCLA 123.591   Houseboats; regulation of sanitation and location by counties. [MSA 5.2965(1)]

MCLA 123.592 Same; designation of enforcement officer.
MSA 5.2965(2)

Sec. 2. *The boards of supervisors in enacting ordinances under the provisions of this act shall designate the proper county and township official or officials whose duty it shall be to cooperate in the administration and enforcement of the provisions of ordinances so enacted.*

MCLA 123.593 Penalty for violation. MSA 5.2965(3)

Act No. 411, P.A. 1919 - Business of Canning and Preserving

AN ACT to regulate the business of canning and preserving; and to prescribe penalties for the violation of the provisions of this act.

MCLA 289.121 Canner's license. MSA 12.911

MCLA 289.122 Same; issuance, fees, renewal; fees credited to general fund. MSA 12.912

MCLA 289.123 Factories, location. MSA 12.913

MCLA 289.124 Disposition of waste, decomposed matter; retention of by-products. MSA 12.914

MCLA 289.125 Buildings and equipment. MSA 12.915

MCLA 289.126 Cans, brining or syruping; potable water.
MSA 12.916

MCLA 289.127 Sterilization; cleanliness of factory; prevention of dust. MSA 12.917

Sec. 7. *... Roadways about the factory shall be sprinkled, oiled or otherwise treated to prevent dust.*

MCLA 289.128 - 289.133 MSA 12.918 - 12.923

Act No. 328, P.A. 1931 - The Penal Code, Chapter LXXX. - Slaughter Houses

MCLA 750.533 Slaughter houses; within 20 rods of highway.
[MSA 28.801]

Sec. 533. ... Any person who shall keep or maintain any slaughter-house, slaughter-yard or slaughter-pen, or any other place for slaughtering or killing any animals, or rendering dead animals as a business, within 20 rods of any public highway within this state, or in any other place except as provided in section 6521 of the Compiled Laws of 1929 and amendments thereto, shall be guilty of a misdemeanor: ...

MCLA 750.534 Same; water supply, sewerage and drainage.
[MSA 28.802]

Sec. 534. ... Any person or his agent who shall keep or maintain ... within 1 mile of the limits of any city or park, or within 30 rods of any highway or street car line, any slaughter-house, slaughter-yard or slaughter-pen or any other place for slaughtering or killing any animals, or for rendering dead animals, unless such place shall be supplied with an adequate supply of water for daily and constant flushing and purifying of the place, and with adequate sewerage and drainage for the speedy removal of all blood and other fluid refuse from such slaughtering, killing or rendering, shall be guilty of a misdemeanor.

Nuisance -- Any person or his agent in charge of any slaughter-house, slaughter-yard or slaughter-pen in or within 1 mile of any city or park, or within 30 rods of any highway or street car line, who shall dispose of any offal, heads, horns, hides or other portions of any dead animals in such manner as to be a nuisance, or contrary to the rules of the local board of health, shall be guilty of a misdemeanor.

Act No. 136, P.A. 1881 - Privies

AN ACT to enlarge the powers of boards of health of townships and villages in certain cases.

MCLA 325.251 Privies; rules of local board; abatement of nuisance.
[MSA 14.431]

Sec. 1. That boards of health in townships ... are hereby empowered to make such rules and regulations in relation to the care and cleansing of privies and water-closets within such townships ... of any of the inhabitants thereof, or such boards may declare any such privy or water-closet a nuisance, and the abatement thereof be by them ordered and enforced.

MCLA 325.252 Penalty. [MSA 14.432]

Act No. 273, P.A. 1939 - Outhouses

AN ACT to protect the public health; to regulate the storage and disposition of sewage; to empower the state commissioner of health to make rules in regard thereto; and to prescribe penalties for the violation of the provisions of this act and said rules.

MCLA 325.271 Outhouse; defined; prohibited unless sanitary. [MSA 14.433(1)]

MCLA 325.272 Same; rules and regulations governing outhouses; publication. [MSA 14.433(2)]

MCLA 325.273 Violation of act, abatement of nuisance. [MSA 14.433(3)]

MCLA 325.274 Exemption of certain outhouses by location. [MSA 14.433(4)]

Act No. 243, P.A. 1951 - Septic Tanks, Servicing

AN ACT to prevent the spread of infectious and contagious diseases; to require persons engaged in servicing and cleaning of septic tanks, seepage pits or cesspools to be licensed and bonded by the commissioner of health; to require solicitors who act on behalf of such persons to be licensed; to provide for the inspection and licensing of vehicles; to provide for the control of dumping wastes; and to provide penalties for the violation of this act.

MCLA 325.281 Definitions. [MSA 14.434(1)]

798

MCLA 325.282 Licenses; bonds. $\boxed{\text{MSA 14.434(2)}}$

MCLA 325.283 License application, filing, contents; license fee; investigation; issuance of license; bond. $\boxed{\text{MSA 14.434(3)}}$

MCLA 325.284 License for vehicles carrying waste; application, contents; fee; issuance; term; lettering. $\boxed{\text{MSA 14.434(4)}}$

MCLA 325.285 Equipment carrying waste; disposal of waste. $\boxed{\text{MSA 14.434(5)}}$

MCLA 325.286 Exemptions from licensing requirements. $\boxed{\text{MSA 14.434(6)}}$

Sec. 6. Nothing in this act shall be construed to require a business license for:
(a) A property owner to clean his own septic tank, seepage pit or cesspool.
(b) A municipality servicing and maintaining a public sewage treatment facility.
(c) A master plumber, ...

MCLA 325.287 Penalty. $\boxed{\text{MSA 14.434(7)}}$

Act No. 136, P.A. 1969 - Liquid Industrial Wastes

AN ACT to require persons engaged in removing liquid industrial wastes from the premises of other persons to be licensed and bonded; to provide for the inspection and licensing of vehicles; to provide for the control of disposal of wastes; and to provide penalties for the violation of this act.

MCLA 323.271 Definitions. $\boxed{\text{MSA 3.533(101)}}$

MCLA 323.272 Licenses and bonds, necessity. $\boxed{\text{MSA 3.533(102)}}$

MCLA 323.273 Removal by non-licensed persons, prohibition. $\boxed{\text{MSA 3.533(103)}}$

MCLA 323.273a Records of waste removals. $\boxed{\text{MSA 3.533(103A)}}$

MCLA 323.274 Municipal waste collection and treatment.
[MSA 3.533(104)]

Sec. 4. The provisions of this act shall not be construed to prevent the removal of liquid industrial waste from the premises of another person by a municipal waste collection and treatment entity nor to prevent a person from contracting or otherwise arranging with a municipal waste collection and treatment entity for such removal.

MCLA 323.275 Licenses, applications, fee; bonds, amount, form, cancellation; deposits in lieu of bonds. [MSA 3.533(105)]

MCLA 323.276 Qualifications for (and issuance of) license.
[MSA 3.533(106)]

MCLA 323.277 Vehicle licenses, necessity, application, fee, transferability, designation on vehicle, expiration, renewal.
[MSA 3.533(107)]

MCLA 323.278 Escape of waste and odors, prevention; disposition of waste; trip records. [MSA 3.533(108)]

MCLA 323.279 Hazardous or nuisance conditions or unlawful pollution; abatement, prevention; notice to licensee; action by commission, indemnification. [MSA 3.533(109)]

MCLA 323.280 Revocation of license, criminal penalties.
[MSA 3.533(110)]

Act No. 226, P.A. 1971 - Cleaning Agents

AN ACT to restrict the content of cleaning agents in order to protect water quality by preventing and controlling growth of algae, weeds and slimes.

MCLA 323.231 Definitions. [MSA 3.533(301)]

MCLA 323.232 Phosphorus, use in cleaning agents, restrictions.
[MSA 3.533(302)]

MCLA 323.233 Rules, promulgation, subject matter; burden of proof, compliance with act and rules; violations of rules. [MSA 3.533(303)]

MCLA 323.234 Unlawful pollution by substance other than phosphorus, determinations, rules, exceptions. [MSA 3.533(304)]

MCLA 323.235 Regulation of cleaning agents by political subdivisions, prohibition. [MSA 3.533(305)]

Sec. 5. A political subdivision shall not enact or enforce an existing or future ordinance or rule with respect to the sale of cleaning agents containing phosphorus or any other substance which is or may be regulated by or pursuant to this act.

MCLA 323.236 Enforcement of act. [MSA 3.533(306)]

Sec. 6. The water resources (mission shall enforce this act and seek court enforcement of its (rs ...

JOINT A   ION
Act No. 41, P.A. 1955   eed Control in Inland Lakes

AN ACT to authorize tc   hip boards to appropriate money for the purpose of cont   ng weeds in inland lakes.

MCLA 41.671 Weed control in ir   d lakes; appropriation by township. [MSA 5.265(1)]

Sec. 1, ... the township b(..., upon receipt of a petition signed by 25 freeholders residi   within the township requesting such work to be done, and they may appropriate money from the contingent or general fund for the purpose of controlling weeds in inland public lakes situated within the township proper.

MCLA 41.672 Same; joint action with other townships. [MSA 5.265(2)]

Sec. 2. ... the township board ... (may) appropriate money from its contingent or general fund for entering into agreements with any other township or townships ... for the purpose of controlling weeds in any inland public lake or public lakes situated within more than 1 township of this state.

MCLA 41.673 Same; use of poison. [MSA 5.265(3)]

Sec. 3. Poison shall not be used for the purpose of weed control in any inland lake unless it is used with the consent of, and under the supervision of, the department of conservation.

JOINT ACTION
Act No. 346, P.A. 1968 - Fluoridation of Water

AN ACT to prohibit a state department, board, commission or agency from authorizing the addition of fluoride to public drinking water; and to require fluoridation of public drinking water in certain cases.

MCLA 325.191 Fluoridation of water; prohibition. [MSA 14.528(101)]

Sec. 1. A state department, board, commission or agency shall not have authority to order any county, city, township or village or any combination thereof supplying water to the public, which may be consumed by humans, to add fluoride.

MCLA 325.192 Fluoridation of water; addition of fluoride within 5 years from effective date of act, rejection by ordinance; submitting question to electors. [MSA 14.528(102)]

Sec. 2. Every county, city, township or village or any combination thereof supplying water to the public, to which water fluoride is not presently added and which may be consumed by humans, shall add fluoride to such water, in a manner and amount to be prescribed by the department of public health, within 5 years after the effective date of this act, unless such addition of fluoride shall have been rejected by an ordinance of the local governing body or by a majority of the electors of such ...(governmental unit)... voting thereon. The question shall be submitted to such electors upon a petition filed with the clerk of the local government and signed by a number of the registered and qualified electors of the local government not less than 5% of the total number of votes cast for all candidates for the office of secretary of state at the last general election held for such purpose.

JOINT ACTION
Act No. 348, P.A. 1965 - Air Pollution Act

AN ACT to control air pollution in this state; to create an air pollution control commission within the state health department; to prescribe its powers and duties; and to provide penalties.

MCLA 336.11 Short title. [MSA 14.58(1)]

MCLA 336.12 Definitions. [MSA 14.58(2)]

MCLA 336.13 Air pollution control commission; members, appointment, qualifications, terms, vacancies, compensation. [MSA 14.58(3)]

Sec. 3. (1) ... (2) Of the 8 citizens so appointed by the governor, ... 2 shall be representatives of local governing bodies, 1 of whom shall be a full-time air pollution control officer; ...

MCLA 336.14 Organization and procedural rules of commission; regular meetings, frequency; special meetings, calling, requests; quorum. [MSA 14.58(4)]

MCLA 336.15 Commission powers and authority. [MSA 14.58(5)]

Sec. 5. The commission may: ... (m) Encourage the formulation and execution of plans by cooperative groups or associations of cities, villages and counties or districts, or other governmental units (townships), industries and others who severally or jointly are or may be the source of air pollution, for the control of pollution. ...

MCLA 336.16 State commissioner of health; authorized agent; duties. [MSA 14.58(6)]

MCLA 336.17 Rules, promulgation, amendments, repeals, purposes. [MSA 14.58(7)]

MCLA 336.18 Violations; complaints; investigations; voluntary agreements or performance contracts to abate pollution, execution, enforcement, hearings and decisions on complaints by aggrieved persons. [MSA 14.58(8)]

MCLA 336.19 Issuance and service of notice, complaint, and proposed order for corrective action; contents; disposition by stipulation or consent order; finality. [MSA 14.58(9)]

MCLA 336.20 Answer to complaint, appearance, hearings, testimony, subpoenas. [MSA 14.58(10)]

MCLA 336.21 Public hearings as to pollution control, presiding officers, qualifications; confidentiality of records, permit applications, quantity or quality of emissions, or other information. [MSA 14.58(11)]

MCLA 336.23 Petition to circuit court for relief from commission's rules or order, venue, verification, contents, proof, demand for relief; petitioners. [MSA 14.58(13)]

MCLA 336.24 Notice to discontinue air pollution, grounds for issuance; hearing. [MSA 14.58(14)]

MCLA 336.24a Annual surveillance fee; purpose; amount, determination, notice; payment; disposition; reports; suspension of act or rules in deference to local controls; allocation of fee proceeds to local agencies; local fees. [MSA 14.58(14A)]

MCLA 336.26 Failure to comply with or obtain permits or commission orders, offense, penalties; jurisdiction; defenses; restraining orders; damages; probation. [MSA 14.58(16)]

Sec. 16. A person who or a governmental unit who fails to obtain or comply with a permit, or comply with a final order or order of determination of the commission made under this act is guilty of a misdemeanor and shall be fined not more than $10,000.00 and in the discretion of the court an additional amount of not more than $2,000.00 per day a violation continues. ...

MCLA 336.27 Action for enforcement. [MSA 14.58(17)]

MCLA 336.28 Violations not proximately caused by negligence or wilful misconduct, penalties or fines not imposed. [MSA 14.58(18)]

MCLA 336.29 Suspension of enforcement. [MSA 14.58(19)]

MCLA 336.30 Variance from rule or regulation, factors to be considered. [MSA 14.58(20)]

MCLA 336.31 Grant of variance; necessary showing. [MSA 14.58(21)]

MCLA 336.32 Variance, period of time; condition. [MSA 14.58(22)]

MCLA 336.33 Revocation of variance; notice. [MSA 14.58(23)]

MCLA 336.34 Purpose. [MSA 14.58(24)]

Sec. 24. It is the purpose of this act to provide additional and cumulative remedies to prevent and abate air pollution. Nothing in this act contained shall abridge or alter rights of action or remedies now or hereafter existing, nor shall any provision of this act or anything done by virtue of this act be construed as estopping individuals, counties, cities, townships or villages or other governmental units from the exercise of their respective rights to suppress nuisances or to prevent or abate air pollution.

MCLA 336.35 Construction. [MSA 14.58(25)]

Sec. 25. This act shall not be construed as repealing any of the laws relating to air pollution which are not by this act expressly repealed, but it shall be held and construed to be as ancillary to and supplementing the laws now in force, excepting as they may be in direct conflict with this act. ...

MCLA 336.36 Effect on existing ordinances or regulations; application or nonapplication. [MSA 14.58(26)]

Sec. 26. (1) Nothing in this act or in any rule or regulation which shall be promulgated pursuant to this act shall be deemed to invalidate any existing ordinances or regulations having requirements equal to or greater than the minimum applicable requirements of this act or prevent any political subdivision from adopting similar provisions if their requirements are equal to or greater than the minimum applicable requirements of this act. ...

Act No. 250, P.A. 1965 - Air Pollution, Tax Exemption

AN ACT to provide for the exemption of air pollution facilities from certain taxes.

MCLA 336.1 Definitions. [MSA 7.793(1)]

MCLA 336.2 Control facility tax exemption certificate; application, contents; approval; notice; hearing; extent of exemption. [MSA 7.793(2)]

MCLA 336.3 Notification of adequacy of facility; certificate, issuance, effective date. [MSA 7.793(3)]

MCLA 336.4 Taxes from which facility exempt. [MSA 7.793(4)]

MCLA 336.5 Tax exemption certificate; sending by mail. [MSA 7.793(5)]

MCLA 336.6 Same; modification or revocation, notice, hearing, grounds, effect. [MSA 7.793(6)]

MCLA 336.7 Same; appeal from issuance or refusal to issue. [MSA 7.793(7)]

MCLA 336.8 State tax commission; adoption of rules and regulations. [MSA 7.793(8)]

Act No. 305, P.A. 1972 - Radiation

AN ACT to provide for control of ionizing radiation emissions; to provide for certain contractual agreements with the federal government for the licensing of radioactive materials; to designate the department of public health as the state radiation control agency; to establish a radiation advisory committee; to adopt rules implementing this act; and to prescribe penalties for violations.

MCLA 325.451 Definitions. [MSA 14.528(301)]

806

MCLA 325.452 Agreements, cooperation with federal government, other states, or interstate agencies. [MSA 14.528(302)]

MCLA 325.453 State department of public health as radiation control agency, designation, duties, licensing and registration rules, programs. [MSA 14.528(303)]

MCLA 325.454 Emergencies; orders, issuance, compliance, continuance, modification, or revocation; hearing. [MSA 14.528(304)]

MCLA 325.455 Permissible entry or warrant to search property and seize source of ionizing radiation, entry upon private or public property. [MSA 14.528(305)]

MCLA 325.456 Environmental monitoring systems, operation, collection and coordination of data. [MSA 14.528(306)]

MCLA 325.457 Rules, contents, promulgation; license fee schedules; disposition of fees. [MSA 14.528(307)]

Sec. 7. ... (7) A municipality or department, agency or official thereof may not license, regulate or require the registration of any radioactive materials or other sources of ionizing radiation. ...

MCLA 325.458 Radiation advisory committee, appointment, membership, compensation, duties. [MSA 14.528(308)]

MCLA 325.459 Violations, injunctions. [MSA 14.528(309)]

MCLA 325.460 Manufacture, transfer, disposition, possession, or use of radioactive material or other source of ionizing radiation, necessity for license or registration; violation, offense; effective date. [MSA 14.528(310)]

MCLA 325.461 Exempted sources or conditions. [MSA 14.528(311)]

MCLA 325.462 Effective date. [MSA 14.528(312)]

PARKS AND RECREATION

When establishing parks and recreation areas, the needs of

both present and future generations must be considered. Walking and driving distances between centers of population, as well as the availability of mass transit, should also be taken into account.

Since individuals in our society tend to go adrift from the normal concerns of others, there must be strict regulations covering such vagaries of human behavior as drunkenness, littering, vandalism and inappropriate use of facilities. Because the parks and many recreational facilities are primarily used by family groups, a municipality has further responsibility to enforce its park ordinances with vigor and consistency, including a curfew and constant police surveillance.

In addition to the following citations, there are additional provisions regarding this subject in several sections of the chapter on Services, Utilities, Contracts and Ordinances.

Act No. 17, P.A. 1921 - Department of Conservation

AN ACT to provide for the protection and conservation of the natural resources of the state; to provide and develop facilities for outdoor recreation; to create a conservation department; to define the powers and duties thereof; to provide rules and regulations concerning the use and occupancy of lands and property under its control and penalties for the violation thereof; to provide for the transfer to said department of the powers and duties now vested by law in certain boards, commissions and officers of the state; and for the abolishing of the boards, commissions and offices the powers and duties of which are hereby transferred.

MCLA 299.1 - 299.2 [MSA 13.1 - 13.2]

MCLA 299.3 Department of conservation; duties; natural resources, outdoor recreation; destruction of timber; reforestation; pollution; protection of game and fish; gifts; acquisition and lease of property. [MSA 13.3]

Sec. 3. The department of conservation shall protect and conserve the natural resources of the state of Michigan; provide and develop facilities for outdoor recreation; prevent the destruction of timber and other forest growth by fire or otherwise; promote the reforesting of forest lands belonging to the state; prevent and guard

808

against the pollution of lakes and streams within the state, and enforce all laws provided for that purpose with all authority granted by law, and foster and encourage the protecting and propagation of game and fish. ...

MCLA 299.3a Conservation commission; rules and regulations for protection of lands and property; misdemeanor. [MSA 13.4]

MCLA 299.3b - 299.4 [MSA 13.4(1) - 13.5]

JOINT ACTION
Act No. 241, P.A. 1972 - Wilderness and Natural Areas Act of 1972

AN ACT to create and regulate wilderness areas, wild areas and natural areas; to prescribe the functions of certain state officers; to require the promulgation of rules; and to prescribe penalties.

MCLA 322.751 Short title. [MSA 13.734(1)]

MCLA 322.752 Definitions. [MSA 13.734(2)]

MCLA 322.753 Wilderness and natural areas advisory board; creation; membership, qualifications, number, terms, compensation; chairman; recommendations; support from other groups.
[MSA 13.734(3)]

MCLA 322.754 Wilderness, wild, and natural areas, annual reviews of state lands, proposed areas, dedication of areas, denial of proposals, alteration or withdrawal of dedications, hearings, notice, exchange of lands. [MSA 13.734(4)]

Sec. 4. ... (4) The commission may exchange dedicated land for the purpose of acquiring other land which, in its judgment, are more suitable for the purposes of this act.

MCLA 322.755 Wild and natural areas in relative proximity to urban centers; private lands or lands controlled by other governmental units, designation as wilderness, wild, or natural areas.
[MSA 13.734(5)]

Sec. 5. (1) The commission shall attempt to provide insofar as possible, wild areas and natural areas in relative proximity to urban centers of more than 100,000 population.

(2) Private land or land under the control of other governmental units may be designated in the same way as a wilderness area, wild area or natural area by the commission and administered by the department under a cooperative agreement between the owner and the commission.

MCLA 322.756 Acts prohibited on state land in wilderness, wild, or natural areas or proposed areas. MSA 13.734(6)

MCLA 322.757 Landing aircraft or operating mechanical transport in wilderness, wild, or natural areas, offense. MSA 13.734(7)

MCLA 322.758 Maintenance and restoration of wilderness, wild, or natural areas. MSA 13.734(8)

MCLA 322.759 Wilderness, wild, or natural area border signs, posting, contents. MSA 13.734(9)

MCLA 322.760 Acquisition of land for inclusion in wilderness, wild, or natural areas. MSA 13.734(10)

Sec. 10. The department may acquire land through purchase, gift or bequest ...

MCLA 322.761 Taxation of wilderness, wild, or natural areas. MSA 13.734(11)

Sec. 11. The local taxing authority shall be entitled to collect from the state a tax on a wilderness, wild or natural area within its jurisdiction at its ad valorem tax rate or $2.00 per acre, whichever is less. The department shall audit the assessments of wilderness, wild or natural areas regularly to insure that such properties are assessed in the same ratio as similar properties in private ownership. The legislature shall appropriate from the general fund for payments under this section.

MCLA 322.762 Saving clause. MSA 13.734(12)

Sec. 12. ... (2) Nothing in this act shall alter the status of

810

land dedicated by the commission before the effective date of this act until dedicated pursuant to section 4 except that tax reverted lands shall be subject to section 11. Purchased land dedicated by the commission before the effective date of this act shall be subject to ad valorem taxes when dedicated pursuant to section 4.

MCLA 322.763 Effective date (July 1, 1972). [MSA 13.734(13)]

Note: The state park commission and various other commissions and offices have been abolished and their powers, duties and records transferred to the department of natural resources.

JOINT ACTION
Act No. 218, P.A. 1919 - State Park Commission

AN ACT to create the Michigan state park commission; to define its rights, powers and duties in acquiring and maintaining state parks; to authorize the commission to rent or lease public service privileges in such parks and to provide for the disposal of revenues received therefrom; making an appropriation and providing a tax to meet the same.

MCLA 318.3 Michigan state park commission; officers, employes; annual report and statement; disbursements. [MSA 13.1011]

MCLA 318.4 Same; supervision of lands; exception; transfer of control. [MSA 13.1012]

MCLA 318.5 Same; acquisition of parks, care; public service privileges; riparian lands; revenue; power to contract, accept deeds; liability of state. [MSA 13.1013]

MCLA 318.6 Same; property held in trust for state, tax exempt; investment by treasurer; state park fund. [MSA 13.1014]

MCLA 318.7 Same; open spaces, agreements with municipalities for care. [MSA 13.1015]

Sec. 7. Any municipality is hereby authorized to transfer the care and control of any open spaces owned or controlled by it to the state park commission upon such terms and for such periods as may be mutually agreed upon, or to enter into an agreement with said commission for the joint care or preservation of open spaces within or adjacent to such municipality, and said commission may in like manner transfer the care and control of any open spaces controlled by it to any local municipality upon such terms and for such periods as may be agreed upon.

MCLA 318.8 Same; rules; posting. [MSA 13.1016]

JOINT ACTION
Act No. 257, P.A. 1968 - Public Recreation Area

AN ACT to authorize the issuance of general obligation bonds of the state of Michigan and to pledge the full faith and credit of the state of Michigan for the payment of principal and interest thereon for public recreation facilities and grants, loans and advances to municipalities of the state for public recreation purposes and facilities; to provide for other matters relating to the bonds and the use of the proceeds of sale of the bonds; and to provide for the submission of the question of the issuance of the bonds to the electors of the state.

MCLA 318.351 Definitions. [MSA 13.1098(51)]

Sec. 1. As used in this act:
(a) "Municipality" or "municipalities" means and includes any county, city, village, township, school district, metropolitan district, port district, drainage district, authority, or other governmental authority, agency or department within or of the state with power to acquire, construct, improve or operate public recreation facilities.
(b) "Public recreation facilities" means and includes the acquisition of lands and the planning, acquisition, construction, equipping and developing of programs and facilities for parks, forest and wildlife areas, fisheries and other facilities used or useful for public recreational purposes hereafter authorized by law.

MCLA 318.352 Determination by legislature. [MSA 13.1098(52)]

Sec. 2. The legislature determines that it is essential for the public health, safety and welfare of the state and the residents *thereof to undertake a complete program of public recreation facilities and to make grants, loans and advances to political subdivisions of the state for such purposes.*

MCLA 318.353 Bonds; issuance, pledge, purpose.
[MSA 13.1098(53)]

MCLA 318.354 - 318.362 [MSA 13.1098(54) - 13.1098(62)]

Note: These sections deal with bond procedures.

JOINT ACTION
Act No. 108, P.A. 1969 - Public Recreation

AN ACT to implement the public recreation bond act by providing for grants, loans and advances from a part of the bond proceeds to local units of government, and for direct use of a part of the bond proceeds by the department of natural resources, in both cases for public recreational purposes.

MCLA 318.371 Definitions. [MSA 13.1098(71)]

MCLA 318.372 Public recreation fund, creation, source of funds.
[MSA 13.1098(72)]

MCLA 318.373 Bond revenues, allocation to local units and department of natural resources, uses. [MSA 13.1098(73)]

Sec. 3. (1) Thirty million dollars of the bond revenues shall be allocated to the local units to be used to initiate local community recreational projects to satisfy deficiencies in community recreational facilities and to provide facilities for future recreational needs as provided in this act.

(2) Seventy million dollars of the bond revenues shall be allocated to the department of natural resources to fund the state's recreation program.

MCLA 318.374 Division of allocation for local units (in 7 regions).
[MSA 13.1098(74)]

MCLA 318.375 Grants to local units, limitations; grant money not allocated to approved projects, disposition. [MSA 13.1098(75)]

MCLA 318.376 Applications for disbursement to local units, terms, conditions, and procedure. [MSA 13.1098(76)]

MCLA 318.377 Grant to local unit; application, approval, representative for unit; recreation plan; priorities. [MSA 13.1098(77)]

MCLA 318.378 Disbursements, form. [MSA 13.1098(78)]

MCLA 318.379 Costs; local, state, and federal portions; payment. [MSA 13.1098(79)]

MCLA 318.380 Financing local portion of costs, loans, advances, interest, payments, security. [MSA 13.1098(80)]

MCLA 318.381 Failure to reasonably progress with approved project, revocation of approval. [MSA 13.1098(81)]

MCLA 318.382 Pre-requisites for disbursement; use not specified in application; availability to general public. [MSA 13.1098(82)]

MCLA 318.383 Records, requirement, access. [MSA 13.1098(83)]

MCLA 318.384 Allocation of funds; reports to legislature. [MSA 13.1098(84)]

MCLA 318.385 Annual status report to legislature and governor. [MSA 13.1098(85)]

MCLA 318.386 Rules. [MSA 13.1098(86)]

MCLA 318.387 Effective date; full implementation date, uncommitted funds, funds subsequently received. [MSA 13.1098(87)]

Sec. 17. This act shall become effective September 1, 1969, and the department shall exert all reasonable efforts to fully implement it within 5 years thereafter. ...

JOINT ACTION
Act No. 326, P.A. 1965 - (State) **Recreation Division**

AN ACT to establish a state recreation division in the department of conservation; to provide technical and advisory services in the development and promotion of recreation programs; to encourage the constructive use of leisure time; to prescribe its powers and duties.

MCLA 299.121 Recreation and cultural arts section; establishment.
MSA 13.1097(1)

MCLA 299.122 Head of section; qualifications. MSA 13.1097(2)

MCLA 299.123 Technical advice and guidance; collection and dissemination of information; duty of section. MSA 13.1097(3)

Sec. 3. The ... section shall provide technical advice and guidance to the political subdivisions of this state and other interested groups and agencies in the planning and development of recreation programs, areas and facilities including but not limited to creative and cultural activities, and programs for senior citizens, the handicapped and the culturally deprived. ...

MCLA 299.125 Advisory committee; appointment, compensation, duties. MSA 13.1097(5)

MCLA 299.126 Existing employees; reassignment. MSA 13.1097(6)

MCLA 299.127 Rules and regulations; promulgation by commission. MSA 13.1097(7)

JOINT ACTION
Act No. 316, P.A. 1965 - Outdoor Recreation

AN ACT to authorize participation by this state and its subdivisions in programs of federal assistance relating to the planning and development of outdoor recreation resources and facilities; and to prescribe the functions of the department of conservation related thereto.

MCLA 299.111 Comprehensive plan, outdoor recreation.
MSA 13.1098(1)

MCLA 299.112 Federal aid programs. MSA 13.1098(2)

Sec. 2. ... In connection with obtaining the benefits of any such program, the department ... shall coordinate its activities with and represent the interests of all agencies and subdivisions of the state having interests in the planning, development and maintenance of outdoor recreation resources and facilities.

MCLA 299.113 Same; federal land and water conservation fund. [MSA 13.1098(3)]

Sec. 3. Grants-in-aid received from the federal land and water conservation fund act shall be deposited in the state treasury and disbursed to agencies and subdivisions of the state upon authorization of the department of conservation. Such apportionments of federal funds received on or before June 30, 1968, shall be made available in the ratio of 50 per centum for state projects and 50 per centum for projects proposed by subdivisions of the state, but the director of the ... department ... may vary said percentages by not more than 10 points either way to meet the current relative needs for recreational lands and facilities as indicated by the comprehensive recreational plan. In the apportionment of funds to subdivisions ... the director ... shall give special consideration to those ... where population density and land and facility needs are greatest.

MCLA 299.114 Same; appropriations; contracts on behalf of state subdivisions. [MSA 13.1098(4)]

Sec. 4. ... such areas and facilities shall be publicly maintained for outdoor recreation purposes. The department ... may enter into and administer agreements with the United States or any appropriate agency thereof for planning, acquisition and development projects involving participating federal-aid funds on behalf of any subdivision of this state, if such subdivision gives necessary assurances ... that it has available sufficient funds to meet its share, if any, of the cost of the project and that the acquired or developed areas will be operated and maintained at the expense of the subdivision for public outdoor recreation use.

MCLA 299.115 Effective date. [MSA 13.1098(5)]

MCLA 299.116 Same; state-appropriated assistance to subdivisions; guidelines and limits on state payments. [MSA 13.1098(6)]

Sec. 6. The department ... is authorized to disburse state appropriated grants-in-aid to political subdivisions of the state to be used in conjunction with P.L. 88-578 which provide financial assistance for outdoor recreation. ...

JOINT ACTION
Act No. 4, P.A. 1921, 2nd Ex. Sess. - Municipal Appropriations (for State Parks)

AN ACT authorizing and empowering counties, cities, and other municipalities to appropriate money for the support, maintenance and improvement of certain state owned parks and zoological grounds; and to authorize such municipalities to contract with the state with respect to the control, management, improvement and up-keep of the same.

MCLA 318.51 State owned parks; appropriations by municipalities. MSA 13.1031

Sec. 1. The board of supervisors of each county, and the legislative body of each city, village and township, are hereby authorized and empowered to appropriate, out of the general or contingent funds ... such sum or sums of money as may by such legislative body be deemed advisable, for the purpose of contributing towards the support, maintenance, up-keep and improvement of any state-owned park or zoological gardens or grounds. ...

MCLA 318.52 Acceptance of gifts by commission; maintenance; contracts. MSA 13.1032

MCLA 318.53 Scope of act; regulation of state parks. MSA 13.1033

MCLA 318.54 Declaration of necessity. MSA 13.1034

Act No. 212, P.A. 1915 - Gifts, Grants and Devises

AN ACT to authorize the public domain commission to accept and receive gifts, grants and devises of real property in trust for the state.

817

MCLA 318.41 Gifts of realty for public parks; supervision.
[MSA 13.1021]

Sec. 1. The public domain commission is hereby authorized to receive and accept gifts, grants and devises of real property which shall by any deed of gift, grant or by will become vested in the state for public park purposes. All such lands shall be under the care and supervision of the public domain commission and it shall be their duty to preserve the property thereon.

Act No. 150, P.A. 1970 - Natural Beauty Roads

AN ACT to designate certain roads as Michigan natural beauty roads; to provide certain powers and duties; and to provide for the development of guidelines and procedures.

MCLA 247.381 - 247.385 [MSA 9.195(61) - 9.195(65)]

Note: For a more complete citation, see the section on Highway Beautification in the chapter on Highways, Roads and Bridges.

JOINT ACTION
Act No. 217, P.A. 1931 - Municipal Forests

AN ACT to provide for the establishment and maintenance of county, township, city, village and school district forests; to provide for commissions to supervise such work; to provide for the sale of state lands for such purposes; and to provide a limitation on the expense of such work.

MCLA 320.201 Definitions. [MSA 13.281]

MCLA 320.202 Municipality; right to carry on forestry. [MSA 13.282]

Sec. 2. Any municipality may acquire by purchase, gift or devise, or may provide lands already in its possession, and use such lands for forestry purposes, either within or without the territorial limits of such municipality, and may carry on forestry on such lands. Any municipality may also receive and expend or hold in trust gifts of money or personalty for forestry purposes.

818

MCLA 320.203 Same; forestry commission, membership, term, vacancy. [MSA 13.283]

Sec. 3. The legislative body ... may appoint a forestry commission ... of 3 members, only 1 of whom shall be a member of the legislative body making such appointment. The members of such commission shall ... Any vacancy shall be filled by appointment by the legislative body at any regular session.

MCLA 320.204 Forestry commission; powers and duties. [MSA 13.284]

MCLA 320.205 Same; reports. [MSA 13.285]

MCLA 320.206 Director of conservation; power to sell certain state lands, reversion. [MSA 13.286]

MCLA 320.207 Cooperation between forestry commissions and department. [MSA 13.287]

MCLA 320.208 Appropriation for forestry purposes, limitation. [MSA 13.288]

Sec. 8. The legislative body ... may appropriate money ... (for) the purposes of this act: Provided, That where such legislative body desires to spend an amount in excess of 1/10 mill per dollar assessed valuation and/or in excess of 5,000 dollars in any 1 year for the purposes of this act, such sum shall not be appropriated unless the electors ... shall agree thereto at any general or special election, by a 3/5 vote.

MCLA 320.209 Accounting. [MSA 13.289]

MCLA 320.210 Special forestry fund; formula for payments in lieu of taxes. [MSA 13.290]

Sec. 10. Any income from forest lands shall be paid into the general fund of the municipality and may be set up in a special forestry fund ... A forestry commission and the townships and school districts in which its municipal forest lies by agreement shall determine a formula under which the commission shall make payments to the townships and school districts in lieu of general property taxes which would otherwise be levied against such lands and forests comprising the municipal forest.

Act No. 86, P.A. 1917 - Private Forestry

AN ACT to encourage private forestry, care and management thereof and to provide for exemption from taxation of such private forest reserves, and to repeal all acts or parts of acts inconsistent with the provisions of this act.

MCLA 320.271 Private forest reservations; proportion of acreage. MSA 13.201

MCLA 320.272 Same; tree quota per acre. MSA 13.202

MCLA 320.273 Same; spacing of trees. MSA 13.203

MCLA 320.274 Same; pasturage. MSA 13.204

MCLA 320.275 Same; maintenance of stock of forest trees. MSA 13.205

MCLA 320.276 Same; restocking. MSA 13.206

MCLA 320.277 Same; varieties of forest trees. MSA 13.207

MCLA 320.278 Same; record of county treasurer; description certified to assessor. MSA 13.208

MCLA 320.279 Same; duty of assessor; oath of owner. MSA 13.209

Sec. 9. It shall be the duty of the supervisor or assessor in each township to keep a record of all private forest reservations within his township as certified to him by the treasurer of said county, and he shall require the owner or his agent to subscribe under oath the extent and description of the land selected as private forest reservation and that the number of trees is as required by this act and that he will maintain the same according to the intent of this act.

MCLA 320.280 Same; form of application and contract. MSA 13.210

MCLA 320.281 Same; examination by assessor; exemption; timber license, fee. ⌈MSA 13.21⌉

Sec. 11. It shall be the duty of the supervisor or assessor to personally examine the various private reservations when the real estate is assessed for taxation, and to ...(extensive responsibilities)...

Act No. 175, P.A. 1903 - Forestry Reserve

AN ACT to create a forestry reserve, to provide for its maintenance, management and regulation, by restoring for sale or homestead entry, lands heretofore reserved in certain counties in this state, to make an appropriation therefor, and to provide for a tax to meet the same.

MCLA 320.101 Forest reserve; creation, location, investigation, control by forest commission; reforestation. ⌈MSA 13.17⌉

MCLA 320.102 - 320.103 ⌈MSA 13.172 - 13.173⌉

MCLA 320.104 Forestry reserve lands; tax assessment; payment by state. ⌈MSA 13.174⌉

MCLA 320.106 Reserve lands, law applicable; short title. ⌈MSA 13.175⌉

MCLA 320.107 Restoration of certain lands (in Roscommon and Crawford counties) **for sale or entry.** ⌈MSA 13.176⌉

Act No. 94, P.A. 1925 - Commercial Forest Reserves

AN ACT to provide for the establishment of commercial forests and for the administration and taxation of them.

MCLA 320.301 Commercial forests, establishment, maintenance, rules, expenses. ⌈MSA 13.221⌉

MCLA 320.301a Intent of act. ⌈MSA 13.221(1)⌉

MCLA 320.302 Definition of commercial forest. ⌈MSA 13.222⌉

MCLA 320.303 Determination and listing as a commercial forest, application (to department of natural resources), **contents, oath, forms.** [MSA 13.223]

MCLA 320.304 Character of land offered, grounds for determination; hearing, date, place, notice; report of determination; application and approval, recording. [MSA 13.224]

MCLA 320.305 Ad valorem general property tax exemption; specific tax, assessment, collection, tax sales, equalization, proceeds. [MSA 13.225]

Sec. 5. Lands ... shall not thereafter be subject to the ad valorem general property tax except as to such taxes as may have been previously levied, but shall be subject to an annual specific tax of 15 cents per acre. The supervisor of the township shall remove from the list of land descriptions assessed and taxed under the ad valorem general property tax the land descriptions certified to him by the department as being commercial forests and shall enter such land descriptions on a roll separate from lands assessed and taxed the ad valorem general property tax and shall spread against such commercial forest lands the specific tax hereinbefore provided, and the township treasurer shall collect such specific tax at the same time and in the same manner as ad valorem general property taxes are collected and subject to the same collection charges. ...

MCLA 320.306 Acres determined and listed, certification; payment of state funds to county, acreage as basis, distribution. [MSA 13.226]

MCLA 320.307 Withdrawal of land; application; fees, disposition; ad valorem general property tax, applicability. [MSA 13.227]

MCLA 320.308 Permits to cut forest products; authorization; applications, contents, verification; issuance; amendments; necessity; stumpage rates, protests, hearings. [MSA 13.228]

MCLA 320.309 Report as to quantity of forest products cut, certification, submission, contents, time; yield or stumpage tax, imposition, rate, unscaled products, disposition of proceeds. [MSA 13.229]

MCLA 320.310 Use lands listed as commercial forests.
[MSA 13.230]

MCLA 320.311 Applications and statements under oath.
[MSA 13.231]

MCLA 320.312 Period for harvesting forest products under permit, extension, shortening, revocation. [MSA 13.232]

MCLA 320.312a Transfers of title to lands listed as commercial forests, effect. [MSA 13.233]

MCLA 320.313 Declassification of land listed as commercial forest, grounds, notice, hearing, fees, taxation. [MSA 13.234]

MCLA 320.313a New laws, lands affected; withdrawal, fees.
[MSA 13.235]

MCLA 320.313b Appeal to circuit court; procedure; interviewers; order. [MSA 13.236]

MCLA 320.313c Conservation department representatives; right of entry on forest lands; access to books and papers. [MSA 13.237]

MCLA 320.314 Penalty. [MSA 13.238]

Act No. 329, P.A. 1969 - Forest Protection and Forest Fires

AN ACT to provide for the protection of forests and forest values in the exercise of the police powers of this state; to assign the responsibility for the prevention and suppression of fires on or endangering forests; to regulate the use of fires; to provide penalties for violation of any of the provisions of this act or any rules adopted thereunder; and to repeal certain acts and parts of acts.

MCLA 320.21 Definitions. [MSA 13.267(1)]

MCLA 320.23 Duties of director; assistants, appointment.
[MSA 13.267(3)]

MCLA 320.24 Burning permits, necessity; conditions as to burning. [MSA 13.267(4)]

MCLA 320.25 Prohibited acts. [MSA 13.267(5)]

MCLA 320.26 Refuse disposal facilities, devices, conditions, rules. [MSA 13.267(6)]

Sec. 6. Any municipality ... maintaining or operating a refuse disposal facility shall provide such devices and conditions as will promote the safe operation and guard against the escape of fire. ... Nothing in this act shall be construed as giving the director authority to allow burning of garbage and refuse disposal facilities contrary to Act No. 87 of the Public Acts of 1965, being sections 325.291 to 325.298 [MSA 14.435(1) TO 13.435(8)] of the Compiled Laws of 1948.

MCLA 320.27 Locomotives and other rolling stock, spark arresters; railroad rights-of-way, clearing; persons liable. [MSA 13.267(7)]

Sec. 7. ... A railroad shall keep its right of way cleared ... to a distance of 50 feet on each side of the center of the track. ...

MCLA 320.28 Forest or grass fires, liability. [MSA 13.267(8)]

Sec. 8. Any person, who in violating any provision of this act, causes a forest or grass fire, is liable for all damages resulting therefrom, including the cost of any governmental unit fighting the fire. ...

MCLA 320.29 Extreme fire hazard, governor's proclamation as to use of fire, prohibited acts. [MSA 13.267(9)]

MCLA 320.30 Emergency assistance; persons subject to call, compensation, penalty for refusal. [MSA 13.267(10)]

Sec. 10. The director or anyone appointed by him may call to his assistance in emergencies any ...

MCLA 320.31 Fire suppression expenses, persons liable, determination and collection of claim, actions, venue, limitation of actions. [MSA 13.267(11)]

MCLA 320.32 Wilfully, maliciously, or wantonly setting or causing fire. [MSA 13.267(12)]

MCLA 320.33 Entry based on reasonable belief as to violations, right, exceptions. [MSA 13.267(13)]

MCLA 320.34 Violations, penalties. [MSA 13.267(14)]

MCLA 320.35 Administration of act, rules, investigations, surveys; other law enforcement agencies, powers; local ordinances and regulations. [MSA 13.267(15)]

Sec. 15.   The director shall administer this act and shall adopt rules necessary to implement this act.   The director may make, conduct or participate in any investigations and surveys designed to establish the cause of a responsibility for a particular forest fire or forest fire conditions generally.   Nothing in this act shall be construed to limit or otherwise impair the jurisdiction or powers of any other department, agency or officer of this state, to investigate, apprehend and prosecute violators of this law nor to obviate local ordinances or to prevent enactment of local regulations which are as restrictive or more restrictive than this act.

MCLA 320.36 Rules, adoption. [MSA 13.267(16)]

MCLA 320.37 Forest fire control, assistance agreements; federal, interstate; personnel training, compensation, other employee benefits. [MSA 13.267(17)]

MCLA 320.38 Repeal. [MSA 13.267(18)]

Act No. 35, P.A. 1955 - Slash Disposal Law

AN ACT to provide for the abatement of forest fire hazards and better protection against the spread of forest fires; to provide for the reduction of fire hazards resulting from right-of-way clearance and maintenance of public roads, telephone, telegraph, and other communication lines, power lines, oil and gas lines, railroads, that are common carriers, or any other utility; to provide a penalty for a violation of any of the provisions of this act; to provide for the disposal of fire hazards from such clearings and maintenance and collection of costs of such disposal; to authorize an action for damages by the owner of property damaged; and to repeal certain acts and parts of acts.

MCLA 320.41 Short title. [MSA 13.270(1)]

MCLA 320.42 Forest cuttings, slash and debris; disposal. [MSA 13.270(2)]

MCLA 320.43 Same; public utilities. [MSA 13.270(3)]

MCLA 320.44 Same; time for disposal, permit for burning. [MSA 13.270(4)]

MCLA 320.45 Same; disposal by director of conservation, reimbursement. [MSA 13.270(5)]

MCLA 320.46   Penalty for violation; civil liability to property owner. [MSA 13.270(6)]

MCLA 320.47 Rules, regulations and specifications. [MSA 13.270(7)]

MCLA 320.48 Repeal. [MSA 13.270(8)]

R.S. 1846, c. 45 - Firing of Woods and Prairies

MCLA 320.392 Assistance by inhabitant in fighting wood or prairie fire; duty of certain public officers to order. [MSA 28.141]

Sec. 2. Whenever the woods and prairies in any township shall be on fire, so as to endanger property, it shall be the duty of the ... supervisor ... of such township ... to order such, and so many of the inhabitants of such township, liable to work on the highways, and residing in the vicinity of the place where such fire shall be, as ...(the supervisor)... shall severally deem necessary, to repair to the place where such fire shall prevail, and there to assist in extinguishing the same, or in stopping its progress.

MCLA 320.393 Same; failure to comply with order; penalty. [MSA 28.142]

Sec. 3. If any person shall refuse or wilfully neglect to comply with such order, he shall forfeit a sum not less than 5, nor more than 50 dollars.

MCLA 320.394 Forest fire prevention; regulation by township board. MSA 28.143

Sec. 4. The township boards of the several townships of this state are hereby authorized and it shall be their duty to prohibit the setting of forest fires or fires for the purpose of clearing lands, and disposing by burning, of refuse material and waste matter within their respective jurisdictions, whenever, in the judgment of a majority of the members of each of said boards, it shall be deemed necessary to prevent the spreading of such fires over the territory of such township, or any part thereof. Each of such boards may make such rules and regulations as they may deem proper for the purpose of carrying this act into effect, which rules and regulations shall be published by posting notices thereof, together with a copy of this act, in 5 of the most public places in such township.

MCLA 320.396 Same; notice to adjoining landowner before starting fire; failure to notify as evidence of negligence. MSA 28.144

The township board acts as the township park commission in all matters regarding parks and recreation until such time as it may receive a petition signed by fifty freeholders of the township. The board at its first meeting thereafter must submit the question of establishing a separate park commission to the qualified electors at the next regular election. If the proposal is approved at that election, the township board then appoints a six-member park commission. Each of the six continues in office until the next township election, at which time two persons are elected for a term of two years, two for four years and two for six years. At each succeeding election, two members are elected for a term of six years.

Act No. 271, P.A. 1931 - Township Park Commission

AN ACT to provide for the acquisition, maintenance, management and control of township parks and places of recreation; to prescribe the powers and duties of the township board in respect thereto; to provide for the creation of a township park commission, and the election, com-

pensation, powers and duties of the members thereof; and to provide for the issuance of bonds and/or the levy of taxes therefor.

MCLA 41.441 Township park commissions; appointment, election, terms. [MSA 5.271]

Sec. 1. On receipt of a written petition signed by 50 free-holders and taxpayers of any township ..., the township board ..., at its first meeting after the receipt of such petition shall submit the question of establishing a township park commission to the registered and qualified electors ... at the next regular election ... If a majority of the electors voting on the question vote in favor of establishing a park commission, the township board shall appoint a township park commission of 6 members, such members to serve until the next biennial township election. At such biennial township election 2 members of such commission shall be elected for a term of 2 years, 2 members for a term of 4 years and 2 members for a term of 6 years, and at each succeeding biennial township election 2 members of such commission shall be elected for a term of 6 years.

MCLA 41.442 Same; acquisition of land; other powers. [MSA 5.272]

MCLA 41.443 Same; compensation and expenses, clerical assistance. [MSA 5.273]

Sec. 3. The members of the township park commission shall receive compensation as fixed by the township board and 10 cents per mile traveling expenses to and from commission meetings. The commission may employ such clerical assistance and incur such other expenses as shall be necessary to carry out the provisions of this act. The compensation and expenses shall be paid from the park maintenance fund hereinafter provided for, or from the township general fund.

MCLA 41.444 Budget, tax, expenditures. [MSA 5.274]

Sec. 4. The township park commission shall submit to the township board at its annual meeting a detailed budget covering ..., such budget not to exceed 1 and 1/2 mill on the assessed valuation of such township. The township board shall ...

MCLA 41.445 Bonds for parks and places of recreation; procedure.
MSA 5.275

Sec. 5.   *The township park commission shall be authorized to submit to the voters of the township at the annual township meeting the question of the issuance of township bonds, the proceeds of which shall be used in the acquisition of lands for township parks and places of recreation.   A 3/5 majority vote of the qualified voters voting thereon shall authorize the issuance of such township bonds.   The issuance ... shall be governed by the provisions of Act No. 202 of the Public Acts of 1943, as amended* (**MCLA 131.1 et seq** MSA 5.3188(1)): *Provided, That where the township, at the time of such annual meeting, has no outstanding indebtedness, bonded or otherwise, and where the amount of the total proposed acquisition cost is less than 1 per cent of the assessed valuation of the township, the voters of the township may, at such annual meeting, authorize and direct the township park commission to purchase or condemn, as the case may be, designated lands for township parks and places of recreation and may, in such case, direct the township board to pay annually to the township park commission such available portions of contingent funds of the township as may be necessary to pay for such acquisition of lands: Provided further, That the voters of the township shall, in such case and at such annual meeting, determine the maximum amount to be paid for such lands and shall also prescribe, where acquisition is made by purchase instead of condemnation, the terms of payment thereof.*

MCLA 41.445a Sale and conveyance of property not needed.
MSA 5.275(1)

MCLA 41.446 Annual report of township park commission.
MSA 5.276

Sec. 6.   *... to the township board and board of state auditors, ... to be filed at the time of the annual meeting of the township board and to be in such form and shall contain such information as the board of state auditors shall direct.*

JOINT ACTION
Act No. 157, P.A. 1905 - Township Parks

AN ACT to authorize a township or townships to ac-

quire by gift or devise real estate and to own and control the same for a public park, resort, bathing beach or other place of recreation; to provide for a board of commissioners therefor and to authorize said township or townships, by a limited tax on the property in such township or townships, to maintain such park or resort and to make rules and regulations for the control and government of the same.

MCLA 41.421 Township parks; board of commissioners; condemnation. [MSA 5.2441]

MCLA 41.422 Same; rules and regulations; leases; liquor; admission charges. [MSA 5.2442]

MCLA 41.423 Board officers, election, duties; treasurer's bond. [MSA 5.2443]

MCLA 41.424 Acquisition plan; disbursements; referendum; adoption, record. [MSA 5.2444]

MCLA 41.425 Tax exempt. [MSA 5.2445]

JOINT ACTION
Act No. 307, P.A. 1941 - Township Park, City or Village Appropriation

AN ACT authorizing cities and other municipalities to appropriate money for the acquisition, support, maintenance and improvement of sites acquired by townships for use as township parks and places of recreation, including bathing beaches.

MCLA 41.461 Township park, right of city or village to appropriate for. [MSA 5.2446]

JOINT ACTION
Act No. 300, P.A. 1939 - Township Parks (to County)

AN ACT to authorize township boards to transfer to county park trustees the title to, or to arrange with county park trustees to improve, maintain, manage and control any lands held for park purposes by any township, in-

cluding all public places vested in any township by virtue of the dedication of any plat duly approved and recorded according to law.

MCLA 41.431 Township parks; conveyance to board of county park trustees or arrangement for maintenance by board. [MSA 5.2438]

Sec. 1. ... the township board ... is hereby authorized to transfer and convey to the board of county park trustees of any county in which said township is located the title to any lands held by such township for park purposes, including ...

Note: Townships should be aware of county prerogatives in the area of recreational facilities.

JOINT ACTION
Act No. 261, P.A. 1965 - County Parks

AN ACT to authorize the creation and to prescribe the powers and duties of county and regional parks and recreation commissions; and to prescribe the powers and duties of county boards of supervisors with respect thereto.

MCLA 46.351 County parks and recreation commission; composition, appointments, vacancies, rules and regulations.
[MSA 5.570(101)]

MCLA 46.352 Regional parks and recreation commission; composition, appointments, vacancies, compensation. [MSA 5.570(102)]

MCLA 46.353 County and regional commissions; officers, elections, treasurer; quorum; bylaws; contracts. [MSA 5.570(103)]

MCLA 46.354 County commission; provision for expenses in annual budget. [MSA 5.570(104)]

MCLA 46.355 Boards of supervisors; provision of funds, commission to present budget. [MSA 5.570(105)]

Sec. 5. ... each county included in a region shall provide funds for ... (its) operations by an appropriation from the general fund of the county, or by a tax levy ... authorized by ...

MCLA 46.356 County and regional commissions; study of facilities and needs. [MSA 5.570(106)]

MCLA 46.357 Same; filing of land ownership records, land acquisition proposals, and development plans. [MSA 5.570(107)]

MCLA 46.358 Same; acquisition of property, consideration of features. [MSA 5.570(108)]

MCLA 46.359 Same; taking of private property. [MSA 5.570(109)]

MCLA 46.359a County and regional commissions; taking of property in another county. [MSA 5.570(109A)]

MCLA 46.360 Same; acceptance of gifts, bequests, grants-in-aid, contributions, and appropriations. [MSA 5.570(110)]

MCLA 46.361 Same; development and operation of facilities. [MSA 5.570(111)]

MCLA 46.362 Same; custody and management of property acquired. [MSA 5.570(112)]

MCLA 46.363 Same; installation and maintenance of roads and parking facilities. [MSA 5.570(113)]

MCLA 46.364 Same; promulgation and amendment of rules; effective date of rules; misdemeanor; park rangers; police services. [MSA 5.570(114)]

Sec. 14. ... (5) A county or regional commission may contract with townships, ... for police services required under this section...

MCLA 46.365 Same; collection of fees, payment to county, uses. [MSA 5.570(115)]

MCLA 46.366 Same; employment of personnel, authorization. [MSA 5.570(116)]

MCLA 46.367 Financing planning, acquisition, construction, and renewal; borrowing money; bonds. [MSA 5.570(117)]

JOINT ACTION
Act No. 287, P.A. 1919 - Hanson Military Reservation

AN ACT to authorize the use of the Hanson Military Reservation by the state, or any municipal subdivision thereof, as a recreational ground; to regulate such use, and to provide an appropriation.

MCLA 32.231 Hanson Military Reservation; recreational uses; control. [MSA 4.791]

MCLA 32.232 Same; use; director, compensation. [MSA 4.792]

Sec. 2. ... under the direction of the state department of health ...

MCLA 32.233 Same; fresh air camps; erection of buildings, etc. [MSA 4.793]

Sec. 3. Any ... township ... desiring to establish fresh air camps or to use such grounds for any other recreational or health giving purpose, may by making application to said board, be assigned space on said grounds for such purpose: Provided, however, That no camps, lodges, cottages or other buildings shall be erected thereon without permission for such erection being granted by the state military board.

MCLA 32.234 Same; water and lights furnished by state. [MSA 4.794]

MCLA 32.235 Same; expense of camps; state may furnish tentage, etc. [MSA 4.795]

Sec. 5. All expense ... shall be borne by the ... municipality ...: Provided, however, That the state military board in its discretion may place at the disposal of such ... municipality any available buildings, tentage or other military stores owned by the state and in the possession of such board.

833

MCLA 32.236 Same; appropriation; revolving fund; initial expense; refund. [MSA 4.796]

JOINT ACTION
Act No. 172, P.A. 1913 - Crawford County Land

AN ACT authorizing the acceptance by the state of a certain tract of land in Crawford county on certain conditions; providing for its control and management when so accepted; making an appropriation for the purpose of making improvements thereon; and providing for payments in lieu of taxes on certain state lands in the counties of Crawford, Kalkaska and Otsego.

MCLA 32.221 Authority of military board to accept certain lands for state. [MSA 4.781]

MCLA 32.222 Same; description. [MSA 4.782]

MCLA 32.223 Same; uses; abandonment; reversion to donors; removal of buildings and timber. [MSA 4.783]

Sec. 3. The said tract of land shall be used for the following purposes: ... For the establishment of fresh air camps, or for other recreational or health giving purposes by any ... township. ...

MCLA 32.223a - 32.225 [MSA 4.783(1) - 4.786]

MCLA 32.226 Military lands; payment from legislative appropriations in lieu of taxes. [MSA 4.786(1)]

JOINT ACTION
Act No. 156, P.A. 1917 - Recreation and Play-grounds

AN ACT authorizing cities, villages, counties, townships and school districts to operate systems of public recreation and playgrounds.

MCLA 123.51 Public recreation system; powers of municipality. [MSA 5.2421]

Sec. 1. Any ... township may operate a system of public recreation and playgrounds; acquire, equip and maintain land, buildings or other recreational facilities; employ a superintendent of recreation and assistants; vote and expend funds for the operation of such system.

MCLA 123.52 Same; powers of school district. MSA 5.2422

MCLA 123.53 Same; operation. MSA 5.2423

Sec. 3. Any city, village, county, township or school district may operate such a system independently or they may co-operate in its conduct in any manner in which they may mutually agree; or they may delegate the operation of the system to a recreation board created by any or all of them, and appropriate money, voted for this purpose, to such board.

MCLA 123.54 Same; location. MSA 5.2424

Sec. 4. Any municipal corporation or board given charge of the recreation system is authorized to conduct its activities on (1) property under its custody and management; (2) other public property, under the custody of other municipal corporations or boards, with the consent of such corporations or boards; (3) private property, with the consent of the owners.

JOINT ACTION
Act No. 90, P.A. 1913 - Parks, Zoological Gardens and Airports

AN ACT authorizing and empowering the boards of supervisors of counties to purchase, acquire by condemnation, accept gifts and devises of real estate for, and to improve and maintain public parks and zoological gardens, airports and landing fields, and to contribute to the improvement and maintenance of public parks and public zoological gardens, airports and landing fields, owned or held in trust by cities, villages or townships or used for the benefit of the public; to authorize the making of reasonable rules and regulations relative to the public use of park property; and to provide penalties for violations of such rules and regulations.

MCLA 123.61 County park, zoological garden or airport; land, acquisition, appropriation. [MSA 5.2431]

MCLA 123.62 Same; appropriation for improvement and maintenance. [MSA 5.2432]

MCLA 123.63 Same; owned or held in trust. [MSA 5.2433]

Sec. 3. It shall be lawful for, and the several boards of supervisors are hereby authorized and empowered to make appropriations by way of contributing toward the improvement and maintenance of any such public parks, public zoological gardens, airports and landing fields, either owned or held in trust by any township ...

MCLA 123.64 Same; county tax. [MSA 5.2434]

MCLA 123.65 Powers construed; boulevards. [MSA 5.2435]

Sec. 5. ... shall be deemed to include boulevards or highways or streets laid out as boulevards and owned or held in trust by the municipalities aforesaid.

MCLA 123.66 County park trustees; board of county road commissioners; rules and regulations, resolution, publication; report to board of supervisors. [MSA 5.2436]

MCLA 123.66a County airport committee; appointment, powers, organization. [MSA 5.2436(1)]

MCLA 123.67 Funds, payment to local treasurer; misapplication penalty. [MSA 5.2437]

MCLA 123.68 Penalty for violation of rules and regulations. [MSA 5.2437(1)]

JOINT ACTION
Act No. 147, P.A. 1939 - Huron-Clinton Metropolitan Authority

AN ACT to provide for the incorporation of the Huron-Clinton metropolitan authority; to permit the counties of

Wayne, Washtenaw, Livingston, Oakland, and Macomb, or certain of such counties, to join in a metropolitan district for planning, promoting, and/or for acquiring, constructing, owning, developing, maintaining and operating, either within or without their limits, parks, connecting drives, and/or limited access highways; to provide for the assessment, levy, collection and return of taxes therefor; to provide for the issuance of revenue bonds; to authorize condemnation proceedings; and to provide a referendum thereon.

MCLA 119.51 Huron-Clinton metropolitan authority; incorporation, counties. [MSA 5.2148(1)]

MCLA 119.52 Definitions. [MSA 5.2148(2)]

MCLA 119.53 Powers; co-operation; charges; succession to rights; vote. [MSA 5.2148(3)]

Sec. 3. The Huron-Clinton metropolitan authority, either acting alone or in cooperation with the department of conservation, the state highway department, any board of county road commissioners, or any federal or other state or local body having authority to construct and maintain parks or highways, shall have the power to ...

MCLA 119.54 Board of commissioners; election and appointment, term. [MSA 5.2148(4)]

MCLA 119.55 Same; meetings; organization; employes. [MSA 5.2148(5)]

MCLA 119.56 Same; records; accounts; treasurer's bond. [MSA 5.2148(6)]

MCLA 119.57 Same; levy of tax, procedure. [MSA 5.2148(7)]

MCLA 119.58 Revenue bonds, issuance; lien. [MSA 5.2148(8)]

MCLA 119.59 Property, purchase, by gift or devise; condemnation, procedure. [MSA 5.2148(9)]

MCLA 119.60 Referendum. [MSA 5.2148(10)]

MCLA 119.61 Same; approval by 2 or more counties; resubmission; governing body. [MSA 5.2148(11)]

JOINT ACTION
Act No. 280, P.A. 1969 - Public Parks and Recreation Areas

AN ACT to prohibit vandalism in state or publicly owned parks and recreation areas; to provide penalties; and to provide for recovery of damages.

MCLA 318.251 Vandalism, prohibition. [MSA 13.1064(1)]

Sec. 1. It is unlawful to destroy, damage or remove any tree, shrub, wildflower or other vegetation, or to destroy, damage, deface or remove any state or publicly owned property in any state or public park or recreation area.

MCLA 318.252 Penalty. [MSA 13.1064(2)]

MCLA 318.253 Reimbursement by vandals; triple damages; judgments, joint, parents; collection. [MSA 13.1064(3)]

MCLA 318.254 Disposition of reimbursement collected. [MSA 13.1064(4)]

MCLA 318.255 Municipal ordinances, penalties, triple damages. [MSA 13.1064(5)]

Sec. 5. ... townships ... may adopt ordinances imposing penalties and providing for the collection of triple damages against any person convicted of an act of vandalism in a park or recreation area owned and operated by the ... township ...

JOINT ACTION
Act No. 58, P.A. 1959 - Control of Swimmers' Itch

AN ACT to authorize the water resources commission to supervise the chemical treatment of certain waters of the state for the control of swimmers' itch; to provide for the lawful use of copper and other chemicals for the purpose; and to provide penalties for the violation of this act.

MCLA 323.221 Chemical treatments; suppression of swimmers' itch; experiments; rules and regulations. [MSA 3.533(11)]

MCLA 323.222 Same; copper, application (is lawful). [MSA 3.533(12)]

MCLA 323.223 Same; permits. [MSA 3.533(13)]

MCLA 323.224 Same; conduct, safeguards. [MSA 3.533(14)]

Sec. 4. ... The commission may provide permits ... where applicants provide at their own expense chemicals and other equipment and services called for in the rules and regulations adopted by the commission.

MCLA 323.225 Same; violation, penalty. [MSA 3.533(15)]

JOINT ACTION
Act No. 230, P.A. 1966 - Public Swimming Pools, Construction and Operation

AN ACT to protect the public health; to place responsibility on the department of public health for supervising the construction and the healthful and safe operation of public swimming pools; to provide for the issuance of construction and operation permits; to authorize rules and regulations to carry out the intent of the act; and to provide penalties and remedies.

MCLA 325.601 Public swimming pools defined; exemptions from act. [MSA 14.447(1)]

MCLA 325.602 Review of design; supervision of construction and operation. [MSA 14.447(2)]

MCLA 325.603 Supervisory and visitorial power. [MSA 14.447(3)]

Sec. 3. The department of public health has supervisory ...

MCLA 325.604 Entry on premises; inspection. [MSA 14.447(4)]

MCLA 325.605 Rules and regulations. [MSA 14.447(5)]

MCLA 325.606 Submission of plans and specifications to department; fees; permit. [MSA 14.447(6)]

Sec. 6. (1) All municipal and private corporations, ...

(2) Nothing in this act nor any action of the department of public health shall relieve the applicant or owner of a public swimming pool from responsibility for securing any building permits or complying with all applicable local codes, regulations or ordinances not in conflict with this act. Compliance with an approved plan shall not authorize the owner constructing or operating a public swimming pool to create or maintain a nuisance or a hazard to health or safety.

MCLA 325.607 Contents of plans and specifications.
[MSA 14.447(7)]

MCLA 325.608 Examination of plans and specifications; issuance or denial of permit for construction; amendments; duration of permit.
[MSA 14.447(8)]

MCLA 325.609 Written approval of changes. [MSA 14.447(9)]

MCLA 325.610 Operation permit; display; expiration; renewal; consent to transfer; fee. [MSA 14.447(10)]

MCLA 325.611 Existing installations; permit without payment of initial operation fee; renewal. [MSA 14.447(11)]

MCLA 325.612 Operation without permit prohibited.
[MSA 14.447(12)]

MCLA 325.613 Notice of reasons for not issuing operation permit.
[MSA 14.447(13)]

MCLA 325.614 Periodic inspections. [MSA 14.447(14)]

MCLA 325.615 Revocation of permit; hearing; reissuance.
[MSA 14.447(15)]

MCLA 325.616 Reports to department. [MSA 14.447(16)]

MCLA 325.617 Order to prohibit use of pool. [MSA 14.447(17)]

840

MCLA 325.618 Payments to city, county and district health departments. [MSA 14.447(18)]

MCLA 325.619 Violation; penalties; prosecution. [MSA 14.447(19)]

MCLA 325.620 Effective date (January 1, 1967). [MSA 14.447(20)]

JOINT ACTION
Act No. 218, P.A. 1967 - Public Bathing Beaches

AN ACT to protect the public health by providing for the supervision and control of bathing beaches open to the public; to prescribe the functions of health agencies; to authorize the establishment of rules for sanitation standards; and to provide penalties for violation of this act.

MCLA 325.631 Water, testing; unsafe water, injunctive and other court relief. [MSA 14.447(101)]

MCLA 325.632 Cooperation between public health department and municipalities. [MSA 14.447(102)]

MCLA 325.633 Minimum sanitation standards, rules; conformance with official state standards. [MSA 14.447(103)]

MCLA 325.634 Penalty for violations. [MSA 14.447(104)]

MCLA 325.635 Authority to enact local regulations.
[MSA 14.447(105)]

Sec. 5. Nothing in this act shall change the authority of local boards of health or health committees or boards of supervisors to enact local regulations in accordance with Act No. 306 of the Public Acts of 1927, as amended (**MCLA 327.201 to 327.208a** [MSA 14.161 TO 14.169]).

JOINT ACTION
Act No. 199, P.A. 1929 - Community Center

AN ACT to authorize and empower villages and townships of this state having a population not exceeding 10,000 inhabitants, to levy a tax for the maintenance or the purchase of lands and maintenance of property for a community center for the benefit of the public, provided the question of such purchase or maintenance, or both purchase and maintenance, as the case may be, is submitted to the duly qualified voters of such villages or townships and is adopted by a majority vote of those participating in said election.

MCLA 123.41 Referendum. [MSA 5.2381]

Sec. 1. The township board ... upon petition of 10 per centum of the qualified voters ... shall submit the question to the people ...

MCLA 123.42 Community center; annual tax levy, credit. [MSA 5.2382]

Sec. 2. ... the legislative body ... is authorized and empowered to levy an annual tax not exceeding 2 mills ... for a community center for the benefit of the public. The said tax shall ...

MCLA 123.43 Same; board of directors, vacancies. [MSA 5.2383]

Sec. 3. After any ... township shall have voted to establish a community center the governing body ... shall appoint 6 directors which shall ... (and) shall receive no compensation as such. Vacancies ...

MCLA 123.44 Board of directors; powers, duties. [MSA 5.2384]

Sec. 4. ... shall on or before the first day of September ... prepare an estimate of the amount of money necessary for the ... ensuing year, and report ...

MCLA 123.45 User of community center. [MSA 5.2385]

Sec. 5. Every community center ... shall be free to the use of the inhabitants where located, always subject to such reasonable rules and regulations as the community board may adopt; ...

MCLA 123.46 Relinquishment of control power by legislative body. [MSA 5.2386]

Sec. 6. ... after a petition signed by 10 per centum of the qualified voters ...

Act No. 97, P.A. 1919 - Recreation Halls in Townships

AN ACT to provide for the issuing of permits by the township board for the conducting of public billiard and pool rooms, dance halls, bowling alleys and soft drink emporiums outside of incorporated cities and villages.

MCLA 41.531 Annual permit for recreation halls. [MSA 18.51 1]

Sec. 1. ... annual permit ... from the township board ...

MCLA 41.532 Same; revocation. [MSA 18.51 2]

MCLA 41.533 Definitions. [MSA 18.51 3]

MCLA 41.534 Penalty. [MSA 18.51 4]

MCLA 41.535 Exceptions. [MSA 18.51 5]

Act No. 53, P.A. 1921 - Recreation Halls in Townships

AN ACT to regulate the establishment, maintenance and conducting of public billiard and pool rooms, dance-halls, bowling alleys and soft-drink emporiums outside of incorporated cities and villages; to provide for the issuance of permits for such places; to prescribe the powers and duties of township boards with relation thereto; and to prescribe the penalty for violation of the provisions hereof.

MCLA 41.501 Recreation hall operating permit; qualifications of grantee. [MSA 18.49 1]

Sec. 1. No public billiard or pool room, dance hall or bowling alley shall be established, maintained or conducted in any place within this state outside of an incorporated village or city, by any person or corporation without first obtaining a permit to operate such place from the township board of the township wherein such

843

place is established or proposed to be operated or established. No person shall be granted a permit ... who is ...

MCLA 41.502 Same; application, contents, fee; management change. [MSA 18.492]

MCLA 41.503 Same; granting; form. [MSA 18.493]

MCLA 41.504   Same; renewal; transferability. [MSA 18.494]

MCLA 41.504a Same; causes for revocation; proceedings. [MSA 18.495]

MCLA 41.505 Powers not abrogated. [MSA 18.496]

Sec. 5. Nothing in this act ... shall be construed as lessening or abrogating the general powers of townships in respect of the regulation and control of places of amusement therein, nor in respect of their general licensing powers as defined by law; nor their general powers of providing by ordinance for the protection of the health and safety of the people thereof.

MCLA 41.506 Penalty. [MSA 18.497]

MCLA 41.507 Exemption of lodges and churches; prosecution. [MSA 18.498]

Act No. 162, P.A. 1915 - Recreation Halls in Townships

AN ACT to provide for the issuing of permits by the township board for the conducting of billiard and pool rooms and bowling alleys outside of incorporated cities and villages.

MCLA 41.541 Annual permit; pool rooms, bowling alleys. [MSA 18.521]

MCLA 41.542 Penalty. [MSA 18.522]

MCLA 41.543 Exceptions. [MSA 18.523]

Act No. 140, P.A. 1963 - Billiard and Pool Rooms

AN ACT to authorize township boards to fix by ordinance the hours of operation of billiard and pool rooms; and to repeal certain acts and parts of acts.

MCLA 41.561 Billiard and pool rooms in townships; hours. MSA 18.499(1)

MCLA 41.562 Repeal. MSA 18.499(2)

Act No. 171, P.A. 1970 - Campgrounds

AN ACT to license and regulate campgrounds; to prescribe the functions of the department of public health; and to provide penalties for violations.

MCLA 325.651 Definitions. MSA 14.447(121)

MCLA 325.652 Construction, alteration, or development of campground; construction permit; necessity; application, submission, contents; state campgrounds. MSA 14.447(122)

MCLA 325.653 Campground license, necessity, applications, submission, contents, fee, term, state campgrounds. MSA 14.447(123)

MCLA 325.654 Facilities, adequacy as prerequisite to approval of license application. MSA 14.447(124)

MCLA 325.655 Issuance of license; display; denial of application, notice, statement of reasons, reconsideration, hearing, appeal. MSA 14.447(125)

MCLA 325.656 Transfers of campground licenses. MSA 14.447(126)

MCLA 325.657 Sanitation and safety, rules. MSA 14.447(127)

MCLA 325.658 Noncompliance with act or rule; notice; specifications; time for compliance; revocation of license, hearing, notice, charges, decision, appeal. MSA 14.447(128)

MCLA 325.659 Advisory committee, purpose, membership, appointment, qualifications, terms. [MSA 14.447(129)]

MCLA 325.660 Inspections and enforcement, access to campgrounds. [MSA 14.447(130)]

MCLA 325.661 Children's camps; housing for seasonal agricultural workers; health officers, enforcement of sanitary controls. [MSA 14.447(131)]

MCLA 325.662 Building permits; ordinances; codes; other regulations. [MSA 14.447(132)]

MCLA 325.663 Violations, penalty. [MSA 14.447(133)]

MCLA 325.664 Injunctive relief. [MSA 14.447(134)]

MCLA 325.665 Effective date. [MSA 14.447(135)]

Note: The campground act does not relieve a person from the provisions of any township ordinance not in conflict with the act. Township zoning and/or building codes would be important in this regard.

Act No. 75, P.A. 1952 - Registration of Persons in Camps, Tourist Homes, etc.

AN ACT to provide for the registration of persons in camps, tourist homes, tourist rooms, cabins, house trailer camps and other sleeping accommodations for transients; and to provide penalties for violation of the provisions of this act.

MCLA 125.781 Registration of persons in camps, tourist homes, etc.; definitions. [MSA 18.1241]

Sec. 1. (a) "Camp"... (b) "Tourist home"... (c) "Tourist room"... (d) "Cabin"... (e) "House trailer camp"...

MCLA 125.782 Register, contents. [MSA 18.1242]

Sec. 2. ... The register shall be available at all times for in-spection by law enforcement officers for a period of not less than 3 years. ...

MCLA 125.783 Misdemeanor. [MSA 18.1243]

MCLA 125.784 Enactment under police power. [MSA 18.1244]

JOINT ACTION
Act No. 48, P.A. 1952 - Registration and Regulation of Campers

AN ACT to require the posting of a registration card by any person or persons camping upon certain state-owned lands; to require the cleaning up of such camp sites; to prescribe penalties for the violation of the pro-visions of this act; and to repeal certain acts and parts of acts.

MCLA 322.601 Camp registration card, posting required; "to camp" defined. [MSA 13.1396(1)]

MCLA 322.602 Duty to obtain and execute card; contents, posting. [MSA 13.1396(2)]

MCLA 322.603 Disposal of rubbish and other articles upon break-ing camp. [MSA 13.1396(3)]

MCLA 322.604 Same; printing and distribution. [MSA 13.1396(4)]

MCLA 322.605 Enforcement (by any peace officer). [MSA 13.1396(5)]

MCLA 322.606 Penalty. [MSA 13.1396(6)]

MCLA 322.607 State park, camp ground, or recreation area admin-istered by department of conservation, exception. [MSA 13.1396(7)]

JOINT ACTION
R.S. 1846, c. 49 - Municipal Police Regulations

MCLA 431.201 Exhibitions; licensing, regulations. [MSA 18.471]

Sec. 1. The township board of any township ... may at any meeting held for that purpose, license theatrical exhibitions, public shows, and such other exhibitions as they deem proper, to which admission is obtained on payment of money, upon such terms and conditions as they shall think reasonable, and may regulate the same in such manner as they shall think necessary for the preservation of order and decorum, and to prevent any danger to the public peace; but no such license shall be in force for a longer time than the officers granting the same shall have been elected to office.

MCLA 431.202 Theatrical exhibitions, public shows, etc.; operating without license, violation deemed separate offense, penalty. MSA 18.472

Act No. 205, P.A. 1939 - Boxing, Sparring and Wrestling Exhibitions

AN ACT to create the Michigan state athletic board of control, for the regulation, control and supervision of boxing, sparring or wrestling exhibitions within this state; to provide for the licensing, taxation, supervision and control of such exhibitions; to prescribe the penalties for the violation of the provisions hereof and to repeal all acts and parts of acts inconsistent with the provisions of this act.

MCLA 431.101 Michigan state athletic board of control; membership. MSA 18.422(1)

MCLA 431.102 - 431.117 MSA 18.422(2) - 18.422(17)

MCLA 431.118 Buildings used for boxing matches; health and fire requirements; compliance with statutes and ordinances. MSA 18.422(18)

MCLA 431.119 - 431.123 MSA 18.422(19) - 18.422(23)

MCLA 431.124 Smoking prohibited; responsibility of promoter; grounds for cancellation of license. MSA 18.422(24)

MCLA 431.125 Gambling prohibited; grounds for cancellation of license. MSA 18.422(25)

MCLA 431.126 Violations, penalty. [MSA 18.422(26)]

JOINT ACTION
Act No. 27, P.A. 1959 - Racing Law of 1959

AN ACT to provide for, regulate and license the conducting of race meetings in this state; to create the office of racing commissioner; to prescribe his powers and duties; to provide for the issuance of track licenses, race meeting licenses and occupational licenses; to provide for the disposition of the fees derived therefrom; to legalize and permit the pari-mutuel method of wagering on the results of races at licensed race meetings in this state; to appropriate the funds derived therefrom; to render inapplicable all acts or parts of acts in conflict herewith; to provide penalties for the violation thereof; and to repeal certain acts and parts of acts.

MCLA 431.31 - 431.39 [MSA 18.966(1) - 18.966(9)]

MCLA 431.40 Statement of receipts, etc.; remittance to state; political contributions; unlicensed events. Licensee's statement of receipts, expenses, disbursements. Remittance to state. Contributions to political parties; revocation of license. Unlicensed horse racing for a stake. [MSA 18.966(10)]

MCLA 431.41 - 431.42 [MSA 18.966(11) - 18.966(12)]

MCLA 431.43 Racing commissioner's receipts; distribution of revenue. [MSA 18.966(13)]

Sec. 13. (1) **Credit to general fund.** *...* *(2)* **Distribution of revenues; municipalities.** *Twenty percent of the revenues received, but not to exceed $600,000.00, from racing license fees from any track shall be returned to the ... township in which the track is located. If the ... township ... has reached the limitation as to amount imposed by the preceding sentence, in addition to such revenues 20% of the revenues received not to exceed $100,000.00, from racing license fees from any meet held before April 16 and after November 15 in any year shall be returned to the ... township ... If the track is located in more than 1 city or township, then the* *revenue shall be divided equally between* (them)... *(3)* **Same; fairs, Michigan bred standardbred harness horses.** ... *(4)* **Same; Michigan bred horses, thoroughbred racing revenue.** ... *(5)* **Same; stadium and parking and other facilities.** *A sum equal to not more than 2%, but not to exceed $2,500,000.00, of the principal amount of bonds issued for a stadium and appurtenant parking and other facilities by an authority organized pursuant to state law before December 1, 1971, from the revenue received from thoroughbred and harness racing shall be returned to a county in or adjoining which a licensed track is located or to a city in such a county, if that county or city has obligated itself to pay more than 1/2 of the annual rental for a stadium and appurtenant parking and other facilities for the conduct of sporting events, exhibitions and other general recreational purposes. ...*

MCLA 431.43a Police, fire, and traffic protection; reports by local governmental units. [MSA 18.966(13A)]

MCLA 431.44 License fees; percentage of wagers; breaks; return of fees. [MSA 18.966(14)]

MCLA 431.45 - 431.53 [MSA 18.966(15) - 18.966(23)]

MCLA 431.54 Political subdivisions not to assess excise or license tax or fee. [MSA 18.966(24)]

Sec. 24. No excise or license tax or fee shall be assessed or collected from any licensee under this act by any political subdivision of the state.

MCLA 431.55 Penal code, application. [MSA 18.966(25)]

MCLA 431.56 Repeal. [MSA 18.966(26)]

JOINT ACTION
Act No. 90, P.A. 1951 - Racing Meets

AN ACT to regulate the conducting of racing meets in the state of Michigan; to provide for the possession, control and disposition of funds held by licensees for the payment of outstanding winning tickets not claimed or demanded by the lawful owners of such funds; and to pre-

scribe penalties for violations of the provisions of this act.

MCLA 431.251 Unclaimed funds held by racing track licensees; past winners. [MSA 18.967(1)]

MCLA 431.252 Same; future winners. [MSA 18.967(2)]

MCLA 431.253 Cashed winning tickets; delivery to racing commissioner. [MSA 18.967(3)]

MCLA 431.254 Delivery of funds and reports relieves from liability, exception. [MSA 18.967(4)]

MCLA 431.255 Funds and receipts delivered to state board of escheats. [MSA 18.967(5)]

MCLA 431.256 Duty of state board of escheats. [MSA 18.967(6)]

MCLA 431.257 Violations, penalty. [MSA 18.967(7)]

Act No. 239, P.A. 1972 - Lotteries

AN ACT to establish and operate a state lottery; to create a bureau of state lottery; to prescribe its powers and duties; to license and regulate sales agents; to provide for an appropriation; and to provide penalties.

MCLA 432.1 Short title. [MSA 18.969(1)]

MCLA 432.3 - 432.18 [MSA 18.969(3) - 18.969(18)]

MCLA 432.19 Personnel, employment; assistance from other governmental subdivisions. [MSA 18.969(19)]

Sec. 19. (1) ... (2) The departments, boards, commissions or other governmental subdivisions of this state shall provide assistance to the bureau upon the bureau's request.

MCLA 432.20 [MSA 18.969(20)]

MCLA 432.23 Licensing of lottery ticket sales agents, person act-

ing exclusively as agent; licenses, issuance factors, assignments, transfers, sales premises, temporary, display, suspension, or revocation; person defined; bonds. [MSA 18.969(23)]

MCLA 432.25 - 432.27 [MSA 18.969(25) - 18.969(27)]

MCLA 432.29 Sales or gifts to persons under 18; violations, penalty. [MSA 18.969(29)]

MCLA 432.30 - 432.33 [MSA 18.969(30) - 18.969(33)]

MCLA 432.34 Tax exemption, proceeds from prize. [MSA 18.969(34)]

Sec. 34. No state or local taxes of any kind whatsoever shall be imposed upon the proceeds from a prize awarded by the state lottery.

MCLA 432.35 Lottery ticket sales proceeds; depositories, designation, services; reports. [MSA 18.969(35)]

MCLA 432.37 Inapplicability of other laws providing penalties or disabilities regarding lotteries. [MSA 18.969(37)]

Sec. 37. Any other law providing any penalty or disability for the sale of lottery tickets or any acts done in connection with a lottery shall not apply to the sale of tickets or shares performed pursuant to this act.

MCLA 432.39 - 432.47 [MSA 18.969(39) - 18.969(47)]

Note: Township officials are advised to consult with the township attorney and/or the county prosecuting attorney before proceeding with the sale of lottery tickets in any township building used for the storage, maintenance and preservation of public records, in view of the statutory provision that such records may not be kept in any place where, among other things, games of chance (including lotteries) take place. Further, proceeds of lottery ticket sales must be maintained in a separate account and not commingled with other township funds. Once sales commissions have been reimbursed to the township by the state, of course, they can be placed in the general fund.

Act No. 382, P.A. 1972 - Bingo

AN ACT to license and regulate the conducting of bingo; and to provide penalties.

MCLA 432.101 Short title. [MSA 18.969(101)]

MCLA 432.102 Definitions. [MSA 18.969(102)]

MCLA 432.103 Definitions. [MSA 18.969(103)]

MCLA 432.104 Application for license to conduct bingo, submission, form, contents. [MSA 18.969(104)]

MCLA 432.105 Issuance of license, grounds, fee, annual reissuance; license, term, number, location, transfer. [MSA 18.969(105)]

MCLA 432.106 Contents and display of license. [MSA 18.969(106)]

MCLA 432.107 Special licenses, application, fee, grounds for issuance; special licenses, contents, term, number, transfer. [MSA 18.969(107)]

MCLA 432.108 Proceeds of fees collected, disposition. [MSA 18.969(108)]

MCLA 432.109 Proceeds of bingo games, disposition. [MSA 18.969(109)]

MCLA 432.110 Management or operation of bingo, members of licensee, compensation, equipment, number of games played, prizes, advertisement. [MSA 18.969(110)]

MCLA 432.111 Taxation, prize. [MSA 18.969(111)]

Sec. 11. State or local taxes of any kind whatsoever shall not be imposed upon any prize awarded by a licensee during a bingo game conducted in conformity with this act.

MCLA 432.112 Enforcement and supervision of administration of act, bureau, personnel, rules; equipment suppliers, licenses; fee. [MSA 18.969(112)]

MCLA 432.113 Rules, promulgation, necessity, purpose, temporary.
[MSA 18.969(113)]

MCLA 432.114 Records of licensees, necessity, inspection, audits; financial statement of receipts and expenses by a licensee, annual, charitable purpose; bingo operations, place, inspection.
[MSA 18.969(114)]

MCLA 432.115 Annual report by commissioner, necessity, contents.
[MSA 18.969(115)]

MCLA 432.116 Suspension or revocation of licenses, grounds, procedure; subpoenas, issuance, contempt. [MSA 18.969(116)]

MCLA 432.117 Violations, offense. [MSA 18.969(117)]

MCLA 432.118 Issuance or reissuance of license after revocation, forfeiture, or suspension; grounds for forfeiture; return of license upon suspension, revocation, or forfeiture; effect of suspension, revocation, or forfeiture. [MSA 18.969(118)]

MCLA 432.119 Applicability of other laws, penalties or disabilities. [MSA 18.969(119)]

Sec. 19. Any other law providing any penalty or disability upon a person who conducts or participates in bingo games, who sells or possesses equipment used in conducting bingo, who permits bingo to be conducted on his premises or who does other acts in connection with bingo shall not apply to such conduct when done pursuant to this act or rules promulgated hereunder.

MCLA 432.120 Effective date (April 1, 1973). [MSA 18.969(120)]

Note: Even though townships are permitted to sell lottery tickets, they are not permitted to conduct other games of chance, such as bingo. Nor should any township building used for the storage, maintenance and preservation of public records be rented to any organization for the conduct of such games because of the statutory provision that township records may not be kept in any place where games of chance take place.

JOINT ACTION
Act No. 207, P.A. 1923 - Acreage Limitation

AN ACT to limit the amount of real estate and the location thereof which can be acquired, held or occupied by any person, partnership, corporation or association for the preservation or propagation of game or fish or for certain sporting purposes.

MCLA 317.261   Limitation on acreage held for sporting purposes. MSA 13.1191

Sec. 1. It shall be unlawful ... for any person, partnership, corporation, or association to acquire, hold or occupy by purchase, lease or other evidence of title, possession or right of occupancy or to enclose by fences or other barriers in 1 tract an amount of real estate within this state exceeding 15,000 acres in extent for the purpose of the preservation or propagation of game or fish, or for use for yachting, hunting, boating, fishing, rowing or any other sporting purpose.

MCLA 317.262   Same; within 2 miles of other lands so held. MSA 13.1192

MCLA 317.263   Penalty. MSA 13.1193

JOINT ACTION
Act No. 159, P.A. 1967 - Hunting Area Control

AN ACT to promote safety in hunting activities; to provide for area closures to hunting and discharge of firearms; to establish a hunting area control committee and to prescribe its powers and duties; to prescribe the powers and duties of the department of conservation, the department of state police, the department of attorney general and the county sheriffs; and to prescribe penalties for violations of this act.

MCLA 317.331   Hunting area control committee, establishment, members, duties; state agency representatives, selection; committee chairman; department of conservation, duties; expenses. MSA 13.1397(101)

Sec. 1. (1) A hunting area control committee, composed of a representative of the department of conservation, ... the department of state police, the township supervisor, or if he declines to serve, a representative selected by the township board, and ... the sheriff's department of the respective counties involved is established and shall perform such duties as are authorized by this act.

MCLA 317.332 Powers of committee, area closures; hearings; investigations; studies; statement of facts; regulations.
[MSA 13.1397(102)]

MCLA 317.333 Submission of committee's findings and recommendations; approval or disapproval; ordinances; regulations; enforcement. [MSA 13.1397(103)]

Sec. 3. ... (2) Local and county law enforcement officers shall enforce ordinances enacted in accordance with this act. State enforcement officers will enforce regulations adopted and made a part of the administrative code in accordance with the provisions of this act.

MCLA 317.334 Closure notice signs, materials, form, placing, maintenance, spacing, publication of notice; rescission of closure.
[MSA 13.1397(104)]

MCLA 317.335 Exceptions to prohibitions against discharge of firearms. [MSA 13.1397(105)]

MCLA 317.336 Penalty. [MSA 13.1397(106)]

Act No. 230, P.A. 1897 - Summer Resort and Assembly Associations

AN ACT to provide for the formation of corporations for the purpose of owning, maintaining and improving lands and other property kept for the purposes of summer resorts or for ornament, recreation or amusement, and to repeal all laws or parts of laws in conflict herewith.

MCLA 455.1 Summer resort associations; incorporation, purposes.
[MSA 21.661]

Sec. 1. That any number of persons, not less than 5, desiring to form a corporation for the purpose of owning, maintaining and im-

proving lands and other property for the purposes of a summer resort or a park for ornament, recreation or amusement, in any ... township ... may, by articles or agreement in writing, under their hands and seals, associate for such purpose under the name to be assumed by them in their articles of association: Provided, That no 2 corporations shall assume the same name.

MCLA 455.2 - 455.18 [MSA 21.662 - 21.678]

MCLA 455.20 Map or plat of lands; record; evidence; streets and public places. [MSA 21.679]

MCLA 455.21 Same; ownership and sale of lots and shares; dissolution, disposition of lots; parks, etc., dedicated to public use. [MSA 21.680]

MCLA 455.22 - 455.24 [MSA 21.681 - 21.683]

Act No. 39, P.A. 1889 - Summer Resort and Assembly Associations

AN ACT to authorize the formation of corporations for the purchase and improvement of grounds to be occupied for summer homes, for camp-meetings, for meetings of assemblies or associations and societies organized for intellectual and scientific culture and for the promotion of the cause of religion and morality, or for any or all of such purposes.

MCLA 455.51 Summer resort and assembly associations; incorporation, purposes. [MSA 21.691]

MCLA 455.52 - 455.57 [MSA 21.692 - 21.697]

MCLA 455.58 Same; powers; control of streets. [MSA 21.698]

MCLA 455.59 - 455.60 [MSA 21.699 - 21.700]

MCLA 455.61 Marshal; compensation, removal, powers and responsibility. [MSA 21.701]

Sec. 11. The board of trustees may, for the preservation of

857

peace and good order, appoint a marshal, whose duties and compensation shall be fixed by such board ...

MCLA 455.62 Same; authority over person arrested. [MSA 21.702]

MCLA 455.63 Injury or destruction of property; penalty.
[MSA 21.703]

MCLA 455.64 Taxation. [MSA 21.704]

Sec. 14. The property of such corporation shall be subject to taxation, except all houses of public worship, and also all school buildings used exclusively for school purposes and the lot upon which they stand, and the furniture therein, which shall be exempt therefrom.

MCLA 455.65 Disposition of property; conflict of powers and duties.
[MSA 21.705]

MCLA 455.66 Assessment of association. [MSA 21.706]

Sec. 16. Whenever the board of trustees of any such association shall serve upon the assessing officer of the township ... in which its real estate is situated a notice in writing, signed by its secretary and under its corporate seal, requesting that all of the cottages and buildings owned by its lessees, situated upon the lands of the association, and not exempt from taxation as hereinbefore provided, be assessed to the association as a part of its real estate, the same as if owned by it, then and thereafter all such real estate and cottages, and buildings thereon, shall be assessed to such association as real estate and taxes paid thereon, by the association the same as if in fact the owner thereof, and no lease had been made.

MCLA 455.67 Same; collection from members. [MSA 21.707]

MCLA 455.68 (Association) **Board of assessors; election, term, vacancy.** [MSA 21.708]

MCLA 455.69 Assessment of members; report to trustees; interest; fees. [MSA 21.709]

MCLA 455.70 Same; additions and corrections by board of trustees. [MSA 21.710]

MCLA 455.71 Same; determination of majority of assessors, effect. [MSA 21.711]

MCLA 455.72 Highway assessments; expenditure. [MSA 21.712]

Act No. 134, P.A. 1905 - Summer Resort and Assembly Associations

AN ACT to authorize any corporation organized under Act No. 39 of the Public Acts of 1889, of this state, entitled "An act to authorize the formation of corporations for the purchase and improvement of grounds to be occupied for summer homes, for camp meetings, for meetings of assemblies or associations and societies organized for intellectual and scientific culture and for the promotion of the cause of religion and morality, or for any or all such purposes," to amend its articles of incorporation.

MCLA 455.91 Summer resort and assembly corporations; amendment of articles. [MSA 21.721]

Act No. 69, P.A. 1887 - Suburban Homestead, Villa Park and Summer Resort Associations

AN ACT to authorize the incorporation of suburban homestead, villa park and summer resort associations.

MCLA 455.101 Suburban homestead, villa park and summer resort associations; incorporation; purposes; corporate life; trustees; number, election. [MSA 21.731]

Sec. 1. That any number of persons, not less than 5, who shall desire to form an association for the purpose of purchasing, holding, improving and disposing of lands or lots for suburban homesteads or residences, or for a villa park or summer resort, may ... (do so)...

MCLA 455.102 - 455.107 [MSA 21.732 - 21.737]

MCLA 455.108 Lots and plots; plat prerequisite to sale.
MSA 21.738

MCLA 455.109 Same; tax assessment; sale for taxes, association as purchaser. MSA 21.739

Sec. 9. All lots or plots sold shall be assessed and taxed to the owners and holders thereof, ...

MCLA 455.110 - 455.113 MSA 21.740 - 21.743

Act No. 137, P.A. 1929 - Summer Resort Owners

AN ACT to authorize the formation of corporations by summer resort owners; to buy, improve, sell and lease lands; to exercise certain police powers over the lands owned by said corporation and within its jurisdiction, and to provide penalties for the violation of by-laws established under police powers.

MCLA 455.201 Summer resort owners; incorporation, purposes.
MSA 21.751

Sec. 1. That any number of freeholders, not less than 10, who may desire to form a summer resort owners corporation for the better welfare of said community and for the purchase and improvement of lands to be occupied for summer homes and summer resort purposes, may, with their associates and successors, become a body politic and corporate, under any name by them assumed ... in the manner herein provided.

MCLA 455.202 - 455.203 MSA 21.752 - 21.753

MCLA 455.204 Corporate powers; liabilities; ownership of land, limitation. MSA 21.754

MCLA 455.205 Sale and disposition of lands. MSA 21.755

MCLA 455.206 Membership; eligibility; jurisdiction of corporation over lands of nonmembers; election. MSA 21.756

MCLA 455.206a Notice of election and registration. MSA 21.756(1)

MCLA 455.206b Registration board; time. [MSA 21.756(2)]

MCLA 455.206c Voters; eligibility. [MSA 21.756(3)]

MCLA 455.206d Election board; polls, hours open. [MSA 21.756(4)]

MCLA 455.206e Adoption, record. [MSA 21.756(5)]

Sec. 6e. If a majority of the said qualified voters of the entire territory comprised in the territorial description contained in the notice of election shall vote in favor of the incorporation under this act, then the said board ...

MCLA 455.207 Grant of authority by members to corporation. [MSA 21.757]

MCLA 455.208 Annual meeting; trustees, election, report. [MSA 21.758]

MCLA 455.209 Board of trustees; officers, quorum, vacancy. [MSA 21.759]

MCLA 455.210 Same; powers. [MSA 21.760]

MCLA 455.211 Corporate jurisdiction; liability for condition of streets. [MSA 21.761]

Sec. 11. Such corporation, through its properly delegated officers, shall have jurisdiction over the lands owned by the corporation and over the lands owned by the members of said corporation for the exercise of the police powers herein conferred. The corporation shall have jurisdiction over the streets and highways passing through ...

MCLA 455.212 By-laws; power to enact. [MSA 21.762]

Sec. 12. The board of trustees shall have the authority to enact by-laws, subject to repeal or modification by the members at any regular or special meeting, calculated and designed to carry into effect ...

MCLA 455.213 Same; effective date, posting. [MSA 21.763]

MCLA 455.214 Same; violation, penalty. [MSA 21.764]

MCLA 455.215 Marshal; powers, compensation, removal.
[MSA 21.765]

Sec. 15. The board of trustees may appoint a marshal, whose duties shall be to enforce the by-laws of said corporation. ...

MCLA 455.216 Same; authority over person arrested. [MSA 21.766]

MCLA 455.217 Water and sewage systems, fire protection, electricity. [MSA 21.767]

Sec. 17. The corporation shall have authority to provide a water system for its members and occupants, a sewage system, fire protection and electric light service.

MCLA 455.218 Annexation to city. [MSA 21.768]

MCLA 455.219 Dues and assessments. [MSA 21.769]

MCLA 455.220 Expiration of term, cessation of jurisdiction.
[MSA 21.770]

Sec. 20. When a corporation, organized under this act, shall dissolve or its term of existence expires by limitation, all jurisdiction over streets, alleys and highways shall cease and the said streets, alleys and highways shall thereupon become dedicated to the use of the public, and in such case the lands of the members shall be cleared of all jurisdiction conferred by the provisions of this act.

Act No. 12, P.A. 1901 - Extension of Corporate Life

AN ACT to provide for an extension of the corporate life of summer resort associations, organized under the laws of the state, whose term of existence would otherwise expire, and to fix the duties and liabilities of such renewal corporations.

MCLA 455.251 Extension of corporate life; procedure, evidence, franchise fee. [MSA 21.781]

862

MCLA 455.252 Renewed corporation; rights and liabilities.
MSA 21.782

Act No. 55, P.A. 1911 - Reorganization of Corporations

AN ACT to provide for the reorganization of corporations for owning, maintaining and improving lands and other property kept for the purposes of summer resorts or for ornament, recreation or amusement, the term of existence of which has heretofore expired or may hereafter expire by limitation, and for the renewal of the corporate term and to fix the rights, duties and liabilities of such renewed corporation.

MCLA 455.281 Reorganization of certain corporations; procedure, evidence, franchise fee. MSA 21.791

MCLA 455.282 Reorganized corporation; rights and obligations.
MSA 21.792

MCLA 455.283 Time limit for reorganization. MSA 21.793

JOINT ACTION
Act No. 161, P.A. 1911 - Parks, Playgrounds, Drives and Boulevards

AN ACT to provide for the formation of corporations with power to acquire, control, own, maintain, improve and convey property for parks, playgrounds, drives and boulevards, and hold the same and the proceeds thereof in trust for municipalities and take private property therefor.

MCLA 455.301 Park, etc., association; incorporation, purposes.
MSA 21.801

Sec. 1. *Any number of persons, not less than 5, who shall desire to form a corporation for the purpose of acquiring, owning, controlling, maintaining and improving lands for the purposes of parks, playgrounds, drives and boulevards, or any 1 or more such purposes, and holding the same in trust for any 1 or more municipal corporations of this state, may, by articles of agreement in writing*

*under their hands and seals, associate for such purposes under a
name to be assumed by them in their articles of association: Provided, That no 2 corporations shall assume the same name.*

MCLA 455.302 - 455.304 [MSA 21.802 - 21.804]

**MCLA 455.305 Corporation not to have shares or be for profit;
directors, election, term, powers.** [MSA 21.805]

MCLA 455.306 Membership. [MSA 21.806]

MCLA 455.307 Powers of corporation; condemnation. [MSA 21.807]

*Sec. 7. Corporations organized under this act shall have power
to govern, manage, control, lay out and improve parks, playgrounds,
boulevards and pleasure drives over which their powers and jurisdiction extend, ...*

**MCLA 455.308 Transfer of realty of municipal corporation; revoca-
tion.** [MSA 21.808]

*Sec. 8. Any municipal corporation, by vote of its governing
body, may transfer to any such corporation in trust as hereinbefore
provided, ...*

MCLA 455.309 Aid from municipal corporation. [MSA 21.809]

*Sec. 9. It shall be lawful for any such municipal corporation to
appropriate, by a vote of its ... governing body, to any such corporation, moneys for the uses and purposes of such corporation.*

MCLA 455.310 Lands held in trust; free access; tax exemption.
[MSA 21.810]

MCLA 455.311 Trustees; appointment by court. [MSA 21.811]

MCLA 455.312 Vesting of property in municipality. [MSA 21.812]

MCLA 455.313 Construction of act. [MSA 21.813]

*Sec. 13. In all proceedings of suits that may arise or be
brought in any of the courts of this state touching or concerning*

corporations under this act, all other acts or parts of acts incon-
sistent herewith shall be interpreted and construed in such manner
as to give full force and effect to all the provisions of this act and
to all the rights and privileges hereby granted.

Act No. 123, P.A. 1929 - Passage of Fish Over Dams

AN ACT to confer power and authority upon the con-
servation commission to provide for the erection and main-
tenance of proper means for the free passage of fish
through and over dams now in existence or which shall
hereafter be erected across rivers, streams or creeks, and
to prohibit the obstruction of rivers, streams and creeks in
such manner as to prevent the free passage of fish up and
down; and to repeal Act No. 295 of the Public Acts of
1909, as amended by Act No. 26 of the Public Acts of
1921.

MCLA 307.1 Free passage of fish, rules; fish ladders.
MSA 13.1651

MCLA 307.2 Inspector of dams; duties; plan, contents, copies.
MSA 13.1652

MCLA 307.3 Same; compliance with order, time. MSA 13.1653

MCLA 307.4 Prosecutions; mandamus. MSA 13.1654

MCLA 307.5 Violations of act. MSA 13.1655

MCLA 307.6 Construction by director; expenses, payment; tax assessment. MSA 13.1656

Sec. 6. ... The board of supervisors ... shall ... order the su-
pervisor of the township ... in which said dam is situated to spread
the amount of such expense upon the assessment roll of such town-
ship ... as a tax against the property to which said dam is appur-
tenant and against the owners of such property to be collected in
the same manner as other township taxes and paid over to the coun-
ty treasurer or returned as delinquent in accordance with law.

MCLA 307.7 Passage of fish through and over dams; unlawful apparatus in rivers, streams or creeks; authority of director of conservation. [MSA 13.1657]

Act No. 350, P.A. 1865 - Contamination of Waters

AN ACT to protect fish and to preserve the fisheries of this state; and to prescribe penalties for violations of the provisions of this act.

MCLA 307.22 Refuse, disposal. [MSA 13.1672]

MCLA 307.28 Transient or non-resident license; fee; forfeiture; moneys, disposition. [MSA 13.1673]

MCLA 307.30 Unlawful dumping into waters; molesting of nets. [MSA 13.1674]

MCLA 307.31 Penalty. [MSA 13.1675]

MCLA 307.32 Unlawful acts; penalty; civil liability. [MSA 13.1676]

Act No. 121, P.A. 1891 - Hook and Line Fishing

AN ACT to secure to the people of the state of Michigan certain rights on any of the navigable or meandered waters of this state where fish have been or hereafter may be propagated, planted or spread at the expense of the people of this state or the United States.

MCLA 307.41 Lawful fishing with hook and line. [MSA 13.1681]

MCLA 307.42 Suits at law; defense. [MSA 13.1682]

Act No. 261, P.A. 1915 - Mussels

AN ACT to regulate the taking, catching or killing of mussels in any of the inland waters of this state, and to provide an open and closed season for taking same; to provide for the issuing of licenses and permits pertaining thereto and the disposition of the moneys derived there-

866

from, and to provide penalties for the violation of the provisions of this act.

MCLA 307.51 - 307.61 [MSA 13.1691 - 13.1701]

Act No. 14, P.A. 1923 - Fishing from Inland Waters

AN ACT to prohibit the taking of fish from the inland waters of this state where the public is excluded from taking fish therefrom and fish have been planted therein at public expense and to provide a penalty for violation of the provisions of this act.

MCLA 307.71 - 307.72 [MSA 13.1721 - 13.1722]

Act No. 84, P.A. 1929 - Commercial Fishing Law

AN ACT to protect fish and to preserve the fisheries of this state; to regulate the taking of fish in the waters of lakes Superior, Michigan, Huron, and Erie, and the bays thereof, and the connecting waters between the lakes within the jurisdiction of this state; to prescribe the powers and duties of the director of conservation; to provide for financial remuneration to this state for fish taken for commercial purposes and disposition of moneys derived therefrom; to provide for establishment of great lakes fishery advisory committee and prescribe its powers and duties; to regulate the transportation, sale and possession of fish in this state; to provide for the issuing of licenses and permits pertaining thereto and the disposition of the moneys derived therefrom; to provide for the confiscation of property used or possessed in violation of this act; and to provide penalties for the violations of the provisions of this act.

GENERAL PROVISIONS

MCLA 308.1 Fish, property of state. [MSA 13.1491]

MCLA 308.1a - 308.21 [MSA 13.1491(1) - 13.1512]

MCLA 308.22 - 308.27 [MSA 13.1513 - 13.1518]

SPECIAL PROVISIONS REGULATING
FISHING IN BAYS AND HARBORS

MCLA 308.29 - 308.30a [MSA 13.1519 - 13.1542(1)]

MCLA 308.31 Public docks or piers, use or setting of nets near, prohibited; exceptions. [MSA 13.1543]

Sec. 31. ... Public docks for the purpose of this act shall be held to include all docks except docks owned by individuals and used exclusively for their own boats: ...

MCLA 308.32 - 308.50 [MSA 13.1544 - 13.1564]

Act No. 196, P.A. 1957 - Game Fish in Private Waters

AN ACT to authorize and regulate the propagation and possession of game fish in private waters, or when lawfully procured from without this state; to regulate the use, transportation and sale of such game fish; to provide for the issuance of licenses and permits pertaining thereto and the disposition of the moneys derived therefrom; and to provide penalties for violations of this act; and to repeal certain acts and parts of acts.

MCLA 308.111 Game fish; definition. [MSA 13.1586(1)]

MCLA 308.112 Same; license for propagation for sale.
[MSA 13.1586(2)]

MCLA 308.113 - 308.119 [MSA 13.1586(3) - 13.1586(9)]

Act No. 105, P.A. 1951 - Signs Prohibiting Hunting, Fishing, or Trespassing

AN ACT regulating the erection of posters, signs and

placards on any state, public or privately owned lands;
and to prescribe penalties for violations of this act.

MCLA 752.821 Erection of posters, etc., on state, public or private lands without permission unlawful. [MSA 13.1484(1)]

MCLA 752.822 Prosecutions, time. [MSA 13.1484(2)]

MCLA 752.823 Enforcement and prosecutions. [MSA 13.1484(3)]

MCLA 752.824 Violations, penalty. [MSA 13.1484(4)]

MCLA 752.825 Resisting arrest. [MSA 13.1484(5)]

Act No. 63, P.A. 1885 - Board of Fish Commissioners

AN ACT to establish a state board of fish commissioners, and to repeal Act No. 124, Session Laws of 1873, Act No. 71, Session Laws of 1875, and Act No. 3, Session Laws of 1882.

MCLA 300.51 Board of fish commissioners; corporate powers.
[MSA 13.1311]

Sec. 1. ...(may take)... conveyances and leases of lands and tenements, ...

MCLA 300.52 Same; fish-breeding duties; property tax exempt; superintendent of fisheries, duties, salary; assistants. [MSA 13.1312]

Sec. 2. ... All property owned or leased by the fish commission shall be exempt from taxation **so long as held and used for state purposes under this act. ...**

MCLA 300.53 - 300.56 [MSA 13.1313 - 13.1316]

Act No. 285, P.A. 1927 - Trespassing by Fishermen and Hunters (and Snowmobilers)

AN ACT to regulate trespass upon any lands or within the limits of the right of way of any public highway ad-

joining or abutting upon such lands, and to prohibit the posting or enclosing of lands except by the owner or lessee of lands or by his authorized agents.

MCLA 317.161 Farm lands and wood lots; hunting or fishing club lands; private waters; fishing, hunting, posting or enclosing without consent prohibited; public highway, definition, possession or discharge of loaded firearm prohibited. MSA 13.1471

MCLA 317.161a Wrongful posting of restrictions; penalty. MSA 13.1471(1)

MCLA 317.161b Hunting without landowner's or lessee's consent, prerequisites to prohibition. MSA 13.1471(2)

MCLA 317.161c Snowmobiles, off road and all terrain vehicles, motorcycles, and motor-driven cycles; lights, entry upon premises, definitions. MSA 13.1471(3)

MCLA 317.162 Prosecutions, form, court, limitations. MSA 13.1472

MCLA 317.163 Enforcement by prosecuting attorneys. MSA 13.1473

MCLA 317.164 Penalty. MSA 13.1474

MCLA 317.165 Unlawful to resist officer. MSA 13.1475

Act No. 230, P.A. 1925 - Regulatory Powers (Conservation)

AN ACT to provide for the better protection and preservation of fish, game and fur-bearing animals and game birds, protected by the laws of this state; to provide a method by which the taking or killing thereof may be regulated and the open season for the taking or killing thereof suspended or abridged in any designated waters or area of this state; to provide for special fisheries research and regulations therefor; to provide a penalty for the violation thereof, and to repeal Act No. 9 of the Public Acts of 1917, as amended by Act No. 156 of the Public Acts of 1921.

MCLA 300.1 Fish, game or birds; regulatory powers of commission.
[MSA 13.1211]

MCLA 300.2 Definitions. [MSA 13.1212]

Sec. 2. As used in this act:

(a) "Waters" means any single or individual inland lake, stream, river, pond or other single or individual body of water including the great lakes and connecting waters or any part or portion thereof, and any and all chains, systems or combinations of the same, in any township or townships, county or counties, within this state and in which any species of fish or waterfowl are protected by the laws of this state.

(b) "Area" means the whole of the state and the whole or any designated portion of any township or townships, county or counties within the state.

MCLA 300.3 Conservation commission orders protecting fish, game or birds; change in open seasons, contents, filing, publication, seal; fisheries research; experimental game management areas.
[MSA 13.1213]

MCLA 300.4 Same; rescission or modification, procedure; exception. [MSA 13.1214]

MCLA 300.5 Misdemeanor; penalty. [MSA 13.1215]

Chapter VIII

PLANNING AND ZONING

Believing that local government does a very poor job with zoning, and planning, federal and state government agencies, along with environmentalists and ecologists, are determined that there will be centralized land use legislation and several plans are being considered now. They say that townships in particular often lack money, know-how and even desire to do anything about the ills that a burgeoning population has brought to land use in Michigan. Zoning too often is a reaction to the effects of development, whereas it should be an attempt to foresee what the future may hold and then make adequate provisions for it.

Regulatory power over land use, for townships, begins with Act No. 144, P.A. 1969 – Codification and Publication of Ordinances (see the section on Ordinances in the chapter on Services, Utilities, Contracts and Ordinances). Authority for planning is found in Act No. 231, P.A. 1931 and Act No. 168, P.A. 1969; and for zoning in Act No. 184, P.A. 1934––all cited in this chapter. These important tools should be thoroughly studied by township officials.

All it takes is a simple resolution on the part of the township board, declaring its intent to adopt a zoning ordinance, then appointment of a zoning board of not less than four nor more than seven members. If a more sophisticated program is desired because of size, degree of development, etc., a township may use the Planning Commission Act, which also is implemented by a resolution of intent. A planning commission has not less than seven nor more than nine members.

872

Government officials need to be aware of modern trends and open to public opinion. A major problem of recent development is that "mini-subdivisions" are springing up because the platting process is considered by many to be time consuming and costly, both to builders and buyers. The law permits an owner to sell four small parcels split off of each large parcel without platting. However, in time these plats will have all the sewage, water and road problems of the big subdivisions, but because of their size and intervening distances, costs will be prohibitive. Also requirements too often are established that provide only for large lots and big homes, or apartment buildings with units of spacious size, in spite of the fact that many people don't want a big home and a big yard to care for or pay for.

Township officials must redouble their efforts to bring about sound, practical land use through good local planning and zoning. They can no longer kid themselves with such negative excuses as "We can't do it," "We're too small to do it," "We don't have the facilities to do it," "Let the city folks do it." What usually happens is that the city folks do—and take the township tax base in order to do it. Furthermore, neighboring governments may have conflicting development plans—there must be more concern with over—all needs and cooperation. The state and federal governments can and will move in and take over if we don't do it.

There are numerous statutes permitting two or more units of government to join together to perform a service or function which is necessary, required or desired by people at the local level. Not the least of these is adequate land use through good planning and zoning, along with provision of necessary services and utilities. An umbrella-type tool may be utilized for a regional concept to guarantee adequate zoning and land use in an area greater than the township. This is done by creating a zoning authority, commission, district or region, to include two or more units of government.

Although this text often emphasizes the many opportunities available for townships to join with other units of government to accomplish various goals, MTA's long-standing policy has been to advocate the regional concept only so long as there is no surrender of political integrity. Regionalism is a fine thing providing it starts on a voluntary basis and continues with total participation and control by local government through representation of the regional board. It should also be pointed out that most local government officials, including those who have formulated basic MTA policy, are perfectly willing and glad to accept guidelines and meaningful standards from state or federal agencies and officials, but are not willing to relinquish local control in matters as important as land use. Most of us feel that local government is more than adequate for the task. We should emphasize here, too, that local government means city, village, township and county——we must stand together to stave off centralization.

The **Handbook Of Michigan Township Zoning And Planning** (written by William R. McTaggart, M.D., B.B.A.; edited by John H. Bauckham, MTA Legal Counsel; and published by the MTA in 1970, with a cumulative supplement in 1972) should be in the hands of every township board member, as well as members of planning commissions, zoning boards and any others who have a part in the administration and enforcement of zoning ordinances.

It is imperative that an attorney be retained to provide competent, professional guidance through the necessary steps to insure that the ordinance complies with and accurately reflects the intent of the particular act being used. Too many times has a township lost litigation over its zoning ordinance because an error was made when it was written or in the way it was adopted. An attorney can help you avoid these pitfalls and will be able to provide a court with legal justification if there is litigation over some of its terms. It is never too early to consult with an attorney versed in real estate and land use.

Finally, and perhaps most importantly, the township board seeks to get citizens to come together and work cooperatively for the growth and development of not only their own township but the neighboring areas as well. As important as legal know-how is, the greatest tangible assets which can be brought to bear on township affairs are the logic, reasoning, common sense and desire to do what is best for a community on the part of concerned citizens.

SUBDIVISION CONTROL

A home usually represents a lifetime of planning and work. It is perhaps the single most important and most expensive item a family will ever own. Therefore the owner needs to know that the land upon which the home will be located has been properly laid out, identified and recorded.

Until 1967 Michigan operated under a very inadequate statute, the Plat Act of 1929, which made it practically impossible for local units of government to satisfactorily regulate the development of subdivisions and plats. The Subdivision Control Act now provides the necessary tools to accomplish this task.

Of utmost importance is a good preliminary plat review. It is at this point that most communities fall into error and commit blunders which eventually lead to litigation. We are, therefore, pointing out some of the pitfalls.

Of prime importance is that lot sizes conform to zoning ordinance requirements, or if there is no local zoning ordinance, that they are (in accordance with state law) at least sixty-five feet wide and 12,000 square feet in area. It is necessary to be sure that the developer's plan conforms to all provisions in the subdivision control ordinance, as well as to any higher standards which may be established by the municipality regarding such things as the installation of sidewalks, curbs, street lights, trees, etc. (In the larger subdivisions, the township board should also consider including requirements for recreational areas.)

Care should be taken to make sure that all necessary approving authorities have approved the preliminary plat sketches and set forth the conditions for final plat approval before granting tentative municipal approval, which is good for one year but may be extended under certain circumstances. Authority for preliminary and final plat approval was given to municipalities because good or bad development directly affects them and thus is the responsibility of their governing bodies. This responsibility accounts for the fact that planning commissions are only advisory. Municipalities which fail to adopt comprehensive plans and then enact the implementing tools of zoning, subdivision control and building codes are not exercising the kind of supervision over land use which is necessary for orderly development.

Township officials embarking upon a planning program need to make sure that the public is kept fully, completely and honestly aware of what is happening. Too often a great deal of time and thousands of dollars are spent in developing well conceived plans and ordinances only to have them go down to defeat at a referendum election because the citizens didn't understand what it was all about. Special interest groups or even an individual often will go to any length to defeat something that might encroach upon a selfish concern, and have a greater chance of succeeding if the township board fails in its public relations, including provisions for in-put from the citizens during the planning process.

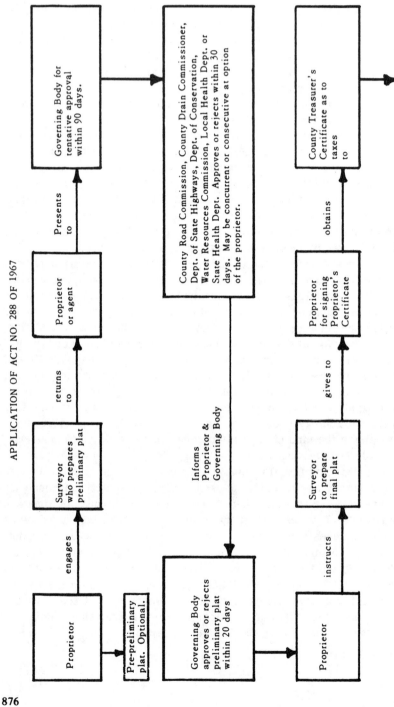

APPLICATION OF ACT NO. 288 OF 1967

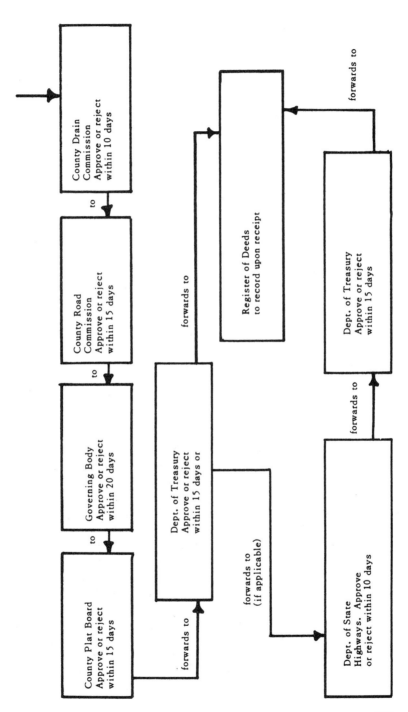

Act No. 288, P.A. 1967 — Subdivision Control Act of 1967

AN ACT to regulate the subdivision of land; to promote the public health, safety and general welfare; to further the orderly layout and use of land; to require that the land be suitable for building sites and public improvements, and that there be adequate drainage thereof; to provide for proper ingress and egress to lots; to promote proper surveying and monumenting of land subdivided and conveyed by accurate legal descriptions; to provide for the approvals to be obtained by subdividers prior to the recording and filing of plats; to establish the procedure for vacating, correcting and revising plats; to control residential building development with floodplain areas; to provide for reserving easements for utilities in vacated streets and alleys; to provide for the filing of amended plats; to provide for the making of assessors plats; to provide penalties for the violation of the provisions of this act; and to repeal certain acts and parts of acts.

MCLA 560.101 Short title. [MSA 26.430(101)]

MCLA 560.102 Definitions. [MSA 26.430(102)]

Sec. 102. ... *(a) "Plat" ... (b) "Land" ... (c) "Preliminary plat" ... (d) "Subdivide" or "subdivision" ... (e) "Parcel" or "tract" ... (f) "Lot" ... (g) "Outlot" ... (h) "Proprietor" ... (i) "Governing body" means the legislative body of a city or village or the township board of a township. (j) "Municipality" means a township, city or village. (k) "County plat board" means the register of deeds, who shall act as chairman, the county clerk, who shall act as secretary, and the county treasurer. ... (l) "Public utility" means all persons, firms, corporations, copartnerships or municipal or other public authority providing gas, electricity, water, steam, telephone, sewer, or other services of a similar nature. (m) "Caption" ... (n) "Replat" ... (o) "Surveyor" means either a land surveyor who is registered in this state as a registered land surveyor or a civil engineer who is registered in the state as a registered professional engineer. (p) "Government survey" ... (q) "Michigan coordinate system" ... (r) "Alley" ... (s) "Health department" means the state, city, county or district health depart-*

ment having jurisdiction. *(t) "Public sewer"* ... *(u) "Public water"* ... *(v) "Topographical map"* ... *(w) "Flood plain"* means that area of land adjoining the channel of a river, stream, water course, lake or other similar body of water which will be inundated by a flood which can reasonably be expected for that region.

MCLA 560.103 Surveys, necessity; plats, submission, approval, recording; plats of retracement or boundary surveys, recording; revision of recorded plat; urban renewal plats. [MSA 26.430(103)]

MCLA 560.104 Replats of recorded subdivision plats, approval, recording. [MSA 26.430(104)]

MCLA 560.105 Preliminary and final plats, approval on conditions. [MSA 26.430(105)]

MCLA 560.106 Approval or rejection conditioned or based on other requirements. [MSA 26.430(106)]

MCLA 560.107 Submission and approval of preliminary plats. [MSA 26.430(107)]

MCLA 560.111 Preliminary plats, submission of copies, contents, scale, form; additional preliminary land development plans. [MSA· 26.430(111)]

MCLA 560.112 Submission of copies of preliminary plat and other data (to municipal clerk); **tentative approval, effect, extension.** [MSA 26.430(112)]

MCLA 560.113 Submission of copies of preliminary plat; county road commission, approval or rejection. [MSA 26.430(113)]

MCLA 560.114 Same; county drain commissioner, approval or rejection; topographic map. [MSA 26.430(114)]

MCLA 560.115 Same; department of state highways, approval or rejection. [MSA 26.430(115)]

MCLA 560.116 Same; conservation department, conditions for submission; approval; objections; adequate plan. [MSA 26.430(116)]

MCLA 560.117 Same; water resources commission of department of conservation, conditions for submission, approval, rejection; flood plain area, determination. [MSA 26.430(117)]

MCLA 560.118 Same; health department, conditions for submission, approval, rejection. [MSA 26.430(118)]

MCLA 560.119 Same; county plat board; public utilities. [MSA 26.430(119)]

MCLA 560.120 Final approval of preliminary plat. [MSA 26.430(120)]

MCLA 560.125 Survey required; monuments, location, form, height, waiver. [MSA 26.430(125)]

MCLA 560.126 Survey by surveyor; error or closure; tolerance; bearings, expression; statement of source of information. [MSA 26.430(126)]

MCLA 560.131 Survey and 5 true plats following approval of preliminary plat; expiration of approvals; acceptance of final plat, time limit; taxation. [MSA 26.430(131)]

MCLA 560.132 Form of plat. [MSA 26.430(132)]

MCLA 560.133 Caption of final plat; form, contents. [MSA 26.430(133)]

MCLA 560.134 Description of land; form, contents. [MSA 26.430(134)]

MCLA 560.135 Map of subdivision; form, contents. [MSA 26.430(135)]

MCLA 560.136 Exterior boundaries shown on plat; contents, form. [MSA 26.430(136)]

MCLA 560.137 Grounds, streets, roads, and alleys; mode of showing on plat. [MSA 26.430(137)]

MCLA 560.138 Flood plain areas; showing on plats.
[MSA 26.430(138)]

MCLA 560.139 Public utility easements; showing on plats.
[MSA 26.430(139)]

MCLA 560.140 Lots and outlots, showing on plats.
[MSA 26.430(140)]

MCLA 560.141 County drains, lagoons, slips, waterways, lakes bays, canals; showing on maps. [MSA 26.430(141)]

MCLA 560.142 Certificates on plats, requirements, form.
[MSA 26.430(142)]

MCLA 560.143 Surveyor's certificates, contents. [MSA 26.430(143)]

MCLA 560.144 Proprietor's certificate, contents. [MSA 26.430(144)]

MCLA 560.145 Signing and dating certificates. [MSA 26.430(145)]

Sec. 145. (1) A certificate shall be signed and dated by the county treasurer relative to paid or unpaid taxes, special assessments and tax liens or titles, as required by section 135 of Act No. 206 of the Public Acts of 1893, as amended (MCLA 211.135)
[MSA 7.194] .

(2) The certificate shall be signed and dated by the treasurer of the municipality, if the municipality does not return delinquent taxes to the state treasurer, as required by section 135 of Act No. 206 of the Public Acts of 1893, as amended (MCLA 211.135)
[MSA 7.194].

MCLA 560.146 Drain commissioner, signing and dating certificates.
[MSA 26.430(146)]

MCLA 560.147 County road commissioners, signing certificates.
[MSA 26.430(147)]

MCLA 560.148 Municipalities; clerk's signing and dating certificates, review of plats, approval by health department, sewer and water service, zoning. [MSA 26.430(148)]

MCLA 560.149 County plat board; signing and dating certificates, review along with county plat engineer. [MSA 26.430(149)]

MCLA 560.150 State highway commission; signing and dating certificates, contents of certificates. [MSA 26.430(150)]

MCLA 560.151 State treasurer; signing and dating certificates, contents of certificates. [MSA 26.430(151)]

MCLA 560.161 Submission of final plat, procedure. [MSA 26.430(161)]

MCLA 560.162 Number of copies submitted to drain commissioner. [MSA 26.430(162)]

MCLA 560.163 Drain commissioner; certification of approval, rejection. [MSA 26.430(163)]

MCLA 560.164 Submission of copies to county road commissioners. [MSA 26.430(164)]

MCLA 560.165 County road commissioners; approval, rejection. [MSA 26.430(165)]

MCLA 560.166 Submission of copies to municipality, filing fees. [MSA 26.430(166)]

MCLA 560.167 Governing body; approval, rejection, record. [MSA 26.430(167)]

MCLA 560.168 Submission to county plat board; review, approval, rejection. [MSA 26.430(168)]

Sec. 168. (1) When approved by the governing body, the clerk shall promptly forward all copies of the plat to the clerk of the county plat board, together with the filing and recording fee. ...

MCLA 560.169 County treasurer, warrant for part of filing and recording fee. [MSA 26.430(169)]

MCLA 560.170 Forwarding plat to state highway commissioner; approval, rejection. [MSA 26.430(170)]

MCLA 560.171   State treasurer; review, approval, rejection.
[MSA 26.430(171)]

MCLA 560.172   Register of deeds; certification, recordation.
[MSA 26.430(172)]

MCLA 560.173 State treasurer; disposition of copies of recorded
plats. [MSA 26.430(173)]

MCLA 560.181 Streets, alleys, roads, and highways; conditions
constituting pre-requisites for approval of plats.
[MSA 26.430(181)]

MCLA 560.182 Same; requirements imposed by municipal governing
body. [MSA 26.430(182)]

MCLA 560.183 Same; requirements imposed by county road commission. [MSA 26.430(183)]

MCLA 560.184 Same; requirements imposed by department of state
highways. [MSA 26.430(184)]

MCLA 560.186 Approval of final plats, conditions.
[MSA 26.430(186)]

MCLA 560.188 Proposed county drains, lagoons, slips, waterways,
lakes, bays, or canals; municipal governing body's imposition of
conditions for approval. [MSA 26.430(188)]

MCLA 560.190 Public utility easements; provision by proprietor,
nature and extent. [MSA 26.430(190)]

MCLA 560.192 County drain commissioner or municipal governing
body, imposition of conditions for approval of final plats.
[MSA 26.430(192)]

MCLA 560.194   Floodplain lying within proposed subdivision,
conditions for approval of final plat. [MSA 26.430.(194)]

MCLA 560.196 General conditions for approval of plats.
[MSA 26.430(196)]

MCLA 560.198 Surveyor's affidavit; recordation, purpose, contents, rejection, evidence, effect. [MSA 26.430(198)]

MCLA 560.201   Assessor's plats; requirements, conditions for ordering. [MSA 26.430(201)]

MCLA 560.202 Captions, contents, and makers of assessor's plats. [MSA 26.430(202)]

MCLA 560.203   Costs of assessor's plats.   [MSA 26.430(203)]

MCLA 560.204 Method of making assessor's plats. [MSA 26.430(204)]

MCLA 560.205 Proprietors' rights to examine maps of proposed assessor's plats, view temporary monuments, and disagree with boundaries; notice. [MSA 26.430(205)]

MCLA 560.206   Reconciliation of discrepancies in making of assessor's plats; boundary agreements; permanent monuments. [MSA 26.430(206)]

MCLA 560.207   Bearings and distances of lines, numbering of lots, surveys, monuments, form and procedure; assessor's plats. [MSA 26.430(207)]

MCLA 560.208   Surveyor's certificates on assessor's plats; necessity, contents. [MSA 26.430(208)]

MCLA 560.209 Filing, notice, revision, and approval of assessor's plats; suits to correct plats. [MSA 26.430(209)]

MCLA 560.210   Acknowledgment, review, rejection, approval, recording, and distribution of assessor's plats. [MSA 26.430(210)]

MCLA 560.211 Notice of recordation of assessor's plat; delinquent taxes or special assessments, notice, apportionment, liens. [MSA 26.430(211)]

MCLA 560.212 Land descriptions based on assessor's plats; sufficience and necessity as to taxation, mortgages, and conveyances, evidence. [MSA 26.430(212)]

MCLA 560.213 Assessing officer's use recorded plat in describing lands and certification as to municipal ownership of highways, streets, alleys, roads, and public places. [MSA 26.430(213)]

MCLA 560.221 Amendment, vacation, correction, alteration, or revision of recorded plats. [MSA 26.430(221)]

MCLA 560.222 Procedure for amending, vacating, correcting, altering, or revising recorded plats. [MSA 26.430(222)]

MCLA 560.223 Petitions for changing, vacating, correcting, or revising plats. [MSA 26.430(223)]

MCLA 560.224 Notice of pendency of petition and time of application. [MSA 26.430(224)]

MCLA 560.225 Mode of service. [MSA 26.430(225)]

MCLA 560.226 Proof of notice; hearing; order. [MSA 26.430(226)]

MCLA 560.227 Title to vacated part. [MSA 26.430(227)]

MCLA 560.228 Recording order; certified copies. [MSA 26.430(228)]

MCLA 560.229 Amended plat setting forth change in recorded plat; filing, recording, distribution of copies. [MSA 26.430.(229)]

MCLA 560.241 Filing and recording fee; deposit, disposition. [MSA 26.430(241)]

MCLA 560.242 File of plats and index; maintenance by state treasurer; fees for copies of plats. [MSA 26.430(242)]

MCLA 560.243 File of recorded plats; maintenance by register of deeds, expense, fees for copies. [MSA 26.430(243)]

MCLA 560.244 Proprietor's copy of final plat; certification, mode of copying, charge for copying. [MSA 26.430(244)]

MCLA 560.245 Abstract of title, title insurance, or other information; attorney's opinion as to ownership and marketability. [MSA 26.430(245)]

MCLA 560.246 Fee schedule ordinance; deposit of fee; governing body's employment of surveyor; limitation on fees. [MSA 26.430(246)]

MCLA 560.247 Compensation for county plat board members. [MSA 26.430(247)]

MCLA 560.248 Fee schedules for plat approvals, adoption by county road commissions, purpose. [MSA 26.430(248)]

MCLA 560.249 Fee schedules for plat approvals, adoption by county supervisor, purpose. [MSA 26.430(249)]

MCLA 560.251 Certified copy of recorded plat as evidence of making and recording. [MSA 26.430(251)]

MCLA 560.252 Recorded plat as pre-requisite to conveyance or encumbrance of subdivision lots. [MSA 26.430(252)]

MCLA 560.253 Conveyance of fee and warranties; lands held by municipalities; mineral or underground gas storage rights. [MSA 26.430(253)]

MCLA 560.254 Enforcement, release, or waiver of restrictions placed by public bodies on platted lands. [MSA 26.430(254)]

MCLA 560.255 Lot descriptions based on plat, use for assessments, taxation, sales, and conveyances. [MSA 26.430(255)]

MCLA 560.256 Opening, vacating, extending, or widening street or alley or changing name; procedure. [MSA 26.430(256)]

MCLA 560.257 Reservation of easements for public purposes upon discontinuance of existing street, alley, or other platted public lands; procedure. [MSA 26.430(257)]

MCLA 560.258 Documents showing manner of maintaining areas reserved for common use of subdivision residents, requiring copies. [MSA 26.430(258)]

MCLA 560.259 Standards for approval of plats; statutory minimums, ordinances imposing stricter requirements, effect. [MSA 26.430(259)]

MCLA 560.261 Sales of land abutting street or road not accepted as public, voidability of contracts of sale. [MSA 26.430(261)]

MCLA 560.262 Removal or disturbance of monuments. [MSA 26.430(262)]

MCLA 560.263 Partition of parcels of land in recorded plats, conformity with ordinances. [MSA 26.430(263)]

MCLA 560.264 Penalties. [MSA 26.430(264)]

MCLA 560.265 Actions to restrain or prevent violations; parties, venue. [MSA 26.430(265)]

MCLA 560.266 Attorney general or county prosecuting attorney as parties; venue. [MSA 26.430(266)]

MCLA 560.267 Sales of land in violation of act; voidability, forfeiture, damages. [MSA 26.430(267)]

MCLA 560.290 Qualifications of employee in charge of plat section in state treasurer's office and employee's chief assistant. [MSA 26.430(290)]

MCLA 560.291 Processing plats approved on or before January 1, 1968, law applicable. [MSA 26.430(291)]

MCLA 560.292 Repeal. [MSA 26.430(292)]

MCLA 560.293 Effective date. [MSA 26.430(293)]

Act No. 184, P.A. 1943 - Township Zoning

AN ACT to provide for the establishment in the unincorporated portions of organized townships of zoning districts within which the proper use of land and natural resources may be encouraged or regulated by ordinance, and within which districts provisions may also be adopted designating the location of, the size of, the uses that may be made of, the minimum open spaces, sanitary, safety and protective measures that shall be required for, and the maximum number of families that may be housed in dwell-

ings, buildings and structures, including tents and trailer coaches, that may hereafter be erected or altered; to provide for a method for the adoption of ordinances and amendments thereto; to provide for emergency interim ordinances; to provide for the administering of ordinances adopted; to provide for conflicts with other acts, ordinances or regulations; to provide penalties for violations; to provide for the assessment, levy and collection of taxes; to provide for the collection of fees for building permits; to provide for petitions, public hearings and referenda; to provide for appeals; and to provide for the repeal of acts in conflict herewith.

MCLA 125.271 Township zoning districts; establishment; provisions. [MSA 5.2963(1)]

Sec. 1. The township board ... may provide by ordinance for the establishment of zoning districts in the unincorporated portions of such township within which districts the use of land for agriculture, forestry, recreation, residence, industry, trade, migratory labor camps, soil conservation, water supply conservation and additional uses of land may be encouraged, regulated or prohibited, and for such purposes may divide unincorporated portions of the township into districts of such number, shape and area as may be deemed best suited to carry out the provisions of this act. For each such district, provisions may also be adopted designating or limiting the location, the height, number of stories, and size of dwellings, buildings and structures that may hereafter be erected or altered, including tents and trailer coaches, and the specific uses for which dwellings, buildings and structures including tents and trailer coaches may hereafter be erected or altered; the area of yards, courts, and other open spaces, and the sanitary, safety and protective measures that shall be required for such dwellings, buildings and structures, including tents and trailer coaches; and the maximum number of families which may be housed in buildings, dwellings and structures including tents and trailer coaches hereafter erected or altered. All such provisions shall be uniform for each class of land or buildings, dwellings and structures, including tents and trailer coaches, throughout each district, but the provisions in one district may differ from those in other districts: Provided, That no township board shall have authority under this act, or under any ordinance adopted as provided by this act, to

888

regulate or control the drilling, completion or operation of oil and/or gas wells, or other wells drilled for oil and/or gas exploration purposes and shall have no jurisdiction with reference to the issuance of permits for the location, drilling, completion, operation or abandonment of such wells, but all such jurisdiction shall be vested exclusively in the supervisor of wells of the state of Michigan.

MCLA 125.272 Same; resolution, notice, petition, vote.
[MSA 5.2963(2)]

Sec. 2. This act shall not become operative in any organized township ... until (a) the township board shall have passed a resolution declaring its intent to proceed under the provisions of this act, and shall have given public notice within 10 days of the passage of its resolution by publication in a newspaper of general circulation in such township, or (b) until a petition signed by 8% of the persons who are residents and property owners in the unincorporated portion of the township, shall have been filed with the township clerk praying the township board to undertake such action. Upon the filing of such petition the township board shall, at the next regular meeting, vote upon a resolution declaring its intent to initiate action under the provisions of this act and give public notice of the resolution as provided in this section.

MCLA 125.273 Same; basis for plan; purposes. [MSA 5.2963(3)]

Sec. 3. The provisions of the zoning ordinance shall be based upon a plan designed to promote the public health, safety, morals and general welfare, to encourage the use of lands in accordance with their character and adaptability and to limit the improper use of land, to avoid the overcrowding of population, to provide adequate light and air, to lessen congestion on the public roads and streets, to reduce hazards to life and property, to facilitate adequate provision for a system of transportation, sewage disposal, safe and adequate water supply, education, recreation and other public requirements, and to conserve the expenditure of funds for public improvements and services to conform with the most advantageous uses of land, resources and properties; and shall be made with reasonable consideration, among other things, to the character of each district, its peculiar suitability for particular uses, the conservation of property values and natural resources, and the general and appropriate trend and character of land, building and population development.

MCLA 125.274 Township zoning board; appointment, terms, vacancies, removal. [MSA 5.2963(4)]

Sec. 4. In each township in which this act becomes operative, there shall be a permanent township zoning board composed of 4 members. The township board may provide by resolution for a zoning board composed of not to exceed 7 members, each to be appointed by the township board. The members of said board shall be selected upon the basis of their respective qualifications and fitness to serve as members of a zoning board and without consideration for their political activities. Of the members first appointed, 2 shall be appointed for terms of 2 years each. The other 2 members shall be appointed for terms of 4 years each; or in case of a township zoning board of more than 4 members, 3 shall be first appointed for 2 years each and the others first appointed for 4 years each. Each member of said board shall serve until his successor is appointed and has qualified. Upon the expiration of the terms of the members first appointed, successors shall be appointed, in like manner, for terms of 4 years each. Vacancies shall be filled in the same manner as is provided for the appointment in the first instance for the remainder of the unexpired term. No elected officer of the township nor any employee of the township board shall serve simultaneously as a member or an employee of the zoning board, and no less than 2/3 of the members of such board shall be electors who reside in and have property assessed for taxes located in the unincorporated portions of the township. Members of the zoning board shall be removable for nonperformance of duty or misconduct in office by the township board upon written charges and after public hearing.

MCLA 125.275 Same; annual meetings; notice; officers, election. [MSA 5.2963(5)]

Sec. 5. The township zoning board shall hold a minimum of 2 regular meetings annually.

MCLA 125.276 Same; compensation, expenses. [MSA 5.2963(6)]

MCLA 125.277 Same; zone plan; basis; administration and enforcement. [MSA 5.2963(7)]

MCLA 125.277a Same; planning expert, compensation. [MSA 5.2963(7A)]

MCLA 125.278 Same; information and counsel furnished. [MSA 5.2963(8)]

MCLA 125.279 Same; tentative zoning plan, hearing, notice. [MSA 5.2963(9)]

MCLA 125.280 Zoning ordinances; approval, county zoning or planning commissions or coordinating zoning committees; committee members, number, appointment; purpose of committee; presumption. [MSA 5.2963(10)]

MCLA 125.281 Same; amendment, adoption, hearing, notice. [MSA 5.2963(11)]

MCLA 125.282 Zoning ordinance referendum; time, petition, signers, filing; election; invalidation of ordinance upon rejection. [MSA 5.2963(12)]

MCLA 125.283 Same; report to township board. [MSA 5.2963(13)]

MCLA 125.284 Same; amendment procedure; conformance to court decree. [MSA 5.2963(14)]

MCLA 125.285 Same; interim ordinance, approval, publication, renewal. [MSA 5.2963(15)]

MCLA 125.286 Existing buildings, dwellings, and land uses. [MSA 5.2963(16)]

MCLA 125.288 Board of appeals; membership, expenses, removals. [MSA 5.2963(18)]

Sec. 18. In each township in which the township board exercises the authority conferred by this act, there shall be a township board of appeals of 3 members. The first member of such board of appeals shall be the chairman of the township zoning board, the

891

second member shall be a member of the township board appointed by the township board; and the third member shall be selected and appointed by the first 2 members from among the electors residing in the unincorporated area of the township. No elected officer of the township nor any employee of the township board may serve simultaneously as the third member of or as an employee of the township board of appeals. The total amount allowed such board of appeals in any 1 year as per diem or as expenses actually incurred in the discharge of their duties shall not exceed a reasonable sum which sum shall be provided annually in advance by the township board. Members of the board of appeals shall be removable by the township board for nonperformance of duty or misconduct in office upon written charges and after public hearing.

MCLA 125.289 Same; meetings, open to public, record of proceedings. [MSA 5.2963(19)]

MCLA 125.290 Same; duties. [MSA 5.2963(20)]

Sec. 20. The township board of appeals shall act upon all questions as they may arise in the administration of the zoning ordinance, including the interpretation of the zoning maps, and may fix rules and regulations to govern its procedures ... It shall hear and decide appeals from and review any order, requirements, decision or determination made by an administrative official charged with enforcement of any ordinance adopted pursuant to the provisions of this act. It shall also ...

MCLA 125.291 Same; appeals. [MSA 5.2963(21)]

MCLA 125.292 Same; restraining order. [MSA 5.2963(22)] ·

MCLA 125.293 Same; hearing; appeal to circuit court. [MSA 5.2963(23)]

MCLA 125.294 Nuisance per se; abatement; enforcement. [MSA 5.2963(24)]

MCLA 125.295 Fees for building permits. [MSA 5.2963(25)]

MCLA 125.296 Prior ordinance effective until new ordinance adopted; deemed adopted under act. [MSA 5.2963(26)]

MCLA 125.297 Townships not subject to act. [MSA 5.2963(27)]

Sec. 27. In the event that an ordinance enacted pursuant to the provisions of this act becomes effective in any township which is located in a county in which Act No. 183 of the Public Acts of 1943, as amended, being sections 125.201 to 125.232 [MSA 5.2961(1) TO 5.2961(32)] *of the Compiled Laws of 1948, the county rural zoning enabling act, has theretofore become or thereafter becomes operative, such township shall not be subject, unless otherwise provided in this act, to the provisions of said Act ..., nor to any ordinance, rule or regulation adopted pursuant thereto.*

MCLA 125.298 Ordinances controlling. [MSA 5.2963(28)]

MCLA 125.301 "Township rural zoning act"; short title. [MSA 5.2963(31)]

Note: A detailed outline of procedure for adoption of a township zoning ordinance and/or amendments thereto under the above statute is provided in the Ordinance section of the chapter on Services, Utilities, Contracts and Ordinances.

Act No. 171, P.A. 1958 - Township Zoning

AN ACT providing for the continuation of zoning regulations in newly incorporated villages or in territories attached to villages.

MCLA 125.311 Annexed property to village; continuation of zoning regulation. [MSA 5.2950]

Sec. 1. Whenever any portion of any township becomes an incorporated village, or whenever any territory is annexed to any village, the then existing zoning regulations for the territory within the newly incorporated village or within the territory attached to a then existing village shall remain in full force and effect for a period of 2 years after incorporation or annexation unless the legislative body of the village shall lawfully adopt other zoning regulations or ordinances.

JOINT ACTION
Act No. 168, P.A. 1959 - Township Planning

AN ACT to provide for township planning; for the creation, organization, powers and duties of township planning commissions; and for the regulation and subdivision of land.

MCLA 125.321   **Township planning commission; definitions.**
MSA 5.2963(101)

Sec. 1. As used in this act:
(1) "Basic plan" ... (2) "Citizen member" means a member of a township planning commission holding no other township office except that he may be a member of a township zoning board of adjustment or appeals. (3) "Planning commission" ...

MCLA 125.322 Same; purpose of plans. MSA 5.2963(102)

MCLA 125.323 Same; creation; referendum; resolution, copies to secretary of state and county or regional planning commission. MSA 5.2963(103)

Sec. 3. The township board ... may create, by resolution, a township planning commission ...

MCLA 125.324 Same; members, qualification, appointment, term, vacancies, compensation; budget; gifts; expenditures. MSA 5.2963(104)

Sec. 4. (1) The planning commission shall consist of not less than 5 nor more than 9 members, who shall be representative of major interests as they exist in the township, such as agriculture, recreation, education, public health, government, commerce, transportation and industry. All members shall be qualified electors and property owners of the township. One member of the township board shall be a member of the planning commission.
(2) All members of the planning commission shall be appointed by the township supervisor with the approval of the township board. Members may be removed by the township supervisor, after a hearing, with the approval of the township board.

(3) The term of each member shall be for 3 years, except that of the members first appointed, 1/3 shall serve for 1 year, 1/3 for 2 years and 1/3 for 3 years. A successor shall be appointed not more than 1 month after the term of the preceding commission member has expired. All vacancies for unexpired terms shall be filled for the remainder of such term.

(4) Members of the planning commission may be compensated for their services as provided by the township board. The planning commission may ...

MCLA 125.325 Same; officers, advisory committees; meetings; director; rules; record; reports. [MSA 5.2963(105)]

MCLA 125.326 Basic plan; consultation with other planning commissions. [MSA 5.2963(106)]

MCLA 125.327 Same; contents. [MSA 5.2963(107)]

MCLA 125.328 Same; adoption procedure, approval by county planning commission. [MSA 5.2963(108)]

MCLA 125.329 Same; hearing, publication of notice. [MSA 5.2963(109)]

MCLA 125.330 Same; approval of public way, space, building or structure. [MSA 5.2963(110)]

MCLA 125.331 Township planning commission; zoning board powers and duties. [MSA 5.2963(111)]

Sec. 11. The township board, by resolution, may transfer to the planning commission all powers, duties and responsibilities provided by ...

MCLA 125.332 Same; approval of plats. [MSA 5.2963(112)]

MCLA 125.333 Inconsistent acts. [MSA 5.2963(113)]

Act No. 285, P.A. 1931 - Municipal Planning

AN ACT to provide for city, village and municipal planning; the creation, organization, powers and duties of

*planning commissions; the regulation and subdivision of
land; and to provide penalties for violation of the provisions
of this act.*

**MCLA 125.31 Definitions; municipality to include cities, villages,
townships, etc.** [MSA 5.2991]

**MCLA 125.32 Municipal planning commission; creation; existing
plan commission.** [MSA 5.2992]

*Sec. 2. Any municipality is hereby authorized and empowered
to make, adopt, amend, extend, add to, or carry out a municipal
plan as provided in this act and create by ordinance a planning
commission with the powers and duties herein set forth.* ...

**MCLA 125.33 Same; members; appointment, compensation, term,
removal, vacancies.** [MSA 5.2993]

*Sec. 3. (1) The commission shall except as provided in
subsection (2) consist of 9 members who shall represent insofar as
is possible different professions or occupations who shall be
appointed by the ... (supervisor) ..., but such appointment shall
always be subject to the approval by a majority vote of the members
elect of the legislative body of such municipality. All members of
the commission may be compensated at a rate to be determined by
the appointing or legislative body and shall hold no other municipal
office except that 1 of such members may be a member of the zoning
board of adjustment or appeals. The term of each member shall be
3 years, except that 3 members of the first commission ... shall
serve for the term of 1 year, 3 for a term of 2 years and 3 for a term
of 3 years. All members shall hold office until their successors
are appointed. Members may, after a public hearing, be removed by
the ... (supervisor) ... for inefficiency, neglect of duty or malfeasance in office.*

*(2) If deemed desirable by the ... (township board) ... such
commission may consist of ...*

MCLA 125.34 Same; chairman, meetings, rules, records.
[MSA 5.2994]

**MCLA 125.35 Same; employees, contracts for services, expendi-
tures.** [MSA 5.2995]

896

MCLA 125.36 Same; adoption of master plan, contents, amendment.
[MSA 5.2996]

MCLA 125.37 Same; surveys for basis, purpose. [MSA 5.2997]

MCLA 125.38 Same; adoption of part or whole of plan; hearing, notice. [MSA 5.2998]

MCLA 125.39 Same; public works; powers of council; failure to act; program. [MSA 5.2999]

MCLA 125.40 Same; rescission of action by legislative body, procedure. [MSA 5.3000]

MCLA 125.41 Same; publicity and education, gifts, cooperation from officials. [MSA 5.3001]

MCLA 125.42 Same; succession to zoning commission. [MSA 5.3002]

Sec. 12. The commission shall have all powers heretofore granted by law to the zoning commission of the municipality, and, from and after the creation of a planning commission in such municipality, all powers and records of the zoning commission shall be transferred to the planning commission: Provided, ...

MCLA 125.43 Same; necessity for approval of plats; street system.
[MSA 5.3003]

MCLA 125.44 Same; regulations governing subdivision of land; bond to secure improvement; publication of regulations.
[MSA 5.3004]

MCLA 125.45 Same; approval or disapproval of plats, procedure, effect. [MSA 5.3005]

JOINT ACTION
Act No. 281, P.A. 1945 - Regional Planning

AN ACT to provide for regional planning; the creation, organization, powers and duties of regional planning commissions; the provision of funds for the use of regional planning commissions; and the supervision of the activities of regional planning commissions under the provisions of this act.

MCLA 125.11 Definitions. [MSA 5.3008(1)]

Sec. 1. ... The terms "local governmental units" or "local units" shall include cities, villages, other incorporated political subdivisions, counties, school districts, special authorities, townships, or any legally constituted governing body responsible for the exercise of governmental functions within a political subdivision of the state.

MCLA 125.12 Regional planning commissions; creation. [MSA 5.3008(2)]

Sec. 2. ... by resolution by 2 or more legislative bodies ...

MCLA 125.13 Same; boundaries. [MSA 5.3008(3)]

MCLA 125.14 Same; compensation; expenses. [MSA 5.3008(4)]

MCLA 125.15 Same; chairman; rules of procedure; records. [MSA 5.3008(5)]

MCLA 125.16 Director and employees. [MSA 5.3008(6)]

MCLA 125.17 Aid from governmental agencies. [MSA 5.3008(7)]

MCLA 125.18 Advisory committees or councils, appointment. [MSA 5.3008(8)]

MCLA 125.19 Research studies, etc.; development plans; advisory services; report. [MSA 5.3008(9)]

MCLA 125.20 Access to records and information. [MSA 5.3008(10)]

MCLA 125.21 Local subdivisions; adoption of plans of regional commission. [MSA 5.3008(11)]

Sec. 11. ... whether active participants in the work ... or not, may adopt all or any portion of the plans ... by following ... proce-

898

dures specified by act of the legislature or by local charter for the adoption of an official master plan.

MCLA 125.22 Same; allocation of funds (and services, etc. by legislative body). [MSA 5.3008(12)]

MCLA 125.23 Gifts, grants. [MSA 5.3008(13)]

MCLA 124.24 Regional planning commissions, transfers of functions, assets, or liabilities; regional council of government, grants-in-aid. [MSA 5.3008(14)]

MCLA 125.25 Research studies and plans (to governor), **review and comment.** [MSA 5.3008(15)]

JOINT ACTION
Act No. 122, P.A. 1965 - Federal Funds Under
Economic Opportunity Act of 1964

AN ACT to authorize local governments to comply with, and accept and match federal funds under certain federal acts.

MCLA 125.1281 Acceptance and expenditure of federal funds; matching funds. [MSA 5.4089]

Sec. 1. Any ... township may take any necessary action consistent with state law to comply with the provisions of Public Law 415 of the 87th Congress, known as the "manpower development and training act of 1962", as amended, and Public Law 452 of the 88th Congress, known as the "economic opportunity act of 1964", as amended, and may accept and expend federal funds available under, and provide matching funds, facilities and services to the extent required by, such laws.

Act No. 218, P.A. 1966 — Professional Community Planners

AN ACT to register and regulate professional community planners; to create a state board of registration for professional community planners, and to prescribe its powers and duties; to impose certain powers and duties upon the state and political subdivisions thereof; to protect public health, safety and welfare; and to provide penalties for the violation of the provisions of this act.

MCLA 338.1351 Professional community planners act; short title. MSA 18.170(1)

MCLA 338.1352 Same; definitions. MSA 18.170(2)

MCLA 338.1353 Use of title "professional community planner" or "community planner". MSA 18.170(3)

MCLA 338.1354 Scope of practice; individuals only entitled to registration; prohibited practice. MSA 18.170(4)

Sec. 4. (1) A registered professional community planner may engage in the preparation of the comprehensive community plan including the preparation of planning studies which assist in the preparation or the implementation of the ... plan. ...

MCLA 338.1355 Seal of professional community planner; use. MSA 18.170(5)

Sec. 5. ... shall place a seal upon his work or the planning work for which he is responsible ...

MCLA 338.1356 Qualifications for registration. MSA 18.170(6)

MCLA 338.1357 Registration without examination; eligibility. MSA 18.170(7)

MCLA 338.1358 State board of registration; creation; membership; appointment; term; vacancies; removal of members; expenses. MSA 18.170(8)

MCLA 338.1359 Powers and duties of state board. MSA 18.170(9)

MCLA 338.1360 Offices and records; custody of funds; roster; notice of expiration of certificate. MSA 18.170(10)

Sec. 10. ... (2) A roster showing the names and business addresses of all professional community planners shall be prepared

900

by the department during the month of February of each year, ... Copies of this roster shall be placed on file with the secretary of state, and furnished at cost to the public upon request. ...

MCLA 338.1361 Application; form; fees; deposit of funds. [MSA 18.170(11)]

MCLA 338.1362 Issuance of certificate; content; duration; renewal. [MSA 18.170(12)]

MCLA 338.1363 Revocation of certificate; grounds; hearing; reissuance. [MSA 18.170(13)]

MCLA 338.1364 Registration in other state or territory; reciprocal privileges. [MSA 18.170(14)]

MCLA 338.1365 Violations; penalty; enforcement. [MSA 18.170(15)]

MCLA 338.1366 Construction of act. [MSA 18.170(16)]

JOINT ACTION
Act No. 62, P.A. 1963 - Industrial Development

AN ACT relating to industrial development; to authorize municipalities to acquire and dispose of industrial buildings and sites and industrial machinery and equipment, including water and air pollution control equipment, and tourist and resort facilities and to lease the same to persons, firms or corporations; to authorize municipalities to acquire and dispose of water and air pollution control equipment and to lease or sell the same to persons, firms, corporations or public utilities; to provide for the financing of such buildings, sites, machinery and equipment or water and air pollution control equipment by the issuance of revenue bonds; to provide the terms and conditions of such bonds; and to prescribe the powers and duties of the municipal finance commission.

MCLA 125.1251 Legislative declaration; short title. [MSA 5.3533(21)]

MCLA 125.1252 Definitions. [MSA 5.3533(22)]

MCLA 125.1253   Municipalities; powers as to industrial sites and buildings. [MSA 5.3533(23)]

MCLA 125.1253a   Industrial and public utility water and air pollution control programs, need, municipal powers. [MSA 5.3533(23A)]

MCLA 125.1254   Same; industrial building revenue bonds, terms. [MSA 5.3533(24)]

MCLA 125.1255   Resolution authorizing issuance of bonds, contents. [MSA 5.3533(25)]

MCLA 125.1256   Redemption of bonds. [MSA 5.3533(26)]

MCLA 125.1257   Default; receiver. [MSA 5.3533(27)]

MCLA 125.1259   Additional bonds, new bonds. [MSA 5.3533(29)]

MCLA 125.1260   Cost of project. [MSA 5.3533(30)]

MCLA 125.1261   Taxation of lessee; liens; recovery. [MSA 5.3533(31)]

Sec. 11. ... the lessee shall be subject to taxation in the same amount and to the same extent as though the lessee were the owner of the property. ...

MCLA 125.1262   Referendum; intention to issue bonds. [MSA 5.3533(32)]

MCLA 125.1263   Municipal finance commission, approval, effect. [MSA 5.3533(33)]

Sec. 13. ... No bonds shall be issued until the municipal finance commission approves the issuance. ...

MCLA 125.1264   Sale of bonds. [MSA 5.3533(34)]

MCLA 125.1265   Industrial buildings and machinery; powers of municipalities. [MSA 5.3533(35)]

Sec. 15. *Nothing herein contained shall be interpreted to grant to any municipality the authority to operate an industrial building or any industrial machinery or equipment for its own use. The prohibition of this section shall not prevent a municipality from conserving and maintaining an industrial building and site and any industrial machinery and equipment acquired hereunder pending lease thereof to a private person, firm or corporation.*

MCLA 125.1266 Cumulative powers. [MSA 5.3533(36)]

Sec. 16. *This act shall be construed as granting cumulative authority for the exercise of the various powers herein conferred, and neither said powers nor any bonds issued hereunder shall be affected or limited by any other statutory or charter provision now or hereafter in force, other than as may be provided herein, it being the purpose and intention of this act to create full, separate and complete additional powers. The various powers conferred herein may be exercised independently and notwithstanding that no bonds are issued hereunder.*

MCLA 125.1267 Liberal construction. [MSA 5.3533(37)]

JOINT ACTION
Act No. 117, P.A. 1963 - Business Development Corporations

AN ACT to provide for the organization and regulation of business development corporations; to provide their rights and powers and to prescribe the conditions on which such corporations may exercise their powers; and to repeal certain acts and parts of acts.

MCLA 487.851 Business development corporations; incorporators. [MSA 23.1189(1)]

MCLA 487.852 Articles of incorporation; copies, filing. [MSA 23.1189(2)]

MCLA 487.853 Contents. [MSA 23.1189(3)]

MCLA 487.854 Purposes of corporations. [MSA 23.1189(4)]

Sec. 4. The purposes ... shall be to assist, promote, encourage and, through the cooperative efforts of the institutions and corporations which, from time to time, shall become members thereof, develop and advance the business prosperity and economic welfare of the state; ...

MCLA 487.855 Powers. [MSA 23.1189(5)]

Sec. 5. In furtherance of the purposes set forth in section 4, and in addition to the powers conferred on corporations by general laws, such corporation, subject to the restrictions and limitations contained in this article, shall have the following powers: **(a) Borrowing power.** *...* **(b) Lending power; surety.** *...* **(c) Real and personal property.** *...* **(d) Good will and other rights; industrial plants; business establishments.** *...* **(e) Stockholding.** *...* **(f) Cooperation with and assistance to governmental agencies.** *To cooperate with and avail itself of the facilities of state departments and other government agencies; and to cooperate with and assist, and otherwise encourage, local organizations in the various communities in the state in the promotion, assistance and development of the business prosperity and economic welfare of such communities and of the state.*

MCLA 487.856 - 487.865 [MSA 23.1189(6) - 23.1189(15)]

MCLA 487.866 Taxation; fees. [MSA 23.1189(16)]

Sec. 16. Any corporation organized hereunder shall be subject to taxation and the payment of fees as a general profit corporation except as may be otherwise provided by law.

MCLA 487.867 Repeal. [MSA 23.1189(17)]

JOINT ACTION
Act No. 144, P.A. 1895 - Abandonment of Business

AN ACT to make it unlawful for any company or corporation to remove, abandon or discontinue any factory, work shop, machine shop, repair shop, office, agency or establishment, or the work, business or industry carried on therein from any village, city, town (township) or place within this state, without repaying and restoring to such town (township), *city, village or place any and all money, bonds, land and other property, with interest, which have been or may hereafter be given or granted as a consideration or inducement for the location, construction, operation, enlargement or maintenance at any such city, village, town, (township) or place, and to provide a remedy by injunction to restrain any such company or corporation from moving, abandoning or discontinuing any such factory, shop, etc. and to provide a penalty for so doing.*

MCLA 445.601 Abandonment of business by municipally aided company without restoration of benefits and interest; unlawfulness. [MSA 19.831]

MCLA 445.602 Same; application of act, benefit given to company office or agent or to predecessor company. [MSA 19.832]

MCLA 445.603 Violation, misdemeanor. [MSA 19.833]

MCLA 445.604 Penalty. [MSA 19.834]

MCLA 445.605 Restoration of benefits; to whom made. [MSA 19.835]

MCLA 445.606 Decree of forfeiture or injunction; rights of municipality when company fails, when company has performed contract. [MSA 19.836]

JOINT ACTION
Act No. 116, P.A. 1963 - Economic Expansion

AN ACT to create a state department of economic expansion and an economic expansion council and to prescribe their powers and duties; and to repeal certain acts and parts of acts.

MCLA 125.1201 Economic expansion department; organization, approval. [MSA 3.540(11)]

MCLA 125.1202 Executive director; deputy executive director; appointment. [MSA 3.540(12)]

MCLA 125.1203 Economic development department, transfer of records, files, property. [MSA 3.540(13)]

MCLA 125.1204 Economic expansion program, activities.
[MSA 3.540(14)]

MCLA 125.1205 Economic expansion department; powers.
[MSA 3.540(15)]

Sec. 5. ... (a) Accept ... grants ... (from) public or private agency ... in this state ... (b) Enter into contracts with boards, commissions and agencies, both public and private, and with individuals to carry out the purposes of this act. ...

MCLA 125.1206 Same; transfer of records, files, property, and employees of department of administration. [MSA 3.540(16)]

MCLA 125.1207 Economic expansion council; members, appointment, term, chairman, officers, quorum, committees, report, compensation, expenses. [MSA 3.540 (17)]

MCLA 125.1208 Repeal. [MSA 3.540(18)]

MCLA 125.1211 Executive Order 1972-1 transferring the Office of Community planning of the Department of Commerce to the Bureau of Programs and Budget within the Executive Office of the Governor. [MSA 3.540(21)]

JOINT ACTION
Act No. 46, P.A. 1966 - Economic Development

AN ACT to create a county or regional economic development commission; and to prescribe the powers and duties thereof.

MCLA 125.1231 County economic development commission; creation, membership. [MSA 5.1193(1)]

MCLA 125.1232 Rules and regulations for commission; compensation. [MSA 5.1193(2)]

MCLA 125.1233 Appointment of employees. [MSA 5.1193(3)]

MCLA 125.1234 Expenses of commission; provision for by board. [MSA 5.1193(4)]

MCLA 125.1235 Economic development and expansion program; activities. [MSA 5.1193(5)]

MCLA 125.1236 Additional powers and duties of commission. [MSA 5.1193(6)]

MCLA 125.1237 Applications for state or federal grants; acceptance, expenditures therefrom. [MSA 5.1193(7)]

Sec. 7. Upon the request of the governing body of any ... township ... for assistance ..., which includes but is not limited to surveys, land use studies, urban renewal plans and technical services. County costs shall be reimbursed to the county or counties by the local units of government. The commission may accept and expend grants from the state and the federal government and other public or private sources, contract with reference thereto, and enter into other contracts and exercise all other powers necessary to carry out the purpose of this act.

JOINT ACTION
Act No. 154, P.A. 1963 - Foreign Trade Zones

AN ACT to authorize the establishment of foreign trade zones; and to provide for their operation and maintenance.

MCLA 447.1 Foreign trade zone act; definitions. [MSA 21.302(1)]

Sec. 1. ... (a) "Act of congress" ... (b) "Public corporation" means the state, or any county, township, city or village within the state, or any state or municipal authority or similar organization financed in whole or in part by public funds. (c) "Private corporation" ...

MCLA 447.2 Establishment of foreign trade zone; application. [MSA 21.302(2)]

Sec. 2. Any public or private corporation ...

MCLA 447.3 Same; board, rules and regulations. [MSA 21.302(3)]

Act No. 24, P.A. 1968 - Division of International
Commerce

*AN ACT to create a division of international commerce
within the department of commerce; and to prescribe its
powers and duties.*

MCLA 447.101 Creation of division; director. MSA 3.542(1.)

MCLA 447.102 Performance of duties within available appropriations. MSA 3.542(2)

MCLA 447.103 Powers and duties. MSA 3.542(3)

*Sec. 3. The division of international commerce shall serve as
the focal point of the state for international activity and shall:* ...

Note: A local foreign trade zone should coordinate through
this agency since it has responsibility for doing research of all
kinds, making said research available to interested agencies and
industries, including port districts, etc.

JOINT ACTION
Act No. 23, P.A. 1968 - Foreign Trade Branch

*AN ACT to create a foreign trade branch of the
marketing section of the department of agriculture; and to
prescribe its powers and duties.*

MCLA 447.121 Creation. MSA 12.90(1)

MCLA 447.122 Performance of duties within available appropriations. MSA 12.90(2)

MCLA 447.123 Powers and duties. MSA 12.90(3)

Note: A local foreign trade zone should coordinate through this
agency since it has responsibility for doing research in the area of
agricultural commodities, making said research available to interested agencies and agricultural businesses.

R.S. 1846, c. 35 - Of the Preservation of Public Health: Quarantine, Nuisances and Offensive Trades

OFFENSIVE TRADES

MCLA 327.46 Designated places; records; supervision. [MSA 14.107]

Sec. 46. The township board ... when they shall judge it necessary, shall, from time to time, assign certain places for the exercising of any trade or employment, offensive to the inhabitants, or dangerous to the public health; and they shall forbid the exercise thereof in places not so assigned; and all such assignments shall be entered in the records ... and they may be revoked when the said township ... officers may think proper.

MCLA 327.47 Same; revocation, removal, conditions authorizing. [MSA 14.108]

MCLA 327.48 Civil damage suit. [MSA 14.109]

JOINT ACTION
Act No. 197, P.A. 1970 - Remodeling Migratory Workers' Housing and Incidental or Appurtenant Facilities

AN ACT to provide for certain remodeling projects; to prescribe certain powers and duties; to create a fund; to provide for certain grants; to provide for the promulgation of rules; and to make certain appropriations.

MCLA 286.611 Definitions. [MSA 17.425(11)]

MCLA 286.612 Grants to employers, amount, matching payments, other aid, sufficiency of remodeling. [MSA 17.425(12)]

Sec. 2. ... (3) A grant shall not be made if the remodeling does not meet the requirements of any law or rule.

MCLA 286.613 Department of public health, powers and duties. [MSA 17.425(13)]

MCLA 286.615 Advisory committee, powers and duties.
[MSA 17.425(15)]

MCLA 286.616 Appropriation establishing migratory labor housing fund. [MSA 17.425(16)]

Note: The above statute will be of direct concern in planning and zoning and health matters.

JOINT ACTION
Act No. 289, P.A. 1965 - Agricultural Labor Camps

AN ACT to protect the public health by licensing and regulating agricultural labor camps; to prescribe the powers and duties of the state health commissioner; and to provide remedies and penalties for the violations of this act.

MCLA 286.621 Definitions. [MSA 17.424(1)]

MCLA 286.622 License for operation of camp; posting. [MSA 17.424(2)]

MCLA 286.623 - 286.634 [MSA 17.424(3) - 17.424(14)]

Note: A member of a local health department may be appointed to an advisory committee, and a local health department may be called upon for assistance in enforcement, etc. of the act and promulgated rules, for which there may be payment of $15.00 for each licensed camp.

AIRPORT ZONING

When man left the ground in a flimsy kite-like apparatus at Kitty Hawk, North Carolina on December 17, 1903, little did he realize the problems that would be created. A costly lesson in foresight over hindsight has been brought into sharp focus, yet it is one generally still unlearned. Pilots warn us over and over again of the tragic consequences of strangling an airport with man-made obstructions, yet we continue to operate with something less than adequacy in zoning laws and controls. Airports usually are found in a conglomerate of all types of industrial, commercial, residential and even recreational facilities. Like the weather, everyone talks about it but no one does anything about it. The fault must be shared by state and federal government officials, who fail to provide adequate funds, and local government officials who are unwilling to establish and enforce zoning which would displace industrial and commercial enterprises or citizens who have the misfortune of living near an airport.

JOINT ACTION
Act No. 23, P.A. 1950, Ex. Sess. - Airport Zoning Act

AN ACT to empower and direct the Michigan aeronautics commission to adopt airport approach plans for publicly owned airports within this state; to empower the Michigan aeronautics commission, municipalities, and other political subdivisions to promulgate, adopt, establish, administer and enforce airport zoning regulations limiting the height of structures and objects of natural growth, and otherwise regulating the use of property in the vicinity of publicly owned airports, and to acquire, by purchase, grant, condemnation or otherwise, air rights and other interests in land; to provide for the establishment of zoning commissions, administrative agencies, and boards of appeals to administer the provisions of this act, and to provide for their organization and procedure and appeals therefrom; and to provide penalties and remedies for violations of this act or any ordinances or regulations made under the authority herein conferred; and to repeal any inconsistent act or parts of acts.

MCLA 259.431 Definitions. [MSA 10.501]

MCLA 259.432 Airport; publicly owned. [MSA 10.502]

MCLA 259.433 Airport hazard. [MSA 10.503]

MCLA 259.434 Airport hazard area. [MSA 10.504]

Sec. 4. The term "airport hazard area", when used in this act means any area of land or water, or both, upon which an airport hazard might be established if not prevented as provided in this act, including any such area which has been declared to be an "airport hazard area" by the Michigan aeronautics commission in connection with any airport approach plan adopted by said commission.

MCLA 259.435 Commission. [MSA 10.505]

MCLA 259.436 Political subdivision. [MSA 10.506]

Sec. 6. The term "political subdivision", when used in this act means any county, city, village or township of this state, and any other political subdivision, public corporation, authority, or district in this state which is or may hereafter be authorized by law to construct, enlarge, improve, maintain, equip, operate and regulate airports.

MCLA 259.437 Person. [MSA 10.507]

MCLA 259.438 State. [MSA 10.508]

MCLA 259.439 Structure. [MSA 10.509]

Sec. 9. The term "structure", when used in this act means any object constructed or installed by man, including, but without limitation, buildings, towers, smoke stacks and overhead transmission lines, but not including highways and their appurtenances.

MCLA 259.440 Tree. [MSA 10.510]

Sec. 10. The term "tree", when used in this act, means any object of natural growth.

MCLA 259.441 Airport hazard declared nuisance, prevention. [MSA 10.511]

MCLA 259.442 Airport approach plan; adoption, considerations. [MSA 10.512]

Sec. 12 The commission shall formulate, adopt and revise, when necessary, an airport approach plan for each publicly owned airport in this state. Each such plan shall indicate and determine the circumstances in which structures and trees are or would be airport hazards, ...

MCLA 259.443 Determination; zoning regulations. [MSA 10.513]

Sec. 13. In order to prevent the creation or establishment of airport hazards, every political subdivision having an airport hazard area wholly or partly within its territorial limits or jurisdiction may make an official determination that ...

MCLA 259.444 Joint airport zoning board; power, membership. [MSA 10.514]

Sec. 14. In each case where (a) an airport is owned, operated, controlled, leased to or leased by a political subdivision and any airport hazard area appertaining to such airport is located wholly or partly outside the territorial limits or jurisdiction of such political subdivision, or (b) an airport hazard area is located wholly or partly within the territorial limits or jurisdiction of 2 or more political subdivisions, whether or not the particular airport in connection with which such airport hazard area exists is owned, operated, controlled, leased to or leased by 1 or more of such political subdivisions, all the political subdivisions involved, including the political subdivision which is the owner, operator, controller, lessee or lessor of such airport, may, by ordinance or by resolution duly adopted, create a joint airport zoning board, which board shall ...

MCLA 259.445 Zoning ordinance; regulations incorporated. [MSA 10.515]

MCLA 259.446 Same; amendment. [MSA 10.516]

MCLA 259.447 Commission to define airport hazard; certification; joint airport zoning board, meeting, powers, compensation, expenditures. [MSA 10.517]

Sec. 17. In each case where an airport hazard area exists in connection with a publicly owned airport and suitable airport zoning regulations have not been adopted, administered and enforced for such airport hazard area in a form and manner deemed reasonably adequate by the commission for the purposes of this act, the com-

mission on behalf of this state shall define and determine such airport hazard area ...

MCLA 259.448 Conflict between zoning regulations, determination by commission. [MSA 10.518]

Sec. 18. In the event of conflict between any airport zoning regulations adopted under this act and any other zoning regulations applicable to the same area, ...

MCLA 259.449 Public hearing; notice. [MSA 10.519]

Sec. 19. No airport zoning regulations shall be adopted, amended, or changed under this act except by action of the governing body of the political subdivision in question, or by action of the joint board provided for in sections 14 or 17, after a public hearing in relation thereto, at which parties in interest and citizens shall have an opportunity to be heard. At least 15 days' notice of the hearing shall be published ...

MCLA 259.450 Airport zoning commission; report; hearings. [MSA 10.520]

Sec. 20. Prior to the initial zoning of any airport hazard area under this act, the governing body of the political subdivision or the joint airport zoning board which is to adopt the regulations shall appoint a body, to be known as the airport zoning commission, to recommend the boundaries of the various zones to be established and the regulations to be adopted therefor. Such airport zoning commission shall make a preliminary report and hold public hearings thereon ...

MCLA 259.451 Regulations to be reasonable, considerations. [MSA 10.521]

MCLA 259.452 Removal, etc., of structure or tree. [MSA 10.522]

MCLA 259.453 Construction permits. [MSA 10.523]

Sec. 23. Any airport zoning regulations adopted under this act shall require that a permit be obtained before any new structure or use may be constructed ...

914

MCLA 259.454 Variances; application, allowance. [MSA 10.524]

Sec. 24. Any person desiring to erect any structure, or increase the height of any structure, or permit the growth of any tree, or otherwise use his property in violation of the airport zoning regulations adopted under this act, may apply to the board of appeals, for a variance ...

MCLA 259.455 Markers and lights. [MSA 10.525]

Sec. 25. In granting any permit ... to indicate to flyers the presence of an airport hazard.

MCLA 259.456 Zoning regulations; administration and enforcement. [MSA 10.526]

Sec. 26. All airport zoning regulations adopted under this act shall provide for the administration and enforcement of such regulations by an administrative agency ...

MCLA 259.457 Board of appeals; powers. [MSA 10.527]

Sec. 27. All airport zoning regulations adopted under the provisions of this act shall provide for a board of appeals to have and exercise ...

MCLA 259.458 Same; appointment, members, officers, removals, rules, meetings, records kept, subpoenas. [MSA 10.528]

Sec. 28. Where a zoning board of appeals already exists it may be appointed as the board of appeals under this act. Otherwise, the board of appeals shall consist of 5 members, each to be appointed for a term of 3 years and until his successor is appointed ...

MCLA 259.459 Appeals; filing, hearing, notice. [MSA 10.529]

MCLA 259.460 Same; petitions for review by court. [MSA 10.530]

MCLA 259.461 Certiorari; jurisdiction of court. [MSA 10.531]

MCLA 259.462 Approach protection; acquisition of property. [MSA 10.532]

MCLA 259.463 Penalty. [MSA 10.533]

MCLA 259.464 Short title. [MSA 10.534]

Act No. 259, P.A. 1959 - Tall Structure Act

AN ACT to promote the safety, welfare and protection of persons and property in the air and on the ground by regulating the height, location and visual and aural identification characteristics of certain structures; and to provide penalties for violation of the provisions of this act.

MCLA 459.481 Tall structure act; definitions. [MSA 10.535(1)]

MCLA 259.482 **Building permit maximum height; proximity to airports.** [MSA 10.535(2)]

MCLA 259.483 **Same; public utility structures, emergency repair.** [MSA 10.535(3)]

MCLA 259.484 **Same; 1000-foot structures.** [MSA 10.535(4)]

MCLA 259.485 **Same; applicant; specification of location.** [MSA 10.535(5)]

MCLA 259.486 **Same; visual or aural identification installation.** [MSA 10.535(6)]

MCLA 259.487 **Same; denial, modification, public hearing.** [MSA 10.535(7)]

Sec. 7. ... Such determination shall become final 20 days after notification thereof is served, unless the applicant within such 20-day period, requests in writing that a hearing be held before the department with reference to the application. All such hearings shall be open to the public. ...

MCLA 259.488 **Public hearings; conduct, controlling statute and rules.** [MSA 10.535(8)]

MCLS 259.489 **Orders, review by Ingham circuit court.** [MSA 10.535(9)]

916

MCLA 259.490 Abatement of violation. ⌐MSA 10.535(10)⌐

MCLA 259.491 Department of aeronautics; rules and regulations; forms. ⌐MSA 10.535(11)⌐

MCLA 259.492 Violation, penalty. ⌐MSA 10.535(12)⌐

MCLA 259.493 Short title. ⌐MSA 10.535(13)⌐

BOUNDARIES AND THE STATE BOUNDARY COMMISSION

Michigan's unique boundary law is implemented by a boundary commission with no right of referendum to the people. Although originally covering only consolidation and incorporation, annexation was added in 1970 "to curtail forever the practice of strip annexation." In fact, a review of MTA's legislative representative's notes of the House of Representative's Committee on Towns and Counties at which MTA, the Michigan Municipal League and the Michigan Boundary Commission entered into discussion and debate, the commission's spokesmen stated they would never permit annexation that was for a tax grab only. Veteran township officials claim more descriptive language would be "ripping the guts right out of the township budgets and plans, and even the future of township government."

History has proven many times over in the last two years that, with the right of referendum denied to the people, greedy city officials are encouraged in their strip annexation practices by a boundary commission which, in our opinion, has flagrantly misinterpreted the law. In the past twenty years there have been seventeen whole townships which prematurely incorporated as cities for defensive purposes only. All comprehensive plans for the future had to be scrapped and efforts concentrated on just one thing-- stopping the neighboring city from annexing the major tax base of the township.

The logical progressive evolution in government is from a general law township to a charter township to a city. Warren Township in Macomb County is the only place in Michigan where this has been allowed to happen and today the city of Warren is one of the fastest growing cities in the nation. It has been concluded there that it enjoys its unique status because of the seven years it was a charter township.

This leads to another part of the dilemma facing township planners. Wherever the local government officials have determined that charter township status would be good for a particular general law township, it is primarily outside interests from nearby cities which tend to influence township residents to turn down the proposal. This is more fully discussed in the chapter on the Charter Township Act.

All township governments should make it a major project to see that the boundary commission law is amended to repeal that part which provides for no referendum if there are less than 100 people resident in the area. The structure of government in a democracy should not rest in the hands of five people through the implementation of veto power.

Act No. 191, P.A. 1968 - State Boundary Commission

AN ACT to create a state boundary commission; to prescribe its powers and duties; to provide for municipal incorporation, consolidation and annexation; and to repeal certain acts and parts of acts.

MCLA 123.1001 Definitions. [MSA 5.2242(1)]

MCLA 123.1002 State boundary commission; creation; members; vacancies; compensation; chairman. [MSA 5.2242(2)]

MCLA 123.1003 State boundary commission; employees and consultants. [MSA 5.2242(3)]

MCLA 123.1004 State boundary commission; office and facilities; rules, regulations and procedures; meetings, records; oaths. [MSA 5.2242(4)]

MCLA 123.1005 State boundary commission; county members, appointment, term, vacancy, compensation and qualifying; municipal boundary adjustment. [MSA 5.2242(5)]

Sec. 5. The presiding probate judge in each county shall appoint 2 persons residing in that county to serve on the commission during such time as the commission shall have under consideration municipal boundary adjustment for territory lying within his county, 1 of whom shall reside in a township and 1 within a city. ...

918

MCLA 123.1006 Petitions and resolutions, processing, disposition, priorities. [MSA 5.2242(6)]

MCLA 123.1007 Proceedings for incorporation of municipalities; census. [MSA 5.2242(7)]

MCLA 123.1008 Review of proposed incorporation; certificate of determination; public hearing; priorities, time period; notice; order for a public hearing, effect. [MSA 5.2242(8)]

MCLA 123.1009 Review of proposed incorporation; criteria. [MSA 5.2242(9)]

MCLA 123.1010 Denial or approval of proposed incorporation; revision of boundaries; submission of question to electors. [MSA 5.2242(10)]

MCLA 123.1011 Succession to property and liabilities; division of properties; sharing in revenues; assessment and collection of taxes. [MSA 5.2242(11)]

MCLA 123.1011a Jurisdiction over petitions or resolutions for annexation. [MSA 5.2242(11A)]

MCLA 123.1012 Petitions for consolidation, filing, signatures; creation of new cities; inclusion of townships; contents and prerequisites of petitions; rejection of petitions. [MSA 5.2242(12)]

MCLA 123.1012a Denial of proposed consolidation, revision of boundaries and approval of proposal, or approval without change, procedure; election, sufficiency of vote, notice, election procedure. [MSA 5.2242(12A)]

MCLA 123.1013 Consolidation including portion of township, municipality defined; charter commissioners, election, qualifications, number. [MSA 5.2242(13)]

MCLA 123.1014 Elections, ballots, expense, canvassing, returns; commissioners, nomination, qualifications, judges of qualifications. [MSA 5.2242(14)]

MCLA 123.1015 Charter commission; meeting, notice; procedure for adopting charter; powers, duties and procedure of commission; adoption of charter. [MSA 5.2442(15)]

MCLA 123.1016 Charter of consolidated city; preparation, contents; effect of adoption of provisions in charter. [MSA 5.2442(16)]

MCLA 123.1017 Corporate status of municipalities, charter taking effect; resubmission of charter for adoption, effect of unfavorable vote. [MSA 5.2442(17)]

MCLA 123.1018 Judicial review. [MSA 5.2442(18)]

MCLA 123.1019 State boundary commission established within department of treasury. [MSA 5.2442(19)]

MCLA 123.1020 Repeal of sections 123.21 and 123.22. [MSA 5.2442(20)]

Act No. 38, P.A. 1883 - Division of Territory

AN ACT to provide for adjustment of rights and liabilities on division of territory of cities and townships.

MCLA 123.1 Division of territory; adjustment of property rights and liabilities. [MSA 5.2221]

MCLA 123.2 Same; sale of lands; division of proceeds. [MSA 5.2222]

MCLA 123.3 Same; burial grounds. [MSA 5.2223]

MCLA 123.4 Same; apportionment of debts. [MSA 5.2224]

MCLA 123.5 Same; joint settlement meeting, notice. [MSA 5.2225]

MCLA 123.6 Same; representation at settlement meeting; duties at meeting. [MSA 5.2226]

MCLA 123.7 Same; institution of proceedings in chancery; decree. [MSA 5.2227]

MCLA 123.8 Liability for pro rata share of indebtedness paid. [MSA 5.2228]

MCLA 123.9 Act construed; scope. [MSA 5.2229]

Sec. 9. This act shall be applied to any change in the boundary of any incorporate village whenever it shall not be a part of any township within this state.

MCLA 123.10 Same; existing change but no settlement. [MSA 5.2230]

MCLA 123.11 New assessment district; assessment and collection; reassessment; apportionment of bonded indebtedness; circuit court, jurisdiction. [MSA 5.2231]

Act No. 123, P.A. 1949 - Disconnection of Land from Cities and Villages

AN ACT to provide for the disconnection of land from cities and villages; and to declare the effect thereof.

MCLA 123.31 Disconnection of farm land from city or village. [MSA 5.3561]

MCLA 123.32 Same; petition, filing, contents; determination of court; denial. [MSA 5.3562]

MCLA 123.33 Same; assessment for bonded indebtedness; division as between municipalities; sale for delinquent taxes. [MSA 5.3563]

MCLA 123.34 Judgment, recording. [MSA 5.3564]

MCLA 123.35 Disconnection of land from city or village; cities and villages excepted. [MSA 5.3565]

MCLA 123.36 Territory annexed to city or village; exemption. [MSA 5.3566]

Act No. 4, P.A. 1955 - Annexation of Submerged Lands

*AN ACT to authorize certain cities and villages to
annex certain lands submerged by waters of the great lakes
or connecting waters; to provide the procedure of annexation; and to declare certain submerged lands part of
political subdivisions without annexation.*

**MCLA 123.581 Great lakes submerged lands; annexation to cities
and villages.** [MSA 5.3571]

MCLA 123.582 Same; consent (by owner), **amendment of charter.**
[MSA 5.3572]

MCLA 123.583 Same; automatic annexation to cities and villages.
[MSA 5.3573]

**Act No. 93, P.A. 1957 - Annexation of State Owned
Land**

*AN ACT to provide for the annexation of state owned
land by cities operating under a special charter.*

**MCLA 123.981 Annexation of state owned land by cities under
special charter. Election** (includes township), **date, manner, costs.**
[MSA 5.3557]

**MCLA 123.982 Prorating of state funds distributable to cities and
townships; stipulation.** [MSA 5.3558]

MCLA 123.983 Same; official special census. [MSA 5.3559]

R.S. 1846, c. 17 - Division of Townships

MCLA 41.111 Division of township; (joint township board meeting)
disposition of land. [MSA 5.2201]

MCLA 41.112 Same; (township board meeting, powers), **annexation.**
[MSA 5.2202]

MCLA 41.113 Same; sale of land; division of proceeds. [MSA 5.2203]

*Sec. 3. If no agreement ... shall be made by the township
boards within 6 months ... then the township board of each township*

... shall ... sell ... (the) ... lands ... included within the ... township; and the proceeds ... apportioned between the ... townships by the township boards ... according to ...

MCLA 41.114   Same; apportionment of personalty (by township boards). [MSA 5.2204]

MCLA 41.115   Meeting of township boards, notice. [MSA 2205]

Sec. 5.   Whenever a meeting of the township boards of 2 or more townships shall be required, in order to carry into effect the provisions of this chapter, such meeting may be called by either of the supervisors; but the supervisor calling the same shall give at least 6 days' notice in writing to all the other officers, of the time and place at which such meeting is to be held.

MCLA 41.116   Burial grounds (remain property of township). [MSA 5.2206]

MCLA 41.117   Debts, apportionment (payment). [MSA 5.2207]

MCLA 41.118 Local boards, failure to act, (subject to suit) **accounting; villages, cities.** [MSA 5.2208]

SURVEYS AND SURVEYORS

Of prime importance to a purchaser of real estate is that the deed reflects the accurate measurements and corners "on the land". Although there is a measure of confidence in receiving a warranty deed in that the seller pledges by law to "warrant and defend" the title to the property, it is nonetheless common sense to have the land surveyed and the closing of the deal done under the capable supervision of an attorney who is knowledgeable in the laws governing property.

The law requires that only registered professional engineers and surveyors, trained in the intricate methods of land measurement, may do this important work.   They are also expert in geological, soil and economic surveys, base maps and utilization of aerial photography, all matters of concern in adequate land use planning. Their training makes them especially adept at assisting township boards in the implementation and enforcement of Act No. 288, P.A.

1968 (the Subdivision Control Act). It is interesting to note that many township boards include attendance of their township engineer and/or surveyor at each of their meetings.

R.S. 1846, c. 14 - County Surveyors

MCLA 54.95 Abolition of office, re-establishment; bond; eligibility. [MSA 5.1021]

MCLA 54.96 Deputies; appointment, revocation, filing; oath. [MSA 5.1022]

MCLA 54.97 Certificates as presumptive evidence. [MSA 5.1023]

MCLA 54.98 Requested surveys. [MSA 5.1024]

MCLA 54.99 Interest disqualification, survey by surveyor of adjoining county. [MSA 5.1025]

MCLA 54.100 Record book, contents; field notes, contents, part of record; fire-proof vault, location; public accessibility; bookkeeping requirement. [MSA 5.1026]

MCLA 54.101 Delivery of records to successor; penalty. [MSA 5.1027]

MCLA 54.102 Federal notes, plats, obtaining certified copies; records of former surveyors, securing; expenses; records on file, evidence. [MSA 5.1028]

MCLA 54.103 Survey principles. [MSA 5.1029]

MCLA 54.105 Corners, relocated, perpetuated; majority petition; expenses, allocation, lien. [MSA 5.1030]

Sec. 105. ... if any person thus benefited, ... shall refuse or neglect to pay his share of such expense, such surveyor shall certify the same and to whom due, to the supervisor of the proper township, who shall ...

MCLA 54.105a Same; surveyor's charges, assessment. [MSA 5.1031]

Sec. 105a. If any person, after having requested ... shall refuse or neglect to pay ... such surveyor shall certify the lawful charges for the same and to whom due to the supervisor of the proper township, who shall ...

MCLA 54.106   County surveyor; compensation, fees; trespass non-liability. [MSA 5.1032]

Act No. 132, P.A. 1970 - Surveys

AN ACT to provide for the filing of surveys in the office of the register of deeds relative to land divisions; and to prescribe the conditions of the survey.

MCLA 54.211   Recording, authorization, necessity. [MSA 13.115(61)]

MCLA 54.212   Registered land surveyors, performance of survey, preparation of map; corners, monumenting. [MSA 13.115(62)]

MCLA 54.213   Maps, form, contents. [MSA 13.115(63)]

Act No. 74, P.A. 1970 - Corner Recordation Act

AN ACT to protect and perpetuate public land survey corners; to require the establishment of monuments and the recording of information concerning public land survey corners; and to prescribe the duties of the register of deeds.

MCLA 54.201   Short title. [MSA 13.115(51)]

MCLA 54.202   Definitions. [MSA 13.115(52)]

MCLA 54.203   Corner record, necessity, form, filing. [MSA 13.115(53)]

MCLA 54.204   Filing corner record. [MSA 13.115(54)]

MCLA 54.205   Contents and form of corner record, rules. [MSA 13.115(55)]

MCLA 54.206   Corner record books, form, numbering, cross index plats, public inspection; filing fees. [MSA 13.115(56)]

MCLA 54.207 Corner monument and accessories, reconstruction or rehabilitation. [MSA 13.115(57)]

MCLA 54.208 Signing, sealing, and certifying corner record. [MSA 13.115.58)]

MCLA 54.209 Previously established, reestablished, or restored corners. [MSA 13.115(59)]

Act No. 149, P.A. 1883 - Section Corners and Quarter Posts

AN ACT to authorize the board of supervisors of the several counties in this state to provide for ascertaining, preserving and maintaining the original section corners and quarter posts, as surveyed and recorded by the original survey, and to repeal Act No. 159 of the session laws of 1877, Act No. 205 of the session laws of 1879 and Act No. 73 of the session laws of 1881.

MCLA 54.221 Section corners, establishment; surveyors' records, evidence; (township election;) **vote; tax levy; limitation.** [MSA 5.511]

MCLA 54.222 Same; marking; penalty. [MSA 5.512]

Act No. 292, P.A. 1907 - Section Corners and Boundaries

AN ACT to provide for the surveying and establishing of section corners and the boundaries of unsurveyed lands in certain cases.

MCLA 322.241 Section corners and boundaries of unsurveyed lands established; appointment of surveyor. [MSA 13.491]

MCLA 322.242 Surveyor; compensation, expenses, payment. [MSA 13.492]

MCLA 322.243 Original notes filed in state land office; effect of corners and boundaries so established. [MSA 13.493]

Act No. 312, P.A. 1921 - Section Corners and Boundaries

AN ACT to provide for the surveying and establishing of section corners and boundaries of lands, and to provide for ascertaining, re-establishing, preserving and maintaining, in certain cases, the original section corners, quarter posts and boundaries as surveyed and recorded by the original survey.

MCLA 322.251 **Section corners, landmarks and shore lines established by department; surveyor; petition; payment of cost; destroyed markers, replacement.** [MSA 13.501]

MCLA 322.252 **Original notes of field work filed with department; record with county surveyor; evidence; not to apply to established surveys.** [MSA 13.502]

Act No. 314, P.A. 1941 - Section, Quarter Section and Center Section Corners

AN ACT to regulate the locating of section, quarter section and center section corners; to require the use of a standard marker therefor; to provide for the furnishing thereof; to provide for the preservation of the records thereof; to provide penalties for violations of the provisions of this act and to repeal all acts and parts of acts inconsistent with the provisions of this act.

MCLA 338.591 **Surveyors to use standard markers; record of survey filed.** [MSA 13.503(1)]

MCLA 338.592 **Standard marker** (in public highway); **construction, lettering, placing.** [MSA 13.503(2)]

MCLA 338.593 **Same; manufacture by prison industries; furnishing at cost.** [MSA 13.503(3)]

MCLA 338.594 **Same; destruction or removal; records as evidence.** [MSA 13.503(4)]

MCLA 338.595 Revocation of surveyor's license for failure to comply. [MSA 13.503(5)]

Act No. 65, P.A. 1869 - Geological Survey

AN ACT to provide for the further geological survey of the state.

MCLA 321.1 Board of geological survey; duties; assistants. [MSA 13.41]

MCLA 321.3 Assistants' salaries; reports. [MSA 13.42]

MCLA 321.4 Character and scope of survey. [MSA 13.43]

MCLA 321.5 Specimens for exhibition. [MSA 13.44]

MCLA 321.6 Annual report; complete report, character. [MSA 13.45]

Sec. 6. ... a complete memoir ... to set forth ... the nature, location, and extent of the geological and agricultural resources of the state: ...

MCLA 321.8 Notes, etc., property of state. [MSA 13.46]

MCLA 321.9 Annual appropriation for expenses; payment; printing reports. [MSA 13.47]

Act No. 373, P.A. 1917 - Soil and Economic Survey

AN ACT to provide for a soil and economic survey of certain lands in this state, to require the making of reports thereon, and to provide an appropriation therefor.

MCLA 321.21 Soil and economic survey. [MSA 13.51]

MCLA 321.22 Same (by county); unit of area; purpose; direction and control; assistants. [MSA 13.52]

MCLA 321.23 Same; detailed report by counties; printing. [MSA 13.53]

MCLA 321.24 Same; report; contents, maps, distribution. [MSA 13.54]

MCLA 321.25 Payment of expenses; statement of unexpended fund.
MSA 13.55

MCLA 321.26 Cooperation with other agencies; purpose of act not to be changed. MSA 13.56

MCLA 321.27 Right of entry on private property. MSA 13.57

MCLA 321.30 Unexpended funds; reduction through federal aid. MSA 13.58

MCLA 321.31 Reports to legislature; progress of work, expenses, recommendations. MSA 13.59

Act No. 248, P.A. 1937 - Aerial Photographing and Base Maps

AN ACT to provide for and authorize aerial photographing and preparing of base maps of certain portions of the state; to authorize cooperation with the federal government and joint contract therewith for certain purposes; to provide for making an appropriation to meet the expenses of the same; and to provide regulations for paying necessary expenses incident to such work.

MCLA 321.151 Aerial photographing and base maps; authorization, federal cooperation. MSA 13.95

MCLA 321.152 Same; features shown; share of expense, right of entry on private lands. MSA 13.96

MOBILE HOMES AND TRAILER COACHES

America, long recognized as a "nation on wheels," is producing all kinds of mobile homes at the rate of 4 to 6 million units a year. Courts, all the way to the U. S. Supreme Court, have more and more supported the theory that it is a person's privilege to live where he wishes, even in a mobile home. New on the scene is the modular dwelling which may be made from varying types of material, including poured concrete, which are mobile only in the sense that they are placed on wheels for delivery to the building site and can be moved to another site in the same manner.

In order to guarantee the rights of both mobile home residents and those who live in more traditional structures, it has become necessary to license and regulate trailer and mobile home parks and prescribe the powers and duties of state and other public officials in this area of concern. Local ordinances based on proper land use may permit mobile homes to be placed in special subdivisions or other suitable areas. In fact, rather elaborate mobile home subdivisions are being laid out in a number of areas of the state, bringing a whole new aspect to township planning and development. The law also makes provision for trailer coaches to be located outside of licensed parks under certain conditions.

The township treasurer collects tax revenues from the licensed parks and the township clerk is responsible for the licensing and regulation of trailer coaches located outside of regular parks.

Act No. 300, P.A. 1949 - Michigan Vehicle Code

MCLA 257.30a (Definition of) **"Mobile home"**. MSA 9.1830(1)

MCLA 257.74 (Definition of) **"Trailer coach"** MSA 9.1874

MCLA 257.719a (Size of mobile home/local ordinance) MSA 9.2419(1)

MCLA 257.801 (Trailer coaches/no exemption for real property taxes) MSA 9.2501

Note: Please refer to the section on Motor Vehicles and Snowmobiles in chapter four for the above citations.

Act No. 243, P.A. 1959 - Mobile Home Park Act

AN ACT to define, license and regulate trailer coach parks; to prescribe the powers and duties of the state health commissioner and other state and local officers; to provide for the levy and collection of specific taxes on occupied trailers in trailer coach parks and the disposition of the revenues therefrom; to provide remedies and penalties for the violation of this act; and to repeal certain acts and parts of acts.

MCLA 125.1001 Short title. [MSA 5.278(31)]

MCLA 125.1002 Definitions. [MSA 5.278(32)]

MCLA 125.1005 Construction or alteration, permit (from commissioner). [MSA 5.278(35)]

MCLA 125.1006 Application for permit, contents. [MSA 5.278(36)]

MCLA 125.1007 Applications for construction permits.
[MSA 5.278(37)]

MCLA 125.1008 Construction plans and specifications.
[MSA 5.278(38)]

Sec. 8. ... Where plans contemplate connections to existing facilities such as water systems, sewers and drains, evidence of authorization ... from ... proper authorities, either on or attached to the plans.

MCLA 125.1009 Application and plans, examination. [MSA 5.278(39)]

MCLA 125.1010 Permit for construction; time, extension.
[MSA 5.278(40)]

MCLA 125.1011 Permits, transferability; prior permits.
[MSA 5.278(41)]

MCLA 125.1012 Permits, notice of issuance (to municipality).
[MSA 5.278(42)]

MCLA 125.1013 Applications, deficiencies, notice, amendment.
[MSA 5.278(43)]

MCLA 125.1014 Affidavit of compliance. [MSA 5.278(44)]

MCLA 125.1015 Examination of construction. [MSA 5.278(45)]

MCLA 125.1016 Compliance with local regulations (required).
[MSA 5.278(46)]

MCLA 125.1021 License; renewal. [MSA 5.278(51)]

MCLA 125.1022 Applications for license to operate park.
[MSA 5.278(52)]

MCLA 125.1023 License fees (units of government exempt).
[MSA 5.278(53)]

MCLA 125.1024 License fee proceeds, disposition, receipts.
[MSA 5.278(54)]

MCLA 125.1025 When licensed. [MSA 5.278(55)]

MCLA 125.1026 Partial completion, licensing. [MSA 5.278(56)]

MCLA 125.1027 Conditions for renewal of license. [MSA 5.278(57)]

MCLA 125.1028 Bonds for payment of taxes (to township clerk before license issued). [MSA 5.278(58)]

MCLA 125.1029 Rent; recovery of a possession of premises.
[MSA 5.278(59)]

MCLA 125.1031 License, issuance, display, transfer. [MSA 5.278(61)]

MCLA 125.1032 Expiration of licenses. [MSA 5.278(62)]

MCLA 125.1033 License, copies, distribution (notice to municipal treasurer by commissioner). [MSA 5.278(63)]

MCLA 125.1034 Notice of deficiencies. [MSA 5.278(64)]

MCLA 125.1035 Located in more than one municipality. [MSA 5.278(65)]

MCLA 125.1041 Specific tax (in lieu of property tax); **collection, exception.** [MSA 5.278(71)]

MCLA 125.1042 Tax revenue, disbursement (by municipal treasurer, to general fund and school district). [MSA 5.278(72)]

MCLA 125.1043 Tax, remittance (on or before 5th day each month); **reimbursement of licensee.** [MSA 5.278(73)]

MCLA 125.1051 Location, general requirements. [MSA 5.278(81)]

932

MCLA 125.1052 Location and identification of trailer coaches. [MSA 5.278(82)]

MCLA 125.1053 Space requirements (from street, alley, park boundary). [MSA 5.278(83)]

MCLA 125.1054 Roadway requirements. [MSA 5.278(84)]

MCLA 125.1055 Water supply. [MSA 5.278(85)]

Sec. 55. The water supply serving any park constructed after the effective date of this act shall be obtained from a municipal supply if it is available ...

MCLA 125.1056 Plumbing. [MSA 5.278(86)]

MCLA 125.1057 Sewage and waste disposal. [MSA 5.278(87)]

MCLA 125.1058 Sewers. [MSA 5.278(88)]

MCLA 125.1066 Garbage and rubbish disposal. [MSA 5.278(96)]

MCLA 125.1067 Electrical service. [MSA 5.278(97)]

Note: Above sections require compliance with applicable codes and ordinances.

MCLA 125.1068 Fire extinguishers. [MSA 5.278(98)]

MCLA 125.1071 Office; registration records (inspection by police officers). [MSA 5.278(101)]

MCLA 125.1072 Management, responsibility and duty. [MSA 5.278(102)]

MCLA 125.1073 Line fences (construction, costs, kind). [MSA 5.278(103)]

MCLA 125.1074 Practices prohibited. [MSA 5.278(104)]

MCLA 125.1075 Streets and driveways. [MSA 5.278(105)]

MCLA 125.1076 Night lighting. [MSA 5.278(106)]

MCLA 125.1077 Attendant in charge. [MSA 5.278(107)]

MCLA 125.1078   Animals at large prohibited.   [MSA 5.278(108)]

MCLA 125.1079   Communicable disease, report.   [MSA 5.278(109)]

MCLA 125.1081   Inspection by health officer.   [MSA 5.278(111)]

MCLA 125.1082   School authorities, inspection.   [MSA 5.278(112)]

MCLA 125.1083   School age children, report.   [MSA 5.278(113)]

MCLA 125.1085 Filing complaints or invoking act, not grounds for evicting tenant or lessee. [MSA 5.278(115)]

MCLA 125.1091 Exclusions. [MSA 5.278(121)]

MCLA 125.1093   Procedure to revoke license.   [MSA 5.278(123)]

MCLA 125.1094   Health and peace officer, duties. [MSA 5.278(124)]

MCLA 125.1095 Injunctive relief. [MSA 5.278(125)]

MCLA 125.1096   Violation of act, penalty.   [MSA 5.278(126)]

MCLA 125.1097 Act repealed. [MSA 5.278(127)]

Act No. 172, P.A. 1958 - Trailer Coaches Outside of Licensed Parks

AN ACT to provide for the payment, collection and disposition of yearly taxes on occupied trailer coaches located outside of licensed trailer parks; and to provide for permits and sanitary regulations of trailers harbored outside of licensed trailer parks.

MCLA 125.741 Trailer coach permit; use outside park.
[MSA 5.278(21)]

Sec. 1. No person shall use or permit the use of any trailer coach as a residence on any site, lot, field or tract of land not

*specifically licensed as a trailer coach park for more than 15 days
except by written permit as hereinafter provided.*

MCLA 125.742 Same; application, contents; fee; renewals.
MSA 5.278(22)

*Sec. 2. (1) All applications ... shall be made to the clerk or
other designated agency within a ... township in which the trailer
coach would be parked. The application shall contain: ... (2) A
registration fee of $5.00 shall accompany the application to the
township clerk ... for ... administrative costs. ... the clerk shall
issue a permit ... (which) ... shall expire and be subject to renewal
12 months from the date issued. Renewals may be limited to 6-month
periods, for which the registration fee shall not exceed $3.00.*

MCLA 125.744 Same; sanitation, zoning, building, fire regulations.
MSA 5.278(24)

*Sec. 4. This act specifically authorizes the county or district
... to make such regulations and bylaws, ... for defining sanitation
requirements for trailer coaches not located in licensed parks.
Nothing in this act or in the regulations or bylaws hereby authorized
shall supersede or be in conflict with local zoning, building, fire
codes or regulations, local ordinances or other legal restrictions
for the protection of the public health and welfare.*

MCLA 125.745 Violation, penalty. MSA 5.278(25)

CONSTRUCTION AND BUILDING CODES

It was only natural that Michigan, with its highly diversified
industrial economy, would take a leading place in the nation in
the building boom that sprang up at the end of World War II.   All
kinds of regulatory building and construction codes were established in municipality after municipality. Builders and contractors
complained that it was impossible to meet the varying restrictions
since seldom were there two alike among the townships, cities and
villages in a county.

The federal government established model codes, and some
local governments, aided by professional groups and consultants,
began to adopt the models with additional regulations to meet

local needs. However, that effort still did not bring about enough voluntary uniformity. In 1972 the state legislature stepped in and set up a nine-member construction code commission to be appointed by the governor, empowered to draw up a mandatory statewide construction code by January 1, 1974, to become legally operative by July 1, 1974.

Provision is made for a local government to exempt itself from the state code by passing an ordinance, effective sixty days thereafter (amendments may be adopted in the same manner) which incorporates the nationally recognized codes. A copy of the ordinance and any amendments to it must be provided to the state construction commission, which will determine if the health, safety and welfare of the people are adequately protected. The local ordinance must be reviewed and updated every three years.

There are two exceptions to local control. First, an ordinance applies to public or non-public schools within the political subdivision **only** by concurrence of the appropriate school authorities. Second, the state will be the only jurisdiction for premanufactured modular housing units, mobile homes and other like construction, which may be issued a certificate of acceptability by the construction code commission at the place of manufacture. Such units will qualify throughout the state without local modification.

Responsibility for administration and enforcement may lie with the governing bodies of the various units of government. If the local unit does not wish to undertake this responsibility, then the county board of commissioners will do so. In the final analysis, if there is a breakdown at the county level, the executive director of the state construction code commission will take over.

Therefore, township boards have several choices with regard to their future in the field of building code enforcement, depending on their present situations. If a township has already adopted nationally recognized building codes, there should be no problem under the new act, providing the three-year updating process is followed. If a township has adopted its own building codes, it should either change to the nationally recognized codes or the new state code when it is finally promulgated and approved, if it wishes to continue in control of its own jurisdiction. Where there is no building code enforcement at present, a township may adopt the national codes or take over administration of the state code. If a township wishes to do nothing, then it will be required to accept administration of the state code within the township by the county.

Local officials are reminded that if a township is small and

936

they believe that administration of national or state codes would be too expensive for the volume of building taking place, the board may elect to act jointly with one or more other townships or units of local government.

JOINT ACTION
Act No. 230, P.A. 1972 - State Construction Code Act of 1972

AN ACT to create a construction code commission and prescribe its functions; to authorize the commission to promulgate rules relating to the construction, alteration, demolition, occupancy and use of buildings and structures; to provide for statewide approval of premanufactured units; to provide for the testing of new devices, materials and techniques for the construction of buildings and structures; to define the classes of buildings and structures affected by the act; to provide that cities, villages and townships may with exceptions elect not to be subject to the act; to provide for administration and enforcement of the act; to establish remedies and fix penalties for violations of the act; and to repeal certain acts and parts of acts.

MCLA 125.1501 Short title. [MSA 5.2949(1)]

MCLA 125.1502 Definitions; references to this act or the code. [MSA 5.2949(2)]

MCLA 125.1503 State construction code commission. Creation; membership, qualifications, appointment, terms, vacancies, removal, disclosures, compensation. Quorum; action by majority vote of members present; meetings, notice, time, place. Officers. Commission within department of labor; independence as to statutory functions. [MSA 5.2949(3)]

MCLA 125.1504 State construction code, promulgation, contents, purpose, divisions. [MSA 5.2949(4)]

MCLA 125.1505 Powers of commission. [MSA 5.2949(5)]

Sec. 5. ... The commission may encourage, support or conduct, either by itself or in cooperation with enforcing agencies, associa-

tions of building code officials, or any other persons, educational and training programs for employees, agents and inspectors of enforcing agencies. ...

MCLA 125.1506 Rules, promulgation (copy to governmental subdivision). [MSA 5.2949(6)]

MCLA 125.1507 Executive director and other officers and employees of commission, appointment; consultants and advisors, appointment or use; effectuation of act. [MSA 5.2949(7)]

MCLA 125.1508 Geographical application of act and code; locally adopted codes; code inclusions or exclusions. Exemptions at election of cities, villages, or townships; locally adopted codes, authorization, periodic updating, effective dates and rejection of amendments. Effective date of code; exemptions, time; locally adopted codes, review of amendments upon elections to be exempt. Administration and enforcement of locally adopted codes. Schools applicability of locally adopted codes. Premanufactured housing and use of particular materials, products, method of manufacture, construction, or installation, applicability of act and code. Inclusions or exclusions by commission. [MSA 5.2949(8)]

MCLA 125.1509 Enforcement of act and code. County responsibility, imposition; assumption of responsibility, cities, villages, townships; enforcing agency, designation; joint enforcement. Failure of county, city, village, or township to enforce code, hearing, determination, remedy. Local laws and ordinances, enforcement of act and construction regulations. [MSA 5.2949(9)]

MCLA 125.1510 Applications for building permits, necessity, form, contents, applicants, filing, custody; site plans; other permits; necessity for building permits. [MSA 5.2949(10)]

MCLA 125.1511 Building permits, necessity, issuance, denial, review, compliance, suspension, revocation, cancellation; changes in plans, approval. [MSA 5.2949(11)]

MCLA 125.1512 Inspection of construction, requirement, consent, time, inspectors; violations, notice, stop orders, injunctions, parties. [MSA 5.2949(12)]

938

MCLA 125.1513 Certificates of use and occupancy, necessity, issuance, contents, applications, inspections, temporary certificates. [MSA 5.2949(13)]

MCLA 125.1514 Construction board of appeals; creation; membership, appointment, terms, qualifications; jurisdiction; decisions, filing, notice, record. [MSA 5.2949(14)]

MCLA 125.1515 Variances; grounds; conditions, granting, breach. [MSA 5.2949(15)]

MCLA 125.1516 Appeals to state construction code commission; parties; time; variance denials, discretion; procedure; appeals to state plumbing and electrical administrative boards, procedure; review by commission. [MSA 5.2949(16)]

MCLA 125.1517 Effect of appeals on stop construction orders, injunctions, or other orders or decisions. [MSA 5.2949(17)]

MCLA 125.1518 Claims of appeals, court of appeals; petitions to review, Ingham county circuit court. [MSA 5.2949(18)]

MCLA 125.1519 Premanufactured units; certificates of acceptability, requirements for issuance; building permits, issuance; objections to use of unit despite certificate, procedure, determination. [MSA 5.2949(19)]

MCLA 125.1520 Examination of plans and specifications, inspections, or performance of other enforcement duties by commission. [MSA 5.2949(20)]

MCLA 125.1521 Particular materials, products, or methods of manufacture, construction, or installation; petitions for approval, acceptance, rejection; certificates of acceptability, granting, conditions, distribution of copies, use for advertising. [MSA 5.2949(21)]

MCLA 125.1522 Fees, establishment, collection, disposition; expenses. [MSA 5.2949(22)]

    Sec. 22. ... (By county) ... Unless otherwise provided by local law and ordinance, ...

MCLA 125.1523 Offenses, penalties. [MSA 5.2949(23)]

MCLA 125.1524 Pre-existing local construction regulations, continuance, repeal, supersedence; building permits and construction based on pre-existing regulations. [MSA 5.2949(24)]

Sec. 24. *Until 6 months after promulgation of the code, construction regulations heretofore or hereafter adopted by a county, city, village or township continue in effect unless repealed by local law or ordinance. Thereafter, ...*

MCLA 125.1525 Licensing or registration of master or journeymen plumbers or electricians, plumbers apprentices, and electrical contractors (not affected). [MSA 5.2949(25)]

MCLA 125.1526 Transfer of functions of state plumbing and electrical administrative boards to commission. [MSA 5.2949(26)]

MCLA 125.1528 Repeals; construction, use of repealed sections; supersedence; saving clause, other statutes. [MSA 5.2949(28)]

MCLA 125.1529 Enforcement of code and construction regulations. [MSA 5.2949(29)]

MCLA 125.1530 Saving clause, construction regulations, proceedings, prosecutions. [MSA 5.2949(30)]

MCLA 125.1531 Effective date (January 1, 1973). [MSA 5.2949(31)]

Act No. 165, P.A. 1966 - Construction Contracts

AN ACT to invalidate certain requirements for indemnity in the construction industry.

MCLA 691.991 Building industry; certain contracts for indemnification void. [MSA 26.1146(1)]

Act No. 240, P.A. 1937 - Architecture, Professional Engineering and Land Surveying

AN ACT to license and regulate the practice of architecture, professional engineering and land surveying; to

940

create separate state boards of registration for architects, professional engineers and land surveyors, and to prescribe their powers and duties; to impose certain powers and duties upon the state and the political subdivisions thereof in connection with public work; and to provide penalties for the violation of the provisions of this act.

MCLA 338.551 Registration of architects, engineers and surveyors (required). [MSA 18.84(1)]

MCLA 338.552 Same; definitions. [MSA 18.84(2)]

MCLA 338.553 - 338.564a [MSA 18.84(3) - 18.84(14A)]

MCLA 338.565 Certificate of registration; issuance, seal (required on plans). [MSA 18.84(15)]

MCLA 338.565a Sealing of plans, plats, drawings, specifications, and reports or index sheets thereof; overlapping of the professions. [MSA 18.84(15A)]

MCLA 338.566 - 338.567 [MSA 18.84(16) - 18.84(17)]

MCLA 338.568 Restrictions by political subdivisions; exception. [MSA 18.84(18)]

Note: Restrictions apply to political subdivisions, including townships, on any project in excess of $5,000.00.

MCLA 338.569 Exemptions; calculated floor area, definition. [MSA 18.84(19)]

MCLA 338.570 - 338.571 [MSA 18.84(20) - 18.84(21)]

MCLA 338.572 Penalty. [MSA 18.84(22)]

Sec. 22. ... All law enforcing officers of this state shall enforce the provisions of this act. ... A person shall not submit to any public official of this state or any political subdivision thereof for approval, a permit or for filing as a public record a plan, specification, report or land survey which does not bear 1 or more seals of a registered architect, registered professional engineer or *registered land surveyor as required by this act, except for public works costing less than $5,000.00 or residential buildings containing not more than 3,500 square feet of calculated floor area as defined herein. ...*

MCLA 338.572a   Unlawful practice of architecture, professional engineering or land surveying; injunction. [MSA 18.84(22A)]

MCLA 338.573 - 338.576 [MSA 18.84(23) - 18.84(26)]

Act No. 126, P.A. 1963 - Landscape Architects

AN ACT relating to landscape architects; to require the registration of landscape architects; to create the board of landscape architects and to prescribe their powers and duties; to prescribe the qualifications of landscape architects; to fix the fees for examination and registration; to prescribe the powers and duties of the director of agriculture and the state agricultural commission; and to provide penalties for the violation of this act.

MCLA 338.1201   Landscape architect act; short title. [MSA 18.84(101)]

MCLA 338.1202   Same; definitions. [MSA 18.84(102)]

MCLA 338.1203 - 338.1217 [MSA 18.84(103) - 18.84(117)]

MCLA 338.1218   Seal of registered landscape architect; permitted (and required) use. [MSA 18.84(118)]

MCLA 338.1219   Violation, penalty. [MSA 18.84(119)]

Act No. 383, P.A. 1965 - Residential Builders, Etc.

AN ACT to provide for the licensing and rights of any person to engage in business as a residential builder or residential maintenance and alteration contractor or salesman; to prescribe the duties and powers of the corporation and securities commission relative thereto; to fix the standards of qualifications and eligibility for the practice thereof; to create a state residential builders' and maintenance and alteration contractors' board; to authorize the

942

collection and expenditure of fees; to provide penalties for the violation of this act; and to repeal certain acts and parts of acts.

MCLA 338.1501 Residences; builders, maintenance and alteration contractors, salesmen, licensing (required). [MSA 18.86(101)]

MCLA 338.1502 Definitions. [MSA 18.86(102)]

MCLA 338.1503 Exemptions. [MSA 18.86(103)]

Note: Act not applicable to any federal or state political subdivision, or any project not exceeding $200.00.

MCLA 338.1503a Exemptions; electrical contractors licensed under sections 338.881 to 338.892. [MSA 18.86(103A)]

MCLA 338.1504 - 338.1508 [MSA 18.86(104) - 18.86(108)]

MCLA 338.1509 Investigation; suspension or revocation, grounds therefor; civil or criminal liability; time limitation for complaints. [MSA 18.86(109)]

Sec. 9. The commission may, upon its motion or upon the complaint in writing of any person made within 18 months after completion, occupancy or purchase of a residential or combination of residential and commercial building, investigate the actions of any ... (license holder) ... and shall ...

MCLA 338.1509a - 338.1516 [MSA 18.86(109A) - 18.86(116)]

MCLA 338.1516a Enforcement of licensing requirements; building permits, showing of license as pre-requisite to issuance. [MSA 18.86(116A)]

MCLA 338.1517 - 338.1518 [MSA 18.86(117) - 18.86(118)]

Act No. 266, P.A. 1929 - Plumbing

MCLA 338.901 - 338.917 [MSA 14.451 - 14.467]

Note: This act has been superseded - see Act No. 230, *P.A. 1972 (MCLA 125.1528 et seq)* [MSA 5.2949(28) ET SEQ].

Act No. 217, P.A. 1956 - Electrical Administrative Act

AN ACT to safeguard persons and property; to provide for licensing of electricians and electrical contractors and the inspection of electrical wiring; to create an electrical administrative board; to exempt certain townships unless the township elects to be covered by this act; and to prescribe penalties for violations of the provisions of this act.

MCLA 338.881 Electrical administrative act; definitions.
MSA 18.204(1)

MCLA 338.882 Electrical administrative board; members, meetings, compensation, expenses, inspection. MSA 18.204(2)

MCLA 338.883 Same; licenses, fees; rules and regulations.
MSA 18.204(3)

MCLA 338.884 New construction (in township); **minimum standards for wiring. Conformity with statutes, ordinances, orders, rules, regulations. Evidence of conformity. Special wiring methods.**
MSA 18.204(4)

MCLA 338.885 Electrical wiring installation; licensed installers (required), **permits.** MSA 18.204(5)

MCLA 338.886 Electrical wiring installation; application of act; municipal regulation, registration, reciprocity. MSA 18.204(6)

Sec. 6. The provisions of this act, except for this section, shall not apply within the jurisdiction of any ... township which has adopted or hereafter adopts an ordinance providing standards for electrical wiring and its installation not less than those prescribed by the 1968 national electrical code and provides inspection service. Nothing contained herein shall be construed as limiting the power of a municipality ...

MCLA 338.886a Municipal regulations; licensing of electrical contractors, master electricians and journeymen. MSA 18.204(6A)

944

MCLA 338.887 Electrical contractor's license; exceptions.
[MSA 18.204(7)]

MCLA 338.888 Municipalities not covered by act. [MSA 18.204(8)]

Sec. 8. *This act shall not apply to municipalities making provisions for inspection and licensing in accordance with the provisions of section 6 if the local requirements are not less than those prescribed by this act, ...*

MCLA 338.888a Licensing without examination. [MSA 18.204(8A)]

MCLA 338.888b Suspension or revocation of licenses.
[MSA 18.204(8B)]

MCLA 338.889 License fees, general fund. [MSA 18.204(9)]

MCLA 338.890 Violation, penalty. [MSA 18.204(10)]

MCLA 338.891 Liability for defective installation or appliances.
[MSA 18.204(11)]

MCLA 338.892 Short title. [MSA 18.204(12)]

Act No. 311, P.A. 1972 - Safety Glazing Materials

AN ACT to require the use of safety glazing materials in hazardous locations in residential, commercial or public buildings; to provide a penalty; and to repeal certain acts and parts of acts.

MCLA 125.1381 Definitions. [MSA 5.2893(11)]

MCLA 125.1382 - 125.1386 [MSA 5.2893(12) - 5.2893(16)]

MCLA 125.1387 Local permits; state or local codes, regulations, or ordinances. [MSA 5.2893(17)]

Sec. 7. *Nothing in this act shall relieve any person from responsibility for securing any local permits or complying with all applicable state or local codes, regulations, or ordinances not in conflict with this act.*

945

MCLA 125.1388 Repeals (effective January 1, 1973).
MSA 5.2893(18)

MCLA 125.1389 Effective date (July 1, 1973). MSA 5.2893(19)

Act No. 1, P.A. 1966 - Utilization of Public Buildings by Physically Handicapped

AN ACT to provide for the accessibility and the utilization by the physically handicapped of certain buildings constructed with funds of the state or its political subdivisions and of certain buildings used by the public and to provide for the enforcement of the act.

MCLA 125.1351 Definitions. MSA 3.447(121)

Sec. 1. ... "Physical handicap" ... "Administrative authority" ... "Public building" means a structure to which the public customarily has access and utilizes and which is constructed, in whole or in part, with funds of the state or its political subdivisions. **(Includes township halls and offices.)** *... "Buildings used by the public" means a building, structure or improved area used primarily by the general public as a place of gathering or amusement, including but not limited to: theaters, restaurants, hotels and stadia.*

MCLA 125.1352 Building construction, remodeling, or rehabilitation, requirements for access and utilization by the handicapped. MSA 3.447(122)

Sec. 2. ... Approval of the (state) administrative authority shall be secured before the awarding of construction contracts for any building covered by this act.

MCLA 123.1353 Administration and enforcement. MSA 3.447(123)

Note: By state building division, state department of education, and the building and inspection departments or agencies of local administrative authority with the responsibility and duty of issuing building permits.

MCLA 125.1354 Rules, promulgation, administration, enforcement. MSA 3.447(124)

946

MCLA 125.1355 Penalty. [MSA 3.447(125)]

MCLA 125.1356 Effective date (July 1, 1971). [MSA 3.447(126)]

JOINT ACTION
Act No. 167, P.A. 1917 - Housing Law

AN ACT to promote the health, safety and welfare of the people by regulating the light and ventilation, sanitation, fire protection, maintenance, alteration and improvement of dwellings; to define the classes of dwellings affected by the act, to establish administrative requirements and to establish remedies and fix penalties for the violation thereof.

ARTICLE I. GENERAL PROVISIONS

MCLA 125.401 Housing law of Michigan; scope of act. [MSA 5.2771]

Sec. 1. ... shall apply to every city and organized village ... (population and territory specifications) ... and extending for a radial distance of 2 1/2 miles beyond such boundaries in all directions. ... and in ... unincorporated areas lying within a radial distance of 1 1/4 miles beyond the boundaries of any city or village ... (between 10,000 and 100,000) ... the provisions of this act relating to private ... and 2 family dwellings may be applied to such unincorporated areas by ordinance of the respective township board adopting such provisions. All ...

Note: Act No. 266, P.A. 1929, (MCLA 338.916) [MSA 14.466] specifically excepted Act No. 617, P.A. 1917, from repeal "except as the same may be in conflict herewith."

MCLA 125.402 Definitions. [MSA 5.2772]

MCLA 125.402a Enforcing agency, defined. [MSA 5.2772(1)]

MCLA 125.407 Sewer connections and water supply. [MSA 5.2777]

MCLA 125.408 Minimum requirements; law not to be modified. [MSA 5.2778].

MCLA 125.409 State board of health; authority. [MSA 5.2779]

MCLA 125.410 Time for compliance. [MSA 5.2780]

ARTICLE II. DWELLINGS HEREAFTER ERECTED

ALTICLE III. ALTERATIONS

Note: These chapters repealed--See now MCLA 125.1501 et seq [MSA 5.2949(1) ET SEQ]

ARTICLE IV. MAINTENANCE

MCLA 125.465 Public halls in multiple dwellings; lighting; exit lights. [MSA 5.2837]

MCLA 125.466 Water-closets in cellars. [MSA 5.2838]

MCLA 125.467 Water-closet accommodations. [MSA 5.2839]

MCLA 125.468 Basement and cellar rooms. [MSA 5.2840]

MCLA 125.469 Kitchen, use of jointly by more than 1 family prohibited. [MSA 5.2841]

MCLA 125.470 Water-closets and sinks, floors under and around. [MSA 5.2842]

MCLA 125.471 Repairs and drainage. [MSA 5.2843]

MCLA 125.472 Water supply. [MSA 5.2844]

MCLA 125.473 Catch-basins. [MSA 5.2845]

MCLA 125.474 Cleanliness of dwellings. [MSA 5.2846]

MCLA 125.475 Multiple dwelling; walls of courts. [MSA 5.2847]

MCLA 125.476 Same; walls and ceilings of rooms. [MSA 5.2848]

MCLA 125.477 Same; wall paper. [MSA 5.2849]

MCLA 125.478 Receptacles for ashes, garbàge and rubbish; chutes prohibited. [MSA 5.2850]

MCLA 125.479 Prohibited uses. [MSA 5.2851]

MCLA 125.480 Combustible materials. [MSA 5.2852]

MCLA 125.481 Same; openings between storage room and public hall. [MSA 5.2853]

MCLA 125.482 Fire prevention and safety requirements. [MSA 5.2854]

MCLA 125.483 Overcrowding; minimum space requirements. [MSA 5.2855]

MCLA 125.484 Multiple dwelling; regulation; application. Lodgers prohibited. [MSA 5.2856]

MCLA 125.485 Health order; infected and uninhabitable dwellings to be vacated. [MSA 5.2857]

MCLA 125.486 Same; repairs to buildings, etc. [MSA 5.2858]

MCLA 125.487 Maintenance of fire escapes. [MSA 5.2859]

MCLA 125.488 Scuttles, bulkheads, ladders and stairs, multiple dwellings. [MSA 5.2860]

MCLA 125.489 Rooms; lighting and ventilation. [MSA 5.2861]

MCLA 125.490 Public halls and stairs, lighting and ventilation, multiple dwellings. [MSA 5.2862]

MCLA 125.491 Plumbing fixtures. [MSA 5.2863]

MCLA 125.492 Privy vaults, school-sinks and water-closets. [MSA 5.2864]

MCLA 125.493 Protection of basements and cellars. [MSA 5.2865]

MCLA 125.494 Shafts and courts; openings. [MSA 5.2866]

MCLA 125.495 Egress; means above first floor. [MSA 5.2867]

MCLA 125.496 Same; other means. [MSA 5.2868]

MCLA 125.497 Roof egress in multiple dwellings. [MSA 5.2869]

ARTICLE VI. REQUIREMENTS AND REMEDIES

Note: This chapter repealed--see now next chapter.

ARTICLE VII. ENFORCEMENT

MCLA 125.523 Administration of act; designation of local officer or agency; joint administration and enforcement agreement.
[MSA 5.2891(3)]

Sec. 123. The governing body of a municipality to which this act by its terms applies, or the governing body of a municipality which adopts the provisions of this act by reference, shall designate a local officer or agency which shall administer the provisions of the act, and if no such officer or agency is designated then the local governing body shall be responsible for administration of the act. Municipalities may provide, by agreement, for the joint administration and enforcement of this act where such joint enforcement is practicable.

MCLA 125.525 Registry of owners and premises. [MSA 5.2891(5)]

MCLA 125.526 Inspection; intervals; basis; inspectors; hours of inspection; fees. [MSA 5.2891(6)]

MCLA 125.527 Inspection; warrants for nonemergency situation; no warrant required in emergency. [MSA 5.2891(7)]

MCLA 125.528 Inspection; policy; records; checklist of recurring violations. [MSA 5.2891(8)]

MCLA 125.529 Certificate of compliance; no occupancy unless certificate issued; hazardous conditions; inspections.
[MSA 5.2891(9)]

MCLA 125.530 Certificate of compliance; vacation of premises while certificate withheld; issuance on condition; suspension of rent; escrow; actions for rent and possession. [MSA 5.2891(10)]

MCLA 125.531 Certificate of compliance; application; fee. [MSA 5.2891(11)]

MCLA 125.532 Violations; recording in registry; notice; order to correct, reasonable time; reinspection. [MSA 5.2891(12)]

MCLA 125.533 Compliance with act; owner; occupant. [MSA 5.2891(13)]

MCLA 125.534 Action to enforce provisions of act; injunction; parties; temporary relief; service of complaint and summons; order; removal of building; expenses of repair or removal. [MSA 5.2891(14)]

MCLA 125.535 Receivership; appointment; bond; purpose; powers and duties; expenses. [MSA 5.2891(15)]

MCLA 125.536 Additional remedies; occupant's action; concurrent remedies. [MSA 5.2891(16)]

MCLA 125.537 Rights of action under this article. [MSA 5.2891(17)]

MCLA 125.538 Dangerous building, prohibition. [MSA 5.2891(18)]

MCLA 125.539 Definition of "dangerous building". [MSA 5.2891(19)]

MCLA 125.540 Notice of dangerous and unsafe condition, issuance, recipient, contents, filing, form, service; hearing officer, appointment. [MSA 5.2891(20)]

MCLA 125.541 Testimony; determination to close proceedings or order building demolished or made safe, compliance, hearing, cost of compliance as lien, collection. [MSA 5.2891(21)]

MCLA 125.542 Review. [MSA 5.2891(22)]

MCLA 125.543 Housing law, adoption by municipalities, necessity. [MSA 5.2891(23)]

Sec. 143. Nothing herein contained shall require any ... township to adopt ... (this act) ...

Act No. 319, P.A. 1929 - Fuel Oil

AN ACT to regulate the use, handling, storage and sale of fuel oil, and the arrangement, design, construction and installation of burners, tanks and other equipment for the burning of fuel oil for heating purposes in cities and villages adopting the provisions of this act.

MCLA 125.551 - 125.575 [MSA 5.2901 - 5.2925]

Note: Although townships are not included in the descriptive title of the above act, a local ordinance might very well be modeled along its terms and conditions. Consult the township attorney.

Act No. 314, P.A. 1921 - Excavated Land

AN ACT to prescribe the duties of an owner or occupant of lands, upon which excavations are made, in reference to the furnishing of lateral and subjacent support to adjoining lands and structures thereon; and to fix remedies for the violation thereof.

MCLA 554.251 Owner or occupant of excavated land, duty to support adjacent land and structures. [MSA 26.1141]

MCLA 554.252 Same; failure, liability for damage to property or business. [MSA 26.1142]

MCLA 554.253 Same; equitable relief. [MSA 26.1143]

MCLA 554.254 Common law duties and remedies. [MSA 26.1144]

Act No. 229, P.A. 1963 - Horizontal Real Property Act (Condominiums)

AN ACT to provide for the establishment of condominium and condominium projects; to define apartments and common elements in such projects; to prescribe the contents of and provide for the recording of master deeds establishing such projects; to define and provide for the identification and description of condominium apartment for purposes of ownership, mortgaging, taxation, possession, sale and other juridic acts; to provide for review and approval of proposed condominium projects and the sale of apartments therein; to provide for certain fees; and to prescribe penalties for violations of this act or regulations and orders issued hereunder.

MCLA 559.1   Short title. MSA 26.50(1)

MCLA 559.2   Definitions. MSA 26.50(2)

MCLA 559.3   Condominium project; establishment. MSA 26.50(3)

MCLA 559.4   Same; apartment as property. MSA 26.50(4)

MCLA 559.5   Apartment; ownership. MSA 26.50(5)

MCLA 559.6   Same; rights of co-owners. MSA 26.50(6)

MCLA 559.7   Master deed, recording; taxes, special assessments. MSA 26.50(7)

Sec. 7.   An approved master deed shall be recorded ... but ... (not) ... without a certification by the treasurer collecting the same that all property taxes and special assessments which have become a lien on the property involved in the project have been paid in full. When recorded, a copy of the master deed and a copy of any subsequently amended master deed must be filed with the local supervisor or assessing officer.

MCLA 559.8   Apartments, conveyances, recording. MSA 26.50(8)

MCLA 559.9   Condominium project; waiver, vacation, merger of records of sole properties. MSA 26.50(9)

MCLA 559.10   Same; subsequent constitution in another project. MSA 26.50(10)

MCLA 559.11 Same; bylaws, recording, amendment, filing. MSA 26.50(11)

MCLA 559.12 Same; bylaws, permissible provisions. [MSA 26.50(12)]

MCLA 559.13 Same; bylaws, mandatory provisions; tax on personal property; destruction. [MSA 26.50(13)]

MCLA 559.14 Same; books and records, examination, audit. [MSA 26.50(14)]

MCLA 559.15 Apartment, contributions for administration, maintenance, and repair; nonuse of common elements, abandonment. [MSA 26.50(15)]

MCLA 559.16 Assessments; lien, enforcement, priority. [MSA 26.50(16)]

MCLA 559.17 Same; liability of mortgagee who forecloses on unit. [MSA 26.50(17)]

MCLA 559.18 Mortgage on project's property; apportionment. [MSA 26.50(18)]

MCLA 559.19 Homestead exemption. [MSA 26.50(19)]

MCLA 559.20 Taxes and special assessments; assessment against project, apartment. [MSA 26.50(20)]

MCLA 559.21 Apartment, sale, payment of assessments for expenses, priority, statement. [MSA 26.50(21)]

MCLA 559.22 Administrator; action on behalf of co-owners. [MSA 26.50(22)]

MCLA 559.23 Condominium subdivision plans, enumeration. [MSA 26.50(23)]

MCLA 559.24 Condominium project; master deed, filing fee; application for permit to sell apartments. [MSA 26.50(24)]

MCLA 559.25 Master deed, examination; inspection of property; expenses; certificate of approval; notice of disapproval. [MSA 26.50(25)]

MCLA 559.26 Permit to sell apartments; application, proposal to sell. [MSA 26.50(26)]

MCLA 559.27 Condominium project, approval of changes, replat. [MSA 26.50(27)]

MCLA 559.28 Misrepresentation, violation of act, penalty. Misrepresentation. Injunction. Prosecution. [MSA 26.50(28)]

MCLA 559.29 Condominium project (is) subject to local laws, ordinances, regulations. [MSA 26.50(29)]

MCLA 559.30 Fees credited to general fund. [MSA 26.50(30)]

MCLA 559.31 Department of commerce; promulgation of rules, forms, forms and orders. [MSA 26.50(31)]

Act No. 188, P.A. 1913 - Hotels, Inns and Lodging Houses

AN ACT relating to the conduct of hotels, inns and public lodging houses.

MCLA 427.1 Hotel; definition. [MSA 18.321]

MCLA 427.2 Same; fire escape equipment, ways of egress and notices in buildings over two stories in height. [MSA 18.322]

MCLA 427.3 Same; fire extinguishers. [MSA 18.323]

MCLA 427.4 Same; rope equipment and notices in two story buildings. [MSA 18.324]

MCLA 427.5 Same; sanitation, water closets. [MSA 18.325]

MCLA 427.6 - 427.15 [MSA 18.326 - 18.335]

Note: These sections have to do with health regulations and inspection.

HOUSING

Engineers trained in the art of projecting future trends generally agree that there will be an estimated need for 30,000 housing units in the next twenty-seven years. This is not just urban renewal or low cost housing as discussed in the chapter on Services, Utilities, Contracts and Ordinances, but is inclusive of all economic levels. It is therefore incumbent upon township officials to study local housing needs, including facilities for senior citizens, the physically handicapped, etc. The statutes which follow are representative of some areas in which townships are expected to become more and more involved in the years ahead.

Competent professional engineers and other consultants must be employed to assist in making decisions reflecting both present and future needs. There are also a number of federal and state agencies which are not only willing to help, but have proven that they welcome inquiry from any level of local government. Very often the federal agencies have offices in major metropolitan areas in each of the states.

Although each of the statutes which follow establish certain basic minimum requirements, local municipalities, including townships, have complete authority to adopt inspection and enforcement ordinances which go beyond the basic scope of federal and state minimums. Townships are encouraged to adopt safety and regulatory ordinances of this type to insure the same degree of protection and services to those who must live in public housing as it does to those in housing which is developed, constructed and maintained by private enterprise.

JOINT ACTION
Act No. 344, P. A. 1945 - Blighted Area Rehabilitation

AN ACT to authorize counties, cities, villages and townships of this state to adopt plans for the rehabilitation of blighted areas; to authorize assistance in carrying out such plans by the acquisition of real property and the disposal of real property in such areas; to prescribe the methods of financing the exercise of these powers, and to declare the effect of this act.

MCLA 125.71 **Rehabilitation of blighted areas.** [MSA 5.3501]

956

Sec. 1. ... blighted areas are detrimental or inimical to the health, safety, morals, and general welfare of the citizens, and to the economic welfare of the municipality; ... in order to improve and maintain the general character of the municipality, it is necessary to rehabilitate such blighted areas; ... public participation in the planning, property, acquisition, disposition and financing thereof; ...

MCLA 125.72 Definitions. [MSA 5.3502]

MCLA 125.73 Power of municipality. [MSA 5.3503]

MCLA 125.74 Definitions; plans, statements, actions, (citizens' and coordinating and) **district council, public hearing, relocation of displaced families, notice and approval.** [MSA 5.3504]

MCLA 125.74a Racial segregation in housing (not permissible); **consultation and assistance of state civil rights commission.** [MSA 5.3504(1)]

MCLA 125.75 Acquisition of property, condemnation; dispossession (limitations). [MSA 5.3505]

MCLA 125.75a Urban renewal plat. [MSA 5.3505(1)]

MCLA 125.76 Acquisition (and disposition) **of property; jurisdiction of public agencies.** [MSA 5.3506]

MCLA 125.77a Municipal bonds payable from income, terms, interest. [MSA 5.3507(1)]

MCLA 125.77b Municipal general obligation bonds, approval, maximum, time of sale, estimated period of usefulness. [MSA 5.3507(2)]

MCLA 125.77c Tax revenues. [MSA 5.3507(3)]

Sec. 7c. As an additional and alternative method of financing part or all of the costs of any project undertaken under this act, any municipality may use general tax revenues levied for the purpose or not otherwise earmarked.

MCLA 125.78 Loans and grants, acceptance, federal assistance, conditions; labor wages and standards. [MSA 5.3508]

MCLA 125.79 Modification of plan; hearing. [MSA 5.3509]

MCLA 125.80 Work done in accordance with plan. [MSA 5.3510]

Sec. 10. ... the local legislative body shall provide by ordinance that the zoning board of appeals, if the municipality has such a board, or if not, then a board of appeals created for the purpose, shall have the power on appeal filed with it by the owner of real property in the area to approve a minor deviation from the plan ... (under certain conditions) ...

MCLA 125.81 Designation of administrative agency. [MSA 5.3511]

Sec. 11. The local legislative body may designate an administrative agency ... or by ordinance may create a commission for that purpose consisting of ...

MCLA 125.82 . Ordinances or resolutions (required); **validation; modification of development plan.** [MSA 5.3512]

MCLA 125.83 Powers deemed additional. [MSA 5.3513]

Sec. 13. The powers granted in this act shall be in addition to powers granted to municipalities, the local legislative bodies thereof and other officials and bodies thereof under the statutes and local charters. Nothing herein contained shall be construed to amend or repeal any of the provisions of Act No. 18 of the Public Acts of 1933 as amended. (MCLA 125.651 et seq) [MSA 5.3011 ET SEQ]

MCLA 125.84 District areas, citizens district and coordinating councils; exemptions, membership, advisory councils, notices of hearings, boundaries, vacancies, validation. [MSA 5.3513(14)]

JOINT ACTION
Act No. 208, P.A. 1949 - Neighborhood Area
Improvements

AN ACT to authorize cities, villages and townships

of this state to designate neighborhood areas for the purpose of planning and carrying out local public improvements for the prevention of blight within such areas; to authorize assistance in carrying out plans for local improvements by the acquisition and disposal of real property in such areas; to provide for the combining of neighborhood improvements that benefit the entire neighborhood into 1 improvement project; to provide for the establishment of local assessment districts coterminous with the neighborhood boundaries; to prescribe the methods of financing the exercise of these powers, and to declare the effect of this act.

MCLA 125.941 Neighborhood areas in municipalities; improvement of, declared to be public use and public purpose. [MSA 5.3521]

MCLA 125.942 Same; definitions. [MSA 5.3522]

MCLA 125.943 Same; betterment plan. Master plan of municipality, approval. Plan of neighborhoods, approval. Neighborhood betterment plan, approval. Improvements. Plats, streets, public utilities, pavement, parks, nonconforming uses; rehabilitation of blighted areas. Relocation of families. Hearing on adoption of area plan; notice, description. [MSA 5.3523]

MCLA 125.944 Same; purchase, etc., of property; condemnation. [MSA 5.3524]

MCLA 125.945 Same; transfers to public agencies; excess land sold or exchanged; special assessment district. [MSA 5.3525]

MCLA 125.946a Bonds payable from project revenue; terms, tax exemption, interest. [MSA 5.3526(1)]

MCLA 125.946b Neighborhood improvement bonds; municipal general obligation bonds, approval, maximum, time of sale, estimated period of usefulness. [MSA 5.3526(2)]

MCLA 125.946c Tax levy; special assessment. [MSA 5.3526(3)]

MCLA 125.947 Gifts, loans, grants from private or public sources; contracts for assistance. [MSA 5.3527]

959

MCLA 125.948 Neighborhood areas in municipalities; modification of plan, hearing. [MSA 5.3528]

MCLA 125.949 Same; permits, withholding. [MSA 5.3529]

Sec. 9. Upon advice of the planning commission that plans for the betterment of a neighborhood are in preparation, the legislative body may establish a date, and for a period of time not to exceed 6 months thereafter, temporarily withhold permits for building construction, sidewalks, drainage systems or other major improvements within the neighborhood.

MCLA 125.950 Same; plans to be officially adopted; board of appeals; hearing, notice, publication. [MSA 5.3530]

Sec. 10. On and after the date when a plan has been approved ... no permit shall be issued for building ... which are not in accordance with the plans ...: Provided, ... That the legislative body shall provide by ordinance that the zoning board of appeals, ... (present or created) ... shall have the power ...

MCLA 125.951 Same; actions to be by ordinance or resolution, procedure. [MSA 5.3531]

MCLA 125.951a Same; designation of administrative agency. (establishment of regulations). [MSA 5.3531(1)]

MCLA 125.952 Powers granted. [MSA 5.3532]

Sec. 12. ... shall be in addition to the powers granted to municipalities, the legislative bodies thereof and other officials and bodies thereof under the statutes and local charters. Nothing herein contained shall be construed to amend or repeal any of the provisions of Act No. 18 of the Public Acts of the Extra Session of 1933. (MCLA 125.651 - 125.698) [MSA 5.3011 - 5.3056(2)]

Act No. 2, P.A. 1935 - National Housing Act

AN ACT to authorize loans, advances of credit and purchases in accordance with the provisions of an act of Congress, entitled "National Housing Act," approved by the President on June 27, 1934, and any acts amendatory thereof or supplemental thereto; and prescribing the effect of this act.

MCLA 487.751 National housing act; investment by state financial institutions; collateral. [MSA 23.181]

MCLA 487.752   Construction of act; state laws.   [MSA 23.182]

MCLA 487.753 Immediate necessity. [MSA 23.183]

Chapter IX

FINANCE AND TAXATION

Taxation in one form or another has had a profound effect on kingdoms and principalities, feudal and totalitarian governments, as well as on democratic government as represented in the United States. Centuries ago someone said, "No two things in life are as certain and sure as death and taxes." It has also been said, "Taxation, or the means to make taxes available, is like a cancerous sore − − once available, there is no cure; taxes just keep growing and growing and growing." Perhaps a little more explicit is the almost indisputable statement, "There is nothing so permanent as a 'temporary' tax."

A simple, basic description of taxation is that it is a means of paying for public services rendered by a governmental body to the citizens of a constituency, whether it be the nation, the state or local government − − or even a private corporation.

Taxes can be levied on income − − many feel this is the only fair tax because it is based upon one's ability to pay the tax on his earnings. They can be intangible taxes, business taxes of all kinds, sales taxes, and the one which affects most people − − the property tax. This chapter deals with these forms of taxation as they apply to township government either directly or indirectly.

The terms "township supervisor" and "assessor" or "assessing officer" are used interchangeably in these citations, since the supervisor has traditionally been the assessing officer in the township. However, reflecting the need to standardize the assessing process, recent legislation has made it mandatory that all assessors be certified by the Michigan State Assessors Board — — making it possible, and sometimes preferable, for a township to employ some other professional assessing officer. The supervisor, in this case, retains responsibilities for preparation of the tax roll and all other administrative and operational requirements of the tax law in the township. Separation of the assessing function from the supervisor's regular duties might well leave that officer more time for dealing with other facets of township government which have increased so much in recent years.

The State Assessors Board employs a professional training officer to see that adequate educational opportunities are available to prepare township supervisors, city assessors, county equalization directors and other individuals who desire to make assessing their profession. Continuing education is also provided to keep assessors abreast of modern methods and changes in the laws. Plans are under way for special classes for individuals who wish to become qualified as an assessor in order to enhance prospects of attaining elective office. As this book goes to press, the new two-volume Assessors' Manual has been published and is available to all assessing officers from the State Assessors Board. The Board meets periodically to review applications and conduct examinations which, although primarily written, may also under certain circumstances be oral, or a combination of both.

If a township finds itself without a certified assessor for one reason or another, there are several alternatives available. The township board may request the State Assessors Board for a temporary certification of a newly elected supervisor while he/she attends assessors' school, it may employ a certified assessor from another township, or a professional assessor/appraiser. Failure by the local unit to comply with the certification law will result in the county equalization director or the state tax commission conducting the annual assessment with the cost charged back to the township.

All assessing officers would do well to become involved in the Michigan Assessors' Association, an organization devoted to the improvement of assessment administration, and which is actively involved in the state educational programs and certification procedures, as well as efforts to promote better tax legislation and in teaching and public relations efforts designed to keep the average student and/or citizen aware of all that is involved in the assessment process. The association's monthly magazine, **Michigan Assessor,** is an invaluable aid to every assessing officer, and the editors solicit suggestions and articles based on experiences.

A township supervisor may be called upon in the matter of appointment of a guardian for a minor under fourteen years of age (see **Act No. 288, P.A. 1939, MCLA 703.2** [MSA 27.3178(202)]), or to serve as an appraiser in court cases dealing with property valuation. Therefore the supervisor/assessor should make it a point to visit the probate court having jurisdiction in his/her county to visit with the judge and become familiar with the various forms he might have to fill out. Although on the surface this may not seem related to a discussion on finance and taxation, it nonetheless imposes upon the supervisor/assessor an additional duty for which he should be prepared if called upon to act.

The successful assessor maintains a high level of proficiency through attending the state assessing classes, reading up on the subject and keeping himself fully informed of revisions in the law. But above all else, the task must be approached as constant effort rather than concentration of activities within a few days and then dumping the whole matter in the lap of the Board of Review. Tax Day (December 31) is merely a cut-off day with no implication that it is the only day assessing is done.

A township's taxing authority depends upon its budgetary requirements and the revenues which may be available to it through the following statutes, with the general property tax act being of prime importance. Additional authority for specific purposes may be granted under other statutes which are found in various other chapters of this book.

STATE TAX AGENCIES

The statutes which follow present a picture of the Michigan power structure under which the assessment of real and personal property is conducted. All problems of grievances, appeals or complaints and all requests for information regarding assessment and taxes ultimately find their way to the assessing office of the state tax commission.

Act 282, P.A. 1905 is included only for informational purposes. Local officers have no concern with this statute except at section 12 wherein certain duties of the local assessing officer and county clerk are required in the implementation of the act.

Act No. 122, P.A. 1941 — Revenue Division of the Department of Treasury

AN ACT to establish a revenue division of the depart-

ment of treasury; to prescribe its powers and duties as the revenue collection agency of the state; to create the position and to define the powers and duties of the state commissioner of revenue; to provide for the transfer of powers and duties now vested in certain other state boards, commissions, departments and offices; to abolish the state board of tax administration; and to declare the effect of this act.

MCLA 205.1 Tax collection agency, creation, purposes; references to department of revenue, meaning. [MSA 7.657(1)]

Sec. 1. ... Any reference to the department of revenue in this act or any other act shall mean the revenue division of the department of treasury.

MCLA 205.2 State commissioner of revenue, operation of position, function, appointments, vacancies, qualifications; deputies and other employees, appointment, qualifications, duties. [MSA 7.657(2)]

MCLA 205.3 Same; powers and duties; testimony, taking; procedure. [MSA 7.657(3)]

MCLA 205.3a Demand for payment of tax; warrant, issuance; levy; sale; cost, penalties, interest; procedure. [MSA 7.657(3A)]

MCLA 205.6a Compromise of tax liability. [MSA 7.657(6A)]

MCLA 205.7 State board of tax appeals; appeals, procedure, costs. [MSA 7.657(7)]

MCLA 205.8 Same; members, appointment of; term, salary. [MSA 7.657(8)]

MCLA 205.9 Same; procedure following decision. [MSA 7.657(9)]

MCLA 205.11 State revenue receipts, reports; divulgence of information by employees prohibited. [MSA 7.657(11)]

MCLA 205.12 Official seal of department. [MSA 7.657(12)]

MCLA 205.13 Administration of laws transferred to department of revenue. [MSA 7.657(13)]

MCLA 205.17 Office space; branch offices; approval of board of state auditors. [MSA 7.657(17)]

Act No. 360, P.A. 1927 — State Tax Commission

AN ACT to create a state tax commission, to prescribe its powers and duties, to provide for the transfer to said state tax commission of the powers now vested by law in the state tax department; to abolish said state tax department, and to repeal all acts and parts of acts contravening any of the provisions of this act.

MCLA 209.101 State tax commission created. [MSA 7.631]

MCLA 209.102 State tax commission; membership and appeals. Membership, qualifications, terms, appointment, chairman, compensation; assistants; removal of commissioners; oath. Appeals; decisions, form, filing, delivery; signing of orders, dissents, record of appeal hearing. [MSA 7.632]

MCLA 209.103 State tax department abolished; transfer of powers, duties and records. [MSA 7.633]

MCLA 209.104 State tax commission, duties, meetings; public officers, duties, failure, penalty. [MSA 7.634]

Sec. 4. The state tax commission shall have general supervision of the administration of the tax laws of the state, and shall render such assistance and give such advice and counsel to the assessing officers of the state as they may deem necessary and essential to the proper administration of the laws governing assessments and the levying of taxes in this state. Said state tax commission shall gather each year, complete information relative to the assessment of property properly classified, the levy of taxes thereon and of the appraised value of the several classes of property exempt from taxation under the laws of this state, and such other information as said state tax commission shall deem to be of public interest. This information shall be embodied in the regular report of the state tax commission. It shall be the duty of all assessing officers of the state and all other public officers, to promptly comply with requests made by said state tax commission for information provided for in this section, and to render all possible assistance in carrying out the provisions hereof. Any assessing officer or other public officer who shall refuse to comply with the requirements of this act or who shall persistently neglect to do so, shall be deemed guilty of a misdemeanor and upon conviction thereof shall be punished by a fine of not less than 50 nor more than 300 dollars.

MCLA 209.105 Signature and seal on papers; inspection of records. MSA 7.635

Sec. 5.... All records of and appraisals made by the state tax commission shall be open to inspection at all reasonable times by any assessing officer in the state of Michigan.

Act No. 282, P. A. 1905 — State Board of Assessors and Assessment of Property of Certain Public Utilities

AN ACT to provide for the assessment of the property, by whomsoever owned, operated or conducted, of railroad companies, union station and depot companies, telegraph companies, telephone companies, sleeping car companies, express companies, car loaning companies, stock car companies, refrigerator car companies, and fast freight companies, and all other companies owning, leasing, running or operating any freight, stock, refrigerator, or any other cars, not being exclusively the property of any railroad company paying taxes upon its rolling stock under the provisions of this act, over or upon the line or lines of any railroad or railroads in this state, and for the levy of taxes thereon by a state board of assessors, and for the collection of such taxes, and to repeal all acts or parts of acts contravening any of the provisions of this act.

MCLA 207.1 — 207.11 MSA 7.251 - 7.261

MCLA 207.12 County clerk, assessing officer, duties; failure to report, penalty; inspection by state board. MSA 7.262

Sec. 12. It shall be the duty of the county clerk ... as soon as possible after the equalization of the board of supervisors ... of the assessment rolls of the several municipalities therein, and not later than the first day of December in each year to make a report, duly certified, to the state board of assessors, ... of the amount of ad valorem taxes to be raised in the several municipalities of such county, for state, county, municipal, township, school and other purposes, also a statement of the aggregate valuation of the property in each of said several municipalities, as taken from the assessment rolls of said municipalities for the year in which such equalization is made, and the equalized valuation of each such municipality. It shall be the duty of the supervisor or other assessing officer of each township, ... to make, within the time above limited, a report to the state board of assessors, upon a form to be provided by said board, of all ad valorem taxes raised in his assessing district for the current year, and of the assessed valuation of real estate and personal property upon which such taxes are levied. In case any county clerk or any supervisor or assessing officer shall neglect or fail to make the report by this section required within the time limited, the said state board of assessors shall inspect and examine or cause an inspection and examination of the records of said board of supervisors or of the proper township ... officers, for the purpose of procuring the information required for the purpose of arriving at the average rate of taxation in this state. Any county clerk, supervisor or assessing officer, who shall fail to make the report required by this section shall be subject to a penalty of 100 dollars, to be recovered in a proper action in the name of the people of the state of Michigan in any court of competent jurisdiction.

MCLA 207.13 State board of assessors; average rate of taxation, public utilities; determination, method. [MSA 7.263]

MCLA 207.14 Tax assessment; tax roll; warrant; time payable, interest; collection; lien. [MSA 7.264]

Sec. 14. Said board shall tax the property of the several companies as assessed by it at the rate as determined by it, and the amount of tax to be paid by each of said companies shall be extended upon said assessment roll, opposite the description of their respective properties. After the completion of said tax roll, and prior to the twentieth day of June, in each year, the said board shall attach thereto a certificate, signed by the members of the board, or a majority thereof, which shall be as follows: ... The said taxes shall be payable on the first day of July following the assessment and levy thereof, and shall be in lieu of all taxes for state and local purposes, not including special assessments on property particularly benefited, made in any county, city, village or township. All taxes not paid before the first day of August in the year in which the same are payable shall bear interest ... The taxes ... shall constitute a lien upon all the property of said companies,

968

real, personal and mixed, which lien shall take precedence of all demands, judgments, assignments by warranty deed or otherwise, or decrees against said companies, which lien and debt may be enforced by seizure, or sale of said property or such portion ...

MCLA 207.15 – 207.16 [MSA 7.265 – 7.266]

MCLA 207.17 Taxes on public utilities, payment into (state) **general fund.** [MSA 7.267]

MCLA 207.18 – 207.21 [MSA 7.268 – 7.271]

Act No. 44, P.A. 1911 – State Board of Equalization

AN ACT to create a state board of equalization; to prescribe its powers and duties; to provide that said board shall be furnished with certain information by the several boards of supervisors and by the state tax commission; to provide for meeting the expense authorized by this act, and to repeal all acts or parts of acts contravening the provisions of this act.

MCLA 209.1 State board of equalization; creation, qualifications of appointees, term, vacancies. [MSA 7.601]

MCLA 209.2 Same; meeting. [MSA 7.602]

Sec. 2. ... in the city of Lansing on the second Monday in May each year for the purpose of equalizing the assessments on all taxable property in this state, except such property as shall be assessed under laws enacted pursuant to sections 4 and 5 of article 10 of the state constitution.

MCLA 209.3 Same; organization; record of proceedings; oath; quorum. [MSA 7.603]

MCLA 209.4 Same; tabular statement of valuation; hearing; equalization of assessments, certified transcript, filing, inspection. [MSA 7.604]

Sec. 4. ... may continue in session until the fourth Monday in May for the purpose of considering the reports from the assessing officers, boards of supervisors and the state tax commission. ...

The secretary of the state tax commission ... shall send a certified transcript thereof to the treasurer of each county, who shall cause the same to be placed on file in his office available for public inspection.

MCLA 209.5 Board of supervisors, April meeting; equalization of assessments, completion date; aggregates of rolls; statement to state board of equalization; excepted property. [MSA 7.605]

Sec. 5. At the regular meeting of the boards of supervisors of the several counties held on the Tuesday following the second Monday in April ... said boards ... shall ... equalize the assessment rolls ... which ... shall be completed prior to the first Monday in May. ...

MCLA 209.6 State tax commission; statement to state board of equalization. [MSA 7.606]

MCLA 209.7 State board of equalization; county representation. [MSA 7.607]

MCLA 209.8 Same; compensation and expenses of appointed members and assistants; copies of proceedings. [MSA 7.608]

Act No. 155, P.A. 1925 — State Tax Department

MCLA 209.152 — 209.154 [MSA 7.621 – 7.623]

Note: This act has been superseded.

TAXATION AS A SOURCE OF REVENUE

There are a great number of statutes which provide the major sources of revenue at both the state and local levels and the system by which taxes are assessed, levied and collected. These, along with the statutes regarding the use of bonded indebtedness or borrowing of money, are the basis for expansion and development of a township.

Years ago Michigan collected a statewide real estate tax, with the citizens evidencing little interest in the mechanism established for assessment, levy and collection of the tax, probably because it was not considered much of a hardship. However, now that the primary source of revenue at the local level is derived from the property tax, most citizens have made it their business to become familiar with and exert .influence upon the taxing authority and structure in the state.

JOINT ACTION
Act No. 206, P.A. 1893 — Assessment, Levy and Collection of Taxes (General Property Tax Act)

AN ACT to provide for the assessment of property and the levy and collection of taxes thereon, and for the collection of taxes heretofore and hereafter levied; making such taxes a lien on the lands taxed, establishing and continuing such lien, providing for the sale and conveyance of lands delinquent for taxes and for the inspection and disposition of lands bid off to the state and not redeemed or purchased; to define and limit the jurisdiction of the courts in proceedings in connection therewith; to limit the time within which actions may be brought; to prescribe certain limitations with respect to rates of taxation; to provide penalties for the violation of this act; and to repeal all acts and parts of acts in anywise contravening any of the provisions of this act.

GENERAL PROVISIONS

MCLA 211.1 Property subject to taxation. [MSA 7.1]

Sec. 1. ... all property, real and personal, ... not expressly exempted, shall be subject to taxation.

MCLA 211.1a Short title. [MSA 7.1(1)]

OF REAL PROPERTY

MCLA 211.2 Real property. [MSA 7.2]

Sec. 2. **Definition for tax purposes.** *For the purpose of taxation, real property shall include all lands within the state, and all buildings and fixtures thereon, and appurtenances thereto, except such as are expressly exempted by law, and shall include all real property owned by the state or heretofore purchased or condemned for public highway purposes by any board, officer, commission or*

971

department thereof and sold on land contract, notwithstanding the fact that the deed has not been executed transferring title.

Tax day, preparation of assessment roll, examination of properties by assessors. *The taxable status of persons and real and personal property shall be determined as of each December 31, which shall be deemed the tax day, ...*

Property acquired by public agency by purchase or condemnation; proration; levy date. *Notwithstanding any provision to the contrary in any law, when real property is acquired for public purposes by purchase or condemnation, all general property taxes, but not penalties, levied during the 12 months immediately preceding, but not including, the day title passes to the public agency shall be prorated in accordance with this paragraph. ... As used in this paragraph "levy date" means the day on which taxes become due and payable. In addition to the portion of taxes for which the public agency is responsible under the provisions of this paragraph, the public agency is also responsible for all general property taxes levied on or after the date title passes and before the property is removed from the tax rolls.*

Responsibility for portion of annual taxes; levy date defined. (Similar regulations re private real estate transactions.)

REAL ESTATE EXEMPTIONS

Note: Sections 7a, 7c and 7f below were repealed effective December 31, 1973. Effective for the 1974 tax roll, see the new chapter nine added to Act No. 281, P.A. 1967 - Income Tax Act, by Act No. 20, P.A. 1973 (MCLA 206.501) MSA 7.557(1501) ET SEQ.

MCLA 211.7 Property exempt from taxation. MSA 7.7 (lists organizations, governmental units).

MCLA 211.7a Real estate used and owned as homestead by blind person, tax exemption; person considered blind; affidavit, filing, contents, inspection; false affidavit; definitions. MSA 7.7(1).

MCLA 211.7b Homestead exemption; specially adapted housing of disabled soldier or sailor; affidavit and certificate, filing, cancellation of tax. MSA 7.7(2).

MCLA 211.7c Persons 65 years of age or over; homestead exemptions. MSA 7.7(4).

MCLA 211.7d Housing for elderly persons owned and operated by nonprofit corporation or state. [MSA 7.7(4A)]

MCLA 211.7e Value of deciduous and evergreen trees, shrubs, plants, bushes and vines growing on agricultural land. [MSA 7.7(4B)]

Note: These items exempted, but growing timber taxation not affected by this section.

MCLA 211.7f Veterans' and servicemen's homestead exemption act. [MSA 7.7(4C)]

OF PERSONAL PROPERTY

MCLA 211.8 Personal property included. [MSA 7.8]

PERSONAL PROPERTY EXEMPTED

MCLA 211.9 Personal property exempt. Charitable, educational and scientific institutions; charitable homes. Libraries. Patriotic, religious, and young peoples associations. Federal pensions. Indians not citizens. Customary equipment of householder, wearing apparel, pictures, books, exceptions. Household furniture, provisions, fuel, limit. Mechanics' tools; definition of mechanic, limit. Fire fighting equipment. Property used in farming. Business property, limit. Products, materials and/or goods in public warehouse, dock or port facility; designated as in transit in interstate commerce; inspection of records; statement, violation or penalty. Definition of warehouse, dock or port facility. Personal property of bank or trust company; exceptions. Farm products in public warehouse, dock or port facility; inspection of records. Sugar, etc., owned or held by processors. [MSA 7.9]

MCLA 211.9a Motor vehicles in stock, exemption from property tax. [MSA 7.9(1)]

MCLA 211.9b Special tools, definition, exemption from taxation. [MSA 7.9(2)]

MCLA 211.10 Annual assessment; nonresident's request for information. [MSA 7.10]

Sec. 10. An assessment of all the property in the state, liable to taxation, shall be made annually in the several townships, ... by the supervisors of the several townships, ... where provision is made in the acts of incorporation or charter for an assessing officer, then by such assessing officer, as hereinafter provided.

MCLA 211.2a Trailer coaches, certain, deemed real property. [MSA 7.2(1)]

Sec. 2a. For all purposes of the preceding section, trailer coaches not under the provisions of Act No. 143 of the Public Acts of 1939, as amended, being sections 125.751 [MSA 5.278(1)] *to 125.768* [5.278(18)] *, inclusive, of the Compiled Laws of 1948, and while located on land otherwise assessable as real property under this act, when such trailer coaches are used as habitations, and whether or not permanently affixed to the soil, shall be deemed to be real property and shall be assessed as part of the real property upon which they are located.*

MCLA 211.3 Real property; parties assessable; persons treated as owner; property of deceased persons. [MSA 7.3]

Sec. 3. Real property shall be assessed in the township ... where situated, to the owner if known, and also to the occupant, if any; ...

MCLA 211.4 Same; licensed homesteads; part-paid state lands; assessment, contents. [MSA 7.4]

Sec. 4. All licensed homestead lands, (etc) ... The taxes, if not paid to the township treasurer, shall be returned and collected as hereinafter provided.

MCLA 211.5 Same; assessment of corporate realty. [MSA 7.5]

Sec. 5. The real property of a corporation shall be assessed to the name of the corporation as to an individual, ...

MCLA 211.6 Same; tenants in common; assessment of undivided interests. [MSA 7.6]

MCLA 211.6a Mineral rights assessed separate from surface rights. [MSA 7.6(1)]

MCLA 211.6b Mineral rights consisting of undeveloped metallic resources; assessment separately from surface rights; exclusions. [MSA 7.6(2)]

Sec. 6b. ... On or before December 31, 1967 owners of surface rights and of mineral rights whose respective rights are subject to separate assessment as herein provided shall file with the assessing officer of the township ... in which the land containing such separate surface or mineral rights is situated an affidavit containing an accurate description of each parcel of land ...

Nothwithstanding any provision to the contrary in the act of incorporation or charter of a village, an assessment for village taxes shall be identical to the assessment made by the township supervisor in which the village is located, and tax statements shall set forth clearly the state equalized value of the individual properties in the village upon which authorized millages are levied.

Whenever a nonresident of the taxing unit against whom an assessment is made shall request in writing information relative to the amount of the assessment against his property, the supervisor or assessing officer, within a reasonable length of time, shall make reply thereto.

MCLA 211.10c State assessor's board; creation; membership, terms, compensation, expenses; courses in assessment practices, examinations. [MSA 7.10(3)]

Sec. 10c. A state assessor's board, hereinafter called the board, to consist of 5 members is created. The members of the board shall be appointed by the governor and shall be composed of 1 member representing the state tax commission, 1 member representing the **township supervisors,** *1 member representing the* **assessors,** *1 member representing the county equalization directors and 1 member representing the public colleges and universities of the state. ... The board shall conduct training courses in assessment practices and review and approve courses in assessment practices offered by schools and colleges and universities as well as courses that are offered by any state or local unit of government in the techniques and practices of assessments. The board shall* prepare and give examinations from time to time to determine if assessing officers possess the necessary qualifications for performing the functions of his office.

MCLA 211.10d Annual property assessments, qualifications required of assessors; schools of assessment practices, establishment, supervision; certificates of qualification; lack of qualified assessor, cost of training. [MSA 7.10(4)]

Sec. 10d. Notwithstanding any provision of any other law to the contrary, the annual assessment of property shall be made by a supervisor, assessing officer or director of an equalization department or bureau who has been certified as qualified by the board by reason of ... may employ an assessor so qualified. If a local assessing district does not have an assessor qualified by certification of the board, and has not employed a certified assessor, the assessment shall be made by the county tax or equalization department or the state tax commission and the cost of preparing the rolls shall be charged to the local assessing district. The local assessing district shall assume the cost of training, if a certification is awarded, to the extent of course fees and recognized travel expenditures.

MCLA 211.11 Corporate property; situs; exemptions. [MSA 7.11]

MCLA 211.12 Copartnership property; taxable situs; liability of each partner. [MSA 7.12]

MCLA 211.13 Personal property; taxable situs, person assessed, basis for assessment. [MSA 7.13]

Sec. 13. All tangible personal property, except as provided in section 14, shall be assessed to the owner thereof, if known, **in the township in which it is located on the tax day.** *If the owner is not known ...*

Inventories ... shall, upon the filing by the owner thereof of a sworn statement with the assessing officer showing the total of such inventories for each of the preceding 12 months ending December 31, be assessed on ...

MCLA 211.14 Same; taxable situs. [MSA 7.14]

Sec. 14. (1) **Goods and chattels situate in township other than**

owner's residence. *All goods and chattels situate in some township other than where the owner resides shall be assessed in the township where situate, and not elsewhere.*

(2) **Animals.** *All animals kept throughout the year in some township other than where the owner resides shall be assessed to such owner or the person in possession in the township where kept.*

(3) **Property subject to guardian.** ... *(4)* **Estates of deceased persons.** ... *(5)* **Property in control of trustee or agent; taxation of possessor.** ... *(6)* **Tangible personal property and buildings on lands of others** ... *(7)* **Tangible personal property of nonresidents; forest products; lien of possessor, release.** *Tangible personal property of nonresidents of the state and all forest products, owned by residents or nonresidents, or estates of deceased persons, shall be assessed in the township ... where the same may be, to the person, persons or corporation having control of the premises, store, mill, dockyard, piling ground, place of storage or warehouse where such property is situated in such township, on December 31, except ...*

MCLA 211.15 Forest products; place of destination; products in transit. [MSA 7.15]

Sec. 15. All forest products in transit on December 31, ...

MCLA 211.16 Same; duty of supervisor. [MSA 7.16]

Sec. 16. It shall be the duty of the supervisor of the township in which any such saw logs, timber, railroad ties, telegraph poles or tanbark, cut prior to the time of taking the annual assessment, may be banked or piled, or that may be in transit, to ascertain the amount of such property ...

MCLA 211.17 Taxable situs of personal property, transfer after tax day. [MSA 7.17]

ASSESSMENT, HOW MADE

MCLA 211.18 Assessing officer; sworn statement of possessor of assessable personal property. [MSA 7.18]

Sec. 18. Each supervisor or other assessing officer, as soon as possible after entering upon the duties of his office, or as may be directed and required by the provisions of any acts of incorporation of any city or village making special provisions for such assessments, shall ascertain the taxable property of his assessing district, and the persons to whom it should be assessed and their residences. For this purpose he shall require ... written statement, under oath ... under the following form ...

Oath of person having no personal property not exempt. *Any person having no personal property which is not exempt, if required to take an oath by the supervisor or assessor, may take the following oath: ...*

Sworn statement as to assessable real property. *Whenever a supervisor, assessing officer or county tax or equalization department, provided for in section 34 of this act, or whenever the state tax commission deems it necessary in the proper administration of this act to require from any person a written statement under oath of real property assessable to such person, it shall notify the person, and every such person, natural or legal, shall make such statement.*

MCLA 211.19   Sworn statement as to assessable property; form, contents. [MSA 7.19]

Sec. 19. The written statement under oath, provided for in section 18 shall be in such form and of such content as may be prescribed by the state tax commission and shall be completed and delivered to the supervisor or assessor on or before February 20 of each year.

MCLA 211.20   Imperfect statements, use. [MSA 7.20]

MCLA 211.21   Wilful neglect to make statement, penalty; complaint. [MSA 7.21]

MCLA 211.22   Incorrect or absent statement, testimony, assessment. Testimony, assessment. Revision of assessment. [MSA 7.22]

MCLA 211.22a   Personal property examiners, certificate of qualification; examination of property or cost records. [MSA 7.22(1)]

Sec. 22a. (1) The state tax commission, upon presentation by representatives of ... townships ... of satisfactory evidence of education, experience, or by passage of a test conducted by the commission, shall certify a successful applicant as a qualified personal property examiner. A certified personal property examiner may ...

978

(2) Upon written request of a ... township assessing officer to examine the property or books of any corporation, firm, or individual, a certified personal property examiner of the county tax or equalization department shall conduct the examination. ...

(3) Where any corporation, firm or individual is subject to personal property assessment in more than 3 counties of the state then the corporation, ...

MCLA 211.23 **Statement** (presentation to board of review); **filing** (with township clerk), **preservation, permissible uses, unlawful use, liability for damages.** [MSA 7.23]

MCLA 211.23a County-wide appraisal of property for assessment; expenses. [MSA 7.23(1)]

Sec. 23a. The board of supervisors of any county may employ an independent appraisal firm to make a county-wide appraisal for the purpose of assisting local assessing officers in arriving at a true cash value for assessment purposes and of assisting the board of supervisors in reviewing and equalizing assessments. The expense of such appraisal, when approved by the board of supervisors, shall be paid from the general fund of the county. The purpose of such appraisal is to provide a uniform basis for the assessment of taxes throughout the county in order to apportion the burden of property taxes fairly and equitably among the owners of taxable property.

OF THE ASSESSMENT ROLL

MCLA 211.24 Property tax assessment roll; time, contents, method. [MSA 7.24]

Sec. 24. **Procedure and form.** *On or before the first Monday in March in each year, the supervisor or assessor shall make and complete an assessment roll, upon which he shall set down the name and address of every person liable to be taxed in his township or assessment district, with a full description of all the real property therein liable to be taxed. If the name of the owner or occupant of any such tract or parcel of real property is known, he shall enter the name and address of such owner or occupant as in this act provided, opposite to the description thereof; in all. other cases the real property described upon such roll shall be assessed as ''owner unknown''. All contiguous subdivisions of any section that are owned by 1 person, firm or corporation, and all unimproved lots in* any block that are contiguous and owned by 1 person, firm or corporation shall be assessed as 1 parcel, unless demand in writing is made by the owner or occupant to have each subdivision of the section or each lot assessed separately; but failure to assess such contiguous parcels as entireties as herein provided shall not invalidate the assessment as made. Each description shall show as near as may be the number of acres contained in it, as determined by the supervisor. It shall not be necessary for the assessment roll to specify the quantity of land comprised in any ... lot. The supervisor shall estimate, according to his best information and judgment, the true cash value of every parcel of real property and set the same down opposite such parcel. He shall also estimate the true cash value of all the personal property of each person, and set the same down opposite the name of such person. In determining the property to be assessed and in estimating such value, he shall not be bound to follow the statements of any person, but shall exercise his best judgment. Property assessed to one other than the owner shall be assessed separately from his property and shall show in what capacity it is assessed to him, whether as agent, guardian or otherwise. Two or more persons not being copartners, owning personal property in common, may each be assessed severally for his portion thereof. Undivided interests in lands owned by tenants in common, or joint tenants not being copartners, may be assessed to the owners thereof.

Metallic mining properties and rights, exemption, assessment, alteration, appeal. ...

MCLA 211.24a Tax rolls, preparation by county, expense.
[MSA 7.24(1)]

Sec. 24a. Notwithstanding any other provisions of this act, a county, by resolution of the board of commissioners, may prepare tax rolls and extend the taxes thereon for the cities and townships in the county at the expense of the county or the local unit.

Note: Although it would seem as if the county usurps the right of the township supervisor and city assessor to prepare a tax roll, note the use of the words "may" and "and." If the county takes over the job it must do it for the whole county.

MCLA 211.24b Assessment based on state equalized valuation, application. [MSA 7.24(2)]

Sec. 24b. ... the tax roll and the tax statement shall clearly set forth the latest state equalized valuation for each item of property. The supervisor or assessor shall spread the taxes on the tax roll on the state equalized valuation for each item of property ...

MCLA 211.24c Increases in assessments; notice, recipients, contents, time, failure to receive, necessity. [MSA 7.24(3)]

MCLA 211.24d Structures or improvements approved for acquisition by governmental units, tax exemption. Term of exemption. Method of obtaining exemption; public inspection of exemption claim. Limitation on number of exemptions claimed; public inspection of exemption claim. Limitation on number of exemptions claimed; public inspection of claims. False statements in exemption affidavits, civil penalties, interest. Reoccupancy, notice, payment of taxes, civil penalties for noncompliance. Vandalism and public nuisance, owners' duties. [MSA 7.14(4)]

MCLA 211.25 Real property, description; mineral rights. [MSA 7.25]

MCLA 211.25a Real estate index number system. [MSA 7.25(1)]

Sec. 25a. An assessing officer, with the approval of the governing body of the ...

MCLA 211.26 Tax roll; description of personal property. [MSA 7.26]

MCLA 211.27 Cash value of property, definition, computation, percentage. [MSA 7.27]

OF THE BOARD OF REVIEW

MCLA 211.28 Township board of review; appointment, vacancy, quorum. [MSA 7.28]

Sec. 28. Three taxpaying electors of the township, who shall be owners of land in the township, appointed by the township board, shall constitute a board of review for the township. The terms ... Members appointed hereafter to the board of review shall serve for terms of 2 years beginning at noon on January 1 of each odd-numbered year. Each member of the board of review shall qualify by taking the constitutional oath of office within 10 days after appointment. *The township board may fill any vacancy which shall occur in the membership of the board of review. No member of the township board shall be eligible to serve on the board or to fill any vacancy. A majority of the board of review shall constitute a quorum for the transaction of business, but a less number may adjourn from day to day and a majority vote of those present shall decide all questions.*

MCLA 211.29   Same; meeting, time; review of assessment roll. [MSA 7.29]

Sec. 29. **Submission and review of roll.** *On the Tuesday next following the first Monday in March, the board of review of each township shall meet ... examine and review ... and ... cause to be done whatever ... may be necessary to make said roll comply with the provisions of this act. The roll shall be ... Notice of the date, time and place of the meeting of the board of review shall be given at least 1 week prior to such meeting by publication in a generally circulated newspaper serving the area. Such notice shall appear in 3 successive issues of the newspaper where available; otherwise, by the posting of such notice in 5 conspicuous places in the township.*

Notice of change of assessment or addition. *Whenever the board of review makes a change in the assessment of property or adds property to the assessment roll, the person chargeable with such assessment shall be promptly notified in such a manner as will assure him opportunity to attend the second meeting of the board of review provided in section 30 of this act.*

MCLA 211.30   Same; meetings, townships of 10,000 or more; examination of objector; indorsement of roll, form. [MSA 7.30]

Sec. 30. Said board of review shall also meet at the office of the supervisor on the second Monday in March at 9 a.m., and continue in session during the day and the day following. Said board of review shall schedule a final meeting whenever the board makes a change in the assessment of property or adds property to the assessment roll. In townships having a population of 10,000 or more, the board shall hold at least 1 of its required sessions for review of assessment rolls beginning at 3 p.m. Such board shall continue its sessions at least 6 hours each day, and at the request of any person whose property is assessed thereon or of his agent, and on sufficient cause being shown, shall correct the assessment as to

982

*such property, in such manner as in their judgment will make the
valuation thereof relatively just and equal.*

MCLA 211.30a Township board of review; completion of review, date. [MSA 7.30(1)]

*Sec. 30a ... the review of assessments by boards of review in
all ... townships shall be completed on or before the first Monday
in April, any provisions of the charter of any ... township to the
contrary notwithstanding: Provided, That the legislative body of
any ... township, in order to comply with the provisions hereof,
may, by ordinance, fix the period or periods for preparing the budget
and for making, completing and reviewing the assessment roll, any
provisions of the charter of such ... township or any law to the contrary notwithstanding.*

MCLA 211.30b Revision of personal property assessments in 1965 (only). [MSA 7.30(2)]

MCLA 211.31 Township board of review; completed roll valid; con- clusive presumption. [MSA 7.31]

*Sec. 31. Upon the completion of said roll and its endorsement
in manner aforesaid, the same shall be conclusively presumed by
all courts and tribunals to be valid, and shall not be set aside except for causes hereinafter mentioned. The omission of such endorsement shall not affect the validity of such roll.*

MCLA 211.32 Same; quorum; conscription of absent members; second meeting alternative. [MSA 7.32]

*Sec. 32. If from any cause a quorum shall not be present at
any meeting of the board of review, it shall be the duty of the supervisor, or, in his absence, any other member of the board present, to
notify each absent member to attend at once, and it shall be the
duty of the member so notified to attend without delay. If from any
cause the second meeting of such board of review herein provided
for is not held at the time fixed therefor, then and in that case it
shall meet on the next Monday thereafter, and proceed in the same
manner and with like powers as if such meeting had been held as
hereinbefore provided.*

MCLA 211.33 Secretary of board of review; record, filing, form. [MSA 7.33]

*Sec. 33. The supervisor shall be the secretary of said board
of review and shall keep a record of the proceedings of the board
and of all the changes made in such assessment roll, and shall file
the same with the township ... clerk with the statements made by
persons assessed. In the absence of the supervisor, the board shall
appoint 1 of its members to serve as secretary. The state tax commission may prescribe the form of the record whenever deemed
necessary.*

EQUALIZATION BY COUNTIES

**MCLA 211.34 Assessment rolls; yearly examination by board of
commissioners; equalization, certification.** [MSA 7.52]

*Sec. 34. (1) The board of commissioners in each county at
its session in April in each year, shall examine the assessment
rolls of the several townships ... and ascertain whether the real
and personal property in the respective townships ... has been
equally and uniformly assessed at true cash value. If, on such examination, it shall ...*

*(2) The board of commissioners of any county shall ... estab-
lish and maintain a department to survey assessments and assist
the board of commissioners in the matter of equalization of assessments, and may employ therein ...*

*Any supervisor of any township ... aggrieved by the action of
the board of commissioners, in equalizing the valuations of the
several townships ... may appeal from such determination to the
state tax commission in the manner herein provided. Whenever any
supervisor ... desires to appeal ... he ... shall within 5 days after
the adoption of the equalization report, file with the clerk of the
board of commissioners a written or printed petition which shall set
forth in detail the reasons for taking the appeal. The petition shall
be signed and sworn to by the supervisor ... shall show that a
certain township ... has been discriminated against in such equalization, and shall pray that the state tax commission proceed at its
earliest convenience to review the action from which appeal is
taken. The clerk of the board of commissioners shall ... In case
the state tax commission shall determine that the equalization
made by the board of commissioners is unfair, unjust, inequitable
or discriminatory, the state tax commission shall notify by mail
the supervisor who has appealed, ... with notice of the time and
place of hearing. At least 7 days but not more than 20 days after
mailing the notice, the commission shall hold a hearing in the*

county. The state tax commission shall also mail a written notice of the time and place of hearing to the county clerk, who shall also notify the members of the board of commissioners ... At the hearing the supervisor ... shall be given the opportunity to submit evidence. Within not less than 5 nor more than 20 days after the hearing, the state tax commission shall make a final determination in writing. If the state tax commission, after the hearing, decides that ...

MCLA 211.34a   Tentative recommended equalization ratios and estimated multipliers, statement, publication, effect. [MSA 7.52(1)]

Sec. 34a. The equalization director of each county shall prepare ... (and) ... publish the tabulation in a newspaper of general circulation within the county on or before the third Monday in February each year and furnish a copy to each of the boards of review in the county and to the state tax commission. All notices of meetings of the boards of review shall ...

MCLA 211.34b   Joint equalization department, two or more counties, authorization, duties. [MSA 7.52(2)]

OF TAXES, HOW AND BY WHOM CERTIFIED

MCLA 211.35   State tax statement; duties of auditor general, of local supervisors; state and county tax apportionment. [MSA 7.53]

Sec. 35. On or before the first day of September in each year, the auditor general shall make and record in his office a statement showing the taxes to be raised for state purposes that year, ... (apportion among several counties per valuation in proportion to taxable property determined by last preceding state board of equalization), ..., and shall before the October session of the board of supervisors in each year make out and transmit to the clerk of each county a statement of the amount of such ... Provided, That such portion thereof, if any, as should be assessed to a particular township, shall be apportioned to and assessed upon such township, ...

MCLA 211.36   Duties of township clerk, supervisor, county clerk, board of supervisors. [MSA 7.54]

Sec. 36. The township clerk ... on or before September 15 of each year, shall make and deliver to the supervisor of his township, a certified copy of all statements and certificates on file, and of all records of any vote or resolution in his office authorizing or direct-ing moneys to be raised therein by taxation for township, school highway, drain, and all other purposes, together with a statement of the aggregate amount thereof, and such certified copies shall, by such supervisor, be delivered to the clerk of the county on or before October 1, and the same shall by said clerk be laid before the board of supervisors at its annual meeting and filed in his office. The board of supervisors shall not levy in the year voted any tax levy voted on or after Sept. 15.

MCLA 211.36a   School levies following millage elections. (1971)
[MSA 7.54(1)]

MCLA 211.36b   School levies following millage elections. (1972)
[MSA 7.54(2)]

MCLA 211.37   Board of supervisors, duties; tax apportionment; prosecuting attorney, duties. [MSA 7.55]

Sec. 37. The board of commissioners, at its annual session in October in each year, shall ascertain and determine the amount of money to be raised for county purposes, and shall apportion such amount, and also the amount of the state tax and indebtedness of the county to the state among the several townships in the county in proportion to the valuation of the taxable property therein, real and personal, as determined by it, or as determined by the board of state tax commissioners upon appeal in the manner provided by law, for that year, which determination and apportionment shall be entered at large on its records. It shall also ... It shall direct that such of the several amounts of money proposed to be raised for town-ship, school, highway, drain and all other purposes as shall be authorized by law, be spread upon the assessment roll of the proper townships, wards and cities.   Such action and direction shall be entered in full upon the records of the proceedings of the board, and shall be final as to the levy and assessment of all such taxes, except when there is a change made in the equalization of any county by the board of state tax commissioners upon appeal in the manner provided by law. Notwithstanding to the contrary in any law, the direction for spread of taxes shall be expressed in terms of millages to be spread against the state equalized values of properties and shall not direct the raising of any specific amount of money.

MCLA 211.37a Appeal to state tax board; assessment of costs; method of reimbursement. [MSA 7.56]

Sec. 37a. *If upon such appeal to the board of state tax commissioners it is determined by said board that the appeal is groundless and not well founded, then the costs made and incurred by the county in defending the same and in the proceedings thereof, shall be paid by the township whose supervisor made such appeal. If the allegations set forth by the said supervisor making such appeal are determined to be well founded, then the said county shall pay the costs of the said township by it expended in making and prosecuting said appeal, but in no case shall more than 75 dollars costs be taxed by either side. The costs shall be ...*

MCLA 211.38 Duplicate apportionment certificates; failure to certify, official notice of records. [MSA 7.57]

Sec. 38. *The clerk of the board of supervisors shall, immediately after the said apportionment, make out 2 certificates showing the millages apportioned to each township for state, county and the various township purposes, each tax being kept distinct, 1 of which he shall deliver to the county treasurer, and the other to the supervisor of the proper township: Provided, That if said clerk fail to make such certificate, the supervisor shall take official notice of all certificates, statements, papers and records in the office of the township and county clerk relating to the levy of taxes in his township, and of the action of the board of supervisors thereon.*

TAXES – HOW TO BE ASSESSED

MCLA 211.39 Assessment of taxes; basis; method; tax receipts. [MSA 7.80]

Sec. 39. *The supervisor of each township ... as provided by law, shall proceed to assess the taxes apportioned to his township, ... according and in proportion to the valuations entered by the board of review in the assessment roll of the township, ... for the year, but if the board of review makes no such entry, then on the valuation therein as entered by the supervisor or assessor. For the purpose of avoiding fractions in computation, the assessor may add to the amount of the several taxes to be raised not more than 1%. The excess shall belong to the contingent fund of the township, ... Such taxes shall be separately assessed and shall be entered in* separate columns, or if authorized by a resolution of the board of supervisors of the county adopted by a majority of the members elect thereof, such taxes in said county shall be entered either as 1 total sum, or in separate columns for each taxing unit. The columns shall be designated, combined county taxes, combined township taxes, combined city taxes, combined school taxes. If such taxes are entered as 1 total sum, or as combined unit taxes there shall be printed upon each tax receipt the percentage, or tax rate which each such tax is of said total sum, or is of each taxing unit sum, in lieu thereof a printed statement showing the tax rate of each separate tax shall be attached to the tax receipt at the time of payment by the officer collecting the tax.

MCLA 211.39a Delay; determination of equalized value, tentative and final levies; additional taxes; tax credits. [MSA 7.80(1)]

Sec. 39a. (1) If the determination of the equalized value is delayed as a result of an appeal taken pursuant to this act and pending before the tax commission, the assessing officer shall levy taxes upon the equalized value of property as determined by the county board of commissioners which is being reviewed by the tax commission. Notwithstanding any contrary provisions of law, the payment of taxes thusly levied, hereinafter called the "tentative levy", shall not constitute a final and ultimate discharge of the taxpayer's obligation.

(2) After the final determination of equalized value by the state tax commission, the assessing officer shall determine the difference in tax, if any, between the tentative levy and a levy made upon the equalized value as finally determined by the tax commission, which levy is hereinafter referred to as the "final levy."

(3) If such determination shows that additional taxes are due, such additional taxes shall be spread upon the next succeeding annual tax roll and collected together with the next succeeding annual taxes upon the property.

(4) If the tax liability is decreased as a result of the tax commission's final determination of equalized value, the taxes collected pursuant to the tentative levy in excess of the tax liability pursuant to the final levy shall be credited against the taxes upon the property for the next succeeding year, together with a proportionate share of any collection fee applicable to said difference.

(5) Additional taxes collected or credits against tax liability made pursuant to the provisions of this section shall inure to the

benefit or detriment of the taxing units in the respective proportions in which they share the proceeds of the final levy.

(6) The state tax commission shall render such technical assistance as is necessary to implement the provisions of this act.

MCLA 211.40 Lien for taxes, priority; statement and receipt for taxes to show taxing unit's fiscal year. [MSA 7.81]

Sec. 40. Notwithstanding any provisions in the charter of any city or village to the contrary, all taxes shall become a debt due to the township, ... from the owner or person otherwise to be assessed on the tax day provided for in sections 2 and 13 of this act, and the amounts assessed on any interest in real property shall, on the first day of December, for state, county, village or township taxes or upon such day as may be heretofore or hereafter provided by charter of a city or village, become a lien upon such real property, and the lien for such amounts, and for all interest and charges thereon, shall continue until payment thereof. Each statement and receipt for taxes on real estate sent or given by any ... township ... treasurer shall contain a statement, which shall ... And all personal taxes hereafter levied or assessed shall also ...

MCLA 211.41 Assessor, duties; local clerk, duties; county clerk, statement to auditor general, contents. [MSA 7.82]

Sec. 41. Before the supervisor or assessing officer shall deliver such roll to the township treasurer or city collector he shall carefully foot the several columns of valuation and taxes, and make a detailed statement thereof, which he shall give the clerk of his township or city, and said clerk shall immediately ...

MCLA 211.41a Statement of land conveyance furnished to township supervisors. [MSA 7.82(1)]

Sec. 41a. In such counties of this state in which the board of supervisors by a majority vote of the members shall vote in favor thereof, the register of deeds of any such county, within 30 days of the recording of any instrument conveying an interest in land, shall furnish the supervisor or supervisors of the township or townships in which the parcel or parcels of land are situated, a statement giving the names of the parties to the instrument recorded, a description of the parcel or parcels of land covered by the instrument recorded, and the interest in land conveyed.

THE TAX ROLL

MCLA 211.42   Tax roll preparation; warrant; township treasurer, accounting; collection period; sale for delinquent taxes; loss of roll; tax roll defined. MSA 7.83

Sec. 42. The supervisor shall thereupon prepare a tax roll, with the taxes levied as hereinbefore provided, and annex thereto a warrant signed by him, commanding the township or city treasurer to collect the several sums mentioned in the last column of such roll but the warrant shall not refer to the total or aggregate of the several sums mentioned in the last column, and to retain in his hand the amount receivable by law into the township treasury for the purpose therein specified, and to pay over to the county treasurer the amounts which shall have been collected for state and county purposes up to and including January 10 next following, and to the treasurer of each school district the amounts which shall have been collected for such school district up to and including January 10 next following, within 10 days thereafter, and notify the secretary or director of each school district of the amount paid to the school district treasurer, and the remainder of the amounts therein specified for said purposes, and account in full for all moneys received on or before March 1 next following.   The warrant shall authorize and command the treasurer, in case any person named in the tax roll shall neglect or refuse to pay his tax, to levy the same by distress and sale of the goods and chattels of such person.   The supervisor may make a new roll and warrant in case of the loss of the one originally given to the township treasurer; the copy of the roll with the warrant annexed shall be known as "the tax roll."

MCLA 211.43   Notice to township treasurer of apportionment of taxes; bond, exception; township tax roll; maximum amount of taxes on hand. MSA 7.84

Sec. 43. The supervisor of each township, on or before the 5th day of November in each year, shall notify the township treasurer of the amount of the state, county and school taxes as apportioned to his township, and such treasurer, on or before the 28th day of November, shall give to the county treasurer a bond running to the county in the actual amount of state, county and school taxes, except such school taxes as are collected through a city treasurer, with sufficient sureties to be approved by the supervisor of the township and the county treasurer, conditioned that ... Provided furthur, That in case the county treasurer and township supervisor

990

shall determine that the bond of the township treasurer recorded with the township clerk and on file with the township supervisor is adequate and sufficient to safeguard the proper accounting of state, county and school taxes as required by law, then the township treasurer shall not be required to file with the county treasurer the bond hereinbefore provided for, and the county treasurer shall deliver to the supervisor on or before the 1st day of December a signed statement of his approval thereof, upon the receipt of which and on or before the 1st day of December the supervisor shall deliver to the township treasurer the tax roll of this township. The county treasurer shall file and safely keep such bond in his office, and shall give to the township treasurer a receipt stating that he has received the bond required, which receipt the township treasurer shall deliver to the supervisor on or before the 1st day of December. The supervisor after the delivery of such receipt and on or before the 1st day of December, shall deliver to the township treasurer the tax roll of his township. Such township treasurer shall at no time have on hand collections of state, county and school taxes in excess of 25 per cent of the amount of such taxes apportioned to his township and from time to time whenever such collections on hand shall reach such percentage he shall immediately account for and turn over to the county treasurer the total amount of such state and county collections on hand and to the several school district treasurers the total amount of such school tax collections on hand and notify the secretary or director of the school districts the total amount of taxes paid to the school district treasurers which notification shall show the different funds for which the taxes were collected.

MCLA 211.43a Delay in receipt of tax roll; fees for unpaid taxes; delinquent tax return. [MSA 7.85]

Sec. 43. That whenever any township ... treasurer does not receive the tax roll within the time specified under the provisions of section 43 of this act by reason of any delay caused by an appeal to the board of state tax commissioners as provided by Act No. 201, Public Acts of 1913 (Sections 211.37, 211.37a. The act also constituted an amendment of section 211.34), *such treasurer shall receive taxes appearing on such roll with the additional charge of 1 per cent for a collection fee for the period of 30 days after the receipt of the tax roll, except in counties, cities or townships where some special provision is made by law for a collection fee the treasurer shall comply with such special provisions during said 30-*

day period. On all taxes unpaid at the expiration of said 30-day period he shall add 4 per cent, and on or before the expiration of 60 days from the receipt of said tax roll by said township ... treasurer he shall make a return to the county treasurer of the uncollected taxes assessed on real and personal property as provided by section 55 of this act.

MCLA 211.43b Public moneys; depository; liability. [MSA 7.86]

Sec. 43b. The governing board ... of every ... township, ... or any other municipal corporation within this state shall provide by resolution for the deposit of all public moneys which shall come into the hands of the treasurer ...

OF THE COLLECTING OF TAXES

MCLA 211.44 Tax collections; statement to taxpayers, time; form; fees; waiver; prevention of tax loss. [MSA 7.87]

Sec. 44. On receiving such tax roll the township treasurer ... shall proceed to collect such taxes. The township treasurer ... shall mail to each taxpayer at his last known address on his tax roll, on the receipt of such tax roll, a statement showing the description of the property against which the tax is levied, the assessed valuation of such property and the amount of the tax thereon. The tax statement shall set forth the state equalized valuation. The expenses of preparing and mailing such statement shall be paid from the county, township, city or village funds. Failure to send or receive such notice shall not in any way prejudice the right to collect or enforce the payment of any tax. The township treasurer shall remain in his office at some convenient place in his township on every Friday in the month of December, from 9 a.m. to 5 p.m. to receive taxes, but he shall receive taxes upon any week day when they may be offered. On all sums voluntarily paid before February 15 of the succeeding year, he shall add 1% for collection fees, and upon all taxes paid on or after February 15 he may add to the tax and 1% fee an additional collection fee equal to 3% of the tax. Taxes collected by the township treasurer after the last day of February and before settlement with the county treasurer shall have added thereto a 4% collection fee and interest on the tax at the rate of ½ of 1% per month, which payment shall be treated as though collected by the county treasurer. Collection fees for years prior to 1964 on taxes which have been paid in full and which have not been heretofore collected *by the township treasurer are deemed waived. If the treasurer shall not mail the statements hereinabove required to be mailed on or before December 30, he shall be limited to 1% for collection fees with respect to taxes collected by him on and after February 15. In townships in which the treasurer receives a salary, the township board only may waive all or part of the collection fees on taxes paid on or before February 15. All fees collected by the township treasurer in townships where the treasurer receives a salary shall be credited to the contingent fund of the township. ... When the bond of the treasurer, as provided in section 43, is furnished by a surety company, the cost of the bond shall be paid by the township from the contingent fund of the township. If the township treasurer is apprehensive of the loss of any personal tax assessed upon his roll, he may enforce its collection at any time, and if compelled to seize property or bring suit in December may add 4% for collection fees.*

MCLA 211.45 Collection, time limit. [MSA 7.89]

Sec. 45. All taxes shall be collected by the several township and city treasurers or collectors, before the first day of March, in each year.

MCLA 211.46 Taxes unpaid January 10; personal demand; use of mails; charter provision exception; receipts. [MSA 7.90]

Sec. 46. For the purpose of collecting the taxes remaining unpaid on the tenth day of January, the said treasurer shall, thereafter during that month, call personally upon each person liable to pay such taxes, if a resident of such township, or at his usual place of residence or business therein, and demand payment of the taxes charged against him. If such person is not a resident of the township, but resides within the county, or an adjoining county, and his residence is known to the treasurer, he shall ...

MCLA 211.47 Unpaid taxes; distraint; sale, notice; surplus; return, unrecovered taxes; power to sue; possessor's recourse; release of levy; audit. [MSA 7.91]

Sec. 47. If any person, firm or corporation shall neglect or refuse to pay any tax ... (The township treasurer) may sell the property seized to an amount sufficient to pay the taxes and all charges, in the place where seized, or in the township ... at public auction, on giving public notice of the same at least 5 days previous to the sale, by posting written or printed notices in 3 public places *in the township, ... where the sale is to be made, which sale may be adjourned from time to time if he shall deem the same necessary; and in case property shall be seized and advertised as herein directed, during the life of the warrant, the sale may take place at any time within 6 days after the expiration thereof. If it becomes necessary to sell personal property ...Provided, further, That in case where levy is made, as hereinbefore provided, for taxes assessed upon land, the levy shall be released if, within 10 days after it is made, the persons having the title to said land shall ...*

MCLA 211.47a Treasurer's bill of sale of property sold for unpaid taxes, contents. [MSA 7.91(1)]

Sec. 47a. The township ... treasurer when requested shall execute, acknowledge and deliver to the purchaser a bill of sale describing the property and setting forth the particulars of the sale.

MCLA 211.48 Collector's fee; statement of personalty removed; evidence; collection; execution levies. [MSA 7.92]

MCLA 211.49 Surplus from sale, contested claim; remedy; treasurer's liability; rule in action. [MSA 7.93]

MCLA 211.50 Township treasurer; appointment to fill vacancy, bond, term, notice of appointment. [MSA 7.94]

Sec. 50. In case any township treasurer shall neglect to give either of the bonds required, or shall die, resign, or remove out of the township or become unable to discharge the duties of his office, the township board shall forthwith appoint a new treasurer, who, on giving the required bonds, shall execute the duties of the office for the remainder of the year and until his successor is elected and qualified. The township clerk shall immediately notify the county treasurer of such appointment.

MCLA 211.51 Same; failure to file bond; sheriff, powers, bond; compensation. [MSA 7.95]

Sec. 51. In case the township treasurer shall neglect or refuse to file his bond with the county treasurer, in the manner and within the time prescribed by law, and the township board shall fail to appoint a treasurer who shall give such bond, and deliver a receipt for the same to the supervisor by the tenth day of December, the supervisor shall ...

MCLA 211.52 Incomplete collection; disbursement of collection funds. [MSA 7.96]

MCLA 211.53 Payment of taxes. Payments in full; partial payments, authorization, certificate; payments under protest, actions for amount paid. Payments of owners of undivided shares, lienholders, and tenants. Payments by owners of surface rights or mineral rights. Realty acquired for highway purposes, separate assessments, allocation of taxes and assessments, removal from tax rolls, tax liens on remainder. [MSA 7.97]

MCLA 211.53a Recovery of excess payments not made under protest. [MSA 7.97(1)]

Sec. 53a. Any taxpayer who is assessed and pays taxes in excess of the correct and lawful amount due because of a clerical error or mutual mistake of fact made by the assessing officer and the taxpayer, may recover the excess so paid, without interest, if suit is commenced within 3 years from the date of payment, notwithstanding that the payment was not made under protest.

MCLA 211.53b Clerical errors and mutual mistakes of fact, corrections, payments and rebates. [MSA 7.97(2)]

Sec. 53b. As an alternative to section 53, whenever there has been a clerical error or a mutual mistake of fact relative to the correct assessment figures, the rate of taxation or the mathematical computation relating to the assessing of taxes, and the error or mutual mistake is verified by the local assessing officer, and approved by the board of review at a meeting held only for such purpose on Tuesday following the second Monday in December. The board of review shall ...

MCLA 211.54 Collected and unpaid taxes, accounting to county treasurer; time. [MSA 7.98]

Sec. 54. Within 20 calendar days after the time specified in his warrant, the township treasurer ... shall ...

MCLA 211.55 Statement delinquent taxes, requirement, contents, delinquent tax roll, affidavit; payment of delinquent taxes, procedure; rejection of tax assessed twice or upon erroneously described parcel. MSA 7.99

Sec. 55. If the township treasurer ... is unable to collect any of the taxes on his roll, assessed on real or personal property, he shall ... (and) ... shall attach his affidavit to the tax roll or delinquent roll stating ... The township treasurer ... upon filing the statement with the county treasurer, or within 5 days thereafter, shall file a duplicate statement with the secretary or director of each school district showing the amount of school taxes collected for the school district and the amount of school taxes remaining unpaid which have been returned delinquent to the county treasurer. The township treasurer or other collecting officer at the time of filing the statement shall ...

MCLA 211.56 Settlement between county and township or city treasurers; discharge of bond; tax roll, filing, evidence; delinquent personal taxes, accounting, collection. MSA 7.100

MCLA 211.56a Personal property taxes unpaid for 5 years; striking from rolls; decree; duties of county treasurer. MSA 7.100(1)

Sec. 56a. On or before the first day of May in the sixth year after any tax upon personal property has been levied which remains uncollected, the township or city treasurer shall make in substantial record books duplicate statements showing such taxes upon personal property remaining unpaid, and the names of the persons against whom assessed, the amount assessed against each which remains uncollected to which shall be added all fees and penalties for which provision is made by this act or by any city charter. The original copy of such statement shall be filed with the circuit court of the county in which such township or city is located together with a petition, which shall ...

MCLA 211.57 Delinquent tax statement; county treasurer, duties; county clerk's certificate; return of delinquent taxes to state treasury department; state treasurer, powers and duties; notice to delinquent taxpayers. MSA 7.101

MCLA 211.57a Auditor general to prescribe practice for county treasurers; failure of treasurer to comply; auditor general may complete work, expense borne by county; auditor general to furnish to county treasurers changes in tax law; duty of treasurer.
[MSA 7.101(1)]

MCLA 211.58 Payments to county treasurer; receipt, numbering, certificate. [MSA 7.102]

MCLA 211.59 Same; collection fee; additional charge; disposition.
[MSA 7.103]

OF THE SALE, REDEMPTION AND CONVEYANCE OF DELINQUENT TAX LANDS

MCLA 211.60 Tax sale; lands to be sold; fee for expenses; collection fee; lien of state [MSA 7.104]

OF THE NOTICE AND LISTS OF LANDS TO BE SOLD

MCLA 211.61 State treasurer's petition for sale; schedules to be annexed, contents; collection and expense fees; record book.
[MSA 7.105]

MCLA 211.61a Notice to taxpayer, treasurer to mail, form; expenses. [MSA 7.106]

MCLA 211.62 County clerk and circuit judge, duties; court order, form. [MSA 7.107]

MCLA 211.63 Designated newspapers; auditor general, duties; notice of tax sale advertising. [MSA 7.108]

MCLA 211.64 Publication by distribution; county treasurer, duties.
[MSA 7.109]

MCLA 211.65 Lands delinquent for taxes; advertisement cost, limit; additional notices. [MSA 7.110]

MCLA 211.66 Publication of petition and order for hearing; jurisdiction, objections, hearing, evidence; order setting aside taxes; decree. [MSA 7.111]

MCLA 211.67 Decree for sale; form; vesting of title in state; disposition of disputed taxes; appeal, condition; rejection and reassessment. [MSA 7.112]

MCLA 211.67a Deed to state of lands bid in; recording; cancellation of taxes; removal from tax roll; subject to taxation; conveyance to state housing development authority. [MSA 7.112(1)]

MCLA 211.67b Lands sold for taxes; easements, right of way, permit, dedication [MSA 7.112(2)]

MCLA 211.68 Unoffered lands; state bid; taxation. [MSA 7.113]

MCLA 211.69 Delinquent tax lands of incompetent persons; equitable relief; state's lien. [MSA 7.114]

OF SALE BY COUNTY TREASURER

MCLA 211.70 Sale; payment of bid; cancellation and forfeiture for failure to make; reoffer, state bid; report and confirmation of sale; setting aside; report to auditor general. [MSA 7.115]

MCAL 211.71 Purchaser's certificate; form. [MSA 7.116]

MCLA 211.72 Tax deed; title conveyed; quieting of title; writ of assistance; loss of certificate. [MSA 7.117]

MCLA 211.73 Same; setting aside or cancellation; 5 year limitation; improvements; refund; taxes. [MSA 7.118]

MCLA 211.73a Same; notice, time; forfeiture and certificate of cancellation, recording; rights prior to amendment; litigation of issues, procedure; chancery jurisdiction. [MSA 7.119]

MCLA 211.73b Certificates and deeds issued prior to September 28, 1907, barred. [MSA 7.119(1)]

OF REDEMPTION AND ANNULMENT

MCLA 211.73c Redemption; notice to owner of expiration of period; form. [MSA 7.119(2)]

Sec. 73c. Not later than 120 days prior to the expiration of the redemption period provided in section 74 of this act, the county treasurer of each county shall send a notice to each person to whom is assessed, according to the records of his office, each piece or parcel of land bid in to the state at the tax sale provided in section 70 of this act, and still held as a state bid. In case the records of his office do not indicate the person to whom the land is assessed or the address of such person, the county treasurer shall notify the several assessing officers of the description of such lands, so bid in to the state in their respective districts. After receiving such list and not later than 60 days prior to the expiration of the redemption period, the several assessing officers shall examine their assessment rolls and shall notify the person to whom is assessed each piece or parcel of land so bid in to the state. The notice to the person to whom such property is assessed shall be in substantially the form prescribed below and shall be sent by registered mail with return receipt demanded, with postage fully prepaid thereon.

Sir:

You are hereby notified that according to the records of this office, the following piece or parcel of land, which is assessed to you, was sold and bid in to the state of Michigan at the annual tax sale of May, 19 ... , for delinquent taxes of 19 ... , and prior years. Unless redeemed from said sale on or before .... 19.... , the title to said land will vest and become absolute in the state of Michigan.

DESCRIPTION OF LAND:

. . . .

Very truly yours,

. . . . County treasurer or

Assessor of . . . .

The cost of mailing the notice herein provided for shall be paid to the county treasurer or the assessing officer by the county, township, city or village as the case may be.

Provided, That failure to receive or serve such notice or any defect therein shall not invalidate the proceedings taken under the auditor general's petition and decree of the circuit court, in foreclosure and sale of such lands for taxes.

999

MCLA 211.74 Same; certificate; duties of county officers; authority of auditor general. [MSA 7.120]

MCLA 211.75 Annulment of certificate of redemption or tax deed, copy, record; notice to auditor general. [MSA 7.121]

MCLA 211.76 Illegal tax; grounds for holding; other taxes sustained. [MSA 7.122]

Sec. 76. *In any suit or proceeding to enforce or set aside any tax before sale, such tax shall be held illegal only for 1 of the following reasons:*
First, That no law authorizes such tax;
Second, That the person or persons appointed to decide whether a tax shall be raised under a given law, have acted without jurisdiction, or have not imposed the tax in question;
Third, That the person or property assessed was exempt from the taxation in question or was not legally assessed;
Fourth, That the tax has been paid;
Fifth, That the supervisor or board of review in assessing a person or property for taxation, or in the apportionment of the tax to the person or property in question acted fraudulently.
If any such illegality, omission or fraud affects the amount of 1 tax only, the tax shall be sustained so far as the same is legal and just.

MCLA 211.77 Competent evidence. [MSA 7.123]

OF TAX LAND HELD BY THE STATE

MCLA 211.83 Loss of certificate of sale or deed; proof; issuance of deed, contents, fee. [MSA 7.137]

MCLA 211.84 Purchase of state bids after tax sale; unpaid taxes; certificate; deed. [MSA 7.138]

MCLA 211.85 Enforcement of remaining unpaid taxes. [MSA 7.139]

MCLA 211.86 Ejectment action, authorized against state; evidence; tax refund. [MSA 7.140]

MCLA 211.87 Adjustment of accounts; interest on delinquent payments; charge back lists. ⌈MSA 7.141⌉

MCLA 211.87a Detailed statement of delinquent taxes to school district, contents; city or township treasurer, duty. ⌈MSA 7.142⌉

Sec. 87a. The township or city clerk shall within 10 days after receiving the notice from the county treasurer of the amount of delinquent taxes and a description of the land upon which said taxes were paid, make out and deliver to the moderator or secretary of the district board or board of education of each school district situated in whole or in part within such township or city to which money may be due from delinquent school taxes as shown by the statement of the county treasurer, a detailed statement showing the amount of such delinquent school tax together with the interest thereon and the year of assessment thereof and deliver a copy of such statement to the township or city treasurer. The township or city treasurer shall forthwith pay all moneys shown by such statement to be due such school district to the proper receiving officer of such district and notify the secretary or director of each respective school district of the total amount paid to the school treasurer.

MCLA 211.87b Delinquent tax revolving fund. Creation; delinquent taxes payable to county. Disposition money in fund. Single school district within a political unit. Interest and collection fees. Surplus. Borrowing, authorization, limitation. Purpose. ⌈MSA 7.142(1)⌉

MCLA 211.88 Tax report (monthly) **of auditor general, contents, time; entries of county treasurer.** ⌈MSA 7.143⌉

MCLA 211.89 Unpaid taxes, fees, charges, disposition. ⌈MSA 7.144⌉

MCLA 211.90 Compensation and expenses, payment. ⌈MSA 7.145⌉

Sec. 90. All compensation of officers in the assessment and collection of taxes in townships and in the return of delinquent taxes to the county treasurer, except fees collected by township treasurers on their tax rolls, shall be paid by the township. ...

MCLA 211.91 Losses by default, allocation. ⌈MSA 7.146⌉

Sec. 91. All losses that may be sustained by the default of any township officer in the discharge of any duty imposed by this act, shall be chargeable to such township. ...

MISCELLANEOUS PROVISIONS

MCLA 211.92   List of part-paid and homestead lands; contents, time. [MSA 7.147]

Sec. 92. The ... (department of conservation) ... shall, during the month of January in each year, furnish to the several county treasurers a list of all part paid state lands, and also of all licensed homestead lands that have been licensed for a term of 5 years and over, and upon which patents have not been issued, together with the date of each license and the name of the licensee, in their counties respectively, and such treasurer shall, on or before the tenth day of February next thereafter, cause to be delivered to the supervisor of each township affected thereby an accurate description of all such lands in his township, with the names of the persons holding the same.

MCLA 211.95   Auditor general withholding sale because of error; taxes charged back; change in boundaries. [MSA 7.148]

Sec. 95. If the auditor general or county treasurer shall discover before the sale of any lands, as aforesaid, that for any reason they should not be sold, he shall cause the same to be withheld from sale; and if the error originated with the township ...

MCLA 211.96 Rejected taxes; list; reassessment. [MSA 7.149]

MCLA 211.97   Same; on detached lands, statement to auditor general; tax credit. [MSA 7.150]

MCLA 211.98 Conveyance, grounds for withholding; 5 year limitation; cancelling of sale; rejection and reassessment of taxes. [MSA 7.151]

MCLA 211.98a Certificate of payment of taxes, certificate of error or cancellation of sale; payment by delinquent treasurer. [MSA 7.152]

Sec. 98a. ... And in case of failure of said delinquent treasurer to pay said amount, as requested, within 30 days of the receipt

1002

of said notice, it shall be the duty of the county treasurer so notify-
ing, to institute suit against delinquent treasurer and his bondsmen
for the recovery of said amount. Upon the receipt of such money so
paid to him, the county treasurer shall at once pay the same over to
the proper township or other officer or fund entitled to the same,
and shall notify the board of supervisors at their annual session in
October of the several amounts thus collected and paid over.

**MCLA 211.98b Withholding of conveyance of lands bid in to state;
certificate of error; inapplicable to lands disposed of under state
land board act.** [MSA 7.152(1)]

**MCLA 211.99 Unprejudicial irregularities; records prima facie evi-
dence; presumption; signing of records; deed unimpeachable.**
[MSA 7.153]

Sec. 99. No tax assessed upon any property, or sale therefor,
shall be held invalid by any court of this state on account of any
irregularity in any assessment, or on account of any assessment or
tax roll not having been made or proceeding had within the time required, by law, or ... Where any statement, certificate, or record is
required to be made or signed by a school district board or a township board, such statement, certificate or record may be made and
signed by the members of such boards, or a majority thereof, and it
shall not be necessary that other members be present when each
signs the same. The provisions of this section shall not be construed to authorize any showing or impeaching the validity of any
deed executed by the auditor general under the provisions of this
act, but such deed shall be held absolute and conclusive as herein
provided.

MCLA 211.100 Prosecuting attorney; duties. [MSA 7.154]

Sec. 100. It shall be the duty of the prosecuting attorney of
each county to give his counsel and advice to the county treasurer,
the township treasurers, and the supervisors of the county whenever
they or any of them may deem it necessary for the proper discharge
of the duties imposed upon them in this act free of charge.

MCLA 211.101 Deed to deceased person; title conveyed.
[MSA 7.155]

MCLA 211.102 Delinquent tax return to ... (department of conservation) **... time, record; failure to pay, forfeiture.** [MSA 7.156]

MCLA 211.103 Same; statement of taxes paid, time; credit.
[MSA 7.157]

Sec. 103. ... and the county treasurer shall credit each township with its share of such amount.

MCLA 211.104 Improvements by dispossessed persons; lien.
[MSA 7.158]

MCLA 211.105 Organization of new county; division of township; effect on assessments; credit. [MSA 7.159]

MCLA 211.106 Payment to county treasurer before sale; part payment, effect. [MSA 7.160]

MCLA 211.107 Application of act; board of review in cities, duties, proceedings, oath of office. [MSA 7.161]

MCLA 211.107a Authority of city to increase rate of taxation; referendum, maximum; reduction, limitation. [MSA 7.161(1)]

MCLA 211.108 Unpaid tax return; ordinance; description rejected by county treasurer; judicial sale, authorization. [MSA 7.162]

MCLA 211.109 Deputies; authorized acts, responsibility.
[MSA 7.163]

Sec. 109. When an officer is authorized to do any act his deputy shall have the same authority, and such officer shall be responsible for the acts of his deputy.

MCLA 211.110 Compensation of county and township officers; powers of cities. [MSA 7.164]

Sec. 110. Supervisors shall be allowed for their services in assessing property, making tax rolls, and for extending taxes thereon, at the rate of 2 dollars for each day actually and necessarily spent in making the same; the members of the board of review shall be paid at the same rate per day for each day actually and necessarily spent in the attendance upon the board; the accounts for such services shall be verified, audited and paid as other township expenses. ...

1004

Note: Care must be exercised in reading the above section. Under MCLA 41.95 and 41.96 [MSA 5.82 and 5.83] there is no dollar limit on the compensation of a township supervisor, clerk, treasurer or trustee in a general law township.

MCLA 211.111 Deputy township treasurer, appointment, responsibility, compensation. [MSA 7.165]

MCLA 211.112 Collected taxes unaccounted, power of supervisor. [MSA 7.166]

Sec. 112. If at any time it shall be discovered that the treasurer of any township has received the tax assessed upon property which has been returned delinquent, the supervisor shall have power, and he is hereby required to collect the same, in the name of his township, from such treasurer or his sureties, together with interest and charges.

MCLA 211.113 Waste; removal of property from lands bid to state prohibited; warrant for seizure and sale of property; agreement; injunctive relief. [MSA 7.167]

MCLA 211.114 Injunctions. [MSA 7.168]

Sec. 114. No injunction shall issue to stay proceedings for the assessment or collection of taxes under this act.

MCLA 211.115 Waste injunction by certificate holder, procedure. [MSA 7.169]

MCLA 211.116 Assessment or review willfully erroneous; penalty. [MSA 7.170]

Sec. 116. If any supervisor or other assessing officer of any township or city shall willfully assess any property at more or less than what he believes to be its true cash value, he shall be guilty of a misdemeanor, and on conviction thereof he shall ...

MCLA 211.117 Failure to record payment; penalty. [MSA 7.171]

MCLA 211.118 Perjury. [MSA 7.172]

Sec. 118. Any person who, under any of the proceedings re-

quired or permitted by this act shall willfully swear falsely, shall be guilty of perjury and subject to its penalties.

MCLA 211.119 Willful neglect; penalty. [MSA 7.173]

Sec. 119. Any officer who shall willfully neglect, or refuse to perform any of the duties imposed upon him by this act shall, when no other provision is made herein, be guilty of a misdemeanor, and upon conviction thereof shall ...

MCLA 211.121 Publication of tax laws, distribution; service claims audit. [MSA 7.175]

Sec. 121. The auditor general shall, from time to time, as he may deem necessary, cause to be printed at the expense of the state, a sufficient number of copies of this act, and such other laws in force relating to the taxation of property, as may be requisite to a full understanding of all the duties of assessing officers, or other state, county or township officers, with proper side notes, index and forms of proceedings, as may be necessary and proper; to furnish 1 copy to each supervisor, assessor, township clerk and county clerk, and 3 copies to each county treasurer. Each copy shall be marked "state property." He shall transmit to each county treasurer, at the expense of the county, a sufficient number of copies for each county, and every county treasurer shall immediately furnish to the township clerk of each township 5 copies, to be distributed by him to the officers entitled thereto. The board of state auditors shall examine and audit all properly certified claims for services rendered and expenses incurred under the provisions of sections 121, 127 and 128 of this act.

MCLA 211.122 Forms and record books; auditor general to prescribe. [MSA 7.176]

Sec. 122. It shall be the duty of the auditor general to prescribe or approve all forms, blanks and record books made necessary by this act, and it shall be the duty of said county clerks and treasurers to use the blanks prescribed or approved by the auditor general, and no others.

MCLA 211.124 Auditor general, duties; completed acts recognized; county treasurer's deeds; new deed; future proceedings. [MSA 7.178]

MCLA 211.125 Vested rights. [MSA 7.179]

MCLA 211.126 Repeal; saving clause. [MSA 7.180]

INSPECTION AND DISPOSITION OF STATE TAX LANDS

MCLA 211.127b Abandoned land; state title absolute; state conveyances to city or village; sale, proceeds. [MSA 7.182(1)]

MCLA 211.130 Taxes canceled; allocation of burden; correction of assessment roll. [MSA 7.185]

MCLA 211.131 Lands withheld from tax sale; minimum price on sale lands; authority of director of conservation and municipalities; distribution of receipts [MSA 7.188]

MCLA 211.131a Delinquent tax lands; conveyance to owner; distribution of moneys received. Conveyance and distribution. Deed, revival of title, liens, encumbrances, priorities. Mining properties; reservation of mineral rights; description, conveyance by department of conservation. Same; redemption from sale for delinquent taxes. Tax deed; conveyance to lessee, interest. [MSA 7.189]

MCLA 211.131b Certain state lands not subject to entry as homestead lands. [MSA 7.190]

Sec. 131b. Hereafter lands which have been or shall hereafter be deeded to the state of Michigan as provided in sections 127 and 127a of this act shall not be subject to entry as homestead lands.

Note: The sections mentioned above have been repealed.

MCLA 211.131c Municipalities may withhold lands from sale; redemption by owner; certificate; when not redeemed. [MSA 7.190(1)]

MCLA 211.131d State lands; tax sale title; management contracts with licensed real estate brokers; commissions and maintenance costs from revenues. [MSA 7.190(2)]

SUPPLEMENTARY

MCLA 211.135 Recording of conveyances; tax certificate; excepted conveyances; register of deeds, violation, penalty. [MSA 7.194]

MCLA 211.137 Writs of assistance. [MSA 7.195]

MCLA 211.138 Treatment of delinquent tax lands prior to 1891; tender of legal charges, effect. [MSA 7.196]

MCLA 211.139 Examination of proceedings; collection of taxes. [MSA 7.197]

MCLA 211.140 Writ of assistance; service of notice; redemption, time and amount; service on corporations; sheriff's return. [MSA 7.198]

MCLA 211.141 Redemption, conditions, amount of payment; effect on tax title; notice; release; reimbursement; title; grantee's lien; writ of assistance. [MSA 7.199]

MCLA 211.142 Notice by tax purchaser to owners; redemption period. [MSA 7.200]

MCLA 211.142a Record, expired notice and service; evidence of ownership; fees. [MSA 7.201]

MCLA 211.143 Failure to redeem, effective bar. [MSA 7.202]

MCLA 211.144 Proceedings to set aside sale; auditor general to be made party; service of petition upon municipalities. [MSA 7.203]

MCLA 211.146 Board of tax commissioners; secretary and chief clerk, salaries, duties. [MSA 7.204]

MCLA 211.147 Oath of office; salaries and expenses of board members. [MSA 7.205]

MCLA 211.148 State tax commission; meetings, access to records and rolls; subpoena, fees; scope of examination; penalties. [MSA 7.206]

MCLA 211.149 Same; regular meetings, time; special meetings. [MSA 7.207]

MCLA 211.150 Same; duties.　Supervision; assessment rolls. Assessing officers, supervision; enforcement of penalties.　Complaints; correction of irregularities.　Reports, statistical data, approval of forms.   Statement to state board of equalization; co-operation. ⌈MSA 7.208⌉

MCLA 211.151 Same; report to governor, contents, time, printed copies. ⌈MSA 7.209⌉

MCLA 211.152 Same; inspection of assessment rolls, time; review procedure; hearing; corrections in roll; finality of action; per diem of assessing officer. ⌈MSA 7.210⌉

MCLA 211.152a Valuation fixed by board of review as basis for tax. Apportionment, levy, equalization, payment, collection. Additional taxes, collection fees; notice of increased tax liability. Decreased tax liability, refunds, collection fee rebates.
⌈MSA 7.210(1)⌉

MCLA 211.154 Assessment roll, taxable property incorrectly reported; notice, hearing, correction, certification of tax due; demand payment notice. ⌈MSA 7.211⌉

MCLA 211.155 Waste and removal of property from tax delinquent lands. ⌈MSA 7.212⌉

MCLA 211.156 Same; warrant to seize and sell property; execution.
⌈MSA 7.213⌉

MCLA 211.157 Same; county treasurer entitled to injunction.
⌈MSA 7.214⌉

Act No. 189, P.A. 1953 - Taxation of Lessees and Users of Tax-Exempt Property

AN ACT to provide for the taxation of lessees and users of tax-exempt property.

MCLA 211.181 Taxation of lessees or users of tax-exempt property; exceptions. ⌈MSA 7.7(5)⌉

MCLA 211.182 Assessment and collection; action of assumpsit.
⌈MSA 7.7(6)⌉

Sec. 2. Taxes shall be assessed to such lessees or users of real property and collected in the same manner as taxes assessed to owners of real property, except that such taxes shall not become a lien against the property. When due, such taxes shall constitute a debt due from the lessee or user to the township, ... for which the taxes were assessed, and shall be recoverable by direct action of assumpsit.

Act No. 117, P.A. 1970 - Exempted Property not used for Tax Exempt Purposes

AN ACT to permit assessing officers to place tax exempt real and personal property on the tax rolls; and to establish the criteria to determine the status of real and personal property for taxation or tax exempt status.

MCLA 211.191 Placing property on tax rolls. [MSA 7.7(15)]

PROPERTY TAX LIMITATION ACT

Checks and balances apply to property taxes as well as to the executive, legislative and judicial branches of government. There are few aspects of government where the average citizen is more concerned than in the field of taxation. Section 6 of article 9 of the Michigan constitution therefore places a fair amount of power in the hands of the people where taxes in excess of the fifteen mill limitation are sought.

Naturally these limitations do not apply to taxes imposed for the payment of principal and interest on bonds or other indebtedness or future payment of assessments or contract obligations in anticipation of which bonds are issued, which taxes may be imposed without limitation as to rate or amount; or to taxes imposed for any other purpose by a local unit of government whose tax limitations are provided by charter or by general law.

Property tax limitations have always caused much controversy between and among counties, school districts and townships, who receive portions of the fifteen mills as follows: for the county -- 3 mills; for school districts -- 4 mills; for community college districts organized after April 15, 1957 -- 1/4 of 1 mill; for intermediate school districts -- 1/10 of 1 mill; for general law townships -- 1 mill. MTA legal counsel has rendered an opinion that a charter township may receive 1 mill the same as general law townships, if the county tax allocation board is inclined to give it; however, it would be counted as part of the 5 mill charter limitation.

Act No. 62, P.A. 1933 - Property Tax Limitation Act

AN ACT to provide limits on the rate of taxation on property, and to provide for a division of the rate of taxation between counties, townships, municipal corporations, school districts and other local units and to earmark funds raised by increasing the total tax limitation; and to repeal all acts and parts of acts and charters and parts of charters of municipal corporations inconsistent with or contravening the provisions of this act.

MCLA 211.201 Short title. [MSA 7.61]

MCLA 211.202 Definitions. [MSA 7.62]

MCLA 211.203 Limit on tax rate; debt service. [MSA 7.63]

Sec. 3. (a) **General limitation.** *Except as hereinafter provided the total amount of taxes levied against property for all purposes in any 1 year shall not exceed the limits provided by or fixed pursuant to section 6 of article 9 of the state constitution, except taxes levied for the payment of interest and principal on obligations incurred prior to December 8, 1932. Taxes levied under this exception shall be known and referred to as debt service tax rates.*

(b) **Charter or general law limitation.** *If any municipal corporation is or shall hereafter be limited, by a provision in its charter or general law, in its power to levy taxes against property for such purposes as may be authorized by law to be supported under the municipal budget, such municipal corporation shall ...*

(c) **Election to raise limits, ballots; declaration of result, filing with county treasurer; notice statement.** *If any local unit shall hold an election for the purpose of increasing the total tax rate limitation, as provided for by section 6 of article 9 of the state constitution, the vote at such election shall be taken by ballot and said ballots shall be cast and counted in the manner provided by the general election laws of this state. Said ballots shall state the amount by which it is proposed that the total tax rate limitation on property in the local unit be increased and the number of years for which it is proposed that said increase shall be effective. Said ballot may also state the purpose for which the funds derived from the voted increase over the constitutional tax rate limitation may be used, and such funds shall not be considered by the county allocation board in dividing the net limitation tax rate among the various*

governmental units entitled thereto under the provisions of this act. Within 5 days after every election held in any local unit to increase the tax rate limitation, a certified copy of the official declaration of the result of the election shall be filed with the treasurer of the county or counties in which such local unit is located. The voted increase in the tax rate limitation shall be effective in such local unit only when such certified copy is filed. The notice of every election in which an increase in the total tax rate limitation is to be voted upon shall contain a statement by the county treasurer of the county or counties in which the local unit so voting is located of the total of all voted increases in the total tax rate limitation, in any local units, affecting the taxable property in the local unit so voting and the years such increases are effective.

MCLA 211.204 State tax rate; operating purposes. ⌐MSA 7.64⌐

MCLA 211.204 State tax rate; operating purposes. Tax rates. Notices; debt service. ⌐MSA 7.64⌐

MCLA 211.205 County tax allocation board; members, selection. ⌐MSA 7.65⌐

Sec. 5. *A county tax allocation board is created for each county and shall be composed of:*
(a) The county treasurer.
(b) The chairman of the board of county auditors if there be such a board, and if not, the chairman of the finance or ways and means committee of the board of supervisors of the county.
(c) The intermediate school district superintendent or his representative.
(d) A member of a school board of a school district in the county maintaining 12 grades of school, who shall be selected by the judge or judges of probate of the county, except that in counties containing 1 or more municipal corporations having a population of 10,000 or more, such member shall be a resident of the county and selected by the board of education of the constituent school district, not an intermediate school district, at least ½ of the area of which lies in the county, and which has the largest number of children in the whole district between the ages of 5 and 20 according to the latest annual school census.
(e) A resident of a municipality within the county who shall be selected by the judge or judges of probate of the county, except that in counties containing 1 or more municipal corporations having

a population of 10,000 or more, such member shall be a resident of such a municipality, except that in counties in which are located municipalities subject to the provisions of this act, such member shall be an official of 1 of such municipalities, and if there be but 1 such municipality within the county, then such member shall be selected by the governing body of such municipality, either from its own members or its municipal officers.

(f) A member not officially connected with any local unit, who shall be selected by the judge or judges of probate of the county.

(g) A member who shall be selected from the members of a township board of 1 of the townships in the county by the county clerk, county treasurer and county sheriff or a majority thereof.

MCLA 211.205a Initiatory petition for separate tax limitation; signatures, filing. [MSA 7.65(1)]

Sec. 5a. A vote on adopting separate tax limitations shall be initiated by petition signed by not less than 4% of the registered electors of each township and city within the county. The petition shall be filed with the county clerk not less than 30 days before the convening of the board in regular session, or any special session called for the purpose of considering the petition.

MCLA 211.205b Same; form, circulators. [MSA 7.65(2)]

Sec. 5b. The petition shall be in substantially the following form:

PETITION INITIATING PROCEDURES FOR THE ADOPTION OF SEPARATE TAX LIMITATIONS

To the county board of supervisors:

We, the undersigned qualified and registered electors and residents of the city or township of ...., in the county of ...., and state of Michigan, hereby petition the county board of supervisors to place before the voters of this county the question of establishing separate tax limitation millage rates (for a period of ....years or for an indefinite period), or until altered by the voters of the county, for the county of .... and the townships and school districts within the county, the aggregate of which shall not exceed .... mills, as follows:

	Mills
County of	. . . .
Townships	. . . .
Intermediate school districts	. . . .
School districts (a school district located entirely within a city or charter township shall receive in addition millage equal to the township millage.)	. . . .
Total	. . . .

WARNING

Whoever knowingly signs this petition more than once, signs a name other than his own, signs when not a qualified and registered elector, or places opposite his signature on a petition a date other than the actual date such signature was affixed, is in violation of the law."

The body of the petition and jurat shall be substantially as provided in section 349a of Act No. 116 of the Public Acts of 1954, as amended, being section 168.349a of the Compiled Laws of 1948. (repealed in 1966)

The circulator of the petition shall be a qualified and registered elector of the county in which he circulates the petition. Petitions shall be signed and acknowledged by the circulator before a person authorized by law to take acknowledgments.

MCLA 211.205c Petition by tax allocation board for separate tax limitation. [MSA 7.65(3)]

MCLA 211.205d Submission of question at general or special election. [MSA 7.65(4)]

MCLA 211.205e County tax allocation board; separate tax limitations. [MSA 7.65(5)]

Sec. 5e. Prior to adoption of a resolution submitting to a vote a question proposed by the initiatory petition of electors, the county board of supervisors shall request the county tax allocation board to submit to the county board of supervisors such separate tax limitations for the county and the school districts and townships therein, aggregating not less than the same number of mills as is in the electors' petition, as a majority of the members of the allocation board deems are best calculated to provide for the financial needs of such local units.

MCLA 211.205f County clerk; transmittal to local clerks for submission of question. [MSA 7.65(6)]

Sec. 5f. The county clerk, within 3 days after passage of a resolution to submit the question to the electors of the county, shall transmit a certified copy of the initiatory petition, the suggested tax rate limitations submitted by the county tax allocation board, and the resolution submitting the questions to a vote, to the clerk of each city and township in the county who shall conduct the election on the question in the same manner as provided by law for other county elections.

MCLA 211.205g Separate tax limitations; submission of question, form. [MSA 7.65(7)]

Sec. 5g. The question of adopting separate tax limitations shall be submitted to the registered and qualified electors of the county in substantially the following form:
"Shall separate tax limitations be established (for a period of . . . . years or for an indefinite period), or until altered by the voters of the county, for the county of . . . . and the townships and school districts within the county, the aggregate of which shall not exceed . . . . mills as follows:

	Mills
County of	*. . . . .*
Townships	*. . . . .*
Intermediate school districts	*. . . . .*
School districts (a school district located entirely within a city or charter township shall receive in addition millage equal to the township millage.)	*. . . . .*
Total	*. . . . .*
Yes ( )	
No ( )"	

MCLA 211.205h Same; adoption of plan [MSA 7.65(8)]

Sec. 5h. At an election upon the question of adopting separate tax limitations, the tax limitations proposed by electors' initiatory petitions and the tax limitations proposed by the county tax alloca-

tion board shall be separately submitted to the voters. If the allocation board has recommended separate tax limitations identical to those proposed by the initiatory petitions, only 1 question shall be submitted to the voters. If more than 1 question receives more "yes" than "no" votes, the set of separate tax limitations which received the greater number of "yes" votes shall be adopted. If more than 1 question receives the same number of "yes" votes being the highest number of "yes" votes, the question adopted shall be the one receiving the greater excess of "yes" votes over "no" votes.

MCLA 211.205i Same; effectiveness. [MSA 7.65(9)]

Sec. 5i. On the filing in the offices of the secretary of state and the county clerk of a copy of the initiatory petition, the separate tax limitations recommended by the county tax allocation board, and of all resolutions thereafter and the certificate of the county board of canvassers showing that a majority of the electors voting on either the separate tax limitations proposed by petition of electors or of the county tax allocation board, or both, has approved thereof, and stating the number of votes cast on the separate questions and the number cast for and against the same, the separate tax limitations for the county and the townships and school districts therein shall be effective and shall thereupon apply to all subsequent tax levies until altered by another vote pursuant to the provisions of this act or expiration of the period for which the separate tax limitations were voted, except that when the election is held after April 1 in any year the adopted limitations shall be first effective in the subsequent calendar year.

MCLA 211.205j Same; adoption, abolition of county tax allocation board, re-establishment. [MSA 7.65(10)]

Sec. 5j. Whenever a majority of the registered and qualified electors of a county voting upon the question adopt separate tax limitations as authorized by section 6 of article 9 of the state constitution, the county tax allocation board created for such county by section 5 is abolished. ...

MCLA 211.205k Same; alteration or extension; county advisory tax limitation committee; election. [MSA 7.65(11)]

Sec. 5k. Whenever an initiatory petition is received by the county board of supervisors to alter or extend within the 18 mill

1016

limitation existing separate tax limitations of the county and the townships and school districts therein, the county board of supervisors shall ...

MCLA 211.205*l* Same; prior voted millage increases; additional millage increases. [MSA 7.65(12)]

Sec. 5-l. *The establishment and alteration of separate tax limitations shall not affect prior voted millage increases or the power of a local unit to vote additional millage increases, pursuant to section 3 or other law.*

MCLA 211.205m Separate millage rates for separate districts. [MSA 7.65(13)]

MCLA 211.206 County tax allocation board; term, officers, assistance. [MSA 7.66]

MCLA 211.207 Same; compensation and expenses. [MSA 7.67]

MCLA 211.208 Same; meetings, examination of local records. [MSA 7.68]

Sec. 8. *The board shall meet for the purpose of organization on the third Monday in April, 1950, and each year thereafter at the office of the county clerk at 1 p.m. and shall hold ...*

MCLA 211.209 Budgets and statements of local units; preparation, form. [MSA 7.69]

Sec. 9. *... Each local unit as defined in this act shall prepare each year a budget containing an itemized statement of its proposed expenditures and estimated revenues, covering all its departments and activities. Such budget shall cover that ...*

MCLA 211.210 Same; filing with county tax allocation board. [MSA 7.70]

Sec. 10. *Such local unit shall file its budget and statements provided for in the preceding section with the board on or before the third Monday in April of each year. Each local unit which has voted to increase the total tax rate limitation as provided in the last sentence of the first paragraph of section 6 of article 9 of the state constitution shall also file with the board a sworn statement ...*

MCLA 211.211 County tax allocation board; powers and duties in establishing tax rates. MSA 7.71

Sec. 11. (a) The board shall examine the budgets and statements of local units which have been filed with it, and shall determine the tax rates exclusive of debt service tax rates which would be required according to its proposed budget. The board may request additional statements and examine financial records to verify the tax rate request of a local unit.

(b) If the board shall find that the total of all such tax rates which would be required to be levied on property located within the area of any local unit does not exceed the net limitation tax rate, it shall approve such tax rates as maximum tax rates, except such tax rates as may be required to be determined under the following subsections.

(c) If the board shall find that the total of all such tax rates which would be required to be levied on property located within the area of any local unit exceeds the net limitation tax rate it shall proceed according to the 3 following subsections.

(d) The board shall approve minimum tax rates as follows: For the county, 3 mills; for school districts, 4 mills; for community college districts organized after April 15, 1957, ¼ of 1 mill; for intermediate school districts, 1/10 of 1 mill; for townships other than charter townships, 1 mill. If the community college district has voted to increase the total tax limitation as provided in section 6 of article 9 of the state constitution, the board during the period the increase is in effect shall not allocate the ¼ of 1 mill minimum tax rate to the community college district, but the community college district shall raise all of its tax revenues from the amount of increase so voted. No local unit shall be allowed a tax rate in excess of what would be required according to its proposed budget. For the year beginning July 1, 1971, exclusively, the allocation for community college districts having a state equalized valuation of $6,000,000,000.00 or more shall be fixed at 18/100 of 1 mill which shall be taken from the millage allocated for the county.

(e) The board shall divide the balance of the net limitation tax rate between all local units after due consideration of the needs of the several local units, the importance to the public of functions of local units which might have to be curtailed, the need of local units for construction or repair of public works, the proposed or accom-

1018

plished transfer of functions from 1 local unit to others, and any other facts or matters concerning the operations of local units which the board may deem relevant. A local unit shall not be allowed a tax rate in excess of what would be required according to its proposed budget. The board shall approve a maximum tax rate for each local unit consisting of the minimum tax rate, if any, provided in subsection (d), added to the tax rate determined under this subsection.

(f) The board shall approve a maximum tax rate for each local unit which has voted to increase the total tax rate limitation as provided in the last sentence of the first paragraph of section 6 of article 9 of the state constitution, and as provided for in this act, which tax rate, with other maximum tax rates which may be levied within the area of such local unit, shall not exceed the limitation voted. In approving a maximum tax rate for the various local units, the board shall not take into consideration any increase of the tax rate limitation voted by any local unit.

(g) The board shall not approve a tax rate for any local unit which has not submitted a budget or statements as required.

(h) The approval by the board of a maximum tax rate for any local unit, which will necessitate a reduction in the total proposed expenditures as listed in the budget of such local unit, shall not be construed as a reduction or elimination of any specific items in such list of proposed expenditures, and the board shall not have the power to reduce or eliminate any such specific items. Any local unit in the budget of which a reduction in the total proposed expenditure is necessitated by the action of the board, or the state tax commission in case of appeal, shall have power to revise its budget and amend and alter its tax levy to the extent made necessary by such action, any law or charter provisions to the contrary notwithstanding. Budgets heretofore prepared to be met from taxes to be levied pursuant to this act may likewise be revised.

MCLA 211.211a Intercounty or intermediate school district; maximum tax rate. [MSA 7.71(1)]

MCLA 211.212 Tax levies, statement in rates, limits; debt service. [MSA 7.72]

Sec. 12. ... In order that the maximum tax rates ordered by the board and tax levies pursuant thereto may not be invalidated by any process of determination or review of assessments subsequent to the allocation of the net limitation tax rate, all tax levies shall hereafter be made by prescribing the rate of taxes and the sums of money to be raised thereby, which shall be imposed upon property. No such levy shall be a rate in excess of the maximum tax rate ordered by the board or by the state tax commission in case of appeal: Provided, That nothing in this act shall be construed to limit or restrict the power of the state or local units to make tax levies separately in excess of such maximum tax rates for the purpose of payment of interest and principal on obligations incurred prior to December eighth, 1932.

MCLA 211.214 District located in more than 1 county; establishment of rate. [MSA 7.74]

MCLA 211.214a Same; establishment of rates in all counties; proposed budget. [MSA 7.74(1)]

MCLA 211.215 County tax allocation board; maximum tax rate, final hearing, redetermination. [MSA 7.75]

Sec. 15. In each year, on the third Monday of May, the board shall make a preliminary order approving a maximum tax rate for the purposes of each local unit and shall give written notice of such order to each local unit. At the same time the board shall give to each local unit written notice of the time and place for final hearing before the board on the maximum tax rate of such local unit, which shall not be less than 8 nor more than 12 days thereafter. At such final hearing any local unit may object by its duly authorized officers or agents to the maximum tax rate as ordered by the board and request a redetermination thereof.

MCLA 211.216 Orders of board; maximum tax rate, final order. [MSA 7.76]

Sec. 16. Within 5 days after the final hearing for each local unit, but not later than the first Monday in June, the board shall make a final order approving a maximum tax rate for the purposes of such local unit and shall give written notice of such order to such local unit. Any local unit, required by any provision of law or city charter, to certify its tax levy for apportionment prior to the first Monday in June may, any provision of such law or charter to the contrary notwithstanding, certify its tax levy on or before the Wednesday following the first Monday in June.

MCLA 211.217 Same; appeal to state tax commission; judicial review. [MSA 7.77]

Sec. 17. Within 15 days after the giving of notice of such final order any aggrieved local unit may appeal in writing to the state tax commission. The commission shall give at least 10 days' written notice to all interested parties of the time and place for a hearing on such appeal, and at the hearing shall give all such parties an opportunity to be heard. The commission shall apply the method provided in section 11 for the division of the net limitation tax rate, and if it finds a material mistake of fact, fraud or an error of law in the proceedings under this act, may make an order increasing or decreasing the maximum tax rate of any local unit as ordered by the board, and adjusting the tax rates of other local units affected by such action. The commission shall give written notice of its order to all interested parties within 15 days after such hearing. The order of the commission, or of the board in case of no appeal, shall be final and shall not be reviewable in any court by mandamus, certiorari, appeal or any other method of direct or collateral attack, nor shall any court of this state issue any injunction to prohibit the carrying out of any order made under this act.

MCLA 211.217a State tax commission's orders, intercounty or intermediate school district; adjustment of tax rates. [MSA 7.77(1)]

MISCELLANEOUS ASSESSING PROCEDURES

Act. No. 218, P.A. 1931 - Civil Remedy, Erroneously Assessed Taxes

AN ACT to provide a civil remedy in the case of the payment of taxes and/or special assessments on real property erroneously assessed.

MCLA 211.381 Payment of taxes and/or special assessments erroneously assessed; assumpsit against owner. [MSA 7.771]

Act. No. 234, P.A. 1929 - Public Improvement Assessments.

AN ACT making the sums of money levied upon any parcel of real estate, as an assessment for benefits de-

rived from the construction of any public improvement, a personal obligation on the part of the owner of such parcel, and to provide for the collection thereof.

MCLA 211.501   Public improvement assessment, personal obligation; recovery. [MSA 7.721]

MCLA 211.502   Same; installments [MSA 7.722]

Act. No. 6, P.A. 1873 - Irregular or Illegal Taxes

AN ACT regarding the payment of irregular or illegal taxes.

MCLA 211.531   Collection process, irregularities; voluntary tax payment; officers not liable. [MSA 7.761]

MCLA 211.532   Same; voluntary payment; officer to account. [MSA 7.762]

Act. No. 122, P.A. 1962 - Manuals for Assessing Officials

AN ACT requiring assessing officials to use manuals prepared by the state tax commission.

MCLA 211.721   Assessment of real and personal property; state tax commission manuals. [MSA 7.40]

Sec. 1. ... all assessing officials, whose duty it is to assess real or personal property on which real or personal property taxes are levied by any taxing unit of the state, shall use only the official manual or manuals, with their latest supplements, as prepared or approved by the state tax commission as a guide in preparing assessments.

Note: For other citations covering assessing records, the reader is referred to the section on Preservation of Township Records and History in the chapter on Services, Utilities, Contracts and Ordinances.

JOINT ACTION

Act. No. 160, P.A. 1972 - Tax Assessment and Collection Agreements

AN ACT to allow units and subdivisions of government to make agreements; and to provide for costs of administration of agreements.

MCLA 211.731 Townships, villages, cities, or counties; purpose and contents of agreements. [MSA 7.1061]

Sec. 1. For the purpose of reducing duplication of effort and to provide for more effective tax administration, a township, village, city or county may enter into an agreement with another township, village, city or county of this state for the assessment and collection of a tax levied by such jurisdictions. The agreement may provide for joint administration or for administration by 1 township, village, city or county on behalf of 1 or more townships, villages, cities or counties that are parties to the agreement and shall provide for the allocation of the cost of the administration among the parties.

Act. No. 162, P.A. 1962 - Special Assessment Procedure

AN ACT to prescribe the method of giving notice of special assessment hearings; to prescribe duties of persons and certain public officials in connection with the keeping and maintaining of tax assessment records; to prescribe the effects of failure to give such notice; and to validate certain special assessment hearings.

MCLA 211.741 Special assessments; notice of hearing, service; local tax assessment records. [MSA 5.3534(1)]

Sec. 1. In all cases where special assessments are made against property, notice of all hearings in the special assessment proceedings shall be given as provided in this act in addition to any notice of such hearings to be given by publication or posting as required by statute, charter or ordinance. The provisions of this act in respect to service of notice by mail shall supersede any existing statutory, charter or ordinance requirements for mailing notice. Notice of hearings in special assessment proceedings shall be given to each owner of or party in interest in property to be assessed, whose name appears upon the last local tax assessment records, by mailing by first class mail addressed to such owner or party at the address shown on the tax records, at least 10 days before the date of such hearing. The last local tax assessment records means the last assessment roll for ad valorem tax purposes which has been reviewed by the local board of review, as supplemented by any subsequent changes in the names or the addresses of such owners or parties listed thereon.

MCLA 211.742 Tax assessment records; filing of names; changes in names and addresses. [MSA 5.3534(2)]

Sec. 2. Where any person claims an interest in real property whose name and correct address do not appear upon the last local tax assessment records, he shall be obligated to file immediately his name and address with the local tax assessing officer. This requirement shall be deemed effective only for the purpose of establishing a record of the names and addresses of those persons entitled to notice of hearings in special assessment proceedings. It shall be the duty of each tax assessing officer to immediately enter on the local tax assessment records any changes in the names and addresses of owners or parties in interest filed with him and at all times to keep such tax assessment records current and complete and available for public inspection.

MCLA 211.743 Notice of hearings; mails. [MSA 5.3534(3)]

Sec. 3. On and after 30 days following the effective date of this act, any officer whose duty it is to give notice of hearings in special assessment proceedings may rely upon the last local tax assessment records in giving notice of hearing by mail. The method of giving notice by mail as provided in this act is declared to be the method that is reasonably certain to inform those to be assessed of the special assessment proceedings.

MCLA 211.744 Same; invalidation of assessment; reassessment. [MSA 5.3534(4)]

Sec. 4. Any failure to give notice as required in this act shall not invalidate an entire assessment roll but only the assessments on property affected by the lack of notice. In no case shall any special assessment be declared invalid as to any property if the owner or said party in interest thereof has actually received notice, has waived notice, or has paid any part of the assessment. If any assessment is declared void by court decree or judgment, a reassessment against the property may be made.

MCLA 211.745 Same; validation of previously held hearings.
[MSA 5.3534(5)]

Sec. 5. Notwithstanding the lack of a statute, charter or ordinance provision for the mailing of notice of hearings, each special assessment hearing heretofore held is validated insofar as any notice of hearing is concerned, if notice was given by mail to the owners or parties in interest whose names appeared at the time of mailing on the last local tax assessment records. Any such special assessment hearing is also validated as to any owner or party in interest who has actually received notice of hearing, has waived such notice, or has paid any part of the special assessment.

Act No. 88, P.A. 1909 - Municipal Bonds, Exemption.

AN ACT to exempt from taxation bonds hereafter issued by any county, township, city, village or school district within the state of Michigan.

MCLA 211.571 Bonds exempted from taxation. [MSA 7.811]

Act. No. 55, P.A. 1956 - Jeopardy Assessment of Personal Property Taxes

AN ACT to authorize the jeopardy assessment of personal property taxes; to establish the terms, limitations and conditions upon which the date for payment of personal property taxes may be accelerated; to provide for the collection of such taxes, and to establish a lien therefor; and to establish the liability of the purchaser of personal property for personal property taxes.

MCLA 211.691 Personal property taxes; jeopardy assessment.
[MSA 7.51(1)]

Sec. 1. The treasurer of any township, city or village is authorized to accelerate the date on which any personal property tax collectible by him would otherwise be due upon the terms, limitations and conditions set forth in this act. Proceedings hereunder shall be known as jeopardy assessment of personal property taxes.

1025

MCLA 211.692 Same; jeopardy assessment affidavit, contents.
[MSA 7.51(2)]

MCLA 211.693 Affidavit, filing, notice to taxpayer. [MSA 7.51(3)]

MCLA 211.694 Acceleration of due date of tax, lien, collection of tax. [MSA 7.51(4)]

MCLA 211.695 Jeopardy assessment tax rate; collection of tax; discharge of affidavit. [MSA 7.51(5)]

Sec. 5. The assessor of any tax collection district shall, upon request of the treasurer thereof, furnish his estimate of the assessed value of any personal property upon which the treasurer proposes to make a jeopardy assessment. Such estimates shall be of the assessed value such property will bear upon completion of the regular personal property assessment procedure for the current year, and such estimate shall be set forth in the treasurer's affidavit as the assessed value of the property described therein. The treasurer shall estimate the tax rate which he believes will be authorized by the taxing unit on whose behalf the jeopardy assessment is made for the current year, which rate shall not be more than 10% in excess of the rate authorized by such unit for the previous year, and the rate so estimated shall be set forth in the affidavit of the treasurer as the jeopardy tax rate. The amount of the jeopardy personal property tax shall be determined therefrom. Upon collection of the amount of the jeopardy tax, the treasurer shall forthwith discharge the jeopardy tax assessment affidavit from the records of the register of deeds. All money received in collection of jeopardy taxes shall be retained by the treasurer in a special account entitled "jeopardy tax account" until receipt of the next regular tax roll of the taxing unit or units on whose behalf the jeopardy assessment was made.

MCLA 211.696 Personal property tax; repayment of excess; collection of unpaid regular tax. [MSA 7.51(6)]

MCLA 211.697 Treasurer, diligence, liability for uncollected taxes. [MSA 7.51(7)]

LANDS FOR PUBLIC PURPOSES

Act No. 107, P.A. 1951 - Tax Lands, Sale After Abandonment of Public Use

AN ACT to authorize the sale and conveyance of certain tax lands, the title to which has revested in the state by reason of abandonment of the public use of said lands.

MCLA 211.641 Sale and conveyance of certain tax lands; deposit of funds. [MSA 7.1051]

Act No. 149, P.A. 1911 - State Agencies and Public Corporations

AN ACT to provide for the acquisition by purchase, condemnation and otherwise by state agencies and public corporations of private property for the use or benefit of the public, and to define the terms "public corporations," "state agencies" and "private property" as used herein.

MCLA 213.21 "Public corporation," "state agencies," defined. [MSA 8.11]

MCLA 213.22 Private property defined. [MSA 8.12]

MCLA 213.23 Authority to take private property. [MSA 8.13]

MCLA 213.23a Scope of act; rights conferred by act. [MSA 8.13(1)]

MCLA 213.24 Condemnation proceedings; necessity declared; authorization; jurisdiction. [MSA 8.14]

MCLA 213.25 Same; resolution; petition, contents; jury to determine necessity, compensation. [MSA 8.15]

MCLA 213.26 Order for hearing on petition; guardian ad litem. [MSA 8.16]

MCLA 213.27 Same; publication, mailing and service; manner; proof. [MSA 8.17]

MCLA 213.28 Jury; order for impanelling; method of selecting; peremptory challenges. [MSA 8.18]

MCLA 213.29 Same; oath; view of property; instructions; written verdict. [MSA 8.19]

MCLA 213.30 Same; verdict; necessity, compensation, apportionment of award. [MSA 8.20]

MCLA 213.31 Same; use of exhibits; blank verdict, entry of descriptions. [MSA 8.21]

MCLA 213.32 Verdict may be set aside; allowance of amendments. [MSA 8.22]

MCLA 213.33 Motion for new trial; confirmation of verdict; appeal, bond, manner of perfecting. [MSA 8.23]

MCLA 213.34 Appeal; duty of clerk, procedure. [MSA 8.24]

MCLA 213.35 Same; hearing; costs; frivolous appeals. [MSA 8.25]

MCLA 213.36 Verdict and confirmance certified; petitioner, compensation for owner, possession. [MSA 8.26]

MCLA 213.37 Fees; officers, juror, witness, attorney. [MSA 8.27]

MCLA 213.38 Condemnation proceedings; discontinuance; expenses and attorney fees. [MSA 8.28]

MCLA 213.39 Ownership, prima facie evidence. [MSA 8.29]

MCLA 213.40 Petition to condemn land; recording of notice; constructive notice to purchaser [MSA 8.30]

MCLA 213.41 Filing of petition; constructive notice to purchaser of personalty; record of notice. [MSA 8.31]

Act No. 379, P.A. 1927 - Service on Unknown Owners or Claimants

AN ACT to provide for service of process or notice on unknown owners or claimants to land in condemnation proceedings.

MCLA 213.261 Condemnation; service of process on unknown claimants. [MSA 8.221]

Act No. 270, P.A. 1931 - Condemnation Awards, Delinquent Taxes.

AN ACT to provide for the application of awards in condemnation proceedings against taxes and/or special assessments, and to prescribe the effect thereof.

MCLA 213.291 Condemnation awards; application to payment of taxes and special assessments. [MSA 8.231]

Act No. 207, P.A. 1965 - Proration of General Taxes on Property Acquired for Public Purposes

AN ACT to provide for the proration of general taxes on real property acquired for public purposes.

MCLA 213.311 Dates of proration. [MSA 7.679(1)]

MCLA 213.312 Taxes to be prorated. [MSA 7.679(2)]

STATE AND FEDERAL LANDS

Michigan has truly been blessed with an abundance of land which by various means has come into the hands of the state, making it a landowner of considerable size. Except for some isolated areas, these statutes are of little concern to many areas of the state. However, they are presented here in abbreviated form using mainly the titles and section headings only. The Department of Natural Resources is now the office responsible for supervision of these lands.

Act No. 155, P.A. 1937 - State Lands; State Land Office Board

AN ACT to create a state land office board, and to prescribe its powers, duties and limitations; to provide for the control and jurisdiction of said board and the department of conservation over certain state owned lands; to provide for the sale and disposition of certain lands held by the state of Michigan, and for the disposition of the moneys received therefrom; to provide for the forfeiture of its contracts and the repossession of property under its jurisdiction; to specify the jurisdiction of courts in actions against the board; to limit the time within which actions to set aside sales made under this act might be brought; and to repeal all acts and parts of acts inconsistent with the provisions of this act.

MCLA 211.355a Definition of terms; validation of previous conveyances and contracts; conveyance to more than 1 as owner. MSA 7.955(1)

MCLA 211.358e Limitation of action to set aside sale or conveyance. MSA 7.958(5)

MCLA 211.358f Vacating of plats; exchange of parcels; conveyances. MSA 7.958(6)

MCLA 211.358g Condemnation of state lands, procedure; payment of award. MSA 7.958(7)

MCLA 211.358h Withholding from sale lands in which persons in military service owned any estate or interest; affidavit, filing. MSA 7.958(8)

MCLA 211.360 Receipts; remittance to tax assessing units; basis; operating expenses; certificate of cancelled taxes. MSA 7.960

MCLA 211.362 Definition(owner). MSA 7.962

MCLA 211.364 Termination of act; land under control of department of conservation; certain rights saved. MSA 7.964

Act No. 92, P.A. 1943 - Withholding Lands from Sale

AN ACT to protect the interest of the public, acquired other than through taxation, in lands under the jurisdiction and control of the state land office board and department of conservation, and to make an appropriation therefor.

MCLA 211.371 **Certain lands, withholding from sale; notice to auditor general.** [MSA 7.965(1)]

MCLA 211.372 **Same; conveyance to grantees; delinquent taxes and special assessments, payment and certification; liens.** [MSA 7.965(2)]

MCLA 211.373 Same; taxes and special assessments subsequently assessed rejected by auditor general and reassessed. [MSA 7.965(3)]

MCLA 211.374 Same; payment of valid taxes and special assessments when interest acquired by state; approval. [MSA 7.965(4)]

MCLA 211.375 Appropriation. [MSA 7.965(5)]

Act No. 260, P.A. 1931 - Governmental Unit Purchases, Delinquent Tax Lands.

AN ACT to authorize counties, cities, villages, townships, school districts and drainage districts to purchase land sold for delinquent taxes and drain assessments.

MCLA 211.421 Lands sold for delinquent taxes and drain assessments, purchase by governmental units. [MSA 7.941]

Sec. 1. The governing body of a ... township, school district or drainage district may appropriate money and purchase lands at the statutory sale of lands for delinquent drain assessments. In case of the purchase of such lands such governing body may also appropriate money and purchase the same lands, if they are tax delinquent, at the statutory sale of lands by county treasurers for delinquent general property taxes, it being the intent of this act to afford protection to the investment that any such local governmental unit may have in drains.

Act No. 130, P.A. 1907 - Refund of Purchase Price and Cancellation of Sale

AN ACT to provide for refunding to purchasers the price paid to the state on sale of land by the commissioner of the state land office, under section 131 of Act 206 of Public Acts of 1893, as amended by Act 141 of Public Acts of 1901, in cases where the land sold did not belong to the class of lands liable to sale thereunder; for cancelling the conveyance of such lands to the state and restoring the tax liens thereon in favor of the state, which were erroneously cancelled.

MCLA 211.451 Purchase price refund; conditions. [MSA 7.671]

MCLA 211.452 Same; circumstances authorizing. [MSA 7.672]

MCLA 211.453 Unrecorded deed, cancellation; release of recorded deed, recording. [MSA 7.673]

MCLA 211.454 Cancellation deed to state; certificate of error, recording; tax liens and state bids restored. [MSA 7.674]

MCLA 211.455 Refund, allocation of burden. [MSA 7.675]

Act No. 223, P.A. 1909 - State Lands, Sale for Public Uses.

AN ACT authorizing the department of natural resources to sell sites to school districts and churches and to sell lands to public educational institutions, to the United States, to governmental units and agencies thereof; and to transfer jurisdiction to departments, boards and commissions of the state from tax reverted state lands under the control of the department.

MCLA 211.461 Authority to sell; purchasers; tax-reverted state lands. [MSA 7.681]

Sec. 1. **School districts, churches, public educational institutions, United States, state governmental units, agencies; tax-reverted state lands, transfers of jurisdiction.** *The department of natural resources may sell sites to school districts and churches and to sell lands for public purposes to public educational institutions; to the United States; and to governmental units of the state and to agencies thereof from tax reverted state lands under the control of the department, at such price as shall be fixed by a formula as determined by the state tax commission. ...*

Reversions; appraised value or nominal fee; proceeds on resale. *The department may sell tax reverted lands to any agency described above, and the transfer of such lands shall not be subject ...*

1032

Act No. 44, P.A. 1883 - Delinquent taxes on Part-paid Lands

AN ACT to provide for the assessment of delinquent taxes assessed on part-paid lands in certain cases.

MCLA 211.481 Unpaid tax list, lands patented after assessment; preparation. [MSA 7.701]

Sec. 1. That it shall be the duty of the ... (department of natural resources) *..., on the first day of October of each year, to prepare lists ... showing the descriptions of lands upon which taxes have been assessed for the current year while the lands were part-paid, but which had been patented by the state, and upon which taxes have not been paid, and forward the same to the supervisor of the township where the lands lie.*

MCLA 211.482 Supervisors to re-assess. [MSA 7.702]

Sec. 2. It shall be the duty of the supervisor of the township receiving such list to re-assess the taxes therein reported upon the same land.

MCLA 211.483 Collection and return. [MSA 7.703]

Sec. 3. It shall be the duty of the township treasurer to collect and return the same in the same manner as provided for the collection and return of other taxes.

Act No. 91, P.A. 1925 - State Game Lands, Payments in Lieu of Taxes

AN ACT to provide for a payment in lieu of taxes to local units of government on certain lands owned by the state of Michigan and controlled by the department of conservation (natural resources) *and to provide for the collection thereof.*

MCLA 211.491 Conservation department lands north and south of township 16 north and Huron county; list furnished state tax commission; annual report of revenues received. [MSA 7.711]

MCLA 211.492 Same; tax evaluation, time; report to assessing districts; spread of tax. [MSA 7.712]

Sec. 2. *The valuation of such lands for the purposes of this act shall be fixed by the state tax commission on or before February 1 of each year and the state tax commission shall on or before February 15 of each year make a report to the several assessing districts of the state in which such lands are located, giving a description of the land in such assessing district so held by the state with the valuation thereof as fixed by the state tax commission. The state tax commission shall furnish a value to the assessing officers which shall ...*

MCLA 211.493 Same; tax statement of assessing district, payment. MSA 7.713

Sec. 3. *The treasurer or other officer charged with the collection of taxes for such assessing district shall forward a statement of such assessment to the Lansing office or the department of conservation, which shall review said ...*

Act No. 223, P.A. 1889 - Waste Injunctions

AN ACT to authorize the issuance of injunctions to restrain waste upon certain lands when the taxes upon the same shall be due and unpaid.

MCLA 211.511 Waste injunction; township treasurer, duties; order of authorized tribunal. MSA 7.741

Sec. 1. *That when any person, co-partnership, company or corporation shall neglect or refuse to pay any tax assessed on the lands of such person, co-partnership, company, or corporation after such tax shall have become a lien upon said lands and before the expiration of the warrant attached to his tax roll, the township treasurer shall make application for and be entitled to an injunction to restrain waste on any of such lands upon which the taxes shall remain unpaid, and to prevent the cutting of any timber standing or growing thereon, or the removal of any timber, wood or logs, or the tearing down or removing of any buildings therefrom. Any circuit judge or ... (district judge) ... of the county in which such lands are situated may on application of such township treasurer make an order restraining any person, co-partnership, company or corporation from committing waste on any such lands by the cutting of any timber standing or growing thereon or the removal of any timber, wood or logs, or the tearing down or removal or any buildings therefrom.*

1034

Act No. 263, P.A. 1897 - Taxes on State Tax Lands

AN ACT to authorize the auditor general to accept payment of taxes and charges from the owner of any description of land held by the state as state tax lands.

MCLA 211.541 Land held as state tax land with other land; tax application; proportionate payment; deed. ⎾MSA 7.78⏋

Act No. 208, P.A. 1913 - Cut-Over and Wild Lands

AN ACT to exempt certain cut-over and wild lands from taxation in certain cases.

MCLA 211.561 Cut-over lands defined; homestead limit; 5-year tax exemption period. ⎾MSA 7.80⏋

MCLA 211.562 Exemption application; treatment on tax roll. ⎾MSA 7.80⏋

Act No. 116, P.A. 1917 - State Tax Homestead and Swamp Lands

AN ACT to provide a tax on state tax homestead and state swamp lands under control and supervision of the department of conservation, and any and all other lands held by the department of conservation except state game farms and certain state park acreage, for county, township and school purposes; to provide for the payment of such tax; and to repeal section 55 of Act No. 59 of the Public Acts of 1915.

MCLA 211.581 Tax on state tax homestead, swamp and department of conservation lands; exceptions, payment, apportionment. ⎾MSA 7.87⏋

Sec. 1. On December 1 of each year, there shall be paid into the treasury of each county in this state in which may be located any state tax homestead or state swamp lands under the control and supervision of the department of conservation, and any and all other lands held by the department of conservation, except that any state game farm, and any state park for which a caretaker is provided, shall be exempt from the provisions of this act up to 1,000 acres, a tax of 20cents per acre, ...

Note: At time of publication this statute was in the process of revision to increase the 20 cents per acre tax.

MCLA 211.582 Same; duty of department of conservation, records, source of payment. MSA 7.872

Act No. 168, P.A. 1966 - Reimbursement for Taxes

AN ACT to provide for reimbursement to local units of government for taxes lost due to the establishment of Sleeping Bear dunes national lakeshore.

MCLA 211.751 Payments to counties within which land acquired by United States for Sleeping Bear dunes national lakeshore; amount, distribution. MSA 7.1041(1)

Sec. 1. The department of treasury shall pay to the treasurer of each county within which land is acquired by the United States after January 1, 1966 for use as Sleeping Bear dunes national lakeshore a sum equal to 1% of the price at which the property was purchased by the United States. The payments shall be made from revenues derived from the sale of state lands to the United States which lie within the boundaries of the Sleeping Bear dunes national lakeshore which sale shall be made in lieu of a gift of the state land to the federal government. Payments shall be made at the close of each fiscal year of the state beginning with the close of the fiscal year following the tax year during which the property was acquired by the United States. The county treasurer shall distribute the payments to the units of government within the county in which the lands are located in the same proportion as are general property taxes in each unit for the fiscal year in which the payment is made.

MCLA 211.752 Review of impact of acquisitions upon tax revenues; report to legislature. MSA 7.1041(2)

Sec. 2. After the close of the fifth fiscal year in which payments are made in accordance with section 1 and before the end of the seventh year of such payments the conservation commission and the state tax commission in consultation with the governing officials in the counties to which payments have been made shall review the impact upon the tax revenue of the counties, townships and school districts as a result of the acquisition of lands for Sleeping Bear dunes national lakeshore and also the tax needs. After the review

1036

the conservation commission shall report to the legislature and make appropriate recommendations before the end of the eighth fiscal year.

MCLA 211.753 Annual payments; limitation on number.
[MSA 7.1041(3)]

Sec. 3. *No more than 8 annual payments shall be made under this act.*

MCLA 211.754 Local units not eligible for payments; conditions.
[MSA 7.1041(4)]

Sec. 4. *Payments under this act shall not be made to any local unit of government eligible to receive payments from the federal government in lieu of taxes for property taken for Sleeping Bear dunes national lakeshore after January 1, 1966.*

STATE REVENUE SHARING FROM SPECIFIC TAXES

In addition to funds from the local property tax and special assessments, fees and regulatory licenses and permits, a considerable portion of state revenues from several specific taxes are shared with local units of government. Although townships do not receive a portion of all of these taxes, the citations are included nevertheless since unpaid taxes in these categories are a lien upon real and personal property. The state sales tax is the only one frozen into the state constitution, which sets the amount at four cents, and provides at section ten of article nine:

> *One-eighth of all taxes imposed on retailers on taxable sales at retail of tangible personal property shall be used exclusively for assistance to townships, cities and villages, on a population basis as provided by law. In determining population the legislature may exclude any portion of the total number of persons who are wards, patients or convicts in any tax supported institution.*

This amounts to one-half cent for townships, cities and villages which is distributed, through the counties, on a population basis. A portion of the intangibles tax and the state income tax are also shared with all local units of government.

The gasoline and weight tax collected by the state is shared, along with the State Highway Department, with all local units of government **except townships.** The watercraft tonnage tax has little or no effect on local financing, although local governments are exempt from taxation under this act.

Act No. 167, P.A. 1933 - General Sales Tax Act

AN ACT to provide for the raising of additional public revenue by prescribing certain specific taxes, fees, and charges to be paid to the state for the privilege of engaging in certain business activities; to provide, incident to the enforcement thereof, for the issuance of licenses to engage in such occupations; to provide for the ascertainment, assessment and collection thereof; to appropriate the proceeds thereof; and to prescribe penalties for violations of the provisions of this act.

MCLA 205.51 Definitions. [MSA 7.521]

MCLA 205.52 - 205.54 [MSA 7.522 - 7.524]

MCLA 205.54a Deductible sales. Sales to schools, hospitals, certain nonprofit institutions; transferee's statement. Sales to churches. Foods at schools not operated for profit. Affixed to and structural part of real estate. Commercial vessels of 500 tons or more, supplies, repairs. Agricultural producing. Industrial processing. Second class mail publications. Radio or television station licensees, component part of film, tape, or recording. Specially registered vehicles. Artificial limbs and eyes. Persons rendering certain communication services. Ambulances and fire department vehicles. Prisoners, purchases by script redeemed by institution. [MSA 7.525]

MCLA 205.54b - 205.62 [MSA 7.525(1) - 7.533]

MCLA 205.63 Tax lien; priority; sale of business, liability of purchaser. [MSA 7.534]

MCLA 205.64 - 205.66 [MSA 7.535 - 7.537]

MCLA 205.66a Duty of assessing, etc., officers. [MSA 7.537(1)]

1038

Sec. 16a. It shall be the duty of each assessing officer of each ... township in preparing the annual property tax roll of personal property to show on the assessment roll ... Any ... township clerk, marketmaster, or any other ... municipal official whose duty it is to issue licenses or permits ... shall ... Any ... township ... officer who shall receive information which ...

MCLA 205.67 - 205.74 [MSA 7.538 - 7.545]

MCLA 205.75 Sales tax revenues; collection costs; distribution, appropriation. [MSA 7.546]

Sec. 25. ... The state disbursing authority shall remit quarterly to county treasurers on a county population basis 1/8 of the balance of the collections. The county treasurer shall remit to the townships, cities and villages in the county on a per capita basis. Population computation shall be based on the last and each succeeding statewide federal census for purposes of division among counties, and upon the same basis or upon any special federal county-wide census, whichever is later, for purposes of division among local units. Fifty percent of the total number of persons who are wards, patients or convicts committed to or domiciled in a city institution located outside the boundaries of the city or committed to or domiciled in a county, state or federal tax supported institution, if such persons were included in the federal census, shall be excluded from the computation. One half of the balance of the collections shall be transferred to the school aid fund created by section 11 of article 9 of the state constitution and distributed as provided by law. The balance in the general fund shall be disbursed only on an appropriation or appropriations by the legislature.

MCLA 205.78 Short title. [MSA 7.549]

Act No. 94, P.A. 1937 - Use Tax Act

AN ACT to provide for the levy, assessment and collection of a specific excise tax on the storage, use or consumption in this state of tangible personal property and certain services; to appropriate the proceeds thereof; and to prescribe penalties for violations of the provisions of this act.

MCLA 205.91 Use tax act. [MSA 7.555(1)]

MCLA 205.92 Definitions. [MSA 7.555(2)]

MCLA 205.93 - 205.93a ⎡MSA 7.555(3) - 7.555(3A)⎤

MCLA 205.94 Exemptions. Sales tax paid. Constitutional provisions. Property for resale, demonstrators, driver education automobiles. Temporary storage, use, or consumption. Reciprocity; tax in other states. Agricultural producing. Industrial processing. Deleted. Sales to United States, Red Cross, state of Michigan and political subdivisions. Sales to schools, hospitals, certain nonprofit institutions. Sales to churches. Commercial vessels of 500 tons or more, supplies, repairs. Property used in certain improvements to real estate. Maximum out-of-state purchases per month. Second class mail publications; films; industrial processing of newspapers. Property sold to commercial radio or television stations for direct use. Purchase of automobile out of state by resident in military service. Specially registered vehicles. Artificial limbs or eyes. Water. Machinery and equipment for certain communication services. Ambulances and fire department vehicles. ⎡MSA 7.555(4)⎤

MCLA 205.94a. - 205.101 ⎡MSA 7.555(4A) - 7.555(11)⎤

MCLA 205.101a. Lien, extent, priority. ⎡MSA 7.555(11A)⎤

MCLA 205.102 - 205.111 ⎡MSA 7.555(12) - 7.555(21)⎤

Act No. 301, P.A. 1939 - Intangibles Tax Act

AN ACT to provide for the imposition and the collection of a specific tax upon the privilege of ownership of intangible personal property; to provide for the disposition of the proceeds thereof; to prescribe the powers and duties of the department of revenue with respect thereto; to prescribe penalties; to make an appropriation to carry out the provisions of this act; and to repeal all acts or parts of acts inconsistent with the provisions of this act.

MCLA 205.131 Definitions. ⎡MSA 7.556(1)⎤

MCLA 205.132 Imposition of tax. Intangible personalty of residents and nonresidents; ownership privilege tax; income producing personalty, rate; corporate stock, value; nonincome producing personalty, rate; moneys, rate. Face value, computation where value changes; ownership for part of tax year; retroactive date, method of determining value; true average method; election of method. Death

1040

or change of domicile, computation of tax. **Exemption from general property tax.** ⌈MSA 7.556(2)⌉

MCLA 205.133 Deductions and exemptions. ⌈MSA 7.556(3)⌉

MCLA 205.133a - 205.135 ⌈MSA 7.556(3A) - 7.556(5)⌉

MCLA 205.136 Remittances; lien against owner. ⌈MSA 7.556(6)⌉

Sec. 6. ... **Bank deposits; stock of bank or trust company; distribution ... Distribution to county treasurers; to cities, townships and villages; uses.** *During the month of July of each year the auditor general shall distribute to the several county treasurers as hereinbefore specified the net revenues received under this act during the previous fiscal year, less 3% of said revenues, which amount shall be credited to the general fund of the state as repayment of the cost of the collection of this tax. The distribution to the county treasurers shall be upon a per capita basis according to the latest or each succeeding federal decennial census. The county treasurer shall distribute the amount received by him among the cities, townships and villages within his county on a per capita basis according to the latest or each succeeding federal decennial census or according to any special federal county-wide census, whichever is later: Provided, That the distribution to townships shall be based on such population outside the corporate limits of incorporated villages in the township. The moneys so returned ... shall be credited to the general fund and shall be available for general fund purposes.*

MCLA 205.137 - 205.147 ⌈MSA 7.556(7) - 7.556(17)⌉

Act No. 48, P.A. 1929 - Severance Tax on Oil or Gas

AN ACT levying a specific tax to be known as the severance tax upon all producers engaged in the business of severing oil and gas from the soil; prescribing the method of collecting the tax; requiring all producers of such products or purchasers thereof to make reports; to provide penalties; to provide exemptions and refunds; to prescribe the disposition of the funds so collected; and to exempt those paying such specific tax from certain other taxes.

MCLA 205.301 - 205.314 [MSA 7.351 - 7.364]

MCLA 205.315 In lieu of other taxes; exceptions. [MSA 7.365]

Sec. 15. The severance tax herein provided for shall be in lieu of all other taxes, state or local, upon the oil or gas, the property rights attached thereto or inherent therein, or the values created thereby; upon all leases or the rights to develop and operate any lands of this state for oil or gas, the values created thereby and the property rights attached to or inherent therein: Provided, however, Nothing herein contained shall in anywise exempt the machinery, appliances, pipe lines, tanks and other equipment used in the development or operation of said leases, or used to transmit or transport the said oil or gas: And provided further, That nothing herein contained shall in anywise relieve any corporation or association from the payment of any franchise or privilege taxes required by the provisions of the state corporation laws.

MCLA 205.316 - 205.317 [MSA 7.366 - 7.367]

Act No. 265, P.A. 1947 - Cigarette Tax

AN ACT to impose an excise and specific tax upon the sale and distribution of cigarettes; to regulate and license manufacturers, wholesalers, vending machine operators, unclassified acquirers, transportation companies, transporters and retailers thereof, as herein defined; to prescribe the powers and duties of the Michigan department of treasury, revenue division with respect thereto; to provide for the collection of such tax and the disposition thereof; to provide for the enforcement of this act; to provide for the appointment of special investigators as peace officers for the enforcement of this act; to make an appropriation; and to prescribe penalties for the violation of this act.

MCLA 205.501 Cigarette tax; definitions. [MSA 7.411(1)]

MCLA 205.502 - 205.513 [MSA 7.411(2) - 7.411(13)]

MCLA 205.514 Tax lien; precedence. [MSA 7.411(14)]

MCLA 205.515 Sales to unlicensed persons, enforcement of act. [MSA 7.411(15)]

Sec. 15. ... *The state police and all local police authorities shall have the authority to enforce, and shall, at the request of the department or duly authorized agent, enforce the provisions of this act.*

MCLA 205.517 - 205.522 [MSA 7.411(17) - 7.411(22)]

Act No. 281, P.A. 1967 - Income Tax Act of 1967

AN ACT to meet deficiencies in the state funds by providing for the imposition, levy, computation, collection, assessment, and enforcement by lien and otherwise of taxes on or measured by net income; to prescribe the manner and time of making reports and paying the taxes, and the functions of public officers and others as to the taxes; to permit the inspection of the records of taxpayers; to provide for interest and penalties on unpaid taxes; to provide exemptions, credits and refunds of the taxes; to prescribe penalties for the violation of this act; to provide an appropriation; and to repeal certain acts and parts of acts.

CHAPTER 1. GENERAL PROVISIONS AND DEFINITIONS

MCLA 206.1 - 206.6 [MSA 7.557(101) - 7.557(106)]

MCLA 206.8 Department, domestic insurer, employee, employer. [MSA 7.557(108)]

MCLA 206.10 - 206.20 [MSA 7.557(110) - 7.557(120)]

MCLA 206.22 Tax. [MSA 7.557(122)]

Sec. 22. *"Tax" includes interest and penalties and further includes the tax required to be withheld by an employer on salaries and wages, unless the intention to give it a more limited meaning is disclosed by the context.*

MCLA 206.24 - 206.36 [MSA 7.557(124) - 7.557(136)]

CHAPTER 2. IMPOSITION OF TAX

MCLA 206.51 - 206.91 [MSA 7.557(151) - 7.557(191)]

CHAPTER 3. ALLOCATION OF TAXABLE INCOME TO MICHIGAN OR OTHER STATES

MCLA 206.102 - 206.195 [MSA 7.557(1102) - 7.557(1195)]

CHAPTER 4. EXEMPTIONS

MCLA 206.201 - 206.221 [MSA 7.557(1201) - 7.557(1221)]

CHAPTER 5. CREDITS AGAINST TAX

MCLA 206.251- 206.271 [MSA 7.557(1251) - 7.557(1271)]

CHAPTER 6. RETURNS AND TAX PAYMENTS

MCLA 206.301 - 206.341 [MSA 7.557(1301) - 7.557(1341)]

CHAPTER 7. WITHHOLDING TAX ON SALARIES AND WAGES

MCLA 206.351 Requirement and amount of withholding; tables; time of payment; liability of employer. [MSA 7.557(1351)]

Sec. 351. ... The commissioner may prescribe withholding tables which may be used by employers in computing the amount of tax required to be withheld.

(2) The taxes withheld under this section shall be returned and paid to the department by the employer within 15 days after the end of any month in which the amount withheld exceeds $100.00. In the case of lesser amounts payment shall be made within 15 days after the end of the quarter period ending in March, June, September and December. ...

MCLA 206.355 Administration, collection, and enforcement of withholding. [MSA 7.557(1355)]

MCLA 206.361 United States, state or political subdivision as employer; offices making return. [MSA 7.557(1361)]

MCLA 206.365 Annual statement of compensation paid and taxes withheld, employees' duplicates; returns by employers; information furnished by employee. [MSA 7.557(1365)]

Sec. 365. (1) Every employer required by this act to deduct and withhold taxes on compensation, shall furnish to each employee on or before January 31 of the succeeding year ...

CHAPTER 8. ADMINISTRATION, COLLECTION, AND ENFORCEMENT

MCLA 206.401 - 206.423 [MSA 7.557(1401) - 7.557(1423)]

MCLA 206.431 Tax lien; property subject; term; priority; notice of lien, recording, fee, form; certificate of discharge of lien, issuance, form, recording, fee. [MSA 7.557(1431)]

MCLA 206.441 - 206.475 [MSA 7.557(1441) - 7.557(1475)]

MCLA 206.481 Disbursement of tax proceeds to counties and municipalities, mode of allocation. [MSA 7.557(1481)]

Sec. 481. (1) ... the state ... shall remit quarterly to county treasurers on a county population basis, a portion of an amount measured by ...

(2) The county treasurer shall allocate 1/2 of the amount received to the credit of the general fund.

(3) The remaining 1/2 shall within 20 days be distributed to the cities, villages, **townships and charter townships in the county** on a per capita basis.

(4) Population computation shall be based on the last and each succeeding statewide federal census, or any special census as provided by law, for purpose of division among counties, and upon the same basis or upon any special federal countywide census, or any special census as provided by law, whichever is later, for purposes of division among local units. Fifty percent of the total number of persons who are wards, patients or convicts committed to or domiciled in a city institution located outside the boundaries of the city or committed to or domiciled in a county, state or federal tax supported institution, if these persons were included in the federal census, or any special census as provided by law, shall be excluded from the computation. The distribution to townships shall

be based on such population outside the corporate limits of incorporated villages in that township.

(5) Any overpayments, underpayments or errors may be adjusted on the subsequent payment date.

(6) The balance in the general fund shall be disbursed only on appropriation of the legislature.

MCLA 206.482 Amounts distributed to each county, lists for legislators. [MSA 7.557(1482)]

MCLA 206.491 - 206.499 [MSA 7.557(1491) - 7.557(1499)]

Act No. 70, P.A. 1911 - Water Craft Tonnage Tax

AN ACT regulating the taxation of certain vessels, boats and other watercraft; to prescribe the powers and duties of the secretary of state and department of conservation with respect thereto; to provide for the disposition of the revenue received therefrom; and to prescribe penalties for violation of the provisions of this act.

MCLA 207.51 Specific tonnage tax on passenger and freight vessels; general tax exemption. [MSA 7.281]

MCLA 207.51a Specific tax on small watercraft; rates; exceptions; license; exemption from general property tax. [MSA 7.281(1)]

Sec. 1a. Every (other) vessel, boat or other water craft ... except those owned or operated by the United States or the State, or by local agencies of government of this state or by ... shall be subject to a specific tax, payable annually, ... levied only on boats operating on the Great Lakes and waters connecting thereto navigable in fact by boats subject to this act.

MCLA 207.52 Annual statement of owners, contents, filing, payment of tax; receipt and license plate, attaching. [MSA 7.282]

Sec. 2. ... Upon receipt of an application from a local agency of government of this state upon a form prescribed by him, the secretary of state may issue such plates at a fee of $1.00 per pair.

MCLA 207.52a Operation without license, or attaching license; penalties. [MSA 7.282(1)]

1046

MCLA 207.53 Revenues; state waterways fund. [MSA 7.283]

MCLA 207.54 Licenses; issuance, compensation; rules and regulations. [MSA 7.284]

Note: The secretary of state makes rules for licensing and the department of conservation for enforcement.

Act No. 150, P.A. 1927 - Motor Fuel Tax

AN ACT to prescribe a privilege tax for the use of the public highways by owners and drivers of motor vehicles by imposing a specific tax upon the sale or use within the state of Michigan, of motor fuel; to prescribe the manner and the time of paying such tax and the duties of officials and others respecting such payment and collection; to provide for the licensing of wholesale distributors and the registration of retail dealers and users as defined herein; to require identification markings upon certain vehicles transporting petroleum products; to fix a time when such tax and interest and penalties thereon become a lien upon the property of persons, firms, associations or corporations, subject to the payment of such tax and to provide for the enforcement of said lien; to permit the inspection and testing of petroleum products; to provide for certain exemptions and refunds and for the disposition of the proceeds of such tax; and to prescribe penalties for the violation of this act.

CHAPTER 1. GASOLINE TAX

MCLA 207.101 - 207.111 [MSA 7.291 - 7.301]

MCLA 207.112 Gasoline tax refund; claim, filing, invoice, assignment; transfer of sales tax. [MSA 7.302]

Sec. 12. The purchaser of gasoline used for any purpose other than the operation of motor vehicles on the public roads, streets and highways of this state, and the state government and the federal government using gasoline in state and federally owned motor vehicles, and persons operating passenger vehicles of a capacity of 10 or more under any municipal franchise, license, permit, agreement or grant, respectively, and the political subdivisions of the state using gasoline in vehicles owned by or leased and operated by the political subdivisions of the state shall be entitled to a refund of the tax paid thereon, upon filing a verified claim with the department of revenue upon forms prescribed and to be furnished by it, within 6 months from the date of purchase, as shown by the invoice. Any claim mailed within the 6 months' period, as evidenced by the postmark, shall, when received by the department of revenue, be considered as filed within the required time. Only 4¢ per gallon shall be refunded to persons operating passenger vehicles of a capacity of 10 or more under any municipal franchise, license, permit, agreement or grant, respectively, and operated over regularly traveled routes expressly provided for in such municipal licenses, permits, agreements or grants. The retail dealer shall furnish any such purchaser with an invoice, showing the amount of gasoline purchased, the date thereof, and the amount of tax paid thereon, and every such dealer shall at the request of the department of revenue forthwith supply the department with a copy of any invoice issued by said dealer during any 6 months' period preceding such request. All claims for refund shall have attached thereto the original invoice received by the purchaser and, when approved by the department of revenue, shall be paid out of the motor vehicle highway fund upon the warrant of the state treasurer. No claims for refund shall be assignable without the prior written consent of the department of revenue. In any case where the verified claim of the purchaser, in form and content as prescribed by the department, shall show or it shall otherwise appear that the amount of gasoline used by the purchaser for purposes on which the taxes under Act No. 167 of the Public Acts of 1933, as amended, being sections 205.51 to 205.78 [MSA 7.521 TO MSA 7.549] of the Compiled Laws of 1948, are deductible pursuant to subsection (f) of section 4a of said act is not the total amount included in the statement of the transferee under said subsection (f), the department of revenue shall deduct from the amount of the refund authorized by this section the rate of sales tax as is established in Act No. 167 of the Public Acts of 1933, as amended, applicable to the retail sales price paid by the transferee on that portion of the gasoline not used for purposes described in subsection (f) of section 4a of Act No. 167 of the Public Acts of 1933, as amended, and shall transfer the sales tax so deducted to the sales tax account of the department of revenue.

MCLA 207.112a Gasoline tax; refund to nonprofit private, parochial or denominational schools. [MSA 7.302(1)]

MCLA 207.112b **Same; claims, false statements in, forfeiture, penalty.** [MSA 7.302(2)]

MCLA 207.113 **In lieu of other taxes.** [MSA 7.303]

Sec. 13. The tax herein provided shall be in lieu of all other taxes imposed or to be imposed upon the sale or use of gasoline by the state or any political subdivision thereof.

MCLA 207.114 **Tax lien.** [MSA 7.304]

MCLA 207.115 - 207.120 [MSA 7.305 - 7.313]

CHAPTER 2. DIESEL MOTOR FUEL TAX

MCLA 207.121 **Definitions.** [MSA 7.316(1)]

MCLA 207.122 **Diesel motor fuel tax; collection, refund, publicly-owned, leased or operated vehicles.** [MSA 7.316(2)]

MCLA 207.123 - 207.123a [MSA 7.316(3) - 7.316(3A)]

MCLA 207.124 **License; issuance, license number, display.** [MSA 7.316(4)]

Sec. 24. ... Every law enforcement officer of this state shall be empowered to halt any motor vehicle which such officer or employee may have reason to believe is using diesel motor fuel as defined in this chapter, for the purpose of ascertaining whether the provisions of this chapter have been complied with.

MCLA 207.125 - 207.128 [MSA 7.316(5) - 7.316(8)]

MCLA 207.129 **Tax to be in lieu of all other taxes.** [MSA 7.316(9)]

MCLA 207.130 **Tax to be lien, priority; secretary of state** (now department of revenue) **may estimate amount of tax payable.** [MSA 7.316(10)]

MCLA 207.131 - 207.134 [MSA 7.316(11) - 7.316(14)]

CHAPTER 3. LIQUEFIED PETROLEUM GAS TAX

MCLA 207.151 Liquefied petroleum gas tax; provisions applicable, definitions. [MSA 7.317(1)]

MCLA 207.152 - 207.159 [MSA 7.317(2) - 7.317(9)]

MCLA 207.160 Tax, lien, precedence, estimate, collection. [MSA 7.317(10)]

MCLA 207.161 - 207.164 [MSA 7.317(11) - 7.317(14)]

CHAPTER 4. RESIDENT OR NONRESIDENT MOTOR VEHICLES AND RECIPROCITY

MCLA 207.181 - 207.186 [MSA 7.318(1) - 7.318(6)]

CHAPTER 5. MACKINAC BRIDGE AUTHORITY BONDS

MCLA 207.191 - 207.194 [MSA 7.319(1) - 7.319(4)]

Act No. 77, P.A. 1951 - Low Grade Iron Ore Tax

AN ACT providing for the specific taxation of low grade iron ore, of low grade iron ore mining property, and of rights to minerals in lands containing low grade iron ores; to provide for the collection and distribution of the specific tax; and to prescribe the powers and duties of the state geologist and township supervisors and treasurers with respect thereto.

MCLA 211.621 Low grade iron ore; definitions (and mining property). [MSA 13.157(1)]

MCLA 211.622 Taxation; preproduction assessment formula. [MSA 13.157(2)]

MCLA 211.623 Same; assessment formula after commencement of production. [MSA 13.157(3)]

MCLA 211.624 Low grade iron ore mining property; minimum specific tax. Minimum tax. Removal of property from general property tax assessment; delinquent taxes; distribution of revenues.

Specific tax in lieu of ad valorem tax on ore, mining property, concentrate and other products. [MSA 13.157(4)]

MCLA 211.625 Purpose of act. [MSA 13.157(5)]

FEDERAL REVENUE SHARING

The most recent method of providing federal funds to local governments is known as "federal revenue sharing." There are restrictions governing uses which may be made of these funds that are important for township officials to understand. They fall into eight major categories: (1) public safety, such as police and fire protection and building inspection, (2) environmental protection, including sewage disposals, solid waste collection and disposal and pollution abatement, (3) public transportation, including transit systems, highways, roads and streets, (4) health programs, (5) recreation programs, (6) social services for the poor and aged, (7) financial administration and (8) libraries.

These monies may be used to supplement state funds but not other federal funds. Certification by local government officials that the money was used only for high priority expenditures and that they were not used for matching any other federal monies will be accepted as proof by the federal government unless the Secretary of the Treasury has reason to believe it is not sufficiently reliable.

There are other qualifications regarding how these funds may be used, including but not limited to the following: (1) They may not be used to reduce the property tax. (2) There may not be any discrimination because of race, color, sex or national origin whenever the funds are used. (3) Two reports to the federal government are required: (a) plans for utilization of the funds, to be submitted after January 1, 1973, and (b) a statement on how the monies have been spent or obligated, due at the end of each fiscal year. **Both reports must be published in a newspaper of general circulation in the local area.**

Because this program has a life span of five years, local government officials are advised to exercise great caution in spending and obligating the funds for anything other than a one-time capital improvement or development project or program which can be terminated, if federal funds are no longer available after 1975, without severely hurting township citizens.

We cannot stress too strongly how important it is for the township clerk to be prompt in filling out and returning the form which must be submitted to the office in Washington. No funds will be forthcoming if this is not done. Inquiries regarding the program may be addressed to Office of Revenue Sharing, U.S. Department of Treasury, 1900 Pennsylvania Av., NW, Washington, DC 20226.

FUNDING THROUGH BONDING AND BORROWING

Inasmuch as ready cash is not always available to local units of government, it becomes necessary to issue bonds or borrow money to bring about improvements, services and utilities which a growing and dynamic state requires to meet the demands and needs of its citizens. Every municipality in the state (cities, villages, townships and counties) must take matters of bonding and borrowing to the Michigan Municipal Finance Commission. Because of the tremendous demands made upon it, the commission takes a long time to process applications. Therefore township officials must allow plenty of time when making plans.

Study of the various bonding acts, along with the Municipal Finance Act, will provide the township officer with a total picture of what bonding, borrowing, notes and certificates of indebtedness, etc., are all about. One of the great tragedies of improper procedures is that thousands of dollars may be spent in preliminary plans for engineering and legal fees, etc., yet the entire project may be held up indefinitely until the entire issue is redone properly. Or it may be negated entirely. This can happen even after a bond issue has been sold. Thus consultation with the township attorney is an absolutely essential requirement to properly facilitate applications before the commission. In fact, many townships direct their attorney also to consult with bond counsel.

JOINT ACTION

Act No. 202, P.A. 1943 - Municipal Finance Act - Definitions

AN ACT relative to the borrowing of money by municipalities, and the issuance of bonds, notes and certificates of indebtedness; to provide for tax levies and sinking funds; to create the municipal finance commission, and to prescribe its powers and duties; to create an advisory tax study committee, and to prescribe its powers and duties; to prescribe penalties; and to repeal all acts and parts of acts inconsistent with the provisions of this act.

1052

CHAPTER I. DEFINITIONS

MCLA 131.1 Short title. ⟦MSA 5.3188(1)⟧

MCLA 131.2 Definitions. ⟦MSA 5.3188(2)⟧

MCLA 131.3 Assessed valuation; definition for taxation or borrowing purposes. ⟦MSA 5.3188(2.1)⟧

Sec. 3. The terms "assessed valuation","valuation as assessed", "valuation as shown by the last preceding tax assessment roll", or similar terms, used in any statute or charter as a basis for computing limitations upon the taxing or borrowing power of any municipality, shall be deemed to mean the valuation as finally determined through the process of equalization. Any municipality, whose electors have heretofore voted to raise by tax or by loan an amount not exceeding the applicable limitation computed in terms of valuation as finally determined through the process of equalization, shall have power to raise such amount by tax or by loan, and any such election is in such respect hereby validated.

CHAPTER II. MUNICIPAL FINANCE COMMISSION

MCLA 132.1 Municipal finance commission; members; records, transferred. ⟦MSA 5.3188(3)⟧

MCLA 132.2 Same; duties and powers. ⟦MSA 5.3188(4)⟧

MCLA 123.3 Complaints by aggrieved party; hearing; review by court. ⟦MSA 5.3188(5)⟧

Sec. 3. If any municipality shall feel aggrieved at any order of the commission, it may notify the commission which shall thereupon set a date, not more than 20 days therefrom, for the hearing of such complaint, which hearing may, in the discretion of the commission, be adjourned from time to time. At such hearing all information in the files of the commission shall ...

MCLA 132.4 Tax study; advisory tax study committee.
⟦MSA 5.3188(5A)⟧

CHAPTER III. GENERAL

MCLA 133.1 Municipal borrowing and obligations payable by taxes or special assessments; purchase contracts, leases, limitation.
MSA 5.3188(6)

Sec. 1. No municipality shall hereafter borrow money and issue any obligations payable out of taxes or special assessments except ...

MCLA 133.1a Municipal borrowing and obligations payable by taxes or special assessments; rate of interest. MSA 5.3188(6A)

Sec. 1a. Notwithstanding the provisions of any other act, any obligations authorized by law to be issued by any municipality may bear any rate of interest which does not exceed 6% per annum.

MCLA 133.2 Same; net interest rate; sale, notice; approval before sale; private sale; applicable to mortgage revenue bonds; sale to federal government. MSA 5.3188(7)

MCLA 133.2a Definitions, obligation, federal government; serial bonds, installment deliveries, payment, interest coupons.
MSA 5.3188(7A)

MCLA 133.3 Same; registry; signatures. MSA 5.3188(8)

MCLA 133.4 Same; order of commission not deemed approval of legality. MSA 5.3188(9)

MCLA 133.5 Reports filed by school and local authorities with commission, contents; failure, penalty. MSA 5.3188(10)

MCLA 133.5a Annual audit report, use as annual report to municipal finance commission. MSA 5.3188(10A)

MCLA 133.6 Same; additional information when obligations sold for cash. MSA 5.3188(11)

MCLA 133.7 Order of permission; implications. MSA 5.3188(12)

MCLA 133.8 New bonds in case of mutilation; coupon bonds.
[MSA 5.3188(12A)]

CHAPTER IV. TAX ANTICIPATION NOTES

MCLA 134.1 Tax anticipation notes. [MSA 5.3188(13)]

Sec. 1. Any municipality may, by resolution of its governing body, and without a vote of the electors, but subject to the prior permission of the commission, borrow money and issue its notes in anticipation of the collection of the taxes for its then next succeeding fiscal year, or the taxes for a current fiscal year, in accordance with the provisions of this chapter.

MCLA 134.2 Same; purpose for which may be used; limitation; newly incorporated city or village, limitation, certification by supervisor; amount set aside, purpose; deficiency in funds; capital improvements; limitation. [MSA 5.3188(14)]

Sec. 2. Where the borrowing is made in anticipation of the collection of the taxes for a next succeeding fiscal year the resolution authorizing such a loan shall contain an irrevocable provision for the levying of a tax in such year for the purpose for which such loan is to be made and the repayment of such loan from the receipts of such taxes. The proceeds of such borrowing shall be used only for the payment of operating expenses and/or capital improvements as hereinafter provided. ...

MCLA 134.3 Same; used solely for purposes expressed; limitation; capital improvement; fund set aside, purpose. [MSA 5.3188(15)]

MCLA 134.4 Same; deposit of moneys in special fund.
[MSA 5.3188(16)]

Sec. 4. The moneys in each special fund required by this chapter shall be deposited in a bank account separate from any other moneys of the municipality and shall be used for no purpose other than to retire the loans for the payment of which such special fund was established.

MCLA 134.5 Same; interest rate. [MSA 5.3188(17)]

Sec. 5. All notes issued under the provisions of this chapter shall bear interest at a rate not to exceed 6 per centum per annum and shall ...

MCLA 134.7 Decision of commission final. [MSA 5.3188(19)]

Sec. 7. The decision of the commission shall be final as to whether any loan subject to the provisions of this chapter may be made and if so to what extent.

MCLA 134.8 Declared general obligations; validations continued in force. [MSA 5.3188(20)]

Sec. 8. Notes heretofore issued under Act No. 26, Public Acts of 1931, or any amendment thereto, and any notes hereafter issued under this act, are hereby declared to be a general obligation of the municipality. ...

MCLA 134.9 Delinquent taxes, use; delinquent tax anticipation notes, issuance, proceeds, full faith and credit obligations, payment; delinquent tax revolving funds, creation, source of funds. [MSA 5.3188(20.9)]

MCLA 134.10 Aggregate principal amounts, interest rates, denominations, date of maturity, prepayment, and sale of delinquent tax anticipation notes; form of notice of public sale, approval. [MSA 5.3188(20.10)]

Sec. 10. The notes issued pursuant to section 9 shall be in such aggregate principal amount, not exceeding the aggregate amount of the delinquent taxes pledged exclusive of interest, fees and penalties; shall bear such interest not exceeding 6% per annum; shall be in such denominations, not less than $1,000.00 each; and shall mature on such date, not exceeding 6 years from their date, ...

MCLA 134.11 Delinquent tax anticipation notes as general obligations. [MSA 5.3188(20.11)]

Sec. 11. Any notes issued under this chapter shall be a general obligation of the municipality notwithstanding a subsequent judicial determination of the invalidity of the taxes pledged thereto by reason of the unconstitutionality or other invalidity of the statute or system of taxation under which such taxes have been or are to be levied. If the taxes pledged are not sufficient to pay the principal and interest of any such notes when due, such notes shall be payable from any funds not otherwise needed for current operations or from general ad valorem taxes imposed without limitation as to rate or amount, but only at rates and in amounts sufficient to make such payments. This section shall only apply to notes issued prior to December 31, 1973.

CHAPTER V. BONDS

MCLA 135.1 Bonds excepted from provisions of chapter, exception.
[MSA 5.3188(21)]

MCLA 135.2 Permission of commission precedent to issue.
[MSA 5.3188(22)]

MCLA 135.3 Maturities. [MSA 5.3188(23)]

Sec. 3. No such bonds shall be issued for a longer time than the estimated period of usefulness of the property or improvement for which issued, as determined by the governing body of the municipality and approved by the commission. ...

MCLA 135.4 Serial bonds with annual maturities; treatment as single issue; premium. [MSA 5.3188(24)]

MCLA 135.5 Special assessment bonds; limitation of amount, equalized assessed valuation. [MSA 5.3188(25)]

Sec. 5. The total amount of special assessment bonds of any township, city or village pledging the full faith and credit of the municipality shall at no time by reason of future issues, other than issues of refunding bonds, exceed 12% of the assessed valuation of the taxable property in the municipality; nor shall such bonds be issued in any calendar year in excess of 3% of such assessed valuation unless authorized by majority vote of the electors, ...

MCLA 135.6 Accrued interest; payment. [MSA 5.3188(26)]

Sec. 6. Interest to accrue on any bond issue before the time of the first collection of the taxes or assessments from which such interest is payable, may be paid from the proceeds of the sale of such bonds.

MCLA 135.7 Municipal finance commission; bonds payable from taxes; information furnished. [MSA 5.3188(27)]

Sec. 7. Before any municipality shall issue any bonds payable from taxes or assessments it shall make sworn application to the commission for permission so to do, on blanks to be provided by the commission and designed to give to the commission such information as it shall ... **Order granting permission, condition, refusal. ...**

MCLA 135.8 Full faith and credit bonds for funding drain special assessments; permission of municipal finance commission, terms. [MSA 5.3188(27.1)]

Any county, township, city or village may by resolution of its governing body and without a vote of its electors, but subject to the prior permission of the commission, issue its full faith and credit bonds for the purpose of funding any part or all of a county or inter-county drain special assessment made against such county, township, city or village at large under the provisions ...

MCLA 135.9 School district debt service funds to belong to debt retirement fund. [MSA 5.3188(27.2)]

MCLA 135.10 Permission to issue school district bonds, prerequisite. [MSA 5.3188(27.3)]

CHAPTER VI. REFUNDING BONDS AND CERTIFICATES OF INDEBTEDNESS

MCLA 136.1 Refunding bonds and certificates of indebtedness; refunding, permission by commission; classes of bonds. [MSA 5.3188(28)]

MCLA 136.2 Powers and duties of commission. [MSA 5.3188(29)]

MCLA 136.3 Indebtedness assumed in part by school district of first class; joint application for refund. [MSA 5.3188(30)]

MCLA 136.3a Public utility refunding bonds, issuance by municipalities authorized. [MSA 5.3188(30A)]

MCLA 136.4 Statutory or charter limitations, inapplicability. [MSA 5.3188(31)]

MCLA 136.5 Drainage bonds continuation of former obligations. [MSA 5.3188(32)]

MCLA 136.6 Maturities; maximum rates of interest; form. [MSA 5.3188(33)]

Sec. 6. Refunding bonds issued hereunder shall mature in not to exceed 30 years from date of issuance, and certificates of indebtedness issued hereunder shall mature in not to exceed 10 years from date of issuance. Subject to ...

MCLA 136.7 Tax reduction. [MSA 5.3188(34)]

MCLA 136.8 Moneys; purposes for which used. [MSA 5.3188(35)]

Sec. 8. Where taxes and/or special assessments have been levied for or pledged to the payment of obligations, all moneys on hand or thereafter received by reason of such taxes and/or special assessments shall, except as otherwise provided in section 16 of this chapter, be used ...

MCLA 136.9 Cancellations; proof furnished to commission. [MSA 5.3188(36)]

MCLA 136.10 Sale or exchange of bonds. [MSA 5.3188(37)]

MCLA 136.11 Delivery to purchaser; redemption or retirement. [MSA 5.3188(38)]

Sec. 11. All refunding bonds issued under this act which are sold for cash, shall not be sold more than 6 months in advance of the first date upon which the refunded bonds may be redeemed or otherwise retired and may, ...

MCLA 136.12 Maturity; interest rate; extension of maturity dates; callability; debt service tax. [MSA 5.3188(39)]

MCLA 136.13 Mortgage bonds; refunding; amending mortgage indentures. [MSA 5.3188(40)]

MCLA 136.14 Additional limitations. [MSA 5.3188(41)]

Sec. 14. The commission shall have power to impose such additional limitations or regulations in connection with the issuance of any refunding obligations authorized herein as shall be reasonable.

MCLA 136.15 Declared legal and valid obligations. [MSA 5.3188(42)]

MCLA 136.16 Debt service money, expenditure. [MSA 5.3188(43)]

MCLA 136.17 Extension of time of payment of special assessments; new roll; division into installments; interest rate. [MSA 5.3188(44)]

Sec. 17. When it is proposed to refund any bonds issued in anticipation of the collection of special assessments, the time of payment of the unpaid portion of such special assessments may, subject to the approval of the commission, be extended. Such extension shall ...

CHAPTER VII. TAX LEVIES, DEBT RETIREMENT AND SINKING FUNDS

MCLA 137.1 Tax levies; debt retirement and sinking funds; definitions. [MSA 5.3188(45)]

MCLA 137.1a Same; what included in; surplus moneys; moneys remaining in debt retirement fund, period held, transfer; portion of tax set aside, division. [MSA 5.3188(45A)]

MCLA 137.1b Separation and use of debt retirement fund. [MSA 5.3188(45B)]

Sec. 1b. All debt retirement funds shall be kept separate from each other and separate from all other moneys of the municipality and shall be used only to retire the funded indebtedness of the municipality for which such debt retirement fund was created.

MCLA 137.1c Retirement of debt; discontinuance of voted tax. [MSA 5.3188(45C)]

Sec. 1c. Whenever any municipality shall have completed the retirement of any outstanding bonds, refunding bonds, notes or certificates of indebtedness or shall have sufficient funds in the debt retirement fund to retire said obligation payable from taxes prior to the final levy of any tax voted to retire the outstanding debt, the governing body of the municipality shall ...

MCLA 137.2 Sinking fund; provisions governing; investment, sale. [MSA 5.3188(46)]

Sec. 2. All sinking funds created for the retirement of term obligations other than refunding bonds and certificates of indebtedness shall be subject to the provisions of this section. All such funds shall ...

MCLA 137.3 Same; retirement of term refunding bonds or certificates of indebtedness; tenders; advertising. [MSA 5.3188(47)]

Sec. 3. Any municipality issuing term refunding bonds or certificates of indebtedness under the provisions of chapter VI hereof shall provide a sinking fund or funds for the retirement thereof, and there shall ...

CHAPTER VIII, REPEAL

MCLA 138.1 Acts repealed. [MSA 5.3188(48)]

Sec. 1. The following acts and all acts and parts of acts amendatory thereto, are hereby repealed, namely: Act No. 273, Public Acts of 1925; Act No. 26, Public Acts of 1931; Act No. 18, Public Acts of 1931; Act No. 13, Public Acts of 1932, First Extra Session; Act No. 1 of the Public Acts of 1932, Second Extra Session. It is not the intent of this act to supersede or repeal any act authorizing loans against revenues but which also pledge the full faith and credit of the municipality.

MCLA 138.2 Hearings, and proceedings; continuation. [MSA 5.3188(49)]

Sec. 2. All hearings, matters and proceedings of whatsoever nature pending before the loan board created by Act No. 26, Public Acts of 1931 (repealed by this act) and the public debt commission created by Act No. 13, Public Acts of 1932, First Extra Session, being section 133.2 [MSA 5.3188(7)] of the Compiled Laws of 1948, shall ...

Act No. 14, P.A. 1926, Ex. Sess. - Public Buildings,
Sinking Fund for Sites

*AN ACT to authorize the board of supervisors of any
county to create a sinking fund for the purpose of purchasing real estate for sites for, and constructing or repairing
public buildings; to authorize such boards to submit the
question of levying a tax to create such sinking fund to
the electors of their certain counties and to provide for
the manner of submission.*

**MCLA 141.51 Creation of sinking fund for public buildings and
sites; tax referendum.** [MSA 5.671]

MCLA 141.52 Tax referendum procedure. [MSA 5.672]

MCLA 141.53 Requisite notice. [MSA 5.673]

*Sec. 3. It shall be the duty of the township clerk ... upon re-
ceipt of the notice herein required, to give notice in writing under
his hand of the time and place when such question will be submitted
to the electors. Such township clerk ... shall ...*

**MCLA 141.54 Ballots, form, contents, distribution, counting; author-
izing vote; levy.** [MSA 5.674]

*Sec. 4. It shall be the duty of the board of election commission-
ers of such county to prepare the necessary ballots for the use ...*

MCLA 141.55 Sinking Fund, control. [MSA 5.675]

JOINT ACTION
Act No. 94, P.A. 1933 - Revenue Bond Act of 1933

*AN ACT to authorize public corporations to purchase,
acquire, construct, improve, enlarge, extend or repair
public improvements within or without their corporate
limits, and to own, operate and maintain the same; to authorize the condemnation of property for such public improvements; to provide for the imposition and collection of
charges, fees, rentals or rates for the services, facilities
and commodities furnished by such public improvements;
to provide for the issuance of bonds and refunding bonds
payable from the revenues of public improvements; to pro-*

1062

vide for a pledge by public corporations of their full faith and credit for the payment of the bonds; to provide for the payment, retirement and security of such bonds; to provide for the imposition of special assessments against properties benefited by such public improvements, and for the issuing of special assessment bonds for the purpose of refunding outstanding revenue bonds; to prescribe the powers and duties of the municipal finance commission relative to such bonds; and to provide for other matters in respect to such public improvements and bonds.

MCLA 141.101 Short title. MSA 5.2731

MCLA 141.102 Construction of act. MSA 5.2732

Sec. 2. This act shall be construed as cumulative authority for the exercise of the powers herein granted and shall not be construed to repeal any existing laws with respect thereto, it being the purpose and intention of this act to create full and complete additional and alternate methods for the exercise of such powers. The powers conferred by this act shall not be affected or limited by any other statute or by any charter, except as otherwise herein provided. The functions, powers and duties of the state commissioner of health in connection with any such public improvement shall remain unaffected by this act.

MCLA 141.103 Definitions. MSA 5.2733

MCLA 141.104 Municipal public improvements; limitations; bonds; acquiring utility for supplying light, heat or power, referendum; powers exercised. MSA 5.2734

MCLA 141.105 Estimate of cost and period of usefulness. MSA 5.2735

MCLA 141.106 Ordinances, adoption, record, publication. MSA 5.2736

Sec. 6. For the purposes of this act, the governing body of any public corporation by the affirmative vote of a majority of its members elect, is authorized to adopt an ordinance or ordinances relating to the exercise of the powers herein granted and to any other matters necessary or desirable to effectuate the full intent and purposes of this act, to provide for the adequate operation of any public improvement established hereunder, and to insure the security of any bonds issued hereunder: *Provided, ...*

MCLA 141.107 Bonds, issuance, form, term, interest, payment, tax exemption, security, indebtedness. [MSA 5.2737]

Sec. 7. (1) For the purpose of defraying the whole or a part of the cost of ... any public corporation may borrow money and issue its negotiable bonds therefor. No such bonds shall be issued unless and until authorized by an ordinance which shall set forth ... (and) shall be serial bonds payable either semiannually or annually with the first installment not more than 5 years from the date thereof and ...

MCLA 141.108 Lien on revenue in favor of bondholders. [MSA 5.2738]

MCLA 141.109 Same; duration, enforcement. [MSA 5.2739]

MCLA 141.110 Receiverships for public improvements. [MSA 5.2740]

MCLA 141.111 Bonds; application of other laws and charters. [MSA 5.2741]

Sec. 11. The bonds authorized hereunder shall not be subject to ...

MCLA 141.112 Same; maximum interest; public and private sale. [MSA 5.2742]

Sec. 12. Bonds issued hereunder shall not be sold at a price which would make the interest cost on the money borrowed after deducting any premium or adding any discount exceeding 6% per annum or sold at a discount exceeding 10% of the principal amount thereof. Except as hereinafter provided, no ...

MCLA 114.113 Same; statement on face. [MSA 5.2743]

MCLA 141.114 Same; qualities of negotiable instruments. [MSA 5.2744]

MCLA 141.115 Same; deposits of proceeds of sale in banks covered by federal deposit insurance; investments, authorization, approval. [MSA 5.2745]

MCLA 141.116 Same; use of proceeds of sale; payment of capitalized interest. [MSA 5.2746]

MCLA 141.117 Same; validity of signatures. [MSA 5.2747]

MCLA 141.118 Charges for services. [MSA 5.2748]

Sec. 18. No free service shall be furnished ... The reasonable cost and value ...

MCLA 141.119 Additional bonds; issuance in separate series, maturities. [MSA 5.2749]

MCLA 141.120 Revenue refunding bonds; maturities, sale or exchange. [MSA 5.2750]

MCLA 141.120a Combined public improvements; bonds; revenues pledged; retirement. [MSA 5.2750(1)]

Sec. 20a. Any public corporation may determine to operate 2 or more public improvements as a combined public improvement and in such case it may ...

MCLA 141.120b Revenue bonds to retire outstanding bonds; validity; premium; sale or exchange. [MSA 5.2750(2)]

MCLA 141.120c Parking revenue bonds, special assessments on benefited properties. [MSA 5.2750(3)]

MCLA 141.121 Rates for service; delinquent charges a lien; enforcement. [MSA 5.2751]

Sec. 21. Rates for services furnished by any such public improvement shall be fixed precedent to the issuance of the bonds. Such rates shall be ...

MCLA 141.122 Disposition of revenues; funds. [MSA 5.2752]

Sec. 22. In the authorizing ordinance the governing body of the borrower shall pledge the revenues of the public improvement for the purposes of the following funds and shall provide that such revenues as collected shall be set aside in a receiving fund and transferred periodically as provided in such ordinance into separate and special funds as follows: ... "operation and maintenance fund" ... "bond and interest redemption fund" ... such additional funds for the public improvement as the ordinance may establish. Revenues remaining in the receiving fund, after satisfaction of the above, at the end of any operating year shall be deemed to be surplus and shall be disposed of by the governing body as hereinafter provided.

MCLA 141.123 Payment of operating expenses from other sources. [MSA 5.2753]

Sec. 23. Nothing in this act shall be construed to prohibit the borrower from appropriating and using any part of its available income or revenues derived from any source other than from the operation of such public improvement in paying any immediate expenses of operation or maintenance of any such public improvement, but nothing in this act shall be construed to require the borrower to do so.

MCLA 141.124 Deposit of moneys in public improvement funds, investment. [MSA 5.2754]

MCLA 141.125 Operating year. [MSA 5.2755]

Sec. 25. The ordinance authorizing the issuance of such bonds shall fix the dates of the beginning and ending of the operating year for such public improvement, subject to the right of the municipal finance commission to require that it correspond with the fiscal year of the borrower.

MCLA 141.126 Receiving fund surplus, disposition. [MSA 5.2756]

Sec. 26. Any moneys remaining in the receiving fund at the end of any operating year, which under the provisions of section 22 shall be deemed to be surplus, may be transferred to other funds of the public improvement or may be used for such purpose or purposes as the governing body may determine to be for the best interests of the borrower, unless some other disposition shall have been made therefor in the ordinance authorizing the issuance of bonds hereunder. In the event that moneys in the receiving fund are insufficient to provide for the current requirements of the operation and maintenance fund or the bond and interest redemption fund, any moneys and/or securities in other funds of the public improvement shall be transferred first to the operation and maintenance fund and second to the bond and interest redemption fund to the extent of any deficits therein.

MCLA 141.127 Permission to issue bonds; approval. [MSA 5.2757]

MCLA 141.128 Order not deemed approval of legality of bond issue. [MSA 5.2758]

Sec. 28. No order of the municipal finance commission permitting the issuance of bonds under this act, shall be deemed an approval of the legality thereof: Provided, ...

MCLA 141.129 Rates not subject to supervision by state agency. [MSA 5.2759]

Sec. 29. Rates charged for the services furnished by any public improvement ... under the provisions of this act shall not be subject to supervision or regulation by any state bureau, board, commission or other like instrumentality or agency thereof.

MCLA 141.130 Same; records, accounts, examination, inspection, statement or audit. [MSA 5.2760]

Sec. 30. Any borrower issuing revenue bonds under the provisions of this act shall install, maintain and keep proper books of record and account, separate entirely from other records and accounts of such borrower, in which full and correct entries shall be made of ... The governing body of such borrower, not later than 6 months after the close of any operating year, shall ...

MCLA 141.131 Calling of bonds before maturity; premium. [MSA 5.2761]

MCLA 141.132 Breach of contract not authorized; pledging of revenues; disconnection of lands not to affect liability under bond issue. [MSA 5.2762]

MCLA 141.133 Governing bodies, powers, issuance of bonds; referendum. [MSA 5.2763]

Sec. 33. Unless otherwise provided in this act, the powers herein conferred upon public corporations shall be exercised by their respective governing bodies; and this act shall be construed as authorizing the issuance of bonds hereunder without submitting the proposition for the approval of the same to the voters of the borrowers. However, if, within 30 days from the publication of a notice of intent to issue the bonds which states the amount of the issue, a petition, signed by not less than 10% of the registered electors residing within the limits of such public corporation, shall have filed with the clerk, or other recording officer, of the borrower, requesting a referendum upon the question of the issuance of ...

MCLA 141.134 Liberal construction of act. [MSA 5.2764]

MCLA 141.136 Immediate necessity. [MSA 5.2766]

MCLA 141.137 Condemnation of property. [MSA 5.2766(1)]

MCLA 141.138 Trustee, appointment. [MSA 5.2766(2)]

MCLA 141.139 Water pollution, prevention or abatement; may accept grants or aid from U.S. government, etc. [MSA 5.2766(3)]

Sec. 39. Any public corporation is hereby authorized to apply for and accept grants or any other aid ... (from) ... the United States government ...

Act No. 200, P.A. 1849 - Emergency Expenses

AN ACT to authorize township boards to raise money by tax, or by borrowing, in certain cases, to defray township expenses.

MCLA 41.131 Emergency expenses, borrowing power. [MSA 5.161]

Sec. 1. Whenever the qualified electors of any township, at the annual township meeting, neglect or refuse to vote such sums of money as may be necessary to defray the ordinary township expenses, or to meet any emergency expenses, the township board, at any regular meeting, may vote such sums as may be necessary for that purpose, not exceeding in any 1 year the sum of 1/2 of 1% of the assessed valuation, and the township board may authorize and direct, by resolution, the supervisor and township clerk to borrow such sum as may be necessary, not exceeding $4,000.00 in any 1 year, for the payment of such expenses and to issue the obligations of the township therefor. In townships having an assessed valuation of $10,000,000.00 or over, the township board may authorize the supervisor and township clerk to borrow not to exceed $12,500.00 in any 1 year.

Act No. 194, P.A. 1929 - Deficiency in Special Assessments

AN ACT to authorize certain townships to borrow money to pay to the county treasurer any deficiency in amounts of special assessments.

MCLA 41.141 Deficiency; township may borrow. [MSA 5.171]

Sec. 1. Any township whose assessed valuation is 1,000,000 dollars or more, may, by a resolution adopted by a majority of the members of its township board, borrow the amount necessary to pay the county treasurer any deficiency in the amount of any special assessments for highway or drain purposes, assessed against the township at large, not to exceed the total of such special assessments returned delinquent.

Act No. 122, P.A. 1915 - Interest Bearing Orders

AN ACT to authorize and empower township boards to issue orders bearing interest at the rate of 6 per cent or less per annum in certain cases.

MCLA 41.151 Authorized orders; interest. [MSA 5.181]

Sec. 1. When a portion of the taxes authorized by the electors of a township at any annual meeting thereof, either for general township purposes or specific purposes, shall be delinquent, the township board is hereby authorized and empowered to issue orders bearing interest at 6 per cent or less per annum, which orders shall not exceed in the aggregate the amounts in the respective funds so authorized.

JOINT ACTION
Act No. 151, P.A. 1933 - Compromise of Municipal Indebtedness

*AN ACT to authorize the state and the municipalities
thereof to compromise, adjust, modify, compound, refund,
or otherwise alter the amount contracted to be paid and the
time within which the same is to be paid under the funded
indebtedness of any municipality or special assessment
district owned and held, in whole or in part, by the state
and/or the municipalities thereof.*

MCLA 141.191 Definitions. [MSA 5.3241]

MCLA 141.192 Compromise of municipal defaulted funded indebtedness owned by state or other municipality. [MSA 5.3242]

*Sec. 2. If the funded indebtedness of any municipality or any
special assessment district, in default as to principal and/or interest, shall be owned and held, in whole or in part, by the state of
Michigan, or any municipality thereof, it shall be lawful for the ...
treasurer of any municipality ... , by and with the consent of the
governing body ...*

Act No. 72, P.A. 1939 - Municipal Debt Adjustment

*AN ACT to authorize taxing agencies and instrumen-
talities in the state of Michigan to proceed under the provisions of the acts of the congress of the United States of
America to secure a composition of their respective debts.*

MCLA 141.201 Taxing agency or instrumentality, procedure under federal municipal debt adjustment act; plan, conditions; retroactive effect. [MSA 5.3464]

*Sec. 1. Any taxing agency or instrumentality in this state as
defined in an act of the congress of the United States of America
entitled "An act to establish a uniform system of bankruptcy throughout the United States," approved July 1, 1898, and acts amendatory
thereof and supplementary thereto, may proceed under the terms and
conditions of such acts to secure a composition of its debts, but
no securities for the refunding of such debts shall be issued until
first approved by the public debt commission (see MCLA 131.1 et
seq [MSA 5.3188(1) et seq]) of this state. The governing authority
... or the officer, board or body having authority to levy taxes to
meet the obligations to be affected by the plan of composition may
file the petition and ... Such plan of composition, when approved by*

the court as provided in said act of congress, shall be binding upon such taxing agency or instrumentality. ...

Act No. 204, P.A. 1933 - Defaulted Municipal Bonds

AN ACT to authorize municipalities to call for and accept tenders of defaulted bonds.

MCLA 141.211 Defaulted municipal bonds. [MSA 5.3251]

Sec. 1. Any ... township ... in this state is hereby authorized to call for tenders of, and accept defaulted bonds of such municipality by complying with the following terms and conditions.

MCLA 141.212 Same; call for tenders. [MSA 5.3252]

Sec. 2. Whenever any bonds of any special assessment district or improvement district of any ... township, ... shall have been or have remained in default as to principal or interest for a period of longer than 6 months and there shall not be, or have been within said period of default, sufficient sums of money on hand belonging to said special assessment district or improvement district to pay the principal and interest of said bonds so in default, the governing body of such municipality may by resolution ...

MCLA 141.213 Same; tenders, acceptance or rejection. [MSA 5.3253]

MCLA 141.214 Same; payment of accepted tenders. [MSA 5.3254]

JOINT ACTION
Act No. 79, P.A. 1937 - Municipal Utility Revenues, Borrowing

AN ACT to authorize any municipality, as herein defined, to borrow money and issue notes in anticipation of the collection of revenues other than taxes and special assessments.

MCLA 141.221 Definitions. [MSA 5.3221]

MCLA 141.222 Bus and street railroad transportation or water supply utility purposes, municipal borrowing. [MSA 5.3222]

MCLA 141.223 Same; municipal finance commission, application, authority. [MSA 5.3223]

MCLA 141.224 Same; borrowing limitations. [MSA 5.3224]

MCLA 141.225 Same; special sinking fund. [MSA 5.3225]

MCLA 141.226 Same; liability of municipality; construction of act. [MSA 5.3226]

Act No. 177, P.A. 1943 - Public Improvement Funds

AN ACT to provide for the creation of a fund or funds in political subdivisions for acquiring, constructing, extending, altering, repairing or equipping public improvements or public buildings; to provide for appropriations, credits and transfers to said fund or funds; and to provide for the disbursement thereof.

MCLA 141.261 Funds for public improvements or buildings. [MSA 5.2770(1)]

MCLA 141.262   Same; transfer or encumbrance. [MSA 5.2770(2)]

MCLA 141.263 Same; allocation of miscellaneous revenues; sale of lands. [MSA 5.2770(3)]

MCLA 141.264 Tax limitation. [MSA 5.2770(4)]

MCLA 141.265 Powers additional; "political subdivision" construed. [MSA 5.2770(5)]

Sec. 5. This act shall be in addition to all powers heretofore granted to political subdivisions by state, law, or by any charter thereof.

The term "political subdivision" as used in this act shall be construed to mean any county, city, village, township, school district or other local unit of this state.

Act No. 297, P.A. 1945 - Public Utility Water Bonds, Validation

AN ACT to validate certain bonds of any municipality incorporated pursuant to Act No. 279 of the Public Acts of 1909, as amended.

MCLA 141.271 Validating certain municipal bonds.
MSA 5.3189(1)

MCLA 141.272 Sale or reinvestment; notice by publication before sale. MSA 5.3189(2)

Act No. 178, P.A. 1931 - Drainage District Bonds, Reports

AN ACT to provide for the keeping of records of highway and drainage district bonds.

MCLA 141.302 Drainage district bonds; report by county drain commissioner. MSA 9.812

Sec. 2. The county drain commissioner ... shall ... file with the township ... treasurer of each township ... assessed at large for any part of the cost of any such drain, a statement of ...

MCLA 141.303 Record of bonds by county and municipal clerks. MSA 9.813

Sec. 3. It shall be the duty of each ... township ... treasurer ... to keep a proper record thereof suitably indexed and open for public inspection.

Act No. 121, P.A. 1969 - Capital Improvements; Bonds, Notes, Pledges of Deferred Income from Sale of Capital Assets

AN ACT to authorize counties, cities, townships and villages to issue bonds or notes, and pledge deferred income from sale of capital assets, due and payable but which has not been received, for the payment of principal and interest thereon; and to authorize the county, city, township or village to pledge its full faith and credit for the payment of the bonds or notes.

MCLA 141.381 Issuance of bonds and notes, resolution, purpose; pledges; use of proceeds; debt limitation; general obligations.
[MSA 5.2769(301)]

Sec. 1. Any ... township ... , by resolution adopted by a majority vote of the members elect of ... (the township board) ...

MCLA 141.382 Form and execution of bonds or notes; principal and interest, maximum, due in one year, due dates; redemption; payment; tax exemption. [MSA 5.2769(302)]

MCLA 141.383 Sale of bonds and notes; approval of issuance.
[MSA 5.2769(303)]

Sec. 3. The bonds or notes shall be sold at public sale for not less than par and notice of sale of the bonds or notes shall be published ...

JOINT ACTION
Act No. 56, P.A. 1962 - Bond Cremation Act

AN ACT to provide for the cremation or disintegration of public obligations and matters incidental and necessary thereto.

MCLA 129.121 Bond cremation or disintegration act; short title.
[MSA 3.996(1)]

MCLA 129.122 Same; definitions. [MSA 3.996(2)]

MCLA 129.123 Cremation or disintegration, authorization, agreements with paying agents. [MSA 3.996(3)]

MCLA 129.124 Same; certificate of cremation; contents, filing.
[MSA 3.996(4)]

Sec. 4. Where obligations and interest coupons are cremated by a public corporation, it shall be done in the presence of the official ... having custody of the financial records of the public corporation, or a representative designated by such official, and in the presence of ...

MCLA 129.125 Same; obligations not considered public records.
[MSA 3.996(5)]

Sec. 5. The powers conferred by this act shall be construed as constituting complete and independent power and authority to do the things herein authorized, the provisions of any other statute or charter to the contrary notwithstanding. Obligations and interest coupons of public corporations for the purpose of this act shall not be considered to be public records within the meaning of any other statute or charter.

JOINT ACTION
Act No. 354, P.A. 1972 - Lost, Destroyed, or Wrongfully Taken Evidences of Indebtedness

AN ACT to authorize the replacement or payment without presentation of lost, destroyed or wrongfully taken bonds or other evidences of indebtedness issued by public corporations.

MCLA 129.131 Definitions. [MSA 3.993(21)]

MCLA 129.132 Replacement obligation, unmatured obligation, payment without presentation of matured obligation; authorization; prerequisites. [MSA 3.993(22)]

MCLA 129.133 Replacement obligations, form, tenor, security, execution, formal requirements, indorsement [MSA 3.993(23)]

MCLA 129.134 Interest coupons. [MSA 3.993(24)]

BUDGET AND ACCOUNTING OF FINANCES

The gateway to proper financing and accounting is the township budget. Without an understanding of the total budget process, it is difficult for local governmental officials to carry out their roles as responsible persons holding the trust and respect of the people. The many factors to be considered in preparing a budget that will meet the township's needs for twelve months require the cooperation and activity of the entire board, from supervisor to trustee and on to the various department heads. If for some reason the necessary funds for normal and ordinary expenses of the township are not provided by the township board and/or the electors at the annual meeting; if there are unexpected emergencies or if there are deficiencies in special assessments, there is statutory provision to borrow money to meet the needs. However, good fiscal responsibility should hold these situations to a minimum.

Although it is almost impossible to prepare a budget for which there will be no criticism, a township board can come very close to doing so if it uses the technique of providing for each fund included in the budget the following information:

1. How much was appropriated for last year.

2. How much was received last year.

3. How much was spent last year.

4. The loss or gain - did the township operate in the red or the black last year?

5. Balance on hand at the beginning of the current fiscal year.

6. Expected income for the year.

7. Expected expenditure for the year.

8. Expected loss or gain - will the township operate in the red or the black next year?

9. An indication of the prospects for the following year.

10. Written justification for both increases or decreases - - this is a statutory requirement for the charter township.

Operating in this manner presents the township board with the greatest opportunity to show people where there have been improvements, where any deficiencies may lie, and what can be done to bring about a greater degree of stability within the township. It will provide a basis upon which the township can decide what additional millage may be required during the coming year. Since much of a township's money comes from taxes allocated by the county allocation board, it is vital that the township board first ascertain whether the county is a fixed millage county, and then whether there may be need for taxes in the township over the fifteen mill limitation. This should be done before any public hearing on the budget in order to avoid calling a second meeting to consider changes which will bring it in line with the county allocation. Further, MTA legal counsel has given an opinion that the budget filed with the county allocation board in April is for the operation of the township during the subsequent fiscal year, since the allocated tax rate is not collected by the township until the December following filing of the budget.

We would suggest that a good place to begin in the budget process is to study the two legal opinions cited below which provide a procedural outline for budget preparation and the public hearing. The board should exercise care that the electors understand they have no authority to make changes or even approve or disapprove the budget, with the exception of compensation of town-

1076

ship officers, but that their opinions and advice are sought and will be given due consideration by the board, which alone has the authority for final approval.

The general law township is governed by Act No. 30, P.A. 1934 and its terms regarding content and filing date (third Monday in April). Charter township officials should refer to Act No. 359, P.A. 1954 (the Charter Township Act) elsewhere in this book for their budget procedures.

In 1968 the legislature brought about one of the greatest regulatory changes in financial accounting in the history of township government. A statute was passed that brought about uniformity in accounting for public moneys and standardization of procedures and report forms, all of which reflect modern systems of finance and accounting. The stipulation that the audit must be done by a Certified Public Accountant is making this an extremely costly process; otherwise, most public officials feel the new system is to their advantage since they realize they must use great diligence and have a high sense of accountability to their constituents.

Anyone who holds public office immediately becomes aware of susceptibility to the grave charge, real or imagined, of misappropriation of public funds. Although bonding companies provide protection for the public interest, nevertheless there is a stigma directted against all government when it happens, even though the money is protected.

MTA, in cooperation with the Institute for Community Development of the Continuing Education Service at Michigan State University, has established classes which will prepare local officials to meet the statutory requirements for accounting for the funds for which they are responsible, and the Michigan Department of the Treasury is always most willing to provide assistance whenever requested.

A well prepared budget, based on the uniform charts of accounts and reports, the proper bonding of public officials, and carefully designated depositories are all essential elements leading to proper accountability and make it easier for township officials and the CPA auditors to prepare the township financial statement. And incidentally, that statement need no longer contain the thousands of line items that were required prior to 1972.

Finally, all budget and other matters of finance shall be expressed in the English language, and legal tender shall be described in terms of dollars, cents and mills.

Township Current Legal Opinions, Vol. I, 1956 to
1969

Opinion 10-10-66: Annual Budgets - Hearings

Opinion 1-9-67: Budget Procedures Outlined

Act No. 43, P.A. 1963, 2nd Ex. Sess. - Budget
Hearings

*AN ACT to provide for public hearings on budgets of
local units of government.*

MCLA 141.411 Local unit of government; definition.
MSA 5.3228(1)

MCLA 141.412 Same; public hearing on proposed budget, notice.
MSA 5.3228(2)

*Sec. 2. Every local unit shall provide for a public hearing to
be held on its proposed budget, notice of such hearing to be given
by publication in a newspaper of general circulation within such unit
at least six days prior to such hearing. Such notice shall include
the time and place of such hearing and shall state the place where
a copy of such budget is available for public inspection.*

MCLA 141.413 Same; final adoption of budget, hearing.
MSA 5.3228(3)

*Sec. 3. Each local unit shall hold such public hearing prior to
final adoption of its budget. Units which submit budgets to a
county tax allocation board shall hold such hearing after its tax rate
allocation has been fixed by such board.*

MCLA 141.414 Same; changes in budget. MSA 5.3228(4)

*Sec. 4. Changes made in its budget by the governing body of a
local unit subsequent to such public hearing shall not affect the
validity of such budget.*

MCLA 141.415 Same; public hearing on budget, charter, statute.
MSA 5.3228(5)

Sec. 5. Local units which provide for a public hearing before adoption of their budgets either in pursuance of charter provision or law shall hold a public hearing in accordance with such provision of charter or law which shall be deemed to be in a manner prescribed by law.

Act No. 140, P.A. 1933 - Budgets, Reopening and Revision

AN ACT to authorize certain municipalities to reopen and revise their budgets to permit deductions from the tax levy of certain debt obligations, and to prescribe certain provisions therefor.

MCLA 211.271 Definitions. [MSA 5.3231]

MCLA 211.272 Revision of municipal budgets for deduction of debt service. [MSA 5.3232]

Sec. 2. Any municipality, which by mutual agreement with creditors has ... and which has heretofore adopted or may hereafter adopt its budget and provided a tax levy for any fiscal year ... may by a 2/3 vote of the members-elect of its legislative body reopen and revise its budget for the purpose only of ...

MCLA 211.273 Same; after approval of refunding by public debt commission. [MSA 5.3233]

Sec. 3. ... the governing body may, by a 2/3 vote of its members elect, by resolution, provide for the revision of its budget for ...

MCLA 211.274 Same; after suspension of moratorium on municipal debt. [MSA 5.3234]

MCLA 211.275 Effect on existing statutes and charters. [MSA 5.3235]

Sec. 5. This act shall not repeal any existing statutory or charter provision for a budget and/or tax levy but shall be construed as an additional grant of power ...

R.S. 1846, c. 16 - Township Boards

MCLA 41.72 Annual meeting; date; claims, auditing, settling, payment. [MSA 5.64]

Sec. 72. The township board shall meet annually on the second Tuesday next preceding the annual township meeting for the purpose of auditing and settling all claims against the township which have not previously been audited and settled ...

MCLA 41.72a Regular meetings, time, place, audit and payment of claims; special meetings, notice, business; publication of proceedings. [MSA 5.64(1)]

R.S. 1846, c. 16 - Township Treasurer

MCLA 41.76 Township treasurer; duties. [MSA 5.68]

Act No. 262, P.A. 1897 - Township Financial Statements

AN ACT to require township boards to make and publish annually a statement of the condition of the finances of the township, in relation to the receipts and disbursements made by the township board.

MCLA 41.171 Township financial statements, publication and distribution. [MSA 5.111]

Sec. 1. The township boards ... shall make and cause to be published annually, immediately upon the settlement of the township board, a statement of first, the amount of in the hands of the township treasurer at the beginning of the fiscal year, specifying the amount in the several funds; second, the amount and source, by type, of all money placed to the credit of the township and the fund to which the same has been credited; third, the total of disbursements of money paid, and for what purposes, and from what fund the same has been paid; fourth, the balance of money remaining to the credit of township, specifying the amount in each of the several funds; fifth, the total of unpaid claims for each fund. The statement shall be written or printed and distributed to each member of the township board and 6 copies shall be posted in 6 conspicuous places within the township. Distribution and posting shall be made at least 10 days prior to every annual township meeting. The board may order further publication of the statement in 1 issue of a newspaper of general circulation in the county. The township clerk shall carry out the provisions as to publication.

MCLA 41.172 Same; expense, payment. [MSA 5.112]

Sec. 2. That the expense ... shall be a charge against and shall be audited and allowed by the township board and paid out of the general fund ...

MCLA 41.173 Penalty. [MSA 5.113]

Sec. 3. The failure ... to comply with the provisions of this act shall be deemed to be a misdemeanor on the part of all the individual members of such township board not voting therefor and shall be punished by ... , upon the complaint of any taxpayer within such township.

Act No. 2, P.A. 1968 - Uniform Charts of Accounts and Reports

AN ACT to provide for the formulation and establishment of uniform charts of accounts and reports in local units of government; to define local units of government; to provide for the examination of the books and accounts of local units of government; to provide for annual financial reports from local units of government; to provide for the administration of this act; to prescribe the powers and duties of the state treasurer and the attorney general; to provide penalties for violation of this act; and to provide for meeting the expenses authorized by this act.

MCLA 141.421 Uniform charts of accounts; standard procedures and forms. [MSA 5.3228(21)]

Sec. 1. The state treasurer shall prescribe uniform charts of accounts for all local units of similar size, function or service designed to fulfill the requirements of good accounting practices relating to general government. ...

MCLA 141.422 Local unit; definition. [MSA 5.3228(22)]

MCLA 141.423 Publication; hearings. [MSA 5.3228(23)]

MCLA 141.424 Annual financial report. ⎡MSA 5.3228(24)⎤

Sec. 4. Each local unit of government shall make an annual financial report which shall be uniform for all accounts of the same class, 3 copies of which shall be filed in the office of the state treasurer and shall contain an accurate statement in summarized form showing, for each fiscal year, the amount of all collections and receipts from all sources and their disposition, the amount of expenditures for each purpose, the amount of indebtedness, balance of funds on hand at the close of each fiscal period, together with such other information as may be required by law. ...

MCLA 141.425 Annual audit; exception. ⎡MSA 5.3228(25)⎤

Sec. 5. (1) All local units of government of less than 1,000,000 population shall have an annual audit of its financial records, accounts and procedures except that in the units of local government having populations of less than 2,000 such audit shall be required not less frequently than biennially. ...

MCLA 141.426 Certified public accounts; cost. ⎡MSA 5.3228(26)⎤

Sec. 6. Local units may retain certified public accountants to perform such audits. If any unit fails to provide for an audit, the state treasurer shall either conduct the audit or appoint a certified public accountant to perform it. The entire cost of any such audits will be borne by the local unit.

MCLA 141.427 Procedures and standards of auditing.
⎡MSA 5.3228(27)⎤

Sec. 7. (1) The state treasurer shall prescribe minimum auditing procedures ...

MCLA 141.428 Contents of audit report. ⎡MSA 5.3228(28)⎤

MCLA 141.429 Public inspection of audit reports. ⎡MSA 5.3228(29)⎤

MCLA 141.430 Orders and subpoenas. ⎡MSA 5.3228(30)⎤

Sec. 10. ... (regarding this audit) ... the state treasurer, or a deputy state treasurer, may issue subpoenas, direct the service thereof by any police officer, and compel the attendance and testimony of witnesses, may administer oaths and examine such persons

1082

as may be necessary, and may compel the production of books and papers. ...

MCLA 141.431 Violations. [MSA 5.3228(31)]

Sec. 11. If ... (such) ... audit or investigation ... d i s c l o s e s statutory violations on the part of any officer, employee or board of any local unit, a copy of such report shall be filed with the attorney general who shall review the report and cause to be instituted such proceeding against such officer, employee or board as he deems necessary. The attorney general, within 60 days after receipt of the report, may institute criminal proceedings as he deems necessary against such officer or employee, ...

MCLA 141.432 Verification of transactions. [MSA 5.3228(32)]

MCLA 141.433 Examiners authority; access to and production of records; confidential information, divulging. [MSA 5.3228(33)]

Act No. 40, P.A. 1932, 1st Ex. Sess. - Deposit of Public Funds

AN ACT to provide for the designation of depositories for public moneys; to prescribe the effect thereof on the liability for such deposits; to suspend the requirement of surety bonds from depositories of public moneys; and to repeal all acts and parts of acts inconsistent with the provisions of this act.

MCLA 129.11 Public moneys; definition. [MSA 3.751]

MCLA 129.12 Same; designation of depositories, liability of sureties. [MSA 3.752]

*Sec. 2. The ... **township board** ... shall provide by resolution for the deposit of all public moneys, including tax moneys, coming into the hands of the ... township treasurer, ... in 1 or more banks or trust companies to be designated therein, and in such proportion and manner as may be therein provided. All such proceedings ...*

MCLA 129.13 Depositories of public funds; requirement of collateral; repeal; suspension of existing laws; severability clause. [MSA 3.753]

Act No. 95, P.A. 1935 - Deposit of Public Funds

AN ACT to relieve all tax collectors, fee collectors, custodians and other officers and former tax collectors, fee collectors, and other officers of the state of Michigan or any of its political subdivisions from liability to any county, township, city, village or school district of the state of Michigan and the state of Michigan, for failure to pay over tax funds, fees and moneys in the possession of such tax collector, fee collector, custodian or other officer but on deposit in a depository designated by or under the the laws of the state of Michigan

MCLA 129.21 Tax collectors relieved from liability for funds in a designated depository. [MSA 3.781]

MCLA 129.22 Fee collectors relieved from liability for funds in a designated depository. [MSA 3.782]

MCLA 129.23 Public officials relieved from liability for funds in a designated depository. [MSA 3.783]

Act No. 29, P.A. 1937 - Unexpended Balances, Township Funds

AN ACT authorizing the township board of the several townships of this state to transfer unexpended balances in special funds to the contingent fund of the township; to provide for the disbursement thereof; to prescribe the powers and duties of the township treasurers with respect thereto; and to repeal all acts and parts of acts inconsistent with the provisions of this act.

MCLA 41.161 Transfers of unexpended balances of special township funds; authority of township board, annual statement. [MSA 5.115]

Sec. 1. The township board ... is hereby authorized at the annual meeting of such township board, (annual settlement day) by resolution, ...

MCLA 41.162 Same; authority of township treasurer. [MSA 5.116]

MCLA 41.163 Same; limitation. [MSA 5.117]

Act No. 7, P.A. 1949 - Unexpended Balances, Transfer

AN ACT to authorize townships, cities and incorporated villages by vote of the electors thereof to appropriate and transfer unexpended balances to the county in which situated to be expended for county purposes.

MCLA 141.351   Transfer of unexpended balances by townships, etc., to county to be expended for county purposes. [MSA 5.1195(1)]

MCLA 141.352 Same; submission to electors; conduct of election. [MSA 5.1195(2)]

Act No. 23, P.A. 1934, 1st Ex. Sess. - United States Securities, Investment In

AN ACT authorizing the investment in bonds of the home owners' loan corporation and bonds of federal home loan banks by the state and all its departments and political subdivisions, including municipal corporations, and instrumentalities, and by any insurance company, building and loan association or company, savings and loan association or company, bank, trust company or other financial institution, and by any executor, administrator, guardian, trustee or fiduciary; authorizing the use of such bonds as security by any depository of funds; and authorizing certain deposits with the state treasurer to be in such bonds.

MCLA 129.81 Public funds, fiduciary funds, investment in bonds of home owners' loan corporation, federal home loan bank, insured banks. [MSA 3.841]

MCLA 129.82 Same; deposit as security. [MSA 3.842]

MCLA 129.83 Construction of act. [MSA 3.843]

Act No. 20, P.A. 1943 - United States Securities, Investment In

AN ACT relative to the investment of surplus funds or (of) political subdivisions of the state; and to validate investments heretofore made.

MCLA 129.91 Surplus funds of municipalities and special assessment districts, investment. [MSA 3.843(1)]

Sec. 1. The legislative ... bodies of ... townships and special assessment districts are hereby authorized to direct the treasurers thereof to ...

MCLA 129.92 School districts, investment sinking funds and insurance moneys. [MSA 3.843(2)]

MCLA 129.93 Investments heretofore made validated. [MSA 3.843(3)]

Act No. 380, P.A. 1913 - Property Gifts

AN ACT to regulate gifts of real and personal property to cities, villages and other municipal corporations, and to validate all such gifts heretofore made.

MCLA 123.871 Gifts, acceptance, terms; informalities; gifts validated. [MSA 5.3421]

Act No. 32, P.A. 1956 - Facsimile Signatures

AN ACT to provide for the use of a facsimile signature or signatures of the person or persons required to sign the same by persons signing checks, drafts or other orders for the payment of money by governmental units, municipal corporations and/or certain other public corporations.

MCLA 129.101 Deposited public funds, facsimile signatures on checks or orders for payment of money. [MSA 3.757]

Sec. 1. Moneys on deposit in any duly designated depository to the credit of any account ... of any township, when so authorized by resolution of its township board, ... or of any other municipal or public corporation within this state, when so authorized by resolution of its governing board, may be drawn upon by checks, drafts or other orders for the payment of money bearing, or purporting to bear, the facsimile signature or signatures of the person or persons required to sign the same; ...

Act No. 19, P.A. 1934, 1st Ex. Sess. - Bonds of Public Officials, Liability of Sureties

AN ACT relative to the bonds of public officials, and the liability of sureties thereon; and to repeal all acts and parts of acts inconsistent therewith.

MCLA 129.51　Bonds of public officials, deputies, assistants, liability of sureties.　[MSA 27.1431]

Sec. 1. If any officer of ... any ... township, ... drainage district, ... or of any other municipal or public corporation within this state, shall be required to file an official statutory bond or bonds, either as additional security or substituted security, the surety or sureties thereon shall not be liable, directly or indirectly, for any acts or defaults committed by such public officer prior to the date of signing of such bond or bonds, or for the failure of any such public officer to pay over on final settlement or to his successor in office, if such failure to pay over be due to an act or default committed prior to the signing of such bond or bonds, or for the failure of such surety or sureties to collect from themselves or from any prior surety or sureties the amount of any loss due to any act or default committed by such public officer prior to the date of the signing of such bond or bonds.　The provisions of this act shall apply to all deputies of any such officer, and to all clerks, agents and servants of any such officer.

Act No. 94, P.A. 1929 - Misappropriation of Public Funds

AN ACT to authorize the institution of suits by taxpayers on behalf of townships or school districts for an accounting or to recover funds misappropriated or unlawfully expended by public officers.

MCLA 129.61　Misappropriation of public moneys; suit by taxpayer. [MSA 5.3281]

Sec. 1. Any person or persons, firm or corporation, resident in any township or school district, paying taxes to such political unit, may institute suits or actions at law or in equity on behalf of or for the benefit of the treasurer of such political subdivision, for an accounting and/or the recovery of funds or moneys misappropriated or unlawfully expended by any public officer, board or commission of such political subdivision. ...

R.S. 1846, c. 34 - Money of Account and Interest

MCLA 438.1 Money of account. [MSA 19.1]

Sec. 1. The money of account of this state, shall be the dollar, cent, and mill; and all accounts in the public offices, and all other public accounts, and all proceedings in courts, shall be kept and had in conformity with this regulation.

MCLA 438.2 Reduction of monetary units to standard units. [MSA 19.2]

MCLA 438.3 Holder in due course, recovery. [MSA 19.3]

Chapter X

MISCELLANEOUS

EMPLOYEE RELATIONS AND FRINGE BENEFITS

Every township, at one time or another and in varying degrees, is involved in the employment of individuals as consultants, advisors, temporary, part-time or full-time employees in many phases of its governing responsibilities. Employer-employee relations are vital concerns, therefore, of the township board. Every member of a township board should be familiar with such important facets of today's labor market as labor relations, civil service, civil rights, fair employment practices, discrimination as to age, color, sex, status, creed, race, etc., and many other matters, if there is to be the close, harmonious relationship at all levels which will bring about an effective administration of services to and for the township residents.

Act No. 133, P.A. 1955 - Military Leaves - Re-employment Protection

AN ACT to provide for the granting of military leaves and providing re-employment protection for officers and enlisted men of the military or naval forces of the state or of the United States.

MCLA 32.271 Members of military or naval forces; discrimination against prohibited. [MSA 4.1487(1)]

MCLA 32.272 Same; employment relations. [MSA 4.1487(2)]

Sec. 2. No employer or officer or agent of any corporation, company, or firm, or other person shall discharge any person from employment because of being or performing his duty as an officer or enlisted man of the military or naval forces of this state, ...

MCLA 32.273 Same; leave of absence from employment, reinstatement. [MSA 4.1487(3)]

Sec. 3. No employee who requests a leave from his employment shall be denied a leave of absence by his employer for the purpose of being inducted into, entering, determining his physical fitness to enter, or performing training duty as an officer or enlisted man of the military or naval forces of the state or of the United States. ...

MCLA 32.274 Violation, penalty. [MSA 4.1487(4)]

Act No. 263, P.A. 1951 - Public Employees Entering Armed Forces, Rights

AN ACT to establish the rights and privileges of officers and employees of the state of Michigan and of civil and political subdivisions thereof who enter into armed forces of the United States; and to provide for enforcement of the rights and privileges created.

MCLA 35.351 Definitions. [MSA 4.1486(1)]

MCLA 35.352 Public employee leaving position to perform military duty, restoration; if position abolished; placement in another department. [MSA 4.1486(2)]

MCLA 35.353 Discharge; restored without loss of seniority; participate in benefits; credit, limitation. [MSA 4.1486(3)]

MCLA 35.354 Leave of absence for induction in military service. [MSA 4.1486(4)]

MCLA 35.355 Enforcement, regulations; compulsory compliance; hearing; officials responsible for reinstatement. [MSA 4.1486(5)]

MCLA 35.356 Laws inapplicable. MSA 4.1486(6)

Sec. 6. Any laws or parts of laws, which are inconsistent with the provisions of this act, or which would serve to defeat the purposes thereof, shall to such extent be deemed inapplicable to public employers and public employees in the exercise of the rights and privileges conferred by this act.

Act No. 205, P.A. 1897 - Preference in Employment

AN ACT to prefer honorably discharged members of the armed forces of the United States for public employments.

MCLA 35.401 Veterans preference for public employment; qualifications; county civil service act. MSA 4.1221

Sec. 1. In every public department and upon the public works of the state and of every county and municipal corporation thereof honorably discharged soldiers, sailors, marines, nurses and members of women's auxiliaries of every war in which the United States of America has been, is, or may hereafter be a participant, shall be preferred for appointment and employment; age, loss of limb or other physical impairment which does not, in fact, incapacitate, shall not be deemed to disqualify them. ...

MCLA 35.402 Same; removal, suspension or transfer from public employment, hearing, protest, waiver, reinstatement. MSA 4.1222

MCLA 35.402a Same; military service counted as period of employment. MSA 4.1222(1)

MCLA 35.403 Penalty. MSA 4.1223

MCLA 35.404 Rejection of application of ex-service man, remedy. MSA 4.1224

Act No. 45, P.A. 1963, 2nd Ex. Sess. - Civil Rights

AN ACT to provide for the protection and enforcement of civil rights; for the organization and functions of the civil rights commission; and to repeal certain acts and parts of acts.

MCLA 37.1 Civil rights commission; bipartisan membership, terms, vacancy. [MSA 3.548(1)]

MCLA 37.2 ₊ 37.3 [MSA 3.548(2) - 3.548(3)]

MCLA 37.4 Same; investigation, enforcement procedure, appeal. [MSA 3.548(4)]

Sec. 4. The commission shall investigate alleged discrimination against any person because of religion, race, color or national origin in the enjoyment of the civil rights guaranteed by law and by the constitution of this state, and shall secure the equal protection of such civil rights without such discrimination. A complaint ...

MCLA 37.5 Same; powers and duties; rules and regulations, reports. [MSA 3.548(5)]

Sec. 5. The commission shall also have the following functions, powers and duties: ... (f) To request the services of all state and local government departments and agencies; ...

MCLA 37.6 - 37.9 [MSA 3.548(6) - 3.548(9)]

Act No. 251, P.A. 1955 - Fair Employment Practices Act

AN ACT to promote and protect the welfare of the people of this state by prevention and elimination of discriminatory employment practices and policies based upon race, color, religion, national origin, sex, age or ancestry; to create a state fair employment practices commission, defining its functions, powers and duties; and for other purposes.

MCLA 423.301 Employment opportunity without discrimination, civil right. [MSA 17.458(1)]

MCLA 423.302 Same; definitions. [MSA 17.458(2)]

1092

MCLA 423.303 Unfair employment practices. ⌈MSA 17.458(3)⌉

MCLA 423.303a Discrimination because of age or sex.
⌈MSA 17.458(3A)⌉

MCLA 423.304 Public contracts; nondiscrimination clauses.
⌈MSA 17.458(4)⌉

Sec. 4. Every contract to which the state or any of its political or civil subdivisions is a party shall contain a provision requiring ...

MCLA 423.304a Same; nondiscrimination because of age or sex; exception. ⌈MSA 17.458(4A)⌉

MCLA 423.307 Prevention of unfair employment practices; powers of commission; procedure. Persuasion, conciliation. Complaint; contents. Same; filing, investigation. Same; service, notice of hearing. Same; amendment, answer. Same; parties, interveners. Same; testimony, criterion for employment. Same; finding of commission, order to cease, declaratory order. Same; order of dismissal; copies. Same; modification of orders. ⌈MSA 17.458(7)⌉

MCLA 423.309 Posted notice of act; violation. ⌈MSA 17.458(9)⌉

MCLA 423.311 Short title of act. ⌈MSA 17.458(11)⌉

Act No. 328, P.A. 1931 - Michigan Penal Code

MCLA 750.556 Discrimination between sexes in payment of wages.
⌈MSA 28.824⌉

Sec. 556. Any employer of labor in this state, employing both males and females, who shall discriminate in any way in the payment of wages as between sexes who are similarly employed, shall be guilty of a misdemeanor. No female shall be assigned any task disproportionate to her strength, nor shall she be employed in any place detrimental to her morals, her health or her potential capacity for motherhood. Any difference in wage rates based upon a factor other than sex shall not violate this section.

Act No. 19, P.A. 1927 - Legal Employment of Minors

AN ACT to provide for the protection and legal employment of minors between the ages of 16 and 18 years.

MCLA 419.301 Legal employment, effect. [MSA 17.61]

Sec. 1. Any minor over 16 and under 18 years of age engaged in an occupation approved by the department of labor and industry as required by section 11 of Act No. 285 of the Public Acts of 1909, as amended (MCLA 408.61) [MSA 17.21], shall, within the meaning of said act, be considered to be legally employed, and shall in all cases be subject to Act No. 10 of the Public Acts of 1912 (extra session), as amended (MCLA 411.1 - 411.17a) [MSA 17.141 - 17.230(4)], known as the workmen's compensation law, provided that the employer has filed the required permit or certificate for said minor.

Act No. 246, P.A. 1965 - Township Civil Service

AN ACT to establish and provide a civil service system in certain townships; to create a civil service commission, and to prescribe the duties thereof; to provide certain exemptions from and classifications in civil service; to prescribe penalties for the violations of the provisions of this act; and to prescribe the manner of adoption of this act by townships.

MCLA 38.451 Civil service; adoption by township, method. [MSA 5.193(1)]

Sec. 1. Upon the adoption of a resolution therefor by a majority vote of the members elect of the township board ..., and the subsequent approval by a majority of the township electors voting thereon, the provisions of this act shall apply in any township now or hereafter having a population of 60,000 or more. The township board may submit the question at any regular election or special election called for some other purpose, and shall submit the question at any such election held not less than 60 days after the filing with the township clerk of petitions for such submission signed by at least 4% of the registered electors of the township.

MCLA 38.452 - 38.464 [MSA 5.193(2) -5.193(14)]

MCLA 38.465 Solicitation for political party prohibited.
[MSA 5.193(15)]

*Sec. 15. No officer or employee of the township in the classi-
fied civil service, directly or indirectly, shall make, solicit or receive, or be in any manner concerned in making, soliciting or receiving any assessment, subscription or contribution for any political party or political purpose whatsoever. Any employee violating
the provisions of this section may be removed from the office.*

MCLA 38.466 - 38.470 [MSA 5.193(16) - 5.193(20)]

**Act No. 78, P.A. 1935 - Firemen and Policemen
Civil Service**

MCLA 38.501 - 38.518 [MSA 5.3351 - 5.3369(1)]

Note: See the section on Fire and Police Protection in the
chapter on Services, Utilities, Contracts and Ordinances.

JOINT ACTION
**Act No. 135, P.A. 1945 - Municipal Employees'
Retirement System**

*AN ACT to provide for a municipal employees' retire-
ment system; to create a municipal employees' retirement
board and prescribe its powers and duties; to establish
certain funds in connection therewith and to require contributions thereto by the participating municipalities and
the municipal employees; and to provide penalties for the
violation of certain provisions of this act.*

MCLA 38.601 Short title. [MSA 5.4001]

MCLA 38.602 Definitions. [MSA 5.4002]

MCLA 38.603 - 38.605 [MSA 5.4003 - 5.4005]

**MCLA 38.606 Election to become participating municipality, mode;
effective date; equality of employees' coverage.** [MSA 5.4006]

Sec. 6. Any municipality, either by a 3/5 majority vote of its governing body or by a majority vote of the qualified electors ..., may ... The clerk ... of the municipality shall certify to the board in the manner and form prescribed by the board, the determination of the municipality within 10 days from the vote of the governing body or canvass of the votes upon such action.

MCLA 38.606a - 38.668a [MSA 5.4006(1) - 5.4068(1)]

JOINT ACTION
Act No. 137, P.A. 1967 - Combined Retirement Systems

AN ACT to authorize 2 or more cities, townships, villages or county road commissions or counties to enter into agreements relative to establishing, combining and financing retirement systems.

MCLA 38.691 Combined retirement systems. [MSA 5.3900(1)]

Sec. 1. Any 2 or more cities, townships, villages or counties or county road commissions or any combination thereof may enter into an agreement to establish, combine and finance retirement systems for their respective employees and officials, elected or appointed.

JOINT ACTION
Act No. 88, P.A. 1961 - Reciprocal Retirement

AN ACT to provide for the preservation and continuity of retirement system service credits for public employees who transfer their employment between units of government.

MCLA 38.1101 Reciprocal retirement; short title. [MSA 4.1601]

MCLA 38.1102 Same; definitions. [MSA 4.1602]

MCLA 38.1103 - 38.1105 [MSA 4.1603 - 4.1605]

Act No. 314, P.A. 1965 - Investment of Funds of Public Employee Retirement Systems

AN ACT to authorize the investment of funds of public employee retirement systems or plans created and established by the state or any political subdivision.

MCLA 38.1121 - 38.1131 [MSA 3.981(101) - 3.981(111)]

Act No. 27, P.A. 1960 - Group Insurance for Officers and Employees

AN ACT authorizing townships to establish retirement systems and make contracts of group insurance and arrangements with prepayment plans for the benefit of its elected or appointed officers and employees; to provide for the deduction of contributions from officers' and employees' compensation; and to permit the exercise of the authority granted without the necessity of a charter amendment.

MCLA 41.901 Group insurance for township officers and employees, contracts. [MSA 5.48(1)]

Sec. 1. Any township may: (a) Establish a retirement system for its employees and provide for ... (b) Make arrangements with any prepayment plans authorized ... (c) Contract with any such company granting annuities or pensions for ...

MCLA 41.902 Same; deduction of premium from pay. [MSA 5.48(2)]

MCLA 41.903 Same; coverage, notice of noncoverage. [MSA 5.48(3)]

MCLA 41.904 Same; previous plans. [MSA 5.48(4)]

MCLA 41.905 Construction of act; additional powers; amendment of charter. [MSA 5.48(5)]

Sec. 5. The authority hereby given shall be in addition to and not in derogation of any power existing in the township under the provisions of any statute or any charter now in effect.

Any township may exercise the powers granted hereunder by ordinance without necessity of amending its charter.

JOINT ACTION
Act No. 205, P.A. 1951 - Social Security for Public Employees

AN ACT to provide for the coverage of certain officers and employees of the state of Michigan, of instrumentalities of the state of Michigan, of interstate instrumentalities jointly created by the state of Michigan and any other state or states, and of local governments of the state of Michigan under the old-age and survivors insurance provisions of title II of the federal social security act, as amended; to prescribe the powers and duties of the state retirement board in respect to such coverage; to provide for the cost of administration of this act by collections from employers above the costs of coverage.

MCLA 38.851   Social security; extension to state and local employees; maintenance of benefits. [MSA 17.801]

MCLA 38.852   Same; definitions. [MSA 17.802]

MCLA 38.853 - 38.871 [MSA 17.803 - 17.821]

JOINT ACTION
Act No. 317, P.A. 1969 - Workmen's Compensation Act of 1969

AN ACT to revise and consolidate the laws relating to workmen's compensation; and to repeal certain acts and parts of acts.

CHAPTER 1. IN GENERAL

MCLA 418.101   Short title. [MSA 17.237(101)]

MCLA 418.111   Persons subject to act. [MSA 17.237(111)]

Sec. 111. Every employer, public and private, and every employee, unless herein otherwise specifically provided, shall be subject to the provisions of this act and shall be bound thereby.

1098

MCLA 418.115 **Private employers, agricultural employers; public employers; applicability of act; relatives as employees.**
MSA 17.237(115)

Sec. 115. This act shall apply to: ... All public employers, irrespective of the number of persons employed. ...

MCLA 418.118 - 418.141 MSA 17.237(118) - 17.237(141)

MCLA 418.151 Employers subject to act, designation.
MSA 17.237(151)

Sec. 151. (1) The following shall constitute employers subject to the provisions of this act:
(a) The state and each ... township, ... and each incorporated public board or public commission in this state authorized by law to hold property and to sue or be sued generally.
(b) Every person, firm and private corporation, including any public service corporation, who has any person in service under any contract of hire, express or implied, oral or written.

MCLA 418.155 Agricultural employer, farm, definitions.
MSA 17.237(155)

MCLA 418.161 Employee, defined; spouses, partners, exclusions from coverage. MSA 17.237(161)

MCLA 418.171 Statutory principals, liability under act, indemnification; contractors; subcontractors; common law recovery prohibited.
MSA 17.237(171)

CHAPTER 2. ADMINISTRATION

MCLA 418.201 - 418.265 MSA 17.237(201) - 17.237(265)

CHAPTER 3. COMPENSATION

MCLA 418.301 Arising out of and in course of employment; time or date of injury. MSA 17.237(301)

Sec. 301. (1) ... (2) Every employee going to or from his work while on the premises where his work is to be performed, and within a reasonable time before and after his working hours, shall be presumed to be in the course of his employment.

MCLA 418.305 - 418.385 [MSA 17.237(305) - 17.237(385)]

CHAPTER 4. DISEASES AND DISABLEMENT

MCLA 418.401 Disability, disablement, and personal injury, definitions. [MSA 17.237(401)]

MCLA 418.405 Firemen, policemen, sheriffs, and deputies, respiratory and heart diseases and illnesses as personal injuries. [MSA 17.237(405)]

Sec. 405. (1) In the case of a member of a full paid fire department of an airport ... or of a ... township ... employed and compensated upon a full-time basis, ... "personal injury" shall be construed to include respiratory and heart diseases or illnesses resulting therefrom which develop or manifest themselves during a period while the member of the department is in the active service of the department and result from the performance of duties as a fire fighter or policeman. ...

MCLA 418.411 - 418.441 [MSA 17.237(411) - 17.237(441)]

CHAPTER 5. SECOND INJURY AND SILICOSIS AND DUST DISEASE FUNDS

MCLA 418.501 - 418.561 [MSA 17.237(501) - 17.237(561)]

CHAPTER 6. CARRIERS, POLICIES, AND COVERAGE

MCLA 418.601 - 418.657 [MSA 17.237(601) - 17.237(657)]

CHAPTER 7. ACCIDENT FUND

MCLA 418.701 - 418.755 [MSA 17.237(701) - 17.237(755)]

CHAPTER 8. PROCEDURE AND MISCELLANEOUS PROVISIONS

MCLA 418.801 - 418.899 [MSA 17.237(801) - 17.237(899)]

CHAPTER 9. VOCATIONALLY HANDICAPPED PERSONS

MCLA 418.901 - 418.941 [MSA 17.237(901) - 17.237(941)]

Act No. 329, P.A. 1937 - Peace Officers Injured in Active Duty

AN ACT providing for compensation to certain peace officers injured in active duty, and payment to dependents in case of death arising from active duty; and to make an appropriation therefor.

MCLA 419.101 - 419.104 [MSA 4.456 - 4.459]

Act No. 9, P.A. 1942, 1st Ex. Sess. - Fireman Injured in Duty

AN ACT providing for compensation to certain firemen injured in the safeguarding of life and property, and payment to dependents in case of death; and to make an appropriation therefor.

MCLA 419.201 - 419.205 [MSA 4.584(1) - 4.584(5)]

Note: See the section on Fire and Police Protection in the chapter on Services, Utilities, Contracts and Ordinances for above citations.

Act No. 119, P.A. 1911 - Occupational Diseases

AN ACT to protect the public health; to require the reporting of occupational diseases to the state department of health; to prescribe the duties and powers of the state department of health with reference thereto; and to prescribe penalties for the violation of the provisions of this act.

MCLA 419.1 Occupational disease; reports, contents; use as public records. [MSA 17.431]

Sec. 1. ... every physician, hospital superintendent, or clinic registrar ... shall within 10 days report ...

MCLA 419.1a Same; definition. MSA 17.431(1)

MCLA 419.1b Same; report blanks. MSA 17.431(2)

MCLA 419.1c Same; investigation of reports. MSA 17.431(3)

MCLA 419.1d Same; statistical summaries. MSA 17.431(4)

MCLA 419.2 Reports; failure to make, falsification, penalty.
MSA 17.432

MCLA 419.3 Violations of act, prosecution. MSA 17.433

Act No. 1, P.A. 1936, Ex. Sess. - Employment Security Act

AN ACT to protect the welfare of the people of this state through the establishment of an unemployment compensation fund, and to provide for the disbursement thereof; to create the Michigan employment security commission, and to prescribe its powers and duties; to provide for the protection of the people of this state from the hazards of unemployment; to levy and provide for contributions from employers; to provide for the collection of such contributions; to enter into reciprocal agreements and to cooperate with agencies of the United States and of other states charged with the administration of any unemployment insurance law; to provide for the payment of benefits; to provide for appeals from redeterminations, decisions and notices of assessment; and for referees and an appeal board to hear and decide any and all issues arising from redeterminations, decisions and notices of assessment; to provide for the cooperation of this state and compliance with the provisions of the social security act and the Wagner-Peyser act passed by the Congress of the United States of America; to provide for the establishment and maintenance of free public employment offices; to provide for the transfer of funds; to make an appropriation for carrying out the provisions of this act; to prescribe penalties for the violation of the provisions of this act; and to repeal all acts and parts of acts inconsistent with the provisions of this act.

MCLA 421.1 Short title. [MSA 17.501]

MCLA 421.2 Declaration of policy. [MSA 17.502]

MCLA 421.3 Michigan employment security commission, members, appointment, terms, vacancy, removal, compensation, policies, purposes; rights reserved, records. [MSA 17.503]

Sec. 3. ... The commission shall ... investigate, recommend, advise and assist in the establishment and operation, by municipalities, counties, school districts, and the state, of reserves for public works to be used in times of business depression and unemployment.

MCLA 421.4 - 421.65 [MSA 17.504 - 17.565]

Act No. 176, P.A. 1939 - Labor Mediation

AN ACT to create a board for the mediation of labor disputes, and to prescribe its powers and duties; to provide for the mediation and arbitration of labor disputes, and the holding of elections thereon; to provide methods for settlement of hospital or public utility labor disputes, including the use of special fact finding commissions, to regulate the conduct of parties to labor disputes and to require the parties to follow certain procedures; to regulate and limit the right to strike and picket; to protect the rights and privileges of employees, including the right to organize and engage in lawful concerted activities; to protect the rights and privileges of employers; to make certain acts unlawful; and to prescribe means of enforcement and penalties for violations of the provisions of this act.

MCLA 423.1 Declaration of policy. [MSA 17.454(1)]

MCLA 423.2 Definitions. [MSA 17.454(2)]

MCLA 423.3 - 423.30 [MSA 17.454(3) - 17.454(30)]

Act No. 336, P.A. 1947 - Public Employees, Strikes

AN ACT to prohibit strikes by certain public employees; to provide review from disciplinary action with respect thereto; to provide for the mediation of grievances and the holding of elections; to declare and protect the rights and privileges of public employees; and to prescribe means of enforcement and penalties for the violation of the provisions of this act.

MCLA 423.201 Strike, defined; rights of public employees.
[MSA 17.455(1)]

MCLA 423.202 Public employee, defined; strike prohibited.
[MSA 17.455(2)]

Sec. 2. No person holding a position by appointment or employment in ... the government of any 1 or more of the political subdivisions thereof, ... or in any public or special district, or in the service of any authority, commission, or board, or in any other branch of the public service, hereinafter called a "public employee," shall strike.

MCLA 423.203 - 423.216 [MSA 17.455(3) - 17.455(16)]

Act No. 312, P.A. 1969 - Compulsory Arbitration of Labor Disputes, Policemen and Firemen

MCLA 423.231 - 423.247 [MSA 17.455(31) - 17.455(47)]

Note: See section on Fire and Police Protection in chapter on Services, Utilities, Contracts and Ordinances.

Act No. 150, P.A. 1962 - Employment of Strikebreakers

AN ACT relating to solicitations for employment; to prohibit recruitment of or advertising for employees to take the place of employees engaged in a labor dispute without stating that the employment offered is in place of employees involved in a labor dispute; to prohibit the importation of strikebreakers; and to provide penalties for violations of this act.

MCLA 423.251 - 423.254 [MSA 17.456(1) - 17.456(4)]

Note: The following citations will be only of indirect interest, since they refer to labor organizations with which the township board may have to negotiate.

Act No. 188, P.A. 1857 - Mechanics' Associations

AN ACT to provide for the incorporation of mechanics' associations.

MCLA 454.1 - 454.11 [MSA 21.581 - 21.591]

Act No. 167, P.A. 1869 - Mechanics' Associations

AN ACT to authorize the incorporation of trades' unions as mechanics' associations under the provisions of Chapter 62 of the Compiled Laws.

MCLA 454.51 - 454.54 [MSA 21.601 - 21.604]

Act No. 13, P.A. 1897 - Labor Associations

AN ACT to provide for the incorporation of labor associations.

MCLA 454.71 - 454.77 [MSA 21.611 - 21.617]

Act No. 42, P.A. 1887 - Arbeiter Bunds (Workmen's Aid Societies)

AN ACT to provide for the incorporation of Arbeiter Bunds.

MCLA 454.101 - 454.106 [MSA 21.621 - 21.626]

Act No. 145, P.A. 1885 - Societies to Promote Trade and Labor

AN ACT to provide for the incorporation of societies to promote the interests of trade and labor.

MCLA 454.151 - 454.159 [MSA 21.631 - 21.639]

Act No. 28, P.A. 1891 - Builders' and Traders' Exchanges

AN ACT to provide for the organization and incorporation of builders' and traders' exchanges.

MCLA 454.201 - 454.205 [MSA 21.651 - 21.655]

AGRICULTURAL, INDUSTRIAL AND OTHER INTERESTS

The following statutes extend from providing an opportunity to advertise the agricultural, industrial and other advantages of the township to those which may bring economic advantages to township citizens through exploitation of the opportunities for individual and amalgamated activities between various agricultural societies and the agencies, boards and commissions of the township.

Act No. 28, P.A. 1968 - Advertising Township

AN ACT to authorize township boards to appropriate funds for purposes of advertising the township.

MCLA 41.991 Appropriations; purpose. [MSA 5.264(11)]

Sec. 1. The board of any township may appropriate moneys or expend funds to be used for advertising agricultural advantages of the state, county or township, or for collecting, preparing or maintaining an exhibition of the products and industries of the township at any domestic or foreign exposition, for the purpose of encouraging immigration and increasing the trade in the products of this state or the township, or advertising the state and any portion thereof for tourists and resorters.

Act No. 33, P.A. 1881 - Crop and Stock Reports

AN ACT to provide for the publication of monthly crop and stock reports.

1106

MCLA 285.21 Monthly crop and stock reports, publication, distribution; cooperation with United States. [MSA 12.31]

Sec. 1. *The secretary of state shall each year obtain monthly statements as to the condition of live stock, condition and prospects of the growing crops, and as soon after the harvest as possible, statements as to the yield of wheat and other farm and fruit products; he shall also ascertain the quantity of wheat, wool, apples and other products marketed, and the quantity remaining in farmers' hands. And ... shall prepare a monthly abstract of the information thus obtained and shall insert therein the number of townships from which reports have been received, and shall publish ... and furnish 1 copy to ... each correspondent furnishing information ...*

MCLA 285.22 Local correspondents, right to receive reports. [MSA 12.32]

Sec. 2. *... the secretary of state, ...(shall)... select not less than 1 person in each township who shall be willing to act as correspondent of the department and furnish the information required by the first section of this act, and such further information as shall be deemed useful. And such person shall thereafter, as long as he shall faithfully perform the duties of a correspondent, be entitled to 1 copy of each of the reports published by the state department relating to agricultural subjects, also to 1 copy of each of the annual reports of the state board of agriculture and of the state horticultural society.*

JOINT ACTION
Act No. 197, P.A. 1956 - Agricultural Interests of Townships

AN ACT to promote the agricultural interests of the various townships of this state; to provide referenda.

MCLA 285.201 Agricultural interests, promotion in townships; extension work agreements, areas, appropriations, special tax. [MSA 5.264(1)]

Sec. 1. *In order to promote agricultural interests of the various townships of this state and to provide for agricultural extension* work for such townships, each township ... through its township board is hereby authorized and empowered to cooperate to said end with the Michigan state university ...; and may enter into agreements with reference thereto. The township board ... may appropriate money, or raise money by taxation, for the purpose hereof. Two or more township boards may act jointly; and a township board may describe an extension area within any township and may levy a special tax from said area to carry out the provisions of this act.

MCLA 285.202 Same; referendum. MSA 5.264(2)

Sec. 2. The provisions of this act shall not become operative in any township ... unless and until it is submitted to a vote of the qualified electors thereof and ratified by a majority ... voting thereon. The question of the adoption ... If a majority ... vote in favor thereof, from and after such determination, the provisions of this act shall be in force.

The township board shall submit such proposition to the electors at the next general or special election whenever petitions ..., signed by 10% of the registered electors of the township as shown by the registration rolls, shall be filed with the township clerk.

MCLA 285.203 Same; discontinuance, referendum. MSA 5.264(3)

Act No. 180, P.A. 1849 - Michigan State Agricultural Society

AN ACT to incorporate the Michigan state agricultural society.

MCLA 453.51 - 453.53 MSA 21.381 - 21.383

Note: This organization is exempt from property tax. See **MCLA 211.7** MSA 7.7.

JOINT ACTION
Act No. 80, P.A. 1855 - County, Town (Township) or District Societies

AN ACT to authorize the formation of local agricultural and horticultural societies.

MCLA 453.231 County, township, city or village societies; organization. [MSA 21.441]

Sec. 1. *Any 10 or more persons, inhabitants of this state, who shall desire to form an agricultural or horticultural society in any county, township, city or village, or in any 2 or more of them, being contiguous, in this state, may make, sign and acknowledge duplicate articles of association, ... and file 1 of the same in the office of the director of agriculture, and the other in the office of the county clerk of the county in which the business of the society is to be conducted. The articles shall state ...*

MCLA 453.232 Body corporate, powers; purchase, etc., real estate, limitation. [MSA 21.442]

Sec. 2. *... shall be capable of purchasing and holding, taking and receiving, by gift, devise or otherwise, exempt from taxation, real estate for the purpose of their incorporation; and they may ...*

MCLA 453.233 Stockholders. [MSA 21.443]

MCLA 453.234 Board of directors; officers; powers. [MSA 21.444]

Sec. 4. *... They shall manage the property and business of the society to best promote the interests of educational, agricultural, horticultural and mechanical arts; they may hold fairs and exhibitions and distribute premiums ...*

MCLA 453.236 Sale of real estate; procedure. [MSA 21.446]

MCLA 453.238 Report to director. [MSA 21.448]

MCLA 453.240 Articles, amendment; procedure, filing. [MSA 21.450]

JOINT ACTION
Act No. 155, P.A. 1889 - County, Town (Township) or District Societies

AN ACT *to enable any town (township), county or district agricultural or horticultural society to re-organize under the act approved February twelfth, 1855, entitled,*

"An act to authorize the formation of county and town (township) agricultural societies" and the several acts amendatory thereof.

MCLA 453.281 - 453.284 ⌈MSA 21.461 - 21.464⌉

JOINT ACTION
Act No. 106, P.A. 1893 - County, Town (Township) or District Societies

AN ACT to enable any town (township), county or district agricultural society, heretofore organized under the laws of this state, whose term of corporate existence has expired, or is about to expire, by limitation, to reorganize for a further period, not exceeding 30 years, and to fix the duties and liabilities of such renewed agricultural corporations, associations or societies.

MCLA 453.291 - 453.294 ⌈MSA 21.471 - 21.474⌉

Act No. 125, P.A. 1871 - Pomological and Horticultural Societies

AN ACT to provide for the incorporation of societies for the promotion of pomology, horticulture, and the kindred sciences and arts, in the state of Michigan.

MCLA 453.301 Pomological, etc., societies; incorporators.
⌈MSA 21.481⌉

Sec. 1. That any 5 or more persons, ... may ... associate together for the purpose of promoting the interests of pomology, horticulture, agriculture and kindred sciences and arts, may become a body corporate, by complying with the requirements of this act.

MCLA 453.302 - 453.306 ⌈MSA 21.482 - 21.486⌉

MCLA 453.307 Local associations; annual report to state association. ⌈MSA 21.487⌉

Sec. 7. District or county, town (township), city, or village associations organized under this act are hereby required to report

1110

*through their secretary, in the month of November in each year, to
the secretary of the state association, ...; such reports ... to be
used as correspondence in compiling the* (state) *report, ...*

MCLA 453.308 Privileges and immunities. ⌐MSA 21.488⌐

JOINT ACTION
**Act No. 188 P.A. 1921 - Societies Receiving Public
Funds**

    *AN ACT to require the secretary of agricultural or
other fair associations receiving aid from public funds to
make, publish and file fiscal reports.*

MCLA 453.341 - 453.343 ⌐MSA 21.511 - 21.513⌐

    Note: See the County Fair section of the chapter on Services,
Utilities, Contracts and Ordinances.

JOINT ACTION
**Act No. 8, P.A. 1862 - Issuance of Bonds, Obliga-
tions and Mortgages**

    *AN ACT to authorize agricultural and horticultural
societies to issue bonds or other evidences of debt and to
mortgage real estate for certain purposes.*

**MCLA 453.351 Agricultural or horticultural societies; issuance of
bonds and obligations.** ⌐MSA 21.521⌐

    *Sec. 1. It shall and may be lawful for any agricultural or horti-
cultural society, ...(to borrow, etc.)... whenever necessary for the
purpose of paying the purchase money of permanent grounds, or for
buildings, or improvements made or to be made thereon; or to secure
any moneys, which have been borrowed to meet the obligations of
said society.*

MCLA 453.352 Former mortgages declared valid. ⌐MSA 21.522⌐

Act No. 121, P.A. 1873 - Protection of Exhibitions

AN ACT to enable agricultural and horticultural societies and horse fairs to extend a more perfect protection to their property and the property of exhibitors at fairs, and to allow the board of managers to appoint police for that purpose.

MCLA 453.361 - 453.362 [MSA 21.531 - 21.532]

Act No. 220, P.A. 1861 - Protection of Exhibitions

AN ACT vesting with police powers, marshals and their deputies at state and county fairs.

MCLA 453.371 Marshals and police at fairs; powers. [MSA 21.541]

Sec. 1. ... during the days of the fairs or exhibitions ... be vested with the police powers of special constables in the township ...(where) held.

REGULATING AND LICENSING OF BUSINESS

The right of a person to choose an avocation, trade or business for a life pursuit is one of the unique guarantees of a democracy. However, the bad conduct of a few makes it necessary for the majority to live within a highly regulated society. Almost without exception, licensing and varying degrees of regulation and supervision are required for business and commercial interests. This is brought about by initiation of a township ordinance intended to specifically regulate a particular business or operation in the township, or enforcement of county, state or federal regulations. This chapter includes citations which did not fit into the various subject matters contained in the other chapters.

Act No. 359, P.A. 1921 - Peddler's License to Veterans

AN ACT to provide for the issuance of veterans' licenses without cost to former members of the coast guard, soldiers, sailors or marines of the military or naval ser-

1112

vice of the United States, to hawk, vend and peddle their own goods, wares and merchandise within this state.

MCLA 35.441 Peddler's license; veterans, term, qualification. [MSA 4.1241]

MCLA 35.442 Same; issuance by county clerk without cost; record; transferability. [MSA 4.1242]

MCLA 35.443 Construction of act. [MSA 4.1243]

Sec. 3. Nothing in this act shall be construed as contravening the provisions of Act No. 191 of the Public Acts of 1901 or Act No. 294 of the Public Acts of 1913, as amended, known as the "itinerant vendors" and "transient merchants" acts.

Note: Repealed; see now **MCLA 445.371 et seq** [MSA 19.691 ET SEQ]

Act No. 68, P.A. 1915 - Solicitation of Public Aid

AN ACT regulating organizations, institutions, associations or persons soliciting from the public for a charitable purpose; and providing a penalty for the violation thereof.

MCLA 400.301 Solicitation of public for charitable purposes; definitions. [MSA 16.71]

Sec. 1. **Definitions. ... Statement filed with state department of social welfare; license, issuance, revocation; local solicitation.** *... the state department shall be authorized to issue to the charitable organization and its agents and representatives, a state license ... authorizing the organization to solicit and receive from the public donations or sell memberships, for the charitable purpose contained in the statement filed with the state department, in any county, city or township in the state. ...*(but person must also obtain any required township license or permit)...

MCLA 400.302 Same; copy of license in possession of solicitor. [MSA 16.72]

MCLA 400.303 Penalty. [MSA 16.73]

MCLA 400.304 Inspection of files; lists. [MSA 16.74]

Act No. 238, P.A. 1879 - Protection of Logs and Timber

AN ACT to protect logs, lumber and timber while floating upon the waters in this state, or lying upon the banks or shores thereof, ...

MCLA 426.151 - 426.159 [MSA 18.251 - 18.259]

MCLA 426.160 Removal of logs drifted on banks; procedure for fixing and recovery of damages, arbitration, lien. [MSA 18.260]

Note: This section makes provision for arbitration of damages, with an arbitration board to be chosen from township freeholders by a court of jurisdiction, and for sale of property involved by certain officials, including constables.

Act No. 8, P.A. 1933, Ex. Sess. - Liquor Law

AN ACT to create a liquor control commission for the control of the alcoholic beverage traffic within the state of Michigan, and to prescribe its powers, duties and limitations; to provide for the control of the alcoholic liquor traffic within the state of Michigan and the establishment of state liquor stores; to provide for the care and treatment of alcoholics; to provide for the incorporation of farmer cooperative wineries and the granting of certain rights and privileges thereto; to provide for the licensing and taxation thereof, and the disposition of the moneys received under this act; to provide for the enforcement and to prescribe penalties for violations of this act; to provide for the confiscation and disposition of property seized under the provisions of this act; to provide a referendum in certain cases; and to repeal certain acts and parts of acts, general, local and special, and certain ordinances and parts of ordinances.

MCLA 436.1 Alcoholic liquors; regulation and control; enforcement, penalty. [MSA 18.971]

Sec. 1. ... On and after the effective date of this act, it shall be lawful to manufacture for sale, sell, offer for sale, keep for sale, possess and/or transport any alcoholic liquor, as hereinafter defined, including alcoholic liquor used for medicinal, mechanical, chemical or scientific purposes and wine for sacramental purposes, subject to the terms, conditions, limitations and restrictions contained herein, and only as provided for in this act.

Except as by this act otherwise provided, the commission shall have the sole right, power and duty to control the alcoholic beverage traffic and traffic in other alcoholic liquor within the state of Michigan, including the manufacture, importation, possession, transportation and sale thereof.

No rule, regulation and/or order made by the commission shall unreasonably discriminate against Michigan manufacturers of alcoholic liquor.

The sheriffs of the several counties and their deputies and the village marshals, constables, officers or members of the village or city police and members of the department of state police, and inspectors of the commission, are hereby empowered and it is hereby made their duty to see that the provisions of this act and the rules and regulations made or authorized by said commission are enforced within their respective jurisdictions. It shall be their special duty to use their utmost efforts to repress and prevent crime and the violation of any of the provisions of this act. Any officer within the above enumeration who shall wilfully neglect or refuse to perform the duties imposed upon him by this section shall be guilty of a misdemeanor and upon conviction shall be fined not to exceed 500 dollars or imprisoned in the county jail not more than 90 days, or both.

MCLA 436.1a Short title. [MSA 18.971(1)]

MCLA 436.2 Liquor control act; definitions. [MSA 18.972]

Sec. 2. The words and phrases used in this act shall be construed as defined in this section and in sections 2a to 2w, inclusive, unless the context shall otherwise require:

"Alcoholic liquor" ... *"Beer"* ... *"Wine"* ... *"Spirits"* ... *"Alcohol"* ...

MCLA 436.2a Same; bar. [MSA 18.972(1)]

MCLA 436.2b Same; brewer. [MSA 18.972(2)]

MCLA 436.2c Same; church. [MSA 18.972(3)]

MCLA 436.2d Same; citizen. [MSA 18.972(4)]

MCLA 436.2e Same; club. [MSA 18.972(5)]

MCLA 436.2f Same; commission. [MSA 18.972(6)]

MCLA 436.2g Same; distiller. [MSA 18.972(7)]

MCLA 436.2h Same; hotel. [MSA 18.972(8)]

MCLA 436.2i Same; license. [MSA 18.972(9)]

MCLA 436.2j Same; manufacturer. [MSA 18.972(10)]

MCLA 436.2k Same; person. [MSA 18.972(11)]

MCLA 436.2*l* Same; residence. [MSA 18.972(12)]

MCLA 436.2m Same; definitions; retailer, vendor, wholesaler, warehouseman. [MSA 18.972(13)]

MCLA 436.2n Same; sale. [MSA 18.972(14)]

MCLA 436.2o Same; special license. [MSA 18.972(15)]

MCLA 436.2p Same; specially designated distributor. [MSA 18.972(16)]

MCLA 436.2q Same; specially designated merchant. [MSA 18.972(17)]

MCLA 436.2r Same; state liquor store. [MSA 18.972(18)]

MCLA 436.2s Same; tavern. [MSA 18.972(19)]

MCLA 436.2t Same; class C license. [MSA 18.972(20)]

MCLA 436.2u Same; vehicle. [MSA 18.972(21)]

MCLA 436.2v Same; warehouse. [MSA 18.972(22)]

MCLA 436.2w Same; wine maker. [MSA 18.972(23)]

MCLA 436.2x Same; cash defined. [MSA 18.972(24)]

MCLA 436.2y Same; school defined; nonincluded institutions.
[MSA 18.972(25)]

MCLA 436.3 Alcoholic liquors; sale and/or delivery by commission; importation by state, persons. [MSA 18.973]

MCLA 436.4 Fruit juices, preparations and other exceptions to act. [MSA 18.974]

MCLA 436.5 Liquor control commission, creation, members, term, oath, removal, salaries, etc. Creation of commission, commissioners' term, oath, removal. Vacancies. Quorum. Salaries, expenses. Designation of chairman. [MSA 18.975]

MCLA 436.5b Liquor control business manager, selection, duty and responsibility. [MSA 18.975(2)]

MCLA 436.6 Liquor control commission; assistants and employees, bonds. [MSA 18.976]

MCLA 436.7 Liquor control commission; rules and regulations; public hearings. [MSA 18.977]

MCLA 436.7a Same; investigations; inspections; searches, seizures and examinations; witnesses, subpoena. [MSA 18.977(1)]

MCLA 436.8 - 436.13 [MSA 18.979 - 18.984]

MCLA 436.14 Specially designated distributors. [MSA 18.985]

MCLA 436.15 Liquor control commission; handling of liquor; gross profit; leasing and purchasing power. [MSA 18.986]

MCLA 436.16 Alcoholic liquor, uniform prices; certain direct sales, gross profit; wine; minimum price. Uniform prices. Discount to licensees; cash sales, exceptions. [MSA 18.987]

MCLA 436.16a Tax rate on wines; incorporation of farm mutual co-operative wineries; sales. [MSA 18.987(1)]

MCLA 436.17 Liquor licenses; discretion of liquor control commission; fees, bonds, insurance. Discretionary issuance of licenses. Stock ownership of corporate manufacturers; expiration of license; construction as contract; death of licensee; court receivers; short term licenses; transfer, approval of retailer by local legislative body; revocation of licenses. State-owned lands; state fair lands. Certain hotels; zones for renewal of retail licenses. [MSA 18.988]

MCLA 436.17a Issuance of liquor licenses; proximity to church or school, method of measurement; exceptions; waiver. [MSA 18.988(1)]

MCLA 436.17c Same; transfer to location farther from church or school. [MSA 18.988(3)]

MCLA 436.17d Same; class "C" or "B" hotel license for state-owned airports. [MSA 18.988(4)]

MCLA 436.17e Licenses; issuance without regard to quota to owner or lessee of certain airport; nontransferability. [MSA 18.988(5)]

MCLA 436.17f Municipal civic centers or auditoriums, issuance of liquor licenses regardless of quota limitations, transferability and use of licenses. [MSA 18.988(6)]

MCLA 436.17g Mackinac Island state park, licenses for state park commission-owned hotels. [MSA 18.988(7)]

MCLA 436.18 Same; law enforcement officers and fraternal organizations as licensees. [MSA 18.989]

MCLA 436.18a Beer and wine, referendum on Sunday sale of; petition; form of ballot. [MSA 18.989(1)]

Sec. 18a.   The sale of beer and wine between the hours of 2:00 a.m. and 12:00 midnight on Sunday may be prohibited in any county, city, village, or township, by a majority vote of the electors voting at a regular state election.   Not oftener than once in every 4 years, upon the filing of a petition with the county, city, village, or township clerk, as the case may be, requesting the submission of the question of the Sunday sale of beer and wine, the clerk shall submit such question ...   The question of the Sunday sale of beer and wine shall be submitted by ballot in substantially the following form:

"Shall the sale of beer and wine within (the county, city, village, or township as the case may be) between the hours of 2:00 a.m. and 12:00 midnight on Sunday be prohibited?
Yes . . . . . .
No . . . . . ."
All votes cast on the question shall ...

MCLA 436.19 Liquor control act; license fees. [MSA 18.990]

MCLA 436.19b Liquor license; transfer fee, exceptions; inspection fee for change of status. [MSA 18.990(2)]

MCLA 436.19c License for consumption of liquor on premises; quota; existing licenses. Quota. Resort area licenses; number, classification. Same; additional for 5-year period, termination or suspension. Veterans. Applicability of section to establishments located at county-owned airports. [MSA 18.990(3)]

MCLA 436.19d Specially designated merchant or distributor licenses, persons eligible; warehousemen and wholesalers, sales and deliveries to consumers. [MSA 18.990(4)]

MCLA 436.19e Prohibited furnishing of alcoholic liquors on Sundays and election days, exception; petition; submission of question to voters; Christmas. [MSA 18.990(5)]

Sec. 19e.   No licensee enumerated under section 19 or any other person shall sell at retail, give away or furnish and no person shall knowingly and wilfully buy any spirits between the hours of

2 a.m. and 12 midnight on any Sunday, except that the legislative body of any county may authorize the sale of spirits, for consumption on the premises, on Sunday after 2 p.m., by resolution approved by a majority of the legislative body voting thereon in any establishment licensed under this act in which the gross receipts derived from the sale of food and other goods and services exceed 50% of the total gross receipts. With respect to any action taken by such legislative body, or, if the legislative body fails to act, a petition may be filed with the county clerk requesting the submission of the question of such sale of spirits for consumption on the premises in addition to beer and wine on Sunday. The petition shall be signed by a number of the registered and qualified electors thereof which shall be not less than 8% of the total number of votes cast for all candidates for the office of secretary of state in the county at the last general election held for such purpose. The question shall not be submitted to the electors of such county more than once every 4 years.

The county clerk shall submit such question at the next regular state election held in such county; provided, that such petitions must be filed at least 60 days prior to said election. The question of the sale of such spirits for consumption on the premises, in addition to beer and wine, on Sunday shall be submitted by ballot in substantially the following form:

"Shall the sale of spirits for consumption on the premises be permitted on Sunday, in any establishment licensed under this act in which the gross receipts derived from the sale of food or other goods and services exceed 50% of the total gross receipts within the county of . . . . under the provisions of the law governing the same?

Yes . . . . .
No . . . . ."
All votes on the question shall ...

MCLA 436.19f Selling spirits on Sunday under section 436.19e; additional license fee; deposit of revenue. [MSA 18.990(6)]

MCLA 436.20   Liquor control commission; licenses, revocation, suspension, penalty, procedure, criminal prosecution.
[MSA 18.991]

MCLA 436.21   Licenses; forfeiture of privileges upon revocation.
[MSA 18.992]

1120

MCLA 436.22 Licensees' bonds; dramshop act. Types of bonds; principal amounts. Form of bonds. Right of action for injuries caused by sales to intoxicated persons, damages, limitations, survival and form of actions, parties; continuance and cancellation of bonds. [MSA 18.993]

MCLA 436.22a Same; retailer's liability insurance policy, approval, minimum limits, bankruptcy. [MSA 18.993(1)]

MCLA 436.22b Consent to service of process, form. [MSA 18.993(2)]

MCLA 436.22c Suit to enforce liability when service of process not effected, affidavit; service upon commission in duplicate; return; copy served on defendant; hearing; duty of commission. [MSA 18.993(3)]

MCLA 436.22d Insurer to file notice of termination or cancellation of contract or policy, effective date. [MSA 18.993(4)]

MCLA 436.22e Judgment, payment; failure to pay, damages; recovery in action of assumpsit. [MSA 18.993(5)]

MCLA 436.22f Insurance policy, coverage, conditions. [MSA 18.993(6)]

MCLA 436.22g False statement or breach of authority; cancellation of insurance. [MSA 18.993(7)]

MCLA 436.23 Liquor license; corporate vendor licensee, qualifications; transfer of stock, sale of assets, permission; renewal of outstanding license. [MSA 18.994]

MCLA 436.24 Vendors; classes. [MSA 18.995]

MCLA 436.25 Printed price list, posting. [MSA 18.996]

MCLA 436.26a Sterilization of glasses. [MSA 18.997(1)]

MCLA 436.26b Sales in hotel rooms. [MSA 18.997(2)]

MCLA 436.26c Unlicensed places, operating, for drinking alcoholic beverages, unlawful; exceptions. [MSA 18.997(3)]

MCLA 436.27 Food; purchasing, giving away. [MSA 18.998]

MCLA 436.28 Removal of liquor from premises where sold for consumption thereon. [MSA 18.999]

MCLA 436.28a Pinball machines. [MSA 18.999(1)]

MCLA 436.29 Gifts; sales to intoxicated person. [MSA 18.1000]

Sec. 29. ... No vendor shall give away any alcoholic liquor of any kind or description at any time in connection with his business except manufacturers for consumption on the premises only. No vendor shall sell any alcoholic liquor to any person in an intoxicated condition.

MCLA 436.30 Aid to liquor vendor; refunding amount of price reductions by manufacturer to specially designated distributor licensees. [MSA 18.1001]

MCLA 436.31 Interest in business of vendor. [MSA 18.1002]

MCLA 436.32 Traffic in wine, spirits, alcohol and liquor by licensees only. [MSA 18.1003]

MCLA 436.33 Sales to minors prohibited; signs, defenses. [MSA 18.1004]

MCLA 436.33a Possessing or transporting alcoholic liquor in motor vehicle by minor. [MSA 18.1004(1)]

MCLA 436.33b Persons under 18, unlawful purchases, consumption, or possession of liquor. [MSA 18.1004(2)]

MCLA 436.34 Consumption of alcoholic liquors; public highways, parks and places of amusement. [MSA 18.1005]

MCLA 436.35 Same; state military reservation. [MSA 18.1006]

MCLA 436.40 Beer; taxation. Discrimination. [MSA 18.1011]

MCLA 436.41 Failure to pay tax, penalties, collection.
[MSA 18.101 2]

MCLA 436.42 Search warrants. [MSA 18.101 3]

MCLA 436.43 Seizures by execution, bankruptcy, payment.
[MSA 18.101 4]

MCLA 436.44 Liability of vendor. [MSA 18.101 5]

MCLA 436.45 False and fraudulent statements. [MSA 18.101 6]

MCLA 436.46 Adulterated and misbranded liquors and refilled liquor bottles; penalty, definitions. [MSA 18.101 7]

MCLA 436.46a Forging, etc., documents, labels, etc.; penalty.
[MSA 18.1017(1)]

MCLA 436.47 Retailers' license fees, disbursement; treatment of alcoholics, fund; exceptions. [MSA 18.101 8]

Sec. 47. Quarterly, upon recommendation of the commission, the state shall pay in the manner prescribed by law to the city, village or township in which a full-time police department or a full-time ordinance enforcement department is maintained, and where no police department or full-time ordinance enforcement department is maintained, then to the counties, to be credited to the sheriff's department in which the license is located 85% of the amount of the proceeds of the retailers' license fees collected therein, for the specific purpose of enforcing the provisions of this act and the rules and regulations of the commission. The legislature shall ...

MCLA 436.48 Handling of moneys, payment monthly to state treasurer. [MSA 18.101 9]

MCLA 436.49 Moneys paid to state treasurer credited to general fund. [MSA 18.1020]

MCLA 436.50 Penalties, intent. [MSA 18.1021]

MCLA 436.51 Revocation of liquor licenses, effect. [MSA 18.1022]

MCLA 436.53 Saving clause. [MSA 18.1024]

MCLA 436.54 Construction of act. [MSA 18.1025]

MCLA 436.56 Sale of spirits for consumption on premises; referendum, petitions, tie vote, resubmission. [MSA 18.1027]

Sec. 56. *Spirits for consumption on the premises, in addition to beer and wine, may be sold by restaurants, hotels and establishments, approved by the commission under this act in ... Provided, ... That with respect to any action taken by ...(township board)..., or, in case ...(it)... shall fail to act within said 60 day period, a petition may be filed with the ... township clerk ... requesting the submission of the question of sale of spirits for consumption on the premises, in addition to beer and wine. ... such petition shall be signed by a number of the registered and qualified electors ... which shall be not less than 35% of the total number of votes cast for all candidates for the office of secretary of state in such ... township at the last general election held for such purpose. ... Provided, That such question shall not be submitted to the electors ... more often than once in every 2 years. ...(Filing and publication provisions)... The question ... shall be submitted by ballot in substantially the following form:*

"Shall the sale of spirits in addition to beer and wine be permitted for consumption on the premises within (the ... township ...) of . . . . under the provisions of the law governing same?

Yes . . . . . .

No . . . . . ."

All votes on the question shall be taken, counted and canvassed in the same manner as votes cast in ... township elections ...

MCLA 436.56a Sale of spirits for consumption on premises; annexation of territory to city prohibiting such sale; continuance of license, referendum. [MSA 18.1027(1)]

MCLA 436.56b Legislative implementation following electors' approval of sale for consumption on premises; unincorporated portions of townships, submission of question to electors. [MSA 18.1027(2)]

MCLA 436.57 Same; county option; form of ballot. [MSA 18.1028]

1124

MCLA 436.58 Warehouse receipts for alcoholic liquor; authority of commission. [MSA 18.1029]

Act No. 204, P.A. 1889 - Peddlers and Pawnbrokers in Upper Peninsula

AN ACT to authorize the township board of any township in the upper peninsula to license hawkers, peddlers and pawnbrokers, and hawking and peddling, and to regulate and license the sale or peddling of goods, wares, merchandise, refreshments or any kind of property or thing by persons going about from place to place in the township, for that purpose, or from any stand, cart, vehicle, or other device, in the streets, highways, or in or upon wharves, docks, open places or spaces, public grounds or buildings in the township, and to provide a forfeiture for every person who, without license, or contrary to the terms of any license granted to him, shall exercise any occupation or trade, or do anything in respect to which any license shall be required by any resolution or regulation of the township board, made or passed under authority of this act.

MCLA 446.101 Regulation and license for peddlers and pawnbrokers in upper peninsula; issuance by township board, limit of license fee. [MSA 19.571]

MCLA 446.102 Same; procedure; resolution of board, posting, affidavit as evidence. [MSA 19.572]

MCLA 446.103 License; term, transferability. [MSA 19.573]

MCLA 446.104 Same; disposal of receipts from fees. [MSA 19.574]

MCLA 446.105 Same; unlawful use, failure to obtain, penalty; exceptions from application of act. [MSA 19.575]

Act No. 85, P.A. 1923 - Drug and Toilet Preparations

AN ACT to provide for the licensing and regulation of the sale of drugs, nostrums, face powders, face creams, face bleaches, face lotions, cosmetics, tooth powders, tooth pastes, dentifrices and other toilet preparations or ointments or applications for the treatment of diseases, injuries or deformities, by itinerant..and traveling vendors or hawkers and to provide a penalty for the violation thereof.

MCLA 446.301 Peddlers of drugs and toilet preparations; license; issuance by board of pharmacy, fee, term. [MSA 19.611]

MCLA 446.302 Same; definition (peddler). [MSA 19.612]

MCLA 446.303 Penalty. [MSA 19.613]

MCLA 446.304 Effect of act on local tax or license. [MSA 19.614]

Sec. 4. Nothing in this act shall be construed to prevent the collection of any tax or license that may be imposed by any ... township ... authority.

MCLA 446.305 Inapplicability of act to certain specified sales. [MSA 19.615]

MCLA 446.306 No necessity for additional state license. [MSA 19.616]

Act No. 285, P.A. 1925 - Credit Unions

AN ACT to provide for the organization, operation and supervision of credit unions; and to provide for the conversion of a state credit union into a federal credit union and for the conversion of a federal credit union into a state credit union.

MCLA 490.1 Credit unions; organization, procedure; approval of commissioner of banking. [MSA 23.481]

MCLA 490.2 - 490.4 [MSA 23.482 - 23.484]

MCLA 490.4a Definitions; cooperative housing, investments, creation, acquisition of realty, consultants, appraisers. [MSA 23.484(1)]

1126

MCLA 490.5 Membership. [MSA 23.485]

MCLA 490.5a - 490.21 [MSA 23.485(1) - 23.501]

MCLA 490.22 Taxation. [MSA 23.502]

Sec. 22. ... A credit union ... shall not be subject to taxation except as to real estate owned. ...

MCLA 490.23 - 490.26 [MSA 23.503 - 23.506]

Act No. 39, P.A. 1961 - License to Conduct Certain Sales

AN ACT to regulate insurance, bankruptcy, mortgage, insolvent, assignee's, executor's, administrator's, receiver's, trustee's removal and closing out sales, and sales of goods, wares and merchandise damaged by fire, smoke, water or otherwise; to provide penalties for the violation hereof; and to repeal certain acts and parts of acts.

MCLA 442.211 Conduct of certain sales; definitions. [MSA 19.401(1)]

MCLA 442.212 Same; application of act; license. [MSA 19.401(2)]

Sec. 2. No person shall advertise, represent or hold out that any sale of goods is an insurance, bankruptcy, mortgage, insolvent, assignee's, executor's, administrator's, receiver's, trustee's, removal or sale, going out of business or sale of goods damaged by fire, smoke, water or otherwise, unless he first obtains a license to conduct the sale from the clerk of the ... township in which he proposes to conduct the sale. This act shall not apply to ...

MCLA 442.213 Same; application for license, contents. [MSA 19.401(3)]

Sec. 3. Any applicant for a license under this act shall file an application in writing and under oath with the ...(township)... clerk setting out the following facts and information ...

MCLA 442.214 - 442.217 [MSA 19.401(4) - 19.401(7)]

MCLA 442.218 Same; application, clerk's records. [MSA 19.401(8)]

Sec. 8. Every ... clerk ... shall indorse upon the application the date of its filing, shall preserve the same as a record of his office, and shall make an abstract of the facts set forth in the application in a book kept for that purpose, properly indexed, containing ... (and) shall indorse on the application the date the license is granted or refused, and ...

MCLA 442.219 - 442.224 [MSA 19.401(9) - 19.401(14)]

MCLA 442.225 Persons not subject to act. [MSA 19.401(15)]

Sec. 15. The provisions of this act shall not apply to sheriffs, constables, or other public or court officers, or to any other person or persons acting under the license, direction or authority of any court, ... in the course of their official duties.

MCLA 442.226 Repeal. [MSA 19.401(16)]

Act No. 180, P.A. 1941 - Collection Agencies

AN ACT to require the bonding of persons, firms and corporations engaged in the business of soliciting accounts for collection or in the collection of accounts; to provide a penalty for the violation of this act, and to repeal Act No. 210 of the Public Acts of 1925, being sections 9728 to 9731, inclusive, of the Compiled Laws of 1929.

MCLA 445.201 Collection agencies; surety bond, approval; bond for each county where business is done; conveyance of real estate listed in personal surety's justification, notice of intent to sell. [MSA 19.655(1)]

MCLA 445.202 - 445.206 [MSA 19.655(2) - 19.655(6)]

MCLA 445.207 Exemptions from application of act, exceptions. [MSA 19.655(7)]

1128

*Sec. 7.   This act shall not apply to ...   Provided, however,
That no ... constable, ... in this state shall engage in the business
of soliciting and collecting of accounts for others on a fee basis
within their legal jurisdiction not provided for under the provisions
of their special authority, and that any such persons shall not be
exempted from the requirements of this act, outside the legal jurisdiction of their office: ...*

MCLA 445.208 - 445.209 [MSA 19.655(8) - 19.655(9)]

Act No. 51, P.A. 1925 - Transient Merchants

*AN ACT to license and regulate the business of
transient merchants, to provide penalties for the violation
of this act, and to repeal certain inconsistent acts.*

MCLA 445.371 Definitions; transient merchant, person. [MSA 19.691]

MCLA 445.372 License; necessity. [MSA 19.692]

**MCLA 445.373 Same; contents of application, consent to service,
deposit of bond, fee, expiration.** [MSA 19.693]

**MCLA 445.374   Deposit; subjection to claims, disposition of
balance.** [MSA 19.694]

*Sec. 4.   Deposits made with such county treasurer as required
by the preceding section shall be subject to claims of creditors and
claims for local license fees on behalf of any ... township in all
cases where a judgment has been obtained against such transient
merchant ...*

MCLA 445.375 - MCLA 445.377 [MSA 19.695 - 19.697]

MCLA 445.378   Effect of act on local license or regulation.
[MSA 19.698]

*Sec. 8.   Nothing in this act contained shall interfere with the
licensing or regulation of said business by any ... township ... in
this state not inconsistent with the provisions hereof.*

Act No. 350, P.A. 1917 - Second Hand and Junk Dealers

AN ACT to regulate and license second hand dealers and junk dealers; and to prescribe penalties for the violation of the provisions of this act.

MCLA 445.401 Second hand or junk dealer; license, certain cities and villages. [MSA 19.711]

MCLA 445.402 Same; issuance by mayor or village president, objection by adjacent property owners, term, transferability, fee. [MSA 19.712]

MCLA 445.403 Same; definition. [MSA 19.713]

MCLA 445.404 Same; display of sign, record of transactions. [MSA 19.714]

Sec. 4. Such ... dealer ... shall post in a conspicuous place in or upon his shop, store, wagon, boat or other place of business, a sign having his name and occupation legibly inscribed thereon, and shall keep a separate book open to inspection by member of a police force, city marshal, constable or other person, in which shall be written ...

MCLA 445.405 - 445.407 [MSA 19.715 - 19.717]

MCLA 445.408 Penalty. [MSA 19.718]

Note: The township attorney should be consulted with regard to township rights under the above act.

Act No. 12, P.A. 1929 - Junk Yards

AN ACT to give power to the township board of any township to license and regulate junk yards and places for the dismantling, wrecking and disposing of junk and/or refuse material of automobiles; to prescribe rules, regulations and conditions for the operation of the same; to provide penalties for the operation of the same without a license and for the violation of any rule, regulation or condition.

MCLA 445.451 - 445.453 [MSA 19.731 - 19.733]

Note: See the Highway Beautification section of the chapter on Highways and Roads.

Act No. 232, P.A. 1937 - Used Car Lots

AN ACT to authorize and require the township board of any township to license and regulate used car lots, as herein defined; to prescribe rules, regulations and conditions for the operation of the same; to prescribe penalties for the violation of the provisions of this act; and to repeal all acts and parts of acts inconsistent with the provisions of this act.

MCLA 445.501 - 445.504 [MSA 19.739(1) - 19.739(4)]

Note: See Highway Beautification section of the chapter on Highways and Roads.

Act No. 224, P.A. 1955 - Public Auctions

AN ACT to regulate sales at public auction; to provide for the issuing of licenses; and to prescribe penalties for violations of the provisions of this act.

MCLA 446.51   Licenses for sale of new merchandise at public auction; territorial application of act. [MSA 19.565(1)]

Sec. 1. It shall be unlawful for any person, ... to sell, dispose of, or offer for sale at public auction at any place outside the limits of any city or village ... that has not by ordinance provided for the licensing of sales by auction, any new merchandise, unless such person ... shall have first secured a license as herein provided and shall have complied with the regulations hereinafter set forth.

MCLA 446.52 Same; application, contents; statement as to reservation. [MSA 19.565(2)]

Sec. 2. Any person, firm or corporation desiring such license shall, at least 10 days prior to ... sale, file with the township clerk ... an application in writing duly verified ... which application shall state the following facts: ...

MCLA 446.53 Same; bond, amount, beneficiaries, conditions, liability. Service of process on principal and surety under bond. Jurisdiction, consent. Joinder of parties. [MSA 19.565(3)]

Note: This section delineates further responsibilities of the township clerk.

MCLA 446.54 Same; fee. [MSA 19.565(4)]

MCLA 446.55 Same; issuance, nontransferability, validity. [MSA 19.565(5)]

MCLA 446.56 Report of sale; inventory of unsold merchandise. [MSA 19.565(6)]

Sec. 6. Within 10 days after the last day of said auction the applicant shall file in duplicate with the township board a listing of all ... The township clerk shall, immediately ... forward a copy thereof to the department of revenue.

MCLA 446.57 Definitions. [MSA 19.565(7)]

MCLA 446.58 Cappers, boosters, shillers, false bids prohibited. [MSA 19.565(8)]

MCLA 446.59 Nonapplication of act as to certain sales. [MSA 19.565(9)]

MCLA 446.60 Violation, penalty. [MSA 19.565(10)]

NOTARIES PUBLIC AND MUNICIPAL LIABILITY

As a matter of convenience and service to township residents, as well as in the conduct of township business matters, it is advisable that at least the township clerk and deputy clerk be appointed notaries public. We are therefore including citations on this subject.

Also, there are two citations that place specific liability upon the township for liability to individuals drafted into service by township officials, or for negligent action on the part of the township.

EXECUTIVE ORDER

MCLA 55.101 Delegation of notaries public functions.

... do hereby transfer and delegate to the Department of State all ministerial and clerical duties and functions relative to process-applications for notaries public.

Note: The above is Executive Reorganization Order No. 1970-1.

R.S. 1846, c. 14 - Notaries Public

MCLA 55.107 Appointment, term (4 years), eligibility; application; revocation; fees; indorsement of application in blank; deposit of fees. [MSA 5.1041]

MCLA 55.108 Commission transmitted, notice. [MSA 5.1042]

MCLA 55.109 Oath; quarterly lists to secretary of state; fee. [MSA 5.1043]

Sec. 109. The person so appointed shall, before entering upon the duties of his office, and within 90 days after receiving notice from the county clerk of his appointment, take and file with the county clerk the oath prescribed by the constitution, and the said clerk shall ... ; and ... for all his services required by this act, shall be entitled to receive the sum of $1.00 from each person so qualifying: ...

MCLA 55.110 Bond, approval. [MSA 5.1044]

Sec. 110. Each notary public shall, also, before entering upon the duties of his office, and within the time limited for filing his official oath, give bond ... with 1 or more sureties, to be approved by the county clerk, in the penal sum of 1,000 dollars, the condition of which bond shall be that such notary shall duly and faithfully discharge the duties of his office, and he shall file the same with said clerk: Provided, ...

MCLA 55.111 Delivery of commission; notice to secretary of state. [MSA 5.1045]

MCLA 55.112 Notary's powers. [MSA 5.1046]

Sec. 112. Notaries public shall have authority to take the proof and acknowledgements of deeds; to administer oaths, and take affidavits in any matter or cause pending, or to be commenced or moved in any court of this state; to demand acceptance of foreign and inland bills of exchange, and of promissory notes, and to protest the same for non-acceptance, or non-payment, as the case may require; and to exercise such other powers and duties, as by the law of nations, and according to commercial usage, or by the laws of any other state, government or country, may be performed by notaries public.

MCLA 55.113   Certificate as presumptive evidence; exception. [MSA 5.1047]

MCLA 55.114   Office vacated, disposition of records; penalty, neglect. [MSA 5.1048]

MCLA 55.115   Destruction or concealment of papers, penalty, civil liability. [MSA 5.1049]

Sec. 115. If any person shall knowingly destroy, deface, or conceal any records or papers belonging to the office of a notary public, he shall ...

MCLA 55.116 Records kept by county clerk; copies, fees. [MSA 5.1050]

MCLA 55.117 Notary's residence; jurisdiction, fees. [MSA 5.1051]

Sec. 117. Notaries public shall reside in the county for which they are appointed, but they may act as such notaries in any part of this state; and they shall receive for their services such fees as are provided by law.

Act No. 18, P.A. 1903 - Expiration Date of Commissions

AN ACT to require notaries public to affix to each affidavit, deposition, certificate and acknowledgment given or taken by them, and to all other instruments signed notarially the date of expiration of their commissions, their commissioned names and the county of authorization.

MCLA 55.221 Notaries public; typing, etc., name, etc., on affidavit, deposition, etc.; expiration date of commission; validity of instrument. [MSA 5.1061]

Sec. 1. Notaries public shall legibly type, print or stamp on each affidavit, deposition, certificate and acknowledgement given or taken by them, and to all other instruments signed notarially, ...: Provided, ...

Act No. 161, P.A. 1871 - Fees for Oaths and Certificates

AN ACT regulating the fees of judges of probate, clerks of courts, justices of the peace and notaries public or other persons authorized to administer oaths in certain cases.

MCLA 35.51 Fees for oaths, certificates; to discharged soldier or sailor. [MSA 4.1111]

Sec. 1. That no ... notary public, or any person authorized to administer oaths under and by the provisions of the laws of this state, shall be allowed to charge any discharged soldier, seaman, or the legal representative of a discharged or deceased soldier or sailor more than 15 cents for administering any oath or giving any official certificate for the procuring or obtaining payment of any pension, bounty or back pay.

MCLA 35.52 Same; to widow of deceased soldier or sailor.
[MSA 4.1112]

Sec. 2. That no ... notary public, or any person authorized to administer oaths under and by the provisions of the laws of this state, shall be allowed to charge any widow of a deceased soldier, or guardian to minor children, or other legal representative of such deceased soldier or sailor, more than 25 cents for the (their) oath ...

MCLA 35.53 Penalty. [MSA 4.1113]

Act No. 203, P.A. 1931 - Drafted Persons, Liability of Municipality

AN ACT to establish the liability of municipalities of this state for injuries sustained by persons drafted into service for such municipalities, and to provide the manner of payment of claims for such injuries.

MCLA 123.401 Definition of municipality and drafted person.
[MSA 5.3431]

Sec. 1. ... "municipality" ... to include any township, ... "drafted person" ... to include any person commanded to assist any municipal official or employe authorized to command the assistance of bystanders in the performance of his duties as such municipal official or employe. In the case of the commanding of assistance in putting out fires, the term "drafted person" shall be construed to include any municipal fire department employe called to aid in putting out a fire in any other municipality, which is not under a fire protection contract with the municipality operating such fire department.

MCLA 123.402 Municipal liability for injuries to drafted persons; basis of compensation. [MSA 5.3432]

MCLA 123.403 Payment of claim, law applicable. [MSA 5.3433]

JOINT ACTION
Act No. 170, P.A. 1964 - Liability for Negligence of State and Political Subdivisions

AN ACT to make uniform the liability of municipal corporations, political subdivisions, and the state, its agencies and departments, when engaged in the exercise or discharge of a governmental function, for injuries to property and persons; to define and limit such liability; to define and limit the liability of the state when engaged in a proprietary function; to authorize the purchase of liability insurance to protect against loss arising out of such liability; to provide for defending certain claims made against public officers and paying damages sought or awarded against them; and to repeal certain acts and parts of acts.

MCLA 691.1401   Governmental functions; liability for negligence; definitions. [MSA 3.996(101)]

Sec. 1.   ...   (a)   "Municipal corporation" means any city, village, township or charter township, or any combination thereof, when acting jointly.

(b) "Political subdivision" means any municipal corporation, county, township, charter township, school district, port district, or metropolitan district, or any combination thereof, when acting jointly, and any district or authority formed by 1 or more political subdivisions.

(c) "State" means the state of Michigan and its agencies, departments, and commissions, and shall include every public university and college of the state, whether established as a constitutional corporation or otherwise.

(d) "Governmental agency" means the state, political subdivisions, and municipal corporations as herein defined.

(e) "Highway" means every public highway, road and street which is open for public travel and shall include bridges, sidewalks, crosswalks and culverts on any highway. The term "highway" shall not be deemed to include alleys.

MCLA 691.1402   Defective highways; liability for injuries; limitations. [MSA 3.996(102)]

MCLA 691.1403   Same; knowledge of defect, repair, presumption. [MSA 3.996(103)]

MCLA 691.1404 Notice of injury and highway defect. Time; form and contents of notice. Service, filing; examination of claimant and witnesses. Injured person under 18 or physically or mentally incapacitated, time for service; determination of capability; effect as to charters, statutes, and ordinances. [MSA 3.996(104)]

MCLA 691.1405 Government owned vehicles; liability for negligent operation. [MSA 3.996(105)]

MCLA 691.1406 Public buildings. Duty to repair and maintain; dangerous or defective conditions, liability; notice, service, contents. Service of notice; filing of notice with state. [MSA 3.996(106)]

MCLA 691.1407 Governmental immunity from tort liability, continuance. [MSA 3.996(107)]

MCLA 691.1408 Action against officer or employee; attorney; compromise and settlement; indemnity by governmental agency. [MSA 3.996(108)]

MCLA 691.1409 Liability insurance; waiver of defenses. [MSA 3.996(109)]

MCLA 691.1410 Claims against state, procedure; against other governmental agencies, courts. [MSA 3.996(110)]

MCLA 691.1411 Limitation of actions. [MSA 3.996(111)]

MCLA 691.1412 Defenses available. [MSA 3.996(112)]

MCLA 691.1413 Proprietary function of state; limitation on actions. [MSA 3.996(113)]

MCLA 691.1414 Repeal. [MSA 3.996(114)]

MCLA 691.1415 Effective date of act. [MSA 3.996(115)]

EDUCATION FOR GOVERNMENTAL FUNCTIONS

Act No. 205, P.A. 1931 - Civics Courses

AN ACT to require the teaching of civics and political science in high schools, county normals and colleges, to prohibit the granting of diplomas, and degrees to students not successfully completing said courses, and to provide penalties for the violation thereof.

MCLA 388.371 Civics courses in high schools (includes township government); **prerequisite to diploma; students in military service.** [MSA 15.1951]

MCLA 388.372   Civics, political science, government, or public administration   courses   as   prerequisite   to   degree   or   diploma. [MSA 15.1952]

Sec. 2. In all county normal schools a course of 4 term hours shall be given in civics, and in all colleges receiving public money, courses of not less than 3 semester hours, or equivalent, shall be given in political science, or in government and public administration, covering the form and functions of our federal and state governments, and of counties, cities and villages. Throughout said course the rights and responsibilities of citizenship shall be stressed. No baccalaureate degree or diploma shall be granted ... unless such student shall have successfully completed said courses.

MCLA 388.373   Recommendation for graduation.   [MSA 15.1953]

Although the above statute includes township government in civics course requirements for Michigan high schools, this viable, potent and active level of government is completely ignored in describing course requirements at the college level. Yet that is where high school teachers are trained and where political science is a major academic discipline.

Township officials are encouraged to offer their services as lecturers and resource persons to universities, colleges, community colleges and high schools for appropriate classes. Perhaps most important is to make this expertise available for teacher education classes and in high schools. Young people are impressionable and especially interested and inquiring about the affairs of all levels of government.

MTA many years ago recognized the need to bring knowledge about township government to the attention of high school students. Out of this interest have come two of the most outstanding and unique programs in the United States--Senior Government Days and Operation Bentley.

Senior Government Days are a series of twenty to twenty-five one-day institutes for 200 to 300 students from government classes of high schools in a particular county or area. These are conducted by a full-time staff of three persons, with governmental officials serving as coaches, resource persons and consultants, and are sponsored by the Michigan Townships Association.

Once a year outstanding participants from Senior Government Days and from high school government classes are provided with mini-scholarships and brought to the Olivet College campus for Operation Bentley (which is sponsored by the Alvin M. Bentley Foundation, the Gerber Foundation and the Michigan Townships Association) at no cost to the students. The young people go through an intensive two-week experience with the entire process of state, county, city, village and township government. There are seven full-time staff members and about forty-five coaches and consultants from all levels of state and local government. The participants work closely with all types of officials from executive, judicial and legislative operations.

Years ago Operation Bentley students adopted the motto: "Bentleyites Never Fail." And the fact is that many of them later reach positions of high trust and responsibility--as judges, lawyers, legislators and officials at all levels of government. Their success is a glowing tribute to the late Congressman Alvin M. Bentley and the Honorable D. Hale Brake, Director of the Education Division of MTA, who never faltered in their faith and confidence in the ability of young people of America.

Appendix A

MICHIGAN TOWNSHIPS ASSOCIATION

The Michigan Townships Association is a non-profit association of all the townships of the State of Michigan, organized in 1953 for the improvement and strengthening of township government through cooperative effort. The association provides information and research facilities for its members and maintains a legislative agent in Lansing during sessions of the Legislature. In addition, a field representative is available to member townships to work on local problems.

Member: NATIONAL ASSOCIATION OF TOWNS AND TOWNSHIP OFFICIALS

Official Publication: MICHIGAN TOWNSHIP NEWS

Motto: "GOOD GOVERNMENT FOR ALL"

HEADQUARTERS OFFICE OF THE ASSOCIATION IS LOCATED AT:

> 3121 W. Saginaw St.
> Lansing, Michigan 48917
> Phone: (517) 371-4133

Appendix B

NATIONAL OFFICERS OF THE STATE OF MICHIGAN

UNITED STATES SENATORS

The Honorable Philip A. Hart (D)	Mackinac Island
The Honorable Robert P. Griffin (R)	Traverse City

UNITED STATES REPRESENTATIVES

1	John Conyers, Jr. (D)	Detroit
2	Marvin L. Esch (R)	Ann Arbor
3	Garry Brown (R)	Schoolcraft
4	Edward Hutchinson (R)	Fennville
5	Gerald R. Ford (R)	East Grand Rapids
6	Charles E. Chamberlain (R)	East Lansing
7	Donald W. Riegle, Jr. (D)	Flint
8	James Harvey (R)	Saginaw
9	Guy Vander Jagt (R)	Cadillac
10	Elford A. Cederberg (R)	Bay City
11	Philip E. Ruppe (R)	Houghton
12	James G. O'Hara (D)	Utica
13	Charles C. Diggs, Jr. (D)	Detroit
14	Lucien N. Nedzi (D)	Detroit
15	William D. Ford (D)	Taylor
16	John W. Dingell (D)	Dearborn
17	Martha W. Griffiths (D)	Detroit
18	Robert J. Huber (R)	Troy
19	William S. Broomfield (R)	Royal Oak

ADDRESS IN WASHINGTON

SENATORS
Senate Office Building, Washington, D.C. 20510

REPRESENTATIVES
House Office Building, Washington, D.C. 20515

OFFICE OF FEDERAL REVENUE SHARING

U.S. Department of Treasury
1900 Pennsylvania Ave., N.W.
Washington, D.C. 20226

Appendix C
STATE OFFICIALS

GOVERNOR
The Honorable William G. Milliken (R)

LIEUTENANT GOVERNOR
The Honorable James H. Brickley (R)

SECRETARY OF STATE
The Honorable Richard H. Austin (D)

ATTORNEY GENERAL
The Honorable Frank J. Kelley (D)

STATE TREASURER
The Honorable Allison Green

AUDITOR GENERAL
The Honorable Albert Lee

SUPERINTENDENT OF PUBLIC INSTRUCTION
The Honorable John W. Porter

DIRECTOR OF THE DEPARTMENT OF STATE HIGHWAYS
The Honorable John P. Woodford

PRESIDENT OFFICER OF THE SENATE
Lieutenant Governor James H. Brickley (R)

SECRETARY OF THE SENATE
Beryl I. Kenyon

SPEAKER OF THE HOUSE OF REPRESENTATIVES
The Honorable William A. Ryan (D)

SECRETARY OF SENATE
Beryl I. Kenyon

ADDRESSES IN LANSING —

SENATORS: The Capitol, Lansing, MI 48902
REPRESENTATIVES: The Capitol, Lansing, MI 48901

STATE OFFICE ADDRESSES
IMPORTANT TO
TOWNSHIP OFFICIALS

Agriculture, Department of	5th Floor, Cass Bldg., Lansing 48913
Civil Rights, Department of	1000 Cadillac Square Bldg., Detroit 48226
Civil Service, Department of	Cass Bldg., Lansing 48913
Commerce Department	Law Bldg., Lansing 48913
Aeronautics Commission	Capital City Airport, Lansing 48906
Cemetery Commission	Law Bldg., Lansing 48913
Office of Economic Expansion	Law Bldg., Lansing 48913
Liquor Control Commission	Box 1260, Lansing 48904
Public Service Commission	Law Bldg., Lansing 48913
Securities Bureau	Law Bldg., Lansing 48913
Bureau of Transportation	113 E. Allegan St., Lansing 48913

Executive (Governor's) Office   Cass Bldg., Lansing 48913
Office of Comprehensive State Health Planning
Intergovernmental Relations Division — for **State Revenue Sharing**

Labor, Department of	Department of Labor Bldg.
Labor Relations Division	300 E. Michigan Ave.
Mediation Division	Lansing 48913

Legislative Service Bureau   4th Floor, State Capitol, Lansing 48902

Licensing and Regulation,	1033 S. Washington Ave., Lansing 48926
Department of	and 200 Lafayette Bldg., Detroit 48226
Executive Office	Lansing
Board of Registration for Architects	Detroit
Board of Community Planners	Lansing
Electrical Administrative Board	Lansing
Board of Registration for Professional Engineers	Detroit
Board of Registration for Land Surveyors	Detroit
Board of Landscape Architects	Lansing
Board of Plumbing	Lansing
Board of Examiners of Sanitarians	Lansing

Mental Health, Department of   Cass Bldg., Lansing 48926

Michigan State University	East Lansing 48824
Institute for Community Development and Services	27 Kellogg Center
School of Labor and Industrial Relations	South Kedzie Hall
Soil Conservation Committee	Natural Resources Bldg.

Natural Resources, Department of   Mason Bldg., Lansing 48926
Bureau of Water Management and Water Resources Commission
Forest Fire Division
Forestry Division
Geological Survey Division
Lands Division
Law Enforcement Division
Parks Division
Recreation Services Division
Tourist Council   300 S. Capitol Ave., Lansing 48933

Public Health, Department of   3500 N. Logan St., Lansing 48914
Bureau of Community Health
Bureau of Environmental Health
     Food Service Sanitation Division
     Solid Waste Management Division
     Wastewater Division
     Water Supply Division
Bureau of Health Care Administration
Bureau of Industrial Health and Air Pollution Control
Bureau of Laboratories

Social Services, Department of   300 S. Capitol Ave., Lansing 48926
Commission on Aging
Office of Youth Services
State Housing Authority

State, Department of   Treasury Bldg., Lansing 48922
Office of Public Information
Bureau of State Services
     Elections Division
     Outstate Elections Specialists
     Michigan History Division   (Att: Archivist)
         208 N. Capitol Ave., Lansing 48933
Bureau of Driver and Vehicle Services   8351 Billwood Hwy. (R. #3),
Vehicle and Watercraft Records Division   Charlotte 48813

State Police, Department of
Executive Bureau   714 S. Harrison Rd., East Lansing 48823
     Highway Safety Planning Division (State Safety Commission), 541 E.
         Grand River, East Lansing 48823
Bureau of Staff Services
     Emergency Services Division (Civil Defense),   714 S. Harrison Rd.
     Fire Marshal Division   416 Frandor Ave., Lansing 48912
     Law Enforcement Officers Training Council,
         Michigan National Bank Bldg., Lansing 48933
     Safety and Traffic Division   416 Frandor Ave., Lansing 48912

Treasury, Department of   Treasury Bldg., Lansing 48922
Municipal Finance Division
Tax Appeals Division
Bureau of Local Government Services
     Local Government Audit Division
     Local Property Services Division
     State Boundary Commission
     Property Tax Division
         State Assessors Board
OTHER ADDRESSES

Olivet College   Olivet 49076
Democratic State Central Committee 900 W.Michigan Ave.,Lansing 48915
Republican State Central Committee 404 E.Michigan Ave.,Lansing 48933

BIBLIOGRAPHY

This manual should not be considered a legal directive nor the final word. It would be dangerous, if not impossible, for a layman to attempt to write such a book since it would have to summarize a whole law library and many related materials amounting to close to a thousand volumes - - from *Robert's Rules of Order* to federal regulations. The contents give only guidelines about how to begin to proceed - - just to get started - - not as authority for making final decisions. For that authority, township officials must always **study the particular law cited,** and always **consult the township attorney regarding any legal procedure.**

Bauckham, John H. *Michigan Township Current Legal Opinions,* Vol. 1 -- 1956 to 1969 and Index, Vol. II -- 1970 to 1972. Michigan Townships Association, Lansing 48917: 1972

Callaghan & Company. *Municipal Legal Forms.* Callaghan & Company, 6141 N. Cicero Ave., Chicago, Illinois 60646: current with yearly supplements.
A comprehensive library of working municipal forms.

Campbell, Henry C. *Black's Law Dictionary,* Revised Fourth Edition. West Publishing Co., St. Paul, Minnesota: 1968

Doubleday Brothers & Co. Forms for Local Government (catalog listing). Doubleday Brothers & Co., Kalamazoo 49001: current.
See page 537 for this list.

McQuillin, Eugene. *The Law of Municipal Corporations,* Volumes 1 through 20. Callaghan & Co., 6141 N. Cicero Ave., Chicago, Illinois 60646: current with yearly supplements.

McTaggart, William R. *Handbook of Michigan Township Zoning and Planning.* Edited by John H. Bauckham. Michigan Townships Association, Lansing 48917: 1970

McTaggart, William R. *Handbook of Michigan Township Zoning and Planning, Cumulative Supplement.* Edited by John H. Bauckham. Michigan Townships Association, Lansing 48917: 1972

Michigan. *Michigan Compiled Laws Annotated,* Volumes 1 through 45. West Publishing Co., St. Paul, Minnesota: 1968 and supplements. These books should always be utilized with the current supplements provided by the publisher on a subscription basis.

Michigan. *Michigan Compiled Laws of 1948,* with Case Annotations. Volumes 1 through 6. Michigan State Compilation Commission, Lansing: 1950 and supplements.

Michigan. *Michigan Compiled Laws of 1970,* Volumes I through VI. Michigan Legislative Council, Lansing: 1971

> A supplement is planned to incorporate 1971 and 1972 Michigan Public Acts.

Michigan. *Michigan Statutes Annotated,* Volumes 1 through 28 and General Court Rules. Callaghan & Co., 6141 N. Cicero Ave., Chicago, Illinois 60646: current and supplements.

> These books should always be utilized with the current supplements provided by the publisher on a subscription basis.

Michigan Attorney General. *Biennial Reports of the Attorney General of the State of Michigan.* Attorney General's Office, Lansing 48913: current and supplements.

Michigan Court of Appeals. *Michigan Appeals Reports,* Cases decided in the Michigan Court of Appeals. Volumes 1 through 42 and Monthly Advance Sheets. The Lawyers Co-operative Publishing Co., Rochester, New York 14614: current and supplements.

Michigan Department of Administration. *Laws Relating to Elections.* Department of Administration, Lansing 48926: 1971 and yearly supplements.

Michigan Department of Administration. *Michigan Manual.* Department of Administration, Lansing 48926: biennially.

> Among other things, this publication, sometimes referred to as "legislative manual," contains the state constitution. It is available free to the township clerk (see **MCLA 24.24** et seq [MSA 4.343 et seq]). The township clerk should consult with the county clerk regarding time and method of distribution. Failure to obtain the copy might result in loss of the privilege.

Michigan Department of Administration. *Public and Local Acts of Michigan.* Department of Administration, Lansing: yearly.

> This publication, which will be of assistance in keeping up to date on current laws cited in this textbook, is available free to the township supervisor and clerk. (see **MCLA 24.2** et seq [MSA 4.322 et seq]). The township clerk should consult with the county clerk regarding time and method of distribution. Failure to obtain the copies might result in loss of the privilege.

Michigan Secretary of State, Elections Division. Manuals, Pamphlets, Supplements. Elections Division, Lansing 48922: as needed.

Michigan Department of Public Health. *Solid Waste Management Plan.* Department of Public Health, Lansing 48914: 1972

Michigan Department of Treasury. *Assessor's Manual,* Volumes I and II. Michigan State Tax Commission, Lansing 48926: current and yearly supplements.

Michigan Department of Treasury. *Uniform Accounting Procedures and Manual.* Local Government Audit Division, Lansing 48926: current and supplements.

Michigan Supreme Court. *Michigan Reports,* Cases decided in the Supreme Court in Michigan. 338 volumes and monthly advance sheets. The Lawyers Co-operative Publishing Co., New York: current and supplements.

Michigan, various departments. Manuals, Pamphlets, Supplements. State of Michigan, Lansing: as needed.
Names and addresses of the various departments of interest to township officials are listed in Appendix D.

Michigan Assessors Association, Inc. *The Michigan Assessor.* Michigan Assessors Association, Donald Hollard, Shelby Township Assessor, 52700 Van Dyke Ave., Utica, MI 48087: monthly.

Michigan State University Cooperative Extension Service. "The Meeting Will Come to Order". Michigan State University, East Lansing 48824: 1973

Michigan State University Department of Labor and Industrial Relations. *The Employment Relations Series.* Michigan State University, East Lansing 48824: current and revisions.
Includes "Michigan Public Employment Relations Act and Procedures" by Hyman Parker.

Michigan State University Institute for Community Development and Services, Continuing Education Service. *Community Development Series of Michigan Legislative Acts.* Michigan State University, East Lansing 48824: as needed.
Includes technical bulletins A–70, "Charter Township Act"; A–71, "Township Planning Commission Act" and A–72, "Township Rural Zoning Act."

Michigan State University Institute for Community Development and Services, Continuing Education Service. *Michigan Local Government Accounting -- Problem Manual and Workbook.* Michigan State University, East Lansing 48824.

Michigan Townships Association. *Michigan Township News.* Michigan Townships Association, 3121 West Saginaw St., Lansing 48917:

monthly.
> Available to township officials as a benefit of membership. Not available to non-member township officials. Available on subscription to other persons or organizations.

Needham, Roger A. *Michigan Lawyer's Manual.* Callaghan & Co., 6141 N. Cicero Ave., Chicago, Illinois 60646: 1964 and supplements.

Parisi, Joseph A. *A Handbook for Township Officials.* Michigan Townships Association, Lansing 48917: 1957

Parisi, Joseph A. *A Manual for Township Officials.* Michigan Townships Association, Lansing 48917: 1963

The Reader's Digest Association, Inc. *Reader's Digest Almanac and Yearbook.* The reader's Digest Association, Inc., Pleasantville, New York: 1973

Robert, Henry M. *Robert's Rules of Order,* Newly Revised. Scott, Foresman and Company, Glenview, Illinois: 1970

United States Office of Management and Budget. *Catalog of Federal Domestic Assistance.* Superintendent of Documents, U.S. Government Printing Office, Washington, D.C.: 1972

VerBurg, Kenneth, Michigan State University Institute for Community Development and Services, Continuing Education Service. *Guide to Michigan County Government.* Michigan State University, East Lansing 48824: 1972 ff.

PREFACE

This is a Subject Index. When looking up a subject or agency, modifying nouns and adjectives should be disregarded, for instance, Board of Health, see Health, Commissioner of Drains, see Drains.
There are also useful cross-references within the index itself.

The following abbreviations are used within the index: J.A., Joint Action; M.C., Michigan Constitution; M.V.C., Motor Vehicle Code; M.P.C., Michigan Penal Code.

Underscored entries under major bold headings are deemed of greater importance to township officials and should be reviewed.

1153

ELECTION(s) - continued

TAX(es) - continued